DICTIONARY OF
American History

Third Edition

EDITORIAL BOARD

DICTIONARY OF
American History

Third Edition

Stanley I. Kutler, *Editor in Chief*

Volume 5
La Follette to Nationalism

CHARLES SCRIBNER'S SONS

New York • Detroit • San Diego • San Francisco • Cleveland • New Haven, Conn. • Waterville, Maine • London • Munich

Dictionary of American History, Third Edition

Stanley I. Kutler, *Editor*

© 2003 by Charles Scribner's Sons
Charles Scribner's Sons is an imprint
of The Gale Group, Inc., a division of
Thomson Learning, Inc.

Charles Scribner's Sons® and Thomson
Learning™ are trademarks used herein
under license.

For more information, contact
Charles Scribner's Sons
An imprint of the Gale Group
300 Park Avenue South
New York, NY 10010

For permission to use material from this
product, submit your request via Web at
http://www.gale-edit.com/permissions, or you
may download our Permissions Request form
and submit your request by fax or mail to:

Permissions Department
The Gale Group, Inc.
27500 Drake Rd.
Farmington Hills, MI 48331-3535
Permissions Hotline:
248-699-8006 or 800-877-4253, ext. 8006
Fax: 248-699-8074 or 800-762-4058

LIBRARY OF CONGRESS CATALOGING-IN-PUBLICATION DATA

Dictionary of American history / Stanley I. Kutler.—3rd ed.
    p.   cm.
Includes bibliographical references and index.
    ISBN 0-684-80533-2 (set : alk. paper)
1. United States—History—Dictionaries.   I. Kutler, Stanley I.
E174 .D52   2003
973′.03—dc21

Printed in United States of America
10 9 8 7 6 5 4 3 2 1

CONTENTS

DICTIONARY OF
American History

Third Edition

LA FOLLETTE CIVIL LIBERTIES COMMITTEE HEARINGS.

From 1936 to 1940, a special committee of the U.S. Senate, known as the La Follette Civil Liberties Committee, held the most extensive hearings in American history to that date into employer violations of the rights of workers to organize and bargain collectively. Conducted by Senator Robert M. La Follette Jr. of Wisconsin, the hearings exposed the heavy-handed, often brutal tactics many of the nation's leading corporations used to prevent their workers from forming unions.

A colorful cast of witnesses, including unrepentant businesspeople and strikebreakers, told how companies had planted spies within the ranks of labor; stockpiled weapons, such as submachine guns, rifles, and tear gas; and subverted local law enforcement by hiring their own police forces. The two most famous sets of hearings both occurred in 1937. In the spring the La Follette committee investigated oppressive conditions in the coal-mining company towns of Harlan County, Kentucky. In the summer the committee staged dramatic hearings into the MEMORIAL DAY MASSACRE, during which police had killed ten strikers and wounded a hundred others outside the gates of Republic Steel's South Chicago factory. In 1939 and 1940 the committee brought its investigations to a close by holding hearings on the plight of migrant farm workers in the fruit and vegetable fields of California.

Business critics accused La Follette and his cochair, Senator Elbert D. Thomas of Utah, of rigging the hearings in favor of labor, and indeed the sympathies of committee members did rest with workers. But most commentators gave the committee high marks for procedural fairness and for safeguarding the rights of witnesses. Although some communists or communist sympathizers served on the committee's staff, no evidence indicated that they significantly influenced the committee's hearings or its voluminous reports and legislative recommendations.

By turning the spotlight on oppressive labor practices, the hearings put corporations on the defensive and helped spur the growth of organized labor during the depression decade. The committee's ninety-five volumes of hearings and reports are one of the best sources of information on labor-management relations in the 1930s.

BIBLIOGRAPHY

Auerbach, Jerold S. *Labor and Liberty: The La Follette Committee and the New Deal.* Indianapolis, Ind.: Bobbs-Merrill, 1966.

Maney, Patrick J. *Young Bob: A Biography of Robert M. La Follette, Jr.* Madison: Wisconsin Historical Society Press, 2002.

U.S. Congress, Senate, Subcommittee of the Committee on Education and Labor. *Hearings Pursuant to S. Res. 266, Violations of Free Speech and Rights of Labor.* 74th–76th Cong., 1936–1940.

Patrick Maney

See also **Collective Bargaining; Labor.**

LA SALLE EXPLORATIONS.

René-Robert Cavelier, Sieur de La Salle, was among the foremost architects of French colonial expansion in North America. Between 1669 and 1687, he traversed the interior of the continent, from the Saint Lawrence River to the Great Lakes to the Gulf of Mexico, and claimed nearly all the territory in between for France. La Salle's prodigious explorations were made possible by the imposition of royal authority over New France, or Canada, in 1663. An imperialist-minded governor, Louis de Buade, Comte de Frontenac et Pallau, gradually reversed the colony's floundering economy and initiated a new era of expansion and growth. La Salle became the principal architect of the imperial designs embodied by Frontenac.

La Salle's beginnings were inauspicious enough. He attended a Jesuit college and was educated for the priesthood in France, but in 1666 he left his homeland and his studies to pursue wealth and adventure in the New World. By 1669, he had established himself as a successful seigneur, or landowner, near Montreal, although he was not content to simply farm the land. He also dabbled in the fur trade, an occupation that brought La Salle into contact with the Native peoples of the region. He soon became enamored with Native accounts of the richness of the lands west of the French settlements. His interests closely coincided with the imperial aspirations of Frontenac, who wanted to expand French influence throughout the Great Lakes region to monopolize the fur trade. In 1672, La Salle sold his land and entered into Frontenac's service as an explorer. He was influential in the establishment of Fort Frontenac (present-day Kingston,

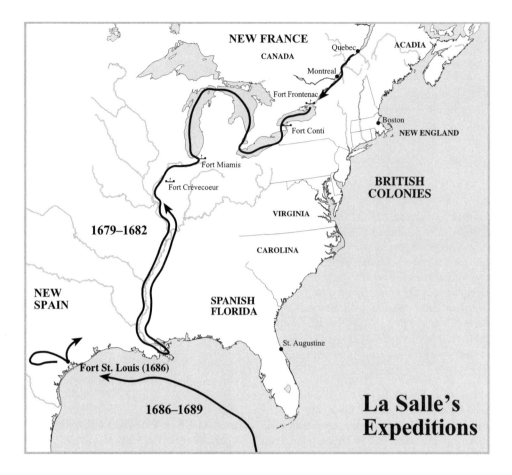

La Salle's Expeditions

Ontario), the centerpiece for the governor's planned initiative against the Iroquois monopoly of the lower Great Lakes fur trade. In 1674, La Salle traveled to France and laid Frontenac's expansionist agenda before an enthusiastic King Louis XIV, who appointed La Salle the seigneur of Fort Frontenac and elevated him to the nobility.

La Salle grew wealthy from trade profits while presiding over Fort Frontenac, but his interest in the interior of North America never waned. He returned to France in 1677 to seek royal permission to explore the territory to the west of New France, to construct forts at advantageous locations, and to facilitate trade with the peoples he encountered. La Salle hoped to establish a new colony and to personally monopolize the extensive trade he expected to come from such an endeavor. The king granted La Salle permission to explore the region, open trade, and build forts, but refused to authorize any new interior colonies that might draw migrants from France and weaken the population base for the army. In addition, the French government refused to finance the expeditions on account of the uncertainty surrounding economic returns. Thus, La Salle had to underwrite his explorations personally, a decision that drained the fortune he had obtained through the fur trade and left him increasingly in debt.

Despite financial difficulties and strong opposition from merchants in Montreal, who believed their profits

would diminish if La Salle transferred the center of trade further to the west, and Jesuit missionaries, who feared his transgression onto uncharted Native lands would anger potential future converts, La Salle began his western explorations in 1679. He set sail aboard the *Griffon*, a small but steady vessel, from a point just above Niagara Falls and entered Lake Erie. Exploring and charting much of the Great Lakes region, La Salle established a trade post on the site of Green Bay, Wisconsin. The *Griffon* soon returned to Fort Frontenac with a full cargo of furs, while La Salle led an expedition to the southern tip of Lake Michigan, where he built Fort Miami, before continuing on to the intersection of the Illinois and Mississippi Rivers. After backtracking a short distance to Lake Peoria, La Salle began the construction of Fort Crèvecoeur and a ship to carry his expedition down the Mississippi.

However, his plans were thrown awry by the failure of the *Griffon* to return from Niagara, leaving his men perilously short of supplies. Unknown to La Salle, the vessel had sunk on Lake Erie. In early 1681, he was forced to endure a treacherous midwinter return to Fort Frontenac, during which time the post at Fort Crèvecoeur was attacked and subsequently deserted. Despite these setbacks, La Salle refused to relinquish his dream of descending the Mississippi River, and by the end of 1681 he had returned to Fort Miami to renew his efforts. Traveling primarily by canoe, he finally reached the Gulf of Mexico on 9 April 1682 and triumphantly claimed the entire Mississippi watershed for France and named the new territory Louisiana in honor of King Louis XIV.

During his return up the Mississippi, La Salle constructed Fort Saint Louis along the Illinois River and organized a colony of several thousand Indians around the post. However, Frontenac was replaced as governor of New France, and his successor quickly proved hostile to La Salle's plans. The explorer was ordered to abandon the western posts and return to Montreal. La Salle refused and instead returned to France, where he once again sought royal permission for his western ambitions. The king upheld La Salle's claims against the governor and even authorized La Salle to establish a military colony in Louisiana at the mouth of the Mississippi River. In return, the king required that La Salle use the site as a base to launch campaigns against Spanish forces in Mexico.

La Salle's final expedition, begun in 1684, proved a disaster. He quarreled incessantly with the French naval officers in charge of the expedition, diseases ravaged his troops, and a nautical miscalculation landed the expedition at Matagorda Bay in Texas, nearly five hundred miles west of the intended destination. Despite repeated attempts, La Salle was unable to rediscover the mouth of the Mississippi River or to effect a junction with French forces in the Illinois country. In the interim, many of his men died. Finally, in 1687 his remaining troops, pushed to mutiny by hunger and privation, murdered the explorer near the Brazos River following yet another failed attempt to locate the Mississippi.

BIBLIOGRAPHY

Galloway, Patricia K., ed. *La Salle and His Legacy: Frenchmen and Indians in the Lower Mississippi Valley.* Jackson: University Press of Mississippi, 1982.

Kellogg, Louise Phelps, ed. *Early Narratives of the Northwest, 1634–1699.* New York: Scribner, 1917. Contains English translations of the original narratives of La Salle's men.

Muhlstein, Anka. *La Salle: Explorer of the North American Frontier.* Translated by Willard Wood. New York: Arcade Publishing, 1994. Modern biography of La Salle.

Parkman, Francis. *La Salle and the Discovery of the Great West.* New York: Modern Library, 1999. Originally published as *The Discovery of the Great West* in 1869; classic study based primarily on the writings of La Salle and his companions.

Daniel P. Barr

See also **Explorations and Expeditions: French; Louisiana; Mississippi River; New France.**

LABOR. As the nearly 4 million Americans recorded in the census of 1790 grew to more than 280 million in 2000, the character of their work changed as dramatically as their numbers. At the beginning of the nineteenth century, most Americans were farmers, farm laborers, or un-

Dolores Huerta. One of the leaders of the international grape boycott, which the United Farm Workers—a union founded in 1966 by Cesar Chávez, its president until the 1990s, and Huerta, its first vice president—began in the late 1960s during a long strike in California to improve conditions for farm laborers, most of them of Mexican or Filipino descent. AP/ WIDE WORLD PHOTOS

paid household workers. Many were bound (as slaves in the southern states, indentured servants elsewhere). Most farmers, craft workers, and shopkeepers were proprietors of family businesses. Most workers were of British origin, though there were large German and African American minorities. Many workers received part or all of their pay in the form of housing, food, and goods. The workday and work year reflected the seasons and the weather as much as economic opportunity or organizational discipline. Two hundred years later, farm labor had become insignificant, employees vastly outnumbered the self-employed, bound labor had disappeared, and child and unpaid household labor had greatly declined. Family and other social ties had become less important in finding work or keeping a job, large private and public organizations employed more than a third of all workers and set standards for most of the others, the labor force had become ethnically diverse, labor productivity and real wages were many times higher, wage contracts and negotiated agreements covering large groups were commonplace, and workplace disputes were subject to a web of laws and regulations.

These contrasts were closely associated with revolutionary changes in economic activity and particularly with the growth of modern manufacturing and service industries. After the middle of the nineteenth century, virtually all new jobs were in these sectors, which were also centers of innovation.

Technology

The changing character of work was closely related to the classic technological innovations of the nineteenth century and the beginning of modern economic growth. Innovations in energy use were particularly influential. Thanks to the availability of numerous waterpower sites in New England and the mid-Atlantic states, industry developed rapidly after the American Revolution. By the 1820s, the massive, water-powered Waltham Mills of northern Massachusetts and southern New Hampshire were among the largest factories in the world. By midcentury, however, steam power had become widespread in manufacturing as well as transportation, and steam-powered factories became the basis of the industrial economy. In 1880, the Census Bureau announced that nonfactory manufacturing had become insignificant. The advent of electrical power at the turn of the century had an even greater impact. It made possible the giant manufacturing operations of the early twentieth century, the smaller, more specialized plants that became the rule after the 1920s, the great versatility in machine use that characterized the second half of the twentieth century, and the mechanization of stores, offices, and homes.

Steam and electrical power and related innovations in machine technology not only made it feasible to create large organizations but gave them an economic advantage over small plants and shops. Workers in the new organizations were wage earners, usually not family members (unlike most nineteenth-century executives), and often they were not even acquainted outside the plant. They rejected payment in kind or in services (company housing and company stores in isolated mining communities became a persistent source of grievances), started and stopped at specific times (the factory bell remained a powerful symbol of the new era), and became accustomed to a variety of rules defining their responsibilities and behavior. Mechanization also led to specialization of function. Factory workers (except for the common laborers, the least skilled and most poorly paid employees) were almost always specialists. Elaborate hierarchies of pay and status grew out of the new ways of work.

The industrial model soon spread to the service sector. Railroad corporations created hierarchical, bureaucratic structures with even stricter lines of authority and more specialized tasks than the largest factories. Insurance companies, department stores, mail-order houses, and large banks followed this pattern, though they typically used only simple, hand-operated machines. The growth of regional and national markets (a result of technological innovations in transportation and communication as well as the expanding economy) made the hierarchical, bureaucratic organization profitable even when power-driven machines played little role in production.

Immigration

Most workers who filled nonexecutive positions in the new organizations were European immigrants or their children. The rapid growth in the demand for labor (confounded by periodic mass unemployment) forced employers to innovate. In the nineteenth century, they often attracted skilled workers from the British Isles or Germany. By the latter decades of the century, however, they hired immigrants mostly to fill low-skill jobs that veteran workers scorned. Although immigration from Britain, Germany, and Scandinavia never ceased, most immigrants increasingly came from the economic and technological backwaters of Europe. By the early twentieth century, more than a million immigrants were arriving each year, the majority from eastern and southern Europe, where most of them had worked as tenant farmers or farm laborers.

An obvious question is why ill-paid American agricultural workers did not respond to the opportunities of industrial and service employment. Several factors apparently were involved. The regional tensions between North and South, where the majority of poor, underemployed agricultural workers were located, and the post–Civil War isolation of the South discouraged movement to industrial centers. Racial prejudice was also influential, though few white southerners moved north before 1915. Lifestyle decisions were also important. In the midwestern states, where industry and agriculture developed in close proximity and where racial distinctions were less important, farm workers were almost as reluctant to take industrial or urban service jobs. (There was, however, significant intergenerational movement, particularly among children who attended high schools and universities.) Consequently a paradox emerged: American farm workers seemed content to eke out a modest living in the country while European agricultural workers filled new jobs in industry and the services.

Mass immigration was socially disruptive. Immigrants faced many hazards and an uncertain welcome. Apart from the Scandinavians, they became highly concentrated in cities and industrial towns. By the early twentieth century, most large American cities were primarily immigrant enclaves. (Milwaukee, perhaps the most extreme case, was 82 percent immigrant and immigrants' children in 1900.) To visitors from rural areas, they were essentially European communities except that instead of a single culture, a hodgepodge of different languages and mores prevailed. It is hardly surprising that observers and analysts bemoaned the effects of immigration and especially the shift from "old," northern and western European, to "new," southern and eastern European, immigrants.

In the workplace, native-immigrant tensions took various forms. The concentration of immigrants in low-skill jobs created a heightened sense of competition—of newer immigrant groups driving out older ones—and led to various efforts to restrict immigrant mobility. These tensions were exacerbated by ethnic concentrations in particular trades and occupations and the perception of discrimination against outsiders. A concrete expression of these divisions was the difficulty that workers and unions had in maintaining solidarity in industrial disputes. The relatively low level of labor organization and the particular character of the American labor movement have often been explained at least in part as the results of a heterogeneous labor force.

The end of traditional immigration during World War I and the low level of immigration during the interwar years eased many of these tensions and encouraged the rise of "melting pot" interpretations of the immigrant experience. World War I also saw the first substantial movement of southern workers to the North and West, a process that seemed to promise a less tumultuous future. In reality, the initial phases of this movement increased the level of unrest and conflict. Part of the problem—repeated in the early years of World War II—was the excessive concentration of war-related manufacturing in a few congested urban areas. The more serious and persistent irritant was racial conflict, with the poorest of the "new" immigrants pitted against African American migrants. Although the wartime and postwar wave of race riots waned by 1921, the tensions lingered. In most northern cities, African Americans were much more likely to live in ethnically homogeneous neighborhoods than were any immigrant groups.

By midcentury, most Americans looked back at immigration as a feature of an earlier age and celebrated the ability of American society to absorb millions of outsiders. Yet at the same time, a new cycle of immigration was beginning. It had the same economic origins and many similar effects, though it differed in other respects. Most of the post–World War II immigrants came from Latin America and Asia rather than Europe. They settled overwhelmingly in the comparatively vacant Southwest and West, areas that had grown rapidly during World War II and continued to expand in the postwar years. In contrast, the Northeast and Midwest, traditional centers of industrial activity, attracted comparatively few immigrants. Most of the newcomers were poorly educated and filled low-skill positions in industry and the services, but there were exceptions. Among the Asian immigrants were many well-educated engineers, technicians, and professionals who quickly rose to important positions, a development that had no nineteenth-century parallel.

Employer Initiatives

Managers of large organizations soon realized that they were dependent on their employees. Turnover, absenteeism, indifferent work, or outright sabotage were signifi-cant threats to productivity and profits. Conversely, highly motivated employees could enhance the firm's performance. Traditional tactics such as threats of punishment and discharge were less effective in a factory or store with numerous work sites and a hierarchy of specialized jobs. Uncertain about how to respond, nineteenth-century employers experimented widely. A handful introduced elaborate services; others devised new forms of "driving" and coercion. Most simply threw up their hands, figuratively speaking, and delegated the management of employees to first-line supervisors, who became responsible for hiring, firing, and other personnel functions. As a result, there were wide variations in wages, working conditions, and discipline, even within organizations, as well as abuses of authority and high turnover. Friction between supervisors and wage earners became a common cause of labor unrest.

Remedial action came from two sources. In the last quarter of the nineteenth century, state governments began to impose restrictions on employers, especially employers of women and children. By 1900, most northern and western states regulated the hiring of children, hours of labor, health and sanitation, and various working conditions. During the first third of the twentieth century, they tightened regulations, extended some rules to male workers, and introduced workers' compensation, the first American social insurance plans. In the late 1930s, the federal social security system added old-age pensions and unemployment insurance, and other legislation set minimum wages, defined the workday and workweek, and restricted child labor. Still, none of these measures directly addressed a variety of shop-floor problems. To remedy this deficiency, as well as to raise wages, the New Deal also promoted collective bargaining, most notably via the NATIONAL LABOR RELATIONS ACT of 1935.

Employers also played an important role in this process. Beginning at the turn of the century, a relatively small number of employers, mostly large, profitable corporations, introduced policies designed to discourage turnover and improve morale. Two innovations were particularly important. The first was the creation of personnel departments that centralized and standardized many of the supervisors' personnel functions. By the 1920s, most large industrial and service corporations had personnel departments whose functions and responsibilities expanded rapidly. The second innovation was the introduction of systematic benefit systems that provided medical, educational, recreational, and other services.

During the 1930s and 1940s, the federal and state governments embraced many features of this "welfare capitalism" in the process of creating a modest welfare state. Government initiatives extended some benefit plans to workers at smaller and less generous firms and encouraged the larger employers to create even more elaborate benefit programs. The spread of collective-bargaining contracts and a more prosperous postwar economy reinforced this trend. The years from the early 1940s to the mid-1970s would be the heyday of corporate benevolence.

Coal Strike of 1902. Two of the 150,000 anthracite coal workers of eastern Pennsylvania who went on strike from May to October, until a sympathetic President Theodore Roosevelt stepped in and set up a commission, which met some of the strikers' demands regarding wages, hours, and a board to resolve disputes. THEODORE ROOSEVELT COLLECTION, HARVARD COLLEGE LIBRARY

Labor Unrest

The growth of industrial and service employment also introduced new forms of unrest and protest. The years from the 1870s to the 1940s witnessed waves of strikes, which were widely viewed as a perplexing and troubling feature of modern society. Yet strikes were only the most visible examples of the many tensions and conflicts characteristic of industrial employment. Dissatisfied wage earners had in fact two basic choices, "exit" and "voice." Unhappy workers could quit, or exit, and search for more satisfying jobs, or they could try to improve their current jobs through the use of their collective "voice," that is, through protests, complaints, and negotiations. Historically, most workers have concluded that quitting is easier than trying to create and maintain a union. Still, the history of organized labor (because it has been carefully documented) is the best available valuable measure of the tensions associated with modern employment and the ability of workers to exercise a "voice" in industry.

Nineteenth-Century Unions

The American labor movement dates from the early nineteenth century, first became an important force during the inflationary prosperity of the 1860s, and flourished during the boom years of the 1880s. During those years a pattern appeared that persisted through the twentieth century. The individuals most likely to organize were so-called autonomous workers, those who had substantial independence in the workplace. Most, but not all, were highly skilled and highly paid. They were not oppressed and with notable exceptions were not the employees of the new institutions most closely associated with American industrialization: the large factories, railroads, and bureaucratic offices. Rather they were the men (with very few exceptions) whose skills made them vital to the production process and who could increase their influence through collective action. Their strategic roles also made employers wary of antagonizing them, another critical factor in union growth. Employers typically countered unions with threats and reprisals. Low-skill employees had to take those threats seriously; autonomous workers could resist employer pressures.

Regardless of their particular jobs, workers were more likely to organize successfully in good times and when they could count on sympathetic public officials. Prosperity and a favorable political climate were important determinants of union growth; recession conditions and state repression often made organization impossible, regardless of other factors.

Two groups dominated the nineteenth-century labor movement. Miners were autonomous workers who were not highly skilled or highly paid. But they worked alone or in small groups and faced extraordinary hazards and dangers. Organization was a way to express their sense of solidarity, increase (or maintain) wages, tame the cutthroat competition that characterized their industries (especially coal mining), and restrict the entrance of even less skilled, lower wage workers. Unions flourished in both anthracite and bituminous coal fields in the 1860s and early 1870s, and they emerged in the western "hard rock" industry in the 1870s. After great turmoil and numerous strikes during the prolonged recession of the mid-1870s, miners' organizations became stronger than ever. Their success was reflected in the emergence of two powerful unions, the UNITED MINE WORKERS OF AMERICA, formed in 1890, and the WESTERN FEDERATION OF MINERS, which followed in 1893. They differed in one important respect: the coal miners were committed to collective bargaining with the goal of regional or even national contracts, while the Western Federation of Miners scorned collective bargaining in favor of workplace activism.

The second group consisted of urban artisans, led by construction workers but including skilled industrial workers such as printers and molders. Some of the unions that emerged in the 1820s and 1830s represented workers in handicraft trades, but in later years, organized workers were concentrated in new jobs and industries, though not usually in the largest firms. Organization was a way to maximize opportunities and simultaneously create buffers against excessive competition. Railroad workers were a notable example. Engineers and other skilled operating employees formed powerful unions in the 1860s and 1870s. Through collective bargaining, they were able to obtain high wages, improved working conditions, and greater security. However, they made no effort to organize the vast majority of railroad workers who lacked their advantages. Most railroad managers reluctantly dealt with the skilled groups as long as there was no effort to recruit other employees.

The limitations of this approach inspired efforts to organize other workers, and the notable exception to this approach was the KNIGHTS OF LABOR, which briefly became the largest American union. The Knights attempted to organize workers regardless of skill or occupation, including those who were members of existing unions. Several successful strikes in the mid-1880s created a wave of optimism that the Knights might actually succeed, and membership rose to a peak of more than 700,000 in 1886. But employer counterattacks, together with the Knights' own organizational shortcomings, brought this activity to an abrupt halt. Thereafter, the Knights of Labor declined as rapidly as it had grown. By 1890, it had lost most of its members and was confined to a handful of strongholds.

Twentieth-Century Unions
After the severe depression of the mid-1890s, which undermined all unions, the labor movement enjoyed a long period of expansion and growing influence. Autonomous worker groups, led by coal miners and construction workers, dominated organized labor for the next third of a century. The debate over tactics was decisively resolved in favor of collective bargaining, though a dissenting group, the INDUSTRIAL WORKERS OF THE WORLD, rallied critics with some success before World War I. Collective bargaining was effectively institutionalized during World War I, when the federal government endorsed it as an antidote for wartime unrest. The other major development of this period was the emergence of an effective union federation, the American Federation of Labor (AFL), which dated from the upheavals of 1886 but only became influential with the membership revival of the early twentieth century. Under its shrewd and articulate president, Samuel Gompers, the AFL promoted the autonomous worker groups while professing to speak for all industrial workers. Gompers and his allies disavowed socialism and efforts to create an independent political party, policies that led to an erroneous perception (encouraged by their many critics) of indifference or hostility to political action. On the contrary, Gompers closely aligned the AFL with the Democratic Party and created aggressive lobbying organizations in the states and in Washington.

Labor's political activism seemed to pay off during World War I, when Gompers was appointed to a high post in the mobilization effort and the federal government directly and indirectly encouraged organization. The greatest gains occurred in the railroad industry, which was nationalized in 1917. Under government control, railroad managers no longer could oppose organization and collective bargaining. By 1920, most railroad employees were union members. Government efforts to reduce unrest and strikes also resulted in inroads in many manufacturing industries. In 1920, union membership totaled 5 million, twice the prewar level.

These gains proved to be short-lived. The end of wartime regulations, the defeat of the Democrats in the 1920 national elections, new employer offensives, and the severe recession of 1920–1922 eliminated the conditions that had encouraged organization. Membership contracted, particularly in industry. The decline of the coal and railroad industries in the 1920s was an additional blow. By the late 1920s, organized labor was no stronger than it had been before the war. The one positive feature of the postwar period was the rapid growth of service sector unionism.

The dramatic recession that began in 1929 and continued with varying severity for a decade set the stage for the greatest increase in union membership in American history. Recessions and unemployment typically reduced the appeal of any activity that was likely to provoke employer reprisals. This was also true of the 1930s. Union membership declined precipitously between 1930 and 1933, as the economy collapsed and unemployment rose. It also plunged in 1937–1938, when a new recession led to sweeping layoffs. Union growth occurred in 1933–1937, and in the years after 1939, when employment was increasing. Yet the generally unfavorable economic conditions of the 1930s did have two important indirect effects. Harsh economic conditions produced a strong sense of grievance among veteran workers who lost jobs, savings, and status. Because the depression was widely blamed on big-business leaders and Republican officeholders, it also had a substantial political impact. The 1932 election of Franklin D. Roosevelt, who had strong progressive and activist credentials as a Democratic politician and especially as governor of New York, proved to be a turning point in the history of the labor movement.

The expansion of union activity after 1933 reflected these factors, particularly in the early years. Roosevelt's New Deal was only intermittently pro-union, but it effectively neutralized employer opposition to worker organization, and with passage of the National Labor Relations Act in 1935 it created a mechanism for peacefully resolving representation conflicts and introducing collective bargaining. Although the ostensible purpose of the legislation was to foster dispute resolution and higher wages, it indirectly promoted union growth by restricting the employer's ability to harass union organizations and members. In the meantime, industrial workers, notably workers in the largest firms such as steel and automobile manufacturing companies, reacted to the new opportunities with unprecedented unity and enthusiasm. The de-

IWW Rally. Members and supporters of the radical Industrial Workers of the World, which preferred confrontational tactics such as strikes over collective bargaining and compromise, meet on 1 May 1914—May Day, the socialist holiday for labor—at New York's Union Square, a gathering place for labor activists in the early twentieth century. LIBRARY OF CONGRESS

pression experience and the New Deal appeared to have sparked a new era of militant unionism. An important expression of this change was the emergence of the Congress of Industrial Organizations, a new labor federation created in November 1938 by John L. Lewis, the president of the United Mine Workers, and devoted to aggressive organizing, especially in manufacturing.

Although the National Labor Relations Act (and other related legislation designed for specific industries) most clearly and explicitly addressed the industrial relations issues of the 1930s, other New Deal measures complemented it. The move to regulate prices and production in the transportation, communications, and energy industries, which began with the National Industrial Recovery Act of 1933 and continued with a variety of specific measures enacted between 1935 and 1938, created opportunities for unions. Regulated corporations had powerful incentives to avoid strikes and cooperate with unions. As a result, about one-third of union membership growth in the 1930s occurred in those industries. If the UNITED AUTOMOBILE WORKERS OF AMERICA and the UNITED STEELWORKERS OF AMERICA were symbols of the new militancy in manufacturing, the equally dramatic growth of the IN-

TERNATIONAL BROTHERHOOD OF TEAMSTERS symbolized the labor upheaval in transportation, communications, and energy.

Government regulations played a more direct role in the equally dramatic union growth that occurred during World War II, when aggregate membership rose from 10 million to 15 million. Most new jobs during the war years were in manufacturing companies that had collective bargaining contracts and in many cases union security provisions that required new hires to join unions. War mobilization thus automatically created millions of additional union members. Government efforts to discourage strikes also emphasized the unions' role in a bureaucratic, intensely regulated economy. By 1945, the labor movement had become a respected part of the American establishment.

Postwar Labor

By the mid-1940s full employment, high wages, and optimism about the future, based on a sense that government now had the ability to manage prosperity (together with awareness of the social safety net that government and business had created since the mid-1930s) replaced the depressed conditions of the 1930s. The experiences of workers in the 1940s and 1950s seemed to confirm the lessons of the New Deal era. With the exception of a few mild recession years, jobs were plentiful, real wages rose, and the federal government continued its activist policies, gradually building on the welfare state foundations of the 1930s. The labor movement also continued to grow, but with less dynamism than in the 1940s. Optimists viewed the merger of the AFL and CIO in 1955, ending the internecine competition that dated from the late 1930s, as a likely stimulus to new gains.

In retrospect, however, those lessons are less compelling. The striking feature of the economy of the 1950s and 1960s was not the affirmation of earlier developments but the degree to which the character of work and the characteristics of the labor force changed. Farming and other natural-resource industries declined at an accelerated rate, and industrial employment also began to decline, but service-industry employment boomed. Formal education became even more important for ambitious workers. Married women entered the labor force in unprecedented numbers. Employers, building on the initiatives of earlier years, extended employee benefit programs, creating a private welfare state that paralleled the more limited public programs. Civil rights laws adopted in the early 1960s banned racial and other forms of discrimination in employment decisions.

One other major development was little noticed at the time. Organized labor stopped growing, partly because it remained too closely wedded to occupations, such as factory work, that were declining, and partly because the employer counterattack that began in the late 1930s at last became effective. A major factor in the union growth of the 1930s and 1940s had been an activist, sympathetic government. Although some postwar employer groups sought to challenge unions directly, others adopted a more subtle and successful approach, attacking union power in the regulatory agencies and the courts and promoting employment policies that reduced the benefits of membership. These attacks gained momentum during the administration of Dwight D. Eisenhower (1953–1961). One additional tactic, locating new plants in southern or western states where there was no tradition of organization, also helped to isolate organized workers.

The impact of these varied trends became inescapable in the 1970s, when the economy experienced the most severe downturns since the 1930s. Manufacturing was devastated. Plant closings in traditional industrial areas were common during the recessions of 1973–1975 and 1979–1982. Well-known industrial corporations such as International Harvester collapsed. Unemployment reached levels that rivaled the 1930s. Productivity declined and real wages stagnated. Exploiting anxiety over the future of the economy, Republican Ronald Reagan ran successfully on a platform that attacked the welfare state and industrial relations policies that emphasized collective bargaining.

A. Philip Randolph. The organizer and head of the Brotherhood of Sleeping Car Porters, which won a long struggle for better working conditions, and the most important labor leader fighting discrimination against African Americans, especially in the workplace and in the military, for a half century. FISK UNIVERSITY LIBRARY

The experience of the 1970s accelerated the changes that were only dimly evident in earlier years, creating a labor force that was more diverse in composition and overwhelmingly engaged in service occupations. The return of favorable employment conditions in the 1980s was almost entirely a result of service-sector developments. Formal education, antidiscrimination laws, and affirmative action policies opened high-paying jobs to ethnic and racial minorities, including a growing number of immigrants. At the same time, industry continued its movement into rural areas, especially in the South and West, and unions continued to decline. Indeed, according to the 2000 census, only 14 percent of American workers belonged to unions.

The results of these complex developments are difficult to summarize. On the one hand, by the 1990s many workers enjoyed seemingly limitless opportunities and accumulated unprecedented wealth. Severe labor shortages in many industries attracted a flood of immigrants and made the United States a magnet for upwardly mobile workers everywhere. On the other hand, many other workers, especially those who worked in agriculture or industry and had little formal education, found that the combination of economic and technological change, a less activist government, and union decline depressed their wages and made their prospects bleak. At the turn of the century, the labor force and American society were divided in ways that would have seemed impossible only a few decades before.

BIBLIOGRAPHY

Bernstein, Irving. *Turbulent Years: A History of the American Worker, 1933–1941.* Boston: Houghton Mifflin, 1970.

Blatz, Perry K. *Democratic Miners: Work and Labor Relations in the Anthracite Coal Industry, 1875–1925.* Albany: State University of New York Press, 1994.

Blewett, Mary H. *Men, Women, and Work: Class, Gender, and Protest in the New England Shoe Industry, 1780–1910.* Urbana: University of Illinois Press, 1988.

Brody, David. *Steelworkers in America: The Nonunion Era.* Cambridge, Mass.: Harvard University Press, 1960. Illini edition, Urbana: University of Illinois Press, 1998.

———. *In Labor's Cause: Main Themes on the History of the American Worker.* New York: Oxford University Press, 1993.

Christie, Robert A. *Empire in Wood: A History of the Carpenters' Union.* Ithaca, N.Y.: Cornell University Press, 1956.

Commons, John R., et al. *History of Labour in the United States.* 4 vols. New York: Macmillan, 1918–1935.

Dubofsky, Melvyn. *We Shall Be All: A History of the Industrial Workers of the World.* 2d ed. Urbana: University of Illinois Press, 1988.

———. *The State and Labor in Modern America.* Chapel Hill: University of North Carolina Press, 1994.

Dubofsky, Melvyn, and Warren Van Tine. *John L. Lewis: A Biography.* New York: Quadrangle, 1977.

Dubofsky, Melvyn, and Warren Van Tine, eds. *Labor Leaders in America.* Urbana: University of Illinois Press, 1987.

Fine, Sidney. *Sit-Down: The General Motors Strike of 1936–37.* Ann Arbor: University of Michigan Press, 1969.

Gitelman, H. M. *Legacy of the Ludlow Massacre: A Chapter in American Industrial Relations.* Philadelphia: University of Pennsylvania Press, 1988.

Gross, James. *Broken Promise: The Subversion of U.S. Labor Relations Policy, 1947–1994.* Philadelphia: Temple University Press, 1995.

Jacoby, Sanford M. *Employing Bureaucracy: Managers, Unions, and the Transformation of Work in American Industry, 1900–1945.* New York: Columbia University Press, 1985.

Kochan, Thomas A., et al. *The Transformation of American Industrial Relations.* New York: Basic Books, 1986.

Lankton, Larry D. *Cradle to Grave: Life, Work, and Death at the Lake Superior Copper Mines.* New York: Oxford University Press, 1991.

Lichtenstein, Nelson. *The Most Dangerous Man in Detroit: Walter Reuther and the Fate of American Labor.* New York: Basic Books, 1995.

Lingenfelter, Richard E. *The Hardrock Miners: A History of the Mining Labor Movement in the American West, 1863–1893.* Berkeley: University of California Press, 1974.

McMurry, Donald L. *The Great Burlington Strike of 1888: A Case Study in Labor Relations.* Cambridge, Mass.: Harvard University Press, 1956.

Montgomery, David. *Beyond Equality: Labor and the Radical Republicans, 1862–1872.* New York: Knopf, 1967.

———. *The Fall of the House of Labor: The Workplace, the State, and American Labor Activism, 1865–1925.* New York: Cambridge University Press, 1987.

Nelson, Daniel. *Managers and Workers: Origins of the Twentieth Century Factory System in the United States, 1880–1920.* Madison: University of Wisconsin Press, 1995.

———. *Shifting Fortunes: The Rise and Decline of American Labor, from the 1820s to the Present.* Chicago: Ivan R. Dee, 1997.

Oestreicher, Richard Jules. *Solidarity and Fragmentation: Working People and Class Consciousness in Detroit, 1875–1900.* Urbana: University of Illinois Press, 1986.

Stockton, Frank T. *The International Molders Union of North America.* Baltimore: Johns Hopkins University Press, 1921.

Voss, Kim. *The Making of American Exceptionalism: The Knights of Labor and Class Formation in the Nineteenth Century.* Ithaca, N.Y.: Cornell University Press, 1993.

Wilentz, Sean. *Chants Democratic: New York City and the Rise of the American Working Class, 1788–1850.* New York: Oxford University Press, 1984.

Zeiger, Robert H. *The CIO, 1935–1955.* Chapel Hill: University of North Carolina Press, 1995.

Daniel Nelson

See also **American Federation of Labor–Congress of Industrial Organizations; Arbitration; Business Unionism; Collective Bargaining; Strikes; Work.**

LABOR, DEPARTMENT OF, established as the tenth executive department by departing President William Howard Taft on 4 March 1913. Demands for a department of labor originated with a conference of labor representatives held in Louisville, Kentucky, in 1865 to deal with post–Civil War labor problems, and the National Labor Union took up the demands. Following the example of Massachusetts in 1869, thirteen other states established bureaus of labor by 1883. In 1884, the Bureau of Labor was established by statute in the Department of the Interior "to collect information upon the subject of labor." The KNIGHTS OF LABOR and the American Federation of Labor continued the pressure for a department. In partial response, the Bureau of Labor was elevated to independent, but noncabinet, status as the Department of Labor in 1888. Legislation in 1903 established the Department of Commerce and Labor with cabinet status, with the Bureau of Labor continuing to study labor conditions. Renamed the Bureau of Labor Statistics, the bureau was installed in the new Department of Labor in 1913.

The mission of the new department was to "foster, promote and develop the welfare of wage-earners, to improve their working conditions, and to advance their opportunities for profitable employment." Besides the Bureau of Labor Statistics, the department included the Children's Bureau and the Bureau of Immigration and Naturalization, with the addition of the Conciliation Service in 1918 and the Women's Bureau by statute in 1920. With labor legislation directed at the problems of economic depression in the 1930s, the department acquired significant administrative responsibilities for the first time. The Wagner-Peyser Act established the U.S. Employment Service in the department in 1933. Administration of working conditions for construction workers was assigned under the Davis-Bacon Act of 1931 and for other workers under the Public Contracts Act of 1936. The FAIR LABOR STANDARDS ACT of 1938 assigned administration of national minimum-wage levels.

From 1958 to 1970, the Labor Department developed to address new post-war problems. Congress passed the Welfare and Pension Plans Disclosure Act and the Labor-Management Reporting and Disclosure Act in 1958–1959. Under the Manpower Development and Training Act of 1962, the department developed national policies to deal with the impact of technology on the growing labor force. Activism by liberal doctors and labor advocates prompted Congress to pass the Occupational Safety and Health Act (OSHA) of 1970, which set and enforced national standards of workplace safety and health. The Department of Labor has grown steadily, as has its functional organization, with assistant secretaries bearing line responsibility for such individual organizations as the Manpower Administration, the Labor-Management Services Administration, the Employment Standards Administration, and the Occupational and Safety Administration. The Bureau of Labor Statistics remains a separate administrative entity.

The role of the Department of Labor as the representative of a specific interest—namely, workers—has been a matter for periodic discussion. Responding to the broad class mandate inherent in its creation in 1913, the U.S. Department of Labor initially—and periodically since—sought to defend workers' rights and mediate labor-management relations. As a result, the department has been one of the federal government's more controversial agencies. Given the volatile combination of class interests and partisan political conflict that it embodies, the department has seen its mission continuously modified by succeeding presidential administrations and each new secretary of labor. Although the first three secretaries of labor—from 1913 to 1933—had been officials of labor unions, since 1933 the backgrounds of the secretaries have been more diverse, including social work; government administration; and legal, academic, and management specialization in labor-management relations.

In the early Cold War period, Congress passed the Taft-Hartley Act in 1947, over President Harry S. Truman's veto; the act attacked the National Labor Relations Board and sought to reconfigure U.S. labor relations in ways more favorable to employers. Taft-Hartley emphasized workers' right *not* to unionize by outlawing closed

shops; authorized the president to intervene in labor disputes with a "national emergency" injunction; required the National Labor Relations Board to seek injunctions against unions involved in secondary boycotts or jurisdictional strikes; and required union officials to sign affidavits swearing they were not and never had been members of the Communist Party. It was viewed by both its advocates and its opponents as a means to limit labor's ability to organize, and it curtailed the Labor Department's ability to protect workers.

In 1977, Democratic President Jimmy Carter installed economist Ray Marshall of the University of Texas as secretary of labor, prompting a change in direction once again. Under Marshall's direction, the Department of Labor became a much more activist agency than it had been in the recent past. A recognized authority on national manpower policy, Marshall devoted much attention to the employment and training problems that accompanied the stagnant economy of the 1970s. He revised and strengthened the Job Corps, created in 1964, and the department's employment and training programs, which had been reorganized in 1973 under the revenue-sharing provisions of the Comprehensive Employment and Training Act (CETA). The Department of Labor also created a substantial array of new programs to provide job training for veterans, retraining for displaced workers, and skills instruction and development to reduce the persistently high rate of youth unemployment. Meanwhile, with some success, business critics urged executive and legislative leaders to limit the mandate of one of the department's most important but controversial agencies—OSHA. Established in 1970 and charged with ensuring safe working conditions for everyone in the United States, OSHA aroused the ire of employers who resented federal intervention in the workplace. With Marshall's encouragement and support, OSHA director Eula Bingham reorganized the agency and streamlined its rules and procedures, leaving it in a stronger position to protect worker health and safety and to withstand the Republican assaults on the department's budget during the 1980s.

However, the department as a whole suffered during the 1980s, when President Ronald Reagan's administration cut its budget and prompted charges that it failed to enforce workers' rights. In 1981, President Reagan used lockout techniques against the Professional Air Traffic Controllers' union, which struck for higher wages and better working conditions. After President Reagan replaced the striking air traffic controllers with nonunion workers (retirees and military workers), other companies increased their use of the lockout, and both workers and employers got the signal that the administration would not be supporting workers' right to organize.

Regulatory relief became the predominant theme of the Republican administrations of Presidents Reagan (1981–1989) and George H. W. Bush (1989–1993). Reflecting the changing political agenda to "less government," the Department of Labor devoted increased attention to reforming or eliminating regulations that employers found cumbersome and coercive. It also devoted more time and energy to developing cooperative programs between government and business to address the problems of unemployment, occupational training and retraining, and U.S. industrial competitiveness. Reflecting this new emphasis, Congress passed the Job Training Partnership Act in 1982, which replaced CETA, and encouraged employers to help design new programs to train the unemployed. In similar fashion, where Democratic administrations had supported and encouraged trade unionism and collective bargaining, Republicans considered the adversarial relationship inherent in such negotiations costly and inefficient. The new emphasis on industrial harmony was institutionalized in the department's renamed Bureau of Labor-Management Relations and Cooperative Programs. New appointments to the Office of Secretary of Labor also reflected the department's changing mandate. Rather than people who considered themselves working-class spokespeople, the Republican appointees tended to be either businesspeople (Raymond Donovan, 1981–1985, and Ann Dore McLaughlin, 1987–1989) or professional politicians (William E. Brock, 1985–1987; Elizabeth H. Dole, 1989–1991; and Lynn Martin, 1991–1993). Democrat Bill Clinton's election in 1992, and his choice in 1993 of Richard Reich to head the Department of Labor, once again produced a significant shift in the agency's policies and procedures. Like Marshall, Reich, an academic economist, embraced the role of working-class advocate in the federal government.

However, the tide turned in the early twenty-first century, when the Labor Department, under President George W. Bush, fell under heavy fire from worker advocates for easing up on workplace enforcement and backing off its commitments. In 2001, a Republican-dominated Congress caused national outcry by overturning the department's ergonomic workplace standards. The decision brought accusations that the Bush administration and Congress cared more about protecting corporations from inconvenient laws than about protecting the nation's workers. A series of forums that the Labor Department called in July 2001 to discuss ergonomic standards drew protesters, and garnered an accusation from Richard L. Trumka, secretary-treasurer of American Federation of Labor and Congress of Industrial Organizations (AFL-CIO), that the Labor Department was holding hearings "designed to lead to no action." Though the forums had more than 100 witnesses, critics pointed to the prevalence of industry participants and the absence of testimony by injured workers as a sign that the department was not committed to worker protection. In the wake of this development, the terrorist bombings of 11 September 2001 led President Bush to redirect funding from numerous domestic programs into the military to fund a "war on terrorism"; one casualty was the Labor Department's funding for such programs as job training and community colleges. The long-term effects of the war

on terrorism upon the Labor Department remain to be seen.

BIBLIOGRAPHY

Ditomaso, Nancy. *The Department of Labor: Class Politics and Public Bureaucracy.* Madison: University of Wisconsin Press, 1977.

Gould, William B. *Labored Relations: Law, Politics, and the NLRB—A Memoir.* Cambridge, Mass.: MIT Press, 2000.

Gross, James A. *Broken Promise: The Subversion of U.S. Labor Relations Policy, 1947–1994.* Philadelphia: Temple University Press, 1995.

Laughlin, Kathleen A. *Women's Work and Public Policy: A History of the Women's Bureau, U.S. Department of Labor, 1945–1970.* Boston: Northeastern University Press, 2000.

McCartin, Joseph A. *Labor's Great War: The Struggle for Industrial Democracy and the Origins of Modern American Labor Relations, 1912–1921.* Chapel Hill: University of North Carolina Press, 1997.

O'Brien, Ruth Ann. *Workers' Paradox: the Republican Origins of New Deal Labor Policy, 1886–1935.* Chapel Hill: University of North Carolina Press, 1998.

Taylor, Benjamin J., and Fred Witney. *U.S. Labor Relations Law: Historical Development.* Englewood Cliffs, N.J.: Prentice Hall, 1992.

Tomlins, Christopher L. *The State and the Unions: Labor Relations, Law, and the Organized Labor Movement in America, 1880–1960.* New York: Cambridge University Press, 1985.

Gary Fink
Joseph P. Goldberg / D. B.

See also **American Federation of Labor-Congress of Industrial Organizations; Child Labor; Clayton Act, Labor Provisions; Conciliation and Mediation, Labor; Contract Labor, Foreign; Lockout; Medicine, Occupational; New Deal; Occupational Safety and Health Act; Work.**

LABOR DAY is observed annually in honor of working people on the first Monday in September in all the states and territories, including Puerto Rico and the Virgin Islands. The day was originally conceived in 1882 by Peter J. McGuire, the radical founder and indefatigable warrior of the Brotherhood of Carpenters and Joiners of New York. On 8 May, McGuire proposed to the New York City Central Labor Union that the first Monday in September, because it fell midway between the Fourth of July and Thanksgiving Day, be set aside annually as a "labor day." His effort bore fruit on Tuesday, 5 September 1882, when workers in New York City held a large parade and a festival sponsored by the Central Labor Union and the Knights of Labor. In 1884, the New Yorkers held a parade on the first Monday of September and designated that day as the annual Labor Day. The agitation in New York City was soon followed by labor unions in other states, which staged vigorous campaigns in their state legislatures for the establishment of Labor Day as a legal holiday. Their earliest victories were in Oregon and Colorado, where Labor Day was declared to be a state holiday in February and March 1887, respectively. The next year the American Federation of Labor passed a resolution for the adoption of a Labor Day at its St. Louis, Missouri, convention. Thirty states had followed the lead of Oregon and Colorado by the time the first Monday in September was made a national holiday by an act of Congress, with the bill signed into law by President Grover Cleveland on 28 June 1894. In the early twenty-first century, Labor Day parades, rallies, festivals, and speeches were still organized by labor unions across the country and often supported by political leaders. Because of the shrinking popular base of traditional labor unions, however, most Americans tended to regard the day merely as the finale of a long summer of fun in which hot dogs, barbecues, and picnics reigned.

BIBLIOGRAPHY

Commons, John R., et al. *History of Labour in the United States.* 4 vols. New York: Macmillan, 1918–1935.

David Park

See also **Holidays and Festivals.**

LABOR LEGISLATION AND ADMINISTRATION.

Labor legislation in America has gone through four distinct periods. Before the late nineteenth century, legislative intervention in the master-servant relationship had been extremely rare and episodic, and common law and court policy had long prevailed as the dominant legal framework. However, in the late nineteenth and early twentieth centuries (especially during the Progressive Era), waves of protective labor legislation swept across the country, providing industrial workers with some protection against flagrantly unfair and inhumane labor practices by employers. Then during the 1930s, labor legislation began to focus on the organization of labor, and leadership was taken over by the federal government. Since the 1960s, labor laws have reached far beyond unions and industrial workers, offering protection against discrimination because of race, gender, age, or disabilities.

In colonial America, when the majority of workers were domestic servants, apprentices, temporary helpers, indentured servants, or slaves, and when wage labor for a livelihood was the exception, the master-servant relationship was hierarchical and mutually obligatory. Many legal commentators and treatise writers of the period noted that the master was supposed to afford the servant provisions and medical care. In colonial Massachusetts, laws and indentures accorded the servant certain rights, such as food, clothing, shelter, safe tools, and the right not to suffer bodily harm or cruel treatment. On the other hand, such paternalistic arrangements often imposed harsh terms on the servant. When the servant failed to measure up to the norms or terms of labor, the servant might be disciplined, even whipped, by the master or imprisoned by a court. In colonial South Carolina (and Massachusetts, to

a lesser extent), the master had statutory permission to put his servant to work for one week—not to exceed a total of two years—for every day the servant was absent from work without consent. In many colonies and localities, voluntary idleness was illegal, and a small number of the "indigent," "vagrant," or "dissolute" persons and criminals were bound to labor for limited terms, usually not exceeding one year. Yet, until the end of the eighteenth century there had been little, if any, legislative action or litigation involving free adult workers.

In the late eighteenth and early nineteenth centuries visible groups of gainfully employed artisans and mechanics appeared in increasing numbers in urban and early industrializing centers and seaports. When those workers envisioned their collective interests and organized as trade societies and brotherhoods, state courts suppressed their efforts by invoking a doctrine of common law that defined such activity as "criminal conspiracy inimical to the general welfare." The leading cases were *Commonwealth v. Pullis* (Pennsylvania, 1806), *State of Maryland v. Powley* (1809), and *People v. Melvin* (New York City, 1809). The judiciary's hostility toward labor would continue until the mid-1930s.

During the first half of the nineteenth century, state courts formulated a new legal framework that viewed the master-servant relationship as a contract between two free and equal parties. The old paternalism persisted for resident servants, juvenile apprentices, and slaves, but a new court policy denied wage workers medical care for injuries resulting from an accident caused by a fellow servant or the injured worker himself. It was also reasoned that an injured worker had assumed the risk of the trade upon entering employment, and that such risk was compensated through wages. Elaborated in the early 1840s, the three so-called employers' defenses would remain until the 1910s. The American judiciary maintained a strong role in subsidizing industrialization—mostly at the expense of workers—by reducing the employers' liability and expenses related to labor organization.

In the 1880s and 1890s, industrialization was in full swing, industrial accidents were mounting, and workers were often treated unfairly and left at the mercy of the marketplace. A growing number of social reformers and public leaders began to lend a sympathetic ear to industrial workers' grievances and to attack the pro-business legal framework. In consequence, a number of state legislatures enacted the first significant labor laws. For example, laws were passed to prescribe safety standards, restrict hours of labor, and regulate methods and terms of wage payment. Although the constitutionality of such laws were sustained by some state courts, most failed to pass judicial muster—most notably *Godcharles v. Wigeman* (Pennsylvania, 1886; struck down an anti-truck act) and *Richie v. People* (Illinois, 1895; struck down an eight-hour law for women).

The legislative initiative and the occasionally favorable judicial response were only a prelude to a full-fledged reform movement of the Progressive Era (c. 1897–1917). During this period, broad interpersonal and interorganizational coalitions developed, dedicated to improving working and living conditions for industrial and mercantile workers. With labor (especially state federations of labor) as the vanguard, the reform coalitions included liberal churches and ministers preaching the "social gospel"; settlement houses and charity organizations; muckraking journalists and popular magazines; reform-minded college professors; progressive public officials and inspectors at bureaus of labor or labor statistics; and pro-labor civic organizations. In addition, dozens of state labor laws were precipitated by a series of industrial calamities, including the 1907 Monongah mine disaster in West Virginia (362 killed); the 1909 Cherry mine disaster in Illinois (259 killed); the 1911 fires at the Triangle Shirtwaist Company in New York City (146 killed); and in 1914, a fire at an Edison lamp factory in West Orange, New Jersey (25 killed).

The confluence of reform coalitions and tragic industrial accidents led to the most rapid and intensive labor legislation in American history, including employers' liability laws; safety laws for factories, workshops, railroads, and mines; hour laws for men and women; laws regulating the terms and conditions of wage payment; prohibition of the trucking (company store) system; convict labor and child labor laws; greater protection for collective bargaining and trade unions; and laws regulating fees and abusive practices by private employment agencies. The most prominent achievement was the passage of workmen's compensation acts, which by 1920 had been enacted by the federal government and by all but six states.

Although most progressive labor legislation was enacted state by state, federal legislation provided the model for many state laws. The Federal Employers' Liability acts of 1906 and 1908 were more liberal than most state counterparts, and earlier than many. The federal government took the initiative in probing the possibility of workmen's compensation, producing the Federal Workmen's Compensation Act of 1908, the earliest viable compensation law in the country. This was also true of the federal eight-hour laws of 1892 and 1912, as well as the Esch Industrial Hygiene and Occupational Disease Act of 1912. A federal law of 1912 even offered postal workers strong union protection and job security. In 1915, Congress eliminated the use of the stopwatch in government plants earlier than any state did. The federal government was also the leader in safety inspection and accident prevention and publicized the need of old age pensions.

Employers' associations vigorously attacked progressive labor laws as too costly, injurious to interstate competition, unconstitutional, and likely to serve as an "entering wedge" for further drastic measures. Yet, despite the major aberration of *Lochner v. New York* (U.S. Supreme Court, 1905; struck down New York's ten-hour law for bakers) courts rejected employers' objections and sustained most progressive laws as a valid exercise of the po-

lice power by the legislature. As shown most dramatically by the *Holden v. Hardy* decision of the U.S. Supreme Court (1898, upheld Utah's eight-hour law for miners and smelters) progressive jurisprudence put the public welfare above private property rights, recognized the unequal power relationship between employer and employee, showed an enormous amount of deference to the will and wisdom of the legislature, adapted law pragmatically to socioeconomic and technological changes, debunked the freedom-of-contract fiction, stripped employers of many of their vested interests in common law, and merged the welfare of workers and the public.

Progressives learned from the past when several "voluntary" labor laws had proved to be only "dead letters," due to employers' noncompliance. Consequently, advocates of progressive legislation equipped the laws with financial and legal penalty clauses—in some cases even criminal penalties with imprisonment terms—and prohibited contracting out of the laws. Many laws were also backed by a newly created or strengthened administrative apparatus with a far greater staff and financial resources than ever before. For example, the Industrial Commissions in several states (most notably in Wisconsin) were given powers to interpret the laws quasi-judicially, write administrative guidelines, issue administrative orders, and penalize or prosecute non-complying employers. Progressive labor legislation, adjudication, and administration occasioned a "radical departure" from the laissez-faire and pro-business past. Furthermore, those progressive ideas would serve as a building block for the labor-relations governance in the following decades.

Progressive labor legislation had a critical flaw, however. While supporting the welfare of industrial workers as an integral part of the broader public welfare, it fell short of recognizing labor's right to organize and promote the exclusive interests of individual unions. In particular, state and federal supreme courts invalidated most measures intended to promote labor organization, and instead they legitimized "yellow-dog contracts" whereby employees signed away the right to unionize as a precondition of employment; held collective action of a union as an antitrust violation; and struck down laws protecting union membership. After a little more than a decade of little progress in protective labor legislation, and even a few setbacks in the 1920s, labor interests emerged as the overarching issue when the very foundation of the nation's economic life and social fabric was in critical jeopardy.

As the first major pro-union measure, the NORRIS-LaGUARDIA ACT (1932) outlawed yellow-dog contracts and banned federal injunctions in labor disputes, except under carefully defined conditions. Pro-union legislation was further amplified by the NATIONAL LABOR RELATIONS ACT (or Wagner Act, 1935), the single most important labor law in American history. Declaring to redress the historical inequality of bargaining power between management and labor, the act guaranteed labor "the right to self-organization, to form, join, or assist labor organizations, to bargain collectively through representatives of their own choosing, and to engage in concerted activities for the purpose of collective bargaining or other mutual aid and protection." It enumerated and prohibited "unfair practices" by employers to undercut labor organization and collective bargaining. The act created a permanent independent agency—the National Labor Relations Board (NLRB)—with the power to conduct and certify union elections and to prevent unfair labor practices by employers. With this epoch-making legislation, organized labor grew from some 3.5 million workers in 1935 to almost 15 million in 1947. These two pro-union measures were followed in 1938 by the FAIR LABOR STANDARDS ACT, which established a minimum wage and a maximum workweek.

After World War II, the public became more conservative and complacent, and legislation reversed some of the more radical legislation of the 1930s. While retaining most of the collective-bargaining provisions of the Wagner Act, the Labor-Management Relations Act (the TAFT-HARTLEY ACT, 1947) prohibited the closed shop (mandatory union membership by employees) and permitted the union shop only on a majority vote of the employees. It also outlawed jurisdictional strikes and secondary boycotts and stipulated a sixty-day "cooling-off" period at the close of a contract. An additional eighty-day cooling-off period might be ordered by the president when the nation's health or safety was deemed at risk. The act also encouraged states to pass right-to-work laws by allowing state anti-union measures to preempt federal legislation. In 1959, the act was amended by the Labor-Management Reporting and Disclosure Act (the Landrum-Griffin Act) to further restrict secondary boycotts and the right to picket, regulate internal financial and managerial affairs of unions, and provide the states with greater freedom to govern labor relations within their jurisdictions.

The 1960s opened a new chapter in the history of American labor law by addressing such entirely new issues as race, sex, age, disability, and family. This was a natural outcome of factors such as the civil rights movement, new social norms, a gradually shrinking trade and industrial workforce, changes in technology, and an increasingly global economy. Since the 1960s, labor laws have come to cover practically all working Americans.

The opening page of this new chapter was the EQUAL PAY ACT (1963). The act prohibited gender-based wage discrimination between workers doing similar kinds of work under similar conditions. The next year saw Title VII of the CIVIL RIGHTS ACT OF 1964—the most sweeping labor measure ever. It barred discrimination in every aspect of employment, based on race, color, ethnic origin, sex, or religion. In 1986 sexual harassment was incorporated into Title VII. In 1967 the Age Discrimination in Employment Act—supplemented by the Age Discrimination Act of 1975—prohibited discrimination against persons forty years of age and older, based solely on age.

For the first time in 1973, with the Rehabilitation Act, Congress prohibited workplace discrimination against employees with disabilities in the federal government or in the private sector receiving federal assistance. The limited scope of the act was greatly extended by the AMERICANS WITH DISABILITIES ACT (ADA) in 1990, which came to cover some 43 million people in the private and nonfederal public sector. In 1999, the Work Incentives Improvement Act made it easier for people with disabilities to return to work by expanding health care coverage and assistance by the Social Security Administration. Also significant was the FAMILY AND MEDICAL LEAVE ACT (1993), which mandated up to twelve weeks of unpaid leave for employees with at least a year of service, so that they could balance the demands of the workplace with their family and medical needs.

The enforcement of many of the labor laws enacted since the 1960s rests with the EQUAL EMPLOYMENT OPPORTUNITY COMMISSION (EEOC), created in 1965. EEOC enforces the Equal Pay Act, Title VII, the Age Discrimination in Employment Act, the Rehabilitation Act, and the ADA by utilizing such enforcement tools as administrative resolution, mediation, outreach, educational and technical assistance, on-site reviews, and litigation in federal court. The agency operates fifty field offices nationwide in cooperation with state and local fair employment practices agencies. The CIVIL RIGHTS ACT OF 1991 provided for both compensatory and punitive damages in cases of willful violations of Title VII, the Rehabilitation Act, and the ADA. And the Occupational Safety and Health Administration (OSHA), created within the Department of Labor, enforces the OCCUPATIONAL SAFETY AND HEALTH ACT (1970), regulating the health and safety conditions in nearly 7 million workplaces for more than 100 million private-sector workers by means of workplace inspections, educational programs, citations, and penalties.

In the final decades of the twentieth century, the enforcement of protective labor laws tended to be relatively strict during Democratic administrations and lax during Republican administrations. Historically, the labor laws since the 1960s have made a remarkable contribution to redressing longstanding injustices and prejudices against minorities, women, and people with disabilities, yet substantial discrimination still exists. Similarly, many basic rights and interests of unskilled, migrant, and low-paid workers have long been largely neglected.

BIBLIOGRAPHY

Commons, John Rogers, et al. *History of Labor in the United States.* 4 vols. New York: Macmillan, 1921–1935.

Dubofsky, Melvyn. *The State and Labor in Modern America.* Chapel Hill: University of North Carolina Press, 1994.

Dubofsky, Melvyn, and Stephen Burwood, eds. *The Law and the New Deal.* New York: Garland, 1990.

Forbath, William. *Law and the Shaping of the American Labor Movement.* Cambridge, Mass.: Harvard University Press, 1991.

Lehrer, Susan. *Origins of Protective Labor Legislation for Women, 1905–1925.* Albany: State University of New York Press, 1987.

Linder, Marc. *The Employment Relationship in Anglo-American Law: A Historical Perspective.* Westport, Conn.: Greenwood Press, 1989.

Montgomery, David. *The Fall of the House of Labor: The Workplace, the State, and American Labor Activism, 1865–1925.* New York: Cambridge University Press, 1987.

Morris, Richard B. *Government and Labor in Early America.* New York: Columbia University Press, 1946.

Steinfeld, Robert J. *The Invention of Free Labor: The Employment Relation in English and American Law and Culture, 1350–1870.* Chapel Hill: University of North Carolina Press, 1991.

Tomlins, Christopher. *The State and the Unions: Labor Relations, Law and the Organized Labor Movement, 1880–1960.* New York: Cambridge University Press, 1985.

David Park

See also **Child Labor; Contract Labor, Foreign; Convict Labor Systems; Injunctions, Labor; Labor; Labor, Department of; Progressive Movement; Trade Unions; Wages and Hours of Labor, Regulation of.**

LABOR PARTIES. The world's first labor parties appeared in a number of American cities after 1828, usually on the initiative of newly founded city labor organizations. They supported a variety of causes important to working men but failed to develop into a national force and did not survive the depression that began in 1837. Since then the city labor party has been a recurring phenomenon. The movement in New York between 1886 and 1888, for instance, attracted national interest by supporting the candidacy of Henry George for mayor. Similar labor parties appeared at the same time in Chicago and other cities and occasionally grew to state level organizations. In 1900 organized labor in San Francisco promoted a Union Labor party.

The first labor organization of national scope, the NATIONAL LABOR UNION, formed a short-lived political party between 1870 and 1872. As well as supporting labor demands such as the eight-hour day, its platform reflected the then-current greenback agitation, demonstrating the connection with farmers' movements that characterized most labor politics in the late nineteenth century. Thus, the Greenback Labor Party, founded nationally in 1878, received the support of the KNIGHTS OF LABOR, whose division into district and local assemblies was admirably suited to political activity. Terence V. Powderly, the best-known leader of the Knights, was elected mayor of Scranton, Pa., on a Greenback Labor ticket in 1878 and later helped found the Populist Party in 1889. By then, however, the American Federation of Labor (AFL) had replaced the Knights as the chief national labor organization. The AFL convention of 1894 refused to support the

labor-wing of the Populist Party, partly owing to the parliamentary tactics of its president, Samuel Gompers.

Meanwhile, some Socialist trade unionists, chiefly of German origin, had founded the SOCIALIST LABOR PARTY in 1877. Their party sometimes participated in the various movements already discussed, but Socialist doctrines often caused dissension, which contributed to the demise of "united labor" parties. After the foundation of the more moderate SOCIALIST PARTY OF AMERICA in 1901, its members within the AFL constantly argued for endorsement of the Socialist Party, but they never succeeded. Had the AFL followed the example of the British Trade Union Council in forming a labor party in 1906, as seemed a possibility after several adverse court decisions, many Socialists would probably have supported it.

After World War I, a labor party finally did emerge. Initiated by several state federations of labor and city centrals, the National Labor Party was formed in 1919, and it renewed the earlier policy of alliance with farmers' groups by organizing the FARMER-LABOR PARTY the following year. The AFL remained aloof. Only in 1924 did it join a coalition of farmers, labor groups, and Socialists in support of Robert M. La Follette's presidential candidacy under the banner of the Conference for Progressive Political Action (CPPA). Disappointing hopes for a new national party, the CPPA disintegrated after the election. The Farmer-Labor Party survived in Minnesota, and small minorities of trade unionists continued to support the Socialist Party of America, the Socialist Labor Party, and the Communist Party (under different names). The AMERICAN LABOR PARTY (now the Liberal Party) was a means by which mainly old-guard Socialists of the garment trades could support Franklin D. Roosevelt and still retain a separate identity from the Democratic Party. In general, the state of the American Left since 1924 has made the traditional "nonpartisan" policy of the AFL seem all the sounder. Adopted in 1906, this policy has aimed at "rewarding friends and punishing enemies" irrespective of party. In practice it has usually involved close alliance with the Democratic party.

BIBLIOGRAPHY

Dick, William M. *Labor and Socialism in America: The Gompers Era.* Port Washington, N.Y.: Kennikat Press, 1972.

McCormick, Richard L. *The Party Period and Public Policy: American Politics from the Age of Jackson to the Progressive Era.* New York: Oxford University Press, 1986.

Montgomery, David. *The Fall of the House of Labor: The Workplace, the State, and American Labor Activism, 1865–1925.* New York: Cambridge University Press, 1987.

*W. M. Dick/*a. g.

See also **American Federation of Labor–Congress of Industrial Organizations; Greenback Movement; Union Labor Party.**

LABOR'S NON-PARTISAN LEAGUE. Established in 1936, Labor's Non-Partisan League was instrumental in garnering worker support in the reelection of President Franklin Roosevelt. In the 1930s, labor militancy and strikes became prevalent across the nation, especially in the years 1934 and 1937. Organizing and union victories created a solidarity among workers that had previously eluded the labor movement in the United States. The emergence of the Congress of Industrial Organizations (CIO), led by the controversial John L. Lewis, symbolized the growth and changes in the labor movement.

In the spring of 1936, International Brotherhood of Teamsters president Daniel J. Tobin, whose union was an American Federation of Labor (AFL) affiliate and who was a leading opponent of Lewis's CIO, was appointed by Roosevelt to head the Democratic Party's National Labor Committee. Fearful of being put at a disadvantage, and realizing the New Deal created opportunity for more extensive labor gains in political policy, CIO leaders John L. Lewis and Sidney Hillman founded Labor's Non-Partisan League (LNPL). The LNPL sought to organize the working class vote for Roosevelt.

The head of the AFL's International Printing Pressmen's and Assistant's Union, George L. Berry, agreed to serve as chairman of the LNPL. Lewis took the position of director in charge of organization and Hillman served as treasurer. The phrase "Non-Partisan" was chosen for the League in order to emphasize that they claimed no ties with either of the two major political parties, and that they were open to union members of whatever faction. Every effort was made to win the support of all unions, with fifty-nine non-CIO unions joining the LNPL in 1936. However, it was Lewis's CIO-affiliated United Mine Workers of America that donated $500,000 to Roosevelt's campaign fund—the largest single contribution ever made at that point to a national political party. In total, the LNPL raised more than $1,500,000 for Roosevelt's 1936 campaign.

Some within labor disagreed with how closely the LNPL affiliated the CIO, and the labor movement, with the Democratic Party. Although most workers supported Roosevelt in the divisive 1936 election, the AFL officially remained uninvolved in politics and more radical elements thought labor should set up a third party rather than work with the country's two capitalist parties. Lewis insisted the LNPL strictly supported Roosevelt as an individual, not the Democratic Party. Consequently, he worked with the LNPL's New York State section to set up its own party, the American Labor Party, with its own line on the ballot.

The efforts of the LNPL and the votes of workers across the country were important in helping Roosevelt sweep the election of 1936, with the American Labor Party delivering New York State to the President. The effort demonstrated the effectiveness of direct labor action in politics. After the 1936 election, the Non-Partisan League made a commitment to ensure the election of other candidates dedicated to labor and progressive issues. In the next few years, the LNPL entered local elections in several states. It also organized support for New Deal legislation and sought to defeat all opponents of the New Deal in the 1938 congressional elections. It was, however, the 1936 election that marked the high point of influence for Labor's Non-Partisan League.

BIBLIOGRAPHY

Dubofsky, Melvyn. *Hard Work: The Making of Labor History.* Urbana: University of Illinois Press, 2000.

Dubofsky, Melvyn, and Foster Rhea Dulles. *Labor in America: A History.* 6th ed. Wheeling, Ill.: Harlan Davidson, 1999.

Goldfield, Michael. *The Decline of Organized Labor in the United States.* Chicago: University of Chicago Press, 1987.

Preis, Art. *Labor's Giant Step: Twenty Years of the CIO.* New York: Pathfinder Press, 1972.

Margaret Keady

See also **American Federation of Labor-Congress of Industrial Organizations; Labor Parties.**

LABORATORIES exist at the nexus of commerce, academic disciplines, and the State in early twenty-first-century America. Laboratories have been, and remain, a source of American military and economic power; their products indispensable elements for everyday life. How these organizations, ostensibly dedicated to the production of new knowledge and technologies, came to occupy such a central place in the landscape of American history is at one with the history of American science and technology as well as the growth of the American state during the twentieth century.

The Nineteenth Century

Although laboratories existed to test materials for railroads and small chemical concerns, as well as in some of the nation's colleges and universities such as Harvard and the Lawrence Scientific School at Yale, laboratories that we might recognize as such date from two distinct events—the 1862 MORRILL Land Grant Act and the establishment of the JOHNS HOPKINS UNIVERSITY in 1876. The Land Grant Act provided each state in the Union with funds to establish an institution of higher learning with an emphasis on practical knowledge. Hopkins followed the German model of higher education, with its reverence for research, albeit with substantial local modification. Uniting these two temporally distinct events was a common recognition that laboratories are sites where the producers and consumers of technical knowledge bargain over a host of meanings.

Prior to World War II (1939–1945), the federal government supported research that might serve to aid in the development of the nation's natural resources. Hence, agriculture was a major beneficiary of Department of Agriculture funding through the experiment station at each state's land grant institution. Successful researchers enrolled local farmers to support research and teaching that might aid the local agricultural economy. Distinctive and important results emerged from these local constellations, ranging from the famous Babcock butterfat test to the development of hybrid corn. Balancing local needs with their own agendas, land grant researchers enacted the American laboratory's dilemma—those charged with the production of knowledge were often the least powerful actors in any given locale.

The founding of the Johns Hopkins University is central for understanding the laboratory's history in America. Until the 1980s, historians viewed the establishment of this new institution in Baltimore as simply an attempt to bring the German model of research to American soil and break with the traditional American college, with its emphasis on the production of morally solid citizens. Under Daniel Coit Gilman's leadership, the new university hired professors trained in European universities, including Henry Rowland (physics), Ira Remsen (chemistry), Henry Newell Martin (biology) and J. J. Sylvester (mathematics). However, far from abandoning the college's traditional function, the new institution's laboratories and seminar rooms became new sites for the production of both knowledge and upstanding citizens, the majority of which became college teachers. Hopkins valued research, but it was inseparable from teaching. As Gilman once explained, "in the hunt for truth we are first men and then hunters"; the antebellum college's moral economy moved to the new university. So great was the connection between research and teaching that Remsen expressed dismay when Gilman left Hopkins to become the first president of the CARNEGIE INSTITUTION OF WASHINGTON (CIW), a private research institution.

Research and No Teaching
Separating research from teaching was among the great social accomplishments of the twentieth century. Private philanthropy and the emergence of the corporate laboratory were crucial in achieving this division. Around 1900, General Electric (GE) and AT&T established the first industrial research laboratories in America. Rather than produce students and theses, these laboratories produced new technologies and patents, the new corporate currency. For example, after many failures, Willis Whitney's group at GE invented the ductile tungsten filament for light bulbs, creating an array of patents that made GE untouchable in this growing market. At AT&T, researchers patented various important aspects of radio so as to maintain the system's monopoly on long distance communication. Far from being a university in exile, the corporate laboratory invented the firm's future and protected its investments. Industrial research was always basic to corporate needs, but that did not mean such work was mundane or less intellectually sophisticated than university-based research. GE's Irving Langmuir won his 1932 Nobel Prize in Chemistry for his explanation of a basic GE problem: why did light bulbs darken over time?

The establishment of the Rockefeller Institute for Medical Research (now ROCKEFELLER UNIVERSITY) and the CIW were also salient in separating research from teaching. Both were the products of the massive fortunes earned by the nineteenth century's great robber barons, but each had different ends. Rockefeller's Institute, founded in 1901, had as its mission the understanding and treatment of disease and the separation of biomedical research from the education of physicians. Sinclair Lewis's *Arrowsmith* offers a fine depiction of Institute life. The CIW, founded in 1902 with $10 million in U.S. Steel bonds, sought to find the "exceptional man" and free him from the distractions of everyday life with financial support. Finding the exceptional man proved difficult, and the CIW settled for the creation of an array of departments under the leadership of recognized leaders in the natural and social sciences as well as the humanities. Only the natural science departments survived into the twenty-first century. Cleaving research from teaching allowed the laboratory to become portable and capable of existing in a variety of contexts.

War and the State
The two world wars facilitated the growth of U.S. laboratories in ways that had been heretofore unthinkable. World War I (1914–1918) provided American science with a new institution, the National Research Council (NRC) of the National Academy of Sciences, which served as the agent for the Rockefeller Foundation's massive postdoctoral fellowship program, which provided American researchers with funds to study at elite institutions in the United States and Europe. These young researchers returned to take up faculty positions, establish laboratories, and effectively end America's reliance on Europe as a source of advanced training in the sciences. The 1920s also featured what one observer called a "fever of commercialized science," as laboratories spread throughout American industry. Although the Great Depression slowed the spread of industrial laboratories, the crisis also acted as a selection mechanism, allowing only those laboratories with independent sources of revenue or outstanding research to survive.

World War II and the massive mobilization of American science led by CIW President Vannevar Bush effectively made the nation's laboratories at one with the nation's security and prosperity. With the federal government's support, the MANHATTAN PROJECT, the American atomic bomb project, created a whole set of laboratories—including Los Alamos, Oak Ridge, and the Metallurgical Laboratory. Equally important were the laboratories established to develop radar (the MIT Radiation Laboratory), the proximity fuze (The Johns Hopkins University Applied Physics Laboratory), and guided missiles (CalTech's Jet Propulsion Laboratory). Government, but more specifically military patronage, heretofore unacceptable to the nation's scientific elite, propelled the laboratory into its central role in American life. Contrary to what many originally believed, American researchers found military problems a rich source of intellectually and technologically important questions. Even more importantly, there was someone eager to pay for answers—the armed services. Bush's famous 1945 report, *Science—The Endless Frontier,* and the visible demonstration of scientific power made at Hiroshima and Nagasaki, made the nation's laboratories and their products essential for America's coming struggle with the Soviet Union as well as the country's future economic growth.

During the Cold War, military patronage supported the largest expansion of the nation's research capabilities in both university and corporate laboratories. Four basic projects dominated the nation's laboratories: the development of the ballistic missile; the various attempts to design and build adequate continental defense systems; the introduction of quantitative methods into the social sciences; and the development of new technologies of surveillance and interpretation for the purposes of intelligence gathering. One basic technology emerging from this quartet was the networked digital computer, a tool now indispensable in so many contexts, including the modern research laboratory. In the biomedical disciplines, the NATIONAL INSTITUTES OF HEALTH (NIH) supported a similar and equally expensive expansion that had as its visible endeavor the human genome project.

In 1990, one-sixth of the nation's scientists and engineers were employed in more than 700 federally funded laboratories, including sixty-five Department of Defense and Department of Energy institutions, having annual budgets ranging from $15 billion to $21 billion, depending on who and what is counted. Even with the Cold War's end and the lessening of federal funds, the nation's laboratories flourished as government and industry rushed to continue the vital business of innovation.

The Present and the Future

As of 2000, industry outspent the federal government as the laboratory's greatest patron, but much of that work involved the laborious and difficult process of developing ideas into viable commercial products. University laboratories still account for the majority of basic research done in the United States. Although the events of 11 September 2001 will undoubtedly affect federal funding of research and lead to an increase in military research, the major areas in which laboratories will play a role will remain roughly as they were in 2000: biotechnology, including the massive private investment by the pharmaceutical industry as well as the ongoing attempts to harvest the work of the human genome project; nanotechnology, the attempt to develop sophisticated miniature technologies to act in a variety of contexts, including the human body and the battlefield; and information technology, as researchers attempt to make computers ubiquitous, easy to use, and capable of mining the vast data archives created by government and industry. In the first and last of these domains, corporate laboratories will play vital roles as individual firms attempt to bring new

therapies and new technologies to market. Nanotechnology will remain a ward of the state as researchers attempt to develop means of manipulating their newfound Lilliputian world effectively. If successful, corporations will adopt that research just as they adopted the biotechnology research originally done in NIH-funded laboratories. The twenty-first century, like the twentieth, will be the laboratory's century.

BIBLIOGRAPHY

Dennis, Michael Aaron. "Accounting for Research: New Histories of Corporate Laboratories and the Social History of American Science." *Social Studies of Science* 17 (1987): 479–518.

Geiger, Roger L. *Research and Relevant Knowledge: American Research Universities Since World War II.* New York: Oxford University Press, 1993.

———. *To Advance Knowledge: The Growth of American Research Universities, 1900–1940.* New York: Oxford University Press, 1986.

Gusterson, Hugh. *Nuclear Rites: A Weapons Laboratory at the End of the Cold War.* Berkeley: University of California Press, 1996.

James, Frank A. J. L., ed. *The Development of the Laboratory: Essays on the Place of Experiment in Industrial Civilization.* Basingstoke, Hampshire: Macmillan Press Scientific and Medical, 1989.

Kevles, Daniel J. *The Physicists: The History of a Scientific Community in Modern America.* New York: Vintage Books, 1979.

Kohler, Robert E. *Partners in Science: Foundations and Natural Scientists, 1900–1945.* Chicago: University of Chicago Press, 1991.

Koppes, Clayton R. *JPL and the American Space Program: A History of the Jet Propulsion Laboratory.* New Haven, Conn.: Yale University Press, 1982.

Leslie, Stuart W. *The Cold War and American Science: The Military-Industrial-Academic Complex at MIT and Stanford.* New York: Columbia University Press, 1993.

Reich, Leonard S. *The Making of American Industrial Research: Science and Business at GE and Bell, 1876–1926.* New York: Cambridge University Press, 1985.

Rhodes, Richard. *The Making of the Atomic Bomb.* New York: Simon and Schuster, 1986.

Rosenberg, Charles E. *No Other Gods: On Science and American Social Thought.* Revised and expanded edition. Baltimore: Johns Hopkins University Press, 1997 [1976].

Michael Aaron Dennis

"LAFAYETTE, WE ARE HERE." These words were spoken during World War I at the tomb of the Marquis de Lafayette during a speech honoring his heroic service in the cause of the American Revolution. On 4 July 1917 Paris celebrated American Independence Day. A U.S. battalion marched to the Picpus Cemetery, where several speeches were made at Lafayette's tomb. The historic words uttered on that occasion, "Lafayette, nous voilà" (Lafayette, we are here), have been popularly, but erroneously, attributed to General John J. Pershing. He stated that they were spoken by Colonel Charles E. Stanton, and "to him must go the credit for coining so happy and felicitous a phrase."

BIBLIOGRAPHY
Pershing, John J. *My Experiences in the World War.* New York: Stokes, 1931.

Smith, Gene. *Until the Last Trumpet Sounds: The Life of General of the Armies John J. Pershing.* New York: Wiley, 1998.

Joseph Mills Hanson / D. B.

See also **French in the American Revolution.**

LAFAYETTE ESCADRILLE, a squadron of volunteer American aviators who fought for France before the United States entered World War I. Formed on 17 April 1916, it changed its name, originally Escadrille Américaine, after German protest to Washington. A total of 267 men enlisted, of whom 224 qualified and 180 saw combat. Since only 12 to 15 pilots formed each squadron, many flew with French units. They wore French uniforms and most had noncommissioned officer rank. On 18 February 1918 the squadron was incorporated into the U.S. Air Service as the 103d Pursuit Squadron. The volunteers—credited with downing 199 German planes—suffered 19 wounded, 15 captured, 11 dead of illness or accident, and 51 killed in action.

BIBLIOGRAPHY
Whitehouse, Arthur George Joseph (Arch). *Legion of the Lafayette.* Garden City, N.Y.: Doubleday, 1962.

Charles B. MacDonald / C. W.

LAFAYETTE'S VISIT TO AMERICA. In February 1824, U.S. President James Monroe, and the U.S. Congress, invited the Marquis de Lafayette, the Revolutionary War hero and American icon, to visit the United States. Lafayette arrived in New York City on 24 August 1824 to an enormous patriotic reception and parade. Over the course of sixteen months, he toured virtually all areas of the country and spent time with Thomas Jefferson at MONTICELLO. Lafayette visited Braddock's Field, Niagara, and other scenes of the Revolution and culminated his trip with a fiftieth anniversary celebration of the Battle of Bunker Hill in Boston. He ended his tour with return visits to New York and Washington, D.C. On 7 December 1825, Lafayette departed for France. Since Lafayette arrived in the United States with little left of his inheritance, Congress rewarded his patriotism with $200,000 in cash and a township of land. At sixty-eight, Lafayette returned to his native home a rich man and an adopted son of America.

BIBLIOGRAPHY
Idzerda, Stanley J. *Lafayette: Hero of Two Worlds: The Art and Pageantry of His Farewell Tour of America, 1824–1825*: Flushing, N.Y.: Queens Museum, 1989.

Karen Rae Mehaffey

See also **Revolution, American: Military History.**

LAFFER CURVE THEORY. The Laffer Curve Theory states that tax revenues are related to the tax rate in such a manner that no revenue is generated at a tax rate of either zero or one hundred per cent, for at one hundred percent taxable activity would effectively cease; somewhere in between these tax rates lies the revenue-maximizing rate. Higher income taxes reduce the tax base by discouraging saving and labor supply. A reduction in after-tax income will reduce savings. An increase in the income tax rate changes the relative price of consumption and leisure, encouraging leisure. Beyond the maximum, higher rates would reduce income so much that revenues would decrease. Lowering tax rates indirectly encourages investment by increasing savings, potentially increasing income and thus tax revenues. The curve need not be symmetric or have a particular maximum. Professor Arthur Laffer and Representative Jack Kemp argued that a large reduction in U.S. income tax rates would reduce the deficit. This implied that previous policymakers were acting against their own true interests, imposing unpopular high tax rates that reduced the amount of revenue they had to spend. The Reagan Administration's tax cuts during the 1980s led to record large deficits, not to reduced deficits.

BIBLIOGRAPHY
Bosworth, Barry P. *Tax Incentives and Economic Growth.* Washington, D.C.: Brookings Institution, 1984.

Canto, Victor A., Douglas H. Joines, and Arthur B. Laffer. *Foundations of Supply-Side Economics: Theory and Evidence.* New York: Academic Press, 1983.

Dunn, Robert M., Jr., and Joseph J. Cordes. "Revisionism in the History of Supply-Side Economics." *Challenge* 36, no. 4 (July/August 1994): 50–53.

Robert W. Dimand

LAISSEZ-FAIRE, a French term that translates loosely as "let things alone," originated in the eighteenth century with a school of French economists, known as the Physiocrats, who opposed trade restrictions that supported older economic systems such as mercantilism. Adam Smith, an eighteenth-century Scottish economist, popularized the term and gave it added influence in later economic thought. He argued that a society's economic well-being and progress are assured when individuals freely apply their capital and labor without state intervention. The theory holds that individuals act out of self-interest and that self-interested action will benefit the larger community's general well-being. Proponents of laissez-faire reject state intervention through measures such as protective social legislation and trade restrictions, viewing them as socially injurious. The doctrine of laissez-faire involves not only a negative social policy of nonintervention but also a positive philosophy that recognizes a harmony between individual and social interests.

The United States has never adhered unconditionally to this doctrine, either theoretically or practically. Tariffs, components of American trade policy almost since the country's independence, contravene the principle of individualism expressed in the doctrine of laissez-faire. Antitrust legislation such as the SHERMAN ANTITRUST ACT (1890) and the Clayton Act (1914) similarly violate laissez-faire principles. Numerous examples of protective labor legislation, such as minimum-wage laws, workers' compensation statutes, hours legislation, and social security laws, belied professed allegiance to laissez-faire principles during the first half of the twentieth century. Since World War II, only a small minority of Americans have espoused laissez-faire theories.

BIBLIOGRAPHY

Bensel, Richard Franklin. *The Political Economy of American Industrialization, 1877–1900.* Cambridge, U.K.: Cambridge University Press, 2000.

Weiss, Thomas, and Donald Shaefer, eds. *American Economic Development in Historical Perspective.* Stanford, Calif.: Stanford University Press, 1994.

Gordon S. Watkins / s. b.

See also **Capitalism; Dartmouth College Case; Tariff.**

LAKE CHAMPLAIN.

More than a hundred miles long and seldom more than ten miles wide, Lake Champlain drains Lake George to the south and parts of New York and Vermont to the west and east. Just south of the Canadian border, it feeds into the Richelieu River—hence into the St. Lawrence River—and protrudes into Quebec as Missisquoi Bay. Easily navigable and situated along the same axis as the Hudson River, to which it was linked by canal in 1823, the lake was a strategic waterway until the late nineteenth century, when more stable geopolitical relations and improved land transport reduced its military and commercial significance.

Some 9,000 years ago, a rising land mass created a lake from what had been a swollen arm of the Champlain Sea. For a brief period around A.D. 1500, eastern Plano hunters probably explored its shores, and northern Iroquoians were the first to establish villages there. In the sixteenth century, the Mohawk Iroquois hunted in the Adirondacks west of the lake, and the Abenakis soon controlled the opposite side. The IROQUOIS, especially the Mohawks, followed what would become known as the Champlain-Richelieu route on northward journeys to raid, make peace, trade, or hunt. Moving in the opposite direction, Samuel de Champlain joined Native allies in 1609 to defeat a Mohawk army near Crown Point, New York, "discovering" and giving his name to the lake.

For close to a century, until the conquest of Canada in 1760, both colonists and Native people used the route to practice an often lively contraband trade, and in the armed conflicts of the turn of the eighteenth century and during the last years of NEW FRANCE, invaders frequently plied these waters. In 1758, at the height of the FRENCH AND INDIAN WAR, the French repulsed General James Abercromby's forces at Fort Carillon (Ticonderoga). After the French had been driven from the lake two years later, the British traced the intercolonial boundary, not suspecting that it would eventually become an international one. In 1775, General Richard Montgomery's army invaded Canada via the lake, and the British controlled the area from 1777 through the end of the American Revolution. Thereafter, European Americans settled both sides of the border. Lake Champlain has, in more recent times, been mainly of recreational significance and has figured in ongoing environmental discussions between the United States and Canada. Thanks to north-south rail and highway links, the regional economy continues to have a strong transborder orientation.

BIBLIOGRAPHY

Lecker, Robert, ed. *Borderlands: Essays in Canadian-American Relations Selected by the Borderlands Project.* Toronto: ECW Press, 1991. See "St. Lawrence Borderlands: The Free Trade Agreement and Canadian Investment in New York and Vermont" by Prem P. Gandhi.

Snow, Dean R. *The Iroquois.* Cambridge, Mass.: Blackwell, 1996.

Sturtevant, William C., ed. *Handbook of North American Indians: Northeast.* Washington, D.C.: Smithsonian Institution, 1978. See especially "Western Abenaki" by Gordon M. Day and "Mohawk" by William N. Fenton and Elizabeth Tooker.

Van de Water, Frederic F. *Lake Champlain and Lake George.* Port Washington, N.Y.: Friedman, 1969.

Thomas Wien

See also **Abenaki; Revolution, American: Military History; Tribes: Northeastern.**

LAKE ERIE, BATTLE OF

(10 September 1813). The victory of Commodore Oliver Hazard Perry's American fleet off Put-in-Bay, Lake Erie, was the major naval engagement on the Great Lakes in the War of 1812 and ensured immediate American control of Lake Erie and thus the freedom to invade Canada. The American and British fleets met in a light afternoon breeze, and, in close fighting, the *Caledonia* was nearly destroyed before the *Niagara* and the tardy *Lawrence* arrived to give support and force Robert H. Barclay, commander of the *Detroit* and the *Queen Charlotte*, to surrender. Perry sent to General William Henry Harrison, commander of the American army in the Northwest, his famous message, "We have met the enemy, and they are ours."

BIBLIOGRAPHY

Bancroft, George. *History of the Battle of Lake Erie, and Miscellaneous Papers*. New York: Bonner, 1891.

Morison, Samuel E. *"Old Bruin": Commodore Matthew C. Perry, 1794–1858; The American Naval Officer Who Helped Found Liberia. . . .* Boston: Little, Brown, 1967.

Skaggs, David C. *A Signal Victory: The Lake Erie Campaign.* Annapolis, Md.: Naval Institute Press, 1997.

*Walter B. Norris/*A. R.

See also **"Don't Give Up the Ship"; Ghent, Treaty of; Great Lakes Naval Campaigns of 1812; Perry-Elliott Controversy; "We Have Met the Enemy, and They Are Ours."**

LAKE OKEECHOBEE. Known at various times throughout history as Laguna del Espiritu Santo, Mayaimi, and Lake Mayaco, Lake Okeechobee—from two Seminole Indian words meaning "big water"—is located in the center of FLORIDA. It covers 730 square miles, has 135 miles of shoreline and an average depth of nine feet, and is the second largest freshwater lake in the continental United States after Lake Michigan. Its existence was mere legend to Americans until 1837, when U.S. Army colonel Zachary Taylor fought with the Creeks and Miccosukees during the Seminole Indian Wars. Even afterward it remained virtually unknown except to the Indians until the early 1880s, when Hamilton Disston dredged a navigable waterway north to Kissimmee River and west to the Gulf of Mexico, facilitating the first steamboat traffic. The first railroad was completed in 1915, and was followed by a major highway in 1924, five drainage canals in 1927, and an eighty-five-mile levee in 1937. Agricultural endeavors in the early decades of the twentieth century included peanuts, nuts, hay, sugar cane, and ramie. The lake and its surroundings provide a unique ecosystem abundant with flora, fish, and wildlife. The 110-mile Lake Okeechobee Scenic Trail was opened by the U.S. Forest Service in 1993 and the lake and its waterways are monitored and managed by the South Florida Water Management District in order to better predict its significant meteorological effects and protect it as a national resource.

BIBLIOGRAPHY

Gross, Eric. L. "Somebody Got Drowned, Lord: Florida and the Great Okeechobee Hurricane Disaster of 1928." Ph.D. diss., Florida State University, 1995.

Hanna, Alfred Jackson, and Kathryn Abbey Hanna. *Lake Okeechobee, Wellspring of the Everglades*. Indianapolis, Ind.: Bobbs-Merrill, 1948.

Christine E. Hoffman

See also **Seminole Wars.**

LAKE PONTCHARTRAIN is in southeastern Louisiana, five miles north of New Orleans. The lake is about 40 miles long and covers about 600 square miles.

It was connected to New Orleans by canal in 1795, by railroad in 1831, and by ship canal in 1921. The Bonnet Carre spillway connects the lake and the Mississippi River thirty-five miles above the city. Two causeways, twenty-three miles in length, cross the lake and form the longest bridge in the world. In the mid-eighteenth century, Lake Pontchartrain served as a link in the British inside passage to the Mississippi. Later, it became part of the overland route to the north and east.

BIBLIOGRAPHY

Colten, Craig E., ed. *Transforming New Orleans and Its Environs: Centuries of Change*. Pittsburgh, Pa.: University of Pittsburgh Press, 2000.

Cowan, Walter G. *New Orleans Yesterday and Today: A Guide to the City*. Baton Rouge: Louisiana State University Press, 2001.

*Walter Prichard/*A. E.

See also **Louisiana; New Orleans; Orleans, Territory of.**

LAKES-TO-GULF DEEP WATERWAY. In 1673, Louis Jolliet noted the favorable possibilities for a canal to connect the GREAT LAKES with the Des Plaines, Illinois, and Mississippi rivers. Both Albert Gallatin and Peter B. Porter, in the early 1800s, urged the actual construction of a canal. Aided by a right-of-way and a land grant provided by Congress, the state of Illinois completed the Illinois and Michigan Canal in 1848. The Chicago Sanitary and Ship Canal, completed in 1900 and extended in 1910, rendered obsolete the first thirty-mile section of this waterway. Sponsored by the Chicago Sanitary District, this new canal had a width of more than one hundred sixty feet and a depth of twenty-four feet. Its construction gave additional impetus to the long-standing movement to develop a Lakes-to-Gulf deep waterway. In 1889, the legislature of Illinois had suggested a channel depth of fourteen feet, but some groups active during the transportation crisis of 1906–1907 and the conservation movement of 1908 demanded the additional ten feet. Congress refused to provide federal support for these proposals. Consequently, in 1921, the state of Illinois started construction, made possible by a $20 million bond issue authorized in 1908, of five locks and four dams between Lockport and Utica. In 1930, the federal government took over the project and completed it three years later with a channel depth of nine feet.

Dredging and construction achieved a similar minimum depth in the Illinois Waterway below Utica and in the MISSISSIPPI RIVER to Cairo, Illinois. Locks and dams at Peoria, La Grange, and Alton, Illinois, were completed during 1938–1939. Near Saint Louis, Missouri, a lateral canal with locks opened in 1953, and a dam was finished in 1964. Improvement of the Calumet-Sag route from the sanitary canal to Lake Calumet, begun in 1955, was scheduled for completion in 1977. This segment is now

Albert Gallatin. Secretary of the Treasury, 1801–1814, and an early advocate of a canal linking the Great Lakes with the Mississippi and other rivers. LIBRARY OF CONGRESS

the primary connection of the Illinois Waterway to Lake Michigan.

Six additional large locks and other improvements are planned for the section of the waterway between Lockport to La Grange. Construction of a new dam and large twin locks at Alton has been proposed. These new authorizations, proposals, and studies are in part related to the great achieved and expected increases in barge traffic. Factors contributing to this growth include the economic expansion of the areas adjacent to the waterway and the substantial improvement in the efficiency of barges, towboats, and related equipment. In the early 2000s, domestic waterborne shipping accounted for about 14 percent of the United States' internal cargo transportation, at less than 2 percent of the annual costs. The waterway created by connecting the Mississippi to Lake Michigan forms a vital link in this transportation network.

BIBLIOGRAPHY

Shaw, Ronald E. *Canals for a Nation: The Canal Era in the United States, 1790–1860.* Lexington: University Press of Kentucky, 1990.

Marcus Whitman / A. E.; S. C.

See also **Canals; Chicago; Sanitation, Environmental.**

LAKOTA. *See* **Sioux.**

LAKOTA LANGUAGE. "Lakota" is a term used in conjunction with a language complex (and therefore derivatively for its speakers) across an area of the Northern Plains extending from western Minnesota to eastern Montana and northward to Alberta. Other terms are used now equivalently, now differentiatingly, with it, including "Sioux" and "Dakota." The former is eschewed by some because it is a French corruption of an Ojibwa term, whereas Lakota and Dakota are autonyms and derive from the root for "friend" or "ally." It should be added, however, that in speaking colloquially in English, the term "Sioux" is often the one used by speakers themselves.

The language complex is differentiated by a systematic correspondence of l~d~n in various speech forms, as seen in Lakota and Dakota, the western and eastern variants, respectively. Because Anglo-American contact was first with the eastern speakers, Dakota was generalized to designate the complex, but recently—because the western speakers who inhabit the large reservations of western South Dakota (Rosebud, Pine Ridge, Cheyenne River, and Standing Rock) are numerically dominant—the choice of terms has shifted to Lakota. There are only a small number of speakers of the n-variety, at least in the main body of speakers, and their speech is closer to that of the d-speakers so that they call the language Dakota also. There are also descendants of two groups of n-speakers who pulled away from the main body in pre-contact times and moved north into present-day Alberta who still call themselves Nakoda, although Lakota calls them Hohe and the common English designations are Assiniboine and Stoney Sioux.

The traditional political alliance of the Sioux, called the Seven Councilfires, is organized linguistically with seven bands of speakers. They consist of four bands of d-speakers (Mdewakanton, Wahpekute, Wahpeton, Sisseton), two of n-speakers (Yankton, Yanktonai), and one of l-speakers (Teton).

Lakota is part of the larger Siouan-Catawban family of languages, which includes Siouan branches of the Mississippi Valley (Winnebago, Iowa-Otoe, Dhegiha), the Missouri River (Crow, Hidatsa, Mandan), the Ohio Valley (Ofo, Biloxi, Tutelo), and the distantly related Catawba. The original home of the Proto-Siouans is debated among specialists, but it must have been considerably east and south of the Lakota homeland of the contact period.

In addition to being the source of a number of large toponyms in the Upper Midwest, Lakota has also contributed to the American vocabulary the word tepee (literally, they live) and the generalized "Indian" expressions "how" (a greeting) and "kola" (friend). There are presently from ten thousand to twelve thousand speakers.

BIBLIOGRAPHY
Rood, David S. "Siouan Languages." In *International Encyclopedia of Linguistics*. Vol. 3. Edited by William Bright. Oxford: Oxford University Press, 1992.

Rood, David S., and Allan R. Taylor. "Sketch of Lakhota, a Siouan Language." In *Handbook of North American Indians*. Vol. 17, *Linguistics*. Edited by Ives Goddard. Washington, D.C.: Smithsonian Institution, 1996.

Gary Bevington

See also **Indian Languages.**

LAME-DUCK AMENDMENT, the name applied to the Twentieth Amendment (1933) to the U.S. Constitution, abolished so-called lame-duck sessions of Congress, which were held from December of even-numbered years until the following 4 March. These sessions acquired their nickname because they included numerous members who had been defeated (the lame ducks) in elections held a month before the session opened. The law permitted them to sit and function until their terms ended in March, while a newly elected Congress, with a fresh popular mandate, stood by inactive and unorganized. Newly elected members usually had to wait thirteen months to take office, because the lame-duck sessions lasted only three months, and Congress did not reconvene until the following December. In the last lame-duck session, which opened in December 1932, 158 defeated members sat in the Senate and House. The amendment, sponsored by Sen. George W. Norris of Nebraska, did away with the lame-duck session by moving back the day on which terms of senators and representatives begin from 4 March to 3 January, and by requiring Congress to convene each year on January 3—about two months after election. The amendment also set back the date of the president's and the vice-president's inauguration from March to 20 January. Other provisions relate to the choice of president under certain contingencies.

BIBLIOGRAPHY
Anastaplo, George. *The Amendments to the Constitution: A Commentary*. Baltimore: Johns Hopkins University Press, 1995.

P. Orman Ray / c. p.

See also **Constitution of the United States.**

LAMP, INCANDESCENT. As early as 1820, scientists all over the world had begun to work on the development of an incandescent lamp, but it remained for Thomas A. Edison at Menlo Park, New Jersey, on 21 October 1879 to make the first successful high resistance carbon lamp, which embodied almost all the basic features of lamps commonly in use today.

The first carbon lamp was inefficient in comparison with present-day lamps, giving only 1.7 lumens (light units) per watt (unit of energy). Inventors, many of them American, gradually improved the carbon lamp through minor changes in construction, so that by 1906 it produced 3.4 lumens per watt. In 1905 Willis R. Whitney, head of the research laboratory of the General Electric Company at Schenectady, New York, succeeded in changing the character of the carbon filament to give it metallic characteristics, and for a few years the Gem lamp, which produced 4.25 lumens per watt, was on the market. In 1904 two Austrian chemists, Alexander Just and Franz Hanaman, patented a remarkably efficient tungsten filament lamp, giving 7.75 lumens per watt; however, it was extremely fragile and could be used only under special conditions. At that time it was believed impossible to draw tungsten wire, but in 1910 William D. Coolidge of the General Electric research laboratory succeeded in making ductile tungsten. Lighting manufacturers quickly saw tungsten's advantages of both efficiency and strength, and the drawn-wire tungsten filament lamp shortly superseded all other forms.

All lamps up to this time operated filaments in a vacuum. In 1913, after much experimentation and fundamental research, Irving Langmuir, one of Whitney's assistants, discovered that with the largest sizes of lamps, if the filaments were coiled and the bulbs filled with inert gases, such as nitrogen or argon, the efficiency could be increased to as high as 20 lumens per watt. Gas filling and double coiling of filament have since been introduced into smaller sizes.

The cost of the incandescent lamp has constantly been reduced and efficiency increased. In 1907 the 60-watt lamp gave 8 lumens per watt and lost 25 percent of this light before burning out. Thirty years later the 60-watt lamp produced 13.9 lumens per watt and emitted 90 percent of its original light at the end of its life. By the 1970s developments had brought the number of lumens produced in a tungsten-filament lamp to 40, the maximum obtainable before the filament melts. In the late–twentieth century, concerns about energy use spurred the manufacture of efficient lamp styles, including "long-life bulbs," with thicker tungsten strands, and the more efficient fluorescent and halogen lamps. (Halogen lights use tungsten filaments, but with halogen added to increase the light output.) Although fluorescent and halogen lamps provide more light with greater efficiency, incandescent lamps continued to be used because of their simplicity and low cost.

BIBLIOGRAPHY
Friedel, Robert D., and Paul Israel with Bernard S. Finn *Edison's Electric Light: Biography of an Invention*. New Brunswick, N.J.: Rutgers University Press, 1985.

Howell, John W., and Henry Schroeder. *History of the Incandescent Lamp*. Schenectady, N.Y.: Maqua, 1927.

A. L. Powell / a. r.

See also **Electric Power and Light Industry; Electrification, Household; Lighting; Manufacturing.**

LAND ACTS. United States land policy has favored putting public lands into private hands, spending income from the sale of public lands to pay public debts and finance public transportation enterprises, adjudicating private land claims in areas acquired by treaty, extinguishing American Indian land titles to a great extent, and enabling tribal management of remaining lands in Indian country. Although these policy goals have evolved and been contested frequently, public policy has favored the wide holding of private property and its productive use.

The Treaty of Paris of 1783 ended the American Revolution and put about 270 million acres of public land in the hands of the Confederation government. The Confederation Congress passed the Land Ordinance of 1785, putting government in the land disposal business. The Land Ordinance of 1785 set the pattern for public land distribution. Public land was to be surveyed, sold at a high minimum price at auction, occupied thereafter—military bounty warrant claimants excepted—and one section set aside for schools. Congress tinkered with the system in 1796, 1800, 1820, and 1841, lowering the price and the minimum lot size to stimulate sales. Preemption by actual settlers on surveyed land, giving them the right to purchase that land before others, became fixed in 1841 and extended to unsurveyed lands in the 1850s. The 1862 Homestead Act offered 160 acres of public land for a transaction fee to an occupier-developer who worked the land for five years. The Timber Culture Act of 1873 and Desert Land Act of 1877 put more public land into private hands for small sums.

Congress gave land away to stimulate enterprise. The Mining Law of 1866 and General Mining Law of 1872 gave claimants to mineral lands on the public domain free use of land for mining purposes. Congress funded the construction of the transcontinental and other railroads with public land grants.

Congress in 1872 turned slightly away from disposal to preservation in withdrawing two million acres for Yellowstone Park. In 1879 it created the Public Land Commission to classify lands and bring the first signs of management to the public domain. In 1891, Congress authorized the president to withdraw forest lands from purchase, and the authority to withdraw public lands for preservation expanded dramatically in the twentieth century.

Congress set a policy of adjudicating private land claims with the acquisition of lands from Great Britain, Spain, France, and Mexico. Most of these lands were along the Detroit River in Michigan, at Vincennes on the Wabash in Indiana, at Cahokia in Illinois, and in Missouri, Louisiana, Mississippi, Florida, California, and New Mexico. The system of adjudication included commissioners who investigated the claims, reviewed documents, and reported to Congress regarding the claims. Specific statutes like the California Land Act of 1851 established such a commission system that heard and decided claims. The parties had the right to appeal decisions to the federal courts.

The policy for American Indian tribal lands in the nineteenth century was extinguishment by treaty or war, or both. Tribal lands were constricted as a result and under constant pressure from federal administrative agencies and state governments until the 1940s, when Congress passed the Indian Claims Commission Act of 1946. Thereunder the tribes started proceedings to recover money for past treaty injustices, at the expense of waiving future claims to land itself. Few tribes recovered land, with the notable exceptions of the Taos Pueblo recovering Blue Lake and acreage within the Kit Carson National Forest and the Zuni recovery of Kolhu/wala:wa in Arizona. Tribal authority over land was confirmed, in part, by the Indian Self-Determination and Education Assistance Act of 1975. The desire of the tribes for greater autonomy and clear sovereignty continues.

BIBLIOGRAPHY

Bakken, Gordon Morris. *Law in the Western United States.* Norman: University of Oklahoma Press, 2000.

Gates, Paul Wallace. *Land and Law in California: Essays on Land Policies.* Ames: Iowa State University Press, 1991.

Gordon Morris Bakken

See also **Homestead Movement; Indian Claims Commission; Land Claims; Land Grants; Land Policy; Public Land Commissions.**

LAND BOUNTIES. Lacking well-filled treasuries but possessing abundant supplies of land, the American colonies and, after the Revolution, the states and the national government, granted land bounties instead of cash subsidies to reward military service in past wars. This was to encourage enlistment in pending wars and to aid various special groups. During the Revolution and the War of 1812, Congress promised land bounties as inducements to enlist and as rewards for service. Many land grants were sold to speculators who used them to accumulate great tracts of property.

BIBLIOGRAPHY

Oberly, James W. *Sixty Million Acres: American Veterans and the Public Lands before the Civil War.* Kent, Ohio: Kent State University Press, 1990.

Paul W. Gates/A. R.

See also **Bounties, Military; Land Grants: Land Grants for Railways.**

LAND CLAIMS. In 1783, Great Britain ceded to the new republic sovereignty over about one-fourth of the land area of the present-day United States. For the next seventy years, the foremost national project was to extend U.S. sovereignty across the continent to the Pacific Ocean. The 1783 territory of the new nation was augmented by seven separate land acquisitions between 1803 and 1853.

25

All of these territorial acquisitions brought real people with real claims to the land. The process of honoring pre-existing private land claims was sufficiently complicated to keep Congress and the courts busy for more than a century. By 1904, the United States had recognized the rights of more than 20,000 claimants to approximately 34 million acres of land.

The first conflict between American sovereignty and prior claims of ownership came in the lands of the Old Northwest Territory, which would become the states of Ohio, Indiana, Michigan, Illinois, and Wisconsin. In that region, French settlers had established trading posts with modest agricultural hinterlands at key sites on the Great Lakes and Ohio and Mississippi valleys. They demanded that the new United States recognize their ownership rights to the lands of their villages. In the 1794 JAY'S TREATY with Great Britain, the United States agreed to uphold the claims of the French in the Northwest, and over the next thirty years almost 3,000 French settlers had their claims validated with clear title recognized by American courts.

The 1803 LOUISIANA PURCHASE resulted in a doubling of the American nation. It also produced many thousands of new private claims to lands around St. Louis and New Orleans on the basis of prior grants from the Spanish and French authorities. The U.S. Congress authorized a special board of commissioners to examine private land claims in the new territory of Missouri and state of Louisiana. The board heard more than 3,000 claims from Missouri but rejected most because of inadequate documentation or because the American commissioners thought the claims conflicted with prior Spanish laws. The rejected claimants turned to Congress for special relief, and they kept the private claims before that body until the late 1870s. In Louisiana, more than 9,000 claimants eventually won title to more than 4 million acres of land.

The purchase of Florida by the United States in 1819 predictably brought a new set of private claims, extending to more than 2.7 million acres. The Florida claims, though large in acreage, were small in number. The confirmation of some of these grants allowed some Florida families to build large estates at key sites around Florida, including around Tampa Bay.

The largest volume of private claims concerned lands acquired by the United States after the annexation of Texas in 1845 and the conquest of Mexico and the resulting Mexican Cession of 1848. In newly acquired California, for example, prior claims were filed for as much as 27 million acres of land. In New Mexico, Colorado, and Arizona, a comparable amount was claimed under prior grants made during Mexican rule, and for this region Congress established a special Court of Private Land Claims in 1891 to hear appeals. That court was kept busy hearing cases through 1904.

The significance of the private land claims in American history is that the United States did not acquire an empty continent. Dealings with American Indians over land were one matter. Dealings with alien residents who claimed private property from a foreign government's grant was another, and the United States set the pattern early on of attempting to deal fairly with the claimants. A title search on property in some of the most valuable real estate in America today, including Los Angeles, San Diego, Tampa, St. Louis, New Orleans, and Detroit, shows the relevance of the private land claims. Their recognition was the result of the accommodation of the new United States to an older, foreign past.

BIBLIOGRAPHY

Gates, Paul W. "Private Land Claims." In *History of Public Land Law Development*. Washington, D.C.: Government Printing Office, 1968.

Keleher, William A. *Maxwell Land Grant: A New Mexico Item*. New York: Argosy-Antiquarian, 1964. Reprint, Albuquerque: University of New Mexico Press, 1983.

James Oberly

See also **Land Acts; Land Grants; Land Patents; Land Policy.**

LAND COMPANIES. From the Virginia Company of 1603 and its grant of land in North America, through the Great Depression of the 1930s, land companies existed as intermediaries between governments seeking to dispose of their lands, and private individuals wishing to settle on the lands. In the original thirteen states, land companies advocated Indian removal and opening lands to white settlement. That often included fraud, as in New York State when the Holland and Ogden Land Companies illegally forced Indians out of the state and into the West or Canada. Some land companies engaged in fraud at the legislative level, as did the group of Yazoo companies involved in buying land from the state of Georgia for less than one cent an acre in the 1790s. The resulting confusion over title to western Georgia lands lasted more than a generation.

The main area of operation for land companies was the public domain of the United States, that is, lands that the United States acquired in spreading from the Atlantic to the Pacific. Alexander Hamilton and George Washington in the 1790s saw a need for land companies as brokers between the federal government, which wanted to sell large tracts of public land, and small farmers looking for new farmland. The first land company in the new Republic was the Scioto Company of Ohio, which bought 5 million acres of land for resale to settlers in the Northwest Territory. Each wave of public land fever brought forth new companies. After the War of 1812, the Boston and Illinois Land Company bought nearly a million acres of land in Illinois. In 1820, the United States stopped selling public land on credit to purchasers, so land companies stepped into the role of seller and creditor.

A new type of land company emerged after 1850, when Congress began granting millions of acres of public land to railroads. Land grant railways used part of their lands to secure loans for construction. Once completed, railroads encouraged settlement by selling some of their land. That way, settlers would grow crops, raise livestock, make journeys, and, in general, use the railway. Railroads sold as much as 100 million acres of land to settlers.

One way to think about land companies is to view them as classic commodity speculators: they tried to buy low and to sell high, and they sought to turn over the inventory as quickly as possible. In this view, land companies were a hindrance to settlement, because they bought up the best land before the average settler could get any, and then withheld that land for resale at higher prices. An alternate view is that land companies were efficient market makers. They provided expertise in locating good lands, and they provided credit that was otherwise nonexistent in many frontier communities.

BIBLIOGRAPHY

Gates, Paul W. *History of Public Land Law Development*. Washington, D.C.: Government Printing Office, 1968.

Hauptman, Laurence. *Conspiracy of Interests: Iroquois Dispossesion and the Rise of New York State*. Syracuse, N.Y.: Syracuse University Press, 1999.

James Oberly

See also **Land Grants: Land Grants for Railways; Yazoo Fraud.**

LAND GRANTS

This entry includes 3 subentries:
Overview
Land Grants for Education
Land Grants for Railways

OVERVIEW

The public lands of the United States consisted of all the land acquired from American Indian tribes, stretching west from the trans-Appalachian region to the Pacific coast, excluding only the original thirteen states, along with Kentucky, Tennessee, Vermont, and Texas. The public domain consisted of about 1.25 billion acres of land. Its potential included some of the following natural resources: the richest farmlands in the world in what became the Corn Belt and Wheat Belt of the Midwest, and the Cotton Belt of the Lower Mississippi Valley; the California gold fields and the Nevada silver fields; the oil and gas lands of Oklahoma; the coal lands of Wyoming; the Iron Range of Minnesota; and the great forests of the Pacific Northwest. In short, the public lands of the United States represented an extraordinary patrimony for the nation. It is no exaggeration to say that the American industrial revolution of the nineteenth and early twentieth centuries was fueled by the enormous riches extracted in one way or another from the public lands.

A Public Trust

The public lands of the United States were (and are) a public trust of the federal government, every bit as much of a trust as the dollars in the U.S. Treasury. So the judgment of history is directed toward determining how well the federal trustees managed their trust. Consider a trustee managing a simple undeveloped parcel of land. The trustee has a number of choices about how to best execute the trust. The trustee can sell the property and try to maximize income for the trust. The trustee can develop the property to promote future revenues. Or the trustee can hold onto the real estate asset for future generations. These three choices were also the ones that the Congress of the United States faced in managing the trust of the public lands. And it exercised all three of those choices from the time that the public lands were established in 1785 through the end of the twentieth century. The focus is rightly on the Congress, for it was the legislative body that set the specific policies for public land management. The Executive Branch, including the president, the secretary of the Treasury, and after 1849, the secretary of the Interior, carried out laws passed by Congress on managing the public lands.

With the benefit of historical perspective, it is possible to see that the Congress exercised its trusteeship of the public lands in three broadly defined chronological eras that correspond with the three abstract choices of a trustee of an undeveloped real estate parcel. First, from 1785 through 1819, the Congress passed a set of public land laws that had the intent of maximizing income to the Treasury through outright sales. Second, from 1820 through about 1902, the Congress made use of the public lands for a host of development projects. Instead of selling land for cash, the Congress established a set of donation programs with the idea that recipients would use their land grants to conduct congressionally approved projects. Finally, beginning about 1900, and especially after 1933, the Congress determined that the public lands should no longer be sold outright, but rather should be held in trust for the long term.

To be sure, there was overlap in policymaking among these three separate historical eras. During the first era, between 1785 and 1820, for example, the Congress legislated the policy that one square mile out of every thirty-six-square-mile township should be dedicated to support public education. After a township was surveyed by federal land surveyors into thirty-six square-mile sections, the sixteenth section was withheld for public education. This policy was later doubled to two square miles per township held from sale or donation, sections 16 and 36 in each township. In practice, this did not mean that the little red schoolhouse was invariably located in section 16 or 36. Rather, the acreage of those sections was turned over to state officials who then became the trustees for the land. Usually, the state land commissions sold the so-called school lands for cash and then used the proceeds to build and maintain public schools.

The Nineteenth Century

The most interesting period of trusteeship was the second phase, the nineteenth-century phase, when Congress passed laws donating public lands for a wide variety of purposes. This was the era of land grants: land-grant universities; land-grant railroads; land-grant old-age pensions; and especially land-grant homesteads for farmers. These land grants were made by Congress to four types of recipients: the states; business corporations; veterans and their dependents; and farmer-settlers.

The land-grant donation from Congress to the states is the element of continuity between the first, or income-producing phase, of public lands policy history and the second phase after 1820. The congressional thinking was that the states were the proper political bodies to carry out national goals, but that the states lacked the resources. For that matter, so did the national treasury lack resources in the form of cash reserves, but the public domain provided a sort of bank account from which to fund what today we would call federal block grants to the states. At first, the form of federal land grants was limited to supporting public primary education in the new states from Ohio on west. But, in 1862, Congress extended the goal of supporting public education to the college and university level with the passage of the Morrill Land Grant Act. The Congress provided the means for each state to build and support a public college that would promote agriculture. In time, these institutions became the state universities that were the pillars of American public higher education in the twentieth century. The funding idea for the Morrill Land Grant Act was simple: each state in the Union was entitled to select undeveloped public land and use that land as a trustee to support the new state agricultural college. Thus, New York, which had no public lands, was able to secure almost 3 million acres of public land from Congress with which to support the new Cornell University. It is no accident that Cornell was named in honor of the state's land agent, Ezra Cornell, who operated so successfully as a land trustee in managing the 1 million acre endowment. In most other states, the land grant college became the University, as in the University of Illinois. States that had a preexising state college or university before 1862, such as the University of South Carolina or the University of Michigan, later established a separate land-grant college specifically for agricultural education, for example respectively, Clemson University and Michigan State University. Overall, Congress granted about 90 million acres in public land grants to the states for primary and higher education.

The nineteenth-century era of congressional land grants to states also coincided with the widespread development of the corporate form of enterprise as the way that Americans conducted business. As the size and scale of corporate enterprises grew, so too did the demand for capital and financing of corporate enterprise. Private capital markets, such as the New York Stock Exchange, supported a limited number of corporate businesses, but private investors shied away from supplying capital to the biggest of projects, the long-distance transportation projects that united the different states into a single national market for production and exchange. Here was a dilemma for congressional policymakers: if they trusted the stock exchange only to underwrite the capital needs of the builders of turnpikes, canals, and railroads, then private business would only construct such projects in the more densely populated parts of the nation. In practice, this meant that transportation would follow population, and not the other way around. So starting in the 1820s, and then increasingly each decade up through 1870, Congress donated grants of public land to private entrepreneurs who pledged to construct the road, canal, or railroad, and then operate it as a private business. The congressional thinking was that land-grant support of transportation would speed the settlement of the West. Especially for railroads, Congress thought that jump-starting transportation connections would speed settlement and subsequent development. Between 1850 and 1870, Congress donated about 91 million acres to numerous private railroad companies. The results were twofold: the transcontinental railroads that linked San Francisco and Omaha, Duluth and Puget Sound, and New Orleans and Los Angeles, were built way ahead of when private enterprise would have done the task. The nation was bound together in a national transportation network and a national market in goods and services developed thereafter. The second result was that almost all the land-grant railroads were unprofitable and defaulted on their obligations and went into bankruptcy by the early 1890s. Yes, the transportation network was completed, but settlement did not occur rapidly enough to make the railways profitable as ongoing private enterprises. "Premature enterprise," as one scholar termed it, had its benefits, but also its costs.

A third type of land grant was made to American veterans of past wars as a sort of old-age pension. This particularly applied to veterans of the War of 1812 (1812–1815) and the host of Indian wars that the United States fought between 1800 and 1860. Pensions in cash were strictly limited to those soldiers who had been wounded and disabled in battle, a relatively small number of individuals. By contrast, more than 400,000 men had done some military service in the War of 1812, and collected little for it. As the surviving War of 1812 veterans became old men in the 1840s and 1850s, they began to demand of Congress that the public lands be used as pension grants. Congress eventually agreed in a series of laws passed in 1850, 1852, and 1855. Some 60 million acres of public land were granted to more than half a million veterans of the various American wars. The old veterans got their land pension in the form of what was called a military bounty land warrant, or certificate for land. Almost invariably, the veterans sold their warrants for cash, which provided them a modest one-time pension. The sold warrants were collected by New York bankers, who in turn sold them with interest to would-be farmer-settlers in western states and territories. In effect, the private capital markets worked very efficiently to turn veterans' land warrants into both pensions for the old men and credit for young farmers.

The fourth and largest type of land grant in the nineteenth and early twentieth centuries was the homestead grant. This was also known as a free-land donation. It, too, was passed as policy by Congress in the year 1862, the same year as the Morrill Land Grant Act. The Homestead Act provided that settlers on the public lands could have five years to live without charge on a parcel of up to a quarter-section of 160 acres (a quarter-mile in area). At the end of five years, if the settler had made improvements to the unimproved quarter-section, then the United States would pass title to the land to that settler. Today, we would call such a policy a "sweat equity" program, where the settler or dweller trades labor today on a property for eventual ownership of an improved property in the future. In America between the Civil War (1861–1865) and World War I (1914–1918), the homestead policy was an enormously popular federal program. The homestead idea combined Jeffersonian veneration for the farmer with the Lincolnian active use of the federal ownership of the public lands to speed development. Some 1.4 million settlers began homestead claims on more than almost 250 million acres of western lands, especially concentrated on the northern Great Plains in Nebraska, the Dakotas, and Montana. Despite droughts, grasshoppers, and sometimes low farm commodity prices, the majority stuck out their five years and earned farm ownership by their own hard work.

By the end of the nineteenth century, much of the arable lands of the West had passed from public ownership into private hands. Congress increasingly had to turn to public monies in the Treasury to fund its development projects rather than public lands.

The historian's judgment is that in the nineteenth century, Congress was determined to support public education, transportation development, veterans' benefits, and new farm settlement. The Treasury simply did not have enough dollars to fund these policies. But the public lands offered a way to convert a wealth in land into material support for congressional policies. So the public lands passed into private ownership by the hundreds of millions of acres between 1820 and 1900. In return, what the modern United States has to show for this spending of its national wealth in land is the establishment of a national commitment to public university education, a national transportation network, a belief that veterans should be supported in old age, and a long-term support for farming as a way of life. That is a fair legacy of trusteeship that the Congress established with its grants of land from the public domain.

BIBLIOGRAPHY

Feller, Daniel. *The Public Lands in Jacksonian Politics.* Madison: University of Wisconsin Press, 1984.

Fogel, Robert William. *The Union Pacific Railroad: A Case in Premature Enterprise.* Baltimore: Johns Hopkins University Press, 1960.

Gates, Paul W. *The Wisconsin Pine Lands of Cornell University: A Study in Land Policy and Absentee Ownership.* Ithaca, N.Y.: Cornell University Press, 1943.

———. *History of Public Land Law Development.* Washington, D.C.: Government Printing Office, 1968.

Oberly, James W. *Sixty Million Acres: American Veterans and the Public Lands before the Civil War.* Kent, Ohio: Kent State University Press, 1990.

Opie, John. *The Law of the Land. Two Hundred Years of American Farmland Policy.* Lincoln: University of Nebraska Press, 1987.

Pisani, Donald J. *To Reclaim a Divided West: Water, Law, and Public Policy, 1848–1902.* Albuquerque: University of New Mexico Press, 1992.

Robbins, William G., and James C. Foster. *Land in the American West: Private Claims and the Common Good.* Seattle: University of Washington Press, 2000.

Souder, Jon A., and Sally K. Fairfax, eds. *State Trust Lands: History, Management, and Sustainable Use.* Lawrence: University of Kansas Press, 1996.

James Oberly

See also **Land Policy; Public Domain; School Lands; Western Lands.**

LAND GRANTS FOR EDUCATION

The American colonies generally followed the practice of making land grants to aid in supporting public schools. The Confederation, borrowing from the New England land system, provided in the Land Ordinance of 1785 that the sixteenth section (640 acres) of each township, or 1/36 of the acreage of the public land states, should be granted to the states for public schools. New states after 1848 were given two sections, or 1,280 acres, in each township. Utah, Arizona, New Mexico, and Oklahoma were given four sections in each township when they entered the Union. At the same time, states were given a minimum of two townships, or 46,080 acres, to aid in founding "seminaries of learning," or state universities. Such great institutions as the Universities of Michigan, Wisconsin, and Indiana benefited from these grants.

The next important step in federal aid to education came in 1862 as the result of an energetic campaign undertaken by Jonathan Baldwin Turner of Illinois, Horace Greeley through the *New York Tribune*, and various farm and labor journals. The Land Grant College Act, generally called the Morrill Act, was fathered in the House of Representatives by Justin Smith Morrill of Vermont. This measure gave each state 30,000 acres of public land for each representative and senator it had in Congress to aid in establishing colleges of agriculture and mechanical arts. States that had no public lands received scrip that could be exchanged for public lands available elsewhere. As a result of this act, agricultural colleges were established in every state, with two in each southern state because of the states' insistence on segregation. Special land grants were made also to endow normal schools, schools of mining, reform schools, and a women's college.

Congress was unusually generous in sharing its public lands with Alaska for education and other purposes upon its admission to the Union in 1959. In place of numerous grants for education, internal improvements, and public buildings, Congress granted a total of 103,350,000 acres to be allocated as the new state wished and promised 5 percent of its net return from all land sales in the state for school use.

This liberal distribution of public lands reflects the ever growing interest of the American people in free public education. It encouraged the states early to create schools, helping to finance them when local resources were unequal to the task. It also made it easier for those of a later generation who favored direct money grants for education by setting a constitutional precedent for the practice of granting land for schools. Altogether, Congress granted to states for public education an area much larger than California. The first public land states recklessly mismanaged their bounty, while others, such as Minnesota, managed theirs so well that they built up a large endowment for education.

BIBLIOGRAPHY

Dick, Everett N. *The Lure of the Land: A Social History of the Public Lands from the Articles of Confederation to the New Deal.* Lincoln: University of Nebraska Press, 1970.

Gates, Paul W. *History of Public Land Law Development.* Washington, D.C.: U.S. Government Printing Office, 1968.

Zaslowsky, Dyan. *These American Lands: Parks, Wilderness, and the Public Lands.* New York: Holt, 1986; Washington, D.C.: Island Press, 1994.

Paul W. Gates / c. w.

See also **Alaska; Education; Morrill Act; Ordinances of 1784, 1785, and 1787; Universities, State.**

LAND GRANTS FOR RAILWAYS

The liberality with which Congress subsidized canal construction by land grants suggested to early railroad promoters that they might also obtain land donations to aid their enterprises. Most persistent were the advocates of a central railroad for Illinois to connect the extreme northwestern and southern parts of the state. When, in 1850, boosters expanded their proposed railroad scheme into an intersectional plan by extending it to the Gulf of Mexico, Congress adopted a measure that gave Illinois, Mississippi, and Alabama a broad right-of-way for the railroad tracks through the public lands. The grant also included alternate sections in a checkerboard pattern for a distance of six miles on both sides of the road, amounting to 3,840 acres for each mile of railroad.

This generosity not only gave railroads the necessary right-of-way but also allowed railroad companies to finance construction by selling adjacent land to prospective farmers. Because the presence of a railroad increased property values, the plan gained approval, even of many strict constructionists, who noted that the government could price its reserved sections within the twelve-mile area at double the ordinary minimum of $1.25 an acre. This assured the government as much return from half of the land as it would receive for all of it without the line. Furthermore, land grants required railroads to provide free transportation for troops and supplies and to offer rate concessions for transporting mail.

Swift completion of the Illinois Central Railroad portion of the intersectional line aided in opening areas to settlement thitherto inaccessible and gave great impetus to immigration, farm and urban development, and rising real estate values in Illinois. This spectacular success produced a scramble for railroad land grants in all existing public land states. The federal government made numerous grants between 1850 and 1871, totaling, with state land grants, 176 million acres, or more than the area of Texas.

Most important and grandest in their conception were the transcontinental railways, which were to connect the Mississippi Valley with the new communities on the Pacific coast. The first of the transcontinentals to be chartered and given land grants, plus loans in 1862, were the Union Pacific, to build west from Omaha, and the Central Pacific, to build east from Sacramento. They met near Ogden, Utah, in 1869. In 1864 the Southern Pacific, the Atlantic and Pacific (a portion of which later became part of the Atchison, Topeka, and Santa Fe), and the Northern Pacific were generously endowed with land, the latter receiving 39 million acres.

All land-grant railroads undertook extensive advertising campaigns at home and abroad to attract immigrants to their lands, which the companies sold on easy credit at prevailing prices. When settlers found it difficult to meet their payments, especially in the poor years after 1873 and in the late 1880s, a chorus of complaints grew against the policies of the land-grant railroads. Critics demanded that the railroads forfeit their undeveloped and unsold lands. Reformers condemned the land grants as inconsistent with the free homestead policy and, in 1871, succeeded in halting further grants. Continued agitation over the large amount of land claimed by railroads that was not in the hands of developers led to the General Forfeiture Act of 1890, which required the return to the government of land along projected lines that had not been built. However, this measure had no effect on the grants earned by construction of the lines. When the railroads succeeded in 1940 in inducing Congress to surrender the government's right to reduced rates for government traffic, it was proposed that the railroads be required to return the unsold portion of their grants to the public domain; Congress did not so provide. Retention of these unsold lands by the railroads was a sore point with many westerners, and agitation for compelling the forfeiture of these lands continued into the twenty-first century.

Land grants encouraged capitalists to invest in railroads and enabled the lines so benefited to advance far beyond the zone of settlement. More than anything else except the free land given to homesteaders by the government, these grants contributed to the rapid settlement of the West.

BIBLIOGRAPHY

Ambrose, Stephen E. *Nothing Like It in the World: The Men Who Built the Transcontinental Railroad, 1863–1869.* New York: Simon and Schuster, 2000.

Gates, Paul W. *History of Public Land Law Development.* Washington, D.C.: U.S. Government Printing Office, 1968; Washington, D.C.: Zenger, 1978.

Mercer, Lloyd J. *Railroads and Land Grant Policy: A Study of Government Intervention.* New York: Academic Press, 1982.

Paul W. Gates / c. w.

See also **Land Policy; Public Domain; Railroads; Transcontinental Railroad, Building of; Western Lands.**

LAND OFFICE, U.S. GENERAL AND BUREAU PLANS MANAGEMENT.

In 1812 the U.S. General Land Office came into existence as a bureau in the Treasury Department intended to manage the public lands of the United States. The increasing burdens of the secretary of the Treasury, who had to provide for surveying western lands, adjudicating the conflicting private land claims arising from the policies of previous foreign governments, and settling conflicting land claims arising from poorly drafted legislation, brought about the creation of the office of commissioner of the General Land Office. The commissioner's responsibility for more than a billion acres of land and for the patenting of tracts to hundreds of thousands of buyers made him a powerful political figure and made the Land Office one of the largest and most important of federal bureaus. The Land Office issued patents, settled contested claims, and drafted instructions amplifying upon, and clarifying, the public acts.

Able and honest administrators, including John Wilson, Joseph Wilson, and William A. J. Sparks, made notable records, but weaker men tolerated inefficiency and corruption. Despite complaints from the West and from Congress, the office received little attention. As revenue from the public land became increasingly less important, the office seemed less related to the Treasury Department. In 1849 it moved to the newly created Department of the Interior, where it worked with the Office of Indian Affairs, the Bureau of Patents, the Bureau of Pensions, and the Office of Agricultural Statistics. Under the Department of Interior, it made detailed reports on minerals, agricultural possibilities, and forests of the West, which constitute a major source for historians of that section.

Consonant with a change in the attitude of Congress, the General Land Office became increasingly settler-minded until the Homestead Act of 1862 provided free lands. No bureaucrats like having their responsibilities and staff reduced. Consequently, when the Forest Reserve Act of 1891 withdrew from entry large timbered areas of the public lands for conservation and public management, which they had never had, the commissioner of the General Land Office was not happy. Yet these reservations remained under his control until 1905, when they transferred to the National Forest Service under Gifford Pinchot in the Department of Agriculture.

In 1916, by the forfeiture of the land grant of the Oregon and California Railroad for failure to conform to the provisions of the granting act, 2,891,000 acres of richly endowed Douglas fir land in Oregon returned to the Department of the Interior, which enabled it to begin its own forestry development policies. After Harold Ickes became secretary of the interior in 1933, the department became ardently conservationist in administering the grazing districts created under the Taylor Grazing Act of 1934 and the Oregon and California Railroad lands. By 1947 the land disposal responsibilities of the General Land Office, which had been chiefly concerned with transferring public lands into private ownership rather than with conserving them in public ownership, were largely over. Its activities transferred to the new Bureau of Land Management. Thereafter, the bureau administered the remaining public lands, the 140 million acres in grazing districts, the Oregon and California Railroad forest lands, and the leasing and sale of mineral rights. The bureau's aims are to protect the public lands from thoughtless exploiters and to develop and preserve the lands for economic use, recreation, wildlife, and scenic beauty.

BIBLIOGRAPHY

Clarke, Jeanne Nienaber. *Roosevelt's Warrior: Harold L. Ickes and the New Deal.* Baltimore: Johns Hopkins University Press, 1996.

Feller, Daniel. *The Public Lands in Jacksonian Politics.* Madison: University of Wisconsin Press, 1984.

Oberly, James Warren. *Sixty Million Acres: American Veterans and the Public Lands before the Civil War.* Kent, Ohio: Kent State University Press, 1990.

Rohrbough, Malcolm J. *The Land Office Business: The Settlement and Administration of American Public Lands, 1789–1837.* New York: Oxford University Press, 1968.

Paul W. Gates / A. E.

See also **Conservation; Interior, Department of the; Public Domain; Public Land Commissions; West, American.**

LAND PATENTS.

In English colonial America, the Crown made large grants of territory to individuals and companies. In turn, royal colonial governors later made smaller grants of land that were based on actual surveys of the land. Thus, in colonial America on the Atlantic seaboard, a connection was made between the surveying of a land tract and its "patenting" as private property.

After the American Revolution and the ratification of the Constitution, the Treasury Department was placed in charge of managing the public lands of the new nation. Public lands came to cover all the territory of the nation except the original thirteen states plus Vermont, Kentucky, Tennessee, and Texas. The Treasury Department, and after 1812, the General Land Office, called the granting of title to a buyer of public land a "patent," so the name continued, even after the end of British rule.

The General Land Office issued more than 2 million patents that passed title to individual parcels of public land. Some patentees bought their land for cash, others homesteaded a claim, and still others came into ownership via one of the many donation acts that Congress passed to transfer public lands to private ownership. Whatever the method, the General Land Office followed a two-step procedure in granting a patent. First, the private claimant went to the land office in the land district where the parcel was located. The claimant filled out "entry" papers to select the parcel, and the land office register (clerk) checked the local books to make sure the parcel was still available. The receiver (bursar) took the claimant's payment, because even homesteaders had to pay administrative fees. Next, the district land office register and receiver sent the paperwork to the General Land Office in Washington. That office double-checked the accuracy of the claim, its availability, and the form of payment. Only then did the General Land Office issue a patent, or title, to the land parcel.

Today some American families, and many more libraries, have land patents from the nineteenth century. They are large parchment documents that bear the signature of the commissioner of the General Land Office and of the president of the United States. Alas, for those possessing an "A. Lincoln" signature on their land patent, it was not actually signed by the Great Emancipator, but rather by a clerk in the General Land Office. The Bureau of Land Management (successor agency to the General Land Office) has an online archive of 2 million patents, containing both the legal descriptions of the parcels and digitized images of the actual patents.

BIBLIOGRAPHY

Land Patents of the General Land Office. Available from www.glorecords.blm.gov.

Rohrbough, Malcolm J. *The Land Office Business: The Settlement and Administration of American Public Lands, 1789–1837.* New York: Oxford University Press, 1968.

James Oberly

See also **Homestead Movement; Land Claims; Land Companies; Land Office, U.S. General and Bureau Plans Management.**

LAND POLICY. Classical microeconomic theory posits "land," or natural resources, as one of the three factors of production, along with labor and capital. Ideally, the business firm optimizes the mix of labor, capital, and land to produce at the highest profit, and the theory describes a point of equilibrium and balance. The history of North America, however, at least since the beginning of the eighteenth century, was one of continual disequilibrium and imbalance due to the rapid growth of the white and black populations, and the parallel rapid decline of the American Indian population. The shift of land from American Indian possession to U.S. government ownership and then into private property was a continuing political issue from the founding of the American Republic to the Great Depression of the 1930s. American policymakers frequently disagreed about some of the methods in this process, but there was a widely held consensus in the electorate that the United States had the right to obtain American Indian lands and to convert them as rapidly as possible into private property.

American policymakers inherited from Great Britain a way of looking at North American land known as the "doctrine of discovery." This legal formula proclaimed U.S. sovereignty over the lands within the defined boundaries of the nation. It did not mean that Americans could simply steal land from the American Indians as needed. Rather, the doctrine of discovery meant that the United States had the exclusive right to negotiate with American Indian nations for the permanent cession of land to U.S. ownership. The Articles of Confederation, the federal Constitution, and the first Congress elected under the Constitution all insisted on federal, national supervision of this land transfer process. The negotiated treaty—not the cavalry—was the instrument by which the United States assembled its public lands patrimony. In the intricate details of more than 350 separate land cession treaties with American Indian nations may be found the history of the American public lands formation.

In 1783, when Great Britain recognized American independence, there was no public land of the American nation, even though its boundaries extended from the Atlantic to the Mississippi, and from the Great Lakes to the Gulf of Mexico. The states had claims to vast lands west of the Appalachian Mountains. That balance changed when the separate states ceded their claims to the lands northwest of the Ohio River to the federal government. In 1785, the original public domain became the NORTHWEST TERRITORY. From the first trans-Ohio settlement at Marietta, all the way to the Pacific Ocean, the lands that passed from American Indian possession to the United States became part of the public domain. And between 1785 and 1934, more than 70 percent of the public lands from Ohio to California passed into private ownership. Only the lands in the original thirteen states, plus Vermont, Kentucky, Tennessee, and Texas, were outside the public domain.

Policymakers in the early Republic contemplated a regular process to transfer land from American Indian nations to private farmers, ranchers, miners, and lumbermen. After Senate ratification of a particular land cession treaty, the lands acquired from that American Indian nation became a part of the public domain and were managed by an extensive federal agency known as the General Land Office (GLO). The GLO had two great functions: first, to apply the rectangular survey to the public domain so that order and predictability could be imposed on the lands; and, second, to manage the transfer by sale, donation, or grant to states, business firms, and private individuals of the lands. The GLO's surveyor-general and his crews took their axes, surveying chains, and pencils and notebooks across each newly acquired tract and subdivided the land into parcels of 160 acres, known as a "quarter-section," because in the language of land, one square mile (640 acres) was known as a section. Congress, meanwhile, was busy creating new public land districts with a GLO agency known as the land office at the center of each district, a ripe source of patronage and politics. After completion of the survey, the surveyor-general turned over the plats to the commissioner of the GLO, who then advised the president of the United States to declare lands in the district open. The president set a date for a public auction, and then land-lookers and would-be buyers examined the papers and sometimes the lands before the day set for competitive bidding on parcels. On occasion, auction day saw so much activity and competition that the phrase "doing a land office business" was coined to describe a scene of frenzied commerce. Those parcels that did not receive a bid at auction then went for sale at the minimum price set by Congress, $1.25 an acre after 1820. Parcels might be claimed at the land office in ways other than cash purchase, such as land grants given as pensions to soldiers of the War of 1812. Some tracts of public land were withdrawn from private selection before the auction, such as the parcels awarded to aid the construction of the great transcontinental railroads. The railroad became the first private owner, seeking settlers to purchase the land, convert it to farmland, and fill the railroad cars with outgoing produce.

And so the process went from American Indian land cession to GLO survey to presidential declaration, and finally the conversion to private property by an individual's entry selection at the district land office. This idealized process often had complications. So-called "squatters," also known as pre-emptors, often claimed land parcels without paying for them. Sometimes the squatters acted even before the surveyor-general had done his work. Too regularly, squatters seized parcels of Native land before the treaty cession, thereby provoking a bloody crisis that made imperative the treaty negotiations to obtain the land cession and prevent more trespassing.

The American political system devoted much attention to land policy issues from the earliest days of independence. The Congress operating under the Articles of Confederation established the basics of the rectangular survey system in the Northwest Ordinance of 1787. The Congress of 1796 set the minimum price and acreage standards for private purchasers: two dollars an acre, and 640 acres. The Democratic-Republican opposition called both minimums into question, and thereafter, the trend in public land policy was toward ever-smaller, ever-cheaper standards. By 1820, the price had dropped to $1.25 an acre for as little a purchase as 40 acres. The Democratic Party of Andrew Jackson made lenient treatment for the squatter its centerpiece of land policy, with Congress repeatedly forgiving prior squatting on the public lands and extending to the squatters extra time to pay for their parcels. In 1841, this became general policy with the Preemption Act that made squatting legal. The opposition Whigs hoped to use some of the revenue generated by public land sales and to return most of it to the older, seaboard states. That same year, their policy became law with the 1841 Distribution Act.

The politics of the public lands also played a part in the emergence of the third party system of Republicans and Democrats between 1854 and 1896. The 1856 Republican slogan of "free soil, free labor, free speech, free men" made the connection between the economics of the firm from an antislavery perspective: the public lands should be given away at no cost to those who pledged to work them with their own labor, also known as the "homestead" idea. Proslavery elements in the Democratic Party in the late 1850s opposed homestead as "squatter sovereignty," and it was not until the Republicans controlled both the Congress and the executive during the Civil War that the homestead bill became law in 1862. And yet the Republicans did not limit their public land policy to the homestead principal. If free land could help a poor but willing laborer build a farm, then free land could also help a poor but willing capitalist build a railroad. And free land could help a state build a land-grant university. Especially during Abraham Lincoln's administration (1861–1865), tens of millions of acres of public land were granted to railroads as an aid in raising capital to complete their construction. Similarly, the Congress and President Lincoln oversaw the granting of millions of acres of the public domain to states for higher education purposes. Some of America's leading colleges, notably Cornell University, were established from the proceeds generated by public land donations to the states. Additional Republican legislation aided miners, ranchers, and lumbermen with generous donations of free lands from the public domain.

After 1862, settlers were slow at first to take advantage of the Homestead Act, but with each passing decade more and more men and women staked their claim to a parcel on the public lands, even as America became a more urban, industrialized nation. The high point for homestead claims came between 1900 and 1920, a time marked by steep commodity prices for farm products. Still, after 1890, it became harder for would-be settlers to find good land for farming. The nation had more than half-a-billion acres in public lands, but much of that acreage was on desert or otherwise inhospitable lands. Congress responded to a perceived shortage in available land in two ways. First, in a bitter irony, it passed various "surplus land acts" that carved 100 million acres from existing American Indian reservations in the West, on the theory that the Indians were not using the lands. Those lands were placed in the public domain for settlers to claim, and a century later gave rise to disputes over jurisdiction between Indians and non-Indians. Second, in 1902, Congress passed the Reclamation Act that established federal assistance to irrigate the dry lands of the West and prepare them for settlers.

The surplus land acts and the Reclamation Act marked the end of congressional efforts to make the public lands available for any settler who wanted a farm. The long slide in farm prices after World War I reduced the number of prospective pioneers. The New Deal's Taylor Grazing Act of 1934 clearly marked the permanent shift in public land policy from sales and grants toward reserving the public lands as federal property to be managed for the benefit of ranchers, other producers, and the general public. Even before 1934, Congress had begun to take lands out of the public domain and place them into permanent reserved status, most notably the national park system and the national forest system. Throughout the twentieth century, and into the twenty-first, both systems grew significantly in size and service area.

As a developing nation in the first century and a half of its existence, the United States used its public lands to assist in economic growth. For much of that time, land policy was designed to extend the value of labor and capital. A developing nation that was often short of funds in its treasury found the public domain an easy source for financing popular endeavors, and the constant goal of federal policy was converting the public lands to private property. By contrast, since 1934, the mature, industrial United States has reserved its public lands for a variety of purposes, including wilderness for its own sake.

BIBLIOGRAPHY

Feller, Daniel. *The Public Lands in Jacksonian Politics.* Madison: University of Wisconsin Press, 1984.

Gates, Paul W. *History of Public Land Law Development.* Washington, D.C.: Government Printing Office, 1968.

Johnson, Hildegard. *Order Upon the Land: The U.S. Rectangular Survey and the Upper Mississippi Country.* New York: Oxford University Press, 1976.

Kappler, Charles. *Indian Affairs: Laws and Treaties.* Vol. 2. Washington, D.C.: Government Printing Office, 1904.

Oberly, James W. *Sixty Million Acres: American Veterans and the Public Lands before the Civil War.* Kent, Ohio: Kent State University Press, 1990.

Opie, John. *The Law of the Land: Two Hundred Years of American Farmland Policy.* Lincoln: University of Nebraska Press, 1987.

Peffer, E. Louise. *The Closing of the Public Domain: Disposal and Reservation Policies, 1900–1950.* Stanford, Calif.: Stanford University Press, 1951.

Pisani, Donald J. *To Reclaim a Divided West: Water, Law, and Public Policy, 1848–1902.* Albuquerque: University of New Mexico Press, 1992.

Robbins, William G., and James C. Foster. *Land in the American West: Private Claims and the Common Good.* Seattle: University of Washington Press, 2000.

James Oberly

See also **Free Soil Party; Indian Land Cessions; Irrigation; Northwest Territory; Reclamation.**

LAND SCRIP and land warrants were certificates from the Land Office granting people private ownership of certain portions of public lands. Congress authorized issues of scrip—some directly, others only after trial of claims before special commissions or the courts. It also placed restrictions on the use of certain kinds of scrip, making them less valuable than scrip with no limitations. Scrip was used primarily to reward veterans, to give land allotments to children of intermarried Native Americans, to make possible exchanges of private land for public, to indemnify people who lost valid land claims through General Land Office errors, and to subsidize agricultural colleges.

The greatest volume of scrip or warrants was given to soldiers of the American Revolution, the War of 1812, the Mexican-American War, and, in 1855, to veterans of all wars who had not previously received a land bounty or who had received less than 160 acres. Warrants of the first two wars were for land located in military tracts set aside for that purpose; those of the Mexican-American War allowed entry to any surveyed public land open to purchase at $1.25 an acre. A total of 68,300,652 acres was thus conveyed to 426,879 veterans, their heirs, or their assignees.

Treaties with the Choctaw (1830) and Chickasaw (1832) Indians of Mississippi and Alabama allocated several million acres in individual allotments and land scrip, all of which became the object of speculation by whites and fell into the hands of powerful white traders and a number of prominent political leaders. For the next thirty years, treaties with Indian tribes were almost impossible to negotiate without the inclusion of similar provisions for allotments and scrip, so powerful were the traders in those negotiations. Three issues of scrip to two bands of Chippewas and Sioux in the 1850s and 1860s, totaling 395,000 acres, similarly fell into the hands of speculators, who used it to acquire valuable timberland in Minnesota and California that they would otherwise have been unable to acquire legally.

In the MORRILL ACT of 1862, Congress granted each state 30,000 acres for each member it had in the House and Senate to aid in the establishment of agricultural and mechanical arts colleges. Land was given to states containing public domain; states with no public lands were given scrip that they had to sell to third parties to enter land in public domain states. As with military warrants, the scrip—totaling 7,700,000 acres—fell well below the basic price of public lands, thereby reducing the cost of that land to settlers and speculators and minimizing the endowment of colleges.

The next major scrip measure was the Soldiers' and Sailors' Additional Homestead Act of 1872, which allowed veterans of the Civil War to count their military service toward the five years required to gain title to a free homestead. It also authorized those homesteading on less than 160 acres to bring their total holdings to 160 acres. The government-issued scrip was greatly in demand as it could be used to enter the $2.50-an-acre reserved land within the railroad land grant areas and to acquire valuable timberland not otherwise open to purchase. In 1877, scrip owners were using it to enter recently ceded Mille Lac Indian lands in Minnesota, worth from $10 to $30 an acre.

Other measures were enacted to indemnify holders of public-land claims that were confirmed long after the land had been patented to settlers. Claimants were provided with scrip equivalent to the loss they sustained. Indemnity scrip for some 1,265,000 acres was issued, most of which was subject to entry only on surveyed land open to purchase at $1.25 an acre. The chief exceptions were the famous Valentine scrip for 13,316 acres and the Porterfield scrip for 6,133 acres, which could be used to enter unoccupied, unappropriated, nonmineral land, whether surveyed or not. These rare and valuable forms of scrip could be used to acquire town and bridge sites, islands, tracts adjacent to booming cities such as Las Vegas, or water holes controlling the use of large acreages of rangelands. Their value reached $75 to $100 an acre in 1888.

Least defensible of all the scrip measures were the carelessly drawn Forest Management Act of 1897 and the Mount Rainier Act of 1899, which allowed land owners within the national forests and Mount Rainier National Park to exchange their lands for public lands elsewhere. Under these provisions it was possible for railroads to cut the timber on their national holdings, then surrender the cutover lands for "lieu scrip" that allowed them to enter the best forest lands in the public domain. It was charged that some national forests, and possibly Mount Rainier National Park, were created to enable inside owners to rid themselves of their less desirable lands inside for high stumpage areas outside. The Weyerhaeuser Company acquired some of its richest stands of timber with Mount Rainier scrip. After much criticism, the exchange feature was ended in 1905.

As public lands rapidly diminished and the demand for land ownership intensified, values of scattered undeveloped land increased. This was accompanied by the increase in value of the various forms of scrip, without which it was impossible to acquire these tracts, because

public land sales were halted in 1889. Peak prices of the nineteenth century seemed small in the twentieth century, when speculators bid up quotations to $500, $1,000, and even $4,000 an acre. By 1966 administrative relaxation had wiped out some distinctions between types of scrip; Valentine, Porterfield, and "Sioux Half-Breed" scrip were all accepted for land with an appraised value of $1,386 an acre, and Soldiers' and Sailors' Additional Homestead and Forest Management lieu scrip could be exchanged for land with a value from $275 to $385 an acre. At that time, 3,655 acres of the most valuable scrip and 7,259 acres of that with more limitations on use were outstanding.

BIBLIOGRAPHY

Gates, Paul W. *History of Public Land Law Development.* Washington, D.C.: U.S. Government Printing Office, 1968.

———. *The Jeffersonian Dream: Studies in the History of American Land Policy and Development.* Albuquerque: University of New Mexico Press, 1996.

Oberly, James W. *Sixty Million Acres: American Veterans and the Public Lands before the Civil War.* Kent, Ohio: Kent State University Press, 1990.

Paul W. Gates / A. R.

See also **Indian Intermarriage; Indian Land Cessions; Land Bounties; Land Grants: Land Grants for Education; Land Policy; Land Speculation; Lumber Industry; Public Domain.**

LAND SPECULATION. The favorite object of speculation in America before the era of big business was public land. Investors could buy it cheaply in large quantities and withhold it from market, if they had sufficient capital to carry it, until rising prices brought profits. Memories of high land values in the Old World and of the social prestige enjoyed by the possessor of broad acres produced in Americans an insatiable lust for land.

Land speculation began with the first settlements in America. The Virginia proprietors, disappointed at the meager returns from their investment, granted themselves great tracts of land from which they hoped to draw substantial incomes. Similarly, the Penns and Calverts in Pennsylvania and Maryland and the early proprietors of New York, New Jersey, and the Carolinas speculated in land in an imperial way. Later in the colonial period, a new crop of land companies composed of English and colonial speculators sought both title to and political control over great tracts in the MISSISSIPPI VALLEY. The Mississippi, the Georgiana, the Wabash, the Indiana, the Loyal, and the Ohio land companies attracted some of the ablest colonial leaders into their ranks, among them George Washington, Richard Henry Lee, Benjamin Franklin, the Whartons, and George Croghan. The struggles of these rival companies for charters and grants played an important role in British colonial policy during the years before the Revolution.

The trival land claims of the colonies matched company rivalries. One of the most notable was the conflict between Connecticut and Pennsylvania for the Wyoming Valley, which Connecticut granted to the Susquehanna Land Company. In western Virginia, Richard Henderson and his Transylvania Company, which claimed title to a great tract received from the Indians, came into conflict with Virginia and were successful in receiving only a small part of the area confirmed to them.

Most influential colonials tried their luck at speculating, either through the land companies or on their own account. George Washington was a large landowner in Virginia, Pennsylvania, and the Ohio country; Robert and Gouverneur Morris, William Duer, Oliver Phelps, Nathaniel Gorham, and William Johnson acquired princely domains in Pennsylvania, New York, and Maine. The Morrises negotiated a number of large purchases and resold tracts to others; perhaps the largest of them went to the Holland Land Company. Dutch capitalists who bought the Holland Reserve in western New York and were busily engaged in settling it during the first third of the nineteenth century made up this company. In the meantime, speculators received parcels comprising most of upstate New York. Among the most prominent of the speculators were the Wadsworths of the Genesee country, John Jacob Astor, and Peter Smith, father of Gerrit Smith. These men, unlike Robert Morris, were able to retain their lands long enough either to resell at high prices or settle tenants on them.

The largest purchase and the most stupendous fraud was the sale in 1795 of 21.5 million acres of western lands in Yazoo River country by the legislature of Georgia to four companies for one and one-half cents an acre. The next legislature canceled the sale, but the purchasers, frequently innocent third parties, waged a long fight to secure justice, claiming that the obligation of the contract clause in the federal Constitution prevented the Georgia legislature from reversing the original sale. The SUPREME COURT, in *Fletcher v. Peck* (1810), agreed with this interpretation. The Yazoo frauds became a *cause célèbre* in which John Randolph, Thomas Jefferson, John Marshall, and other notables took prominent parts.

Undeveloped Lands

When donations by states with western land claims created the public domain of the United States, speculative interests converged upon Congress with requests to purchase tracts of land north of the OHIO RIVER. In fact, the land speculation craze was partly responsible for the adoption of the Northwest Ordinance of 1787, which set up a government for the ceded territory north of the Ohio. A group of New England capitalists known as the Ohio Company of Associates wished to buy a tract of land in southeastern Ohio for a New England settlement. To get the measure through Congress, it seemed necessary to enlarge the original project and to create a second organization, the Scioto Company, which consisted of members of Congress and other influential people who planned to buy some 5 million acres of land. The formation of the Scioto Company increased support for the enactment of the Northwest Ordinance, but the company itself was a failure because it could not fulfill its contract with the government. The Ohio Company of Associates did, however, succeed in planting a little New England outpost at Marietta on the Ohio River. In 1788 John Cleves Symmes of New Jersey also bought a large tract from Congress. These purchases virtually defeated the purpose of the Land Ordinance of 1785, which authorized the sale of land at $1.00 an acre, or a third more than the Scioto Company paid, and the Land Act of 1796, which raised the price to $2.00 an acre, because the speculators whom Congress had allowed to acquire large tracts of land at lower prices than were offered to individual settlers were able to undersell the government.

There were three land speculation periods after the creation of the public domain: 1817–1819, 1834–1837, and 1853–1857. Easterners such as Daniel Webster, Caleb Cushing, Edward Everett, Amos Lawrence, Moses and John Carter Brown, and James S. Wadsworth and southerners such as John C. Breckinridge, John Slidell, Eli Shorter, and William Grayson bought western lands in large quantities. Speculators again organized land companies, and they entered tracts embracing entire townships. The New York and Boston Illinois Land Company acquired 900,000 acres in the Military Tract of Illinois; the American Land Company had estates in Indiana, Illinois, Michigan, Wisconsin, Mississippi, and Arkansas; and the Boston and Western Land Company owned 60,000 acres in Illinois and Wisconsin.

The Homestead Act of 1862 did not end land speculation; some of the largest purchases occurred after it was passed. William S. Chapman alone bought over 1 million acres of land in California and Nevada; Henry W. Sage, John McGraw, and Jeremiah Dwight, benefactors of Cornell University, entered 352,000 acres of timberland in the Northwest and the South; and Francis Palms and Frederick E. Driggs bought 486,000 acres of timberland in Wisconsin and Michigan. Not until 1889 did the federal government take effective steps to end large speculative purchases, and by that date it had parted with its best lands. At the same time, the canal and railroad land grants and the lands given to the states for drainage and educational purposes were also attracting a great deal of speculative purchasing.

The accumulation of vast quantities of land in advance of settlement created many problems for the West, some of which remain unsolved. The Indians lost their lands more rapidly than the needs of the population dictated, and more social control of westward expansion and land purchases might have prevented the frequent clashes between settlers and Indians. In some places, absentee proprietors who withheld large amounts of land from development while waiting for higher prices created "speculators' deserts." Settlers were widely dispersed because they could not find land at reasonable prices close to existing settlements. This settlement pattern consequently aggravated the problem of providing transportation facilities, and as a result of the importunities of settlers, developers built thousands of miles of railroads through sparsely settled country, which could provide but little traffic for the roads.

Nevertheless, the speculators and land companies were an important factor in the development of the West. Their efforts to attract settlers to their lands through the distribution of pamphlets and other literature describing the western country lured thousands from their homes in the eastern states and the countries of northern Europe to the newly developing sections of the West. They also aided in building improvements, such as roads, canals, and railroads, to make the life of the immigrant easier. Land speculators were often unpopular and regarded unfavorably in newly opened areas because they often left their holdings undeveloped. By contrast, local people, actively selling and improving their holdings and thus contributing to the growth of the town and country, were shown every favor, were popular, and were frequently elected to public office.

The land reform movement, with its corollary limitation of land sales, had as its objective the retention of the public lands for free homesteads for settlers. Beginning in 1841, new land acts, such as the Preemption Act (1841), the Graduation Act (1854), the Homestead Act (1862), the Timber Culture Act (1873), and the Timber and Stone Act (1878) restricted sales to 160 or 320 acres. Nevertheless, the cash sale system continued, although after 1862 very little new land became open to unrestricted entry, and large purchases were made only in areas previously opened to sale. Although reformers had tolerated the granting of land to railroads in the 1850s and 1860s, they later turned against this practice and began a move to have forfeited the grants unearned by failure to build railroads. In the midst of a strong revulsion against what were called "monopolistic" landholdings by railroads, cattle kings, and lumber companies in 1888–1891, Congress adopted the Land Forfeiture Act of 1890, which required the return of unearned grants to the public domain, and enacted other measures to end the cash sale system, to limit the amount of land that an individual could acquire from the government to 320 acres, and to make it more difficult to abuse the settlement laws. However, through the use of dummy entrymen and the connivance of local land officers, land accumulation continued.

Urban Property
Speculation in urban property was not so well structured as was speculation in rural lands, but investors widely indulged in it and found it subject to the same excesses in periods of active industrial growth and to a similar drastic deflation in values following the economic crises of 1837, 1857, 1873, and 1930–1933. During the boom years, prices for choice real estate in New York and other rapidly growing cities skyrocketed, only to decline when depression brought economic activity to a grinding halt. Old-line families made fortunes in New York, Philadelphia, and Chicago from swiftly rising real estate values. Among the parvenus, the best known is John Jacob Astor; the great wealth he accumulated enabled his family to rise to the top of the social ladder. With remarkable prescience, between 1800 and 1840, Astor invested $2 million, made from his trade with China and from returns in his land business, in land in Greenwich Village and elsewhere in Manhattan, but outside New York City limits. He acquired the fee simple to the land bought from Aaron Burr and George Clinton and took long-term leases on land from Trinity Church. After dividing the acreage bought from Clinton into blocks and lots, he waited until the demand rose and then began selling. His profit from these sales was substantial, but in later years he concentrated on granting long leases on his property. By his death, his rent roll alone was bringing in $200,000 annually. His estate, valued at from $18 million to $20 million, mostly invested in real estate that was rapidly appreciating, had made him the richest man in the country. In two successive generations, the family fortune, still concentrated in Manhattan real estate, increased to $50 million and $100 million. Other New York families were enjoying like successes in the burgeoning real estate market. The purchase in 1929 by John D. Rockefeller Jr. of a long-term lease from Columbia University for the 11-acre tract on which he built Rockefeller Center was the most spectacular real estate transaction up to that point. He was able to get an eighty-seven-year lease for a ground rent of $3.3 million a year. With other city property, this acquisition placed the Rockefeller family among the largest owners of New York property.

In every growing city, similar increases in land values occurred, to the profit of those whose families by wisdom or good luck acquired land early. In Chicago, for example, lots on State Street between Monroe and Adams climbed from $25 per front foot in 1836 to $27,500 in 1931, a depression year. The families of Potter Palmer, Walter L. Newberry, and George M. Pullman were representative of the new rich in the Windy City.

Each generation produced its new millionaires: those who had the foresight to buy land in promising urban centers when prices were low. The spendthrift lifestyle of the new millionaires and their children aroused resentment, especially among the followers of Henry George. To tax the unearned increment in rising land values for the social good, George proposed a single tax on land so that the enhanced value of land that stemmed from society's growth would benefit the government directly. He also criticized the concentration of rural land ownership in a few hands, a situation most evident in California. Appropriately, George had his largest following in New York, where economic pressures had pushed up land values. To further his reforms, George offered himself as an independent candidate for mayor in New York in 1886.

Without any party machine to fight for him and protect his interests at the polls, he still won 30 percent of the vote, against 41 percent for Tammany's candidate and 23 percent for Theodore Roosevelt, the Republican candidate. By that time, George was the best-known economist in the country. Few people in America or Great Britain were unaware of his single-tax proposal and his strictures on the unearned increment that was creating so many millionaires.

For everyone who turned to land and tax reform there were several who tried to emulate, on a smaller scale, the achievements of the Astors, the Schermerhorns, and the Hetty Greens by getting in on the ground floor of promising municipalities. In some states, particularly Illinois, eastern Iowa, and Kansas, town-site promoters took up hundreds of quarter sections of public land; laid out their blocks and lots; prepared alluring lithographed maps showing imagined buildings, factories, and homes; and peddled their towns, blocks, and lots in older communities that had long since given up the prospect of becoming miracle cities. Most of these dream cities never flourished, but a few, with aggressive leadership, managed to become the county seat, the territorial or state capital, or a railroad center, or managed to acquire the U.S. land office, a religious college, or a state university or other public institution. These few grew moderately.

Among the major promoters of towns and cities were the land-grant railroads, which created station sites every ten or fifteen miles along their routes and offered numerous advantages to persons and institutions for locating in the vicinity. The officers of the Illinois Central alone laid out thirty-seven towns in Illinois, and the transcontinental railroads created far more communities around their stations. In fact, the struggle of town promoters to bring railroads and state and federal institutions to their communities constitutes one of the central themes of western American history. Some of these once-flourishing cities or towns have become ghost towns; few have gone on to flourish and grow.

The United States did not accept Henry George's view that profits from rising land values should be used for the public good, but it has increasingly sought to restrict property owners' rights by zoning regulations in both rural and urban areas. The outstanding illustration of such action is New York State's Adirondack Park Agency Act of 1971, intended to protect the wild character of the Adirondacks. The law curbs the creation of subdivisions with numerous small sites for second homes.

BIBLIOGRAPHY
Feller, Daniel. *The Public Lands in Jacksonian Politics.* Madison: University of Wisconsin Press, 1984.

Gates, Paul Wallace. *The Jeffersonian Dream: Studies in the History of American Land Policy and Development.* Albuquerque: University of New Mexico Press, 1996.

Hyman, Harold M. *American Singularity: The 1787 Northwest Ordinance, the 1862 Homestead and Morrill Acts, and the 1944 G.I. Bill.* Athens: University of Georgia Press, 1986.

Oberly, James Warren. *Sixty Million Acres: American Veterans and the Public Lands before the Civil War.* Kent, Ohio: Kent State University Press, 1990.

Williams, Frederick D. *The Northwest Ordinance: Essays on Its Formulation, Provisions, and Legacy.* East Lansing: Michigan State University Press, 1989.

Paul W. Gates / A. E.

See also **Financial Panics; Land Policy; Ordinances of 1784, 1785, and 1787; Public Domain; Single Tax; Wyoming Valley, Settlement of; Yazoo Fraud.**

LANDSCAPE ARCHITECTURE is both the art and profession of landscape design, in which topographical, horticultural, and other elements are arranged to suit human use. While humans have shaped landscapes since antiquity, landscape architecture developed as a profession only in the mid-1800s, and the term was first used in 1858 by Frederick Law Olmsted and Calvert Vaux, who were then designing and constructing New York's Central Park.

Olmsted and Vaux may have coined the term, but they did not originate the art. Americans had long intentionally shaped landscapes to suit various needs, particularly in streetscapes, garden designs, and park construction. Colonial Americans borrowed heavily from European landscape design, particularly in creating classical, rectilinear gardens, with straight paths and square beds of formal plantings. Although regional differences developed early, as the southern climate and plantation culture encouraged the development of larger gardens, formal design remained a constant. George Washington's Mount Vernon gardens represent the grand gardens of the late 1700s—the long bowling green provided a striking vista, and the symmetrical garden plots provided both beauty and produce. The University of Virginia and the grounds of Monticello remind us of the importance of landscape design to Thomas Jefferson, who built them with an eye to both attractiveness and efficiency.

Andrew Jackson Downing's *A Treatise on the Theory and Practice of Landscape Gardening, Adapted to North America* (1841) was the first major work on gardening by an American. Downing attempted to describe a growing uniqueness of American landscape design. While the work marked the movement away from the classical style and toward a picturesque aesthetic, Downing's book also revealed the continuing debt American landscape design owed to Europeans. Deeply influenced by Romanticism, itself of European origins, the picturesque style emphasized more natural landscapes, with variety, irregularity, and informality. The picturesque style played to America's growing appreciation of its distinctive wilderness. In essence, picturesque gardens could capture a bit of the wildness and preserve it in accessible spaces. Since gaining popularity in the 1850s, the picturesque style has continued to dominate landscape design, with formal gardens playing a smaller role in American landscape architecture.

The profession of landscape architecture developed with the growing urban demand for parks after 1850. After Olmsted and Vaux set the standard with their designs for Central Park and Brooklyn's Prospect Park, most American cities sought their own landscaped parks. Olmsted became the premiere landscape architect and, as that new term implied, he intended to design the landscape as fully as architects design buildings. Natural elements, such as trees, shrubs, and water, would be among his tools, but his creations would be primarily cultural. Mixing open spaces, formal walks, rustic architecture, and naturalistic woodlands, these picturesque landscapes offered variety to increasingly regularized lives.

Even as landscaped parks provided relief from monotonous city life, some visionaries sought to provide more pervasive relief by designing picturesque neighborhoods and communities. In the mid-1850s Alexander Jackson Davis, a protégé of Downing, designed the first picturesque suburb, Llewellyn Park in New Jersey. With its curvilinear streets and planned open "ramble," Llewellyn Park became a model for future suburban developments, including Olmsted's Chicago suburban design, Riverside, built in the following decade. In addition to the movement to create new, planned, landscaped communities, late in the 1800s, the City Beautiful Movement encouraged a greater level of planning throughout cities. While not strictly concerned with landscape design, the City Beautiful Movement did emphasize urban beauty as created by streetscapes, vistas, and architectural design. Inspired in part by the great success of the 1893 World's Columbian Exposition, held in Chicago, reformers demanded more beauty in their cities, particularly in the form of Beaux Arts architecture, open civic plazas, and striking street vistas. These ideals made their way into the 1902 plan for Washington, D.C., with its long, formal mall, neoclassical architecture, and formally placed monuments. Many other cities initiated redevelopment on a smaller scale, including Denver's civic center, created by 1921. By that date most large American cities had transformed some significant public space to fit the City Beautiful vision.

The World's Columbian Exposition and the City Beautiful Movement marked the return of formal landscape design, as suited the renewed interest in neoclassical architecture. Private development also witnessed a turn toward classical design, particularly in the gardens of America's new castles, built for the growing number of superrich robber barons. These massive estates often included a range of landscape designs, but by the early 1900s the mansions of Newport, Rhode Island, and other refuges for the extremely wealthy, were surrounded by well-trimmed hedges, straight paths, and formal fountains.

Despite the return of classical design, the picturesque continued to dominate city planning, particularly as cities spread out along railroad lines and increasingly important roadways. The curvilinear roads, ample tree plantings, and open spaces of the early planned suburbs continued into the twentieth century. John Nolen's 1923 Mariemont, Ohio, design, for example, relied on European ideas of the garden city, as is evident in the Tudor architecture of the town center, the large central commons, and abundant open and wooded spaces. Mariemont residents, just fifteen minutes from downtown Cincinnati, could think themselves living in the English countryside. The picturesque suburban ideal persisted, influencing the United States Resettlement Administration's design of several "greenbelt" cities in the 1930s, including Greenbelt, Maryland, in 1936. The lush landscapes of these communities, and other less planned suburbs around the nation, contrasted markedly with dense urban cores. They also hid the numerous and necessary connections between suburban and urban landscapes.

After World War II, American landscape architecture revealed a greater diversity of influences, including Asian gardens and massive modern art. Particularly on corporate campuses, where the picturesque could be inappropriate or impossible, modern landscape designs turned again to straight lines, but often at a tilt or on multiple levels, and natural components often found themselves extremely confined, as waterfalls clung to rectangular walls and trees sat upon pavement in large pots. Modern landscape designs created deceptively complex visual spaces, more accepting of artificiality than the picturesque designs of previous decades.

BIBLIOGRAPHY

Major, Judith. *To Live in the New World: A. J. Downing and American Landscape Gardening.* Cambridge, Mass.: MIT Press, 1997.

Newton, Norman T. *Design on the Land: The Development of Landscape Architecture.* Cambridge, Mass.: Harvard University Press, 1971.

Rybczynski, Witold. *A Clearing in the Distance: Frederick Law Olmsted and America in the Nineteenth Century.* New York: Scribners, 1999.

David Stradling

See also **Central Park; City Planning; Suburbanization.**

LARAMIE, FORT, originally constructed in 1834 by fur traders, served as a meeting place for economic exchange between traders, trappers, and Indians. During the 1840s, the post's strategic location near the intersection of the Laramie and North Platte Rivers made it an important way station for emigrants moving west along the Oregon and Mormon Trails. When the increasing flow of westward migrants created conflicts with American Indian peoples, specifically the Northern Cheyennes and the Lakota Sioux, the U.S. Army purchased Fort Laramie and expanded the small log structure into a major military post.

After 1849, Fort Laramie was an important conduit in the U.S. government's western policy. While no major military engagements occurred within its immediate vicinity, the post served as a major staging ground for army expeditions against Indian nations in the Dakotas and Montana during the 1860s and 1870s. The fort was also a crucial hub in the civilian transportation and communication network that linked the Pacific coast with the eastern states. The Pony Express, Deadwood Stagecoach, and Trans-Continental Telegraph all used the fort at one time or another. However, Fort Laramie's most significant contribution to the conquest of the American West was its diplomatic role in the confinement of the Plains Indian tribes onto reservations. Two treaties signed at the fort, the first in 1851 and the second in 1868, paved the way for the transfer of vast expanses of Indian territory to the U.S. government and the relocation of thousands of Cheyennes, Sioux, and other Plains Indian peoples onto permanent reservations.

With the abatement of the western Indian wars during the 1880s, the army abandoned the fort in 1890 and auctioned its buildings to civilians. The federal government reacquired the surviving structures in 1938 and proclaimed the site a national monument, administered by the National Park Service.

BIBLIOGRAPHY

Hafen, Le Roy R., and Francis Marion Young. *Fort Laramie and the Pageant of the West, 1834–1890.* Glendale, Calif.: Arthur H. Clarke, 1938.

Hedren, Paul L. *Fort Laramie in 1876: Chronicle of a Frontier Post at War.* Lincoln: University of Nebraska Press, 1988.

Lavender, David. *Fort Laramie and the Changing Frontier: Fort Laramie National Historic Site, Wyoming.* Washington, D.C.: Department of the Interior, 1983.

Daniel P. Barr

See also **Frontier; Mormon Trail; Oregon Trail.**

LARAMIE, FORT, TREATY OF (1851), represented an attempt to halt intertribal warfare and safeguard travel routes to California and Oregon. Emigration along the Oregon Trail had aggravated conflicts between tribes over access to the fur trade and increasingly scarce resources. Fears that emigrants' destruction of game would provoke Indian retaliation led the Upper Platte agent Thomas Fitzpatrick in 1849 to request funds for a general treaty council. In February 1851 Congress responded with a $100,000 appropriation. Couriers were sent to the Indians appointing a council for 1 September at Fort Laramie in what would become Wyoming. More than 10,000 Indians representing the Lakota, Cheyenne, Arapaho, Shoshoni, Crow, and other tribes gathered for twenty days of negotiations, feasting, and visiting. In the treaty, Indians agreed to allow emigration along the Oregon Trail and to permit the government to build forts to protect the trail. Signatories also pledged to maintain intertribal peace

and respect the territorial boundaries set by the treaty. In return, the government agreed to distribute a $50,000 annuity to cooperating tribes for fifty years. In ratifying the treaty the Senate unilaterally reduced the annuity provision to ten years, with an option for an additional five at the discretion of the president. Although the treaty succeeded in reducing conflict—both between tribes and between Indians and whites—for a time, competition for resources and the militaristic, decentralized nature of Plains Indian communities undercut the effectiveness of the treaty. More importantly, the treaty marked the end of the concept of a "permanent Indian frontier" separating Native Americans and whites, and set the stage for future treaties that confined Indian communities to legally defined reservations.

BIBLIOGRAPHY

Trennert, Robert A., Jr. *Alternative to Extinction: Federal Indian Policy and the Beginnings of the Reservation System, 1846–1851.* Philadelphia: Temple University Press, 1975.

Utley, Robert M. *The Indian Frontier of the American West, 1846–1890.* Albuquerque: University of New Mexico Press, 1984.

Frank Rzeczkowski

See also **Oregon Trail; Tribes: Great Plains;** *and vol. 9:* **Fort Laramie Treaty of 1851.**

LARAMIE, FORT, TREATY OF (1868). Established in 1863 and running through some of the richest game lands on the Northern Plains, the Bozeman Trail (an emigrant trail linking Fort Laramie, Wyoming, to the Montana gold fields) sparked renewed conflict between the United States and Lakota, Cheyenne, and Arapaho bands in the region. In 1866 the United States attempted to negotiate an agreement with the tribes to permit use of the trail, but the arrival of troops sent to occupy the trail before the conclusion of negotiations led to a walkout of prominent Indian leaders and a collapse of the proceedings. In the subsequent conflict—often termed "Red Cloud's War"—hostile Indians inflicted heavy casualties on U.S. troops, particularly in the Fetterman Fight, but were unable to force the abandonment of the forts along the trail. Peace advocates in the East, however, proved unwilling to support a protracted Indian war. In 1867 and 1868 commissioners were sent out to attempt to end the conflict. The 1868 commission drafted a treaty calling for the abandonment of the Bozeman Trail and the recognition of the country north of the North Platte River and east of the Bighorn Mountains in northern Wyoming as "unceded Indian territory" in which no whites might settle. Additionally, all of present-day South Dakota west of the Missouri River was defined as the Great Sioux Reservation. The treaty also provided for the creation of a "civilization" program for the Sioux. It promised annuities, including food, clothing, and educational and technical assistance, to Indians who settled on the new reservation.

The treaty also stipulated that any future land cession by the Lakotas would need to be ratified by three-fourths of all Lakota males. The failure of the United States to obtain the required three-fourths consent following the discovery of gold in the Black Hills in the 1870s and the subsequent invasion of the Hills by whites would spark renewed fighting and become the basis for an ongoing Lakota grievance against the federal government.

BIBLIOGRAPHY

Gray, John S. *Custer's Last Campaign: Mitch Boyer and the Little Big Horn Reconstructed.* Lincoln: University of Nebraska Press, 1991.

Lazarus, Edward. *Black Hills/White Justice: The Sioux Nation Versus the United States, 1775 to the Present.* New York: Harper-Collins, 1991.

Frank Rzeczkowski

See also **Black Hills War; Sioux; Sioux Wars.**

LAS VEGAS.   A tourist economy and federal largesse made Las Vegas, Nevada, the only American metropolitan area founded in the twentieth century to reach one million in population. Yet its past and present are more complex and connected than its "sin city" image suggests.

Before the Neon

Native Americans lived in southern Nevada for thousands of years. Southern Paiutes were the only residents when Rafael Rivera, scouting for Mexican traders, became the first non-Native visitor in January 1830. In May 1844, John Frémont's mapmaking expedition named the area "Las Vegas," Spanish for "the Meadows," for its water and grass.

Aware of Frémont's description, the Mormon leader Brigham Young chose Las Vegas for a mission. Arriving on 14 June 1855, missionaries built a fort, part of which still stands. They left within three years. The miner Octavius Gass started buying land in 1865 and eventually owned nearly 1,000 acres, until old debts cost him his holdings. After the new owner, Archibald Stewart, died in a gunfight in 1884, his widow, Helen, ran the ranch until 1902, selling all but 160 acres to Senator William Clark, a Montana copper baron planning a Los Angeles-to-Salt Lake railroad. When the Union Pacific threatened to compete, they became partners.

After Clark auctioned land on 15 May 1905, Las Vegas became a railroad town, serving passengers and servicing trains. A railroad subsidiary, the Las Vegas Land and Water Company, controlled municipal improvements while limiting growth. Named Clark County seat in 1909 and incorporated as a city in 1911, Las Vegas catered to sin with the red-light district known as Block 16, which offered drinking, gambling, and prostitution despite laws to the contrary.

Dorothy Dandridge. The African American singer-dancer performs at a Las Vegas nightclub in 1955, the year after her role in the movie musical *Carmen Jones* earned her an Academy Award nomination for best actress. LIBRARY OF CONGRESS

The Prewar and Postwar Boom

Hoover Dam construction, begun in March 1931, changed Las Vegas forever. Depression victims poured in, seeking jobs. The federal government built Boulder City to house workers, whose trips downtown boosted the economy—as did the dam's visitors, prompting Las Vegas to market itself as a tourist venue with the annual Helldorado, with parade and rodeo. The New Deal promoted growth: Nevada led the nation in per capita federal spending, and Las Vegas received such projects as a school and parks.

Democratic control of the presidency and Congress aided Las Vegas. Nevada Senator Pat McCarran, elected in 1932, used his seniority and power to obtain federal projects, thereby infusing payroll and attracting new residents. An Army Air Corps gunnery school opened in 1941 and became Nellis Air Force Base, still a key source of jobs and spending. To the southeast, the Basic Magnesium plant refined manganese for the war; the surrounding town, Henderson, housed southern Nevada's only heavy industry as the plant moved into chemical production and research. Northwest of town, the Nevada Test Site opened in 1951 and began conducting aboveground (later underground) atomic tests; while testing was discontinued, the site still supported research at the beginning of the twenty-first century.

Las Vegas increasingly relied on gambling, which the state legalized in 1931. The downtown area benefited, especially in the late 1930s, and many illegal gamblers driven out of California relocated to Las Vegas. During World War II, Benjamin "Bugsy" Siegel, representing gangster Meyer Lansky, invested in downtown casinos

Old Las Vegas. A view of sleepy Fremont Street from the railroad depot, photographed before the dramatic changes in the 1930s. LIBRARY OF CONGRESS

and took over construction of the Flamingo on the nascent "strip." The El Rancho Vegas became the Las Vegas Strip's first resort in 1941, followed in 1942 by the Hotel Last Frontier—both were ranch-style. The Flamingo, Las Vegas's first luxury resort, opened late in 1946, but proved unprofitable. Its turnaround came too late for Siegel, who was killed in July 1947.

The Flamingo's profits inspired more organized crime investment, while for their part gamblers relished practicing their trade legally. A spate of hotel-casinos opened in the 1950s and 1960s, often with loans from the Teamsters and the Bank of Las Vegas, the first bank to loan to casinos; most lenders disdained gambling and feared that mobsters would refuse to repay loans. A disproportionate number of casino owners were Jewish, expanding an already thriving Jewish community.

Las Vegas's image suffered not only for its criminal connections but also for its reputation as the "Mississippi of the West." Banned from patronizing resorts where they performed, black entertainers stayed in segregated West Las Vegas until the late 1950s. While a National Association for the Advancement of Colored People chapter formed in the late 1920s, it was not until the 1950s and 1960s—by which time the black population had grown larger and had gained an organized, educated leadership—that discrimination was overcome. Thus, Las Vegas reflected the national civil rights movement, complete with unrest and lawsuits.

The Age of Legitimacy?

The last third of the century brought corporatization to Las Vegas and casinos to new jurisdictions. State laws passed in 1967 and 1969 enabled publicly traded companies to buy casinos; previously, every stockholder would have been licensed. Thus, Kirk Kerkorian built the International, bought the Flamingo, and sold both to Hilton; he subsequently built the MGM Grand. Steve Wynn parlayed a Bank of Las Vegas loan and a small piece of Strip property into ownership of the Golden Nugget. Aided by junk bond trader Michael Milken, Wynn built the Mirage, Treasure Island, and Bellagio, and owned other properties outside Las Vegas, before Kerkorian took over his Mirage Resorts in 2000. Local operators such as the Boyd Group, Station Casinos, and Harrah's became publicly traded, invested elsewhere, or teamed with Indian reservations operating casinos.

Las Vegas also reinvented itself. "Theming" went back to the 1930s, when operators patterned casinos on the Old West; Caesars Palace's Roman statuary restored the idea in the 1960s. Megaresort builders in the 1990s imploded old resorts, often replaced by replicas—the Luxor (Egypt), Excalibur (medieval castles), Paris, and New York, New York—and enormous properties that were almost cities unto themselves, such as the 5,000-plus-room MGM Grand and the Venetian. By 2001, Las Vegas boasted more than 120,000 hotel rooms, filled annually by millions of tourists.

The city fueled and benefited from this growth. Each census revealed Las Vegas as one of the fastest-growing American cities, if not the fastest, with the population doubling or nearly doubling every decade. The once physically small city expanded as the Howard Hughes Corporation developed Summerlin to the northwest. Green Valley helped Henderson evolve from an industrial city into a suburb. Three Sun City communities attracted "snowbirds" escaping cold winters or retirees seeking an active lifestyle and moderate cost of living. Latinos grew in influence and topped 20 percent of the population in the 2000 census. That same census showed Las Vegas to be home to 1,375,765 of Nevada's 1,998,257 residents, and more ethnically diverse than the rest of the state.

Understandably, problems accompanied growth. Growing suburban communities prompted white flight from the inner city. Schools were overcrowded. Newcomers understandably lacked a sense of community and history, prompting apathy about local affairs and difficulties in developing a cultural community—no performing arts center and classical music companies beset by financial troubles. Downtown declined and redevelopment proved difficult, while the county government controlled prime land, including the Strip. Gaming and other businesses sometimes clashed over economic diversification, yet shared ample political power. Las Vegas enjoyed a large majority in the state legislature, but its delegation voted more by party than region.

While obtaining water from Arizona's allotment from the Colorado River appeared to ease concern over Las Vegas's ability to maintain an adequate water supply, debates still raged over air quality, education, traffic, the tax structure, and concentrated political power. Neither Las Vegas's success, nor its troubles, seemed likely to abate as the twenty-first century began.

BIBLIOGRAPHY

Denton, Sally, and Roger Morris. *The Money and the Power: The Making of Las Vegas and Its Hold on America, 1947–2000.* New York: Knopf, 2001.

Elliott, Gary E. *The New Western Frontier: An Illustrated History of Greater Las Vegas.* Encinitas, Calif.: Heritage, 1999.

Gottdiener, M., Claudia Collins, and David R. Dickens. *Las Vegas: The Social Production of an All-American City.* London: Blackwell, 1998.

Hopkins, A. D., and K. J. Evans, eds. *The First 100: Portraits of the Men and Women Who Shaped Las Vegas.* Las Vegas: Huntington Press, 1999.

Moehring, Eugene P. *Resort City in the Sunbelt: Las Vegas, 1930–2000.* 2d rev. ed. Reno and Las Vegas: University of Nevada Press, 2000.

Michael S. Green

See also **Crime, Organized; Gambling; Nevada; Resorts and Spas.**

LASER TECHNOLOGY. The word "laser" is an acronym for light amplification by stimulated emission of radiation and refers to devices that generate or amplify light through that principle. Lasers are used whenever a directed, sometimes very intense, beam of monochromatic (single wavelength) light is required. For a laser to function, the gas or solid of which it is composed must be excited into a non-equilibrium condition wherein the number of atoms or molecules in a highly energetic state is greater than the number in a less energetic state, a so-called inverted population. If a photon of light with energy equal to the difference between the two energy levels is introduced into the excited substance, either from the outside or by spontaneous decay of one of its own excited atoms or molecules, it can stimulate other excited atoms or molecules to decay to the less energetic state with release of additional photons. Emitted photons travel in the same direction, at the same wavelength, and in phase with the original photon, producing coherent radiation. Often mirrors (one fully reflecting and the other partially reflecting) are placed parallel to each other on opposite sides of the laser material so that each photon is likely to make many transits of the laser, stimulating release of other photons, before escaping. Lasers may operate in the continuous wave mode or in the pulsed mode, in which they store energy and suddenly release a burst of photons. Since the first lasers were reported in the early 1960s, many thousands of different atoms, ions, and molecules, pure or in combinations, have been used. Each generates light at its characteristic wavelengths, which may lie in the energetic X-ray region of the spectrum; the ultraviolet, visible, and infrared regions; or the low-energy microwave region (in which case it becomes a maser).

Applications of lasers increased rapidly. The unique properties of laser beams allow them to be focused into tiny spots, travel long distances without diverging, and be turned on and off rapidly, making them ideal for many uses, including rapid transmission of digital information. In the 1990s lasers were used regularly in scientific research, military weapons, medical diagnosis and surgery, communications, air quality analysis, surveying and seismology, barcode scanners, CD and video disc scanners, printers, welding, etching, and micromachining. Chemists explored the use of lasers to trigger parts of molecules to react while other normally more reactive sites are unaffected, which may allow inexpensive commercial production of molecules that are difficult or impossible to synthesize with other processes. George W. Bush's election to the presidency in 2000 revived Ronald Reagan's dream of a Strategic Defense Initiative (popularly dubbed "Star Wars"), renewing the debate about the technical feasibility using airborne or space-based laser systems to shoot down enemy missiles. Finally, intense laser beams were also being used to heat molecules to the extremely high temperatures needed to initiate nuclear fusion. If achieved, controlled nuclear fusion could create virtually limitless energy, reducing or eliminating dependence on nonrenewable fossil fuels and nuclear fission. A more likely outcome is suggested by a report in March 2001 that petroleum industry researchers had begun exploring the use of high-energy lasers to explore and drill for more oil.

BIBLIOGRAPHY

Bromberg, Joan L. *The Laser in America, 1950–1970.* Cambridge, Mass.: MIT Press, 1991.

Perin, Monica. "Drilling with Lasers." *Houston Business Journal* (March 2, 2001).

Townes, Charles H. *How the Laser Happened.* New York: Oxford University Press, 1999.

David K. Lewis/A. R.

See also **Compact Discs; Fiber Optics; Physics; Physics: Solid-State Physics; Strategic Defense Initiative.**

LATIN AMERICA, COMMERCE WITH. U.S. commerce with South America originated in the intercourse of the thirteen colonies with ports in the Spanish Indies. Shortly after the United States acknowledged the independence of the Spanish-American republics, it began to negotiate treaties of commerce with them. During the period from 1825 to 1850 large quantities of cotton goods were exported from the United States to Colombia, Chile, and Brazil. South America sent to the United States hides, wool, sugar, guano, and copper. After 1850, because of the Civil War and the increasing competition from European countries, the export trade of the United States with South American nations declined. Although in 1867 the United States made purchases of coffee and rubber from Brazil and of sugar, spices, fruits, chemicals, and woods from other nations of South America, its sales of manufactured goods to these countries amounted to scarcely one-third of the total of its purchases from them.

During the years from 1900 to 1914 a marked development took place in the commerce of the United States with South American nations. In particular, there was an increase in the volume of imports from Argentina, Brazil, Chile, Peru, Colombia, and Venezuela.

During World War I, leading nations of South America sent larger shares of their products to the United States and purchased more manufactured goods in this country. Imports into the United States from South America in 1916 were nearly 100 percent in excess of those in 1914, while exports from the United States to that continent showed a gain of 140 percent during the two-year period, 1914–1916. By 1917 the United States enjoyed about one-half of the total trade of South America.

The years immediately following World War I were distinguished by a great expansion of commercial life in South America. After the construction of the Panama Canal (1904–1914), the trade of the United States with countries on the west coast of South America increased considerably. The chief exceptions to this tendency were countries in the basin of Rio de la Plata, where the staple products were the same as those of the United States. Import duties levied by the U.S. tariff on wheat as well as the stringent application of sanitary regulations to meat provoked resentment in Argentina, which made that country turn more and more toward English marts and markets.

During World War II and immediately thereafter South America was the most important source of U.S. imports and the second most important market for U.S. exports. But in the late 1940s the South American share of U.S. trade began to decline steadily as Europe and Japan rapidly recovered from the devastation of the war and together with Canada became the major U.S. trading partners. Nevertheless in 1973 the region was still the fourth largest market for U.S. goods and the fourth largest U.S. supplier.

The United States provided about half of South America's imports around 1950, but only about one-third in 1970. During those two decades the U.S. market for South American products declined in similar fashion. Nevertheless, although South America reoriented its trade to Europe and Japan, the United States remained South America's most important single trading partner by far.

After 1968, as the region's industrialization accelerated, South American demand for U.S. products increased more sharply than its exports to the United States. South American trade formed a triangular pattern, the region being a net exporter to Europe and Japan and a net importer from the United States.

By the late 1960s Brazil surpassed Venezuela as the largest market for U.S. exports to South America, importing nearly $2 billion from the United States in 1973, nearly double Venezuela's purchases. As U.S. suppliers, however, the importance of these two countries was reversed: U.S. imports originating from Venezuela were more than double those from Brazil in 1973.

Argentina—the country with the highest standard of living in South America and, after Brazil, the region's largest in terms of population, national income, and degree of industrialization—has had a relatively weak commercial relationship with the United States. From World War II until 1975 its trade with the United States was consistently exceeded by that of Venezuela and Brazil and in some years also by Colombia, Peru, and Chile, economically much less developed countries than Argentina.

About 75 percent of U.S. exports to South America has traditionally consisted of manufactured goods, but the kinds of manufactured goods exported changed during the post–World War II period from primarily finished consumer products to primarily machinery, equipment, industrial raw materials, and supplies. This change coincided with the acceleration of industrialization based on import substitution in the major South American countries. The production of most of the manufactured consumer goods that had been formerly imported from the United States began in Argentina, Brazil, Chile, and Uruguay and then developed in Colombia, Peru, and Venezuela. This industrialization process required imports of investment goods for the establishment and operation of South America's new factories. In 1970 the United States supplied between 33 and 50 percent of the manufactured imports of South American countries.

Because the emphasis of U.S. aid shifted from donations to loans during the mid-1960s, a significant part of South America's imports from the United States was financed through increasing indebtedness. The external public debt of South American countries became a serious burden on their economies during the 1960s, surpassing $15 billion in 1971, nearly five times the earnings from their exports to the United States in that year. Interest payments on their external public debt amounted to nearly one-third of their 1971 exports to the United States.

Natural resource products have been the traditional U.S. imports from South America. Between World War I and World War II coffee and petroleum were the most important single imports. After World War II, crude oil and petroleum products began to outweigh coffee in the value of U.S. imports from South America. It is estimated that their import value amounted to about $2 billion in 1972, nearly all the petroleum imports originating in Venezuela. More than one-third of this amount came to the United States via the Netherlands Antilles, where much Venezuelan crude oil was refined after the 1950s. The value, but not the quantity, of petroleum imports from South America quadrupled in 1974 because of the sharp price increases imposed by the Organization of Petroleum Exporting Countries (OPEC), of which Venezuela and Ecuador were members. Crude oil imports from Ecuador did not become significant until 1973.

Brazil and Colombia provided by far the largest share of U.S. coffee imports immediately after World War II, supplying almost 1 million metric tons a year, or about 90 percent of U.S. consumption. U.S. coffee imports from South America declined thereafter, as Africa became an important U.S. supplier. By the end of the 1960s South America was shipping to the United States about 650,000 metric tons yearly, which amounted to roughly two-thirds of the U.S. market.

Copper has been the third most important U.S. import from South America, with most copper imports coming from Chile, which shipped to the United States over 200 million metric tons of refined copper and about 50 million metric tons of the unrefined product ("blister" copper) a year during the early 1950s. By 1960 nearly all U.S. copper imports from Chile were in unrefined form, as Chile shifted its refined copper exports to Western Europe. During the second half of the 1960s Chilean refining capacity increased, and U.S. imports of refined copper resumed. During the 1950s Peru became another South American source of U.S. copper imports. Peruvian production increased rapidly during the 1960s, primarily in the form of concentrates, but exports to the United States remained far below those of Chile. Until the early 1970s most copper output in Chile and Peru was produced by U.S. subsidiaries, which, except for one in Peru, were subsequently expropriated by the respective governments.

After World War II, South American iron ore production increased rapidly and, aside from sugar, was the only other commodity of which the export value to the United States began to exceed $100 million. Venezuela, Brazil, Chile, and Peru supplied over 22 million metric tons of iron ore for the U.S. market by 1960, but after that time most of the increase in South American production for export was sold to Japan.

Other important U.S. imports from South America have been sugar, primarily from Brazil and Peru; bananas, primarily from Ecuador; cocoa from Brazil and Ecuador; fishmeal from Peru; tin from Bolivia; manganese from Brazil; tungsten from Peru and Brazil; zinc ores from Peru; and processed meats from Argentina. As late as 1970 the U.S. import value from the region for any of these products, except sugar, still remained below $100 million, although these imports from South America accounted for significant proportions of U.S. consumption. The elimination of the U.S. import quota for sugar in 1974 benefited South American exports.

Of all South American countries, Argentina's exports of temperate zone agricultural products have competed most directly with U.S. production, which may explain the relatively low level of United States–Argentine trade. As U.S. consumption of beef began to outstrip domestic production after World War II, the United States imported increasing quantities of beef, Argentina's most important export commodity beginning in the mid-1950s. Although U.S. imports of fresh and frozen beef reached $1 billion in 1973, none of it came from any South American country because of the strict enforcement of U.S. sanitary regulations.

Manufactured products accounted for about 5 percent of South American exports to the United States in 1950 and about 12 percent in 1970. Exports of manufactures continued to rise, reaching 20 percent of Argentine exports, 12 percent of Brazilian, and 13 percent of Colombian exports in 1972. A significant part of this increase was the result of the expanded role of U.S. and other foreign investments in South American manufacturing production.

By 1970 the industrialization of South American countries had become increasingly dependent on the import of U.S. technology and capital and had led to a large foreign indebtedness. Subsequently the prices of the region's raw material exports increased more than the prices of its imports, and the value of South American exports grew faster than its external debt to the United States as shortages of raw materials made themselves felt during the economic boom of 1973 in industrial countries. As a result of the ensuing economic recession in the United States and other developed countries, South America's raw material prices had weakened again by the end of 1974. Nevertheless, the first half of the 1970s brought into sharp focus what was already apparent: a growing economic interdependence had become a fact of United States–South American relations.

Hyperinflation plagued South American economies in the 1980s, and the region's economic instability continued into the 1990s. Nevertheless, American investment in South America grew rapidly, spurred in no small part by the spread of democratic governments across the continent. By 2000 U.S. direct investment in South America reached $80 billion. Brazil alone received $35 billion in U.S. investment, a sum greater than the total of U.S. investment in First World economies such as Australia, Italy, and Sweden. The United States is now the largest trading partner of Brazil, Columbia, Ecuador, and Peru, and one of the top three trading partners of virtually every other South American country. Moreover, the U.S. dollar operates as the de facto currency in many parts of South America. Most economists expect that the early twenty-first century will see an expansion of the North American Free Trade Agreement to Latin America, and thus the creation of the world's largest free trade zone.

BIBLIOGRAPHY

Baily, Samuel L. *The United States and the Development of South America, 1945–1975.* New York: New Viewpoints, 1976.

Friedman, Thomas. *The Lexus and the Olive Tree.* New York: Anchor Books, 2000.

Grunwald, Joseph. *Latin America and World Economy: A Changing International Order.* Beverly Hills, Calif.: Sage, 1978.

Haring, Clarence. *South America Looks at the United States.* New York: Arno Press, 1970.

Kraus, John. *The GATT Negotiations: A Business Guide to the Results of the Uruguay Round.* Paris: ICC Publishing, 1990.

Weaver, Frederick. *Class, State, and Industrial Structure: The Historical Process of South American Industrial Growth.* Westport, Conn.: Greenwood Press, 1980.

Whitaker, Arthur P. *The United States and the Southern Cone: Argentina, Chile, and Uruguay.* Cambridge, Mass.: Harvard University Press, 1976.

Yergin, Daniel. *Commanding Heights: The Battle Between Government and the Marketplace That Is Remaking the Modern World.* New York: Simon and Schuster, 1999.

William Spence Robertson / A. G.

See also **Agricultural Price Support; Balance of Trade; Dollar Diplomacy; Foreign Investment in the United States; Good Neighbor Policy; Latin America, Relations with; Reciprocal Trade Agreements; Roosevelt Corollary.**

LATIN AMERICA, RELATIONS WITH. The United States and the Latin American nations have been linked geographically since colonial times, and in the late-eighteenth century, U.S. merchants began trading with Spain's New World colonies. During this period, Latin American revolutionaries increasingly looked to the United States as a political model, a successful example of a colony throwing off the yoke of the European power and establishing a republic. Despite strong pressures from some U.S. leaders such as Henry Clay, who supported the Latin American revolutions, many Americans looked southward with apprehension, fearful of upsetting the Spanish, from whom they wanted Florida. Nevertheless, with some U.S. support, almost all of the Latin American republics won their independence by the middle of the 1820s.

The first major U.S. pronouncement regarding the Western Hemisphere and Latin American nations came in 1823. British officials approached U.S. diplomats about issuing a joint declaration that would deliver a warning to European powers conspiring with the Spanish crown to reimpose Madrid's control over Latin American nations. Instead, Secretary of State John Quincy Adams pushed President James Monroe to issue a unilateral statement (see MONROE DOCTRINE). The two-part document argued that the Europeans could no longer colonize the New World or seek to reimpose their rule. It also stated that a European nation could not transfer an existing colony to another European nation. While the British navy was the real force preventing the Europeans from acting, the Monroe Doctrine became the cornerstone of U.S. actions in Latin America for more than a century.

Initially, efforts to cooperate against foreign incursions failed. The Latin American nations unsuccessfully sought U.S. assistance against foreign interventions, principally the Falklands/Malvinas crisis in Argentina in 1831 and the Baker's War in Mexico in 1838. Most of the exchanges that occurred were economic. While the British remained the dominant economic power in the region, U.S. merchants and bankers made significant inroads. Brazilian coffee, Cuban sugar, and Mexican mining materials flowed northward while U.S. finished and agricultural goods flowed southward. The two regions became increasingly interdependent.

Over time, tensions developed between the United States and the Latin American nations over U.S. territorial expansion. The primary target of U.S. intentions was Mexico. In 1835, Americans living in Texas overthrew Mexican control and established a republic. In 1846, following the U.S. annexation of Texas, a war erupted over boundary disputes (see MEXICAN-AMERICAN WAR). The United States defeated Mexico. In the TREATY OF GUADALUPE HIDALGO of 1848, the United States took more than one-third of Mexico's territory, including California, which provoked anger in Latin America and fears of territorial dismemberment.

The efforts of individual Americans in the 1850s further caused problems. Filibusters such as General Narciso López and William Walker tried to annex new lands including Cuba and Nicaragua. They ultimately met their deaths, but the perception of Americans as land- and power-hungry became the common stereotype among Latin Americans. Some positive relations developed during the 1860s. The United States finally recognized the republic of Haiti once Southern congressmen left during the U.S. Civil War. More important, Washington pressured Napoleon III to withdraw his troops from Mexico. Ultimately Benito Juárez's forces expelled the French and executed Emperor Ferdinand Maximilian in 1867.

In the aftermath of the U.S. Civil War, the focus returned in both regions to internal development. As U.S. industrial might grew, American entrepreneurs and bankers spread throughout Latin America looking for investment opportunities. These included men such as Minor Keith, who established the forerunner of the United Fruit Company in Central America, and W. R. Grace, involved in mining in Chile. With the assistance of compliant Latin American elites who provided optimal investment and labor conditions, U.S. businessmen became the most important foreigners in Latin America by the end of World War I.

As economic investment increased, so did U.S. government efforts to create a favorable business environment in Latin America. In October 1889, President Benjamin Harrison and Secretary of State James G. Blaine invited the Latin American republics to Washington, D.C., for a conference. Blaine presided over the meetings, which included discussion of reduced tariffs, the arbitration of disputes, and the construction of a Pan American railroad. Remembering past U.S. transgressions, Latin Americans suspiciously questioned American motives. The conference's only major accomplishment was the establishment of the Commercial Bureau of the American Republics (forerunner of the Pan American Union) to collect and distribute economic and technical information. Still, the Washington conference established a precedent that eventually implemented many of the ideas of Blaine and others regarding the hemisphere.

In the aftermath of the Washington conference, the United States began flexing its newfound strength, developed as a result of rapid industrialization and the building of a modern navy. In 1891, its navy had a showdown with Chile over a riot involving U.S. sailors on leave and then influenced the outcome of a rebellion in Brazil in 1893. Two years later, Washington forced London to negotiate with Venezuela a disputed boundary along the Orinoco River.

The most significant event of the 1890s was the U.S. intervention in Cuba. In 1895, the Cubans rose in revolt against the Spanish under the leadership of José Martí and General Máximo Gómez. The vicious fighting and sensationalistic reporting in the United States raised American concerns about the rebellion. In 1898, President William McKinley asked for a declaration of war following the publication of a private letter written by the Spanish minister in Washington, Enrique Dupuy de Lôme, that made derogatory comments about the U.S. president, and the sinking of the battleship *Maine*, which exploded in Havana harbor.

The war went well for the United States and produced victory in a short time (see SPANISH-AMERICAN WAR). The United States took possession of Puerto Rico and control of Cuba. Ultimately U.S. troops withdrew from Cuba in 1902, but only after imposing the PLATT AMENDMENT, which effectively gave the United States control over an independent Cuba. It prohibited the Cuban government from entering into treaties with foreign nations, provided for U.S. military bases, and conceded Washington the right to intervene in Cuban affairs to preserve stability.

The victory in the Spanish-American War cemented U.S. hegemony over the Caribbean. In the presidency of Theodore Roosevelt, the United States exercised what he called a "big stick." In 1903, he helped the Panamanians win independence from Colombia and won the United States the right to build and control the PANAMA CANAL (completed in 1914). U.S. troops intervened in the Dominican Republic (1904) and Cuba (1906), following the issuing of the ROOSEVELT COROLLARY to the Monroe Doctrine that granted the United States the right to intervene in periods of crisis to maintain order and stability and prevent European intervention. In the eyes of many Latin Americans, such paternalism made the United States as repressive as the Europeans.

The situation did not improve as Roosevelt's successors intervened in Latin America. President William Howard Taft (1909–1913) practiced "Dollar Diplomacy" and Woodrow Wilson (1913–1921) promised greater respect for democratic principles in relations with Latin America, but his rhetoric failed to match his actions. During Wilson's term, U.S. troops occupied the Dominican Republic, Haiti, Mexico, and Nicaragua. U.S. threats against other nations led many Latin Americans to denounce the United States for violating basic ideas of democracy, self-determination, and international law. Mexico's constitution of 1917 reflected a growing anti-Americanism by limiting U.S. ownership of lands and protecting the rights of its workers.

Despite Latin American disillusionment with the United States, World War I ensured more hemispheric interdependence. Great Britain, France, and Germany lost substantial ground during the conflict. More American entrepreneurs flooded into Latin America looking for investment opportunities, despite efforts by Latin American nationalists to stem the tide through industrialization and the development of internal markets. In addition, American culture, especially popular culture, became a fixture in Latin America. American movies and music increasingly became popular with Latin Americans. Similarly, Latin Americans increasingly influenced American culture.

The United States continued to play a significant role in Latin American politics in the 1920s. While U.S. troops remained in Haiti and Nicaragua, they were withdrawn from the Dominican Republic in 1924, but not before putting in place the machinery for the rise of the dictatorship of Rafael Leónidas Trujillo Molina (who ruled until 1961). In 1929, President Herbert Hoover finally began to withdraw troops from Nicaragua and Haiti. In the case of the former, the United States left in place a National Guard under the control of Anastasio Somoza García, who established a family dictatorship that ruled until 1979.

President Hoover set in motion the events that led to the rise of the GOOD NEIGHBOR POLICY proclaimed by President Franklin D. Roosevelt in 1933. In his inaugural address, he called for a Latin American policy based on the "good neighbor" that respects the rights of other nations and in turn receives the respect of those nations. Soon after, at the Seventh International Conference of American States meeting in Montevideo, Uruguay, Secretary of State Cordell Hull backed a resolution disavowing intervention in the internal affairs of other nations. The administration followed its words with deeds, refusing to directly intervene in Cuba in 1933, although the ultimate result was the establishment of the dictatorship of Fulgencio Batista.

U.S. efforts to create better relations paid significant dividends during World War II. With the exception of Argentina, whose leaders harbored strong profascist sympathies, Latin American nations wholeheartedly supported the Allied war effort. Mexico and Brazil sent troops to fight, and the others provided valuable natural resources. At the end of the war, the majority of these countries helped create the United Nations in 1945.

With the death of Roosevelt and his replacement by Harry Truman, U.S. policy began to change. While Latin Americans clamored for economic assistance such as Washington was providing to Europe, U.S. policymakers focused more on creating a solid defensive front against a perceived Soviet threat. At the Rio conference in August 1947, American and Latin American delegates created a regional security organization. The Rio Pact provided that an attack on any nation in the Western

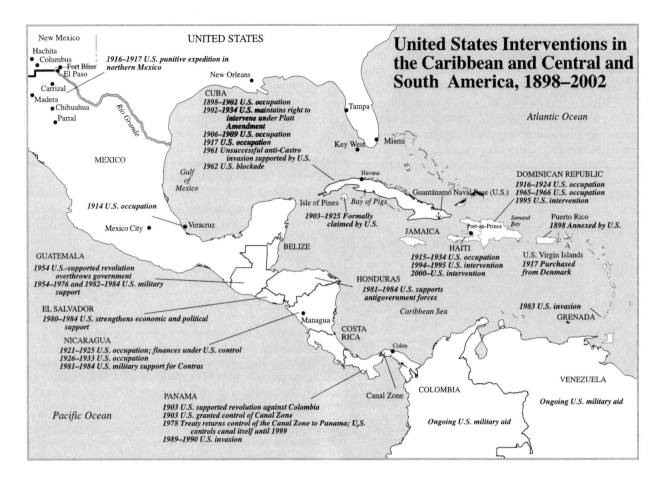

United States Interventions in the Caribbean and Central and South America, 1898–2002

Hemisphere by another state, including other regional states, would prompt action by all signatories.

A year later, the nations convened in Bogotá, Colombia, and created the Organization of American States (OAS). It established an administration for hemispheric consultation and the Advisory Defense Committee to coordinate military activities. Over U.S. objections, the Latin Americans voted for several articles that reflected a fear of a return to old ways. Articles 15 and 16 of the charter prohibited intervention—including economic and diplomatic coercion—into the affairs of other signatory nations.

Despite such pronouncements, the United States grew increasingly apprehensive about possible communist takeovers in Latin America, especially after the fall of China and Soviet explosion of the atomic bomb in 1949, and the Korean conflict that began in 1950. When President Dwight Eisenhower took over in 1953, the United States moved closer to Latin American dictators including Somoza, Trujillo, Batista, and Venezuela's Marcos Pérez Jiménez. Many U.S. officials believed that these dictators provided stability and a welcoming climate for U.S. investors.

The Eisenhower administration faced a dilemma in Guatemala, where nationalists had been in power since 1944. Fears of communist influence increased, especially after the government of Jacobo Arbenz nationalized prop-

erties held by the powerful United Fruit Company. The company had powerful friends in the White House including Secretary of State John Foster Dulles. Soon the administration instructed the Central Intelligence Agency to overthrow the Arbenz government. In June 1954, a mercenary air force and Guatemalan exile army successfully replaced Arbenz with a dictatorship dominated by Carlos Castillo Armas. The event created a great deal of hostility toward the United States throughout the region.

Two events caused the Eisenhower administration to intensify its focus on Latin America. Visiting Peru and Venezuela in 1958, Vice President Richard Nixon encountered angry crowds upset over U.S. support of dictators in their countries. (In Caracas, he barely escaped from one group.) In addition, in early 1959, Fidel Castro overthrew the Batista government in Cuba and established a socialist state aligned with the Soviet Union, the first in the Western Hemisphere. In the wake of these events more U.S. economic assistance began to flow into Latin America in an attempt to assuage the anger and resentment.

The administration of John F. Kennedy continued the change in orientation started by the Eisenhower administration. In 1961, Kennedy inaugurated the Alliance for Progress to pump billions of dollars in public and private investment into Latin America. Determined to attack poverty, illiteracy, and social injustice, the administration wanted to improve living conditions for the majority of Latin Americans and thereby undermine their anti-Americanism and support for Castro or other communist insurgents. Peace Corps assistance and massive military spending also flowed into the region.

With Kennedy's death, Lyndon B. Johnson continued some of Kennedy's programs in Latin America, although he shifted attention primarily to Vietnam and domestic programs. In 1965, Johnson ordered U.S. troops into the Dominican Republic to stabilize a situation in which U.S. policymakers believed that a Castro-style government was about to be established. OAS cooperation with the effort undermined its credibility (because the OAS was perceived as unquestioningly following the United States) and led to hostile denunciations in all quarters.

U.S.–Latin American relations continued to deteriorate under President Richard Nixon. He and his primary foreign policy adviser, Henry Kissinger, did not want to devote much time to Latin America. Nevertheless, the CIA helped overthrow the democratically elected government of Chilean president Salvadoran Allende, whose nationalist-socialist policies alarmed U.S. officials. Military conspirators led by General Augusto Pinochet murdered Allende and more than ten thousand others in a coup in September 1973. The action severely damaged U.S.–Latin American relations.

Nixon's successor, Gerald Ford, had little interest in the region, as attention remained focused on Southeast Asia and the Middle East. The OPEC crisis, and the role Venezuela and Mexico played in the oil shortage by taking advantage of the increase in prices, brought some attention to the region, but not a great deal. By this period, U.S.–Latin American relations had reached a very low point.

When Jimmy Carter took office in 1977, he promised a new U.S. foreign policy that would focus on human rights and reject cooperation with military dictatorships. Immediately Carter helped establish the position of assistant secretary of state for human rights. Washington began to put economic and diplomatic pressure on countries with records of human rights abuses, including Argentina, Nicaragua, and El Salvador.

Carter also focused on reorienting U.S. policy toward Latin America so as to create more favorable perceptions of the United States. This included negotiating the PANAMA CANAL TREATY that returned sovereignty to Panama by 2000. Washington also tried to improve relations with Cuba. It eased travel restrictions and the two countries opened preliminary talks on normalization of relations.

By the second half of his administration, Carter found himself drifting back toward the policies of his predecessors. The efforts at reconciliation with Cuba deteriorated over Cuba's interventions in Africa. When Washington

criticized Cuba's human rights record, Castro allowed a massive exodus of Cubans to the United States. In Nicaragua, after having criticized the Somoza dictatorship, the Carter administration tried unsuccessfully to prevent a Sandinista victory. It found itself in a similar situation in El Salvador. In its efforts on human rights, it backed off from criticizing the dictatorships and applied pressure inconsistently. By the time Carter left office, his policies were much like the old versions of U.S. responses.

Carter's successor, Ronald Reagan, never tried to change U.S. policy. He and his advisers, including Jeane Kirkpatrick, criticized Carter's human rights policy, calling it impractical. As a result, the United States closed ranks with such men as Pinochet and Manuel Noriega in Panama. It also began a massive effort to undermine revolutions in Nicaragua and El Salvador. In the former, financing of the right-wing Nicaraguan contra rebels became a major debate in the United States. While Reagan called them the equivalent of the American founding fathers, opponents criticized their tactics and ties to the Somoza dictatorship.

The Reagan administration's strong anticommunist crusade led to some experiments such as the Caribbean Basin Initiative to address economic problems, but most of its efforts focused on covert and military operations to prevent the spread of communism in the region. In 1983, the United States invaded Grenada to stop the construction of an airport that it feared would endanger strategic shipping lines. It continued to funnel money to the contras, even after a congressional prohibition, resulting in the IRAN-CONTRA AFFAIR.

As Reagan left office and George H. W. Bush took over in 1989, conditions in Latin America began to change. In Argentina, Brazil, Chile, and Central America, the military governments began to surrender control to civilians. The Bush administration supported these initiatives as well as those designed to end years of state control of industries and utilities and to promote a free-market model. The high point of the Bush administration's efforts was the negotiation and signing of the NORTH AMERICAN FREE TRADE AGREEMENT (NAFTA) in 1992. Bush also increasingly focused on the Latin American drug trade. In 1989, U.S. troops invaded Panama and removed Noriega for his role in facilitating the drug trade.

Bush left office before the final Senate approval of NAFTA. His successor, Bill Clinton, pushed the treaty through Congress despite dogged opposition from labor unions and environmentalists. The administration also pushed the open market model and dealt with a crisis in Haiti in 1994 when Washington forced out General Raoul Cédras and his allies and installed the legally elected president, Jean-Bertrand Aristide.

During the Clinton administration, most Americans shifted their attention from security issues to those of the drug trade, immigration, and the environment, including the signing of the Kyoto Protocols designed to reduce greenhouse gases. While problems erupted over Cuba regarding illegal immigration and the downing of a Cuban exile plane in 1994, leading to passage of the Helms-Burton Act (1996) that tightened U.S. trade and exchanges with the island, the Clinton administration devoted relatively little attention to the region.

At the turn of the twentieth century, it appeared that similar cycles would continue, with periodic outbursts of U.S. interest and conflict in Latin America followed by periods in which policymakers focus on other regions or on domestic issues.

BIBLIOGRAPHY

Coerver, Don M., and Linda B. Hall, *Tangled Destinies: Latin America and the United States.* Albuquerque: University of New Mexico Press, 1999.

Gilderhus, Mark T. *The Second Century: U.S.–Latin American Relations since 1889.* Wilmington, Del.: Scholarly Resources, 2000.

Kyrzanek, Michael J. *U.S.–Latin American Relations.* New York: Praeger, 1985.

Langley, Lester D. *America and the Americas: The United States and the Western Hemisphere.* Athens: University of Georgia Press, 1989.

Longley, Kyle. *In the Eagle's Shadow: The United States and Latin America.* Wheeling, Ill.: Harlan-Davidson, 2002.

Lowenthal, Abraham F. *Partners in Conflict: The United States and Latin America.* Baltimore: Johns Hopkins University Press, 1987.

Pastor, Robert A. *Whirlpool: U.S. Foreign Policy toward Latin America and the Caribbean.* Princeton, N.J.: Princeton University Press, 1992.

Pike, Frederick B. *The United States and Latin America: Myths and Stereotypes of Civilization and Nature.* Austin: University of Texas Press, 1992.

Poitras, Guy. *The Ordeal of Hegemony: The United States and Latin America.* Boulder, Colo.: Westview Press, 1990.

Schoultz, Lars. *Beneath the United States: A History of U.S. Policy Toward Latin America.* Cambridge, Mass.: Harvard University Press, 1998.

Smith, Peter H. *Talons of the Eagle: Dynamics of U.S.–Latin American Relations.* New York: Oxford University Press, 1996. 2d edition, 2000.

Kyle Longley

See also vol. 9: **The Monroe Doctrine and the Roosevelt Corollary.**

LATIN AMERICAN WARS OF INDEPENDENCE

(1808–1826). The wars of independence in Latin America were watched with considerable interest in North America. Apart from the prospective commercial benefits that might flow from the end of Spain's trade monopoly, U.S. sympathy for an independent Latin America was grounded in the view that the wars of independence reflected the same republican ideals of freedom and liberty that had animated the creation of the United States.

Historians looking for long-term causes of the war of independence usually start in the middle of the eighteenth century with a series of reforms launched by the Spanish Bourbons aimed at gaining greater administrative control over, and increased tax revenue from, its possessions. By this period most of the positions in the Spanish bureaucracy in the Americas were held by Creoles (people of Spanish or European descent born in the Americas). However, under the Bourbons, Creole officials were increasingly replaced by Spanish-born (*peninsulares*) administrators.

Almost all layers of society in the Americas were antagonized by the Bourbon reforms. However, the colonial pact between the Creoles and the Spanish, which rested on a mutual wariness of the Indian, mestizo, and African majorities, ensured that a number of major revolts, such as the Tupac Amaru Rebellion of the early 1780s, came to nothing. Furthermore, the example of Haiti in the early 1790s, where a full-scale slave revolt had overthrown the French government and the planter elite, made many Creoles in Spanish America even more wary of calls for independence. Nonetheless, liberal, republican, and antimonarchist ideas, which would underpin the full-scale wars of independence in the early nineteenth century, were gaining ground by the end of the eighteenth century.

The more immediate origins of the wars of independence in Latin America are usually traced to the 1807 alliance between the Spanish crown and Napoleon Bonaparte, who placed his brother Joseph on the Spanish throne the following year. Spanish nationalists opposed to his ascendance responded by setting up a Central Junta in Seville. The Central Junta decreed that the Spanish territories in the Americas were free, and representatives from Spanish America were invited to Spain to participate in a reformed *Cortés* (parliament). However, the Junta collapsed in 1810, sowing confusion in both Spain and Spanish America.

Local and regional juntas in the Americas had initially aligned themselves with the Central Junta, and they took over the Spanish colonial administration in the name of Ferdinand VII. In 1810 the junta in Caracas (in the Captaincy-General of Venezuela), still claiming loyalty to Ferdinand, went a step further and rejected the authority of the Spanish Council of Regency that had succeeded the Central Junta in Cádiz. Similar revolts in Chile, Argentina, and New Spain came in the wake of events in Caracas.

The most socially progressive movement for independence at this point was one that was emerging in the Viceroyalty of New Spain, and was led by the priest Miguel Hidalgo y Costilla. Hidalgo succeeded in mobilizing the Indian and mestizo population of central Mexico, killing at least 2,000 *peninsulares*. The specter of a "race" war quickly united the Creoles and the Spanish authorities, and Hidalgo's revolt was brought under control. The leadership mantle then passed to another priest, José María Morelos, who organized a particularly effective

CHRONOLOGY

1700: The Habsburgs are replaced by the Bourbons on the Spanish Throne.

1776: The Viceroyalty of Río de la Plata is established.

1778: The system of monopoly ports is brought to an end in Spanish America following the "Decree of Free Trade" (*comercio libre*).

1780–1781: Tupac Amaru Rebellion in Peru.

1789: The Portuguese bring an end to an independence conspiracy in Brazil.

1806: Francisco de Miranda launches an independence bid for Venezuela; first British defeat in Buenos Aires.

1807: Second British defeat in Buenos Aires; Napoleon Bonaparte invades Portugal; the Portuguese monarchy and government flee to Brazil.

1808: Ports in Brazil are opened to British trade; Joseph Bonaparte ascends the Spanish throne; Central Junta of Seville coordinates anti-French effort; the members of the elite in Montevideo (Uruguay) organize a junta loyal to the Central Junta; the Viceroy in Mexico leads an attempted revolt.

1809: Juntas established in Bolivia and Ecuador are defeated.

1810 (January): Central Junta of Seville defeated and replaced by the Spanish Council of Regency.

1810 (April): Junta in Venezuela assumes power and overthrows the Captain-General.

1810 (May): Junta ousts Viceroy in Buenos Aires.

1810 (July): Junta takes power in Paraguay and in Colombia.

1810 (September): The Hidalgo Revolt begins in Mexico; junta becomes the government in Chile.

1811: Congress in Venezuela declares independence; Miguel Hidalgo y Costilla is captured and executed in Mexico; a triumvirate assumes power in Buenos Aires; the United Provinces of New Granada is established; José Gervasio Artigas retreats from Uruguay following a threat of Portuguese invasion from Brazil.

1812: A new constitution is promulgated in Spain; Spanish forces crush the independence movement in Venezuela.

1813: The French Army is driven from Spain by the British Army and Spanish guerrillas; José Gervasio Artigas reinvades Uruguay.

1814: Ferdinand VII is restored to the Spanish throne; Montevideo is occupied by insurgents fighting for independence; Spanish forces defeat insurgents in Chile.

1815: José María Morelos is captured and executed by Spanish forces; Simón Bolívar writes the Jamaica letter that lays out his political philosophy.

1816: Bogotá is occupied by Spanish forces; the Congress of Tucumán is convened in Argentina; a new Viceroy arrives to reconsolidate Spanish rule in Mexico.

1818: José San Martín decisively defeats the Spanish army in Chile.

1819: Simón Bolívar is victorious against the Spanish army at Boyacá.

1820: Liberal revolts in Spain and Portugal; Agustin Iturbide unifies independence forces in Mexico around the Three Guarantees.

1821 (April): John VI transfers control of Brazil to his son, Pedro, and returns to Portugal.

1821 (July): Independence leader José San Martín takes control in Lima.

1821 (August): Mexico becomes independent.

1822 (July): An independent Gran Colombia is established under Simón Bolívar's leadership; Ecuador is formally decreed to be part of Gran Colombia.

1822 (September): Brazil is declared an independent empire by Pedro I.

1823: Portuguese forces are driven from Brazil.

1824: Battle of Ayacucho leads to an independent Peru.

1825: Bolivia liberated by José Antonio de Sucre.

1828: Uruguay gains independence from Brazil.

1830: Simón Bolívar dies; Gran Colombia breaks into Venezuela, Colombia, and Ecuador.

SOURCE: Adapted from Graham, *Independence in Latin America,* first edition, pp. 137–138.

military force, outlined a political program that included major political and social reforms, and managed to hold out against Spanish forces until 1815.

The death of Morelos highlighted the fact that, within a year of Ferdinand VII's restoration to the Spanish throne in 1814, Spanish military forces in the Americas had put down virtually all resistance. However, Britain and the other main powers in Europe were worried that Spain's repressive measures would make things worse in the Americas and also stimulate republican revolution in Europe. As a result Spain was encouraged to make political and economic concessions to its possessions. The latter were particularly favored by Great Britain and the United States because of the anticipated commercial opportunities that this might open up. At the same time, the loosening of Spanish control only encouraged those, such as Simón

Bolívar, who were advocating complete independence from Spain.

By the beginning of the 1820s, Britain's foreign secretary, George Canning, and U.S. President James Monroe were competing in an effort to give support to, and gain influence in, an increasingly independent Latin America. This rivalry was symbolized by the promulgation of the MONROE DOCTRINE of 1823, under the terms of which the United States warned Britain and the other European powers to stay clear of Latin America; however, its significance for much of the region was minimal until the twentieth century. This was particularly apparent, for example, in the case of the move to independence in Portuguese-ruled Brazil. The movement for independence there was a relatively brief affair that led to the establishment of a monarchy in 1822 under Pedro I, the son of the Portuguese king who had been exiled in Brazil from 1807 until 1821. This particularly conservative transition to independence attracted limited U.S. interest, while Britain was a key player in Brazil throughout this period.

While Brazil had emerged as an independent monarchy by the 1820s, the Spanish empire in the Americas had fragmented into a number of independent republics. These new nation-states were often connected economically more to the expanding world market than to each other. England's thirteen colonies in North America, for geographical and commercial as well as political reasons, had earlier managed to break the bonds of British rule while remaining united as a political unit. However, politics, economics, and geography were not conducive to the emergence of the united polity in Spanish America that had been envisioned by Simón Bolívar, the region's most prominent leader.

BIBLIOGRAPHY

Graham, Richard. *Independence in Latin America: A Comparative Approach.* 2d ed. New York: McGraw-Hill, 1994. The original edition was published in 1972.

Kinsbruner, Jay. *Independence in Spanish America: Civil Wars, Revolutions, and Underdevelopment.* 2d rev. ed. Albuquerque: University of New Mexico Press, 2000. The original edition was published in 1994.

Langley, Lester D. *The Americas in the Age of Revolution 1750–1850.* New Haven, Conn.: Yale University Press, 1996.

Lynch, John. *The Spanish American Revolutions 1808–1826.* 2d rev. ed. New York: Norton, 1986. The original edition was published in 1973.

Rodríguez O., Jaime E. *The Independence of Spanish America.* Cambridge: Cambridge University Press, 1998. The original edition was published in Spanish in 1996.

Mark T. Berger

See also **Colonial Administration, Spanish; Republicanism.**

LATIN SCHOOLS, the first educational institutions in the American colonies, were patterned on the Latin schools of England. Boston's Latin school, established in 1635, served for nearly a half century as that city's principal school to prepare the sons of elite families for college. The Massachusetts law of 1647 requiring a grammar school in every town of fifty families stimulated these schools; they also appeared in neighboring colonies and in the South. Tuition fees were charged, and the curriculum consisted primarily of Latin and Greek with a smattering of religion and mathematics. The Latin schools began to give way to the academies in the middle of the eighteenth century.

BIBLIOGRAPHY

Middlekauff, Robert. *Ancients and Axioms: Secondary Education in Eighteenth-Century New England.* New Haven, Conn.: Yale University Press, 1963.

Edgar W. Knight / A. R.

See also **Colonial Society; Education; School, District; Schools, Private.**

LATINOS. *See* **Hispanic Americans.**

LATITUDINARIANS were members of the Church of England in the seventeenth and eighteenth centuries who subscribed to a school of thought that emphasized the fundamental principles of the Christian religion rather than any specific doctrinal position. In early America, latitudinarianism influenced the "catholick Congregationalists," who broke with more traditional Puritans in the early eighteenth century and emphasized general Christian principles rather than specific Calvinist doctrine. Since that time, latitudinarians have included religious leaders and groups who have placed less emphasis on the interpretation of a creed and have been liberal in their tolerance of diverse religious perspectives and viewpoints.

BIBLIOGRAPHY

Corrigan, John. *The Prism of Piety: Catholick Congregational Clergy at the Beginning of the Enlightenment.* New York: Oxford University Press, 1991.

May, Henry F. *The Enlightenment in America.* New York: Oxford University Press, 1976.

Shelby Balik
William W. Sweet

See also **Church of England in the Colonies; Congregationalism; Episcopalianism.**

LATROBE'S FOLLY, the name given by engineers to the Thomas Viaduct, the Baltimore and Ohio Railroad's stone arch bridge over the Patapsco River, near Relay, Md., designed by and constructed under the direction of Benjamin H. Latrobe Jr., in 1832. His engineering contemporaries insisted that the bridge could not be built, that it would not stand up under its own weight, let alone the weight of the six-ton locomotives then in service, with their trains. But the viaduct was a complete success, to the extent that a century after its construction 300-ton engines were passing over it in safety.

BIBLIOGRAPHY

Hungerford, Edward. *The Story of the Baltimore & Ohio Railroad, 1827–1927.* New York: Putnam, 1928.

Julius H. Parmelee / A. R.

See also **Allegheny Mountains, Routes Across; Bridges; Maryland; Railroads.**

LATTER-DAY SAINTS, CHURCH OF JESUS CHRIST OF.

The Mormon Church traces its origins to founder Joseph Smith's vision of 1820, which upheld the view that no existing church had "right" doctrine. Mormonism avowed a belief in the Trinity but denied original sin. It stressed faith in Jesus Christ, baptism by immersion for the remission of sins, and the laying on of hands for the gift of the Holy Spirit. While it accepted the Bible as the word of God, Smith's discovery of an alternative scripture, the Book of Mormon, provided an ac-

Joseph Smith. The founder of the Mormon Church, who was murdered by a mob in 1844. LIBRARY OF CONGRESS

count of an Israelite prophet, Lehi, who was commanded by God in 600 B.C. to lead a small group of people to the American continent. It also recorded the appearance of Christ, after his Resurrection, to the people in America. Early Mormonism held that there would be a literal gathering of Israel to the United States and that Zion would be built upon the American continent. The Church of Jesus Christ of Latter-day Saints (LDS) was organized on 6 April 1830.

The Early Years

The new Church settled in Ohio, where it fostered a communitarian lifestyle, created a collective religious leadership, and launched the first mission to England in 1837. It then moved to Missouri, where political and religious controversy led to the MORMON WAR of 1838. The Saints withdrew to Illinois where they established the new city of Nauvoo in 1840, an agricultural rather than a commercial center. At Nauvoo, the Relief Society was established in 1842 to improve community morals. During this period, Joseph Smith also received a revelation, enjoining members of the Church to practice plural marriage (polygamy), based on precedents from the Old Testament.

Nauvoo and the Migration

While the Mormons engaged in Illinois politics, sympathy for the idea of a Mormon kingdom in the West increased during the early 1840s. After the governor of Illinois ordered a trial of the Church leadership for the destruction of the press of a newspaper critical to Mormonism, Joseph Smith and his brother were murdered in Carthage, Illinois, on 27 June 1844. The state legislature revoked the Nauvoo charter in January 1845 and the Church announced plans for removal in September 1845. In 1846, 12,000 Saints left Illinois, dedicating the Nauvoo Temple before their departure, and the Pioneer Company reached the Salt Lake Valley on 24 July 1847. The state of DESERET was established in January 1849 as the civil government of the territory.

Settling Utah

In 1850, LDS Church President Brigham Young sought statehood within the United States, but this was blocked in Congress, and territorial status was accepted in 1851. Young encouraged colonization to the south of Salt Lake City and along the Wasatch Front, where communities were organized to encourage community life and religious activity, with common pastures and the cooperative raising of grain. Missionaries were sent to Latin America and Europe, and the notion of the Gathering of Zion (the migration of converts to UTAH) was fostered by means of the Perpetual Emigrating Fund in the late 1850s. Given the Church's political dominance, tensions soon arose with federally appointed officials. President James Buchanan sent a force to Utah in 1857, in the face of protests about Brigham Young's dictatorial rule. Young recalled distant colonists, declared martial law, and forbade the entry of federal troops and in June 1858 a peace formula was negotiated.

The Church in the Nineteenth Century
During the Civil War the Latter-day Saints remained generally loyal to the Union. After the war, mining and cotton production developed in southern Utah and railroad connections in 1869 broke down the territory's isolation. A new Mormon cooperative system discouraged trade with outsiders, and after the depression of 1873, an effort was made to foster strongly collectivist cooperative organizations, called the United Orders, but these did not endure. A movement to Arizona and Wyoming took place in the late 1870s, and Mormons settled in Mexico in 1886. By 1880, the Church had 134,000 members, 80 percent of whom lived in Utah. Missionary work was pursued in Mexico, Polynesia, and the domestic United States, though Mormons faced violent reprisals in the American South. Missions increased between 1890 and 1900, as 6,125 missionaries were sent out, but immigration to Utah was discouraged after 1890.

The War Against Polygamy
In the late 1860s, a war against polygamy was unleashed in Utah Territory and other parts of the West inhabited by Latter-day Saints. The anti-Mormon Liberal Party was formed in Utah in 1870 to oppose LDS political and economic dominance, while James McKean, chief justice of Utah Territory, launched a campaign to prosecute those who practiced polygamy, including Brigham Young. In *Reynolds v. United States* (1879) the U.S. Supreme Court upheld the constitutionality of the Anti-Bigamy Act of 1862. Non-Mormons in Utah called for resolute action on polygamy and the Edmunds Act of 1882 assured penalties for polygamy and disenfranchised twelve thousand Saints. Over one thousand men were sent to jail in Utah, and similar prosecutions took place in Idaho and Arizona. Five years later, the Edmunds-Tucker Act threatened to destroy the Church by dissolving it as a legal corporation, a move upheld by the Supreme Court in 1890. Fearful that all members of the Church would be disenfranchised, President Wilford Woodruff issued the Manifesto against polygamy in 1890, accepted willingly by most Mormons, and a new understanding was reached with the federal authorities.

The Church in the Progressive Era
In the early twentieth century, the LDS Church displayed a greater readiness to become involved in the affairs of the nation. In 1903, Apostle Reed Smoot was elected to the Senate despite charges of disloyalty to the nation. The Church solved its debt problem with bond issues and curtailed its direct involvement in business ventures. Established missions were strengthened and a new training system for missionaries established. Signs of Mormon integration came with the increasing national popularity of the Mormon Tabernacle Choir, the Church's support for national prohibition after 1916, and its contributions to

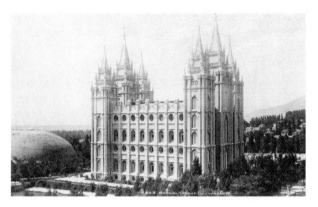

Mormon Temple. A photograph of the prominent Salt Lake City structure, built between 1853 and 1893. LIBRARY OF CONGRESS

the war effort. During World War I, twenty-four thousand Latter-day Saints enlisted in the armed forces, the Church and its auxiliaries bought $1.4 million worth of Liberty bonds, and the Relief Society sold its store of wheat to the government.

The Response to the Depression
During the 1920s, the agricultural depression drove many Saints to the cities and made them a more urban people. The Church's Relief Society created a Social Welfare Department in 1919, and the Church began to undertake more intensive studies of social problems and foster cooperation with some secular agencies. The coming of the Great Depression in 1929, therefore, did not catch the Church entirely unprepared. Although opposed to the dole, it did not condemn federal work relief. A survey of need was carried out in 1933 and local units were urged to create community enterprises. In 1936, the Church launched the Welfare Plan under Harold B. Lee, reviving the idea of the bishop's storehouse and calling on local units to establish coordinating committees. An exchange system was formed and make-work projects created where necessary, based around agriculture. This provided positive publicity for the Church, and even progressive periodicals like *Time* and *The Nation* started to reflect a more positive view of Mormon life.

An International Church
During World War II, one hundred thousand Mormons entered the armed forces, and the LDS Serviceman's Committee was organized to provide programs and guidelines for them. Missionary activity was resumed in 1946, and by 1950, there were five thousand missionaries, twelve hundred of them in Europe. A new sense of internationalism was evident, with the shift of missionaries to Asia. Efforts also were made to keep young men and women involved in church life through recreational activity, and seminary involvement grew from 28,600 to 81,400. Student wards were created in university towns, enabling stu-

dents for the first time to hold church offices. A new churchwide home teaching program was begun in 1964, with priesthood holders expected to get to know the families in their charges, and the family home evening program was launched in 1965. By the end of the 1960s, the church had achieved a membership of 2.8 million, with new growth in Latin America and seventeen thousand missionaries in the field.

The Latter-day Saints Today

In politics, the Church shifted sharply to the right during the 1960s, although Apostle Hugh Brown supported some social welfare programs and was a Democratic candidate for U.S. senator. By the late 1970s, however, the Church eschewed direct political participation in favor of taking stands opposed to the Equal Rights Amendment, legalized abortion, and gambling. In 1978, LDS Church President Spencer Kimball received a revelation extending the priesthood to all worthy male believers (prior to this date, black males had been excluded from the otherwise universal male priesthood), solving the problem of the priesthood in South America and Africa as well as the United States. In 1998, LDS Church President Gordon B. Hinckley stated that church members who practiced polygamy risked excommunication, but the Church was drawn uncomfortably into the spotlight in 2000 when Tom Green of Utah was prosecuted on charges of polygamy. The Church in the 1990s, led by President Hinckley since 1995, was an expanding force, though more outside the United States than within it, with over five million members in 1998.

BIBLIOGRAPHY

Alexander, Thomas G. *Mormonism in Transition: A History of the Latter-Day Saints, 1890–1930.* Urbana: University of Illinois Press, 1986.

Allen, James B., and Glen M. Leonard. *The Story of the Latter-day Saints.* Salt Lake City, Utah: Deseret Books, 1992.

Bushman, Claudia L., and Richard L. Bushman. *Building the Kingdom: a History of Mormons in America.* New York: Oxford University Press, 2001.

Gottlieb, Robert, and Peter Wiley. *America's Saints: The Rise of Mormon Power.* San Diego, Calif.: Harcourt Brace Jovanovich, 1986.

Mauss, Armand L. *The Angel and the Beehive: The Mormon Struggle with Assimilation.* Urbana: University of Illinois Press, 1994.

Quinn, D. Michael, ed. *The New Mormon History: Revisionist Essays on the Past.* Salt Lake City, Utah: Signature Books, 1992.

Shipps, Jan. *Mormonism: The Story of a New Religious Tradition.* Urbana: University of Illinois Press, 1985.

Jeremy Bonner

See also **Mormon Battalion; Mormon Expedition; Mormon Trail; Nauvoo, Mormons at.**

LAUSANNE AGREEMENT. At a 1932 conference in Lausanne, Switzerland, the European allies of World War I agreed to eliminate the last remaining German reparations debt originally imposed under the Treaty of Versailles. They conditionally canceled nine-tenths of the obligations still in effect under the YOUNG PLAN, dependent on cancellation of their own debts to the United States. The U.S. government never accepted the arrangement; but at President Herbert Hoover's suggestion in 1931 an all-around moratorium for one year on international debts, including those to the United States, was agreed to, for the purpose of easing a desperate economy. At the expiration of the year all debtor nations defaulted, except Finland.

BIBLIOGRAPHY

Leffler, Melvin P. *The Elusive Quest: America's Pursuit of European Stability and French Security, 1919–1933.* Chapel Hill: University of North Carolina Press, 1979.

Wilson, Joan Hoff. *American Business and Foreign Policy, 1920–1933.* Boston: Beacon Press, 1973.

Samuel Flagg Bemis / A. G.

See also **Dawes Plan; Moratorium, Hoover; World War I; World War I War Debts.**

LAW. See **Constitution of the United States; Military Law;** *and individual cases, courts, and legislatures.*

LAW SCHOOLS. The history of American legal education, like that of other professions, is deeply intertwined with the history of the social, economic, and political experiences of the United States, the history of higher education, and the history of the profession itself. Law schools supply graduates to meet society's demand for attorneys. Thus, legal education is not autonomous but rather is the product of its social contexts.

Apprenticeships

American legal education has its origins in the early colonial period. European settlers brought with them their legal systems, but innovation and adaptation characterized the development of the laws and legal procedures in each colony. Despite the early hostility the Puritans and some of the other first colonists displayed toward lawyers and their use of more informal dispute-settling mechanisms, the need for lawyers' services soon developed. As urbanization increased and both intercolonial and transatlantic trade grew, more formal means of dispute settlement and more lawyers were needed. Prior to the American Revolution, there were three sources for lawyers in the English colonies: lawyers who received legal training in England prior to immigration, colonists who returned to England to apprentice and become admitted to one of the Inns of Courts and then returned to the colonies; and colonists who apprenticed in the colonies with a colonial lawyer. These first two sources were important during the seventeenth century, but by the eighteenth century most colonial lawyers received their training through the apprenticeship system. Famous examples of Revolutionary heroes who had been legal apprentices are Thomas Jefferson, Alexander Hamilton, John Adams, John Marshall, John Jay, and James Wilson.

Apprenticeship as a means of legal education was quite variable during the colonial era. In some instances the apprentice did little more than occasionally read books on his own, copy from form or pleading books, or other drudgery required in law practice. Other masters, however, were excellent teachers who provided their students with a broad education in both law and letters. Following an apprenticeship a successful student was required to be admitted to practice before the courts of the colony where he resided. These requirements also differed considerably from colony to colony.

After the American Revolution, apprenticeship, or "reading law" on one's own, continued to be the dominant forms of legal education. For example, Abraham Lincoln read law, while the leading late-nineteenth-century U. S. Supreme Court justice Stephen Field gained admission to the bar following an extensive apprenticeship. Following the U.S. Civil War, apprenticeship began to decline, and by the twentieth century it was highly unusual for a lawyer to be admitted to the bar who had been apprenticed. In the twenty-first century it is possible in only a few states to apprentice and then sit for the bar.

Law Schools

American law schools developed primarily out of the apprentice system. Some of the masters who were excellent teachers expanded their training by establishing a training school. Tapping Reeve, a Connecticut lawyer with an excellent reputation in the courtroom and as a teacher, founded the first such school in Litchfield, Connecticut, in 1784. The school was most successful and attracted students from every state in the country. When the school disbanded in 1833, it had trained more than 1,000 lawyers. Many other schools became modeled on Litchfield.

The second strand of the history of American law schools also began shortly after the Revolution. In 1777 Yale's president added courses in law to the undergraduate education, and in 1799 the College of William and Mary made Thomas Jefferson's former tutor, George Wythe, the first professor of law in the United States. Over the first half of the next century more universities such as Yale and Pennsylvania added either professors of law or schools of law. In most of these universities law remained an undergraduate field of study, while in the others the education was similar to the apprenticeship schools.

The modern American law school took shape in the 1870s at Harvard. It was a product of the movement for professionalization both within the university and within the legal profession. Harvard had established its first chaired professorship in law in 1816 and its law school

followed the Litchfield model during the 1840s. But when Charles Elliot became president of Harvard in 1869 he sought to adapt the German university model of a scientifically based curriculum organized into departments. He believed that law fit within this model, and he hired Christopher Columbus Langdell as Harvard's dean in 1875 to implement this vision. Over the next two decades Langdell moved Harvard away from a school that emphasized the practical training of lawyers to a postgraduate school that hired scholars rather than practitioners to teach students the science of the law. By 1899 Harvard had raised its requirements for a bachelor of laws degree (LL.B.) to a three-year course of study following a bachelor's degree. During the last quarter of the nineteenth century both private and public universities, such as Columbia, Northwestern, Iowa, and Cincinnati, adopted the Harvard model.

The Harvard model did, however, continue to compete with the Litchfield model. Urban schools, such as the YMCA Law School and Suffolk in Boston, George Washington University in Washington, D.C., Chicago-Kent, and the University of Buffalo, resisted the emphasis on scholarly training, and instead emphasized the acquisition of practical skills through lectures by judges and practitioners, which emphasized local rather than national law and work in law offices. Many of these schools were independent of universities and almost all had part-time and evening programs.

Throughout the twentieth century the competition between these models continued. Harvard, however, dominated. Its victory was in large measure assured by the founding of two organizations, the AMERICAN BAR ASSOCIATION (ABA) in 1878 and the Association of American Law Schools (AALS), as well as the continued push by public and private universities to emphasize research and scholarship as the measure of their prestige and greatness. The Harvard model fit the ABA's ambitions of increasing the prestige and power of the legal profession because Harvard required more schooling (two years as an undergraduate—later increased to four—plus three as a law student) and it promoted the idea of law as a science, not a trade to be learned by apprenticeship. The goals of the AALS were to establish minimum standards for admissions to law school, for facilities such as libraries, and for qualifications to take the bar. The two organizations worked successfully throughout the first half of the twentieth century to become the regulators of legal education. Crucial to that effort was to first give the ABA the authority to accredit law schools to ensure that the schools met the standards that the organizations set, and then persuade state supreme courts, which established the requirements for admission to the bar of each state, to restrict admissions only to graduates of schools that could meet the standards.

The 1920s was the pivotal decade in the two organizations' efforts. The number of law schools increased by 25 percent, but fewer of the new schools met the standards of accreditation. The percentage of all law students attending accredited law schools fell. The ABA and AALS organized on the state and national level to fight these trends—first by attacking the independent night schools that could not meet standards, and then by slowly convincing the state supreme courts to tighten admissions requirements. By the end of the 1930s the ABA and the AALS had made substantial progress toward their goals of dominance in legal education, as almost two-thirds of all law school students were attending the approximately 100 ABA-approved law schools. The combination of the increasing importance of accreditation, the costs of operation of a school that met standards, and the decline in interest in attending law school caused by the Great Depression and World War II produced a decline in the number of law schools. Some of the independent schools were taken over by both public and private universities, while other independents, such as the John Marshall School of Law and the Suffolk School of Law, acknowledged that they must meet accreditation to survive and sought ABA approval in the 1950s. Thus, after the 1960s the Harvard model of university-based legal education was in complete ascendance, and the ABA and AALS controlled the regulation of legal education. As of 2002, 164 of the 185 ABA-approved law schools were members of the AALS.

During the late twentieth century, some new schools started to challenge the regulatory monopoly that the ABA enjoyed. One in suburban Virginia and one outside Boston were low-cost weekend or evening schools that had no intention of meeting ABA standards. The Massachusetts School of Law unsuccessfully sued the ABA under the Sherman Antitrust Act for being in restraint of trade. However, the ABA later reached an antitrust settlement with the Justice Department that changed some of its accreditation procedures. Since then the federal government has also taken an increasingly hard look at the accreditation procedures.

Curriculum

Before Langdell transformed legal education at Harvard, all curricula were pretty much the same. The student learned by reading or by lecture (if attending a school) or by observing the rules and procedures necessary to practice law in the student's local area. Subjects were not taught in any particular order. There were no exams except perhaps for the court-administered bar exam.

When Langdell brought the idea for the study of law as a science, he totally reformed the law school curriculum. First, he ordered the study into a first-year curriculum that introduced students to the main subjects of the common law: contracts, property, torts, criminal law, and procedure. Second, since the students were to learn the scientific principles of the law, not how to practice in their locality, the focus was on national law. Third, the faculty members selected appellate court decisions from which the principles could be derived. Rather than presenting a lecture, faculty members used the Socratic method of questioning students and then leading them to the principles through further questions and answers. The Harvard curriculum spread because its national approach and promise of scientific principles matched well with the national ambitions for prestige and prominence of the universities. The curriculum also fit the legal profession, which included a growing number of large urban nationally focused law firms.

Throughout the late nineteenth and early twentieth centuries the Harvard curriculum and its methodology remained supreme, yet it faced challenges. The first sustained effort of attack began in the early twentieth century when a group of legal scholars, called Legal Realists, sought to replace the Harvard curriculum with one that emphasized policy analysis informed by social science. The group had success at Yale and Columbia law schools, and their theories gained support as President Franklin D. Roosevelt led an attack on the U.S. Supreme Court for its reactionary views in blocking New Deal reforms. World War II sent the Legal Realists into retreat because many law professors believed that their theories undercut the rule of law, which was necessary to fight fascism and communism. Despite Realism's failure to dislodge the Harvard curriculum, many law schools introduced some "law and" courses, such as legal history or law and sociology. A few schools, such as the University of Wisconsin, Northwestern, and the University of Denver, established reputations as leading interdisciplinary law schools. More social science was introduced into legal studies during the last quarter of the twentieth century as law and economics began to be offered, most notably at the University of Chicago. At the century's end, almost all law schools had some version of the Harvard first-year curriculum together with either first-year "perspective" (law and) courses or upper level interdisciplinary courses.

Law school curriculum has responded to socio-political-economic developments, as well as technology. Beginning in the 1920s, labor law, securities regulation, environmental law, civil rights law, and sex discrimination became regular staples of students' selections in their last two years. The political activism of the civil rights and anti-poverty movements of the 1960s led schools to adopt clinical education, whereby small groups of students were assigned to a clinical faculty member who would supervise their representation of an indigent client. To these live-client clinics were added simulation courses, such as trial advocacy and externships, where students were placed in public or not-for-profit agencies. As the Watergate scandal shocked the nation in the 1970s, law schools responded with an increased focus on ethics courses. The development of computers led to online legal research, as well as an increase of courses in intellectual property and e-commerce. As critics of the legal profession criticized lawyers for making America a litigious society, law schools responded by adding courses in alternative dispute resolution.

Students and Faculty

Until the early twentieth century, admission to law school was somewhat open. Reading law, apprenticeship, or tuition fees at part-time independent law schools were relatively inexpensive and most white males who wanted to practice law could do so. A few women were able to receive legal education during this period, although the numbers remained small because courts were reluctant to admit women and employment opportunities were very limited. There were also very few blacks or other racial minorities. However, Jewish and Catholic males began to be admitted in larger numbers during the 1920s and 1930s.

The major transformation in the composition of the law student population occurred in the last half of the twentieth century. The demand for legal education soared following the return of soldiers after World War II. In 1947 about 47,000 students were enrolled in law school. By 2000 there were over 135,000. This demand was fueled in part by the tremendous growth in the size of law firms in the last quarter of the century, and the gradual removal of discrimination in hiring male Jewish and Catholic lawyers. The civil rights movement and the feminist revolution also expanded opportunities for women and religious and racial minorities. In 1950, the first year Harvard admitted women to the school, there were approximately 1,200 women enrolled. By 2000 women comprised almost half of the law student population. In 1971 there were fewer than 6,000 minorities; by 2000 there were over 25,000. During that same period the African American law student population grew from approximately 3,000 to 9,000; Hispanics from 1,000 to 7,500; and Asians from 500 to 8,000. Large law firms both increased the demand for law school education among women and minorities by hiring them in greater numbers, and responded to the pressure to hire more minorities once they were in school.

Another important factor in the growth and changing composition of the student population was the Law School Admissions Test (LSAT), which was devised by the elite law schools, such as Harvard and Yale, in 1948. Within a short period it was required of all students who wanted to attend law school. The standardized test allowed schools to make the admissions process more rational, and increased the chances that women and racial and religious minorities could succeed in that process. A second factor was the increased federal and private financial aid available. Law schools raised large endowments from their alumni in order to be able to assist students to graduate with manageable debt.

Full-time law school faculty did not become professionalized until Langdell established the Harvard model. Until then faculty were part-time practitioners who did not engage in scholarship. However, given the case method for teaching, faculty scholarship began by assembling cases and materials for courses. In 1887 the *Harvard Law Review* was established as a student-edited journal that published faculty scholarship, analyzed and criticized doc-trinal developments in case law, and published student notes analyzing recent court decisions. Each law school soon started its own review. Faculty scholarship became more varied as groups such as law and economics scholars, or members of Critical Legal Studies, pursued interdisciplinary work. With more law schools having university affiliation, scholarship became a hallmark of the American law school. Norms for hiring, tenure, and promotion became heavily influenced by those in the physical and social sciences and the humanities, and faculty members that held a doctor of philosophy degree became more and more desirable, especially in the late twentieth century.

The demographic composition of the faculty mirrored that of the student body, in part because faculty at the elite law schools tended to be hired from the pool of former students. For many years the typical pattern followed Langdell's hiring of James Barr Ames, a future dean of Harvard Law School: he was the best in his class and was hired upon graduation. Over the twentieth century, faculty, in addition to excelling in school, had usually clerked for the U.S. Supreme Court or for a prominent judge on a state supreme court or lower federal court. A few had graduated from non-elite schools and then gone to an elite school for a master's degree (LL.M.) or doctorate (S.J.D.) in law. They probably had practiced in a large firm or with the government for several years before teaching. In the 1960s there were fewer than a dozen women who were tenured professors, and very few minorities. As the student body diversified so did the professorate: by 2000 about 25 percent of law teachers were women and 12 percent were minority group members.

BIBLIOGRAPHY

Auerbach, Jerold S. *Unequal Justice: Lawyers and Social Change in Modern America*. New York: Oxford University Press, 1976.

Feldman, Marc, and Jay M. Feinman, "Legal Education: Its Cause and Cure." *Michigan Law Review* 92 (1984): 914–931.

Friedman, Lawrence M. *A History of American Law*. New York: Simon and Schuster, 1973.

Kalman, Laura. *Legal Realism at Yale, 1927–1960*. Chapel Hill: University of North Carolina Press, 1986.

LaPiana, William P. *Logic and Experience: The Origin of Modern American Legal Education*. New York: Oxford University Press, 1994.

Schlegel, John H. *American Legal Realism and Empirical Social Science*. Chapel Hill: University of North Carolina Press, 1995.

Stevens, Robert. *Law School: Legal Education in America from the 1850s to the 1980s*. Chapel Hill: University of North Carolina Press, 1983.

Rayman L. Solomon

LAWRENCE, SACK OF, occurred when tensions mounted in Kansas between free-state and proslavery forces after the passage of the Kansas-Nebraska Act. While Nebraska was to be a free state, the position of

Kansas remained unclear, and the rival factions began to populate the state. Both sides began extralegal actions, fraudulent voting practices, and arms distribution. When proslavery forces won the legislature in the first Kansas election, they began to prosecute free-state organizations. They indicted several free-state leaders and their publications and began legal action against the New England Emigrant Aid Company, one of the earliest and largest free-state organizations.

On 21 May 1856 a U.S. marshal arrived in Lawrence with a posse of seven hundred to eight hundred men to serve arrest warrants. He relinquished his posse to the proslavery sheriff, S. J. Jones, who sought the destruction of this "hotbed of abolitionism." Led by Jones and former Senator David R. Atchison of Missouri, the mob entered the town, burned the Emigrant Aid Company's Free State Hotel, and wrecked the newspaper offices. A few days later, fanatical abolitionist John Brown retaliated with the Pottawatomie Massacre, a brutal attack on the proslavery settlement at Pottawatomie Creek. At the request of Governor Wilson Shannon, troops were sent to Topeka to effect the dispersal of a free-state legislature. News of the sack aroused the entire North, led to the formation of the National Kansas Committee, and provided the Republican Party with the issue of "Bleeding Kansas."

BIBLIOGRAPHY
Castel, Albert E. *Civil War Kansas: Reaping the Whirlwind.* Lawrence: University Press of Kansas, 1997.
Goodrich, Thomas. *Bloody Dawn: The Story of the Lawrence Massacre.* Kent, Ohio: Kent State University Press, 1991.
Nichols, Alice. *"Bleeding Kansas."* New York: Oxford University Press, 1954.
Rawley, James A. *Race and Politics: "Bleeding Kansas" and the Coming of the Civil War.* Philadelphia: Lippincott, 1969.

Samuel A. Johnson
Honor Sachs

See also **Border War; Kansas-Nebraska Act; Pottawatomie Massacre.**

LAWRENCE SCIENTIFIC SCHOOL, established at Harvard University in 1847 by a gift of $50,000 from industrialist Abbott Lawrence, who wished to support applied science in eastern Massachusetts. The school existed until 1906 but enjoyed only mixed success, since Harvard presidents Edward Everett and Charles W. Eliot did not favor applied subjects in their liberal arts university. Everett thought the school would be a means for bringing a German university to Cambridge and from the start tried to direct the school into advanced studies of pure science. He hired Eben N. Horsford to teach pure and applied chemistry and Louis Agassiz, the eminent Swiss naturalist, to teach zoology and geology. The school was most popular as an engineering school under Henry L. Eustis. Many of his students went on to have important careers in railroading and mining around the world. Other scientists, such as Simon Newcomb, Harvey W. Wiley, Charles F. Chandler, John D. Runkle, and Thomas M. Drown, also attended the school.

The school had an uneven history. It began with high hopes but had only modest enrollments in the 1850s, declined in the 1860s, and did not recover until the late 1890s. As it was unable to compete with the Sheffield Scientific School at Yale and the Massachusetts Institute of Technology (MIT), then in Boston, Eliot tried repeatedly to transfer its programs to MIT. Nathaniel S. Shaler, a Lawrence alumnus and Agassiz's successor on the faculty, became dean in 1891 and devoted himself to building up the school. Despite his success (the enrollment reached 584 in 1902, an all-time high) and a 1903 bequest of approximately $30 million from manufacturer Gordon Mc-Kay, Eliot tried another merger with MIT in 1904. To protect the new endowment and to preserve a place for applied science at Harvard, Shaler agreed in 1906 to dissolve the Lawrence Scientific School and send its remaining undergraduate programs to Harvard College in return for a new Graduate School of Applied Science, which survives.

BIBLIOGRAPHY
Elliott, Clark A., and Margaret W. Rossiter, eds. *Science at Harvard University: Historical Perspectives.* Bethlehem, Pa.: Lehigh University Press, 1992.
Hawkins, Hugh. *Between Harvard and America, The Educational Leadership of Charles W. Eliot.* New York: Oxford University Press, 1972.

M. W. Rossiter/A. R.

See also **Education, Higher: Colleges and Universities; Engineering Education; Harvard University; Science Education.**

LAWRENCE STRIKE began in Lawrence, Massachusetts, in 1912, when textile mill owners cut workers' wages in response to a state law that lowered the maximum workweek for women and children to fifty-four hours. The strike lasted from 11 January until 14 March, and was initiated by a group of Polish women who discovered the unannounced pay cut and immediately walked off their jobs. The initial strike by more than 10,000 men, women, and children was largely peaceful, and workers only wanted to have their previous pay levels restored. The walkout first drew national attention through the presence of the Industrial Workers of the World (IWW), a primarily western labor organization that proclaimed the necessity of "one big union." The IWW represented only about 1 percent of Lawrence's 30,000 textile workers before the strike, but thousands more joined during the work stoppage, particularly after the IWW's New York headquarters sent organizers Joseph Ettor and Arturo Giovannitti to help coordinate strike activities. The companies refused to negotiate, and used their political and economic influence to convince judges, politicians, and police to help break the strike. By the end of the first week, twelve companies of state militia, the Massachusetts state police, Lawrence police, and company guards squared off against approximately 15,000 strikers. Dynamite discovered by police was later proven to have been planted by mill owners, who sought to discredit the workers. The violence escalated, and the Italian striker Anna Lo Pizzo was shot and killed during a confrontation with police on 29 January. Ettor and Giovannitti were charged with murder, although authorities admitted they were elsewhere when Lo Pizzo was killed. The IWW sent William Haywood and Elizabeth Gurley Flynn to take control of the strike.

To help alleviate hardship for their families, many workers began sending their children to relatives and supporters in other states. The first 119 children left the train depot on 10 February, followed on 17 February by another 138 children. The companies used their political connections to fight back. City police occupied the train station on 24 February, with orders to prevent any striker's children from leaving Lawrence. When the adults accompanying 40 children insisted on their right to travel peacefully, police responded by attacking both adults and children with clubs. This unprovoked brutality sparked national outrage, and the Massachusetts legislature and Congress began investigations. As their political allies dissolved, mill owners finally began negotiating. By 12 March, owners offered significant improvements in wages, including overtime pay, and promised that strikers would not be singled out for retribution. Workers approved the offer at a mass meeting on 14 March and began returning to work the following day. The Lawrence victory also helped win increases for workers in mills across New England.

Still, the strike was not over, because Ettor and Giovannitti were still imprisoned. When the trial began on 30 September, 15,000 Lawrence workers staged a one-day strike. The trial recommenced in Salem, Massachusetts, on 14 October and lasted fifty-eight days. Amid misplaced evidence and questionable witnesses, the jury on 26 November returned a verdict of not guilty. After more than ten months in prison, Ettor and Giovannitti were freed, and the Lawrence strike was over.

Strike in Lawrence, Mass. Members of the state militia hold strikers at bay. LIBRARY OF CONGRESS

"A Little Child Shall Lead Them." Accompanied by evocative banners, children of Lawrence, Mass., strikers take part in a New York City parade in support of the workers. LIBRARY OF CONGRESS

BIBLIOGRAPHY

Cameron, Ardis. *Radicals of the Worst Sort: Laboring Women in Lawrence, Massachusetts, 1860–1912.* Urbana: University of Illinois Press, 1993.

Dubofsky, Melvyn. *We Shall Be All: A History of the I.W.W.* Chicago: Quadrangle Books, 1969.

Meltzer, Milton. *Bread and Roses: The Struggle of American Labor, 1865–1915.* New York: Knopf, 1967.

John Cashman

See also **Industrial Workers of the World; Strikes; Textiles.**

LEAD INDUSTRY first became commercially important to the United States in 1750 when sustained lead mining and smelting began in Dutchess County, New York, and at what later became known as the Austinville mine in Virginia. The demand for lead bullets and shot in the Revolutionary War prompted the working of several small deposits in Massachusetts, Connecticut, Maryland, Pennsylvania, and North Carolina. The domestic availability and relative ease of smelting of lead ores greatly contributed to early frontier development and to sustaining the revolt against the English Crown.

Although reports exist of some petty lead production in connection with a 1621 iron furnace project in Virginia, later investigators have never found evidence of lead occurrences in the vicinity. French trappers discovered lead in the upper Mississippi Valley about 1690, and by 1763 the district near Galena, Illinois, had become a regular lead producer. The French-Canadian, Julien Dubuque, arrived in 1774 and made peace with the local Indians. He operated lead mines and furnaces in Iowa, Wisconsin, and Illinois until his death in 1810. The Fox and Sauk Indian tribes continued to mine and smelt the ore until the 1820s, when white venturers, using black slaves and under strong military protection, largely dispossessed them. This situation, in part, caused the Black Hawk War.

In 1797, Moses Austin migrated from the Virginia district bearing his name (Austinville) to southeast Missouri, where lead had been mined sporadically since about 1724 at Mine La Motte and other mines by early French explorers. Austin set up a large furnace and shot tower on the banks of the Mississippi River in 1798 and by 1819 was producing 3 million pounds of lead per year. With the Louisiana Purchase in 1803, these areas came under the control of the United States.

The simple log furnace—consisting of a crib of logs piled with lead ore, topped by more logs—was of poor smelting efficiency. Thus, when Peter Lorimier built a Scotch hearth in 1834 near Dubuque, Iowa, this new technology greatly lowered production costs and improved productivity within the lead industry. The frontier lead region from Galena into southern Wisconsin and Dubuque developed rapidly, so that by 1845 the district had a population of nearly 10,000 people and reportedly produced 54,495,000 pounds of lead, which was shipped by boat to New Orleans, or by prairie schooner to the Erie Canal and then by boat to eastern markets. Perhaps more than any other factor, early mining and commerce in lead accounted for opening the upper Midwest to American settlers.

From 1845 until the 1860s, domestic lead production continued primarily from shallow galena (lead sulfide) workings within three districts: Austinville, Wisconsin-Illinois-Iowa, and southeast Missouri. Deeper mining had to await renewed exploration during the war periods of the twentieth century. Throughout the Civil War, all these areas were largely controlled by the Confederacy, so that the Union had to melt lead gutters, pewter housewares, and lead pipe for its lead supplies, along with purchasing lead from foreign sources.

In the 1860s and early 1870s, new developments rapidly shifted the locus of the lead industry. With the westward surge of miners and prospectors to the Rocky Mountains following the gold rush of the 1850s came discoveries of lead as a host mineral for some silver and gold. In 1863, lead associated with silver was discovered in Little Cottonwood Canyon in Utah. Completion of the transcontinental railroad in 1869 gave the needed impetus to the growth of the intermountain lead-silver industry, including several smelters in Montana, Idaho, Utah, Nevada, California, and Colorado. Rich silver-lead ore was discovered at Leadville, Colorado, in 1876, and, for a time, this was the world's largest lead-producing area. The large high-grade ore body found at Bunker Hill, Idaho, in 1885 was the basis for the development of the Coeur d'Alene as an important lead-silver-zinc–producing area.

Mining these western lead carbonate ores proved to be much more hazardous to health than mining the lead sulfide ores of the central and eastern states. The human body assimilated carbonate dust more easily than lead in its traditional forms, causing "lead colic," which was most debilitating. In response to the problem, the lead industry initiated the practice of industrial hygiene, using dust respirators and providing a free ration of milk daily to the mine and smelter workers.

At the same time that prospectors were making many new discoveries of lead ore in the West, the shallow occurrences in the southeast Missouri district began to run out. In 1869, the first diamond drill used in the United States arrived from France to the Missouri district, where engineers used it to locate deeper, horizontally bedded deposits of lead ore with thicknesses of up to 500 feet at depths of 120 feet and more. This area of nearly pure lead ore was destined to become one of the largest in the world and a source of great strength to the United States through the wars of the twentieth century. Since 1904, southeast Missouri has been the leading lead-producing area in the United States.

The completion in 1872 of a railway linking Saint Louis and Joplin, Minnesota, in the vicinity of which new ore bodies had been discovered, caused zinc-lead mining activity to accelerate. About 1895, natural gas discoveries were made in the Kansas and Oklahoma part of the Joplin, or tristate, district, providing cheap fuel for zinc smelting and further stimulating mining activities. Since lead was a coproduct of zinc in the ore, lead production also grew, allowing several smelters to be constructed in the area and in the vicinity of Saint Louis.

The lead blast furnace first came into use in the United States in the late 1860s in areas of Nevada, Utah, and Montana, where lower-grade and more-complex lead ores required new technology. Gradually, in the older mining regions, the old furnace, reverberatory, and hearth methods of smelting became outdated. With new concentrating methods of tabling, jigging, and selective flotation, the fine grinding of the ore required to permit upgrading produced unsuitable feed material for the smelters. Adoption of a new technique—sintering (desulfurizing and agglomerating) the fine ore concentrate, then reducing it to lead bullion in a blast furnace—solved the new problems and again gave the lead industry an economic boost. Because the new technologies required greater amounts of capital, they acted as catalysts for a period of consolidation into a few large companies within the lead mining and smelting industry around the turn of the century.

Having provided the lead needs of the nation during the first half of the twentieth century, the older mining districts (Illinois-Wisconsin, Joplin, southeast Missouri "Old Lead Belt," Austinville) gradually became depleted, so that a new find was most welcome. Such was the case with the discovery of a "New Lead Belt" (some 50 miles from the Old Lead Belt) called the Viburnum Trend in southeast Missouri during the late 1950s. As companies developed the mines and came into full production between 1966 and 1974, Missouri lead output more than tripled, approaching a half million tons, or 80 percent of the total U.S. lead production. Two new lead smelters were built in Missouri and the capacity of a third was doubled, while two historic western smelters were being abandoned, indicating the extent of this major shift in mine production.

Once made into a metal, lead is almost indestructible. Water pipes, cisterns, and baths of the pre-Christian era in Rome, and artifacts of the earlier Egyptian and Phoenician civilizations, have been found almost completely intact. Large-scale peacetime reuse of lead became significant in the United States about 1907. Since the 1960s, secondary recovery has accounted for half the domestic lead supply. In 1974, the United States used 1.5 million short tons of lead, which was supplied by 510,000 tons recycled from scrap, 670,000 tons from domestic mines, and the remainder from imports (31 percent from Peru, 26 percent from Canada, 18 percent from Mexico, 11 percent from Australia, and 14 percent from other countries). By the year 2000, more than 60 percent of the industry's production came from recycled materials, primarily because of the large number of scrapped lead batteries.

Historically, lead has been widely used in a variety of consumer products, such as lead-acid storage batteries and organic lead gasoline additives in automobiles. Lead-tin alloys are used for soldering radiators, electrical connections, and tin cans. Sheet lead appears in shielding from nuclear and X-ray radiation and from noise. The corrosion resistance of lead to acids, moisture, and atmosphere accounts for its use in chemical process equipment, electrical cable sheathing, plumbing, and architectural units. Lead compounds have been used as paint pigments, metal primers, ceramic glazes, and insecticides. Because of its density, metal use varies from ballast in the keel of sailboats to shot and bullets for military and sporting ammunition.

Lead and lead compounds can constitute a biological hazard if not properly handled, however, and with the rise of the environmental and consumer movements, this fact has given lead something of a bad reputation. Excessive ingestion and inhalation of lead compounds can result in illness or even death in humans. As a result, increasingly strict regulations have been established for permissible levels of lead in paints and emissions into the atmosphere, particularly in leaded automotive gasoline. This resulted in a dramatic shift in consumer use of lead. As demand for lead in paints, gasoline, and water systems has declined, the use of lead in all battery types expanded to account for 88 percent of the market by the early 2000s. The next-largest demands for the metal are for ammunition and oxides in glass and ceramics—both of which account for about 3 percent of the market.

BIBLIOGRAPHY

Blaskett, Donald R. *Lead and Its Alloys.* New York: Ellis Horwood, 1990.

Cotterill, Carl H., and J. M. Cigan, eds. *Proceedings of AIME World Symposium on Mining and Metallurgy of Lead and Zinc.* Vol. 2, *Extractive Metallurgy of Lead and Zinc.* New York: American Institute of Mining, Metallurgical, and Petroleum Engineers, 1970.

Rausch, D. O., F. M. Stephens, Jr., and B. C. Mariacher, eds. *Proceedings of AIME World Symposium on Mining and Metallurgy of Lead and Zinc.* Vol. 1, *Mining and Concentrating of Lead and Zinc.* New York: American Institute of Mining, Metallurgical, and Petroleum Engineers, 1970.

Carl H. Cotterill / c. w.

See also **Electricity and Electronics; Leadville Mining District; Mining Towns; Recycling.**

LEADVILLE MINING DISTRICT, Colorado's longest lived, is located at the headwaters of the Arkansas River. In 1860, gold placers discovered in California Gulch spurred the first rush, but the gold was exhausted by 1865. A much bigger boom followed in the 1870s with the discovery that the local lead carbonate ore was rich in silver. Leadville, incorporated in 1878, became a celebrated silver and smelter city. In 1893, however, the silver crash and subsequent labor troubles ended Leadville's heyday. Molybdenum was the main product in the twentieth century; the giant Climax mine, twelve miles north of Leadville, produced 60 percent of the world's supply by the late 1950s. This era ended when Climax shut down in 1982. It has reopened only for brief periods.

BIBLIOGRAPHY

Griswold, Don L., and Jean Harvey Griswold. *History of Leadville and Lake County, Colorado: From Mountain Solitude to Metropolis.* Denver: Colorado Historical Society, 1996.

Philpott, William. *The Lessons of Leadville.* Denver: Colorado Historical Society, 1995.

William Philpott

See also **Colorado; Gold Mines and Mining; Mining Towns; Silver Prospecting and Mining.**

LEAGUE OF NATIONS. The name of this organization is generally traced to the 1908 book *La Société des Nations* by the influential French peace negotiator Leon Bourgeois. During WORLD WAR I a growing number of political leaders, including Lord Robert Cecil in Britain, Jan Christian Smuts in South Africa, and the former U.S. president William Howard Taft, pointed to the need for an international organization that would facilitate greater security and cooperation among nations. The U.S. president Woodrow Wilson, whose name would become most closely associated with the League of Nations, had also repeatedly proposed such an organization. Wilson's concern to set up an international organization to secure and maintain peace between nation-states was laid out in a number of speeches and public addresses before and after the United States entered World War I in April 1917. On 8 January 1918, in a major address to the U.S. Congress, he outlined his proposal to end the war and provide a framework for a new postwar international order. Wilson's address centered on his so-called FOURTEEN POINTS, which, with some revision, provided the overall framework for the negotiation of an armistice in Europe by 11 November 1918. Of particular importance was his fourteenth point, which called for the establishment of an organization that would protect the independence and sovereignty of all nations. Wilson certainly played an important role in the establishment of the League of Nations, even if the notion that he was its veritable "father" is exaggerated.

63

Origins

In a more general way the League of Nations was grounded in the rise and fall of the practice of consultation among the European powers, which was increasingly formalized as the Concert of Europe after 1815. By the late nineteenth century the Concert of Europe was breaking down in the context of the rise of imperial Germany. The emergence of the United States as an increasingly important player also weakened the balance of power on which the Concert of Europe rested, as did the wider social and political changes in Europe itself. However, the central idea of the Concert of Europe—that the Great Powers had particular rights and duties in international relations—underpinned the creation of the Council of the League of Nations. This was the organization's supreme decision-making body and included only the major powers.

Despite the influence of the Concert of Europe, a more immediate and equally important catalyst for the League of Nations was World War I. The war stimulated a general dissatisfaction with the management of interstate relations and encouraged growing interest in a new international system of collective security. In May 1916 Woodrow Wilson publicly spoke of the need to reform the international order. This gave the whole idea greater legitimacy and encouraged European political leaders to examine the idea. This interest was further strengthened when the Russian Revolution of 1917 brought pressure to bear on the old international system. A number of draft versions of the constitution for the League of Nations were produced by the United States and by the European governments. The actual peace conference in 1919 focused on a draft produced jointly by the United States and Britain.

Establishment and Organization

By 1918 there was general agreement that a League of Nations should be established. The key articles of the actual covenant (constitution) spelled out the role of the league in identifying and addressing threats to peace, the settlement of disputes, and the imposition of sanctions against states violating international agreements. These articles occasioned limited disagreement. Participating nations also generally agreed that the league should be made up of an executive council, a deliberative assembly, and an administrative secretariat, but they disagreed over the exact function and makeup of these bodies. In an early draft of the covenant, membership of the council was restricted to the Great Powers and any smaller nation-states that the Great Powers chose to invite. However, the formulation that eventually prevailed designated the Great Powers as permanent members of the council while small powers had nonpermanent membership. The operation and membership of the assembly, which was the model for the General Assembly of the UNITED NATIONS after 1945, was also a subject of some debate. In fact its overall operation and significance was really only worked out in subsequent years.

The administrative secretariat, set up as a coordinating and administrative body, was a less divisive issue. Its power was grounded entirely in the council and the assembly. The headquarters of the league were in Geneva, Switzerland, where the secretariat prepared reports and agendas. The assembly, which was made up of representatives of all the member governments, set policy and met on an annual basis. Britain, France, Italy, and Japan held permanent membership in the council, which met more regularly than the assembly. It had been expected that the United States would be the fifth permanent member of the council. At the same time, the assembly elected another four (eventually nine) temporary members to the council to serve three-year terms. All decisions taken by the council and the assembly had to be unanimous if they were to be binding. The league also included a number of subsidiary organizations. One of these, the International Labor Organization (ILO) was a specific response to the Russian Revolution. It was hoped that the ILO would appease some of the more radical tendencies within the trade union movement in various parts of the world and curtail the attractions of international communism. A Permanent Court of International Justice was also set up, as well as a range of commissions that dealt with issues such as refugees, health, drugs, and child welfare. At the time of its foundation in 1919 the league had forty-two member governments. This increased to fifty-five by 1926; however, the failure of the United States to become a member contributed significantly to the decline of the organization by the 1930s. Meanwhile, Germany only became a member in 1926 and withdrew in 1933, while the Soviet Union was only a member from 1934 to 1939. The Japanese government departed in 1933, and the Italian government ended its association with the league in 1937.

Operations and Activities

The prevention and settlement of disputes between nation-states in order to avoid another conflagration like World War I was central to the operations and activities of the league. Although it did not have a military force of its own, the league prevented or settled a number of conflicts and disputes in the 1920s. In fact, it was the activities of the league in the 1920s that made it appear to many people that it had some long-term prospects for success. The league played a major role in the resolution of a dispute over the Aaland Islands between the governments of Finland and Sweden. In 1925 it got the Greek government to withdraw from Bulgaria and resolved a border dispute between the governments of Turkey and Iraq. The league's inability to settle a conflict between the governments of Bolivia and Paraguay at the beginning of the 1930s demonstrated that the league's sphere of influence was centered on Europe. It also showed that the league's activities in Latin America were hampered by Washington's lack of support for, or membership in, the organization. During its entire history, none of the disputes that the league successfully resolved affected the interests of the Great Powers.

It is generally argued that the limitations of the league were manifested most obviously in the Manchurian crisis of the early 1930s. The Chinese government requested help from the league following Japan's invasion of Manchuria in 1931, but the league failed to prevent the ensuing Sino-Japanese conflict. None of the other major powers in the league were able or willing to take a strong stand against Japan, and the league moved slowly on what little action it did take, following well behind the unfolding situation. By early 1932 the Japanese government had set up the puppet state of Manchukuo in Manchuria. It was not until February 1933 that the league discussed and adopted the report of the Lytton Commission, which had been dispatched earlier to look into the affair. Although the report was a relatively mild document, it did recommend that Manchuria be given autonomous status within China. Within a month of the adoption of the report of the Lytton Commission, the Japanese government had withdrawn from the League of Nations.

In the wake of the league's failure in Manchuria, the crisis that clearly signaled its waning influence in the 1930s was the invasion of Ethiopia by Italy in October 1935. This led to the imposition of economic sanctions on war-related materials that were, in theory, carried out by all members of the league. These sanctions soon proved insufficient. But the ability of the league, or more particularly of Britain and France, to move to more significant actions, such as closing the Suez Canal to Italian shipping and the cutting off of all oil exports to Italy, was constrained by the fear that such action would provoke war with Italy. The situation was further undermined because Britain and France tried, unsuccessfully, to negotiate a secret deal with Mussolini (the Hoare-Laval Pact) that would settle the dispute peacefully by allowing Italy to retain control of some Ethiopian territory.

The End of the League of Nations

In broad terms the decline of the League of Nations in the 1930s reflected the unwillingness or inability of Britain, France, and the United States to oppose the increasingly nationalist-imperialist and militaristic trajectories of Nazi Germany, Fascist Italy, and imperial Japan. The post-1919 international order that resulted from the Treaty of Versailles was fragile, and the league embodied that fragility. Following the Ethiopian crisis the league was more or less irrelevant. It failed to respond to the direct military intervention of Germany and Italy in the Spanish Civil War (1936–1939). Meanwhile, Turkey's capture of part of Syria, Hitler's occupation of Czechoslovakia, and Mussolini's invasion of Albania in the late 1930s also produced virtually no response from the league. Its final, and largely symbolic, action was the expulsion of the Soviet Union following its invasion of Finland in 1939. The League of Nation's numerous shortcomings ensured that it never played the role in international affairs that its early promoters had hoped it would. In a somewhat circular fashion it is clear that the lack of cooperation and collective action between nation-states that encouraged

political leaders to call for a League of Nations in the first place was the very thing that undermined the league once it was created. The League of Nations was dissolved in 1946. However, World War II also led to the reinvention of the League of Nations, insofar as the United Nations, which was first suggested in the Atlantic Charter in 1941 and formally established in late 1945, built on the earlier organization.

BIBLIOGRAPHY

Armstrong, David. *The Rise of the International Organisation: A Short History.* London: Macmillan, 1982.

Gill, George. *The League of Nations: From 1929 to 1946.* Garden City Park, N.Y.: Avery, 1996.

Knock, Thomas J. *To End All Wars: Woodrow Wilson and the Quest for a New World Order.* New York: Oxford University Press, 1992.

Ostrower, Gary B. *The League of Nations: From 1919 to 1929.* Garden City Park, N.Y.: Avery, 1996.

Thorne, Christopher G. *The Limits of Foreign Policy: The West, the League, and the Far Eastern Crisis of 1931–1933.* New York: Putnam, 1973.

Walters, F. P. *A History of the League of Nations.* 2 vols. London: Oxford University Press, 1952.

Mark T. Berger

See also **Versailles, Treaty of.**

LEAGUE OF WOMEN VOTERS. When the victory for suffrage was won, Carrie Chapman Catt was president of the National American Women's Suffrage Association. Catt was determined that women would use the vote and envisioned the League of Women Voters to forward this goal. On 14 February 1920, the organization came to life with Maud Wood Park, a leading suffragist, as president.

The League focused on educating women to vote. The method they used became a hallmark of the organization: members studied issues closely at the local level, and took a stance when consensus was achieved.

In the first blush of women's suffrage, many goals of women's groups seemed attainable. The League lobbied for the Sheppard-Towner Act, to provide funding for maternal and child health clinics. The act passed in 1921. In 1922, the League supported the Cable Act. It too passed, establishing independent citizenship for women who married foreigners. The League then advocated a child labor amendment; however, it was not ratified by enough states to be added to the Constitution. The League also worked for membership in the League of Nations and the World Court.

In 1923, the NATIONAL WOMAN'S PARTY introduced the EQUAL RIGHTS AMENDMENT, granting legal equality to women under the Constitution. Social feminists who dominated the League of Women Voters opposed the amendment, believing it imperiled protective labor legislation, based on women's special needs. The amendment did not pass.

By the mid-1920s, Congress realized that the woman's vote was not as large or as influential as anticipated, and began to retreat from women's legislation such as the Sheppard-Towner Act, allowing it to expire in 1929.

During the depression, the League lobbied for the development of a publicly owned power system in the Tennessee River Valley. The league sponsored national forums, conferences, and debates to influence lawmakers, who passed the legislation needed for the establishment of the Tennessee Valley Authority. When Eleanor Roosevelt, an early member of the League, called a conference on the emerging needs of women, the League participated. The League also contributed to formulation of the Social Security Act of 1935.

Before World War II began, the League advocated an internationalist program and supported the Lend-Lease Act of 1941. In 1945, the League acted in support of the United Nations charter, the World Bank, and the International Monetary Fund. During the postwar red scare, the League pressed for individual liberties.

The president of the League served on the Committee on the Status of Women from 1961 to 1963. The report issued from the Committee made recommendations for improvement of women's status. The committee did not support the Equal Rights Amendment. (It was not until 1972 that the League would support the Equal Rights Amendment.) The 1964 Civil Rights Act nullified special legislation for working women undermining the basis for opposition.

In the 1960s and 1970s, the League studied issues of poverty, unemployment, and racism, supporting fair housing, fair employment, and integration. It also took a strong position on environmentalism.

More recently, the League has advocated gun control, streamlined voter registration or motor-voter laws, the right to reproductive choice, campaign finance reform, and health care reform.

During its eighty years, the League has become known for its careful study of issues and earned a reputation for citizen participation. It maintains a non-partisan status. In 1998, the League elected its first African American president, Carolyn Jefferson-Jenkins. In 2001, membership was 130,000.

BIBLIOGRAPHY

Perry, Elisabeth Israels. *Women in Action: Rebels and Reformers, 1920–1980.* Washington, D.C.: League of Women Voters Education Fund, 1995.

Young, Louise M. *In the Public Interest: The League of Women Voters, 1920–1970.* New York: Greenwood Press, 1989.

Bonnie L. Ford

See also **Suffrage; Women's Rights Movement: The Twentieth Century.**

LEARNED SOCIETIES are voluntary organizations of individuals dedicated to scholarship and research, often focused on a particular subject or method. Although this form has ancient antecedents and European exemplars such as the British Royal Society and the French Academy, it has taken on a distinct form in the United States and has played a critical role in the evolution of American higher education. The history of learned societies can be divided into three phases. The earliest societies, founded before the Revolution, were local collections of literate and inquiring minds. In the mid-nineteenth century, a new model emerged: broad-based organizations often dedicated to popularizing new knowledge and promoting social reform. With the development of the American research university, learned societies in the United States developed their present form.

The first learned society founded in what was to become the United States was the American Philosophical Society, founded in 1743 in Philadelphia by Benjamin Franklin and reorganized and put on a firmer footing by incorporating offshoot organizations in 1769. The Society began publishing a journal, *Transactions of the American Philosophical Society*, in 1771, and organized the systematic observation and documentation of the transit of Venus in 1769. John Adams of Massachusetts, aware of the work of the American Philosophical Society from time spent in Philadelphia at the Continental Congress, was concerned lest Boston cede intellectual prestige to Philadelphia. He convinced the Massachusetts General Court to charter the American Academy of Arts and Sciences in 1780 with its seat at Boston.

The Boston and Philadelphia examples were reproduced throughout the early nineteenth century in smaller, newer cities. While these early learned societies aspired to national prominence (Thomas Jefferson was president of the American Philosophical Society while he was also president of the United States), they were primarily vehicles of local elites. The original statutes of the American Academy of Arts and Sciences required that the preponderance of its members be drawn from the immediate vicinity of Boston. Composed of gentlemen chosen by honorific election, these societies were defined initially by an Enlightenment commitment to general moral and intellectual cultivation, not to scholarly research as we now define it.

In the mid-nineteenth century, new national societies emerged that were both more focused and more inclusive than the local organizations. The American Association for the Advancement of Science (AAAS), founded in 1848, and the American Social Science Association, founded in 1865, were open to all who supported their broad aims. The AAAS evolved from a more specialized society of geologists and sought to provide a national forum wherein all scientists could announce discoveries and educate the public on scientific progress. The American Social Science Association was concerned not with abstract theory and methodology, but with the systematic approach to the solutions of social problems. The ethos of these societies, like that of their contemporary institution, the lyceum, reflected a conception of learning and science as elements of a shared civic culture and not as the esoteric pursuits of a few professionals. Less inclusive was the National Academy of Sciences, chartered by Congress in 1863 to help organize knowledge to support the Union cause in the Civil War. The National Academy of Sciences was limited originally to fifty distinguished scholars, who would elect all future members.

What became the predominant form of learned society—an open organization of scholars seeking to establish standards and to advance research in a particular arena of academic inquiry—was coeval with the development of the American research university. Beginning in the 1880s, scholars, often trained in German universities and eager to develop in America the type of research institutions with which they had become familiar abroad, established new societies frankly devoted to developing academic research in particular fields as professions. Three of the leading learned societies in the humanities and social sciences were founded within three years of each other by faculty of Johns Hopkins University, the first American institution founded as a research university: the Modern Language Association (1883), the American Historical Association (1884), and the American Economic Association (1885). The scholarly journals established by these new societies quickly became the principal arena for establishing standards and intellectual authority in the emerging scholarly disciplines. University presidents immediately saw and supported the professionalizing project of these nascent societies, since these new organizations provided them with a means of measuring scholarly credentials when deciding on faculty appointments and promotions. Universities provided offices, publication support, and other facilities to the new societies. Although many larger, discipline-based societies eventually developed independent offices, most of the smaller learned societies continue to rely on university support for their operations. The two strands of departmental organization of universities on the one hand and the professional authority of learned societies on the other together formed the DNA of the scholarly disciplines in modern American academia.

Even though the aims and membership of these new societies were narrower than those of those of their mid-nineteenth-century predecessors, the new academic professional organizations were generally more inclusive in their membership than the societies founded in the eighteenth century with elected memberships. Membership in research-oriented societies is usually open to all, but the overwhelming majority of members are faculty and students from colleges and universities. There has always been a tension between the academic and the occupational roles of learned societies. Many societies, committed to professionalizing scholarly research, initially es-

chewed engagement with pedagogy and occupational aspects of teaching.

The emergence of learned societies made possible in turn the creation of national organizations that could advance scholarly research through and with universities. While the American Association for the Advancement of Science continued to have individuals as its constituent members, it developed a complementary aspect as a federation of the more specialized, disciplinary-based scientific societies. In 1918, the National Academy of Sciences, supported by the nascent Rockefeller and Carnegie Foundations, established the National Research Council as a means of mobilizing the scientific expertise manifested in the new learned societies, which were to nominate scholars for membership in the new Research Council. The American Council of Learned Societies (ACLS), founded in 1919 with a constituent membership of thirteen societies, soon became the means by which the foundations could support research in the humanities and related social sciences. Since its founding, the ACLS has also sought to strengthen relations among its member societies, now numbering sixty-six. Activist social scientists drew together representatives of seven societies to form the Social Science Research Council (incorporated in 1924) as a vehicle for supporting policy-oriented research on contemporary social issues.

The number and size of learned societies increased during the epochal expansion of American higher education after World War II. The role of learned societies in establishing professional authority became all the more important in managing the growth of academia, especially as the larger, disciplinary societies provided the structure for the academic employment market, at least for junior faculty, by publishing lists of open academic positions and promoting their annual conventions as sites for the interviewing of job candidates. The increasing specialization of scholarship brought the founding of many new societies with interdisciplinary, topical, and sometimes highly focused interests. At the same time, the earlier, honorific societies begun in the eighteenth century became more national in their membership, selecting new fellows for their scholarly and institutional prominence, not for their local social positions. While many newer, smaller societies were directed by volunteers, usually taking time from other academic employment, the management of larger learned societies became more professionalized, with a permanent staff led by full-time executive directors.

The social and political turmoil of the late 1960s and 1970s deeply affected learned societies. Insurgent factions within large societies rejected a limited, academic definition of their society's mission and sought greater engagement with public issues. Many societies altered their methods of governance to allow for more competitive elections and broader representation of the demographic and institutional diversity of their membership. The retrenchment in the academic sector in the late 1970s obliged many learned societies to focus anew on the occupational issues concerning their members. Concern for the conditions of the academic workforce persists in many societies, along with activities aimed at the development of their fields not only in higher education, but also in primary and secondary education, and in the public realm.

While membership size, financial structure, and range of operations vary greatly among contemporary learned societies, a few generalizations are possible. The larger, disciplinary societies and the smaller, interdisciplinary societies often complement, rather than compete with, each other. Many scholars are members of more than one society, seeking different types of community in each organization. Most societies are financed though a combination of membership dues, meeting registrations, publication revenues, and donations. The membership of most societies extends beyond the United States, and many, especially those concerned with the study of world areas, have increasingly international constituencies. The rise of digital information technology poses special challenges and opportunities to learned societies, as electronic versions of their journals are distributed easily through the servers of university libraries and listservs and electronic discussion groups provide for virtual scholarly meetings.

BIBLIOGRAPHY

Bender, Thomas. *Intellect and Public Life: Essays of the Social History of Academic Intellectuals in the United States.* Baltimore: Johns Hopkins University Press, 1993.

Bledstein, Burton J. *The Culture of Professionalism: The Middle Class and the Development of Higher Education in America.* New York: Norton, 1976.

Geiger, Roger L. *To Advance Knowledge: The Growth of American Research Universities, 1900–1940.* New York: Oxford University Press, 1986.

Kiger, Joseph Charles. *American Learned Societies.* Washington, D.C.: Public Affairs Press, 1963.

Steven C. Wheatley

See also **American Academy of Arts and Sciences; American Association for the Advancement of Science; American Association of University Professors; American Association of University Women; American Historical Association; American Philosophical Society; Engineering Societies.**

LEATHER AND LEATHER PRODUCTS INDUSTRY.

Leather industries in North America date from early European settlement. Tanneries were established in New England, Virginia, and the middle colonies before 1650. Shoemaking began as quickly.

Leather Crafts

Leather and leather products were important crafts through 1850, employing 15.7 percent of all workers in manufacturing, with shoemakers outnumbering workers in any other industry. European handicraft techniques adopted by colonists persisted with minor modifications throughout the mid-nineteenth century. In leather making, hides were soaked in lime and water, and loosened hair was scraped off. After this cleaning, hides were tanned in large vats by the chemical action of the tannin-bearing bark of hemlock, sumac, or oak trees. Finishing improved the suppleness of the leather, enabling the leather to be worked into a variety of products. The most important, boots and shoes, were made by cutting leather pieces with a knife, sewing upper-leather pieces, forming the upper around a foot-shaped device called a last, and stitching the soles to the upper with awls and waxed thread.

Initially, tanning was undertaken on a small scale and often on a part-time basis. Using local materials and targeting local markets, it was widely dispersed. Capital costs were modest, and skills were acquired experientially. Tanneries in the United States and the colonies that came to make it up grew with the population, passing 1,000 by 1750, 4,000 by 1810, and 8,000 by 1840. Early shoemakers were widespread; over 11,000 establishments operated in 1850. Saddlers and harness makers, numbering about 3,500 in 1850, were equally common. There was little guild activity in these trades. Although tanners secured legislation to control their trade, it had little effect.

The most important changes in the industry until 1850 were organizational. Emerging regional leather markets led to the growth of larger tanneries, the separation of merchants from tanners, and some concentration of tanning in cities, where hides were available, and in the Catskill Mountains in New York, where hemlock trees abounded. Nineteenth-century wholesale shoemakers sold ready-made shoes in regional and increasingly national markets. To supply shoes, they organized a "putting-out system" in which upper pieces were cut in central shops, put out to women who sewed them, and then put out again to men who bottomed the shoe. This system was concentrated in Massachusetts, which in 1850 employed almost half of shoemaking workers, in establishments averaging thirty-seven workers. New products originated, including morocco and patent leathers, leather belting used to transmit power in factories, and pegged shoes, made by using wooden pegs to attach soles to uppers. Except for shoemaking's central-shop system, these changes little affected the size of establishments, which in 1850 averaged 3.8 workers in leather making; 4.5 in saddlery, harnesses, and other products; and 5.4 in shoemaking outside Massachusetts.

Mechanization and the Factory System

By 1850, some mechanization had already occurred in auxiliary occupations that ground bark for tanning or turned shoe lasts. Over the second half of the nineteenth century, the mechanized factory eliminated most hand labor in leather industries. Tanners and leather-machinery firms developed machines to unhair, scrape, beat, split, tan, dry, and finish leather, including steam-driven mechanisms to feed tannin and stir hides. Chemical processes changed more slowly. Tannin extract substituted for bark after 1890. Building on German inventions, Augustus Schultz, a New York dye salesman, and Martin Dennis, a scientifically trained tanner, developed chrome tanning, which substituted chromic acid for tannin, reducing tanning time and overcoming the dependence on bark. Based on these successes, firms invested modestly in industrial research, leather chemists organized nationally, and universities formed industry-supported leather research centers.

Leatherworking was also mechanized, most importantly through the sewing machine, which had initially been used to make clothing. First used to stitch shoe uppers in 1852, the sewing machine increased productivity in factories and subcontractors' shops and was adopted widely by 1860. The most revolutionary machine, the McKay bottom-stitcher, attached uppers to soles. Patented by Lyman Blake, a shoe manufacturer, and developed by Gordon McKay, a machinery producer, it bottomed two-fifths of U.S. shoes in 1871, largely in factories employing machine operatives and some hand laborers. Machines to last, heel, and finish shoes followed, as did the Goodyear stitcher, which duplicated hand-sewn shoes. The sewing machine was also adapted to stitch saddles, harnesses, gloves, and books.

Leather mechanization succeeded around the Civil War (1861–1865) because it both supported the growth of mechanizing firms selling in wholesale markets and built on techniques of machine design and production that originated in other sectors. Tanners, shoemakers, and machinists were the principal inventors. Leather machinery firms diffused machines, spread knowledge of machine design, and thus fostered invention. Shoemaking patents quadrupled from 1860 to 1900, and seven-eighths were issued to machinists, professional inventors, and shoemakers.

As mechanization proceeded, firms grew in size. The average leather-making firm grew from five employees in 1860 to forty in 1900 and one hundred in 1925, led by firms in Massachusetts, New York, Pennsylvania, and Wisconsin. As large firms grew, many smaller firms closed; the 5,200 leather-making firms in 1860 had fallen to 530 in 1925. Shoemaking firms specialized in factory production or in custom-making shoes and repair; the average factory employed 57 workers in 1880, 89 in 1900, and 141 in 1925. Massachusetts remained the center of shoe firms, shoe machinery firms, and shoe invention.

Glove-making firms were somewhat smaller and even more localized; half of all leather gloves were made around Gloversville, New York, where localized knowledge provided a great advantage. Firms making leather and its products never attained the size or complexity of the managerial firms arising in more capital-intensive sectors. The large machinery firms did; Singer and United Shoe Machinery became diversified transnational corporations spreading American techniques to Europe and elsewhere since the late nineteenth century. The growth of factory

TABLE 1

Employment in U.S. Leather Industries (in thousands)

Year	Leather Manufacturing	Boots and Shoes	Other Products	Total	Total, Share of all Manufacturing
1850	26	105	17	148	15.7%
1860	26	123	17	167	12.7%
1880	40	137	37	215	7.9%
1900	52	159	55	266	5.0%
1925	53	214	39	307	3.7%
1954	39	227	55	321	2.6%
1997	12	28	22	62	0.5%

Note: Data is for production workers, but changing census definitions make precise comparison impossible.

SOURCE: U.S. censuses of manufacturing.

production was associated with the polarization of classes and efforts at unionization. These efforts had only localized success until the 1930s and World War II (1939–1945), when successful unions were organized in leather and shoe industries.

Decline

American leather industries experienced great changes in the twentieth century. The growth of demand decreased. Leather-shoe purchases per capita did not grow from 1900 to 1987. Though total employment in leather industries doubled from 1850 to 1954, the share of manufacturing workers decreased from 15.7 to 2.6 percent. Technical change undercut markets for harnesses, saddles, and industrial belting. Alternative materials cut into the use of leather to make products. Rubber and plastics came to be used in shoe soles and heels. Introduced by rubber companies around 1900, athletic shoes have grown rapidly in popularity since then. In 1963, DuPont introduced Corfam, a synthetic leather.

Changing techniques after World War II improved tanning machinery and methods; created leathers that were waterproof, washable, or scuff resistant; and introduced computer-aided design, injection molding, and laser cutting to shoemaking. However, these changes diffused erratically and did not alter the production process fundamentally. Automation was limited by the heterogeneity of leather and shoes.

Globalization after 1950 brought radical changes. While the United States was largely self-sufficient in both leather and shoe production in 1954, imports skyrocketed over the next several decades. Italy became the leader in fine leather and shoes and the machinery to make them. Italy's leather industries are decentralized, and networks of producers, contractors, suppliers, and skilled labor quickened turnover and improved product quality and responsiveness to style changes. The greatest growth occurred in developing countries, the source of four-fifths of U.S. leather and leather product imports by the early 2000s. This growth rested on the transfer of labor-intensive technology via subcontracting and joint ventures to economies with far lower wages, longer hours, antiunion practices, and little social and environmental regulation. As a result, U.S. imports of leather shoes rose from 30 percent of pairs purchased in 1975 to 82 percent in 1995. Domestic shoe manufacturing employment fell by 88 percent from 1954 through 1997. The decline in other leather industries was less severe; employment in tanning fell by 38 percent from 1954 through 1997, and in other leather industries by 54 percent. Once key crafts, then important centers of industrialization, the leather industries largely left the United States by the end of the twentieth century.

BIBLIOGRAPHY

Dawley, Alan. *Class and Community: The Industrial Revolution in Lynn.* Cambridge, Mass.: Harvard University Press, 1976.

Ellsworth, Lucius F. *The American Leather Industry.* Chicago: Rand McNally, 1969.

Hazard, Blanche Evans. *The Organization of the Boot and Shoe Industry in Massachusetts Before 1875.* Cambridge, Mass.: Harvard University Press, 1921.

Hoover, Edgar M. *Location Theory and the Shoe and Leather Industries.* Cambridge, Mass.: Harvard University Press, 1937.

Thomson, Ross. *The Path to Mechanized Shoe Production in the United States.* Chapel Hill: University of North Carolina Press, 1989.

Welsh, Peter C. *Tanning in the United States to 1850: A Brief History.* Washington, D.C.: Museum of History and Technology, Smithsonian Institution, 1964.

Ross D. Thomson

See also **Boot and Shoe Manufacturing; Manufacturing.**

LEATHERSTOCKING TALES.

James Fenimore Cooper's *Leatherstocking Tales*, featuring the adventures and exploits of independent frontiersman Natty Bumppo, were tremendously popular in the antebellum era and helped to define both American literary culture and the emerging nation's self-image. There were five tales in all: *The Pioneers* (1823), *The Last of the Mohicans* (1826), *The Prairie* (1827), *The Pathfinder* (1840), and *The Deerslayer* (1841). From the beginning, Cooper's works met with success, and he was hailed as America's first major author. Contemporary readers found in the *Leatherstocking Tales* both reassurance that American writers could produce significant literary work and an inspiring patriotic portrayal of the United States. Many of Cooper's characters went on to become stock figures or stereotypes of American popular culture, such as the tragically noble Indian and the loyal slave. However, it was the rugged, manly, and lawless Natty Bumppo, or "Leatherstocking," who truly captured the public imagination. Cooper romanticized the frontier as a place of wild adventure where Americans lived beyond the reach of corrupt, restrictive society and tested themselves against nature. By writing on such themes, he helped overcome an earlier American bias against novels as feminine and trivial. He also began a tradition of depicting the country's unsettled lands as places of purity, honor, and integrity, and hence of identifying the frontier as a key component of American identity. Despite this celebration of rugged individualism, later commentators have pointed out the ambiguity of Cooper's message. While he clearly admired the colorful lives of men like Leatherstocking, Cooper's novels also insisted that such radical independence would have to give way to social cooperation and the rule of law if America was to survive and prosper. Ultimately, the *Leatherstocking Tales* taught that hard-fought American liberty could only be sustained if the best qualities of the frontiersman were brought into the mainstream of society.

BIBLIOGRAPHY

Klein, Kerwin Lee. *Frontiers of Historical Imagination: Narrating the European Conquest of Native America, 1890–1990.* Berkeley: University of California Press, 1997.

Smith, Henry Nash. *Virgin Land: The American West as Symbol and Myth.* New York: Vintage Books, 1950.

Taylor, Alan. *William Cooper's Town: Power and Persuasion on the Frontier of the Early American Republic.* New York: Knopf, 1995.

Jennifer Burns

See also **Literature: Popular Literature.**

LEAVENWORTH EXPEDITION.

On 2 June 1823 a party led by General William Henry Ashley, sponsored by the Rocky Mountain Fur Company, was attacked at the Arikara villages on the upper Missouri. Thirteen men were killed. Colonel Henry Leavenworth promptly started up the Missouri from Fort Atkinson, at Council Bluffs, Nebraska, with six companies of the Sixth Infantry and some artillery. Joined on the way by Joshua Pilcher's party of the Missouri Fur Company, by Ashley's survivors, and by 750 Sioux, Leavenworth reached Grand River on 9 August. The next day, he attacked the Arikara villages, forcing their submission.

BIBLIOGRAPHY

Clokey, Richard M. *William H. Ashley: Enterprise and Politics in the Trans-Mississippi West.* Norman: University of Oklahoma Press, 1980.

Dale, Harrison Clifford. *Explorations of William H. Ashley and Jedediah Smith, 1822–1829.* Lincoln: University of Nebraska Press, 1991.

Krause, Richard. *The Leavenworth Site: Archaeology of an Historic Arikara Community.* Lawrence: University of Kansas, 1972.

Joseph Mills Hanson / T. D.

See also **Fur Trade and Trapping; Indian Trade and Traders; Missouri River Fur Trade.**

LEAVES OF GRASS is a major work by the poet Walt Whitman, and is known as a strikingly original masterpiece that introduced Whitman's own poetic form, the lyric epic. First published in 1855, the text was expanded, revised, and reissued in six subsequent editions, the last in 1892. Because Whitman's poem was so original and different, it at first met with a mixed critical reception, although Ralph Waldo Emerson immediately recognized Whitman's genius. Contemporaries were unsure of how to react to *Leaves of Grass* because both its form and content departed markedly from poetic conventions of the day. Whitman wrote entirely in free verse, and combined the traditional historical subject matter of epic poetry with the personal, subjective focus of lyric poetry. His themes were especially notable: Whitman celebrated the creation and restless spirit of America, particularly its westward expansion, and embraced the different experiences of the country's diverse population, including slaves and recent immigrants in his vision. *Leaves of Grass* was also remarkable for its frank depiction of sexuality and its overtly sensual imagery, which troubled and embarrassed critics in Whitman's day. However, over time Whitman attracted a growing number of readers who appreciated both his artistic achievement and his depiction of a multicultural and truly democratic America.

BIBLIOGRAPHY

Allen, Gay Wilson. *The Solitary Singer: A Critical Biography of Walt Whitman.* Chicago: University of Chicago Press, 1985.

Klammer, Martin. *Whitman, Slavery, and the Emergence of Leaves of Grass.* University Park: Pennsylvania State University Press. 1995.

Jennifer Burns

LEBANESE AMERICANS.

Almost 3.2 million people of Arab descent make their home in the United States. Of that number, approximately 56 percent are of Lebanese descent, making them the largest single group of Arab immigrants in the United States. Although relative latecomers to this country, Lebanese Americans have become fully integrated into American society and have made numerous contributions in many fields.

Lebanese Americans can be found throughout the United States, but the largest concentrations are in the Midwest, especially in Chicago, Cleveland, Detroit, and Toledo. Detroit is home to more Lebanese Americans—125,000—than any other city in the country. Lebanese American communities are also growing in the South and the West, particularly in Southern California, and a number of communities have emerged in smaller American cities.

Early Immigration

Between 1881 and 1925, approximately 100,000 Lebanese immigrants came to the United States. A small minority compared to other immigrant groups, their departure from Lebanon was significant because their number represented a quarter of the country's population. The majority of the immigrants were Christian Lebanese from the area known as Mount Lebanon.

By 1914, the first wave of Lebanese immigration had peaked. On the eve of World War I (1914–1918), about 9,000 Lebanese made their way to the United States. Difficulties in travel during wartime reduced the number of Lebanese immigrants. By 1921, however, the numbers again rose, with approximately 5,000 Lebanese immigrants coming to the United States. But the new immigration quotas put into place during the 1920s virtually eliminated Lebanese immigration.

Because many of the first Lebanese immigrants hoped to return to their homeland, they turned to a profession that with hard work could yield great profits—peddling. Historians estimate that as many as 90 percent of Lebanese immigrants became peddlers. These peddlers traveled across the country offering a wide variety of wares to people, particularly those who lived in rural communities. The more enterprising earned upwards of $1,000 a year, almost three times the average national income.

One result of the Lebanese peddlers' efforts was the creation of an extensive network that also was beneficial to American export trade. Through their contacts with the many merchants in the Middle East, a variety of goods were sent to the United States. Lebanese peddlers also helped American small businesses by introducing their products to people who otherwise might not know of them. Another effect of the Lebanese peddling was the creation of Lebanese-owned banking and financial institutions, such as the one established by the Faour brothers in Manhattan in 1891.

Other immigrants went to work in the automobile and steel factories of Detroit and other midwestern cities or in the textile and garment industries of New York and New Jersey. Lebanese Americans at work in the garment trade revived the silk industry during the 1920s; by 1924, fifteen Lebanese American silk factories were in operation.

The Second Wave of Immigration

The end of the Arab-Israeli War in 1967 sparked the second wave of Lebanese immigration, when approximately 13,000 Lebanese came to the United States. The number of Lebanese immigrants increased when civil war between Muslims and Christians broke out in 1975. Between 1975 and 2002, some 46,000 Lebanese arrived in the United States.

The second wave of Lebanese immigrants had a greater political awareness than their predecessors, and were especially active in shaping U.S. policy toward Lebanon. The new immigrants also exerted a new interest in, and a revival of, Lebanese customs and culture in the United States.

Lebanese American Culture

One of the most enduring Lebanese contributions to American culture is cuisine. In many large cities there are a number of Lebanese restaurants and bakeries that count many Americans who are not of Lebanese descent among their regular customers.

While many of the first Lebanese to arrive in the United States were Christians, by the late twentieth century a growing number of immigrants were Muslims. Lebanese American Muslims established a number of mosques throughout the country. Two of the more elaborate mosques were located on the Upper East Side of Manhattan, and another was near the University of Southern California in Los Angeles.

Lebanese Americans also worked hard to combat negative images of and discrimination against all Arab peoples. In 1980, two Lebanese Americans, former U.S. Senator James Abourezk and professor of political science James Zogby, established the American Arab Anti-Discrimination Committee (ADC). By the 2000's the ADC was the largest Arab American organization in the United States.

Prominent Lebanese Americans

Perhaps the most famous Lebanese American is the poet and writer Kahlil Gibran, whose book *The Prophet*, published in 1923, has provided inspiration for thousands around the world. Although Gibran died in 1931, his fame endures and his writings continue to find an audience.

A number of other Lebanese Americans have made important contributions to American culture, business, and life. They include singer and songwriter Paul Anka, screenwriter Callie Khoury, who won an Oscar for the hit movie *Thelma and Louise*, actresses Kathy Najimy and Marlo Thomas, and actor, director, and screenwriter Harold Ramis. In politics, Lebanese Americans have occupied offices from the mayor of Waterville, Maine (Ruth Joseph) to the governor of Oregon (Victor Aityes) to the Secretary of Energy (former U.S. Senator Spencer Abraham).

John Elway, the former quarterback of the Denver Broncos, the Maloof Brothers, who owned the Sacramento Kings of the National Basketball Association, Bobby Rahal, who won the Indianapolis 500 in 1986, and Faud Ruebiz, the former kicker for the Minnesota Vikings, are Lebanese Americans. In business, the Lebanese American community has been well represented. Camille Chebeir was president of SEDCO Services, an investment firm owned by the Bin Mahfouz family of Saudi Arabia. Chebeir also served as president of the Arab Bankers Association of North America. Raymond Debbane was president of the Invus Group, a multimillion dollar private equity firm specializing in buyouts and venture capital. Richard Debs is former president of Morgan Stanley International. Ned Mansour was president of Mattel, and Jack Nasser is the former president of the Ford Motor Company.

BIBLIOGRAPHY

Abinader, Elmaz. *Children of the Roojme: A Family's Journey from Lebanon.* Madison: University of Wisconsin Press, 1997.

Abraham, Sameer Y., and Nabeel Abraham, eds. *Arabs in the New World: Studies on Arab-American Communities.* Detroit, Mich.: Center for Urban Studies, Wayne State University, 1983.

Kayal, Philip M. *The Syrian-Lebanese in America: A Study in Religion and Assimilation.* New York: Twayne, 1975.

Meg Greene Malvasi

See also **Arab Americans.**

LEBANON, U.S. LANDING IN. In May 1958 President Camille Chamoun of Lebanon appealed to the United States for military forces to prevent a civil war. By directive of President Dwight D. Eisenhower, U.S. forces landed on Lebanese beaches and secured port facilities and the international airport at Beirut. Only an occasional minor encounter occurred between dissidents and American troops. On 31 July the Lebanese Chamber of Deputies elected General Fuad Shehab as president, but Chamoun refused to resign for several weeks, and Shehab was not inaugurated until 23 September. At that point, the Lebanese army acted firmly to restore and maintain order, and the last U.S. forces departed on 25 October.

BIBLIOGRAPHY

Alin, Erika G. *The United States and the 1958 Lebanon Crisis: American Intervention in the Middle East.* Lanham, Md.: University Press of America, 1994.

Korbani, Agnes G. *U.S. Intervention in Lebanon, 1958 and 1982: Presidential Decision Making.* New York: Praeger, 1991.

Charles B. MacDonald/E. M.

See also **Arab Nations, Relations with; Intervention.**

LECOMPTON CONSTITUTION. When the Kansas territory was ready to seek admission to the Union in 1857, the key issue was whether it would be a free state or a slave state. The pro-slavery forces won control of the constitutional convention, which met in the town of Lecompton in September of that year. The complicated fight over the pro-slavery Lecompton Constitution manifested the sectional tension that would erupt in the CIVIL WAR three years later.

The pro-slavery majority at Lecompton knew that most Kansans preferred to enter the Union as a free state, so the delegates resolved to send a pro-slavery document to Washington without putting it to a fair vote. The referendum on the Lecompton Constitution claimed to let voters decide between a "constitution with slavery" and a "constitution with no slavery," but they were given no real choice: the "constitution with no slavery" prohibited only the importation of new slaves, not the maintenance of slaves already established in the territory.

In December the "constitution with slavery" and the "constitution with no slavery" went to a vote, but anti-slavery forces boycotted the election. The "constitution with slavery" passed (6,226 to 569). Two weeks later, however, the territorial legislature, which unlike the constitutional convention was controlled by the antislavery forces, organized an "up or down" vote on the Lecompton Constitution. This time the pro-slavery forces refused to participate, and the constitution was voted down (10,226 to 162).

In February the drama moved to Washington, where Congress could either grant statehood under the Lecompton Constitution or deny it altogether. President James Buchanan pledged his support to the pro-slavery constitution. The Republican minority in Congress opposed it. The decisive figure was Stephen Douglas, the powerful Democratic senator from Illinois. He had long served as the bridge between the northern and southern wings of his party (he engineered the Kansas-Nebraska Act of 1854), but he believed strongly in the tenets of popular sovereignty and was convinced that Kansans had not been allowed to vote. Douglas broke with southerners and organized the congressional opposition to the Lecompton Constitution. After bitter debate, it passed the Senate but was rejected in the House.

In the end the two houses struck a compromise to make what had become a crisis go away. In an election ostensibly having nothing to do with slavery, Kansans went to the polls to vote on whether to accept a smaller land grant. If they accepted the revised grant, Kansas would become a state under the Lecompton Constitution. If they refused it, Kansas would remain a territory. The issue of the land grant became a safe proxy for the dangerous issue of slavery. In August, Kansans voted no on the land grant (11,300 to 1,788), implicitly rejecting the Lecompton Constitution.

Though disaster was averted, the split between Douglas and the southerners made it clear that as long as slavery remained the dominant political issue, the Democratic Party could no longer be a national organization. The party convention actually broke in two in 1860, and disunion and war followed the next winter.

BIBLIOGRAPHY

Johannsen, Robert W. *Stephen A. Douglas.* New York: Oxford University Press, 1973.

Nevins, Allan. *The Emergence of Lincoln.* New York: Scribners, 1950.

Jeremy Derfner

See also **Kansas; Kansas-Nebraska Act.**

LEGAL PROFESSION. Known as "the bar," after the railing in courtrooms, the legal profession is the vocation of the law, and its practitioners include essentially those who hold licenses to practice law granted by states or particular courts, but also those who through legal education or vocation participate in the culture or institutions of the law. Law is a profession, and, as such, it requires special knowledge and skill acquired under the supervision of a practitioner and is subject to standards of admission and regulation by an elite within the profession.

There were lawyers of various sorts in ancient Greece and Rome, but the legal profession in its current sense was a medieval invention. The development of a professional bench and bar in England began in the twelfth and thirteenth centuries, shortly after the rediscovery of the texts of classic Roman law led both to more sophisticated forms of legal education and to a more complex system of national and Church laws. In early medieval England, university instruction prepared young men to practice canon and admiralty law, while a loose band of full-time lawyers consolidated into various London houses or "inns" in which the older lawyers who pled before the Courts taught younger lawyers. These inns became the basis for both the schooling and the management of the bar. By the dawn of the American colonial era, English lawyers usually studied the liberal arts at a college or university and then studied law in one of the London Inns of Court. Scotland maintained a similar institution in the College of the Faculty of Advocates.

Early America

American colonists who acted as judges or lawyers initially had no legal education but acted from their consciences and such law books as they had, to the degree they understood them. By the late 1600s, a few attorneys traveled to England to study in the Inns of Court, being called to the bar in London and returning to the United States. Although this practice began in Massachusetts, by 1770 most colonial lawyers trained in England were in the southern colonies. Throughout the eighteenth century, a few quite influential lawyers emigrated to the colonies from England, Ireland, and Scotland. Moreover, the number of lawyers with legal training had grown large enough for successive generations to be taught through apprenticeships. On the eve of the Revolution, several colleges occasionally taught law as an academic pursuit, although only the College of William and Mary had a law professor.

Lawyers were active during the Revolution and in the early Republic. Twenty-four of the forty-six signers of the Declaration of Independence were lawyers, and its drafter, lawyer Thomas Jefferson, wrote it in the form of a legal petition. Indeed, many leaders of the early states were lawyers, as were Jefferson, John Adams, Alexander Hamilton, and other leaders of the young national government.

With independence, different states and the federal courts had varied approaches to the bar. Until 1801 the U.S. Supreme Court required a distinction between attorneys, who appeared in court, and counselors at law, who provided legal advice, a division similar to the English distinction between barristers and solicitors, and one followed in various ways by some states. This practice died early in the 1800s, since which time all U.S. lawyers have been considered eligible to perform either role.

On the other hand, in 1790 Massachusetts passed a law attempting to end the legal profession, by allowing any person to represent another in court. Many states embraced this legal deprofessionalization. In 1842 New Hampshire declared that any adult could act as an attorney, a law copied by Maine, Wisconsin, and Indiana. A similar mood had already led to popular elections of judges in which candidates were not required to be lawyers; this practice began in 1832 and eventually spread to thirty-eight states, in many of which it still continues.

Even so, the growing complexity of the law and the legalistic nature of the national culture spurred both evolution and enlargement in the bar. The expansion of commercial, industrial, canal, road, and railroad concerns, growing personal wealth, and increased state and federal regulation all led to a swelling demand for lawyers. Moreover, law came to be seen as the tool to balance power between the state and the citizen. As Alexis de Tocqueville noted, Americans "prize freedom much, they generally value legality still more: they are less afraid of tyranny than of arbitrary power."

Throughout the nineteenth century, most attorneys read law in the office of an experienced lawyer, who would appear before a judge to move the student be sworn into the practice of law. Occasionally, judges would interrogate the applicant, but usually the word of the older lawyer alone was sufficient, and the attorney was launched on a career. The result was a loose-knit fraternity of lawyers with greatly varying levels of skill and professionalism.

The Enhancement of Professional Standards

After the Civil War, lawyers concerned with the bar's poor reputation formed institutions to improve the standards of both the profession and the existing body of law. Bar associations were created to establish standards for lawyer admission and conduct, as well as to promote law reform, commencing with the Association of the Bar of the City of New York in 1870, and the American Bar Association in 1878. These associations pressed state legislatures and courts to hold law schools to standards of accreditation and to promote law reform projects, such as the American Law Institute, formed in 1923 to encourage modernization and uniformity among state laws.

Two nineteenth-century innovations led to greater restrictions on entry to the practice. The first was the growth of legal education, which became a requirement to practice in most states by the end of the century (see LAW SCHOOLS). The second was the advent of formal examinations as a condition of licensure. In the 1850s the Massachusetts Court of Common Pleas instituted written exams for all candidates, rather than oral exams administered by individual judges. This practice spread slowly, although it blossomed in the 1870s and 1880s. Although some states conferred licenses on graduates of their state

Belva Lockwood. The first female attorney admitted to practice before the U.S. Supreme Court, in 1879, as well as the first woman to run for president (with the Equal Rights Party, in 1884 and 1888) and later a delegate to peace congresses in Europe. ARCHIVE PHOTOS, INC.

law schools, every state employed some form of bar examination by the mid-twentieth century. At the start of the twenty-first century, both legal education and the bar exam remain significant steps toward entry of the profession. By 2000 almost every applicant for the bar had graduated from law school. Of 72,704 people examined that year to enter the bar in the fifty states, only 59 had read for the bar rather than taking law degrees. The bar examination remains a formidable barrier to entry of the profession; only 47,160 of those examined, or 65 percent, passed.

Two restrictions on entry into the profession, however, ended in the 1800s. Until 1844, the legal profession, like most professions in the United States, was open only to men descended from Europeans; women and members of other races were excluded. The first lawyer of African descent, a native of Indiana named Macon Bolling Allen, was admitted in 1844 to practice law in Maine. In 1847 he became a justice of the peace in Massachusetts. Myra Bradwell, arguably the first American woman lawyer, was a law publisher in Chicago who passed the Illinois bar examination in 1869 but was initially denied a license by that state and by the U.S. Supreme Court. She was admitted to practice in 1890, and her admission was back-dated by the state supreme court to 1868. Lemma Bar-kaloo appears to be the first female law student, admitted to St. Louis Law School in 1868. In 1872 Charlotte E. Ray became the first black woman lawyer in the United States and the first woman lawyer in the District of Columbia. Despite these initial inroads, the law remained a largely white, male domain, and large numbers of both women and minorities began to enter the profession only in the later twentieth century.

The Growing Size of Law Firms

The twentieth century saw a dramatic increase in the size of law firms and the degree of specialization of legal practice. In a trend that began with New York firms, such as Cravath, large numbers of young lawyers were hired to work as associates for a smaller number of partners, selected from among the associates who were not culled out over a seven-year period; this pyramidal structure had the effect of increasing the fees earned by partners. It also allowed a partnership to have hundreds of specialists and to provide a broader range of services to large multinational clients. By the close of the century, many firms had hundreds of lawyers, working from multiple cities. These firms expect their associates to work very long hours, though for very high pay. Despite this high pay for associates, in the year 2000 partnership shares reached as high as $3.2 million per partner and averaged just over $800,000 in the richest one hundred U.S. law firms.

As law firms grew, a gulf widened between lawyers representing plaintiffs and those representing defendants. Except for suits initiated by corporations, most large firms specialized in corporate defense and the support of commercial activities. Plaintiffs' work generally fell to lawyers in solo practice or to small firms without conflicts arising from work for clients like those they sued, with less overhead, and with less of the liability risk faced by large firms with work done by many partners. This division was heralded in 1946, with the formation of an association for lawyers representing claimants for workman's compensation, which later became the American Trial Lawyers Association.

Changes in information technology, especially the growth of electronic information archives and communications systems, growing competition from organizations besides law firms, increased reliance on non-legal treatments for criminal behavior, an increasingly global economy, and greater specialization and enlargement of the profession will all alter the legal profession in the twenty-first century. Still, lawyers will continue to perform a variety of unique tasks, particularly in managing the criminal justice system, assisting in government, managing complex commercial transactions, and resolving disputes.

The bar has grown faster than the population as a whole. In 1850 there were 23,900 lawyers; in 1900 there were 114,700. In the year 2000, the U.S. Census Bureau estimated that 955,300 lawyers and judges were primarily

employed in legal practice in the United States. An additional 15,000 were law teachers and another 80,000 lawyers were inactive, engaged in non-legal work, or retired. There are expected to be 1,355,000 U.S. lawyers by 2005. The legal profession has become an important part of the U.S. economy, not only by facilitating commercial transactions and dispute resolutions but also as an industry. In 1999 the U.S. Census Bureau estimated that legal services in the United States generated $157 billion in revenues.

BIBLIOGRAPHY

Abel, Richard. *American Lawyers.* New York: Oxford University Press, 1989.

Dos Passos, John. *The American Lawyer: As He Was—As He Is—As He Can Be.* Reprint. Littleton, Colo.: Rothman, 1986. The original edition was published in 1907.

Pound, Roscoe. *The Lawyer from Antiquity to Modern Times, with Particular Reference to the Development of Bar Associations in the United States.* St. Paul, Minn.: West, 1953.

Reed, Alfred Z. *Training for the Public Profession of the Law.* New York: Arno, 1976.

Steve Sheppard

See also **American Bar Association; National Lawyers Guild.**

LEGAL TENDER is anything that, by law, a debtor may require his creditor to receive in payment of a debt in the absence of the appearance in the contract itself of an agreement for payment in some other manner. The tender is an admission of the debt and, in some jurisdictions, if refused, discharges the debt.

There were two periods of American history when the question of legal tender was an important political issue. Between 1776 and 1789, during and after the turmoil of the Revolution, the question was whether the states should be permitted to print CURRENCY and require its acceptance by creditors regardless of its severe depreciation in value. Later, in the years following the Civil War, the question was whether Congress had power, under the Constitution, to cause the issuance of paper MONEY (greenbacks) that would be legal tender in payment of private debts.

The amount of circulating financial medium in the newborn states was insufficient to finance a costly war. Early on, nearly every state had recourse to printing presses to meet its own expenses and the quota levies made by the Continental Congress. At first, these monetary issues were small, and notes passed at their face value. Soon, however, they began to depreciate, and the state legislatures resorted to creating laws requiring acceptance of state bank notes at par. In Connecticut, for example, in 1776 the legislature made both Continental and state notes legal tender and ordered that anyone who tried to depreciate them should forfeit not only the full value of the money they received but also the property they offered for sale. Attempts were made also at price regulation. The South, in particular, went to excess in the abuse of public credit. Virginia, for example, practically repudiated its paper issues at the close of the Revolution.

Leaders in business and finance in the states hoped to avoid a repetition of this financial chaos. Therefore, when the Constitutional Convention met in 1787, there was general agreement on the need for a single national system of currency and for laws prohibiting note issues by the states. Accordingly, Article I, Section 10, of the Constitution contains the following prohibitions: "No state shall . . . coin Money; emit Bills of Credit; make any Thing but gold and silver Coin a Tender in Payment of Debts; pass any . . . ex post facto Law or Law impairing the obligation of Contracts."

The question raised after the Civil War related to the constitutionality of the Legal Tender Act passed by Congress in 1862. It was alleged that Congress, in requiring the acceptance of greenbacks at face value, was violating the Fifth Amendment, which forbade the deprivation of property without due process of law. However, the Supreme Court had the power to make paper money legal tender, since the Constitution clearly denied such powers to the states.

BIBLIOGRAPHY

Ferguson, E. James. *The Power of the Purse: A History of American Public Finance, 1776–1790.* Chapel Hill: University of North Carolina Press, 1961.

Harvey Walker / A. R.

See also **Greenbacks; Legal Tender Act; Revolution, American: Financial Aspects.**

LEGAL TENDER ACT (1862). To provide funds to carry on the Civil War, Congress found it necessary to issue fiat money. By the act of 25 February 1862, and by successive acts, the government put into circulation about $450 million of paper money dubbed "greenbacks." These acts did not set aside any specific gold reserve to back the paper issue, nor did they announce any date when greenbacks could be redeemed for hard currency. To insure the negotiability of the new paper currency, Congress declared these notes legal tender in "payment of all taxes, internal duties, excises, debts, and demands of every kind due to the United States, except duties on imports, and of all claims and demands against the United States . . . and shall also be lawful money and legal tender in payment of all debts, public and private, within the United States." Wall Street and the metropolitan press opposed this measure, fearing runaway inflation. On the Pacific coast people frequently evaded the law through the passage of acts allowing exceptions on the basis of specific contracts. By imposing a wide range of taxes, however, Congress generated a steady stream of revenue into the federal treasury, inspiring confidence in the Union's ability to pay its debts and offsetting some of the

inflationary characteristics of paper currency. In 1870 the Supreme Court declared the Legal Tender Act unconstitutional and void in respect to debts contracted prior to its passage, but after two vacancies were filled, the Court reversed its decision.

BIBLIOGRAPHY

Ellison, Joseph. "The Currency Question on the Pacific Coast During the Civil War." *Mississippi Valley Historical Review,* June 1929.

Unger, Irwin. *The Greenback Era.* Princeton, N.J.: Princeton University Press, 1964.

J. W. Ellison / C. W.

See also **Greenbacks; Hard Money; Legal Tender; Legal Tender Cases.**

LEGAL TENDER CASES involved the question of the constitutionality of the measures enacted by the U.S. Congress during the CIVIL WAR for the issue of treasury notes to circulate as money without provision for redemption. The constitutional question hinged not on the power of the government to issue the notes, but on its power to make them LEGAL TENDER for the payment of debts, particularly debts contracted before the legislation. The Supreme Court first ruled on the question on 7 February 1870 in the case of *Hepburn v. Griswold* (8 Wallace 603). The majority held that Congress had no power to enact the legal-tender provisions. The vote of the Court members was five to three, with the obvious senility of Justice Robert C. Grier, one of the majority, casting doubt on the weight of his opinion. He retired before the Court announced the decision, which left the alignment four to three. Chief Justice Salmon P. Chase, who, as the secretary of the Treasury had shared responsibility for the original enactments, wrote the opinion against the constitutionality of the legislation.

Nominations of two new members of the Supreme Court arrived in the Senate on the day on which the Court announced the decision. At the ensuing term, the Court heard the reargument of the constitutional question in another case. On 1 May 1871, the Court reversed the *Hepburn* decision in *Knox v. Lee* and *Parker v. Davis* (12 Wallace 457). The question of whether President Ulysses S. Grant deliberately packed the Court to bring about a reversal of the original decision is still a matter of debate.

The Treasury withdrew some of the notes but reissued others under a later statute enacted without reference to wartime conditions. The Supreme Court upheld this statute on 3 March 1884, in *Juilliard v. Greenman.*

BIBLIOGRAPHY

Dunne, Gerald T. *Monetary Decisions of the Supreme Court.* New Brunswick, N.J.: Rutgers University Press, 1960.

Kutler, Stanley I. *Judicial Power and Reconstruction Politics.* Chicago: University of Chicago Press, 1968.

Niven, John. *Salmon P. Chase: A Biography.* New York: Oxford University Press, 1995.

Schwartz, Bernard. *A History of the Supreme Court.* New York: Oxford University Press, 1993.

Carl Brent Swisher / A. E.

See also **Legal Tender Act; Repudiation of Public Debt.**

LEGIONNAIRES' DISEASE,

an acute infection manifested principally by pneumonia, takes its name from its first known victims—military veterans who attended the Pennsylvania state convention of the American Legion in Philadelphia, 21–24 July 1976. Within days after the convention, reports reached the legion's headquarters that a number of attendees who stayed at the Bellevue-Stratford Hotel had died of pneumonia. Before the epidemic subsided, 221 cases had been found—182 Legionnaires and 39 others who had been near the hotel—and 34 had died. The cause at first was unknown, although speculation centered on a chemical toxin or sabotage. In December 1976 Joseph McDade at the Centers for Disease Control in Atlanta, Georgia, demonstrated that a previously unknown bacterium, *Legionella pneumophila*, was the causative agent.

Although *Legionella* will not grow in the usual diagnostic media of the laboratory, it is hardy and common in nature. It grows in fresh water, preferring a temperature close to that of the human body and an atmosphere laden with carbon dioxide. It is found in potable water systems on the hot water side and in recirculating towers of heat-exchange systems. At the Bellevue-Stratford it was probably spread through the air-conditioning system. There are many strains of *Legionella*, which cause diseases of varying severity, including 1 to 2 percent of all pneumonia cases in the United States. At the other end of the *Legionella* spectrum is Pontiac fever, a nonfatal disease in which pneumonia does not occur.

BIBLIOGRAPHY
Fraser, David W. "Legionnaires' Disease." In *The Cambridge World History of Human Disease.* Edited by Kenneth F. Kiple. Cambridge; New York: Cambridge University Press, 1993.

Lattimer, Gary L., and Richard A. Ormsbee. *Legionnaires' Disease.* New York: Marcel Dekker, 1981.

Elizabeth W. Etheridge / C. W.

See also **Centers for Disease Control and Prevention; Epidemics and Public Health.**

LEGISLATIVE REORGANIZATION ACT
(1946). This Act, also known as the Congressional Reorganization Act, was the most comprehensive reorganization of Congress in history to that date. The need to modernize the national legislature became evident during the Great Depression of the 1930s and World War II. During those years of economic crisis and global war, the federal government took on vast new responsibilities—responsibilities that stretched to the breaking point the capacity of the national legislature, as it was then structured, to cope with a vastly increased workload. At the same time the power and prestige of Congress were rapidly eroding. During the depression and even more so during the war Congress delegated to the administration of Franklin D. Roosevelt sweeping authority to implement legislation as he and his agents in the executive branch saw fit. In addition the war caused Congress a severe loss of prestige. Suddenly it seemed legislators became the whipping boys for all the pent up frustrations and anxieties of war. Some influential commentators charged that Congress's antiquated traditions, cumbersome procedures, and long delays in considering legislation rendered it incapable of meeting the needs of the modern world. The future, they said, rests with the president.

By the end of the war many legislators had concluded that the only way to recapture their lost stature was to reform the Congress. A key leader of the reform movement was the veteran Wisconsin senator Robert M. La Follette Jr., scion of Wisconsin's famous political dynasty. In 1945 he and Oklahoma representative A. S. "Mike" Monroney cochaired a joint committee of Congress to consider what might be done to make the body more efficient and effective. The following year the committee recommended sweeping reforms, and the committee's cochairs incorporated many of those reforms into a reorganization measure.

The key provisions of the measure proposed streamlining Congress's cumbersome committee system by reducing the number of standing committees and carefully defining their jurisdictions; upgrading staff support for legislators; strengthening congressional oversight of executive agencies; and establishing an elaborate procedure to put congressional spending and taxation policies on a more rational basis. The bill also required lobbyists to register with Congress and to file periodic reports of their activities.

Final passage was something of a tour de force for La Follette. Although practically all legislators wanted reform of some sort, entrenched interests, especially among southern Democrats, resisted efforts to reform the existing committee system, which they dominated. Nevertheless, the measure passed by large margins in both houses with the key provisions more or less intact.

The Legislative Reorganization Act produced mixed results. Probably its greatest success was in equipping legislators and their committees with staffs of experts to help draft bills and analyze the complex issues that come before Congress. Legislative oversight of the executive branch also improved as a result of reorganization. In other areas reorganization fell short. The positive effects of reducing committee numbers was at least partly counterbalanced by the unexpected proliferation of subcommittees, which were not regulated in the act. Many lobbyists exploited loopholes in the act to avoid full compliance. The ambitious reform of the budget process failed to work and was abandoned after a couple of years. Above all the act failed to achieve its major objective. It slowed but did not reverse the flow of power and prestige from the legislative branch to the executive branch.

BIBLIOGRAPHY
Davidson, Roger. "The Legislative Reorganization Act of 1946." *Legislative Studies Quarterly* 15 (August 1990): 357–73.

Galloway, George B. *The Legislative Process in Congress.* New York: Crowell, 1953.

———. *Congressional Reorganization Revisited.* College Park: Bureau of Governmental Research, University of Maryland, 1956.

Maney, Patrick J. *Young Bob: A Biography of Robert M. La Follette, Jr.* Madison: Wisconsin Historical Society Press, 2002.

Patrick Maney

See also **Congress, United States.**

LEGISLATURES, BICAMERAL AND UNICAMERAL.

In the United States, legislatures at the federal, state, and local levels may be bicameral (consisting of two houses) or unicameral (one house). Even before adoption of the U.S. Constitution in 1789, the bicameral legislature—modeled on the example of the British Parliament and exemplified later by the U.S. Congress—was more common among colonial, and then state, governments. But unicameralism, which now is widely used only by local governments, has occasionally been employed by states and even at the national level: the first organizational law of the United States, the Articles of Confederation of 1781, prescribed a unicameral Congress.

This changed when delegates met at the Constitutional Convention in the summer of 1787. They adopted Edmund Randolph's plan for a three-branch government and a bicameral legislature based on population after a weeklong debate dismissing an alternative proposal by William Paterson of New Jersey for a unicameral legislature in which each state would have one vote. Paterson's plan had been supported by the smaller states, which feared that a legislature apportioned according to population would lead to dominance by the larger states. Distrusting democracy, many of the delegates were afraid that in a single house only the members' "virtue and good sense" would prevent legislative despotism. This seemed an inadequate check. The only possible restraint was to divide the legislative authority within itself. Ideas about an upper house, where men of property and great wisdom would take care of issues that were beyond the grasp of the masses, merged with the need to find a compromise that would provide the smaller states with a satisfactory input in the legislative process. Accordingly the convention compromised to propose a House of Representatives, in which members were apportioned among the states according to population, and a Senate, in which each state had an equal vote.

Before the Revolution, most individual colonies had followed the bicameral model in their governments, with an upper house, generally called the council, representing the interests of the proprietor or the Crown, and a lower house, generally called the assembly, representing the settlers. However, Pennsylvania and Delaware (which had been part of Pennsylvania until 1701) both had unicameral legislatures. Delaware adopted a bicameral legislature at the time of the Revolution, though Pennsylvania did not convert to bicameralism until 1790. Georgia went the other way, converting to unicameralism in 1777 and then back to bicameralism eleven years later. Vermont adopted a unicameral legislature in 1777 and retained this system when it entered the union in 1791. For forty-five years, Vermont remained the only state with a unicameral legislature within the United States, until a tie vote for governor that could not be resolved under this system led to the change to bicameralism in 1836.

On the local level, bicameral legislatures were most common until the reform movement at the turn of the twentieth century made unicameral city councils the norm by the 1930s. While distrust of the masses and the "need" for a propertied elite to guide them has clearly vanished as an argument for a bicameral system, this is not reflected in the set-up of the legislatures at the state or federal levels. Only Nebraska changed its system when, during the Great Depression and due to the energetic campaigning of the "New Deal Republican" George Norris, the state implemented a unicameral legislature in 1937, making it more efficient and less costly.

BIBLIOGRAPHY
Keefe, William J., and Morris S. Ogul. *The American Legislative Process: Congress and the States.* 10th ed. Upper Saddle River, N.J.: Prentice Hall, 2001.

Kurland, Philip B., and Ralph Lerner, eds. *The Founders' Constitution.* 5 vols. Indianapolis, Ind.: Liberty Fund, 2000.

Moschos, Demitrios, and David Katsky. "Unicameralism and Bicameralism: History and Tradition." *Boston University Law Review* 45 (1965): 250–270.

Wood, Gordon S. *The Creation of the American Republic, 1776–1787.* Chapel Hill: University of North Carolina Press, 1998.

Michael Wala

See also **Congress, United States; Separation of Powers.**

LEGISLATURES, STATE.

Citizens of the states have long struggled with the issue of how powerful their legislatures should be. Power in this context has two important dimensions: authority relative to governors, and the ability to enact laws and oversee their implementation.

The First States

The constitutions of the first states clearly designated the legislative bodies as the dominant institution of state government. To avoid the kind of rule previously imposed by colonial governors, legislatures were empowered to enact laws, to appoint key administrators of state agencies, to levy taxes, and to determine how public monies were to be spent. Over one-half of the initial state legislatures acted without fear of gubernatorial vetoes.

Similarly, the U.S. Constitution initially recognized state legislatures as the key unit of democracy and legitimacy. State legislators, not voters, elected individuals to the U.S. Senate, and electors designated by each state's legislative body chose the president. Ratification of the Seventeenth Amendment to the Constitution, providing for direct election to the Senate, did not occur until 1913, although a few progressive states adopted the change on their own a decade earlier. State legislatures still have the authority to determine who will be their representatives in the Electoral College, although all now let that be decided by the popular vote for president.

Despite the relative dominance of the legislatures in state governments, these bodies had limited capabilities. Members were, by design, amateurs. Those elected to state legislatures served part-time and met infrequently—typically once every two years for a period of two or three months. Legislators usually had no offices and no staff. There were virtually no resources available to aid in the analysis of proposed policy or to help evaluate the performance of state agencies. On the other hand, the scope of operations of state governments was very limited in the early days of the republic.

Regional Differences

Regional differences among the states began to emerge after the Civil War. Those states that had joined the Confederate States of America had to adopt new constitutions that banned slavery, disenfranchised those active in the Confederacy, and reconstituted their state governments. In the decade following the Civil War, eleven southern states adopted twenty-seven different constitutions as they struggled with the transition back to the Union. The end result was state governments that were generally weak. Governors were limited to two-year terms and could not succeed themselves. Legislatures were restricted to meeting for as little as two months once every two years.

Western states joined the Union during the height of the Progressive Era, during which time there was much concern about the power of the political machines. Their constitutions provided for relatively weak legislatures by allowing citizens to bypass the legislature through the Direct Initiative—which allows for the enactment of laws in statewide referenda. These states also adopted primaries to let voters, not bosses, nominate party candidates. Citizens could recall elected officials from office.

Representation

Throughout the first half of the twentieth century, state legislatures increasingly became marginal because urban areas were not fully represented. The boundaries of legislative districts remained constant throughout most of this period despite the rapid growth of cities and suburbs. Tennessee, for example, based its districts on a 1901 statute and by 1954 had one representative with nineteen times as many voters as another legislator coming from a more rural area. In 1962 the United States Supreme Court, in *Baker v. Carr* 369 U.S. 186 (1962), ruled that such discrepancies violated the Fourteenth Amendment. The Court mandated that state legislatures must adhere to the principle of one-person-one-vote and must draw boundaries in such a manner that each district has the same number of eligible voters.

In a 1977 ruling, the U.S. Supreme Court added another principle of representation. In *United Jewish Organization of Williamsburg, Inc. v. Hugh L. Carey* the Court prohibited gerrymandering intended to minimize the chances of electing a member of an ethnic minority group. This decision did, however, allow state legislatures to draw boundaries that made minority representation probable. The challenge of ensuring minority representation without relying solely on race when drawing legislative district boundaries has led to subsequent litigation.

The effect of making state legislatures more representative was profound. Prior to *Baker v. Carr*, state legislatures tended to be irrelevant to many of the major issues facing a state. Misrepresentation meant that the agendas of these bodies did not include the needs and concerns of growing urban areas. Decisions, similarly, did not reflect the values of the majority of the state's electorate. However, once the principles of equal representation were implemented, legislative agendas included urgent contemporary issues and attracted candidates for office who were serious, capable people.

Professionalization

In the aftermath of *Baker v. Carr*, state legislatures became more professionalized. In states such as New York, California, Michigan, and Ohio, the job of state legislator became full-time and was compensated accordingly. In all states, professionalization meant getting staff to help with the tasks critical to deliberative policymaking.

Only eight state legislatures met annually in 1960. By 1969 that number grew to eighteen and in 2002 only seven state legislatures did not meet annually. The average salary of state legislators in 1960 was only $3,738—a clear indication of the part-time, amateur status of this position. By 1970 the average rose to $7,248 and by 2000 it was $24,489. Salaries in 2000 varied from $100 in New Hampshire to $99,000 in California. In addition, legislators in every state received from $50 to $125 for each day that they were in session or in legislative hearings.

In some states, legislators have their own personal assistants, who aid in clerical and analytical work. Another pattern is the employment of staff agencies for legislative committees, partisan caucuses, and the legislature as a whole. Since the mid-1960s, thirty-one state legislatures have established audit bureaus, which help evaluate the work of administrative agencies, and reference bureaus, which do research much like that done by the Library of Congress. From 1968 to 1973, staff of state legislatures grew 134 percent, and expansion has continued at an annual rate of about 4 percent since then. Since the mid-1970s, state legislators have also been able to draw upon the staff resources of two major national organizations: the Council of State Governments and the National Conference of State Legislatures.

Term Limits

In part as a response to the professionalization of state legislatures and in part as a way of dislodging longtime incumbents from office, a movement began in the 1980s to limit the number of terms an individual could serve. Term limits applied to governors in twenty-four states in 1960 and in thirty-three in 2000, but this concept has traditionally not applied to legislators. Proponents argued that states are best served by citizen legislatures that are part-time and have regular turnover of people and ideas. Opponents cite the advantages of professionalism, especially in light of the workload of state legislatures and the need to match the strength of governors, bureaucracies, and interest groups. The concern is that a lack of continuity may lead to a loss of institutional memory and the advantages that come with experience.

Proponents have been most successful in getting the adoption of term limits in states that allow the Direct Initiative. Their efforts first succeeded when California and Colorado voters endorsed term limits for their state legislators in 1990. Eventually twenty states took similar action by 2000, although the state courts in Massachusetts, Washington, and Oregon voided the action as unconstitutional. In nine states, no one can serve in the state legislature for more than eight years. Five have a limit of twelve years and three allow six years for the lower chamber and eight years for the upper chamber.

Although term limits took effect in Maine in 1996, most other states set 2000 or later as implementation dates. In 2002 71 percent of the Senate seats in Michigan became vacant because of term limits. In Missouri, 46 percent of its House seats were opened and in six other states the turnover was 25 percent. These figures contrast with normal turnover rates of 20 to 35 percent in states without term limits. The requirement to leave office after a specified period of time guarantees a minimum turnover rate that is only slightly higher than the rate in states without term limits. The major effect of term limits has been to ensure that no single legislator stays in office for a long period of time.

Party Control

The partisan composition of a state's legislature has generally been consistent with how the electors in that state vote for president and members of Congress. The major exception to this principle is that when a state changes its party preference, the state legislature tends to lag behind. The major reason for this is that incumbents are usually successful in their bid for reelection, regardless of whether their party is in favor.

Democrats dominated southern state legislatures throughout the twentieth century. Since the 1950s, however, the Democratic Party in the South has not had the same policy preferences as the national Democratic Party. Increasingly, southern states began voting for Republican presidential candidates and sent Republicans to Congress. Republican gubernatorial candidates began winning. State legislatures were not affected until 1994, when Republicans won 37 percent of the state legislative races in the South and took control of three chambers. Republicans increased their representation in subsequent elections, and southern states, like most others, became very competitive for the two major parties.

Through increasing professionalization, state legislatures have generally become very competent policy makers, with access to expertise and analysis. They have become more representative and more reflective of the values of state voters. In relative terms, however, legislatures have lost the clear position of dominance they had in the first states. The office of Governor has acquired considerable authority, and, in some states, the electorate can circumvent the legislature and enact laws through the Direct Initiative.

BIBLIOGRAPHY

Benjamin, Gerald, and Michael J. Malbin, eds. *Limiting Legislative Terms.* Washington, D.C.: Congressional Quarterly Press, 1992.

Bowman, Ann O'M., and Richard C. Kearney. *The Resurgence of the States.* Englewood Cliffs, N.J.: Prentice-Hall, 1986.

Council of State Governments. Home page at www.csg.org.

Dresang, Dennis L., and James J. Gosling. *Politics and Policy in American States and Communities.* 3d edition. New York: Longman, 2002.

Hickok, Eugene W., Jr. *The Reform of State Legislatures and the Changing Character of Representation.* Lanham, Md.: University Press of America, 1992.

Jewell, Malcolm E. *Representation in State Legislatures.* Lexington: University Press of Kentucky, 1982.

Key, V. O., Jr. *American State Politics.* New York: Knopf, 1956.

Miewald, Robert D. *Nebraska Government and Politics.* Lincoln: University of Nebraska Press, 1984.

National Conference of State Legislatures. Home page at www.ncsl.org.

O'Rourke, Timothy. *The Impact of Reapportionment.* New Brunswick, N.J.: Transaction, 1980.

Rosenthal, Alan. *Legislative Life: People, Process, and Performance in the States.* Cambridge, Mass: Harper and Row, 1981.

Smith, T. V. *The Legislative Way of Life.* Chicago: University of Chicago Press, 1940.

Uslaner, Eric M., and Ronald E. Weber. *Patterns of Decision Making in State Legislatures.* New York: Praeger, 1977.

Dennis Dresang

See also **Legislatures, Bicameral and Unicameral; Proportional Representation;** *and vol. 9:* **Congress Debates the Fourteenth Amendment.**

LEISLER REBELLION. The revolution in England that forced King James II to abdicate was followed by uprisings in America. On 1 August 1689 a convention of civil and military officers met in Albany to set up an emergency government. Fearful of attack by the French, the Albany Convention sought a promise of aid from the revolutionary regime of Jacob Leisler. That May, Leisler, a merchant backed by Dutch laborers and artisans, had seized Fort James on Manhattan Island and usurped complete control of southern New York. In the spring of 1690, Leisler schemed with representatives from Albany, as well as Massachusetts and Connecticut, to invade Canada. The plan fell apart after Leisler insisted on being recognized as commander in chief. After King William appointed a royal governor to reassert British control over the colony, Leisler was tried for treason, and on 16 May 1691 he and his son-in-law were executed.

BIBLIOGRAPHY

Reich, Jerome R. *Leisler's Rebellion: A Study of Democracy in New York, 1664–1720.* Chicago: University of Chicago Press, 1953.

Voorhees, David W. "The 'Fervent Zeale' of Jacob Leisler." *William and Mary Quarterly* 51, no. 6 (July 1994): 447–472.

*A. C. Flick/*A. R.

See also **Colonial Society; New York City; New York Colony.**

LEND-LEASE, a program of providing U.S. military and economic assistance to nations fighting the Axis powers in World War II. After the fall of France in June 1940, President Franklin D. Roosevelt worried that if Great Britain were defeated by Nazi Germany, the United States would stand virtually alone against the fascist powers. Isolationist sentiment and unpreparedness for war discouraged American entry into the conflict directly, while U.S. law (the Johnson Debt-Default Act of 1934) required nations at war to pay cash for American military supplies. When Prime Minister Winston Churchill warned Roosevelt that Britain would not survive without further military assistance but was running out of funds, Roosevelt developed the idea of "lending" the British the necessary supplies. On 17 December 1940 he explained the

Leisler Rebellion. Jacob Leisler, captain of one of the colonial militia companies known as trainbands, is shown standing in the center of this woodcut as others support his declaration that he is acting lieutenant governor of New York. © CORBIS

principle to newsmen using the famous analogy of lending one's garden hose to a neighbor whose house is on fire, before the fire should spread. On 29 December he sought to build public support by arguing in a national radio address that America should become "the great arsenal of democracy." Congress debated the Lend-Lease Act, named House Resolution 1776 to lend it a patriotic aura, and passed the measure on 11 March 1941.

The Lend-Lease Act greatly increased executive power by authorizing the president to "sell, transfer title to, or otherwise dispose of" military supplies to countries selected by the president. Roosevelt had sought such broad language in order to be able to extend the program to the Soviet Union, which his cabinet expected would soon be attacked by Germany. Repayment was to be in kind or in the form of any "indirect benefit" to the United States. By eliminating the need for cash payments, Lend-Lease made it possible to deliver large quantities of vital matériel for the fight against the Axis powers while avoiding the kind of recriminations over unpaid war debts that lingered after World War I.

Under the Lend-Lease program, from 1941 to 1945 the United States provided approximately $50 billion in military equipment, raw materials, and other goods to thirty-eight countries. About $30 billion of the total went to Britain, with most of the remainder delivered to the Soviet Union, China, and France. The program was administered by top Roosevelt aide Harry L. Hopkins until October 1941, then formalized under the Office of Lend-Lease Administration under Edward R. Stettinius. In September 1943, Lend-Lease was placed under the Foreign Economic Administration, headed by Leo T. Crowley. The program was terminated by President Harry S. Truman in August 1945 at the end of the war, an action resented by Soviet leaders, who believed the cutoff in aid was intended to gain diplomatic concessions.

The provision of large quantities of aid to Great Britain accelerated American involvement in the conflict with Germany because it constituted a declaration of economic warfare against Germany, and it led to the organization of naval convoys to deliver the aid, convoys that came into direct confrontation with German submarines. Whether this was Roosevelt's secret intention is a subject of debate. While Churchill gratefully described Lend-Lease as "the most unsordid act in the history of any nation," the program clearly served American interests by allowing other countries to do the actual fighting against the Axis while the United States improved its own military readiness.

The Lend-Lease program substantially bolstered the military efforts of both Britain and the Soviet Union, although in the Soviet case, the overall importance of Lend-Lease has been disputed. Soviet histories tend to play down the value of the American contribution, while some American histories have argued that the Soviet Union would have been defeated without Lend-Lease aid (even though the threat of collapse was greatest in 1941–1942, before the bulk of Lend-Lease aid arrived). Whether or not American assistance was indispensable to Soviet survival and success on the battlefield, it does seem to have improved Soviet offensive capabilities against the German military after 1942.

The United States negotiated on a bilateral basis with individual countries to determine the form of repayment, if any, for Lend-Lease aid. Approximately $10 billion in goods, in kind and in cash, was repaid to the United States, chiefly by Great Britain. The Roosevelt and Truman administrations considered the fighting carried out by their allies to have been sufficient "indirect" repayment for the bulk of the assistance, and the cost of other aid was simply written off. Lend-Lease assistance was provided to some countries for political ends, as in the case of those Latin American nations that were not directly involved in the war effort but received limited quantities of military equipment as an inducement to side with the Allies. With its conversion of loans to grants and the use of aid for diplomatic or political purposes, Lend-Lease helped create a precedent for U.S. foreign aid programs in the postwar era.

BIBLIOGRAPHY

Dobson, Alan P. *U.S. Wartime Aid to Britain, 1940–1946.* New York: St. Martin's Press, 1986.

Kimball, Warren F. *The Most Unsordid Act: Lend-Lease, 1939–1941.* Baltimore: Johns Hopkins University Press, 1969.

Van Tuyll, Hubert P. *Feeding the Bear: American Aid to the Soviet Union, 1941–1945.* New York: Greenwood Press, 1989.

Max Paul Friedman

See also **Foreign Aid; World War II.**

LEOPOLD-LOEB CASE. Few murders in American history were as notorious or sensational as the "thrill" slaying of fourteen-year-old Bobby Franks in the summer of 1924. Two of his Chicago neighbors, eighteen-year-old Richard Loeb and nineteen-year-old Nathan Leopold, pleaded guilty.

What made the crime puzzling was its motive. Both of the killers were born to wealth and were intellectually gifted. Loeb apparently wanted to prove that he was capable of committing the perfect crime (which included kidnapping), and needed an accomplice. Leopold wore eyeglasses that were extremely rare, and had mistakenly left them near the culvert where police discovered the corpse. Trapped by such evidence, the pair confessed. Their families hired Clarence Darrow, a canny criminal defense attorney who never lost a client to the gallows. Arguing that the minds of his clients were not normal, though not insane, Darrow secured for them a judicial sentence of life imprisonment, plus an additional ninety-nine years. So remarkable an evasion of capital punishment attracted as much international attention as the trial itself. Loeb was murdered in prison in 1936; Leopold was eventually released, after submitting to dangerous medi-

Nathan Leopold (*right*) and Richard Loeb. The murder they committed in 1924 was one of the most notorious of the twentieth century. AP/WIDE WORLD PHOTOS

cal experiments and demonstrating contrition. He died in 1971. The case inspired Meyer Levin's best-selling novel *Compulsion* (1959).

BIBLIOGRAPHY

Higdon, Hal. *The Crime of the Century: The Leopold and Loeb Case.* Urbana: University of Illinois Press, 1999.

Stephen J. Whitfield

See also **Capital Punishment; Crime.**

LEPROSY, or Hansen's disease, is a chronic infectious disease caused by the microorganism *Mycobacterium leprae*, which mainly affects the skin, the peripheral nerves, and the upper respiratory tract. A complex affliction, Hansen's disease manifests itself through skin discoloration and loss of sensation in minor cases to disfigurement and physical debilitation in the most severe and advanced cases. Equally devastating have been the social stigma, rejection, and exclusion that sufferers of Hansen's disease have endured throughout history. Although popularly regarded as incurable, contagious, and mutilating, the disease is curable, it is not highly contagious, and mutilation occurs only in the most severe cases and is not an inevi-

table feature of the disease's course. Because of the stigma associated with the terms "leprosy" and "leper," the disease has since the 1950s been alternatively called Hansen's disease, named after Gerhard Armauer Hansen, the Norwegian physician who identified *Mycobacterium leprae* in 1873.

The fear of leprosy's importation by immigrants played an important role in anti-immigrant policies and racist rhetoric directed against Chinese immigrants in the 1870s and 1880s. Notable American efforts to combat leprosy abroad were led by Victor Heiser, director of health in the American colonial administration in the Philippines, and by Joseph de Veuster (Father Damien), a Belgian priest on the Hawaiian island of Molokai. Also leprosy was endemic in regional pockets of Louisiana and the upper Midwest among French Acadian and Norwegian immigrants, respectively.

Immigrants diagnosed with leprosy were often deported to their native countries. Those who could not be deported and native-born patients with leprosy were forcibly isolated in the few leprosy hospitals that existed. The Louisiana Leper Home in Carville, Louisiana, opened in 1893 and in 1921 the federal government assumed control and designated it the national leprosarium, to which all states subsequently sent patients. It became the leading American center for medical research on leprosy, culminating in the discovery in 1941 that sulfones (sulfa-based drugs) could effectively treat the disease. The leprosarium operated continuously until June 1999, when it was closed and the care of patients with leprosy moved to outpatient centers throughout the United States. Therapeutic regimens that relied exclusively on sulfones have been supplanted by multidrug therapy programs, which the World Health Organization expected will lead to the total eradication of leprosy by 2005.

BIBLIOGRAPHY

Gussow, Zachary. *Leprosy, Racism, and Public Health: Social Policy in Chronic Disease Control.* Boulder, Colo.: Westview Press, 1989.

Joseph, D. George. "Americans Confront the 'Loathsome' Disease: Leprosy and Tropical Medicine in Progressive Era Massachusetts." Ph.D. diss., Yale University, 2002.

Kalisch, Philip A. "Lepers, Anachronisms, and the Progressives: A Study of Stigma, 1889–1920." *Louisiana Studies: An Interdisciplinary Journal of the South* 12 (1973): 489–531.

Moran, Michelle T. "Leprosy and American Imperialism: Patient Communities and the Politics of Public Health in Hawai'i and Louisiana." Ph.D. diss., University of Illinois, Urbana-Champaign, 2002.

D. George Joseph

See also **Health Care.**

LET US NOW PRAISE FAMOUS MEN: *Three Tenant Families*, text by James Agee, photographs by

George Gudger is a human being, a man, not like any other human being so much as he is like himself. I could invent incidents, appearances, additions to his character, background, surroundings, future, which might well point up and indicate and clinch things relevant to him which in fact I am sure are true, and important, and which George Gudger unchanged and undecorated would not indicate and perhaps could not even suggest. The result, if I was lucky, could be a work of art. But somehow a much more important, and dignified, and true fact about him than I could conceivably invent, though I were an illimitably better artist than I am, is that fact that he is exactly, down to the last inch and instant, who, what, where, and when and why he is. He is in those terms living, right now, in flesh and blood and breathing, in an actual part of a world in which also, quite as irrelevant to imagination, you and I are living. Granted that beside that fact it is a small thing, and granted also that it is essentially and finally a hopeless one, to try merely to reproduce and communicate his living as nearly as exactly as possible, nevertheless I can think of no worthier and many worse subjects of attempt.

SOURCE: From *Let Us Now Praise Famous Men,* pp. 232–233.

Walker Evans, is the culminating achievement of the Great Depression's documentary art and media and one of the few classics of world journalism. Overlong, self-conscious, and often infuriating, it is also brave, poetic, morally challenging, and for many readers a secular holy book. In August 1936, Agee, twenty-seven years old, and Evans, thirty-two years old, stayed with a white Alabama sharecropper family to prepare an article for *Fortune* magazine. When *Fortune* turned the article down, Agee expanded it into a book for Harper and Brothers. In 1939, Harper refused to publish it. The book finally appeared in September 1941, by which time the sharecropper problem was old news, and the nation was transfixed by the war in Europe. The first edition sold six hundred copies and disappeared. When Agee's posthumous *A Death in the Family* won the 1957 Pulitzer Prize, Houghton Mifflin, the original publisher of *Let Us Now Praise Famous Men*, brought out a second edition with an expanded selection of Evans's photographs. The book's anguished inquiry into how those privileged with money and education relate to society's unfortunates made it must reading in the socially conscious 1960s, and it entered the twenty-first century second only to John Steinbeck's novel *The Grapes of Wrath* (1939) as the most popular literary introduction to the hardships and complexities of the 1930s.

BIBLIOGRAPHY
Stott, William. *Documentary Expression and Thirties America.* 2d ed. Chicago: University of Chicago Press, 1986.

William Stott

See also **Great Depression.**

LEVER ACT. Congress passed the Lever Food and Fuel Control Act on 10 August 1917 to mobilize food and fuel resources for World War I. Among other things, the Lever Act prohibited "unfair" trade practices and authorized price fixing of commodities and the licensing of producers and distributors. Subsequently, the president, by executive orders, created the Price-Fixing Committee, the Food and Fuel Administrations, and the Grain Corporation to administer the law. The Lever Act reflected Progressive Era faith in bureaucracy and expanded federal lawmaking authority.

BIBLIOGRAPHY
Harries, Meirion, and Susie Harries. *The Last Days of Innocence: America At War, 1917–1918.* New York: Random House, 1997.
Painter, Nell Irvin. *Standing at Armageddon: The United States, 1877–1919.* New York: Norton, 1987.

Martin P. Claussen / c. p.

See also **Fuel Administration; Progressive Movement; World War I, Economic Mobilization for.**

LEVERAGED BUYOUTS. A leveraged buyout (LBO) is one method for a company to acquire another. In an LBO, the acquiring firm typically borrows a large percentage of the purchase price by pledging the assets of the acquired firm as collateral for the loan. Because the assets of the target company are used as collateral, LBOs have been most successfully used to acquire companies with stable cash flows and hard assets such as real estate or inventory that can be used to secure loans. LBOs can also be financed by borrowing in the public markets through the issuance of high-yield, high-risk debt instruments, sometimes called "junk bonds."

An LBO begins with the borrower establishing a separate corporation for the express purpose of acquiring the target. The borrower then causes the acquisition corporation to borrow the funds necessary for the transaction, pledging as collateral the assets it is about to acquire. The target company is then acquired using any number of techniques, most commonly through a public tender offer followed by a cash-out merger. This last step transforms the shares of any remaining shareholder of the target corporation into a right to receive a cash payment, and merges the target corporation into the acquisition corporation. The surviving corporation ends up with the obligation to pay off the loan used to acquire its assets.

Levittown. The Long Island original in 1947. AP/Wide World Photos

This will leave the company with a high amount of debt obligations on its books, making it highly "leveraged," meaning that the ratio of debt to equity will be high. Indeed, in the average LBO during the 1980s, when they were most popular, the debt-to-assets ratio increased from about 20 percent to 90 percent.

Following an LBO, the surviving company may find that it needs to raise money to satisfy the debt payments. Companies thus frequently sell off divisions or portions of their business. Companies also have been known to "go public" again, in order to raise capital.

Many LBOs are "management buyouts," in which the acquisition is pursued by a group of investors that includes incumbent management of the target company. Typically, in management buyouts the intent is to "go private," meaning that the management group intends to continue the company as a privately held corporation, the shares of which are no longer traded publicly.

Management buyouts were particularly popular during the 1980s, when they were used in connection with the purchase of many large, prominent firms. Public tender offers by a corporation seeking to acquire a target company were frequently met with a counterproposal of a leveraged buyout by the target company management. One of the most famous takeover battles was the 1988 battle for RJR Nabisco between a management team led by F. Ross Johnson and an outside group led by the takeover firm Kohlberg Kravis Roberts & Company (KKR). Both groups proposed to take the company private using LBOs. This contest, eventually won by KKR when it purchased RJR Nabisco for $31 billion, is the subject of the book and movie *Barbarians at the Gate*. At the time, it was the most expensive corporate acquisition in history.

In the later years of the 1980s, LBOs became so popular that they were used in situations in which they were poorly suited, and the deals were poorly structured. Beginning in 1989, the number of defaults and bankruptcies of companies that had gone through LBOs increased sharply. As a result, the number of LBOs declined significantly.

BIBLIOGRAPHY

Burrough, Bryan, and John Helyar. *Barbarians at the Gate: The Fall of RJR Nabisco.* New York: Harper and Row, 1990.

Carney, William J. *Mergers and Acquisitions: Cases and Materials.* New York: Foundation Press, 2000.

Hamilton, Robert W., and Richard A. Booth. *Business Basics for Law Students: Essential Terms and Concepts.* 2d ed. New York: Aspen Law and Business, 1998.

Kent Greenfield

See also **Mergers and Acquisitions.**

LEVITTOWN. A mass-produced suburban housing development on Long Island, New York, the first Levittown came to symbolize post–World War II suburbanization. The product of the builders Levitt and Sons, Levittown was constructed between 1947 and 1951 on seven square miles of Nassau County, about thirty miles east of Manhattan. Responding to a postwar housing shortage, the Levitts built the four-room look-alike dwellings at the rate of 150 per week, eventually producing 17,447 houses. The first 6,000 units, all Cape Cod–style, were offered for rental. But exploiting the availability of low-cost, insured mortgages offered by the Federal Housing Administration and the Veterans Administration, the Levitts soon abandoned their role as landlords and chose instead to sell the houses. Veterans could purchase a two-bedroom, one-bath house on a six-thousand-foot lot with no money down and payments of only $60 a month. In 1949, Levitt and Sons discontinued the Cape Cod model and introduced ranch-style houses, all of which were for sale. The Levitts also built seven small shopping centers, known as village greens, and nine public swimming pools to serve the subdivision's residents.

Although most of the new home owners praised Levittown, outside critics claimed the community's cheap structures were destined to become the slums of the future. Moreover, the rows of virtually identical houses became a target for those who feared the suffocating homogeneity that supposedly characterized suburban culture. Levittown became synonymous with working-class and lower-middle-class suburbanization and an object of contempt for all those who deplored that phenomenon. In fact, the Levitt houses were well constructed and appreciated in value. Furthermore, through extensive remodeling, the once-identical units developed an individuality. By the beginning of the twenty-first century, houses that originally cost $7,500 were selling for $250,000. In 2000, 53,067 residents called the massive subdivision home.

BIBLIOGRAPHY

Kelly, Barbara M. *Expanding the American Dream: Building and Rebuilding Levittown.* Albany: State University of New York Press, 1993.

Jon C. Teaford

See also **Housing; Suburbanization.**

LEVY, a British project in the early years of the nineteenth century to recruit recent British arrivals in the United States and Canada for an enterprise against Napoleon's French possessions in the West Indies. In 1803 Charles Williamson, a British officer captured during the American Revolution and former agent of the Pulteney Associates, received orders to organize the Levy. He proposed cooperating with Francisco de Miranda in an attack against Spanish possessions in Florida, Mexico, and South America. The British may have offered the Levy to Aaron Burr, but no organization ever emerged. Miranda failed, and Williamson returned to Great Britain.

BIBLIOGRAPHY

Kennedy, Roger G. *Burr, Hamilton, and Jefferson: A Study in Character.* New York: Oxford University Press, 2000.

Thomas Robson Hay/A. E.

See also **British Empire, Concept of; Conscription and Recruitment; Great Britain, Relations with.**

LEWIS AND CLARK EXPEDITION. In 1803, President Thomas Jefferson purchased from France the extensive Louisiana Territory, a vast tract of land comprising nearly two-thirds of the present trans-Mississippi United States. Jefferson was a leading proponent of scientific expansion, a program of planned westward growth that called for the systematic exploration and mapping of new territory prior to settlement. Believing the Louisiana Territory held nearly unlimited potential for the future growth of the United States, Jefferson appointed his personal secretary, a twenty-nine-year-old army captain named Meriwether Lewis, as commander of an expedition to explore the vast region and to locate a water route to the Pacific Ocean. Lewis in turn chose Lieutenant William Clark, a thirty-three-year-old army officer and fellow Virginian, as his cocaptain. Late in 1803, Lewis and Clark established their headquarters at St. Louis, where they spent the winter gathering supplies and training the twenty-five soldiers under their command for the arduous journey.

The expedition set out for the unknown in the spring of 1804. Most of the first summer was spent making a difficult ascent up the Missouri River to present-day North Dakota, where the expedition wintered among the villages of the Mandan Sioux. When the expedition moved out the next spring, it was joined by the French-Canadian fur trader and interpreter Toussaint Charbonneau and his Shosone Indian wife, Sacagawea, who emerged as the party's principal guide. With Sacagawea in the lead, carrying her infant son much of the way, Lewis and Clark reached the headwaters of the Missouri and then pushed westward across the Bitterroot Mountains in Montana and Idaho late in the summer of 1805. That autumn the expedition crossed the Continental Divide and descended the Clearwater and Snake Rivers. On 7 November 1805, their canoes reached the mouth of the Columbia River, and the explorers at last laid eyes upon the Pacific Ocean. They built a small wooden post, Fort Clatsop, along the Columbia River as their winter headquarters and embarked upon the return voyage the following March. After recrossing the Rocky Mountains, Lewis and Clark divided the expedition into three groups to map more territory and reunited near the convergence of the Yellowstone and Missouri Rivers. Finally, after nearly twenty-eight months of exploration and travail, the weary expedition arrived to a hero's welcome at St. Louis on 23 September 1806.

In accordance with Jefferson's detailed instructions for the expedition, Lewis and Clark brought back a multitude of scientific information, including maps, the bones and hides from animal specimens, and caged birds and prairie dogs. Of the utmost value were their voluminous journals and diaries, which provided detailed firsthand de-

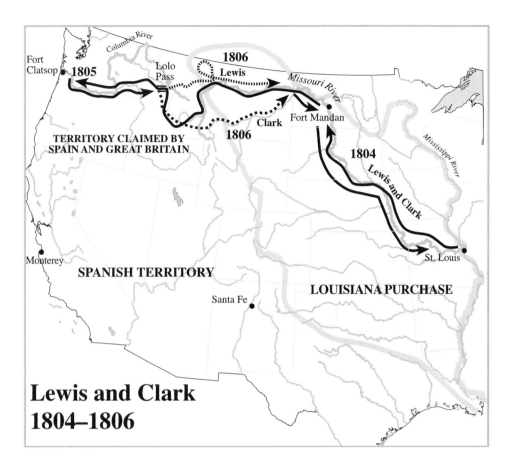

**Lewis and Clark
1804–1806**

scriptions of the plant and animal life, geography, and Native peoples encountered during the journey. Although Lewis and Clark failed to locate a convenient water passage to the Pacific Ocean, they were nonetheless handsomely rewarded for their efforts. The U.S. government awarded both men 1,600 acres of land, while each member of the expedition received 320 acres and double pay. Lewis was later appointed governor of the Louisiana Territory, while Clark held a similar post in the Missouri Territory. Their most lasting achievement, however, was their contribution to the opening, both figurative and real, of the American West.

BIBLIOGRAPHY

Ambrose, Stephen E. *Undaunted Courage: Meriwether Lewis, Thomas Jefferson, and the Opening of the American West.* New York: Simon and Schuster, 1996.

Duncan, Dayton. *Lewis and Clark: An Illustrated History.* New York: Knopf, 1997.

Moulton, Gary E., ed. *The Journals of the Lewis and Clark Expedition.* 13 vols. Lincoln: University of Nebraska Press, 1983–2001.

Ronda, James P., ed. *Voyages of Discovery: Essays on the Lewis and Clark Expedition.* Helena: Montana Historical Society Press, 1998.

Daniel P. Barr

See also **Explorations and Expeditions: U.S.; Louisiana Purchase;** *and vol. 9:* **Message on the Lewis and Clark Expedition; The Journals of the Lewis and Clark Expedition.**

LEXINGTON, a name given to four American ships: (1) A Continental brig that, under Capt. John Barry, captured the British sloop *Edward* in April 1776, off Chesapeake Bay. In 1777 it cruised about Ireland under Henry Johnson, but was captured in September of that year. (2) A store ship that, under Lt. Theodorus Bailey, captured San Blas, Mexico, in 1848, in the final naval operation of the Mexican War. (3) A Union sidewheeler, later armored, that fought at Belmont, Miss., Fort Henry, Tenn., and on the Red River, 1861–1863. At Shiloh it saved Gen. Ulysses S. Grant's army from being driven back in utter defeat the first day of the battle. (4) A World War II aircraft carrier that participated in the Battle of the Coral Sea, 7–9 May 1942, the first major check to Japan's advance in the Pacific. The *Lexington* was so badly damaged that it had to be sunk by an American destroyer.

BIBLIOGRAPHY

Johnston, Stanley. *Queen of the Flat-Tops: The U.S.S. Lexington and the Coral Sea Battle.* New York: Dutton, 1942.

Walter B. Norris / A. R.

Lexington. In this contemporary illustration by F. Godefroy, Massachusetts minutemen confront British regulars at the very beginning of the American Revolution. © CORBIS

See also **Aircraft Carriers and Naval Aircraft; Coral Sea, Battle of the; Mexican-American War; Shiloh, Battle of.**

LEXINGTON AND CONCORD, BATTLES OF.

On the evening of 18 April 1775 the British military governor of Massachusetts sent out from Boston a detachment of about 700 regular troops to destroy military stores collected by the colonists at Concord. Detecting the plan, the Whigs in Boston sent out Paul Revere and William Dawes with warnings. At sunrise on 19 April, the detachment found a part of the minuteman company already assembled on the Lexington green. At the command of British Major John Pitcairn, the regulars fired and cleared the ground. Eight Americans were killed and 10 were wounded. The regulars marched for Concord after a short delay.

At Concord the outnumbered Americans retired over the North Bridge and waited for reinforcements. The British occupied the town, held the North Bridge with about 100 regulars, and searched for stores to burn. The smoke alarmed the Americans, and, reinforced to the number of about 450, they marched down to the bridge, led by Major John Buttrick. The regulars hastily reformed on the far side to receive them and began to take up the bridge planks. Buttrick shouted to them to desist. The front ranks of the regulars fired, killing 2 Americans and wounding more. Buttrick gave the famous order, "Fire, fellow soldiers, for God's sake, fire!" The American

counterattack killed 2 and forced the British from the field. The Americans did not pursue, however, and the British marched for Boston about noon.

At Meriam's Corner their rear guard was fired upon by rebels from Reading, and from there to Lexington the British were under constant fire from snipers. By the time they reached Lexington, the regulars were almost out of ammunition and completely demoralized. They were

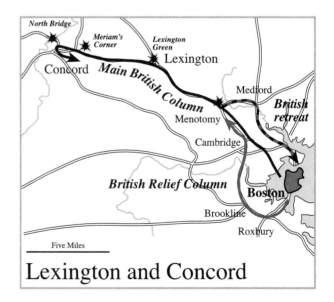

Lexington and Concord

saved only by the arrival of Sir Hugh Percy with a column from Boston and two fieldpieces. When they marched on again, the militia dogged them all the way to Charlestown, where, before sundown, the regulars reached safety under the guns of the fleet.

The casualties of the day bear no relation to its importance. Forty-nine Americans and 73 British were killed; the total of those killed and wounded of both sides was 366. But the fighting proved to the Americans that by their own method they could defeat the British. In that belief, they stopped the land approaches to Boston before night, thus beginning the siege of Boston.

BIBLIOGRAPHY

Cress, Lawrence D. *Citizens in Arms: The Army and the Militia in American Society to the War of 1812.* Chapel Hill: University of North Carolina Press, 1982.

Martin, James K., and Mark E. Lender. *A Respectable Army: The Military Origins of the Republic, 1763–1789.* Arlington Heights, Ill.: Davidson, 1982.

Shy, John. *Toward Lexington: The Role of the British Army in the Coming of the American Revolution.* Princeton, N.J.: Princeton University Press, 1965.

———. *A People Numerous and Armed: Reflections on the Military Struggle for American Independence.* New York: Oxford University Press, 1976.

Allen French / A. R.

See also **Boston, Siege of; Bunker Hill, Battle of; Minutemen; Revere's Ride;** *and vol. 9:* **Battle of Lexington, American and British Accounts.**

LEYTE GULF, BATTLE OF (23–25 October 1944). As the first step in recapturing the Philippines, a huge American armada descended on Leyte Island in mid-October 1944. The invasion force, Vice Admiral Thomas C. Kinkaid's Seventh Fleet, included some seven hundred vessels and five hundred aircraft. Supporting it was the Third Fleet, under Admiral William F. Halsey, with nearly one hundred warships and more than one thousand planes. Japan's sixty-four warships, operating under a defensive plan called *Sho* (Victory), immediately countered. From the north, aircraft carriers under Vice Admiral Jisaburo Ozawa would lure Halsey away so that Vice Admiral Takeo Kurita's battleships and Vice Admiral Kiyohide Shima's cruisers could attack the exposed American amphibious assault units in Leyte Gulf.

Kurita's force left Borneo on 22 October in two groups. The larger group, under Kurita, would pass through the San Bernardino Strait and enter Leyte Gulf from the north. A smaller force, under Vice Admiral Shoji Nishimura, moved through the Sulu Sea toward Surigao Strait—the southern entrance to Leyte Gulf—which he planned to enter simultaneously with Kurita. Early on 23 October, two American submarines attacked Kurita, sinking two heavy cruisers and badly damaging a third. Planes from Halsey's carriers assaulted Kurita the next day, sink-

ing the 64,000-ton superbattleship *Musashi* and crippling a heavy cruiser. Simultaneously, land-based Japanese aircraft sank one of Halsey's carriers. Kurita, badly shaken, returned to Leyte Gulf too late for his planned rendezvous with Nishimura and Shima.

To the south, Kinkaid intercepted Nishimura in Surigao Strait. The American battleships and cruisers formed a line across the northern end of the strait, while destroyers and torpedo boats were stationed ahead to attack the Japanese flanks. First contact came about midnight of 24–25 October, and, within a few hours, Nishimura was destroyed. Of seven Japanese vessels entering Surigao Strait, only a damaged cruiser and destroyer managed to escape. Only one U.S. destroyer was damaged, mistakenly struck by American fire. Shima's force, arriving shortly thereafter, was also warmly greeted but escaped with only slight damage. Pursuing American ships and planes sank another cruiser and destroyer before the surviving Japanese force could get away.

Meanwhile, before dawn on 25 October, Kurita's force steamed for Leyte Gulf. Halsey, who should have intercepted him, had rushed north to attack Ozawa, in the mistaken belief that Kurita was crippled and that Ozawa's carriers now constituted the main threat. Shortly after sunrise, Kurita struck Kinkaid's northernmost unit, a small force of escort carriers and destroyers. The tiny American force fought off the powerful Japanese fleet, while American destroyers made repeated attacks to cover the fleeing escort carriers. Suddenly, Kurita broke off his attack. Although he had sunk one escort carrier and three destroyers, he had suffered considerable damage. Aware of the destruction of Nishimura and Shima, and believing that he could no longer reach Leyte Gulf in time to do significant damage, the Japanese commander elected to escape with the remnants of his fleet. Far to the north, on the afternoon of 25 October in the final action of the battle, Halsey struck Ozawa's decoy force, sinking four Japanese carriers, a cruiser, and two destroyers.

The lopsided American victory destroyed the Japanese fleet as an effective fighting force. It also ensured the conquest of Leyte and cleared the way for the invasion and ultimate recapture of the Philippine Islands.

BIBLIOGRAPHY

Cannon, M. Hamlin. *Leyte: The Return to the Philippines.* Washington, D.C.: Office of the Chief of Military History, Department of the Army, 1954.

Falk, Stanley L. *Decision at Leyte.* New York: Norton, 1966.

Morison, Samuel Eliot. *Leyte, June 1944–January 1945.* Vol. 12, *History of United States Naval Operations in World War II.* Boston: Little, Brown, 1958.

Stanley L. Falk / A. R.

See also **Navy, United States; Philippine Sea, Battle of the; Task Force 58; World War II; World War II, Navy in.**

LIBEL refers to a highly technical common-law concept concerning defamation that has broad political implications and a lengthy, confusing history. In its seventeenth-century form, libel covered any written statement, whether true or false, that tended to damage the opinion which "right-thinking" people might otherwise hold of the government, public officials, or ordinary citizens.

The seminal early libel case in America occurred in 1735, when John Peter Zenger, publisher of the *New York Weekly Review*, stood trial for seditious libel for articles criticizing New York's colonial governor. Andrew Hamilton, Zenger's attorney, argued that truth should constitute a sufficient defense against such charges. At the time, the strict common-law rule, as reiterated by Sir William Blackstone, rejected truth as a defense and held that "the greater the truth, the greater the libel." Yet, the jurors agreed with Hamilton, used their power of nullification, and found Zenger not guilty.

The Federalist Party's Sedition Act of 1798 incorporated these "Zengerian Principles," truth as a defense and a jury's power to determine whether or not a statement was libelous. Although the law was never tested in the courts, Jeffersonians, especially those targeted for prosecution, complained that the Zengerian principles provided little protection in libel cases marked by partisan passion.

In the aftermath of the Sedition Act, debate over legal-constitutional protections for political expression became closely connected to the rules of libel law. During the nineteenth century, most states adopted specific constitutional provisions on criminal libel that resembled the Zengerian principles. Thus, most of the controversy over libel during the nineteenth and early twentieth centuries involved civil suits by political figures, especially those against newspapers.

In civil suits, in addition to the absolute defense of truth, defendants could invoke other "conditional privileges" that could excuse a libelous publication. "Fair comment," for example, covered libelous opinions about issues of general public interest, such as the quality of artistic works. A privilege, not a right, fair comment did justify libelous factual statements or any defamatory comment made with malice. A few states adopted a "minority rule" that did extend protection to libelous falsehoods published without malice.

The law of libel operated within this doctrinal framework for much of the twentieth century. The situation changed during the 1960s and 1970s. Libel suits by segregationists against civil rights activists and northern media outlets, and a perceived increase in other types of political libel litigation, led the activist majority of the U.S. Supreme Court, in *Times v. Sullivan* (1964) and *Garrison v. Louisiana* (1964), to bring both civil and criminal libel within the structure of constitutional law. In effect, the Court belatedly declared the Sedition Act of 1798 unconstitutional and adopted the minority rule on falsehoods as

the new First Amendment standard in both civil and criminal actions. Unless a case involved libelous falsehoods published knowingly with actual malice, such as with "reckless disregard" of their veracity, the law of libel violated the principle that public debate should be "uninhibited, robust, and wide open." The Court also rejected the venerable common-law rule that required defendants, rather than plaintiffs, to bear the greater evidentiary burden and held that, at least in cases involving public officials and the media, even the most outrageous opinion could not become the basis for a libel suit.

Changes in the law of libel intensified debate over the overly complex nature of specific doctrines. Even so, libel seemed an area of the law that—as an earlier commentator had observed about the pre-Sullivan situation—looked much worse in theory than it actually operated in practice.

BIBLIOGRAPHY

Lewis, Anthony. *Make No Law: The Sullivan Case and the First Amendment*. New York: Random House, 1991.

Rosenberg, Norman L. *Protecting the "Best Men": An Interpretive History of the Law of Libel*. Chapel Hill: University of North Carolina Press, 1985.

Smolla, Rodney. *Jerry Falwell vs. Larry Flynt: The First Amendment on Trial*. New York: St. Martin's Press, 1988.

Norman Rosenberg

See also **Common Law; First Amendment;** *New York Times v. Sullivan;* **Sedition Acts; Zenger Trial.**

LIBERAL REPUBLICAN PARTY was the result of a revolt of the reform element in the Republican party during President Ulysses S. Grant's first administration (1869–1873). It advocated a conciliatory policy toward the white South and civil service reform and condemned political corruption. Some members of the party favored tariff revision. The movement was led by B. Gratz Brown, Horace Greeley, Carl Schurz, Charles Sumner, and Charles Francis Adams. The party nominated Greeley for president in 1872, and he subsequently won the Democrats' endorsement. In the ensuing campaign, however, Grant overwhelmingly defeated Greeley and the party disbanded soon thereafter.

BIBLIOGRAPHY

Foner, Eric. *Reconstruction: America's Unfinished Revolution, 1863–1877*. New York: Harper and Row, 1988.

Lunde, Erik S. *Horace Greeley*. Boston: Twayne, 1981.

Glenn H. Benton / A. G.

See also **Civil Service; Corruption, Political; Radical Republicans; Reconstruction; Republican Party.**

LIBERALISM. For centuries the word "liberal" has carried multiple meanings, on the one hand meaning generous or broad-minded, on the other dissolute or undisciplined. In American history the concept of liberalism has been similarly multivalent despite its champions' and critics' efforts to narrow or simplify its significance. Despite an enduring myth that a single "liberal tradition" has dominated American history, the central liberal values of generosity toward the poor and toleration of diversity have always been contested. Contemporary critics of liberalism fall into two distinct camps. Conservatives, including many Republican Party loyalists, accuse liberals of mobilizing the resources of big government in a futile effort to engineer equality without respecting individual property rights. Academic cultural radicals, by contrast, accuse liberals of neglecting the egalitarian aspirations of marginalized Americans and paying too much attention to individual property rights. Can the ideas of liberalism, assailed from the right and the left, be salvaged?

Varieties of Liberalism

Viewed historically, liberalism in America bears little resemblance to today's stereotypes. From the seventeenth century onward, liberals have tried to balance their commitments to individual freedom, social equality, and representative democracy. Until recently, most American liberals conceived of individual rights within the ethical framework provided by the Christian law of love. Puritan John Winthrop, for example, was neither an egalitarian nor a pluralist, but in 1630 he characterized "liberallity" toward the least fortunate members of the community as a duty Christians must observe. Massachusetts pastor John Wise, writing in 1707, invoked the German philosopher of natural law Samuel von Pufendorf rather than the Englishman John Locke to bolster his claim that the principles of sociability and love of mankind operate alongside the principle of self-reservation. Similar combinations of religious, ethical, and traditional restraints on personal freedom provided the vocabularies employed when Americans began to challenge different aspects of British rule after 1767. The resulting discourses of protest culminated first in local and state declarations of independence, then in state constitutional conventions, and finally in the United States Constitution, complete with its Bill of Rights. As all these documents stipulated, what Thomas Jefferson termed the rights to "life, liberty, and the pursuit of happiness" could be pursued legitimately only within boundaries established "by certain laws for the common good," as John Adams put it in the 1779 Constitution of Massachusetts. Whether that concern for the public interest derived from the Christian law of love or the Scottish common-sense philosophers' principle of benevolence, from the English common law or colonial legal practice, from classical republicanism or Renaissance civic humanism, from Pufendorf or Locke, the concept of justice as a goal transcending the satisfaction of individuals' personal preferences pervaded the founding documents that secured the rights of citizens in the new nation.

But what about those denied citizenship? Proclamations of the common good clashed with the fact that a majority of Americans did not enjoy equal liberties. In response, some mid-nineteenth-century liberal reformers such as Sarah Grimké and Frederick Douglass began to clamor for women's rights and the abolition of slavery. A few invoked the principle of toleration to protest the removal of Indians from their ancestral lands. Others invoked the language of liberty on behalf of a campaign for economic enterprise that extended Enlightenment convictions about the civilizing effects of commerce and economic growth. But local and state laws continued to circumscribe much economic activity with regulations premised on the common-law doctrine of the people's welfare, a principle invoked to justify laws controlling the use of waterways, the operation of stables and slaughterhouses, and the licensing of butchers, bakers, grocers, physicians, and lawyers. Many of those who clamored for the right of all to own property justified their claims by invoking egalitarian ideals rather than more individualist concepts of natural rights. The notion of laissez-faire never succeeded in uprooting such practices and traditions. In the decade prior to the Civil War, contrasting appeals to equal rights assumed strikingly different meanings in the North and the South. When Lincoln succeeded in tying the expansion of slavery to the degradation of free labor, he bound the political, economic, and religious strands of liberal reform sentiment into a fragile but impressive coalition perceived by the South as a threat to slaveholders' property rights.

Setting a pattern for times of peril, during the Civil War the restriction of civil liberties was justified by the goal of securing liberty. Afterward the sacrifice of the freed slaves' rights and the postponement of women's rights were both justified by the goal of restoring a Union rededicated to the principle of liberty for white men. Lincoln's more generous and more broad-minded vision of the national purpose faded from view.

For a brief moment in the late-nineteenth century, gangs of greedy industrialists and politicians hijacked liberal principles to rationalize the unchecked exploitation of people and resources, but by the turn of the century agrarian and labor activists were working to bring that anomalous period to a close. Some coalitions of progressive reformers sought to restore the earlier liberal balance between rights and obligations, invoking the eighteenth-century concept of the common good to justify restoring the authority of government as a counterweight to the assertion of private prerogatives. Their "new liberalism" sought to harness the techniques of science to regulate an industrializing and urbanizing America in order to secure effective freedom for all instead of protecting empty, formal rights that enabled "the interests" to oppress "the people." Thinkers such as John Dewey and W. E. B. Du Bois and reformers such as Louis Brandeis and Jane Addams yoked the language of liberty and justice to the philosophy of pragmatism and the energetic engagement of public authority to address social and economic problems.

Although business interests protested at first, during and after World War I they learned how to live with government because it promised to secure and legitimate the stability they prized. The Great Depression shattered their hopes and altered their strategy. Although large enterprises continued to depend on the state's cooperation, the business community developed an ideology of implacable opposition to "liberal" government intrusions into the "private" sector.

The New Deal emerged from the chaos of the depression, established a new social vision, then ended in retreat in the late 1940s when its opponents in both parties joined forces to defend hierarchies of race and privilege. Although Franklin D. Roosevelt initially lacked a coherent program of national recovery, by the end of World War II he and his advisers had transformed the meaning of liberalism. When he declared in 1944 that the Allies were fighting to secure a "Second Bill of Rights," including the rights to higher education, a job, a living wage, decent housing, and health care for all citizens, he established an agenda that has continued to drive liberal politics ever since. During the Cold War, critics derided such programs as being antithetical to an "American way of life" that sanctified the individual rights of a privileged majority, and interpreted invocations of a shared common good as evidence of dangerous communist sympathies.

Recent Debates

In the wake of World War II, renewed efforts to secure rights for African Americans and women culminated in legal and legislative milestones but failed to achieve social and economic equality. Many liberals who championed the rights of blacks and women in the 1960s eventually also allied themselves with campaigns against discrimination stemming from sexuality, age, and physical and mental disability. Such movements have proliferated since 1980, when Ronald Reagan became president, by proclaiming that government is the problem rather than the solution. Since then many liberals abandoned FDR's ambitious plans for a more egalitarian form of social democracy and turned instead toward a strategy that emphasized the rights of individuals who are members of disadvantaged groups. As a result, liberalism seemed to many Americans in the twenty-first century nothing more than a catalog of complaints asserted on behalf of minorities asserting themselves against the traditions and the will of the majority.

Although the proclamation of equal rights for aggrieved groups has been an important part of liberalism ever since theorists such as Locke and Jefferson asserted the importance of religious toleration, liberals surrender precious resources from their heritage when they narrow their discourse to rights talk. They risk appearing as narrowly self-interested as those conservatives who, following in the path of Thomas Hobbes, have tried to reduce politics to the protection of individual rights, particularly the right to property. The historical record indicates that

Americans drawn to liberalism have tried instead to balance liberty, equality, and the common good. They have understood, as James Madison wrote to James Monroe in 1786, that the idea of self interest must be "qualified with every necessary moral ingredient" or else it can be used to justify all sorts of injustice. Insofar as liberals neglect the ideas of ethical responsibility, social obligation, and justice that animated the writings and reform activities of many of their predecessors, they will find themselves vulnerable to such criticism.

Sturdier versions of liberal theory emerged in the late twentieth century through the efforts of scholars influenced by John Rawls, whose monumental work *A Theory of Justice* (1971) provided a rationale for keeping alive the spirit of FDR's Second Bill of Rights. Rawls argued, in the tradition of theorists such as Locke, Wise, Jefferson, Adams, Madison, and Dewey, that a liberal society must balance the values of liberty and equality. Rawls reasoned that individuals entering a hypothetical social compact, ignorant of their own gifts and goals, would choose two principles of justice. First, and for Rawls this principle takes precedence over the second, they would provide each person with the most extensive set of liberties compatible with an equally extensive set of liberties for others. Second, any social or economic inequalities in the society would be attached to positions open to everyone and must be in the interest of the least advantaged members of the society. Rawls's theory, which updates the original liberal injunctions to protect liberty and provide for the weak, sparked a lively controversy and prompted Rawls to refine his views in *Political Liberalism* (1993). Critics from the right charged Rawls with overstating the redistributive claims of the community against the rights of the individual. Some imagined a "night watchman state," a chimera that has bewitched conservatives who overlook the dependence of market economies on the (government-enforced) rule of law and the (government-funded) provision of social services. Critics from the left challenged Rawls's abstract, rights-bearing individuals, reasoning that real human beings are influenced more by the cultural traditions they inherit and the aspirations they cherish than by any abstract rights they might envision.

Many early twenty-first century liberal theorists emphasized the importance of such cultural traditions, whether religious, ethnic, national, or civic, in shaping the debates that yield liberal democratic ideals and procedures. Some, such as Richard Rorty, insisted that liberalism could no longer rest on solid footing in the universal principles that earlier liberal thinkers invoked. Others, such as Michael Walzer, continued to turn to the Western tradition itself for the religious, philosophical, and political resources necessary to renew liberalism through democratic deliberation in a pluralist and contentious age. Thus liberalism, best understood as a fluid discourse concerning the meaning and relative importance of the ideals of generosity and broad-mindedness, still attracted adherents. Against competing conservative values such as hierarchy and tradition, and against radical doubts about norms such as reason and fairness, liberalism continued to assert itself as a rich and important constellation of ideas in the highly charged atmosphere of American culture.

BIBLIOGRAPHY

Galston, William. *Liberal Purposes: Goods, Virtues, and Diversity in the Liberal State.* Cambridge, U.K.; New York: Cambridge University Press, 1991.

Glendon, Mary Ann. *Rights Talk: The Impoverishment of Political Discourse.* New York: Basic Books, 1991.

Hartz, Louis. *The Liberal Tradition in America.* New York: Harcourt, 1955.

Kloppenberg, James T. *The Virtues of Liberalism.* New York: Oxford University Press, 1997.

Rawls, John. *A Theory of Justice.* Cambridge, Mass.: Harvard University Press, 1971.

Walzer, Michael. *Spheres of Justice: A Defense of Pluralism and Equality.* New York: Basic Books, 1983.

James T. Kloppenberg

See also **Conservatism.**

LIBERATION THEOLOGY.

Liberation theology emerged from a long process of transformation in post-Enlightenment Christian theological reflection. As science and historical criticism challenged the findings of traditional metaphysical foundations of theology, theologians were widely expected to reconcile their findings with modern principles of analysis and criticism. Where theological reflection was previously focused on the metaphysical and supernatural, it became increasingly concerned with pragmatic and concrete problems.

Liberation theology originated in the 1960s in North and South America, although it was rooted in works by post–World War II European theologians like Rudolf Bultmann, Jürgen Moltmann, and Johann-Baptiste Metz. Among its foundational texts was *The Secular City* (1965), by the U.S. Protestant theologian Harvey Cox. It argued that, for religion to retain vitality in a secularized environment, theological reflection must conform to the concrete social and political challenges of the modern secular world; for example, he argued that contemporary problems like racism and poverty must be treated as theological problems as well as social problems. Selling a million copies in numerous languages, Cox was especially influential in Latin America, and with the 1971 Spanish-language publication of *A Theology of Liberation: History, Politics, and Salvation* by the Peruvian Catholic theologian Gustavo Gutiérrez (the book was published in English in 1973), liberation theology was given its name and became a new branch of theological reflection. By the mid-1970s, many exponents of liberation theology emerged in North and South America, including Catholics (Leonardo Boff, Mary Daly, Rosemary Radford Ruether, Juan Luis Segundo, Jon Sobrino) and Protestants (Robert McAfee

Brown, James H. Cone). Thereafter, the influence of liberation theology expanded, becoming mainstream within the international community of theologians, especially influencing theological reflection in Africa and Asia.

Liberation theology had a mutually supportive relationship with important developments in the post–World War II era. First, it emerged amidst the European decolonization of Africa and Asia, supporting and drawing strength from the discourse around third-world poverty and global politics spurred by decolonization. Second, liberation theology both helped to affirm and was, in turn, affirmed by innumerable liberation movements, including the black power and sexual liberation movements in the United States in the late 1960s and 1970s, popular guerrilla movements in Latin American nations like Nicaragua and El Salvador in the 1980s, and the popular anticommunist movement in Central and Eastern Europe during the 1980s. Third, given its use of theological reflection as a means to "human liberation," liberation theology promoted the idea that theology should be political and activist in its goals; in the process, it was often distinguished from post–World War II fundamentalist theologies that generally placed a higher premium on metaphysical and supernatural concerns. In recent years, liberation theology has helped to promote a multiculturalist and human rights–based critique of contemporary politics, society, and culture.

BIBLIOGRAPHY

Casanova, José. *Public Religions in the Modern World.* Chicago: University of Chicago Press, 1994. Treats the global influence of theological thought from liberationist to fundamentalist theologies in the late twentieth century.

Cox, Harvey. *The Secular City: Secularization and Urbanization in Theological Perspectives.* 1965. New York: Collier, 1990. Twenty-fifth anniversary edition with a new introduction by the author.

Tracy, David. *The Blessed Rage for Order: The New Pluralism in Theology.* 1975. Chicago: University of Chicago Press, 1996. Includes a learned, concise treatment of modern theology's relation to developments in the sociology of knowledge.

James P. McCartin

See also **Catholicism; Fundamentalism; Protestantism.**

LIBERIA, RELATIONS WITH.

Liberia lies on the western coast of Africa and is the continent's oldest republic. The area is approximately 43,000 square miles, mostly dense tropical rain forest. Nearly the entire population is indigenous, comprising about twenty ethnic groups. Two percent belong to the Americo-Liberian elite, descended from liberated slaves and black American freedmen repatriated to Africa in the nineteenth century through the efforts of the American Colonization Society.

Since the founding of Liberia in 1822, the United States has maintained a policy of relative detachment. The colony declared itself independent in 1847, but the

United States, embroiled in controversy over slavery, withheld recognition until 1862. American naval vessels occasionally assisted Liberian colonists in police actions against recalcitrant indigenes. In 1909 and 1915 the U.S.S. *Chester* was sent to rescue American missionaries and Liberian officials during Kru rebellions.

Relatively prosperous during the mid-nineteenth century, Liberia became territorially overextended and declined disastrously when faced with European commercial and colonial competition. British and French traders and diplomats reduced Liberian territory by one-third before the United States quietly applied pressure around 1900 to preserve Liberian independence. Germany and even Poland cast covetous eyes on the struggling republic. By 1912 Liberia was badly in default to European creditors, and in return for a loan from the United States agreed to accept American customs officers and a military mission. Heavy investment by the Firestone Tire and Rubber Company in Liberian rubber plantations after 1926 partially alleviated financial strains. The United States suspended diplomatic relations from 1930 to 1935 over alleged forced labor abuses and cooperated with Liberian and League of Nations authorities in investigating the charges. United States influence peaked during World War II when the Liberian capital, Monrovia, became a major supply depot. Exports of high-grade iron ore began to revolutionize the country in the 1960s. European and Asian influence and capital now compete heavily with American.

The Liberian constitution replicates the U.S. form: a bicameral legislature with the lower house apportioned somewhat according to the population in nine counties and four territories. Legislative and judicial branches have atrophied and power has been concentrated in the executive, especially under President William V. S. Tubman (1944–1971). Tubman's National Unification Plan, supposed to close the gap between the oligarchy and indigenous peoples, was only a marginal success.

BIBLIOGRAPHY

Chester, Edward W. *Clash of Titans: Africa and U.S. Foreign Policy*. Maryknoll, N.Y.: Orbis Books, 1974.

Duignan, Peter, and Lewis H. Gann. *The United States and Africa: A History*. New York: Cambridge University Press, 1984.

Ronald W. Davis / A. G.

See also **Africa, Relations with; African Americans; Slavery.**

LIBERTARIANS. *See* **Third Parties.**

LIBERTY, CONCEPT OF. "Give me liberty, or give me death!" cried Patrick Henry in 1775. His words still resound, warning potential tyrants at home and abroad of liberty's place in the hearts of Americans. Noth-

Liberty Poster. This 1918 poster, humanizing the country's most enduring symbol of liberty, was created by Z. P. Nikolaki as part of the drive to sell Liberty Bonds to finance American involvement in World War I. LIBRARY OF CONGRESS

ing is as dear to them as liberty—not even equality. But what does liberty entail, who is entitled to it, and what is the proper role of government in securing it? Broadly speaking, the answers to these questions cluster around the concepts of negative and positive liberty. The tension between the two has been central to debates surrounding ratification of the Constitution, the abolition of slavery, the "second revolution" in civil rights after World War II, and other turning points in American politics.

Negative liberty is freedom from unwarranted restrictions on belief, action, or movement. "Unwarranted" is the operative word here. Without some restrictions there is no liberty for anyone; anarchy reigns. Without additional restrictions, liberty would not be universal; only the strong would enjoy it. Yet every restriction, no matter how necessary or desirable it may be, is also a limit on freedom and forecloses opportunities that may be important or even essential for the pursuit of happiness as some individuals understand it. Therefore, those who value negative liberty insist that restrictions be minimized so as not to undermine freedom.

Positive liberty is the right to pursue happiness as a person thinks best. This right involves guarantees that ensure no person is denied opportunities on the basis of race, gender, ethnicity, or creed. Such guarantees are political in origin and presume the existence of another guarantee: the right to participate in political decisions that shape the structure of opportunities in American society. But the exercise of liberty depends on more than guaranteed opportunities: it also requires some capacity for using these opportunities to full advantage. Advocates of positive liberty argue that the development of this capacity is what enables individuals to enjoy the benefits of freedom. The two senses of liberty obviously give rise to competing notions of government and its proper role in social and economic life. Those who emphasize freedom from unwarranted restrictions believe with Jefferson "that government is best which governs least." Government ought to provide for the common defense and maintain law and order, thereby protecting us from each other. Beyond this, government cannot function without diminishing the liberty of some, if not all, citizens. This is true even, or perhaps especially, when governments pursue the public good or the general welfare, which may be so broadly defined as to require massive amounts of regulation and proscription.

Proponents of positive liberty take a more expansive view of government. For them, government exists not only to protect liberty, but also to promote freedom by empowering individuals. Hence, government is much more than a "night watchman"; it is also the provider of goods and services essential for the realization of success, such as public education. In the twentieth century, the list of goods and services has grown to include unemployment insurance, social security, health services, and environmental protection. Some would expand it still further, adding affirmative action and similar policies intended to overcome the legacy of previous discriminations and abridgements of liberty.

Reconciling these opposing views of liberty is the principal problem of constitutional government. As James Madison noted: "It is a melancholy reflection that liberty should be equally exposed to danger whether Government have too much or too little power." Efforts to strike the right balance between too much and too little government define the history of liberty in the United States.

BIBLIOGRAPHY

Berlin, Isaiah. *Four Essays on Liberty*. London: Oxford University Press, 1969.

Foner, Eric. *The Story of American Freedom*. New York: Norton, 1999.

Kammen, Michael G. *Spheres of Liberty: Changing Perceptions of Liberty in American Culture*. Madison: University of Wisconsin Press. 1986.

Mill, John Stuart. *On Liberty*. New York: Viking Press. 1983.

Russell L. Hanson

See also **Antislavery; Personal Liberty Laws; Religious Liberty.**

Liberty Bell. The famous symbol of American independence, in its place of honor near Philadelphia's Independence Hall. PHILADELPHIA CONVENTION AND VISITORS BUREAU

LIBERTY BELL. The bell was commissioned by the Pennsylvania Assembly in 1751 to commemorate the fiftieth anniversary of William Penn's 1701 CHARTER OF PRIVILEGES. Whitechapel Foundry produced the bell, which cracked as it was being tested. The bell is inscribed with the words from Leviticus 25:10 "Proclaim liberty throughout all the land unto all the inhabitants thereof." It tolled for the reading of the Declaration of Independence on July 8, 1776. During the British occupation of Philadelphia in 1777, the bell was hidden away. After it was rung for Washington's birthday in 1846, the crack widened, rendering the bell unringable. It is now ceremoniously tapped each Fourth of July.

BIBLIOGRAPHY

Kramer, Justin. *Cast in America*. Los Angeles: J. Kramer, 1975.

Connie Ann Kirk

See also **Independence Hall; Philadelphia.**

LIBERTY **INCIDENT.** The USS *Liberty* (AGTR-5), a U.S. Navy communications intelligence ship, was attacked by Israeli air and sea forces on 8 June 1967 while cruising in international waters in the Mediterranean Sea off the coast of the Sinai Peninsula. The Israeli attack occurred on the fourth day of the Israeli-Arab Six Day War, just prior to Israel's assault of the Golan Heights in Syria. In addition to the extensive damage to the *Liberty*, its crew suffered 34 dead and 171 wounded. To preserve the ship's non-hostile status, the *Liberty*'s commander, Captain William L. McGonagle, directed the crew not to return fire. Except for a brief episode of unauthorized machine gun fire at attacking Israeli torpedo boats, the

Liberty offered no armed defense. For his heroism under fire, Captain McGonagle was awarded the Medal of Honor in June 1968.

Israeli motivation for the attack and the official response of the administration of President Lyndon B. Johnson have been shrouded in secrecy and controversy. Israel deemed the attack accidental, claiming the *Liberty* was mistaken for an Egyptian craft. The Johnson administration accepted this explanation and Israeli apologies, and Israel subsequently paid compensation to the victims and for ship damages. Some American officials and members of the *Liberty*'s crew contended that Israel's actions were intentional, possibly to prevent the United States from learning of Israel's plans to attack Syria, and that the Johnson administration aborted efforts by American aircraft to assist the vessel.

BIBLIOGRAPHY

Borne, John E. *The USS "Liberty": Dissenting History vs. Official History*. New York: Reconsideration Press, 1995.

Ennes, James M., Jr. *Assault on the "Liberty": The True Story of the Israeli Attack on an American Intelligence Ship*. New York: Random House, 1979.

Vincent H. Demma

See also **Israel, Relations with.**

LIBERTY LOANS.

Upon the entry of the United States into WORLD WAR I in April 1917, it at once became apparent that large sums in excess of tax receipts would be needed both to provide funds for European allies and to conduct the war activities of the nation. To obtain the necessary funds, the Treasury resorted to borrowing through a series of bond issues. The first four issues were known as liberty loans; the fifth and last was called the victory loan.

The issues were brought out between 14 May 1917 and 21 April 1919 in the total amount of $21,478,356,250. The disposal of this vast amount of obligations was accomplished by direct sales to the people on an unprecedented scale. Liberty loan committees were organized in all sections of the country, and almost the entire population was canvassed. Four-minute speakers gave high-powered sales talks in theaters, motion picture houses, hotels, and restaurants. The clergymen of the country made pleas for the purchase of bonds from their pulpits. Mass meetings were held on occasion, and the banks assisted by lending money, at a rate no higher than the interest on the bonds, to those who could not afford to purchase the bonds outright. In this way it was possible to secure the funds wanted and to obtain oversubscriptions on each issue.

BIBLIOGRAPHY

Cornbise, Alfred E. *War as Advertised: The Four Minute Men and America's Crusade, 1917–1918*. Philadelphia: The American Philosophical Society, 1984.

Gilbert, Charles. *American Financing of World War I*. Westport, Conn.: Greenwood, 1970.

Kennedy, David M. *Over Here: The First World War and American Society*. New York: Oxford University Press, 1980.

Frederick A. Bradford/A. G.

See also **Budget, Federal; War Costs; World War I, Economic Mobilization for.**

LIBERTY PARTY.

The Liberty Party emerged in 1839 as an abolitionist political organization in upstate New York. Organized abolitionism was divided along several fault lines, one of which involved the constitutionality of slavery. William Lloyd Garrison, who took control of the American Anti-Slavery Society, denounced the Constitution as a "covenant with death and an agreement with hell." Garrison insisted that the founders had embraced the sin of slavery, and that reformers must divorce themselves from the authority of the Constitution. The Liberty Party organized in opposition to this view. Gerrit Smith, William Goodell, and other leaders of the original party turned to the arguments of Alvan Stewart and Lysander Spooner, insisting that law could not be divorced from morality, and that the Constitution must be interpreted to sustain abolitionist goals.

In the 1840 presidential campaign, the Liberty Party nominated James G. Birney as its candidate. A Kentucky-born lawyer and former slaveholder, Birney had become a celebrated convert to the abolitionist cause. By the mid 1830s, the threat of mob violence convinced Birney to relocate to Cincinnati, Ohio. There, with the assistance of Gamaliel Bailey (formerly a lecturer at nearby Lane Seminary), he edited an abolitionist newspaper, *The Philanthropist*. Birney attracted further national attention in the Matilda Lawrence case, when the state of Ohio successfully prosecuted him for giving shelter and employment to a fugitive slave woman. The future Liberty Party leader Salmon P. Chase served as Birney's defense attorney. In the 1840 presidential election, Birney received about seven thousand votes.

Chase and Bailey collaborated to expand the western Liberty Party based on moderate antislavery constitutional principles. In contrast to the New York Liberty Party, Chase and Bailey distinguished between morality and law. Although they acknowledged that the Constitution permitted slavery in existing states, they insisted that it denied slavery beyond those states. The principle of freedom, Chase argued, defines the nation; slavery has no national standing. Expressing these views, at the party's Buffalo, New York, convention in August 1843, Chase drafted the Liberty Resolutions defining the party's principles.

As the presidential election of 1844 approached, the party again nominated Birney for president. It did so over the mild opposition of Chase, who wanted a candidate with wider popular appeal. As Chase expected, the electorate—excited by the agitation to annex Texas—delivered substantial support to the Liberty Party. Birney received more than sixty thousand votes. The election left Chase convinced that the time had come to form a more broadly based antislavery party.

Chase's influence in antislavery politics grew after 1844. He sponsored the Southern and Western Liberty Convention in Cincinnati in 1845. In 1848, Chase led the bulk of the Liberty Party into the new FREE SOIL PARTY coalition. With a handful of followers, Gerrit Smith opposed the Free Soil fusion. The antiabolitionist background of the Free Soil presidential nominee, Martin Van Buren, angered Smith, as did Chase's willingness to accept the constitutionality of slavery in existing states. Smith formed the short-lived Liberty League in a final attempt to maintain the moral principles of the Liberty Party.

BIBLIOGRAPHY

Gerteis, Louis S. *Morality and Utility in American Antislavery Reform.* Chapel Hill: University of North Carolina Press, 1987.

Sewell, Richard H. *Ballots for Freedom: Antislavery Politics in the United States, 1837–1860.* New York: Norton, 1980.

Louis S. Gerteis

See also **African Americans; Antislavery; New England Antislavery Society; Slavery.**

LIBERTY POLES. Soon after the appearance of William Hogarth's 1763 print of John Wilkes holding a liberty pole topped with a liberty cap, American colonists embraced the symbols to represent their own views of political liberty. Liberty poles with various banners were raised in numerous towns to protest the STAMP ACT of 1765 and to celebrate its repeal in 1766. In New York, British troops on at least four occasions destroyed the liberty pole erected by the SONS OF LIBERTY, leading to a minor skirmish in January 1770. Soon the liberty pole became the public symbol of American opposition to king and Parliament; suspected Tories were sometimes forced to kiss the liberty pole, and tax collectors were hung in effigy from them. In response to such events, British troops purposefully cut down Concord's liberty pole before the battle began there in April 1775.

The enduring political importance of the symbol was reflected in the first design for the Great Seal of the United States in 1776, depicting the goddess of liberty holding a liberty pole and cap, and it also was represented on U.S. coins from 1793 until 1891. The icon is still found today on the state flag of New York and the state seals of New Jersey, North Carolina, and Arkansas.

After the American Revolution, the raising of liberty poles continued as a form of protest against policies of the new national government. Liberty poles were raised by insurgents during the WHISKEY REBELLION and FRIES' REBELLION against federal taxes and by Republicans protesting the Alien and Sedition Acts of 1798. As early as 1792, depictions of the liberty pole and cap also became associated with the critique of slavery. During the nineteenth century, the term "liberty pole" came to mean practically any flagpole, whether permanently erected in a community or raised to support particular issues.

BIBLIOGRAPHY

Olson, Lester C. *Emblems of American Community in the Revolutionary Era: A Study in Rhetorical Iconography.* Washington, D.C.: Smithsonian Institution, 1991.

Schlesinger, Arthur M. "Liberty Tree: A Genealogy." *New England Quarterly* 25 (1952): 435–457.

Stephen A. Smith

See also **Flags; Liberty-Cap Cent; Seal of the United States.**

LIBERTY-CAP CENT, a U.S. coin, about an inch in diameter, struck by the U.S. mint at Philadelphia, 1793–1796. On the obverse is a bust of Liberty with a pole over the left shoulder surmounted by a round hat called a liberty cap. The image of the liberty cap was borrowed from France, where it had symbolized the egalitarian spirit in the late eighteenth century.

BIBLIOGRAPHY

Department of the Treasury, Bureau of the Mint. *Domestic and Foreign Coins Manufactured by Mints of the United States, 1793–1980.* Washington, D.C.: Department of the Treasury, Bureau of the Mint, 1981.

Taxay, Don. *The United States Mint and Coinage: An Illustrated History from 1776 to the Present.* New York: Arco Publishing, 1966.

Thomas L. Harris/A. R.

See also **Currency and Coinage; Liberty, Concept of; Liberty Poles; Mint, Federal; Treasury, Department of the.**

LIBRARIES. What distinguishes libraries in the United States from all others in the world is their emphasis on access. While libraries in many countries collect and preserve those books and other materials that document national heritage, libraries in the United Sates have focused on building collections to meet their patrons' needs. Consequently, American libraries are unrivaled in their ease of use. But the history of the library cannot be told in a single story because there are three distinct types in the United States: academic, special or corporate, and public. Academic libraries are subsets of educational institutions, and their histories reflect the principles and philosophies of their parent organizations. Similarly, the history of special libraries, established by individuals with a particular interest in certain topics, or of corporate libraries, created to support researchers in an organization, parallel the histories of their founders and funders. Only the public library has a history of its own.

University libraries were the first to appear in America (beginning with the Harvard College Library in 1638). The availability of books for the young men who attended universities was an indication that the new nation valued education and knowledge. The presence of books was valued much more than services, but books were scarce, and more than a few British travelers wrote back to their fellow countrymen that the collections found in the United States were not worthy of the name of a library. Since the librarians were most often faculty members who had the assignment of looking after the books, university libraries were poorly funded and unevenly administered.

The history of libraries in America is essentially the story of public libraries. Public libraries grew in countless communities as a response to a growing democracy, but it was not until the nineteenth century that libraries became ubiquitous.

The public library that developed in the United States in the late nineteenth century was a prime example of the democratic institutions created to assimilate and integrate the diverse ethnic and cultural groups that had come to constitute America. By 1900 there were approximately two thousand public libraries in the United States. Most were either social libraries, supported by individual philanthropists with a special interest in the community, or subscription libraries, supported by fees paid by those patrons who wished to use the circulating collections.

It is no coincidence that the public library came onto the scene at the same time that large corporations came into existence. Mercantile libraries, especially in the East, were founded by and run for the benefit of businesspeople, and they became a source of great pride for many cities during the nineteenth century. Most library historians who have studied these institutions argue that the libraries served, primarily, an educational purpose. The self-improvement campaign that was evident in the middle class during much of the nineteenth century was exemplified by the belief that no knowledge should be foreign to the merchant, and therefore that the reading of books, newspapers, and magazines touching on any subject was professionally useful. These mercantile libraries also became the locus of informational lectures on a wide range of topics.

The Enoch Pratt Free Library in Baltimore, established in 1886, exemplified the type of library that was becoming common in many cities. Successful individual businessmen—such as Enoch Pratt, who called the library a symbol of democracy—established libraries in an effort to repay the community. The wealthy and well educated men who served on Pratt's board of trustees proclaimed that his new library was to be an institution "where neither wealth nor poverty, high nor low position in society nor any other distinction entitles the individual to special privileges before the law." Even if the rules were applied universally, the library was more a symbol of personal success than an open institution for information. The library in Baltimore was built as a closed-stacks institution, which could be used only with permission. Letters of reference had to be submitted to the head librarian.

The modern public library—the type that emphasizes access to information—emerged first in the guise of the Boston Public Library, established in 1852 as the first tax-supported municipal library. Even though it is popular among library historians to refer to the "public library movement," states and communities were reluctant to tax themselves to provide free library services. In 1849 New Hampshire was the first state to pass enabling legislation that allowed communities to levy taxes for public libraries. It took another fifty years for thirty-seven additional states to pass similar legislation.

Andrew Carnegie's PHILANTHROPY did more than anything else to accelerate the development of public libraries in towns across the country. In 1881 Carnegie made the first of a series of gifts that would link his name permanently to public library buildings. Motivations for Carnegie's philanthropy are sharply debated. Some argue that Carnegie's own experience as a self-made man led him to the recognition that access to books can lead to education, and, ultimately, wealth. Other historians have argued that Carnegie used library development as a form of social control, seeing in the library a way to instill standards of behavior and an appreciation of culture. Whatever the reason, between 1881 and 1919 Andrew Carnegie made grants for the construction of 1,679 public libraries in the United States.

His particular form of philanthropy had enormous influence: Carnegie gave money to municipal governments to build library buildings. The town or city had to promise to buy books and provide library staff. The latter requirement resulted in the growth of library education programs in universities and the creation of a professional organization—the American Library Association—that would campaign for universal library service in the United States. The topic most forcefully debated by the new organization was the nature of library collections. Many of the early professionals who worked in public libraries recognized that most readers had the greatest interest in books and magazines that entertained. Yet, the leaders of the profession argued that the role of the librarian was to encourage the reading of "good" books. The founders of the Boston Public Library, Edward Everett and George Ticknor, held opposing views on the type of collections the public library should contain. Ticknor believed that collecting and circulating the "pleasant literature of the day" would result in the cultivation of higher tastes in reading among the library patrons. Everett, who ultimately lost the battle, argued that the library should be a reference (noncirculating) library for scholarly purposes. The compromise reached at the Boston Public Library— a compromise between the "best books" and "the best that people will read"—was copied by libraries across the country throughout the nineteenth and early twentieth centuries.

From the mid-nineteenth century until 1956, public libraries were guided by state legislation and professional principles. Reference services and children's services grew as more funding was applied to public libraries. In 1956 the federal government began to support the expansion of library services into rural communities. Federal funds were made available for professional training, construction of new library facilities, and research into library problems. By the 1970s, states began to think in terms of developing uniform library services that were administered by the main state library. Since then, technology-based networks have allowed states to offer more library services at less cost.

In the opening years of the twenty-first century, one aspect of the public library that is assuming more importance is its role as a place where members of a community can come together. Computer-based services are offered to all socioeconomic groups, but as home computers become more popular, the public library increasingly serves as a social safety net by ensuring access to information for those from lower economic levels, seeing this access as a right of all citizens. At the same time, many of the largest university libraries are deeply engaged in developing digital, or virtual, libraries, making resources for research and scholarship available through the INTERNET. To modern-day librarians, building collections of material that are available to anyone who has access to a computer is a natural extension of earlier services. It is uncertain how the availability of Web-based research materials will affect the concept of the library, but it does cause one to reflect on the extent to which the history of the library, until now, has been a history of buildings. As libraries move into a new era, there will be greater emphasis on information services available to scholars, researchers, and the general public.

BIBLIOGRAPHY

Carpenter, Kenneth E. *Readers and Libraries: Toward a History of Libraries and Culture in America*. Washington, D.C.: Library of Congress, 1996.

Shera, Jesse H. *Foundations of the Public Library: The Origins of the Public Library Movement in New England, 1629–1855*. Chicago: University of Chicago Press, 1949.

Van Slyck, Abigail. *Free to All: Carnegie Libraries and American Culture, 1890–1920*. Chicago: University of Chicago Press, 1995.

Deanna B. Marcum

See also **Harvard University.**

LIBRARIES, PRESIDENTIAL. Established to concentrate archival materials relating to individual U.S. presidents and to collect pertinent artifacts for research and public viewing, the presidential libraries have become significant archival repositories and museums. Most presidential libraries are federally and privately funded and are operated by the National Archives and Records Admin-

John Fitzgerald Kennedy Library and Museum. A 1995 photograph of the Boston building, designed by I. M. Pei and dedicated on 20 October 1979. © CORBIS

istration (NARA). Two are not part of NARA: the Rutherford B. Hayes Library and Museum in Fremont, Ohio, and the Richard Nixon Library and Birthplace in Yorba Linda, California. Established in 1916 the Hayes Library is the oldest presidential library and receives some funding from the state of Ohio. The Nixon Library, opened in 1992, operates largely as a museum because of legal disputes over the custody of Nixon's presidential records. Since passage of the 1974 Presidential Recordings and Materials Preservation Act, Nixon's presidential papers have been processed and housed by NARA, which began to open them to the public in 1987, under the name Nixon Presidential Materials Project.

In 1939 Congress authorized the Franklin D. Roosevelt Library in Hyde Park, New York, thus making it the first federally administered presidential library. The land and the initial building were privately donated. Roosevelt deeded his official records, personal papers, and many artifacts, which the government agreed to maintain, along with the library structure, for research and museum purposes. The Roosevelt Library opened to the public in 1941. Fund-raising for Harry S. Truman's library began before Truman left office in 1953. Efforts also soon began to establish a library for the new president, Dwight D. Eisenhower. The National Archives consequently sought legislation to regularize the creation of presidential libraries. In 1955 Congress passed the Presidential Libraries Act, allowing the government to accept historical materials, donated land, and buildings for the establishment of presidential libraries and to maintain and operate them. The Truman Library opened in Independence, Missouri, in 1957, and the Eisenhower Library in Abilene, Kansas, in 1962. Similar institutions have been created in the names of Herbert Hoover in West Branch, Iowa; John F. Kennedy in Boston; Lyndon B. Johnson in Austin, Texas; Gerald R. Ford in Ann Arbor and Grand Rapids, Michigan; Jimmy Carter in Atlanta, Georgia; Ronald Reagan in Simi Valley, California; and George Bush in College Station, Texas. William Clinton's library will be in Little Rock, Arkansas. Since passage of the 1978 Presidential Records Act, no president can claim private ownership of his papers, but he can restrict access to them for up to twelve years, after which they can be subject to release under the FREEDOM OF INFORMATION ACT.

In 1992 the federal presidential libraries had in their custody 218 million pages of records and papers and 263,000 artifacts. That year the libraries had 1,534,281 visitors and, with the Nixon records in federal custody, attracted 13,409 daily research visits and 55,906 written and oral inquiries. The availability of such holdings has increased the quantity and quality of research connected with recent presidents and served as a valuable instrument of public education. Private support organizations affiliated with the libraries have also financed conferences, research grants, publications, lectures, and other program aspects of the presidential libraries.

BIBLIOGRAPHY

McCoy, Donald R. *The National Archives: America's Ministry of Documents, 1934–1968.* Chapel Hill: University of North Carolina Press, 1978.

Schick, Frank L., Renee Schick, and Mark Carroll. *Records of the Presidency: Presidential Papers and Libraries from Washington to Reagan.* Phoenix, Ariz.: Oryx Press, 1989.

U.S. National Archives and Records Administration. *Annual Report for the Year Ended September 30, 1992.* Washington, D.C.: National Archives and Records Administration, 1993.

Veit, Fritz. *Presidential Libraries and Collections.* New York: Greenwood, 1987.

Donald R. McCoy/F. H.

See also **Archives; Federal Agencies; Libraries; Watergate.**

LIBRARY OF CONGRESS. The Library of Congress is the largest repository of human knowledge and creativity in the world. Located primarily in three buildings on Capitol Hill in Washington, D.C., its collections have grown from the original 740 volumes and 3 maps acquired from a London dealer in 1801 to over 120 million items. Its mission is to make those collections available to the Congress of the United States, to the offices of the Federal Government, and to the American people and researchers from around the world.

History and Evolution of the Collections

The Library was created by two acts of Congress. The first, on 24 April 1800, in appropriating funds to relocate the national government from Philadelphia to the District of Columbia, allocated $5,000 for the purchase of books and provided for the "fitting up of a suitable apartment for containing them." The second, on 26 January 1802, provided that the president should appoint a Librarian of Congress, overseen by a Congressional joint committee. The same act granted borrowing privileges to the president and vice president.

The early collection appears to have stretched beyond "the purpose of reference" specified by President Jefferson in his recommendation to the first Librarian, John James Beckley. The initial purchase was limited to books on law, political science, economics, and history, but gifts from members of Congress and others seem to have added materials in geography, natural history, medicine, and literature. By 1812 the Library possessed three thousand volumes. Soon thereafter dramatic events forever altered the Library. The British occupied Washington, D.C., in August 1814 and burned the Capitol, destroying much of the Library's collection. After some debate, Congress agreed to replace the loss by purchasing the personal library of Thomas Jefferson, 6,487 volumes, at the cost of $23,950. The resulting Library of Congress was both twice the size of its predecessor and contained a rich selection of philosophy, classical literature, and scientific material, probably the finest collection in the country. The Library also acquired President Jefferson's method of classification, which would continue to be applied to the collections until the close of the nineteenth century.

The collections grew slowly before the Civil War. Access was broadened to include cabinet members, and in 1832, a separate law collection was created and access was given to justices of the Supreme Court. But there were losses, too. Two-thirds of the collection was destroyed by fire on Christmas Eve, 1851. Later in that decade, Congress took away the Library's role in distributing public documents, giving it to the Bureau of the Interior, and at the same time transferred the role of exchanging books with foreign institutions from the Library to the Department of State. In 1859 registration of copyrights was moved to the Patent Office, depriving the Library of the depository function that had done much to build its collections.

Significant growth in the Library began only with the appointment of Ainsworth Rand Spofford as Librarian, 1865–1897. The copyright depository program returned that same year, and the Smithsonian Institution's library was purchased the next. Spofford organized an international document exchange program and also took in several important acquisitions and gifts. The Library's 80,000 volumes of 1870 became 840,000 volumes by 1897, 40 percent of that growth coming from the copyright depository. The growth necessitated the Library's move out of the Capitol in 1897 into its new building, now called the Thomas Jefferson Building. In that same year, Congress enacted a new organization for the Library, giving the Librarian full control over the institution and subjecting his appointment to Senatorial approval.

Spofford's immediate successors, John Russell Young, 1897–1899, and Herbert Putnam, 1899–1939, continued to build the collections and undertook innovations appropriate to the Library's growing national significance. Young inaugurated national service to the blind and physically disabled. His catalogers, Charles Martel and J. C. M. Hanson, also undertook a new classification scheme, finally abandoning Jefferson's method. Putnam, the first professionally trained Librarian, initiated interlibrary loan service and began sale and distribution of the Library's printed catalog cards. He greatly expanded the Library's international exchange programs and brought in major collections of Hebrew, Indic, Chinese, and Japanese materials. In 1930 he convinced Congress to allocate $1.5 million to acquire the Vollbehr Collection of incunabula, bringing the Library one of three existing perfect vellum copies of the Gutenberg Bible. In 1914, influenced by Progressive-Era developments in state libraries, Putnam created the Legislative Reference, now the Congressional Research Service, to serve the specific reference needs of the Congress.

In recognition of the Library's growing contribution to the national culture, Congress created the Library of Congress Trust Fund Board in 1925, providing a mechanism for the receipt of private money gifts. Finally, as he was leaving office, Putnam bequeathed to the Library its second building. Opened in 1939 as the Annex, it is now named for President John Adams.

The Library entered a new era under the administrations of Archibald MacLeish (1939–1944), Luther Evans (1945–1953), and L. Quincy Mumford (1954–1974). As the United States became an international superpower, the Library dramatically increased its own acquisition of international documents and publications and undertook structures to assist other libraries across the country in building their international resources. Evans established a Library mission in Europe to acquire materials, inaugurated a program of blanket orders with foreign dealers around the globe, and expanded the Library's exchange program for foreign government documents. Mumford oversaw the implementation of Public Law 480, permitting the Library to use U.S.–owned foreign currency to purchase foreign publications for its own and other American library collections. In 1961 the Library established its first overseas acquisition centers in New Delhi and Cairo. Mumford also enjoyed two successes that would bear fruit under his successors: approval to build a third building, the James Madison Memorial, which opened in 1980; and establishment of the Machine Readable Cataloging (MARC) standard, which would provide a foundation for the computer catalogs and national databases of the next generation.

Library of Congress. *The Evolution of Civilization* (1895–1896), a mural by Edwin H. Blashfield in the rotunda dome, includes this section of allegorical figures representing Science (America), Written Records (Egypt), and Religion (Judea). LIBRARY OF CONGRESS

With the appointment of Daniel J. Boorstin as Librarian (1975–1987) the Library's focus returned to the national sphere, building stronger ties to Congress and expanding its relationship with the scholarly and business communities. Boorstin held luncheons, lectures, and concerts. He created a Council of Scholars to advise the Librarian, and he inaugurated the Center for the Book, a privately funded forum for discussion of the book's place in national culture. These initiatives were continued and expanded under Librarian James H. Billington (1987–). To increase private funding and enhance the Library's national visibility, Billington created the James Madison Council, an advisory board of business, philanthropic, and cultural leaders. He established an Education Office and began the use of technology to bring the Library out into the nation, digitizing the Library's resources and delivering them over the Internet.

Funding

The Library is an agency of Congress. Its primary funding derives from the annual Legislative Branch Appropriations Act, from which its various operations received more than $300 million for fiscal year 2002. But private funds represent an increasing share of the budget. The $60 million launch of the National Digital Library, for instance, received $15 million in Congressional support, the remaining $45 million raised from private donors. Annual gifts averaged $1 million in 1987, when the Library's Development Office was created. By 1997 they were exceeding $14 million.

The Collections and Their Acquisition

The Library's holdings stretch across every medium and historical age. More than 120 million items occupy approximately 530 miles of shelves. The collections include more than 18 million books, 2.5 million recordings, 12 million photographs, 4.5 million maps, 54 million manuscripts, a half-million motion pictures, and over 5,600 incunabula. Outside the fields of agriculture and medicine, where it defers to the national libraries in those fields, its stated mission is to build "a comprehensive record of American history and creativity" and "a universal collection of human knowledge." While its greatest strengths lie in American history, politics, and literature, it also possesses extraordinary collections in the history of science, the publications of learned societies around the world, and bibliography in virtually every subject. Two-thirds of its books are in foreign languages. Its Chinese, Russian, Japanese, Korean, and Polish collections are the largest outside those countries, and its Arabic holdings are the largest outside of Egypt.

The Library's collections are built from a complex network of sources. More than 22,000 items arrive each day. About 10,000 are retained for the permanent collections. Gifts, an important component of the Library's growth from the beginning, remain significant. The copyright depository program is the largest single feature of the acquisitions program. The depository does not generate a national collection of record, as Library selectors are not bound to retain all copyrighted items received. Current practice retains approximately two-thirds of copyright receipts. There are over 15,000 agreements with foreign governments and research institutions, and the library also receives publications from the governments of all fifty states and from a wide range of municipal and other government units. Overseas offices acquire materials from over sixty countries for the Library and for other American libraries through the Cooperative Acquisition Program. Approval plans, blanket and standing orders with foreign vendors complete the collection.

Place in National Culture and Education

The Library has been at the center of national library culture at least since 1901, when it began distributing its catalog cards to libraries around the nation. Recent changes in cataloging practices have reduced the Library's near-complete domination of cataloging, but its role in setting national bibliographic standards remains pivotal. The Library has also played a central role in the development of standards for the presentation and exchange of digital information.

Yet, however expansive the vision of Librarians like Spofford, Putnam, MacLeish, and Mumford, the Library was the realm of researchers fortunate enough to visit its Washington home and long stood remote from the broader national culture. That situation changed dramatically in the last decades of the twentieth century. From Daniel Boorstin's creation of the Center for the Book in 1977 to his appointment of Robert Penn Warren as the nation's first poet laureate in 1986, the Library took a place at the center of national intellectual life. That role has expanded dramatically under Billington with the emergence of the Internet as a vehicle for making the Library's collections accessible to Americans in their homes and offices. Thomas, the Library's legislative information service, provides ready access to Congressional documents. The American Memory exhibit has made many of the Library's historical documents, photographs, and sound and video collections available to every citizen with computer access. America's Story is a web site designed specifically for young people, putting the Library's resources in a form even young children can enjoy. Together these resources have revolutionized the Library and its relationship with the nation.

BIBLIOGRAPHY

Cole, John Y. *Jefferson's Legacy: A Brief History of the Library of Congress.* Washington: Library of Congress, 1993. Also available on the Library's web site, at: http://www.loc.gov/loc/legacy/.

Cole, John Y., ed. *The Library of Congress in Perspective: A Volume Based on the Reports of the 1976 Librarian's Task Force and Advisory Groups.* New York: R.R. Bowker, 1978.

Conaway, James. *America's Library: The Story of the Library of Congress, 1800–2000.* New Haven, Conn.: Yale University Press, 2000.

Goodrum, Charles A., and Helen W. Dalrymple. *The Library of Congress.* Boulder: Westview, 1982.

Highsmith, Carol M., and Ted Landphair. *The Library of Congress: America's Memory.* Golden, Colo.: Fulcrum, 1994.

Mearns, David C. *The Story Up to Now: The Library of Congress, 1800–1946.* Washington, D.C.: Library of Congress, 1947.

U.S. Library of Congress. *Annual Report of the Librarian.* Washington, D.C.: Library of Congress, 1886– .

Michael E. Stoller

See also **Libraries.**

LICENSE CASES (*Thurlow v. Massachusetts, Fletcher v. Rhode Island, Peirce v. New Hampshire*), 5 How. (46 U.S.) 504 (1847). In six opinions, with no majority, the United States Supreme Court upheld state statutes regulating the sale of alcoholic beverages that had been brought in from other states. The statutes were quadruply controversial: they involved temperance and prohibition, they impinged on interstate commerce, they interfered with property rights, and they were surrogates for the states' power to control enslaved persons and abolitionist propaganda. All eight sitting justices sustained the statutes on the basis of the states' police powers, but they disagreed on the problems of conflict between Congress's dormant power to regulate interstate commerce and concurrent state regulatory authority.

BIBLIOGRAPHY

Swisher, Carl B. *The Taney Period, 1836–1864.* New York: Macmillan, 1974.

William M. Wiecek

See also **Interstate Commerce Laws.**

LICENSES TO TRADE in colonial times regulated the "common callings," such as innkeeping, carrying goods and persons, or operating a bridge. By the nineteenth century the scope of licenses to trade extended to a wider variety of occupations and included professions such as medicine and architecture. The growing concern after the Civil War over regulating businesses led many states to rely on licenses to trade for such diverse industries as ice manufacture and the operation of grain elevators. As late as the early 1930s, the U.S. Supreme Court used the due process clause of the Constitution to bar much state regulation, including restrictive licenses to trade. However, it retreated in the 1930s, and by the 1970s state licensing affected wide areas of the economy without serious constitutional doubts.

The growth of huge corporations weakened the effectiveness of state licensing of trade, however, making federal licensing of trade increasingly important, particularly in areas such as banking, electric power, gas distribution, telecommunications, and various forms of inter-

state transport. At the municipal level, licenses have tended to reflect local concerns with sanitation, orderly trade, and protecting local tradespeople from outside competition, rather than with generating revenue. In many states, local licensing of trade is frequently subject to state laws and increasing state supervision.

BIBLIOGRAPHY

Frese, Joseph R., S. J. Judd, and Jacob Judd, eds. *Business and Government.* Tarrytown, N.Y.: Sleepy Hollow Press and Rockefeller Archive Center, 1985.

Goldin, Claudia, and Gary D. Libecap, eds. *The Regulated Economy: A Historical Approach to Political Economy.* Chicago: University of Chicago Press, 1994.

William Tucker Dean
Christopher Wells

See also **Elevators, Grain; Government Regulation of Business; Public Utilities.**

LIFE EXPECTANCY at birth is defined as the average number of years that a newborn would live under mortality conditions prevailing at that time. For example, life expectancy for females born in the United States in 1900 was forty-nine years. This means that if mortality conditions existing in 1900 did not change, baby girls born at that time would have lived, on average, until they were forty-nine. In addition to life expectancy at birth, one can also examine life expectancy at other ages. For example, life expectancy at age sixty (which was fifteen years for women in 1900) is the average number of years of life remaining for someone who survives to age sixty, under mortality conditions prevailing at that time. A life table provides information on life expectancy at various ages. When correctly understood, life expectancy provides a useful summary measure of mortality conditions at a particular time in history.

Although life expectancy is a good starting point for discussing mortality patterns, it is important to note two significant limitations of this measure. First, mortality conditions often change over time, so this measure may not reflect the actual experience of a birth cohort. (A birth cohort consists of all individuals born in a particular time period.) To illustrate this point, females born in the United States in 1900 actually lived for an average of fifty-eight years. The discrepancy between life expectancy in 1900 and the average years lived by those born in 1900 occurred because mortality conditions improved as this cohort aged over the twentieth century. The second limitation of life expectancy as a mortality index is its failure to reveal anything about the distribution of deaths across ages. Relatively few of the girls born in 1900 actually died around age forty-nine; 20 percent died before reaching age ten, and over fifty percent were still alive at age seventy. In other words, the average age at death does not mean that this was the typical experience of individuals. Given the limited information contained in the life expec-

103

tancy statistic, a satisfying discussion of changing mortality experiences in American history must use additional information on the timing and patterning of deaths.

To calculate the life expectancy for a population, one would ideally have a complete registration of deaths by age and a complete enumeration of the population by age. With these data, it is a straightforward exercise to calculate age-specific death rates and to construct the life table. In the United States, mortality and population data of good quality are available for most of the twentieth century, so we can report with confidence life expectancy patterns over this period. Because of data limitations, there is less certainty about mortality conditions in earlier American history. However, a number of careful and creative studies of the existing death records for some communities (or other populations) provide enough information to justify a discussion of changing mortality conditions from the colonial era to the present.

Colonial America

The first life table for an American population was published by Edward Wigglesworth in 1793, and was based on mortality data from Massachusetts, Maine, and New Hampshire in 1789. Until the 1960s, this life table, which reported an expectation of life of about thirty-five years for New England, was the primary source of information on the level of mortality in America prior to the nineteenth century. Since the 1960s, however, quantitative historians have analyzed a variety of mortality records from various sources, providing a more comprehensive and varied picture of mortality conditions in the colonial era.

These historical studies have presented conflicting evidence regarding the trend in life expectancy between the founding of the colonies and the Revolutionary War (1775–1783)—some reported a significant decline over time, while others argued that life expectancy was increasing. One explanation for the different findings is that there were large fluctuations in death rates from year to year (as epidemics broke out and then rescinded) and significant variations across communities. Based on the most reliable data, it seems likely that overall conditions were not much different around 1800 than they were around 1700. After considerable work to analyze data from various sources, the Wigglesworth estimate of life expectancy around thirty-five years in New England during the colonial period appears reasonable. Although this is an extraordinarily low life expectancy by contemporary standards, it reflects a higher survival rate than the population of England enjoyed at that time. Life expectancy in the Southern and Mid-Atlantic colonies, where severe and frequent epidemics of smallpox, malaria, and yellow fever occurred throughout the eighteenth century, was significantly lower than in New England.

There are two primary reasons life expectancy was so low in colonial America. First, the average years lived reflects the impact of many babies dying in infancy or childhood. Studies from various communities found that between 10 and 30 percent of newborns died in the first year of life (now only seven out of 1,000 die before age one). Those who survived the perilous early years of life and reached age twenty could expect, on average, to live another forty years. The second factor was that, lacking public health and medical knowledge of how to prevent or treat infectious diseases, the population was extremely vulnerable to both endemic diseases (malaria, dysentery and diarrhea, tuberculosis) and epidemics (smallpox, diphtheria, yellow fever). An indication of the deadly potential of epidemics is seen in Boston in 1721, when 10 percent of the population died in one year from a smallpox outbreak, and in New Hampton Falls, New Hampshire, in 1735, when one-sixth of the population died from a diphtheria epidemic. Despite the dramatic effects of epidemics, it was the infectious endemic diseases that killed most people in colonial America.

Nineteenth Century

Life expectancy increased significantly over the nineteenth century, from about thirty-five years in 1800 to forty-seven years in 1900. However, this increase was not uniform throughout the century. In fact, death rates may have increased during the first several decades, and by midcentury, life expectancy was not much higher than it had been at the beginning of the century. After the Civil War (1861–1865) there was a sustained increase in life expectancy, and this upward trend would continue throughout the twentieth century.

Two conflicting forces were influencing mortality patterns prior to the Civil War. On one hand, per capita income was increasing, a trend that is generally associated with increasing life expectancy. On the other hand, the proportion of the population living in urban areas was also increasing, and death rates were higher in urban than in rural environments. An examination of data from 1890, for example, found death rates 27 percent higher in urban areas than in rural areas. This excess mortality in urban areas was common in almost all societies before the twentieth century, and is explained by the greater exposure to germs as population density increased. Studies of nineteenth century death rates in such cities as New York, Philadelphia, Baltimore, Boston, and New Orleans document the high risks that urban residents had of contracting such infectious diseases as tuberculosis, pneumonia, cholera, typhoid, and scarlet fever. It was not until after the 1870s that the health picture in American cities improved and life expectancy for the entire population began its steady ascent.

It is clear that increasing life expectancy in the last third of the nineteenth century was due to decreasing death rates from infectious diseases. But why did death rates decline? Medical historians have given considerable attention to three possible explanations: improving medical practices, advances in public health, and improved diet, housing, and personal hygiene. Most agree that medicine had little to do with the decline in infectious diseases in the nineteenth century (although it later played an important role when penicillin and other antibiotic drugs became widely used after 1940). Physicians in the nineteenth century had few specific remedies for disease, and some of their practices (bleeding and purging their patients) were actually harmful. Some evidence suggests that diet and personal hygiene improved in the late nineteenth century, and these changes may account for some decline in diseases. The greatest credit for improving life expectancy, however, must go to intentional public health efforts. With growing acceptance of the germ theory, organized efforts were made to improve sanitary conditions in the large cities. The construction of municipal water and sewer systems provided protection against common sources of infection. Other important developments included cleaning streets, more attention to removal of garbage, draining stagnant pools of water, quarantining sick people, and regulating foodstuffs (especially the milk supply).

Twentieth Century

The gain in life expectancy at birth over the twentieth century, from forty-seven to seventy-seven years, far exceeded the increase that occurred from the beginning of human civilization up to 1900. This extraordinary change reflects profound changes both in the timing of deaths and the causes of deaths. In 1900, 20 percent of newborns died before reaching age five—in 1999, fewer than 20 percent died before age sixty-five. In 1900, the annual crude death rate from infectious diseases was 800 per 100,000—in 1980 it was thirty-six per 100,000 (but it crept back up to sixty-three per 100,000 by 1995, because of the impact of AIDS). At the beginning of the twentieth century the time of death was unpredictable and most deaths occurred quickly. By the end of the century, deaths were heavily concentrated in old age (past age seventy), and the dying process was often drawn out over months.

In 1999, the Centers for Disease Control ran a series in its publication *Morbidity and Mortality Weekly Report* to highlight some of the great public health accomplishments of the twentieth century. Among the most important accomplishments featured in this series that contributed to the dramatic increase in life expectancy were the following:

Vaccinations. Vaccination campaigns in the United States have virtually eliminated diseases that were once common, including diphtheria, tetanus, poliomyelitis, smallpox, measles, mumps, and rubella.

Control of infectious diseases. Public health efforts led to the establishment of state and local health departments that contributed to improving the environment (clean drinking water, sewage disposal, food safety, garbage disposal, mosquito-control programs). These efforts, as well as educational programs, decreased exposure to micro-

organisms that cause many serious diseases (for example, cholera, typhoid, and tuberculosis).

Healthier mothers and babies. Deaths to mothers and infants were reduced by better hygiene and nutrition, access to prenatal care, availability of antibiotics, and increases in family planning programs. Over the century, infant death rates decreased by 90 percent and maternal mortality rates decreased by 99 percent.

Safer workplaces. Fatal occupational injuries decreased 40 percent after 1980, as new regulations greatly improved safety in the mining, manufacturing, construction, and transportation industries.

Motor vehicle safety. Important changes affecting vehicle fatalities include both engineering efforts to make highways and vehicles safer and public campaigns to change such personal behaviors as use of seat belts, use of child safety seats, and driving while drunk. The number of deaths per million vehicle miles traveled was 90 percent lower in 1997 than in 1925.

Recognition of tobacco use as a health hazard. Antismoking campaigns since the 1964 Surgeon General's report have reduced the proportion of smokers in the population and consequently prevented millions of smoking-related deaths.

Decline in deaths from coronary heart disease and stroke. Educational programs have informed the public of how to reduce risk of heart disease through smoking cessation, diet, exercise, and blood pressure control. In addition, access to early detection, emergency services, and better treatment has contributed to the 51 percent decrease since 1972 in the death rate from coronary heart disease.

Despite the advances in life expectancy between 1900 and the present, several striking differences in longevity within the population have persisted. Researchers have given a lot of attention to three differentials in life expectancy—sex, race, and social class. The female advantage over males in life expectancy increased from 2.0 years in 1900 to 7.8 years in 1975. Most of this increasing gap is explained by the shift in cause of death from infectious diseases (for which females have no survival advantage over males) to degenerative diseases (where the female advantage is large). Also, the decline in deaths associated with pregnancy and childbearing contributed to the more rapid increase in life expectancy of females. After 1975, the gender gap in life expectancy decreased, and by 2000 it was down to 5.4 years. The primary explanation for the narrowing gap in the last decades of the twentieth century is that female cigarette smoking increased rapidly after mid-century and became increasingly similar to the male pattern. In other words, females lost some of the health advantage over males that they had when they smoked less.

The racial gap in life expectancy was huge in 1900—white Americans outlived African Americans by an average of 14.6 years. This gap declined to 6.8 years by 1960 (when the civil rights movement was beginning), but declined only slightly over the rest of the century (in 2000 the racial gap was still 5.6 years). A particularly telling indicator of racial inequality is the infant mortality rate, which continues to be more than twice as large for African Americans as for white Americans (13.9 per 1,000 versus 6.0 per 1,000 in 1998). Much of the racial disparity is explained by the persistent socioeconomic disadvantage of African Americans (lower education and lower income). Social resources are related to individual health behavior (diet, exercise, health care), and to the environment within which individuals live (neighborhood, occupation). After adjusting for family income and education, African Americans still experience some excess deaths compared to white Americans. A possible cause of this residual difference may be racial discrimination that causes stress and limits access to health care.

Active Life Expectancy

The marked declines in death rates that characterized the first half of the twentieth century appeared to end around the early 1950s, and life expectancy increased by only a few months between 1954 and 1968. A number of experts concluded that we should not expect further increases in life expectancy. They reasoned that by this time a majority of deaths were occurring in old age due to degenerative diseases, and there was no historical evidence that progress could be made in reducing cardiovascular diseases and cancer. But this prediction was wrong, and life expectancy continued its upward climb after 1970. As death rates for older people began to fall, a new concern was expressed. Were the years being added to life "quality years," or were people living longer with serious functional limitations? Would we experience an increasingly frail older population?

The concern over quality of life in old age led demographers to develop a new measure, active life expectancy. Using data on age-specific disability rates, it is possible to separate the average number of years of life remaining into two categories—active years (disability-free years) and inactive years (chronic disability years). Using data since 1970, researchers have tried to determine whether gains in life expectancy have been gains in active life, gains in inactive life, or gains in both. There is some uncertainty about the 1970s, but since 1980 most of the gains have been in active life. Age-specific disability rates have been declining, so the percentage of years lived that is in good health is increasing. Two factors have contributed to increasing active-life expectancy. First, over time the educational level of the older population has risen, and disability rates are lower among more highly educated people. Second, medical advances (for example, cataract surgery, joint replacement) have reduced the disabling effect of some diseases. Thus, the good news is that at the end of the twentieth century, individuals were living both longer and healthier lives than ever before in history.

BIBLIOGRAPHY

CDC. "Ten Great Public Health Achievements—United States, 1900–1999." *Morbidity and Mortality Weekly Report* 48 (1999): 241–243.

Crimmins, Eileen M., Yasuhiko Saito, and Dominique Ingegneri. "Trends in Disability-Free Life Expectancy in the United States, 1970–90." *Population and Development Review* 23 (1997): 555–572.

Hacker, David J. "Trends and Determinants of Adult Mortality in Early New England." *Social Science History* 21 (1997): 481–519.

Kunitz, Stephen J. "Mortality Change in America, 1620–1929." *Human Biology* 56 (1984): 559–582.

Leavitt, Judith Walzer, and Ronald L. Numbers, eds. *Sickness and Health in America: Readings in the History of Medicine and Public Health*. 3d ed. Madison: University of Wisconsin Press, 1997.

Vinovskis, Maris A. "The 1789 Life Table of Edward Wigglesworth." *Journal of Economic History* 31 (1971): 570–590.

Peter Uhlenberg

LIFE STAGES. *See* **Adolescence; Childhood; Old Age.**

LIFESAVING SERVICE. In 1789 the Massachusetts Humane Society began erecting huts on dangerous portions of that state's coast for the shelter of persons escaped from shipwrecks. The practice was made more permanent in 1807 when the society established the first lifesaving station in America in the area of Boston Bay. Thirty years later, Congress authorized the president to employ ships to cruise along the shores and render aid to distressed navigators, and in 1870–1871, Congress authorized the organization of a government lifesaving service. On 28 January 1915 this service merged with the Revenue Cutter Service to form the U.S. Coast Guard.

BIBLIOGRAPHY

Noble, Dennis L. *That Others Might Live: The U.S. Life-Saving Service, 1878–1915*. Annapolis, Md.: Naval Institute Press, 1994.

Alvin F. Harlow / F. B.

See also **Coast Guard, U.S.; Lighthouse Board; Navy, United States; River and Harbor Improvements.**

LIGHTHOUSE BOARD. Navigational aids were nominally under federal control beginning in 1789, but they did not come under organized government control until the creation of the Lighthouse Board in 1851. Two naval officers, two army engineers, and two civilians made up the board, which operated through committees supervising particular aspects of its work. In 1910 the board was supplanted by the Bureau of Lighthouses within the Department of Commerce. Congress limited military control over the bureau and civilians oversaw most light-

Gaslights. A street scene in 1911, as street lighting was shifting from gas to electricity. LIBRARY OF CONGRESS

houses. In 1939 the bureau became part of the U.S. Coast Guard, which continues to oversee lighthouses and other maritime navigational aids.

BIBLIOGRAPHY

Noble, Dennis L. *Lighthouses and Keepers: The U.S. Lighthouse Service and Its Legacy.* Annapolis, Md.: Naval Institute Press, 1997.

Nathan Reingold / F. B.

See also **Coast Guard, U. S.; Lifesaving Service; Navy, United States; River and Harbor Improvements.**

LIGHTING in America prior to about 1815 was provided by a variety of devices, including lamps fueled by oil derived from animal or vegetable sources, tallow or bayberry CANDLES, and pinewood torches. The late eighteenth-century chemical revolution associated with Antoine Lavoisier included a theory of oxidation that soon stimulated dramatic improvements in both lamp design and candle composition. These included a lamp with a tubular wick and shaped glass chimney invented in the early 1780s by Aimé Argand, a student of Lavoisier, and introduced into the United States during the administration of George Washington. The Argand lamp was approximately ten times as efficient as previous oil lamps and was widely used in lighthouses, public buildings, and

homes of the more affluent citizens. European chemists also isolated stearine, which was used in "snuffless candles," so called because they had self-consuming wicks. The candles became available during the 1820s and were produced on a mass scale in candle factories.

After European scientists discovered an efficient means of producing inflammable gas from coal, a new era of lighting began during the first decade of the nineteenth century. Baltimore became the first American city to employ gas streetlights in 1816, but the gaslight industry did not enter its rapid-growth phase until after 1850. Capital investment increased from less than $7 million in 1850 to approximately $150 million in 1880. The central generating station and distribution system that became standard in the gaslight industry served as a model for the electric light industry, which emerged during the last two decades of the century. Improvements such as the Welsbach mantle kept gas lighting competitive until World War I. Rural residents continued to rely on candles or oil lamps throughout most of the nineteenth century because coal gas could not be economically distributed in areas of low population density. The discovery of petroleum in Pennsylvania in 1859 soon led to the development of the simple and comparatively safe kerosene lamp, which continued as the most popular domestic light source in isolated areas in the United States until the mid-twentieth century.

Electric Lamps. Miners began switching in the early twentieth century to lamps such as these, which were brighter and safer than earlier flame safety lamps. LIBRARY OF CONGRESS

Certain deficiencies of the gaslight, such as imperfect combustion and the danger of fire or explosion, made it seem vulnerable to such late nineteenth-century electric inventors as Thomas A. Edison. Two competing systems of electric lighting developed rapidly after the invention of large self-excited electric generators capable of producing great quantities of inexpensive electrical energy. The American engineer-entrepreneur Charles F. Brush developed an effective street-lighting system using electric arc lamps beginning in 1876. One of Brush's most important inventions was a device that prevented an entire series circuit of arc lamps from being disabled by the failure of a single lamp. Brush installed the first commercial central arc-light stations in 1879. Because of the early arc light's high intensity, it was primarily useful in street lighting or in large enclosures such as train stations.

Edison became the pioneer innovator of the incandescent-lighting industry, which successfully displaced the arc-light industry. Beginning in 1878, Edison intensively studied the gaslight industry and determined that he could develop an electric system that would provide equivalent illumination without some of the defects and at a competitive cost. His reputation attracted the finan-

cial backing needed to support research and development. Crucial to his success was the development of an efficient and long-lived high-resistance lamp, a lamp that would allow for the same necessary subdivision of light that had been achieved in gas lighting but not in arc lighting. Edison and his assistants at his Menlo Park, New Jersey, laboratory solved this problem by means of a carbon filament lamp in 1879.

Edison also proved skillful as a marketer. By 1882 his incandescent lamp system was in use on a commercial scale at the Pearl Street (New York City) generating station. All the components—not only the lamp but also the generator, distribution system, fuses, and meters—needed for an effective light-and-power system were in place.

The thirty-year period after 1880 was a time of intense market competition between the gaslight, arc light, and incandescent light industries and between the direct-current distribution system of Edison and the alternating-current system introduced by George Westinghouse. Each of the competing lighting systems made significant improvements during this period, but incandescent lighting with alternating-current distribution ultimately emerged as the leader. The General Electric Company, organized in 1892 by a consolidation of the Edison Company and the Thomson-Houston Company, became the dominant lamp manufacturer, followed by Westinghouse.

The formation of the General Electric Research Laboratory under Willis R. Whitney in 1900 proved to be an important event in the history of electric lighting. In this laboratory in 1910, William D. Coolidge invented a process for making ductile tungsten wire. The more durable and efficient tungsten filaments quickly supplanted the carbon filament lamp. Irving Langmuir, also a General Electric scientist, completed development of a gas-filled tungsten lamp in 1912. This lamp, which was less susceptible to blackening of the bulb than the older high-vacuum lamp, became available commercially in 1913 and was the last major improvement in the design of incandescent lamps.

Development of a new type of electric light began at General Electric in 1935. This was the low-voltage fluorescent lamp, which reached the market in 1938. The fluorescent lamp had several advantages over the incandescent lamp, including higher efficiency—early fluorescent bulbs produced more than twice as much light per watt as incandescent bulbs—and a larger surface area, which provided a more uniform source of illumination with less glare. It also required special fixtures and auxiliary elements. This lamp came into wide usage, especially in war factories during World War II, and then spread quickly into office buildings, schools, and stores. Homes proved much more reluctant to adopt fluorescent lighting, however, in part due to the more complicated fixtures they required and in part because incandescent bulbs produced much warmer colors. Following the energy crisis that began in 1973, designers made a number of breakthroughs that boosted the efficiency of fluorescent lamps, primarily by improving the "ballasts," which regulated the flow of energy through the bulb, and by developing new, even more efficient, compact fluorescent bulbs. Many businesses also used dimmers, timers, and motion detectors to reduce energy costs.

The energy crisis beginning in 1973 little affected the lighting habits of American homeowners, unlike its effects on American business. (Household energy costs account for only about 6 percent of the lighting energy used in the United States as compared to the roughly 50 percent used by commercial establishments.) Although some installed dimmers and timers and others paid closer attention to turning off unused lights, home consumption of energy for lighting remained relatively stable. Indeed, though energy-efficient lamps became increasingly available in the 1980s and 1990s, their gains were offset by new uses for lighting, particularly with the growth of outdoor lighting in the 1990s.

BIBLIOGRAPHY

Bright, Arthur A. *The Electric-Lamp Industry: Technological Change and Economic Development from 1800 to 1947.* New York: Macmillan, 1949; New York: Arnco Press, 1972.

Nye, David E. *Electrifying America: Social Meanings of a New Technology, 1880–1940.* Cambridge, Mass.: MIT Press, 1990.

Tobey, Ronald C. *Technology as Freedom: The New Deal and the Electrical Modernization of the American Home.* Berkeley: University of California Press, 1996.

James E. Brittain / A. R; C. W.

See also **Electric Power and Light Industry; Electrification, Household; Kerosine Oil; Lamp, Incandescent; Natural Gas Industry.**

LINCOLN HIGHWAY. The idea of a coast-to-coast highway originated with Carl G. Fisher of Indianapolis in 1912, when the AUTOMOBILE was in comparative infancy and when there was no system of good roads covering even one state. In September 1912, Fisher laid the proposition before the leaders of the automobile industry, and, giving $1,000 himself, obtained pledges of more than $4 million for construction. To add a patriotic touch, he gave the name "Lincoln" to the proposed road in 1913, and the Lincoln Highway Association came into existence to further the project. States and individuals the country over made contributions, and cement manufacturers donated material for "demonstration miles." By an act of 1921, the federal government increased its aid to states in road building, which greatly helped this project. From Jersey City, the route chosen passed through Philadelphia, Gettysburg, and Pittsburgh, Pennsylvania, and Fort Wayne, Indiana; near Chicago; through Omaha, Nebraska, Cheyenne, Wyoming, Salt Lake City, Utah, and Sacramento, California. It ended in San Francisco. The original course was 3,389 miles, later cut by more than 50 miles. Work began in October 1914 but proceeded slowly. When the association closed its offices on 31 De-

cember 1927, after $90 million in expenditures, travelers could use the road throughout its length, although there were still sections of gravel and some even of dirt, which were slowly improved thereafter. In 1925, the road became U.S. Highway 30. In 1992, Lincoln Highway enthusiasts reestablished the Lincoln Highway Association, which now strives to preserve the road and promote it as a tourist attraction and topic of historical inquiry.

BIBLIOGRAPHY

Hokanson, Drake. *The Lincoln Highway: Main Street across America.* Iowa City: University of Iowa Press, 1999.

Lackey, Kris. *RoadFrames: The American Highway Narrative.* Lincoln: University of Nebraska Press, 1997.

Patton, Phil. *Open Road: A Celebration of the American Highway.* New York: Simon and Schuster, 1986.

Alvin F. Harlow / A. E.

See also **Federal-Aid Highway Program; Roads.**

LINCOLN LOGS. John Lloyd Wright (1892–1972), son of noted "Prairie Style" architect Frank Lloyd Wright, invented Lincoln Logs in 1916, began manufacturing them in Chicago, and patented them in 1920. The sets of tiny, notched, redwood logs fostered construction skills while playing on the pioneer myth in an era of rugged individualism popularized by Theodore Roosevelt. With the "Lincoln Cabin" trademark, Wright advertised them as "America's National Toys." Yet, he got the idea from the earthquake-resistant foundation of Tokyo's Imperial Hotel designed by his father.

Wright recognized the sudden popularity of the stonemason Charles Pajeau's Tinkertoys (1913), invented in Evanston, Illinois. Their colored sticks and eight-holed spools were used to build abstract constructions. The toys came packaged in cylindrical boxes for storage, and by 1915, had sold 900,000 sets. With the rise of new, mass-produced, and nationally marketed toys aimed at teaching construction skills in the Progressive Era, both became classics.

Wright expanded his line of miniature construction materials in the 1920s with Lincoln Bricks, Timber Toys, and Wright Blocks, some sets even included mortar and wheels. Like the contemporary invention of the Erector Set, Lincoln Logs appealed to parents and educators who heeded John Dewey's dictum that playing is essential to learning.

Blanche M. G. Linden

See also **Erector Sets; Toys and Games.**

LINCOLN TUNNEL. Linking midtown Manhattan (at West Thirty-Ninth Street) and central New Jersey (in Weehawken), the Lincoln Tunnel provided a key element

Lincoln Tunnel. A test drive through the first tube, eight days before it opened in December 1937. © Bettmann/corbis

for the mid-twentieth-century expansion of the interstate metropolitan region centered in New York City. New York City Mayor Fiorello La Guardia and powerful political leader Robert Moses identified the project as part of a regional development plan and as a depression-era source of employment. By allowing for more car and bus traffic, the Lincoln Tunnel (along with the Holland Tunnel, opened in 1927, and the George Washington Bridge, opened in 1931) reduced residents' dependency on commuter railroads and ferries and promoted the automobile as a central factor in the region's growth.

Construction of the first tube of the three-tube tunnel under the Hudson River began on 17 May 1934. Workers confronted claustrophobic and dangerous conditions, including floods and high pressures in a work zone as deep as ninety-seven feet below the river's surface. The first tube opened on 22 December 1937. The Port Authority of New York and New Jersey responded to increasing traffic by opening a second tunnel in 1945 and a third in 1957. The total cost of the structure reached $75 million. At the beginning of the twenty-first century, the Port Authority reported that nearly 21 million vehicles used the tunnel annually, making it the busiest vehicular tunnel in the world.

BIBLIOGRAPHY

Caro, Robert A. *The Power Broker: Robert Moses and the Fall of New York.* New York: Knopf, 1974.

Lankevich, George J. *American Metropolis: A History of New York City.* New York: New York University Press, 1998.

Sarah S. Marcus

LINCOLN-DOUGLAS DEBATES, seven joint debates between Abraham Lincoln and Stephen A. Douglas during the 1858 senatorial election campaign in Illinois. The debates marked the culmination of a political rivalry that had its origin twenty-five years before, when both were aspiring politicians in the Illinois legislature. Their careers had followed divergent tracks in the political culture of nineteenth-century America—Lincoln, the Henry Clay Whig espousing a broad program of national centralization and authority and distrustful of the new mass democracy, and Douglas, the Andrew Jackson Democrat standing for local self-government and states' rights, with an abiding faith in the popular will. By 1858, both had become deeply involved in the sectional conflict between the slave and free states over the status of slavery in the creation of western territories and the admission of new states. Douglas, seeking reelection to a third term in the U.S. Senate, had fifteen years of national experience and notoriety behind him and was widely known for his role in the passage of the Compromise of 1850 and his authorship of the Kansas-Nebraska Act of 1854. Lincoln, a spokesman for the new antislavery Republican Party, whose experience save for one term in the House of Representatives had been limited to several terms in the Illinois legislature, was virtually unknown outside the boundaries of the state.

From the beginning, the campaign assumed national significance. Douglas, with Republican support, was at that moment leading the opposition in Congress to the southern effort to admit Kansas as a slave state under the fraudulent Lecompton Constitution. To the southern slave power and its ally in the White House, President James Buchanan, Douglas's defeat for reelection was essential to the extension of slavery, a cause recently given constitutional sanction by the Supreme Court in the Dred Scott decision. At the same time, influential Republican leaders in the eastern states regarded Douglas's reelection as necessary to the success of their effort to keep slavery from expanding into new territories. Because the stakes were high, the contest between Douglas and Lincoln attracted widespread attention.

Lincoln opened the campaign in Springfield, the state capital, on 16 June 1858, when he delivered what has been hailed as the most important statement of his career, the "House Divided" speech. It was a strident call for Republican unity against what he described as a slave power conspiracy, of which Douglas was the principal conspirator, to extend slavery throughout the territories and free states of the Union. Moving away from his earlier conservative position, opposing the extension of slavery while tolerating it in the states where it already existed, Lincoln assumed a more radical stance. The conflict between freedom and slavery, he argued, was irrepressible and incapable of compromise, and would not cease until slavery should be placed in the course of "ultimate extinction," an abolitionist argument in everything but name. "A house divided against itself cannot stand."

Douglas returned to Illinois from his Senate seat in Washington, where he had been leading the fight against the Lecompton Constitution, and on 9 July, in Chicago,

Lincoln-Douglas Debates. Republican senatorial candidate Abraham Lincoln towers over Stephen A. Douglas, the Democratic incumbent, in this illustration of one of their seven debates across Illinois in 1858. Douglas won reelection, but Lincoln gained national prominence. ARCHIVE PHOTOS/FILMS

Rarely, if ever, had two candidates for the position of U.S. senator taken their arguments directly to the people, for senators were elected by the state legislatures until 1913.

The debates elicited little that was new and unexpected. Each spent considerable time in accusations and denials, typical of nineteenth-century stump speaking, their arguments often ambiguous and inconsistent. Lincoln repeated his conspiracy charge against Douglas, while at the same time dramatizing the split between Douglas and the South on the Lecompton issue. When he pointed out the inconsistency of Douglas's popular sovereignty with the Dred Scott decision, Douglas responded with what became known as the Freeport Doctrine, the right of a territory to exclude slavery by "unfriendly legislation" regardless of what the Supreme Court might decide. When Douglas charged Lincoln with harboring views of racial equality, Lincoln replied with emphatic denials. For Lincoln, slavery was a moral, social, and political evil, a position he reinforced with an appeal to the equality clause of the Declaration of Independence. The contest was but part of the eternal struggle between right and wrong that would not cease until the evil—slavery—was restricted and placed on the path toward extinction. Douglas found a dangerous radicalism in Lincoln's stand that would lead to disunion and a disastrous sectional war. Only by treating slavery as a matter of public policy, to be decided by the right of every community to decide the question for itself, could the Union be saved.

On 2 November 1858, Illinois voters gave the Democrats a legislative majority, which in turn elected Douglas to a third term in the Senate. Lincoln, although defeated, won recognition throughout the North that by 1860 placed him on the path to the presidency. Douglas, in winning reelection, alienated the South and weakened his power in the Senate. The debates—the specter of Lincoln's "ultimate extinction" of slavery and Douglas's threat to slavery's expansion in the territories—intensified the conflict between the slaveholding states and the free states of the North, placing the cherished Union itself in jeopardy. Douglas's worst fears were about to be realized.

BIBLIOGRAPHY

Angle, Paul M., ed. *Created Equal: The Complete Lincoln-Douglas Debates of 1858.* Chicago: University of Chicago Press, 1958.

Donald, David Herbert. *Lincoln.* New York: Simon and Schuster, 1995.

Johannsen, Robert W. *Stephen A. Douglas.* New York: Oxford University Press, 1973.

Robert W. Johannsen

See also **Compromise of 1850; Dred Scott Case; House Divided; Kansas-Nebraska Act; Lecompton Constitution; Slavery;** *and vol. 9:* **A House Divided.**

he opened his campaign for reelection. In defense of his role in the struggle to keep slavery out of Kansas, Douglas cited the "great principle of self-government" upon which he had based his political beliefs, "the right of the people in each State and Territory to decide for themselves their domestic institutions" (including slavery), or what he called popular sovereignty.

Lincoln's House Divided speech and Douglas's Chicago speech provided the themes and arguments for the debates that followed. Seven joint debates were agreed upon, one in each of the state's congressional districts except the two in which the candidates had already spoken. Beginning in late August and extending to the middle of October, debates were scheduled in Ottawa, Freeport, Jonesboro, Charleston, Galesburg, Quincy, and Alton. Thousands of spectators flocked to the debate sites to hear the candidates, railroads offered special excursion tickets, and the pageantry of election campaigns was provided by parades, brass bands, and glee clubs. On the platforms, Lincoln and Douglas offered a striking contrast, Lincoln standing six feet four inches tall, with patient humility, serious and persuasive, and Douglas a foot shorter at five feet four inches, animated, bold, and defiant.

LINCOLN'S SECOND INAUGURAL ADDRESS.

Abraham Lincoln delivered his second inaugural address on 4 March 1865. As Lincoln prepared to speak, the Civil War was drawing to a close. Newspapers were filled with reports of the armies of William T. Sherman and Ulysses S. Grant. As late as August 1864, neither Lincoln nor his Republican Party believed he could win reelection. Now Lincoln would be the first president inaugurated for a second term in thirty-two years. The crowd of thirty to forty thousand was greeted by an ongoing rain that produced ten inches of mud in the streets of Washington. Sharpshooters were on the rooftops surrounding the ceremony. Rumors abounded that Confederates might attempt to abduct or assassinate the president.

What would Lincoln say? Would he speak of his reelection, report on the progress of the victorious Union armies, lay out policies for what was being called "Reconstruction"? How would he treat the defeated Confederate armies? And what about the liberated slaves?

Lincoln addressed none of these expectations. He did not offer the North the victory speech it sought, nor did he blame the South alone for the evil of slavery. Rather, he offered a moral framework for reconciliation and peace. The speech was greeted with misunderstanding and even antagonism by many in the Union.

Lincoln's address of 703 words was the second shortest inaugural address. Five hundred and five words are one syllable. Lincoln mentions God fourteen times, quotes Scripture four times, and invokes prayer four times. The abolitionist leader Frederick Douglass, who was in the crowd that day, wrote in his journal, "The address sounded more like a sermon than a state paper" (*Autobiographies*, 802).

Lincoln began his address in a subdued tone. In the highly emotional environment of wartime Washington, it is as if he wanted to lower anticipations. At the beginning of his speech, he sounded more like an onlooker than the main actor. Lincoln directed the focus of his words away from himself by using the passive voice.

In the second paragraph Lincoln began the shift in substance and tenor that would give this address its remarkable meaning. He employed several rhetorical strategies that guided and aided the listener. First, Lincoln's overarching approach was to emphasize common actions and emotions. In this paragraph he used "all" and "both" to include North and South.

Second, Lincoln used the word "war" or its pronoun nine times. The centrality of war is magnified because the word appears in every sentence. Previously war had been used as the direct object, both historically and grammatically, of the principal actors. In his speech, however, war became the subject rather than the object. The second paragraph concludes, "And the war came." In this brief, understated sentence, Lincoln acknowledged that the war came in spite of the best intentions of the political leaders of the land.

When Lincoln introduced the Bible, early in the third paragraph, he entered new territory in presidential inaugural addresses. Before Lincoln there were eighteen inaugural addresses delivered by fourteen presidents. Each referred to God or the deity. The Bible, however, had been quoted only once.

The insertion of the Bible signaled Lincoln's determination to think theologically as well as politically about the war. The words "Both read the same Bible, and pray to the same God; and each invokes His aid against the other" are filled with multiple meanings. First, Lincoln affirmed the use of the Bible by both South and North. In a second meaning he questioned the use or misuse of the Bible or prayer for partisan purposes.

With the words "The Almighty has His own purposes" Lincoln brought God to the rhetorical center of the address. In quick strokes he described God's actions: "He now wills to remove"; "He gives to both North and South this terrible war"; "Yet, if God wills that it continue. . . ."

In September 1862 Lincoln had put pen to paper during one of the darkest moments of the war: "The will of God prevails. In great contests each party claims to act in accordance with the will of God. Both may be, and one must be wrong. . . . In the present civil war it is quite possible that God's purpose is something different from the purpose of either party ("Meditation on the Divine Will").

In the address Lincoln uttered a blistering biblical quotation: "Woe unto the world because of offences" (Matthew 18:7). When he defines American slavery as one of those offenses, he widened the historical and emotional range of his address. Lincoln did not say "Southern slavery" but asserted that North and South must together own the offense.

Lincoln carried the scales of justice to his speech. He did so knowing that Americans had always been uncomfortable facing up to their own malevolence. Lincoln suggested that the war was a means of purging the nation of its sin of slavery. The images reach their pinnacle in "until every drop of blood drawn with the lash, shall be paid by another drawn with the sword." His words sound more like the romantic language of Harriet Beecher Stowe than the legal language of the lawyer who delivered the first inaugural address.

The first eight words of Lincoln's last paragraph proclaim an enduring promise of reconciliation: "With malice toward none, with charity for all." These words immediately became the most memorable ones of the second inaugural address. After his assassination they came to represent Lincoln's legacy to the nation. Lincoln ended the address with a coda of healing: "to bind up . . . to care for . . . to do all which may achieve and cherish a just, and a lasting peace. . . ." In this concluding paragraph he offered the final surprise. Instead of rallying his followers, in the name of God, to support the war, he asked his listeners, quietly, to emulate the ways of God.

BIBLIOGRAPHY

Basler, Roy S., et al., eds. *The Collected Works of Abraham Lincoln*. 8 vols. New Brunswick, N.J.: Rutgers University Press, 1953. Also index vol., 1955, and supplements, 1974 and 1990.

Donald, David Herbert. *Lincoln*. New York: Simon and Schuster, 1995.

Douglass, Frederick. *Autobiographies*. New York: Library of America, 1994. Reprint of 1893 ed.

White, Ronald C., Jr. *Lincoln's Greatest Speech: The Second Inaugural*. New York: Simon and Schuster, 2002.

Wills, Gary. *Lincoln at Gettysburg: The Words That Remade America:* New York: Simon and Schuster, 1992.

Ronald C. White Jr.

See also vol. 9: **President Lincoln's Second Inaugural Address.**

LINDBERGH KIDNAPPING CASE.

What the media of the depression era hailed as "the crime of the century" began on the night of 1 March 1932, when someone abducted Charles Lindbergh Jr., twenty-month-old son of aviator hero Charles A. Lindbergh, from his New Jersey country home. A month later, the Lindbergh family paid $50,000 in ransom through an intermediary, but the baby, whose body was finally found in May, was not returned. In response, Congress passed the Lindbergh Kidnapping Law of 1932, which made it a federal crime to take a kidnap victim across state lines. Two years later, police arrested a German-born carpenter, Bruno Hauptmann. A New York City tabloid hired the flamboyant attorney Edward J. Reilly to represent Hauptmann, whose 1935 trial produced a six-week media spectacle. Though he called more than 150 witnesses, including Hauptmann himself, Reilly could not shake crucial evidence against his client, including about $14,000 in traceable ransom bills in his possession and a ladder (used in the kidnapping) that had been repaired with a board from his house. Rebuffing all entreaties to confess, Hauptmann insisted that a now-deceased friend had given him the money. Convicted in February 1935, Hauptmann was executed on 3 April 1936. Until her own death in 1994, his widow Anna Hauptmann championed his cause. Ironically, as Lindbergh's reputation suffered, in part because of his pro-Hitler and anti-Semitic stances during the late 1930s, thinly documented arguments for Hauptmann's innocence gained currency.

BIBLIOGRAPHY

Fisher, Jim. *The Ghosts of Hopewell: Setting the Record Straight in the Lindbergh Case*. Carbondale and Edwardsville: Southern Illinois University Press, 1999.

Lindbergh Kidnapping Victim. Anne Morrow Lindbergh, the wife of the world's most famous aviator, poses with her son, Charles A. Lindbergh Jr., for this photograph taken not long before the baby was kidnapped in March 1932 and murdered, in one of the twentieth century's most sensational crimes. © CORBIS

Hixson, Walter L. *Murder, Culture, and Injustice: Four Sensational Cases in U.S. History*. Akron: University of Akron Press, 2001.

Norman Rosenberg

See also **Kidnapping.**

LINDBERGH'S ATLANTIC FLIGHT.

The first nonstop flight from New York to Paris and the first solo flight across the Atlantic Ocean, 20–21 May 1927. When Charles Lindbergh, a handsome and charming airmail pilot, landed in Paris after a thirty-three-and-a-half-hour journey, he instantly became an international superstar and America's most-loved living hero. At Le Bourget Air Field, he was cheered by 150,000 Parisians, some of whom stole pieces of his plane, the *Spirit of St. Louis*

Lucky (and Skillful) Lindy. Charles Lindbergh stands next to the *Spirit of St. Louis* in New York, shortly before his historic 1927 transatlantic flight. © BETTMANN/CORBIS

dia technology. News outlets were able to follow the odyssey almost in real time, and the newsreels of the take-off were some of the first to synchronize picture and sound.

Few observers expected Lindbergh to succeed. In 1919, a wealthy flying enthusiast offered a $25,000 prize to the first aviator to fly from New York to Paris or vice versa without stopping, and dozens of famous pilots had tried and failed. Just two weeks before Lindbergh took off, a pair of Frenchmen bound for New York disappeared somewhere over the Atlantic. Moreover, while most attempts involved teams of pilots and massive aircrafts, Lindbergh flew alone and with only one engine. He wanted control over every aspect of the flight, fewer moving parts that could malfunction, less total weight, and more fuel capacity.

BIBLIOGRAPHY

Berg, A. Scott. *Lindbergh*. New York: Putnam, 1998.

Lindbergh, Charles A. *An Autobiography of Values*. New York: Harcourt Brace Jovanovich, 1978.

Jeremy Derfner

See also **Air Transportation and Travel; Mass Media.**

LINE-ITEM VETO. *See* **Veto, Line-Item.**

LINEN INDUSTRY. This industry originated in colonial America, where farmers raised flax to make linen clothing. Some colonies subsidized linen's manufacture into sailcloth. For two centuries, dressed flax and yarn were common articles of barter—homespun was familiar merchandise in country trade, and linsey-woolsey, made of flax and wool, was a common clothing fabric.

The cotton gin and Arkwright machinery helped cotton displace flax, for, after their invention, few large linen mills succeeded. Most of those that survived manufactured thread and canvas. Civil War cotton shortages stimulated efforts to revive the industry, but high costs prevented its extension. While some linen goods still are manufactured in the United States, most are imported.

BIBLIOGRAPHY

Hoke, Donald. *Ingenious Yankees: The Rise of the American System of Manufacturers in the Private Sector*. New York: Columbia University Press, 1990.

Victor S. Clark / c. w.

See also **Cotton Gin; Industrial Revolution; Textiles.**

LINGAYEN GULF, situated on the northwest coast of Luzon Island in the Philippines, suffered two invasions during World War II: the first, in 1941, was by the Japanese; the second, three years later, was by the returning

(named by his financial backers from that city). Three weeks later, on "Lindbergh Day" in New York, the city closed the stock exchange and public schools, and more than four million people lined the parade route.

Transatlantic flight captured the Western imagination for several reasons. In the golden age of mass entertainment, Lindbergh's attempt had the feel of a great sporting event. Fans held their breath during the suspenseful fifteen-hour Atlantic crossing, and they followed Lindbergh's progress in exhilarating stages as the *Spirit of St. Louis* was sighted over Ireland, then England, and finally France. Lloyd's of London put odds on the flight. Transatlantic air travel also marked another step in the march of scientific advancement. The Wright brothers had pulled off the first minute-long flight at Kitty Hawk, North Carolina, just twenty-four years earlier, and already an aviator had made the New York to Paris run.

Most importantly, however, Lindbergh seemed to embody true heroism—one brave man risking his life for the sake of human progress. F. Scott Fitzgerald wrote that Lindbergh resurrected the "old best dreams" of a culture infatuated with "country clubs and speak-easies." Lindbergh's accomplishment took on even greater heroic proportions because it coincided with improvements in me-

American forces. In December 1941, Lingayen Gulf was defended by General Douglas MacArthur's force of poorly equipped Filipinos and some American troops. Japanese victories in the initial weeks of the war denied the defenders vital air and naval support. In contrast, Lieutenant General Masaharu Homma's invasion force was well trained, adequately supplied, and supported by strong naval and air units. Homma's troops began landing before dawn on 22 December along the east shore of Lingayen Gulf. A few artillery rounds and ineffective attacks by a handful of American submarines and bombers were all the defenders could muster. Homma quickly began to drive inland. A day later, MacArthur issued the order to abandon Luzon and withdraw to Bataan.

Three years later, the situation was reversed. The Japanese force, commanded by General Tomoyuki Yamashita, was numerous and strong but lacked air and naval support. They were totally outmatched by the combined forces MacArthur had marshaled for his return to Luzon. Other than Japanese suicide planes that punished the American convoys, there was no opposition to the invasion. After a devastating pre-assault bombardment, the landing began at 9:30 A.M. on 9 January 1945 on the south shore of Lingayen Gulf. The shores of Lingayen Gulf soon became a vast supply depot to support the American drive on Manila.

BIBLIOGRAPHY

Breuer, William B. *Retaking the Philippines: Americans Return to Corregidor and Bataan, July 1944–March 1945.* New York: St. Martin's Press, 1986.

Morison, Samuel Eliot. *The Liberation of the Philippines: Luzon, Mindanao, The Visayas, 1944–1945.* Vol. 13, *History of United States Naval Operations in World War II.* Boston: Little, Brown, 1959.

Smith, Robert Ross. *Triumph in the Philippines, United States Army in World War II. The War in the Pacific.* Washington, D.C.: Office of the Chief of Military History, Department of the Army, 1963, 1991.

Stanley L. Falk / A. R.

See also **Bataan-Corregidor Campaign; Navy, United States; Philippines; World War II.**

LINGUISTICS.

The early discipline of linguistics in the United States consisted in large part of the work of three eminent scholars—Franz Boas, who studied Native American languages; Edward Sapir, the most prolific of Boas's students; and Leonard Bloomfield, who was trained in Germanic philology and taught languages. Boas, Sapir, and Bloomfield were among the founders in 1924 of the Linguistic Society of America, the leading professional organization and publisher of the discipline's journal.

Bloomfield and Sapir were leaders in descriptive linguistics, now often referred to as structural linguistics. According to them, languages should be described as interlocking assemblages of basic units and as functioning wholes independent of earlier developmental stages. Such descriptions might then form the basis for comparing related languages and reconstructing their common origin. Sapir identified the phoneme as a basic unit of sound patterning and offered evidence for its psychological reality. Bloomfield, on the other hand, advocated indirect observation to identify the distinct meanings associated with units of form. His followers developed a mandatory set of discovery procedures for all valid analyses that built upon the sequential distribution of units of sound. These procedures, and strictures against mixing comparison with description, were in practice often violated, with good reason. Linguists were prepared to assume that languages might differ from one another without limit; thus, one could assume no commonalities. They were reacting in part to clumsy attempts to superimpose categories of classical grammar on descriptions of New World languages. Many of them thought that the grammatical categories of language might shape perceptions of reality.

Beginning in the mid-twentieth century, Noam Chomsky revised these ideas—including the supposed necessity of phonetically based discovery—in what became known as generative grammar. Language was for him a hypothetico-deductive system centered about *Syntactic Structures*, the title of his 1957 treatise. According to Chomsky, language and human cognition evolve together. Language is innate, its categories universal among humankind. It is part of children's normal development, rather than a skill learned by some and not by others, such as playing a musical instrument or driving a car. Children must ascertain the particular sound-meaning combinations and parameter settings used in their environment. The linguist can learn more about this innate capability from probing a single language rather than surveying multiple languages.

Whereas generative grammar was autonomous, with many of its constructs presuming homogeneous speech communities of identical idealized hearer-speakers, William Labov developed methods for sampling and quantifying the variation in usage by members of actual communities and by given individuals on different occasions. He showed the influence of social attitudes on language within speech communities. Some of his studies using the sound spectrograph demonstrated that speakers perpetuate distinctions they are unable to recognize.

Even as they considered the existence of a universal grammar, however, linguists in the 1990s became concerned with the high rate of language death in the modern world. An increasing number of young linguists committed themselves to studying language ecology, in hopes of preventing or curtailing the incidence of language death, and to recording and analyzing little-studied endangered languages to preserve at least a record of what had been lost. It was almost as if the discipline had come full circle from the efforts of Boas and his students nearly a century earlier.

BIBLIOGRAPHY

Hymes, Dell, and John Fought. *American Structuralism*. The Hague and New York: Mouton, 1981.

Newmeyer, Frederick J. *Linguistic Theory in America*. 2d ed. Orlando, Fla.: Academic Press, 1986.

Newmeyer, Frederick J., ed. *Linguistics: The Cambridge Survey*. 4 vols. New York: Cambridge University Press, 1988.

Byron W. Bender / c. w.

See also **Behaviorism; Post-structuralism; Psychology.**

LIQUOR INDUSTRY. *See* **Spirits Industry.**

LIQUOR LAWS. *See* **Alcohol, Regulation of.**

LITCHFIELD LAW SCHOOL was established in 1784 in Litchfield, Conn., by Tapping Reeve, who was its only teacher until 1798. In that year he was succeeded by James Gould, who developed an institution that in the early years of the nineteenth century gave legal training to hundreds of young men from almost every state in the Union and numbered among its graduates some of the most prominent men in the public life of the next generation, including Henry Clay. Before it closed its doors in 1833, the Litchfield school had sent out more than a thousand graduates.

BIBLIOGRAPHY

McKenna, Marian C. *Tapping Reeve and the Litchfield Law School*. New York: Oceana, 1986.

Francis R. Aumann / a. r.

See also **Law Schools.**

LITERACY TEST refers to the government practice of testing the literacy of potential citizens at the federal level, and potential voters at the state level. The federal government first employed literacy tests as part of the immigration process in 1917. Southern state legislatures employed literacy tests as part of the voter registration process as early as the late nineteenth century.

As used by the states, the literacy test gained infamy as a means for denying the franchise to African Americans. Adopted by a number of southern states, the literacy test was applied in a patently unfair manner, as it was used to disfranchise many literate southern blacks while allowing many illiterate southern whites to vote. The literacy test, combined with other discriminatory requirements, effectively disfranchised the vast majority of African Americans in the South from the 1890s until the 1960s. Southern states abandoned the literacy test only when forced to by federal legislation in the 1960s. In 1964, the Civil Rights Act provided that literacy tests used as a qualification for voting in federal elections be administered wholly in writing and only to persons who had not completed six years of formal education. The VOTING RIGHTS ACT OF 1965 suspended the use of literacy tests in all states or political subdivisions in which less than 50 percent of the voting-age residents were registered as of 1 November 1964, or had voted in the 1964 presidential election. In a series of cases, the SUPREME COURT upheld the legislation and restricted the use of literacy tests for non-English-speaking citizens. Since the passage of the civil rights legislation of the 1960s, black registration in the South has increased dramatically.

Dennis Ippolito / a. g.

See also **Civil Rights Act of 1964; Primary, White; Suffrage: Exclusion from the Suffrage; White Citizens Councils.**

LITERATURE

This entry includes 5 subentries:
Overview
African American Literature
Children's Literature
Native American Literature
Popular Literature

OVERVIEW

The first Europeans in America did not encounter a silent world. A chorus of voices had been alive and moving through the air for approximately 25,000 years before. Weaving tales of tricksters, warriors and gods; spinning prayers, creation stories, and spiritual prophesies, the First Nations carved out their oral traditions long before colonial minds were fired and flummoxed by a world loud with language when Leif Ericsson first sighted Newfoundland in A.D. 1000. Gradually the stories that these first communities told about themselves became muffled as the eminences of the European Renaissance began to contemplate the New World. One of them, the French thinker and father of the essay, Michel de Montaigne, was not loath to transform the anecdotes of a servant who had visited Antarctic France (modern Brazil) into a report on the lives of virtuous cannibals. According to his "On Cannibals" (1588), despite their predilection for white meat, these noble individuals led lives of goodness and dignity, in shaming contrast to corrupt Europe. Little wonder that on an imaginary New World island in Shakespeare's *The Tempest* (first performed in 1611), the rude savage Caliban awaits a conquering Prospero in the midst of natural bounty.

Pioneers to Puritans

Whether partially or entirely fanciful, these visions of paradise on Earth were not much different from Sir Thomas More's *Utopia* (1516), itself partly inspired by the Italian Amerigo Vespucci's voyages to the New World. Wonders of a new Eden, untainted by European decadence, beck-

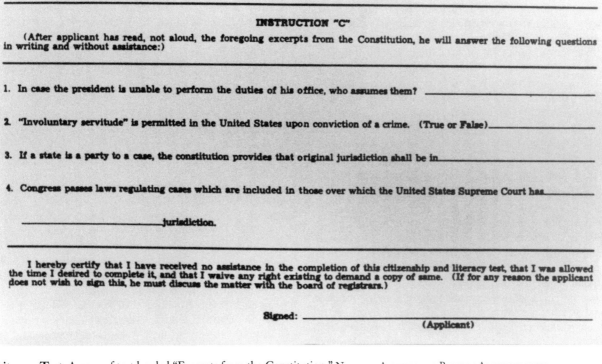

EXCERPTS FROM THE CONSTITUTION

Part 1. In case of the removal of the president from office, or of his death, resignation, or inability to discharge the powers and duties of the said office, the same shall devolve on the vice-president, and the congress may by law provide for the case of removal, death, resignaton or inability, both of the president and vice-president, declaring what officer shall then act as president, and such officer shall act accordingly, until the disability be removed, or a president shall be elected.

Part 2. In all cases affecting ambassadors, other public ministers and consuls, and those in which a state shall be a party, the supreme court shall have original jurisdiction.

Part 3. In all the other cases before mentioned, the supreme court shall have appellate jurisdiction, both as to law and fact, with such exceptions, and under such regulations as the congress shall make.

Part 4. Neither slavery nor involuntary servitude, except as a punishment for crime whereof the party shall have been duly convicted, shall exist within the United States, or any place subject to their jurisdiction.

INSTRUCTION "C"

(After applicant has read, not aloud, the foregoing excerpts from the Constitution, he will answer the following questions in writing and without assistance:)

1. In case the president is unable to perform the duties of his office, who assumes them? _____

2. "Involuntary servitude" is permitted in the United States upon conviction of a crime. (True or False)_____

3. If a state is a party to a case, the constitution provides that original jurisdiction shall be in_____

4. Congress passes laws regulating cases which are included in those over which the United States Supreme Court has_____

_____jurisdiction.

I hereby certify that I have received no assistance in the completion of this citizenship and literacy test, that I was allowed the time I desired to complete it, and that I waive any right existing to demand a copy of same. (If for any reason the applicant does not wish to sign this, he must discuss the matter with the board of registrars.)

Signed: _____
(Applicant)

Literacy Test. A page of text headed "Excerpts from the Constitution." NATIONAL ARCHIVES AND RECORDS ADMINISTRATION

oned to those who would venture to America, even as others spared no ink to paint accounts of the savagery of this hostile, unknown world. Between these extremes lay something approaching the truth: America as equal parts heaven and hell, its aboriginal inhabitants as human beings capable of both virtue and vice. While wealth, albeit cloaked in Christian missionary zeal, may have been the primary motive for transatlantic journeys, many explorers quickly understood that survival had to be secured before pagan souls or gold. John Smith, himself an escaped slave from the Balkans who led the 1606 expedition to Virginia, wrote of his plunders with a raconteur's flair for embellishment, impatient with those who bemoaned the rigors of earning their colonial daily bread. His twin chronicles, *A True Relation of Virginia* (1608) and *The General History of Virginia, New England, and the Summer Isles* (1624), differ in at least one suggestive detail: the Indian maiden Pocahontas appears only in the latter, betraying the free-

dom with which European imagination worked on some "facts" of this encounter.

Competing accounts of the American experiment multiplied with Thomas Morton, whose Maypole paganism and free trade in arms with the natives raised the ire of his Puritan neighbors, Governor William Bradford, who led *Mayflower* Pilgrims from religious persecution in England to Plymouth Rock in 1620, and Roger Williams, who sought to understand the language of the natives, earning him expulsion from the "sanctuary" of Massachusetts. More often than not, feverish religiosity cast as potent a spell on these early American authors as their English literary heritage. The terrors of Judgment Day inspired Michael Wigglesworth's *The Day of Doom* (1662), a poem so sensational that one in twenty homes ended up harboring a copy. Equally electrifying were narratives of captivity and restoration, like that of Mary Rowlandson

(1682), often cast as allegories of the soul's journey from a world of torment to heaven. Beset by fragile health and religious doubt, Anne Bradstreet captured in her *Several Poems* (1678) a moving picture of a Pilgrim mind grappling with the redemptive trials of life with a courage that would later bestir Emily Dickinson.

It seems unlikely that two college roommates at Harvard, Edward Taylor and Samuel Sewall, would both come to define Puritan literary culture—yet they did. Influenced by the English verse of John Donne and George Herbert, Taylor, a New England minister, became as great a poet as the Puritans managed to produce. Sewall's *Diary* (begun 12 August 1674) made him as much a rival of his British counterpart Samuel Pepys as of the more ribald chronicler of Virginia, William Byrd. While it is easy to caricature the Puritans as models of virtue or else vicious persecutors of real or imagined heresy, the simplicity of myth beggars the complexity of reality. A jurist who presided over the SALEM WITCH TRIALS, Sewall was also the author of *The Selling of Joseph* (1700), the first antislavery tract in an America that had accepted the practice since 1619.

The GREAT AWAKENING, a period in which the Puritan mindset enjoyed a brief revival, is notable for the prolific historian and hagiographer Cotton Mather. *The Wonders of the Invisible World* (1693) afforded a glimpse of his skepticism about the prosecutors of the witch trials, while his *Magnalia Christi Americana* (1702) provided a narrative of settlers' history of America, regularly illuminated with the exemplary "lives of the saints." Moved equally by dogmatic piety and the imperatives of reason and science, Jonathan Edwards delivered arresting sermons that swayed not only his peers, but also centuries later, William James's *Varieties of Religious Experience* (1902). True to form, Edwards's *A Faithful Narrative of the Surprising Work of God* (1737) is a celebration not only of spiritual reawakening, but of the empiricism of John Locke as well.

Enlightenment to Autonomy
If anyone embodied the recoil from seventeenth-century Puritan orthodoxy toward the Enlightenment, it was the architect of an independent, modern United States, Benjamin Franklin (1706–1790). Printer, statesman, scientist, and journalist, he first delighted his readers with the annual wit and wisdom of *POOR RICHARD'S ALMANAC* (launched in 1733). In 1741, in parallel with Andrew Bradford's *The American Magazine*, Franklin's *General Magazine and Historical Chronicle* marked the beginning of New England magazine publishing. But it was his best-selling *Autobiography* (1791) that revealed the extent to which his personal destiny twined with the turbulent course of the new state. Ostensibly a lesson in life for his son, the book became a compass for generations of Americans as it tracked Citizen Franklin's progress from a humble printer's apprentice, through his glory as a diplomat in the Revolutionary War (1775–1783), to the exclusive club of the founding fathers who drafted the Declaration of Independence and ratified the Constitution.

The Revolution that stamped Franklin's life with the destiny of the nation found its most brazen exponent in Thomas Paine. Author of *COMMON SENSE* (1776) and *The American Crisis* (pamphlet series, 1776–1783), Paine was a British expatriate who came to Philadelphia sponsored by Franklin and galvanized the battle for independence. His fervid opposition to the British social order, slavery, and the inferior status of women made him a lightning rod of the Revolution, helping to create an American identity in its wake. America's emergence as a sovereign power became enshrined in the Declaration of Independence, drafted by Thomas Jefferson. Harking back to Montaigne in *Notes on the State of Virginia* (1784–1785), this patrician statesman idolized the purity of agrarian society in the fear that the closer the New World edged toward the satanic mills of industrial Europe, the more corrupt it would become. The founder of the University of Virginia, whose library would seed the Library of Congress, Jefferson was elected president in 1800 and again in 1804.

Literature after the Revolution
After the Revolution, American literary culture grew less dependent on British models, and the popular success of poets like the Connecticut Wits, including Timothy Dwight, composer of an American would-be epic, *The Conquest of Canaan* (1785), only confirmed this point. The broad appeal of novels like *The Power of Sympathy* (1789) by William Hill Brown and *Charlotte Temple* (1791) by Susanna Haswell Rowson, both tales of seduction that spoke to what future critics would call a pulp fiction sensibility, signaled the growing success of domestic authors (Rowson's novel, *the* best-seller of the eighteenth century, would do equally well in the nineteenth). Modeled on *Don Quixote*, the comic writings of Hugh Henry Brackenridge and the gothic sensibilities of Charles Brockden Brown also won a degree of popular and critical laurels, the latter presaging the dark strains of Poe and Hawthorne.

Knickerbockers to Naturalists
The career of Washington Irving marked a categorical break with the past, inasmuch as this mock-historian succeeded where the poet/satirist Philip Freneau and others had failed by becoming the first professional American writer. Affected by the Romantics, Irving created folk literature for the New World: *A History of New York* (1809), fronted by the pseudonymous Diedrich Knickerbocker, would be synonymous thereafter with American folklore and tall tales, while *The Sketchbook of Geoffrey Crayon, Gentleman* (1819–1820) introduced the immortal "Rip Van Winkle" and "The Legend of Sleepy Hollow." Admired on both sides of the Atlantic, Irving's prose did for America's literary prestige what the Romantic poetry of William Cullen Bryant did for its verse, while James Fenimore Cooper worked a similar alchemy on the novel. While critics from Twain to the present have belittled

Cooper's cumbersome prose, he gripped the imagination with books of frontier adventure and romance, collectively known as the LEATHERSTOCKING TALES (after the recurrent hero). *The Pioneers* (1823), *The Last of the Mohicans* (1826), and *The Prairie* (1827) still captivate as narrative testimonies to American frontier clashes: civilization against savagery, pioneers against natives, apparent goodness versus moral rot.

The flood of creative energy unleashed by these no longer apologetic American authors crested with the birth of TRANSCENDENTALISM, overseen by the sage Ralph Waldo Emerson. This minister, essayist, and philosopher renounced the theological and literary dogma of the past, striving to nurture and encourage new American muses. It is for no other reason that his essays, including "Nature" (1836) and "Representative Men" (1850), and his Harvard address, "The American Scholar" (1837), amount to America's declaration of literary independence. The more reclusive Henry David Thoreau beheld in the tranquility of the pond at WALDEN (1854) the difference between false liberty and herd consciousness, while his *Civil Disobedience* (1849) made nonviolent resistance to tyranny a new and powerful weapon in the hands of Gandhi, King, and Mandela. Singing himself and America, Walt Whitman cultivated his LEAVES OF GRASS (1855) over nine ever-grander editions, confirming him as the poet that Emerson tried to conjure: a giant clothed in the speech of the people. Emily Dickinson would lift her voice along with Whitman, though her startling hymns were made for the chambers of the solitary mind, minted to miniature perfection.

The same fertile season saw Herman Melville complete *MOBY-DICK* (1851), a multilayered sea epic whose White Whale incarnates the essence of evil and otherness and everything that the human will cannot conquer. Its deranged pursuer, Ahab, may be the doomed part of us all that vainly rejects that "cannot." Exhausted by this beast of a novel, Melville produced nothing to rival its scope and complexity, languishing forgotten until the Hollywood decades. Nathaniel Hawthorne revisited an allegorical world in which vice masqueraded as virtue, staining the Puritan snow with blood from "Young Goodman Brown" (1835) to *The Scarlet Letter* (1850). The shadows explored by Hawthorne became the abode of Edgar Allan Poe, a legendary editor, poet, and literary critic, as well as a short story giant, inventor of the detective novel, and father of modern horror and science fiction. Tied to "The Fall of the House of Usher" (1839), "The Purloined Letter" (1845), or "The Raven" (1845), Poe's worldwide influence is bound to endure evermore.

Civil War to World War

The events of the Civil War (1861–1865) made it possible for the literature written by African Americans to receive a measure of attention and acclaim, the torch passing from Olaudah Equiano and Phillis Wheatley to Frederick Douglass. With the advent of Lincoln's Emancipation Proclamation, black Americans would finally secure basic liberties and a literary voice. Some of the abolitionist zeal, both at home and abroad, may be credited to Harriet Beecher Stowe: no less than 1.5 million pirated copies of her UNCLE TOM'S CABIN (1852) flooded Britain weeks after its publication. Though a powerful storyteller, she was certainly no Joel Chandler Harris, whose acute ear for dialect and fearless sense of humor made his tales of *Uncle Remus* (1880–1883) as entertaining as morally astute. In some of their writings, Booker T. Washington and W. E. B. Du Bois would continue to offer differing remedies for the gross inequities still imposed on their black countrymen.

The end of the nineteenth century was the playing field for Bret Harte and his regional tales of a harsh, untamed California, for the crackling wit of William Sydney Porter, a.k.a. O. Henry (1862–1910), and for the scalding satire of Samuel Langhorne Clemens, better known as Mark Twain (1835–1910). A national masterpiece, Twain's *The Adventures of HUCKLEBERRY FINN* (1884) has been universally admired since its publication, though it continues to stir controversy in politically correct circles. Just because the author permits his protagonist to speak the mind of his age and call his runaway slave friend, Jim, "a nigger," some readers miss the moral metamorphoses that Huck undergoes, and the salvos Twain launches against ignorance and prejudice. What looks like interpretive "safe water" (Clemens's pseudonym meant "two fathoms of navigable water under the keel"), can prove very turbulent, indeed.

Twain's unflinching representation of "things as they were," whether noble or nasty, shared in the realism that reigned in the novels and stories of Henry James (1843–1916). Lavish psychological portraits and a keen eye for the petty horrors of bourgeois life allowed James to stir controversy, and occasionally, as in *The Turn of the Screw* (1898), genuine terror. Edith Wharton (1862–1937), who added the gray agonies of *Ethan Frome* (1911) to the canon of American realism, garnered a Pulitzer in 1921, and in 1923 she became the first woman to receive the degree of Doctor of Letters from Yale. Stephen Crane (1871–1900) used his short life to produce extraordinary journalism about New York's daily life and a gory close-up of warfare in *The Red Badge of Courage* (1895).

Naturalism

Fidelity to life along realistic lines, combined with a pessimistic determinism concerning human existence, dominated NATURALISM, a somewhat later strain in American fiction. Heavily under the influence of Marx and Nietzsche, Jack London was more fascinated by the gutter than the stars—his *The People of the Abyss* (1903), a study of the city of London's down and out, merits as much attention as *The Call of the Wild* (1903). Theodore Dreiser (1871–1945) gave a Zolaesque account of sexual exploitation in the naturalist classic *Sister Carrie* (1900), and similarly shocking scenes of deranged dentistry in *McTeague* (1899)

119

allowed Frank Norris to show the mind cracking under the vice of fate, symptoms that would become more familiar as the next anxious century unfolded.

Modernists to Mods

According to Jonathan Schell, antinuclear activist and author of the harrowing *Fate of the Earth* (1982), the "short" twentieth century extended from the Great War (1914–1918) to the collapse of the Berlin Wall in 1989. World War I forms another historical dam, between the (if only by comparison) placid nineteenth century and the turmoil of modernism that raced to supersede Romantic and/or realist art with a mosaic of manifesto-armed movements. Germinating in fin de siècle Germany and Scandinavia, the modernist period spawned a palette of programmatic "isms" underpinning most of early twentieth-century poetry and painting (the novel formed the secondary wave): impressionism, expressionism, cubism, symbolism, imagism, futurism, unanimism, vorticism, dadaism, and later surrealism.

In the United States, the changing of the guard coincided with the New York Armory Show of 1913, a defiant exhibition of European cubists, from the enfant terrible Marcel Duchamp to the already famous Pablo Picasso. On their geometrically condensed and contorted canvas lay the heart of modernism. Order, linearity, harmony were out. Fragmentation, collage, and miscellany were in. Continuities ceded to multitudes of perspectives; classical unities to clusters of "days in the life"; moral closure to open-ended, controlled chaos. *The Sun Also Rises* (1926), Ernest Hemingway's story of Jake Barnes, a war-emasculated Fisher-King vet, captures not only this literary generation but also its poetics of arbitrary beginnings, episodes bound only by the concreteness of imagery and the irony of detachment, and the endings dissolving with no resolution. The prose is sparse, the narrator limited in time, space, and omniscience, the speech colloquial and "unliterary," in accord with Papa Hemingway's dictum that American literature really began with *Huckleberry Finn*.

Hard and terse prose was in part a legacy of the muckrakers, a new breed of investigative journalists who scandalized the public with the stench of avarice, corruption, and political "muck." An early classic was Upton Sinclair's (1878–1968) *The Jungle* (1906), an exposé of economic white slavery in the filth of the Chicago stockyards. An instant celebrity, its socialist author, who conferred with President Theodore Roosevelt and later came within a heartbeat of winning the governorship of California, forever rued hitting the country in the stomach while aiming for its heart. The same vernacular, mean street–savvy style became the trademark of Dashiell Hammett, James M. Cain, and Raymond Chandler, hard-boiled founders of the American *noir* which, together with the western, science fiction, and the romance, began its long ascent out of the literary gutter into the native voice and dominant vehicle of American culture.

Novelistic modernism—less international, more involved with domestic, social themes—flourished in the period of 1919 to 1939. It stretched from the Jazz Age, during which American literature caught up with the world, to the end of the radical, experiment-heavy decade of the Great Depression—from Sinclair Lewis's broadsides against conformism and Babbitry in *Main Street* (1920) and *Babbitt* (1922), to the controversial breast-feeding finale of John Steinbeck's proletarian *The Grapes of Wrath* (1939). In between there was Sherwood Anderson's impressionistic *Winesburg, Ohio* (1919), John Dos Passos's urban etude, *Manhattan Transfer* (1925), Dreiser's naturalistic *An American Tragedy* (1925), Thornton Wilder's philosophical *The Bridge of San Luis Rey* (1927), Hemingway's tragic *A Farewell to Arms* (1929), Thomas Wolfe's autobiographic *Look Homeward, Angel* (1929), and the first volumes of William Faulkner's symbolic southern chronicles. There was also F. Scott Fitzgerald, whose masterpiece *The Great Gatsby* (1925) told of a man in search of the elusive bird of happiness, fatally beguiled by America's materialist Dream.

The obscure symbolism of T. S. Eliot's *The Waste Land* (1922) was interpreted by the culturati as a rallying cry against a nation that, in accord with the presidential "the business of America is business," lost its soul amid advertisements for toothpastes, laxatives, soft drinks, automobiles, and household gadgets without which families might become un-American. Trying to make sense of these freewheeling times was Van Wyck Brooks's *America's Coming of Age* (1915), which mythologized the nation's "usable past" while assaulting its puritanism and stagnation. This harsh diagnosis was seconded by a crop of polemical columnists, running the gamut from arch-conservatives like H. L Mencken to the more proletarian Walter Lippmann and Joseph Wood Krutch, and from harangues against the cultural "booboisie" to campaigns against the establishment.

In poetry a pleiad of older and rising stars, many part-time expatriates in London and Paris, burst on the scene: from the CEO of the modernist risorgimento (revolution), Ezra Pound, to H. D. (Hilda Doolitle), Robert Frost, and the typographically untamed e. e. cummings. Despite colossal internal differences, the entire prewar generation—both the expatriates and those who, like Wallace Stevens or Marianne Moore, never saw Paris—rallied around a modern poetic idiom. Joined by William Carlos Williams, Conrad Aiken, Edgar Lee Masters, and Carl Sandburg, they self-consciously pursued Whitman's legacy in a more concrete, layered, and allusive style.

The era whose dawn coincided with *Tender Buttons* (1913), an experimental volume by the prose lyricist Gertrude Stein, came to a climax in 1930, when Sinclair Lewis became America's first Nobel winner. Lewis attributed his personal triumph to the renaissance of American fiction in the 1920s, even as Eugene O'Neill, Nobel laureate for 1936, brought the American theater to the world stage, boldly experimenting with dramatic structure and production methods. Maxwell Anderson, Lillian Hellman, Robert E. Sherwood, Elmer Rice, and Sidney Kingsley steered contemporary drama even further away from the vaudeville and music hall of Broadway, as did Clifford Odets in his Marxist *Waiting for Lefty* (1935).

The stock market crash of 1929 wiped out the nation's savings accounts and its faith in freestyle capitalism. The literary scene may have been titillated by Henry Miller's *Tropics*, racy enough to be banned in the United States until the 1960s, but away from Gay Paris, the depression spelled poverty so acute that some papers suggested the popular song "Brother, Can You Spare a Dime" as the new national anthem. Economically and culturally the period could not have been worse for black artists, whose dazzling if brief Harlem Renaissance of the 1920s, led by the jazz-inspired Langston Hughes and Zora Neale Hurston, gave way to Richard Wright's *Native Son* (1940), a brutal book about Bigger Thomas's execution for the "almost accidental" murder of a white woman.

The wave of experimentation bore Faulkner's novel-as-multiple-point-of-view, *As I Lay Dying* (1930), the scandalous *Sanctuary* (1931)—which in violence and sensationalism vied with William Randolph Hearst's yellow journalism of the era—and the James Joyce–influenced *Light in August* (1932). John O'Hara's shard-edged short stories rose alongside James Thurber's and Erskine Caldwell's. James T. Farrell released his socionaturalistic Studs Lonigan trilogy, while James M. Cain's *The Postman Always Rings Twice* (1934) and *Double Indemnity* (1936) stunned with brevity and pith equaled only by Nathanael West's *Miss Lonelyhearts* (1933) and *The Day of the Locust* (1939). In that same year Raymond Chandler, one of the foremost stylists of the century, inaugurated his career with *The Big Sleep*, while Thornton Wilder, having won the highest accolades for his prose, turned to drama in *Our Town* (1938) and the convention-busting *The Skin of Our Teeth* (1942).

Robert Penn Warren, poet, New Critic, and self-declared leader of the Southern Agrarian movement against the conservatism and sentimentality of the literary Old South, won the country's highest honors, notably for his panoramic *Night Rider* (1939) and *All the King's Men* (1946). But the national epic—majestic in scope, flawless in execution, as eloquent in politics as in aesthetics—came from a writer who made the cover of *Time* a full year before Hemingway: John Dos Passos. Distributed over three volumes—*The 42nd Parallel* (1930), *1919* (1932), and *Big Money* (1936)—his *U.S.A.* trilogy spans the twentieth-century United States from coast to coast and from the topmost to the most wretched social lot. Slicing the rapacious American colossus to the bone, Dos Passos's saga displays the symbolic finesse of Herman Melville and the narrative fervor of Jack London combined.

If the United States arose from World War I secure as a superpower, it emerged from World War II (1939–1945) looking up the Cold War nuclear barrel. Artists recoiled in horror, writing of war with contempt, of nu-

clear doom with dread, and of consumerist suburbia with contempt mixed with dread. Norman Mailer's *The Naked and the Dead* (1948), Irwin Shaw's *The Young Lions* (1948), Herman Wouk's *Caine Mutiny* (1951), James Jones's *From Here to Eternity* (1951)—war novels that were almost all antiwar novels—achieved celebrity even before becoming Hollywood films, just as Joseph Heller's epochal CATCH-22 (1961) and Kurt Vonnegut's *Slaughterhouse 5* (1969) did a decade later. As captured in a cinematic jewel, *The Atomic Café* (1982), written and directed by Jayne Loader, Kevin Rafferty, and Pierce Rafferty, the 1950s were the years of Cold War retrenchment, of Nixon and McCarthy–stoked Communist witch-hunts, of the H-Bomb frenzy and the MAD (Mutual Assured Destruction) military-political doctrine. The literary response, often in a grotesque/satirical vein, formed an axis stretching from Walter M. Miller Jr.'s *Canticle for Leibowitz* (1959), Eugene Burdick and Harvey Wheeler's *Fail-Safe* (1962), and Vonnegut's *Cat's Cradle* (1963) to more contemporary postapocalyptic science fiction.

In a more canonical vein, John Updike's decades-spanning series of novels about Harry "Rabbit" Angstrom, the angst-ridden suburban man—Vladimir Nabokov's metaphysically complex novels/riddles—and the diamond-cutter short prose of John Cheever, Flannery O'Connor, and J. D. Salinger, all defied the country going ballistic. Ralph Ellison's rumble from America's tenement basement, INVISIBLE MAN (1952), together with James Baldwin's *Go Tell It on the Mountain* (1953), marked the coming-of-age of the African American, even as between his comedies/caricatures *Goodbye Columbus* (1959) and *Portnoy's Complaint* (1969), Philip Roth deplored the dwindling powers of fiction to do justice to the world that was fast overtaking writers' imaginations. Little wonder that the 1950s were also a time of social and sociological reckoning. Warning against the closing of the American mind, David Riesman's *The LONELY CROWD* (1950) and Malcolm Cowley's *The Literary Situation* (1954) pinned the mood of the nation: atomized, "other-directed," looking for a fix in the religious existentialism of Paul Tillich, in the social criticism of C. Wright Mills's *The Power Elite* (1956), or even—anticipating the eclectic 1960s—in Asiatic mysticism.

One of the most distinct regional voices was the New York Jewish elite, congregated around intellectuals from the *Partisan Review*. Saul Bellow, Bernard Malamud, and Philip Roth are independently famous as novelists, but Delmore Schwartz (subject of Bellow's Nobel-winning *Humboldt's Gift*, 1975), Lionel and Diana Trilling, Philip Rahv, Irving Howe, Arthur Miller, Hannah Arendt, Alfred Kazin, E. L. Doctorow, and Isaac Bashevis Singer all gave the East Coast establishment its legendary clout and verve. As the encroaching 1960s would not be complete without the Beatles, so would not the 1950s without the Beats. Their eclectic "howls" (from the title of Allen Ginsberg's linchpin poem) fueled the junk fiction of William S. Burroughs, the social protest of Lawrence Ferlinghetti, and Jack Kerouac's *On the Road* (1957), an "easy-rider" write-up of his picaresque travels across the United States and still a gospel for circles of modish, black-clad, bearded intellectuals in quest of Emersonian ideals.

Flower Power to Popular Fiction

Starting with the 1960s all labels and historical subdivisions become increasingly haphazard, not to say arbitrary. Styles, influences, and ideologies mix freely as 40,000, and then 50,000 new titles are published annually in multi-million editions, glutting the literary market. Day-Glo colors mask the culture of black humor, forged among the Vietnam genocide, political assassinations, drug and sexual revolutions, and race riots spilling out of inner-city ghettos. Where Ken Kesey's *One Flew Over the Cuckoo's Nest* (1962) branded America as an oppressive mental institution in a fit farewell to the 1950s, Malamud's *God's Grace* (1982) may have contained the key to the two literary decades that followed. In turn ironic and savagely funny, awash in intertextual and intercultural allusions, at once sophisticated and vernacular, this realistic fantasy was a melting pot of genres, techniques, and modes in the service of art that gripped readers with the intensity of the scourge of the 1980s: crack cocaine.

With traditions and conventions falling left and right, fiction writers invaded the domain of history and reportage, creating—after the MO of Truman Capote's sensational real-crime account *In Cold Blood* (1966)—"nonfiction novels." As the award-winning docufiction of Norman Mailer, William Styron, or Robert Coover made clear, history could be profitably (in both senses) melded with the techniques and best-selling appeal of the novel. In turn, media-hip journalists such as Tom Wolfe, Joan Didion, Gay Talese, Jimmy Breslin, and the gonzo-prodigy Hunter S. Thompson smashed all records of popularity with their hyped-up, heat-of-the-moment pieces that eroded inherited distinctions between literary and popular culture. A generation of confessional poets, from John Berryman, Theodore Roethke, and Robert Lowell, to Anne Sexton and Sylvia Plath, stood emotionally naked after casting the innermost aspects of their lives in verse, defying the distinction between art and real life much as today's poetry "slams" and the rhyming art of rap do. Popular fiction and literature worthy of attention by the academic canons began to blur in Edward Albee's drama *Who's Afraid of Virginia Woolf?* (1962), Ira Levin's *Boys from Brazil* (1976), or Paul Auster's *New York Trilogy* (1987).

Even with Faulkner, Hemingway (by now Nobel winners), the dramatist Tennessee Williams, and other heavyweights still at work, with Vonnegut, Heller, and Roth fertile with tragicomedies and satires, with Bellow, Malamud, and Mailer reaping national and international awards, the times—as Bob Dylan forewarned—were a-changin'. A new wave of crime novelists, from Ed McBain to Chester Himes to Joseph Wambaugh, elevated the genre to rightful literary heights. Science fiction enjoyed

a meteoric rise on bookstands and university curricula, romances and erotica—though few as stylish as Erica Jong's *Fanny* (1980)—smashed all readership records, and Stephen King single-handedly revived the horror story. Theory-laden postmodern fiction sought refuge in universities which, funding writers-in-residence, cultivated a new crop of professionally trained "creative writers."

American literary theory was not born with structuralism. As the nineteenth century bled into the twentieth, C. S. Peirce and John Dewey proposed a pragmatic view of reading as an ongoing transaction with the reader, while formalists like Pound and Eliot defended classical standards with an opaqueness that left some readers scratching their heads. By the early 1950s, René Wellek, Robert Penn Warren and John Crowe Ranson made fashionable the art of "close reading," at the expense of historicism and historical context. Soon thereafter, New Criticism itself was overshadowed by structuralist theories drawn in part from the work on the "deep structure" of language by the politically outspoken MIT professor Noam Chomsky. More recently, Richard Rorty and Stanley Fish have turned back to reader response, albeit without the philosophical elegance of the pragmatists. While Susan Sontag argued against too much tedious analysis of hallowed art, deconstruction, neo-Marxism, feminism, and post-colonialism began to vie for their fifteen minutes of fame. Today unorthodox, even wildly counterintuitive, readings remain in vogue, proving that the understanding of art—to say nothing of enjoyment—is more often than not compromised by obscure jargon and capricious thinking.

Much affected by these interpretive battles, postmodern authors dug convoluted trenches, cutting "truth" and "reality" loose and getting lost in a maze of fictional and metafictional simulacra. The bewildering "novel" *The Recognitions* (1955), by William Gaddis, orbited around issues of authenticity and counterfeiting, plotting the trajectory for many works to follow. John Barth launched several of these language- and self-centered voyages, from the early stories of *Lost in the Funhouse* (1968) to his exhaustive effort at throwing everything—including himself and postmodernist fiction—to the demons of parody and self-reflexivity: *Coming Soon!!!* (2001). It is equally difficult to get a fix on the fiction of Thomas Pynchon: from *Gravity's Rainbow* (1973) to *Mason & Dixon* (1997), whose compulsion for detail and antinarrative paranoia throw conventional techniques and characters out the window. Robert Coover charted hypertext and cyberspace with guru patience, while Don DeLillo gave much of the last century's history the zoom of a fastball in his gargantuan *Underworld* (1997). Alongside the postmodern pyrotechnics, the 1980s' minimalism—sometimes disparaged as K-mart or "dirty" realism—exerted its populist fascination with social "lowlifes" addicted to alcohol, drugs, welfare, trailer park blues, or intellectual malaise. In a style stripped of excess, with plots in abeyance and moral judgments suspended, Marilyn Robinson, Anne Beattie, and

Richard Ford aired the kitchen side of America, though none as successfully as Raymond Carver, exquisitely filmed in 1993 in Robert Altman's *Short Cuts.*

A splintering mosaic of ethnic and cultural communities gained unprecedented readership and critical applause as Toni Morrison, an African American winner of the 1993 Nobel Prize, summoned in *Beloved* (1987), a ghost story about the abominable history of slavery. Joining a chorus of black artists such as Alice Walker, the poet Maya Angelou, Imamu Baraka, Ishmael Reed, Clarence Major, Ernest J. Gaines, and John A. Williams, Asian Americans also gained ground, with the best-sellers of Amy Tan, from *The Joy Luck Club* (1989) to *The Bonesetter's Daughter* (2001), lamenting conformity and the loss of cultural moorings. Shirley Lim's memoir, *Among the White Moon Faces* (1996) detailed her suffering as a girl in Malaysia, while Frank Chin's gadfly antics in *Donald Duk* (1991) are sure to shock and delight. Hispanic prose and poetry of Gary Soto, Ana Castillo, Richard Rodriguez, Denise Chavez, and a phalanx of others record the humor, wisdom, and socioeconomic discontents of their communities. From John Okada's scorching treatment of Japanese anguish over World War II internment or military service, *No-No Boy* (1957), to Jhumpa Lahiri's Pulitzer-winning tale of the limbo between her Bengali heritage and Western upbringing, *Interpreter of Maladies* (1999), the number of ethnic voices in American literature is legion and growing.

With belles lettres now accounting for only 3 percent of literature disseminated through the United States, popular fiction made substantial gains in prestige and legitimacy, gradually spawning a nobrow culture, indifferent to rhetorical tugs-of-war between aesthetic highs and genre lows. The comic gems of Woody Allen, the literary horror of Thomas M. Disch, the Texan regionalism of Larry McMurtry, the survivalist thrillers of James Dickey, the black neo-noir of Walter Mosley, or the existential best-sellers of Walker Percy (*Love in the Ruins*, 1971; *The Thanatos Syndrome*, 1987), and a host of yet unknown but worth knowing genre artists set a fresh course for American literature in the new millennium.

BIBLIOGRAPHY

Baym, Nina, et al., eds. *The Norton Anthology of American Literature.* 2 vols. New York: Norton, 1986. An invaluable resource containing works by most of the eminent authors in American history as well as immaculately researched introductions that serve as models of pithy exegesis.

Bercovitch, Sacvan, et al., eds. *The Cambridge History of American Literature.* Cambridge, U.K.: Cambridge University Press, 1994. A more thorough historical study, these volumes are part of a projected, complete history and set the standard for scholarly rigor. Volumes 1 (1590–1820) and 2 (1820–1865) contain histories of prose writing, while Volume 8 covers contemporary poetry and criticism (1940–1995).

Elliott, Emory, ed. *Columbia Literary History of the United States.* New York: Columbia University Press, 1988. Divided into short, discrete sections on various subjects, this source is not as complete or useful as might have been hoped. Of special interest, however, is the opening piece on Native Literature.

Hart, James D., ed. *The Oxford Companion to American Literature.* New York: Oxford University Press, 1995. Arranged alphabetically by author, this is an extremely useful, well-organized research tool. Given the format, the relative brevity of the entries is understandable, even refreshing.

Jones, Howard Mumford, and Richard M. Ludwig. *Guide to American Literature and Its Background since 1890.* Rev. and Exp., 4th ed. Cambridge, Mass.: Harvard University Press, 1972. A carefully researched bibliography of American literature that is easy to use.

Knippling, Alpana S., ed. *New Immigrant Literatures in the United States: A Sourcebook to Our Multicultural Literary Heritage.* Westport, Conn.: Greenwood Press, 1996. Covers an enormous array of material, with sections on everything from Filipino American to Sephardic Jewish American literature.

Ruland, Richard. *From Puritanism to Postmodernism: A History of American Literature.* New York: Viking, 1991. An eminently readable, lively history of American literature, rich in observations about connections between periods and authors.

Swirski, Peter. *From Lowbrow to Nobrow.* Toronto: University of Toronto Press, 2003. Irreverent humor and rigorous scholarship (including discussions of topics as diverse as sociology and aesthetics) are combined in this trenchant analysis of the relationship between highbrow and lowbrow literatures.

Tindall, George B. *America: A Narrative History.* 2d ed. New York: Norton, 1988. A lucid history characterized by a wealth of detail: the time lines and indexes are particularly useful.

Trachtenberg, Stanley, ed. *Critical Essays on American Postmodernism.* New York: G. K. Hall; Toronto: Maxwell Macmillan, 1995. For the most part fair-minded and informative, this study neither rhapsodizes about postmodernism nor dismisses its influence among academics.

Walker, Marshall. *The Literature of the United States of America.* London: Macmillan, 1983. Although not as comprehensive as others, it is written with style and humor and gives a human face to many authors of interest.

David Reddall
Peter Swirski

See also vol. 9: **Untitled Poem (Anne Bradstreet).**

AFRICAN AMERICAN LITERATURE

The struggle to establish African American writing in both the world of popular literature and the more academic world of letters has largely been won. With a remarkably growing black audience and increased interest from white readers, black writers of pop fiction such as E. Lynn Harris and Terry McMillan routinely sell hundreds of thousands of copies. On the other hand, African American literature has become part of the highbrow literary establishment with the Nobel Prize for literature being conferred on Toni Morrison, and with such critically acclaimed writers as Jamaica Kincaid, August Wilson, Carl Phillips, James Alan McPherson, John Edgar Wideman, and Charles Johnson.

Two movements coincided to increase dramatically not only the public's interest in African American literature but also the quantity and dissemination of professional African American literary criticism. The first of these movements was the establishment of black studies programs at white-majority universities in the late 1960s and early 1970s, an intellectual and ideological offshoot of the civil rights movement. The second was the feminist movement of the early 1970s. At that moment, a number of important black women writers appeared: Nikki Giovanni, Toni Cade Bambara, Toni Morrison, Alice Walker, and Ntozake Shange. Their emergence was accompanied by the rediscovery of an earlier black woman writer, Zora Neale Hurston. With the rise of African American studies—despite the dominance of social science in this field—came increased awareness of black American literature and a growing number of highly trained people who could analyze it. With the sudden visibility of black women authors, came both critical controversy and the core audience of American literature: women. It can safely be said that, as a result of these social and political dynamics, African American literary scholars could achieve two important ends: the recognition of African American literature within the American literary canon and the creation of an African American literary canon. Both goals have been served through the construction of a usable black literary past.

African American Literature during Slavery
Because of the prohibition against teaching slaves to read, the acquisition of literacy among African Americans before the Civil War was something of a subversive act, and certainly the earliest writings by African Americans were meant—explicitly or implicitly—to attack the institution of slavery and to challenge the dehumanized status of black Americans.

The earliest significant African American writers were poets. Phillis Wheatley, a slave girl born in Senegal, was taught by her owners to read and write. Her poetry, published in 1773, was celebrated in various circles, less for its quality than for the fact that a black woman had written it. Jupiter Hammon, a far less polished writer, was a contemporary of Wheatley and, like her, was deeply influenced by Methodism. And in 1829, George Moses Horton published *The Hope of Liberty*, the first poetry that plainly protested slavery.

Without question, however, the most influential black writing of the period emerged during the antebellum period (1830–1860) and was explicitly political: the slave narrative—accounts of slavery written by fugitive or former slaves—was a popular genre that produced hundreds of books and tracts. Several of these books have become classics of American literature, such as Frederick Douglass's *Narrative of the Life of Frederick Douglass, An American Slave* (1845), William Wells Brown's *Narrative of William Wells Brown, a Fugitive slave* (1847), and Harriet Jacobs's *Incidents in the Life of Slave Girl* (1861). Brown, a

full-fledged man of letters, also wrote the first African American travelogue, *Three Years in Europe: Or, Places I Have Seen and People I Have Met* (1852); the first play published by a black, *Experience: Or, How to Give a Northern Man Backbone* (1856); and the first black novel, *Clotel: Or, The President's Daughter: A Narrative of Slave Life in the United States* (1853). Other important black novels of the period are Harriet E. Wilson's *Our Nig* (1859), Frank J. Webb's neglected *Garies and their Friends* (1857), and the recently discovered *Bondwoman's Narrative* by Hannah Crafts (1853/60).

From Reconstruction to World War I
Paul Laurence Dunbar, Pauline Hopkins, Charles Waddell Chesnutt, and Frances Ellen Watkins Harper—who had established her career before the Civil War—were the principal black writers to emerge during the GILDED AGE, the nadir of race relations in the United States, when strict racial segregation was established by law and custom, and enforced by violence. It was a time when dialect and regional (local color) writing was in vogue, and the southern plantation romance was being cranked out as slavery suddenly became nostalgic. Watkins wrote both poetry ("Bury Me in a Free Land," 1854) and fiction, most notably *Iola Leroy* (1892). Hopkins, editor of *The Colored American* (1893), wrote the novel *Contending Forces* (1900), now considered an important work. Dunbar and Chesnutt were the two major writers of that period, both of whom used dialect and local color in their writings. Dunbar became the first black poet to achieve real fame and critical notice. He also wrote novels and lyrics for black Broadway shows. Chesnutt was a short story writer and novelist who used black folklore and the trappings of the old plantation to great, often ironic effect. His novel, *The Marrow of Tradition* (1901), about the Wilmington, North Carolina riot of 1898 was one of the more uncompromising works by a black author of the time—and uncomfortable for many white readers who had come to enjoy Chesnutt's early, more subtle work. Probably the best selling book of the period was Booker T. Washington's *Up From Slavery: An Autobiography* (1901).

W. E. B. Du Bois's *The Souls of Black Folks* (1903), a highly unified collection of essays, remains the single most influential book by a black author from this period. James Weldon Johnson's novel, *Autobiography of an Ex-Colored Man* (1912), used the theme of racial "passing" in a fresh way. Both books explored the idea of a unique African American "double consciousness."

The Harlem Renaissance
Several occurrences made the HARLEM RENAISSANCE possible, including the large migration of African Americans from the south to northern cities during World War I; the creation of interracial, progressive organizations, such as the NATIONAL ASSOCIATION FOR THE ADVANCEMENT OF COLORED PEOPLE (1909) and the NATIONAL URBAN LEAGUE (1911); the emergence of Marcus Garvey and the mass attraction of BLACK NATIONALISM as a political movement;

the growing interest among black intellectuals in socialism and communism; and the rise of jazz and a modernist sensibility among black artists. This renaissance largely coincided with the 1920s and was midwived by such eminent figures as Charles S. Johnson; W. E. B. Du Bois; Alain Locke, who, in 1925, edited the seminal anthology *The New Negro: An Interpretation*; and James Weldon Johnson, who wanted to create an identifiable school of black writing. Poets such as Langston Hughes and Countee Cullen came to public attention at this time, as well as poet/novelist Claude McKay, novelists Jessie Fausett, Nella Larsen, Wallace Thurman, and Rudolph Fisher, and the relatively unknown but brash Zora Neale Hurston. Probably the most artistically accomplished work of the period was Jean Toomer's evocative novel-cum-miscellany, *Cane* (1923).

The Depression and After

The depression signaled the end of the Harlem Renaissance, as white publishers and readers became less interested in the works of blacks, and as the fad of primitivism faded. Also, Black Nationalism and pan-Africanism lost traction as mass political movements, although they continued to affect black thinking. The impact of communism on black writers became more pronounced, particularly after the role communists played in the Scottsboro trial (1931). But black writers retained their interest in exploring the folk roots of their culture. Zora Neale Hurston, who had already made a name for herself during the Harlem Renaissance, published some of her major works during the depression, including her first novel *Jonah's Gourd Vine* (1934) and the anthropological study *Mules and Men* (1935). Her second novel, *Their Eyes Were Watching God* (1937), is considered her masterpiece, one of the major feminist works by a black woman author. Other noteworthy novels of the 1930s include George Schuyler's *Black No More* (1931) and Arna Bontemps's *God Sends Sunday* (1931) and *Black Thunder* (1936).

A year after Hurston's great novel of black southern folk life, Richard Wright, a communist from Mississippi, published *Uncle Tom's Children* (1938)—intensely violent and political short stories with a decidedly different take on the black South. He became the first black writer to have his book selected by the Book-of-the-Month Club when, two years later, he published the most celebrated black novel in American literary history at the time, *Native Son*, with its stark naturalism and unappealing protagonist. Wright became, without question, the first true black literary star. In 1945, he published his autobiography *Black Boy: A Recollection of Childhood and Youth*, another highly successful book—an uncompromising and unsentimental examination of his family and life in the Deep South. He influenced a cadre of significant black writers including William Attaway (*Blood on the Forge*, 1941), Chester Himes (*If He Hollers Let Him Go*, 1945), and Ann Petry (*The Street*, 1946).

Langston Hughes. A photograph by Nickolas Muray of the admired and influential poet and writer, one of the leading lights of the Harlem Renaissance. GETTY IMAGES

By the end of the 1940s, Wright's influence was waning, and black writers turned to less naturalistic and less politically overt themes. William Demby's *Beetlecreek* (1950), with its existentialist theme, is a good example of this new approach. Wright went to Europe in 1947, never to live in the United States again, and though he continued to publish a steady, mostly nonfiction stream of books in the 1950s, including the outstanding collection of short fiction *Eight Men* (1961), he never enjoyed the level of success he had in the late 1930s and 1940s.

By the early 1950s, black writers went much further in their crossover appeal, achieving greater acclaim than even Wright had done. In 1950, Gwendolyn Brooks became the first black to win the Pulitzer Prize for poetry for her book *Annie Allen* (1949). Ralph Ellison's 1952 novel *Invisible Man* won the National Book Award and has been judged the most impressive and the most literary of all black American novels. Some consider it not only the greatest of all black novels but also arguably the greatest post–World War II American novel. Finally, there is James Baldwin, son of a Harlem preacher, who began writing highly stylistic and penetrating essays in the late 1940s, and whose first novel, the highly autobiographical *Go Tell It On the Mountain* (1953), was well received. All these writers were trying to show dimensions of black life they felt were lacking in the works of Wright and other black naturalistic writers.

After the 1960s

By the late 1950s, two black women writers gained recognition for their work: Paule Marshall for her coming-of-age novel *Brown Girl, Brownstones* (1959), and Lorraine Hansberry for the play about a working-class black family in Chicago, *A Raisin in the Sun* (1959), which has become the most famous drama written by a black playwright.

In the 1960s, James Baldwin became a major force in American letters, publishing novels such as *Another Country* (1962) and *Tell Me How Long the Train's Been Gone* (1968), as well as his meditation on the NATION OF ISLAM and the state of race relations in America, *The Fire Next Time* (1963), his most popular book. He also wrote the play *Blues for Mister Charlie* (1964). Propelled by the civil rights movement and the momentous sense of political engagement taking place in America in the 1960s, blacks began to make their presence in a number of genres. Best-sellers of the period include *The Autobiography of Malcolm X* (1965), the compelling life story of the Nation of Islam minister; *Manchild in the Promised Land* by Claude Brown (1965), about growing up in Harlem; and Sammy Davis Jr.'s *Yes I Can* (1965), about the life of the most famous black entertainer of the day. Maya Angelou's *I Know Why the Caged Bird Sings* (1970) remains one of the best-selling black autobiographies of all time. John A. Williams, a prolific writer during this period, wrote, unquestionably, the major novel of this period, *Man Who Cried I Am* (1967), a roman à clef about post–World War II black writers. It deeply reflected the feelings of many blacks at the time, who felt they lived in a society on the verge of a "final solution," and was one of the most talked about books of the 1960s.

Probably the most influential writer of this period was LeRoi Jones, who became Imamu Amiri Baraka. He was a poet of considerable significance (*Preface to a Twenty-Volume Suicide Note*, 1961, and *The Dead Lecturer*, 1964); a music critic (*Blues People*, 1963, is still one of the enduring studies of black music); a dramatist (*Dutchman*, 1964, was the single most famous play of the period); and an essayist (*Home: Social Essays*, 1966). As he became more involved in the cultural nationalist politics of the middle and late 1960s, the quality of his writing deteriorated, as he focused more on agitprop. Nevertheless, he helped spawn the black arts movement, which produced poets such as Nikki Giovanni, Don L. Lee (Haki Matabuti), Lucille Clifton, Sonia Sanchez, June Jordan, and Etheridge Knight. Much of this work, too, was agitprop, though several of these writers developed their craft with great care.

In the 1970s, more black novelists appeared: the satirist Ishmael Reed (*Mumbo Jumbo*, 1972); Ernest Gaines (*The Autobiography of Miss Jane Pittman*, 1971); and the highly intense work of Gayl Jones (*Corregidora*, 1975).

With the rise of interest in black women's work, Toni Morrison and Alice Walker appeared, along with writers like Gloria Naylor (*The Women of Brewster Place*, 1982). David Bradley's groundbreaking novel about remembering slavery and the impact of its horror, *The Chaneysville Incident* (1981), foreshadowed Morrison's highly acclaimed *Beloved* (1987).

In the realm of children's and young adult literature, the late Virginia Hamilton (*M. C. Higgins the Great*, 1974) is the only children's author to win the coveted MacArthur Prize. Mildred Taylor (*Roll of Thunder, Hear My Cry*, 1976) and Walter Dean Myers (*Fallen Angels*, 1988) have also produced major works for young people.

BIBLIOGRAPHY

Andrews, William L. *To Tell A Free Story: The First Century of Afro-American Autobiography, 1760–1865*. Urbana: University of Illinois Press, 1986.

Baker, Houston A. *Modernism and the Harlem Renaissance*. Chicago: University of Chicago Press, 1987.

Bell, Bernard W. *The Afro-American Novel and Its Tradition*. Amherst: University of Massachusetts Press, 1987.

Carby, Hazel V. *Reconstructing Womanhood: The Emergence of the Afro-American Woman Novelist*. New York: Oxford University Press, 1987.

Foster, Frances Smith. *Written by Herself: Literary Production by African American Women, 1746–1892*. Bloomington: Indiana University Press, 1993.

Gates, Henry Louis. *Signifying Monkey: A Theory of Afro-American Criticism*. New York: Oxford University Press, 1988.

Gilroy, Paul. *The Black Atlantic: Modernity and Double Consciousness*. Cambridge, Mass.: Harvard University Press, 1993.

Holloway, Karla F. C. *Moorings and Metaphors: Figures of Culture and Gender in Black Women's Literature*. New Brunswick, N.J.: Rutgers University Press, 1992.

Huggins, Nathan I. *Harlem Renaissance*. New York: Oxford University Press, 1971.

Lewis, David L. *When Harlem Was In Vogue*. New York: Penguin, 1997.

McDowell, Deborah E. *"The Changing Same": Black Women's Literature, Criticism, and Theory*. Bloomington: Indiana University Press, 1995.

North, Michael. *The Dialect of Modernism: Race, Language, and Twentieth-Century Literature*. New York: Oxford University Press, 1994.

Posnock, Ross. *Color and Culture: Black Writers and the Making of the Modern Intellectual*. Cambridge, Mass.: Harvard University Press, 1998.

Gerald Early

See also **African American Studies; African Americans;** *Autobiography of Malcolm X;* **Harlem;** *Invisible Man; Souls of Black Folk.*

CHILDREN'S LITERATURE

The genre of children's literature in the United States was not named as such until the middle of the twentieth century, when libraries and bookstores began placing books they believed to be of special interest to children in separate sections of their establishments. Publishers caught on to this trend and began producing and selling books specifically to the children's market, further dividing the audience by age and reading levels. These groupings include picture books, easy readers, beginning readers, middle grade, and young adult. The categories overlap and disagreement over what books belong in what category are frequent and ongoing among professionals in the field. Late-twentieth-century scholarship questioned the practice of separating this literature from the mainstream and targeting it strictly for children. Interestingly, American children's literature has come full circle from its earliest days, when it taught culture and history through didactic texts. Afterward, it went through several decades of emphasis on entertaining and literary fiction, followed by a renewed interest in nonfiction, and then—to the turn of the twenty-first century—a stress on accounts of historical people and events, with an emphasis on multiculturalism.

Indian and Early American Literature

American children's literature originated with the oral tradition of its Native peoples. When stories and legends were told by Native Americans, children were included in the audience as a means of passing on the society's culture and values to succeeding generations. This oral literature included creation stories and stories of chiefs, battles, intertribal treaties, spirits, and events of long ago. They entertained as they instructed, and were often the most important part of sacred ceremonies.

The Puritans and other British settlers in New England brought with them printed matter for children to be used for advancing literacy, teaching religion, and other didactic purposes. British works were imported and reprinted in the American colonies, beginning a trend of European imports that would continue for some time. A number of the earliest known children's works written in the colonies borrowed heavily from these imports in theme and purpose. These include John Cotton's *Spiritual Milk for Boston Babes* (1646). Probably the best-known Puritan book that children read at the time was the *New England Primer*, originally published sometime between 1686 and 1690. It contained lessons in literacy and religious doctrine in verse form with pictures, not for the purpose of entertaining children but because Puritans believed children learned best that way. Other common books in early America included John Bunyan's *Pilgrim's Progress* (1678) and American schoolbooks such as Noah Webster's *Webster's American Spelling Book* (1783) and George Wilson's *American Class Reader* (c. 1810).

The Emergence of an American Children's Literature

Imported books for children began losing their appeal after the War of 1812 and American themes expanded from religious doctrine to a more general moral stance that was viewed as important to the establishment of the character of the new nation. Jacob Abbott's "Rollo" stories, about a little boy named Rollo who gets older with succeeding stories, are a good example. The Congregationalist minister published the first Rollo story in 1835 and went on to write more than two hundred moralistic tales for children.

Moralistic teaching carried over into the general education system established by a nation desiring a literate democracy. The most commonly used textbook series from before the Civil War to the 1920s was the McGuffey Reader. It concerned itself as much with right and wrong as it did about reading. An exception to this kind of writing for children in the pre–Civil War period is the poem probably written by Clement Moore, "A Visit from St. Nicholas"—later known as "The Night before Christmas"—published in 1823 in a New York newspaper. This poem carried a new purpose, that of pure entertainment.

A well-known publisher and writer of the antebellum era was Samuel Goodrich, who founded *Parley's Magazine* in 1833 after a successful round of books featuring his popular storyteller character, Peter Parley. Goodrich's magazine mixed information about the world, much of which would be questioned today, with enjoyable entertainment for children. Other well-known American children's periodicals of the nineteenth century include *The Youth's Companion* (1827–1929), *Juvenile Miscellany* (1826–1834), and *Our Young Folks* (1865–1873). Each periodical had its own character and emphasis and dealt with the timely issues of the day such as slavery, the Civil War, and Reconstruction.

Late-Nineteenth- and Twentieth-Century Literature

As it was in Britain, the late nineteenth century in the United States was an era rich in book-length fiction for American children, producing some of the best-known classics enjoyed by children and adults. These include Louisa May Alcott's *Little Women* (1868), along with its subsequent related novels, and Samuel (Mark Twain) Clemens's *The Adventures of Tom Sawyer* (1876) and *The Adventures of HUCKLEBERRY FINN* (1884). The turn of the century brought L. Frank Baum's fantasy *The Wonderful Wizard of Oz*, published in 1900.

The twentieth century saw a shift in American children's literature so that domestic authors and titles finally won preeminence over imported titles. Readers became interested in subjects of American history and series like Laura Ingalls Wilder's Little House books—beginning with *Little House in the Big Woods* (1932)—drew dedicated fans. Classic novels involving the American theme of nature also appeared, including E. B. White's *Charlotte's Web* (1952).

The mid-twentieth century was marked by advances in printing technology that allowed for high-quality reproductions of artwork, leading to the mass production of thousands of picture books for children each year, a practice that continues. This created an even more important role for illustrators, who now wrote many of the books they illustrated. One of the earlier classics of this form is *Goodnight Moon* (1947), by Margaret Wise Brown and illustrated by Clement Hurd. Probably the best-known author-illustrator is Maurice Sendak, whose *Where the Wild Things Are* (1963) became an instant classic. Picture books have also provided a new venue where children can enjoy poetry, since many picture books are illustrated poems or prose poems.

In the late twentieth century, American children's literature began to turn toward multicultural themes. Works of fiction, nonfiction, drama, and poetry illustrated and promoted an understanding of the diversity of the population of the United States and the richness and struggles of its people.

BIBLIOGRAPHY

Avery, Gillian. *Behold the Child: American Children and Their Books, 1621–1922.* Baltimore: Johns Hopkins University Press, 1994.

Carpenter, Humphrey, and Mari Prichard. *The Oxford Companion to Children's Literature.* Oxford: Oxford University Press, 1984.

Hunt, Peter. *Children's Literature: An Illustrated History.* Oxford: Oxford University Press, 1995.

Kirk, Connie Ann, ed. *Encyclopedia of American Children's and Young Adult Literature.* Westport, Conn.: Greenwood Press, 2003.

Connie Ann Kirk

See also **Childhood; Webster's Blue-Backed Speller.**

NATIVE AMERICAN LITERATURE

In the course of their adaptation to a largely Anglo-American presence in North America, Native Americans blended the literary and linguistic forms of the newcomers with their own oral-based traditions. Native American authors who have achieved widespread acclaim since the middle twentieth century have drawn not only on the rich tension between these two traditions but also on several centuries of Native American writing in English. Before the American Revolution, Native American literature followed the history of Euro-American movement across the continent; where explorers and settlers went, missionaries could be found converting and educating indigenous peoples. Samson Occom studied English with missionaries and earned the honor of being the first Native American to publish in English with his *A Sermon Preached at the Execution of Moses Paul* (1772) and *Collections of Hymns and Spiritual Songs* (1774).

White attitudes toward Native American literature changed at the end of the WAR OF 1812. After the United States defeated the tribes of the trans-Appalachian frontier, the dominant culture began to romanticize Native American culture, celebrating its nobility and mourning its imminent demise. The Indian removal policy of the 1830s only added to this nostalgia, which manifested itself most clearly in the popularity of Native American auto-

biography. Autobiography writers, working primarily as Christian converts, modeled their books on the popular format of spiritual confession and missionary reminiscence. In 1829, William Apes published the first of these personal accounts, *A Son of the Forest.* This work reflects the temperance theme of the time, decrying destruction of the Indians at the hand of alcohol. George Copway proved an ideal native model for white society; he illustrated the nobility of his "savage" past as he integrated it with Euro-American religion and education. His *The Life, History, and Travels of Kah-ge-ga-gah-bowh* (1847) used personal episodes to teach English-speaking audiences about his tribe and culture. He published the first book of Native American poetry, *The Ojibway Conquest*, in 1850. One year later, with publication of the book by white ethnologist Henry Rowe Schoolcraft, entitled *Historical and Statistical Information Respecting the History, Condition, and Prospects of the Indian Tribes of the United States*, native poetry garnered a wider audience. In 1854 John Rollin Ridge broke away from autobiography and published the first novel by an American Indian, *The Life and Adventures of Joaquin Murieta*.

The second half of the nineteenth century marked the defeat and humiliation of Native Americans west of the MISSISSIPPI RIVER and the solidification of the reservation system. The Dawes General Allotment Act of 1887 attempted to force Americanization by abolishing communal landholding and instituting individual property ownership. Many Native Americans feared that their oral traditions would disappear under the reservation system, so they began to write down legends and folktales, as did Zitkala Sa, who published *Old Indian Legends* (1901). Between 1880 and 1920, other Native American writers were distinctly integrationist, asserting that only through assimilation could their people survive. Publishers hid the racial identity of John M. Oskison, the most popular Indian writer of the 1920s, while the novels of Simon Pokagon, John Joseph Mathews, and Mourning Dove continued to educate readers about tribal ways. D'arcy McNickle, considered by many the first important Native American novelist, published *The Surrounded* in 1936. He foreshadowed the use of alienation as a theme in post–World War II Native American literature.

The Termination Resolution of 1953 undid John Collier's NEW DEAL policy of Indian cultural reorganization by terminating federal control and responsibility for those tribes under the government's jurisdiction. Termination attempted, again, to Americanize native peoples by breaking up what was left of tribal cultures. With service in WORLD WAR II, poverty, and termination, many Native Americans were cut loose from their moorings, alienated from both the dominant Euro-American culture and their own tribal roots. It was not until 1970 that the U.S. government officially ended the policy of tribal termination.

Encouraged by civil rights activism, Native American voices appeared in the 1960s, including Duane Niatum and Simon Ortiz. These writers rejected assimilation as the only viable means of survival and asserted a separate native reality. N. Scott Momaday, with his 1968 novel *House Made of Dawn*, won the Pulitzer Prize for fiction in 1969 and brought Native American literature newfound respect. The year 1969 proved a turning point, not only because of Momaday's prize but also because Indian activism became more militant. The work of Gerald Vizenor, James Welch, and Leslie Marmon Silko asserted Indian identity. Vizenor wrote two novels, *Darkness in Saint Louis Bearheart* (1978) and *Griever: An American Monkey King in China* (1987), and the latter won the American Book Award in 1988. Welch received a National Endowment for the Arts grant in 1969 and then wrote his first book of poetry. He also wrote many novels, including *Winter in the Blood* (1974), joining oral traditions and the English language. Silko published her best-known work, *Ceremony*, in 1977, also combining the mythic past and the English literary tradition.

The best-known Native American writer of the mid-1990s was Louise Erdrich, author of the award-winning *Love Medicine* (1984). Like most Native American authors who published in English, Erdrich used her talents to decry the toll that white religion, disease, and industrialization took on native cultures. Like Welch and Silko, she weaves tribal mythology with English literary forms. Sherman Alexie also distinguished himself as one of the nation's best new writers. Most widely known for his collection of short stories, *The Lone Ranger and Tonto Fistfight in Heaven* (1993)—the basis for the 1998 film *Smoke Signals*—he has distinguished himself as a poet and novelist who explores the questions of love, poverty, and Native American identity in a sharp but often humorous manner. The English language, used for so long by white society to remove Native Americans from their "uncivilized" ways, was used in the final decades of the twentieth century by Native American writers to assert their distinct cultural heritage.

BIBLIOGRAPHY

Fleck, Richard F., ed. *Critical Perspectives on Native American Fiction.* Washington, D.C.: Three Continents Press, 1993; Pueblo, Colo.: Passeggiata Press, 1997.

Larson, Charles R. *American Indian Fiction.* Albuquerque: University of New Mexico Press, 1978.

Owen, Louis. *Other Destinies: Understanding the American Indian Novel.* Norman: University of Oklahoma Press, 1992.

Wiget, Andrew, ed. *Critical Essays on Native American Literature.* Boston: Hall, 1985.

Kristen Foster/J. H.

See also **Indian Oral Literature; Indian Oratory; Indian Reservations; Termination Policy.**

POPULAR LITERATURE

While Edgar Allan Poe (1809–1849) is often called the father of popular literature because of his seminal role in the development of three popular genres (detective fiction, science fiction, and horror fiction), the world of mass-market popular literature did not emerge until toward the end of the nineteenth century. When it did, its themes and preoccupations appeared to owe little to Poe.

The First Literary Boom (1830–1900)

As a result of a variety of socioeconomic factors, the United States experienced its first literary boom in the years between 1830 and 1900. Romances by the likes of Mary Johnston (1870–1936) and Laura Jean Libbey (1862–1925), and westerns by writers such as E. Z. C. Judson ("Ned Buntine," 1821–1886) and Edward S. Ellis (1840–1916) appeared in biweekly or weekly "dime novels," the most famous of which were those published by Erastus Beadle and Robert Adams, whose firm began publication, as Beadle's Dime Novel series, in 1860.

Unapologetically commercial in intent, the dime novels avoided any potentially difficult questions raised by either their subject matter or their literary antecedents. This tendency was most notable, perhaps, in the dime novel western, which, while being derived almost exclusively from the work of James Fenimore Cooper (1789–1851), managed to ignore completely the conflicts between the American East and the West discernible in Cooper's image of the frontier.

New Genres Appear in the Pulps (1900–1925)

While the next generation of the western did engage itself with the kind of question Cooper had asked, it rarely delved more deeply than nostalgia. In 1902, this added dimension, however slight, helped give the fledgling genre a cornerstone: *The Virginian*, by Owen Wister (1860–1938). Zane Grey (1872–1939), whose *Riders of the Purple Sage* appeared in 1912, was among the most prominent of Wister's many imitators.

Pulps (the term being derived from the cheap paper on which the magazines were printed) appeared as new postal regulations rendered prohibitively expensive the publication and distribution of dime novels. Their appearance was accompanied by that of detective fiction and, in the form of the romantic fantasy of Edgar Rice Burroughs (1875–1950), the germ of an as-yet unnamed genre, science fiction.

Fantasy Dominates Depression-Era Popular Literature (1925–1938)

As the country entered the Great Depression, popular taste turned to fantasy. The most popular detective fiction, for example, was no longer a dream of order, which is how some critics describe the early form, but rather a fantasy of power accompanied by a pervasive sense of disillusionment. In 1929, Dashiell Hammett (1894–1961) published the first such "hard-boiled" detective fiction novel, *Red Harvest*, which, as it owes much to Wister's *The Virginian*, is basically a western set in the city. Raymond Chandler (1888–1959), Erle Stanley Gardner (1889–1970),

129

and Rex Stout (1896–1975) were other notable practitioners of this new detective subgenre.

Fantasy of an altogether different kind also entered the pulps of this era in the form of a hyperrealist school of science fiction founded by Hugo Gernsback (1884–1967). In its own way no less fantastic than the Burroughsian mode, the new form remained distinguishable by its thoroughly unromantic obsession with the scientific and otherwise technical elements it brought to the genre.

An Explosion of New Forms (1938–1965)

During the war and postwar years, aside from some works by the likes of the western's Ernest Haycox (1899–1950) and Jack Schaefer (1907–1999), detective and science fiction remained the dominant popular genres of the day, albeit transformed by the war and a few signal figures.

John W. Campbell (1910–1971), who assumed the editorship of the pulp *Astounding* in 1937, helped bring about a revolution within the genre. He broke with tradition by publishing original work by Isaac Asimov (1920–1992) and Robert Heinlein (1907–1988), two writers who helped bring about a synthesis of the Gernsbackian and Burroughsian schools. This helped to make possible science fiction's eventual graduation from the pulps, as is evidenced by the later mainstream success of Ray Bradbury (b. 1920), author of *Fahrenheit 451* (1953).

Detective fiction fairly exploded in this period, with new subgenres and fresh takes on established forms reflecting not only the impact of the war on the public consciousness, but also wartime advances in technology and the sciences. Espionage and other war-related subjects were incorporated (the "Cold War novel," appearing first in the 1960s and taken up beginning in the 1970s by writers such as James Grady, Ross Thomas, Robert Ludlum, and Tom Clancy, had its roots in the detective fiction of this era), and a more sophisticated reading public embraced a hitherto unimaginably cynical variation: Mickey Spillane's *I, the Jury* (1947). In this brutish exercise in misogyny, sadism, and gore, the main character, Mike Hammer, metes out his own peculiar form of justice in a lawless urban dystopia that bears little resemblance to either Hammett's Poisonville or Chandler's Los Angeles.

The Romance and the Western Are Reborn (1965–)

Spillane's reinvention of hard-boiled detective fiction anticipated by a full generation the widespread inclusion in popular forms of graphic depictions of sex and violence. The appearance of the adult western is perhaps the most obvious manifestation of this trend, but sex also became an almost obligatory element of the modern form of the "category romance," which reappeared in the last third of the century.

In the 1960s, Harlequin, which began publishing romances in 1957, took full advantage of new methods of marketing and distribution to resurrect a genre that had lain largely dormant, with few exceptions, since the turn of the century. Prominent writers of the modern category

romance include Elizabeth Lowell, author of *Tell Me No Lies* (1986), and Jane Anne Krentz, author of *Sweet Starfire* (1986).

Notable variations on the genre, however, such as Margaret Mitchell's *Gone with the Wind* (1936), an anti-romance, appeared with some consistency prior to Harlequin's ascendance, and the gothic revival of the 1940s and 1950s saw the reappearance of many themes familiar to readers of the romance. (The work of Mary Higgins Clark, Stephen King, and William Peter Blatty, author of *The Exorcist* [1971], lies in the shadow of the gothic tradition.) Novels with historical settings or themes, ranging from James Branch Cabell's *The Cream of the Jest* (1917) to John Jakes's *North and South* (1982), also bear strong traces of the romance.

The western experienced a similar rejuvenation in this period, with wide notice of the work of Louis L'Amour (1908–1988) and Larry McMurtry (b. 1936), among others, ensuring the popularity of the later, iconoclastic detective fiction of Tony Hillerman (b. 1925) and Elmore Leonard (b. 1925).

BIBLIOGRAPHY

Aldiss, Brian W. *Billion Year Spree: The True History of Science Fiction.* Garden City, N.Y.: Doubleday, 1973. Thorough and opinionated.

Cawelti, John G. *The Six-Gun Mystique.* 2d ed. Bowling Green, Ohio: Bowling Green State University Press, 1984.

Ohmann, Richard M. *Selling Culture: Magazines, Markets, and Class at the Turn of the Century.* London: Verso, 1996.

Prince, Gerald. "How New Is New?" In *Coordinates: Placing Science Fiction and Fantasy.* Edited by George E. Slusser, Eric S. Rabkin, and Robert Scholes. Carbondale: Southern Illinois University Press, 1983. Places science fiction in the context of literary history.

Pyrhönen, Heta. *Murder from an Academic Angle: An Introduction to the Study of the Detective Narrative.* Columbia, S.C.: Camden House, 1994.

Radway, Janice. *Reading the Romance: Women, Patriarchy, and Popular Literature.* With a New Introduction by the author. Chapel Hill: University of North Carolina Press, 1991. Concerned with the socioeconomic origins of the category romance.

Unsworth, John. "The Book Market II." In *The Columbia History of the American Novel.* Edited by Emory Elliott et al. New York: Columbia University Press, 1991. Good introduction to the economics of popular culture production.

Michael Robinson

See also **Dime Novels; Magazines; Publishing Industry.**

LITTLE BIGHORN, BATTLE OF (25 June 1876). The Sioux Indians in Dakota Territory bitterly resented the opening of the Black Hills to settlers, which occurred in violation of the Treaty of Fort Laramie of 1868. Owing also to official graft and negligence, they faced starvation in the fall of 1875. They began to leave their reservations contrary to orders, to engage in their annual buffalo hunt. They were joined by tribespeople from other reservations until the movement took on the proportions of a serious revolt. The situation was one that called for the utmost tact and discretion, for the Sioux were ably led, and the treatment they had received had stirred the bitterest resentment among them. But an order originating with the Bureau of Indian Affairs was sent to all reservation officials early in December, directing them to notify the Indians to return by 31 January under penalty of being attacked by the U.S. Army. This belated order could not have been carried out in the dead of winter even if the Indians had been inclined to obey it.

Early in 1876 Gen. Philip H. Sheridan, from his headquarters at Chicago, ordered a concentration of troops on the upper Yellowstone River to capture or disperse the numerous bands of Dakotas who hunted there. In June, Gen. Alfred H. Terry, department commander, and Col. George A. Custer, with his regiment from Fort Abraham Lincoln, marched overland to the Yellowstone, where they were met by the steamboat *Far West* with ammunition and supplies. At the mouth of Rosebud Creek,

Sitting Bull. The holy man and principal leader of the Sioux resistance to whites, which culminated in his warriors' short-lived triumph at the Little Bighorn in 1876; he was killed in 1890 during the Ghost Dance revival, just before the massacre at Wounded Knee, S. Dak. © CORBIS

George Armstrong Custer. The Civil War hero and post–Civil War lieutenant colonel on the frontier is shown (*seated at center*) surrounded by some of his scouts in Montana Territory, just a few years before he and every man under his command were killed at the Little Bighorn on 25 June 1876.
© BETTMANN/CORBIS

a tributary of the Yellowstone, Custer received his final orders from Terry—to locate and disperse the Indians. Terry gave Custer absolutely free hand in dealing with the situation, relying on his well-known experience in such warfare.

With twelve companies of the Seventh Cavalry, Custer set out on his march and soon discovered the Sioux camped on the south bank of the Little Bighorn River. He sent Maj. Marcus Reno with three companies of cavalry and all the Arikara scouts across the upper ford of the river to attack the southern end of the Sioux camp. Capt. Frederick Benteen, with three companies, was sent to the left of Reno's line of march. Custer himself led five companies of the Seventh Cavalry down the river to the lower ford for an attack on the upper part of the camp. One company was detailed to bring up the pack train.

This plan of battle, typical of Custer, was in the beginning completely successful. Suddenly faced by a vigorous double offensive, the Indians at first thought only of retreat. At this critical juncture, and for reasons still not fully explained, Reno became utterly confused and ordered his men to fall back across the river. Thereupon the whole force of the Indian attack was concentrated upon Custer's command, compelling him to retreat from the river to a position at which his force was later annihilated. The soldiers under Reno rallied at the top of a high hill overlooking the river where they were joined by Benteen's troops and, two hours later, by the company guarding the pack train.

In 1879 an official inquiry into Reno's conduct in the battle cleared him of all responsibility for the disaster. Since that time the judgment of military experts has tended to reverse this conclusion and to hold both Reno and Benteen gravely at fault. In Sheridan's *Memoirs* it is stated: "Reno's head failed him utterly at the critical moment." He abandoned in a panic the perfectly defensible and highly important position on the Little Bighorn River. Reno's unpopularity after the battle was one of the reasons he was brought up on charges of drunkenness and "peeping tomism" and court-martialed. Reno was found guilty and dishonorably discharged. However, in December 1966 Reno's grandnephew, Charles Reno, asked the Army Board for the Correction of Military Records to review the court-martial verdict, citing disclosures in G. Walton's book *Faint the Trumpet Sounds*. In June 1967 the secretary of the army restored Reno to the rank of major and the dishonorable discharge was changed to an honorable one. The action was taken on the grounds that the discharge had been "excessive and therefore unjust." However, the guilty verdict still stands. In September 1967 Reno was reburied in Custer Battlefield National Cemetery in Montana.

As to Benteen, he admitted at the military inquiry following the battle that he had been twice ordered by Custer to break out the ammunition and come on with his men. Later, at 2:30 P.M., when he had joined Reno, there was no attacking force of Indians in the vicinity, and he had at his disposal two-thirds of Custer's entire regiment, as well as the easily accessible reserve ammunition. Gen. Nelson A. Miles, in his *Personal Recollections*, found no reason for Benteen's failure to go to Custer's relief. He asserted, after an examination of the battlefield, that a gallop of fifteen minutes would have brought reinforcements to Custer. Miles's opinion contributes to the mystery of why, for more than an hour—while Custer's command was being overwhelmed—Reno and Benteen remained inactive.

BIBLIOGRAPHY

Ambrose, Stephen. *Crazy Horse and Custer: The Parallel Lives of Two American Warriors.* Garden City, N.Y.: Doubleday, 1975; New York: New American Library, 1986; New York: Anchor Books, 1996.

Connell, Evan S. *Son of the Morning Star.* San Francisco: North Point Press, 1984; New York: Harper & Row, 1985.

McMurtry, Larry. *Crazy Horse.* New York: Lipper/Viking Books, 1999.

Sajna, Mike. *Crazy Horse: The Life Behind the Legend.* New York: Wiley, 2000.

Welch, James. *Killing Custer: The Battle of the Little Bighorn and the Fate of the Plains Indians.* New York: W. W. Norton, 1994.

O. G. Libby / A. G.

See also **Army, United States; Black Hills War; Cavalry, Horse; Frontier Defense; Indian Claims Commission; Literature: Native American Literature;** *and vol. 9:* **Account of the Battle at Little Bighorn.**

LITTLE BIGHORN NATIONAL MONUMENT.

On 25 June 1876, in the tranquil valley of the Little Bighorn River near Crow Agency, Montana, General George A. Custer led his Seventh Cavalry in a surprise attack on an enormous village of some seven to ten thousand Sioux, Cheyenne, and Arapaho. Chiefs Sitting Bull, Crazy Horse, Rain in the Face, Gall, Two Moons, and Kicking Bear led warriors in a counterattack, circling Custer's forces and killing them all.

The Indians removed their dead while U.S. soldiers were buried where they had fallen and later moved to a mass grave. The battle site was designated a national cemetery on 29 January 1879 and a national monument on 22 March 1946. Originally called Custer Battlefield National Monument, it was renamed Little Bighorn National Monument on 10 December 1991. In addition, a memorial to the Indian men, women, and children who died defending their homeland and traditional way of life was planned for the site. The "Peace through Unity" Indian Memorial was dedicated in the fall of 2002 and established an integral relationship with the Seventh Cavalry oblique that guards the mass grave.

BIBLIOGRAPHY

Josephy, Alvin M. Jr. *500 Nations: An Illustrated History of North American Indians.* New York: Knopf, 1994.

Veda Boyd Jones

LITTLE LEAGUE

originated in Williamsport, Pennsylvania, in 1938, when Carl Stotz, while playing catch with his nephews, conceived of a baseball game for boys between the ages of eight and twelve. In order to create a game with the physical dimensions and rules appropriate to their ages, Stotz used sixty-foot base paths, thirty feet less than the base paths used in adult leagues. At first thirty-eight feet separated the pitcher from the catcher; this was later changed to the present distance of forty-six feet, fourteen feet, six inches shorter than in the adult game. Base runners were not allowed to take a lead and not allowed to steal until the ball crossed the plate, nor could batters advance to first when the catcher dropped a third strike. A game lasted just six innings.

Little Red Schoolhouse. The teacher gives a lesson to children sitting near the heat in this one-room schoolhouse. GRANGER COLLECTION, LTD.

In 1939, with local business support and adult volunteers, a three-team Little League organized by Stotz began play. Rosters came from school districts to prevent recruiting from outside local communities. Recruitment was later limited to populations of a certain size, a policy that often angered adults eager to win.

Following World War II Little League grew. In 1947, the first league outside Pennsylvania began and the first tournament, later called the Little League World Series, was held. The tournament was held in Williamsport, still the site for the annual event. Press stories on Little League helped spread its popularity and in 1951 leagues began in Canada, Cuba, and the Panama Canal Zone. In 1957, Monterrey, Mexico, became the first non-U.S. team to win the World Series. ABC televised the last game of the World Series for the first time in 1960.

The success of Little League created concerns about commercialism and competition for Stotz and he resigned in 1955, after a bitter struggle with his successors. Little League, nonetheless, continued to grow, reaching 4,000 leagues by 1956. In 1959, Dr. Creighton J. Hale, then vice president of Little League, designed a protective helmet with double earflaps, later used by adults. Though in 1950, Kathryn Johnston posing as a boy, played in Little League, it was not until 1973, following a court decision, that girls were officially allowed to participate.

In 1969, Taiwan won its first of seventeen World Series. By 1975, concern over foreign domination and rules violations prompted Little League to ban non-U.S. teams, for one year. It also created two divisions that year to guarantee there would always be a U.S. team in the finals. Taiwan withdrew from Little League in 1997. Little League was played in over one hundred countries by 2000. In August 2001, Little League suffered the news that a player who had pitched a perfect game for a United States team was two years older than his father had claimed.

BIBLIOGRAPHY

Frommer, Harvey. *Growing Up at Bat: Fifty Years of Little League Baseball.* New York: Pharos Books, 1989.

Van Auken, Lance, and Robin Van Auken. *Play Ball: The Story of Little League Baseball.* University Park: Pennsylvania State University Press, 2001.

Wills, Garry. *Certain Trumpets: The Call of Leaders.* New York: Simon and Schuster, 1994.

John Syrett

See also **Baseball.**

LITTLE RED SCHOOLHOUSE. From the eighteenth century well into the twentieth, the country school stood as a symbol of American democracy and civilization founded upon the "three R's." The small, one-room school building, usually located on a small piece of wasteland that farmers could readily spare, was painted, if at all, with red or yellow ochre, the cheapest possible paint. Such schoolhouses were found along country roads throughout New England and states further west, serving several farm families in a central place. Pictures of such buildings became a sort of patriotic fetish with the American Protective Association, successor of the Know-Nothing party, at the close of the nineteenth century.

BIBLIOGRAPHY
Daugherty, Mary Lee. "The Little Red Schoolhouse," in Ray B. Brown and Marshall Fishwick, eds., *Icons of America.* Bowling Green, Ohio: Popular Press, 1978.

Robert P. Tristram Coffin/A. R.

See also **American Protective Association; Education; Old Field Schools; School Lands.**

LITTLE ROCK is on the Arkansas River some 150 miles above its confluence with the Mississippi River. The place name was identified in 1721 by the French explorer Benard LaHarpe with his journal entry noting a "point of rocks" on the south bank of the river. Little Rock, a derivative of that name, was established in 1821. Decisions by the territorial legislature to designate the city as the seat of government and in 1836 the state capital secured the city's future.

The Civil War left the city unscathed, and in the last quarter of the nineteenth century investments in railroads and natural resources led to steady economic growth. This pattern, coupled with a growing presence of state and federal agencies, continued in the twentieth century. Employment opportunities stimulated by World War II accelerated a population boom that continued a full decade following the war. Growth was curtailed by the Little Rock school crisis in 1957. The city became an international symbol for racial prejudice when some of its citizens supported the governor's attempts to stop INTEGRATION at the city's Central High School. Major reform efforts to improve the city's image and national demographic changes fueled by interests in recreation, retirement, and an energy crisis allowed the city to regain its momentum. Governor Bill Clinton's election as president brought added attention to the city. By the year 2000 Little Rock's population exceeded 180,000.

Little Rock. Federal troops enforce court-ordered desegregation by escorting African American students to Central High School in 1957. AP/WIDE WORLD PHOTOS

BIBLIOGRAPHY

Herndon, Dallas Tabor. *Why Little Rock Was Born*. Little Rock, Ark.: Central Printing, 1933.

Lester, Jim, and Judy Lester. *Greater Little Rock*. Norfolk, Va.: Donning, 1986.

Roy, F. Hampton, Sr., and Charles Witsell Jr. *How We Lived: Little Rock as an American City*. Little Rock, Ark.: August House Publishers, 1984.

C. Fred Williams

See also **Arkansas; Segregation.**

LIVESTOCK INDUSTRY. The livestock industry has played an important role in America's economic development. It involves raising the animals, which include cattle, swine, sheep, horses, and to a lesser extent, goats and mules, and the processing of the animal products for consumers. (Fowl and fur animals are not considered livestock.) The history of American livestock begins with the European exploration of the New World, but the place and date usually accepted for the start of an organized effort to maintain herds is the establishment of Jamestown in 1607.

Early America

In colonial times livestock was dependent on free grazing. Animals were allowed to roam and forage in the forest. Despite the presence of predators the domestic animals thrived; only sheep needed constant care. Swine did particularly well in the New World, and by the eighteenth century they were classified as vermin in some areas.

After the Revolution the free range evolved into a more stable farming environment, and science and technology began to change agriculture. Agricultural state societies were formed, colleges began to include agricultural studies, and several related journals appeared. The Ohio Valley emerged as the center of the livestock industry, although the South and Northeast were still important livestock areas. Most farmers hired men to drive their livestock to market even after railroads began to appear because the rail rates were expensive and dangerous for the livestock. Further, they often used the slow trip east to allow their stock to fatten.

As the frontier moved west, so did the livestock industry. Not everyone succeeded: the industry was reliant on the environment and weather. A bad corn harvest meant less food for swine, resulting in earlier butchering and lower prices. Diseases such as hog cholera or tick fever in cattle could decimate entire herds. Events such as the California gold rush also created boom-bust cycles. Mining towns sprang up and created a demand for livestock, but many of the towns dried up just as fast.

Meatpacking

The slaughtering, butchering, and packing aspects of the livestock industry developed along the same lines. Besides slaughtering on an as-needed basis, people slaughtered excess animals every winter, usually animals they could not support through the winter. People used hooves, tallow, and hides for trade items and made jerky from some of the meat, but a good deal of the animal went to waste. Pork preserved the best. The earliest pork packer, William Pynchon, began his business in Springfield, Massachusetts, in 1660. The pork was rubbed with salt, molasses, and black gunpowder and stored in barrels called hogsheads. These activities also shifted west as the frontier moved.

The livestock industry began to change after the Civil War due to the differences between farming and ranching and also because of technological advances. Most of the myths and lore of the West are rooted in the image of the ranch and the cattle drive. Ranchers, sometimes called cattle barons, held huge tracts of land and animals. (Robert Kleburg's 1940 Texas ranch was over 900,000 acres, making it larger than Rhode Island.) Among the technological advances of the late 1800s were barbed wire, the gas tractor, silage, and improved veterinary medicine. Scientists discovered that certain disease-carrying insects, such as the cattle tick, operated in vectors.

As the demand for beef increased, a distribution system developed to move beef east. Some attempted to take advantage of the railways, which had expanded at a rapid pace, and the new types of refrigerated cars. Georgia Hammond, in Chicago, made the first refrigerated shipment in 1869, and by 1877 Gustavus Swift had joined the refrigerated shipping business. By the turn of the century the largest packers were Swift, Philip and Simeon Armour, Nelson Morris, and two relative newcomers in the Midwest, Cudahy Packers, and Schwarschild and Sulzberger. The five companies' control over the meatpacking industry attracted the notice of the Department of Justice, which launched a number of antitrust violation investigations.

The meatpacking industry also suffered from some of the worst working conditions in American history. Workers held spontaneous walkouts throughout the 1890s to lobby for better conditions and wages. Efforts to organize meat workers were common. At an 1896 American Federation of Labor (AFL) convention, four men organized the Amalgamated Meat Cutters and Butcher Workmen of North America, the meatpacking industry's first example of organized labor. The Fair Labor Standards Act (1938) improved working conditions, and by 1941 workers received time and a half for working more than forty hours a week. By 1945 collective bargaining was established. Many of the trials of the meat workers can be found in Upton Sinclair's muckraking novel *The Jungle* (1906), which set out to expose the abuses and conditions in meatpacking. Despite rebuttals by companies, Sinclair's book helped lead to the Pure Food and Drug Act and the Meat Inspection Act, both in 1906.

During the Great Depression, the government helped the livestock industry by initiating tariffs and opening public lands for grazing. Livestock producers also began

Chicago Stockyards. A complex of pens and walkways for holding livestock before the animals were killed and processed, c. 1947. NATIONAL ARCHIVES AND RECORDS ADMINISTRATION

to experiment with cross breeding. In the late 1930s, for example, Texas rancher Thomas Lasater crossbred shorthorns, Herefords, and Brahmans, creating the Beefmaster breed.

Postwar Developments

World War II brought economic recovery but also rationing and price freezes. The postwar boom, however, meant prosperity and improvements in transportation, including the refrigerated truck, which helped suppliers meet consumer demand. Preservation methods also improved. In 1940, the U.S. Department of Agriculture (USDA) approved the use of nitrates, Hormel developed a canned ham, and prepackaged sliced bacon was introduced.

Feedlots also grew in the postwar years. Ranchers and farmers realized that cattle that are fed grains yield a higher-grade beef than grazing produces. As a result, companies built huge feeding complexes that handled as many as 50,000 animals a year. By 1963 the USDA estimated that 9 million cattle were on feed. Slaughterhouses also benefited from technology and automation. However, the industry remains subject to the same dangers. In the 1970s the fluctuations in the economy and bad weather forced the price of grain to rise. Disease continues to play a role in the livestock industry. In the late twentieth century mad cow disease (bovine spongiform encephalopathy) and foot-and-mouth disease decimated English stockyards.

Livestock industries have also come under fire by animal rights groups for a variety of reasons. Further, the industries' use of chemicals, such as growth hormones, to preserve and generate greater yields has generated concern and condemnation from health organizations. Despite its checkered history the livestock industry remained strong through the 1990s.

BIBLIOGRAPHY

Corey, Lewis. *Meat and Man: A Study of Monopoly, Unionism, and Food Policy.* New York: Viking, 1950.

Skaggs, Jimmy M. *Prime Cut: Livestock Raising and Meatpacking in the United States, 1607–1983.* College Station: Texas A&M University Press, 1986.

Lisa A. Ennis

See also **Agriculture; Cattle; Cattle Associations; Cattle Drives; Hogs; Horse; *Jungle, The*; Meat Inspection Laws; Meatpacking; Sheep.**

LOBBIES, groups of individuals acting for themselves or others who seek to influence the decisions of government officials, primarily by informal off-the-record communications and exchanges. Their tactics range from such high-pressure techniques as bribery, threats of electoral retaliation, and mass mailings to such low-pressure methods as supplying research and information in support of their views or testifying before Congressional committees. Intermediate forms of influence include campaign contributions and persuasion.

The objects and tactics of lobbying have shifted sharply in American history. In the nineteenth and early twentieth centuries the typical lobbyist focused on the legislative arena and used high-pressure methods, including bribery, to influence legislators. The most notorious examples of illicit lobbying in the nineteenth century involved railroad lobbyists, who brazenly handed out checks to legislators on the floor of the House and Senate. By the 1950s many lobbyists had enlarged their focus to include the executive branch and shifted to soft-sell tactics. This shift in technique was a response to exposure of lobbying scandals at both state and national levels.

Congress began investigating lobbies in 1913 with a study of the National Association of Manufacturers (NAM). Since that time there has been at least one major investigation in every decade. The investigations were followed first by piecemeal legislation and then, in Title III of the Legislative Reorganization Act of 1946, by general legislation to regulate lobbies. These acts and subsequent legislation aim at control primarily through publicity, but many loopholes remain that permit lobbies such as the NAM and Washington, D.C. law firms to avoid registration and others to avoid full disclosure of their activities. While not eliminating lobbies, the investigations and legislation have encouraged lobbies to seek a lower profile by moving away from high-pressure methods.

With the rise of the executive branch as initiator of legislation and the growth of the administrative bureaucracy, the focus of lobbyists began to shift from legislative bodies to executive offices. As a corollary, the growing proportion of lobbying that occurs outside the legislative limelight reduces its overall visibility. Increasingly, chief executives and bureaucratic agencies lobby for legislative passage of bills they have initiated. They often appear to be the sole influence on legislation, even though it is not uncommon for regulatory agencies to be lobbying in the interests of the clientele they are supposed to be regulating. These changes have led critical observers to question the validity of distinguishing between private and public lobbies.

In the 1970s most lobbyists were still acting for associations with an economic interest—business, farm, labor, and the professions. Over half of all registered lobbyists in Washington, D.C. are specialized business associations such as the American Petroleum Institute and Aerospace Industries Association. Although multiinterest peak associations such as the AFL-CIO, the Farm Bureau Federation, and the NAM continue to lobby on a variety of congressional issues, critics of lobbying have moved on to new targets—for example, the "military-industrial complex" and the impact of corporate campaign contributions on executive policymaking. In addition to primarily economic lobbies, the twentieth century has seen major lobbying efforts by prohibition groups like the Anti-Saloon League, civil rights groups like the National Association for the Advancement of Colored People (NAACP), reform groups like Common Cause, and peace groups like the National Peace Action Committee.

In the 1980s and 1990s social issues became a major focus of lobbying activity in Washington. For example, Christian evangelical organizations such as the Moral Majority lobbied Congress to outlaw abortion and legalize school prayer. In contrast, civil liberties groups such as People for the American Way lobbied Congress to maintain a strict separation of church and state, and the National Abortion and Reproductive Rights Action League (NARAL) lobbied Congress to preserve abortion rights. The overall number of lobbies proliferated and included groups as diverse as teacher's unions, policemen, and scientists. Along with the rise in the number of lobbies, the amount of money spent by lobbies on political campaigns escalated enormously.

The late twentieth century also saw a dramatic increase in the role of lobbies in the Senate confirmation process. In 1987 the American Civil Liberties Union, NARAL, and other liberal lobbies vigorously opposed the Supreme Court nomination of Robert Bork. The lobbying campaign created a media firestorm, and after weeks of contentious hearings, the Senate rejected Bork's nomination. In the aftermath of the Bork controversy, lobbying organizations have become regular participants in Senate confirmation hearings.

By the 1990s public outcry against lobbies focused on their role in campaign finance. Virtually every major candidate for federal office in the United States relied on contributions from lobbies to finance their campaigns. The massive infusion of money into the political process led many Americans to conclude that lobbies and other political pressure groups threatened to corrupt democracy itself. By the early twenty-first century, the effort to reign in lobbies and reduce the role of money in politics had emerged as one of the principal issues in American political life.

BIBLIOGRAPHY

Birnbaum, Jeffrey H. *The Lobbyists: How Influence Peddlers Get Their Way in Washington*. New York: Times Books, 1992.

Deakin, James. *The Lobbyists*. Washington, D.C.: Public Affairs Press, 1966.

Hayes, Michael T. *Lobbyists and Legislators: A Theory of Political Markets*. New Brunswick, N.J.: Rutgers University Press, 1981.

Edward S. Malecki / A. G.

See also **Government Regulation of Business; Interests; Majority Rule; Petroleum Industry; Pharmaceutical Industry; Pro-Choice Movement; Pro-Life Movement; Trucking Industry.**

LOCAL GOVERNMENT is the designation given to all units of government in the United States below the state level. During the colonial period, the pattern of local government was not uniform throughout the thirteen colonies. In New England the town was the principal unit of local rule, responsible for poor relief, schooling, and roads. The primary governing body was the town meeting, an assembly of all the enfranchised residents, though the popularly elected selectmen seem to have assumed increasing authority over town affairs. In the southern colonies, the parish vestry and county court were the chief elements of local government. Appointed by the royal governor, the members of the county court exercised both administrative and judicial powers, supervising road construction as well as presiding over trials. The parish vestry of the established Church of England administered poor relief. In the middle colonies, local government was a mix of the New England and southern elements. Both county governments and towns were significant, sharing responsibility for local rule. In the middle colonies and in Maryland and Virginia as well, the colonial governors granted municipal charters to the most prominent communities, endowing them with the powers and privileges of a municipal corporation. Although in some of these municipalities the governing council was elected, in Philadelphia, Norfolk, and Williamsburg the city council was a self-perpetuating body, with the incumbent councilors filling vacancies. In marked contrast to the direct democracy of the town meeting tradition of New England, these were closed corporations governed by a self-chosen few.

Change After the American Revolution

The closed corporations, however, did not survive the wave of government change unleashed by the American Revolution. By the 1790s the electorate chose the governing council in every American municipality. Moreover, the state legislatures succeeded to the sovereign prerogative of the royal governors and thenceforth granted municipal charters. During the nineteenth century, thousands of communities became municipal corporations. Irritated by the many petitions for incorporation burdening each legislative session, nineteenth-century state legislatures enacted general municipal incorporation laws that permitted communities to incorporate simply by petitioning the county authorities.

Meanwhile, the newly admitted states west of the Appalachians were replicating the local government structure of the Atlantic seaboard states. Most of the trans-Appalachian South followed the example of Virginia and North Carolina and vested local authority in county courts that exercised both judicial and administrative powers. With the disestablishment of the Church of England during the Revolutionary era, however, the parish vestries lost all secular governing authority. The new midwestern states imitated New York, Pennsylvania, and New Jersey, dividing local responsibilities between counties and townships. Nowhere west of the Appalachians was the township as significant as in New England, but it survived as a major element of rural government in the states north of the Ohio River.

To administer public education, the nineteenth-century states added a new unit of local government, the school district. These districts exemplified grassroots rule run amuck. By the early 1930s there were 127,531 such districts in the United States. There was a district for vir-tually every one-room school, and in some districts the number of school board members exceeded the number of pupils. With an average of 118 districts per county, Illinois had the largest number of school governments. One Illinois district comprised only eighty acres.

Reducing Grassroots Power

In the late nineteenth and early twentieth centuries the nation's cities, however, were the most criticized units of local government. Although they were responsible for the creation of grand parks, well-stocked public libraries, up-to-date fire departments, and the world's most advanced water and sewerage systems, the major American municipalities fell short of the expectations of prosperous city dwellers who rallied behind a growing body of good-government reformers. Members of the urban elite resented the clout of plebeian councilmen representing immigrant constituencies and cited well-publicized examples of political corruption in their crusades for reform. To weaken the grip of the supposedly venal political party organizations, reformers called for the introduction of a civil service system and a nonpartisan municipal bureaucracy. Moreover, they urged the adoption of nonpartisan elections. They also sought to curb the power of ward-based politicians from working-class neighborhoods by introducing at-large election of council members and by strengthening the role of the mayor, who was usually a figure of citywide distinction chosen by a citywide electorate.

Some cities discarded the mayor-council scheme and experimented with new forms of government. In 1901 reformers in Galveston, Texas, introduced the commission form of municipal rule. Under this plan, a small commission elected at large exercised all legislative and executive authority. During the first two decades of the twentieth century, hundreds of cities adopted the commission option, but after 1915 it fell from favor and reformers rallied instead in support of the city manager plan. This scheme of government originated in Staunton, Virginia, in 1908 and spread rapidly until by the end of the twentieth century more than half of all American cities had adopted it. Its major feature was a strong, centralized, professional executive branch under a city manager who was hired by the city council. Council-manager government made little headway among the largest cities of the Northeast and Midwest, where voters preferred strong mayors with the political skills necessary to mediate clashing ethnic and economic interests. But many communities embraced the notion of a nonpartisan, expert administrator at the helm of government.

During the twentieth century there was also reform in those bastions of grassroots rule, the school district and the New England town. In an attempt to upgrade rural education, the states restructured school government, eliminating eighty thousand redundant school districts between 1940 and 1960. Consolidated school districts replaced existing minuscule units of government, and one-room schools yielded to graded institutions with students bused in from a five- or ten-mile radius. In twentieth-century New England a number of the largest towns deviated from the town meeting tradition and adopted an institution known as the representative town meeting. In these communities an assembly of usually over two hundred elected representatives determined town policy. No longer could every enfranchised townsperson vote in the town meeting; that became a prerogative belonging to the elected representatives.

Special Districts

Meanwhile, thousands of new special districts were adding to the complexity of American local government. Between the early 1950s and late 1980s the number of such districts rose from twelve thousand to thirty thousand. Most of these local governments were established to provide a single service or perform a single function. The functions included fire protection, water, sewerage, mosquito abatement, parks and recreation, airports, and a variety of other activities. In a few instances, special districts were created for multiple purposes such as water and sewerage, but all were limited in scope. The governing boards of special districts were often appointed rather than elected, and this gave rise to some concern over the degree of popular control possible in these governments. Two major reasons existed for the rapid growth of special districts. First, many potential service areas did not coincide with the boundaries of existing local governments, and special districts could be created to fit these service areas. Second, many local governments had exhausted the taxing and bonding authority granted to them by the state legislatures, and each special district could begin with a new grant of authority to tax and borrow.

Merged Government and Its Alternatives

The growing number of special districts in metropolitan areas as well as the proliferation of suburban municipalities gave rise to new concerns about duplication of effort and inefficient delivery of services. From the 1920s on, metropolitan reformers decried the multitude of conflicting governments and offered schemes for unifying the fragmented American metropolis. The most far-reaching of these proposals would have merged counties and city into a single unit of metropolitan government. During the 1960s this option, with some modification, was adopted in Nashville, Tennessee; Jacksonville, Florida; and Indianapolis, Indiana. Elsewhere, reformers proposed federative structures that would preserve existing municipalities but assign certain regional responsibilities to an overarching metropolitan government. Voters repeatedly rejected such schemes, though in 1957 something resembling a federative plan was adopted for Miami-Dade County in Florida.

Local governments and their citizens generally resisted sweeping reforms that would alter the basic structure of government in metropolitan areas. Instead, many local governments sought other means to avoid duplication and inefficiency in the provision of services. One increasingly popular device was the intergovernmental agreement. By utilizing contractual agreements, existing governments could band together to provide services that single units were unable to afford. In other cases, as in California's Lakewood Plan, cities could contract for services with an urban county that already provided such services to unincorporated areas. During the second half of the twentieth century, such agreements were popular because they permitted existing governments to continue operation and allowed local citizens to maintain mechanisms for local control of policy.

Americans have, then, opted to adjust to fragmentation rather than embrace consolidation or a radical restructuring of government. Thousands of school districts disappeared during the mid-twentieth century, but townships survived in the Northeast and Midwest, as did a myriad of little municipalities in metropolitan and rural areas.

BIBLIOGRAPHY

Daniels, Bruce C., ed. *Town and County: Essays on the Structure of Local Government in the American Colonies.* Middletown, Conn.: Wesleyan University Press, 1978.

Pollens, John C. *Special District Governments in the United States.* Berkeley: University of California Press, 1957.

Stone, Harold A., Don K. Price, and Kathryn H. Stone. *City Manager Government in the United States: A Review After Twenty-five Years.* Chicago: Public Administration Service, 1940.

Teaford, Jon C. *The Unheralded Triumph: City Government in America, 1870–1900.* Baltimore: Johns Hopkins University Press, 1984.

Teaford, Jon C. *Post-Suburbia: Government and Politics in the Edge Cities.* Baltimore: Johns Hopkins University Press, 1997.

Wooster, Ralph A. *The People in Power: Courthouse and Statehouse in the Lower South, 1850–1860.* Knoxville: University of Tennessee Press, 1969.

John H. Baker
Jon C. Teaford

See also **City Manager Plan; Commission Government; County Government; Metropolitan Government; Municipal Government; Municipal Reform; Town Government.**

LOCHNER V. NEW YORK, 198 U.S. 45 (1905). Lochner, proprietor of a Utica, New York, bakery, had been arrested, tried, and convicted for violation of a state law setting maximum work hours for workers in the baking industry at ten hours per day and sixty hours per week. Seven years earlier, in *Holden v. Hardy,* the Supreme Court had upheld a Utah law regulating hours for workers in dangerous industries. But in *Lochner,* the Court argued that such protections were unnecessary in industries that required care in cleanliness and sanitation. The Court, rejecting the New York law's stated intent to safeguard public health, held the act void as a violation of freedom of contract.

BIBLIOGRAPHY

Gillman, Howard. *The Constitution Besieged: The Rise and Demise of Lochner Era Police Powers Jurisprudence.* Durham, N.C.: Duke University Press, 1993.

Kens, Paul. *Judicial Power and Reform Politics: The Anatomy of Lochner v. New York.* Lawrence: University Press of Kansas, 1990.

———. *Lochner v. New York: Economic Regulation on Trial.* Lawrence: University Press of Kansas, 1998.

W. Brooke Graves
Andrew C. Rieser

See also **Labor Legislation and Administration; Wages and Hours of Labor, Regulation of;** *West Coast Hotel Company v. Parrish; and vol. 9:* **Women in Industry (Brandeis Brief).**

LOCKE'S POLITICAL PHILOSOPHY. The legacy of John Locke's ideas in American history derives from the complexity of Locke's own life and writings. John Locke (1632–1704) was an Oxford-educated physician drawn into English politics by his association with dissenting Whigs who eventually helped achieve the Glorious Revolution of 1688. Locke's three most influential books (*A Letter Concerning Toleration, Two Treatises of Government,* and *An Essay Concerning Human Understanding*) appeared in 1689; *Some Thoughts Concerning Education* followed in 1693, and *The Reasonableness of Christianity* in 1695. Locke's devout Christian faith informed everything he wrote. Most nineteenth- and early-twentieth-century scholars stressed Locke's challenges to religious orthodoxy, royal absolutism, and the doctrine of innate ideas. This portrait of Locke as a champion of tolerance, individual rights (especially the right to property), and philosophical empiricism emphasized important features of his thought but neglected his profound Puritan asceticism.

When American historians identified Locke as the most important source of their nation's political ideas, they too accentuated certain themes: his protest against religious orthodoxy, his idea that government originates when individuals leave the state of nature to form a social compact in order to protect their natural rights, and his conviction that knowledge comes from—and must be verified in—experience. If the United States was a nation dedicated to pluralism, liberty, and experimentation, then Locke could be designated its official philosopher, a tendency that reached its apex in Louis Hartz's *The Liberal Tradition in America* (1955).

The late twentieth century witnessed the unraveling, then reconstituting, of such ambitious claims. First, historically minded political theorists following the lead of Peter Laslett reconstructed the profoundly Calvinist framework within which Locke conceived his philosophy. Locke advised resisting religious orthodoxy because he believed genuine faith must be voluntary, not because he prized

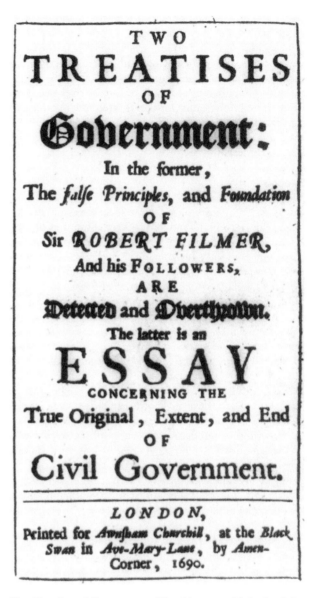

Two Treatises of Government. The title page of John Locke's landmark book of political philosophy, which had a profound—if sometimes misinterpreted—impact on the founding fathers. LIBRARY OF CONGRESS

religious skepticism or tolerated atheism. Locke valued independence and industriousness not because he endorsed the unchecked pursuit of wealth or the emergence of capitalism but because slavery of the mind (to an absolute authority) or slavery of the body (to sinful impulses such as the desire for pleasure) prevented individuals from developing, through self-discipline, the Christian virtues of self-sacrifice and love. Locke emphasized experience not because he was a materialist or relativist but because he wanted to establish on a firm basis the compatibility of the exercise of human reason with the will of God.

Equally significant challenges to the simple equation of American politics with the right to property came when

140

historians discovered that eighteenth-century Americans spoke of equality as well as freedom, of duties as well as rights, and of the common good as well as individual liberty. The generation that founded the United States drew its political ideals from a number of sources in addition to Locke's liberalism, including Christianity, the English common law, the Scottish Enlightenment, and ancient, Renaissance, and eighteenth-century writers in the tradition of classical republicanism. Now that Locke's own deep commitment to an ascetic ethic of Protestantism has been recovered, it is easier to see how and why so many Americans ranging from the old-fashioned, sober-sided John Adams to the forward-looking, Enlightenment-drenched Thomas Jefferson invoked Locke's writings more often than any other single source except the Bible.

BIBLIOGRAPHY

Hartz, Louis. *The Liberal Tradition in America: An Interpretation of American Political Thought since the Revolution.* New York: Harcourt, 1955.

Huyler, Jerome. *Locke in America: The Moral Philosophy of the Founding Era.* Lawrence: University Press of Kansas, 1995.

Locke, John. *Two Treatises of Government.* Edited by Peter Laslett. Cambridge, U.K.; New York: Cambridge University Press, 1988.

James T. Kloppenberg

LOCKOUT, in management-labor relations, is the tactical action of the employer in refusing work to unionized and/or organizing employees and either forcing them to leave the workplace, while hiring replacement workers, or closing down production altogether. The goal is to force the unionized employees into making concessions. Employers have utilized the lockout numerous times since the 1870s, although the 1947 Labor-Management Relations Act (see TAFT-HARTLEY ACT) and subsequent rulings by both the National Labor Relations Board (NLRB) and the courts have imposed some legal restrictions on use of this tactic. Under the law, employers may use the lockout to protect their companies against economic injury and/or to protect themselves at the bargaining table.

Striving for recognition and collectively bargained contracts, unions in many industries during the last third of the nineteenth century struggled intensely with employers across the nation, many of whom had formed antiunion trade associations. Trying to gain advantage in negotiations with companies that belonged to multiemployer trade associations, unions on occasion organized whipsaw strikes, targeting one or more of the employers in such groups for strikes organized specifically to pressure the companies suffering economic losses to appeal to all employers in the respective trade associations to yield to union demands at the bargaining table. Employers developed an arsenal of counter-strategies, including the lockout, to break the whipsaw strikes.

In the common-law tradition, employers were assumed to have virtual autonomy in conducting their businesses, except when constrained by contracts with unions. The persistent efforts of workers in many industries, from iron and steel to railroads, to organize unions prompted employers during the post–Civil War era into the twentieth century to use the lockout. Thus, after locking out workers affiliated with the Knights of Labor during spring 1886, the Chicago-based McCormack Harvester Company hired 300 replacement workers who were guarded by a force of 350 to 500 police officers. Most spectacularly, a strike against Carnegie Steel at Homestead, Pennsylvania, erupted in 1892 when management refused to renegotiate a three-year contract with the Amalgamated Association of Steel and Iron Workers and locked out all employees. Blood flowed when hundreds of Pinkerton guards and 8,000 state militia soldiers tried to escort "scabs" (strikebreakers) past 10,000 striking workers and into the plant.

Legislation enacted during the mid-twentieth century attempted to defuse such labor strife, through institutionalizing the principles of industrial relations that legally sanctioned negotiation and enforcement of contractual rights and responsibilities of management and labor. Accordingly, passage of the NATIONAL LABOR RELATIONS ACT (NLRA) in 1936 affirmed workers' rights both to organize unions and to negotiate and enforce contracts through their exclusive COLLECTIVE BARGAINING agents. Though it broke new ground in protecting workers' rights to unionize, the NLRA did not address the lockout. The Taft-Hartley Act, however, did establish particular parameters governing the legality of the lockout. The act prohibits use of either strikes or lockouts to force modification of contracts prior to expiration, and it instructs the director of the Federal Mediation and Conciliation Service to press for negotiated settlements before strikes or lockouts are utilized by either party. Other provisions authorize the president to impose a sixty-day "cooling-off" period in case of stalled collective bargaining negotiations heading toward strikes or lockouts that threaten to become national emergencies.

In findings of the NLRB and the rulings of the federal circuit courts as well as various state courts, the right of employers to use the lockout has been upheld. Moreover, decisions in three cases heard in the U.S. Supreme Court—*NLRB v. Truck Drivers Local 449* (1957), *NLRB v. Brown* (1965), and *American Ship Building Co. v. NLRB* (1965)—have affirmed the constitutionality of the lockout.

BIBLIOGRAPHY

Gregory, Charles O., and Harold A. Katz. *Labor and the Law.* 3d ed. New York and London: Norton, 1979.

Peterson, Florence. *Strikes in the United States, 1880–1936.* United States Department of Labor, Bureau of Labor Statistics, Bulletin 651. Washington, D.C.: GPO, 1938.

Wolff, Leon. *Lockout, The Story of the Homestead Strike of 1892: A Study of Violence, Unionism, and the Carnegie Steel Empire*. New York: Harper and Row, 1965.

Jonathan W. McLeod

See also **Homestead Strike; Labor; Strikes.**

LOCOFOCO PARTY. In the decade before the panic of 1837, discontent among artisans in eastern cities found expression in the Working Men's movement. Disparities in wealth and a tendency toward centralized manufacturing threatened the artisan ideal of equality in a republic of independent producers. Particularly offensive to wage-earning journeymen were state-chartered banks, through which a wealthy elite manipulated a "paper system" of currency and credit. Antibank sentiments gained political support in the Democratic Party. The New York editor William Leggett argued that banks provided an "aristocracy" with exclusive privilege and transferred wealth "from the many to the few."

The bank issue and the Working Men's movement divided New York Democrats. Meeting in Tammany Hall in October 1835, conservatives pushed through the nomination of probank candidates and tried to end the meeting by turning out the gas lights. Forewarned, the antibank men illuminated the room with candles lit with new "locofoco," or scratch-ignited, matches. The Locofoco Party briefly agitated for antibank candidates in New York City. Like the Working Men's movement to which it appealed, the Locofoco Party did not survive the depression of the late 1830s. However, Whigs continued to use the term "locofoco" to describe Democrats across the country as enemies of economic stability.

BIBLIOGRAPHY

Watson, Harry L. *Liberty and Power: The Politics of Jacksonian America*. New York: Hill and Wang, 1990.

Wilentz, Sean. *Chants Democratic: New York City and the Rise of the American Working Class, 1788–1850*. New York: Oxford University Press, 1984.

Louis S. Gerteis

See also **Democratic Party.**

LOCOMOTIVES. Locomotives first came into use in the United States in the early nineteenth century, inspired by the steam-powered locomotives that had appeared on England's first common-carrier railroads and roads for coal mines. In 1825 Col. John Stevens of Hoboken, New Jersey, built an experimental locomotive and demonstrated it on a circular track. The Baltimore and Ohio Railroad, chartered in 1827 as the first common-carrier railroad in the United States, faced the question early on of what form of power to use. Peter Cooper of New York City, a director of the railroad, built the Tom Thumb for demonstration purposes. Success was suffi-

cient to lead the railroad to sponsor a competition to secure a commercially useful locomotive. Phineas Davis, of York, Pennsylvania, won the competition in 1831. His York was the predecessor of a considerable group of vertical-boiler locomotives called "grasshoppers" that had walking-beam power transmission. Meanwhile, the West Point Foundry in New York built Best Friend of Charleston, the first locomotive intended for commercial service, for the South Carolina Canal and Railroad Company.

Some companies imported locomotives from England during the early experimental period, notably for service on the Camden and Amboy Railroad and for tests on the gravity railroad of the Delaware and Hudson Canal Company. These imports proved ill adapted to the light and uneven track of early American railroads and to the sharp curvature and heavy grades that often were encountered. To adapt to these conditions, American locomotive design began to depart from British practice. American designers used a leading truck to improve track-keeping qualities, applied headlights and cowcatchers, and developed various devices such as the Baldwin "flexible beam" truck to lend curve-keeping ability to freight locomotives of six- and eight-coupled design.

The early locomotive builders—Matthias W. Baldwin and William Norris of Philadelphia, as well as Davis—began as jewelers and shifted to machine-shop practice. Baldwin and Norris proved to be highly inventive contributors to locomotive development. The Baldwin works, first in Philadelphia and later in Eddystone, Pennsylvania, became the nation's largest locomotive builder. Norris developed some early export business: one of his locomotives proved to have the ability to haul a train up the inclined plane of the Great Western of Great Britain; others supplied power for the first railroad built in Russia.

Numerous small locomotive works operated in the early period, ranging from the William Mason Company at Taunton, Massachusetts, to the Richmond Locomotive Works at Richmond, Virginia. Some of these ultimately disappeared; a number were merged to form the American Locomotive Company, headquartered at Schenectady, New York, second of the country's great locomotive builders. Several railroads built locomotives in their own shops but none so many as the Pennsylvania Railroad, principally at Altoona, Pennsylvania. The Pennsylvania also pioneered the standardization of locomotives beginning in the 1870s and contributed much to the improvement of locomotive design.

The steam locomotive demonstrated its speed capabilities early, having attained sixty miles an hour by 1848. Hauling capability developed more slowly. The typical locomotive for freight and passenger work in the 1870s had four driving wheels (4-4-0, or American type) and a tractive effort of 8,000 to 12,000 pounds. Locomotives for heavy freight work were built with six or eight driving wheels. The Consolidation type (2-8-0), first built for the Lehigh Valley Railroad in 1866, became the most popular. Tractive efforts of leading specimens of this locomotive type increased from 24,000 pounds in the 1870s to 46,000 pounds by the end of the century. Apart from gradual perfection of design, improvement of materials, and increase of boiler pressures and weight on driving wheels, the greatest early post–Civil War challenge was the development of suitable grates and fireboxes for burning coal in place of wood.

Unlike stationary or marine plants, locomotive power plants needed to fit into a small space and have a weight that tracks and bridges could carry. They also had to function while exposed to the weather and the vibration encountered in moving over the road. By the end of the century, at a time when railroad traffic was burgeoning, the locomotive had attained close to its maximum capacity under conventional design practice. Between 1895 and 1910, a series of innovations—trailing wheels that allowed a wide firebox to be carried behind the rear drivers and the boiler to be lengthened, the brick arch, piston valves, and outside valve motion—enabled engineers to more than double the locomotive's tractive power.

Most important was the introduction of superheating, which delivered very hot, dry steam to the cylinders, reducing condensation and increasing cylinder horsepower within existing dimensions. In 1904, the first Mallet type of articulated locomotive came into service on the Baltimore and Ohio Railroad. This method utilized two systems—one of compounding (use of steam first in high-pressure cylinders, then a second time in low-pressure cylinders), developed in Europe; and one of attachment, in which the front engine and driving wheel were set by a pin to the main frame so it could swing with curvature. Of particular use on lines of heavy gradient, the articulated locomotive increased rapidly in size, and, by 1920, some models exerted 120,000 pounds of tractive effort when working single expansion. The mechanical stoker, essential for firing such locomotives, had been perfected by then. Improved lateral-motion devices made the ten-coupled nonarticulated locomotive more practical, and typical examples of the 2-10-2 on eastern roads developed up to 84,000 pounds of tractive effort prior to World War I.

The need for greater horsepower to permit sustained high-speed operation with heavy loads led to a series of experiments from which emerged the first "superpower" locomotive, completed by the Lima Locomotive Works in 1925. This locomotive combined the elements already noted with a feedwater heater and four-wheel trailing truck to permit a much larger firebox. It became the prototype for hundreds of locomotives of the 2-8-4, 2-10-4, and, ultimately, 4-8-4 types that allowed for a major acceleration of freight service with greatly improved efficiency.

By this time, the manufacture of locomotives for main-line railroad service was confined to three outside builders: Baldwin, American Locomotive, and Lima. Railroad shops, especially those of the Pennsylvania, Norfolk and Western, and Burlington Railroads, continued to build new power. Railroads that built power also procured lo-

Locomotive. A diesel-electric engine—the most common type of locomotive after the steam era—on the New York, New Haven, and Hartford Railroad. LIBRARY OF CONGRESS

comotives from outside builders. Railroad motive-power departments and the outside builders shared in the engineering, from which improved design emerged. But the manufacture of specialty items—such as superheaters, feedwater heaters, stokers, and boosters—moved more and more into the hands of the supply industries.

The Great Depression of the 1930s brought a near-paralysis of locomotive building during the years 1932–1935. The revival of railroad purchasing, although slow, was marked by the development of a new generation of locomotives—single-expansion articulated models specially made for service on the western transcontinental roads and several of the coal-hauling roads in the East. These locomotives combined the starting tractive effort of the Mallets with the speed capabilities of the later superpower locomotives. In these designs, the steam locomotive reached its peak of development in the United States. Locomotives of this genus, differentiated somewhat in design to meet intended service conditions, could haul 18,000 tons or more in coal or ore service, or move a 7,000-ton manifest freight at seventy miles per hour.

World War II interrupted steam locomotive development. So great had been the progress in diesel locomotive development that many railroads never bought steam-powered locomotives again. There were exceptions, especially the coal-hauling railroads of the Northeast, and several advanced designs were engineered for them. Locomotives built to those specifications, however, had a short life, as the superior efficiency of the diesel locomotive in all service classes was recognized. The last steam locomotives built by Baldwin for service in the United States were delivered in 1949, and Lima's last locomotive for an American railroad was the same year.

The steam locomotive was rugged, long-lived, and capable of being designed for any type of service. Hundreds of steam locomotives operated for forty years and more, often with few modifications. But the steam locomotive was never a particularly efficient machine, delivering, at the peak of its technical development, power at the drawbar equivalent only to 12 to 13 percent of the energy latent in the fuel. Since the greatest energy losses were in the cylinders of the reciprocating machine, late experiments were undertaken on three of the coal-hauling roads with steam turbine locomotives. This effort was made obsolete by the proven success of the diesel.

Straight electric locomotives were never extensively employed on American railroads. Although the Baltimore and Ohio used them after 1895 in its Baltimore tunnels, the Pennsylvania electrified the approaches to Pennsylvania Station in New York City in 1908, and the suburban lines out of Grand Central Station were electrified in the period 1906–1913, use of electric locomotives was always confined to special circumstances. The Milwaukee employed them over 641 route miles across the Rocky, Bitter Root, and Cascade mountain ranges; the Great Northern between Skykomish and Wenatchee, Washington; and the Norfolk and Western and the Virginian on heavy-grade lines. The outstanding electrification was that of the Pennsylvania between New York and Washington, which was later extended over the main line to Harrisburg. The first segment, between New York and Philadelphia, was opened in 1932. Exceptionally heavy traffic density was considered to justify the investment in power transmission and distribution. Of the several types of locomotives employed on this 11,000-volt alternating current electrification, the GG-1 was outstanding, developing 8,500 horsepower on short-period rating and working both freight and passenger trains. Most of these locomotives were still in service forty years after the prototype was delivered.

Changes in technology resulted in renewed consideration of the advantages of electric propulsion. The mercury arc and, later, the ignitron rectifier, superseded the motor-generator set in locomotives powered by alternating current. The use of commercial frequencies became possible, and several western roads instituted studies of electrification of their more heavily trafficked main lines.

In the 1970s, except over the limited electrified mileage and on a few short lines, all American railroad service was powered by diesel-electric locomotives. These used diesel engines to power generators that supplied direct current to the traction motors. The first such locomotives were delivered for switching service in 1925 and Baldwin and American Locomotive both began manufacturing them. However, the electric motive division of General Motors pioneered the application of the diesel to both passenger and freight road service in the late 1930s. In the 1970s, the business was dominated by General Motors and General Electric, the latter a past supplier of components to other manufacturers.

The diesel locomotive has the advantage of high efficiency and availability compared with the steam locomotive. It can operate in multiple units, with any number

of locomotives being controlled by a single engineer. Mid-train helper locomotives are controlled from the head locomotive, making for a better distribution of power in long and heavy trains. The problem of water supply—a serious issue for steam locomotives in many parts of the country—was eliminated. Unlike steam locomotives, diesels have been standardized by manufacturers, and traction motors and other components can be removed and replaced by standby units to keep the locomotives in service. Although the first diesel road-freight unit was tested in 1940, third-generation diesels were coming into service in the 1970s. Single units could generate more horsepower than four units of the original 5,400-horsepower freight diesel; however, locomotives in the 2,500-horsepower range remained popular because of their versatility in the systemwide locomotive pools that most railroads employed in the mid-1970s.

Always in need of advanced data processing techniques, railroads were a leader in adopting computerized "total information" systems. Such systems use computers at each terminal or freight-yard office to report the action of every car to headquarters, which then generates reports on a variety of aspects of locomotive activities. By the end of the 1980s, most major North American railroads were developing systems that would allow their freight customers to transact business electronically, and passengers can reserve seats and berths electronically as well. Computerization allows railroads to track the mileage and maintenance requirements of each locomotive so overhauls can be based on need rather than at arbitrarily chosen intervals (as was the case). Overall, computers have facilitated significant advances in railroad operations, cost efficiency, and service.

BIBLIOGRAPHY

Bianculli, Anthony J. *Trains and Technology: The American Railroad in the Nineteenth Century.* Newark: University of Delaware Press, 2001.

Bohn, Dave, and Rodolfo Petschek. *Kinsey, Photographer: A Half Century of Negatives by Darius and Tabitha May Kinsey.* Vol. 3. *The Locomotive Portraits.* San Francisco: Chronicle Books, 1984.

Bruce, Alfred W. *The Steam Locomotive in America: Its Development in the Twentieth Century.* New York: Norton, 1952.

Collias, Joe G. *The Last of Steam: A Billowing Pictorial Pageant of the Waning Years of Steam Railroading in the United States.* Berkeley: Howell-North, 1960.

Reutter, Mark, ed. *Railroad History, Millennium Special: The Diesel Revolution.* Westford, Mass.: Railway and Locomotive Historical Society, 2000.

White, John H. *American Locomotives: An Engineering History, 1830–1880.* Baltimore: Johns Hopkins University Press, 1968; 1997.

Ernest W. Williams Jr. / D. P.

See also **Railroad Brotherhoods; Railroads; Railroads in the Civil War; Railways, Interurban; Railways, Urban, and**

Rapid Transit; Steam Power and Engines; Transcontinental Railroad, Building of; Transportation and Travel.

LOG CABIN.

Origins of the log cabin remain obscure. Historians asserted that Swedes on the lower Delaware introduced such construction in 1638. Others cited a log blockhouse, McIntyre Garrison (York, Maine), built between 1640 and 1645, as evidence that New England colonists had learned log construction for themselves, though some might have seen log buildings in Scandinavia and northern Germany. Native Americans did not build log structures. Such construction increased rapidly in the seventeenth century, and the one- or two-room log cabin became the typical American pioneer home, supplemented by log outbuildings. For dwellings, spaces between logs were filled with flat stones or wood chips embedded in clay. In stables, the crevices were usually left unfilled. As the frontier pushed westward, small log buildings became the first churches, schools, mills, stores, hotels, courthouses, and seats of town and county government. In the South, tall tobacco barns were built of long logs with wide, unfilled chinks between the logs, letting the wind blow through to dry the leaf tobacco. Many built their little huts single-handed or with the aid of family members; in settlements, a house-raising became a pioneer social function, as neighbors gathered and completed the essential structure in one day. More prosperous farmers or villagers might erect two-story log houses of several rooms, shingled on the outside (New England) or often weather-boarded farther west; in Pennsylvania they were occasionally stuccoed. Today bookstores sell construction plans.

The log cabin became a potent political icon. In December 1839, a pro-Democratic Party columnist belittled the Whig Party presidential candidate, William Henry Harrison, by saying he lived in a log cabin. Whigs seized upon the snobbery inherent in the remark, and Harrison rode to victory in the 1840 election as the "log cabin candidate." Other "log cabin presidents" followed: James Polk, James Buchanan, Millard Fillmore, Abraham Lincoln, Andrew Johnson, and James Garfield. Ironically, Harrison was born in a frame dwelling. Theodore Roosevelt sought a log cabin connection by noting how he lived in a log structure as a cowboy in the Dakota Badlands. Log cabins symbolized individualism, the pioneer spirit, humble beginnings, and hard work—proof that in America even someone from a poor background could become president. In 1989, Gay and Lesbian GOP members formed the Log Cabin Republicans.

Politics flowed to popular culture. In 1887, Log Cabin syrup first appeared, as did the earliest log cabin quilt pattern. Children could play with LINCOLN LOGS.

BIBLIOGRAPHY
Kniffen, Fred, and Henry Glassie. "Building in Wood in the Eastern United States: A Time-Place Perspective." In Thomas J. Schlereth, ed., *Material Culture Studies in America*. Nashville, Tenn.: AASLH Press, 1982.

Pessen, Edward. *The Log Cabin Myth: The Social Backgrounds of the Presidents*. New Haven, Conn.: Yale University Press, 1984.

Weslager, C. A. *The Log Cabin in America: From Pioneer Days to the Present*. New Brunswick, N.J.: Rutgers University Press, 1969.

Alvin F. Harlow
Shelby Shapiro

LOGISTICS

is the application of time and space factors to war. If international politics is the "art of the possible," and war is its instrument, logistics is the art of defining and extending the possible. In short, it is the economics of warfare. Literally, it provides the substance that physically permits a military force to "live and move and have its being." As the U.S. Army's *Field Service Regulations* puts it, "It envisages getting the right people and the appropriate supplies to the right place at the right time and in the proper condition."

The word itself is derived from the Greek *logistikos*, meaning "skilled in calculating." Logistics has been a recognizable part of military science, together with strategy and tactics, since ancient times. Nonetheless, Baron Henri Jomini, the French writer on military affairs, appears to have been the first to have made systematic use of the term in this sense, in about 1838. One of the first to use the term in this way in a book in the United States was Henry B. Harrington in *Battles of the American Revolution 1775–1781*, published in 1876.

In the triad of war, a more or less sharp distinction exists for each segment. Military leaders usually see strategy as the planning and management of campaigns toward achieving the object of the war, tactics as the planning and waging of battles or engagements toward achieving strategic objectives, and logistics as the planning and management of resources to support the other two. Nevertheless, in a broader sense, these are all branches of the same entity. Frequently, the objectives of strategic operations and tactical engagements are themselves aimed at weakening the enemy's logistics, whether through bombing an industrial center, mining a harbor, or seizing key terrain to threaten a line of supply.

It can be argued, for instance, that most of the major strategic decisions of World War II, such as Europe first, the cross-Channel invasion of 1944, the landings in southern France, the return to the Philippines, and the bypassing of Formosa for Okinawa, were essentially logistic decisions. That is, military leaders based the timing, location, scale, and very purposes of those operations mainly upon logistic considerations. They evaluated comparative resources and determined that the seizure of Normandy or Marseilles or Luzon or Okinawa would facilitate further the support of forces by opening the way for additional bases and supply lines.

145

Logistics may be thought of in terms of scale as paralleling the scale of military operations. "Grand strategy" refers to national policy and the object of the war; "strategy," to the planning and management of campaigns; and "tactics," to the planning and management of battles or engagements. Parallel terminology may also apply to logistics. Thus, "grand logistics" refers to the national economy and industrial mobilization. "Strategic logistics" relates to the analysis of requirements and logistic feasibility of proposed campaigns, a determination of requirements to support a particular strategic decision, and to the follow-up mobilization and assembly of forces and the moving of them—with their supplies and equipment—to the area, with provision for effective resupply. "Tactical logistics" refers to the logistics of the battlefield: the movement of troops to the battlefield and the supplying of these troops with the ammunition, food, fuel, supplies, and services needed to sustain them in combat.

As a calculation of logistic efficiency, one may speak of "primary logistics" as those needed for the support of combat units, and of "secondary logistics" as those required to support the means to meet the primary requirements, or what the satisfaction of requirements in one category may create for requirements in another. Thus, in delivering a given amount of gasoline to an armed force, for instance, the amount of fuel and other resources needed to deliver that gasoline must be taken into account. During the American Civil War, Gen. William Tecumseh Sherman reckoned that an army could not be supplied by horses and wagons at a distance greater than 100 miles from its base, for in that distance, the horses would consume the entire contents of their wagons. Air transportation occasionally creates greater logistic problems than it solves. During the KOREAN WAR, for each five tons of cargo that a C-54 air transport carried across the Pacific Ocean, it consumed eighteen tons of gasoline. To move a given 15,000 tons of cargo from San Francisco to Yokohama by sea required two Victory ships. By contrast, to move it by air required 3,000 air flights plus eight ships to carry the gasoline for the airplanes. On the other hand, other secondary logistic requirements are built up in the maintenance of long supply lines and multiple storage facilities. At times, a supply base, given to continuous proliferation, reaches the point at which it consumes more supplies than it ships out, and thus becomes a net drain on the logistic system. Another aspect of secondary logistics arises in the acceptance and manufacture of a new weapon or in the choice of one weapon over another for expanded production, in terms of the effect of the decision on the problem of ammunition supply.

BIBLIOGRAPHY

Jessup, John E., ed. *Encyclopedia of the American Military: Studies of the History, Traditions, Policies, Institutions, and Roles of the Armed Forces in War and Peace*. New York: Scribners, 1994.

Leonard, Thomas C. *Above the Battle: War Making in America from Appomattox to Versailles*. New York: Oxford University Press, 1978.

Lynn, John A., ed. *Feeding Mars: Logistics in Western Warfare from the Middle Ages to the Present*. Boulder, Colo.: Westview Press, 1993.

Van Creveld, Martin L. *Supplying War: Logistics from Wallenstein to Patton*. Cambridge, U.K.; New York: Cambridge University Press, 1977; 1980

James A. Huston/A. E.

See also **Air Force, United States; Army, United States; Demobilization; Navy, Department of the; World War II, Navy in.**

LOGROLLING is the term used when members of congress support each other's hometown projects not for the merit of the project but simply as a reciprocative exchange. The first known use of the term was by Congressman Davy Crockett, who said on the floor in 1835, "my people don't like me to log-roll in their business, and vote away pre-emption rights to fellows in other states that never kindle a fire on their own land." Logrolling is closely akin to, and results in, pork barrel legislation that loads up spending bills with hometown project money, often directed toward suspect causes or construction. It is an affliction of the democratic process that seems incurable.

BIBLIOGRAPHY

Oxford English Dictionary. 2nd ed., s.v. "Logrolling." New York: Oxford University Press, 1989.

Carl E. Prince

See also **Pork Barrel.**

LONDON, DECLARATION OF. This was a code of laws relating to maritime warfare drafted on 26 February 1909 by the London Naval Conference. Conspicuous in the declaration were the issues of contraband and continuous voyage. The parties reached agreement on lists of contraband and on the classification of goods that could not be declared contraband. They restricted continuous voyage in application to contraband.

The declaration illustrates the strength and weakness of international legislation. Although the declaration was never ratified, the United States tried to make it an important instrument of policy. Secretary of State Robert Lansing secretly tried to persuade Britain to follow the declaration during World War I. Britain rejected the plan, and the United States fell back on the traditional principles of international law.

BIBLIOGRAPHY

International Naval Conference. *The Declaration of London, February 26, 1909: A Collection of Official Papers and Documents Relating to the International Naval Conference Held in London, December 1908–February 1909*. New York: Oxford University Press, 1919.

Perkins, Bradford. *The Great Rapprochement: England and the United States, 1895–1914.* New York: Atheneum, 1968.

Pyke, Harold Reason. *The Law of Contraband of War.* Oxford: Clarendon Press, 1915.

Honor Sachs
Richard W. Van Alstyne

See also **International Law; World War I.**

LONDON, TREATY OF

LONDON, TREATY OF (1604), brought to an end the formal warfare that had been waged since 1585 between England and Spain, endangering all English colonizing projects in the New World. The treaty temporarily eradicated this danger and, among other things, reopened "free commerce" between the two kingdoms "where commerce existed before the war." Spain intended this clause to exclude English merchants from its colonies overseas, but the English gave it the opposite interpretation, causing continued warfare "beyond the Line" and the rise of the buccaneers. Three years later, with the Spanish threat no longer pressing, King James I authorized the first permanent English settlement in the New World.

BIBLIOGRAPHY
Andrews, Charles M. *The Colonial Period of American History.* New Haven, Conn.: Yale University Press, 1934.

Davenport, Frances G. *European Treaties Bearing on the History of the United States and Its Dependencies to 1648.* Washington, D.C.: Carnegie Institution, 1937.

Raymond P. Stearns/A. G.

See also **Colonial Policy, British; Colonial Settlements; Colonial Wars; Piracy.**

LONDON NAVAL TREATIES

LONDON NAVAL TREATIES. Two conferences in London sought to continue and extend naval armaments pacts initially agreed upon at the Washington Naval Conference of 1921–1922. At this conference, the United States, Great Britain, Japan, France, and Italy agreed on ratios for battleship and aircraft carrier tonnage in a successful effort to halt what might have been an expensive arms race; the resulting treaty also allowed the British to let the Anglo-Japanese Treaty of 1902 terminate. Britain thus avoided being caught in a possible future Japanese-American conflict as an ally of each power.

As the industrialized world slid into the Great Depression, the five nations met in London from late January to late April 1930. The United States, Great Britain, and Japan agreed to extend the Washington naval accord for battleships (and aircraft carriers) and established a new 10:10:7 ratio for small cruisers and destroyers while permitting Japan parity in submarines. France and Italy, both of which considered themselves to be ill-used, did not officially accept these new ratios but, given the depression, all five powers agreed to defer construction of new capital ships until 1937. These new agreements were to continue to 1936, with the signatories pledged to meet again in five years to re-open the discussions.

In December 1935, the naval powers met again in London to continue and extend naval disarmament from earlier Washington (1922) and London (1930) naval treaties. A threat loomed on the horizon—in 1934, Japan had announced its intention not to extend the treaties past 1936, their expiration date, and began planning on the super battleships of the "Yamato" class. The United States and Great Britain would not grant Japan parity in warship tonnage (and hence in the number of capital ships), and Japan withdrew from the conference. The United States, Great Britain, and France signed a naval treaty on 25 March 1936 to limit cruisers and destroyers to 8,000 tons and battleships to 35,000 tons (and 14-inch guns) but, without Japanese, German, and Italian concurrence, this London naval treaty was powerless.

By 1938, as word of super battleships under construction in Japan and Germany spread, the signatories revised treaty limits on the size of major warships, and in 1939 with the German invasion of Poland and the subsequent British and French declarations of war against Germany, the treaty was scrapped.

However well intentioned, the treaties failed in their larger goal of preventing war. While Japan signed the 1930 London Naval Treaty, eighteen months later it used the Mukden Incident to take over China's rich province of Manchuria and generally begin to expand on the Asian mainland. Meanwhile, the naval treaties had no impact on Germany's plan for a war of conquest and aggression on the European mainland.

BIBLIOGRAPHY
Borg, Dorothy. *The United States and the Far Eastern Crisis of 1933–1938.* Cambridge, Mass.: Harvard University Press, 1964.

Crowley, James B. *Japan's Quest for Autonomy: National Security and Foreign Policy, 1930–1938.* Princeton, N.J.: Princeton University Press, 1966.

Doenecke, Justus D., and Edward Wilz. *From Isolation to War, 1931–1941* 2d ed. Arlington Heights, Ill.: Harlan Davidson, 1991.

Pelz, Stephen.E. *Race to Pearl Harbor: The Failure of the Second London Naval Conference and the Onset of World War II.* Cambridge, Mass.: Harvard University Press, 1974.

Charles M. Dobbs

LONE WOLF V. HITCHCOCK

LONE WOLF V. HITCHCOCK, 187 U.S. 553 (1903). Article 5 of the U.S. Constitution places American Indian affairs and policies solely in the hands of the federal government, and throughout the nineteenth century the Supreme Court rearticulated and affirmed this "government to government" relationship. Treaties between the federal government and Indian nations became the primary mechanism for adjudicating differences, ending wars, and ceding lands. Once ratified by Congress, treaties became law, the foundation for Indian rights. In *Lone Wolf v. Hitchcock*, the Supreme Court undermined the legal supremacy of Indian treaties and placed Indian affairs under the plenary power of the U.S. Congress.

The Kiowas and Comanches dominated the southern Plains for much of the Spanish, Mexican, and early American periods. Following increased white migration and conflict, the Kiowas and Comanches signed the Treaty of Medicine Lodge in 1867, which created a sizable reservation for them in Indian Territory. Article 12 of the treaty states that no further land cessions would occur "unless executed and signed by at least three fourths of all the adult male Indians" within the reservation and that no individuals would lose access to their existing treaty lands. With the passing of the Dawes General Allotment Act of 1887, Congress systematically attacked the communal land base of all Indian reservations, and in Indian Territory government agents pressured Comanche and Kiowa groups to allot their reservation lands. Government agencies lacked the signatures of a three-fourths majority of Indians, and Lone Wolf and other Kiowa-Comanche landholders who had lost access to their treaty lands following allotment sued. In *Lone Wolf v. Hitchcock*, the Supreme Court affirmed the rulings of the lower courts and ruled that Congress has "the power . . . to abrogate the provisions of an Indian treaty" and that Article 12 of the Medicine Lodge Treaty did not protect the Kiowa-Comanches from congressional rulings.

Placing Indian affairs under the power of Congress, the Supreme Court set the landmark precedent that treaties were not immune from congressional acts. Throughout the twentieth century, Congress passed numerous acts that violated Indian treaties, including the termination era laws of the 1950s and the 1960s, which attempted to "terminate" the federal trust status of Indian lands and communities.

BIBLIOGRAPHY

Clark, Blue. *"Lone Wolf" v. "Hitchcock": Treaty Rights and Indian Law at the End of the Nineteenth Century*. Lincoln: University of Nebraska Press, 1994.

Prucha, Francis Paul. *The Great Father: The United States Government and the American Indian*. Lincoln: University of Nebraska Press, 1984.

Ned Blackhawk

See also **Dawes General Allotment Act; Indian Treaties.**

LONELY CROWD, THE. David Riesman's book *The Lonely Crowd: A Study of the Changing American Culture* (1950), coauthored with Nathan Glazer and Reuel Denney, was one of the most influential works of twentieth-century American SOCIOLOGY. It asserted that the prevailing social character of Americans had changed dramatically since the nineteenth century in response to changing demographics and the emergence of a service- and consumption-based economy. The change was from an "inner-directed" personality type, a self-reliant and purposeful person who was able to navigate through a changing world by relying upon the firm principles implanted by parents, to an "other-directed" type, exquisitely attentive to the cues of others—particularly peer groups, coworkers, and mass media—in finding its way in the world. This change reflected the larger transformation in American life, the causes of which range from the increasingly abstract and corporate structure of the modern economy to the social homogeneity of the postwar suburbs, to the amorphousness of the modern democratic family. The book's popularity derived from a widespread concern that the American ethos of self-reliant freedom was vanishing as the newly prosperous nation became a land of anxious, oversocialized, glad-handing personality mongers and empty suits. Hence the paradox captured in the title: a throng whose individual members nevertheless felt themselves painfully alone, unable to claim independent meaning for their lives.

In fact, the book's actual arguments were more nuanced than many of its readers noticed. Far from calling for a restoration of the past, Riesman readily conceded the highly compulsive quality of much "inner directedness" and saw considerable merit in an "other directedness" that enhanced Americans' capacity for empathy. Nevertheless, the book's most salient message was its warning against the perils of conformism, expressed in a closing admonition that Americans "lose their social freedom and their individual autonomy in seeking to become like each other." That message still resonates today.

BIBLIOGRAPHY

McClay, Wilfred M. *The Masterless: Self and Society in Modern America*. Chapel Hill: University of North Carolina Press, 1994.

Pells, Richard H. *The Liberal Mind in a Conservative Age: American Intellectuals in the 1940s and 1950s*. New York: Harper and Row, 1985.

Wilfred McClay

See also **Existentialism.**

LONG BEACH. Located in the southern portion of Los Angeles County, the 2000 census placed Long Beach's population at 461,522, making it the fifth largest city in California. Long famous as a tourist destination, the city has also become an important commercial hub, with the port of Long Beach handling more container traffic than any other U.S. harbor. The city was originally established in the 1880s as a beachside resort, but its economy quickly diversified. Improvements on its harbor, completed in 1924, facilitated the expansion of commerce and fishing. The 1920s also witnessed the discovery of land petroleum deposits in Long Beach and surrounding communities that made Long Beach a major center of oil production. Struck by a devastating earthquake in 1933, the city's economy quickly rebounded, thanks in part to the emerging AIRCRAFT INDUSTRY. During World War II federal investments in aircraft production and the creation of the Long Beach Naval Shipyards further strengthened the economy. Military spending spurred by the Cold War sustained Long Beach's prosperity, with the McDonnell-Douglas Corporation becoming the city's largest employer. In the late twentieth century the oil industry waned and federal investments slackened, forcing the closure of the naval shipyards and causing a decline in aerospace employment. However, the city remains a major convention and tourism center and the growth of trade with Asia and Latin America has facilitated the port's commercial prosperity.

BIBLIOGRAPHY

DeAtley, Richard. *Long Beach: The Golden Shore, a History of the City and Port.* Houston, Tex.: Pioneer Publications, 1988.

Malone, Myrtle D., ed. *Long Beach: A 21st Century City by the Sea.* Houston, Tex.: Pioneer Publications, 1997.

Daniel J. Johnson

See also **Petroleum Industry.**

LONG DRIVE. At the close of the Civil War, large herds of longhorn cattle roamed freely throughout Texas. High meat prices in eastern cities attracted a variety of entrepreneurs and prompted cattlemen to search for a way to bring them to market. The building of the first transcontinental railroads offered a solution by providing an inexpensive mode of transporting cattle to large urban markets. Beginning in 1866, cowboys drove herds of cattle, numbering on average twenty-five hundred head, overland to railheads on the northern Plains, which typically took from six weeks to two months. Gradually, however, the westward spread of homestead settlement, expanding railroad networks, and shrinking free-range cattle herds pushed the trails farther west. By 1890, long drives to reach railroad stations had become unnecessary, and professional ranchers had replaced the early entrepreneurs in supplying urban America with beef cattle.

BIBLIOGRAPHY

Dale, Edward E. *The Range Cattle Industry: Ranching on the Great Plains from 1865 to 1925.* Norman: University of Oklahoma Press, 1960.

Everett Dick / c. w.

See also **Cattle Drives; Trail Drivers; Transcontinental Railroad, Building of.**

LONG ISLAND, located in the Atlantic Ocean, constitutes the easternmost point of New York State. The island is 118 miles long and 12 to 23 miles wide and splits into two peninsulas at its ends. The northern peninsula ends at Orient Point, and the southern peninsula ends at Montauk Point. At 1,723 square miles, it is the fourth largest island of the United States and the largest outside of Hawaii and Alaska.

Delaware and Montauk Indians inhabited Long Island. European settlement began with the Plymouth Company, and the title was conveyed to William Alexander of Great Britain in 1635. Nonetheless the island became a part of the Dutch West India Company, which established numerous settlements, including Bruekelen (now Brooklyn). English settlers continued to arrive and founded communities such as Southampton, Hempstead, and Flushing. In 1650 New Netherland and the New England Confederation entered into the Treaty of Hartford, which drew a demarcation line on Long Island, giving the Dutch the western end and the British the part east of Oyster Bay.

In this unsettled period of European colonization, control of Long Island continued to shift. In 1664 the island became part of the lands Charles II gave to James, duke of York, who later became King James II. The British militarily defeated the Dutch, who ceded New Amsterdam to the British. New Amsterdam became a part of Yorkshire, with the local administrative seat of the territory located in Hempstead. In 1683 Long Island was subdivided into administrative units called "counties," including Kings, Queens, and Suffolk Counties. The county-level politics and administration of New York and Long Island remained powerful into the twenty-first century.

Both the patriots and the Loyalists hotly contested Long Island during the American Revolution. The island's strategic location and its function as a wood and food supply point made it the target of frequent raids by both military units and privateers. Indeed the Battle of Long Island was the first battle of the 1776 Revolutionary War campaign.

The evolution of Long Island as a commercial center after independence centered on its proximity to New York City, which emerged as a major metropolitan area. In 1844 the Long Island Railroad was completed, giving New York efficient access to the industries of Long Island, including farming, whaling, oystering, and fishing. Bridges and highways, in particular the Long Island Expressway, accelerated the growth and transformation of Long Island.

The manufacture of electrical equipment and aircraft made Long Island an important industrial center. After World War II many of the communities close to New York City experienced rapid residential growth. At that time Long Island became the site of an experiment in suburban housing, identical, inexpensively constructed single-family, stand-alone homes. William J. Levitt started these developments and between 1947 and 1951 constructed 17,447 houses in LEVITTOWN. These inexpensive family homes, affordable to middle-class Americans, began a national trend that eventually became synonymous with suburban "sprawl."

As New York City grew, important infrastructures, such as La Guardia and Kennedy International Airports, were built on the western tip of Long Island. Coney Island, Jones Beach, and Fire Island near New York City became popular summer destinations. Fire Island was one of the first communities in the United States associated with homosexual community life. On the far east end the Hamptons (Southampton and East Hampton) became synonymous with wealth and summer mansions. Southampton is the venue of F. Scott Fitzgerald's novel *The Great Gatsby* (1925). Long Island achieved a significant place in American popular culture.

BIBLIOGRAPHY

Bookbinder, Bernie, and Harvey Weber. *Long Island: People and Places, Past and Present*. New York: Abrams, 1998.

Newsday Staff. "Long Island Our Story." *Newsday*, 1998. http://www.lihistory.com/

Steffen W. Schmidt

See also **Dutch West India Company; New Amsterdam; New York City.**

LONG ISLAND, BATTLE OF (27 August 1776).

On 27 August 1776, British general William Howe embarked from Staten Island in New York, with all but one of his brigades, for Gravesend Bay beach on the southwestern tip of Long Island. General George Washington's outpost line, from Brooklyn Heights along the shore from the Narrows, was quickly reinforced with nearly a third of the entire American army. On the night of 26–27 August, Howe struck Washington's main position. Had this attack been pushed, all American forces on Long Island could have been captured. As it was, realizing his danger, Washington withdrew to Manhattan on the night of 29–30 August without interference from the British.

BIBLIOGRAPHY

Gruber, Ira D. *The Howe Brothers and the American Revolution*. New York: Atheneum, 1972.

Tiedemann, Joseph S. "A Revolution Foiled: Queens County, New York, 1775–1776." *Journal of American History* 75, no. 2 (September 1988): 417–444.

Robert S. Thomas / A. R.

See also **Harlem, Battle of; Long Island; New York City; Revolution, American: Military History.**

LONG, STEPHEN H., EXPLORATIONS OF.

Major Stephen H. Long (1784–1864), army topographical engineer, commanded a scientific expedition that explored portions of the Rocky Mountains and the Platte, Arkansas, and Canadian Rivers during the summer of 1820. His party departed Pittsburgh on 5 May 1819 as the scientific arm of a larger expedition with orders to explore the Upper Missouri by steamboat. Technical dif-

ficulties, disease, delay, and lack of funding compelled the abandonment of this venture during the winter of 1819–1820. As an alternative, Secretary of War John C. Calhoun ordered Long's party to travel overland from its winter quarters at Engineer Cantonment near Council Bluffs to explore the Arkansas and Red Rivers.

Long's party, which included the entomologist Thomas Say, the artists Titian Peale and Samuel Seymour, and the physician-naturalist Edwin James, began its journey on 6 June 1820. They moved westward along the Platte and arrived in early July at the Rocky Mountains, where James and other members of the party made the first recorded ascent of Pike's Peak. The party then divided into two groups that turned south and east. One group was ordered to travel down the Arkansas River, and the other, led by Long himself, intended to find the source of the Red River. It failed to do so, mistaking the Canadian River for the Red. Exhausted by hunger and thirst, the two groups reunited at Belle Point on the Arkansas River on 13 September 1820.

Though Long failed to make any significant contributions to formal geographical knowledge of the region, his party gathered extensive scientific and ethnographic data, recording their observations of the Pawnees and identifying numerous new plant and animal species. In 1823 James published a compilation of the expedition's journals, which brought the results of the expedition to a wider audience. Some historians have chastised Long for characterizing the Great Plains in present-day Kansas, Nebraska, and Oklahoma as a "Great American Desert" in his report to Calhoun. However, others have pointed out the accuracy of Long's description of the arid plains as unsuitable for agriculture, given the technological resources of his era. Long undertook another major exploration, this one of the Minnesota River and the Great Lakes, in 1823. This expedition concluded his career as an explorer, though he remained an active member of the army engineers until a few years before his death.

BIBLIOGRAPHY

Benson, Maxine, ed. *From Pittsburgh to the Rocky Mountains: Major Stephen Long's Expedition, 1819–1820*. Golden, Colo.: Fulcrum, 1988. Edited and annotated version of the James report.

Goetzmann, William H. *Army Exploration in the American West, 1803–1863*. Austin: Texas State Historical Association, 1991. A reprint of the 1959 edition with a new introduction by the author.

———. *Exploration and Empire: The Explorer and the Scientist in the Winning of the American West*. Austin: Texas State Historical Association, 1993. Originally published in 1966. With Goetzmann's other works, the most comprehensive discussion of Long's expeditions within the wider context of American history.

James, Edwin. *Account of an Expedition from Pittsburgh to the Rocky Mountains*. March of America Facsimile Series, no. 65. Ann Arbor, Mich.: University Microfilms International, 1966. Reprint of the 1823 edition in its entirety.

Nichols, Roger L., and Patrick L. Halley. *Stephen Long and American Frontier Exploration*. Newark: University of Delaware Press, 1980.

Monica Rico

See also **Explorations and Expeditions: U.S.; Great American Desert.**

LONG TELEGRAM. *See* **"X" Article.**

LOOKOUT MOUNTAIN, BATTLE ON (24 November 1863), also known as the "battle of the clouds," an action in which Union Gen. Joseph Hooker, commanding the right wing of Gen. Ulysses S. Grant's army of about 56,000 men, cleared Lookout Mountain, Tennessee, of the disheartened Confederate troops who had held it since the Battle of Chickamauga two months earlier. The withdrawal of Gen. James Longstreet's corps from Lookout Mountain had left the Confederate left wing dangerously weak. Hooker's troops, scrambling up the mountain, drove off the remaining Confederates, swept on across Chattanooga Creek, and the next day fought at Missionary Ridge to the east. The battle marked the beginning of Union triumph in the Chattanooga campaign.

BIBLIOGRAPHY

Bowers, John. *Chickamauga and Chattanooga: The Battles That Doomed the Confederacy*. New York: HarperCollins, 1994.

Sword, Wiley. *Mountains Touched with Fire: Chattanooga Besieged, 1863*. New York: St. Martin's Press, 1995.

Woodworth, Steven E. *Six Armies in Tennessee: The Chickamauga and Chattanooga Campaigns*. Lincoln: University of Nebraska Press, 1998.

Alfred P. James / A. R.

See also **Chattanooga Campaign; Chickamauga, Battle of; Civil War; Cumberland, Army of the.**

LORDS OF TRADE AND PLANTATION, an administrative body organized by Charles II in 1675 to create stronger administrative ties between the colonial governments and the Crown. Previously, constitutional practice provided that English provinces outside the realm were charges of the Privy Council. Beginning in 1624, special committees advising the Privy Council directed British colonial administration. As these committees were short-lived and often unskilled, confusion and inefficiency in imperial control resulted. To create an informed personnel with vigor and continuity in colonial policy, Charles II organized the Lords of Trade and Plantation, a body of twenty-one privy councillors, nine of whom held "the immediate Care and Intendency" of colonies, with any five constituting a quorum. The lords held no formal power and were only advisory to the Privy Council. But because they were men of informed ability and great administrative

capacity, and because they served for twenty years with relatively few changes in personnel, they achieved more systematic administration than any previous agencies for colonial affairs, serving as a transition to and a model for the BOARD OF TRADE AND PLANTATIONS, which succeeded them in 1696. They held 857 meetings (1675–1696) and maintained permanent offices in Scotland Yard. They also established a permanent, salaried secretary (Sir Robert Southwell), assistant secretary (William Blathwayt), and clerical staff to handle colonial correspondence; became a bureau of colonial information by sending inquiries to colonial governors and agents (notably Edward Randolph) to colonies; recommended appointees as royal governors to crown colonies and prepared their commissions and instructions; developed the technique of judicial review of colonial cases appealed to the Privy Council; assaulted, in the interests of unity and efficiency, the charters of colonies—forcing surrender of two and instituting quo warranto proceedings against five others by 1686—and instituted the policy of consolidating colonies (the Dominion of New England). Although vigorous in its early years, the Popish Plot (1678—a conspiracy by Roman Catholics to kill Charles II and replace him with his Roman Catholic brother, James, Duke of York) lessened activity, and, as death took older members and political disorders (1685–1689) interfered, the Lords of Trade became weak and ineffective. Their last meeting was on 18 April 1696, a month before the Board of Trade was instituted.

BIBLIOGRAPHY

Lawson, Philip, ed. *Parliament and the Atlantic Empire*. Edinburgh, Scotland: Edinburgh University Press, 1995.

Lovejoy, David S. *The Glorious Revolution in America*. Cambridge, Mass.: Harvard University Press, 1985; Middletown, Conn.: Wesleyan University Press, 1972; 1987.

Smuts, R. Malcolm. *Culture and Power in England, 1585–1685*. New York: St. Martin's Press, 1999.

Raymond P. Stearns / s. b.

See also **Colonial Agent; Colonial Policy, British; Colonial Settlements; Dominion of New England; Mercantilism; Parliament, British.**

LOS ANGELES. Located in Southern CALIFORNIA, Los Angeles is a world-class city featuring a diverse economy based on international trade, high-technology production, and the entertainment and tourist industry. As of the 2000 census, Los Angeles had a population of 3,694,820, making it the second largest city in the United States, as well as one of the most culturally, ethnically, and racially diverse places in the world.

Early History

The region was originally the home of Native American peoples such as the Tongvas and the Chumashes. A Spanish expedition led by Gaspar de Portolá passed through

151

Early Los Angeles. In 1880 the city of Los Angeles had only 11,183 residents, but by 1920 that number had exploded to 576,673. Founded by the Spanish, the city retained its Hispanic heritage until the coming of the Southern Pacific (1875) and Santa Fe (1886) railroads, which brought diversity to the city's population. A land boom in the 1880s led to rapid growth and many new buildings, as can be seen in this bird's-eye view picture of Los Angeles, c. 1880–1890. LIBRARY OF CONGRESS

the area in late July and early August of 1769. On 2 August they crossed the local river and named it after the Franciscan feast day celebrated on that date: El Rio de Nuestra Señora la Reina de los Angeles de la Porciúncula (The River of Our Lady the Queen of the Angels of Porciuncula). In 1781 the Spanish founded an agricultural pueblo, naming it after the river. By the 1830s the city had become the principal urban center of Mexican California. Los Angeles's dominance was shattered by the discovery of gold in Northern California in 1848 and the subsequent gold rush, events that made San Francisco the leading city in California.

Well into the 1870s Los Angeles retained strong elements of its Hispanic past and a modest economy rooted in cattle raising and viticulture. However, the arrival of the Southern Pacific Railroad in 1876 and the Santa Fe Railroad in 1886 sparked explosive development. During the 1880s Los Angeles experienced a speculative land boom. While the initial boom collapsed fairly quickly, it left a solid infrastructure of development that supported the extraordinary population growth of the next few decades. Having only 11,183 residents in 1880, in 1920 Los Angeles boasted a population of 576,673. The largest number of settlers were from the midwestern states, relatively affluent and overwhelmingly native born and Protestant. They were drawn to the city by the promise of a pleasant, temperate climate and a more relaxed lifestyle. Many people also flocked to the region as tourists and health seekers, similarly drawn by the city's unique climate and location. While tourism and demographic growth fueled economic expansion, many civic leaders remained concerned about the lack of industrial diversity

and the potential limitations upon continued population expansion.

Economic Expansion in the Twentieth Century

In the late nineteenth and early twentieth centuries the city witnessed significant infrastructure development; the city greatly improved its public transportation system through massive federal and local investments in the harbor at San Pedro and the creation of a far-flung system of interurban streetcars. At the same time, the city engaged on an ambitious quest to secure an adequate water supply. Faced with limitations imposed by a relatively arid climate, the municipality sought to exploit the water resources of the Owens Valley, located over two hundred miles to the north. With the completion of the Los Angeles Aqueduct in 1913, the city successfully obtained the water needed for future growth. The utilization of the aqueduct as a source of hydroelectric power also gave the city a plentiful supply of cheap electricity.

Continuing population growth and an increasingly diversified economy promoted Los Angeles's emergence as a key urban center for California. The discovery of major petroleum deposits in the 1890s led to the creation of refineries and the spread of drilling operations. At the turn of the century, the burgeoning movie industry took root there and quickly became a major employer. Equally significant were the factories established by national corporations. In 1914 Ford established a branch manufacturing plant in the region and other automobile and tire manufactures soon followed. The Southern California region also became the center of the emerging AIRCRAFT INDUSTRY, including firms such as Hughes, Douglas, Lockheed, and Northrop. Even during the Great Depression of the 1930s Los Angeles continued to grow, with continued supplies of cheap water and power being guaranteed by the completion of Hoover Dam in 1936. To take advantage of these resources, the city helped create the Metropolitan Water District of Southern California.

Government spending associated with World War II and the subsequent Cold War offered even greater opportunities. The growing demand for military airplanes sparked a huge expansion of the aircraft industry. By the 1950s federal monies also flowed into businesses manufacturing rockets and electronics, leading to the evolution of a complex and profitable aerospace and high-technology sector. During this same period the development of an extensive freeway system facilitated the continued suburbanization of population and industry.

Diversity, Conflict, and Modern Problems

Over the course of the twentieth century, Los Angeles increasingly developed a complex social mosaic of cultures and peoples. By the 1930s Los Angeles had 368,000 people of Mexican origin, more than any city except Mexico City. At the same time Los Angeles became home to a large Japanese population, and after World War II, growing numbers of African Americans. While these communities enjoyed the economic opportunities available in the region, they were also often subjected to con-

Entertainment Industry. As Los Angeles grew, many movie studios, television studios, and record companies began to call Southern California home. Readily available labor and the fantastic weather were strong lures, and soon the Los Angeles area—specifically Hollywood—became the entertainment capital of the world. Grauman's Chinese Theater, shown here hosting a movie premiere in 1927, has remained a prime tourist attraction. Outside the theater, hundreds of entertainers have added to the Walk of Fame by placing their handprints and autographs in the concrete sidewalks. LIBRARY OF CONGRESS

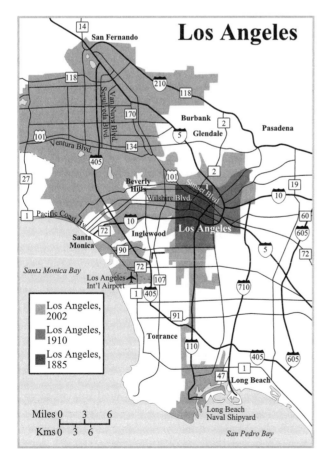

Los Angeles, 2002
Los Angeles, 1910
Los Angeles, 1885

siderable discrimination. Residential segregation helped create overcrowded minority communities that suffered from minimal access to basic public services, including education and health care, and limited access to political representation.

The 1940s saw rising levels of social and cultural tension. During the war years the city's Japanese American communities were profoundly disrupted by a 1942 federal order to exclude people of Japanese origin from the West Coast. Forced to abandon or sell their homes and businesses, they were relocated to hastily built inland camps. Wartime tensions were manifested as well in two ugly outbursts that targeted the city's growing Hispanic population, the Sleepy Lagoon Trial and the Zoot Suit Riots. In the postwar years the city's African American community became particularly frustrated by de facto segregation and declining economic opportunities. The growing suburbanization of industry and the lack of public transportation made it difficult for African Americans to find jobs, leading to relatively high levels of unemployment. This was compounded by a hostile relationship with the Los Angeles Police Department. These frustrations exploded in 1965 with the WATTS RIOTS, which left large parts of South Central Los Angeles in ruins.

There were other troubling undercurrents to the city's rapid development. Located in a geologically active region, EARTHQUAKES have long been a concern, but increasing population density progressively increased the

East Los Angeles. By 1930, when this photo was taken, Los Angeles was a world-class city and the largest in the western United States. Even during the Great Depression, when the rest of the country had ground to an economic halt, Los Angeles continued to grow, as businesses were drawn to the city by its climate and its cheap supplies of water and electricity. In turn, people continued to move to the city to take advantage of the new jobs that those businesses were providing. LIBRARY OF CONGRESS

possibility for a truly massive disaster. Following the 1933 Long Beach earthquake the city reevaluated local building codes; changes were made that helped limit the destruction caused by the Sylmar earthquake in 1971 and the Northridge earthquake of 1994. However, there remain intrinsic limits to what engineering can accomplish.

Explosive population growth, coupled with a reliance on the automobile and a strong preference for single-family detached homes, contributed to growing problems of AIR POLLUTION, traffic congestion, and spiraling housing costs. Efforts to cope with these problems have seen mixed results. The creation of the South Coast Air Quality Management District in 1975 undoubtedly helped ease problems of air pollution, but Los Angeles's environment remains seriously contaminated. Beginning in 1990 the city also began an ambitious project to improve its public transportation infrastructure by building a light-rail system, but this project has been repeatedly plagued by delays and cost overruns. The growing strain on public services, particularly on police protection and education, inspired significant civic discontent, highlighted by the efforts of the San Fernando Valley to gain municipal autonomy; a movement that, if successful, could halve the city's population and area.

The 1992 riots in South Central Los Angeles similarly indicate continued social tension within the city's racial and ethnic communities. Compounding these problems have been setbacks to the economy. Declining military spending in the late 1980s forced the downsizing of many aerospace firms, while growing competition from other high-tech manufacturing centers, such as Silicon

Valley, and the rising cost of living have discouraged some businesses from locating in Los Angeles and have even prompted their flight to other locales. At the same time, the branch automobile and tire factories established in the 1920s and 1930s have been closed.

Continued Promise and Growth

Despite these persistent problems, Los Angeles still remains a city of opportunity for many people. Since the 1960s the city has become a key gateway for immigrants entering the United States. Much of this migration derives from Latin America and Asia, but it includes people from virtually every corner of the world. In some instances this extraordinary diversity has fueled social tensions, but the city has also benefited from the labor, knowledge, and capital provided by immigrants. The overt discrimination of the early twentieth century has waned and minority groups have gained a greater public voice. Indicative of this was the election of Mayor Tom Bradley in 1973. One of the first African Americans to serve as a mayor of a major U.S. city, Bradley held this position for twenty years until he retired in 1993. Since the late 1940s Mexican Americans have similarly gained increasing recognition in local government although by the 2000s they, like the population of Asian origin, remained somewhat underrepresented.

Economically, high-technology manufacturing continues to play an important role, although it has been supplemented in part by low-tech industries that take advantage of the city's deep pool of immigrant labor. The entertainment and tourism industries also remain important employers in the region, while the city's strategic location has made it a major financial and commercial nexus for the emerging Pacific Rim economy. The volume of container traffic handled by Los Angeles's harbor facilities has steadily grown, making this one of the largest ports in the world. Los Angeles has truly become a world-class city, reflecting both the hopes and frustrations of the age.

BIBLIOGRAPHY

Davis, Mike. *City of Quartz: Excavating the Future in Los Angeles*. New York: Vintage Books, 1992.

Fogelson, Robert M. *The Fragmented Metropolis: Los Angeles, 1850–1930*. Cambridge, Mass.: Harvard University Press, 1967.

George, Lynell. *No Crystal Stair: African-Americans in the City of Angels*. New York: Verso Press, 1992.

Klein, Norman, and Martin G. Schiesel, eds. *20th Century Los Angeles: Power, Promotion, and Social Conflict*. Claremont, Calif.: Regina Books, 1990.

Ovnick, Merry. *Los Angeles: The End of the Rainbow*. Los Angeles: Balcony Press, 1994.

Pitt, Leonard, and Dale Pitt. *Los Angeles A to Z: An Encyclopedia of the City and County*. Berkeley: University of California Press, 1997.

Reiff, David. *Los Angeles: Capital of the Third World*. New York: Simon and Schuster, 1991.

Waldinger, Roger, and Mehdi Bozorgmehr, eds. *Ethnic Los Angeles*. New York: Russell Sage Foundation, 1996.

Daniel J. Johnson

See also **Immigration; Japanese American Incarceration; Riots, Urban; Urbanization; Water Supply and Conservation;** *and vol. 9:* **Pachucos in the Making.**

LOS ANGELES RIOTS,

an uprising that occurred in May 1992 following the acquittal of four white police officers in the 1991 beating of Rodney King, a black man who had led Los Angeles police on a high-speed automobile chase. The beating was videotaped by a bystander and broadcast repeatedly by news organizations. Most observers were shocked when the jury did not convict the officers, who had been shown savagely beating a prostrate King. The riots ravaged inner-city Los Angeles, killing at least fifty-three people and injuring twenty-four hundred. Rioters burned and looted stores—in some neighborhoods, shops owned by Korean Americans were targeted—leaving twelve hundred businesses destroyed. Cost estimates climbed to more than $1 billion. A white truck driver, Reginald Denny, became a national symbol of the riots when he was pulled from his vehicle in south-central Los Angeles and severely beaten by a group of young black men, leaving him unconscious and critically injured. That beating was also caught on videotape and dominated national news for some time. Another group of black residents came to Denny's rescue and took him to a hospital. In 1993 two of the acquitted officers were convicted on federal civil rights charges of assault with a deadly weapon and brutality. A commission investigating the riots concluded that the Los Angeles Police Department, then under police chief Daryl Gates, was inadequately prepared for violence. Rampant poverty, unemployment, and social decay were also blamed for igniting the uprising.

Los Angeles Riots. After the height of the violence in May 1992, a National Guardsman stands in front of a wall bearing the message "For Rodney King." © CORBIS

BIBLIOGRAPHY

Abelmann, Nancy. *Blue Dreams: Korean Americans and the Los Angeles Riots.* Cambridge, Mass.: Harvard University Press, 1995.

Gooding-Williams, Robert, ed. *Reading Rodney King, Reading Urban Uprising.* New York: Routledge, 1993.

Hunt, Darnell M. *Screening the Los Angeles "Riots": Race, Seeing, and Resistance.* New York: Cambridge University Press, 1997.

*Kathleen B. Culver/*A. R.

See also **Riots; Riots, Urban.**

LOST BATTALION,

a misnomer applied to part of the U.S. Seventy-seventh Division that was surrounded by German troops in Charlevaux Ravine during the Meuse-Argonne offensive in World War I. Under the command of Major Charles W. Whittlesey, the force comprised six companies from the 308th Infantry, one from the 307th Infantry, and two platoons from the 306th Machine Gun Battalion. Adjoining French and American attacks launched on 2 October failed, whereas Whittlesey penetrated to his objective and was promptly encircled. For five days, from the morning of 3 October until the evening of 7 October, he maintained a heroic defense against great odds until American relief troops broke through.

BIBLIOGRAPHY

Krohn, Charles A. *The Lost Battalion: Controversy and Casualties in the Battle of Hugh.* Westport, Conn.: Praeger, 1993.

*Robert S. Thomas/*C. W.

See also **American Expeditionary Forces; Meuse-Argonne Offensive.**

"LOST CAUSE"

refers to the shared public memory constructed by late–nineteenth-century white southerners of a romantic pre-Civil War South and a noble Confederate crusade. The central institutions of the "Lost Cause" were postwar Confederate organizations that conducted ceremonial rituals, sponsored writings and oratory, and erected Confederate monuments that shaped southern perceptions of war and defeat. The name for this tradition came from the title of Edward A. Pollard's 1866 book *The Lost Cause.*

BIBLIOGRAPHY

Foster, Gaines M. *Ghosts of the Confederacy: Defeat, the Lost Cause, and the Emergence of the New South.* New York: Oxford University Press, 1987.

Gallagher, Gary W., and Alan T. Nolan, eds. *The Myth of the Lost Cause and Civil War History.* Bloomington: Indiana University Press, 2000.

Horwitz, Tony. *Confederates in the Attic: Dispatches from the Unfinished Civil War.* New York: Pantheon, 1998.

Cynthia R. Poe

See also Civil War; Richmond; Sectionalism.

LOST GENERATION

LOST GENERATION refers to a group of early-twentieth-century American writers, notably Hart Crane, e. e. cummings, John Dos Passos, William Faulkner, F. Scott Fitzgerald, Ernest Hemingway, Thornton Wilder, and Thomas Wolfe. The writings of these authors were shaped by World War I and self-imposed exile from the American mainstream. Malcolm Cowley, a chronicler of the era, suggested that they shared a distaste for the grandiose patriotic war manifestos, although they differed widely in their means of expressing that distaste. The influence of T. S. Eliot, James Joyce, and Gertrude Stein, as well as encouragement of editors and publishers of magazines such as *Dial*, *Little Review*, *transition*, and *Broom*, were significant in the development of their writings.

BIBLIOGRAPHY

Cowley, Malcolm. *A Second Flowering: Works and Days of the Lost Generation.* New York: Viking Press, 1974.

Dolan, Marc. *Modern Lives: A Cultural Re-reading of the "Lost Generation."* West Lafayette, Ind.: Purdue University Press, 1996.

Sarah Ferrell/D. B.

See also Generational Conflict; Literature: Popular Literature.

LOTTERIES

LOTTERIES. State-sanctioned lotteries have a long history as a way of raising "painless" revenue for "good" causes. Most European countries (France, Holland, England) utilized lotteries to finance capital improvements, such as roads, harbors, and bridges. For the original European immigrants to the United States, lotteries were an established method of raising the funds to build the infrastructure a developing country needed. Hence lotteries often are seen by American legislators as the harmless form of gambling that can be harnessed for the common good. The United States has experienced three waves of lottery activity.

The First Wave: State-Sanctioned Lotteries (1607–1840s)

The first wave of gaming activity in North America began with the landing of the first European settlers but became much more widespread with the outbreak of the Revolutionary War. A few of these lotteries were sponsored by colonies to help finance their armies, but most lotteries were operated by nonprofit institutions, such as colleges, local school systems, and hospitals, to finance building projects or needed capital improvements. For example, both Yale and Harvard used lotteries to build dormitories. In 1747 the Connecticut legislature gave Yale a license to raise £7,500, while Harvard waited until 1765 for approval from the Massachusetts legislature to conduct a lottery worth £3,200. The primary reason for the failure of Harvard's lottery was that it had to compete with lotteries to support British troops fighting the French and Indian War. It should also be noted that, during this wave of lottery activity, no colony ever operated its own lottery. Private operators conducted lotteries. An organization or a worthy project, such as the Erie Canal, received permission from state legislatures to operate a lottery to support its "worthy" cause.

But these private operators often were less than honest in conducting lotteries. One famous lottery scandal occurred in Washington, D.C. In 1823 Congress authorized a Grand National Lottery to pay for improvements to the city. Tickets were sold, and the drawing took place. But before anyone could collect winnings, the private agent that organized the lottery for the District fled town. While the majority of winners accepted their fates with resignation, the winner of the $100,000 grand prize sued the government of the District of Columbia, and the Supreme Court ruled that the District had to pay the winner. It was a sober reminder to local officials that authorizing lotteries could be potentially dangerous, and the movement to ban lotteries began. From 1840 to 1860 all but two states prohibited lottery activity due to various scandals that occurred in the 1820s and 1830s. However, less than forty years later lotteries once again exploded onto the national scene.

The Second Wave: National Lotteries (1860s–1890s)

With the conclusion of the Civil War, the South had to find some method to finance the construction of roads, bridges, school buildings, and various other social capital projects to recover from war damage. One way was to permit private operators to conduct lotteries to raise revenue for reconstruction. The primary difference between this period of lottery activity and the previous period was the scale of ticket sales. Whereas in the previous lottery boom, sales of tickets were confined to local regions, these southern lotteries took on a national scope and, ironically, were particularly popular in the North. The most famous southern lottery, known as the Serpent, was conducted in Louisiana. In the late 1880s almost 50 percent of all mail coming into New Orleans was connected with this lottery.

As was the case with the first wave of lottery activity, controversy surrounding lotteries eventually led to a federal government ban. In 1890 the charter that authorized the running of the lottery in Louisiana was about to expire. The operators bribed various state officials with offers of up to $100,000 to renew the Serpent's charter, and this was reported throughout the country. Various state legislatures passed resolutions calling on Congress and President Benjamin Harrison to stop this lottery. In late 1890 Congress passed the primary piece of legislation that crippled the Louisiana lottery by denying the operators the use of the federal mail. If customers could no longer mail in their requests for tickets, then the lottery's life would be short-lived. By 1895 the Louisiana lottery had vanished, and as the twentieth century dawned, gaming activity in the United States had ceased. But like a phoenix lotteries were resurrected as governments searched for additional sources in the late twentieth century.

The Third Wave: State Operated Lotteries (1964–)
In 1964 New Hampshire voters approved a lottery. The rationale used by proponents to justify its legalization was strictly economic. Proceeds from the lottery were to fund education, thereby averting the enactment of either a sales or an income tax for New Hampshire. The lottery was an instant success, with 90 percent of the lottery tickets purchased by out-of-state residents. But this lesson was not lost on neighboring northeastern states, and in the next ten years every northeastern state approved a lottery.

However, the greatest growth of state lotteries occurred in the period between 1980 and 1990. By 2001 only three states (Utah, Hawaii, and Tennessee) did not have some form of legalized gaming. Lotteries and associated forms of "gaming" had gained a social acceptance that had not occurred in previous waves of lottery activity.

This third wave of lottery activity was quite different from those that preceded it. First, the breadth or the widespread use of gambling as a source of revenue for state governments was greater. Thirty-eight states plus the District of Columbia sponsored a lottery by the twenty-first century.

Second, the depth of gambling taking place was unprecedented. No longer was lottery play confined to a monthly or even a weekly drawing. Most states offered three types of lottery games. First was a daily number game that involved selecting a three- or four-digit number for a fixed-amount prize. The second type of game fits the general rubric of "lotto." These games involved picking six numbers of a possible forty or forty-eight numbers. The game was usually played twice a week, and jackpots can build up quite enormously, sometimes up to $90 million. The final lottery innovation was the "instant" or scratch tickets, in which the players know immediately if they have won. The odds and the sizes of the prizes for these games varied greatly.

The third difference in the third wave of gambling activity involved both the state-authorization and the state-ownership of the lottery operations. Previously the actual operation of the lottery itself was given to private brokers. In the third wave the state itself became the operator and sole beneficiary of lotteries. While some states, such as Georgia, Nebraska, West Virginia, Maine, and Texas, have permitted private concerns, such as Scientific Games and G-Tech, to operate the instant game portion of their lotteries, the vast majority of lottery operations were conducted by the state at the beginning of the twenty-first century.

The final difference deals with the "good" causes lottery proceeds are used to support. In the two previous waves, the good causes were onetime events, and lottery proceeds supported building canals, waterworks, bridges, and highways. Once the good cause was complete, the lottery ceased. While the state needed the lottery to finance these projects, it did not depend on lottery proceeds to fund daily services, By the twenty-first century many states, such as California, Illinois, Florida, and New Jersey, used lottery proceeds to fund education. In other states lottery proceeds have funded Medicare (Pennsylvania), police and fire departments in local communities (Massachusetts), and a host of other day-to-day operations of government.

State lotteries are no longer one-shot affairs. They must provide the sponsoring state with a consistent source of revenue to fund various good causes in order to justify their approval.

BIBLIOGRAPHY
Fleming, Alice. *Something for Nothing.* New York: Delacorte Press, 1978.

Richard McGowan

See also **Gambling.**

LOUISBURG EXPEDITION. Louisburg, a French fortress and naval station on Cape Breton Island, threatened British dominance in the North Atlantic. New Englanders especially resented attacks by pirates and privateers on their commerce and fishing. Knowing that France had neglected the settlement, Massachusetts governor William Shirley organized regional support for an attack on the fortress in the spring of 1745. Colonists, joined by British naval ships, captured the settlement on 15 June 1745. The colonists held Louisburg despite ill-fated attempts at recapture and were embittered when, by the Treaty of Aix-la-Chapelle of 1748, England sacrificed Louisburg for Madras, although England's financial reimbursement to Massachusetts energized its flagging economy.

BIBLIOGRAPHY
Anderson, Fred. *A People's Army: Massachusetts Soldiers and Society in the Seven Years' War.* Chapel Hill: University of North Carolina Press, 1984.

Leckie, Robert. *A Few Acres of Snow: The Saga of the French and Indian Wars.* New York: Wiley, 1999.

Sosin, Jack M. "Louisburg and the Peace of Aix-la-Chappelle, 1748." *William and Mary Quarterly* 14 (1957): 516–535.

Raymond P. Stearns/T. D.

See also **Aix-la-Chapelle, Treaty of; French and Indian War; King George's War.**

LOUISIANA

LOUISIANA, a southeastern state bordered on the west by the Sabine River, Texas, and Oklahoma; on the north by Arkansas; to the east by the Mississippi and Pearl Rivers and the state of Mississippi; and to the south by the Gulf of Mexico. Louisiana's French and Spanish history endowed the state with a rich and unique cultural heritage, while its geographic location at the mouth of the Mississippi River profoundly affected its historical development.

The Colonial Period

Humans reached present-day Louisiana some ten thousand years ago, at the end of the last ice age. By approximately 1,000 B.C., the area's Paleo-Indian peoples had constructed systems of large, earthen mounds that still exist at Poverty Point and elsewhere in the state. At the time of European contact, Louisiana's Indian population included the Caddos, Attakapas, Muskegons, Natchez, Chitimachas, and Tunicas. During the eighteenth century, other Indian groups from the British colonies to the east, such as the Choctaws, relocated in Louisiana.

During the sixteenth century, Spanish conquistadores, including Hernando De Soto, explored present-day Louisiana but did not settle it. European colonization of Louisiana began as an extension of French Canada, established as a fur-trading center in the early seventeenth century. As the century progressed, French control extended throughout the Great Lakes region. In 1672, Father Jacques Marquette explored the Mississippi River as far south as Arkansas, heightening interest in a Gulf Coast colony. By the early 1680s, the French nobleman René-Robert Cavelier, Sieur de La Salle, attempted to realize the French vision of a colony at the mouth of the Mississippi River anchoring a central North American empire. Retracing Marquette's route in spring 1682, La Salle arrived at the river's mouth in early April. He claimed the entire Mississippi basin for France and named the area Louisiana

for King Louis XIV. In 1684, La Salle attempted to establish a permanent colony, but his ill-fated expedition failed to locate the Mississippi River from the open sea and landed in present-day Texas. The settlement foundered, and in 1687 La Salle's own men murdered him.

Not until the late 1690s did France again attempt to establish a colony in Louisiana. This time the leader was the Canadian nobleman and French military officer Pierre Le Moyne, Sieur d'Iberville. Joined by his brother Jean Baptiste Le Moyne, Sieur de Bienville, and succeeding where La Salle had failed, Iberville located the Mississippi River from the open sea in spring 1699 and established a series of coastal settlements during the next several years. Whereas Iberville did not spend much time in Louisiana, succumbing to yellow fever in 1706, Bienville participated in colonial affairs for the next forty years, serving as military governor several times and founding New Orleans in 1718.

Initially a royal colony, Louisiana soon burdened the treasury and in 1712 became a proprietary colony under Antoine Crozat, who failed to make the colony profitable and in 1717 relinquished his charter. The crown then selected the Scotsman John Law as the new proprietor. An innovative financier, Law devised a plan in which the Royal Bank of France would underwrite Louisiana through Law's Company of the Indies. This MISSISSIPPI BUBBLE burst in the early 1720s, and Law fled France. A reorganized Company of the Indies led Louisiana to modest growth, but prosperity eluded the colony. The company surrendered its charter in 1731, and Louisiana remained a royal colony until French rule ended.

Louisiana's relatively late founding, semitropical climate, and undeserved reputation as a refuge for undesirables inhibited population growth. The oldest permanent European settlement in present-day Louisiana, Natchitoches, was founded in 1714. During the 1720s, several hundred German and Swiss immigrants settled along what is still called the Mississippi River's "German Coast." Baton Rouge was also founded in the 1720s but languished until the 1760s. Despite slow demographic growth, a distinct group of Creoles—native-born descendants of European settlers—eventually emerged, but by the 1760s, only about 5,000 whites inhabited Louisiana.

Problems of government compounded those of population. Louisiana chronically suffered from neglect by France and from lack of regular communication. Unclear lines of authority led to frequent quarrels among officials. Most importantly, as the product of an absolute monarchy, Louisiana failed to develop representative institutions, such as a colonial legislature, that could limit either the prerogatives or the abuses of royal appointed officials. Consequently, corruption and centralized power have historically characterized Louisiana government.

The 1763 Peace of Paris ended the French and Indian War and compelled France to relinquish its North American empire. France surrendered Louisiana east of the Mississippi River to England, and land west of the river to Spain, a French ally. Word of Spanish rule prompted discontent in New Orleans, a situation worsened by delay and confusion over the formal transfer of power. Resentment increased until 1768, when New Orleans revolted against Spanish rule. Authorities suppressed the insurrection the next year and executed several leaders.

Despite this difficult transition, Spanish Louisiana enjoyed stability and progress. Effective governors provided strong leadership, and generous land grants encouraged immigration. The free white population increased to more than 20,000 by 1800 and displayed much ethnic diversity, as Spaniards, Canary Islanders, Britons, Americans, Acadian exiles (today's Cajuns), and refugees from the French Revolution of the 1790s settled in Louisiana. The Spanish colony also enjoyed economic growth. The main crops during French rule had been tobacco and indigo, which brought little profit. During the 1790s, invention of the cotton gin and production of sugar in Louisiana precipitated an economic revolution.

Slave labor drove the new economic prosperity. Under French rule the colony's slave population had been small, about 4,000 by the early 1760s, and ethnically unified, as most slaves originated from West Africa's Senegambia region. Under Spanish rule the slave population increased to more than 16,000 and displayed ethnic complexity, as slaves were imported from various points throughout Africa. By the late eighteenth century, a distinct "Afro-Creole" culture combining African, Indian, and European influences had developed.

During the American Revolution, with Spain aiding the colonies, Governor Bernardo de Galvez led attacks against British East and West Florida that secured Spanish control of the lower Mississippi Valley and the Gulf of Mexico. After American independence, tensions grew between Spain and the United States over American access to the Mississippi River and the northern border of West Florida. These issues were resolved in 1795 with Pinckney's Treaty, in which Spain acquiesced to American demands.

Napoleon Bonaparte's 1799 ascension to power in France revived dreams of a French New World empire, and the following year Napoleon forced Spain to retrocede Louisiana. News of this development prompted President Thomas Jefferson to initiate negotiations for the purchase of New Orleans. Talks went slowly, but by April 1803, Napoleon decided to sell all of Louisiana to the United States, resulting in the Louisiana Purchase Treaty.

The Nineteenth Century

American acquisition of Louisiana provoked Creole resentment and confronted the United States with the challenge of incorporating territory and people from outside the British tradition. Jefferson appointed W. C. C. Claiborne territorial governor and granted him broad powers to handle this unprecedented situation. Americans and

their slaves swarmed into Louisiana: between 1803 and 1820 the white population increased from 21,000 to 73,000, and the slave population from 13,000 to 34,000. This migration transformed the Creoles into a distinct minority and sparked Anglo-Creole conflict over language, legal traditions, religion, and cultural practices. Although the Creoles eventually became reconciled to American rule, tensions lingered for many years.

In 1804, Congress created the Territory of Orleans—the future state of Louisiana—and later authorized election of a territorial legislature, which divided the territory into parishes (counties) and created local government. In 1810, the overwhelmingly American residents of Spanish West Florida rebelled and petitioned for U.S. annexation. Congress granted the request, and the area west of the Pearl River became part of the Territory of Orleans. The next year, Congress authorized a constitutional convention, half the delegates to which were Creoles, indicating their accommodation to American rule and republican government. Louisiana's 1812 constitution was a conservative document, reflecting its framers' suspicion of direct democracy and their belief in private property as the basis for citizenship. Congress admitted Louisiana as the eighteenth state on 30 April 1812, and Claiborne was elected the first governor, demonstrating further Creole reconciliation. Louisiana's geographical boundaries were finalized with the 1819 Adams-Onís Treaty, which set the boundary between the United States and Spanish Mexico and defined Louisiana's western border.

Soon after Louisiana's statehood, the United States declared war on Britain. The War of 1812 culminated with General Andrew Jackson's victory in the Battle of New Orleans, which occurred before news of an armistice arrived from Europe. Jackson's triumph made him a national hero and guaranteed American westward expansion, but many New Orleanians resented Jackson for his declaring martial law and for his enlisting free black men to fight. Nonetheless, the Place des Armes was later renamed Jackson Square in his honor.

Before the Whig and Democratic parties emerged nationally during the late 1820s, state politics revolved around Louisiana's cultural, geographic, and economic divisions: Anglo-Creole, north-south, cotton-sugar, city-country. Organized parties partially redefined political alignments. Sugar planters, New Orleans professionals, and personal opponents of Jackson supported the Whigs, while cotton planters, the New Orleans working classes, and small farmers endorsed the Democrats. Louisiana's economic and demographic growth between 1820 and 1840 exacerbated political divisions and made the 1812 constitution obsolete. The white population grew from 73,000 to 158,000, while the slave population jumped from nearly 70,000 to more than 168,000. Much of northern Louisiana—previously sparsely populated—was settled, cotton and sugar production mushroomed, and New Orleans became a major commercial center. These changes, combined with the nationwide advance of Jacksonian Democracy, prompted Democratic calls for political reform, which the Whigs initially resisted but assented to by the early 1840s. The 1845 constitution heralded Jacksonian Democracy by inaugurating universal manhood suffrage, reining in the power of banks and corporations, and moving the capital from New Orleans to Baton Rouge, which was closer to the state's geographic center.

Before the Civil War, free African Americans further enhanced Louisiana's uniqueness. Resulting from Spanish manumission law, miscegenation, and the arrival of several thousand free-black refugees fleeing the Haitian slave revolt of the 1790s, Louisiana's free-black population was the Deep South's largest, peaking in 1840 at more than 25,000. Although relegated to second-class citizenship and largely impoverished, the free people of color nonetheless included a racially mixed elite, also called "Creoles," many of whom were French-speaking, wealthy, educated, and active in cultural and intellectual circles. After 1840, legal restrictions on manumission caused a decline in the number of free black people, who nonetheless would provide important leadership within the black community after the abolition of slavery.

The question of slavery consumed the nation during the 1850s, and, following Abraham Lincoln's election as president in 1860, Louisiana seceded on 26 January 1861, the sixth state to do so. By late April 1862, federal forces had captured New Orleans, and the city became a Unionist and Republican stronghold during the Civil War and Reconstruction. The Union triumph also prompted thousands of slaves to flee from nearby plantations and to seek protection from occupying federal forces, thereby helping to redefine the Civil War as a war against slavery. Under Lincoln's wartime Reconstruction plan, a Unionist state government was formed in early 1864 that formally abolished slavery. However, Confederate troops defeated a Union attempt to capture the Confederate state capital at Shreveport in 1864, and Louisiana remained politically and militarily divided until the war ended.

The Confederacy's defeat brought Reconstruction to the South. Even by the standards of the time, Louisiana was rife with violence. The New Orleans riot of 30 July 1866, in which white mobs killed black and white Republicans, helped scuttle President Andrew Johnson's restoration plan. The 1868 constitution instituted black suffrage and brought the Republican Party to power. Republicans attempted to fashion a biracial coalition that would implement economic and political reforms and achieve racial equality, but they could not overcome corruption, factionalism, and violent white opposition. The 1873 Colfax massacre, in which more than one hundred black men were slain, was the bloodiest event in the Reconstruction South and resulted in a U.S. Supreme Court ruling that undermined federal enforcement of black civil rights. By 1876, Louisiana Republicans were in retreat, and the state's electoral votes were contested in that year's presidential election, a dispute decided by the Compromise of 1877 that ended Reconstruction and returned Louisiana Democrats to power.

Reconstruction's demise inaugurated the state's Bourbon period, characterized by the rule of a wealthy, reactionary oligarchy that retained power until the 1920s and relegated Louisiana to economic underdevelopment. White supremacy, fiscal conservatism, electoral fraud, and contempt for the public good were the hallmarks of Bourbon rule, as even the modest gains of Reconstruction, such as creation of a state education system, were undone. Nothing reflected the Bourbon mindset better than the notorious Louisiana lottery, the corrupting influence of which attracted national opprobrium, and the convict-lease system, which sometimes subjected the overwhelmingly black inmates to annual mortality rates of twenty percent. The Bourbons' crowning achievements were the segregationist laws enacted during the 1890s, the blatant electoral fraud that prevented a Populist-Republican coalition from taking power in 1896, and the property and literacy requirements and poll tax provision of the 1898 constitution that deprived almost all blacks, and thousands of poor whites, of the right to vote, thus completely overturning Reconstruction. The U.S. Supreme Court's 1896 *Plessy v. Ferguson* decision, which sanctioned legal segregation, originated as a challenge to Louisiana's 1890 law requiring racially segregated accommodations on railroad cars in the state.

The Twentieth Century

The history of Louisiana was profoundly altered with the 1901 discovery of oil in the state. For the rest of the century, Louisiana's economic fortunes were pinned to those of the oil industry. The Progressive movement of the early twentieth century brought little change to Louisiana, dominated as it was by the Bourbon elite, except for implementation of the severance tax—a tax on natural resources that are "severed" from the earth—and creation of the white party primary system.

Louisiana experienced a political revolution with the 1928 election of Huey P. Long as governor. Long employed populistic rhetoric in appealing to the common people and in promising to unseat the entrenched elites. As governor and, after 1932, as United States senator, Long oversaw a vast expansion in public works and social services, building roads, bridges, schools, and hospitals, and providing free medical care and textbooks, all funded by increases in the severance tax and the state's bonded debt. In 1934, Long created the Share-the-Wealth movement, with its motto "Every Man a King," in which he promised to tax the wealthy in order to provide economic security for all American families. Intended as an alternative to President Franklin D. Roosevelt's New Deal, Share-the-Wealth won over millions of impoverished Americans and raised the possibility of Long challenging Roosevelt's 1936 reelection. However, Long's undemocratic methods, which included using the state's coercive power to stifle political dissent, combined with his presidential aspirations, provoked opposition and heightened fears of his becoming an American dictator. Long was assassinated in September 1935, allegedly by a political opponent, although controversy has continued to surround this event. Long left an ambiguous legacy: he improved daily life for common people, but his dictatorial tactics, corrupt practices, and centralization of power were in keeping with Louisiana traditions, and, despite Long's successes, Louisiana remained amongst the nation's poorest states.

For the next twenty-five years, contests between Longite and anti-Longite—or reform—factions of the Democratic Party characterized Louisiana politics. In 1939, a series of exposés revealing widespread corruption sent many leading Longites to prison and brought the reformers to power. Between 1940 and 1948, the reformers continued the popular public works and social services of Longism while also implementing changes, including civil service, designed to end Longism's abuses. Military spending during World War II and, later, the expansion of the petrochemical industry along the Mississippi River financed much of the reform program. In 1940, war games known as the Louisiana Maneuvers greatly improved U.S. military preparedness, and during the war, the New Orleans businessman Andrew Jackson Higgins designed and built military transport boats that proved essential to the Allied war effort.

From 1948 to 1960, Earl K. Long, Huey's younger brother and himself a formidable historical figure, dominated Louisiana politics. Long, who finished the unexpired gubernatorial term of Richard Leche, 1939–1940, quickly became a political power in his own right. During two nonconsecutive gubernatorial terms (1948–1952, 1956–1960), Earl Long continued the public works and social services aspects of Longism; he also engaged in some of Longism's abuses but nothing near those of his brother.

Earl Long was also progressive on the question of race. As the civil rights movement gained momentum after World War II, and as the U.S. Supreme Court's 1954 *Brown v. Board of Education* decision invalidated segregated schools, Earl Long strongly supported black civil rights by permitting black voter registration, ensuring that black people benefited from his economic programs, and trying to persuade white Louisianians to abandon segregation. Despite these efforts, white support for legal segregation remained strong, and the desegregation of public schools and of Louisiana as a whole proceeded slowly. Legal segregation had been dismantled in Louisiana by the early 1970s, but as the twentieth century ended, desegregation in certain local school systems, including Baton Rouge, remained under federal court supervision.

During the last third of the twentieth century, Louisiana experienced some of the same trends that affected the rest of the South, including the reemergence of the Republican Party, suburbanization, and cultural homogenization, but the state also continued to be plagued by many of its traditional difficulties, including political corruption and economic underdevelopment. Louisiana's fortunes during these years were greatly reflected in those of Edwin W. Edwards, who served an unprecedented four full gubernatorial terms (1972–1980, 1984–1988, 1992–1996). The charismatic Edwards followed in the populistic, big-government traditions of Longism while involving himself in many legally questionable activities. Edwards's first two terms witnessed major increases in state spending, financed by oil revenues, but the 1980s oil bust had devastating consequences for Louisiana's economy and for Edwards's third term. Edwards won a fourth term in 1992, but only because his opponent was David Duke, a former member of the Ku Klux Klan and the American Nazi Party whose meteoric political rise was propelled by economic distress and white resentment. After the 1980s, the state government slowly weaned itself off oil as its primary source of revenue, a process helped by the adoption of a state lottery and legalized gambling during the early 1990s and by the national economic growth of the following years. Nonetheless, the state's regressive tax system—sales taxes became the main sources of revenue while the popular homestead exemption enables most homeowners to pay little or no property taxes—resulted in chronic funding problems. Louisiana's 2000 population of 4,468,976 marked only a 5.9 percent increase from 1990, less than half the national increase of 13.1 percent, and the early twenty-first century witnessed a continuing "brain drain," as many of the state's younger, educated residents pursued better economic opportunities elsewhere.

BIBLIOGRAPHY

Hair, William Ivy. *Bourbonism and Agrarian Protest: Louisiana Politics, 1877–1900*. Baton Rouge: Louisiana State University Press, 1969.

Hall, Gwendolyn Midlo. *Africans in Colonial Louisiana: The Development of Afro-Creole Culture in the Eighteenth Century*. Baton Rouge: Louisiana State University Press, 1992.

Kurtz, Michael L., and Morgan D. Peoples. *Earl K. Long: The Saga of Uncle Earl and Louisiana Politics*. Baton Rouge: Louisiana State University Press, 1990.

Sanson, Jerry Purvis. *Louisiana during World War II: Politics and Society: 1939–1945*. Baton Rouge: Louisiana State University Press, 1999.

Sitterson, J. Carlyle. *Sugar Country: The Cane Sugar Industry in the South, 1753–1950*. Lexington: University of Kentucky Press. 1953.

Taylor, Joe Gray. *Negro Slavery in Louisiana*. Baton Rouge: Louisiana Historical Association, 1963.

———. *Louisiana Reconstructed, 1863–1877*. Baton Rouge: Louisiana State University Press, 1974.

———. *Louisiana: A Bicentennial History*. New York: Norton, 1976.

Tregle, Joseph G. *Louisiana in the Age of Jackson: A Clash of Cultures and Personalities*. Baton Rouge: Louisiana State University Press, 1999.

Wall, Bennett H., ed. *Louisiana: A History*. 4th ed. Wheeling, Ill.: Harlan Davidson, 2002.

Williams, T. Harry. *Huey Long.* New York: Knopf, 1969.

Winters, John D. *The Civil War in Louisiana.* Baton Rouge: Louisiana State University Press, 1963.

John Rodrigue

See also **Bourbons; New Orleans; Orleans, Territory of; Share-the-Wealth Movements;** *and vol. 9:* **Police Regulations of Saint Landry Parish, Louisiana.**

LOUISIANA PURCHASE.

A watershed event in American history, the purchase of the Louisiana Territory from France in 1803 nearly doubled the land mass of the young nation: for a purchase price of $15 million, the United States increased its size by some 828,000 square miles. The region included the Mississippi River and its tributaries westward to the Rocky Mountains, and extended from the Gulf of Mexico at New Orleans up the Red River to the Canadian border.

Natural and Political History of the Territory before the Purchase

The central portion of North America was considered prime land for settlement in the early days of the republic. The Missouri and Red Rivers drained the region east of the Rocky Mountains into the massive Mississippi Valley, offering navigation and fertile farmlands, prairies, pastures and forests. The region also held large deposits of various minerals, which would come to be economic boons as well. Buffalo and other wild game were plentiful and offered an abundant food supply for the Native Americans who peopled the region as well as for later settlers.

From the mid-fifteenth century, France had claimed the Louisiana Territory. Its people constituted a strong French presence in the middle of North America. Always adamant in its desire for land, France engaged the British in the Seven Years' War (1754–1763; also known as the FRENCH AND INDIAN WAR because of the alliance of these two groups against British troops) over property disputes in the Ohio Valley. As part of the settlement of the Seven Years' War, the 1763 Treaty of Paris called for France to turn over control of the Louisiana Territory (including New Orleans) to Spain as compensation for Spanish assistance to the French during the war.

By the early 1800s, Spain offered Americans free access to shipping on the Mississippi River and encouraged Americans to settle in the Louisiana Territory. President Thomas Jefferson officially frowned on this invitation, but privately hoped that many of his frontier-seeking citizens would indeed people the area owned by Spain. Like many Americans, Jefferson warily eyed the vast Louisiana Territory as a politically unstable place; he hoped that by increasing the American presence there, any potential war concerning the territory might be averted.

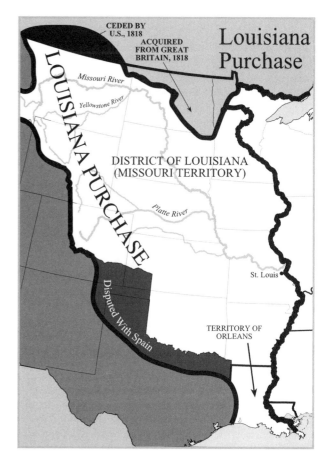

The Purchase

In 1802 it seemed that Jefferson's fears were well founded: the Spanish governor of New Orleans revoked Americans' privileges of shipping produce and other goods for export through his city. At the same time, American officials became aware of a secret treaty that had been negotiated and signed the previous year between Spain and France. This, the Treaty of San Ildefonso, provided a position of nobility for a minor Spanish royal in exchange for the return of the Louisiana Territory to the French.

Based on France's history of engaging in hostilities for land, Jefferson and other leaders were alarmed at this potential threat on the U.S. western border. While some Congressmen had begun to talk of taking New Orleans, Spain's control over the territory as a whole generally had been weak. Accordingly, in April 1802 Jefferson and other leaders instructed Robert R. Livingston, the U.S. minister to France, to attempt to purchase New Orleans for $2 million, a sum Congress quickly appropriated for the purpose.

In his initial approach to officials in Paris, Livingston was told that the French did not own New Orleans and thus could not sell it to the United States. However, Livingston quickly assured the negotiators that he had seen the Treaty of San Ildefonso and hinted that the United States might instead simply seize control of the city. With

Louisiana Purchase Exposition. A panoramic view of the 1904 world's fair in Saint Louis, photographed from the top of Festival Hall. LIBRARY OF CONGRESS

the two sides at an impasse, President Jefferson quickly sent Secretary of State James Monroe to Paris to join the negotiations.

Napoleon Bonaparte (1769–1821), who had come to power in France in 1799, planned in 1801 to use the fertile Mississippi Valley as a source of food and trade to supply a French empire in the New World. However, in 1801 Toussaint L'Ouverture led a slave revolt that eventually took control of Haiti and Hispaniola, the latter of which Napoleon had chosen as the seat of his Western empire. French armies under the leadership of Charles LeClerc attempted to regain control of Haiti in 1802; however, despite some successes, thousands of soldiers were lost in battle and to yellow fever. Realizing the futility of his plan, Napoleon abandoned his dreams for Hispaniola. As a result, he no longer had a need for the Louisiana Territory, and knew that his forces were insufficient to protect it from invasion. Furthermore, turning his attentions to European conquests, he recognized that his plans there would require an infusion of ready cash. Accordingly, Napoleon authorized his ministers to make a counteroffer to the Americans: instead of simply transferring the ownership of New Orleans, France would be willing to part with the entire Louisiana Territory.

Livingston and Monroe were stunned at his proposal. Congress quickly approved the purchase and authorized a bond issue to raise the necessary $15 million to complete the transaction. Documents effecting the transfer were signed on 30 April 1803, and the United States formally took possession of the region in ceremonies at St. Louis, Missouri on 20 December.

Consequences of the Louisiana Purchase

The Louisiana Purchase has often been described as one of the greatest real estate deals in history. Despite this, there were some issues that concerned Americans of the day. First, many wondered how or if the United States could defend this massive addition to its land holdings. Many New Englanders worried about the effect the new addition might have on the balance of power in the nation. Further, Jefferson and Monroe struggled with the theoretical implications of the manner in which they carried out the purchase, particularly in light of Jefferson's previous heated battles with Alexander Hamilton concerning the interpretation of limits of constitutional and presidential powers. In the end, however, the desire to

purchase the territory outweighed all of these practical and theoretical objections.

The increases in population, commerce, mining, and agriculture the Louisiana Purchase allowed worked to strengthen the nation as a whole. The opportunity for individuals and families to strike out into unsettled territory and create lives for themselves helped to foster the frontier spirit of independence, curiosity, and cooperation that have come to be associated with the American character.

BIBLIOGRAPHY

Ellis, Joseph J. *American Sphinx: The Character of Thomas Jefferson.* New York: Knopf, 1997.

Kastor, Peter J., ed. *The Louisiana Purchase: Emergence of an American Nation.* Washington, D.C: Congressional Quarterly Books, 2002.

Kennedy, Roger. *Mr. Jefferson's Lost Cause: Land, Farmers, Slavery, and the Louisiana Purchase.* New York: Oxford University Press, 2002.

Labbé, Dolores Egger, ed. *The Louisiana Purchase and Its Aftermath, 1800–1830.* Lafayette: Center for Louisiana Studies, University of Southwestern Louisiana, 1998.

Barbara Schwarz Wachal

See also **Manifest Destiny; Mississippi River; Westward Migration.**

LOUISIANA PURCHASE EXPOSITION was organized to commemorate the centenary of the Louisiana Purchase of 1803. Civic leaders in Saint Louis, led by the former mayor and Missouri governor David R. Francis, planned a world's fair. They chose the city's largest park as the site and May to December 1904 as the time. (The ceremony of the transfer of Upper Louisiana Territory had taken place in Saint Louis in 1804.) All major nations except war-torn Russia took part, as did all U.S. states and territories, including the newly annexed Philippine Islands. Native Americans including the Sioux, Apaches, and Osages participated.

While earlier fairs had stressed products, the fair in Saint Louis stressed methods of production. The participants compared techniques and exchanged experiences. Automobiles and trains shared attention. Fourteen palaces designed for such fields as education, agriculture, transportation, mining, and forestry provided 5 million square feet of exhibit space. Sunday closings typified the Victorian tone that dominated entertainment.

Scholars and scientists sponsored conferences in conjunction with the fair, and the International Olympic Committee chose Saint Louis for the first games held in America. Close to 20 million visitors attended, among them in late November the newly reelected president Theodore Roosevelt, who invited the Apache warrior Geronimo to ride in his inaugural parade.

BIBLIOGRAPHY

Faherty, William Barnaby, and NiNi Harris. *The St. Louis Portrait*. Tulsa, Okla.: Continental Heritage Press, 1978.

Fox, Timothy J., and Duane R. Sneddeker. *From the Palaces to the Pike: Visions of the 1904 World's Fair*. St. Louis: Missouri Historical Society Press, 1997.

William B. Faherty

See also **Louisiana Purchase; Saint Louis; World's Fairs.**

LOVE CANAL has become synonymous with environmental mismanagement and was why the federal government created the Environmental Protection Agency's Superfund in 1980 to pay for the cleanup of environmental disasters. In the 1890s William Love wanted to build a town near Niagara Falls in upstate New York. He designed a canal to connect two branches of the Niagara River and provide the town with electricity from the power of the rapids just before the falls. But economic difficulties forced Love to abandon the project. All that was left was the canal, which was acquired by Niagara Falls in 1927.

Around 1940 the city allowed the Hooker Chemical Company to use the canal as a dumping ground for chemical waste. For the next thirteen years Hooker buried more than twenty thousand tons of chemicals, including

Love Canal. A youngster looks at some of the hundreds of abandoned houses in this environmental disaster area near Niagara Falls, N.Y. GREENPEACE PHOTO

dioxin. In 1953 Niagara Falls announced it intended to build an elementary school on the canal site. After the school was built, parents reported burns on children who played in the area. By the mid-1970s Love Canal's residents were reporting cases of miscarriages, birth defects, liver abnormalities, and cancer. In 1978 the Love Canal Homeowners Association demanded action and relief. The federal government and the state of New York purchased over eight hundred houses and relocated one thousand families. Legal action also began, as the federal government, Hooker Chemical, and the city of Niagara Falls fought over liability issues. In 1995 Hooker agreed to pay the Superfund and the Federal Emergency Management Agency a total of $129 million for the environmental cleanup of the site.

BIBLIOGRAPHY

Ferrell, O. C., and John Fraedrich. *Business Ethics*. Boston: Houghton Mifflin, 1991.

John A. Morello

See also **Hazardous Waste; Superfund.**

LOVE MEDICINE, a novel by Louise Erdrich, was first published in 1984 and republished in an expanded version in 1993. Among the first works by a Native American woman to portray modern Indian life, *Love Medicine* depicts several generations of three families whose members search for an identity that fuses their Native and European American roots. Erdrich, whose ancestry includes both Ojibwa and German Americans, is a member of the Turtle Mountain community of the Chippewa Nation. She drew on memories of childhood visits to North Dakota reservations for the book. The novel interlaces the narratives of the families, who live on a fictionalized reservation, offering multiple authentic "Indian" points of view through sharply individual characters.

Academic critics have praised *Love Medicine* for its lyrical prose, complex nonlinear narrative, Native and European tropes, and themes including both opposing heritages and cultural hybridity. It won the National Book Critics Circle Award in 1984. Some Native American writers, however, have asserted that Erdrich's novels have become the dominant representation of Native life, rather than one facet of a diverse culture. Some Turtle Mountain readers have objected to Erdrich's stylistic flourishes and impoverished, despairing characters. Nonetheless, *Love Medicine* has been a groundbreaking text, generating wider appreciation for works representing Natives as contemporary Americans rather than romanticized noble savages.

BIBLIOGRAPHY

Stookey, Lorena L. *Louise Erdrich: A Critical Companion*. Westport, Conn.: Greenwood, 1999.

Wong, Hertha D. Sweet. *Louise Erdrich's* Love Medicine: *A Casebook*. New York: Oxford University Press, 2000.

Jane Weiss

See also **Literature: Native American Literature.**

LOVEJOY RIOTS. Elijah P. Lovejoy, an abolitionist clergyman, established *The Observer* in Saint Louis in 1833. Threatened with violence by proslavery men in 1834, he refused to back down, citing his rights to free speech and free press. He moved his press to free soil in Alton, Illinois, in 1836, where it was smashed on the dock by locals. When Lovejoy spoke out for immediate abolition and a state antislavery society (July 1837), a mob destroyed a second press in August, smashed a third on 21 September, and, in an effort to destroy yet another (7 November), killed Lovejoy, who was immediately canonized as a martyr to the cause.

BIBLIOGRAPHY

Dillon, Merton L. *Elijah P. Lovejoy, Abolitionist Editor.* Urbana: University Press of Illinois, 1961.

Smith, Kimberly K. *The Dominion of Voice: Riot, Reason, and Romance in Antebellum Politics.* Lawrence: University Press of Kansas, 1999.

Raymond P. Stearns/A. R.

See also **Antislavery; Newspapers.**

LOVING V. VIRGINIA, 388 U.S. 1 (1967). In *Loving v. Virginia* the Supreme Court of the United States held that laws prohibiting interracial marriage violate the equal protection clause and the due process clause of the Fourteenth Amendment. Richard Loving, a white man, and Mildred Jeter, an African American woman, were arrested when they returned to Virginia following their marriage in Washington, D.C. They were convicted for violating Virginia's antimiscegenation laws, which made the marriage "between a white person and a colored person a felony." Virginia's antimiscegenation laws, however, did not formally ban marriage between any other races. The trial courts and the Supreme Court of Virginia had upheld the Lovings' convictions.

Previously the U.S. Supreme Court had been hesitant to address the constitutionality of antimiscegenation laws. The Court had refused to review the constitutionality of a conviction under a state antimiscegenation law shortly after *Brown v. Board of Education of Topeka* (1954), the landmark school desegregation case. Surprisingly the *Loving* decision did not provoke the angry controversy that followed the *Brown* decision. The ban on interracial marriages was one of the last vestiges of legal racial discrimination. At the time this case was heard by the Supreme Court, fifteen states still had prohibitions against interracial marriage. The ruling in *Loving*, however, was not difficult to predict. In the 1964 case *McLaughlin v.*

Florida the Court had held unconstitutional bans on interracial cohabitation.

In previous cases the Court held that state-mandated racial discrimination, in order to pass constitutional muster, would have to meet a "strict" standard of review. The strict standard of review requires a state to demonstrate that its laws mandating racial discrimination are necessary to the accomplishment of a "permissible state objective." The Court, in a unanimous opinion written by Chief Justice Earl Warren, found that Virginia's antimiscegenation laws did not pass this strict test. The Court did not accept Virginia's argument that the antimiscegenation laws applied equally among races by punishing both the white and the black person attempting to marry and therefore did not discriminate based on race. The Court determined that marriage is a basic civil right in the United States, and the denial of this fundamental right on the basis of race violates the Fourteenth Amendment of the Constitution.

BIBLIOGRAPHY

Baer, Judith A. *Equality under the Constitution.* Ithaca, N.Y.: Cornell University Press, 1983.

Mezey, Susan Gluck. *In Pursuit of Equality.* New York: St. Martin's, 1992.

Moran, Rachel F. *Interracial Intimacy: The Regulation of Race and Romance.* Chicago: University of Chicago Press, 2001.

Sollors, Werner, ed. *Interracialism: Black-White Intermarriage in American History, Literature, and Law.* Oxford: Oxford University Press, 2000.

Spann, Girardeau A. *Race against the Court: Supreme Court and Minorities in Contemporary America.* New York: New York University Press, 1993.

Akiba J. Covitz
Esa Lianne Sferra
Meredith L. Stewart

See also **Brown v. Board of Education of Topeka; Miscegenation.**

LOWER EAST SIDE of Manhattan in New York City lies east of the Bowery and north of Fulton Street. Its northern boundary is less clear. Some commentators draw it at Fourteenth Street. Others set it further south on Houston Street. The latter is more accurate, but many sites associated with eastern European Jews in New York City—the Yiddish theater district; the Hebrew Technical School; Union Square; Cooper Union; and the Asch Building, home of the Triangle Shirtwaist factory—are north of Houston. The name "Lower East Side" was not used regularly before the end of the 1930s. In the 1960s it became fixed with capital letters. Previously it was "downtown, "the east side," "the ghetto," or "the Hebrew quarter."

The Lower East Side is associated primarily with the large wave of eastern European Jewish immigration to the United States starting in the 1880s. The descendants of

Orchard Street. A historical view of the Lower East Side; this street was usually lined with vendors' carts lining the curbs outside these tenements. ARCHIVE PHOTOS, INC.

those immigrants, few of whom lived there, consider it special and have memorialized it in fiction, film, pageantry, and tours. Before that, however, the area was home first to free black settlers in the seventeenth century. Their small holdings were consolidated into larger ones, the largest owned by James De Lancey, a loyalist who lost his land at the end of the American Revolution. The area then became a magnet for petty artisanal and shopkeeper families. By the 1830s, Irish immigrants settled there. In that decade the first tenement buildings went up to accommodate them.

German immigrants, including Jews, arrived next. The neighborhood, which became known as Kleindeutschland (Little Germany), was a center of Jewish religious and retail life. In 1843 a group of Jewish men who had been rejected for membership by the Masons met on Essex Street and founded a benevolent society, the forerunner of the B'nai B'rith. In the middle decades of the nineteenth century, central European Jews from Hungary, Bohemia, and Posen (a Polish province annexed by Prussia) moved to the Lower East Side. The first Russian Jewish congregation, Beth Hamedrash Hagadal, was established in 1852 on Bayard Street. In 1852, Reb Pesach Rosenthal opened the Downtown Talmud Torah, offering instruction in Yiddish.

The greatest influx of newcomers were Russian, Lithuanian, Polish, Romanian, Hungarian, and Galician Jews. Italians, Greeks, Chinese, and other non-Jews from eastern Europe also arrived in the 1880s. The immigrant Jews, including some from Turkey, Greece, and Syria, made up about half the neighborhood's residents. In 1892

about 75 percent of all New York City Jews lived in the Seventh, Tenth, and Thirteenth Wards, which constituted the Lower East Side. In 1910, the peak of Jewish residence, over 500,000 Jews lived there. Thereafter, new immigrant Jews settled elsewhere in New York City. By 1920 the neighborhood's Jewish population had dipped to 400,000, declining with each decade. Yet even as Jews moved to other neighborhoods, they returned to the Lower East Side for Yiddish plays and films. They also went there to purchase Jewish foods, including bread, pickles, and fish, as well as Jewish books and ritual objects.

Considered one of America's worst slums, the Lower East Side inspired Jacob Riis to write *How the Other Half Lives* (1890). Reformers initiated projects to help residents. Lower East Side housing conditions improved somewhat with municipal legislation in 1878 and 1901. Settlement houses, like the Education Alliance and the Henry Street Settlement, encouraged painting, theater, and dance. The Jewish immigrant community sponsored artistic, journalistic, literary, dramatic, and political endeavors.

Not all Jews left the neighborhood after the 1930s. The older, poorer, and more religiously observant remained. Other Jews stayed on in the Amalgamated Clothing Workers Union cooperatives. Some Jewish institutions like the Eldridge Street Synagogue and the Educational Alliance continued to function.

The 1950s brought change. Puerto Ricans moved in, as did immigrants from the Dominican Republic, Korea, the Philippines, India, and China. In the 1980s, young

166

people discovered the Lower East Side's low rents. With this, musicians, painters, clothing designers, and performance artists made the neighborhood a cultural and artistic zone.

BIBLIOGRAPHY

Diner, Hasia R. *Lower East Side Memories: A Jewish Place in America*. Princeton, N.J.: Princeton University Press, 2000.

Rischin, Moses. *The Promised City: New York's Jews, 1870–1914*. Cambridge, Mass.: Harvard University Press, 1962.

Hasia Diner

See also **Jews; New York City; Poverty; Triangle Fire; Urbanization.**

LOWER SOUTH, or the Deep South, is that part of the southern United States lying wholly within the cotton belt, including South Carolina, Georgia, and the Gulf states of Florida, Alabama, Mississippi, Louisiana, and Texas. Before the Civil War, the Border States and the Middle South states (Arkansas, North Carolina, Tennessee, and Virginia) had more diversified economies than did the Lower South states, which relied more heavily on cotton and sugar as their main cash crops and on slave labor. In the later antebellum period, these states (Florida excepted) secured political leadership in the South and led the drive for secession.

Freehling, William W. *The Road to Disunion: Secessionists at Bay, 1776–1854*. New York: Oxford University Press, 1990.

Morris, Christopher. *Becoming Southern: The Evolution of a Way of Life, Warren County and Vicksburg, Mississippi, 1770–1860*. New York: Oxford University Press, 1995.

Haywood J. Pearce Jr./c. p.

See also **Cotton Kingdom; Secession; Slavery; South, the: The Antebellum South.**

LOYALISTS were colonials who took the British side during the American Revolution. "Tories" often is used as a synonym but refers in the eighteenth-century context to believers in an unrestrained monarchy. Most Loyalists believed in Parliament's supremacy over the Crown and the colonies alike. Revolutionaries used "the disaffected" to describe not only active opponents but also people who tried to stay out of the conflict, including religious objectors like Quakers.

Estimates of the number of Loyalists have varied widely. John Adams supposedly said that one-third of colonials favored the Revolution, one-third opposed, and one-third stayed neutral, but that no longer commands credence. The historian Robert R. Palmer demonstrated that roughly sixty thousand people emigrated rather than accept the Revolution's triumph, a larger proportion of the actual population than emigrated from revolutionary France.

But many who opposed the Revolution did not leave, and some eventually rose to prominence in the young Republic. Moreover neither the supposed Adams estimate nor Palmer's figure takes into account the numerous enslaved blacks who chose the British side to win the British guarantee of freedom. Nor do the numbers include Indians who saw Britain as their only ally against land-hungry white colonials. For their own part British officials believed the vast majority of colonials would prove loyal if only the revolutionary leadership could be overthrown.

Without a general head count all arguments about absolute numbers are moot. A better approach is to understand that once independence was declared people might experience either conversion or persecution, in either direction, but no compromise or hope that the next election would change the state of affairs existed. The Revolution was not an era of normal politics. In principle the choice of king or Congress was absolute.

In practice Loyalists' strength depended not so much on numbers as on political and military situations. As the American movement moved from resistance to Revolution, Loyalists at the top of the old political and social structure could slow it down. These included native-born royal governors, such as Benjamin Franklin's son William Franklin in New Jersey or Thomas Hutchinson in Massachusetts; royal councilors and high judges in most provinces; Anglo-American politicians, like the Mohawk baronet Sir William Johnson and his son Sir John; and some political groups, such as the De Lancey party in New York. They also included individuals who had helped begin the movement, such as the lawyer Daniel Dulany of Maryland, the lawyer William Smith Jr. of New York, and the merchant Isaac Low of New York. But during the independence crisis they all were driven from the political arena. Their patriot compeers and the nucleus of a new elite displaced them.

At the popular level few white Loyalists lived in New England or Virginia. In New York, however, Staten Islanders and Long Islanders favored the king over Congress by an overwhelming majority. People in the Hudson and Mohawk Valleys divided, leading to disruption and outright civil war. Many Loyalists lived in New Jersey, and a significant number lived on Maryland's eastern shore. They resisted the Revolution, even to the point of guerrilla warfare, but they remained clandestine unless British soldiers were nearby. Until 1780 it seemed that the Lower South was secure for the Revolution. But when the British captured Charles Town, South Carolina's governor renewed his allegiance and many backcountry people rallied to the British forces. As in the Mohawk Valley, civil war ensued.

After initial efforts to convert the "disaffected," political police, such as New York's Commissioners for Detecting and Defeating Conspiracies, hauled suspects in, paying little regard to procedure. A few Loyalists were executed. Others were imprisoned in dismal places like Connecticut's Simsbury Mines. States confiscated Loyalists' property, and Loyalists were deprived of "the protection of the laws" and exiled with the penalty of death upon return. Victorious patriots could sue them despite the requirement in the Treaty of Paris of 1783 that the persecution end. Black Loyalists feared and often suffered reenslavement until British vessels finally bore them away. Indians who had chosen and fought on the British side were treated as conquered people whose land and liberties were forfeited unless they moved to Canada.

BIBLIOGRAPHY

Bailyn, Bernard. *The Ordeal of Thomas Hutchinson.* Cambridge, Mass.: Harvard University Press, 1974.

Calhoon, Robert M. *The Loyalists in Revolutionary America, 1760–1781.* New York: Harcourt Brace Jovanovich, 1973.

Frey, Sylvia R. *Water from the Rock: Black Resistance in a Revolutionary Age.* Princeton, N.J.: Princeton University Press, 1991.

Hodges, Graham Russell. *The Black Loyalist Directory.* New York: Garland, 1996.

Hoffman, Ronald, Thad W. Tate, and Peter J. Albert, eds. *An Uncivil War: The Southern Backcountry during the American Revolution.* Charlottesville: University Press of Virginia, 1985.

Kelsay, Isabel Thompson. *Joseph Brant, 1743–1807: Man of Two Worlds.* Syracuse, N.Y.: Syracuse University Press, 1984.

Norton, Mary Beth. *The British-Americans: The Loyalist Exiles in England, 1774–1789.* Boston: Little, Brown, 1972.

Edward Countryman

See also **Confiscation Acts; Indians in the Revolution; Revolution, American.**

LOYALTY OATHS administered by colonial, revolutionary, confederate, federal, state, and municipal governments have asked pledgers to swear allegiance to the governing bodies. The contents of such oaths have varied, reflecting the political climates of their times, and often have been required only of particular individuals or groups, such as public officials and employees, persons feared to be subversives, residents of Confederate states, and educators. The best-known loyalty oath is the "Pledge of Allegiance," recited by schoolchildren and at many public events. Francis Bellamy wrote the original version of the Pledge of Allegiance in 1892. His version read, "I pledge allegiance to my Flag and the Republic for which it stands, one nation, indivisible, with liberty and justice for all." Congress's addition of the words "under God" in 1954 came under attack by those objecting that it violated the separation of government and religion.

During World War II (1939–1945), the War Relocation Authority administered loyalty questionnaires to interned Japanese Americans, citizens as well as noncitizens. One of the questions asked respondents whether they would swear loyalty to the United States and renounce allegiance to the Japanese emperor or any other foreign power. Those who responded "no," or who qualified their answers—out of suspicion that the question was intended to trick them into admitting allegiance to Japan, or as an expression of bitterness about their confinement—were classified as "disloyal" and subsequently segregated from the 65,000 internees who had responded in the affirmative.

The red scares following World War I (1914–1918) and World War II fueled fears of plots against the U.S. government. Anticommunist panic surged after World War II as the Cold War developed. In 1947, President Harry Truman's Executive Order 9835 created a loyalty-security program that subjected federal employees and job applicants to loyalty and security checks and allowed the firing of employees found to be members of, or sympathetic to, the Communist Party or other groups characterized as subversive. In the 1930s and 1940s, some states, including New York and California, enacted legislation requiring educators to swear allegiance to the state and the nation, and to uphold their constitutions. In the late 1950s, two out of three states compelled loyalty oaths, with some schools and universities augmenting the loyalty requirement, essentially for the purpose of purging communists. For example, in 1949 the Regents of the University of California required all faculty and staff to swear that they were not members of the Communist Party or otherwise aligned with allegedly subversive organizations. The Board of Regents fired thirty-one professors who refused to take the anticommunist oath on the grounds that it violated principles of political and academic freedom.

Laws requiring loyalty oaths did not necessarily entail investigations into the actual beliefs, political associations, and fidelities of oath-takers. Although controversial, into the twenty-first century governments and educational institutions have asked employees to take such oaths. Critics have asserted that loyalty oaths were by themselves ineffective measures of a person's allegiances; that they were so vague as to be subject to broad and possibly capricious interpretations; or that they resulted from the political opportunism of legislators, and from governments' attempts to suppress dissent.

BIBLIOGRAPHY

Daniels, Roger. *Prisoners without Trial: Japanese Americans in World War II.* New York: Hill and Wang, 1993.

Heale, M. J. *American Anti-Communism: Combating the Enemy Within, 1830–1970.* Baltimore: Johns Hopkins University Press, 1990.

Hyman, Harold M. *To Try Men's Souls: Loyalty Tests in American History.* Berkeley: University of California Press, 1959.

Schrecker, Ellen W. *No Ivory Tower: McCarthyism and the Universities.* New York: Oxford University Press, 1986.

Donna Alvah

Timothy Leary. The persistent advocate of widespread LSD use was arrested several times during the decade after the U.S. government made the hallucinogen illegal. © CORBIS-BETTMANN

LSD is the abbreviation for lysergic acid diethylamide, a synthetic hallucinogenic drug discovered by Albert Hofmann in 1938. By disrupting the action of serotonin in the brain, LSD produces markedly abnormal behavior, including psychotic episodes that can last anywhere from hours to several days. The drug is usually administered through the tongue, although it can be absorbed through any of the mucous membranes.

Medical experimentation with LSD began in the 1950s, soon after the Swiss pharmaceutical firm Sandoz Laboratories began legally manufacturing the drug. Early investigators included Oscar Janiger, a Los Angeles psychiatrist who administered LSD to approximately 1,000 volunteers between 1954 and 1962, and Timothy Leary, a Harvard psychology professor, who experimented with LSD during the early 1960s. Leary administered the drug to Harvard students, helping to spark an interest in it on college campuses around the nation. Like Janiger, Leary also gave the drug to a number of celebrities. Harvard fired Leary in 1963, but he continued his experiments and advocacy of what had come to be called psychedelic drugs. While the United States government had initially sponsored covert investigations into the utility of LSD for the military and other agencies, in response to mounting public concern and a Senate inquiry, the government outlawed LSD in 1966.

LSD moved rapidly from medicinal to recreational use. Interest in the drug was greatly stimulated by accounts of celebrities, including the actor Cary Grant, and artists who reported remarkable psychological insights and transformations after using LSD. The drug was touted as an aphrodisiac and as a chemical adjunct to the "hippie" movement. It was widely distributed through illegal channels during the 1960s to those eager to follow Leary's siren call to "turn on, tune in, drop out." When LSD was outlawed by most countries and abandoned by legal pharmaceutical manufacturers, any early promise it had as a therapeutic drug was lost in a wave of bad experiences associated with its illegal use and unregulated production.

BIBLIOGRAPHY

Lee, Martin, and Bruce Shlain. *Acid Dreams: The Complete Social History of LSD: The CIA, the Sixties, and Beyond.* New York: Grove Press, 1985.

Montagne, Michael. "LSD at 50: Albert Hofmann and His Discovery." *Pharmacy in History* 35 (1993): 70–73.

Stevens, Jay. *Storming Heaven: LSD and the American Dream.* New York: Grove/Atlantic, 1998.

Ulrich, Robert F., and Bernard M. Patten. "The Rise, Decline, and Fall of LSD." *Perspectives in Biology and Medicine* 34 (1990–1991): 561–578.

Loren Butler Feffer

See also **Counterculture; Substance Abuse.**

LUDLOW MASSACRE. One of the bloodiest labor conflicts that shook the early twentieth-century American West, the Ludlow Massacre marked the end of Colorado's "thirty years' war." While relations between coal miners and mining corporations in Colorado had been poor for more than a decade, the direct origins of this event were in the United Mine Workers' organizing efforts, begun in the fall of 1913. The refusal of John D. Rockefeller's Colorado Fuel and Iron Company and several smaller mine operators to recognize the budding union sparked a strike by more than eight thousand miners in September 1913. Evicted from company-owned housing, the striking miners, comprised mostly of Slavic, Greek, and Italian immigrants, formed their own tent colony. Workers demanded union recognition, a 10 percent wage increase, and rigorous enforcement of existing state laws, especially the eight-hour day. Over the next several months sporadic violence between miners and the state militia marred the coalfields. Despite federal mediation efforts, John D. Rockefeller Jr. refused to budge and followed the unfolding conflict from his New York office some two thousand miles way.

On 20 April 1914 a day-long gun battle broke out between the state militia and miners, culminating in an attack on the tent colony that took the lives of ten male strikers and a child. The militia and local deputies eventually overran the camp and torched it. When the smoke cleared two women and eleven children were found suffocated in a dugout beneath a burned tent. Over the next several days the miners retaliated by burning mining operation buildings and confronting company guards. By the end of April, President Woodrow Wilson ordered federal troops to Ludlow and began more than six months of unsuccessful mediation before striking miners called off the strike. The Ludlow Massacre engendered a great deal of debate about the deteriorating relations between capital and labor on the eve of World War I.

Workers throughout the nation rallied to the cry of Ludlow, while the U.S. Commission on Industrial Relations undertook an extensive investigation of the event. One long-term impact of the massacre was Rockefeller's decision to hire labor experts to devise an employee representation plan. By the early 1920s more than a million American workers belonged to such company unions.

BIBLIOGRAPHY

Gitelman, H. M. *Legacy of the Ludlow Massacre: A Chapter in American Industrial Relations.* Philadelphia: University of Pennsylvania Press, 1988.

McGovern, George S., and Leonard F. Guttridge. *The Great Coalfield War.* Niwot: University Press of Colorado, 1996.

John C. Putman

See also **Labor; Strikes; United Mine Workers of America.**

LUDLOW RESOLUTION, a proposed constitutional amendment introduced by Rep. Louis Ludlow of Indiana in 1935. It was a by-product of the Senate munitions investigation of 1934 and the keep-America-out-of-war movement, which culminated in the Neutrality Acts of 1935, 1936, and 1937. This proposal limited the power of Congress by requiring a popular referendum to ratify a declaration of war except in case of actual attack on the United States or its outlying territories. The resolution gained considerable popularity, and only strenuous efforts by the administration of President Franklin D. Roosevelt prevented its coming to a final vote in the House of Representatives in January 1938.

BIBLIOGRAPHY

Cole, Wayne S. *Roosevelt and the Isolationists, 1932–45.* Lincoln: University of Nebraska Press, 1983.

Devine, Robert. *The Illusion of Neutrality.* Chicago: University of Chicago Press, 1962.

Harold H. Sprout/T. M.

See also **Isolationism; Munitions; Neutrality; War and the Constitution.**

LUDLOW'S CODE. A common complaint of the early American colonists was that, in the absence of an established body of laws, the decisions of magistrates tended to be capricious. To correct this situation, in 1646 the general court of Connecticut asked Roger Ludlow, a member of the court and trained in the English law, to compile a body of laws for the commonwealth. The result was Ludlow's Code of 1650, which established the law of the colony. Although revised many times, this code remains the foundation of Connecticut's laws.

BIBLIOGRAPHY

Main, Jackson Turner. *Society and Economy in Colonial Connecticut.* Princeton, N.J.: Princeton University Press, 1985.

R. V. Coleman/A. E.

See also **Colonial Society; Connecticut.**

LUMBEE. Numbering over 54,000 enrolled members, the Lumbees are the largest Indian tribe east of the Mississippi River. Located mainly in southeastern North Carolina along the Lumber River, the Lumbees have lived among the river swamps for almost three centuries. There are numerous theories regarding the historical tribal origin of the Lumbees. In the late nineteenth and early twentieth centuries, the prevailing theory was that the Lumbees were the descendants of the coastal Algonkian tribes of North Carolina and the English colony that mysteriously disappeared from Roanoke Island in 1587. More recent theories suggest significant tribal influence from the many Siouan-speaking tribes from the Piedmont and coastal plain, particularly the Cheraws, who had long lived in this area. Regardless of tribal origin, archaeological evidence indicates a continuous indigenous presence in the area for at least 14,000 years.

A number of events in Lumbee history have forced the tribe to assert its rights. The decade of the Lowry War (1864–1874) saw unbounded violence against the white establishment throughout Robeson County. Led by the Lumbee outlaw Henry Berry Lowry, the Lowry gang waged war for ten years in an effort to fight the injustices perpetrated against the Lumbees by the Confederacy and local militia. Because of his unrelenting struggle, Lowry, who mysteriously disappeared in 1872, has become the legendary hero of the present-day Lumbee people.

By the late 1800s, reform had come to North Carolina. In 1885 the state legislature created a separate educational system for the Indians of Robeson County. In 1887 an Indian normal school was established to train the Lumbee people to be teachers in their own schools. For many years, this was the only higher educational institution available for the Lumbees, and from 1940 to 1953, Pembroke State College (which grew out of the early normal school) was the only state-supported four-year college for Indians in the United States. Pembroke State College is now the University of North Carolina at Pembroke, one of the sixteen constituent campuses of the University of North Carolina, and serves a multicultural student body.

In 1956 the federal government officially recognized the Lumbees but withheld customary Indian benefits and services. Through administrative and legislative efforts, the Lumbees have continually tried to remove the restrictive language of the 1956 law but have not yet been successful. On 7 November 2000, the Lumbees elected a twenty-three-member tribal government, part of whose focus is on achieving full federal status as a tribe.

Lumbee Athletes. Members of the girls' basketball team at the Indian normal school, 1928.

BIBLIOGRAPHY

Dial, Adolph L., and David K. Eliades. *The Only Land I Know: A History of the Lumbee People.* Syracuse, N.Y.: Syracuse University Press, 1996.

Sider, Gerald M. *Lumbee Indian Histories: Race, Ethnicity, and Indian Identity in the Southern United States.* New York: Cambridge University Press, 1993.

Starr, Glenn Ellen. *The Lumbee Indians: An Annotated Bibliography with Chronology and Index.* Jefferson, N.C.: McFarland, 1994.

Linda E. Oxendine

See also **Tribes: Southeastern.**

LUMBER INDUSTRY. The production of lumber, wood split or sawed for use as boards, beams, planks, and the like, has been a critical economic activity throughout American history. Whereas Indian peoples altered North America's woodlands through the extensive use of fire, European colonists introduced the first mass cuttings of trees for both trade and subsistence purposes. Although most felled trees were cut to provide firewood and to open fields for agriculture, timber products were important commodities for trade with Europe from the inception of British North America. Indeed, the Pilgrims' first shipment home in 1621 was dominated by milled wood for their comparatively timber-starved mother country. Lumber from North America was consumed and shipped to other British colonies and to Europe for a wide variety of uses, including barrel staves, building construction, furniture, and shingle manufacture. Colonial society was comparatively lumber rich. European travelers were often staggered by the colonists' unwillingness to use any but the finest of wood for even the most pedestrian purposes. As one observer wrote of eighteenth-century New Englanders:

> The richest and straightest trees were reserved for the frames of the new houses; shingles were rived from the clearest pine; baskets, chair bottoms, cattle bows, etc., were made from brown ash butts; all the rest of the timber cleared was piled and burned on the spot. . . . All the pine went first. Nothing else was fit for building purposes in those days. Tables were 2½ feet wide from a single board, without knot or blemish.

The white pine, the largest of New England's trees, was the most important tree for export. Indispensable for ship masts and increasingly scarce in Europe, the pines were actively sought by the Royal Navy, which by the end of the seventeenth century mandated fines for unauthorized cutting of large specimens.

Because of their abundant stands of large white pine, Maine and New Hampshire were the most important commercial lumbering centers in colonial times. More than two dozen sawmills were in operation in southern Maine by the 1680s. Lumbermen used draft animals to pull downed trees over frozen winter ground to the nearest waterway, where they floated to sawmills in the spring. Although many logs were sawed by hand throughout the colonial period, New England's mills resorted to waterpower more extensively than did their English counterparts.

Private Timberlands

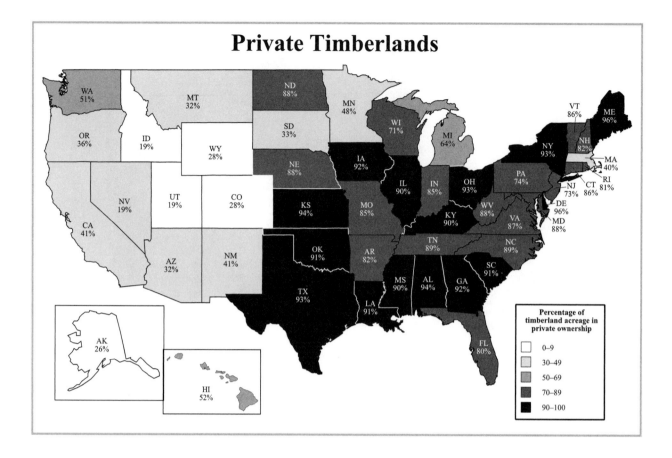

WA 51%
MT 32%
ND 88%
MN 48%
VT 86%
ME 96%
OR 36%
ID 19%
WY 28%
SD 33%
WI 71%
MI 64%
NY 93%
NH 82%
MA 40%
NV 19%
UT 19%
CO 28%
NE 88%
IA 92%
IL 90%
IN 85%
OH 93%
PA 74%
NJ 73%
CT 86%
RI 81%
CA 41%
AZ 32%
NM 41%
KS 94%
MO 85%
KY 90%
WV 88%
VA 87%
DE 96%
MD 88%
OK 91%
AR 82%
TN 89%
NC 89%
TX 93%
MS 90%
AL 94%
GA 92%
SC 91%
LA 91%
FL 80%
AK 26%
HI 52%

Percentage of timberland acreage in private ownership

0–9
30–49
50–69
70–89
90–100

The nineteenth century brought an intensification of lumbering as the new nation grew in size. For a time, Maine held its dominant position in the industry. By one estimate, Bangor was the world's largest lumber-producing site in the early nineteenth century. But soon the industry began to move westward on the "timber frontier" in search of relatively unharvested forests, particularly the still valuable white pine. By 1840, upstate New York and Pennsylvania had supplanted northern New England as the largest producers of lumber. In the 1850s, lumbermen began cutting the large pine forests of the Great Lakes states, and by 1880, Michigan produced more lumber than any other state. White pine remained the single most important commercial tree in the nineteenth century, accounting for about half of all lumber sawed each year through the 1870s. By the early twentieth century, however, the enormous redwood, pine, and fir forests of the Far West and the South's piney woods provided most of the nation's lumber. While different regions produced their own owners, firms, and laborers, many New Englanders moved westward with the industry and continued to wield disproportionate influence over it well into the twentieth century. At the height of the Great Lakes white pine harvest, for example, four-fifths of the 131 most influential lumber entrepreneurs hailed from the northeastern United States or eastern Canada, as did many of their most experienced laborers.

The nineteenth century lumber industry was part and parcel of the industrialization of the United States. Before the widespread use of coal after the Civil War, wood likely supplied more than 90 percent of the nation's energy needs for heat, light, and rail and steamship transportation. Rapid population growth on the timber-poor Great Plains helped make timber production a true industry, with operators harvesting and milling wood near the Great Lakes and shipping wood to build homes in Kansas and Nebraska. The burgeoning railroad network made such transportation possible even as it increased demand for timber. Railroads needed lumber to construct rail cars, stations, fences, and cross ties in addition to the massive amounts of wood they burned for fuel. Each year railroads needed some 73 million ties for the construction of new rail lines and the maintenance of old ones, estimated by the magazine *Scientific American* in 1890. From the 1870s to 1900, railroads used as much as a fourth of national timber production. The mining industry similarly used large amounts of lumber to support underground diggings and to maintain its own rail beds. Indeed, many mining companies ran their own local logging and sawing operations.

The internal structure of the lumber industry changed to meet these economic circumstances. Individuals and families had operated single sawmills to make lumber of

Timber. A patch in Northern California after clear-cutting, May 1972. NATIONAL ARCHIVES AND RECORDS ADMINISTRATION

raw logs, either for the direct use of the log provider or for sale to wholesalers. In the 1850s, many operators began buying multiple mills, acquiring their own timberlands, and operating their own lumberyards in market centers such as Chicago. The rise of the Weyerhaeuser timber company epitomized this consolidation. Starting in 1860 with a single sawmill on the Mississippi River in Rock Island, Illinois, the German immigrant Frederick Weyerhaeuser directed the energies of some 20,000 employees a decade later. By the early twentieth century, he and his business partners owned more than 2 million acres of forest and perhaps 15 billion feet of valuable pine. The "lumber king," a private man in comparison with other industrial giants of the era, may have been the world's richest man by his death in 1914.

Consolidating ownership led to other changes in the production and marketing of timber. Operations like Weyerhaeuser's had significant advantages over their smaller and less-capitalized competitors. The exhaustion of timber stands near waterways large enough to drive lumber created the need for railroad spurs to connect inland sawmills to the national rail network. The companies that constructed their own rail lines, an expensive proposition, were for the first time also able to ship mass quantities of hardwoods, especially oak, hickory, ash, and maple, all of which were too heavy to easily float, to market, allowing for a more intensive and profitable cutting of woodlands.

Away from the timber harvest sites, corporate lumberyards began sorting lumber into standardized categories to ensure higher prices for finer products. By the 1890s, regional grading schemes were in place. Firms in urban timber markets began shipping manufactured building components, such as doors and sashes and in some cases entire structures, as early as the 1860s. Standardization and reliable transportation by rail allowed for the extensive use of the distinctly American "balloon-frame" construction technique, in which light, mass-produced boards were nailed together to create a strong building skeleton. The balloon frame allowed fewer and less-skilled workers to follow easily repeatable plans in the erection of even large buildings.

After the Civil War, the production of lumber thus became a modern and highly specialized industry. In Chicago, the nation's largest lumber market, for example, twelve miles of docks were devoted exclusively to unloading lumber. Enormous piles of stacked wood dominated entire blocks of the city. "The timber yards are a considerable part of the city's surface," wrote a British traveler, "there appearing to be enough boards and planks piled up to supply a half-dozen states." The city's lumber wholesaling was such an important business that by 1880 its operators owned several times more capital than did all of Chicago's banks combined.

The very size of the industry raised the prospect that it would cut over the nation's woodlands, leaving nothing of value to replace the once majestic pine forests. As early as 1876 the Canadian lumber entrepreneur James Little argued that those cutting the Great Lakes forests were "not only burning the candle at both ends . . . but cutting it in two, and setting the match to the four ends to enable them to double the process of exhaustion." In the next three decades, the spread of such fears, reflected in increasing prices and decreasing sawlog size, prompted the development of professional forestry and the creation of what became the national forest system. Although federal lands never accounted for more than one-fifth of the national timber harvest, their existence reflected the concern that private enterprise was unable to use timber resources on a sustainable basis.

The industry's rapid growth also created a large demand for labor. Logging itself remained a winter activity until the twentieth century. Work crews, consisting largely of farmers idled by the season, moved into place in late fall and early winter, working until spring thawed the waterways and called them home to plant their fields. Before the Civil War, crews consisted of around a dozen men, but the postwar florescence gave rise to camps of as many as several hundred. Loggers lived amidst the trees to be harvested, generally in temporary wooden structures. Their isolation and the perennial cash flow problems for the still seasonal cutting meant that many were paid in company store scrip or abruptly were fired in economic downturns and periods of low stumpage price. Work in the mills and yards was year-round by contrast. By the dawn of the twentieth century, immigrants made up most of the lumber industry's workforce. Large waves of strikes swept through timber country in the 1910s, resulting in sporadic wage increases and amelioration of working conditions. Organized labor secured an institutional presence in the industry in the 1930s and 1940s.

The development of new technologies created some changes in the nature of timber labor. Sawmills became increasingly mechanized. In the early nineteenth century, the machine-driven circular saw replaced the water-driven "muley saw," but the circular saw was replaced later by the more efficient and more expensive band saw, essentially a giant chainsaw fixed in place. The process of logging continued to rely on axes and handsaws to fell trees well into the twentieth century, until the post–World War II mass adoption of portable chainsaws. Trucks and forest roads allowed the cutting of less accessible areas, especially in the mountainous West. In the last decades of the century, the most heavily capitalized logging outfits began using large machines able to cut trees, delimb them, and stack them for transport to the mill. With such equipment, loggers were able to cut ten times more stumpage than their predecessors.

In the twentieth century, the lumber industry lost most of its frontier characteristics. Although Alaskan forests began to produce large volumes of timber, the exhaustion of most of the continent's uncut woods forced companies to make already-cut lands productive again. Remaining stands of old-growth forest were still lucrative targets for cutting, but by the 1960s, federal lands policies and environmentalist opposition removed many of these tracts from timber harvesting. Forest nurseries, tree farms, and reforestation efforts became essential to the industry's survival. Indeed, in the South intensively managed tree plantations largely replaced the management of natural forests for timber production. Moreover new wood products, such as pulp for paper manufacture, plywood, and wood fibers for wallboard and insulation, allowed companies to shift their focus from cutting large softwoods such as the white pine to using a much greater variety of trees, particularly the species that replaced pines in the most heavily cut regions. At the end of the twentieth century, the Southeast and Northwest were the most important lumber-producing regions, and imports accounted for nearly one-third of national softwood consumption.

BIBLIOGRAPHY

Chase, Alston. *In a Dark Wood: The Fight over Forests and the Rising Tyranny of Ecology.* Boston: Houghton Mifflin, 1995.

Cronon, William. *Changes in the Land: Indians, Colonists, and the Ecology of New England.* New York: Hill and Wang, 1983.

———. *Nature's Metropolis: Chicago and the Great West.* New York: Norton, 1991.

Hidy, Ralph W., Frank Ernest Hill, and Allan Nevins. *Timber and Men: The Weyerhauser Story.* New York: Macmillan, 1963.

Holbrook, Stewart. *The American Lumberjack.* New York: Collier, 1962.

Larson, Agnes M. *History of the White Pine Industry in Minnesota.* Minneapolis: University of Minnesota Press, 1949.

Williams, Michael. *Americans and Their Forests: A Historical Geography.* New York: Cambridge University Press, 1989.

Benjamin H. Johnson

See also **Conservation; Forestry.**

LUSITANIA, SINKING OF THE. On 7 May 1915, a German submarine sank without warning the *Lusitania*, killing 128 Americans. Since Germany had warned travelers against sailing on British or Allied ships, many believed that the sinking was premeditated. The log of the submarine shows, however, that it was not.

President Woodrow Wilson resisted considerable popular clamor for war but demanded that Germany make reparation for and disavow the sinking. The German government agreed to make reparation and eventually promised that it would not sink liners without warning, but it steadfastly refused to disavow the sinking of the *Lusitania*.

BIBLIOGRAPHY

Hickey, Des. *Seven Days to Disaster: The Sinking of the Lusitania.* New York: Putnam, 1982.

Lusitania. The German government placed this ad in New York newspapers just before the final sailing of the Cunard liner *Lusitania*, warning travelers not to sail on Allied ships or enter the "war zone" around the British Isles. The sinking, on 7 May 1915, killed nearly 1,200 people, including more than 100 Americans. © CORBIS

Ramsay, David. *Lusitania: Saga and Myth.* London: Chatham, 2001.

Bernadotte E. Schmitt / A. E.

See also **Meuse-Argonne Offensive; Submarines; World War I.**

LUTHER V. BORDEN, 7 Howard (48 U.S.) 1 (1849). The United States Supreme Court resolved some constitutional questions raised in Rhode Island's Dorr Rebellion (1842). After suffrage reformers adopted a new state constitution by extralegal popular referendum and elected a new state government to redress severe problems of disfranchisement and malapportionment, the extant state government, backed covertly by President John Tyler, declared martial law and crushed the new government. Chief Justice Roger B. Taney rejected a challenge to the old regime based on the clause guaranteeing the states a republican form of government. He declared that to be a political question to be resolved by Congress and/or the president.

BIBLIOGRAPHY

Gettleman, Marvin E. *The Dorr Rebellion: A Study in American Radicalism, 1833–1849.* New York: Random House, 1973.

Dennison, George M. *The Dorr War: Republicanism on Trial, 1831–1861.* Lexington: University Press of Kentucky, 1976.

William M. Wiecek

See also **Dorr's Rebellion; Suffrage.**

LUTHERANISM in America traces its heritage to the Reformation of the sixteenth century in Germany and northern Europe, stressing justification by faith and the sacraments of Baptism and the Eucharist. While Lutherans may have resided in the Dutch settlements of New Netherland beginning in the mid-1620s, the first Lutheran-majority community was a Swedish colony established on the Delaware in 1638 and subsequently captured by the Dutch in 1655. During the eighteenth century, however, many German Lutherans settled in Pennsylvania and the southern colonies. In 1742, Henry M. Muhlenberg was sent from Germany and helped unite most Lutheran pastors in North America into the Ministerium of North America in 1748. At the close of the American Revolution, there were 120,000 Lutherans in 300 congregations throughout the new nation.

The Rise of the General Synod

In the new Lutheran world, English-speaking synods revealed a willingness to participate in mainstream Protestant culture, showing sympathy for the temperance and antislavery movements. Many German-speakers, by contrast, preferred Lutheran exclusivity and encouraged the establishment of German newspapers and schools. The

Henry M. Muhlenberg. The German-born clergyman is known as the patriarch of American Lutheranism for his key role in uniting most Lutheran congregations in North America by 1748. LIBRARY OF CONGRESS

changing character of American Lutheranism was epitomized by Samuel Schmucker, who was instrumental in the founding of Gettysburg Seminary in 1826—a bastion of American Lutheranism in the nineteenth century. In 1834, Schmucker published his *Elements of Popular Theology*, which defended unity with all orthodox Christian bodies who held a common faith based on the "fundamental doctrines of Scripture," and extolled the Augsburg Confession as a model because it left certain theological questions open. After 1820, most Lutheran synods coalesced into the new General Synod, which was given authority to devise plans for seminaries, give missionary instruction, and provide aid to poor ministers and families. A network of orphanages, homes for the aged, and hospitals also began to appear in the Lutheran community, and several new colleges were founded.

The Challenge of Confessionalism
During the 1830s and 1840s, many Lutherans fled from Prussia, Saxony, Norway, and Sweden for a variety of political, religious, and economic reasons. Settling in the Midwest, they brought with them a theology of confessionalism, which stressed adherence to the historic confessions of the Lutheran tradition, most notably the *Book of Concord* (1580). The greater numbers of European Lutherans helped to cut off Lutheranism in the United

States from other Protestant denominations. Most prominent of the new German synods was the Missouri Synod, formed in 1847, which took a confessional stance and opposed Americanization. Its vision was that of super-congregationalism, in which a synod had no authority over individual congregations. Other German and Scandinavian synods took less dogmatic stands, but inclined more to the theology of Missouri than that of the General Synod.

Theological Disputes
In the 1850s, a distinct theological division emerged between advocates of confessionalism and Neo-Lutherans who held to the Augsburg Confession only insofar as it conformed ostensibly to the Bible, rejecting unbiblical teachings such as original sin, private confession, baptismal regeneration, and the "real presence." Samuel Schmucker, the acknowledged leader of the Neo-Lutherans, was a vocal evangelical regarded with scorn by opponents of American Lutheranism. When he issued his Definite Synodical Program in 1855, which sought to rework the Augsburg Confession to conform to American values, it was rejected even by several eastern synods and American Lutheranism suffered a defeat from which it never recovered during the nineteenth century. Throughout the nineteenth century, moderates continued to search for an acceptable basis on which to unite the synods in the East and the Midwest. In 1867, they formed the General Council, which adopted the Akron Rule in 1872, reserving Lutheran pulpits for Lutheran pastors and Lutheran altars for Lutheran communicants. The issues of the Civil War provoked another division: five southern synods withdrew from the General Synod to form what in 1886 would become the United Synod, South. Advocates of confessionalism in the Midwest responded to the withdrawal of the southern synods by forming the Synodical Conference in 1872 to coordinate their activities.

Lutheranism in the Late Nineteenth Century
After the Civil War, German and Scandinavian immigration continued, with the high point being reached in 1882, but the motivations for this were now more economic than religious. Church growth occurred in the East as well as the Midwest, with the General Council's membership being one-third English, one-third German, and one-third Swedish. The Missouri Synod also made gains in the East, although most of their new members were migrants to the Midwest. Twenty-eight institutions of higher education were established between 1870 and 1910. Lutheran church life was influenced by the pietistic strain in Protestant America, but was unaffected by the Social Gospel. All its energy was devoted to home missions and evangelical outreach, for the focus of Lutheran interest was on personal not social ethics.

Renewed Doctrinal Controversy
Biblical criticism had only a slight impact on nineteenth-century Lutheranism. Instead, Lutherans focused on con-

fessionalism and predestination. Divisions arose between those who favored inclusive confederation (the General Synod), confessional subscription (the General Council and the United Synod, South), and complete unity in doctrine and practice (the Synodical Conference). The General Synod acquired a new appreciation for its Lutheran heritage in the last quarter of the nineteenth century and committed itself to the Augsburg Confession, but nevertheless continued a good relationship with evangelical denominations and enacted no bar on altar or pulpit fellowship. Despite this, closer relations did develop between the General Synod, the General Council, and the United Synod, South, at the end of the century. During the 1870s, the Synodical Conference was itself divided over predestination (or the "election of grace"). The Lutheran doctrine of election applied only to salvation, not damnation, and was never a central aspect of the faith. Nevertheless, Friedrich A. Schmitt of the Norwegian Synod accused the Missouri Synod's president, C. F. W. Walther, of Calvinistic leanings. After acrimonious debate, several synods left the Synodical Conference with a consequent decline in funding for education and missionary work.

The First Steps Toward Lutheran Unity
Efforts to celebrate the four-hundredth anniversary of the Reformation in 1917 united Lutherans in the United States and led them to establish the Lutheran Bureau to provide ordinary Americans with information on the Lutheran heritage. The outbreak of war that year provided a further opportunity for Lutheranism to acquire national prominence. The entry of Lutherans into military service led to the creation of the National Lutheran Commission for Soldiers' and Sailors' Welfare, a trans-synodical body that established camps, recruited pastors, and raised $1.35 million. The National Lutheran Council (NLC) handled problems on the home front and aided reconstruction in Europe. Even the midwestern synods worked with the National Lutheran Council, though conflict did erupt over cooperation with other Protestant churches. The drive toward Lutheran unity was cemented by the creation of the Norwegian Lutheran Church in America (NLCA) in 1917, and the formation the following year of the United Lutheran Church in America (ULCA), which united most of the eastern-based synods into one body. Significantly, the ULCA was much more centralized than any of its predecessor synods, with much less congregational autonomy.

Depression and War
Lutheranism remained a conservative force in the 1920s and Lutherans remained rural-oriented, though there was a shift in mission work toward recovering unchurched Lutherans in the cities and the Northwest. After disputes within the National Lutheran Council, moderate midwestern synods formed the American Lutheran Conference, banning cooperation with other Protestants and restricting altars and pulpits, and in 1930 they merged into the American Lutheran Church. The Great Depression of 1929 dramatically reduced budgets and prompted calls for collective social responsibility. The Lutheran Home Missions Council of America was formed to transcend ethnic boundaries and allow for a degree of altar and pulpit fellowship, but most Lutheran churches in the mid–twentieth century remained committed to the confessional viewpoint. The outbreak of war in 1941 gave new life to the National Lutheran Council, which recruited chaplains, supported orphan missions, and ministered to armed forces personnel.

The Postwar World
During the 1950s, the Lutheran churches saw great growth, though Lutheran evangelism was based on a sacramental emphasis rather than revivalism, and Lutherans came closer together in ecumenical ventures. The ALC and ELC (formerly the NLCA) completed merger in 1960 to form The American Lutheran Church and the ULCA and the Augustana Synod united in 1962 to form the Lutheran Church in America (LCA). New types of ministry were initiated to address contemporary social problems, as theologians tried to enunciate a Lutheran doctrine that allowed for engagement in social justice without denying the action of grace in making a Christian. Throughout these mergers, however, the Lutheran Church–Missouri Synod stood apart, insisting that doctrinal conformity was the prerequisite for Lutheran unity.

Lutheranism Today
For Lutherans other than the Missouri Synod, merger became an end in itself and in 1987 the Evangelical Lutheran Church in America (ELCA) was formed from a merger of the American Lutheran Church and the Lutheran Church in America. In 2000 the ELCA endorsed a concordat with the Episcopal Church, U.S.A., allowing for a high degree of altar and pulpit fellowship. In 1999, membership in the Evangelical Lutheran Church in America stood at 5,149,668 members compared with 2,582,440 for the Lutheran Church–Missouri Synod and 722,754 for the Wisconsin Evangelical Lutheran Synod. Some smaller groups include the Association of Free Lutheran Congregations with 32,984, the American Association of Lutheran Churches with 18,252, the Evangelical Lutheran Synod with 16,734, the Latvian Evangelical Lutheran Church in America with 15,012, and the Church of the Lutheran Brethren in America with 13,920.

BIBLIOGRAPHY

Avery, William O. *Empowered Laity: The Story of the Lutheran Laity Movement for Stewardship*. Minneapolis, Minn.: Fortress Press, 1997.

Bachmann, E. Theodore, with Mercia B. Bachmann. *The United Lutheran Church in America, 1918–1962*. Minneapolis, Minn.: Fortress Press, 1997.

Nelson, E. Clifford, ed. *The Lutherans in North America*. Philadelphia: Fortress Press, 1980.

Nelson, E. Clifford, and Eugene L. Fevold. *The Lutheran Church Among Norwegian-Americans: A History of the Evangelical Lutheran Church.* Minneapolis, Minn.: Augsburg, 1960.

Todd, Mary. *Authority Vested: A Story of Identity and Change in the Lutheran Church-Missouri Synod.* Grand Rapids, Mich.: W. B. Eerdmans, 2000.

Trexler, Edgar R. *Anatomy of a Merger: People, Dynamics, and Decisions That Shaped the ELCA.* Minneapolis, Minn.: Augsburg, 1991.

Jeremy Bonner

See also **German Americans; Protestantism; Religion and Religious Affiliation; Religious Thought and Writings; Scandinavian Americans.**

LYCEUM MOVEMENT, an important phase of the early adult education and public school movements, utilizing, principally, lectures and debates. It began with an article in the *American Journal of Education* (October 1826) by Josiah Holbrook, containing a plan for "Associations of Adults for Mutual Education." Holbrook organized the first lyceum society in November 1826 at Millbury, Mass. Within a year more than a dozen lyceums had sprung up in Worcester County, Mass., and in Windham County, Conn. The movement was endorsed by a meeting of eminent Bostonians, presided over by Daniel Webster, in 1828. By 1831 lyceums existed in all the New England states and in northern New York. State lyceums were organized in 1831 in Massachusetts, Maine, and New York, and in the same year the New York State Lyceum called a meeting in New York City to organize a national lyceum. Pressure from Lyceum organizers contributed to the Massachusetts legislature's decision to commence taxation for a public school system in 1834 and to install Horace Mann as its first Superintendent of the State Board of Education in 1837.

Holbrook journeyed as far west as Missouri and found active interest in the western states, including Kentucky and Tennessee. National lyceums were held each year until 1839, although often poorly attended. The town lyceums, estimated by Holbrook at 3,000 in 1835, were the heart of the movement. The Lyceum's much-touted utopian vision of *Lycenia* invoked Thomas Jefferson's pre-industrial utopia of educated yeoman farmers. After 1840 the main emphasis was on self-education in science, literature, and morality. At first apolitical, the lyceums often developed interest in topics that later became political issues, such as slavery and prohibition.

Besides improving the public schools and giving a supplementary education to those unable to attend high school or college, the early lyceums led to certain permanent institutions, such as Lowell Institute in Massachusetts and Brooklyn Institute in New York. The Lyceum Village was founded at Berea, Ohio, in 1837. Holbrook conducted the Central Lyceum Bureau from 1842 to 1849, and in 1867–1868 a number of commercial lecture bureaus were founded, among them the Boston Lyceum Bureau of James Redpath, whose successor, J. B. Pond, was a successful lecture promoter. Some lyceums developed into historical or literary societies, public libraries, or museums. A variant of the lyceum idea took different shapes in the Chautauqua movement and women's clubs of the late nineteenth century. The lyceums continued to grow until the early twentieth century. In 1915 their number was estimated at 12,000. By the 1920s they existed mostly in small towns and consisted mainly of popular music and "sanitized vaudeville."

BIBLIOGRAPHY

Bode, Carl. *The American Lyceum: Town Meeting of the Mind.* Carbondale: Southern Illinois University Press, 1968.

Mead, C. David. *Yankee Eloquence in the Middle West: The Ohio Lyceum, 1850–1870.* East Lansing: Michigan State College Press, 1951.

Scott, Donald M. "The Popular Lecture and the Creation of the Public in Mid-Nineteenth-Century America." *Journal of American History* 66 (1980).

W. C. Mallalieu/A. R.

See also **Book-of-the-Month Club; Chautauqua Movement; Education; Franklin Institute; Libraries; Mechanics' Institutes; Science Education.**

LYME DISEASE, an infectious disease transmitted by the deer tick, was first identified conclusively in 1975 in New England. The cause initially eluded investigators, who found inconsistencies in the symptoms affecting inhabitants of Old Lyme, Connecticut, where it was first observed, and neighboring communities. The illness manifested itself in one or more symptoms, including fever, chills, lethargy, headaches, muscle aches, backaches, sore throats, nausea, and stiff necks. Some, but not all, victims incurred a rash that resembled a bull's-eye roughly six centimeters in diameter. While most recovered, about 15 percent were left with neurologic problems and a few with life-threatening cardiac conditions.

The disease initially appeared most frequently in the northeastern, north-central, and northwestern United States, in woods and transitional areas between woods and grassy fields. Investigators eventually traced the disease to ticks that transmitted the disease into the bloodstream by burying themselves in human skin. In 1982 Willy Burgdorfer of the Rocky Mountain Laboratories in Hamilton, Montana, identified the spiral-shaped bacteria, *Borrelia burgdorferi*, that causes Lyme disease. By 1987 physicians had detected the disease in the southern United States. Reported cases grew from 545 in 1989 to 8,000 in 1993. Symptoms seldom linger in victims who obtain early treatment with antibiotics, although as of 2001 doctors disagreed about how easy it is to diagnose the disease and about what to do for patients whose symptoms last beyond the typically effective four-week antibiotic treatment. Some fear that using additional antibiotics too readily will expose patients to uncomfortable side effects and, worse, engender resistant bacterial strains of the disease.

BIBLIOGRAPHY

Barbour, Alan G. *Lyme Disease*. Baltimore: Johns Hopkins University Press, 1996.

Kantor, Fred S. "Disarming Lyme Disease." *Scientific American* 271 (September 1994): 34–40.

Lang, Denise V. *Coping with Lyme Disease*. 2d ed. New York: Henry Holt, 1997.

Ruth Roy Harris/c. w.

See also **Medical Research.**

LYNCHING.   Defined as an act of violence perpetrated for the purpose of punishment (usually torture and death) for an alleged crime carried out by an extralegal mob, lynching has a long history in the United States. Historians have traced its roots to seventeenth-century Ireland; the American Revolutionary War Colonel Charles Lynch, from whose name the term derives, was said to have indiscriminately meted out the punishment of flogging for Tory sympathizers. Lynch law, or mob rule, became part of the fabric of the United States; lynchings took place in every geographic section of the nation, and victims included African Americans, immigrants, and native-born whites. Alleged crimes varied, but most lynchings involved a perceived transgression of community values or a violation of societal honor codes.

During the antebellum period, lynch mobs across the country preyed upon individuals and groups deemed dangerous because they were political, religious, or racial "others." Abolitionists, Catholics, Mormons, Asian, Mexican, and European immigrants and African Americans all were targets. The pattern of mob violence and lynching changed after the Civil War. During the five decades between the end of Reconstruction and the New Deal, there were three specific transformations in the character of American lynching: increased numbers over all; increased likelihood that African Americans would fall victim to lynch mobs; and a concentration of lynchings in the South, particularly after 1886. The Tuskegee Institute started recording statistics on lynchings in 1882 (later, the *Chicago Tribune* and the NATIONAL ASSOCIATION FOR THE ADVANCEMENT OF COLORED PEOPLE [NAACP] also collected statistics). The first decade of those statistical findings best illustrates the transformation of lynching patterns. In 1882, 113 people were lynched, sixty-four whites and forty-nine African Americans. The year 1885 was the last during which more whites than African Americans were lynched, and 1892 witnessed the largest number of lynchings in U.S. history (230). From 1882 to 1903, there were approximately one to two hundred lynchings annually. Between 1882 and 1968, there were 4,742 recorded lynchings (3,445 of the victims were African American, or approximately seventy-five percent). During World War I

"Gruesome Spectacle." Photographs such as this one were used by the National Association for the Advancement of Colored People and other organizations in the decades-long effort to persuade the federal government to take action against lynching, which primarily targeted blacks. GETTY IMAGES

and the postwar red scare, race riots swept the country, wreaking havoc in Chicago, St. Louis, Tulsa, Omaha, Washington, D.C., and other cities. Lynchings decreased dramatically during the New Deal era, and the period between 1952 and 1954 was the longest during which no lynchings were recorded. But lynch mobs did not disappear completely. As civil rights workers stepped up their campaigns for desegregation and voting rights, they were beaten, killed, and tortured. Although some argue that race relations have improved, the tragedy of American lynching has not been completely eradicated. The dragging death of James Byrd, in Texas, and the beating and crucifixion murder of Matthew Shepard in Wyoming have been called late twentieth-century lynchings.

There was, however, clearly a decline in lynching during the twentieth century, and this was a result of long and hard-fought battles of anti-lynching crusaders. In 1892, after three prominent Memphis businessmen were lynched, Ida B. Wells, the renowned journalist, began speaking out about the violence. She used Memphis newspaper, the *Free Speech*, to spread her outrage. She was soon joined by other prominent individuals and organizations. The founders of the NAACP in 1909 cited lynching as key to its formation and agenda. The organization was joined by the ASSOCIATION OF SOUTHERN WOMEN FOR THE PREVENTION OF LYNCHING in the 1930s. Wells's research did the most to destroy the myths about the causes of lynching, though it took decades for her findings to permeate mainstream American consciousness. In her pamphlet, "Southern Horrors: Lynch Law in All Its Phases," Wells argued that the majority of alleged rape charges were not only impossible to prove—that sexual liaisons between many black men and white women might have been consensual—but that rape was not even cited by mobs as the cause of lynching. Retribution for alleged homicide and assault were the most common reasons for the formation of lynch mobs. Legislation was a key goal of those who fought to punish the violence. Although many had tried to use the Fourteenth Amendment to prosecute lynchers, most efforts failed. In 1922, the House of Representatives passed the Dyer Anti-Lynching Bill, which had been sponsored by the NAACP. The bill died in the Senate, however, thanks to a filibuster by southern senators. Similar tactics were used to kill bills in 1937 and 1940. President Truman's Committee on Civil Rights recommended anti-lynching legislation but was ignored by Congress. Finally, in 1968, under the Civil Rights Act, the federal government could take action against mob violence and lynching.

BIBLIOGRAPHY

Brundage, W. Fitzhugh. *Lynchings in the New South: Georgia and Virginia, 1880–1930.* Urbana: University of Illinois Press, 1993.

Raper, Arthur F. *The Tragedy of Lynching.* New York: Dover, 1970.

Schechter, Patricia A. *Ida B. Wells-Barnett and American Reform, 1880–1930.* Chapel Hill: University of North Carolina Press, 2001.

White, Walter. *Rope and Faggot: A Biography of Judge Lynch.* Notre Dame, Ind.: University of Notre Dame Press, 2001.

Williamson, Joel. *The Crucible of Race: Black-White Relations n the American South since Emancipation.* New York: Oxford University Press, 1984.

Caroline Waldron Merithew

See also **Civil Rights Act of 1964; Civil Rights and Liberties; Civil Rights Movement.**

LYNG V. NORTHWEST INDIAN CEMETERY ASSOCIATION,

485 U.S. 439 (1988). The Supreme Court ruled that the AMERICAN INDIAN RELIGIOUS FREEDOM ACT (AIRFA) of 1978 and the FIRST AMENDMENT of the U.S. Constitution do not protect the rights of American Indians to practice their religions at off-reservation public lands held by the U.S government. Beginning in the 1960s, the Yurok, Karok, and Tolowa Indians of northern California began protesting attempts by the U.S. Forest Service to build roads through Indian sacred sites in California's National Forests. AIRFA stipulates that federal agencies examine their practices in an attempt "to protect and preserve Native American religious cultural rights and practices," and during the lower court hearings, Forest Service experts agreed that their proposed road threatened the "ceremonies . . . of [Indian] religious beliefs and practices." Overturning the Court of Appeals for the Ninth Circuit, which had affirmed the U.S. district court's decision, the Supreme Court ruled that unless there was direct government intent to infringe upon Indian religious practices or direct government coercion of individuals to act against their religious beliefs, then the First Amendment offered no protection against governmental action that impacted upon, or even threatened to destroy, an American Indian sacred site. This ruling severely weakened the AIRFA and the legal basis for American Indian religious freedoms.

BIBLIOGRAPHY

Davis, Mary B., ed. *Native America in the Twentieth Century: An Encyclopedia.* New York: Garland, 1994.

Prucha, Francis Paul. *Documents of United States Indian Policy.* 3d ed. Lincoln: University of Nebraska Press, 2000.

Ned Blackhawk

M

MacARTHUR FOUNDATION, formally known as The John D. and Catherine T. MacArthur Foundation, is a private general-purpose foundation created in 1978 and headquartered in Chicago. At the time of his death, John D. MacArthur (1897–1978) was one of the three wealthiest men in America and the owner of the nation's largest privately held insurance company, Bankers Life and Casualty Company. Catherine T. MacArthur (1909–1981) worked closely with her husband and was a director of the Foundation until her death.

One of the nation's ten largest foundations, the MacArthur Foundation's assets are around $4 billion and it distributes approximately $180 million in grants annually. It is organized into four divisions: Human and Community Development, focused on public education, juvenile justice, mental health policy and neighborhood development, with special emphasis upon Chicago and Florida; Global Security and Sustainability, with grants for conservation, international peace, population and reproductive health, with special initiatives in Russia, south Asia and sub-Saharan Africa; the General Program, which provides institutional grants to such organizations as National Public Radio; and the controversial MacArthur Fellows Program, which awards between twenty and forty five-year fellowships, or "genius grants," of around $500,000 to "talented persons" who "show exceptional merit and promise of continued and enhanced creative work." The Foundation has field offices in Florida, Mexico, Brazil, Nigeria, India, and Russia.

BIBLIOGRAPHY

MacArthur Foundation Web site. Home page at www.mac found.org.

The Work Ahead: New Guidelines for Grantmaking. John D. and Catherine T. MacArthur Foundation: Chicago, 1998.

Fred W. Beuttler

See also **Foundations, Endowed; Philanthropy.**

McCARRAN-WALTER ACT (1952). The act revised and consolidated all previous laws regarding immigration, naturalization, and nationality. It retained the national-origin system of the Immigration Act of 1924, which gave preference to immigrants from the United Kingdom, Ireland, and Germany. But it also removed race as a bar to immigration and naturalization, so that countries whose citizens were previously ineligible were assigned annual quotas of not fewer than 100 persons. In addition, it removed gender discrimination; gave preference to aliens with special skills; and provided for more rigorous security screening. The law aroused much opposition, mainly on the grounds that it discriminated in favor of northern and western European nations. It passed over President Harry S. Truman's veto and remained in effect until the Immigration and Nationality Act of 1965.

BIBLIOGRAPHY

Hing, Bill Ong. *Making and Remaking Asian America through Immigration Policy, 1850–1990.* Stanford, Calif.: Stanford University Press, 1993.

Ueda, Reed. *Postwar Immigrant America.* Boston: St. Martin's Press, 1994.

Charles S. Campbell Jr.
Andrew C. Rieser

See also **Immigration; Immigration Restriction; Naturalization.**

McCARTHYISM has been misnamed. Often identified with the bizarre antics of the Wisconsin senator Joseph McCarthy, the anticommunist political repression to which he gave a name had been in operation for years before he appeared at a Republican banquet in Wheeling, West Virginia, in February 1950. And it was to continue for several years after he self-destructed before the nation's television viewers at the Army-McCarthy hearings in the spring of 1954. There was nothing unique about McCarthy's charges of subversion in high places. Ever since the 1930s, conservative politicians and journalists had been attacking the New Deal administrations of Franklin Roosevelt and Harry Truman for being "soft on communism." But it took the Cold War to bring the originally partisan issue of anticommunism from the margins into the political mainstream.

Although McCarthyism came in many flavors, all its adherents agreed that it was essential to eliminate the danger of American communism. They differed, however, in their assessment of what that danger was. Right-wingers, hostile to everything on the left, attacked liberals

Senator Joseph McCarthy. The Wisconsin Republican's own actions in pursuit of communism in the early 1950s played only one part in the longer Cold War period of excessive zeal named for him. AP/WIDE WORLD PHOTOS

as well as communists, while moderates, who were willing to purge actual Communist Party members, tried to protect noncommunists from unfounded persecution. They did not always succeed. In the supercharged atmosphere of the early Cold War, the anticommunist crusade spun out of control, creating the most widespread and longest lasting episode of political repression in American history.

By the time that repression sputtered to an end in the late 1950s, thousands of men and women had lost their jobs, hundreds had been deported or sent to prison, and two—Ethel and Julius Rosenberg—had been executed. Most, but not all, of these people had once been in or near the American Communist Party. Because that party had been the most dynamic organization on the American left during the 1930s and early 1940s, thousands of activists gravitated into its orbit, attracted by its opposition to war and fascism and its support for the labor movement and racial equality. Most of these men and women were idealistic individuals who had not anticipated that their political activities would get them into trouble years later, when anticommunism came to dominate American politics.

What made McCarthyism so powerful was that so many different agencies and individuals took part in its operations. It functioned in accordance with a two-stage procedure. The supposed communists were first identified; then they were punished—usually by being fired. Most of the time, an official body like the Federal Bureau of Investigation or the House Un-American Activities Committee (HUAC) handled the first stage, while a public or private employer took care of the second. Because it was common to identify McCarthyism only with the initial identification stage of the procedure, many other-

wise moderate and even liberal Americans were able to collaborate with it. Claiming to deplore the excesses of the congressional investigations, they nonetheless applied sanctions against the people McCarthy and his allies had fingered.

They now realize they were wrong. The sanctions imposed on thousands of school teachers, longshoremen, film directors, union officials, civil servants, automobile workers, and housewives during the late 1940s and 1950s seriously violated those people's constitutional rights. But at the time, most Americans believed that communists were Soviet puppets who might subvert the government, steal official secrets, or sabotage defense plants whenever their Kremlin masters gave the word. Since some American communists had spied for the Soviet Union during World War II, that demonized stereotype, though exaggerated, was quite plausible. The highly publicized cases of Alger Hiss and the Rosenbergs reinforced the stereotype, convincing liberals and conservatives alike that communists were so dangerous they did not deserve the same rights as other Americans. That consensus made it possible for a wide range of government officials and private employers to punish people for their political views and affiliations.

Washington led the way. Not only did the federal government create and carry out some of the earliest anticommunist purges, but it also developed the ideological justification for them. The FBI and its militantly anticommunist director, J. Edgar Hoover, oversaw the process. Much of the information about communism that fed the loyalty-security investigations, criminal prosecutions, and congressional hearings that dominated the McCarthy era came from the FBI and reflected that organization's distorted view of the red menace. In addition, because Hoover and his men were so eager to eradicate American communism, they supplemented their normal operations with a wide range of unauthorized and even illegal activities, including wiretaps, break-ins, and leaks to right-wing journalists and politicians.

HUAC and the other congressional investigators were among the main recipients of those leaks. Not only did the committees identify specific individuals as communists, but they also helped disseminate the anticommunist scenarios that fueled the purges. Friendly witnesses told stories about their experiences in the Communist Party and identified its members, while unfriendly witnesses remained silent. Most of them would have been willing to talk about their own political activities, but they balked at describing those of others. However, because the Supreme Court did not protect people accused of communism during the late 1940s and early 1950s, witnesses who did not want to name names had to rely on the Fifth Amendment's privilege against self-incrimination and refuse to answer any question that might subject them to prosecution. Although they did not go to prison, most of these "Fifth Amendment" witnesses lost their jobs.

The most well-known unfriendly witnesses were the so-called Hollywood Ten, a group of screenwriters and directors who had defied HUAC on First Amendment grounds in 1947. Even before they went to prison, the Ten were on the street, early victims of an informal but highly effective blacklist that kept hundreds of men and women out of the entertainment industry during the 1950s. Similar blacklists emerged in other sectors of the economy, thus ensuring that most of the people who tangled publicly with an anticommunist investigation or were targeted by the FBI would lose their jobs. As the repression spread, unorthodox opinions or controversial activities could also invite dismissal.

The threat of unemployment was a powerful deterrent. People shrank from involvement in anything that could conceivably be linked to the left. Because of the stigma and secrecy that surrounds McCarthyism, it is hard to assess its impact. If nothing else, it narrowed the political spectrum, marginalizing if not silencing all critics of the status quo.

BIBLIOGRAPHY

Ceplair, Larry, and Steven Englund. *The Inquisition in Hollywood: Politics in the Film Community, 1930–1960.* Garden City, N.Y.: Anchor Press/Doubleday, 1979.

Oshinsky, David M. *A Conspiracy So Immense: The World of Joe McCarthy.* New York: Free Press, 1983.

Schrecker, Ellen. *Many Are the Crimes: McCarthyism in America.* Boston: Little, Brown, 1998.

Theoharis, Athan G., and John Stuart Cox. *The Boss: J. Edgar Hoover and the Great American Inquisition.* Philadelphia: Temple University Press, 1988.

Ellen Schrecker

See also **Anticommunism; Blacklisting; Communist Party, United States of America; Federal Bureau of Investigation; Hiss Case; House Committee on Un-American Activities; Rosenberg Case;** *and vol. 9:* **Censure of Senator Joseph McCarthy; Senator Joseph McCarthy: The History of George Catlett Marshall.**

McCLELLAN COMMITTEE HEARINGS.

The McClellan Committee opened Senate hearings on 26 February 1957 to investigate corruption, criminal infiltration, and illegal activities in the nation's labor unions. Chaired by Democrat John McClellan, the committee included John F. Kennedy and Barry Goldwater, along with Robert Kennedy as chief counsel. The committee's investigation focused on the International Brotherhood of Teamsters, Teamster president Dave Beck, and Beck's successor Jimmy Hoffa. In televised hearings watched by 1.2 million American households, the committee detailed the Teamsters' misuse of union funds and ties to labor racketeers and organized crime. While the inquiry led to the conviction of more than twenty individuals including Beck, it failed to convict Hoffa and in fact, strengthened his leadership. The investigation also led to the Teamsters' expulsion from the American Federation of Labor and Congress of Industrial Organizations in December 1957.

The McClellan Committee's efforts culminated in the Labor-Management Reporting and Disclosure Act of 1959, which established for the first time close regulation of unions by the federal government. The law created requirements for union elections and for annual financial reports to the Labor Department, banned convicted criminals from holding union office, and established union members' rights against coercive labor practices.

BIBLIOGRAPHY

Hearings before the Select Committee on Improper Activities in the Labor or Management Field. 85th Congress, 1st session, 1957; 85th Congress, 2nd session, 1958; and 86th Congress, 1st Session, 1959.

Kennedy, Robert F. *The Enemy Within.* New York: Harper and Row, 1960.

McClellan, John L. *Crime Without Punishment.* New York: Duell, Sloan and Pearce, 1962.

Petro, Sylvester. *Power Unlimited: The Corruption of Union Leadership: A Report on the McClellan Committee Hearings.* New York: Ronald Press, 1959.

James Tejani

McCORMICK REAPER.

The machine with which the name of Cyrus Hall McCormick has always been associated had many inventors, notably Obed Hussey, who patented his machine in 1833, a year before the first McCormick patent. Hussey's machine was the only practicable one on the market before 1840. It was the McCormick reaper, however, that invaded the MIDWEST, where the prairie farmer was ready for an efficient harvester that would make extensive WHEAT growing possible. In 1847 McCormick moved from the Shenandoah Valley in Virginia, where the first machine was built, to CHICAGO.

Perhaps, as his biographer contends, McCormick (or his father, Robert McCormick) did most effectively combine the parts essential to a mechanical grain cutter. Other improvements came in the 1850s and 1860s—the self-raker, which dispensed with the job of raking the cut grain off the platform, and then the binder, first using wire to bind the sheaves and later twine. The first self-raker was sold in 1854, seven years before McCormick produced such a machine. The first wire binder was put on the market in 1873, two years before the McCormick binder. Through effective organization the McCormick reaper came to dominate the field. The invention helped facilitate the rapid economic development of the rural Midwest, and the McCormick Harvesting Machine Company's massive factories in Chicago helped transform that city into an industrial giant.

BIBLIOGRAPHY

Hutchinson, William T. *Cyrus Hall McCormick.* New York: Da Capo Press, 1968.

McCormick, Cyrus. *The Century of the Reaper.* Boston: Houghton Mifflin, 1931.

Ozanne, Robert W. *A Century of Labor-Management Relations at McCormick and International Harvester.* Madison: University of Wisconsin Press, 1967.

Ernest S. Osgood / A. R.

See also **Agricultural Machinery.**

McCRAY V. UNITED STATES   (1904), 195 U.S. 27.

In this 6 to 3 decision, the U.S. Supreme Court sanctioned Congress's use of its taxing power for purposes of economic regulation. It upheld a prohibitive tax on artificially colored oleomargarine despite challenges based on the Article 1 tax clause, the Fifth Amendment's due process and takings clauses, and the Tenth Amendment. Justice Edward D. White held that Congress could tax for regulatory as well as for revenue purposes. Together with *Champion v. Ames* (1903), also known as the Lottery Case, *McCray* sustained what is sometimes called a "national police power." The court narrowed McCray's permissive reach in the Child Labor Tax Case (1922).

BIBLIOGRAPHY

Gordon, David. "McCray v. United States." In *Encyclopedia of the American Constitution.* Edited by Leonard W. Levy. Volume 3. New York: Macmillan, 1986.

William M. Wiecek

See also **Child Labor Tax Case; Taxation.**

McCULLOCH V. MARYLAND,   4 Wheaton 316

(1819), was decided by the Supreme Court of the United States on 6 March 1819. Congress had incorporated the second BANK OF THE UNITED STATES, a branch of which was established in Baltimore. The state of Maryland required all banks not chartered by the state to pay a tax on each issuance of bank notes. When James W. McCulloch, the cashier of the Baltimore branch of the bank, issued notes without paying the tax, Maryland brought suit. Two questions were at issue: first, whether Congress had power under the Constitution to establish a bank and, second, whether Maryland could impose a tax on this bank.

Chief Justice John Marshall wrote the opinion for a unanimous court upholding the power of Congress to charter a bank as a government agency and denying the power of a state to tax the agency. Marshall's discussion, broadly interpreting the powers of Congress, is still a classic statement of the IMPLIED POWERS of the federal government. Since the Constitution empowers the government to tax, borrow, and engage in war, Congress, by incorporating a bank, was creating the means to attain the goals of these powers. The chief justice phrased the basic point as follows: "Let the end be legitimate, let it be within the scope of the Constitution, and all means which are appropriate, which are plainly adapted to that end, which are not prohibited, but consist with the letter and spirit of the Constitution, are constitutional." Along with

this principle, Marshall expounded the notion of federal supremacy, noting that the national government, "though limited in its powers, is supreme within its sphere of action."

Having reaffirmed the principle of federal supremacy, Marshall responded to the second question, which was whether the state of Maryland could legally tax a branch of the U.S. bank located in that state. The power of the federal government to incorporate a bank had been established; the supremacy of the federal government in legal conflicts with state authority had likewise been set forth; and there was agreement that "the power to tax involves the power to destroy." It followed from all of this that an admittedly legal function of the federal government could not be subjected to possible destruction by an inferior government through taxation. The state tax was void.

BIBLIOGRAPHY

Gunther, Gerald, ed. *John Marshall's Defense of McCulloch v. Maryland.* Stanford, Calif.: Stanford University Press, 1969.

Kelly, Alfred H., Winfred A. Harbison, and Herman Belz. *The American Constitution: Its Origins and Development.* 7th ed. New York: Norton, 1991.

White, G. Edward. *The Marshall Court and Cultural Change, 1815–1835.* New York, 1988.

Paul C. Bartholomew / A. R.

See also **Banking;** *Cohens v. Virginia;* **Judiciary Act of 1789;** *Osborn v. Bank of the United States.*

McDONALD'S,   the world's leading fast food restau-

rant chain. In 1948, the brothers Maurice and Richard McDonald converted their San Bernardino, California, drive-in to a take-out restaurant serving mainly inexpensive hamburgers and French fries prepared assembly-line style. Ray A. Kroc (1902–1984) became the brothers' franchising agent in 1954, and expanded the company nationwide, opening his first McDonald's in Des Plaines, Illinois, the next year. Using business-format franchising, Kroc maintained strict corporate-level control of the McDonald's concept, service, and products. Kroc's chief financial officer, Harry Sonneborn, created a system of carefully choosing sites for new stores, then leasing them to franchisees, making rents an important source of corporate revenue and the company the world's largest owner of commercial real estate.

McDonald's mass-marketing strategy emphasized family-oriented and "all-American" themes, "quality, service, cleanliness, and value," and continual innovations, such as the Big Mac in 1968, a line of breakfast foods in the mid-1970s, child-oriented Happy Meals in 1979, and Chicken McNuggets in 1982. In 2001, McDonald's, with 30,000 stores and 395,000 employees serving 46 million people each day in 121 countries, achieved sales of

$14.9 billion—over 60 percent of that outside the United States—earning $1.6 billion in net income. The international expansion of McDonald's has made its logo, the golden arches, a leading symbol of globalization and American culture.

BIBLIOGRAPHY

Kroc, Ray, with Robert Anderson. *Grinding It Out: The Making of McDonald's.* Chicago: Regnery, 1977.

Love, John F. *McDonald's: Behind the Arches.* Rev. ed. New York: Bantam, 1995.

Mariani, John. *America Eats Out: An Illustrated History of Restaurants, Taverns, Coffee Shops, Speakeasies, and Other Establishments That Have Fed Us for 350 Years.* New York: Morrow, 1991.

Jeffrey T. Coster

See also **Food, Fast.**

McFADDEN BANKING ACT

McFADDEN BANKING ACT of 25 February 1927 permitted national banks to operate home-city branch offices in cities where state banks had similar privileges. Its provisions barring state bank members of the Federal Reserve System from establishing such branches, and stipulating that no nonmember banks might join the Federal Reserve System without relinquishing their out-of-town branches, tended to delimit the growth of out-of-town branches. The act also changed the restrictions on real estate loans of national banks and provided indeterminate charters for national and Federal Reserve banks.

BIBLIOGRAPHY

Degen, Robert A. *The American Monetary System.* Lexington, Mass.: Lexington Books, 1987.

Frederick A. Bradford
Christopher Wells

See also **Banking; Federal Reserve System.**

McGUFFEY'S READERS

McGUFFEY'S READERS formed a series of textbooks that molded American literary taste and morality, particularly in the Middle West, from 1836 until the early twentieth century. The total sales reached 122 million copies by 1920. Only the Bible and *Webster's Spelling Book* have enjoyed equal acceptance in the United States.

William Holmes McGuffey prepared the Eclectic Series of school readers at the request of a Cincinnati publisher interested in books adapted to the western schools. The books followed the conventional pattern of readers, teaching the principles of religion, morality, and patriotism through literary samples and pictures. They included considerable lore about nature, games and sports, manners, and attitudes toward God, relatives, teachers, companions, unfortunates, and animals. The lessons simplified complex problems so that, in the end, right always conquered and sin or wrong was always punished.

The earlier editions of McGuffey's Readers were intended for primary school students. Later readers, for older pupils, completed the series. These contained fewer pictures and focused more on British and American literature and skills in oral reading and presentation. In 1879 the books were completely remade, and in 1901 and 1920 the series was recopyrighted with slight changes. During this time, the McGuffey's Readers' popularity extended far beyond their intended frontier audience, and they eventually had a considerable impact on curricula throughout the country.

BIBLIOGRAPHY

McClellan, B. Edward. *Moral Education in America: Schools and the Shaping of Character from Colonial Times to the Present.* New York: Teachers College Press, 1999.

Westerhoff, John H. *McGuffey and His Readers: Piety, Morality, and Education in Nineteenth-Century America.* Nashville, Tenn.: Abingdon Press, 1978.

Harry R. Warfel / s. b.

See also **Curriculum; Education; Literature, Children's; Publishing Industry.**

McHENRY, FORT

McHENRY, FORT, built in 1799 on a small island in the Baltimore harbor at the time of the Quasi-War with France, was named for Secretary of War James McHenry. During the War of 1812 a British fleet in Chesapeake Bay bombarded the fort (13 September 1814). A spectator, Francis Scott Key, who watched through the night, was moved to write "The Star-Spangled Banner," which later became the national anthem of the United States. Subsequently, the fort was used as a storage depot and an army headquarters post.

BIBLIOGRAPHY

Coles, Harry L. *The War of 1812.* Chicago: University of Chicago Press, 1965.

Steiner, B. C., ed. *The Life and Correspondence of James McHenry.* Cleveland, Ohio: Burrows Bros., 1907.

Thomas Robson Hay / a. r.

See also **Baltimore; France, Quasi-War with; "Star-Spangled Banner"; War of 1812;** *and picture (overleaf).*

MACHINE GUNS

MACHINE GUNS. The first machine gun, the *mitrailleuse*, was designed in 1851 in Belgium, but the weapon is largely a product of American inventors. In 1862 Dr. Richard J. Gatling patented a gun with six barrels that rotated around a central axis by a hand crank. Conservative officers rejected Gatling's invention during the Civil War, but the army purchased 100 improved Gatling guns in 1866. The Gatling gun nevertheless occupied only a minor position as an auxiliary artillery weapon. Hiram S. Maxim, an American engineer, patented the first automatic machine gun in 1884. Maxim's gun—smaller,

Fort McHenry. A July 1954 aerial view of the historic fort, looking north. LIBRARY OF CONGRESS

lighter, and easier to operate than the Gatling—proved to be an excellent infantry weapon. In 1890 John M. Browning introduced the principle of gas operation, the last basic development in machine-gun design.

The Spanish-American War rekindled the army's interest in machine guns, but only in 1916 did the army authorize a regimental machine-gun company. By November 1918 each infantry regiment had a twelve-gun company, and each division included three machine-gun battalions—a total of 168 weapons. Entering World War I equipped with obsolescent machine guns, the army finished the war partially equipped with superb Brownings, which remained standard equipment during World War II and the Korean War. During World War II Browning guns also served as the principal armament for fighter aircraft and as antiaircraft weapons for tanks and other vehicles. During the mid-1950s American ordnance officers replaced the Browning .30 caliber guns with the new M60, which they distributed at the infantry platoon level. Through continued physical and doctrinal development, the machine gun gradually shifted from classification as an artillery weapon to the backbone of infantry firepower.

BIBLIOGRAPHY

Armstrong, David. *Bullets and Bureaucrats: The Machine Gun and the United States Army, 1861–1916.* Westport, Conn.: Greenwood Press, 1982.

Ellis, John. *The Social History of the Machine Gun.* New York: Pantheon Books, 1975; Baltimore: Johns Hopkins University Press, 1986.

David Armstrong/c. w.

See also **Artillery; Munitions; Rifle.**

MACHINE, POLITICAL.

To its critics a political machine is a corrupt urban regime ruled by a boss and his cronies. To its defenders, the machine steps in where city government has failed to provide essential services to its residents.

In New York during the 1860s, William Marcy Tweed built an organization of DEMOCRATIC PARTY functionaries and building contractors that became known as the "TWEED RING." The city had experienced extraordinary growth over the previous several decades, as Irish and German immigrants streamed into Manhattan. New York's infrastructure was totally unequipped to deal with this population surge. With his allies in the state legislature, Tweed engineered a new city charter that gave New York City control over its own budget. An advocate of labor unions and the Catholic Church, Tweed gained the support of immigrants, particularly the Irish—the largest foreign-born group in the city—although he was neither Catholic nor Irish. He leveraged the city heavily with municipal bonds and embarked on a massive, and very corrupt, campaign of public works to modernize the city. Al-

Richard Daley. A 1966 photograph of the powerful mayor of Chicago from 1955 to 1976. LIBRARY OF CONGRESS

though Tweed was arrested in 1871 and cast from power, machine politics continued in New York and developed elsewhere.

The Irish and the Democratic Party would dominate this form of politics in many cities, including New York, Chicago, and San Francisco, until reforms in both civil service and elections over the course of the twentieth century brought about its demise. The Irish were the first immigrant group to arrive in American cities in large enough numbers to challenge the leadership of the British-descended colonial elites. Irish politicians made a populist appeal to immigrants that came after them, offering cultural tolerance and a voice in government in return for political loyalty. The Democratic Party made much greater efforts to court urban immigrants than the Republicans, so it often became a vehicle to power for local bosses.

As immigration grew from the 1880s to the 1910s, cities became very ethnically diverse and newcomers dominated some of the largest. New York was three-quarters foreign-born by 1920. The Irish clung tenaciously to the power they had won, but stinginess in handing out favors to newly arrived ethnic groups gave reformers an edge against them. Progressives struggled to centralize urban government to eliminate the ward system that divided cit-

ies into fiefdoms controlled by vassals of a machine boss. They wanted experts to expand infrastructure rationally and honestly and hoped to eliminate vice.

During the New Deal in the 1930s, when the federal government vastly expanded the social services it offered to urbanites, opponents of machine politics hoped the patronage of bosses would be eclipsed. In some cases, however, city control over distributing federal money only further entrenched a boss.

The style of urban politics developed by Boss Tweed in New York during the 1860s, died with Mayor Richard Daley in Chicago in the 1970s. In 1970, only one-third of Chicago's population was first or second-generation immigrant. But its African American population was about thirty-three percent, and these Chicagoans demanded power. The politics of race would supersede the politics of ethnicity in the postindustrial city, and declining urban populations and wealth undermined the patronage basis for new machines.

BIBLIOGRAPHY

Allswang, John M. *Bosses, Machines, and Urban Voters.* Baltimore: Johns Hopkins University Press, 1986.

Adam Hodges

See also **Bosses and Bossism, Political; Corruption, Political; Irish-Americans; Political Cartoons; Tammany Hall.**

MACKEREL FISHERIES have been almost as important to New England's economic and social development as cod fisheries. The first public free school, opened in 1671, received aid directly from the profits of the Cape Cod mackerel fishery. Later, mackerel supplemented codfish as an important commodity in the profitable trade with the West Indies. Mackerel fishing lagged far behind that of cod, however, until after the United States concluded the Convention of 1818 with England. But even this instrument initially failed to provide facilities for the mackerel fisheries, which led Americans to send large mackerel fleets to the Gulf of Saint Lawrence.

In 1840, Gloucester surpassed Boston as the leading mackerel port. Gloucester fishers introduced such improvements as the clipper fishing schooner and the purse seine, a large fishing net that enabled mackerel vessels to fish profitably off the Atlantic coast. The fisheries reached their height in the decade from 1880 to 1890, after which they suffered an abrupt decline. With the settlement of the Pacific coast and ALASKA, the Pacific mackerel became a commercially important product, and the annual catch gradually surpassed that of the Atlantic mackerel. Later in the twentieth century, Japanese and Norwegian fishing vessels overtook the United States in mackerel fishing and exportation.

BIBLIOGRAPHY

Garland, Joseph E. *Down to the Sea: The Fishing Schooners of Gloucester.* Boston: David R. Godine, 2000.

Vickers, Daniel H. *Farmers and Fishermen: Two Centuries of Work in Essex County, Massachusetts, 1630–1850*. Chapel Hill: University of North Carolina Press, 1994.

F. Hardee Allen / s. b.

See also **Cod Fisheries; Colonial Commerce; Conservation; Fishing Bounties; Food and Cuisines; Industries, Colonial; Massachusetts.**

MACKINAC, STRAITS OF, AND MACKINAC ISLAND.

The waters of lakes Michigan and Superior unite with Lake Huron by the Straits of Mackinac and the Saint Marys River. Lying at the crossroads of the upper Great Lakes, in the middle of the straits and within striking distance of the outlet of the Saint Marys, is Mackinac Island, widely famed for its scenic beauty and as a summer resort. When waterways were the chief highways of travel, it was renowned as a strategic center of military and commercial operations.

Historically, the Indian name Michilimackinac, and its shortened form, Mackinac, applies not only to the straits and to the adjacent mainland, but also specifically to three distinct place sites: the island, Saint Ignace on the northern mainland, and Mackinaw City on the southern mainland. In modern times, the final syllables of both island and mainland names—*nac* and *naw*—are pronounced alike to rhyme with "paw," but originally the French pronounced *nac* as they spelled it, to rhyme with "pack."

Before the establishment of French rule in Mackinac in the 1660s, Ottawa, Chippewa, and Huron Indians inhabited the area. Almost immediately upon arrival, the French began to intermarry with Indian women, which resulted in the creation of a Métis society that combined both French and Indian ways into a new culture. Within a century, most babies born on Mackinac Island were of mixed heritage.

The French missionary, Claude Dablon, wintered in 1670 with the Huron, and, in 1673, Louis Jolliet launched his successful search for the Mississippi River from Mackinac. The first marine disaster on the Great Lakes occurred at Mackinac in 1679, when the *Griffon*, the ship of Robert Cavelier, Sieur de La Salle, vanished. British rule arrived in 1761, and during the American Revolution, the British moved their fort from Mackinaw City to Mackinac Island. The United States gained possession of Mackinac by the Treaty of Paris of 1783, and, in 1795, the United States and various local Indian tribes agreed to the Treaty of Greenville, which gave the United States possession of the area in exchange for annuities. During the War of 1812, however, the British forced the surrender of the garrison, and Fort Mackinac fell into British hands until 1815.

After the war and until the 1830s, Mackinac Island was the center of John Jacob Astor's fur trading business. The advent of the railroad and the decline of the fur trade,

Mackinac Island. A 1903 photograph by Frances Benjamin Johnston of two Indian women. LIBRARY OF CONGRESS

however, wrought the doom of Mackinac as a military and commercial center. Since then, it has been promoted as a summer resort. In 1895, most of Mackinac Island became a state park, and it has retained its turn-of-the-century setting by banning automobiles from the island.

Construction of the Mackinac Bridge, from Mackinaw City over the straits to a point near Saint Ignace, began in July 1954, and the bridge opened in November 1957. It connects the upper and lower peninsulas of Michigan. Residents also depend on airplanes to travel to the mainland. In addition, by mid-February, an ice bridge often forms over the straits, which temporarily allows islanders to walk or snowmobile to Saint Ignace. The year-round population of Mackinac Island in 2002 was about 550.

BIBLIOGRAPHY

Burley, David V., Gayel A. Horsfall, and John D. Brandon. *Structural Considerations of Métis Ethnicity: An Archaeological, Architectural, and Historical Study*. Vermillion: University of South Dakota Press, 1992.

Rubin, Lawrence A. *Bridging the Straits: The Story of Mighty Mac*. Detroit, Mich.: Wayne State University Press, 1985.

White, Richard. *The Middle Ground: Indians, Empires, and Republics in the Great Lakes Region, 1650–1815*. Cambridge, U.K.: Cambridge University Press, 1991.

Widder, Keith R. *Battle for the Soul: Métis Children Encounter Evangelical Protestants at Mackinaw Mission, 1823–1837.* East Lansing: Michigan State University Press, 1999

M. M. Quaife / A. E.

See also **Ferries; Fox-Wisconsin Waterway; Fur Companies; Fur Trade and Trapping; Indian Intermarriage; Indian Missions; Jolliet-Marquette Explorations; Michigan; Portages and Water Routes.**

McKINLEY ASSASSINATION. *See* **Assassinations, Presidential.**

McNAMARA CASE.

On 1 October 1910 an explosion set off by a dynamite bomb destroyed the Los Angeles Times building, killing twenty people. City officials and business leaders insisted that the bomb had been planted by labor activists upset by the virulently anti-union sentiments of the newspaper and its owner, Harrison Gray Otis. Union leaders heatedly rejected this accusation. The arrests of James McNamara and his brother John, secretary-treasurer of the International Association of Bridge and Structural Iron Workers, further infuriated trade unionists, who became convinced that the arrests represented an attempt to discredit organized labor by framing them for the crime. For a brief moment disparate elements of working-class America were drawn together in a common cause: to defend the McNamara brothers. Clarence Darrow, one of America's most prominent defense attorneys, was hired to head their legal team, and the case quickly attracted national attention. Shortly before their trial began in the fall of 1911, however, the brothers confessed. This shattering revelation was a serious setback for the labor movement in Los Angeles, in California, and in the nation at large. This case was also the precursor for the Indianapolis Dynamite Conspiracy trials in 1912, where thirty-nine other union officials were convicted. These trials further damaged the reputation of the American labor movement.

BIBLIOGRAPHY

Adams, Graham, Jr. *Age of Industrial Violence, 1910–15: The Activities and Findings of the United States Commission on Industrial Relations.* New York: Columbia University Press, 1966.

Cowan, Geoffrey. *The People v. Clarence Darrow: The Bribery Trial of America's Greatest Lawyer.* New York: Times Books, 1993.

Greenstein, Paul, Nigey Lennon, and Lionel Rolfe. *Bread and Hyacinths: The Rise and Fall of Utopian Los Angeles.* Los Angeles: California Classic Books, 1992.

Daniel J. Johnson

See also **Assassinations and Political Violence, Other.**

McNARY-HAUGEN BILL,

a plan to rehabilitate American agriculture by raising the domestic prices of farm products. By the end of 1920 the decline of foreign markets, the effects of the protective tariff, and the burdens of debt and taxation had created a serious agricultural depression. It grew steadily worse in the mid-1920s. The McNary-Haugen plan proposed that farm products for domestic sale be segregated from exports. The former would be sold at the higher domestic price (world price plus the tariff), and the latter at the world price. Farmers of each commodity would meet the difference between the higher domestic price and the world price by levying an "equalization fee" on themselves and distributing the proceeds. The legislation, before Congress from 1924 to 1928, received vigorous support from agricultural interests. In 1927 and in 1928 it passed both houses, only to meet two vetoes by President Calvin Coolidge.

BIBLIOGRAPHY

Harstad, Peter T., and Bonnie Lindemann. *Gilbert N. Haugen: Norwegian-American Farm Politician.* Iowa City: State Historical Society of Iowa, 1992.

Hoffman, Elizabeth, and Gary D. Libecap. "Institutional Choice and the Development of U.S. Agricultural Policies in the 1920s." *Journal of Economic History* 51 (1991).

Thomas S. Barclay / A. R.

See also **Agricultural Price Support; Agriculture; Export Debenture Plan; Wheat.**

MACON'S BILL NO. 2,

"An Act concerning the commercial intercourse between the United States and Great Britain and France and their dependencies, and for other purposes," was enacted by Congress on 1 May 1810, during the period preceding the War of 1812. The objective was to compel Great Britain and France to stop their restrictions against U.S. shipping. Designed as a substitute for the unsuccessful Nonintercourse Act, it prohibited British and French armed vessels from entering American waters and ports unless forced in by distress or to deliver dispatches. The measure reopened American trade to the entire world. The act stated that if either France or Britain removed its restrictions on American commerce by 3 March 1811 and the other failed to do so within three months, the president would revive the restrictions of nonintercourse against that other nation.

BIBLIOGRAPHY

Eagan, Clifford L. *Neither Peace nor War: Franco-American Relations, 1803–1812.* Baton Rouge: Louisiana State University Press, 1983.

George D. Harmon
Michael Wala

See also **France, Relations with; Great Britain, Relations with; Nonintercourse Act.**

MACY'S.

In 1858, Rowland Hussey Macy opened a fancy dry goods store in New York City that evolved into

Macy's. Christmas shoppers crowd the sidewalks outside the famous New York City department store. © CORBIS

one of the world's largest and most famous department stores. After running unsuccessful stores in Massachusetts and in California during the gold rush, Macy employed a low price strategy and aggressive advertising to develop a fast-growing business. In 1874, he rented space in the basement to Lazarus Straus, his supplier of china, glass, and silverware. The member of a rich European Jewish family, Straus came to the United States after the revolution of 1848. He moved to Georgia, became a peddler, and eventually operated a store, before moving to New York. After R. H. Macy died in 1877, his successor took Straus as a partner in 1888 and sold him the entire store in 1896.

The Straus family moved the store to Herald Square (34th Street and Broadway) in 1902. With the completion of its Seventh Avenue expansion in 1924, Macy's became the largest store in the world (2,200,200 square feet). The company built its reputation by advertising heavily and consistently selling merchandise for less than the competition. The company advertised "We sell goods cheaper than any house in the world," and "Save 6% at Macy's." The term "Macy's basement" became a metaphor for crowds and "Macy's window" a synonym for a public place to be seen.

The Strauses became one of the richest families in America. Family patriarch Isidor and his wife Ida died on the voyage of the Titanic. His brother Jesse became Ambassador to France.

Macy's started one of the first in-store employee training programs in 1914 and began the famous executive training program in 1919. Many successful executives received their training at Macy's. Movie stars Carol Channing and Burgess Meredith as well as Mayor Jimmie Walker also worked at Macy's. The world-famous Macy's New York Thanksgiving Day Parade began in 1924. The corporation expanded outside of New York, buying stores in Toledo, Ohio (1923), Atlanta, Georgia (1925), Newark, New Jersey (1929), San Francisco (1945), and Kansas City, Missouri (1949).

In the 1980s the executives of Macy's purchased the company in a leveraged buyout. When sales did not meet estimates in 1992, the company incurred a large debt, forcing it into bankruptcy. Two years later, Federated Department Stores acquired control of Macy's and consolidated other Federated stores into new Macy's East and Macy's West divisions.

BIBLIOGRAPHY

Harris, Leon. *Merchant Princes: An Intimate History of Jewish Families Who Built Great Department Stores.* New York: Harper & Row, 1979.

Hower, Ralph M. *History of Macy's New York, 1858–1919: Chapters in the Evolution of the Department Store.* Cambridge, Mass.: Harvard University Press, 1943.

International Directory of Company Histories. Vols. 5, 30. Chicago: St. James Press, 1988, 1999.

Jerry Brisco

See also **Department Stores; Leveraged Buyouts; Retailing Industry.**

MADISON SQUARE GARDEN. William Vanderbilt opened New York's Madison Square Garden in 1879 at Twenty-Sixth Street and Madison Avenue. The structure was a former railroad shed, first employed for mass entertainment in 1874 by P. T. Barnum. Vanderbilt replaced it in 1890 with Stanford White's $3 million arena, the city's second tallest building. It became the preeminent American indoor sports facility, featuring bicycle races, long distance footraces, boxing matches, an annual horse show, and the Westminster Kennel Club dog show, and was the site of the seventeen-day Democratic national

Madison Square Garden. The exterior of the third incarnation of New York City's famous sports and entertainment facility, located at Fiftieth Street and Eighth Avenue from 1925 until the next one was built farther downtown in 1968. AP/WIDE WORLD PHOTOS

convention in 1924. However, the second Garden was not profitable until Tex Rickard leased the building in 1920. A great promoter, he made the edifice the mecca for prizefighting, six-day bicycle races, and the circus. In 1925, a new $6 million Garden was built at Fiftieth Street and Eighth Avenue and became an immediate success. Profitable new attractions included professional hockey, the Ice Show, and college basketball doubleheaders. After World War II, the building was busier than ever with the addition of the Knickerbockers professional basketball team. However, the 1951 basketball scandal curtailed intercollegiate basketball, and boxing began to decline at the end of the 1950s because of antitrust violations, underworld influence, and television overexposure. A new, more modern $116 million facility was built in 1968 atop Pennsylvania Station between Thirty-First and Thirty-Third Streets on Seventh Avenue. It has been the scene of three Stanley Cup hockey finals, four National Basketball Association championship series, and momentous boxing events such as the 1971 match between Muhammad Ali and Joe Frazier.

BIBLIOGRAPHY

Durso, Joseph. *Madison Square Garden: 100 Years of History.* New York: Simon and Schuster, 1979.

Steven A. Riess

MAFIA. *See* **Crime, Organized.**

MAFIA INCIDENT. On 15 October 1890, during a police crackdown on the local Sicilian Mafia, New Orleans chief of police David C. Hennessey was assassinated. Nineteen men were indicted. The evidence marshaled against the first nine defendants was overwhelming, yet no one was convicted. The acquittals were denounced the following morning at a mass meeting of more than six thousand people. The mob marched on downtown New Orleans and lynched eleven of the accused. The Italian government vehemently protested the lynchings. In April 1892 President Benjamin Harrison, seeking an end to the brewing diplomatic crisis with Italy, offered a $25,000 indemnity to the families of the victims and expressed his regrets for the incident. Full diplomatic relations were restored.

BIBLIOGRAPHY

Coxe, John E. "The New Orleans Mafia Incident." *Louisiana Historical Quarterly* 20 (October 1937).

Higham, John. *Strangers in the Land: Patterns of American Nativism, 1860–1925.* New Brunswick, N.J.: Rutgers University Press, 1988.

Pierce Butler / A. R.

See also **Crime, Organized; Nativism.**

MAGAZINES were the dominant mass medium in the United States from the late nineteenth to the mid-twentieth century. They helped create a national culture of shared references, information, perspectives, and literature, and as the premier venue for advertising nationally available products, created a national material culture as well. In 2000, despite the rise of competing media, more than 17,000 consumer magazines were published in the United States. The 758 of those titles tracked by the Audit Bureau of Circulations, an industry group, reported over 378 million in aggregate circulation that year.

Barely differentiated from newspapers in the eighteenth century, magazines soon functioned as more durable anthology and miscellany, defining national literature and national identity. Initially, ties to England were strong. The term "magazine" itself originates with British monthlies, beginning in 1731 with the *Gentleman's Magazine*, adopting the word's sense of storehouse. Names of early-nineteenth-century American magazines continued to suggest a collection of miscellaneous but precious contents, with such words as "museum," "repository," "casket," or "cabinet" in their titles. Eighteenth-century American magazines were largely reprints from books, newspapers, and other magazines, often from England, though some editors sought out original contributions. In a country that lacked a class of professional writers, these were often hard to obtain. Nineteenth-century magazines likewise maintained strong ties to England's literary production. As they reprinted British literature—pirated or paid for—they did less than they might have to foster American literature, until changes in copyright law made piracy a less attractive alternative to paying American authors. While periodical circulations remained small, however, reprints and exchanges among newspapers and magazines effectively distributed news, literature, and information nationwide.

Individual eighteenth-century magazines circulated locally to only a few hundred and were short lived; the publishing historian Frank Luther Mott calls it unlikely that the aggregate circulation of all the magazines for any given period in the eighteenth century was ever more than five thousand. Many were church affiliated, and they included a children's magazine, a music magazine, and women's magazines. Like newspaper producers of the time, magazine publishers accepted fuel and produce as payment for subscriptions, and continued to accept such payment for advertising into the late nineteenth century.

Nineteenth Century

Successful women's magazines, such as *Godey's Lady's Book* (1830–1898), had large readerships, with *Godey's* circulation reaching 150,000 in the 1860s. Men and children read women's magazines too; despite its name, sailors exchanged bundles of *Godey's* when their ships met at sea and created scrimshaw based on its fashion illustrations, while wounded soldiers later requested *Ladies' Home Journal* and other women's magazines. The label "ladies" reassured readers that the work would be concerned with matters of the home, and would not be improper or controversial. *Godey's* published a combination of fiction (usually with a moral), fashion illustration, sermons, and household advice, all in a friendly tone, and ignored the Civil War. Other nineteenth century women's magazines of this type included, at mid-century, the *Home Journal, Arthur's Home Magazine*, and, by the end of the century, *Ladies' Home Journal, Women's Home Companion, Good Housekeeping, Delineator,* and fashion magazines such as *Harper's Bazaar.*

Although women's magazines such as *Frank Leslie's Chimney Corner* frequently offered support for elements of women's equality, and other magazines did so more sporadically, suffragist and feminist political magazines were a smaller separate category, lacking the advertising support that came to dominate the women's magazines. But numerous suffrage publications appeared throughout the country: Amelia Bloomer's *The Lily* and Susan B. Anthony and Elizabeth Cady Stanton's *Revolution* in Seneca Falls, New York; Lucy Stone's *Woman's Journal* in Boston; and Colorado's *Queen Bee.* The *Lowell Offering*, a literary magazine edited and published by the female workers in the Lowell cotton mills, was another type of women's magazine.

Book and magazine publishing were closely entwined. *Appleton's, Atlantic Monthly, Scribner's, Harper's Monthly, Harper's Weekly,* and others were owned by book publishers, which used them to promote their books and authors and fostered a sense of an American literary center. Book reviews in magazines helped to promote individual books and to shape public conversation about books and reading.

Gift books or annuals, widely popular in the middle of the nineteenth century, served some of the same functions as magazines. The same people, such as Nathaniel P. Willis, could be found wearing both magazine and gift book editorial hats. Often issued specifically as Christmas or New Year gifts, they nurtured the vogue for holiday-related stories. The monthlies branched out to make not only Christmas but also Thanksgiving and Independence Day stories a reliable topic for magazine writers.

Much U.S. literature, especially essays, first appeared in magazines, with book reprints following. Through midcentury, book publishers worried that magazine publication of a work competed with book sales. Low postal rates for periodicals and high ones for books helped the magazine industry, and also attracted publishers who pirated British and European authors to sell their works cheaply. The 1830s and 1840s saw an explosion of fiction made available in the form of extraordinarily cheap weekly newspapers in a gigantic format, such as *Brother Jonathan*, with fiction-filled pages sometimes over four feet long—a format that mimetically enhanced their claims to hold the "whole unbounded universe," as *The New World*, another elephantine paper, put it. Blurring boundaries between book, magazine, and newspaper, such weeklies issued "extra" editions containing entire pirated novels by popular authors such as Dickens, sold for eighteen or twenty cents, and directly competed with book publishers. A post office decision labeling them pamphlets rather than newspapers, and therefore requiring higher postage, helped kill them off, but they had reached audiences of up to 60,000. By the late nineteenth century, however, publishers found that magazine serialization had the effect of publicizing a work and building book sales. These papers, and several dollar-a-year magazines, established that a low-priced periodical could be profitable. While eighteenth-century magazines cost the equivalent of two to three days of labor in wages for a year's subscription, by the mid-nineteenth century prices were relatively lower, at between one and five dollars per year.

Although the women's magazines and the largest of the general magazines at midcentury, such as *Graham's* and *Harper's*, avoided or ignored the major political controversies of the day, other general magazines did espouse positions, with *Atlantic Monthly*, for example, known for its abolitionist sympathies. Numerous noncommercial magazines sponsored by organizations and societies took stands. Antislavery magazines blossomed from the 1820s on, while southern magazines such as the *Southern Quarterly Review* of Charleston championed the proslavery position. Others promoted such causes as women's rights, temperance, and later socialism, anarchism, and birth control. Many late-eighteenth-century magazines were church affiliated, and church-related magazines continued into the nineteenth century, with many children's magazines produced by denominations or connected to the Sunday school movement. Weekly magazines such as *Frank Leslie's, The Independent,* and *Harper's Weekly* provided readers with battlefield news and pictures during the Civil War.

Specific racial and ethnic communities produced magazines as well. The *Literary Voyager, or Muzzeniegun* (1826–1827), was the first of a small number of Native American magazines that made brief appearances. The category grew enormously with the rise of the American Indian Movement in the 1960s. Spanish-speaking communities of Texas, California, and the Southwest along with immigrant communities produced extensive publications in languages other than English, though most of these were daily or weekly newspapers rather than magazines. An estimated 3,444 publications in languages other than English were launched between 1884 and 1920, with a combined circulation of 6 million in 1910. Hundreds of magazines lived brief lives and folded, succumbing to the problems of finding a readership and an economical means of distribution; those without sufficient capital were particularly vulnerable.

Late Nineteenth Century

The so-called "class monthlies" of the 1880s and 1890s—*Harper's, Atlantic Monthly, Century,* and *Scribner's*—were read by the well off and more educated people and helped to create or consolidate the reputations of such writers as Henry James, Constance Fenimore Woolson, Mark Twain, Sarah Orne Jewett, and William Dean Howells (also editor of *Atlantic Monthly*, 1871–1881). The role these monthlies played in shaping literary opinion and their connection to other publishing enterprises has led literary scholars and historians to consider these four the most prominent and important magazines of the late nineteenth century. They were not, however, the most widely read.

The appearance of cheap, mass circulation magazines in the United States has often been linked to the "magazine revolution" of the early 1890s, when three monthlies—*Munsey's, Cosmopolitan*, and *McClures*—dropped their price to ten cents, shifted the basis of their enterprise from the sale of the magazine to the sale of advertising, and began to achieve circulations in the hundreds of thousands. But this development was more gradual than revolutionary. Ten-cent and even five-cent monthlies that depended on advertising for their revenues already existed. Known as mail-order monthlies, they advertised goods available by mail, assuming their readers would be out of reach of stores. These newspaper-sized magazines were far more widely distributed than the class monthlies, with circulations above half a million, though such figures were notoriously based on continuing to send papers to nonpaying subscribers. Many, such as the *People's Literary Companion, Ladies' World*, and *Youth's Companion*, were addressed to a largely rural, poorer readership; others, such as *Ladies' Home Journal*, saw their readers as genteel town people, if not the upper-class elite that *Harper's, Atlantic Monthly*, and *Century* drew at thirty-five cents a copy (four dollars a year), or *Scribner's* at twenty-five cents a copy. Although the three big new ten-cent monthlies of the 1890s looked like heavily illustrated versions of the elite magazines, resembling them in size, and in sequestering ads to the front and back of the magazines, their content addressed a new white-collar audience of professionals and managers. Their version of "progressivism" embraced and promoted new developments in technology and consumer goods. In achieving such large circulations, they necessarily reached readers who had not previously subscribed to magazines. The new magazines also followed the elite magazines in their sale and promotion of single issues of the magazine, rather than inviting readers to join a community of readers as the mail-order monthlies did through their emphasis on subscriptions and subscription clubs.

The new readership cultivated by the ten-cent magazines, if only because of its size, was a less homogeneous group than the mainly northeastern elite readers of the quality class publications. These readers sought magazines about their own regions as well, and supported new regional magazines: San Francisco's *Overland Monthly* beginning in 1868, *Honolulu* in 1888, *Brooklyn Life* in 1890, *Delestry's Western Magazine* of Minnesota in 1897, and *Sunset Magazine* in 1898. Regional and city-based magazines proliferated in the 1960s and 1970s.

While promising something new every month, each magazine provided a familiar, reliable set of experiences—columns to be followed, stories and poems catering to a particular taste or range of tastes, features and service articles for a defined audience. Editors of the new magazines of the 1890s actively solicited work, rather than waiting in the more genteel and leisured fashion for suitable writing to drop in over the transom. *McClures*, for example, commissioned muckraking articles. And the magazines both defined and created communities of readers.

The most crucial distinction between the new ten-cent magazine and the older elite magazines was the reliance of the new magazines on advertising rather than sales, and soon the pinning of advertising rates to circulation figures. Publishers had shifted from directly selling magazines to readers to selling their readership to advertisers. Nationally circulated magazines were attractive to the new burgeoning advertising trade as the best way to reach readers, now thought of principally as consumers. The editor's new role was to attract and keep readers interested in the magazine's pages, including its advertising pages. As Edward Bok, editor of *Ladies' Home Journal*, explained in 1921, "The making of a modern magazine is a business proposition; the editor is there to make it pay."

The magazines themselves advertised in order to draw more readers. Authors became celebrities and their names became promotional tools, advertised and listed on magazine front covers and posters, instead of hidden by the anonymity and pseudonymity common early in the century.

Advertising did not help all magazines thrive, however. Magazines addressed to specific communities such as African Americans were financially precarious, since they competed with the far-better-capitalized mass-circulation magazines for both readers and advertisers, while national advertisers largely refused to see African Americans as consumers. Newspapers such as the *Chicago Defender* and *Pittsburgh Courier* long served as the national publications for African Americans, while the longest lived African American magazines were those sponsored by organizations: *Crisis* (1910–1996) issued by the National Association for the Advancement of Colored People (NAACP) and edited by W. E. B. Du Bois from 1910 to 1934, and the Urban League's *Opportunity*, begun in 1923. The first African American commercially based magazine to achieve substantial success was *Ebony*, founded in 1945, which persuaded advertisers that African Americans could be lucrative targets.

Twentieth Century

From the 1920s through the 1960s, surveys found that about 60 percent of Americans regularly read a magazine—generally more than read books, and fewer than read newspapers. Magazine circulations reached millions. Mass-market magazines of the early to mid-twentieth century were the place for authors to establish themselves and to make money. Mainstream magazines such as *Sat-*

urday Evening Post, Life, and Look were for decades the most attractive medium for advertisers wishing to reach Americans all over the country. (An exception to the connection between mass circulation and advertising was the immensely popular conservative Reader's Digest, which began in 1922 by reprinting articles from other publications, and refused advertising, in order to keep its high circulation figures secret from the sources it paid for reprints.) The mass-circulation news magazines, born in the 1920s and 1930s, influenced political policy. Henry Luce's powerful Time, Life, and Fortune empire tested the potential of multimedia with its newsreels. But radio and then television proved far more effective media than magazines for reaching the largest possible audience. Since the 1960s, many mass magazines folded, while others retooled to address more specialized demographic groups than broadcast television could reach. At the same time, magazines arose that catered to the new medium: TV Guide continued to have one of the highest magazine circulation rates in the twenty-first century.

In contrast to the general mass-circulation magazines, eventually known as the "slicks," because of the photograph-enhancing, shiny paper on which they were printed, "little" or literary magazines appeared in the early twentieth century and defined themselves by their difference from the commercial magazines, publishing fiction, poetry, and essays that would not be acceptable in the slicks. Little magazines were often produced as labors of love to house new or experimental writing. Literary monthlies of the 1910s and 1920s, such as Little Review and Poetry, defined themselves as upholding high art against commercial publishing, offering access to a purer art, and maintaining a personal editorial vision against the increasingly bland fare of the commercial magazines.

Such magazines are widely credited with nurturing the principal figures of modernism. Sherwood Anderson, H. D., T. S. Eliot, Ernest Hemingway, Marianne Moore, Ezra Pound, and others first appeared or had their first significant publication in such magazines as Little Review, Poetry, Lyric, Glebe, and Dial of the 1920s, usually without pay. Some faced censorship. The Little Review's editor Margaret Anderson serialized James Joyce's novel Ulysses for three years, though the post office seized and burned four of the issues, charging obscenity. W. H. Auden celebrated the feeling that the small press was an embattled force, in this case a bulwark against both utilitarianism and politics he saw contaminating intellectual life in the postwar university: "Our intellectual marines, / Landing in little magazines / Capture a trend" ("Under Which Lyre," 1946).

But noncommercial periodicals often did have a political focus. Progressive magazines such as The New Masses (1926) became increasingly prominent in the 1930s, and reappeared in greater numbers in the 1960s. Magazines such as Freedomways emerged from the civil rights era, along with black arts movement periodicals such as Umbra (1962) and Nommo (1969), whose antecedents also in-

cluded the independent black arts periodical Fire!! (1926). New feminist policy and criticism-oriented periodicals such as Chrysalis, Heresies, and Quest appeared in the 1970s, along with an outpouring of feminist literary magazines such as Aphra, Conditions, Common Lives, Lesbian Lives, and Sinister Wisdom. The commercial magazine Ms. achieved substantial circulation both with and without advertising.

A few small press magazines had sponsors. By the 1940s, many literary magazines were situated in and subsidized by universities. The Sewanee Review, for example, was reinvigorated in the 1940s by the University of the South as a way of raising the school's prestige and attracting prominent writers and scholars. On the other end of the economic spectrum, Beat poets of the 1950s and poets allied with or following them created a rich lode of low-budget publications, in what was known as the Mimeograph Revolution.

Magazines such as The New Yorker (begun 1925), Smart Set: A Magazine of Cleverness (1900–1930), Vanity Fair in its 1913–1936 version, and the influential American Mercury, begun by H. L. Mencken and George Jean Nathan (1924–1950) defined a niche more sophisticated than the slicks but less esoteric than the small press magazines. Another alternative to the slicks were the pulps, printed on rough wood-pulp paper, which began in the 1890s and flourished most dramatically between the wars, with an estimated two hundred titles in circulation at any point during that period. They picked up characters, writers, and readers from the older dime novels. Librarians refused to order these garishly covered magazines, which primarily appealed to readers who were young, immigrant, poor, uneducated, and working class. Early pulps such as Frank Munsey's Argosy published general fiction, but specialized titles soon concentrated on romance, boxing, war, detective, western, aviation, science fiction, fantasy, and "spicy" stories. The romance titles targeted women readers and the adventure magazines went after men, but readers crossed over, as they had for Godey's Lady's Book. Authors, too, crossed over, with writers such as Dashiell Hammett and Raymond Chandler writing for both pulps and slicks. Pulps ultimately lost their readership to television, paperbacks, and comic books, and most were gone by the mid-1950s. With the exception of the small press magazines, fiction in general was a rarity in most magazines by the twenty-first century.

By the early twenty-first century, new magazines were aimed at increasingly specialized markets, nearly always niches organized around specific consumer interests or an audience defined by demographics that magazine founders expected to attract advertisers. For example, magazines for brides, an attractive readership for advertisers selling household goods as well as wedding and honeymoon accoutrements, include not only Bride's magazine (begun 1935), but the more specialized Destination Weddings and Honeymoons, Latina Bride, Christian Bride, Houston Bride, Manhattan Bride, and Mother of the Bride, all begun in 2000. Other advertiser-generated categories included airlines' in-flight magazines or new niche market magazines, such as *American Windsurfer, Dub: Automotive Lifestyles Magazine*, and Mary Beth's *Teddy Bears and More*. New forms of periodical publishing created new fusions of advertising and editorial matter, seen in periodicals such as *Simple Living, Flair, Unlimited*, and *CML: Camel Quarterly* produced by magazine publishing conglomerates on special order for cigarette companies.

The anticommercial opposition likewise became more specialized, with the proliferation of zines, homemade photocopied magazines often with tiny circulations on topics like working at temporary jobs, 1970s nostalgia, grrrlpower, and neopaganism. Many zines and other magazines, such as *Salon*, abandoned the printed page to appear solely on the World Wide Web.

The Internet

The Internet promised to change the face of magazines, and briefly seemed likely to eliminate them altogether. As commercial (rather than educational or nonprofit) concerns moved onto the Web, they rapidly discovered the potential to support their publications with advertising, just as magazines do, and to target the reader/consumer more precisely than magazines aimed at even the most specialized of niches. Amazon.com, for example, in this sense functioned as a magazine: offering reading matter by selling services at a loss, and aiming to make up the shortfall by selling advertising.

The very low cost of producing an attractive Web site, in contrast to the costs of paper, printing, and binding incurred even with desktop publishing, drew many independent "content producers" to the Web, disrupting established earmarks of professionalism that told magazine readers whether they were holding a well-financed professional production or an amateur periodical issued from a basement. Such contrasts reemerged as media conglomerates moved onto the Web, but then distinctions between a Web site connected to a television station and one for a magazine blurred, just as their ownerships did, resulting in such combinations as AOL (America Online) Time Warner magazines.

Most commercial print magazines developed Web sites, typically promoting the current issue, offering a sample of its contents, special Web-only content, and sometimes offering options for interacting with the magazine (and its advertisers) such as chat rooms, e-mail discussion lists, and shopping links. Trade magazines for specialized business niches often displayed the table of contents, but offered full access only to subscribers, or sold access to specific articles by the piece. Long-established print magazines capitalized on their past publications through the Web as well, with the *New Yorker*, for example, republishing old covers and old articles of general interest on its Web site's "From the Archive" section and selling its historic stock of cartoons—on T-shirts, in frames, or for use in presentations.

Other sites, more closely resembling traditional magazines, with departments and columns, appeared entirely on the Web. Some Web publications like *Salon*, originally offered without a fee, continued offering a selection of free matter while creating a "premium" site for a fee as well, offered with exclusive content, fewer ads, and "galleries of erotic art." Such sites cultivated online discussion groups based on common interests of readers, which, once established, might shift to charging a fee.

The World Wide Web also emerged as an extraordinary resource for research using magazines, as educational groups have scanned lengthy runs of defunct magazines in the public domain (generally into the 1920s) and made searchable archives available for free. Owners of active magazines scanned their archives and, often after an initial period of free access, sold access to them.

BIBLIOGRAPHY

Anderson, Elliott, and Mary Kinzie, eds. *The Little Magazine in America: A Modern Documentary History.* Yonkers, N.Y.: Pushcart Press, 1978.

Chielens, Edward E., ed. *American Literary Magazines: The Eighteenth and Nineteenth Centuries.* New York: Greenwood Press, 1986.

———. *American Literary Magazines: The Twentieth Century.* New York: Greenwood Press, 1992.

Duncombe, Stephen. *Notes from Underground: Zines and the Politics of Alternative Culture.* London: Verso, 1997.

Friedman, R. Seth. *The Factsheet Five Zine Reader: The Best Writing from the Underground World of Zines.* New York: Three Rivers Press, 1997.

Garvey, Ellen Gruber. *The Adman in the Parlor: Magazines and the Gendering of Consumer Culture, 1880s to 1910s.* New York: Oxford University Press, 1996.

Hoffman, Fredrick John, Charles A. Allen, and Carolyn Farquhar Ulrich. *The Little Magazine.* Princeton, N.J.: Princeton University Press, 1946.

Kaestle, Carl F., et al. *Literacy in the United States: Readers and Reading since 1880.* New Haven, Conn.: Yale University Press, 1991.

Mott, Frank Luther. *A History of American Magazines.* 5 vols. Cambridge, Mass.: Belknap Press, 1938–1966.

Ohmann, Richard M. *Selling Culture: Magazines, Markets, and Class at the Turn of the Century.* New York: Verso, 1996.

Oxbridge Communications. *National Directory of Magazines.* New York: Oxbridge Communications, 2001.

Peterson, Theodore. *Magazines in the Twentieth Century.* Urbana: University of Illinois Press, 1964.

Smith, Erin A. *Hard-Boiled: Working-Class Readers and Pulp Magazines.* Philadelphia: Temple University Press, 2000.

Tebbel, John, and Mary Ellen Zuckerman. *The Magazine in America, 1741–1990.* New York: Oxford University Press, 1991.

Wilson, Christopher P. *The Labor of Words: Literary Professionalism in the Progressive Era.* Athens: University of Georgia Press, 1985.

Ellen Gruber Garvey

See also Advertising; *Atlantic, The; Godey's Lady's Book;* Magazines, Women's; Magazines and Newspapers, African American; *Nation, The; New Yorker, The; Reader's Digest; Saturday Evening Post; Time.*

MAGAZINES, MEN'S.

The definition of a men's magazine is capacious and variable. In the nineteenth century, it was sometimes assumed that anything that was not specifically a women's or "family" periodical, but rather encompassed serious reflection on the world, was primarily a men's magazine with women as only incidental readers. Particular subject matter, such as sports, hunting, adventure, and, for many years, sex, business, and automobiles, have been classified as of specifically male interest. Magazines such as *Scientific American* or *Popular Mechanics* have similarly often been classified in this way. The category arguably includes the labor press of male-only or largely male occupations, the military and clergy, and the magazines of men's social and fraternal organizations like the Masons, Woodmen, and Knights of Pythias.

Since many subscription magazines were likely to arrive in the name of the man of the house, and men were more likely to be newsstand customers, other magazines also may have appeared to be primarily for a male audience, though actually reaching a more evenly distributed readership. The publisher Cyrus Curtis, for example, conceived of the *Ladies' Home Journal* and the SATURDAY EVENING POST as a gendered pair, with the *Post* addressed to the businessman who anticipated success, and full of such features as the serial begun in 1901, "Letters of a Self-Made Merchant to His Son." Similarly, *Vanity Fair* (1913–1936, revived in 1983) had, according to one magazine historian, a masculine focus, pitched to a male elite, although it certainly had women readers, and the African American magazine *Ebony* (1945–) promoted a specifically African American version of success to men.

Sports and Men's Bodies

The *National Police Gazette* (1845–1932) exemplified the cultivation of a specifically male magazine audience. At its start it was filled with sensational crime stories and exposés of the police. After the Civil War, the focus shifted to sex scandals and sex crimes, all heavily illustrated, with advertising to match. It later focused on the theater, with numerous pictures of actresses. It also covered sports, including prizefighting and baseball. More specialized magazines published news of sports, minus the scandals and pictures of actresses. Baseball magazines got their start in 1867 with *The Ballplayers' Chronicle*. A magazine with broader interests, *Sporting Life*, began sixteen years later and lasted until 1926.

In the mid-twentieth century, as a generation of American men returned from military service, the postwar era brought great growth in hunting, fishing, mechanical, and handyman magazines. *Field and Stream* began in 1896 but was revitalized in this period; *Sports*

Illustrated, part of Henry Luce's magazine empire with *Time, Life,* and *Fortune,* began in 1954.

Magazines on sports and athletics divided between covering the reader's favorite teams and addressing the development of the reader's own body. *Physical Culture: Weakness a Crime* (1899–1947), advocated bodybuilding and avoidance of tobacco, alcohol, and meat. Unlike men's physique magazines, it anxiously insisted that the male bodies on display were not meant to appeal sexually to other men. A late-twentieth century variation on magazines focused on the development of the reader's own body were magazines like *Men's Health* (begun in 1988). These mirrored women's magazines in campaigns to cultivate insecurity about the reader's body, though the solutions offered were most likely to be abdominal exercises rather than the wider variety of cosmetics and diets found in the women's magazines.

General Interest Magazines

General interest men's magazines developed alongside the sense that men would spend money on leisure and appearance. *Esquire* began in 1933 and became an immediate hit despite its high price, even in the depths of the Great Depression. It published well-known authors like Ernest Hemingway, Dashiell Hammett, Thomas Mann, F. Scott Fitzgerald, Thomas Wolfe, and Ezra Pound, some of them picked up at bargain rates from other magazines' piles of materials they found too daring to publish.

Pulp magazines for men, specializing in action, adventure, and he-man heroes, were popular among workingclass men from the 1920s through the 1940s. Absorbing and continuing such titles as *Railroad Man's Magazine,* Frank Munsey's *Argosy* was the first, developing in various incarnations from 1896 on, and rapidly followed by *The Shadow, Dime Detective, Western Story,* and *Detective Fiction Weekly. Black Mask* was published by H. L. Mencken and George Jean Nathan, better known for their work on *The Smart Set.* Pulp magazines had little reliance on advertising, but instead depended on cheap production to keep prices down. They published writers like Erle Stanley Gardner, Raymond Chandler, Hammett, and scores of others now forgotten. Rising post–World War II production costs and competition from paperback books, comic books, and later television brought the pulp magazine era to a close.

Some magazines descended from the pulps found new popularity, however. *True: The Man's Magazine* (1937–1976) was based on the assumption that men preferred ostensibly factual material to fiction; it became the first men's magazine with over one million in circulation. *Argosy* took a different tack in its development from a pulp to a magazine with a circulation over one million: it became an all-story magazine in 1943, and later encompassed true adventure, hunting, fishing, crime, and science.

Picking up from *Esquire's* emphasis on fashion and good (bachelor) living, men's fashion magazines like *GQ,* originally *Gentleman's Quarterly,* infused the clothing con cerns of women's fashion magazines with an air of after-shave, and thus tapped new advertising markets. Other slick magazines with an advertising base eager to reach men's spending on leisure emerged: *Details* (1982–) and *Maxim* (1997–) were written in a wiseguy style infused with casual misogyny. Some, like *Cigar Aficionado* (begun 1992), pushed masculine consumption even more directly.

Skin Magazines

Late-nineteenth-century magazines like *Broadway Magazine* (1898–1912, with some title changes) featured bathing beauties and burlesque stars, modestly clad by today's standards, and then, under the editorship of Theodore Dreiser and others, developed a muckraking side. A variety of girlie magazines included those that specialized in cartoons and sexual innuendo, like the 1920s *Hot Dog: A Monthly for the Regular Fellows.*

Playboy launched in 1953 with a centerfold of Marilyn Monroe. Its founder, Hugh Hefner, sought to create a sophisticated magazine like *Esquire*, and although its explicit nude display of women's bodies remained a main draw, it published well-known authors like Norman Mailer, Evelyn Waugh, and Jack Kerouac. The somewhat raunchier *Penthouse* (1969–), by contrast, sold mainly on newsstands, as did *Oui* (1972–), the *Playboy*-owned magazine which attempted to recapture the *Penthouse* readership. *Hustler* began in 1974, addressed to a blue-collar readership, and took sexual explicitness and sometimes demeaning treatment of women further, inspiring protests and imitators. *Players* began in 1973 addressing a largely African American readership.

Gay Men's Magazines

"Physique" magazines from the late 1940s to the 1970s featured male models completely nude from the back or covered with a posing strap. They included *Physique Pictorial*, *Tomorrow's Man*, *Grecian Guild Pictorial*, and *Adonis*, with the first two routinely reaching circulations of forty thousand each. This was a far higher circulation than the nascent gay rights movement publications *ONE* (begun 1953) and the *Mattachine Review* (1955–1966), though the publisher of *Physique Pictorial* and other titles urged readers to join homophile organizations and demand their rights.

Physique magazine publishers had been imprisoned for obscenity, and in one case indicted for "excessive genital delineation." But by 1969, the legal obscenity standards were loosened; full-frontal male nudes could be shown, and openly gay magazines like *Drum* published male nude photos.

Conclusion

Men's magazines from the nineteenth through the twentieth century continued to define a community of readers and tie that community to a three-dimensional space, whether it be a barbershop, a gay bar, or the great outdoors. Although pornography on the Internet may have cut into the revenues of skin magazines, other men's magazines have thrived by cultivating insecurity about appearance—strategies adapted from women's magazines.

BIBLIOGRAPHY

Cohn, Jan. *Creating America: George Horace Lorimer and the* Saturday Evening Post. Pittsburgh, Pa.: University of Pittsburgh Press, 1989.

Hooven, F. Valentine, III. *Beefcake: The Muscle Magazines of America, 1950–1970.* New York: Taschen America, 1996.

Mott, Frank Luther. *A History of American Magazines.* 5 vols. Cambridge, Mass.: Harvard University Press, 1938–1968.

Pendergast, Tom. *Creating the Modern Man: American Magazines and Consumer Culture, 1900–1950.* Columbia: University of Missouri Press, 2000.

Peterson, Theodore. *Magazines in the Twentieth Century.* Urbana: University of Illinois Press, 1964.

Smith, Erin A. *Hard-Boiled: Working-Class Readers and Pulp Magazines.* Philadelphia: Temple University Press, 2000.

Tebbel, John, and Mary Ellen Zuckerman. *The Magazine in America, 1741–1990.* New York: Oxford University Press, 1991.

Ellen Gruber Garvey

See also **Magazines; Pornography.**

MAGAZINES, WOMEN'S. Within days of each other in 1741 the first two indigenous magazines were published in the American colonies. Largely aimed at men and at establishing a reputable product in the face of British imports, these and subsequent American magazines focused from the start on social life, politics, manners, and what might seem an unlikely topic, women. Article after article debated women's roles in and outside the home, eventually tying together notions of loyalty, morality, and family with larger political ideals of citizenship and then nation. In the postrevolutionary period, periodicals aimed directly at women emerged. The best known of these was the *Lady's Magazine and Repository of Entertaining Knowledge*, founded in Philadelphia in 1792. Primarily literary, the *Lady's Magazine* contained no information about what later came to distinguish women's magazines, the topic of household work. The magazine's most notable feature in fact was a nine-page tribute to Mary Wollstonecraft's *Vindication of the Rights of Women*, which was also first published in 1792.

By 1830 over forty women's magazines, all short-lived, had appeared. Unlike men's magazines, women's magazines paid little attention to current events and focused instead on fashion, beauty, and fiction. They demonstrated little editorial coherence but provided an important outlet for women writers and editors, paving the way for mass publications aimed at women. Nathaniel Hawthorne's famous remark about the "damned mob of scribbling women" who wrote for these publications illustrates both the public presence of women writers and the debates they engendered about magazines as popular discourse.

The most successful of the early women's magazines, *GODEY'S LADY'S BOOK,* stated in its first issue that it was dedicated to "female improvement." Sarah Josepha Hale, who edited the magazine from 1837 to 1877, used the pages of *Godey's* to promote her causes, chief among them women's education. The magazine was not overtly political, however. Hale managed to interweave discussions of women's issues with a great deal of sentimental and romantic fiction and poetry. She never challenged nineteenth-century notions of women's place, viewing women's domestic roles and their education as entirely compatible. *Godey's* largely avoided politics, carrying only a brief mention of the suffrage convention at Seneca Falls in 1848. It even failed to comment on the Civil War throughout its duration.

Godey's Lady's Book laid the foundation for the "big six" women's magazines that emerged in the late nineteenth century. Three of these publications—*Ladies' Home Journal, Woman's Home Companion,* and *Good Housekeeping*—started as women's pages of popular periodicals or as publications directed at the home. The *Ladies' Home Journal,* for example, began as "Women and Home," a column in the *Tribune and Farmer.* The second three of the big six—*Delineator, McCall's,* and *Pictorial Review*—started as fashion publications. These six general interest magazines quickly came to share editorial approaches, focusing on women and the home and targeting a white, middle-class audience. They also quickly advanced in circulation. The *Ladies' Home Journal,* known as the "monthly Bible of the American home," reached a circulation of one million by January 1904.

Circulation rates of women's magazines grew at the same time that advertising increasingly financed magazine production. It was not enough that women purchased the magazines, they had to be convinced to purchase the goods advertised in the pages of those magazines. Magazines depended on advertisers to support their efforts in producing and distributing high-quality products, and advertisers depended on magazines to reach female audiences, who by the early twentieth century were estimated to have purchased over 80 percent of all consumer goods. The relationship between the two industries proved mutually beneficial and allowed magazine and advertising production to become increasingly more sophisticated technically and culturally. In fact women's magazines, using a strategy Mary Ellen Zuckerman identified as "low price, advertising underwriting and targeting of female consumers" (*History of Popular Women's Magazines,* p. 25), led the magazine field in general and laid the framework for the expansion of this popular medium for the rest of the twentieth century.

The consumer culture promoted in women's magazines presented what Jennifer Scanlon called "a unified and powerful vision of satisfaction not through social change but through consumption" (*Inarticulate Longings,*

p. 230). As a result few of these early women's magazines attempted to or succeeded in breaking out of the pattern of addressing white, middle-class housewives. When they recognized problems in the idealized family, the magazines suggested that women's sphere was that of influence rather than action. At the same time, however, by giving voice to reader complaints and concerns, the magazines revealed women's dissatisfactions as they struggled to live up to cultural standards of womanhood.

Not until the 1960s did more diverse publications aimed at women achieve a secure level of commercial success. One of the most notable of these was *Cosmopolitan,* a fiction magazine initially published in the early twentieth century then revamped in 1965 to address the needs and desires of single women. The editor, Helen Gurley Brown, and the advertisers who supported the magazine recognized that single women had disposable income and a desire to see themselves, or at least their fantasies, reflected in the pages of a magazine. The *Advocate,* which started as a weekly in 1967, created the space for a series of publications aimed at gay and then lesbian audiences. *Essence,* the first mass magazine aimed at African American women, hit the newsstands in 1970 and finally challenged advertisers' reluctance to acknowledge the purchasing power of black Americans. More recent publications like *Latina* and *Moderna* followed the lead of *Essence* and targeted women by race and ethnicity. Another challenger was *Ms.,* which hit the newsstands in 1972. *Ms.* responded to and helped popularize the women's liberation movement by publishing articles about politics, child care, women's health, lesbian issues, and violence against women. *Working Woman,* founded in 1976, brought to the fore workplace, financial, and career issues. A magazine targeting older women, *Lear's,* opened another market but itself came and went. Magazines targeting young women continued to thrive into the twenty-first century primarily because they recognized and exploited the purchasing power of the young. *Seventeen* boasted to advertisers, for example, that its readers were "branded for life," indicating that brand loyalty is deemed worthy of pursuit in the young, even in a demographically diverse market. Newsstand publications primarily targeted young women, with an emphasis on fitness and beauty.

One development in the world of women's magazines was the "zine," the noncommercial, nonprofessional, small-circulation magazine produced by do-it-yourself publishers. Zines like *Bust,* for example, have proliferated, offering more explicit discussions of sexuality and feminist politics than advertising-driven women's magazines. Zines and more mainstream women's magazines increasingly have relied on the Internet as a means of distribution and gauging reader satisfaction. Women's magazines in the twenty-first century have been marketed through a curious combination of appeals to women as individuals, as members of distinct demographically definable groups, and as members of a community of women. For the most part, however, the "essential" woman in the mass magazines has been white, middle-class, and heterosexual. Alternative publications respond and react to the mission and the marketing of those mass "women's" magazines.

BIBLIOGRAPHY

Farrell, Amy Erdman. *Yours in Sisterhood: Ms. Magazine and the Promise of Popular Feminism.* Chapel Hill: University of North Carolina Press, 1998.

Garvey, Ellen Gruber. *The Adman in the Parlor: Magazines and the Gendering of Consumer Culture, 1880s to 1910s.* New York: Oxford University Press, 1996.

Karp, Marcelle, and Debbie Stoller, eds. *The Bust Guide to the New Girl Order.* New York: Penguin, 1999.

Marchand, Roland. *Advertising the American Dream.* Berkeley: University of California Press, 1985.

Scanlon, Jennifer. *Inarticulate Longings:* The Ladies' Home Journal, *Gender, and the Promises of Consumer Culture.* New York: Routledge, 1995.

Tebbel, John, and Mary Ellen Zuckerman. *The Magazine in America, 1741–1990.* New York: Oxford University Press, 1991.

Zuckerman, Mary Ellen. *A History of Popular Women's Magazines in the United States, 1792–1995.* Westport, Conn.: Greenwood Press, 1998.

Jennifer Scanlon

See also **Advertising**; *Ms.* **Magazine**.

MAGAZINES AND NEWSPAPERS, AFRICAN AMERICAN.

The first black newspaper in the United States, *Freedom's Journal*, was established in 1827 by John Russwurm, the first African American to graduate from a university, Bowdoin in Maine, and Samuel Cornish, a militant clergyman in New York City. In the first issue, dated 16 March, the youthful editors boldly stated their objectives: "We wish to plead our own cause. Too long have others spoken for us. Too long has the public been deceived by misrepresentation in things which concern us dearly." Their manifesto captured the spirit and mission of thousands of black newspapers that followed. The editors were in part reacting to the racist propaganda put forth by the white journals of the period. Later, other black newspapers also assumed a corrective and assertive role.

Popular Press

The viability of *Freedom's Journal* and the other papers launched in the mid-nineteenth century was compromised by the relatively small black population that could financially support newspapers in the North and by substantive intragroup differences over issues like emigration to Africa and the merits of violence in the struggle against southern slavery. In 1828, Russwurm resigned, having abandoned his hopes for freedom in the United States, and he channeled his energy into the African emigration cause. The next year *Freedom's Journal* folded.

The noted black abolitionist Frederick Douglass launched the *North Star* in Rochester, New York, in 1847. In his editorials Douglass carefully distanced himself from Oswald Garrison, his former mentor, who grounded his antislavery crusade in moralism. Douglass, like many other black abolitionists, was skeptical about the effectiveness of moral appeals and retained hope in the U.S. Constitution as a lever for abolition. Despite attracting only a small number of black subscribers, the *North Star* (renamed *Frederick Douglass' Monthly* in 1851) survived until 1861, largely through the contributions of white patrons in the abolitionist movement.

While slavery, African emigration, and racist practices in the North dominated the thinking of blacks, several persons recognized the need for outlets that featured creative work as well as political material. The *Anglo-African Magazine*, founded in 1859 by Thomas Hamilton, offered readers poems, essays, and creative writing along with stirring political pieces by writers like Martin Delaney and John Langston.

After the Civil War, Reconstruction policies and the optimism and rhetoric that accompanied them spawned dozens of black newspapers across the country. However, the hopeful mood could not offset the economics of publishing. For most free blacks toiling for basic essentials, newspaper subscriptions were out of the question financially. White newspapers depended on commercial advertising for operating revenue, but embryonic black business enterprises were in no position to invest resources in advertising. By the 1890s a majority of these early publications had closed down.

At the beginning of the twentieth century, blacks continued their migration to northern cities, where discriminatory laws and custom patterns limited them to segregated enclaves. As the African American population embraced self-help strategies, the need for newspapers to educate and communicate was apparent. Literally every city harbored a black newspaper. Among the more stable and influential papers were Robert Abbott's *Chicago Defender* (1905), William Monroe Trotter's *Boston Guardian* (1901), and T. Thomas Fortune's *New York Age* (1887). The activist Ida Wells (who later married and became Ida Wells-Barnett) coedited *Free Speech* in Memphis. The tension between her militant views and the southern political climate peaked in 1892, when gangsters vandalized the offices of *Free Speech*. Fearful for her safety, Wells moved to New York and continued to write some of the most forceful antilynching journalism of the era.

The influential black leader Booker T. Washington recognized the growing influence of black papers and adroitly dangled financial assistance to those who supported his political views. Washington's manipulation of organs like the *Colored American* infuriated W. E. B. Du Bois, whose views challenged Washington's conservative outlook. However, Du Bois could offer none of the largesse available to editors who endorsed Washington's accommodationist politics. Despite Washington's manipulation of the black press, three magazines emerged that rekindled the protest traditions of the nineteenth-century papers. Du Bois's *Crisis* (1910), Charles S. Johnson's *Opportunity* (1923), and A. Phillip Randolph and Chandler Owen's *Messenger* (1917) profoundly shaped the thinking of their black readers. All three magazines included political and nonpolitical works, and each was subsidized by an organization—the *Messenger* by the Brotherhood of Sleeping Car Porters, *Crisis* by the National Association for the Advancement of Colored People, and *Opportunity* by the Urban League. Girded by institutional backing, all three magazines enjoyed a longer publishing life than any of the earlier magazines.

Claude Barnett, a journalist with the *Chicago Defender*, recognized the need for an agency to serve the black press and started the Associated Negro Press (ANP) service in 1919. In addition to collecting and distributing news about black Americans, Barnett traveled to Africa and set up an informal network of correspondents to funnel news about the continent to African and black domestic outlets. The highest number of domestic subscribers in one year was 112 in 1945. In 1964 more than two hundred papers in Africa had signed up with the ANP. Unable to compete with the resources marshaled by the major news services, the agency closed in 1964.

Scholarly Journals
Serious historical scholarship about blacks found an outlet when Carter G. Woodson, a Washington, D.C., teacher, established the *Journal of Negro History (JNH)* in 1916. The journal was affiliated with the Association for the Study of Negro Life and History, an organization Woodson and several other black educators had created to promote interest in and knowledge about black history. The Harvard-trained Woodson insisted on rigorous scholarship, and the pages of *JNH* were open to all able contributors. Remarkably, Woodson managed to publish *JNH* regularly despite often-contentious relationships with sponsoring foundations and donors. *JNH* survived into the twenty-first century but appeared irregularly.

Three other important scholarly journals were initiated by blacks during the first half of the century, and all enjoyed success. The *Journal of Negro Education* founded by Charles Thompson at Howard University focused on education and social conditions and featured the work of scholars like Horace Mann Bond, E. Franklin Frazier, and Ralph Bunche. The university-subsidized publication remained viable in the twenty-first century and enjoyed a fine reputation in scholarly circles. *Phylon* and the *College Language Association Journal* (*CLA Journal*) appeared in 1940 and 1957, respectively. *Phylon*, with links to Atlanta University, concentrated on the social sciences, while the *CLA Journal* published literary criticism. Both helped fill significant gaps in American scholarship.

A National Focus
Through the first half of the twentieth century, nationally focused papers like the *Pittsburgh Courier*, the *Baltimore*

Afro-American, and the *Chicago Defender* effectively exposed racial injustice and offered news of special interest to the black community. The *Defender* in particular was a consistent advocate of southern black migration to the North from 1917 to 1923. Several decades later the black press successfully fended off attempts by President Franklin Roosevelt and J. Edgar Hoover to use wartime sedition powers to suppress their publication during World War II. Long before white papers discovered the civil rights and black power movements, the black press was gathering and distributing information about the trends.

The legal and political victories of the 1960s civil rights struggles had paradoxical implications for the black press. As more blacks made their way into the American mainstream, the need for an ethnically focused fourth estate came into question. Talented black editors and reporters were hired by white papers, and many thrived in the new environment. Circulation figures for the traditionally black dailies and weeklies dwindled, and few were viable into the twenty-first century. With a circulation of 600,000 in the 1960s, *Muhammad Speaks*, published by the Nation of Islam, reigned as the most widely read black newspaper. The *Black Scholar*, another independent quarterly, was founded in 1969 and in the twenty-first century continued to publish research and commentary on black studies.

Several general-interest magazines, like *Jet* and *Ebony*, founded in Chicago by John L. Johnson in the 1950s, survived into the twenty-first century and served the mass market for black society and entertainment items. Specialty magazines like *Essence* (1970), directed toward black women readers, and *Black Enterprise*, a monthly on black businesses, successfully reached the growing market of young urban Americans.

BIBLIOGRAPHY

Banks, William M. *Black Intellectuals: Race and Responsibility in American Life*. New York: Norton, 1996.

Dann, Martin E., ed. *The Black Press 1827–1890: The Quest for National Identity*. New York: Putnam, 1971.

Johnson, Abby Arthur, and Ronald Mayberry Johnson. *Propaganda and Aesthetics: The Literary Politics of Afro-American Magazines in the Twentieth Century*. Amherst: University of Massachusetts Press, 1979.

Pride, Armistead S., and Clint C. Wilson II. *A History of the Black Press*. Washington, D.C.: Howard University Press, 1997.

Washburn, Patrick S. *A Question of Sedition: The Federal Government's Investigation of the Black Press during World War II*. New York: Oxford University Press, 1986.

Wolseley, Roland E. *The Black Press, U.S.A.* 2d ed. Ames: Iowa State University Press, 1989.

William M. Banks

See also **African Americans; Literature: African American Literature; Newspapers; Publishing Industry.**

MAGNA CARTA, or Magna Charta, is the thirteenth-century document regarded as the foundation of English constitutional liberty. By early spring of 1215, England was in the throes of a civil war. King John's blundering foreign policy had disrupted the Angevin Empire and had alienated a considerable number of his former followers. His clash with Rome over the vacant See of Canterbury outraged the nation's religious leaders. More significant were his repeated violations of feudal and common law. These abuses caused most of John's barons to revolt. John capitulated at Runnymede on 15 June 1215. Here he gave his consent to the Magna Carta.

No document in all of English history equals the Magna Carta, although none has been more misunderstood or misinterpreted. The "great charter" was a treaty won by a victorious barony from a defeated king. In its essence, the charter simply meant that John, like all the English, was to be subject to the spirit and letter of the law. His past conduct was condemned; in the future he was to rule in accordance with law and custom. The charter was not a document of human liberties. Although it did stipulate that personal liberty and private property could be taken away, the document contained no explicit reference to habeas corpus, jury trial in criminal cases, or Parliament's control over taxation. Several centuries were to pass before these basic rights became an integral part of England's organic law.

Between the thirteenth and seventeenth centuries, the Magna Carta was largely forgotten. The civil conflicts attending the War of the Roses and the strong arm of the Tudors blotted out the memory of the Magna Carta. Contemporary literature of the Tudor period (1485–1603) is strangely silent about the charter, and William Shakespeare in *King John* made no reference to what probably was the most important event in the life of that monarch. Had the great dramatist known of the charter, he would hardly have passed over so significant an episode.

It remained for the Puritans, lawyers, and members of Parliament of the seventeenth century, in their contest with the Stuarts, to resurrect the Magna Carta and interpret it as an impregnable bulwark of democracy. Although they misunderstood the intent of the charter and thus laid the foundation of the myth of the Magna Carta, they fashioned it into an obstacle to arbitrary government and paved the way for the present constitutional monarchy. When the Puritans migrated to the New World, they embedded their ideas in American political philosophy. The Magna Carta was viewed in the United States as a priceless heritage, never to be lost sight of, and to bravely be defended. As historical research has removed much of the myth and fancy that have surrounded the charter, its essential truths have become more significant than when John reigned: human rights, individually or collectively, are not to be destroyed by arbitrary and despotic government; the law of the land is supreme and inviolable and must be respected; and no individual or government may transcend law.

BIBLIOGRAPHY

Cantor, Norman F. *Imagining the Law: Common Law and the Foundations of the American Legal System.* New York: HarperCollins, 1997.

Holt, James C. *Magna Carta.* 2d ed. New York: Cambridge University Press, 1992.

Pallister, Anne. *Magna Carta: The Heritage of Liberty.* Oxford: Clarendon Press, 1971.

W. E. Galpin/c. p.

See also **Bill of Rights in U.S. Constitution; Due Process of Law; Habeas Corpus, Writ of.**

MAGNET SCHOOLS gained popularity in the 1970s, when the federal courts accepted such schools as a method of desegregation, as in *Morgan v. Kerrigan* (1976). They were proposed in an effort to make desegregated schools more attractive to parents, educators, and students. Magnet schools, the most widespread form of public school choice, are typically characterized by four qualities: a thematic curriculum (such as arts or technology) or unique method of instruction (such as Montessori); admission to facilitate voluntary desegregation; choice of school by families; and access to pupils beyond neighborhood attendance zones.

Magnet schools are typically established in urban school districts with large student enrollments (over 10,000). Fifty-three percent of large urban school districts include magnet school programs as part of their desegregation plans. More than half of all magnet programs are located in low socioeconomic districts. School districts establish admission processes for magnet schools because they usually have more students than spaces. Most districts use a lottery format, while others rely upon a first-come, first-served arrangement. Magnet schools have been supported with considerable investments of resources to serve as incentives for parental choice. On average, expenditures per student are 10 percent higher in districts with magnets. Magnet schools are funded through state desegregation funds and grants through the federal Magnet Schools Assistance Program (MSAP).

Magnet schools have met with mixed success. They attract students of different racial and socioeconomic backgrounds with similar educational interests, provide unique sets of learning opportunities, encourage innovation, and promote academic gains for some students. Critics charge that magnets tend to select the most motivated and academically able students as well as the most innovative and effective teachers, lead to socioeconomic segregation because middle-class parents are more motivated and more informed regarding the availability of educational options and choices, and divert resources that should be used for systemwide improvements.

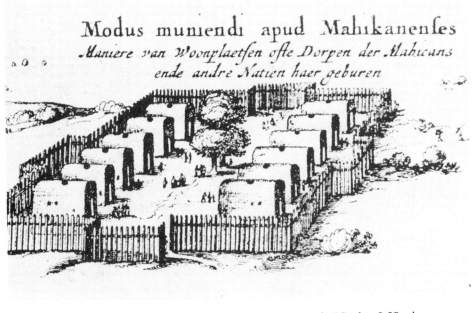

Modus muniendi apud Mahikanenses
Maniere van Woonplaetsen ofte Dorpen der Mahicans
ende andre Natien haer geburen

Mahican Village. This illustration is from a map of the Northeast by Nicolaes J. Visscher, published in Amsterdam c. 1655—before the tribe began decades of trying to find a permanent home after being repeatedly uprooted and forced to move on. LIBRARY OF CONGRESS

BIBLIOGRAPHY

Eaton, Susan E., and Elizabeth Crutcher. "Magnets, Media, and Mirages." In *Dismantling Desegregation: The Quiet Reversal of "Brown v. Board of Education."* Edited by Gary Orfield and Susan Eaton. New York: New Press, 1996.

Metz, Mary Heywood. *Different by Design.* New York: Routledge, 1986.

Smrekar, Claire, and Ellen Goldring. *School Choice in Urban America: Magnet Schools and the Pursuit of Equity.* New York: Teachers College Press, 1999.

Steel, Laurie, and Roger Levine. *Educational Innovation in Multiracial Contexts: The Growth of Magnet Schools in American Education.* Washington, D.C.: American Institutes for Research, 1994.

Ellen Goldring

See also **Desegregation; Education, Parental Choice in.**

MAGNETIC RESONANCE IMAGING (MRI), first used for medical purposes in 1976, is based on the phenomenon of nuclear magnetic resonance reported in 1946 by Felix Bloch of Stanford University and Edward Purcell of Harvard University, physicists awarded the Nobel Prize in 1952. Using complicated equipment to measure resonating frequencies emitted by tissue components, images of those tissues are constructed in much the same way as in CAT (computerized axial tomography) scanning. Information can be obtained about the soft tissues of the body—such as the brain, spinal cord, heart, kidneys, and liver—but not bone. MRI does not involve ionizing radiations and is noninvasive.

Scientists developed the functional MRI (fMRI) in 1993. This technique allows for more accurate mapping of the human brain, especially those regions that control thought and motor control. Other developments include machines that have open sides, so that patients need not be enclosed in a chamber, as they are for an MRI; faster machines that can take full-body scans in minutes; machines that can provide real-time images during surgical procedures; machines with stronger, superconducting magnets; and finally, diffusion-weighted MRI, a scanning sequence that allows doctors to identify strokes by detecting the minute swelling of brain tissue that accompanies such attacks.

BIBLIOGRAPHY

Lee, Joseph K. T., et al., eds. *Computed Body Tomography with MRI Correlation.* 3d ed. Philadelphia: Lippincott-Williams, 1998.

Peter H. Wright/ A. R.

MAHICAN. When Henry Hudson first met the Mahicans in 1609, the Eastern Algonquian-speaking tribe occupied both sides of the Hudson River from Catskill Creek to the mouth of Lake Champlain. By the end of the seventeenth century colonial pressures on their land and conflicts with the Mohawks forced the Mahicans to move eastward into the Berkshire Mountains, where they were joined by other Indians from the lower Hudson Valley. Others moved west to join Oneidas living at Oquaga,

The Overland Mail

New York, and the Delaware in the Wyoming Valley in Pennsylvania.

In the 1730s, led by the missionary John Sergeant, they founded a village at Stockbridge, where they remained until the 1780s. During the Revolutionary War, they fought on the side of the colonies; their loyalty was rewarded with the loss of their land at Stockbridge. They then moved to Oneida lands in New York, where they received a ten-mile-square tract. They were joined by a Delaware group from New Jersey called the Brotherton. Here they remained through the first two decades of the nineteenth century, when pressures from the state forced them to sell their lands in New York in violation of the Trade and Intercourse Acts. This time they moved to land held by the Munsee Delaware in Indiana. By the time they arrived, however, the land had been purchased by the United States, and they and the Munsee Delaware moved to the Lake Winnebago area in Wisconsin. There they came to be known as the Stockbridge-Munsee tribe. Their stay in the Lake Winnebago area was short. In 1843, the United States granted the tribal members citizenship and divided the land in severalty. While some of the tribe accepted the act, many refused and eventually were given land in Shawano County, Wisconsin, where they now reside.

The tribe re-established itself and under the 1934 Indian Reorganization Act is federally recognized. The Mahicans are governed by an elected council that administers a 46,080-acre reservation, of which approximately 15,000 acres are in trust.

BIBLIOGRAPHY

Brasser, T. J. "Mahican" In *Handbook of North American Indians*, Vol. 15: *Northeast*. Edited by Bruce G. Trigger. Washington, D.C.: Smithsonian Institution, 1978.

Frazier, Patrick. *The Mohicans of Stockbridge*. Lincoln: University of Nebraska, 1992.

Jack Campisi

See also **Indian Trade and Intercourse Act; Tribes: Northeastern.**

MAIL, OVERLAND, AND STAGECOACHES.

Overland mail and stagecoaches followed the covered wagon into the trans-Missouri West. Monthly government mail services were established from Independence, Missouri, to Santa Fe and to Salt Lake City in 1850. Thirty days were allowed for the one-way trip on each line. A similar service between Salt Lake City and Sacramento, California, began in 1851. These routes paid poorly, so only one team was usually employed for the trip. No way stations were maintained, making the carriers' journey lonely and sometimes perilous. Because of these limited facilities, practically all mail for California went by steamer, via Panama, with a thirty-day schedule from New York to San Francisco.

Proponents of overland mail service lobbied for increased subsidies for the maintenance of stations and changes of teams. In 1858 the semiweekly Southern, or Butterfield, Overland Mail Company began carrying mail between El Paso and Tuscon. The choice of a southern route, however, angered proponents of the central route (via Salt Lake City). The postmaster general defended the southern route as the only one feasible for year-round travel. To disprove this contention, William H. Russell, of the firm Russell, Majors, and Waddell, in 1860 inaugurated the PONY EXPRESS, which carried mail on a semimonthly schedule. With the outbreak of the CIVIL WAR, the Southern Overland Mail was moved to the central route in Union-controlled territory, further strengthening Russell's position as the leading candidate for government mail contracts.

The Pony Express, with its legendary relay system and record delivery times, was a popular sensation. But the more important development of the 1860s was the gradual expansion of an efficient mail and stagecoach system in the West. In February 1860 the Kansas legislature chartered a daily service, the Central Overland California and Pikes Peak Express, also run by William H. Russell. It absorbed the stage lines running from St. Joseph, Missouri, to Denver and to Salt Lake City; service was extended to California in May 1860. Letter mail on this system traveled from the Missouri River to California in an unprecedented twenty days.

Revenues never met expenses, however, and the Pony Express failed after eighteen months of operation. Ben Holladay purchased the line and contract in 1862. A vigorous organizer, he improved the line and extended branches to Oregon and Montana. Some Native American tribes interrupted the coaches and destroyed stations in 1864, but the distribution of additional soldiers cleared the road. Wells Fargo purchased Holladay's lines in 1866 and continued operations until the completion of the first transcontinental railroad in 1869. Coaches continued for many years to serve localities not reached by rail.

The Concord stagecoach, manufactured by Abbot, Downing, and Company of Concord, New Hampshire, was the great overland carrier of passengers, mail, and express before 1869. Its frame rested on leather thoroughbraces in lieu of springs and it accommodated nine passengers inside and others on the top. A team of four or six horses or mules powered the coach, which usually made a hundred miles in twenty-four hours. Although replaced by the railroad in the late nineteenth century, the stagecoach lived on as a symbol of conquest, progress, and opportunity for Americans heading west.

BIBLIOGRAPHY

Hafen, LeRoy R. *The Overland Mail, 1849–1869: Promoter of Settlement, Precursor of Railroads.* New York: AMS Press, 1969.

Holmes, Oliver Wendell, and Peter Rohrbach. *Stagecoach East: Stagecoach Days in the East from the Colonial Period to the Civil War.* Washington, D.C.: Smithsonian Institution Press, 1983.

Ormsby, Waterman L. *The Butterfield Overland Mail.* San Marino, Calif.: Huntington Library, 1991.

Morris F. Taylor, *First Mail West: Stagecoach Lines on the Santa Fe Trail.* Albuquerque: University of New Mexico Press, 1971.

LeRoy R. Hafen / A. R.

See also **Carriage Making; Overland Trail; Postal Service, U.S.; Stagecoach Travel; Taverns and Saloons.**

MAIL, SOUTHERN OVERLAND,

also known as the Butterfield Overland Mail, was the first land mail route from the East to California. On 3 March 1857, Congress authorized a semiweekly service on a twenty-five-day schedule at $600,000 per year. Postmaster General Aaron V. Brown, a native of Tennessee, chose a southern route, running from St. Louis and Memphis to San Francisco. Service began 15 September 1858 and lasted until the outbreak of the Civil War, when the line was moved to a more northerly route.

BIBLIOGRAPHY

Hafen, LeRoy R. *The Overland Mail, 1849–1869: Promoter of Settlement, Precursor of Railroads.* Cleveland, Ohio: A. H. Clark, 1926. Reprint, New York: AMS Press, 1969. Reprint, Mansfield Center, Conn.: Martino, 2002.

Tallack, William. *The California Overland Express.* Los Angeles: Historical Society of Southern California, 1935.

Leroy R. Hafen / A. R.

See also **Postal Service, U.S.; Stagecoach Travel.**

MAIL-ORDER HOUSES.

Mail-order houses, along with DEPARTMENT STORES and chain stores, were the most important innovations in retailing institutions during the late nineteenth century. Unlike the other two, however, mail-order houses were essentially a unique American phenomenon in their extent and significance. Indeed, because the majority of Americans still lived in rural settings before the 1920s, they often first experienced the emerging national consumer culture through the medium of the mail-order catalog—or, as many called it, the "wish book."

Montgomery Ward and Sears

Before the 1860s a few firms (for example, patent medicine vendors) advertised the availability of their wares by mail in newspapers and agricultural journals, but general

Mail-Order Giant. The cover of the 1902 Sears, Roebuck and Co. general merchandise catalog; editions were published from 1893 to 1993.

merchandise mail-order houses were first established after the Civil War. During the 1870s Augusta, Maine, became host to a number of nationally circulated periodicals, like E. C. Allen's *People's Literary Companion* and P. O. Vickery's *Comfort*. These were known as mail-order magazines because they were read mostly for—and derived the bulk of their income from—advertisements; many of these magazines flourished for decades. More important, however, was Montgomery Ward, the first mail-order house to use catalogs as its primary promotional tool. Founded by Aaron Montgomery Ward and his brother-in-law in 1872 and based in the railroad hub of Chicago, where it was able to take full advantage of the burgeoning national transportation infrastructure, Montgomery Ward's was closely affiliated with the Patrons of Husbandry, better known as the Grange movement. A widespread animus against local merchants and their country stores, which usually featured overpriced, small, and limited inventories, prompted agrarian attempts to avoid "parasitic middlemen" in the retail trade. By the early 1890s the Montgomery Ward general catalog had become hundreds of pages long and offered nearly 25,000 items for sale.

Of the many firms that quickly followed Montgomery Ward into the mail-order trade, its most important competitor was the company founded by Richard W. Sears. Beginning in 1886 as a vendor of watches and reorganized several times through the early 1900s, in 1893 Sears began offering a general merchandise catalog that soon rivaled Ward's in size and variety. Moreover, Richard Sears was a master of promotional copy. Bucking the trend, he filled every available inch of ad space with text as well as illustrations. His catalog instructions were designed to make the farmer feel comfortable and secure, emphasizing liberal return policies ("Satisfaction Guaranteed"). With the addition of Julius Rosenwald as a partner in 1895, the company's administration and operations were increasingly systematized, and by the time it occupied a new forty-acre Chicago facility in 1906, Sears's sales were nearly $40 million annually, surpassing Ward's in total sales. The two leading mail-order houses would remain major national rivals for much of the twentieth century.

Some urban department stores, such as Macy's, followed suit with their own catalog sales departments, although with mixed results. Other mail-order houses specialized in particular types of goods, like the Larkin Company, a Buffalo, New York, soap manufacturer that began distributing nonperishable groceries by mail beginning in 1885, or National Bellas Hess, a Chicago clothing apparel concern. Spiegel, May, and Stern was founded in 1882 as a Chicago furniture retailer and moved into the mail-order trade in 1904; the company would gain national renown for its sales on installment credit (a practice previously known to rural folk mainly through the auspices of the itinerant peddler), helping prompt other mail-order houses to follow suit.

Improvements in Postal Service

Indispensable to the growth of the mail-order industry were improvements in the federal postal service. In 1875 a more favorable rate for bulk mailings of periodical and other "educational" literature was established and was lowered by half again a decade later—a boon to mail-order magazines and smaller catalogs. During his tenure as postmaster general in the early 1890s, the department store magnate John Wanamaker authorized the first experiments with rural free delivery (RFD) of mail, a system that became fully national by 1902. Even more important, Wanamaker and others campaigned for the creation of a parcel post system to ease the restrictions on rural deliveries. Most shipments were still handled by a small number of powerful express companies, whose welter of regulations and high prices hampered growth and efficiency, and farm customers had to make the often arduous trek into town to pick up goods that they had ordered. The steadfast opposition of local merchants and the express companies to a federal parcel post system, however, delayed its adoption until 1913.

In an age sensitive to the charge of monopolistic privilege, the major mail-order houses carefully avoided leading the push toward parcel post, but the system proved doubly beneficial to them: not only was it less expensive and more convenient for customers, but it also significantly dropped the cost of distributing catalogs. Parcel post reform combined with rising farm incomes to make the period from 1910 to 1925 the golden age of mail order. Taken together, Sears and Montgomery Ward sold over $400 million of goods annually by 1925, and that same year Sears's mail-order sales alone accounted for over 2 percent of total farm cash income.

Retail Outlets and Specialized Mail Order

The two mail-order giants, however, saw the writing on the wall. The increasing personal mobility made possible by the automobile, the incursion of chain stores like J. C. Penney's into small-town markets, and the demographic trend toward an increasingly urban-based population all meant that rural mail-order sales had probably peaked. Beginning in the mid-1920s, each began to diversify operations to include retail outlets; by the 1950s, these stores would become their leading sources of income.

Mail-order retailing remained big business through the end of the twentieth century, but companies tended to thrive with more specialized niche marketing. The Sharper Image, L. L. Bean, and Victoria's Secret were all examples of using upscale mail-order appeals as a successful entering wedge into the enormous American consumer market. Although e-commerce barely accounted for 1 percent of total retail sales at the end of the century, its reliance on shipping goods ordered online using credit cards represented a lucrative new form of mail-order industry. Still, signaling the end of an era for many, Montgomery Ward and Sears discontinued their general merchandise catalogs in 1985 and 1993, respectively; when

Ward's went out of business in 2000, the mail-order industry had lost its pioneer.

BIBLIOGRAPHY

Cronon, William. *Nature's Metropolis: Chicago and the Great West.* New York: Norton, 1991. A wide-ranging book with excellent sections on the significance of the mail-order industry for Chicago and its hinterlands.

Emmet, Boris, and John E. Jeuck. *Catalogues and Counters: A History of Sears, Roebuck and Company.* Chicago: University of Chicago Press, 1950. A still-classic work based on extensive research in company archives.

Smalley, Orange A., and Frederick D. Sturdivant. *The Credit Merchants: A History of Spiegel, Inc.* Carbondale: Southern Illinois University Press, 1973.

Strasser, Susan. *Satisfaction Guaranteed: The Making of the American Mass Market.* New York: Pantheon Books, 1989. Places mail-order houses in the context of the late-nineteenth-century revolution in retailing.

Scott P. Marler

See also **Postal Service, U.S.; Retailing Industry.**

MAINE. For many, Maine appears on the map as a peninsula, the northeasternmost extension of the United States. However, there is nothing peninsular about Maine. In fact, geographically, it is the southern edge of a much larger land mass that extends south from Hudson Bay and the Canadian shield and from the east through the great timber lands of eastern Canada and the complex coastline of the western North Atlantic. Maine's history has been shaped by these natural characteristics and the social and economic conditions spawned by its unique positioning. Maine is at once at the center of a vibrant natural corridor that produces staple products and on the outermost edge of a great political institution.

Maine's first inhabitants, the Paleoindians (a term used to describe early inhabitants of America, not yet distinguished into modern tribal groups), arrived in the area in the wake of the retreating glaciers 11,000 to 10,000 years ago, where they encountered a relatively barren landscape. The changing environment brought about a new culture, known as the Archaic, between 10,000 and 8,500 years ago. This new culture exploited new resources based on changing forest and sea conditions and developed advanced woodworking skills. Agriculture arrived in what is now New England a few hundred years before European contact. The Native peoples in Maine developed the common corn–beans–squash regimen of crop production. However, those east of the Kennebec River remained dependent upon hunting and gathering.

The Colonial Period

The first documented case of European exploration in the Gulf of Maine was by Giovanni da Verrazano in 1524. This was followed by a series of failed colonizing attempts between 1602 and 1607. Most Europeans were unable to adapt to the harsh environment and the lack of familiar natural resources. The first successful settlements along the Maine coast were those established by European fishing ventures, which supplied winter residents in order to lay claim to the best fishing grounds earlier in the season. By 1610, the Jamestown Colony began to send fishing vessels to the Maine coast. As the activities increased, year-round fishing stations were established at Damariscove Island, Cape Piscataque, Monhegan Island, Pemaquid, and Richmond Island.

European activity in Maine began to increase as more settlers began to recognize the wealth that could be produced from Maine's forests, rivers, and seas. Both internal conflict within England, France, and among Natives, and external conflict between the colonies characterized the settlement of the Maine territory. In order to extend their territorial control, the Massachusetts Bay Colony set up townships at York (1630), Cape Porpus (ca. 1630), Saco (1630), Kittery (ca. 1631), Scarborough (ca. 1631), Falmouth (1633), North Yarmouth (1636), and Wells (1642). The restoration of Charles II to the throne of England was accompanied by further territorial claims from France. By 1670, Maine's settlers moved from a subsistence agriculture base to a profitable export trade of cattle, corn, fish, and lumber products. Both the English and the French inhabitants of Maine lived within a family-based economy with men working in the fields, upon the seas, and in the lumber camps, while women and children worked at home to provide foodstuffs such as milk, butter, and eggs, as well as clothing and tools.

French activities in Maine increased after 1670 when they reoccupied a fort at the mouth of the Penobscot River. For the French, Maine remained primarily a fishing, lumbering, and, most importantly, fur trading center; however, internal conflict between rival French claims hindered French settlement efforts. By the mid-1600s, nearly 75 percent of Maine's original Native inhabitants had died, mostly from European diseases. The survivors were often uprooted and forced to relocate. The arrival of a European-based fur trade further altered the Natives' traditional relationship with the environment. Competition among tribal bands for fur-bearing animals and friction with the colonizing nations transformed the region into a volatile political area, bringing an era of brutal warfare. The Wabanakis in Maine comprised about 20,000 people before contact. Relations with Europeans began to sour early when explorers captured natives for slaves. Conflicting alliances with Europeans fractionalized the Wabanakis and plagues further weakened the solidarity of the "People of the Dawn." As Natives further became dependent upon European firearms and ammunition, the fur trade took on a desperate tone. Beavers grew scarce, forcing the Wabanakis to expand into rival lands. This competition resulted in a series of violent clashes between the tribes known as the "Beaver Wars."

The internal Native conflicts overlapped with a series of European conflicts. Native–English violence during

King Philip's War (1675–1676), King William's War (1689–1697), and Queen Anne's War (1702–1713) brought a universal declaration of war by Massachusetts on all Maine Indians in August 1703. Drummer's War (1721–1727) saw the collapse of Wabanaki military and political power and a dramatic extension of English settlement. The French and Indian War (1754–1763) brought the final collapse of both Native and French military presence in the Maine territory. In May 1759, Massachusetts Governor Thomas Pownall led a force of 400 militia up the Penobscot River to attack Native settlements and construct Fort Pownall near the mouth of the river at Stockton Springs, ending the long land rivalry in Maine. Native families resettled upon ancestral lands, but in small, separate villages. Peace brought further English settlement eastward along the coast and up river valleys.

The American Revolution and Statehood
Maine's participation in the American Revolution reflected its maritime traditions. Tension first appeared over British regulations on timber use and the Royal Navy's monopoly on timber for shipbuilding. Friction over enforcing the Nonimportation Agreement led to the arrival of the British man-of-war *Canceaux* in Falmouth port. Militia captured its captain and some crew, but the men were quickly released. HMS *Margaretta* was captured by militia in Machias in June 1775. In October, the *Canceaux* returned to Falmouth and after warning the residents, bombarded the town and destroyed two-thirds of its structures. The power of the Royal Navy prevented most of Maine's inhabitants from participating directly in the American Revolution.

Maine's location as a borderland between the American colonies and the British holdings in Canada and Nova Scotia led to its use as a launching point of invasion into pro-British territories. Benedict Arnold marched his troops through Maine on his ill-fated attempt to capture Quebec. As they advanced up the Kennebec River in the fall of 1775 and north and west across the heights of land to the Chaudiere River, they encountered harsh weather and difficult travel. Many turned back, weakening the strength of the expedition. In October 1776 and May 1777, pro-American refugees from Nova Scotia launched two raids on Nova Scotia hoping to spark rebellion in the British colony. In the summer of 1779, a British expedition from Halifax arrived in Penobscot Bay and constructed Fort George at present-day Castine. Massachusetts maritime interests reacted by sending an armada of about forty vessels, which arrived on 25 July. Wracked by internal conflict and poor organization, the armada faltered and eventually was trapped by the Royal Navy. The Americans beached and burned their own vessels. The peace treaty of 3 September 1783 renounced British claims on Maine territories, but no definitive line was established as a border between Maine and the British colonies of Nova Scotia, New Brunswick, and Quebec. Nor was any answer found for the fishing disputes that John Adams brought up during negotiations. Continued conflict over these issues persisted for generations, and even reappear today.

Internal friction began as soon as the Revolution concluded. The political debate quickly turned toward the issue of statehood. Maine's chief economies still relied on the sea, and therefore maritime interests took precedence over others. If Maine became a state independent of Massachusetts, the shippers would be forced to pay additional port charges as they entered Boston and New York. Challenging these maritime interests were backcountry settlers, who sought more political power through statehood. These backcountry radicals were spurred on by national events such as Shay's Rebellion (1786–1787). Early test votes showed this division of interests, but equally important, these popular votes demonstrated the indifference many Mainers felt toward the issue: in one significant poll, only 4,598 bothered to vote.

The separatist movement gained momentum after the War of 1812. Maine's role in this conflict was again primarily a maritime one. Maine's economy was deeply affected by the Jeffersonian embargo and smuggling became a chief source of wealth for many small down-east towns that had, over the course of a century, built strong economic and social ties with their neighbors in the British Atlantic colonies. Maine ports also served as launching points for many wartime privateers who raided British shipping. During the war years, Eastport and Castine were invaded and held by British troops and naval vessels. By controlling the northern region of New England, Britain was able to perfect its blockade of the coast of the United States. By war's end, British troops occupied much of the settled area of the state. Britain, however, was eager to end the conflict and return to a profitable trade relation and therefore returned the occupied territory (along with northern Michigan and western New York).

The failure of Massachusetts to protect its Maine district touched off an emotional defense of the separatist movement. The economic rationale for remaining a part of Massachusetts crumbled when Congress passed a new coasting law in 1819, allowing American vessels to sail to any port from Maine to Florida without paying additional port charges or taxation. But the timing of Maine statehood placed it squarely within the sectional issue of slavery extension. In 1820 Congress adopted the Missouri Compromise, as part of which Maine, a free state, and Missouri, a slave state, were admitted to the union.

Economic Development
Following statehood, Maine entered a phase of rapid economic development. The state's wealth was still tied to its ability to produce staple products, but unlike earlier production, this new phase incorporated commercial production and industrial production. As early as 1785, Acadian families from southern Quebec and northern New Brunswick began to migrate to the rich lands of the St. John Valley. For most of its early history, Maine's agricultural production was small-scale subsistence produc-

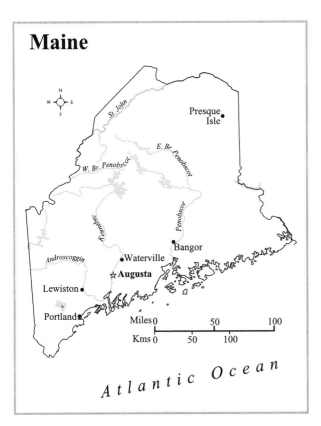

Maine

ness forced many smaller companies out of business, concentrating control in the hands of a few major players. Their wealth would not last for long; by 1915, the industry was in a decline as Canadian, Great Lakes states, and, later, southern producers entered the market. Natural depletion and substitute products shifted lumbering interest out of the state to southern and western regions of the nation.

While Maine had many staple economies, including potatoes, blueberries, ice, granite, and others, timber and seafood production proved to be the two most influential in Maine's history. Like the timber trade, the production of marine food products underwent significant changes during the nineteenth century. Traditionally, Maine specialized in salt cod production, but in the late nineteenth century Maine fishermen began to diversify their catch, marketing mackerel, menhaden, herring, sardines, and lobster. The southern plantations in the West Indies and later the American South provided early markets for North Atlantic seafood. But Maine's sea fisheries were part of a larger global economy that included most of the British colonies in the North Atlantic and in the West Indies. Urban expansion drastically increased the domestic market for fish products and Maine fishermen began to provide fish for the growing Catholic population of Boston and New York. During the early years, Maine's sea fisheries were conducted by small family-owned firms. Fish and fish products were carried by small vessels to larger ports in Portland, Gloucester, and Boston and from there to distant markets. This tie to out-of-state distributors characterized Maine's fisheries even more so during the second half of the nineteenth century.

Spurred by transportation developments like railroads, ice-cars, and larger schooners, the production and distribution of marine resources increased and took on an industrial form. Expensive trawl lines and nets replaced traditional forms of fishing. The fisheries became more capital-intensive and fishing production was concentrated in a handful of major firms in Gloucester and Boston. By the 1860s and 1870s, vessels were owned by large corporations. Huge wholesaling corporations were able to use price fixing to manipulate the market in their favor and limit competition. The repeal of government bounties and the replacement of the share system by a wage-labor system further hindered small-scale fishermen and created an industrial economy of fishing.

tion based on a village economy. Spurred on by outside capital investment and new transportation networks in the form of superior roads and railroads, Maine's farms began to commercialize. As elsewhere in the United States, agricultural production was concentrated into larger farms, and specialized production became part of the national market economy.

Forestry also shifted from a small-scale side business of village farmers into a massive industry concentrated in the hands of a few corporations. Lumbering operations expanded as new networks were developed and larger trees could be transported from the deep interior over friction-free snow-and-ice roads. With the introduction of modern sawmill technology in the 1840s, Bangor became the center of Maine's lumbering industry, exporting more wood product than any other port in the world.

The second half of the nineteenth century saw the continuation of this trend as the lumber industry followed national trends in monopoly capitalism. In the 1880s, the wood-product industry shifted from lumber to pulp and paper. This new capital-intensive industry brought more out-of-state investment. Mill towns appeared in Maine's interior, most notably at Millinocket, built and run by the Great Northern Paper Company. Exemplifying the principles of monopoly capitalism, the Portland businessman Hugh J. Chrisholm and several other bankers and businessmen merged more than a score of New England and New York paper producers to form the International Paper Company. The changing costs of the lumbering busi-

The Civil War and Postwar Politics

The Civil War played an important part not only in the state's history, but also in its modern folklore. Joshua Chamberlain of Brewer, a Bowdoin College graduate, commanded the Twentieth Maine at a pivotal moment on Little Round Top during the battle of Gettysburg, for which he received a Medal of Honor. Chamberlain went on to become a general and was wounded several times. Approximately 73,000 Mainers saw action during the war and many Maine women served as nurses, including Dorothea Dix of Hampden, who served as superintendent of women nurses during the war.

Maine state political leaders had been important players in the formation of the Republican Party in the 1880s, and their leadership was carried through the war and into reconstruction. Hannibal Hamlin won a strong following as an antislavery candidate in 1850 and later served as Abraham Lincoln's first vice president; William Pitt Fessenden served first as a senator and later as secretary of the Treasury; and James G. Blaine served as speaker of the U.S. House of Representatives, was elected senator in 1876, and served as secretary of state in 1881 and from 1889 to 1892.

The legacy of the Civil War cemented Maine's loyalty to the Republican Party. The Republicans held state political power throughout the rest of the nineteenth century and oversaw the expansion of Maine's natural resource production and the concentration of industrial capitalism discussed earlier. The economic collapse of 1929 called into question Republican leadership and the Democratic lawyer and mayor of Lewiston, Louis J. Brann, was elected to the governor's office in 1932. However, Maine and Vermont were the only two states not to vote to reelect Franklin Roosevelt.

The Twentieth Century
President Roosevelt's New Deal brought in much-needed federal aid and the creation of numerous job opportunities. Although Maine's traditionalist culture accepted these changes slowly, the Civilian Conservation Corp recruited about sixteen thousand young men and women to work alongside the Maine Forest Service and proved to be an exceptional labor source for the creation of the Appalachian Trail. Under the Works Progress Administration, many women found employment in the canning industry and Maine farmers received funding for improvements in irrigation. The Passamaquoddy Tidal Power Project, intended to provide hydroelectric power, was never completed, but during its planning stage it employed several hundred Maine workers.

Maine's maritime focus again proved to be of national significance during World War II. Maine had always had a strong shipbuilding tradition and during the war Bath Iron Works, on the Kennebec River, put this tradition into action by constructing 266 ships. In cooperation with Todd Shipbuilding in South Portland, the two firms employed more than 30,000 people, including 4,000 women.

Maine's postwar economic situation was grim, marked by textile mill closures, heavy migration from the state, and decline in its staple production. Rural poverty became endemic and the state's social services fell well behind the national average. In the 1950s, the Republican ascendancy was shaken, and under the leadership of Frank Morey Coffin and Edmund S. Muskie, the Democratic Party took control of the state government in 1954. Muskie's liberal agenda included environmental reform, minimum wage increases, hospital and school reform, and highway construction. During the 1960s, Mainers assumed a leading role in the nation's new environmental movement. As a U.S. senator, Muskie distinguished himself as the champion of national clean air and water legislation.

Maine's tourist industry became a profitable venture in the decades following the Civil War. The industry was a unique mixture of small-scale shops and folk traditions and large promotional developments launched by railroad, steamship-line, and hotel firms, including the Ricker family's Poland Spring House and spring water bottling company. Visitors were attracted by Maine's reputation for natural beauty, a healthy atmosphere, abundant fish and game resources, and its outdoor activities. A national obsession with an outdoor life quickened interest in Maine's wildlands, rivers, and lakes. The state government slowly became involved in the industry after 1870 with a series of legislative acts protecting Maine's natural wilderness and animal populations, while at the same time encouraging further road and hotel construction in previously remote areas.

The tourist industry gathered momentum during the nineteenth century and played a part in Maine's emergence as a leader in environmental protection in the 1960s. Maine residents have often accepted this tourist industry only reluctantly. Some of the biggest debates in its political arena stem directly from the tourist industry. As tourists flooded into southern Maine, many decided to stay and build vacation homes. This influx of wealthy "out-of-staters" drastically increased land taxes, forcing many long-term residents off their land. The conflict in land management between park land and commercial forest remains one of the most important political debates and few Mainers would shy away from offering their opinion.

Maine's economy continues at an uneven pace—strong in the southern cities and much weaker in the north and east. Maine political leaders have encouraged growth based on new communications, new technology, and an advanced service industry. However, traditionalist sentiment is difficult to overcome and the new technological service industry has not yet taken hold in many parts of Maine.

BIBLIOGRAPHY
Clark, Charles E., James S. Leamon, and Karen Bowden, eds. *Maine in the Early Republic: from Revolution to Statehood.* Hanover, N.H.: University Press of New England, 1988.

Clifford, Harold B. *Maine and Her People,* with a supplement by Charlotte L. Melvin on The Story of Aroostook, Maine's Last Frontier. 4th ed. Freeport, Me.: Bond Wheelwright, 1976.

Cronon, William. *Changes in the Land: Indians, Colonialists, and the Ecology of New England.* New York: Hill and Wang, 1983.

Duncan, Roger. *Coastal Maine: A Maritime History.* New York: Norton, 1992.

Judd, Richard W. *Common Lands, Common People: The Origins of Conservation in Northern New England.* Cambridge, Mass.: Harvard University Press, 1997.

Judd, Richard W., Edwin Churchill, and Joel W. Eastman, eds. *Maine: The Pine Tree State from Prehistory to Present.* Orono: University of Maine Press, 1995.

Longacre, Edward G. *Joshua Chamberlain: The Soldier and the Man.* Conshohocken, Pa.: Combined, 1999.

O'Leary, Wayne, M. *Maine Sea Fisheries: The Rise and Fall of a Native Industry, 1830–1890.* Boston: Northeastern University Press, 1996.

Sanders, Michael S. *The Yard: Building a Destroyer at the Bath Iron Works.* New York: HarperCollins, 1999.

Smith, David C. *A History of Lumbering in Maine, 1861–1960.* Orono: University of Maine Press, 1972.

Taylor, Alan. *Liberty Men and Great Proprietor: The Revolutionary Settlement on the Maine Frontier, 1760–1820.* Chapel Hill: University of North Carolina Press, 1990.

Ulrich, Laurel Thatcher. *A Midwife's Tale: The Life of Martha Ballard, Based on Her Diary, 1785–1812.* New York: Knopf, 1990.

Brian Payne

See also **Aroostook War; Kennebec River Settlements; King Philip's War; King William's War; Passamaquoddy/Penobscot; Wilmot Proviso.**

MAINE, **SINKING OF THE**   (15 February 1898). In January 1898, the second-class battleship *Maine,* under the command of Capt. Charles D. Sigsbee, was ordered from Key West, Florida, to Havana, Cuba, during that island's revolt against Spanish rule, as an "act of friendly courtesy." Spanish authorities in Havana objected to the arrival of the *Maine.* For three weeks, the ship lay moored to a buoy 500 yards off the Havana arsenal. There was considerable ill feeling against the United States among Spanish citizens on the island, but no untoward incident took place until 9:40 P.M. on 15 February, when two explosions threw parts of the *Maine* 200 feet in the air and illuminated the whole harbor. A first dull explosion was followed by one much more powerful, probably that of the forward magazines. The forward half of the ship was reduced to a mass of twisted steel; the after section slowly sank. Two officers and 258 of the crew were killed or died soon afterward. Most of these were buried in Colón Cemetery, Havana.

American and Spanish authorities soon made separate investigations. Their conclusions differed: the Spaniards reported that an internal explosion, perhaps spontaneous combustion in the coal bunkers, had been the cause; the Americans, that the original cause had been an external explosion that in turn had set off the forward magazines.

News of the disaster produced great excitement in the United States, and newspapers such as the *New York Journal* accused the Spanish of complicity in the disaster. Without doubt, the catastrophe stirred up national feeling over the difficulties in Cuba and crystallized in the slogan "Remember the *Maine.*" After two months of deteriorat-

ing relations, the United States declared war on Spain in April 1898.

The wreck remained in Havana harbor until 1911, when U.S. Army engineers built a cofferdam about the wreck, sealed the aft hull of the ship (the only part still intact), and floated it out to sea. There, on 16 March 1912, appropriate minute guns boomed as the *Maine* sank with its flag flying. The remains of sixty-six of the crew found during the raising were buried in Arlington National Cemetery, Virginia. During the removal of the wreck, a board of officers of the navy made a further investigation. Their report, published in 1912, stated that a low form of explosive exterior to the ship caused the first explosion. "This resulted in igniting and exploding the contents of the six-inch reserve magazine, A–14–M, said contents including a large quantity of black powder. The more or less complete explosion of the contents of the remaining forward magazine followed." The chief evidence for this was that the bottom of the ship had been bent upward and folded over toward the stern. European experts, perhaps influenced by several internal explosions in warships in the intervening years, still maintained the theory of an internal explosion. Subsequent investigations drew suspicion to a faulty boiler as the explosion's cause, but no conclusive evidence has ever been found to solve the mystery.

BIBLIOGRAPHY

Gould, Lewis L. *The Spanish-American War and President McKinley.* Lawrence: University Press of Kansas, 1982.

Healy, David F. *The United States in Cuba, 1898–1902: Generals, Politicians, and the Search for Policy.* Madison: University of Wisconsin Press, 1963.

Hoganson, Kristin L. *Fighting for American Manhood: How Gender Politics Provoked the Spanish-American and Philippine-American Wars.* New Haven, Conn.: Yale University Press, 1998.

Trask, David F. *The War with Spain in 1898.* New York: Macmillan; London: Collier Macmillan, 1981.

Walter B. Norris / A. G.

See also **Jingoism; Minesweeping; Spanish-American War; Spanish-American War, Navy in; Warships; Yellow Journalism;** *and picture (overleaf).*

MAJORITY RULE.   A fundamental American concept, evolved from the principle of the sovereignty of the people, is that when two candidates are running for an office, the one who receives more than half of the total votes cast shall be elected, and that person's policies shall be entitled to a fair trial. If three or more candidates are seeking the same office, the concept holds that an absolute majority is not required but that the one who receives a mere plurality, or more votes than any other candidate, shall be elected.

Sinking of the *Maine*. Tabloid headlines such as these in the *New York World* inflamed public opinion and pressured the U.S. government into declaring war on Spain. LIBRARY OF CONGRESS

The operation of majority rule was well illustrated when the election of Thomas Jefferson to the presidency was accepted as sufficient warrant for refusing to approve Federalist changes in the judiciary. Majority rule is limited somewhat by the Constitution. Civil liberties are specifically protected by the fundamental law and cannot be suppressed by a temporary majority. The Constitution itself cannot be amended without the consent of three-fourths (thirty-eight) of the states. Because of constitutional guarantees of freedom of speech and of the press and other liberties, minority groups in the United States are able to oppose the majority. Minority criticism and the ever present possibility that the minority will become the majority have operated to make majority rule work well.

BIBLIOGRAPHY

Bowen, Catherine Drinker. *Miracle at Philadelphia: The Story of the Constitutional Convention.* Boston: Little, Brown, 1966.

Maier, Pauline. *American Scripture: Making the Declaration of Independence.* New York: Knopf, 1997.

Rakove, Jack. *Original Meanings: Politics and Ideas in the Making of the Constitution.* New York: Knopf, 1996.

Tocqueville, Alexis de. *Democracy in America*. London: Saunders and Otley, 1838.

Erik McKinley Eriksson / A. G.

See also **Constitution of the United States; Elections; Elections, Presidential; Judiciary Act of 1801.**

MAKAH is a Native American tribe that resides at the extreme northwestern corner of Washington State, where the Pacific Ocean meets the Strait of Juan de Fuca. Together with the Nuu-chah-nulth bands of Vancouver Island, Canada, the Makah form the Nootkan subgroup of Northwest Coast Native cultures. The first recorded European contact was in 1790 with the Spanish ship *Princesa Real*. The 1855 Treaty of Neah Bay established the reservation while preserving hunting and fishing rights in "usual and accustomed" areas. The aboriginal population of perhaps 2,000 was reduced to 654 by 1861, largely through smallpox epidemics. Tribal enrollment at the beginning of the twenty-first century was approximately 2,300, and 70 percent of tribal members lived on the 44-square-mile reservation, mostly at the settlement of Neah Bay.

Prior to European colonization, Makahs lived in five autonomous villages, Diah't (now Neah Bay), Ba'adah, Wa'atch, Tsooyes, and Ozette. A strong reliance on halibut and marine mammals (whales and seals) distinguished Makahs from the salmon-oriented tribes of Washington State. Accumulation of material wealth and private property ownership were important factors in Makah society, with hierarchies of rank and class characterizing social relationships. Potlatch ceremonies reinforced these social positions and continue into the twenty-first century.

Archaeological excavations at Ozette in the 1970s yielded the most comprehensive collection of Indian artifacts on the Northwest Coast, sparking a cultural revival and renewed pride in tribal identity. Artifacts are displayed at the Makah Cultural and Research Center in Neah Bay, which also teaches Qwiqwidichchuk (the Makah language) and traditional arts.

In 1999 the tribe drew international attention for its resumption of subsistence whale hunting. The Treaty of Neah Bay is the only U.S.–Indian treaty that specifically mentions whaling rights, a reflection of the importance of whaling in local culture. Tribal whaling ended in the 1920s, after non-Indian commercial hunters decimated whale populations. The California gray whale was removed from the endangered species list in 1994, and the tribe began controversial preparations to resume hunting this species. In 1997 the International Whaling Commission approved a subsistence quota that included up to five gray whales per year for the Makah. On 17 May 1999, amid protests, media attention, and Coast Guard protection, a single whale was taken using a combination of ancient and modern technology. Whale meat and blubber

Makah Crafts. A Makah woman displays cedar bark baskets at the Makah reservation in northwestern Washington. NATIONAL ARCHIVES AND RECORDS ADMINISTRATION

were consumed by Makah families for the first time in decades, and indigenous representatives from around the world attended a ceremonial potlatch feast. The tribe at that time made clear its intention to continue subsistence hunting as long as the whale population can support a sustainable harvest.

BIBLIOGRAPHY

Colson, Elizabeth. *The Makah Indians: A Study of an Indian Tribe in Modern American Society*. Manchester, U.K.: Manchester University Press, 1953.

Sullivan, Robert. *A Whale Hunt*. New York: Scribner, 2000.

Swan, James Gilchrist. "The Indians of Cape Flattery, at the Entrance to the Strait of Fuca, Washington Territory." *Smithsonian Contributions to Knowledge* Vol. 16, article 8. Washington, D.C.: Smithsonian Institution, 1870.

Jennifer Sepez

See also **Ozette; Washington, State of; Whaling.**

MALARIA is a disease characterized by chills and fever that recur at regular intervals, anemia, and an enlarged spleen. It is caused by four species of *Plasmodium*, a protozoan. Long prevalent in Europe and Africa, malaria was probably brought to the Americas by colonists and slaves. By 1700 it had become established from South Carolina to New England. Malaria spread into the Mississippi Valley with the American settlers, where it became a commonly accepted part of life. Generally chronic and debilitating to all ages and often fatal, it placed a heavy burden of ill health on settlers, especially along the waterways that formed the chief routes of commerce.

Malaria reached its height in New England in the eighteenth century and after 1800 appeared only sporadically. In the Midwest it reached its peak about 1875, de-

Aid against Malaria. This 1939 photograph by Marion Post Wolcott shows a public health doctor handing out medicine to a tenant family near Columbia, S.C.; both the medical care and the photography were New Deal programs of the Farm Security Administration. LIBRARY OF CONGRESS

clining thereafter quite rapidly in the north. Associated with marshes, malaria in the United States tended to rise with the initial clearing of land and to fall with cultivation and drainage, as Benjamin Rush noted in 1785. Better housing and the development of railroads moved settlement out of the river bottoms, contributing to the decline of malaria.

Cinchona bark, used to treat malaria, was brought to Europe in the 1630s from Peru, and by the eighteenth century was widely used, although often incorrectly. Well into the nineteenth century, American doctors also relied on bloodletting and cathartics. The isolation of quinine by French chemists in 1820 made treatment more practicable, and from the 1850s, quinine was also used to prevent malaria from developing. In 1880 a French army surgeon, Alphonse Laveran, demonstrated the parasitic cause of the disease in the blood of humans. Dr. A. F. A. King of Washington, D.C., correctly speculated on its transmission by mosquito in 1882, and William George MacCollum added significantly to knowledge of the complex life history of the plasmodium in 1897. British physician Ronald Ross made the crucial demonstration of mosquito transmission in 1898. Using anti-mosquito measures and prophylactic quinine, William C. Gorgas in 1901 initiated a campaign that reduced the malaria rate in Havana from 909 per 1,000 in 1899 to 19 per 1,000 in 1908. Later he obtained comparable results in the Canal

Zone, which made possible the building of the PANAMA CANAL.

A decline in antimalaria programs in the 1920s, followed by the depression, led in the early 1930s to a resurgence of the disease in the United States, which was curbed under New Deal relief programs. During World War II, both the Public Health Service and the army increased antimalaria programs in the United States, while overseas actions brought home the global importance of the disease. After the war, the Public Health Service, using the newly developed insecticide DDT, inaugurated a program to eradicate malaria in the United States. In 1935, there were about 4,000 malaria deaths in the country, in 1945 about 400, and by 1952 only 25. Since World War II the United States has also participated in antimalaria campaigns in other countries. Although these efforts have greatly reduced the incidence of malaria, it remains a major health problem in many of the less developed countries.

BIBLIOGRAPHY

Ackerknecht, Erwin Heinz. *Malaria in the Upper Mississippi Valley, 1760–1900.* Baltimore: John Hopkins Press, 1945; New York: Arno Press, 1977.

Jaramillo-Arango, Jaime. *The Conquest of Malaria.* London: W. Heinemann, 1950.

Russell, Paul Farr. *Man's Mastery of Malaria*. London, New York: Oxford University Press, 1955.

Shuler, Alexandria V. *Malaria: Meeting the Global Challenge*. Boston: Oelgeschlager, Gunn, and Hain, 1986.

John B. Blake / h. s.

See also **Epidemics and Public Health; "Silent Spring."**

MALLS, SHOPPING. The rapid, post–World War II ascendancy of the shopping center—of which malls are the largest and most important type—represented the confluence of demographic, technological, and institutional trends affecting the retailing of goods and services that had been under way since the late nineteenth century. A long-term demographic shift toward the concentration of population in urban areas, as well as a steady rise in per capita income, had culminated in the exodus of many middle-class households from increasingly crowded inner cities to the more spacious suburban developments that began to surround metropolitan areas. SUBURBANIZATION, in turn, was only possible because of Americans' increasing reliance on the automobile for personal transportation and the publicly subsidized road and highway infrastructure that supported it. Finally, the success of mass marketing techniques and organizations—especially the advent of regional and national department and chain stores—steadily changed the nature of retail distribution and helped to achieve the economies of scale that facilitated the emergence of a full-blown consumer culture in the postwar United States.

Early Shopping Centers

At the heart of this culture was the shopping mall—a centrally owned and managed cluster of architecturally unified retailing spaces designed to accommodate automobile access on its periphery while restricting traffic to pedestrians in its core. Malls had their precursors in the public marketplaces of the colonial and early national periods and the enclosed arcades of mid-nineteenth-century Europe. The malls' design, construction, and management, however, reflected not only the symbiosis of peculiarly American circumstances, but also the rise of an aggressive new breed of entrepreneur who flourished in the postwar suburban landscape: the real estate developer.

Perhaps the earliest planned shopping district in the United States was built in 1916 in Lake Forest, Illinois, a Chicago suburb, but more influential was Country Club Plaza in Kansas City, Missouri, designed by J. C. Nichols in 1922 as an integral part of a wider suburban community. Although some shopping centers were built in the 1930s (Highland Park Village, Dallas, 1931; River Oaks Center, Houston, 1937), and a few visionary developers like Don M. Casto of Columbus, Ohio, promoted them as the wave of the future, the Depression and World War II delayed their full emergence.

MALLS AND THE DEATH OF MAIN STREET, U.S.A.

In 1985 William Severini Kowinski described the effect of two suburban shopping malls on his hometown of Greensburg, Pennsylvania:

> Now the department stores of Main Street were gone, including Troutman's, which held on as a forlorn and somewhat tawdry three floors of merchandise until early 1985, when it closed completely. Most of the old shops and nearly all the restaurants, coffee shops, and tearooms had closed. But there was a brand-new Troutman's (now owned by a national department store chain) opening at Westmoreland Mall. Sears had already moved there; Penney's and Royer's had long since been at Greengate [Mall]. Two of the five-and-tens had closed, and the other—Murphy's—had new stores at both malls. Many other small businesses relocated at the malls, including a women's store called La Rose Shop, which left after fifty-five years on Main Street under the going-out-of-business-sale banner of THE FUTURE DECIDED. . . . The train station was boarded up and abandoned, and the hotels were empty. The fate of downtown retailing was more than symbolized one spring day shortly after I came back, when the facade of the long-abandoned Bon Ton [department store] literally fell onto Main Street.
>
> It's a short drive from Main Street to Greengate Mall, especially if the driver takes the Route 30 bypass just west of downtown. This east-west bypass was built in the 1960s to make it possible to zip from Ligonier to Pittsburgh without passing through Greensburg's downtown. Few at the time thought it was going to affect Greensburg except for the better. There were too many stoplights in town that slowed the efficient traffic flow, and the impatient cars wanting to get through made walking on Main Street more dangerous than before. But now the sad truth was obvious: Main Street had been totally bypassed. People can drive from Westmoreland Mall to Greengate without crossing Main Street at all, and they do.

SOURCE: William Severini Kowinski, *The Malling of America: An Inside Look at the Great Consumer Paradise* (New York: William Morrow and Company, 1985), p. 43.

Enclosed Regional Malls

At war's end there were only a few hundred shopping centers in existence. By 1958, just a little over a decade later, there were nearly three thousand, although the overwhelming majority (then as half a century later) were what later became known as strip centers: a row of shops with parking in front, usually anchored by a major store, such as a supermarket or a large "five-and-dime." Many large DEPARTMENT STORES, nearly all of which were located in

Shopping Mall. A 1973 photograph of the Old Arcade in downtown Cleveland, built in 1890—the first indoor shopping mall in the United States. NATIONAL ARCHIVES AND RECORDS ADMINISTRATION

the central business districts (CBDs) of cities or on Main Street in smaller towns, were at first reluctant to establish major branches on the suburban periphery, preferring to let customers travel to their long-established locations instead. The man who broke this deadlock and thus pioneered the next stage of shopping center design was Victor Gruen, an Austrian-born Nazi refugee.

Gruen belonged to a reform-minded wave of urban design theorists who were helping to plan many new suburban communities like Levittown, New York, and after the war he quickly became known as the nation's premier designer of shopping centers. Having identified shopping as a vital part of public experience in modern America, Gruen designed shopping centers that were intended to be, as he put it, "crystallization points for suburbia's community life," both as functional marketplaces and as nodes of cultural and recreational activity. From the outset, however, Gruen relied on department stores to assume a key role in shopping center development. He designed his first shopping center for a department store, Milliron's, in suburban Los Angeles in 1947, and in 1954 his innovative two-level, open-air design for Northland Mall in Detroit was underwritten by a development consortium of two major Midwestern department store chains, Dayton's of Minneapolis and Hudson's of Detroit. The Dayton-Hudson Company also financed Gruen's next project, in Edina, Minnesota, outside of Minneapolis. The Southdale Mall opened there in 1956, and Gruen designed it to feature not one but two department stores, each anchoring opposite ends of the two-level mall and separated in the middle by a central court. But even more portentously, Gruen's Southdale was the first completely enclosed mall, sealing consumers inside a controlled and secure shopping environment.

Southdale was a huge success, and over the next two decades its basic layout was duplicated by hundreds of new enclosed malls around the country. Department stores quickly overcame their earlier qualms about suburbia and some chains established their own shopping center development companies, led most notably by Sears, Roebuck's Homart. Relatively cheap land with minimal zoning restrictions, in combination with generous federal tax code changes in 1954 that allowed accelerated depreciation write-offs for new commercial construction, quickly attracted many venture capitalists into lucrative suburban shopping center development. A new generation of real estate developers like Edward J. DeBartolo of Youngstown, Ohio, Melvin Simon of Indianapolis, Indiana, and California's Ernest Hahn began constructing ever-larger shopping malls in advance of existing suburban development, usually near the junctures of highways being built as part of the federal government's ambitious interstate highway system.

Urban Malls

Such regional malls—featuring 300,000-plus square feet of space—sought to attract customers from wide geographic areas, and their rapid proliferation in the 1960s represented competition that overwhelmed older downtown retail districts. (See sidebar.) By the 1970s, however, critics of suburban mall development (who by now included Victor Gruen) helped spur a trend toward locating new malls back in CBDs as centerpieces of urban revitalization projects. Sunbelt developers like John Portman of Atlanta (the Omni) and Gerald D. Hines of Houston (the Galleria) pioneered in the design and construction of multi-use mall facilities that included offices, hotels, and atrium shops. Long-time designer-developer James Rouse's successful renovations of Boston's Faneuil Hall Marketplace (1976), Baltimore's Harborplace (1980), and New York City's South Street Seaport (1983) received national acclaim despite criticism of the apparent commercial gentrification they propelled.

A Questionable Future

By the 1990s, with nearly forty thousand shopping centers—of which almost two thousand were regional malls—signs of an oversaturated and changing market became evident: older malls were in decline; discount retailers like Wal-Mart and the advent of e-commerce were making deep inroads into mall sales; and the shift of women into the workplace had eroded malls' customer base. Hailed as the signature structures of postwar American affluence not long before, these cathedrals of consumption thus entered the new millenium facing an uncertain future.

BIBLIOGRAPHY

Cohen, Lizabeth, Thomas W. Hanchett, and Kenneth T. Jackson. "AHR Forum: Shopping Malls in America." *American Historical Review* 101 (1996): 1049–1121. Three articles discuss aspects of the postwar shopping center boom.

Gillette, Howard, Jr. "The Evolution of the Planned Shopping Center in Suburb and City." *Journal of the American Planning Association* 51 (1985): 449–460.

Harris, Neil. "Spaced Out at the Shopping Center." In his *Cultural Excursions: Marketing Appetites and Cultural Tastes in Modern America*. Chicago: University of Chicago Press, 1990.

Kowinski, William Severini. *The Malling of America: An Inside Look at the Great Consumer Paradise*. New York: Morrow, 1985. Nonscholarly, but still a thoughtful and detailed account.

Scott P. Marler

See also **Consumerism; Retailing Industry.**

MALMÉDY MASSACRE

MALMÉDY MASSACRE (17 December 1944). During the Battle of the Bulge, the First SS Panzer Division under Lieutenant Colonel Joachim Peiper overran a convoy of Battery B, 285th Field Artillery Observation Battalion, in the Belgian Ardennes near the town of Malmédy. On 17 December 1944, the Germans marched approximately one hundred unarmed American prisoners into a field and systematically shot them. A few feigned death and escaped; eighty-six died. Peiper and seventy-two others were subsequently tried and convicted by an American tribunal. Forty-three, including Peiper, were sentenced to death by hanging, the others to imprisonment ranging from ten years to life. The death sentences were later commuted, and none of the convicted served a full prison sentence. Peiper was paroled after ten years.

BIBLIOGRAPHY

Bauserman, John. *The Malmédy Massacre.* Shippensburg, Pa.: White Mane, 1995.

Gallagher, Richard. *The Malmédy Massacre.* New York, 1964.

Weingartner, James J. *Crossroads of Death: The Story of the Malmédy Massacre and Trial.* Berkeley: University of California Press, 1979.

Whiting, Charles. *Massacre at Malmédy: The Story of Jochen Peiper's Battle Group, Ardennes, December, 1944.* New York: Stein and Day, 1971.

Charles B. MacDonald / A. R.

See also **Atrocities in War; Bulge, Battle of the; Violence; War, Laws of.**

MAMMALOGY

MAMMALOGY is a subdivision of vertebrate ZOOLOGY, and its practitioners specialize in the scientific study of the biology of those species included in the class mammalia. Mammalogy as a discipline grew out of the study of the natural history of terrestrial vertebrates; a renewed interest in natural sciences began in Europe during the sixteenth century. In America the scientific study of living and fossil organisms was fostered by President Thomas Jefferson. His description of fossil mammal remains led him to hope that living representatives survived in the interior of North America. The expeditions of Lewis and Clark (1804–1806) and Zebulon Pike (1805–1807) were charged with recording data on the flora and fauna encountered during their travels. Subsequent expeditions sponsored by the U.S. government were staffed in part by scientists, who made important collections of birds and mammals. During the 1820s Thomas Say accompanied Major Stephan Long to the Rocky Mountains; William Keating was the naturalist on Long's Mississippi expeditions. The work of the U.S. Topological Survey led by John C. Fremont in the 1840s and 1850s resulted in many important discoveries of new vertebrate species.

The first major work on North American mammals, written by John James Audubon and J. Bachman, was published between 1846 and 1854. This work was followed by the scholarly work of Spencer Baird in 1859. The scientific study of mammals involved the description of new species and the preservation of reference specimens. The need for a repository for biological materials, such as a museum, became obvious; a reference library to house scientific literature published worldwide was also necessary. The first public museum in what was to become the United States was founded at Charleston, South Carolina, in 1773, and Charles Willson Peale founded his private museum in Philadelphia in 1785, but the national collection of artifacts and specimens began with the establishment of the SMITHSONIAN INSTITUTION in 1846. Within the Smithsonian, Baird organized the U.S. National Museum in 1879. Under the guidance of C. Hart Merriman, the Bureau of Biological Survey was organized in 1886 within the U.S. Department of Agriculture. The collections resulting from the survey were housed at the Smithsonian. The efforts of Merriam and his coworkers greatly advanced knowledge of mammal species and their distributions.

To increase communication among North American mammalogists, the American Society of Mammalogists was founded in 1919 under the leadership of Hartley H. T. Jackson of the Biological Survey. The Society initiated *The Journal of Mammalogy*, which has published articles dealing in a broad manner with studies on the biology of mammals. The society has also fostered research and the publication of results of research continuously since its founding, and it has served, through its annual meetings, as a forum for reviewing research results and addressing national and international issues.

Taxonomic Advances

The description and naming of species and their classification is termed "taxonomy." The collections of the U.S. Biological Survey and other museums' collections have contributed greatly to this endeavor. In 1959 E. Raymond Hall and Keith Kelson published *The Mammals of North America*, a two-volume synthesis of taxonomic and biogeographical information. The volumes offered range maps of the species and subspecies, thus providing an empirical basis for advances in biogeographical theory. This work also laid the groundwork for the 1999 natural history synthesis of the mammalian fauna of North America, *The Smithsonian Book of North American Mammals*.

Studies of the physiological and anatomical structure of mammals have contributed much information to our understanding of how mammalian bodies function. The applications of such knowledge to human medicine is incalculable. The standard laboratory mammals, the mouse, rat, and guinea pig, have made possible many medical advances and breakthroughs. The contribution of mammalian studies to genetics and cytogenetics is also vast. Studies of mammal populations have led to a significant understanding of how ecological communities are organized and function. The study of life history and reproduction has been essential to the formulation of plans for the management and conservation of wildlife populations. The bacteria, viruses, and parasites of non-human mammals are often capable of infecting human hosts, thus causing serious outbreaks of disease. The study of mammalian populations and their diseases has been a focus of public health studies for decades. Rabies, tularemia, plague, Lyme disease, and hemorrhagic fevers are carried by a variety of mammalian hosts, and the study of mammalian populations is necessary to control disease outbreaks.

The fossil mammals of North America have long been studied. The richness of the fauna and the history of episodic extinctions have supplied data and fueled speculation about events leading to a faunal collapse. Extinctions in the last 12,000 years have been linked to human occupation of North America. The ancient mammal fauna of North America was summarized in *Evolution of Tertiary Mammals* (1998), edited by C. M. Janis, K. Scott, and L. L. Jacobs.

Conservation

Conservation concerns in the late nineteenth century focused on North American species: the American bison, pronghorned antelope, beaver, big horned sheep, and grizzly bear. The New York Zoological Society and the National Zoological Park were involved early on in the propagation of endangered species. World concern with vanishing wildlife led to the publication of two important volumes—*Extinct and Vanishing Mammals of the Western Hemisphere* (1942) by G. M. Allen and *Extinct and Vanishing Mammals of the Old World* (1945) by F. Harper—assessing the status of wild mammal populations: Work on endangered species continues to be a priority for CONSERVATION efforts. The scientific study of mammals touches on many related disciplines in biology. Mammalogy is taught as a college-level discipline at most major universities. Collections for study are supported at most major state and university museums.

BIBLIOGRAPHY

Allen, Glover Morrill. *Extinct and Vanishing Mammals of the Western Hemisphere*. New York: New York Zoological Park, 1942.

Audubon, John J., and John Bachman. *The Viviparous Quadrupeds of North America*. 3 vols. New York: J. J. Audubon, 1846–1854.

Baird, Spencer Fullerton. *Mammals of North America*. Philadelphia: J. B. Lippincott, 1859.

Birney, Elmer C., and Jerry R. Choate, eds. *Seventy-Five Years of Mammalogy*. Provo, Utah: American Society of Mammalogists, 1994.

Hall, E. Raymond. *The Mammals of North America*. 2d ed. 2 vols. New York: Wiley, 1981.

Janis, Christine M., Kathleen Scott, and Louis L. Jacobs, eds. *Evolution of Tertiary Mammals in North America*. New York: Cambridge University Press, 1998.

Martin, Paul S., and Richard G. Klein, eds. *Quaternary Extinctions*. Tucson: University of Arizona Press, 1984.

Sterling, Keir B. *Last of the Naturalists: The Career of C. Hart Merriam*. New York: Arno Press, 1977.

Wilson, D. E., and John F. Eisenberg. "Origin and Applications of Mammalogy in North America." In *Current Mammalogy*, edited by Hugh Genoways. New York: Plenum, 1990.

John F. Eisenberg

See also **Endangered Species; Zoological Parks.**

MANAGEMENT. *See* **Scientific Management.**

MANASSAS, BATTLE OF. *See* **Bull Run, Battles of.**

MANCHURIA AND MANCHUKUO. Manchuria, a region in China roughly coincident with the present-day provinces of Liaoning, Jilin, and Heilongjiang, first became a focus of U.S. policy in East Asia in the late 1890s. The accelerating encroachment of foreign powers undermined the territorial integrity of China, impeded free access to Chinese markets, and threatened American interests. Secretary of State John Hay's Open Door Notes of 1899 and 1900 articulated a general policy that favored equal commercial opportunity throughout China, but Russian activity in Manchuria was his primary target. Between 1900 and 1905, the United States made common cause with Japan, which saw Russian power in Manchuria as a strategic threat, and provided Tokyo with diplomatic and financial support in the Russo-Japanese War (1904–1905). Friendship between the United States and Japan suffered after the latter took over Russian holdings in the southern part of Manchuria. Japanese claims to special rights in this part of China became a persistent irritant in U.S.-Japan relations for the next twenty-five years.

The United States launched a number of diplomatic initiatives aimed at dislodging Japan from southern Manchuria, most notably between 1907 and 1910 and between 1918 and 1922. They met with little success, in part because of Japanese intransigence but also because of the limits of American interest in settling the problem. Enforcing the Open Door in Manchuria was not worth the costs of alienating the Japanese, whose cooperation was essential to American policy goals elsewhere in China and in the Pacific.

This calculus continued to operate to a significant degree even after the Japanese army occupied Manchuria outright in 1931 (Manchurian Incident) and established the puppet state of Manzhouguo (Manchukuo) in 1932. The United States condemned the invasion and refused to recognize any changes in the status quo in China that violated existing treaties, but it took no further action. Not until well after the outbreak of the second Sino-Japanese War in 1937 did the United States begin a program of economic sanctions against Japan. Between 1938 and 1941, some Japanese officials, alarmed at the steady deterioration of relations with the United States, initiated attempts at reconciliation, but American diplomats made it clear that no settlement in China that failed to restore the status quo ante 1931, including the return of Manchuria to China, would be acceptable. Even Japan's most conciliatory leaders were unable to concede Manzhouguo, and this impasse dashed any hopes for averting a Japanese-American confrontation. Manchuria ceased to be a separate consideration for U.S. policy toward China and East Asia after Japan's defeat in World War II (1945), despite a brief period of uncertainty associated with the outbreak of civil war in China (1946–1949).

BIBLIOGRAPHY

Cohen, Warren I. *America's Response to China: A History of Sino-American Relations*. 4th ed. New York: Columbia University Press, 2000.

Hunt, Michael H. *Frontier Defense and the Open Door: Manchuria in Chinese-American Relations, 1895–1911*. New Haven, Conn.: Yale University Press, 1973.

Iriye, Akira. *Pacific Estrangement: Japanese American Expansion, 1897–1911*. Cambridge, Mass.: Harvard University Press, 1972.

LaFeber, Walter. *The Clash: U.S.-Japanese Relations*. New York: W.W. Norton, 1997.

Yoshihisa Tak Matsusaka

See also **China, Relations with; Japan, Relations with; Open Door Policy; Russia, Relations with; Sino-Japanese War.**

MANDAN, FORT. Constructed in November 1804 near present-day Bismarck, North Dakota, Fort Mandan served as winter quarters for the Lewis and Clark Expedition (1804–1806). A fortified encampment in the rough-hewn style of other seasonal military installations, the fort's location near the Mandan and Hidatsa Indian villages was a matter of crucial importance. These horticultural peoples were situated at the center of a vast trading network that extended over much of central North America; thus, frequent councils with Native leaders and European traders provided Meriwether Lewis and William Clark with abundant information on the lands and peoples to the west. The expedition left Fort Mandan in April 1805, and passed the site again in August 1806, but by

this time a prairie fire of unknown origin had destroyed the fort.

BIBLIOGRAPHY

Appleman, Roy E. *Lewis & Clark: Historic Places Associated with Their Transcontinental Exploration (1804–1806)*. Washington, D.C.: National Park Service, 1975.

Ronda, James P. *Lewis and Clark among the Indians*. Lincoln: University of Nebraska Press, 1988.

Mark David Spence

See also **Lewis and Clark Expedition.**

MANDAN, HIDATSA, ARIKARA. The tribes known today as the Three Affiliated Tribes of Fort Berthold Indian Reservation had separate origins but shared a village lifestyle in the Missouri River Valley. They built fortified towns of circular earth lodges on the river terraces, and lived by hunting buffalo and farming corn, squash, melons, beans, and tobacco. In the eighteenth and nineteenth centuries their villages were commercial hubs; at annual trade fairs they exchanged agricultural produce, horses, and goods, such as flint tools and fine quillworks for the products of the Sioux, Cheyennes, Pawnees, Arapahos, Crees, Assiniboines, and Crows. Village life was organized around age-grade societies, which had ceremonial, social, and civic duties, and matrilineal clans. Both individuals and clans attained power through ownership of sacred bundles, the oldest of which were linked to mythic cycles that were periodically re-enacted in spectacular ceremonies. The most famous ceremony, the Mandan's Okipa, was a weeklong observance that culminated in the SUN DANCE.

The languages of the three tribes were mutually incomprehensible. The languages of the Mandans and the Hidatsas were both Siouan, but dissimilar. The Arikaras (Sahnish) spoke a Caddoan language and were closely related to the Pawnees of Nebraska, where they probably originated. By the 1600s, the Mandans lived in a cluster of villages around the Heart River near present Bismarck, North Dakota, where they were first visited in 1738 by Pierre Gaultier de Varennes, sieur de la Vérendrye. The Hidatsas were comprised of three village groups—the Awatixa, Awaxawi, and Hidatsas—with disparate origins to the north and east, who were living near each other on the Knife River near Stanton, North Dakota, by the eighteenth century. Early visitors referred to them confusingly as Gros Ventres, Big Bellies, or Minitarees.

The movement of Sioux tribes onto the Plains in the eighteenth century gave the village Indians a formidable new enemy. A smallpox pandemic from 1780 to 1782 decimated the villages and left them vulnerable.

The Mandans and Hidatsas consolidated for mutual defense. In the 1830s, they were made famous by artists George Catlin and Karl Bodmer, who visited the flourishing Knife River Villages and their attendant trading

219

Arikaras. A photograph by Edward S. Curtis of a family on the Fort Berthold Reservation, N.D. LIBRARY OF CONGRESS

post, Fort Clark. Yet, a new smallpox epidemic in 1837 reduced the Hidatsas by half and nearly wiped out the Mandans, including their great leader Four Bears. Again the tribes moved north to found a single village named Like-a-Fishhook, to which was attached the AMERICAN FUR COMPANY post of Fort Berthold. There, traditional life again took hold. The Arikara joined them in 1860s.

The Fort Laramie Treaty of 1851 defined over 12.6 million acres of western North Dakota as Mandan Hidatsa land, but executive orders in 1870 and 1880 reduced that to 1.2 million without tribal consent. Starting in 1886 the Fort Berthold Reservation was allotted to individual tribal members, breaking up the age-old village lifestyle and scattering families on 160-acre farms. Unallotted land was sold; by 2000 the reservation was still 53% owned by non-Indians. Farming and ranching gave the tribe a measure of prosperity by 1934, when an elected tribal business council was established under the Indian Reorganization Act.

In the 1940s, the U.S. Army Corps of Engineers devised the Pick-Sloan plan to build a chain of massive dams on the Missouri River. When the Garrison Dam was completed in 1954, all the arable bottomland on Fort Berthold Reservation, where 90% of the tribe lived, was covered by Lake Sakakawea—ironically named for the Indian heroine Lewis and Clark had met among the Hidatsas. Only the arid, rugged uplands remained. The result was instant poverty.

The years after 1954 were spent in recovery from the dam's devastating effects. New towns such as New Town, Mandaree, and White Shield replaced older communities. The tribe developed the Four Bears Recreation Area, the Four Bears Casino, and the Fort Berthold Community College to provide training, employment, and cultural renewal. Tribal enrollment in 2000 was 8,400, of which 3,776 lived on the reservation.

BIBLIOGRAPHY

Gilman, Carolyn, and Mary Jane Schneider. *The Way to Independence: Memories of a Hidatsa Indian Family, 1840–1920.* St. Paul: Minnesota Historical Society Press, 1987.

Meyer, Roy W. *The Village Indians of the Upper Missouri: The Mandans, Hidatsas, and Arikaras.* Lincoln: University of Nebraska Press, 1977.

Schneider, Mary Jane. *North Dakota Indians: An Introduction.* Dubuque, Iowa: Kendall/Hunt, 1986.

Carolyn Gilman

See also **Tribes: Great Plains.**

MANGEURS DE LARD, or "pork eaters," was a term applied to each year's new crop of recruits for the fur trade. While en route from Canada, they were fed on pea soup, bread, and pork, but chiefly on the latter. They were scorned by veteran trappers and assigned only the most menial tasks. New workers were only bound for a period of five years' service, but their wages were so low that they customarily ended the apprenticeship in debt to the company and were forced to remain as employees. The term was frequently applied to any newcomer.

BIBLIOGRAPHY

Lavendar, David. *The Fist in the Wilderness.* Garden City, N.Y.: Doubleday, 1964; Lincoln: University of Nebraska Press, 1998.

Ray, Arthur. *Indians and the Fur Trade: Their Role as Trappers, Hunters, and Middlemen in the Lands Southwest of Hudson Bay, 1660–1870.* Toronto; Buffalo, N.Y.: University of Toronto Press, 1974.

Carl L. Cannon / T. D.

See also **Fur Companies; Fur Trade and Trapping; Voyageurs.**

MANHATTAN. Geography largely shaped the character and development of Manhattan, the acknowledged heart of New York City. An island, Manhattan was only linked to the "outlet" boroughs by bridges and tunnels in the late nineteenth century. Its location, dominating New York Harbor, ensured that it would emerge as one of the major centers of colonial and national commerce. Originally settled around its southern tip (the Battery), Manhattan expanded northward to Canal Street by the American Revolution, continued to Greenwich Village by the Age of Jackson, and encompassed the upper East and West Sides above Herald Square (Thirty-third Street) in the mid- and late nineteenth century. The fields of Harlem and beyond, above Central Park, were settled at the end of the nineteenth century and just after.

Manhattan's economic centricity in turn guaranteed its political clout and helped shape its national claim to cultural prominence. This island has always had an enormous impact on American literature, theater, and art. Writers centered on Manhattan, for example, included the Algonquin Round Table, GREENWICH VILLAGE bohemia, and the HARLEM RENAISSANCE. Broadway and later off BROADWAY dominated the landscape of American drama. Manhattan's great museums, particularly the famed "museum mile" along upper Fifth Avenue, became among the best in the world. Its prominent role along the entire spectrum of human endeavor has not always made Manhattan beloved by Americans, but it is a place most Americans want to visit.

BIBLIOGRAPHY

Burrows, Edwin G., and Mike Wallace. *Gotham*. New York: Oxford University Press, 1999.

Jackson, Kenneth T., ed. *The Encyclopedia of New York City*. New York: New-York Historical Society, 1995.

Carl E. Prince

See also **New York City.**

MANHATTAN PROJECT, the secret American effort during World War II to construct an atomic bomb. Following the discovery of nuclear fission in Nazi Germany in late 1938, physicists the world over recognized the possibility of utilizing the enormous energy released by the splitting of an atom. If enough neutrons could be emitted by any given "broken" atom, such that at least one neutron struck another atom, causing it to break apart, a self-perpetuating "chain reaction" would result. Such a process, if controlled at a suitable rate, could serve as a power source, or "reactor." If a chain reaction proceeded unchecked, it could result in an explosion of unprecedented magnitude.

Several European scientists who had fled Nazi persecution in Europe felt it was their duty to alert the U.S. government to this new danger. In August 1939, the Hungarian émigré physicist Leo Szilard convinced Albert Einstein to write President Franklin D. Roosevelt and urge increased government support for research on the element most likely to support a chain reaction, uranium. By early 1940, government funding had commenced on a variety of related subjects, and in 1941 a series of studies confirmed the potential that uranium research held to create a usable weapon before the end of the war. In Jan-

uary 1942—only weeks after the Japanese attack on Pearl Harbor—Roosevelt gave the go-ahead to proceed with a full-scale effort to develop the atomic bomb.

By this time it was obvious that large factories would eventually have to be built. Because the work was now being done in secrecy, and considerable construction was foreseen, the Manhattan Engineer District of the U.S. Army Corps of Engineers was created in August 1942 to oversee the entire atomic bomb program. (It was initially headquartered in New York in order to be close to the fission research then being conducted at Columbia University.) The following month, Colonel Leslie R. Groves was promoted to brigadier general and given command of what was coming to be known as the Manhattan Project. Groves quickly brought in major contractors such as Stone and Webster and the Dupont Chemical Company. Less than four years after the discovery of fission, the program to build an atomic bomb had grown from a primarily academic pursuit to what was becoming, by September 1942, a prototypical example of what Dwight D. Eisenhower would later dub the "military-industrial complex." At its height a mere three years later, the Manhattan Project employed more than 130,000 men and women, having already spent more than $2 billion.

The most pressing problem immediately facing Groves was the acquisition, in an extremely short amount of time, of a quantity of fissionable material sufficient first for experimentation and thereafter for the production of at least one bomb. The kind of uranium needed to generate a chain reaction, the isotope U-235, comprised only 0.7 percent of all naturally occurring uranium, and a variety of exotic and unproven techniques were proposed for "enriching" uranium, or increasing the amount of U-235 contained in a sample. Following a period of intense debate, the scientists in November 1942 made their best guess as to which of these methods showed the most promise, choosing gaseous diffusion and electromagnetic separation. Groves immediately ordered the construction of two massive, full-scale uranium-enrichment plants. In less than three years their site at Oak Ridge, Tennessee, grew from remote farmland to the fifth largest town in the state.

In early 1941, a second path to the atomic bomb was pioneered by the discovery of a new element: plutonium. This substance did not occur in nature but could be created by irradiating common uranium. In December 1942, Enrico Fermi demonstrated this by producing the world's first controlled nuclear chain reaction in a "pile," or reactor, constructed beneath the west stands of the University of Chicago's Stagg Field. Soon, three gigantic reactors were under construction on the banks of the Columbia River near Hanford, Washington, to mass produce plutonium.

The final task remaining was to devise the actual means by which these "special nuclear materials" could be transformed into practical weapons. In late 1942, Groves placed J. Robert Oppenheimer in charge of the

J. Robert Oppenheimer. The physicist and educator who led the scientific team that created the first atomic bomb; he later raised moral concerns about the spread and use of atomic energy, and during the Cold War he was suspended as an adviser to the U.S. Atomic Energy Commission, which regarded him as a security risk. NATIONAL ARCHIVES AND RECORDS ADMINISTRATION

18,000 tons of TNT. Oppenheimer later reported that the blast reminded him of a line from the *Bhagavad-Gita:* "Now I am become Death, the destroyer of worlds." The reaction of the test director, Kenneth Bainbridge, was more succinct: "Now we are all sons of bitches." On the morning of 6 August 1945, an American B-29 bomber dropped the uranium bomb on the Japanese port city of Hiroshima; three days later the second, plutonium device "Fat Man," was dropped on Nagasaki. Japan offered to surrender the following day. Although estimates vary, it is likely that by the end of 1945, there were at least 200,000 deaths directly attributable to the two bombings. Most were civilians. The total number of deaths after five years, including radiation and other secondary effects, may have been well over 300,000. At the beginning of 1947, control of the growing U.S. nuclear arsenal was formally transferred to the civilian Atomic Energy Commission, and in August of that year, the Manhattan Engineer District was formally disbanded.

BIBLIOGRAPHY

Gosling, F. G. *The Manhattan Project: Making the Atomic Bomb.* Washington, D.C.: History Division, Department of Energy, 1999.

Hewlett, Richard G., and Oscar E. Anderson Jr. *A History of the United States Atomic Energy Commission.* Vol. 1: *The New World, 1939–1946.* University Park: Pennsylvania State University Press, 1962. Comprehensive official history.

Rhodes, Richard. *The Making of the Atomic Bomb.* New York: Simon and Schuster, 1986. Pulitzer Prize–winning account focusing on the activities at Los Alamos.

David Rezelman
Lawrence Badash

See also **Nuclear Weapons; World War II.**

new weapons laboratory to be built on an isolated mesa in the desert at Los Alamos, New Mexico. Oppenheimer soon managed to assemble a virtual "dream team" of scientists drawn from around the world. Relatively little difficulty was encountered in the design of a uranium weapon. One piece of U-235 could be fired at another in a gun barrel, such that together they would form a critical, or explosive, mass. For technical reasons this crude method was unsuitable for plutonium, however, and, ultimately, a new technique called implosion was conceived, wherein a small sphere of plutonium was rapidly compressed to critical mass by conventional high explosives.

There had never been much doubt that "Little Boy," the gun-type uranium weapon, would work, and on 14 July 1945 it was shipped from Los Alamos to begin its journey westward toward Japan. Because the implosion process was so novel, however, a test of the plutonium design was held near Alamagordo, New Mexico, on 16 July 1945. This test, named "Trinity" by Oppenheimer, exceeded the expectations of almost every scientist at Los Alamos by exploding with a force equivalent to more than

MANIFEST DESTINY. In 1845 John L. O'Sullivan coined the term "manifest destiny" in reference to a growing conviction that the United States was preordained by God to expand throughout North America and exercise hegemony over its neighbors. In the *United States Magazine and Democratic Review* (July–August 1845, p. 5) he argued for "the fulfillment of our manifest destiny to overspread the continent allotted by Providence for the free development of our yearly multiplying millions." Around the time of O'Sullivan's writing, the United States saw an extraordinary territorial growth of 1.2 million square miles, an enlargement of more than 60 percent. Most of this growth occurred at the expense of the newly independent Mexico and the Native American nations. The expansion happened at such an accelerated pace that people like O'Sullivan thought that even larger expansions were inevitable, necessary, and desirable—hence the origin of the concept of manifest destiny.

Manifest destiny was obviously a defense of what is now called IMPERIALISM. It was a complex set of beliefs that incorporated a variety of ideas about race, religion, culture, and economic necessity. Some people, like the land speculators that settled in Florida, Texas, and Native American lands, wanted more land to get rich. Some fled poverty in Europe and eastern metropolitan centers. Some assumed that without spreading out to fresh lands the nation would languish. Some sought to perpetuate the institution of slavery by expanding it to new territories. Some believed that expansion into "uncivilized" regions would spread progress and democracy. It was convenient for all to think that they had the divine right to acquire and dominate because they had the proper economic system and the most developed culture and belonged to the most advanced race.

Origins of the Idea

This conviction of a destined glorious future for the United States had roots in colonial times. The influential Puritan John Winthrop wrote, "We shall be as a City upon a Hill, the eyes of all people are upon us." Many colonial leaders adopted time-honored expansion imagery from the Bible, portraying northern European Protestant colonists as the new Israelites and North America as the new Promised Land to justify conquering new lands and dominating other cultures.

When colonists attempted emancipation from Britain, the rebellion heightened the importance of the idea that the North American colonists were special individuals selected by God to rule over an extended territory. Insurgent leaders purposely sought Promised Land imageries for the new nation's symbols. The British forces were seen as the Egyptian soldiers, the Atlantic Ocean was the new Red Sea, and George Washington became the "American Moses."

With independence came new ideas that encouraged the desire to extend the country beyond the original perimeter of the thirteen colonies. Expansionist patriots reasoned that expansion was linked to the survival of republicanism. Not only did the new nation have the divine assignment of spreading the true religion of Protestantism by example and enlargement, but it also had the responsibility of spreading its political tenets in the same manner. An upsurge in births and immigration was directly tied to the promises of expansion, which included cheap land and economic opportunities west of the Appalachian Mountains. The country's population grew from about 5 million in 1800 to more than 23 million by midcentury. The frontier offered relief in the form of land, resources, and commercial opportunities to those affected by the economic downturns of 1818 and 1829. Seizing Native American and Spanish lands would allow the national economy to expand, acquire more raw materials for fledgling industries, and secure new commercial outposts, particularly those of the Far East. Expansion would ensure new markets for an increasing U.S. industrial output. The expansionists saw no contradiction between advancing their capital and improving the world by

stimulating economic activity. Popular bourgeois values of self-sufficiency and self-rule received unexpected support from the general public as it tried its luck in the new lands. These expansions, however, also created a permanent economic and cultural underclass composed of the Native Americans and Hispanics who had been living in those territories.

Manifest Destiny in Practice

The MONROE DOCTRINE exemplified the mood and ideas behind manifest destiny. President James Monroe said that the Americas were "not to be considered as subjects for future colonization by any European powers," paving the way for an increasing United States hegemony over its neighbors by attempting to cut off European influence in the Western Hemisphere. The gradual inroads of English-speaking settlers from the United States into the Mexican province of Texas, starting in 1823, is one of the clearest examples of manifest destiny's coming of age. Mexico opened the land for colonization, but the response was so overwhelming that Mexican authorities lost control of the province. Motivated by ideas of manifest destiny, the new English-speaking settlers rebelled in 1835 in an attempt to form an independent state. A series of reactions led to the annexation of Texas in 1845 and war between Mexico and the United States in 1846. The war ended on 2 February 1848 with the Treaty of Guadalupe Hidalgo ceding to United States the present-day Arizona, California, New Mexico, Texas, and parts of Colorado, Nevada, and Utah. The goal of reaching the Pacific coast was accomplished.

The Civil War of 1861–1865 did not cool the expansionist impulses completely. The military strength built during the war was now used against Native Americans to gain their land in the Northwest. Expansionists, now freely using the term manifest destiny to justify their wishes, also turned their attention to the Caribbean, Central America, and the Pacific. Times had changed since the antebellum period, and now the ideologies behind manifest destiny contained elements of Darwinism and beliefs in social and climatic determinism. North Americans felt they had "the white's man burden" in the Americas and it was their responsibility to lead the inferior races in the south to better lives. These new expressions of the principles behind O'Sullivan's manifest destiny inspired the United States' intervention in the Cuban War for Independence in 1895 and in Panama in 1903. Military and technical successes in these enterprises led to a transoceanic North American empire. Altered ideas of manifest destiny, combined with other forces of the time, continued to determine international relations through the twentieth century.

Notwithstanding the popularity of the principles advanced by the different expressions of manifest destiny, not everyone accepted the expansionism they entailed. The Whig Party opposed expansion, believing that the republican experiment in the United States would fail if

Manifest Destiny. Ever since independence, most Americans believed that it was their God-given right to expand the country's borders as far as possible across the North American continent. In this nineteenth-century illustration, an angelic woman oversees and protects pioneers as they head westward across America. © ARCHIVE PHOTOS, INC.

the nation grew too large. Politicians from the Northeast felt they would lose political power in Congress if the United States admitted more states into the union. Attempts to expand further into Mexico were defeated by racism toward Mexicans. The abolitionists also opposed expansion, particularly if it would bring slave territories into the union. Pacifists became gravely concerned with the casualties of expansion and opposed its violence. Yet the overall opposition to the ideas of manifest destiny was modest. Most people gladly embraced the concept that they belonged to a superior culture and race, and that Providence or genetics had preordained the people of the United States for greatness. Even black leaders like Frederick Douglass accepted the principles of manifest destiny when he supported the annexation of Santo Domingo.

Native Americans and Hispanics, however, were not passive victims of the expansion. The stories of Native American and Mexican resistance to Anglo-Saxon occupation are well known. Yet some local elites seeking opportunities for profit adapted their interests to the new circumstances, even when other members of their own ethnic groups opposed their moves.

BIBLIOGRAPHY

Cherry, Conrad. *God's New Israel: Religious Interpretations of American Destiny.* Englewood Cliffs, N.J.: Prentice Hall, 1971.

Johannsen, Robert Walter, Sam W. Haynes, and Christopher Morris, eds. *Manifest Destiny and Empire: American Antebellum Expansionism.* College Station: Texas A&M University Press, 1997.

Joseph, Gilbert M., Catherine C. LeGrand, and Ricardo D. Salvatore, eds. *Close Encounters of Empire: Writing the Cultural History of U.S.–Latin American Relations.* Durham, N.C.: Duke University Press, 1998.

Koning, Hans. *The Conquest of America: How the Indian Nations Lost Their Continent.* New York: Monthly Review Press, 1993.

Owsley, Frank Lawrence, Jr., and Gene A. Smith. *Filibusters and Expansionists: Jeffersonian Manifest Destiny, 1800–1821.* Tuscaloosa: University of Alabama Press, 1997.

Weinberg, Albert Katz. *Manifest Destiny: A Study of Nationalist Expansionism in American History.* New York: AMS Press, 1976.

Dennis R. Hidalgo

See also **Westward Migration; "City on a Hill."**

MANILA BAY, BATTLE OF (1 May 1898). Upon the declaration of war with Spain in April 1898, George Dewey, commander of the U.S. Asiatic Squadron, received orders to attack the Spanish squadron under Adm. Patricio Montojo y Pasarón at Manila. On 30 April, Dewey reached Manila Bay and entered at midnight, disregarding serious risks from shore batteries and mines. Off Manila at dawn, he sighted Montojo's force ten miles westward. At 5:41 A.M. Dewey opened fire and by early afternoon every Spanish ship, to quote Dewey's report, "was sunk, burned, or deserted." The Spanish suffered 381 casualties, the Americans but nine wounded. Manila surrendered on 13 August.

BIBLIOGRAPHY

Spector, Ronald H. *Admiral of the New Empire: The Life and Career of George Dewey.* Baton Rouge: Louisiana State University Press, 1974; Columbia: University of South Carolina Press, 1988.

Trask, David F. *The War with Spain in 1898.* New York: Macmillan; London: Collier Macmillan, 1981; Lincoln: University of Nebraska Press, 1996.

Allan Westcott / A. R.

See also **Imperialism; Navy, United States; Philippines; Spanish-American War; Spanish-American War, Navy in.**

MANN ACT. Congress passed the White Slave Traffic Act on 25 June 1910. Commonly known as the "Mann Act" in honor of the bill's sponsor, Illinois Representative James Robert Mann, the act was designed to eliminate "white slavery," broadly understood as forced female prostitution. The act makes it a felony to transport in interstate or foreign commerce or in the District of Columbia "any woman or girl for the purpose of prostitution or debauchery, or for any other immoral purpose." Conviction under the original law was punishable by a "fine not exceeding five thousand dollars" and/or "imprisonment of not more than five years."

The act was inspired, and possibly drafted, by Mann's friend Edwin W. Sims, United States District Attorney for the Northern District of Illinois (1906–1911), an early anti–white slavery crusader. Reform groups such as the American Purity Alliance and the Woman's Christian Temperance Union were influential in its passage, as were "purity journals" such as *Vigilance* and *The Light.* The dramatic rhetoric used to describe white slavery during the early twentieth century has led some historians to explain the law as a response to moral hysteria. The actual prevalence of white slavery in 1910 is a matter of debate.

PROSTITUTION was traditionally considered a matter for the state and local police power; indeed, in 1910 every state had laws regulating prostitutes and "bawdy houses." Beginning in the early twentieth century, however, some crimes, like white slavery, were considered too widespread and insidious for states to handle without federal assistance. Congress passed the Mann Act under its power to regulate interstate and foreign commerce. It is one of several federal police power statutes enacted under the COMMERCE CLAUSE during the Progressive Era (Pure Food and Drug Act, 1906; Harrison Narcotic Drug Act, 1914). The act met little opposition, despite some federalism objections. The Department of Justice and its newly formed investigative unit, the Bureau of Investigation (now known as the FBI), were primary enforcement agencies.

The act was passed with a narrow purpose: to allow federal prosecution of those who force women into prostitution. It has been used to punish both commercial and noncommercial sexual behavior. In the first few years after enactment, police officers and Bureau agents used the act to track prostitutes and drive brothels underground. In the late teens and 1920s noncommercial offenses, such as interstate adultery, were prosecuted with some enthusiasm. Under the leadership of FBI Director J. Edgar Hoover (1924–1972) the law was generally used to convict racketeers involved in prostitution; on occasion, it was used to convict noncommercial offenders and/or political miscreants. Prosecution plummeted during the 1960s and 1970s. Since the 1980s, prosecutors have used an amended version of the law, among other things, to combat rape, male prostitution, pornography, child abuse, and international human trafficking.

Federal judges have been largely sympathetic to the act, upholding it against federalism and right-based challenges. The law was first validated by the Supreme Court in *Hoke v. United States* (1913). *Caminetti v. United States* (1917) has become famous (and infamous) for its application of the ejusdem generis rule of statutory construction.

BIBLIOGRAPHY

Bristow, Edward J. *Prostitution and Prejudice: The Jewish Fight against White Slavery, 1870–1939.* New York: Schocken, 1983.

Connelly, Mark T. *The Response to Prostitution in the Progressive Era.* Chapel Hill: University of North Carolina Press, 1980.

Langum, David J. *Crossing over the Line: Legislating Morality and the Mann Act.* Chicago: University of Chicago Press, 1994.

Kimberly A. Hendrickson

See also **Police Power.**

MANNERS AND ETIQUETTE go hand in hand, but are not the same. Etiquette is a set of rules dealing with exterior form. Manners are an expression of inner character. According to Emily Post, perhaps the most influential American writer on etiquette in the twentieth century, "manners are made up of trivialities of deportment which can be easily learned if one does not happen to know them; manner is personality—the outward manifestation of one's innate character and attitude toward life." Manners are common sense, a combination of generosity of spirit and specific know-how. Rules of etiquette are the guiding codes that enable us to practice manners.

Most commentators would agree with Emily Post and add that rather than being stiff, rigid rules, proper etiquette is meant to help people get along with each other and avoid conflict. Respect, kindness, and consideration form the basis of good manners and good citizenship. Etiquette becomes the language of manners. Rules of etiquette cover behavior in talking, acting, living, and moving; in other words, every type of interaction and every situation.

History

Proper codes of behavior have been a concern for thousands of years. The first known book on appropriate behavior was a guide that Ptah-hotep, a government official in Egypt in 2500 B.C., wrote for his son. Several Greeks and Romans wrote behavior guides, including Aristotle, Horace, Cicero, and Plutarch. In thirteenth-century Europe, the chivalric code established precisely and minutely the proper behavior for knights regarding the Christian church, their country, and the treatment of women. During the reign of Louis XIV (1638–1715) in France, the term "etiquette" came into use. Based on the French word "ticket," which denoted the proper paths for nobility to follow in the gardens of the palace of Versailles, the rules of etiquette came to provide a daily, very precise list of functions related to times, places, and proper dress and behavior. Thus, proper etiquette came to be associated with the upper classes and those trying to emulate their behavior.

Nevertheless, proper manners were a concern even of leaders in the more democratic society of eighteenth-century America. At age fourteen, George Washington transcribed his own "Rules of Civility." William Penn published collections of maxims on personal and social conduct. Benjamin Franklin's very popular *Poor Richard's Almanac* was full of comments on proper behavior. During the nineteenth century, hundreds of books on etiquette were published in the United States. These were designed for the common person and schoolchildren as well as the upper classes. One of the most popular, which has survived to the twenty-first century, is the *Youth's Educator for Home and Society*, published in 1896, which covered a wide variety of situations, including the usual—parties, traveling, weddings, parents and children, letter writing, and personal hygiene—but also, cycling.

As society has changed, so have rules for proper behavior. After World War I (1914–1918), society became more open as roles of women began to change. Many believed that proper manners would become less important. In 1922, Emily Post published the most popular book on etiquette for society, business, politics, and home and family. Her book became the model for thousands of others since then. The sixteenth edition of *Etiquette* was published in 1997. Instead of decrying the lack of etiquette among Americans, Post applauded their youthful enthusiasm and sought only to refine it. She claimed that improvements in taste in home decoration were evidence of progress. She also pointed out other examples of improvements; for instance, unlike earlier times, weddings no longer had to be set by noon for fear that the bridegroom would no longer be sober after that hour.

There are still many writers on etiquette and manners. Some of the most popular include Miss Manners, or Judith Martin, who presents her comments in several types of media; Letitia Baldridge, who was particularly influential during the late 1900s; Sue Fox, who joined the "dummies" series with her *Etiquette for Dummies* (1999); and Emily Post's great granddaughter-in-law, Peggy Post.

The Present

Many manners commentators agree that although society and manners changed before World War II (1939–1945), the changes since then have amounted to nearly a revolution, and writers have created etiquette rules for the new situations. One way to describe the difference is that rules of etiquette are no longer for how to behave properly in a restricted society, but to provide knowledge of ways to put others at ease. Few people now have to deal with servants, mansions, or elaborate entertainment, but they still have to deal with difficult or unknown situations in business or the community. American society has also become much less formal. One simple yet indicative example of the change is the proper greeting. Instead of the formal "How do you do," "hello" is now considered appropriate. Also, earlier it was not considered proper for a girl or woman to walk alone. Etiquette delineated when she should be accompanied by a woman her age, by an older woman, or by a man. Today, the advice not to walk alone would be a safety concern.

Probably the greatest change since the 1960s has been in the relationship between men and women toward greater equality. Lord Chesterfield once declared that no provocation whatever could justify any man not being civil to any woman. "It was due them and the only protection women had against a man's superior strength." Men are no longer expected to protect women in every instance; rather, they are to treat them equally and with the consideration due every person. However, as folk singer Joan Baez is credited with saying, "If I have a baby in one arm and a guitar in the other, I'm not going to say no to a man who offers to open the door for me."

There are etiquette books and Web sites for nearly every subject imaginable. The arena of most concern appears to be the proper manners and etiquette for weddings. A large bookstore may carry over 200 titles related to wedding planning, the event, and the honeymoon. Other titles reflect changes in American society and cover everything: singles in the city, all sports (not just cycling), proper computer "netiquette" and use of cellphones, and multicultural situations. The coverage demonstrates the changes in society but also demonstrates the continued concern about how to behave appropriately. As many people believe, good manners may be dead, but certainly the curiosity and concern about rules of etiquette are alive and well.

BIBLIOGRAPHY

Baldridge, Letitia. *Letitia Baldridge's Complete Guide to the New Manners for the 90s.* New York: Rawson Associates, 1990.

Fox, Sue. *Etiquette for Dummies.* Indianapolis, Ind.: IDG Books, 1999.

Post, Emily. *Etiquette.* New York: Funk and Wagnalls, 1922.

Diane Nagel Palmer

MANUFACTURING. Rather than undergoing a single, rapid "industrial revolution," manufacturing in America has evolved over four centuries of European settlement. While the first colonists introduced some manufacturing processes to their "new world," manufacturing did not become a vital part of the economy until the achievement of national independence. Over the first half of the nineteenth century, all forms of manufacturing—household, artisanal, and factory based—grew and expanded, and textile manufacturing in particular spawned important new technologies. From the Civil War through the early twentieth century heavy industry grew rapidly, transforming the national economy and the very nature of society. After a period of manufacturing prosperity due, in part, to World War II, heavy industry began to decline and Americans suffered from deindustrialization and recession. The growth of high technology and the service sector in the final decades of the century offered both challenges and opportunities for American manufacturing.

The Colonial Era to 1808

Both of the major early English settlements hoped to establish manufacturing in America. The Virginia Company attempted to set up iron foundries and glass manufactories on the James River while the Puritans built several iron foundries in Massachusetts. As colonization proceeded, however, manufacturing became increasingly peripheral to the economy. With quicker and easier profits to be made from cash crops and trans-Atlantic trade, colonists exerted little effort toward manufacturing. Beginning in the late-seventeenth century, colonial manufacturing was further hindered by mercantilistic restrictions imposed by the English, most notably the Woolen Act (1699), Hat Act (1732), and Iron Act (1750). All three of these acts were designed to limit nascent colonial competition with English manufacturers in keeping with the developing mercantilistic perception that colonies should serve the empire as producers of raw materials and consumers of finished products from the mother country. While large-scale iron and steel manufacturing continued to have a presence in the colonies, most colonial manufacturing would still be performed in the farm household and, to a lesser extent, within craft shops.

It was only after the French and Indian War (1689–1763) that Americans, propelled by their new quest for independence from England, began to turn toward manufacturing in a systematic way. Colonial resistance to the Sugar Act (1764), Stamp Act (1765), Townshend Duties (1767), and Coercive Acts (1774/1775) all involved economic boycotts of British goods, creating a patriotic imperative to produce clothing, glass, paint, paper, and other substitutes for British imports. Empowered by this movement and increasingly politicized by the resistance, urban artisans began to push for a permanently enlarged domestic manufacturing sector as a sign of economic independence from Britain.

The Revolution itself offered some encouragement to domestic manufacturing, particularly war materiel such as salt petre, armaments, ships, and iron and steel. But it also inhibited manufacturing for a number of reasons. Skilled laborers, already scarce before the war, were now extremely difficult to find. Wartime disruptions, including the British blockade and evacuation of manufacturing centers such as Boston, New York City, and Philadelphia further hindered manufacturing.

In the years immediately following the war, manufacturing began to expand on a wider scale. Lobbying efforts by urban mechanics as well as some merchants swayed state governments and later the new federal government to establish mildly protective tariffs and to encourage factory projects, the most famous of which was Alexander Hamilton's Society for Establishing Useful Manufactures in Patterson, New Jersey. New immigrants brought European industrial technologies. The best known case was that of Samuel Slater, who established some of the new nation's first mechanized textile mills in Rhode Island in the 1790s. But the great majority of manufacturing establishments still relied on traditional technologies to perform tasks such as brewing beer, refining sugar, building ships, and making rope. Moreover, craft production and farm-based domestic manufacturing, both of which grew rapidly during this period, continued to be the most characteristic forms of American manufacturing.

From 1808 to the Civil War

Factory production, particularly in the textile industries, became an important part of the American economy during the Embargo of 1808 and the War of 1812. During these years imports were in short supply due to the United States' efforts to boycott European trade and disruptions caused by the British navy during the war. Economic opportunity and patriotic rhetoric pushed Americans to build their largest textile factories to date, from Baltimore's Union Manufactory to the famous establishments financed by the Boston Associates in 1814 in Waltham and in 1826 in Lowell, Massachusetts. America's first million-dollar factories, they used the latest technologies and employed thousands of workers, many of them women and children. After the war promanufacturing protectionists pushed for high tariffs to ensure that manufacturing would continue to flourish. These efforts culminated with the so-called Tariff of Abominations of 1828, which included rates of 25 percent and more on some imported textiles. Protectionism was a vital part of the Whig Party's American System, consisting of tariffs, improved transportation, and better banking. But after 1832, as Southerners successfully fought to lower tariffs, government protection of manufacturing waned.

During these years the proportion of the workforce involved in manufacturing grew more rapidly than in any other period in America's history, rising from only 3.2 percent in 1810 to 18.3 percent by 1860. Growth in textile manufacturing led the way. Cotton production capacity alone increased from 8,000 spindles in 1808 to 80,000 by 1811 and up to 5.2 million by the dawn of the Civil War. By 1860 the United States was, according to some calculations, the world's second greatest manufacturing economy, behind only England. Spectacular as this growth was, it did not come only from the revolution in textile manufacturing. In fact, American manufacturing was extremely varied. While even Europeans admired American inventors' clever use of interchangeable parts and mechanized production, traditional technologies also continued to flourish. Household production, although declining relative to newer forms, remained a significant element of American manufacturing. Many industries other than textiles, and even some branches of textiles, relied on more traditional processes. Established urban centers such as New York City experienced metropolitan industrialization that relied more on the expansion and modification of traditional craft processes than on construction of large vertically integrated factories on the Lowell model.

From the Civil War to World War II
During the latter part of the nineteenth century the United States became the world's leading industrial nation, exceeding the combined outputs of Great Britain, France, and Germany by 1900. Between 1860 and 1900 the share of manufacturing in the nation's total production rose from 32 percent to 53 percent and the number of workers employed in manufacturing tripled from 1.31 million to 4.83 million. Heavy industry, particularly steel, played the most dramatic role in this story. Between 1873 and 1892 the national output of bessemer steel rose from 157,000 to 4.66 million tons. Geographically, the trans-Appalachian midwest was responsible for a disproportionate amount of this growth. Major steel-making centers such as Pittsburgh, Cleveland, and Chicago led the way. The combined population of these industrial metropolises grew by more than 2,500 percent between 1850 and 1900. Yet, even smaller

midwestern towns rapidly industrialized; by 1880 60 percent of Ohio's population was employed in manufacturing, and ten years later Peoria County, Illinois, was the most heavily industrialized in the United States. To a far lesser extent manufacturing also extended into the New South after the Civil War. Here industries based on long-time southern agricultural staples such as cotton manufacturing and cigarette making led the way, following some mining and heavy industry.

Besides the growth of heavy industry and large cities, this era marked the onset of big business. The railroad industry, which benefited from the ease of coordination offered by large units, set the pace, but it was in the steel industry that bigness really triumphed, culminating in the creation of United States Steel, America's first billion-dollar firm (it was capitalized at $1.4 billion in 1901). By 1904, 318 large firms controlled 40 percent of all American manufacturing assets. Firms grew due to vertical integration (incorporating units performing all related manufacturing functions from extraction to marketing) as well as horizontal integration (incorporating new units providing similar functions throughout the country). Such growth was hardly limited to heavy industry; among the most famous examples of vertical integration was the Swift Meat Packing Corporation, which, during the 1870s and 1880s, acquired warehouses, retail outlets, distributorships, fertilizer plants, and other units that built on its core businesses.

While consumers welcomed the increasing availability of mass-produced goods ranging from dressed meat to pianos, the growth of big industry also worried many Americans. Concerns that the new colossuses would serve as monopolies spurred government concern, beginning with state actions in the 1880s and the federal Sherman Antitrust Act of 1890 and followed by a number of largely ineffectual efforts by federal courts to bust trusts such as those alleged in the whiskey and lumber industries to keep the market competitive for smaller players. Perhaps more importantly, workers were also frightened by the increasing amount of economic power in the hands of a few industrial giants who were able to slash wages at will. Major labor actions against railroad and steel corporations helped to build new unions such as the Knights of Labor (established 1869), the United Mine Workers (1890), and the American Federation of Labor (1886). In the 1890s there were an average of 1,300 work stoppages involving 250,000 workers per year. Such actions sometimes ended in near-warfare, as in the famous case of the 1892 strike at Carnegie Steel's Homestead, Pennsylvania, plant.

The most important new manufacture of the twentieth century was the automobile. In 1900 the United States produced fewer than $5 million worth of automobiles. Only sixteen years later American factories turned out more than 1.6 million cars valued at over half a billion dollars. Henry Ford's assembly line production techniques showcased in his enormous River Rouge factory transformed industry worldwide. Automobile production also stimulated and transformed many ancillary industries such as petroleum, rubber, steel, and, with the development of the enclosed automobile, glass. Automobiles also contributed significantly to the growth of a consumer culture in the era before World War II, leading to new forms of commuting, shopping, traveling, and even new adolescent dating rituals. While the development of new forms of consumption kept the economy afloat during good times, reluctance to purchase goods such as automobiles and radios during the Great Depression would intensify the economic stagnation of the 1930s.

World War II to 2000

After the fallow years of the depression, heavy industry again thrived during and after World War II, buoyed by defense spending as well as consumer purchases. Due partly to the politics of federal defense contracts and partly to lower labor costs, the South and West experienced more rapid industrial growth than the established manufacturing centers in the Northeast and Midwest. While workers in the Pacific coast states accounted for only 5.5 percent of the nation's manufacturing workforce in 1939, by 1969 they accounted for 10.5 percent of the total. Manufacturing employment in San Jose, Phoenix, Houston, and Dallas all grew by more than 50 percent between 1960 and 1970.

Industrial employment reached its peak in 1970, when 26 percent of Americans worked in the manufacturing sector. By 1998 the percentage had plunged to 16 percent, the lowest since the Civil War. Deindustrialization struck particularly hard during the 1970s when, according to one estimate, more than 32 million jobs may have been destroyed or adversely affected, as manufacturing firms shut down, cut back, and moved their plants. Due to increasing globalization, manufacturing jobs, which previously moved from the northern rust belt to the southern and western sun belt, could now be performed for even lower wages in Asia and Latin America. These developments led some observers to label the late twentieth century a post-industrial era and suggest that service industry jobs would replace manufacturing as the backbone of the economy, just as manufacturing had superseded agriculture in the nineteenth century. They may have spoken too soon. In the boom years of the 1990s the number of manufacturing jobs continued to drop, but increased productivity led to gains in output for many industries, most notably in the high technology sector. Additionally, other economic observers have argued that manufacturing will continue to matter because the linkages that it provides are vital to the service sector. Without manufacturing, they suggest, the service sector would quickly follow our factories to foreign countries. Thus, at the dawn of the twenty-first century the future of manufacturing and the economy as a whole remained murky.

BIBLIOGRAPHY

Bluestone, Barry, and Bennett Harrison. *The Deindustrialization of America*. New York: Basic Books, 1982.

Clark, Victor. *History of Manufactures in the United States, 1893–1928*. 3 vols. New York: McGraw Hill, 1929.

Cochran, Thomas. *American Business in the Twentieth Century*. Cambridge, Mass.: Harvard University Press, 1972.

Cochran, Thomas, and William Miller. *The Age of Enterprise: A Social History of Industrial America*. New York: Macmillan, 1942.

Licht, Walter. *Industrializing America: The Nineteenth Century*. Baltimore: Johns Hopkins University Press, 1995.

Porter, Glenn. *The Rise of Big Business, 1860–1910*. New York: Caswell, 1973; Arlington Heights, Ill.: Harlan Davidson, 1973.

Tryon, Rolla M. *Household Manufactures in the United States, 1640–1860*. Chicago: University of Chicago Press, 1917. Reprint, New York: Johnson Reprint Company, 1966.

Lawrence A. Peskin

See also **Automobile; Automobile Industry; Cotton; Demography and Demographic Trends; Great Depression; Iron and Steel Industry; Labor; Textiles.**

MANUFACTURING, HOUSEHOLD. In the colonial and early national periods, many rural households conducted their own manufacturing activities in conjunction with farming, making yarn, cloth, soap, candles, tools, and other items. Farm families manufactured such items partly to avoid purchasing them and partly to exchange them with neighbors or merchants for other goods. Estate inventories reveal the existence of spinning wheels, looms, and other equipment connected with textile production, as well as carpenters' tools and other implements. Usually employing the labor of women, children, servants, and slaves, household manufacturing was somewhat correlated with wealth. It became increasingly important in the later eighteenth century, when the American Revolution spurred domestic production and "homespun" became a patriotic symbol of both family and national virtue.

Household manufactures were never comprehensively enumerated. Incomplete returns at the 1810 census reported more than 72 million yards of household-made fabrics valued at almost $38 million, or roughly $5 per head of population. The expansion of factory production, which had already begun by this time, substantially replaced household textile manufactures in subsequent decades, so that while total family-made goods of all kinds were valued at $25 million in 1860, this now represented less than $1 per capita. However, the decline of "homespun" masked some important changes in the character of household manufacturing. In New England especially, merchants organized networks of "outworkers" in shoemaking, straw- and palm-leaf braiding (for hats), and the manufacture of brooms, buttons, and suspenders. Most of these activities employed women and child workers; as many as 51,000 Massachusetts women worked at straw- or palm-leaf braiding in 1837. In some regions, men also worked part-time making parts for tools and implements, or, in southwestern Connecticut, they worked in the production of wooden-movement clocks that flourished in that region from the 1810s to the 1840s. Outwork constituted an American example of "protoindustrialization," a stage in the introduction of factory and mechanized manufacturing techniques. It posed problems for the entrepreneurs who organized it: it was hard to supervise, control quality, or accurately record. Manufacturers often resolved these difficulties by moving the work into larger workshops or factories. By the later nineteenth century, most remaining rural outwork was in marginal trades and was conducted by poor families.

Household manufacture did not die out with industrialization, however; it just took new forms. Although production shrank, farm families continued to make foodstuffs, clothing, and other goods for their own use or for sale. Urban household production also grew: clothing manufacturers put out sewing and dressmaking to homeworking seamstresses, and the mid-nineteenth century development of the sewing machine fostered the expansion of sweatshop production, particularly among poorer and immigrant populations of large cities. Indeed, although its relative economic contribution dwindled, household manufacture remained a significant activity throughout the twentieth century. It even experienced elements of a resurgence in the early twenty-first century—to meet tourist demand for craft-produced items in poor but scenic rural regions such as Vermont or New Mexico, or with the spread of electronic information technology that fostered new patterns of home-working in both manufacturing and service occupations.

BIBLIOGRAPHY

Boris, Eileen. *Home to Work: Motherhood and the Politics of Industrial Homework in the United States.* Cambridge, U.K.: Cambridge University Press, 1994.

Boydston, Jeanne. *Home and Work: Housework, Wages, and the Ideology of Labor in the Early Republic.* New York: Oxford University Press, 1990.

Dublin, Thomas. *Transforming Women's Work: New England Lives in the Industrial Revolution.* Ithaca, N.Y.: Cornell University Press, 1994.

Ulrich, Laurel Thatcher. *The Age of Homespun: Objects and Stories in the Creation of an American Myth.* New York: Knopf, 2001.

Christopher Clark

See also **Candles; Soap and Detergent Industry; Textiles.**

MANUMISSION. The legal term for the freeing of a slave, the word "manumission" is sometimes used interchangeably with "emancipation," although the latter implies a more universal and unconditional release of slaves.

Manumission of American slaves was achieved by a variety of means, including state-ordered manumission as well as private manumission of individuals. In 1777, Ver-

mont became the first state to mandate manumission within its borders through a constitutional ban on slavery. By the early nineteenth century, New Jersey, New York, and Pennsylvania were phasing out slavery by providing for the gradual manumission of the children of current slaves; and Delaware and Maryland had enacted liberal manumission laws that made it easier for slaves to acquire their freedom.

By 1792, manumission societies were active in New York, Virginia, and Massachusetts. Such societies, of which some 143 were established in the United States by the early nineteenth century (including more than 100 in the South), called for the gradual manumission of slaves. While less radical than the abolitionism movement that emerged in the 1830s, manumission societies served as the foundation for future antislavery organizations.

Individual slaves could also gain manumission directly from their owners, who occasionally freed their slaves out of acts of conscience, but more often provided for their manumission in their wills—as did George Washington. Slaves who were fortunate enough to win a lottery or otherwise save up the required sum could purchase their own freedom, and in many cases, would then work to free their families. And religious groups (notably the Quakers) and antislavery activists sometimes purchased the manumission of slaves.

Many moderate antislavery proponents found gradual, or conditional, manumission more palatable than the idea of universal emancipation, which they feared would overwhelm white society with difficult-to-assimilate former slaves.

Such was the case with supporters of the American Colonization Society, founded in 1817, which, over the course of two decades, helped establish a nation-state of former slaves in Liberia, West Africa. Supporters of the society—which was led by such eminent white Americans as Daniel Webster, James Madison, Andrew Jackson, and Francis Scott Key—advocated manumission with the condition that, once freed, the former slaves would be "repatriated" back to Africa.

During the Civil War (1861–1865), the contrasting strategic and political value of controlled manumission versus universal emancipation became apparent when General John Charles Frémont, commander of the Department of the West, instituted martial law in Missouri in September 1861, and proclaimed manumission for the slaves of rebel owners in that state. Despite his desire to free the slaves, President Lincoln, still fighting what seemed like a losing war, annulled Frémont's order (but not before a number of Missouri slaves had already been freed).

In a similar unilateral move in 1862, General David Hunter, commander of the Department of the South, issued an order freeing the slaves of Florida, Georgia, and South Carolina. Again, Lincoln forced a retraction, explaining that his military commanders were not empowered to enact such sweeping policy initiatives. Nonetheless, the manumission orders of Frémont and Hunter tested the waters of public approval for universal emancipation and set the stage for Lincoln's Emancipation Proclamation of 1863.

BIBLIOGRAPHY

Beyan, Amos. *The American Colonization Society and the Creation of the Liberian State: A Historical Perspective, 1822–1900.* Lanham, Md.: University Press of America, 1991.

Foner, Eric. *Nothing But Freedom: Emancipation and Its Legacy.* Baton Rouge: Louisiana State University Press, 1983.

Library of Congress Special Collections: Records and Photographs of the American Colonization Society. Available at http://www.loc.gov/rr/print/coll/007.html.

McClelland, Peter D., and Richard J. Zeckhauser. *Demographic Dimensions of the New Republic: American Interregional Migration, Vital Statistics, and Manumissions, 1800–1860.* New York: Cambridge University Press, 1982.

Staudenraus, P. J. *African Colonization Movement, 1816–1865.* New York: Octagon Books, 1980.

Whitman, Stephen T. *The Price of Freedom: Slavery and Manumission in Baltimore and Early National Maryland.* Lexington: University Press of Kentucky, 1997.

University of North Carolina, Greensboro: Race and Slave Petitions Project. Available at http://history.uncg.edu/slavery petitions/index.html.

Laura A. Bergheim

MAPLE SUGAR was familiar to Native Americans, who drank maple sap fresh or boiled it down to syrup and sugar in bark troughs. French settlers in Canada learned of its merits early, well before English settlers discovered it. The sugar rapidly became an article of food and commerce in the late seventeenth century, especially in the northern colonies. By 1794, Vermont's total output was estimated at 1,000 tons, and in 1809 probably two-thirds of the state's population worked in spring at making sugar and syrup.

Shallow pans replaced traditional iron kettles in the mid-nineteenth century, revolutionizing production. On the frontier, with cane sugar and molasses scarce, the maple tree provided the pioneers' confection. By 1900, Ohio's production rivaled Vermont's, but thereafter, cheaper cane sugar gradually replaced maple sugar in popularity. Although maple sugar production declined in the nineteenth century, syrup production rose. Maple sugar production is now confined to the northeast, particularly in Vermont and New York, and takes place from February to April.

BIBLIOGRAPHY

Fox, William Freedman, and W. F. Hubbard. *The Maple Sugar Industry.* Washington, D.C.: U.S. Government Printing Office, 1905.

Pendegrast, James F. *The Origin of Maple Sugar.* Ottawa: National Museums of Canada, National Museum of Natural Sciences, 1982.

Alvin F. Harlow/c. w.

See also **Fur Trade and Trapping; Industries, Colonial; Sugar Industry.**

MAPS AND MAPMAKING. Maps are inextricably linked to how humans know the world as well as to the means by which spatial relationships can be depicted with specific tools and techniques. Thus, the history of cartography in the United States reflects human history—exploration, political change, and wars as well as technological change from designing maps on bark and vellum to creating cartographic displays with computers. The history of cartography in America is a history of making spatial knowledge visible.

Native American Maps

Any discussion of cartography in America must begin with the maps created and used by the peoples indigenous to North America. Native Americans did not have a system of writing like their European contemporaries, but they possessed meticulous methods for keeping records. These were almost entirely oral systems that depended on human memory to pass knowledge between generations. Although the first maps of America are typically considered European in origin, historians have demonstrated that these maps could have only been created with Native American assistance.

The first testament to this cartographic knowledge is documented in a story concerning an interview between the king of Portugal and Columbus in 1493. The records speak of the Native Americans who made the return trip to Europe with Columbus and who accompanied him to visit the king. The king, trying to determine just where Columbus had ventured, questioned one of the Native Americans and had him assemble a map of the Caribbean region with dried beans. The Native American cartographer expertly clustered the beans to represent Cuba and Hispaniola and used single beans to depict the smaller Bahamas and Lesser Antilles. The king asked a second Native American to do the same; he reassembled the bean map and added even more detail to the region than the first. A detailed map published in a 1511 book by Peter Martyr (in Seville) is indicative of the influence of Native American knowledge. The map depicts areas and coastlines that, at the date of publication, had yet to be traversed by Europeans. This map remains the first printed Spanish map showing any part of the Americas.

Several European cartographers noted the influence of Native American spatial knowledge on their maps. Samuel de Champlain created a map of the New England and Nova Scotia coasts in 1607. This map, now in the Library of Congress, is thought to be "one of the great cartographical treasures of America." On his survey trip near present-day Cape Ann in Massachusetts, Champlain encountered a group of Native Americans and asked them to show how the coast trended. The Native Americans took a piece of charcoal and drew a large bay, now known as Massachusetts Bay. Additionally, they drew a long river with shoals, which represented the Merrimac River. This indigenous knowledge is reflected by Champlain's beautiful chart drawn on vellum with outlines in brown ink. Captain John Smith, Virginia's first published cartographer, attributed much to native cartographers and informants.

Early Mapping of America by Europeans

Early European maps of America were often used as documents of power, denoting areas of control. Cartography at this time, however, was an inexact science and most of the early European maps of the Americas were based on relatively few explorations. Many of them depended almost entirely on Native American knowledge. Although it is thought that several maps of the New World were made before 1500, none have been authenticated. The most widely accepted "first map" of North America is known as the "Portolan World Chart" (1500, Juan de la Cosa). Many historians identify Juan de la Cosa as a Basque cartographer who accompanied Columbus on his first two voyages. Another important early map was that of Martin Waldseemüller in 1507 titled "Universalis Cosmographic." Two aspects are of note concerning this woodcut world map. First, Waldseemüller was the first to depict the land reached by Columbus as an entirely new continent, not attached in any way to Asia. Second, it is the earliest known work to label "America" as part of the New World.

At that time, most geographers continued to see the world as described by Ptolemy's (120–150 A.D.) *Geographia* and struggled to incorporate new knowledge of locations in the Western Hemisphere. It was not until the late 1500s that cartography began to challenge the supremacy of Ptolemy's worldview, mainly due to the greater understanding of locations in the New World. Two important atlases published in Europe reflect the changing worldview. Abraham Ortelius compiled new maps of the world based on contemporary charts and maps in his "Theatrum Orbis Terrarum" in 1570. A significant map in this collection was his "New Description of America or the New World." Fifteen years later, Gerardus Mercator's collection of 107 maps clearly signified a new view of the world invoking a new map projection that was essentially for navigation. The Wytfliet altas of 1597 was the first atlas dedicated exclusively to the Americas, with 19 copper-engraved maps.

Many of the early maps were either hand drawn or created using the Chinese technique of xylography (wood block printing), which allowed maps to be reproduced mechanically. Wood block printing was the most common method through the fifteenth century because it was relatively inexpensive. Early in the 1400s, however, cal-cography was invented. This method involved incising lines on a copper surface rather than carving them in wood. The engraving tool created finer lines, thereby depicting a more detailed image. This engraving process changed with the addition of a wax coating on the copper. The map was sketched lightly onto the copper through the wax and then the plate was dipped into nitric acid. The acid would not permeate the wax, but, rather, would etch the copper that had been left exposed.

Although some maps of this time were in color, most of this was done with hand tinting after the printing process. Map coloring was, for many of the period, a hobby, and manuals were produced that detailed the process. An interesting outcome of these manuals was the prescription of some "traditional" cartographic conventions such as representing political boundaries with dotted lines and symbolizing major cities with red circles.

Colonial Mapping

Colonial rivalries played out cartographically in the New World. To celebrate the Dutch recapture of New Amsterdam (New York) from the English in 1673, Hugo Allard created the "New and Exact Map of All New Netherland." Other colonial period maps were used to depict the extent of control in North America, such as Guillaume Delisle's "Carte de la Lousiiane et du Cours du Mississipi" (1718), which showed the Mississippi Valley and delta region as possessions of France totally surrounded by British settlement. Another example is William Popple's (1733) twenty-sheet "Map of the British Empire in America with the French and Spanish Settlements adjacent thereto," which reflected the extent of known North America and the degree to which Britain controlled it.

The year 1755 is known as a year of great maps. Considered the most notable map of this year was John Mitchell's "A Map of the British and French Dominions in North America with the Roads, Distances, Limits, and Extent of the Settlements." Essentially, this map served as a rebuttal to French boundary claims in the New World. The information used to create the map was as sophisticated as possible for the day, with latitude determined with the quadrant and longitude remaining slightly less precise. This map was taken to the Treaty of Paris in 1783 and was used well into the twentieth century to resolve boundary disputes. Because of its accuracy in depiction of locations and its completeness, it is often noted by cartographic historians as the most important map in the history of American cartography.

Mapping the New Nation

The first map compiled, engraved, and completed by an American was Abel Buell's (1784) "A New and Correct Map of the United States of North America Layd down from the latest Observations and best Authority agreeable to the Peace of 1783." This map, in many ways, represents the end of an era. By the early 1800s, cartography had begun to move from works of art based on geographic knowledge to works of science based on known geographic fact. Earlier maps, often incorrect, were no longer tolerated; too many people had knowledge of the world. Beginning in the early 1800s, maps became quite similar in appearance, often seen as a triumph of science over art.

Cartography During the Nineteenth Century

By 1800, several atlases of the new nation had already been created (*The American Pilot*, 1792, and *Casey's American Atlas*, 1795). However, the publication of Henry Schenk Tanner's *New American Atlas* (1823) indicated a change in cartography now based on rigorous scientific surveying. Surveyors used distinct color and uniform symbology, indicated cultural features, and retained the "received" names of places. This atlas marks the first comprehensive analytical compilation of American cartographic data, and maps of each state were of a uniform size and scale.

There are several notable maps in the history of American cartography in the first half of the nineteenth century. William Maclure's 1809 map, considered by many as the origin of thematic cartography, depicts the known geology of the United States imprinted over a topographic map. Exploration maps such as "Lewis and Clark's Track Across the Western Portion of North America . . ." (1814) greatly enhanced knowledge of the continent. The earliest American publication of an ethnographic map was Albert Gallatin's (1836) representation of Native Americans classified by linguistic family. Elias Loomis's maps, many designed during the 1840s, are considered to be the earliest maps based entirely on scientific data. Considered the origin of weather maps, most of these depict meteorological phenomena.

Between 1814 and 1830, a revolution occurred in the printing of maps. Lithography was a new printing technology that was based on the chemical repellence of oil and water. Instead of an image being cut into a plate, maps were drawn with greasy ink or crayons on a specially prepared stone. The stone was then moistened with water (repelled in the areas with greasy ink) and the printing ink was rolled onto the stone, adhering to only the mapped (inked) areas. The map was then made by pressing the paper against the inked drawing. Lithography significantly lowered the cost and increased the speed of map production. A few years later, wax engraving (cerography) began to have a large influence on American cartography. The map image was engraved on wax rather than on copper or stone. This image was then used to create a mold on a thin metal plate that could be used on a letterpress printing machine. With this method, type could be inserted in the wax mold rather than engraving each letter by hand. These two new printing processes, along with the lower cost of wood pulp paper and a shift in production from individual maps to maps published in sets based on systematic surveying and mapping, dramatically increased the number and use of maps in the United States.

During the second half of the 1800s, maps were designed for development, population statistics, war, ownership, health, westward expansion, and protection of property. County maps were commercially produced to show land ownership by 1850. Notable and widely used maps were those of the Sanborn Map and Publishing Company (begun in 1865). These large-scale maps depicted the locations and dimensions of buildings and included the structural materials of each in order for insurance companies to determine fire risk. General Land Office Maps standardized the format and content of maps. During the Civil War (1861–1865), map accuracy was critical. Many of the topographic maps of the southeastern United States made during the war were used well into the twentieth century because of their high level of accuracy. A uniquely American cartographic form emerged after the Civil War. Panoramic views of U.S. cities using an oblique perspective became a common and popular map form that lasted into the early twentieth century. A map representing the distribution of slave population in 1860 is often noted as the first map of census data in the United States. Rand McNally, a small commercial printing firm at the time, found that their addition of small strip maps to accompany their railroad guide became enormously popular. By 1874, the *First Statistical Atlas of the United States* was published. This prompted an increase in thematic and statistical maps that incorporated more diverse political and social data. By this time, physicians began using cartographical-statistical methods to document diffusion and distribution of major epidemics of tuberculosis, pneumonia, malaria, and typhoid fever. By 1879, the U.S. Geological Survey (USGS) had mapped the entire nation by quadrilateral tracts. The initial scale of these maps was 1:250,000. The USGS maps used standardized symbology, colors, and place names. The simplified cartographic design made the maps accessible to the general public.

Published at the turn of the century (1898), *The Statistical Atlas of the United States Based on the Results of the Eleventh Census* represents the most comprehensive and analytical cartography in the United States to date. This atlas incorporated four main thematic mapping methods that were devised during the nineteenth century: dot maps (uniform symbols represent a quantity), choropleth maps (different shadings represent different values in different areas), flow lines (indicate direction and amount of a flow), and graduated symbols (varying sizes of symbols represent different values).

Twentieth-Century Cartography

A significant change in transportation from rail to automobiles in the early part of the twentieth century influenced the demand for practical and accurate road maps and prompted a boom in commercial cartography. In the academic world, the Hart American History Series of maps (1918–1921) reflected the influence of James Harvey Robinson's emphasis on "totality" in historical study in his *New History* (1916). Additionally, a significant volume, C. O. Paulin's *Atlas of the Historical Geography of the United States*, compiled more than 600 maps documenting American history.

Scientific mapping techniques were well established by the beginning of the twentieth century. A national inventory of soils by county was undertaken by the U.S. Department of Agriculture in order to assist American farmers. By 1940, there were well over 1,500 maps just depicting different aspects of soils in the United States. This type of survey was a common "New Deal" government practice during which time there was an enormous expansion in maps of the United States, representing statistics such as population, manufacturing, climate, agriculture, and urban housing conditions.

Many changes in cartographic techniques evolved during the twentieth century. Representing the earth's third dimension had always been a cartographic challenge. Erwin Raisz's "Physiographic Provinces of North America" was published in 1939, and demonstrated a realistic depiction of relief through numerous physiographic symbols that he developed. Aerial photography, a technique employed in both world wars of the twentieth century, influenced mapping dramatically by allowing cartographers to view the earth from a planar perspective (the perspective of most maps) for the first time. Three-dimensional terrain models and negative scribing both had their roots in war as well and contributed to advances in cartographic techniques in midcentury.

However, it is the period from 1950 to 1990 that is classified as revolutionary in cartography, with numerous innovations and developments for representing spatial relationships. During the 1950s, air photos and maps were merged to create what is now known as orthophoto maps. On these maps, traditional map symbols are placed on rectified air photos. In the early 1960s, Howard Fisher, a Harvard sociologist, developed a mapping technique known as SYMAP that used an early computer to create maps depicting density data. Computer cartographic techniques made mapping quicker and more accurate. Data sources such as rectified air photos, satellite images (early 1970s), and digital databases all helped to usher in a new period in cartography in the United States. Mapping software based on Geographic Information Systems (GIS) created a system in which spatial data and attribute data could be linked. This new method of managing spatial data permitted numerous different maps to be created for just one specific purpose rather than as a general map meeting many needs. By the end of the twentieth century, people could access data and mapping software via the Internet to create a map of nearly any place and show any available statistical relationship. Additionally, virtual maps have allowed cartographers to show temporal relationships, how places have changed over time. No longer do maps show a frozen moment in time. By using animation techniques, cartography is reaching into new areas of research called cartographic visualization. *The National Atlas of the United States* exemplifies the rapid change in car-

tography during the last thirty years of the twentieth century. Initially a huge volume of 765 maps representing the history of cartography in America (1970), by 2001 it was available online with an infinite number of maps available to each individual user.

Cartography has experienced dramatic change in methodology and presentation from the Columbian encounter to present day. Once created as ornate works of art by specially trained individuals, maps by the end of the twentieth century could be created by anyone with access to data and mapping software. Maps, however, remain representations of reality. Maps represent how individuals see and interpret the world, whether they are maps from the 1500s on vellum or those that animate on a computer screen.

BIBLIOGRAPHY

De Vorsey, Louis Jr. "Silent Witnesses: Native American Maps." *Georgia Review* (1992): 709–726.

Portinaro, Pierluigi, and Franco Knirsch. *The Cartography of North America, 1500–1800.* New York: Facts on File, 1987.

Schwartz, Seymour I., and Ralph E. Ehrenberg. *The Mapping of America.* New York: H. N. Abrams, 1980.

Thrower, Norman J. W. *Maps and Civilization: Cartography in Culture and Society.* 2d ed. Chicago: University of Chicago Press, 1999.

Tooley, R. V., and Charles Bricker. *Landmarks of Mapmaking.* Ware, Hertfordshire, U.K.: Wordsworth Press, 1989.

Janet S. Smith

MARATHONS. The long-distance foot race known as the marathon is named after the celebrated Athenian victory over Persian invaders near the Bay of Marathon in Greece in 490 B.C. It commemorates the feat of the Greek soldier who ran twenty-five miles from the battlefield to Athens with tidings of the victory, only to die of exhaustion. A marathon was incorporated into the Olympic Games when the modern series began in Athens in 1896 and has retained an important place in them. The first victor was a Greek, Spiridon Loues, who won in two hours, fifty-eight minutes, and fifty seconds. A year later, the Boston Marathon was established and is held annually on Patriots' Day; by the 1990s, it was attracting 10,000 competitors. The New York Marathon, founded in 1970 by Fred Lebow, head of the New York Road Runners Club, draws about 25,000 entrants each year. The length of the marathon was fixed at twenty-six miles, three hundred eighty-five yards in 1908 when the British Olympic Committee determined that the race should commence at Windsor Castle and finish in front of the royal box at Shepherds Bush in London. Although no official records of marathons are kept because the courses are of varied difficulty, by 1995 the fastest recorded times were about two hours and seven minutes for a man and about two hours and twenty minutes for a woman. Violet Percy of Great Britain became the first woman to officially enter a marathon—the London Marathon—in 1926. In 1970, the Road Runners Club of America organized the first championship marathon for women, although it was not until 1984 that a women's race was included in the Olympic Games. In 1970, two women in the New York Marathon became the first to break three hours.

Marathons grew in popularity in the United States after Frank Shorter won the marathon in the 1972 Olympic Games. The New York Marathon began to be televised in 1979, and the following year, after fraudulent finishes in both Boston and New York by Rosie Ruiz, videotaping became routine. Triathlons, such as the Ironman Triathlon World Championship held on the Kona coast of Hawaii that began in 1978, incorporate a marathon, a 2.4-mile swim, and a 112-mile bicycle race. A related sporting challenge is the endurance marathon, in which the length of uninterrupted participation is the determining factor in any number of activities, from tiddlywinks to trampolining.

BIBLIOGRAPHY

Higdon, Hal. *Boston: A Century of Running: Celebrating the 100th Anniversary of the Boston Athletic Association Marathon.* Emmaus, Pa.: Rodale Press, 1995.

Robert Garland/A. R.

See also **Olympic Games, American Participation in; Sports.**

MARBURY V. MADISON, 1 Cranch (5 U.S.) 137 (1803), the case that established the constitutional doctrine of judicial review in the United States, according to which the federal courts would declare void statutes that conflict with the Constitution.

The concept of judicial review had long existed in the common law. The judicial power to declare void statutes that were contrary to right and reason had been asserted by the English Chief Justice Edward Coke in *Dr. Bonham's Case* (1610). This doctrine was well known in the American colonies and had been employed in both state and lower federal courts in actions dealing with state statutes. Still, the text of the U.S. Constitution, Article III, which declares the right of the federal courts to hear all cases "arising under this constitution," does not clearly confer this authority.

The dispute leading to *Marbury v. Madison* arose when William Marbury, Dennis Ramsay, Robert Townsend Hooe, and William Harper were not given their commissions as federal justices of the peace, appointments made by John Adams in the waning days of the Federalist Congress (see MIDNIGHT JUDGES). They sued in the original jurisdiction of the U.S. Supreme Court, seeking a writ of mandamus against James Madison, the new secretary of state, asking the Court to order Madison to deliver their commissions.

In the heated atmosphere of Thomas Jefferson's new presidency, the Court was faced with granting an order that could be ignored or could cause a constitutional crisis between the Anti-Federalist Congress and the Federalist Supreme Court. Not to grant it, however, would be a capitulation.

The responsibility for dealing with this quagmire fell to the new Chief Justice, John Marshall, himself a last-minute Adams appointee. Indeed it was Marshall who, as the former Secretary of State, had left the disputed commissions with his clerk for delivery just before Madison assumed office.

Marshall's opinion framed three questions: Did the plaintiffs have a right to the commission? If so, and if that right had been violated, did the laws afford them a remedy? If they did, was it a mandamus issuing from the Supreme Court?

Marshall found that the commissions having been sealed, the plaintiffs had a right to delivery, and, under the ancient common-law principle that a right denied must have a remedy, the plaintiffs should have a writ of mandamus to deliver the commission. This was allowed under the Judiciary Act of 1789, which authorized the Supreme Court "to issue writs of mandamus, in cases warranted by the principles and usages of law, to any courts appointed, or persons holding office, under the authority of the United States."

Marshall compared this statutory authority to Article III of the U.S. Constitution: "in all cases affecting ambassadors, other public ministers and consuls, and those in which a state shall be a party, the Supreme Court shall have original jurisdiction. In all other cases . . .the Supreme Court shall have appellate jurisdiction." A case in the Court's original jurisdiction that neither affects the representatives of a foreign state nor has a state of the union as a party is outside the powers conferred on the Court in the Constitution, and the act giving such jurisdiction exceeded Constitutional limits.

Marshall held that the judicial oath of office to defend the Constitution requires that a judge refuse to act according to a law that violates it. He concluded that "a law repugnant to the constitution is void; and that courts, as well as other departments, are bound by that instrument." Thus, he refused to enforce that part of the Judiciary Act, much of the rest of which remains in force.

The case initially provoked outrage from Jefferson and his party, not for the claim to judicial review but for the presumptions that the plaintiffs had been harmed and that the Court might have granted the mandamus. The doctrine of judicial review, expanded to include acts of states and of the federal executive, grew considerably through the twentieth century.

BIBLIOGRAPHY

Nelson, William E. *"Marbury v. Madison": The Origins and Legacy of Judicial Review.* Lawrence: University Press of Kentucky, 2000.

Newmyer, R. Kent. *John Marshall and the Heroic Age of the Supreme Court*. Baton Rouge: Louisiana State University Press, 2001.

Steve Sheppard

See also **Judicial Review; Judiciary Act of 1789.**

MARCH OF DIMES.

President Franklin D. Roosevelt established the March of Dimes in January 1938 to save America's youth from polio. The agency was officially known as the National Foundation for Infantile Paralysis. Roosevelt, a polio survivor, created the partnership between scientists and volunteers to conquer poliomyelitis.

Eddie Cantor, a comedian and entertainer, coined the phrase "March of Dimes." It reflected the first grassroots fundraising campaign he started when he asked Americans to send dimes to the president.

The first president of the March of Dimes, Basil O'Connor, directed the foundation's early activities, including providing the first iron lung to assist polio victims in 1941. A year later Dr. Jonas Salk began leading research on the poliovirus. In 1953, Salk confirmed that a killed-virus vaccine for polio could stop the epidemic. In 1954, the foundation ran field trials of the Salk vaccine on 1,830,000 schoolchildren. The vaccine was declared safe the next year.

Virginia Apgar, an anesthesiologist and creator of the "Apgar Score" for newborns, was president of the foundation from 1959 to 1973. The foundation established the Salk Institute for Biological Studies in La Jolla, California in 1960. In 1962, the government licensed an oral polio vaccine developed by Dr. Albert Sabin with March of Dimes funding.

In 1958 the March of Dimes initiated its first efforts to save babies from birth defects. Subsequently, the foundation funded research on the in-utero treatment of birth defects, prenatal diagnosis of sickle cell anemia, spina bifida, and Marfan and Fragile X syndromes. In 1994 it began its successful folic acid campaign, which promoted the B vitamin to women of childbearing age for the prevention of birth defects of the brain and spinal cord called neural tube defects.

The March of Dimes has helped pass several national acts: the Mothers and Newborns' Health Protection Act (1996), the State Children's Health Insurance Program (S-CHIP) (1997), and the Birth Defects Prevention Act (1998). It also worked to enact the Children's Health Act of 2000. Nearly 3 million Americans volunteer with the March of Dimes.

BIBLIOGRAPHY

Gould, Tony. *A Summer Plague: Polio and its Survivors*. New Haven, Conn.: Yale University Press, 1995.

Sills, David L. *The Volunteers, Means and Ends in a National Organization*. Glencoe, Ill.: Free Press, 1957. Reprint, New York: Arno Press, 1980.

Smith, Jane S. *Patenting the Sun: Polio and the Salk Vaccine*. New York: William Morrow and Company, Inc., 1990.

Rebecca Tolley-Stokes

See also **Medical Research; Poliomyelitis; Volunteerism.**

MARCH OF TIME.

The *March of Time* presented dramatizations and reports of contemporary news events on network radio from 1931 through 1945. The show imitated the style of the movie newsreel, complete with inflated narration and urgent musical accompaniment. Before the advent of communication satellites, live broadcasts from remote locations were difficult, unpredictable, and often impossible. The *March of Time*, in response, employed an ensemble of actors to dramatize the news. Sponsored and produced by *Time* magazine, the show relied on *Time*'s global staff of reporters, many of whom were on call for last-minute script changes. The *March of Time* was, in essence, a breaking news docudrama. *Time* aggressively retained editorial control over the show's content, even when other sponsors joined the program.

For most of its run, the *March of Time* was narrated by Westbrook Van Voorhis. His authoritative, stentorian voice became a trademark of the show, as did his closing declaration: "Time—marches on!" Among the wide variety of news stories covered, the Great Depression and the events leading to and during World War II dominated the reports. Among the figures dramatized regularly were Franklin Roosevelt, Winston Churchill, Adolf Hitler, and Joseph Stalin. Actors who provided voices included Orson Welles, Agnes Moorehead, Jeanette Nolan, and in the role of FDR, Art Carney.

The *March of Time* aired on CBS from 1931 through 1937, on NBC from 1937 through 1944, and on ABC from 1944 to 1945. It was a half-hour live weekly broadcast except during the 1935–1936 season, when it was heard for fifteen minutes nightly. As the show matured and technology advanced, the *March of Time* became a more conventional news broadcast, offering in some important ways a model for the contemporary news show. Dramatizations became less and less frequent, and when they were used they were approached with an almost scholarly attention to detail. More documentary sound was employed through reports from correspondents in the field.

Even from its beginning in 1931, however, the *March of Time* was considered a news program, and millions of Americans learned of the events of the turbulent times through this series. By later standards, of course, dramatizations and synthesized sound effects would be considered unacceptable by legitimate news operations. It should be remembered, however, that the standards of broadcast journalism had not yet been established in 1931. Even into the late 1940s, for example, NBC's early TV news broadcasts bore the name of the sponsors: the *Esso Newsreel*, the *Camel Newsreel Theatre*, and the *Camel News Car-*

avan. Just as a news broadcast today bearing the name of an oil or tobacco product would be unthinkable, so too would be some of the techniques used by the *March of Time.* The docudrama style is now primarily employed in made-for-TV movies and tabloid newsmagazines.

ABC revived the *March of Time,* renamed the *March of Time through the Years,* for prime-time television in 1951 with some significant changes. The program now relied upon historical documentary film footage and live guests. Westbrook Van Voorhis returned as host of the show in 1952, replacing John Daly, but the series ended in December of that year.

BIBLIOGRAPHY

Dunning, John. *Tune in Yesterday: The Ultimate Encyclopedia of Old-Time Radio. 1925–1976.* Englewood Cliffs, N.J.: Prentice-Hall, 1976.

Fielding, Raymond. The March of Time, *1935–1951.* New York: Oxford University Press, 1978.

Robert Thompson

See also **Radio.**

MARCH ON WASHINGTON. In June 1941, Asa Philip Randolph, president of the Brotherhood of Sleeping Car Porters, informed President Franklin D. Roosevelt that 100,000 protesters would march on the nation's capital unless the president acted to end racial discrimination in federal government and defense industry employment. Roosevelt issued Executive Order 8802 (barring discrimination in the government and defense industry), thereby averting the march.

Randolph revived his idea for a mass march in 1963. The March on Washington for Jobs and Freedom, as it came to be known, addressed issues including high unemployment rates for African Americans, school integration, violence against civil rights activists, and a proposed civil rights bill. Randolph selected Bayard Rustin, a civil rights veteran whom Randolph had mentored, to organize the march. The planners brought together major civil rights groups and leaders from religious organizations and labor unions. President John F. Kennedy, unable to dissuade organizers from carrying out their plans, hesitantly sanctioned the march.

On 28 August 1963, 250,000 people walked from the Washington Monument to the Lincoln Memorial, where they listened to speeches from representatives of the various organizations. At the day's end, the Reverend Martin Luther King Jr. delivered his powerful and memorable "I Have a Dream" speech. The interracial, peaceful assembly demonstrated to the public the influence, unity, and optimism of the civil rights alliance.

BIBLIOGRAPHY

Levine, Daniel. *Bayard Rustin and the Civil Rights Movement.* New Brunswick, N.J.: Rutgers University Press, 2000.

March on Washington for Jobs and Freedom. On 28 August 1963, 250,000 African Americans and supporters of civil rights marched from the Washington Monument to the Lincoln Memorial in Washington, D.C., where they heard numerous speakers call out for racial justice, school integration, and a proposed civil rights bill. The highlight of the day came when the Rev. Dr. Martin Luther King gave his legendary "I Have a Dream" speech.

Pfeffer, Paula F. *A. Philip Randolph, Pioneer of the Civil Rights Movement.* Baton Rouge: Louisiana State University Press, 1990.

Donna Alvah

See also **Brotherhood of Sleeping Car Porters; Civil Rights Movement; Civil Rights Act of 1964.**

MARCHING BANDS, using mostly percussion and wind instruments, originally served the military by providing communication and music in the field as troops marched from one locale to another. Broader instrumentation was eventually added for parades, ceremonies, and review, especially after brass instrument valves were patented in 1818, which allowed a bigger "outdoor" sound to be projected before crowds.

The brass band first became important in America during the Civil War. Union Army Bandmaster Patrick S. Gilmore's band instrumentation is still the model for the concert band. It was John Philip Sousa (1854–1932), however, who took this music to its zenith. After twelve years as the leader of the U.S. Marine Band, he formed his own "Sousa's Band" in 1892 and began touring the United States and Europe. His marches are considered a distinctively American music, and his "Stars and Stripes Forever," written in 1896, is his most popular piece. As professional touring bands began to disappear in the early twentieth century, American schools filled the void. Beginning with the bandmaster A. A. Harding at the University of Illinois, school bands across the country conducted by both former professional band directors and academically trained teachers participated in nationwide playing and marching contests. Municipal and military bands continued, but colleges and universities clearly had gained the spotlight. In the mid-twentieth century, band music finally received the attention of world class European and American composers such as Robert Russell Bennett, Morton Gould, Vincent Persichetti, and William Schuman.

BIBLIOGRAPHY
Smith, Michelle K. *Band Music in American Life: A Social History, 1850–1990.* Amawalk, N.Y.: Jackdaw, 1993.

Christine E. Hoffman

See also **Football; Music: Popular.**

MARCY, R. B., EXPLORATION OF

(1852). This expedition was ordered by the War Department for the purpose of exploring the Red River to its source. The government chose Capt. Randolph B. Marcy, a seasoned veteran of explorations in the southwest and California, to command the expedition. His report of 1853 disclosed that there were two main branches of the Red River; earlier treaties, including the one between Mexico and Texas, admitted but one. Between the two stretched valuable lands, which were made the object of protracted litigation between the United States and Texas in 1896 (sometimes referred to as the Green County dispute).

BIBLIOGRAPHY
Foreman, Grant, ed. *Adventure on Red River: Report on the Exploration of the Red River.* Norman: University of Oklahoma Press, 1937; 1968.

Hollon, W. Eugene. *Beyond the Cross Timbers: The Travels of Randolph B. Marcy, 1812–1887.* Norman: University of Oklahoma Press, 1955.

Carl L. Cannon / A. R.

See also **Explorations and Expeditions: U.S.; Mexican-American War; Texas.**

MARDI GRAS

is the elaborate series of outdoor pageants and indoor tableau balls held annually during the winter social season in the United States, especially in New Orleans and Mobile. The carnival culminates on Fat or Shrove Tuesday, the day before Ash Wednesday, the first day of Lent. Rooted in European pre-Lenten revelries, the carnival tradition in the United States began in the colonial period and developed in tandem with racial policies and practices and survives as an extravagant spectacle of excess, decadence, and burlesque. The pageants, each sponsored by one of the many exclusive carnival organizations, are based upon themes drawn from mythology, history, or fiction and are often satiric of contemporary social issues.

BIBLIOGRAPHY
Kinser, Samuel. *Carnival, American Style: Mardi Gras at New Orleans and Mobile.* Photographs by Norman Magden. Chicago: University of Chicago Press, 1990.

Walter Prichard
Kristen L. Rouse

See also **Holidays and Festivals.**

MARIA MONK CONTROVERSY

originated in 1836 with the publication of *Awful Disclosures of the Hotel Dieu Nunnery of Montreal,* which, although purportedly Maria Monk's autobiography, was actually written by a group of New York clergymen. Its stress on Catholic immorality aroused a storm of controversy that persisted even after several committees investigated the Hotel Dieu Convent and pronounced Maria Monk a fraud. She retained some notoriety until after her death in 1849 in a Five Points brothel. *Awful Disclosures,* an immediate bestseller, was one of the most influential pieces of nativistic propaganda ever printed in the United States.

BIBLIOGRAPHY
Franchot, Jenny. *Roads to Rome: The Antebellum Protestant Encounter with Catholicism.* Berkeley: University of California Press, 1994.

Ray Allen Billington / F. B.

See also **Nativism.**

MARIEL BOATLIFT

of late April 1980 was named for the northern Cuban port from which thousands joined an unprecedented exodus to the United States, and was rooted in Fidel Castro's earlier announcement that anyone who wanted to leave Cuba could do so. The crisis began when Peruvian patrol boats sank two Cuban fishing vessels off the Peruvian port of Callao, worsening relations between Lima and Havana, and inspiring groups of would-be Cuban emigrants to seek refuge in Havana's Peruvian Embassy. Castro then ordered his police to cease guarding the embassy. After someone died in an accidental shooting, the police retreated, and hundreds and then thousands of Cubans entered the embassy grounds to seek asylum and assistance in emigrating. Within days, more than 10,800 desperate Cubans lacking food and water jammed the embassy. Thousands of others camped out in the swamps around the port of Mariel, waiting for permission to leave. Embarrassed and resentful, Cuban officials opened the door for emigration, although many dissidents seeking to leave were harassed, sometimes viciously, mostly by police and civilians at the port of Mariel.

Hundreds of boats, large and small, headed across the Florida Straits to pick up passengers and bring them to the United States. Some refugees in Miami sold possessions or took out second mortgages on their homes to buy a boat. Perhaps fittingly, the man who took command of the flotilla that eventually brought 125,000 Cubans to Florida was Napoleón Vilaboa, a car salesman and one of the members of the 1978 Committee of 75 that had journeyed to Havana as part of a Jimmy Carter administration–backed people-to-people "dialogue."

Having grown up under communism, the new arrivals assumed the U.S. government would give them jobs, housing, and sustenance, as they had come to expect in Cuba. South Florida's militant exile community, by then nearly half a million strong, distanced themselves from the new arrivals, and recoiled when the mostly young and mostly dark-skinned *marielitos*, some named Vladimir or Vassily or Irina because of Cuba's cultural relationship with the Soviet bloc, used socialist words like *compañero* (comrade). In response, the Carter administration released $10 million in emergency refugee funds to reimburse the voluntary agencies that were working night and day to take care of the newcomers.

Robert M. Levine

See also **Cuba, Relations with; Cuban Americans.**

MARIETTA, the first settlement made under the provisions of the Ordinance of 1787, was settled on 7 April 1788, when forty-eight men under the leadership of General Rufus Putnam of the Ohio Company of Associates concluded their journey from Massachusetts to the mouth of the Muskingum River in the present state of Ohio. It was at first named Adelphia, but on 2 July 1788, in honor of Queen Marie Antoinette of France, the name was changed to Marietta. The machinery of government in the Northwest Territory first functioned here, when General Arthur St. Clair, governor of the territory, arrived on 9 July 1788.

BIBLIOGRAPHY

Reginald Horsman. *The Frontier in the Formative Years, 1783–1815.* New York: Rinehart and Winston, 1970.

T. N. Hoover/A. R.

See also **Miami Purchase; Northwest Territory; Ordinances of 1784, 1785, and 1787.**

Marijuana Protest. The poet Allen Ginsberg takes part in a demonstration outside the Women's House of Detention in New York on 10 January 1965, calling for the release of prisoners arrested for marijuana possession or use. LIBRARY OF CONGRESS

MARIJUANA, also spelled "marihuana," whose scientific name is *cannabis sativa*, is a drug obtained from the stems and leaves of the Indian hemp plant. Marijuana is one of the most commonly used drugs in the world: a 1999 survey on drug abuse showed that 75 percent of illicit drug dealers smoked it. It has several intrinsic virtues: it is an analgesic, an anesthetic, an antibiotic, an antidepressant, and a sedative, depending on its dosage.

Marijuana was introduced into India from China and from there it spread to North Africa and Europe as early as A.D. 500. The Spanish introduced it to the New World in 1545. The English settlers at Jamestown (1611) used hemp produced from the marijuana plant's fibers to make clothes. The hemp industry started in Kentucky in 1775 (in 1860, 40,000 tons were produced). The Harrison Narcotics Act became law in 1914 and aimed at controlling the sale of narcotics. Utah became the first state to pass an anti-marijuana law in 1915, and by 1931 twenty-nine states had criminalized the non-medical use of marijuana. Congress then passed the 1937 Marijuana Tax Act which prohibited its non-medical use while requiring the people producing, distributing, and using it for medical reasons to register and to pay a tax. In 1942, marijuana was removed from the *American Pharmacopoeia* because of its addictive qualities, and side effects such as anxiety, sleeplessness, paranoia, and altered time perception.

Evaluations of marijuana and its effects vary radically. In the 1950s the beatniks praised it (as would the hippies of the 1960s) as a gesture of protest against materialistic society and as a possible means of attaining enlightenment, though this assumption was later declared mistaken by such a counter-cultural figure as Allen Ginsberg. The 1970 Controlled Substances Act classified it as extremely dangerous and harmful. Until the 1970s marijuana came mostly from Mexico. By 1975 Colombian marijuana had inundated the American market. Because of drastic measures adopted under the Reagan and Bush administrations, such as the 1986 Anti-Drug Abuse Act, marijuana consumption and imports dropped sharply. Some Americans, young and old, however, continued to cultivate it at home, mainly in California and Hawaii. In 1992, the National Institute of Drug Abuse estimated that 67 million Americans—about one out of three—had smoked marijuana at least once in their lives. In 1996 California adopted Proposition 215, which allowed seriously ill people to obtain and consume marijuana for medical purposes. Connecticut, Louisiana, New Hampshire, Ohio, Vermont, and Wisconsin adopted such laws in 1998. Hawaii became the first state to decriminalize marijuana in June 2000. On 14 May 2001 the Supreme Court ruled eight to zero against authorizing the medicinal use marijuana under federal law.

BIBLIOGRAPHY

Bonnie, Richard J., Charles H. Whitebread, and Dana L. Farnsworth. *The Marijuana Conviction: A History of Marijuana Prohibition in the United States*. New York: The Lindesmith Center. 1999.

Mathre, Mary Lynn. *Cannabis in Medical Practice: A Legal, Historical, and Pharmacological Overview of the Therapeutic Use of Marijuana*. Jefferson, N.C.: McFarland and Company, 1997.

Sloman, Larry R. *Reefer Madness: The History of Marijuana in America*. Griffin Trade Paperback, 1998.

Frédéric Robert

See also **Drug Trafficking, Illegal.**

MARINE BIOLOGY. Study of life along the seashore, which became known as marine biology by the twentieth century, was first developed and institutionalized in the United States at the end of the nineteenth century. Two distinct traditions contributed to its modern disciplinary form.

First to emerge was marine biology as a summertime educational activity, chiefly designed to instruct teachers of natural history about how to study nature within a natural setting. The notion was first suggested to Louis Agassiz, the Harvard zoologist and geologist, by his student Nathaniel Southgate Shaler. Shaler had conducted highly successful summer field experiences for geology students, and felt that similar experiences could be valuable for biology students. Encouraged by his wife, Elizabeth—a longtime advocate for educational opportunities for the largely female teaching community—Agassiz obtained funding and opened the Anderson School of Natural History in 1873 on Penikese Island, located not too distant from Cape Cod. Following this school, several others offered similar experiences. The Summer School of the Peabody Academy of Sciences (Salem, Massachusetts) sponsored instruction for teachers in marine botany and zoology in 1876, and the Boston Society of Natural History, with the support of the Women's Education Association (WEA) of Boston, started its summer station north of Boston at Alpheus Hyatt's vacation home in Annisquam.

The second tradition was European, where several marine stations operated by 1880, most notably the Stazione Zoologica in Naples. This marine biology laboratory was founded by Anton Dohrn in 1872. The "Mecca for marine biology," as Naples was soon known, attracted scholars from throughout the world. Agassiz's son, Alexander Agassiz, imported Dohrn's notion to his summer home near Newport, Rhode Island, offering the latest microscopical tools for researchers. William Keith Brooks, a student of the elder Agassiz, accepted the invitation and completed his doctoral research with the younger Agassiz in 1875. Then, when Brooks obtained a position at America's first graduate university, Johns Hopkins University, one of his first tasks was to create a research laboratory in marine biology. Thus, the Chesapeake Zoological Laboratory was opened in 1878

The first U.S. marine biology laboratory to incorporate both traditions was the Marine Biological Laboratory (MBL), which opened in Woods Hole, Massachusetts, in 1888. It originally offered courses in marine botany and marine zoology for beginning students and teachers. But its original director, C. O. Whitman, had spent time at Naples and, like his colleague Brooks, wanted to create research opportunities in marine biology for more advanced students and researchers. To accomplish the task, Whitman initiated advanced courses in embryology, invertebrate zoology, cytology, and microscopy, all of which began to attract more sophisticated students. By the early twentieth century, the MBL welcomed only advanced students and investigators.

Similar marine biology LABORATORIES were founded on the Pacific Coast. Stanford University established the Hopkins Marine Station in Pacific Grove, California, in 1892. To the north, the University of Washington opened a marine station near Friday Harbor (San Juan Islands, Washington) in 1904. Henry Chandler Cowles, an ecologist from the University of Chicago who had done pioneering studies on the sand dunes of Lake Michigan started a course in intertidal ecology, the first such course in the United States.

One additional West Coast laboratory played a critical role in defining the new field of marine biology, albeit by exclusion. William Emerson Ritter, an embryologist from Berkeley, created a laboratory near San Diego, initially named the San Diego Marine Biological Laboratory, in 1903. But Ritter was interested in a more global approach to investigations by the seashore, an approach he never successfully defined. He was successful, however, in attracting the financial resources of the Scripps family, and soon the Scripps Institution for Biological Research was built north of the village of La Jolla. Ritter specifically stated that he had no intention of forming another MBL on the West Coast, preferring to emphasize a comprehensive study of the sea. After he retired, without creating an educational base for the institution similar to the other stations, he was replaced by Thomas Wayland Vaughan in 1924. The La Jolla station was renamed the Scripps Institution of Oceanography, and marine biology disappeared as a focus.

The three major American marine biology stations throughout the twentieth century and into the twenty-first century are the MBL, Hopkins Marine Station, and Friday Harbor Laboratories. By the end of World War I (1914–1918), the stations defined marine biology as the study of life in the littoral zone (also known as the intertidal zone), or the area that serves as an interface between the marine and terrestrial environments. Courses at the laboratories helped to divide marine biology into several specialty areas, including invertebrate zoology, ecology, algology, embryology, and invertebrate physiology. Following World War II (1939–1945), this focus shifted somewhat as more research funding was available in the biological sciences, especially in terms of research questions with an application to medicine and to the exciting field of molecular biology. Woods Hole's MBL, for example, has all but abandoned the traditional areas of marine biology for specialized medical and genetic research. Most investigations at the MBL by the end of the twentieth century were laboratory-based studies of cellular and molecular processes, with little fieldwork or studies of marine life. At the same time, largely because the West Coast has a more robust intertidal fauna and flora that is largely unaffected by human intervention, Hopkins and Friday Harbor retain a traditional focus on marine biology.

For the most part, marine biology does not include investigations of the open seas, studies of freshwater marine systems, or inquiries into the country's fisheries. Biological oceanography, a subdiscipline of oceanography, examines biological questions in the oceans, including studies of marine mammals, marine fisheries, and freshwater sources for the ocean (limnology).

BIBLIOGRAPHY

Benson, Keith R. "Laboratories on the New England Shore: The 'Somewhat Different Direction' of American Marine Biology." *New England Quarterly* 56 (1988): 53–78.

————. "Summer Camp, Seaside Station, and Marine Laboratory: Marine Biology and Its Institutional Identity." *Historical Studies in the Physical and Biological Sciences* 32, no. 1 (2001).

Maienschein, Jane. *100 Years Exploring Life, 1888–1988: The Marine Biological Laboratory at Woods Hole.* Boston: Jones and Bartlett Publishers, 1989.

Keith R. Benson

See also **Science Education; Zoology.**

MARINE CORPS, UNITED STATES,

one of the four armed services of the U.S. military. Originally, its function was to supply guards to warships. Over the twentieth century, however, the corps transformed into a multifunction organization that combines ground and air combat units into a maritime force, trained to come from the sea to fight on land (littoral warfare).

The history of the Marine Corps traditionally dates from 10 November 1775, when the Continental Congress authorized the raising of "two Battalions of Marines." These first marines executed a successful amphibious raid into the Bahamas in March 1776; joined George Washington at Princeton, New Jersey, in January 1777; wintered at Morristown, New Jersey; participated in the defense of the Delaware River and Philadelphia in the autumn of 1777; and joined the unsuccessful Penobscot expedition in the summer of 1779. At sea, marines—Continental, state, or privateer—served on virtually all armed ships of the embattled colonies. Both the Continental navy and the marines disbanded at the war's end.

Congress resurrected both the marines and the navy before the century's end. In 1794, spurred by the depredations of Algerian pirates, Congress authorized the building of six frigates, the complements of which included marine quotas. On 11 July 1798, concomitant with the separation of the navy from the War Department, Congress authorized "a Marine Corps." In the Quasi-War with France (1798–1800), the new U.S. Marines fought in virtually all sea actions and performed some minor landings, including those in Santo Domingo in 1800. Next came operations against the Barbary pirates (1801–1815), including the celebrated march of eight marines "to the shores of Tripoli" as part of the polyglot "army" that moved 600 miles across the Libyan desert from Alexandria to Derna (1805).

In the War of 1812, the chief service of the U.S. Marines continued to be at sea, notably in the great frigate duels and in the *Essex*'s cruise to the Pacific (1812–1814). A provisional battalion fought well at Bladensburg, Maryland (1814), as did another battalion at New Orleans (1815), but neither resources nor opportunities justified significant amphibious employment. The next three decades saw operations against the pirates in the Caribbean (1822 to the 1830s), landings in such diverse places as the Falkland Islands (1832) and Sumatra (1831–1832), and patrolling off West Africa to suppress the slave trade (1820–1861). An improvised marine regiment participated in the Seminole War of 1836–1842.

In the Mexican-American War (1846–1848), marines conducted many amphibious operations on both the Gulf and Pacific coasts. A marine battalion drawn from the Gulf Squadron executed raids against Frontera, Tampico, and Alvarado (1846–1847) and landed with Gen. Winfield Scott at Veracruz (9 March 1847). A second marine battalion joined Scott at Puebla and marched with him to the "halls of Montezuma" in Mexico City (13 September 1847). In the West, marine landing parties from the Pacific Squadron participated in the conquest of California (1846) and in raids on Mexico's west coast ports (1847).

In the CIVIL WAR (1861–1865), a marine battalion fought at the first Battle of Bull Run (1861), but primarily served with the navy. Overshadowed by the larger scope and drama of the land campaigns, the series of amphibious operations in which marines participated—beginning with the capture of Fort Clark on Hatteras Inlet, North Carolina, on 28 August 1861 and ending with the assault of Fort Fisher, a guardian of Wilmington, North Carolina, on 15 January 1865—has been largely overlooked.

The U.S. Marines were in China with the East India Squadron as early as 1844 and accompanied Commodore Matthew C. Perry when he forced open the doors of Japan to foreign commerce in 1853. In the last third of the nineteenth century, marine involvement in the Orient and in the Caribbean increased. From 1865 until 1898, marines participated in some thirty-two landings, including Formosa (1867), Japan (1867 and 1868), Mexico (1870), Korea (1871, 1888, and 1894), Colombia (1873), Hawaii (1874 and 1889), Egypt (1882), Panama (1885 and 1895), Samoa (1888), Haiti (1888), China (1894 and 1895), and Nicaragua (1894 and 1896). In the Spanish-American War (1898), a marine battalion seized an advanced base at Guantánamo Bay, Cuba, in support of the American blockade of the Spanish squadron at Santiago de Cuba, and a regiment formed for service in the Philippine Insurrection (1899–1904). Between the turn of the century and World War I, the corps continued to participate in landings and expeditions in Central America, Africa, and China.

In World War I, the Fifth Marine Regiment was in the first convoy to sail for France (14 June 1917). Along with the Sixth Marine Regiment, it became the Fourth Brigade, Second U.S. Division, which fought at Belleau Wood (June 1918), Soissons (July 1918), Saint-Mihiel (September 1918), Blanc Mont (October 1918), and in the final Meuse-Argonne offensive (November 1918). Four marine squadrons, forming the day wing of the navy's northern bombing group, operated primarily over Belgium in support of the British. Marine involvement in the occupation of Haiti and Santo Domingo continued through these war years. The marines served along the Mexican border, participated in the sugar intervention in Cuba (1917–1919), and conducted minor expeditions to Siberia

(1918–1920). After the war, they renewed large-scale involvement in Nicaragua (1926–1933) and China (1926–1941).

When the Japanese struck Pearl Harbor on 7 December 1941, the U.S. Marines were there helping defend the islands. The marines were also in the Philippines and at Guam, Wake, and Midway islands. Beginning with Guadalcanal (August 1942), marine divisions or corps conducted amphibious assaults at Bougainville (November 1942), Tarawa (November 1942), New Britain (December 1943), Kwajalein (January 1944), Eniwetok (February 1944), Saipan (June 1944), Guam (July 1944), Tinian (July 1944), Peleliu (September 1944), Iwo Jima (February 1945), and Okinawa (April 1945). Marine aviation, in addition to providing air defense and close air support incident to these and other operations, contributed to the neutralization of bypassed Japanese-held islands. During World War II the Marine Corps reached a peak strength of 485,113; almost 87,000 were killed or wounded.

Marine units took part briefly in the occupation of Japan (1945–1946) and for a longer term in the occupation of northern China (1945–1949). Immediately after the outbreak of the KOREAN WAR (June 1950), a marine brigade moved to reinforce the Pusan perimeter. Joined by the remainder of the First Marine Division and supported by the First Marine Aircraft Wing, these marines executed the assault at Inchon and the subsequent recapture of Seoul (September 1950). The marines also joined the United Nations forces in the counteroffensives of spring and summer 1951 until reaching the truce line. Two years of trench warfare followed. More then 25,000 marines were killed or wounded during the Korean conflict.

Involvement in Vietnam began with the assignment of U.S. Marine advisers to the Vietnamese Marine Corps in 1954. Marine transport helicopter units arrived in 1962 and, in 1965, the landing of the Ninth Marine Expeditionary Brigade at Da Nang marked the first significant introduction of U.S. ground forces. Marine ground operations concentrated in the First Corps Tactical Zone, the northern five provinces of South Vietnam. By the summer of 1968, Marine Corps strength reached a peak of more than 85,000, more than the number who fought at Iwo Jima or Okinawa during World War II. This force completely left Vietnam by June 1971. In reaction to the North Vietnamese Easter offensive of 1972, two marine aircraft groups returned to Vietnam but without any marine ground forces. They helped evacuate embassy staff, U.S. citizens, and refugees from Saigon and Phnom Penh in 1975.

During the 1980s, the Marine Corps participated in several efforts to restore stability in countries threatened by war or by political disintegration. Lebanon presented a particularly difficult situation. In August 1982, marine security guards went to Beruit, Lebanon, as part of a multi-national peacekeeping force to oversee evacuation of Palestine Liberation Organization (PLO) guerillas un-

Marines on Guam. As with so many other islands across the Pacific, U.S. Marines played a pivotal role in recapturing Guam, after nearly three weeks of heavy fighting in July–August 1944. NATIONAL ARCHIVES AND RECORDS ADMINISTRATION

der Israeli siege. They remained in Lebanon after the PLO evacuation to train Lebanese soldiers and prevent the outbreak of war. On 23 September 1983, a suicide truck bomber destroyed the Marine Corps barracks, killing 241 and wounding 70. The marines and American civilians evacuated Beruit in February 1984. For the rest of the decade, marines remained stationed on ships in the Mediterranean.

The August 1990 Iraqi invasion of Kuwait lead to the largest mobilization of marine forces since World War II. More than 92,000 marines, including more than 1,000 women, were deployed to the Persian Gulf as part of Operations Desert Shield and Desert Storm in 1990–1991. Since the end of Desert Storm, the Marine Corps has increasingly been involved in "military operations other than war." These operations include providing relief after a devastating cyclone in Bangladesh (1991); safeguarding humanitarian relief efforts in Somalia (1993–1994); evacuating embassy staff and civilians from countries torn by civil strife; helping residents of Dade County, Florida, who were displaced by Hurricane Andrew (1992); providing relief at Guantanomo Bay to Haitians fleeing political upheaval (1992), and to Cubans fleeing economic hardship (1993–1994); assisting with drug interdiction efforts along the U.S.-Mexico border; and supporting the efforts of civilian authorities to combat forest fires. But the marines began the twenty-first century in a familiar role as the forward deployed units in Afghanistan as part of Operation Enduring Freedom.

The Gulf War was a watershed event in terms of the participation of enlisted women in an armed conflict. However, women had been offering to serve in the marines for many years before that conflict. According to legend, the first woman marine was Lucy Brewer, who donned men's clothing, took on the name of George Baker, and saw action on the USS *Constitution* during the War of 1812. Officially, Opha Mae Johnson was the first woman marine. She and some 300 other women enlisted in 1918 to take over stateside clerical duties from battle-ready male marines. After the war was over, the Marine Corps separated all women from the service. During World War II, women came back to "free a man to fight" when the corps formed the Women Marine Corps Reserve on 13 February 1943. During the war, women not only handled clerical duties, but also worked as map makers, mechanics, parachute riggers, radio operators, and welders. A total of 23,145 women served as reserves in the corps during World War II.

After Japan surrendered, the Marine Corps demobilized the Women's Reserve. However, some women returned to the service as regulars under the 1948 Women's Armed Services Integration Act. At the height of the Vietnam War, there were about 2,700 women marines on active duty. During this period, the Marine Corps began to expand training and opportunities for women within the service. It took some time, however, for the training of women to closely resemble that of men. Firing rifles became part of training for all marine women in 1980; testing on combat rifles began in 1985. By the year 2000, training and testing standards for women were almost identical to that of men. At the beginning of the twenty-first century, women made up six percent of Marine Corps ranks. Ground combat was still off limits, but women were near the heat of battle—flying planes in combat and serving on combat ships during the war in Afghanistan. In January 2002, Sgt. Jeannette L. Winters became the first woman marine killed in a hostile-fire zone when a tanker plane crashed in Pakistan.

Hidden within this combat history is another story—that of the Marine Corps's institutional changes and its changing role in U.S. military and foreign policy. During the nineteenth century, the main function of the corps was to supply ships guards for naval warships. These guards provided internal security aboard ships and infantry for ship battles or landing operations. At the end of the nineteenth century, the corps became a colonial infantry force for use in prolonged interventions in the Pacific and Latin America. Between the turn of the century and World War I, the Marine Corps expanded gradually and became structured more permanently into companies, regiments, and brigades for this expeditionary service, which ended in the 1940s. At the same time, the corps acquired an amphibious assault function as it began to provide forces to defend advanced naval bases. This mission led to the creation of the Fleet Marine Force in 1933 and the development of ship-to-shore movement tactics and equipment used in the amphibious campaigns in the Pacific during World War II. Since the end of World War II, the Marine Corps has expanded its mission even further as development of air support technology allowed the corps to acquire rapid intervention capabilities that made it the nation's principal "force in readiness" for the twenty-first century.

BIBLIOGRAPHY

Alexander, Joseph H., Don Horan, and Norman C. Stahl. *A Fellowship of Valor: The Battle History of the United States Marines.* New York: HarperCollins, 1997.

Heinl, Robert D., Jr. *Soldiers of the Sea: The United States Marine Corps, 1775–1962.* Annapolis, Md.: U.S. Naval Institute, 1962.

Millett, Allan Reed. *Semper Fidelis: The History of the United States Marine Corps.* New York: Macmillan, 1980; New York: Free Press; Toronto: Maxwell Macmillan Canada; New York: Maxwell Macmillan International, 1991.

Moskin, J. Robert. *The U.S. Marine Corps Story.* New York: McGraw-Hill, 1977; 1987; Boston: Little, Brown, 1992.

Sherrod, Robert. *History of Marine Corps Aviation in World War II.* Washington: Combat Forces Press, 1952; 1979; San Rafael, Calif: Presidio Press, 1980; Baltimore: Nautical and Aviation Publishing Co. of America, 1987.

Simmons, Edwin H. *The United States Marines: A History.* Annapolis, Md.: Naval Institute Press, 1998.

Simmons, Edwin H., and J. Robert Moskin, eds. *The Marines.* Quantico, Va.: Marine Corps Heritage Foundation, 1998.

Stremlow, Mary V. *A History of the Women Marines, 1946–1977.* Washington, D.C.: U.S. Marine Corps, 1986.

Edwin H. Simmons/c. w.; c. p.

See also **Barbary Wars; Lebanon, U.S. Landing in; Navy, United States; Perry's Expedition to Japan; Persian Gulf War; Philippine Insurrection; Seminole Wars; Spanish-American War; Vietnam War; Women in Military Service.**

MARINE SANCTUARIES, created by Title III of the Marine Protection, Research, and Sanctuaries Act of 1972, and amended and reauthorized every four years beginning in 1980. Congress was responding in large part to pressure from the growing environmental movement for environmental protection. Books such as *The Sea Around Us* (1951, rev. 1961) by Rachel Carson and television documentaries by the French undersea explorer Jacques Cousteau enchanted a wide popular audience with descriptions of marine organisms. Their works carried the message that the human impact on marine ecosystems directly and adversely affects human health. The 1972 legislation not only provided the mechanism for protecting the ecosystems of the U.S. coast through ocean sanctuaries but also mandated a federal marine research program and enabled the Environmental Protection Agency to regulate industrial and municipal disposal of wastes at sea.

Thirty years later, the National Marine Sanctuary System, administered by the National Oceanic and Atmospheric Administration, comprises thirteen designated sanctuaries, including unique and threatened areas in both coastal and offshore locations. Seven of the designated sanctuaries have been incorporated into the system since 1990, and together the sanctuaries comprise nearly 18,000 square miles of protected area—an area almost as large as Vermont and New Hampshire together. They are located from American Samoa to California to Florida, and protect a wide range of environmentally sensitive phenomena, from corridors for migrating whales to deep-sea canyons, coral reefs, and historically significant shipwrecks. Although the government regulates the use of the sanctuaries, it encourages many different uses, including recreation, shipping, and even commercial fishing.

BIBLIOGRAPHY

Hays, Samuel P. *Beauty, Health, and Permanence: Environmental Politics in the United States, 1955–1985.* New York: Cambridge University Press, 1987.

Shabecoff, Philip. *A Fierce Green Fire: The American Environmental Movement.* New York: Hill and Wang, 1993.

Dennis Williams/c. w.

See also **Conservation; Conservation Biology; Environmental Protection Agency; Marine Biology; Whaling.**

MARION, BATTLE AT (18 December 1864). Union Gen. George Stoneman, raiding southwestern Virginia from eastern Tennessee, struck the Confederates under John C. Breckinridge at Marion, Virginia. During the battle, Stoneman detached a force that moved back to Saltville, Virginia, and destroyed the salt works there. This was his original purpose, even though he could gain no decision against Breckinridge.

BIBLIOGRAPHY

Hattaway, Herman, and Archer Jones. *How the North Won: A Military History of the Civil War.* Urbana: University of Illinois Press, 1982; 1991.

Johnson, Robert Underwood, and Clarence Clough Buel, eds. *Battles and Leaders of the Civil War, Vol. IV: Retreat with Honor.* Seacaucus, N.J.: Castle, 1989.

Robert S. Thomas/a. r.

See also **Civil War; Southern Campaigns.**

MARITIME COMMISSION, FEDERAL, a regulatory agency charged with protecting the interests of shippers, carriers, and passengers sailing under the U.S. flag. The Commission investigates anticompetitive practices in the maritime transport business and reviews the records of service contracts and rates. It issues licenses to ocean transportation intermediaries to guard against unqualified, insolvent, or dishonest companies; requires companies to maintain bonds against financial loss; and ensures that passenger cruise operations take financial responsibility when found liable for personal injury, death, or nonperformance of a voyage.

Today's Federal Maritime Commission is a fragment of a once huge network of government agencies created by legislation including the Shipping Act of 1916 and the Merchant Marine Acts of 1920 and 1936. On the eve of World War I, with American ships carrying only 2 percent of the nation's foreign trade, policymakers moved to reverse the nation's vulnerability to shortages in vital supplies. With the help of massive government subsidies, by the end of World War II the United States had one of the largest maritime fleets in the world and U.S. merchant ships carried 60 percent of the world's tonnage.

In the decades after the war, U.S.-flagged shipping began a continuing decline as air traffic took over passenger service previously provided by ocean liners, containerization technology made managing cargo more efficient, and U.S.-owned ships transferred registration to foreign countries such as Liberia to avoid higher costs associated with U.S. regulation.

In 1950 the U.S. Maritime Commission, which had presided over the fleet's buildup, was dismantled and its responsibilities shifted to the Maritime Administration and the Federal Maritime Board. In 1961 the Board was renamed the Federal Maritime Commission and its nonregulatory responsibilities were given to the Maritime Administration. Regulatory provisions of the Shipping Act of 1984 and the Ocean Shipping Reform Act of 1998 reflect the recent era of diminished government involvement in the ocean transportation industry.

BIBLIOGRAPHY

Federal Maritime Commission. *39th Annual Report for Fiscal Year 2000.* Washington, D.C.: Federal Maritime Commission, 2001.

Labaree, Benjamin W., et al. *America and the Sea: A Maritime History.* Mystic, Conn.: Mystic Seaport Museum, 1998.

Jennifer Maier

See also **Merchant Marine; Shipping, Ocean; Shipping Board, U.S.**

MARKETING is the multifaceted, systematic approach to selling goods, adopted by every business and not-for-profit agency and group with a message. It attempts to optimize an organization's ability to make a profit, whether monetary (profits or donations) or electoral.

Marketing encompasses advertising, promotions, product design, positioning, and product development. Marketing tools include elements such as focus groups, gap analysis, concept testing, product testing, perceptual maps, demographics, psychographics (lifestyles), and choice modeling. It is powerfully aided by market research, a science that has become increasingly complex and sophisticated over the past century or more.

Market research embraces qualitative and quantitative methods. Environmental analysis gives companies key information about economic conditions, consumer demographics, consumer lifestyles, industry trends, distribution channels, new technology, employee relations and supply, foreign markets, corporate image, political and regulatory changes, and key players in the business. Sophisticated data collection and analysis investigate market segmentation and target selection, product and advertising positioning, product design, pricing, mass media advertising, direct marketing, promotion, distribution channels, and sales force allocation.

Market research rarely has a direct impact on income, but provides the essential data to prove or disprove client preconceptions, resolve disagreements, expose threats, quantify a population, and qualify an opportunity. The ways that research is used for strategic decision making determines its relationship to profit and market advance. Marketing has existed in every age and culture. In the United States, marketing reached its high level of sophistication as a result of the mass market.

Three overlapping stages have marked the history of our republic. Until roughly the 1880s, the economy was characterized by market fragmentation. Geographical limitations were reinforced by the absence of a transportation and communications infrastructure that spanned the continent. There were hundreds of local markets and very few national brand names. Profit was determined by low sales volume and high prices.

Mass Marketing

Spurred by a communications revolution and the completion of a national railroad network that by 1900 consisted of more miles of track than the rest of the world combined, a national mass market emerged. Technological innovation mushroomed, and a small number of firms realized economies of scale previously undreamed of. Giant corporations (or a small cluster of corporations) dominated single industries. Companies were able to produce goods in high volume at low prices. By 1900, firms followed the logic of mass production as they sought to create a "democracy of desire" by universalizing the availability of products.

Mass production required the development of mass marketing as well as modern management, a process spurred by analysis of the depression of the 1870s, when unsold inventory was blamed in part for the depth of the crisis, and the depression of the 1890s, when the chaos of market competition spurred efforts to make the market more predictable and controllable.

As the mass market emerged, manufacturers and retailers developed a range of instruments to shape and mold the market. National brand names like the Singer Sewing Machine from the 1860s, Coca-Cola from the 1890s, Wrigley's Chewing Gum after 1907, and Maxwell House coffee around the same time heralded the "golden age of brand names." Advertising also came into its own during the early decades of the twentieth century. The first advertising agency was established in 1869 as N. W. Ayer and Son. John Wanamaker placed the first full-page advertisement in a newspaper in 1879. Advertising media were powerfully supplemented by the use of subway cars, electric trolleys, trams, billboards, and the explosion in magazine sales. Further developments came after the 1890s with flashing electric signs, and in 1912 "talking signs" that allowed copy to move swiftly along boards from right to left first appeared on Broadway in New York City. By 1910, photo technology and color lithography revolutionized the capacity to reproduce images of all kinds.

Forward integration into wholesaling also aided mass marketing, beginning in the 1870s and 1880s with meat packers like Gustavus Swift. Franchise agreements with retailers were one key to the success of companies such as Coca-Cola. Another feature in the success of mass marketing was the creation and implementation of sales programs made possible by the spread of modern management structures and the division of corporate functions. In 1911, with the appointment of its first director of commercial research, the Curtis Publishing Company instituted the systematic analysis of carefully collected data. Hart, Shafner, and Marx became the largest manufacturer of men's suits in America by the 1910s through research that suggested producing suits for fourteen different male body types and psychographic appeals in its advertising. During and after the 1920s, as the social sciences matured, sweeping improvements in statistical methodology, behavioral science, and quantitative analysis made market research more important and accurate. Through these means—as well as coherent production and marketing plans—a mass market was created by World War II. However, consumerism as understood in the beginning of the twenty-first century did not triumph until after 1950.

Market Segmentation

The final stage of the twentieth-century market in America has been characterized as "market segmentation." Fully developed in the 1970s and 1980s, firms sought competitive advantage through the use of demographics and psychographics to more accurately pinpoint and persuade consumers of their products. Price was determined not so much by how cheaply something could be sold, but more by the special value a particular market placed upon the goods, independent of production costs.

General Motors (GM) pioneered market segmentation in the 1920s, as it fought and beat Ford for the biggest market share of the booming automobile business. Henry Ford was an exemplar of mass marketing. He had pioneered the marketing of the automobile so that it could be within the reach of almost all Americans. Standardized models were produced quickly, identically, and only in black, which dropped the cost of car buying from $600 in 1905 to $290 by 1924. In nineteen years of production, his Model T sold to 15.5 million customers. By 1924, thanks largely to Ford, the number of cars produced in the United States was greater than 4 million, compared

to 180,000 in 1910. Due to his methods, by 1921 Ford sold 55 percent of all new cars in America. In trying to compete with Ford, GM first tried merging with rivals to create a larger market force, but then embraced individuality. It was in the 1920s that annual modifications to automobile models were introduced. GM made not one model to suit all, but a number of different models to suit differing pocketbooks. It looked at the market not as an undifferentiated whole, but as a collection of segments with differing requirements and desires to be satisfied. GM made the ownership of automobiles both a status symbol and stylish. By 1927, Ford's market share had been cut to 25 percent, and Ford was forced to retool and try to catch up with GM.

By the 1960s, as consumer values shifted because of social change, marketers and advertisers sought ways to reach a more segmented society. Generational differences became much more important. Further changes, after 1970, meant that marketers needed to be much more sensitive to the differences between groups of Americans and their values. Serious foreign competition in American markets during the 1970s and 1980s also spurred innovation in market research, product design, and marketing generally. Television's Nielsen ratings offered one instrument, and more sophisticated polling techniques another. The ability to identify who watched what shows according to age, gender, and ethnic background led to more targeted advertising and a leap in TV advertising, from $12 billion in 1960 to $54.5 billion in 1980. By 1985, advertisers had developed eight consumer clusters for women alone, and over forty lifestyle groups.

By the 1990s, children, teens, and seniors were similarly analyzed. In 1997, it was estimated that "kid power" accounted for sales of over $200 billion per year. Age segmentation among children received particular attention, as researchers took into account neurological, social, emotional, and moral development. Testing determined the relative perception of visual and verbal information at different ages and developmental stages. Humor and gender differences were also studied to make marketing more successful. Deregulation of children's programming in the 1980s led to cartoons becoming merchandising vehicles. By 1987, about 60 percent of all toys sold in the United States were based on licensed characters from television, movies, or books.

Market research also determined the kinds of junk mail that went to each individual and how advertising would appear on the Internet or on television. During the 1980s and 1990s, more sophisticated research developed as patterns of credit card spending were analyzed, television was deregulated into cable and satellite channels, and Internet usage was identified.

Despite the end of a long post–World War II economic expansion, after 1970 consumer spending continued to grow, largely the result of consumerism; newer, easier forms of obtaining credit; and segmented marketing; which seized a generation of Americans who were born into the first generalized age of affluence in America. Consumer spending jumped from $70.8 billion in 1940 to $617 billion in 1970. The U.S. Census Bureau reported in 2001 that retail sales just for the fourth quarter accounted for $861 billion, a remarkable figure, given the slowdown in economic growth in the preceding thirty years.

The development of marketing during the twentieth century matched and aided American economic growth and was symbiotic with the triumph of consumerism. The creation of a "democracy of desire" came to characterize American society and its values. It was a distinctive quality that influenced the attitudes of the rest of the world toward the United States, as the strength of marketing smoothed its economic dominance around the planet.

BIBLIOGRAPHY

Acuff, Dan S. *What Kids Buy and Why: The Psychology of Marketing to Kids.* New York: Free Press, 1997.

Beacham, Walton, et al., eds. *Beacham's Marketing Reference: Account Executive-Market Segmentation.* 2 vols. Washington, D.C.: Research Publishing, 1986.

Burwood, Stephen. "Advertising and Consumerism." In *Beacham's Encyclopedia of Social Change: America in the Twentieth Century.* Edited by Veryan B. Khan. Osprey, Fla.: Beacham Publishing, 2001.

Clancy, Kevin J., and Robert S. Shulman. *The Marketing Revolution: A Radical Manifesto for Dominating the Marketplace.* New York: HarperBusiness, 1991.

Tedlow, Richard S. *New and Improved: The Story of Mass Marketing in America.* Boston: Harvard Business School Press, 1996.

Zollo, Peter. *Wise Up To Teens: Insights into Marketing and Advertising to Teenagers.* 2d ed. Ithaca, N.Y.: New Strategist Publications, 1999.

Stephen Burwood

See also **Advertising; Consumerism; Direct Mail; Mass Production; Marketing Research; Radio; Television: Programming and Influence.**

MARKETING RESEARCH evolved as the U.S. economy shifted from a production-driven one to a market-driven one. As the American production of goods and services, plus imports, was beginning to satiate American demand, marketers needed to learn how to tailor their products to the needs and likes of an increasingly discerning public. This tailoring resulted in increased market demand and, for successful companies, increased market share.

Formal marketing research was initiated in 1911 when the Curtis Publishing Company appointed its first director of commercial research. Early practitioners were inspired by the efforts of Frederick W. Taylor, famous for his time and motion studies, and others to employ disciplines of "scientific management" to improve business processes and thereby improve results. Marketing research has evolved into an industry consisting of large and small firms worldwide as well as dedicated market research departments in all large and many small companies. Expenditures for marketing research in the United States exceeded $1 billion in 2000.

The American Marketing Association defines marketing research as "the function that links the consumer, customer, and public to the marketer through . . . information used to identify and define marketing opportunities and problems; generate, refine, and evaluate marketing actions; monitor marketing performance; and improve understanding of marketing as a process." Marketing research "specifies the information required to address these issues, designs the method for collecting information, manages and implements the data collection process, analyzes the results, and communicates the findings and their implications."

Marketing research consists of gaining consumer input and data. It is the lifeline between companies and customers, and it allows the application of scientific methods to gain knowledge about consumers, buyers, competitors, markets, and marketing.

In general terms, marketing research is either primary research or secondary research. Primary research is either qualitative or quantitative. Qualitative research explores, defines, and describes. It involves in-depth studies of limited samples of people. Use of focus groups is a popular tool of qualitative research. In this format, participants are prescreened to assure that they match the sociodemographic profile of the brand or company performing the research (that is, they are either customers or potential target customers). Once screened, groups of eight to twelve customers participate in a group discussion, with a company-hired moderator, to discuss the topic at hand: new products, reaction to advertising or packaging, or assessment of goods or services. Use of one-on-one interviews is another popular tool of qualitative research. Often these are conducted in shopping malls (mall intercepts), where shoppers are approached, screened to match a predetermined sociodemographic profile, and escorted to a facility for a thirty-minute to one-hour interview.

Quantitative research measures, estimates, and quantifies. It generally involves polling of a broad sample of people. This choice is necessary when statistically significant results are required. Large companies and well-known packaged-goods brands use this type of research when they want to be certain that consumer opinions are representative of the population at large. In the last decade especially, political opinion polls have become popular for U.S. presidents and others to assure that they are taking the public's point of view into consideration in policymaking and that they remain popular among their constituents.

Specific research objectives may require a mix of qualitative and quantitative research. Examples include awareness and attitude surveys, brand image surveys, advertising tracking, promotion testing, media mix evaluation, new products research, marketing optimization research, and customer loyalty evaluation.

Secondary research entails gathering information from already published data and sources. Some applications for secondary research include competitive intelligence (where one company wants to monitor its competitors, their spending, their new product introductions, their staffing, or their financial performance) and trend assessment. As an example, Albing International Marketing, a global home furnishings consultancy, used secondary research data to prepare a market study, *Windows on the Millennium—Across the Threshold to the New Century* (2001), which cited ten key trends expected to shape and impact the home furnishings industry in the subsequent decade. The trends were listed under the following headings: Home and Family, Leisure, The Aging Population, The Ethnic Influence, The Spiritual Search, Information and Technology, The Environment, The Wealth Effect, Globalization and Nationalism, and The Value Mentality.

New methodologies and new technologies are continually being adopted by the marketing research industry. New research techniques provide deeper insight into buyer behavior, even using predictive models of how their behavior will change under alternative scenarios. The computer has been integrated into nearly every phase of research, from computer-assisted telephone and personal interviews to disk-by-mail data collection to Internet sampling. The Internet has become the key portal for gathering secondary research. In addition to access to public library databases, several sites exist exclusively to sell market research reports on a broad variety of subjects (for example, Profound, Factiva, MarketResearch.com). It is only a matter of time until Web-based survey research becomes an industry norm.

BIBLIOGRAPHY

Mendelsohn, Susan. "In Search of Market Research." *Information World Review* (March 2002).

Neal, William D. "Getting Serious about Marketing Research." *Marketing Research* (Summer 2002).

Thomas, Jerry W. "Marketing Research." *Executive Excellence* (November 2001).

Wade, A. Kenneth. "Focus Groups Research Role is Shifting." *Marketing News* (4 March 2002).

Nancy P. Neumann

See also **Advertising; Business Forecasting; Polling.**

MARKETS, PUBLIC. When the New World was being settled, every European town of any importance had its public market, and so in laying out their towns it was not unusual that the early settlers provided for them. There was a marketplace in Jamestown as early as 1617 and one in New Amsterdam as early as 1647. As in Eu-

rope, forestalling, regrating, and engrossing were generally prohibited. The sale of meats and vegetables was permitted only in the public market. Sale of these articles at any other place was illegal. The system was quite general in America in the colonial and early national periods. By the time of the Civil War, the public market system was well on its way to disintegration. It was inconvenient for the householder to travel some distance to make daily purchases. As a result, meat shops were established closer to the householder. The public market buildings were then either abandoned or converted into predominantly wholesale markets. Although the public market no longer exists, echoes of it remain in the form of pedestrian malls, farmers' markets, and massive retail attractions, such as Boston's redeveloped Faneuil Hall, often conceived as part of a larger urban renewal project and built with taxpayer support.

BIBLIOGRAPHY

Bailyn, Bernard. *The New England Merchants in the Seventeenth Century.* Cambridge, Mass.: Harvard University Press, 1955.

Fred M. Jones / A. R.

See also **Colonial Commerce; Malls, Shopping; Merchant Adventurers.**

MARQUE AND REPRISAL, LETTERS OF, are papers from a belligerent government authorizing privately owned vessels, called privateers, to engage in warfare against enemy commerce. The Constitution gives Congress power to "grant Letters of Marque and Reprisal, and make Rules concerning Captures on Land and Water" (Article I, Section 8). Prize courts typically decided the legality of captures, and the profits went chiefly to the privateer and crew. During the Revolution, Congress and state governments issued letters to 1,150 vessels. In the War of 1812, 515 privateers captured about 1,450 prizes. European nations abolished privateering in 1856. The South briefly used this practice in the Civil War. In subsequent wars the destruction of enemy commerce was limited to government-owned vessels.

BIBLIOGRAPHY

Buel, Richard. *In Irons: Britain's Naval Supremacy and the American Revolutionary Economy.* New Haven, Conn.: Yale University Press, 1998.

Butler, Lindley S. *Pirates, Privateers, and Rebel Raiders of the Carolina Coast.* Chapel Hill: University of North Carolina Press, 2000.

Swanson, Carl E. *Predators and Prizes: American Privateering and Imperial Warfare, 1739–1748.* Columbia: University of South Carolina Press, 1991.

Allan Westcott / H. S.

See also **Privateers and Privateering; War of 1812.**

MARRIAGE as an institution in America has changed in a variety of ways over the last three centuries. From early colonial days, the differing marital practices and understandings of Native Americans, of Africans, of European peasants, and eventually of all the peoples who brought their marriages to North America mixed with the more settled expectations and understandings that church and governmental authorities thought they were bringing from England. By the late eighteenth century, America was already understood as a society in which parental power was notably weak, a society in which children, including daughters, were genuinely free to choose who, when, and whether to marry. Geographical mobility often meant the movement of children away from parental homes and increased the isolation of married couples from their familial and ethnic communities. Couples forced to depend on each other might grow closer, become more interdependent; but hatred and the terrors of having to depend on an incompatible companion was also a possibility for couples living across America. Mobility and distance also made leaving a marriage—whether in the form of abandonment, separation, divorce, or bigamy—a possibility and a temptation, one that men in particular often found hard to resist. By the early nineteenth century, particular U.S. states were recognized as the easiest places in the world to obtain a divorce; and throughout the twentieth century, demographers and sociologists identified the United States as the world leader in its divorce rate.

American Marriage: Theory and Practice

For early modern Protestant theologians and political theorists, both in England and in the North American colonies, marriage had modeled the state. Within marriage, the relation of husband and wife offered the primordial example of the "law of persons," the dyadic hierarchical relations (parent and child, master and servant, guardian and ward, king and subject were other examples) out of which the "constitution" of a legitimate political realm was formed. The good Christian should know himself or herself as like the "bride of Christ," that is, he or she should submit to the governance of a loving savior. For civic republican theorists, including some, like James Harrington, whose writings framed the ideas of the makers of the American Revolution, the idea of a citizen, of a man capable of participating in the government of the realm was intimately tied to the idea of a husband, one who properly governed his dependents and properties. A man who ruled his household as a good man should became someone capable of participating in the governance (rulership) of the state.

What was the "marriage" that played these roles in early modern thought? It was a contractual relationship, given by God, free in its entry, but fixed in its terms. By entering in to marriage, men and women were transformed, though differentially so. They became wives and husbands, beings of a new order, though men also remained men as well as husbands. The antinomic relationship of wife and husband depended on a series of coercive metaphors and images drawn both from the English common law and from Protestant theology. Husband and his wife became "one flesh," united at least during the duration of their lives. A wife became a "femme" or "feme" "covert," a being covered over by her husband during her life as a wife, during her "coverture." Wife and husband were locked into a non-negotiable relationship of reciprocity, in which a husband's obligation to support a wife was conditioned on her dutiful obedience and sexual availability, and vice versa.

These images had real power in the world, and a good deal of the law of marriage was taken up with elaborations of logical implications drawn from these images. Thus, to take one example, a wife's settlement, the town in which she could receive poor relief if her husband abandoned her (or in other cases of need), was her husband's town, the town of his birth, not the town of her birth. For the duration of her marriage, her home was by definition her husband's, though if he died or if she violated the terms of the marriage relationship by disobeying him or deserting him, once her coverture was at an end, then her settlement of birth became the place from which she could claim poor relief. As a second example, marital rape was something close to an oxymoron. As late as the 1950s, a standard definition of the crime of rape was when a man had "illicit sexual intercourse with a woman not his wife without her consent." And though a husband's sexual coercion might give his wife grounds for separation or divorce, and an order granting her alimony and custody of their children, it would not subject him to criminal punishment.

These images were formalisms, often radically inconsistent with the real lives led by American couples. Yet they were no longer united in fact, and such couples worked out the terms of their lives, often understanding themselves as separate individuals, sometimes holding on to the idea of being married. When men sought gold in California or signed on to shipping expeditions and wives remained behind caring for children and taking care of households, they were still understood as legally united, though separated by a continent or an ocean. How resources were distributed, who held practical power, how relationships evolved over time, and who did what within a relationship were improvisational narratives of particular marriages shaped by changing cultures, extended family networks, economic circumstances, and the individuals themselves.

Marital Law and its Effects

From a legal standpoint, what most shaped marriage as an institution was the peculiar structure of American federalism, which left the governance of marriage to the individual states. Different states had the power to institute their own distinctive marital laws. And by the second third of the nineteenth century, significant differences appeared between various states, particularly in the rules for obtaining a divorce and in the ability of a wife to secure her own property. A few jurisdictions even adopted a version of a European civil law tradition of community property, rejecting the English common law understanding that nearly all property within a marriage would come under the effective ownership of the husband. The continuing experiments of various states with laws that allowed divorce on a variety of grounds and with marital property reforms that authorized married women to hold property produced endless legal complexities and enormous quantities of litigation, as mobile Americans moved from jurisdiction to jurisdiction across the political landscape of American federalism. Did they move because of the diversity of marital regimes? Perhaps the most important reason for the litigation this diversity produced were uncertainties about liability in law suits between husbands (and sometimes wives) and creditors and other "third parties" to the marriage. In addition, we should not exaggerate the variation in the marital laws the different states produced. To be a husband in a community property jurisdiction, for example, still meant that one had full managerial control over all property held by the community. Marriage as an institution remained recognizable in its structure and in the structured relationship it offered and imposed.

Received images of marriage played a part in some national enterprises and controversies. The fact that no North American slave jurisdiction recognized the legitimacy of slave marriages—putting all slave relationships on the wrong side of the bright line between marriage and sin—became for abolitionists a core and politically potent feature of the wrongs of slavery, and for proslavery apologists, a continuing embarrassment. From the 1850s through the 1890s, the control of Mormon polygamists over territorial Utah created a long constitutional dilemma in a national political culture that regarded any deviation from monogamy as abusive to women and inconsistent with republican virtue. (To the Republican Party it became in 1860, along with slavery, one of the "twin relics of barbarism.") By the end of the nineteenth century, the triumph over Mormonism had implicated and changed American federalism and the law of church and state, although not the commitment to state control over domestic relations.

Immigration law constituted one area of continuing national responsibility where marriage and marital status was (and has remained) of crucial concern. The 1858 immigration law passed by Congress reversed an earlier understanding, identified with the writings of Joseph Story, which separated citizenship from the institution of marriage. Thereafter, a non-American woman who married an American would become an American. She would take on a political identity derived from her husband, because of the nature of marriage. There were racial exceptions to this conclusion. During the era of Chinese exclusion, from the 1880s to the 1920s, a Chinese woman who married an American was likely to be labeled a prostitute, not a wife. But what of the converse situation: would an American woman who married a non-American lose her political identity? Federal courts went back and forth on the question for the next half century. In 1912 the Supreme Court finally decided the logic of marriage would be sustained: a native-born American woman would become an alien if she married an alien, a conclusion that held until after the passage of the Nineteenth Amendment, when citizenship was again separated from marriage within legal doctrine and administrative practice.

Changing Perceptions

Beginning in the middle of the nineteenth century, there were voices that challenged understandings of marriage as a hierarchy and as the responsibility of individual states. Drawing from abolitionism, anti-Calvinist strains of Protestantism, and a universalistic reading of egalitarian texts like the Declaration of Independence, woman's rights activists, the first generation of American feminists, formulated a critique of orthodox marriage as an unjust institution. They sometimes compared it to chattel slavery, and they insisted on an individual Christian woman's direct relationship with God, unmediated by a husband. In novels and in prescriptive texts, middle-class readers found a romantic remaking of marriage, one that denied hierarchy and alternately insisted that marriage be understood as a partnership or as an ecstatic union between apparent equals. "Free lovers" (a term that can only make sense in a culture where marriage was defined as "unfree") created alternative models of sexual relationships, at first in rural utopian communities, later in Bohemian enclaves like GREENWICH VILLAGE of the early twentieth century. On the other side, conservatives unhappy with the messiness of marital life in America, and in particular with the relative ease of divorce, would regularly issue calls for national laws that would recreate discipline and national virtue.

Still, the foundational understanding of marriage as a fixed hierarchical relationship governed by the states did not change over nearly two centuries of American history. After the Civil War, when Republican congressional leaders defended the new FOURTEENTH AMENDMENT against claims that it was destroying the fabric of American life, they assured Democrats and others the egalitarian and transforming provisions of the amendment would not apply to marriage, which would remain a distinctive responsibility of the states and within a protected private sphere of male life. Woman's rights activists like Elizabeth Cady Stanton, who since the 1840s had challenged legislators and theologians by describing orthodox marriage as a radically unjust institution, were outraged. To them the Fourteenth Amendment ought to have been understood as having made a new departure in American constitutionalism, one that required subjected existing institutions, even longstanding ones like marriage, to a standard of substantive equality. It would be a century, however, before their claims would be revived, and a constitutional reconsideration of marriage would occur.

The Late Twentieth Century

In 1968, when David Schneider published *American Kinship*, his now-classic portrayal of the structure of the American family, it was still possible to portray heterosexual marriage as the linchpin of family life and the embodiment of American culture. Perhaps 1968 was the last possible moment when such a portrait could have been presented as descriptive truth. Within two years, California's revision of its divorce law would provide a model for no-fault divorce that would soon sweep across the nation. The increasingly widespread availability of contraception, combined with a cultural sexual revolution, was already making sex outside of marriage "normal," no longer shameful, criminal, and destructive to the respectability of young, unmarried women. By 1972, in *Eisenstadt v. Baird*, the Supreme Court held that allowing distribution of contraceptives to married, but not to unmarried, people violated the equal protection clause of the U.S. Constitution. Along the way to that decision, Justice Brennan marked the revolution underway in marital identities, asserting that "the married couple" was "not an independent entity with a mind and heart of its own, but an association of two individuals each with a separate intellectual and emotional makeup." The year before Schneider's study appeared, in *Loving v. Virginia*, the U.S. Supreme Court had declared unconstitutional state antimiscegenation laws, definitively interposing the antisubordination concerns of the equal protection clause of the Fourteenth Amendment against the claimed exclusive authority of the states to legislate the terms of marriage within their borders. In later decisions, federal and state courts, influenced by second-wave feminism, applied Fourteenth Amendment equal protection standards to marital identities, making constitutionally problematic the gendered identities once central to marriage. Other decisions, under the heading of sex discrimination law, made illegal many of the traditional understandings that had excluded women from many remunerative occupations, understandings that had long made marriage the plausible and economically acceptable choice for young women. Meanwhile, a trail of state cases, following the California Supreme Court's landmark decision in *Marvin v. Marvin* (1976), gradually recognized that non-marital cohabitation of a variety of forms could produce economic obligations only barely distinguishable from those imposed by marital union.

By the 1980s, the "fact" that more than 50% of all marriages ended in divorce (a figure that had been reached after more than a century of growth in the divorce rate) had become one of the clichés of public discourse. The divorce rate was then of a piece with, though some thought it an explanation for, the greater diversity of family forms found across late-twentieth-century America, filled as it was with children born outside of marriage, stepparents, joint-custody arrangements, complex open adoptions, and fluidity and renegotiation in what some still assumed were traditional roles and obligations.

Many still married; indeed, many reproduced the marital forms of their parents' and grandparents' marriages. And many voices pressed on those contemplating parenthood that a "two parent" household was a necessity for healthy childrearing. And for gay men and lesbian women, historically excluded from the privileges that marriage retained, single-sex marriage became an aspirational rights claim and a focus for political and legal struggles. But all those who married or aspired to marriage at the end of the twentieth century did so in a culture that had accepted the separation of marriage from sexual expression and (more reluctantly) from childrearing. Marriage had become a private choice, an act of private freedom.

BIBLIOGRAPHY

Clark, Elizabeth Battelle. "Matrimonial Bonds: Slavery, Contract and the Law of Divorce in Nineteenth-Century America." *Law and History Review*, 8:1 (Spring 1990): 25–54.

Cott, Nancy. *Public Vows: A History of Marriage and the Nation*. Cambridge, Mass.: Harvard University Press, 2000.

DuBois, Ellen. "Outgrowing the Compact of the Fathers: Equal Rights, Woman Suffrage, and the United States Constitution, 1820–1878." *Journal of American History*, 74 (December 1987): 836–862.

Grossberg, Michael. *Governing the Hearth: Law and Family in Nineteenth-Century America*. Chapel Hill: University of North Carolina Press, 1985.

Hartog, Hendrik. *Man and Wife in America, a History*. Cambridge, Mass.: Harvard University Press, 2000.

Lystra, Karen. *Searching the Heart: Women, Men, and Romantic Love in Nineteenth-Century America*. New York: Oxford University Press, 1989.

Schneider, David M. *American Kinship: A Cultural Account*. 2nd ed. Chicago: University of Chicago Press, 1980.

Stanley, Amy Dru. *From Bondage to Contract: Wage Labor, Marriage, and the Market in the Age of Slave Emancipation*. New York: Cambridge University Press, 1998.

Hendrik Hartog

See also **Defense of Marriage Act; Divorce and Marital Separation; Family; Indian Intermarriage; Kinship;** *Loving v. Virginia;* **Miscegenation.**

MARRIED WOMEN'S PROPERTY ACT, NEW YORK STATE.

In the mid-nineteenth century, various states adopted statutes intended to diminish the economic consequences of the common law idea of coverture. In general, the common law doctrine required that the property of a married woman went to her husband. English law responded by permitting the creation by the father of a trust—a separate estate at equity—of which his daughter (about to become a married woman) would be the beneficiary. Trustees named by the father controlled and managed the property for the benefit of the daughter. The property was thus kept free of the husband's claims, without necessarily enhancing the authority of the daughter. This trust device was also used in America.

Mississippi adopted the first married women's property act in 1839. New York passed a much better known statute in 1848. Although this also was the year of the Seneca Falls Meeting, often identified as the starting point of the American women's suffrage movement, married women's property issues were not high on the agenda of nineteenth-century feminism. The push for married women's property acts apparently came primarily from creditors interested in clarifying issues relating to property used to secure commercial loans or other transactions.

The statutes were construed narrowly, and various specific issues arising from the economic relations of husbands and wives were resolved by additional legislative action. Some residual aspects of the inferior status of women under coverture were dealt with legislatively in the twentieth century. In 1974, for example, Congress passed the Equal Credit Opportunity Act forbidding discrimination in credit because of marital status or sex. This statute was broadened in 1976 to ban discrimination based on race, religion, and other characteristics.

BIBLIOGRAPHY

Basch, Norma. *In the Eyes of the Law: Women, Marriage and Property in Nineteenth Century* New York: Cornell University Press, 1982.

Carol Weisbrod

See also **Women's Rights Movement: The Nineteenth Century.**

MARSHALL ISLANDS, a group of coral atolls and reefs located 2,000 nautical miles southwest of Hawaii. Seized by Japan in 1914, the Marshall Islands were granted as a mandate to Japan after World War I by the League of Nations. After taking the neighboring Gilbert Islands in November 1943 to provide bases for bombing the Marshalls, Admiral Chester W. Nimitz, Central Pacific Area commander, focused on Kwajalein atoll, which was located in the center of the Marshalls and served as headquarters for Japanese defense of the islands. Heavy naval and air bombardment began on 29 January 1944. Two days later, landing craft carried the Fourth Marine Division under Major General Harry Schmidt toward the causeway-connected islands of Roi and Namur in the north of the atoll and the Seventh Infantry Division under Major General Charles H. Corlett toward Kwajalein in the south. The marines cleared Roi in one day and Namur in two. U.S. Army troops encountered more resistance on Kwajalein but cleared it on 4 February. A battalion of the army's 106th Infantry occupied nearby Majuro Island unopposed. The marines took the islands of Engebi and Parry in one day each, 18 and 22 February, respectively. Resistance again was stouter for army infantry on Eniwetok, requiring four days, until 21 February, to reduce.

Total American losses in the Marshalls were 671 killed, 2,157 wounded; the Japanese dead totaled 10,000.

The airfields and fleet anchorages that subsequently were established facilitated advance to the Caroline and Mariana Islands and neutralization of a strong Japanese base on Truk Island. In 1947 the Marshall Islands became part of the U.S. Trust Territory of the Pacific.

BIBLIOGRAPHY

Crowl, Philip A. *Campaign in the Marianas.* Washington, D.C.: Office of the Chief of Military History, Department of the Army, 1960.

Crowl, Philip A., and Edmund G. Love. *Seizure of the Gilberts and Marshalls.* Washington, D.C.: Office of the Chief of Military History, Department of the Army, 1955.

Charles B. MacDonald / A. R.

See also **Gilbert Islands; Task Force 58; Trust Territory of the Pacific.**

MARSHALL PLAN, formally called the European Recovery Program (ERP) even though it was later extended to Japan and (southern) Korea, was named after Secretary of State George C. Marshall, who announced it in a speech at Harvard University on 5 June 1947. The plan was unique, offering U.S. assistance for recovery efforts designed and implemented by the still war-ravaged nations of Europe.

Historians continue to argue the main thrust of the plan. The main arguments are that the plan was (1) humanitarian in seeking to ameliorate postwar economic suffering; (2) anti-communist in that it sought to rebuild the economies of western European countries to resist communism; and (3) designed to help the American economy since participating nations had to spend these dollar-denominated grants in the United States (and later Canada) for purchases of goods and services.

Regardless of the motives behind it, the ERP, which lasted from 1948 to 1952, was a phenomenal success. The Soviet Union and its eastern European satellites declined to participate, but the Marshall Plan provided approximately $13.5 billion in economic assistance to seventeen countries, including Great Britain, France, Italy, and western Germany, and resulted in a 25 percent increase in western European GNP.

BIBLIOGRAPHY

Donovan, Robert J. *The Second Victory: The Marshall Plan and the Postwar Revival of Europe.* New York: Madison Books, 1987.

Killick, John. *The United States and European Reconstruction, 1945–1960.* Edinburgh: Keele University Press, 1997.

Schain, Martin, ed. *The Marshall Plan: Fifty Years After.* New York: Palgrave, 2001.

Charles M. Dobbs

MARTHA GRAHAM DANCE COMPANY. Launched in 1929 in New York City, the Martha Graham

Martha Graham Dance Company. George White Jr. performs in the sexually explicit "Phaedra's Dream," with set design by Isamu Noguchi. © Beatriz Schiller 1997

Dance Company represented the fulfillment of a dream for its original principal ballerina, director, and choreographer, Martha Graham. She felt that ballet should express extreme emotion; through spastic movements, tremblings, and one-count falls, she and her dancing expressed a range of emotion on stage. She often sought a visceral response from the audience to her explicitly sexual and violent performances. Graham's dancers followed her lead with techniques of breathing and muscle control that she referred to as "contraction and release," originating in the tension of the contracted muscle and culminating in the release of energy from the body as the muscles relaxed.

Graham was the first modern dance choreographer to actively seek collaboration with other artists, using Isamu Noguchi, the Japanese American sculptor, to design her sets, and Aaron Copland to create the musical scores. This is perhaps best seen in her performance of "Appalachian Spring" in 1944, considered to be the apex of her career. Graham continued to dance until 1969 and then worked as a choreographer until her death in 1991. Prone to controversy, including her relationship with artistic director Ron Protas, Graham's radicalism continued after her death. The March 2000 firing of Protas, who owned the rights to the Graham Company name, demonstrated that Graham's memory was still alive.

BIBLIOGRAPHY

Aloff, Mindy. "Family Values: The Legacy of Martha Graham Dwindles." *The New Republic* 213, no. 11 (1995): 30–36.

Hering, Doris, and Gia Kourlas. "Two Views of the Martha Graham Company Season." *Dance Magazine* 73.5 (1999): 66–70.

Philip, Richard. "The High Cost of Conflict." *Dance Magazine* 74.6 (2000): 12–13.

Jennifer Harrison

MARTHA'S VINEYARD, an island off the southwestern coast of Cape Cod, Massachusetts, was visited by Giovanni de Verrazano, Samuel de Champlain, and possibly Norse explorers. The island was given its name in 1602 by Bartholomew Gosnold. It was bought in 1641 by Thomas Mayhew, an English merchant who also acquired the rights of government. The first settlement was founded at Edgartown within a year. The Mayhew family held manors and offices for life until the American Revolution put an end to hereditary pretensions. Formerly an important whaling center, since the mid-nineteenth century Martha's Vineyard has been a well-known summer resort.

BIBLIOGRAPHY

Banks, Charles Edward. *The History of Martha's Vineyard*. Dukes County, Mass.: Dukes County Historical Society, 1966. 3 vols. The original edition was published in 1911–1925.

Hare, Lloyd Custer Mayhew. *Thomas Mayhew, Patriarch to the Indians (1593–1682): The Life of the Worshipful Governor and Chief Magistrate of the Island of Martha's Vineyard*. New York, London: D. Appleton, 1932.

Railton, Arthur R. *Martha's Vineyard Historical Society's Walking Tour of Historic Edgartown, Including a Brief History from 1602: Rare Old Photographs, Maps, Facts, and Legends About its Oldest Buildings.* Edgartown, MA: The Society, 1998.

Lloyd C. M. Hare
Michael Wala

See also **Massachusetts**.

MARTIAL LAW is most easily defined as the application of military force to control all or part of an area where civilian authority is ineffective or in defiance of higher authority. Martial law often applies to battle theaters where army commanders require control of civilian resources close to front lines. In this vein, Andrew Jackson imposed martial law in New Orleans in 1814. More recently, martial law has been used to support civilian authorities in times of natural disaster. Americans traditionally view martial law with great suspicion because of the power it grants to the army and its commanders. The Declaration of Independence condemned George III's use of the British army to "render the military independent of, and superior to, civil power." The Constitution's guarantee of the right of habeas corpus protects U.S. citizens from potential arbitrary excesses of martial law. Only the president can declare martial law on the federal level and only governors may do so on the state level.

Despite American ideals opposing martial law, presidents have used it to deal with crises since the founding of the nation. George Washington declared martial law to quell the Whiskey Rebellion in 1794. Washington set an important American precedent by ordering the army to turn the rebels over to civil courts for trial. By not making the rebels subject to military law, Washington established the ideal that martial law should be used to bolster, not supersede, legally constituted local powers.

In order to avoid the often-unpopular step of declaring martial law, authorities have frequently called out troops without a formal declaration. Several governors used this tactic during the late nineteenth century in order to deploy local militia and guard units to quell railroad and mining strikes. These incidents raised questions about the proper chain of command for local militia, with governors seeking to maintain control of their militia without federal interference. In 1877, the governors lost the struggle when the National Guard Act made local militia subject to federalization in the event of a national emergency, as declared by the president.

On other occasions, presidents have used martial law when local authorities appeared unwilling or unable to enforce the law. During the 1950s and 1960s, Presidents Dwight Eisenhower, John Kennedy, and Lyndon Johnson used federal troops or federalized National Guard troops to enforce civil rights laws against the will of state governors, most notably at Little Rock, Arkansas, in 1957, Oxford, Mississippi, in 1962, and Selma, Alabama, in 1965.

In these cases, martial law effectively negated the power of recalcitrant local authority. In cases where local authority simply breaks down or cannot control an urban disturbance or natural disaster, martial law can be used to support local law enforcement.

Nevertheless, American suspicion of concentrated power has meant that martial law has only been declared thirty times, usually in localized areas and for brief time periods. Furthermore, the Supreme Court has limited the legal scale and scope of martial law. In the 1866 case *Ex Parte Milligan*, the court ruled that the military may not try civilians when civil courts are still functioning. In 1932, in *Sterling v. Constantin*, the Supreme Court asserted the right of judicial review over martial law.

Controversial uses of the military in domestic incidents, such as General Douglas MacArthur's 1932 eviction of the Bonus Army from Washington, D.C., have undermined the public's faith in martial law except in extraordinary circumstances. Excessive uses of martial law for purely political purposes have also tarnished the legitimacy of martial law. In 1935, the governor of Arizona tried unsuccessfully to impose martial law in order to stop a federal project on federal land. Two years later, the governor of Rhode Island used martial law to enforce a ban on horse racing. To American sensitivities, these incidents did not warrant the drastic step of imposing martial law, whether at the state or federal level.

The regular military has normally been reluctant to participate in martial law situations. The army has not traditionally been trained to handle domestic disturbances, and it has not historically seen itself as a national police force. Moreover, declarations of martial law sometimes carry political overtones that the army prefers to avoid, as in the declaration of martial law by Indiana's Republican governor to head off a Copperhead movement in 1862 or the struggle in the wake of riots in Detroit in 1967 between President Johnson and Governor George Romney of Michigan, a potential Republican rival for the presidency in the 1968 election.

In practice, martial law in the United States usually involves the careful blending of military and civilian authorities. U.S. military authorities rarely completely take over situations, with the civil rights era being an important exception. More commonly, the military follows the Whiskey Rebellion model of deploying to support and assist local officials. This tradition fits in with perennial American fears of standing armies and concentrated power.

BIBLIOGRAPHY

Coakley, Robert. *The Role of Federal Military Forces in Domestic Disorders, 1789–1878.* Washington, D.C.: Center of Military History, 1988.

Higham, Robin, ed. *Bayonets in the Streets: The Use of Troops in Civil Disturbances.* 2d ed. Manhattan, Kans.: Sunflower Press, 1989.

Neely, Mark, Jr. *The Fate of Liberty: Abraham Lincoln and Civil Liberties.* New York: Oxford University Press, 1991.

Michael S. Neiberg

See also **Military Law;** *Ex Parte Milligan;* **National Guard.**

MARTIN V. HUNTER'S LESSEE.

Justice Joseph Story's opinion in this 1816 case upheld the power of the U.S. Supreme Court to review decisions of all state courts on federal questions as defined in the 1789 Judiciary Act, and upheld the constitutionality of that statute. Story insisted that the framers of the 1787 Constitution had intended the Supreme Court to be supreme in interpretation of the federal Constitution, laws, and treaties to correct "state prejudices" of local judges and assure "uniformity of decisions throughout the whole United States" on such federal questions.

BIBLIOGRAPHY

Warren, Charles. *The Supreme Court in United States History.* Boston: Little, Brown, 1932.

White, G. Edward. *The Marshall Court and Cultural Change, 1815–1835.* New York: Macmillan, 1988.

William M. Wiecek

See also **Judiciary Act of 1789; Supreme Court.**

MARTIN V. MOTT,

12 Wheaton (25 U.S.) 19 (1827). During the War of 1812, a New York militia private was ordered to report for duty and refused. A court martial seized his property as a penalty, which he challenged, testing the power of the President to call out the militia. Justice Joseph Story, for the U.S. Supreme Court, held that the Constitution authorizes the president alone to determine when to call out the militia against actual or imminent invasion, in which case his decision is final. This decision set in place the president's power to federalize state national guards as well as to allow for integrated reserve and standing forces.

BIBLIOGRAPHY

Story, Joseph. *Commentaries on the Constitution of the United States, With a Preliminary Review of the Constitution.* Reprint. New York: Da Capo, 1970. The original edition was published in 1833.

Steve Sheppard

See also **Militias.**

MARYLAND.

A small state on the Atlantic coast, midway between the northern and southern boundaries of the United States, Maryland embraces the Chesapeake Bay and extends narrowly westward into the Appalachian Mountains. When the first European settlers arrived in the area, there were a dozen or more Native American tribes, each with 200 or more members crisscrossing the land, living mostly on the seafood from the Chesapeake. For sixty years after European settlement, relations between the Indians and the settlers were tense but short of war, and during the 1690s most of the Indians of the area moved south or west.

Seventeenth-Century Settlement

Explorers arrived in the 1580s, and in 1607 the London Company, with a British title to the land that is now Maryland, settled at Jamestown. The Virginians mapped the Chesapeake, traded with the Indians, and in 1631 William Claibourne from Jamestown established a fur-trading settlement at Kent Island. Maryland's existence as a separate colony, however, emerged from the Calvert family. George Calvert was a personal friend of King James I, liked by the king for his Roman Catholic faith and his devotion to conservative feudal ideals. King James elevated him to the peerage as Lord Baltimore and gave him title to lands in Newfoundland. From 1620 to 1629, Calvert invested in the colony that he called Avalon, but the climate was too severe and the colony failed. In 1632, Calvert persuaded King Charles I to reclaim from the London Company the Potomac River and the Virginia lands to the north, and to transfer this land to him. Calvert diplomatically named the grant for the king's wife.

George Calvert died before settlement could proceed, but his sons ably took up the project. The oldest son Cecil became the second Lord Baltimore and managed colonization from London. The second son Leonard led the expedition of the *Arc* and *Dove* that landed at St. Clement's Island in the Potomac on 25 March 1634 and proceeded a few days later to settle permanently at St. Mary's. The first settlers included about seventeen gentlemen-investors who were mostly Catholic, about thirty freemen, and about eighty indentured servants who were mostly Protestant. The expedition also included two Africans who boarded the ship in the Caribbean, presumably as indentures. The Calverts gave at least 2,000 acres to investors who paid the way of five or more servants, and they gave 100 acres to freemen who paid their own way. The Calverts sold additional land, and they collected quitrents on the lands they gave away or sold.

Within a few years the settlers were widely scattered, cultivating corn for subsistence and tobacco for sale to England. At least until the end of the century, life was extremely rude. The ratio of men to women was three to one, and life expectancy was far below that in England. Still, there was easy upward mobility for those who survived, and for those who bought servants and collected the land bounty for them, and newcomers kept arriving. In 1649 the Calverts made the most of their settlers' religious diversity, accepting an Act of Religious Toleration to encourage more settlers. It was one of the first such acts in the history of Christianity.

Life was harsh enough on this outer edge of civilization, and eight decades of intermittent warfare made it

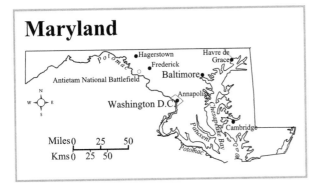

Maryland

harsher. From 1645 to 1660 Maryland repulsed at least three expeditions of attacking Virginians who proclaimed fear of their Catholic-led neighbors and who sought booty for themselves in the wilderness. Then, periodically, especially from 1689 to 1715, the colony was torn by civil war as younger planters revolted against the Calvert proprietors and their appointed governors. The rebellions expanded the power of the General Assembly over the governor, moved the capital from Catholic-leaning St. Mary's to Puritan-leaning Annapolis (1694), and repealed the Toleration Act in order to establish the Anglican Church (1702). The chastened Calverts—there were six generations from George Calvert to the American Revolution—joined the Anglican Church and regained most of their authority over the governor.

The Eighteenth Century and the American Revolution

The transition from rudeness to prosperity—from a population of 30,000 in 1700 to 340,000 in 1800—came largely with slavery. The Calvert proprietors and the settlers increasingly saw permanent bondage as an avenue toward stability and prosperity, and tolerance of slavery grew into active promotion. When slavery became fully legal in 1664, Africans numbered no more than 2 percent of the population, but their numbers surged to 20 percent in 1710, and 30 percent in 1750. The result was an economic takeoff—a surge in tobacco exports, and the rise of a money economy. A rich and stable planter class emerged, and fine Georgian country houses appeared. Scotch-Irish and Germans poured in, moving into the backcountry to establish new towns like Frederick and Hagerstown. Wheat came to supplement tobacco as an export crop, and BALTIMORE grew as a trade center. Artisan industry emerged and iron manufacturing began.

The new prosperity gave way to new tensions, less between settlers and proprietor than among classes, sections, ideas, and especially between America and the British Empire. New ideas found expression in a newspaper, the *Maryland Gazette*, and in able local leaders like Daniel Dulaney, Dr. Alexander Hamilton, Charles Carroll of Carrollton, Samuel Chase, and William Paca. Maryland planters and merchants howled against the British Stamp Act of 1765, and in June 1774, the anti-British faction in

the General Assembly picked a fight with the proprietary governor who was enforcing the British laws. The patriot-secessionists formed a Provisional Convention that assumed control of the government. They drew up a conservative constitution that they adopted in 1776 without a referendum. It reestablished toleration for all Christians, and shifted taxes from a per capita base to land assessment, but it retained property qualifications for voting, limited voting to the election of delegates to the General Assembly, and actually increased property qualifications for holding office.

The General Assembly hesitated in calling out the state militia for its loyalty was doubtful, but numerous volunteers, encouraged by a state bounty, joined the Continental Army and gained renown as the "Maryland Line." Slave masters sometimes collected the bounty for enlistment, sent off their slaves to serve, and usually freed the slaves when the war ended. Maryland shipbuilders built warships for the Continental Navy, and Maryland shippers, with a subsidy from the General Assembly, armed their vessels to prey on British commerce.

Tobacco production declined after the Revolution, but otherwise the economy flourished and new institutions burgeoned—state banks, state-supported turnpikes and canals, organized medical and legal professions, and a multitude of colleges. In 1784 the Methodist Church was born in Maryland, the first formal separation from its Anglican parent. Marylanders were leaders in the establishment of American branches of the Catholic, Episcopal, Presbyterian, and African Methodist Churches. Maryland was a leader in calls for a stronger central government, a United States Constitution, and in the formation of political parties. Maryland happily ceded land for the new District of Columbia.

The Nineteenth Century and the City

The nineteenth century brought urbanization, democracy, industry, and the end of slavery. State population grew from 340,000 in 1800 to 1,200,000 in 1900, and Baltimore City grew from 8 percent of the total to 43 percent. The size and wealth of the city overwhelmed Annapolis and the state's long-established plantation culture.

The city—with its merchant, professional, artisan, and proletarian classes—led the statewide movement toward democracy and party politics. Property qualifications for voting ended in 1802; property qualifications for holding office ended in 1809; a public school system began, at least in theory, in 1825; Jews were allowed to vote in 1826; popular election of the governor came in 1837, election of city and county officials in 1851; African Americans were enfranchised in 1870; the secret ballot came in 1901; and women gained the vote in 1920. Actually, Maryland tended to lag behind other states in most of these reforms.

The city won its first notable struggle with the planters in the War of 1812. Federalist planters, eager to maintain their profitable trade with Great Britain, opposed the war, but Baltimore relished the alliance with France and another chance to loose its privateers on British commerce. When the British landed at Bladensburg in 1814, the planter-led militia let them pass; but three weeks later when the British attacked Baltimore, the city militia held firm. Francis Scott Key, watching the British bombardment, wrote a poem celebrating the victory over the British that became the words to the National Anthem. The planter-led Federalist party of Maryland never recovered.

Especially from the 1820s to the 1850s, Maryland's General Assembly, dominated by Whigs, promoted a frenzy of capital formation and construction projects. First came the turnpikes. The assembly gave rights-of-way to private companies to improve the roads, establish stagecoaches, and charge tolls. Most famous was the National Pike that, with its extensions, stretched from Baltimore to Ohio. Then came a craze for canals, the most famous of which was the Chesapeake and Ohio Canal, designed to reach from Washington to Cincinnati. It nearly bankrupted the state and never got beyond Cumberland. The grandest and most successful of the projects were the railroads. The line from Baltimore to Ohio was one of the first and busiest in the country, and by 1840 other lines extended to Washington, Philadelphia, and central Pennsylvania.

Eventually urbanization, democracy, and capitalism came up against the continued existence of slavery. After the collapse of tobacco, slavery was barely profitable in Maryland, and by midcentury there were almost as many free blacks as slaves. African Americans like Richard Allen, Harriet Tubman, and Frederick Douglass were leaders of their people. Still, battered Maryland planters clung desperately to the institution. Roger B. Taney of Maryland, chief justice of the United States Supreme Court, was a powerful spokesman for slavery's expansion.

By the 1850s change was coming too fast and tensions were too great, and Maryland drifted toward chaos. Party structure collapsed, rioting turned Baltimore into mobtown, and for a while the Know-Nothings ruled the state with a platform that made a scapegoat of immigrants.

When the Civil War came, Maryland was overwhelmingly pro-slave; in the presidential election of 1860 only 2 percent of the votes went to Abraham Lincoln. But the state was also mostly opposed to secession. After his inauguration, Lincoln intervened forcibly, arresting some 3,000 community leaders who were Southern sympathizers and allowing many more to be disfranchised. Southern sympathy waned. About 50,000 Marylanders eventually enlisted in the Union army, including 9,000 African Americans. About 20,000 Maryland whites fled to join the army and navy of the Confederacy.

From 1864 to 1867, with pro-Southern Marylanders disfranchised, the state launched its own radical reconstruction, foreshadowing what was to come in the South. The radicals abolished slavery, threatened to seize slaveholders' property to pay for the war, and established an authoritarian and far-reaching school system for whites and former slaves. As the war ended, however, and as Southern sympathizers returned home, radicalism collapsed and conservative leadership reasserted itself.

After the war people were concerned mainly with things economic. The railroads, led by the aggressive John W. Garrett, spread into every county. Coal mining expanded in the western counties, oystering expanded on the Eastern Shore, and in Baltimore came vast steel mills, copper and tin smelting, a ready-to-wear clothing industry, canning, and meat packing. Immigrants poured into the city and state—Germans, Irish, Italians, Poles, Jews, and others—often into crowded tenements. Industry and labor sometimes fought; scores died in the Great Railroad Strike of 1877. Many people still lived on farms, although the farms were usually small and poor. The very rich provided grand philanthropies—the Garrett State Forests, the Enoch Pratt libraries, the Walters Art Gallery, and the great JOHNS HOPKINS UNIVERSITY. The two political parties—Democrats and Republicans—were nearly balanced after the war, both run by bosses who were closely allied with business, both offering generous patronage to faithful followers.

Twentieth-Century Suburbanization
Twentieth-century change was measurable in a demographic shift—the rise of the suburbs and the corresponding decline of the city and farm. Maryland population grew from 1,200,000 in 1900 to 5,200,000 in 2000, and the suburbs grew from 2 percent to about 80 percent of that total. People moved from factory and farm into middle-class, white-collar, and service occupations.

As the century began, the rising middle classes—doctors, lawyers, managers, engineers, accountants, bureaucrats—were asserting themselves as a Progressive movement, less concerned with creating new wealth than with its management, by people like themselves, for the benefit of all society. Working through both political parties, the Progressives forced through a mass of new laws in the 1900s and 1910s establishing nonpartisan citizen boards to replace politicians in control of the schools, parks, hospitals, and libraries. Other citizen boards gained control over rates charged by electric, water, telephone, railroad, and shipping companies. In 1904, in the midst of these reforms, much of Baltimore burned in what was until then the greatest conflagration in American history, but this only stimulated city planning and new housing codes. Progressivism, however, also had its dark side. The middle class was eager to disfranchise illiterate voters, especially African Americans. Disfranchisement failed in Maryland as blacks and immigrants joined to protect their right to vote, but the reforms succeeded in legalizing racial segregation in most public and commercial facilities. World War I provided a culmination of Progressivism as citizen commissions promoted war production and patriotism with equal fervor.

By the 1920s people were tired of reform and eager to enjoy themselves. Local police refused to enforce the national prohibition laws that lasted from 1919 to 1933, and illegal booze may have flowed more freely in Maryland than in any other state. Eubie Blake and Cab Calloway played in the local jazz clubs. Marylanders like H. L. Mencken, F. Scott Fitzgerald, and Ogden Nash caught the mood of the times. Baseball was the rage, and its greatest hero was Baltimore's Babe Ruth, even if he played for New York. Maryland became famous for its horse racing and slot machines. Albert Ritchie was the state's all-time most popular governor, serving from 1919 to 1934. Aristocratic and autocratic, he believed in state rights and unfettered capitalism. Three times he tried to gain the Democratic nomination for president, arguing that Presidents Coolidge and Hoover were spendthrift radicals.

The Great Depression descended relentlessly, first to the farms, then to the city and suburbs. From 1929 to 1933, Maryland's per capita income dropped 45 percent, industrial production dropped 60 percent. Maryland received less from the New Deal than most states because of its unwillingness to provide matching funds. The New Deal built the model town of Greenbelt in Maryland, with cooperative housing and stores. The town was a success but opponents scuttled its experiment in socialism.

In World War II, Maryland, because of its location, became a center of military training, arms and aircraft production, and shipments abroad. African Americans and women made major inroads into the labor market, where they would remain. After the war, prosperity continued but politics grew shrill. A liberal governor, William P. Lane, enacted a sales tax and built airports and a spectacular bridge across the Chesapeake Bay; but a conservative General Assembly enacted the Ober Law, the country's most far-reaching loyalty oath and a forerunner of McCarthyism.

Meanwhile, burgeoning suburbanization was transforming the state's economic and political landscape. The movement began with the trolley lines of the 1890s and the automobile of the 1920s, mostly into affluent enclaves out from Washington and Baltimore. Then the suburban population doubled in the late 1940s, this time mostly into inexpensive housing tracts, bringing shopping strips and drive-in movies; it doubled again in the 1950s and 1960s with planned bedroom cities like Bowie and Columbia; it doubled again in the 1970s and 1980s, bringing beltways and malls; and it continued after that, bringing office towers, mass transit, and ethnic diversity.

The other side of suburban growth was urban and rural decline. Baltimore reached its peak about 1920 with half the state's population and by far its highest per capita income; but in 2000 it had fallen to 12 percent of the state population and by far the lowest per capita income. Urban renewal programs lurched forward by trial and error. In the 1970s, Mayor Donald Schaefer built a sparkling Harborplace development that attracted tourists into the city for spending and recreation.

Suburbanization provided a liberal tilt to Maryland politics, and Maryland kept pace and occasionally offered leadership to the civil rights movement of the 1950s and 1960s. African American leaders like Lillie Mae Jackson and Thurgood Marshall worked comfortably with Governors Theodore McKeldin and Millard Tawes. Baltimore was the first major segregated city to integrate its schools, a year before court requirements, and state laws were ahead of federal laws in promoting civil rights. The state suffered from race riots in the late 1960s, but the civil rights movement did not go backward for state agencies promoted school busing and affirmative action, and an ever larger portion of the African Americans entered the middle class.

Idealism slumped into malaise in the 1970s. Two successive governors, Spiro Agnew and Marvin Mandel, plus many other local officials, pled guilty to accepting bribes. They were caught between the old politics of favors and the newer middle-class ethic that was tinged with hostility to politics of all sorts.

The last decades of the century, however, were happy as personal income soared, especially for those already prosperous. Government and business bureaucracies expanded and clean high-tech industries grew. Government in the 1980s and 1990s was mostly corruption-free and progressive, with abundant funding for education and for the environment. Women increasingly entered politics. Universities, claiming to be the engines of the new economy, especially flourished. As the century ended, optimism prevailed.

BIBLIOGRAPHY

Argersinger, Jo Ann E. *Toward a New Deal in Baltimore: People and Government in the Great Depression.* Chapel Hill: University of North Carolina Press, 1988.

Baker, Jean H. *The Politics of Continuity: Maryland Political Parties from 1858 to 1870.* Baltimore: Johns Hopkins University Press, 1973.

Brugger, Robert J. *Maryland, A Middle Temperament, 1634–1980.* Baltimore: Johns Hopkins University Press, 1988. A full and excellent history.

Callcott, George H. *Maryland and America, 1940 to 1980.* Baltimore: Johns Hopkins University Press, 1985.

Carr, Lois Green, Russell R. Menard, and Louis Peddicord. *Maryland—At the Beginning.* Annapolis, Md.: Department of Economic Development, 1978.

Evitts, William J. *A Matter of Allegiances: Maryland from 1850 to 1861.* Baltimore: Johns Hopkins University Press, 1974.

Fields, Barbara Jeanne, *Slavery and Freedom on the Middle Ground: Maryland During the Nineteenth Century.* New Haven, Conn.: Yale University Press, 1985.

Hoffman, Ronald. *Spirit of Dissension: Economics, Politics, and the Revolution in Maryland.* Baltimore: Johns Hopkins University Press, 1973.

Kulikoff, Alan. *Tobacco and Slaves: The Development of Southern Cultures in the Chesapeake.* Chapel Hill: University of North Carolina Press, 1986.

Land, Aubrey C. *Colonial Maryland: A History.* Millwood, N.Y.: KTO Press, 1981.

Main, Gloria L. *Tobacco Colony: Life in Early Maryland, 1650–1720.* Princeton, N.J.: Princeton University Press, 1982.

George H. Callcott

See also **Chesapeake Colonies; Know-Nothing Party; Toleration Acts.**

MARYLAND, INVASION OF

MARYLAND, INVASION OF (September 1862). The defeat of Union General John Pope in the second Battle of Bull Run, and his retreat to the Washington, D.C., lines forced General Robert E. Lee to adopt a new plan of operations. He wrote Confederate President Jefferson Davis, "The present seems to be the most propitious time . . . to enter Maryland." Regardless of objections, Lee added, "We cannot afford to be idle." Aggressive movements, he thought, would insure the safety of Richmond, Virginia.

On 2 September 1862 marching orders were issued. Within a week troops were concentrating at Frederick, Maryland. Union General George B. McClellan, who had been restored to command, began organizing a force to defend Maryland. Meantime, Lee detached General Thomas J. ("Stonewall") Jackson to capture Harpers Ferry (in present-day West Virginia), while he led his army westward to an expected junction with Jackson in the vicinity of Hagerstown, Maryland. Once across South Mountain, Lee's line of supply would be through the Shenandoah Valley.

On 13 September McClellan reached Frederick. He hurried troops after Lee. Sharp fights took place at gaps in South Mountain; Lee sent reinforcements but by nightfall, finding the positions no longer tenable, he directed a retirement toward Sharpsburg, Maryland. McClellan advanced slowly, diverted by Jackson's movement against Harpers Ferry. As soon as that place surrendered, Jackson hurried to Sharpsburg, leaving A. P. Hill to dispose of captured property and prisoners and then follow promptly.

McClellan reached Sharpsburg on 16 September and spent the day testing Lee's line. His attacks the following day brought on the Battle of Antietam, characterized by more hard fighting than any other battle of the war. Lee, outnumbered, remained in possession of the field, but severe losses and heavy odds made it inadvisable to stay. McClellan did not attack again. On the night of 18 September Lee recrossed the Potomac "without loss or molestation," ending the campaign.

Johnson, R. U., and C. C. Buel, eds. *Battles and Leaders of the Civil War.* Vol. 2. Edison, N.J.: Book Sales, 1985.

McPherson, James M. *Battle Cry of Freedom: The Civil War Era.* New York: Oxford University Press, 1988.

Thomas Robson Hay / A. R.

See also **Antietam, Battle of; Bull Run, Second Battle of; Civil War; Fredericksburg, Battle of; Harpers Ferry, Capture of.**

MASHPEE

MASHPEE. The Mashpee Wampanoag tribe, which is located on Cape Cod, spoke an Eastern Algonquian language. The first known contact occurred in 1602, and by the 1650s the Mashpees were made a self-governing Christian Indian town and then an Indian district. In 1869–1870, Massachusetts converted Mashpee into a town and made its land alienable. However, the tribe continued to control the town until the 1970s. In 1976, the tribe filed suit in federal court to recover the land. The tribe lost because it was not federally recognized, but instead of discouraging tribal members, the ruling heightened their determination, and in 1990 they petitioned the Interior Department for recognition. The tribe's 1,500 members await a decision.

Campisi, Jack. *The Mashpee Indians: Tribe on Trial.* Syracuse, N.Y.: Syracuse University Press, 1991.

Conkey, Laura E., Ethel Boissevain, and Ives Goddard. "Indians of Southern New England and Long Island: Late Period." In *Handbook of North American Indians.* Edited by William C. Sturtevant et al. Vol. 15: *Northeast,* edited by Bruce G. Trigger. Washington, D.C.: Smithsonian Institution, 1978.

Jack Campisi

See also **Tribes: Northeastern; Wampanoag.**

MASON-DIXON LINE

MASON-DIXON LINE is the southern boundary line of Pennsylvania, and thereby the northern boundary

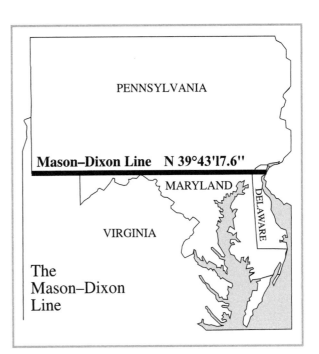

The Mason–Dixon Line

Mason-Dixon Line. Established by surveyors Charles Mason and Jeremiah Dixon in 1767 to settle a boundary dispute between Pennsylvania and Maryland, this was considered the dividing line between slavery and free soil in the Civil War. This stone marker in Adams County, Pennsylvania, indicated the line's location. LIBRARY OF CONGRESS

line of Delaware, Maryland, and West Virginia, formerly part of Virginia. It is best known historically as the dividing line between slavery and free soil in the period of history before the Civil War, but to some extent it has remained the symbolic border line—political, cultural, and social—between North and South.

The present Mason and Dixon line was the final result of several highly involved colonial and state boundary disputes. The first dispute was between Maryland and Pennsylvania. The Maryland Charter of 1632 granted to the Calvert family lands lying north of the Potomac River and "under the fortieth degree of Northerly Latitude." Almost fifty years later (1681), Charles II issued a charter making William Penn proprietor of lands between latitudes 40° N and 43° N and running west from the Delaware River though five degrees in longitude. The terms of the two charters were inconsistent and contradictory. A full century of dispute with regard to the southern boundary of Pennsylvania was the result. Had all Pennsylvania claims been substantiated, Baltimore would have been included in Pennsylvania, and Maryland reduced to a narrow strip. Had all Maryland claims been established, Philadelphia would have been within Maryland.

In 1760, after years of conferences, appeals to the Privy Council, much correspondence, attempted occupation, forced removal of settlers, and temporary agreements, the Maryland and Pennsylvania proprietors reached an agreement to resolve the dispute. Under its terms, two

English surveyors, Charles Mason and Jeremiah Dixon, surveyed the boundary line. In 1767, after four years' work, Mason and Dixon located the boundary line between Maryland and Pennsylvania at 39° 44' north latitude. The crown ratified the results in 1769.

In the meantime Virginia claimed most of what is now southwestern Pennsylvania. Both colonies tried to exercise jurisdiction in the area, which led to conflicts in 1774 and 1775. That dispute ended when joint commissioners of the two states agreed to extend the Mason and Dixon line westward, a settlement not completed until 1784. Historically the Mason-Dixon line embodies a Pennsylvania boundary triumph.

BIBLIOGRAPHY

Buck, Solon J., and Elizabeth H. Buck, *The Planting of Civilization in Western Pennsylvania*. Pittsburgh, Pa.: University of Pittsburgh Press, 1939.

Danson, Edwin. *Drawing the Line: How Mason and Dixon Surveyed the Most Famous Border in America*. New York: John Wiley, 2001.

Gray, Richard J. *Writing the South: Ideas of an American Region.* New York: Cambridge University Press, 1986.

Illick, Joseph E. *Colonial Pennsylvania: A History.* New York: Scribners, 1976.

Morrison, Charles. *The Western Boundary of Maryland.* Parson, W. Va.: McClain Print Co., 1976.

Alfred P. James / c. p.

See also **Boundary Disputes Between States; Maryland; Pennsylvania; Sectionalism; South, the: The Antebellum South; Surveying; Virginia.**

MASONS. *See* **Freemasons.**

MASS MEDIA. The term "mass media" refers to various audiovisual culture industries that send content from a particular source to a wide audience—for example, recorded music and television. The twentieth century in the United States was characterized by the transformation of artisanal, local hobbies and small businesses into highly centralized, rationalized industries working like production lines, and the entertainment and informational media were no different. In the process, pleasure was turned into profit. And when governments occasionally intervened to regulate, or alternative technologies destabilized established forms and interests, ways were found of accommodating threats or capitalizing on others' innovations, resulting in renewed corporate control over each medium. For instance, when newspapers were confronted with radio and then television, they bought into these sectors as quickly as possible, where cross-ownership laws permitted. Even the Internet, initially celebrated as a source of freedom from centralized control, has gradually come under corporate domination.

These tensions are played out in the history of radio and motion pictures. Radio began in the 1920s as a means of two-way communication, a source of agricultural stock-price and weather information, a boon to military technology, and a resource for ethnic cultural maintenance. Then radio became a broadcast medium of networked mass entertainment dominated by corporations in the 1930s that was confronted with wartime censorship and the advent of television as an alternative in the 1940s. It was transformed by popular music and the Top Forty in the 1950s; saw the emergence of college radio and frequency modulation as sites of innovation in the 1960s; and felt the impact of Spanish-language and right-wing talk stations in the increasingly deregulated environment of the 1980s and 1990s.

For its part, the motion picture industry began among textile merchants in New York City, who made films as segments of vaudeville shows. Around the time of World War I (1914–1918), the cinema shifted from depicting actual events and tricks to fictional narratives told in longer forms. This coincided with the rise of trade unions in New York, which, together with climatic considerations, encouraged the industry to shift to California. Filmmaking enterprises emerged and became fully integrated companies, called studios. Each studio owned the labor that made the films, the places where they were shot, the systems by which they were distributed, and the places where they were watched. The federal government intervened after World War II (1939–1945) because this vertical integration was seen to jeopardize competition, and the studios were required to sell off many of their assets. Combined with the advent of television and the suburbanizing movement of population in the late 1940s away from the inner cities (where most theaters were located), this posed a threat to Hollywood. But it managed to reduce costs, sell its product to television, and survive, later becoming linked to other cultural sectors and diverse industries from banking to gin.

Various debates about the mass media have recurred since the beginning of the twentieth century. Most of the U.S. population learned to read with the spread of public schooling. At that point, newspapers divided between those appealing to the middle and ruling classes (today's broadsheets) and the working class (today's tabloids). Ever since, there has been controversy about appeals to popular tastes versus educational ones (that the press will print, and people will prefer rap versus opera and sex crime versus foreign policy). This division is thought to exacerbate distinctions between people who have power and knowledge and other groups. There has also been a debate about concentration of media ownership, which has often generated conflicts of interest and minimized diverse points of view. The most consistent disagreements have been about what are called hypodermic-needle effects on audiences. This concept assumes that what people read, hear, and see has an immediate and cumulative impact on their psyches. Beginning with 1930s panics

about movies affecting young people, this perspective became especially powerful with the advent of television. There have been vast numbers of academic studies and public-policy debates on the topic of violence in the media ever since. Such debates reach the headlines whenever an individual embarks on a killing spree—but never when the U.S. military invades another country or engages in covert action and the media accept images and stories provided by the government itself, as per conflicts in Panama and Afghanistan.

Another recurring debate, which began in the 1960s, has been over the extraordinary success of the United States in dominating the media around the world. Accusations have been made of U.S. cultural imperialism, a process whereby the political imperialism of the nineteenth and twentieth centuries has been superseded by the ideological capture of subordinate populations—this time through advertising and popular culture as much as guns and government, with the United States developing into a mass exporter of media products and a prominent owner of overseas media. And when the United States became a more and more indebted nation as a consequence of corporate welfare and military programs favored by successive federal governments, the mass media provided key sources of overseas revenue and capital to offset this crisis.

The twentieth century saw the U.S. mass media multiply in their technological variety but grow ever more concentrated in their ownership and control. The twenty-first century promises more of the same, with an aggressively global strategy to boot.

BILBIOGRAPHY

Bordwell, David, Janet Staiger, and Kristin Thompson. *The Classical Hollywood Cinema: Film Style and Mode of Production to 1960.* New York: Columbia University Press, 1985.

Herman, Edward S., and Robert W. McChesney. *The Global Media: The New Missionaries of Global Capitalism.* London: Cassell, 1997.

Hilmes, Michele, and Jason Loviglio, eds. *Radio Reader: Essays in the Cultural History of Radio.* New York: Routledge, 2002.

Miller, Toby, ed. *Television: Critical Concepts,* 5 vols. London: Routledge, 2002.

Schiller, Herbert I. *Culture Inc.: The Corporate Takeover of Public Expression.* New York: Oxford University Press, 1989.

———. *Mass Communications and American Empire.* 2d ed. Boulder, Colo.: Westview Press, 1992.

Sklar, Robert. *Movie-Made America: A Cultural History of American Movies.* 2d ed. New York: Vintage Books, 1994.

Toby Miller

See also **Communications Industry;** and vol. 9: **The New Right: We're Ready to Lead.**

MASS PRODUCTION is a system of manufacturing based on principles such as the use of interchangeable parts, large-scale production, and the high-volume as-

SEMBLY LINE. Although ideas analogous to mass production existed in many industrialized nations dating back to the eighteenth century, the concept was not fully utilized until refined by Henry Ford in the early twentieth century and then developed over the next several decades. Ford's success in producing the Model T automobile set the early standard for what mass production could achieve. As a result, mass production quickly became the dominant form of manufacturing around the world, also exerting a profound impact on popular culture. Countless artists, writers, and filmmakers used the image of the assembly line to symbolize either the good or the evil of modern society and technological prowess.

Background

British inventors pioneered the earliest use of machine tools. Early inventors like Richard Arkwright and Henry Maudslay built precision machines necessary for mass production. Many of England's early machine tool artisans worked as apprentices, then later crafted precision lathes, plane surfaces, and measuring instruments. Even with the early successes in Europe, scholars of technology attribute the widespread adoption of mass production to trailblazers in the United States. With its abundant waterpower, coal, and raw material, but shortage of workers, America was the ideal place for building skill into machinery. From the start, American leaders attempted to mechanize production of barrels, nails, and other goods. In the early 1800s, the American inventor Thomas Blanchard used mechanized production to make rifles and muskets for the federal armory in Springfield, Massachusetts. Blanchard's efforts were supported by the War Department, which also backed other applications of mass production.

The distinct system developed in the United States became known as the AMERICAN SYSTEM of manufacturing. In the nineteenth century, the nation witnessed the rise of innovators such as Eli Whitney, Samuel Colt, and Cyrus McCormick. These leaders were committed to interchangeability and mechanized production. By 1883, the Singer Manufacturing Company sold over 500,000 sewing machines. McCormick, whose machine enabled farmers to double crop sizes, produced thousands of grain reapers in the mid-1800s and spurred additional innovation in agriculture. These early innovators, however, depended on skilled machinists to properly fit parts together. Only later, when parts were completely interchangeable, did true mass production occur.

Impact

Many factors came together in the early twentieth century to make mass production possible. Henry Ford's decision to produce an inexpensive automobile that working people could afford was a gamble. He succeeded in convincing his financial partners to back his idea through sheer determination. Detroit's history of mechanical innovation also played an important role. The city's many skilled engineers and designers helped refine Ford's early attempts

and later helped build large factories to showcase his ideas. The abundant talent—similar to California's Silicon Valley in the late twentieth century—allowed Ford to recruit talented employees. The immigration boom in Michigan provided Ford's company with the unskilled workers for the assembly lines.

Ford's determination to make Model T's and only Model T's helped in the development of mass production techniques based on the moving belt assembly line. Each process was broken down into its smallest parts. As the components moved down the line, the pieces were fitted to form the whole. Throughout the process, Ford emphasized accuracy; experts noted the durability and soundness of his automobiles. Ford devised an assembly line that delivered parts moving by hooks, overhead chains, or moving platforms to workers in the exact order in which they were required for production.

The assembly line gave Ford factories a fluid appearance and dramatically increased productivity. Without the assembly line, Ford would not have been able to keep pace with consumer demand. At the same time, Ford hoped to maximize economies of scale by building large factories. Most important for consumers, the increased efficiency brought with it a reduced cost. Model T prices quickly dropped from more than $800 to $300. As a result of these innovations, workers were soon able to produce a new Model T every two minutes. The company sold 11,000 cars from 1908 to 1909, a 60 percent increase over the previous year. Ford then outdid himself with the 1910–1911 model, selling 34,528. Sales skyrocketed in 1914, reaching 248,000, or nearly half the U.S. market. The heavy demand forced Ford to continue innovating. He built the largest and most modern factory in America on a sixty-acre tract at Highland Park, north of Detroit. Ford's net income soared from $25 million in 1914 to $78 million by 1921.

Another essential facet of Ford's mass production system was his willingness to adopt resourceful means of finding labor to work the assembly lines. The sheer size of the workforce Ford needed to keep pace combined with the monotony of the assembly line led to great turnover in the factories. Early in 1914, Ford introduced the "five dollar day" to deal with labor shortage. He paid workers the then-outrageous sum of $5 a day for an eight-hour workday. The basic wage eclipsed the industry standard of $1.80 to $2.50 a day on a longer shift. The five dollar day program transformed Ford from a business leader into a legend.

Because of mass production and Ford's high wages, company workers were given the ability to elevate themselves above working-class means, contributing to the growing consumer culture in the United States. With the extra pay, they participated in the accumulation of material items previously out of their reach. In turn, other mass producers, especially of middle-class luxuries, were given another outlet for goods. The five dollar day ensured the company that it would always have the workers

Mass Production. Employees work on the flywheel assembly line—the first automatic conveyor belt production line—at the Ford Motor Company plant in Highland Park, Mich., 1913. AP/WIDE WORLD PHOTOS/FORD MOTOR COMPANY

needed to produce, while at the same time allowing working-class families a means to participate in America's consumer culture.

Even the decline of the Model T did not affect the demand for automobiles. Mass production techniques spread to other car manufacturers. Alfred P. Sloan of General Motors introduced the annual model change in the 1920s. The changing look of automobiles, made affordable by mass production, mirrored the changing national landscape. A sweeping car craze prompted the desire for material abundance that would mark the genesis of modern America after World War II.

Advertisers, artists, and writers used the factory and assembly line to symbolize life in the United States. Often, they associated manliness with technology and engineering. Many looked upon the factories that linked American cities with an attitude akin to romanticism. Corporate marketing, advertising, and public relations staffs and outside agencies developed to massage this message into the public's subconscious. Many factories even began offering tours to show off production capabilities. Ford's Highland Park factory received more than 3,000 visitors a day before 1920. General Electric, National Cash Register, and Hershey Chocolate established tours

as well. They were a new form of public relations and left visitors with a deep, positive impression of the company. Over the next several decades, the influence and dominance of mass production solidified around the world. In preparing for World War I and then World War II, nations intensified mass production of arms and ammunition. The efficiencies of mass production allowed American businesses to switch from consumer goods to war stuffs quickly. The amount of armaments brought to the war effort by the United States turned the tide in both wars.

After World War II, American industry shifted back to consumer goods, but did not slow the pace. The rise of suburban living and the subsequent baby boom kept assembly line production at phenomenal rates. The growth of the middle class, both its wages and desire for material goods, can be traced to the development and dominance of mass production. Mass production also bears great responsibility for the manipulation and exploitation of workers, particularly unskilled labor. The process made workers dispensable and increased the power of the foremen, managers, and department heads that wielded power over them. These influences were mocked across the popular culture spectrum, from Upton Sinclair's muckraking novel

THE JUNGLE (1906) to the 1936 film by Charlie Chaplin, *Modern Times.*

Mass production techniques maximized the profit-making ability of corporations, but it dehumanized the lives of workers. Frederick W. Taylor introduced SCIENTIFIC MANAGEMENT at the beginning of the twentieth century, which used time and motion studies (often timing them with a stopwatch) to measure workers' output. Taylor's goal was to find the ideal process and then duplicate it over and over. In the abstract, scientific management was a giant leap forward, but in reality, mass production led to worker unrest, turnover, and social conflict. Unionization efforts, particularly the struggles to organize unskilled workers by the Congress of Industrial Organizations (CIO) in the 1930s and 1940s, and battles between management and employees intensified as workers became more alienated because of the factory setting.

BIBLIOGRAPHY

Cowan, Ruth Schwartz. *A Social History of American Technology.* New York: Oxford University Press, 1997.

Hounshell, David A. *From the American System to Mass Production, 1800–1932: The Development of Manufacturing Technology in the United States.* Baltimore: Johns Hopkins University Press, 1984.

Kranzberg, Melvin, and Joseph Gies. *By the Sweat of Thy Brow: Work in the Western World.* New York: Putnam, 1975.

Nye, David E. *American Technological Sublime.* Cambridge, Mass.: MIT Press, 1994.

Bob Batchelor

See also **Consumerism; Ford Motor Company; Industrial Management; Industrial Relations; Manufacturing.**

MASSACHUSETTS.

One of the oldest settlements in British North America, Massachusetts was the site of the outbreak of the American Revolution (1775–1783), and later the state most closely associated with the movements to promote public education, to reform the care of the mentally ill, to abolish slavery, and to restrict immigration. Massachusetts's people refer to it either as "the state" or "the Commonwealth." At the close of the twentieth century, Massachusetts continued to be a national leader in business, politics, higher education, medicine, high technology, environmental protection, and the arts and sciences.

Topography

Massachusetts is the center of New England, as it is the only state that shares a border with four of the other states in the region. It is south of New Hampshire and Vermont, east of New York, and north of Connecticut and Rhode Island. Maine, which was part of the Commonwealth until it achieved its independence in 1820, is separated from Massachusetts by less than twenty miles of New Hampshire's Atlantic coast. The state's land area is 7,840 square miles, and it ranks forty-fifth among the states. Its highest

point is Mount Greylock, 3,491 feet, which is in the northwest corner of the state, near Williamstown. Significant on the Atlantic coast is the state's highest drumlin, the Great Blue Hill, south of Boston, used for hiking, skiing, and as a nature preserve.

The Atlantic coastline is nearly 1,500 miles long, and includes Cape Ann, north of Boston; Cape Cod, south of Plymouth; and Buzzard's Bay, which washes the shores of New Bedford and Fall River, two venerable former textile mill towns, whose fame is derived from their participation in the whaling industry. In the Atlantic, south of Cape Cod, are the islands Martha's Vineyard (106 square miles) and Nantucket (46 square miles.)

The Connecticut River flows from north to south across the west central portion of the state and passes the industrial cities of Holyoke, Chicopee, and Springfield. The Taunton River in the southeastern corner of the state flows into an arm of Rhode Island's Narragansett Bay. The Merrimack, which flows from north to south within New Hampshire, flows from west to east after it enters Massachusetts. In this northeast corner of the state, the border with New Hampshire was set ten miles north of the Merrimack so that the communities situated along its banks could tend to their river without the complication of two separate state governments. The urban and suburban Charles River is eighty miles long, flows from south to north through some of the western suburbs, and empties into Boston Harbor. During the 1990s. the Metropolitan District Commission, a state agency, began reclaiming the banks of the Charles River—once abandoned public lands upon which adjacent residential and industrial property owners had encroached—by restoring the natural river banks and building a set of park-like pedestrian and bicycle pathways.

Perhaps equal in importance to the state's natural waterways is the system of manmade reservoirs and aqueducts that bring fresh water from the rural west to the state's urban east. During the 1930s, a dam on the Swift River near Ware created the Quabbin reservoir, under which four rural towns were submerged. The Quabbin water joins the older Wachusett water system. On its way to Boston the aqueduct crosses the Charles River on the high Echo Bridge at the river's spectacular Hemlock Gorge.

Population

The state's population at the turn of the twenty-first century continued to grow, but at a rate much lower than the nation as a whole. The population reached 6,349,097 in 2000 and the state ranked thirteenth (in size) among all the states. It ranked third in population living in urban areas and third in per capita income. The state ranked third in population density, and second in the percentage of foreign-born residents. It ranked eighth in the number of undocumented (illegal) immigrants. African Americans constituted 5.4 percent of the state's population and included large numbers from the Carribean, including

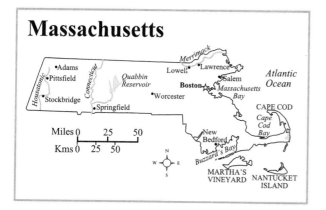

Massachusetts

French-speaking Haitians. Hispanics made up 6.8 percent, Asians 3.8 percent, and people of mixed race 2.3 percent of the state's population.

With a highly concentrated population, Massachusetts nonetheless developed an awkward division between a predominantly white, financially comfortable, highly educated population in urban and suburban areas, and a poor and less educated population in the older neighborhoods and in manufacturing cities and former mill towns. The continuation of this division may be one of the state's most significant social problems. Massachusetts has in effect two separate and unequal societies, one marked by people with excellent housing, schools, libraries, and hospitals, with modern office buildings and laboratories; and other communities plagued by poor housing, modest schools, and many of the economic and social problems that stem from poverty. The state ranks first in the percentage of the population possessing college degrees, first in attracting out-of-state students to its colleges and universities, second in state spending for the arts, and third in per capita library holdings. But it is fiftieth in per capita state spending for public higher education, thirty-seventh in state aid per pupil for elementary and secondary schools, and among youths joining the military, the state ranked thirty-fourth on scores in the Armed Forces Qualification Test.

History

The history of the Commonwealth can be divided into four periods: colonial, federal, industrial, and the present era, high technology and services.

The first successful English settlement north of Virginia was that of the Pilgrim Separatists, who had been religious refugees in Holland. Their party, consisting of 101 passengers, which included hired (non-Separatist) workmen, arrived at the site of Plymouth in late December 1620. The group was quartered on the anchored *Mayflower* during a hard winter in which half of their number died. In the spring they were joined by Squanto, an English-speaking Native American who had been a victim of Spanish slavers but was able to return to the site of his youth, where he found that his tribe had been wiped

out by a plague. He joined the Pilgrims and taught them how to hunt, fish, and farm. He helped in the construction of Plymouth Plantation but died two years after joining the colony. After a supply ship arrived at Plymouth in 1621, the Pilgrims were able to trade with the Native Americans one hundred miles along the coastline.

The success of the Pilgrims encouraged other English settlers to visit, trade, and establish towns, and early trading posts and settlements were established at Salem, Weymouth, Wollaston, and Gloucester. The most important settlement came with the chartered Massachusetts Bay Company. Its first wave included 800 settlers together with livestock and building materials. These Puritans initially chose Charlestown as the site of their capital, but before a year passed they moved to the Shawmut peninsula, where a spring was found. If the Puritans had remained in Charlestown, situated at the junction of two rivers, with plenty of space and good overland routes to the interior, they would have engaged in agriculture, fishing, and timber harvesting, as well as trade. But the move to Boston on the small peninsula forced their colony to grow as a seaport and trading center.

This early Boston was a theocracy in which the ministers instructed the civil officers. Those like Anne Hutchinson, whose orthodoxy was questioned, were exiled, while troublesome Quakers like Anne Dyer were put to death. Literacy was important and a printing press was set up. Primary schools were followed by the founding of the Boston Latin School, and Harvard College one year later. Located at the midpoint of British North America, Boston became the region's largest city and chief transshipment point. The Congregational churches were self-governing and merchants overtook ministers as the leaders of the colony, yet church and state were unified until 1833, and in most towns the same buildings were used both for worship and for town meetings.

The cultural achievement of the Bay Colony was significant. Boston became a center of fine furniture production. John Singleton Copley and Gilbert Stuart painted great portraits, and Paul Revere's silver bowls are widely admired. The Old State House, the Old North Church, the Old South Meeting House, the King's Chapel, Harvard's Massachusetts Hall, and Christ Church, Cambridge are exemplary and surviving works of architecture. Also important were the newspapers and pamphlets, which together with discussions in taverns, led to the coming of the American Revolution.

The Federal period was a time of great population growth and achievements in many fields. Shays' Rebellion (1786) was a result of a post–Revolutionary War recession. Many of the farmers in the Connecticut Valley were in debt and faced foreclosures of their properties. Shays, a Revolutionary War veteran, led an unsuccessful raid on the United States arsenal in Springfield in an attempt to arm the threatened farmers so that they could shut down the courthouses where foreclosures would take place, before the legislature could meet and enact a moratorium on foreclosures. The rebellion and the threat of a mortgage moratorium frightened well-to-do citizens throughout the nation; historians connect this rebellion with the calling of the Philadelphia Convention of 1787, which wrote the second (present) U.S. Constitution, which created a stronger central government and forbids the states from enacting laws impairing the obligations of contracts.

The land area of Boston grew through the filling-in of the peninsula's tidal basins. The top sixty feet of rock and soil of the steep Beacon Hill was leveled to create a site for the nation's oldest prestige neighborhood. The debris from this project was dumped into the millpond to create the West End. Later the South End, and still later the Back Bay, were graceful neighborhoods built on filled land.

Charles Bullfinch was the outstanding architect and developer of this period. His Tontine Crescent combined town houses with a public library. His New State House (1797), Massachusetts General Hospital (1823), the First Harrison Gray Otis House (1796), and his North Hanover Street Church (1804) are all on the National Registry of Historic Places. Alexander Parris's Cathedral of Saint Paul (1820), Quincy Marketplace adjacent to Faneuil Hall (1826), and the Unitarian Church of the Presidents in Quincy are all noteworthy. Also important are the African Meeting House (1806), the first church and social center in the nation that a black community built for its own use, and the Abiel Smith School (1835), the first publicly supported school for black children. In 1855, the Legislature outlawed racial segregation in the public schools of the Commonwealth.

Massachusetts leadership in the antislavery movement was crucial. William Lloyd Garrison of Newburyport founded the American Anti-Slavery Society in 1833. Amos Adams Lawrence financed members of the antislavery movement who moved to Kansas in an attempt to bring that territory into the Union as a free state. Lawrence also financed John Brown, a Springfield woolen merchant, in his trips to Kansas, where five slavery advocates were put to death, and to Harpers Ferry, Virginia, where a United States arsenal was attacked in 1859.

The creation of the Massachusetts State Board of Education in 1837, with Horace Mann as its leader, provided for publicly supported schools throughout the state, and two years later the nation's first public teachers' college was founded here. Mount Holyoke College, the nation's first women's college, was founded in 1837.

From 1845 to 1945 the United States became the greatest industrial, financial, and military power in the world, and in the first half of that period, New England, and especially Massachusetts, was the chief focus of these developments.

In 1813, in Waltham, the Boston Manufacturing Company built the first factory where raw cotton was processed into finished cloth in a single building. Four decades later, the Waltham Watch Company began the manufacture of machine-made watches, which prospered there for nine decades. The textile industry took a major step with the formation of the Merrimack Manufacturing Company and the establishment of Lowell as a company-owned, cotton-weaving town in 1822. Downstream, in 1845, Boston financiers founded Lawrence, which quickly became the nation's most important worsted (woolen) weaving center. The great Lawrence strike of 1912 was widely recognized as a major victory for the American working man. Brockton was the leading center for shoe manufacturing before the Civil War (1861–1865), and the site of an experimental electric streetcar line. Lynn was also a leading shoe-producing city, and it had General Electric's major engine facility. Worcester could boast of a variety of wire-making, metal machine tool, and shoe factories. The United States Armory at Springfield produced small arms for the military services for nearly eighteen decades until its closing in 1968. Its existence provided work for scores of metalworking and machine shops in Springfield and adjacent towns.

By the 1860s, two hundred mills, most situated at waterpower sites within a hundred miles of Boston, made Massachusetts the most important industrial state in the union. In the early decades of the twentieth century, General Electric was the state's largest industrial employer. Raytheon was the leader of the state's large electronics industry. This entry could be filled with a listing of American industries that had their beginnings or early expansion in the Commonwealth.

The decades following the Civil War were an era of accomplishment for the fine arts. Boston's Museum of Fine Arts built its first home at Copley Square, which opened to the public in 1876. The Worcester Art Museum dates from 1896. The Isabella Stewart Gardner Museum in Boston, and the Sterling and Francine Clark Art Institute in Williamstown, house magnificent personal art collections. Important art museums are found on the campuses of Harvard, Williams, Smith, and other colleges and universities in the state. The Boston Symphony was endowed in 1881 and its magnificent hall was opened in 1900. The Boston Public Library was the first of the large city libraries in the nation. Its McKim building, named for its architect, was opened in 1895 and remains one of the great treasure houses of the nation.

The first digital computer was built at Harvard University in 1944. Massachusetts is second only to California in the high-technology industry. More than 30,000 scientists and engineers, all with advanced degrees, live and work in the Boston region. Their efforts are matched by perhaps 60,000 technically trained blue-collar workers.

Immigration

Immigration, emigration, and social mobility have changed what was once called the tribal nature of the Commonwealth's social system. The historic enmity between wealthy Protestants of English ancestry and working-class Irish Catholics that existed in the nineteenth and early twentieth centuries is difficult to detect today. Relations among and between other immigrant groups are friendly and respectful. In 1975, the controversy over the busing of students to remedy racial segregation in the Boston public schools caused violence to occur in several blue-collar Irish-identified older neighborhoods and heightened tensions throughout the region. But the city and the state entered the twenty-first century with these tensions much reduced, if not entirely eliminated. The only evidence of racial negativism in the political sphere may be detected in the failure of the black and Hispanic populations to win citywide elections in Boston and Democratic Party nominations to county and statewide offices. Immigration during the last quarter of the twentieth century brought many new people from nations not previously settled here to the state and its cities and towns. The number of foreign-born residents rose from 573,733 in 1990 to 756,165 in 2000. (The economic prosperity of the 1990s may have played an important role here.)

Economics

Economic trends that began in the decades prior to World War II continued in the closing decades of the century. There was the almost complete displacement of the textile, garment, shoe, machinery, and food-processing industries. Overfishing is a major threat to the state's ocean fishing fleet. High costs associated with cold winters, lack of fossil fuels, failure to develop sustainable power sources, and a location distant from national markets and raw materials, together with unionized workers and a relatively high state minimum wage scale, made competition in manufacturing with Sunbelt states and the less industrialized nations difficult. The state's prosperity rests on its high-technology, electronics, investment (finance), higher education, medical research, and service industries, which replaced the older manufacturing industries.

During the recessions of the early 1970s and the late 1980s, state government was plagued by unbalanced budgets, high unemployment, and increases in public assistance spending. The recovery of the 1980s was called the "Massachusetts miracle." High technology took root in the 1960s and, supported by military research and breakthroughs in electronics and miniaturization, produced the economic turnaround. Expansion of architecture and engineering firms, centers for medical treatment and research, and graduate and professional education also were important. Within the post-1960 economic revival, unemployment soared to 11.2 percent in 1975 but dropped to 3.2 percent in 1987. During the 1990s, unemployment ranged from 9.6 percent in 1991 to 2.5 percent in 2000.

Important to the economic revival was the scientific and technologic excellence of the state's research universities, especially the Massachusetts Institute of Technology (MIT) and Harvard. Government-sponsored research conducted here during World War II and the Cold War decades produced many military breakthroughs, some with civilian applications. Another factor was the region's skilled manpower, especially in machine tools, which provided an abundance of trained technicians. Massachusetts has entered the twenty-first century with several other strong and large research universities moving into positions of national prominence. Included here are Boston University and Boston College, whose assets exceed $1 billion each. Northeastern University has pioneered in placing its students in a vast array of work experiences. Important smaller research universities include Tufts in Medford and Somerville, Brandeis in Waltham, and Clark and Worcester Polytechnic Institute in Worcester. Also significant is the five-campus University of Massachusetts system that includes a large graduate school in Amherst and a medical school in Worcester.

Office and hotel construction in Boston and elsewhere in the state was meager in the decades between 1920 and 1960, but in response to the business revival after 1960 many office, apartment, and hotel towers were built in Boston, and were matched by numerous office buildings, factories, laboratories, warehouses, hotels, and shopping malls erected at almost every interchange of the Boston region's pioneering circumferential highway, Route 128. The area adjacent to this highway, west of the research universities in Cambridge, contains one of the nation's most important concentrations of high-technology industries. Within the city of Boston, Mayor John Collins (1960–1968) and redevelopment director Edward Logue pursued one of the largest and boldest redevelopment programs in the nation, which focused on both the city's business and government office building centers and a cross-section of older neighborhoods.

Transportation

Prior to the 1970s the state government may have been antiquated, burdened by patronage, and unable to plan and coordinate continued economic development, but in the last three decades of the twentieth century there were several notable achievements. The Massachusetts Port Authority expanded and modernized Boston's Logan Airport, the eighth largest in the nation in terms of the number of passengers served. In 1970 Governor Francis Sargent, in a prophetic move, declared a moratorium on highway construction within the Route 128 perimeter. Two years later, the Boston Transportation Planning Review proposed major extensions and improvements of the region's rail-oriented Massachusetts Bay Transportation Authority, including both the rapid transit system serving Boston and its immediate suburbs, and the region's commuter rail system. Entering the twenty-first century, the rapid transit system's four major lines carried 250,000 passengers on the average workday. The bus system carried 170,000 passengers, commuter rail lines carried 33,000 passengers, and commuter boats carried 2,000. (These figures assume that passengers take two trips each day.)

The decade of the 1990s witnessed the restoration of the Old Colony commuter rail line serving suburban communities south of Boston. The region's first "busway" (highway lanes and paved transit tunnels built to accommodate certain types of buses) will serve a corridor in one of Boston's oldest residential neighborhoods, the new U.S. courthouse, and a planned business, hotel, and convention area in the South Boston waterfront, and is scheduled for completion in 2003. Planning is under way for a circumferential transit ring, approximately two miles from the business core, which will connect several low-income neighborhoods to two major medical centers, the airport, and declining warehouse and industrial areas. This wealth of public transportation facilities serves to preserve the historic and business areas of Boston as perhaps the most walk-friendly city center in the nation.

Boston's Central Artery and Tunnel project, a ghost of the 1950s automobile-oriented highway mind-set, is scheduled for completion in 2005, and is expected to cost nearly $15 billion, making it the nation's most expensive highway project. Called "The Big Dig," it includes replacing an elevated expressway with an eight-lane underground roadway, the world's widest bridge to carry traffic across the Charles River, a four-lane harbor tunnel connecting the downtown with the airport, and a vast amount of highway spaghetti providing links to all the downtown area's highways and expressways. A significant failure of this project is the lack of a one-mile rail link between the city's two major rail terminals. This causes passengers from Maine and the New Hampshire coastal towns to have to take a taxi or a complicated transit trip if they intend to proceed by rail south or west of Boston.

Politics

Massachusetts voters may be the most liberal in the nation. Democratic presidential candidates carry the state by the widest margins, or lose it by the narrowest margins, in the nation. The state's delegation in Congress is entirely composed of liberal Democrats. Democrats control both houses of the legislature with overwhelming majorities. Michael Dukakis, a Democrat, was the only governor to serve more than seven years. He served three full four-year terms. Democrats also have had success in winning election to the state's four lesser constitutional offices (attorney general, treasurer, auditor, and secretary of state). But Republicans and conservative Democrats had remarkable success in winning the governorship during the last quarter of the century. In 1978 a conservative Democrat, Edward J. King, was elected governor, and in 1990 a moderate Republican, William Weld, was elected over a conservative Democrat, John Silber. Weld was reelected in 1994, but chose not to serve his full second term. In 1998, his successor, Lieutenant Governor Paul Cellucci, was elected to a full term, but when nominated to be ambassador to Canada, he vacated the governorship to his lieutenant governor, Jane Swift, who assumed office at age thirty-six, making her the youngest woman ever to serve as one of the nation's governors. Upon leaving office, both King and Weld have pursued their careers outside of the state.

Massachusetts's political party organizations may be among the weakest in the nation. On even-numbered years the use of the office block form, which scatters party nominees almost at random across the ballot, weakens party awareness. Nonpartisan local elections deprive party organizations of needed exercise during odd-numbered years, when local officials are elected. In 2000, 36 percent of voters were enrolled Democrats, 14 percent were enrolled Republicans, and 50 percent chose not to enroll in either party. Almost all candidates in both partisan and nonpartisan elections must build personal political organizations for raising campaign funds and for getting out the vote on Election Day. In a referendum in 1998 the voters, by a two-thirds margin, enacted a system of state-financed election campaigns, but the legislature has failed to provide funds for the system, and the issue is being argued in the state courts.

Culture and the Arts

Massachusetts is the home of an unrivaled array of cultural and educational institutions. The Boston Symphony Orchestra is admired around the world. In addition to its traditional season of concerts in Symphony Hall, its summer activities include the Boston Pops, free concerts on the Esplanade, and Tanglewood, its vacation home in the Berkshires. The state has other magnificent music halls and conservatories. Down the street from the Symphony is Berklee, the only four-year college in the nation devoted solely to jazz and contemporary popular music. In the field of the visual arts, the collections and galleries of the Museum of Fine Arts rival the world's greatest museums, but the state also has major collections of art displayed in magnificent buildings in Worcester, Williamstown, Salem, North Adams, and at several sites on the Harvard campus in Cambridge. Smith and Wellesley Colleges have important fine arts museums on their campuses. Boston's outstanding Children's Museum shares a former warehouse with the Computer Museum. Brookline is the host to a museum of transportation, and New Bedford has its whaling museum. The large and popular Museum of Science is located adjacent to a dam on the Charles River. Harvard has several important science museums and is most famous for its collection of glass flowers.

Land and Conservation

From the Berkshires to Cape Cod, Massachusetts is a place of natural beauty, and the need to safeguard this resource for healthy environments and spiritual delights is well understood. Boston's historic Common may be the nation's oldest public park. All levels of government and a variety of citizens' organizations share in protecting the Commonwealth's lands and waters. The National Park Service maintains fourteen parks and historical sites in Massachusetts, including the Cape Cod National Seashore. The state system of parks and forests consists of 170 properties (298,000 acres). The Boston Metropolitan Park System, designed by Frederick Law Olmsted and

Charles Eliot, is known as the Emerald Necklace and comprises 20,000 acres of parks, woodlands, wetlands, and beaches, and 162 miles of landscaped parkways, all located within fifteen miles of the statehouse in Boston.

The Trustees of Reservations was organized by private parties to protect the Massachusetts landscape in 1891. It owns 91 reservations (22,545 acres) that are open to the public, and it protects 202 additional properties (13,314 acres) with conservation restrictions. Massachusetts Audubon (independent of the national organization) owns 60 sanctuaries (25,794 acres). The Charles River Watershed Association, supported by membership contributions of 5,200 individuals and organizations, serves as a guardian of this valued resource. No other citizens' group focused on a river valley has attracted and held the support of so many dues-paying people. Massachusetts is first among the states in the number of local and regional conservation land trusts. These include 143 trusts, which own and protect 210,000 scenic acres.

BIBLIOGRAPHY

Bluestone, Barry, and Mary Huff Stevenson. *The Boston Renaissance: Race, Space, and Economic Change in an American Metropolis.* New York: Russell Sage Foundation, 2000.

Dukakis, Michael S., and Rosabeth Moss Kanter. *Creating the Future: The Massachusetts Comeback and Its Promise for America.* New York: Summit Books, 1988.

Encyclopedia of Massachusetts, Biographical—Genealogical. New York: The American Historical Society, 1984.

Hovey, Kendra A., and Howard A. Hovey. *CQ's State Fact Finder 2000: Rankings Across America* Washington, D.C.: Congressional Quarterly Books, 2000.

Keating, Raymond J., and Thomas Keating. *US by the Numbers: Figuring What's Left, Right, and Wrong with America State by State.* Sterling, Va.: Capital Books, 2000.

Kennedy, Lawrence W. *Planning the City Upon a Hill: Boston Since 1630.* Amherst: University of Massachusetts Press, 1992.

Lampe, David, ed. *The Massachusetts Miracle: High Technology and Economic Revitalization.* Cambridge, Mass.: MIT Press, 1988.

Lukas, J. Anthony. *Common Ground: A Turbulent Decade in the Lives of Three American Families.* New York: Knopf, 1985.

Rand, Christopher. *Cambridge, USA: Hub of a New World.* New York: Oxford University Press, 1964.

Roger Feinstein

MASSACHUSETTS BALLOT.

Before 20 July 1629, all voting in New England was by acclamation or by the uplifted hand, but on that date the Salem church used the BALLOT in choosing a pastor. By 1634 the ballot was used in electing the governor of Massachusetts. In 1645 Dorchester ordered that all "elections be by papers," that is, by ballots. Paper being scarce, kernels of wheat and Indian corn were sometimes used, the wheat for the affirmative and the corn for the negative. The Australian, or secret, ballot was introduced into the United States by Massachusetts in 1878.

BIBLIOGRAPHY

Fredman, Lionel E. *The Australian Ballot: The Story of an American Reform.* East Lansing: Michigan State University Press, 1968.

Miller, Perry. *The New England Mind: From Colony to Province.* Cambridge, Mass.: Belknap Press of Harvard University Press, 1983.

R. W. G. Vail / A. G.

See also **Colonial Assemblies; Council for New England; Massachusetts Body of Liberties; New England Way; Suffrage: Colonial Suffrage.**

MASSACHUSETTS BAY COLONY.

Established under the aegis of the New England Company, Massachusetts Bay Colony was first established by a group of Puritan merchants in 1630. The merchants had obtained their initial charter from the Council for New England in 1628. Wary of the validity of that document, the company reorganized, secured a modified royal charter, and renamed itself the Governor and Company of Massachusetts Bay. The charter, which ceded lands from three miles south of the Charles River to three miles north of the Merrimack, allowed the company to establish its own government for the colony, subject only to the king.

In the face of mounting tensions in England—constricting economic opportunities, an increasingly corrupt Anglican Church, the dissolution of Parliament by Charles I, and the jailing of prominent Puritan leaders—settlement in American grew ever more attractive. And though members maintained an interest in the trading company's economic potential, they recognized too the religious and political benefits of establishing an American colony. The colony would be a religious refuge, a "holy experiment," where devout Puritans and their families would settle far from England's corruption. In a daring move that contributed to their governmental, religious, and economic autonomy, the Company decided to move its entire operation to MASSACHUSETTS, out of range of the Crown's watchful eye. In October 1629 the General Court of the Massachusetts Bay Company chose lawyer, gentleman, and devout Puritan John Winthrop to be the colony's first governor. Winthrop began the arduous task of raising money, locating and provisioning ships, and attracting a range of passengers interested in participating in the "holy experiment."

Though most immigrants were motivated in part by the promise of economic stability in a colony rich in natural resources, including land, many were guided by a commitment to the tenets of Puritanism, a religion that stressed the individual's personal covenant with God and community. In New England they would plant the seeds for a godly colony where the congregants themselves would shape their religious institutions. Not all of those immigrants attracted to the mission, however, were devout Puritans. Winthrop and the other Company leaders took pains to ensure that the colony would include settlers with the skills necessary to ensure its success—craftsmen, doctors, servants, and laborers—regardless of the depth of their religious commitment.

The Company pointedly assured those they left behind that they were not Separatists; from aboard their ship the *Arbella*, they published a written public statement proclaiming their allegiance to the Crown and Church of England. Unlike their brethren who had abandoned the Church to establish a Separatist colony in Plymouth, Massachusetts, in 1620, the members of the Bay Company intended instead to plant the seeds for a pure church that would in turn spark the continued reformation of the church in England. On 8 April 1630 the *Arbella* and three other ships set sail with some four hundred men, women, and children.

Though the ships initially made land at the small settlement at SALEM, where eighty people had died during the previous harsh winter, Winthrop and the other Company officers encouraged their band to settle new land south of Salem, on the bay. Concerns about the Salem settlement went beyond its limited resources: several of Salem's settlers had developed a reputation for sympathy with the Separatists in Plymouth. Seeking to escape that branding, the new colonists established plantations in towns around the bay, including Charlestown, Newtown, Roxbury, and Dorchester. Winthrop eventually settled in Boston.

The first winter in the colony tested the mettle of the settlers. Starvation and disease took the lives of two hundred people, and another two hundred returned to England in the spring. The task of not only protecting colonists but also ensuring the economic stability of the colony fell to Winthrop and his officers. Aided by a steady stream of immigrants who continued to flee England and arrived with fresh supplies, including window glass, cooking tools, guns and powder, and cloth and clothing, by 1631 the colony had attained a level of economic equilibrium.

In the fall of 1630 the Company called the first General Court in Massachusetts Bay. Though franchise (being able to vote) was not considered the right of Englishmen, and the colony's charter did not demand that the magistrates address this issue, the Court opened freemanship (the rights of citizenship) to all male residents. At the same time, the Court limited the power of freemen to the right to choose the colony's assistants; all legal and judicial powers were retained by the assistants themselves, who on their own elected the governor and deputy governor.

In acknowledgment of the colony's religious mission, in 1631 the Court restricted franchise to only those freemen who were church members. In spite of that limitation, by so doing the Court extended franchise to more men than would have had that right in England. The Court recognized that a covenanted people would be more inclined to accept their leadership if they had participated in the process of establishing the government. Though the new government was explicitly not a theoc-

racy—ministers were prohibited from holding public office—the decision to limit franchise to church members also made the colony's theocratic underpinnings abundantly clear. A religious commonwealth, Massachusetts Bay established Puritanism as the state-supported religion, and made it clear that no other faiths would be tolerated in the colony.

At its session in May, the Court enfranchised 118 men. By the following year, the Court decided to turn the election of the governor over to freemen rather than the assistants. Winthrop and the majority of the original assistants were reelected in each of the first few years of the colony.

The original settlers of Massachusetts Bay implemented laws designed to create communities that capitalized on broadly based franchise; they sought to avoid a society ruled by a few wealthy landowners, typical of that which they had left behind in England. Though property ownership was and remained the primary ingredient in the Puritan recipe for godly communities, for the most part the colony took pains to ensure equitable distribution of that essential resource. The Bay Colony government deeded title for townships to groups of male settlers. These proprietors distributed the land among themselves. And though proprietors made land grants reflecting the current wealth and status of town leaders—men of the highest rank received the largest plots—all proprietors received enough land to support their families.

Moreover, all men participated in the central governmental organ, the town meeting. Each year the town meeting chose selectmen, passed ordinances, and levied and collected local taxes. Each town elected its own representatives to the General Court, which soon assumed a greater authority in colonial politics than the governor and magistrates.

Colonists recognized the centrality of their holy covenant with God and each other. As regenerate Christians, it was their duty to monitor the purity of their political leaders, their spouses and children, their neighbors, and even the very clerics who instructed them in the path to a godly life and community. Though the governor, deputies, and assistants did not always agree on the extent to which the government should control behavior—resulting in an almost constant legal battle over laws governing everything from dress to alcohol consumption—all colonists were wary of behavior perceived to be outside of accepted definitions of pious conduct and demeanor.

Over the course of the first generation of settlement in Massachusetts Bay, tensions surrounding the colony's religious establishment erupted into outright disputes. On several occasions those disputes resulted in attempts to purge the community of people who put into practice controversial religious beliefs. Roger Williams, minister of the church in Salem, condemned the legal establishment of the Puritan church in Massachusetts Bay, advocating instead the separation of church and state the

Pilgrims had instituted in the Plymouth Colony. The government, he claimed, had no authority over the spiritual lives of the settlers. In addition, he objected to the Puritans' practice of seizing rather than purchasing Indian lands. In the face of mounting tension, the magistrates banished Williams from the colony in 1635. He settled with his followers in Rhode Island, where they established the town of Providence.

Anne Hutchinson was another target in the magistrates' attempts to control dissidence in the colony. Hutchinson, a midwife of some renown in England, mother of seven children, and wife of a prominent merchant, held prayer meetings for as many as sixty women in her home following church services. There she led discussions about the minister's sermons, and questioned the emphasis they seemed to her to place on good behavior—a covenant of works rather than one of faith. An antinomian, Hutchinson believed that faith and the resulting grace came through direct revelation from God, clearly threatening to the authority of the colony's ministers. Moreover, as a woman, Hutchinson's actions challenged traditional belief that only men should be responsible for religious teaching.

In 1637 Massachusetts Bay's magistrates tried Anne Hutchinson for heresy. Though she defended herself before the judges with courage and no small amount of skill, they found her guilty and banished her from the colony. Hutchinson followed Roger Williams to Rhode Island.

Other religious dissidents left Massachusetts Bay of their own volition. In search of both greater religious freedom and the opportunity to acquire more land, one hundred Puritans led by Thomas Hooker left the colony in 1636 to settle in the Connecticut River Valley, establishing the town of Hartford. Others established Wethersfield, Windsor, and New Haven.

In addition to religious dissent, political and economic controversy shaped the colony's development. With three thousand miles separating Massachusetts Bay from mother England, the colony considered itself an independent commonwealth. That assumption came into direct conflict with the Crown's mercantilist expectations. In 1660, on his ascent to the throne, Charles II established a committee to gain control of British colonial resources. The LORDS OF TRADE AND PLANTATION oversaw colonial commerce. It monitored adherence to Parliament's new NAVIGATION ACTS of 1660 and 1663, reining in colonial merchants trading with foreign countries in sugar, tobacco, and indigo, and instituting additional laws regulating European exports to America.

New England merchants bristled at the Crown's efforts to reassert control. The Bay Colony's government chose to ignore the Navigation Acts, and persisted in importing and exporting goods as it saw fit, claiming that the royal charter exempted it from the new trade regulations. The Crown responded by sending troops to the colony to enforce compliance. In 1684, on the recommendation of the Lords of Trade, the English court re-

voked the colony's charter. Two years later, it created the DOMINION OF NEW ENGLAND, effectively eliminating a number of existing colonial governments, Massachusetts Bay's among them. James II appointed Edmund Andros Governor of the Dominion. Andros banned town meetings, dismissed the assembly, and questioned the validity of all land titles filed under the original charter. The Puritan colonists of Massachusetts Bay petitioned the Crown for Andros's dismissal, but their protests fell on deaf ears.

In the wake of the ouster of James II in the Glorious Revolution of 1688, however, Massachusetts Bay successfully revolted against Andros, who returned to England. The Bay Colony asked for the restoration of its original charter. Though the recently enthroned William and Mary agreed to the dissolution of the Dominion, they did not fully restore the colony's independent authority. Instead, they created a new colony of Massachusetts, under a royal charter established in 1691. Plymouth and Maine were absorbed into Massachusetts Bay. Though the charter restored the Massachusetts assembly, it undermined the colony's theocratic underpinnings; all male property owners, not just Puritan church members, were guaranteed the right to elect representatives. The charter also gave the Crown the right to appoint the governor. The government established by the 1691 charter existed for the next seventy years. In spite of the Crown's influence under the new charter, the Bay Colony's government grew increasingly independent.

BIBLIOGRAPHY

Allen, David Grayson. *In English Ways: The Movement of Societies and the Transferal of English Local Law and Custom to Massachusetts Bay in the Seventeenth Century.* Chapel Hill: University of North Carolina Press, 1981.

Bremer, Francis J. *The Puritan Experiment: New England Society from Bradford to Edwards.* New York: St. Martin's Press, 1976.

Morgan, Edmund. *The Puritan Dilemma: The Story of John Winthrop.* Boston: Little, Brown, 1958.

Leslie J. Lindenauer

See also **Antinomian Controversy; Plymouth Colony; Providence Plantations, Rhode Island and; Puritans and Puritanism;** *and vol. 9:* **Evidence Used Against Witches; Massachusetts School Law; Trial of Anne Hutchinson at Newton, 1637.**

MASSACHUSETTS BODY OF LIBERTIES.

To curb the power of the magistrates, deputies in the Massachusetts General Court agitated for a code of laws. In November 1639 a committee adopted a code presented by Nathaniel Ward, formerly an English lawyer. The General Court submitted it to the towns for review, then shortened and adapted the code, which was adopted as law in 1641. Similar to bills of rights and based largely on English common law, the Massachusetts Body of Liberties invested the magistrates with considerable authority.

Therefore, after a probationary period of three years, deputies replaced the code with *The Book of the General Lawes and Libertyes.*

BIBLIOGRAPHY

Dufour, Ronald P. *Modernization in Colonial Massachusetts, 1630–1763.* New York: Garland, 1987.

Kammen, Michael G., ed. *Politics and Society in Colonial America: Democracy or Deference?* New York: Holt, Rinehart, and Winston, 1967; Huntington, N.Y.: Krieger, 1978.

Raymond P. Stearns / s. b.

See also **Assemblies, Colonial; Colonial Councils; General Court, Colonial.**

MASSACHUSETTS CIRCULAR LETTER

MASSACHUSETTS CIRCULAR LETTER was written by Samuel Adams in 1768 as a response to the Townshend Acts passed by the English Parliament taxing colonists on the goods they imported from England. In 1768, the legislature of Massachusetts approved Adams's letter for circulation to all the other American colonial legislatures to form the basis of a united response to the English taxes. This quote from the letter offers a sense of its content: "imposing Duties on the People of this province with the sole & express purpose of raising a Revenue, are Infringements of their natural & constitutional Rights . . . as they are not represented in the British Parliament."

BIBLIOGRAPHY

Alexander, John K. *Samuel Adams.* New York: Rowman and Littlefield, 2002.

King, Peter. "Documents on the Townshend Acts and Period 1767–1768." Available at http://www.carleton.ca/~pking /docs/440docs1.htm

Kirk H. Beetz

See also **Townshend Acts;** *and vol. 9:* **Massachusetts Circular Letter.**

MASSACHUSETTS GOVERNMENT ACT

MASSACHUSETTS GOVERNMENT ACT of 20 May 1767 was one of the Coercive Acts (see also Intolerable Acts) passed by Parliament in response to the Boston Tea Party. The act was draconian in nature, and its justification lay in the sweeping claim to sovereignty codified by the Declaratory Act of 1767. The Massachusetts Government Act effectively ended nearly a century and a half of virtual democracy in the Bay Colony. The Massachusetts charter was suspended, and the upper house of the legislature was henceforth to be appointed by the governor, loyalist Thomas Hutchinson. Judges and sheriffs were also to be appointed, and all officials were to be paid by the crown, not by the democratically elected and decidedly Whig lower house of the Assembly. Town meetings were severely circumscribed as to when they could meet and what they could do.

When taken in context with the other two measures of the Coercive Acts, the Massachusetts Government Act was part of a punitive effort to teach rebellious Massachusetts Bay a lesson meant for all of the American colonies with revolution on their minds. The acts did not merely strip the colony of its sovereignty, it destroyed its economy by closing the port of Boston; the Government Act was complicit in this by denying colonials in the Bay Colony any evident means of redress. But as punitive as the Government Act was, it failed in one important instance: it allowed the freely elected lower house of the Assembly to survive intact, and it, along with the Sons of Liberty in the streets, became the focal point of resistance to the British crown. Massachusetts revolutionaries were able to utilize this apparatus for elections to the lower house to call for a Continental Congress made up of representatives from twelve colonies and to elect Massachusetts delegates to that First Continental Congress, convened on 5 September 1774.

BIBLIOGRAPHY

Namier, Louis B. *England in the Age of the American Revolution.* 2d ed. New York: St. Martin's Press, 1962. The original edition was published in 1930.

Rakove, J.N. *The Beginnings of National Politics: An Interpretive History of the Continental Congress.* New York: Knopf, 1979; Baltimore: Johns Hopkins University Press, 1982.

Carl E. Prince

MASSACHUSETTS INSTITUTE OF TECHNOLOGY

MASSACHUSETTS INSTITUTE OF TECHNOLOGY (MIT) was founded in the late 1850s as part of a broad American effort to provide superior technical training that combined advanced theoretical education with practical industrial problem solving. William Barton Rogers, a distinguished geologist and natural scientist, expressed the initial concept for MIT as a school of such intellectual rigor that it "would soon overtop the universities of the land." On 10 April 1861 the Boston Society of Natural History and associated organizations proposed that the Massachusetts legislature charter "a society of Arts and a School of Industrial Science" to be located on real estate in Back Bay Boston made available through reclamation. Rogers became president of the institution and spent the next four years preparing his plan of organization and instruction, visiting European technical schools and laboratories, selecting building designs, and raising funds. His astute fund-raising secured the initial federal college grant to Massachusetts under the Morrill Act of 1862.

When the first student, Eli Forbes, enrolled, the regular classes were held in rented space in the Mercantile Building in downtown Boston. In 1866 the new building designed by William Preston was completed on the Back Bay campus. The classes were to be "suited to the various professions of the Mechanician, the Civil Engineer, the Builder and Architect, the Mining Engineer, and the practical chemist." The MIT faculty, under the auspices of the Lowell Institute, provided evening classes for both men and women. 1866 saw the first graduating class of fourteen, the establishment of the physics laboratory, and the first of several proposals to merge the new MIT into Harvard. Over the next decade, the institute admitted its first female student, Ellen H. Swallow, who graduated with an S.B. in chemistry; Alexander Graham Bell studied at the physics laboratory; and the first student publication, the *Spectator*, was founded. The last decades of the nineteenth century saw the completion of the original Back Bay campus. At the same time, the institute established a new electrical engineering laboratory and initiated efforts to work with industry on specific technical problems.

The importance of technology and engineering to American industry fostered ties between MIT and industrial corporations from the institute's inception. Chemical and electrical engineering were a continuing focus of cooperation between the institute and industry, starting in the 1880s. Fueled by the expansion of American industry in the early twentieth century and the accompanying importance of engineering academics, MIT built a new campus on 154 acres that spread for a mile along the Cambridge side of the Charles River. The architect W. Welles Bosworth, an 1889 graduate of MIT, designed the central group of interconnecting buildings to permit easy communication among departments and schools. These buildings were dedicated in 1916.

The school's close links with industry and its ability to manage large-scale technology and engineering projects prompted Alfred P. Sloan, chairman of General Motors, to endow the Sloan School of Management for special research and education in management in 1928. During World War I and especially during World War II major military projects were located and managed at MIT. The radiation laboratory for research and development of radar was established in 1940. The school's Lincoln Laboratory for research and development of advanced electronics was established with federal government sponsorship at Lexington, Massachusetts, where the Whirlwind project began the initial developmental work on computers. During the Vietnam War the institute was the site of major protests; consequently, MIT reduced its direct role in military research. In 1983, in response to the burgeoning role of the computer, the school founded the Media Laboratory to examine the processes and consequences of all media and their interactions with technology.

In the second half of the twentieth century MIT evolved into one of the premier research universities in the United States. It is organized into five schools—the School of Architecture and Planning, the School of Engineering, the School of Humanities and Social Sciences, the Sloan School of Management, and the School of Science—which contain twenty-one academic departments and sixty-two programs, laboratories, and research centers. While clearly strong in its traditional disciplines of engineering and technology, the school's academic structure provides breadth and strength in other areas, such as economics, political science, and urban studies. The

stated mission of the institute is "to advance knowledge and educate students in science, technology and other areas of scholarship that will best serve the nation and the world in the twenty-first century." During the 2000–2001 academic year MIT enrolled 9,972 students; 4,300 were undergraduates, and 5,672 were graduate students. Thirty-four percent were women. Also in that academic year the institute's endowment reached $6.6 billion.

BIBLIOGRAPHY

Brand, Stewart. *The Media Lab: Inventing the Future at MIT.* New York: Viking Press, 1987.

Garfinkel, Simson L. *Architects of the Information Society: Thirty-five Years of the Laboratory for Computer Science at MIT.* Cambridge, Mass.: MIT Press, 1999.

Guerlac, Henry E. *Radar in World War II.* Los Angeles: Tomash Publishers, 1987.

Hapgood, Fred. *Up the Infinite Corridor: MIT and the Technical Imagination.* Reading, Mass.: Addison-Wesley, 1993.

Johnson, Howard Wesley. *Holding the Center: Memoirs of a Life in Higher Education.* Cambridge, Mass.: MIT Press, 1999.

Killian, James R., Jr. *The Education of a College President.* Cambridge, Mass.: MIT Press, 1985.

Wildes, Karl L., and Nilo A. Lindgren. *A Century of Electrical Engineering and Computer Sciences at MIT, 1882–1982.* Cambridge, Mass.: MIT Press, 1985.

Michael Carew

See also **Computers and Computer Industry; Engineering Education.**

MATERNAL AND CHILD HEALTH CARE.

The story of maternal and child health care in America parallels major changes not only in medical science, but also in society at large. Colonial Americans continued European practices of obstetrics and midwifery, while child health care remained largely undifferentiated from adult treatments. Complications from childbirth were the leading killers of young women, and infant and toddler mortality was high. In 1789, 40 percent of all deaths were among children under age five. Infants frequently succumbed to dysentery, diarrhea, and cholera, while epidemics of smallpox, scarlet fever, typhoid, yellow fever, and diphtheria often killed older children.

Maternal health was threatened by postpartum bleeding as well as by deadly ailments such as puerperal ("childbearing") fever, a bacterial infection contracted during childbirth. Labor pain went largely untreated until 1853, when Queen Victoria of England demanded chloroform while delivering her eighth baby. The smallpox inoculation was introduced to America in 1721, and a greatly improved smallpox vaccination became available in 1800; still, infant and child mortality rates remained high well into the mid-nineteenth century.

By 1850, nearly 17 percent of deaths nationwide were among infants, although they accounted for less than 3 percent of the total population. Cities were particularly deadly: between 1854 and 1856, children under age five accounted for more than 60 percent of New York City's deaths. Yet the roots of pediatrics and obstetrics were taking hold. In 1825, William P. Dewees of the University of Pennsylvania published the first comprehensive treatise on children's health. Philadelphia opened the first children's hospital in 1855, and in 1860, Dr. Abraham Jacobi, who became known as the "father of pediatrics," was appointed to head the first children's clinic at the New York Medical College. Before long, the American Medical Association had departments devoted to obstetrics and pediatrics, and in 1888 the American Pediatric Society was formed.

Meanwhile, the problem of child labor was reaching a crisis point. In 1870, some 764,000 children—about 13 percent of the nation's 10- to 15-year-olds—were working in America's factories, mines, and fields. Within 30 years, the child workforce had mushroomed to 1.75 million. Child labor abuses, however, also spawned child welfare programs. In 1874, the Society for the Prevention of Cruelty to Children was founded, modeled after the Society for the Prevention of Cruelty to Animals, which had been established in 1866. By the end of the century, the "sanitary milk movement" had become a powerful force in combating diarrheal diseases brought on by spoiled milk, the leading cause of death among young children at the time. The advent of pasteurization further aided the cause, allowing for wide distribution of safe milk to fight disease and malnutrition.

As the Progressive Era ushered in the new century, reform movements such as the "crusade for children" promoted a range of maternal and child health issues. Public schools took an active role in preventative care by introducing school nurses and instituting general health and eye exams for students. New York City piloted programs that became national models, including, in 1908, the first public school lunch program, as well as the establishment of the first Bureau of Child Hygiene. In 1909, President Theodore Roosevelt hosted the first White House Conference on Children. He called for the establishment of what, in 1912, became the Federal Children's Bureau. Its mission: to "investigate and report upon all matters pertaining to the welfare of children and child life among all classes of our people."

The 1921 Maternity and Infancy Care Act provided health services funding for mothers and children, particularly in rural communities. The act, though not renewed in 1929, inspired the 1935 Social Security Act Title V maternal and child health care funding programs. Later in the century, federal legislation and programs for maternal and child health care ranged from the Special Supplemental Nutrition Program for Women, Infants, and Children (WIC), permanently established in 1974, to the Family and Medical Leave Act (FMLA) of 1993.

In the private sector, the National Easter Seal Society (formed originally as the National Society for Crippled

Children in 1921; the first such association was the Ohio Society for Crippled Children, formed in 1919) and the March of Dimes Birth Defects Foundation (created as the National Foundation for Infantile Paralysis in 1938) were among the many organizations formed to promote maternal and child health through prevention and treatment.

One of the century's most significant medical advances was Dr. Jonas Salk's introduction of the polio vaccine in 1952. Salk's fame also paved the way for a new breed of superstar doctor, including pediatricians-turned-authors Dr. Benjamin Spock and, a generation later, Dr. T. Barry Brazelton. Best-sellers written by and for women, including *Our Bodies, Ourselves* (first published in 1970) and the "What to Expect" series, gave women a common, personal point of reference on reproductive health and child rearing.

The evolution of women's roles in society also had a significant impact on maternal health care in the twentieth century, with reproductive health issues sparking frequent national debate. Early in the century, women's rights advocates such as the Planned Parenthood founder Margaret Sanger fought to overturn the nineteenth-century Comstock laws (named for anti-vice crusader Anthony Comstock), which banned contraceptives and related information as obscene materials. In 1936, a U.S. Circuit Court of Appeals ruling liberalized the interpretation of the Comstock laws as they applied to contraceptives; a year later, the American Medical Association officially recognized the importance of birth control in medical education and practice. The patenting of the birth control pill in 1960, which quickly became women's birth control method of choice, kicked off the sexual revolution. The 1960s and 1970s also spawned natural childbirth and Lamaze movements, which gave fathers a more prominent role during delivery.

The most bitter war over reproductive rights stemmed from the 1973 Supreme Court decision in *Roe v. Wade*, which effectively legalized first- and second-trimester abortions in the United States, using the same privacy standard the court had applied in overturning *Griswold v. Connecticut* (1965), which dealt with state bans on contraceptives. *Roe* set off a firestorm between "pro-life" abortion opponents and "pro-choice" advocates of a woman's right to end a pregnancy.

Medical science also stretched toward the other end of the spectrum near the end of the century with the advent of fertility treatments such as *in vitro* fertilization and other methods of assisted reproductive therapy. As the twenty-first century began, the ethical debates about everything from prenatal gene therapy to human cloning hinted at a new century of cutting-edge science and social discourse about maternal and child health care.

BIBLIOGRAPHY

American Pediatric Society/Society for Pediatric Research. Web site http://www.aps-spr.org.

King, Charles R. *Children's Health in America: A History.* New York: Twayne, 1993.

Kotch, Jonathon B., ed. *Maternal and Child Health: Programs, Problems, and Policy in Public Health.* Gaithersburg, Md.: Aspen, 1997.

Luker, Kristin. *Abortion and the Politics of Motherhood.* Berkeley: University of California Press, 1984.

McCann, Carole R. *Birth Control Politics in the United States, 1916–1945.* Ithaca, N.Y.: Cornell University Press, 1994.

Meckel, Richard A. *Save the Babies: American Public Health Reform and the Prevention of Infant Mortality, 1850–1929.* Baltimore: Johns Hopkins University Press, 1990.

Quiroga, Virginia Anne Metaxas. *Poor Mothers and Babies: A Social History of Childbirth and Child Care Hospitals in Nineteenth-Century New York City.* New York: Garland, 1990.

Wollons, Roberta, ed. *Children at Risk in America: History, Concepts, and Public Policy.* Albany: State University of New York Press, 1993.

Laura A. Bergheim

See also **Child Care; Child Labor; Family and Medical Leave Act; Society for the Prevention of Cruelty to Children; Women's Health.**

MAY DAY. Although May Day was observed as a rite of spring in Europe for centuries, it became associated in the late nineteenth century as a workers' holiday. In 1889 an International Socialist Congress selected the first day of May as a world labor holiday to show support for labor activism in the United States. After the Haymarket Square Riot in early May 1886, the labor activists around the world followed the lead of American workers and began to agitate for an eight-hour work day. May Day was first celebrated in 1890, and many countries continue the tradition today, though the United States does not, and only recognizes LABOR DAY in September.

BIBLIOGRAPHY

Foner, Philip S. *May Day: A Short History of the International Workers' Holiday, 1886–1986.* New York: International Publishers, 1986.

Panaccione, Andrea, ed. *The Memory of May Day: An Iconographic History of the Origins and Implanting of a Workers' Holiday.* Venice, Italy: Marsilio Editori, 1989.

Alvin F. Harlow / h. s.

See also **Haymarket Riot; Labor; Socialist Movement.**

MAYAGUEZ INCIDENT. On 12 May 1975, Cambodian gunboats acting on the orders of a local Khmer Rouge commander seized the American cargo ship *Mayaguez* while it cruised in the Gulf of Thailand some sixty miles south of Cambodia. Forty American sailors were captured and taken to Koh Tang, a small island about seven miles away. The United States regarded this region of the gulf as international waters, but the new Khmer Rouge government claimed a ninety-mile zone from the mainland and had been detaining foreign ships for the past ten days. The administration of President Gerald Ford saw the incident as a deliberate challenge to American credibility, badly weakened after the collapse of the pro-U.S. regimes in South Vietnam and Cambodia less than one month earlier. On 15 May a force of 175 marines assaulted Koh Tang to rescue the *Mayaguez* hostages, while the aircraft carrier USS *Coral Sea* launched air strikes against the Cambodian airfield at Ream and the port of Kompong Som. In the ensuing battle for Koh Tang, fifteen Americans died, three were reported missing (later declared dead), and fifty were wounded. The marines claimed to have killed fifty-five Khmer soldiers. Several hours after the battle began, the U.S. destroyer *Wilson* found and rescued the *Mayaguez* crew aboard a fishing vessel, which had been set adrift by the Cambodians earlier in the day. The Ford administration defended the use of military force as a necessary step to deter communist aggression.

BIBLIOGRAPHY

Guilmartin, John F., Jr. *A Very Short War: The Mayaguez and the Battle of Koh Tang.* College Station: Texas A&M University Press, 1995.

Hersh, Seymour M. *The Price of Power: Kissinger in the Nixon White House.* New York: Summit Books, 1983.

Isaacson, Walter. *Kissinger: A Biography.* New York: Simon and Schuster, 1992.

Erik B. Villard

MAYFLOWER, a three-masted, double-decked merchant ship of 180 tons, chartered in London to take the PILGRIMS to America. The *Mayflower* left Holland on 31 July 1620, joining the *Speedwell* in Southampton, England, for the voyage to America. The two ships sailed on 15 August but returned because of the leaky condition of the *Speedwell.* The *Speedwell* was eventually abandoned, and on 16 September, 102 passengers and crew aboard the *Mayflower* finally sailed from England, sighted Cape Cod on 19 November, and arrived in what is now the harbor of Provincetown, Cape Cod, MASSACHUSETTS, on 21 November. Repairs kept them there until 21 December 1620. The *Mayflower* followed the land-exploring party and sailed into Plymouth, Massachusetts, harbor on 26 December, where it remained until houses could be built for the new settlement. It sailed for England on 5 April 1621, reaching London safely.

BIBLIOGRAPHY

King, H. Roger. *Cape Cod and Plymouth Colony in the Seventeenth Century.* Lanham, Md.: University Press of America, 1994.

Langdon, George D., Jr. *Pilgrim Colony: A History of New Plymouth, 1620–1691.* New Haven, Conn.: Yale University Press, 1966.

R. W. G. Vail / a. r.

See also **Colonial Ships; Plymouth Colony.**

MAYFLOWER COMPACT, signed aboard the *May-flower* on 11 November 1620 by the ship's forty-one free adult men, served as the basis for Plymouth Colony's government throughout its history. As the *Mayflower*'s passengers had settled in New England, their patent for establishing a colony in Virginia was useless. The Pilgrim colony thus had no legal foundation, and some non-Pilgrim passengers talked of striking out on their own, ignoring Governor John Carver's now ambiguous authority. If the Pilgrims were to have a colony at all, they needed to establish a government based on some sort of consensus, and they turned to the model of their own congregational churches for guidance. The colonists would form a "body politic," which would select and wholly submit to leaders chosen by the majority, just as members of Pilgrim congregations each elected their own ministers and governed themselves. Thus, in the name of King James I, did the settlers "Covenant and combine ourselves together into a civil body politic, for our better ordering and preservation." The compact was put into practice when John Carver was confirmed as the colony's first governor.

The Mayflower Compact provided Plymouth with a simple constitution. The "General Court" of all freemen (nearly all adult men, excluding servants) met several times a year, elected the governor and his assistants, and passed laws for the colony. Voting directly in assembly or through representatives, asserted as fundamental right of Englishmen in the colony's 1636 legal code, also carried responsibilities. Freemen were expected to attend all General Court sessions, and those who did not faced heavy fines. Since the General Court was an assembly of citizens that was not in regular session, the governor dominated Plymouth's politics until the General Court was transformed into a representative assembly. Because the colony's expansion into several settlements made meetings of all freemen impractical, the 1638 General Court voted to allow freemen to assemble in individual towns and select deputies to attend General Court sessions in Plymouth town. All freemen were still expected to meet in Plymouth town for the June session, at which the governor and his assistants were chosen, but the General Court voted to allow colonywide proxy voting in 1652, finally doing away with colonywide meetings of all freemen. A now formal representative assembly holding regular sessions, the General Court stole the initiative from the governors. While the governor remained a powerful figure, charged with executing laws and having powers of arrest, the General Court claimed the sole right to tax, declare war, and frame legislation.

Voting rights became more restrictive as the colony grew and diversified. By 1670 property requirements excluded about 25 percent of adult men from voting, but the franchise still remained relatively open. Plymouth's governmental system was modified as the colony grew and the population changed, but the basic foundation established by the Mayflower Compact—that Plymouth would have self-government based on majority rule—remained intact. The colony never did receive legal recognition or a royal charter from England, apart from two patents issued by the Council for New England in 1621 and 1630. Failure to obtain a charter eventually led to Plymouth's annexation by much larger and more populous Massachusetts in 1691.

BIBLIOGRAPHY

Bradford, William. *History of Plymouth Plantation, 1620–1647.* Edited by Samuel Eliot Morrison. 2 vols. New York: Russell and Russell, 1968.

Cushing, John D., ed. *The Laws of the Pilgrims: A Facsimile Edition of The Book of the General Laws of the Inhabitants of the Jurisdiction of New Plymouth, 1672 and 1685.* Wilmington, Del.: Michael Glazer, 1977.

Langdon, George D. "The Franchise and Political Democracy in Plymouth Colony." *William and Mary Quarterly*, 3d ser., 20 (October 1963): 513–526.

———. *Pilgrim Colony: A History of New Plymouth, 1620–1691.* New Haven, Conn.: Yale University Press, 1966.

Shurtleff, Nathaniel B., and David Pulsifer, eds. *Records of the Colony of New Plymouth in New England.* 12 vols. 1855. Reprint, New York: AMS Press, 1968.

Aaron J. Palmer

See also **Assemblies, Colonial; Plymouth Colony;** *and vol. 9:* **The Mayflower Compact.**

MAYO FOUNDATION is a charitable, nonprofit corporation based in Rochester, Minnesota. Established in 1919, the foundation controls the Mayo Clinic and its associated institutions, furthering their missions of patient care, medical research, and education.

The Mayo Clinic evolved from the medical practice of William Worrall Mayo (1819–1911) and his two sons William J. Mayo (1861–1939) and Charles H. Mayo (1865–1939). In 1889 they joined with the Sisters of St. Francis to found St. Mary's Hospital, the first general hospital in southeastern Minnesota. Over the next two decades the Mayo brothers invited others to join their practice, developing an integrated medical team of clinicians, specialists, and laboratory workers. In 1915 they organized one of the world's first formal graduate programs for physicians, the Mayo Graduate School of Medicine, which by 2001 offered over one hundred specialties.

On 8 October 1919 the Mayo brothers turned over the clinic's name and assets to the Mayo Properties Association, which later changed its name to the Mayo Foundation. All net earnings from the practice were reserved for medical education and research. At the beginning of the twenty-first century all of Mayo's staff, including 2,500 physicians and over 35,000 allied health professionals, were salaried with no profit sharing.

The Mayo Foundation is governed by a thirty-member board of trustees composed of fourteen Mayo physicians and administrators and sixteen public members. The foundation controls the Mayo Clinic in Rochester, clinics in Jacksonville, Florida, and in Scottsdale, Arizona, four hospitals affiliated with the clinics, a retirement community, and the Mayo Health System in the upper Midwest. The foundation treats half a million patients annually. In addition, the foundation runs five medical educational schools, including the highly selective Mayo Medical School, which opened in 1972.

In 2001 the total assets of the Mayo Foundation were approximately $5 billion, including over $100 million in contributions from around 50,000 donors. Research expenditures total around $250 million annually, roughly half of which is funded through the foundation and the remaining through federal and other sources.

BIBLIOGRAPHY

Clapesattle, Helen. *The Doctors Mayo.* Minneapolis: University of Minnesota Press, 1941.

Mayo Foundation for Medical Education and Research. Home page at http://www.mayo.edu.

Nelson, Clark. *Mayo Roots: Profiling the Origins of the Mayo Clinic.* Rochester, Minn.: Mayo Foundation, 1990.

Fred W. Beuttler

See also **Medical Education; Medical Profession; Medical Research.**

MAYSVILLE VETO, the veto of a bill to allocate federal funds for a road from Maysville to Lexington in Kentucky, was cast by President Andrew Jackson on 27 May 1830. While significant Jacksonians in Congress favored the bill, Vice President Martin Van Buren argued for a veto, and Jackson ultimately agreed with him. In his veto message, which was a product of Van Buren's pen, Jackson repeated the constitutional arguments on which Van Buren and his Virginia allies had erected their Democratic Party in the 1820s. As Thomas Jefferson and James Madison had done before him, Jackson coupled his denial of the constitutionality of federal expenditures for "purely local" public works with a call for a constitutional amendment to legitimize such projects.

BIBLIOGRAPHY

Cole, Donald B. *The Presidency of Andrew Jackson.* Lawrence: University Press of Kansas, 1993.

K. R. Constantine Gutzman

See also **Constitution of the United States; Veto Power of the President.**

MAZZEI LETTER, a letter written by Thomas Jefferson to Phillip Mazzei on 24 April 1796, in which the former secretary of state offered a characteristically hyperbolic and Manichean appraisal of the state of American public affairs. Jefferson asserted that the ruling Federalist Party was dominated by corrupt men who intended to assimilate the U.S. government to the British government. (The recent Jay's Treaty, which he and other Republicans read as an ignominious surrender of just American claims to the British, had reinforced Jefferson's appraisal.) Within a short time of its receipt in Italy, the letter appeared in Italian translation in a Florentine paper, from whence it made its way into the French press and, soon enough, across the sea. In America, the letter's publication caused great controversy. Among its fruits was the final rupture of the friendship between Jefferson and President George Washington, who joined his fellow Federalists in seeing an insult to the president in Jefferson's reference to "men who were Samsons in the field & Solomons in the council, but who have had their heads shorn by the harlot England."

BIBLIOGRAPHY

Banning, Lance. *The Jeffersonian Persuasion: Evolution of a Party Ideology.* Ithaca, N.Y.: Cornell University Press, 1978.

Malone, Dumas. *Jefferson and the Ordeal of Liberty.* Volume 3 of *Jefferson and His Time.* Boston: Little, Brown, 1948–1981.

K. R. Constantine Gutzman

See also **Republicans, Jeffersonian.**

MEAT INSPECTION LAWS. In 1906, Upton Sinclair published *The Jungle,* a novel about unsanitary conditions in Chicago meat-packing plants and the social inequalities suffered by the laboring classes working there. While the social commentary was largely ignored, the public was outraged at the grisly descriptions of meat production, including how the packers treated diseased beef with kerosene to hide its foul smell before placing it on the market. Sinclair claimed that such "EMBALMED BEEF" had killed more American soldiers in the Spanish-American War than had died in battle.

The health horrors described in *The Jungle* cut the sale of meat products almost in half. The push for regulation thus came not only from the public, but also from some meat-packing companies that believed food quality regulation was necessary to restore public confidence in processed meat products. Prompted by such pressures, President Theodore Roosevelt ordered a secret investigation of Sinclair's charges. After less than three weeks in Chicago, Roosevelt's investigators substantiated Sinclair's claims. In response to these findings, Congress passed two important laws, the Pure Food and Drug Act of 1906, which regulated food and drug processing, and the Federal Meat Inspection Act (FMIA) of 1907, which focused on the meat industry.

FMIA, which remains in effect today, requires the inspection of all animals before slaughtering to prevent the commercial use of adulterated meat and meat products. The Act also requires the postmortem inspection of all carcasses and animal parts to determine their fitness

Meat Inspection. At the Hormel meat-packing plant in Austin, Minn., inspectors examine pork innards in this 1940s photograph by John Vachon. LIBRARY OF CONGRESS

for human consumption. The Act also includes provisions for the proper labeling of meat, and it imposes strict sanitation standards for slaughtering and packing plants.

FMIA was among the nation's first consumer protection measures, and it established a basis for broad government oversight. More than one thousand pages of the Code of Federal Regulations now govern animal inspection, processing, and commerce. The Food Safety and Inspection Service (FSIS), an agency within the U.S. Department of Agriculture, currently inspects and regulates all meat and poultry moving in interstate commerce, pursuant to FMIA.

The FSIS has been criticized as using obsolete and inflexible methods that cannot effectively identify, monitor, and control food-related illnesses. Almost a century after the passage of FMIA, more than 9,000 people were still dying each year in the United States due to food-related illnesses, and another 6.5 to 33 million people were still developing nonfatal food-borne sicknesses.

BIBLIOGRAPHY

Sinclair, Upton. *The Jungle.* New York: Doubleday, Page, 1906.

Young, James Harvey. *Pure Food: Securing the Federal Food and Drug Act of 1906.* Princeton, N.J.: Princeton University Press, 1989.

Kent Greenfield

See also **Chicago; Meatpacking.**

MEATPACKING began as a local business in the colonial era, but by the dawn of the twenty-first century it had become a huge industry. The first meatpacking business began in 1692, when John Pynchon of Springfield,

Massachusetts, began buying hogs and shipping the meat to Boston for the growing city population and the provisioning of ships. Colonial farmers at first marketed their surplus meat in coastal towns and in the West Indies, and later the growing cities and the plantations of the South provided additional outlets. Early meatpackers were given that name because they literally packed cuts of pork and beef into barrels with brine. Meatpacking in those days was essentially a seasonal industry; there was no mechanical refrigeration to aid in keeping the meat from spoiling. Even when salt treatment was used, operations were confined almost entirely to the winter months. The custom was to pack meat through the winter, pile the barrels on the ground outside, and then sell in the spring.

Packinghouses were originally concentrated in New England and on the western frontiers of the Atlantic states. The shift westward began in the nineteenth century with the development of the livestock industry in the Middle West. Settlers found that the new land grew corn abundantly, but that there was no way to sell the grain to the growing industrial centers of the East; shipment overland cost more than the grain was worth. Ohio settlers found the answer in feeding their corn to cattle that were driven over the Alleghenies to the seaboard, or by stuffing some fifteen bushels of corn into a pig and subsequently packing the pork into a barrel. Prior to 1825, most beef, pork, and mutton from the Middle West moved eastward on the hoof, since the era of canals and railroads and a major meatpacking industry was yet to come. Local butchers predominated in the meat business. Slaughter took place close to the ultimate consumers because of the impossibility of storing fresh meat or shipping it any considerable distance—except occasionally during the winter in the northern areas—though the introduction of ice allowed for curing in the summer months.

Commercial meatpacking came into existence around 1818 in Cincinnati, soon called "Porkopolis" because by 1850, it hosted 27 percent of meatpacking in the West. Chicago, Louisville, and Saint Louis soon became rivals. During the Civil War, Chicago reached first rank, largely because of favorable rail and water transportation facilities. Beef had come to equal pork in importance, and competition developed in Kansas City, Omaha, Sioux City, and Saint Paul, in particular. As the livestock population grew in the West and the human population increased in the East, refrigerated packing plants were built to bridge the meat gap from the farm to the table. In the 1870s, several large packing firms with headquarters at Chicago came to dominate the U.S. meatpacking industry, namely Armour and Company, Swift and Company, and Libby, McNeill and Libby. After the Civil War, the vast western rangelands became a new major center for beef cattle because of the advancing railroads. Until 1865, meat-canning establishments, which had originated in Massachusetts and Maine in 1815, were small and located in the East. Meat-canning got a considerable boost through the Civil War in providing for the army, and after

1868, P. D. Armour and others developed a canned corned beef and roast beef trade. Other companies packed ox and pork tongues and potted meats, chicken, rabbits, ham, and soups.

Numerous technical and transportation improvements pushed the development of meatpacking. After 1880, packers could use efficient railroad refrigerator cars to transport fresh meat from as far west as Omaha to New York City without spoilage. Improvements in refrigeration allowed the marketing of less salty ham and bacon, less heavily smoked meat, and glandular meats throughout the United States and year-round by 1900. Freezing later became a method for bulk storage of raw material for subsequent production of canned and dried items, as well as sausages, meat dishes, and soups. Efficient motor trucks, and the extension of hard-surfaced roads, facilitated the trucking of livestock. Other cost changes largely eliminated the locational advantage of large rail terminals, and slaughter became feasible at almost any location. The industry further profited by using an ever-increasing number of by-products, such as fertilizers, leather, wool, glue, and many pharmaceuticals, including hormones and sterols. Furthermore, meatpackers hired poor immigrants and African Americans, who had few other work opportunities, and paid them poorly to work in often brutal conditions; such labor practices boosted profits for the industry.

Meatpacking House. Workers at Swift and Company, Chicago, use large axes to split the backbones on hog carcasses, 1906. LIBRARY OF CONGRESS/© CORBIS

In 1906 Upton Sinclair's novel *The Jungle* focused attention on unsavory conditions in the packing plants and led to the federal Meat Inspection Act of 1906. *The Jungle* may have led to some reforms, but working conditions in meatpacking plants remained dangerous and often wretched, though they improved for a few decades. Employers squashed unionization efforts in 1919–1920, but in the 1930s, the United Packinghouse Workers of America formed to represent meatpacking workers. The union made great strides from the 1930s into the 1950s, surviving the political oppression that turned many unions rightward during the McCarthy period, and making efforts to break down racial segregation in plants. However, in the 1950s, conditions began to turn worse again for workers. On the one hand, meatpacking corporations began moving out of the great industrial centers; on the other, new firms arose that used labor-saving technology, reducing the need for workers. A 1986 strike at the Hormel plant in Austin, Minnesota, mobilized tens of thousands of supporters throughout the region, and garnered nationwide attention. However, without the backing of its national leadership, the local union that struck, P-9, could not withstand the combined efforts of the company's use of strikebreakers and the state governor's deployment of the National Guard. By the end of the twentieth century, meatpacking work was done mostly by an immigrant and impoverished workforce laboring in dirty, dangerous surroundings, as the decline of organized labor and the rise of government deregulation pushed the industry into a state not so different from the days of Sinclair's *The Jungle*.

BIBLIOGRAPHY

Halpern, Rick. *Down on the Killing Floor: Black and White Workers in Chicago's Packinghouses, 1904–1954.* Urbana: University of Illinois Press, 1997

Horowitz, Roger. *"Negro and White, Unite and Fight!" A Social History of Industrial Unionism in Meatpacking, 1930–90.* Urbana and Chicago: University of Illinois Press, 1997.

Georg Borgstrom / D. B.

See also **Food and Drug Administration; Labor; Pure Food and Drug Movement; Trade Unions; Work;** and vol. 9: **Conditions in Meatpacking Plants, 1906.**

MECHANICS' INSTITUTES. Along with lyceums, apprentices' libraries, and other organizations that emphasized self-improvement through education in science, mechanics' institutes grew out of the reform spirit of the early nineteenth century. Many institutes—including the New York Scientific and Mechanic Institution (1822) and others in Baltimore, Philadelphia, and Cincinnati—employed academics in their evening lecture programs. Other societies, the Boston Mechanics' Lyceum in particular, argued for a system in which artisans educated themselves. Still others stressed their LIBRARIES. Philadelphia's FRANKLIN INSTITUTE carried on all these activ-

ities as well as major programs in technical research and publication.

By midcentury, mechanics' institutes had lost much of their original mission—to provide low-cost technical education to the poor. Colleges took over the function of technical instruction, while evening lectures tended increasingly to be patronized by the middle classes, who wanted general talks on a miscellany of topics. In time, some institutes were absorbed into temperance societies, lyceums, museums, town libraries, new agencies for vocational training, or simply disappeared.

BIBLIOGRAPHY

Bode, Carl. *The American Lyceum: Town Meeting of the Mind.* New York: Oxford University Press, 1956; Carbondale: Southern Illinois University Press, 1968.

Royle, Edward. "Mechanics' Institutes and the Working Class, 1840–1860." *The Historical Journal*, 14 (June 1971): 305–321.

Sinclair, Bruce. *Philadelphia's Philosopher Mechanics: A History of the Franklin Institute, 1824–1865.* Baltimore: Johns Hopkins University Press, 1974.

Bruce Sinclair / A. R.

See also **Lyceum Movement.**

MECKLENBURG RESOLVES (MECKLENBURG DECLARATION OF INDEPENDENCE). *See* **Charlotte Town Resolves.**

MEDALS, MILITARY. *See* **Decorations, Military.**

MEDICAL EDUCATION. Pain, suffering, and premature death from disease have ravaged human beings from the beginning of recorded time. This harsh fact was as true for colonial America, where life expectancy as late as 1800 was only twenty-five years, as for every other known society. Yet the aspiration for health and the desire to explain the mysteries of disease have also characterized all known human societies. Thus, inhabitants of colonial America sought medical care from a variety of practitioners of folk, herbal, and Indian medicine. In addition, some members of the clergy, such as the Protestant New England clergyman Cotton Mather (1663–1728), incorporated the healing art in their services to the colonists.

In the eighteenth century, practitioners of "regular," or "allopathic," medicine began to become more commonplace. A small number of elite practitioners obtained medical degrees, primarily by studying medicine in Edinburgh, Leiden, or London. This mode of study was not economically feasible for more than a few. Of necessity, the apprenticeship tradition became the dominant system of medical training, with the typical preceptorial period lasting three years. Apprentice physicians would study medicine with a practicing physician, who would allow the apprentice the opportunity to participate in his practice in exchange for a fee and the performance of various menial chores.

In the early nineteenth century, the "proprietary" medical school became the dominant vehicle of medical instruction in America. In 1800, only four medical schools existed: the University of Pennsylvania (founded in 1765), King's College (1767), Harvard (1782), and Dartmouth (1797). Between 1810 and 1840, twenty-six new schools were established, and between 1840 and 1876, forty-seven more. In the late nineteenth century, dozens of additional schools sprouted. Originally, these schools were intended to be a supplement to the apprenticeship system. However, because they could more readily provide systematic teaching, by the middle of the nineteenth century they had superseded the apprenticeship as the principal pathway of medical education.

Though the first schools were created with lofty ambitions, the quality of instruction at the proprietary schools rapidly deteriorated, even based on the standards of the day. Entrance requirements were nonexistent other than the ability to pay the fees. Disciplinary problems arising from outrageous student behavior were commonplace. The standard course of instruction in the mid-nineteenth century consisted of two four-month terms of lectures during the winter, with the second term identical to the first. The curriculum generally consisted of seven courses: anatomy; physiology and pathology; materia medica, therapeutics, and pharmacy; chemistry and medical jurisprudence; theory and practice of medicine; principles and practice of surgery; and obstetrics and the diseases of women and children. Instruction was wholly didactic: seven or eight hours of lectures a day, supplemented by textbook reading. Laboratory work was sparse, and even in the clinical subjects, no opportunity to work with patients was provided. Examinations were brief and superficial; virtually the only requirement for graduation was the ability to pay the fees. Students who wished a rigorous MEDICAL EDUCATION had to supplement what they learned in medical school in other ways, such as through enrollment at non-degree-granting extramural private schools, study in Europe, or work in hospitals as "house pupils."

The mid-nineteenth-century proprietary schools, such as Bennett Medical College and Jenner Medical College in Chicago, were independent institutions. University or hospital affiliations, in the few cases in which they existed, were nominal. The faculties were small, typically consisting of six or eight professors. The professors owned the schools and operated them for profit. A commercial spirit thus pervaded the schools, for the faculty shared the spoils of what was left of student fees after expenses. The mark of a good medical school, like that of any business, was considered its profitability. Since an amphitheater was virtually the only requirement to operate a medical school, physical facilities were meager. The second floor above

the corner drugstore would suffice; a school that had a building of its own was considered amply endowed.

The Creation of the Modern Medical School

While American medical education was floundering in the mid-1800s, the reform of the system was already beginning. At the root of the transformation was a series of underlying events: the revolution in experimental medicine that was proceeding in Europe; the existence of a cadre of American doctors traveling to Europe (particularly Germany) to learn laboratory methods; the emergence of the modern university in America; the development of a system of mass public education to provide qualified students for the university; and the cultivation of a habit of philanthropy among some very rich industrialists. Together, these developments provided the infrastructure for a new system of medical education soon to appear.

The creation of America's current system of medical education occurred in two overlapping stages. In the first stage, which began in the middle of the nineteenth century, a revolution in ideas occurred concerning the purpose and methods of medical education. After the Civil War, medical educators began rejecting traditional notions that medical education should inculcate facts through rote memorization. Rather, the new objective of medical education was to produce problem-solvers and critical thinkers who knew how to find out and evaluate information for themselves. To do so, medical educators deemphasized the traditional didactic teaching methods of lectures and textbooks and began speaking of the importance of self-education and learning by doing. Through laboratory work and clinical clerkships, students were to be active participants in their learning, not passive observers as before. A generation before John Dewey, medical educators were espousing the ideas of what later came to be called "progressive education."

At the same time, a revolution occurred in the institutional mission of medical schools. The view emerged that the modern medical school should not only engage in the highest level of teaching but also should be committed to the discovery of new knowledge through research. This meant that medical schools could no longer remain freestanding institutions. Rather, they had to become integral parts of universities and hire scientifically trained, full-time faculty who, like all university professors, were researchers as well as teachers.

In the early 1870s, the first lasting reforms occurred, as Harvard, Pennsylvania, and Michigan extended their course of study to three years, added new scientific subjects to the curriculum, required laboratory work of each student, and began hiring full-time medical scientists to the faculty. In the late 1870s, the plans for the new Johns Hopkins Medical School were announced, though for financial reasons the opening was delayed until 1893. When the school finally did open, it immediately became the model by which all other medical schools were measured,

281

much as the JOHNS HOPKINS UNIVERSITY in 1876 had become the model for the modern American research university. A college degree was required for admission, a four-year curriculum with nine-month terms was adopted, classes were small, students were frequently examined, the laboratory and clinical clerkship were the primary teaching devices, and a brilliant full-time faculty made MEDICAL RESEARCH as well as medical education part of its mission. In the 1880s and 1890s, schools across the country started to emulate the pioneering schools, and a campaign to reform American medical education began. By the turn of the century, the university medical school had become the acknowledged ideal, and proprietary schools were already closing for lack of students.

Nevertheless, ideas alone were insufficient to create the modern medical school. The new teaching methods were extremely costly to implement, and hospitals had to be persuaded to join medical schools in the work of medical education. Thus, an institutional as well as an intellectual revolution was needed. Between 1885 and 1925 this revolution occurred. Large sums of money were raised, new laboratories were constructed, an army of full-time faculty was assembled, and clinical facilities were acquired. Medical schools, which had existed autonomously during the proprietary era, became closely affiliated with universities and teaching hospitals.

No individual contributed more dramatically to the institution-building process than Abraham Flexner (1886–1959), an educator from Louisville who had joined the staff of the Carnegie Foundation for the Advancement of Teaching. In 1910, Flexner published a muckraking report, *Medical Education in the United States and Canada*. In this book, he described the ideal conditions of medical education, as exemplified by the Johns Hopkins Medical School, and the deficient conditions that still existed at most medical schools. Flexner made no intellectual contribution to the discussion of how physicians should be taught, for he adopted the ideas that had developed within the medical faculties during the 1870s and 1880s. However, this report made the reform of medical education a cause célèbre, transforming what previously had been a private matter within the profession into a broad social movement similar to other reform movements in Progressive Era America. The public responded by opening its pocketbook, state and municipal taxes were used to fund medical education, private philanthropists, George Eastman and Robert Brookings among them, and philanthropic organizations all contributed significant sums to support medical education. In the two decades that followed the public provided the money and clinical facilities that had long eluded medical schools. In addition, an outraged public, scandalized by Flexner's acerbic depiction of the proprietary schools still in existence, brought a sudden end to the proprietary era through the enactment of state licensing laws, which mandated that medical schools operated for profit would not be accredited.

Graduate Medical Education

Through World War I, medical education focused almost exclusively on "undergraduate" medical education—the years of study at medical school leading to the M.D. degree. At a time when the great majority of medical school graduates entered general practice, the four years of medical school were considered an adequate preparation for the practice of medicine. Abraham Flexner's 1910 report did not even mention internship or other hospital training for medical graduates.

By World War I, however, medical knowledge, techniques, and practices had grown enormously. There was too much to teach, even in a four-year course. Accordingly, a period of hospital education following graduation—the "internship"—became standard for every physician. By the mid-1920s the internship had become required of all U.S. medical graduates.

The modern internship had its origins in the informal system of hospital appointments that dated to the early nineteenth century. Until the end of the century, such positions were scarce, available only to a tiny handful of graduates. Though such positions allowed the opportunity to live and work in a hospital for a year or two, they were saddled with considerable education deficiencies. Interns had limited clinical responsibilities, and the positions involved a considerable amount of nonmedical chores like maintaining the hospital laboratories. During the first two decades of the twentieth century, the internship was transformed into a true educational experience. Internship now provided a full schedule of conferences, seminars, rounds, and lectures as well as the opportunity to participate actively in patient management.

Internships came in three forms. The most popular was the so-called "rotating" internship, in which interns rotated among all the clinical areas. Some hospitals, particularly those associated with medical schools, offered "straight" internships in medicine or surgery, in which interns spent the entire time in that field. The third type was the "mixed" internship, a cross between the rotating and straight internship. Mixed internships provided more time in medicine and surgery and less in the various specialties than rotating internships. Typically, internships lasted one year, though some were as long as three years. All forms of internship provided a rounding-out clinical experience that proved invaluable as a preparation for general medical practice.

Medical education in the early twentieth century faced another challenge: meeting the needs of individuals who desired to practice a clinical specialty (such as ophthalmology, pediatrics, or surgery) or to pursue a career in medical research. To this end the "residency"—a several-year hospital experience following internship—became the accepted vehicle.

The modern residency was introduced to America at the opening of the Johns Hopkins Hospital in 1889. Based upon the system of "house assistants" in the medical clinics of German universities, the Hopkins residency was designed to be an academic experience for mature scholars. During World War I, the Hopkins residency system began to spread to other institutions, much as the Hopkins system of undergraduate medical education had spread to other medical schools the generation before. By the 1930s, the residency had become the sole route to specialty training. In doing so, it displaced a variety of informal, educationally unsound paths to specialty practice that had preceded it, such as taking a short course in a medical specialty at a for-profit graduate medical school or apprenticing oneself to a senior physician already recognized as a specialist.

Residency training before World War II had three essential characteristics. First, unlike internship, which was required of all medical school graduates before they could receive a license to practice medicine, residency positions were reserved for the elite. Only one-third of graduates were permitted to enter residency programs following the completion of an internship, and only about one-quarter of first-year residents ultimately completed the entire program. Second, the defining educational feature of residency was the assumption of responsibility by residents for patient management. Residents evaluated patients themselves, made their own decisions about diagnosis and therapy, and performed their own procedures and treatments. They were supervised by—and accountable to—attending physicians, but they were allowed considerable clinical independence. This was felt to be the best way for learners to be transformed into mature physicians. Lastly, the residency experience at this time emphasized scholarship and inquiry as much as clinical training. The residency system assumed many characteristics of a graduate school within the hospital, and residents were carefully trained in clinical research. Residency came to be recognized as the breeding ground for the next generation of clinical investigators and medical scholars.

Evolution and Growth

Scientific knowledge is continually growing. In addition, the diseases facing a population are constantly changing, as are medical practices, cultural mores, and the health care delivery system. Thus, of necessity, medical education is always evolving to reflect changing scientific and social circumstances.

After World War II, medical educators continued to emphasize the importance of "active learning" and the cultivation of problem-solving skills. However, the postwar period witnessed several important curricular innovations: the development of an organ-based curriculum by Western Reserve (1950s); the invention of "problem-based" learning by McMaster (1970s); the introduction of a primary care curriculum by New Mexico (1980s); and the establishment of the "New Pathway" program at Harvard Medical School (1980s). In addition, all medical schools reduced the amount of required course work, increased the opportunity for electives, and began to pro-

vide early clinical experiences during the first and second years of medical school.

Reflecting changes in the broader society, medical schools also became more representative of the diverse population they served. Religious quotas against Jewish and Catholic students, established at many medical schools in the early 1920s, disappeared in the 1950s following the revelation of Nazi atrocities and changes in civil rights laws. The admission of African American students, though still short of target levels, roughly tripled from 2.7 percent of enrolled medical students in the 1960s to around 8 percent in the 1990s. Greater success was achieved in the enrollment of women, whose numbers increased from roughly 7 percent of students in the 1960s to about 50 percent in the 1990s.

Graduate medical education also changed significantly following World War II. In the late 1940s and 1950s, residency training became "democratized"—that is, it became available to all medical graduates, not merely the academic elite as before. Between 1940 and 1970, the number of residency positions at U.S. hospitals increased from 5,796 to 46,258. Thus, the number of residents seeking specialty training soared. At the same time, the academic component of residency training diminished. Residency became an exclusively clinical training ground rather than a preparation point for clinical research as before. Most physicians desiring research training now had to acquire that through Ph.D. programs or postgraduate research fellowships.

In addition, the stresses of residency training also increased substantially after Word War II. In the 1960s, intensive care units were introduced, as were new, life-sustaining technologies like ventilators and dialysis machines. Hospitalized patients tended to be much sicker than before, resulting in much more work. In the 1980s, following the death of nineteen-year-old Libby Zion at the New York Hospital, the public began to demand shorter hours and greater supervision of house officers. Ironically, after extensive investigation, Libby Zion's death appeared not to be the result of poor care provided by fatigued or unsupervised house officers. Nevertheless, the movement to regulate house staff hours gained strength.

As medical education was changing, it also grew longer. In the 1960s and 1970s, in response to the public's demand for more doctors, existing medical schools expanded their class size, and forty new medical schools were established. Between 1960 and 1980, the number of students entering U.S. medical schools increased from 8,298 to 17,320. Following World War II, the research mission of medical schools expanded enormously, mainly because of the infusion of huge amounts of research funding from the NATIONAL INSTITUTES OF HEALTH. The number of full-time faculty at U.S. medical schools grew from 3,500 in 1945 to 17,000 in 1965. After 1965, medical schools grew larger still, primarily because of the passage of Medicare and Medicaid legislation that year and the resultant explosion in demands on the schools to provide clinical care. By 1990, the number of clinical faculty at U.S. medical schools had grown to around 85,000, with most of the increase occurring in the clinical departments. By that time one-half of a typical medical school's income came from the practice of medicine by the full-time faculty. By the 1990s, the "academic health center"—the amalgam of a medical school with its teaching hospitals—had become an extremely large and complex organization with many responsibilities besides education and research. By the late 1990s, a typical academic health center could easily have a budget of $1.5 billion or more and be the largest employer in its community.

The Challenge of Managed Care

Though medical schools prospered and served the public well during the twentieth century, a cautionary note appeared at the end of the century. Academic health centers had grown strong and wealthy, but they had become dependent for their income on the policies of the third-party payers (insurance companies and government agencies) that paid the bills. During the managed care era of the 1990s, the parsimonious payments of many third-party payers began causing academic health centers considerable financial distress. For instance, in 2000 the University of Pennsylvania Health System suffered a $200 million operating loss. (All hospitals were threatened financially by managed care, but teaching centers, because of their higher costs, were particularly vulnerable.) In addition, the emphasis of managed care organizations on increasing the "throughput" of patients—seeing as many patients as possible, as quickly as possible—eroded the quality of educational programs. Students and residents no longer had as much time to learn by doing or to study their patients in depth. Hopefully, the desire of the profession and public to maintain quality in education and patient care will allow these difficulties to be surmounted in the years ahead.

BIBLIOGRAPHY

Bonner, Thomas N. *American Doctors and German Universities: A Chapter in International Intellectual Relations, 1870–1914.* Lincoln: University of Nebraska Press, 1963.

Fleming, Donald. *William H. Welch and the Rise of Modern Medicine.* Boston: Little, Brown, 1954.

Ludmerer, Kenneth M. *Learning to Heal: The Development of American Medical Education.* New York: Basic Books, 1985.

———. *Time to Heal: American Medical Education from the Turn of the Century to the Era of Managed Care.* New York: Oxford University Press, 1999.

Norwood, William F. *Medical Education in the United States before the Civil War.* New York: Arno, 1971.

Kenneth M. Ludmerer

MEDICAL INSURANCE. *See* **Health Insurance.**

MEDICAL PROFESSION. Before the Civil War, physicians directly competed for access to patients within a weak marketplace. The income from practice was limited, and physicians struggled to maintain control over the provision of medical services. Many states had licensing laws, but these were rarely enforced and did little to limit the activities of lay and sectarian practitioners. The care the physician provided therefore represented only one of a variety of options available to the sick in early America, including regular recourse to self-treatment with home medical guides or folk remedies. The profession lacked the cultural authority and political clout to stop patients from seeking out these alternatives, and the little authority they did have came to be further eroded as the populist spirit of the Jackson Era ushered in distrust for all forms of orthodox medical expertise.

The conflict between the interests of the patient and those of the profession culminated in the 1830s with the repeal of medical licensing in a number of states. This shift was coupled with the growth of a variety of populist medical movements—notably Thomsonianism—which provided botanical alternatives to the mercurial compounds and bleeding many doctors relied upon. The development of professional control was also impeded by an overproduction of doctors and a lack of effective occupational oversight. The proliferation of proprietary medical schools and the corresponding increase in the number of graduates intensified competition during the middle years of the nineteenth century. No national standards existed governing the educational quality these schools provided, and there was significant variation in the length of training and expectations of cognitive competence. As a result, the profession lacked a shared intellectual base or a sense of proper conduct, impeding the growth of professional associations, which might have provided medical practice with oversight and common identity.

This situation began to change with the founding of the AMERICAN MEDICAL ASSOCIATION (AMA) in 1847. The AMA initially had little power to influence the behavior of its small number of members. By 1910, however, overall membership had swelled to 50 percent of all practicing doctors, making it by far the largest medical society in the nation and providing it with an adequate working budget. The period from 1870 to 1900 also saw a renewed concern with medical licensing, and by 1901, twenty-five states required doctors to present a diploma and pass an independent exam in order to practice. Medical schools began to standardize their curricula and introduce more stringent requirements, limiting the number of new graduates. This led to the closure of many proprietary medical schools, which were unable to cover the costs of the new standards. Although these events strengthened the social and political position of the profession, the authority of orthodox medicine remained constrained by the persistence of alternative sources of treatment until the turn of the twentieth century. This threat decreased gradually between 1880 and 1900, as homeopathic and eclectic med-

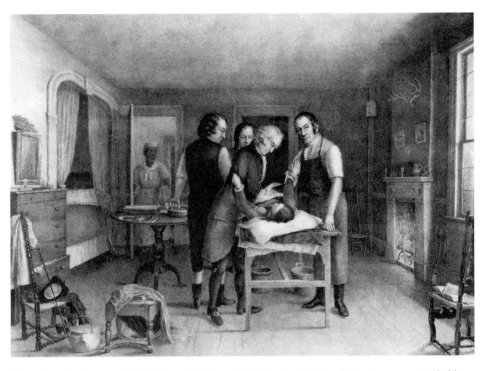

First Ovarian Surgery. This lithograph shows Dr. Ephraim McDowell *(in a brown coat)*, aided by assistants, removing a twenty-two-pound tumor in the first known operation of this kind, in December 1809 in Danville, Ky. GRANGER COLLECTION, LTD.

icine gained some acceptance among regular members or the profession. The incorporation of these practitioners into the AMA allowed the association to regulate their education and practice, transforming them from excluded opponents into active consultants. The growing strength of regular medicine was also fostered by changes to the association's organizational structure in 1901, making local membership a prerequisite for national membership. The new organization promoted local involvement with the association, and improved collegiality of doctors working in close proximity. As association membership increased, the AMA progressively came to represent and reflect the interests of the profession as a whole, setting standards for practice and laying down professional guidelines governing the relations between physicians. It also increasingly came to control access to the medical technologies necessary for treatment, since membership was often a prerequisite for using hospital facilities.

The fee-for-service model of care, which arose in the wake of AMA reorganization, placed significant emphasis on the autonomy of the individual practitioner. Patients were free to choose any doctor they wished and were directly billed for the services they received. Doctors were generally self-employed, allowing them to maintain personal control over the treatment and services they provided. This approach to medical care prevailed throughout the first half of the twentieth century, and represents the height of professional control. Supported by successes

in surgical practice and public health, which enhanced the cultural authority of the profession, fee-for-service allowed doctors to monopolize access to patients and limit their ability to seek out alternatives. The control doctors wielded was reflected in improvements in the average annual income, which jumped from between $750 and $1,500 in 1900 to $6,000 in 1928.

While fee-for-service benefited doctors financially, it led to significant increases in the overall cost of medical care. Public concern over these costs grew throughout the 1950s and 1960s, culminating in the passage of Medicare in 1965. This legislation resulted in increased profits for health care providers, thereby making medical management attractive to investors and giving rise to large-scale corporate involvement in medicine. In order to limit medical expenditures and thereby increase profits, many corporations have implemented systems of managed care, in which doctors receive a fee directly from the corporation with which they are contracted. Oversight is high, and most doctors are limited in the number and type of procedures they may perform, and in the drugs they may prescribe. The introduction of cost management controls has meant decreased economic independence for many doctors, and while the cultural authority of the profession remains strong, its autonomy in diagnosis and treatment has been eroded as a result of corporate involvement.

The professionalization that took place following the Civil War resulted in greater internal control over edu-

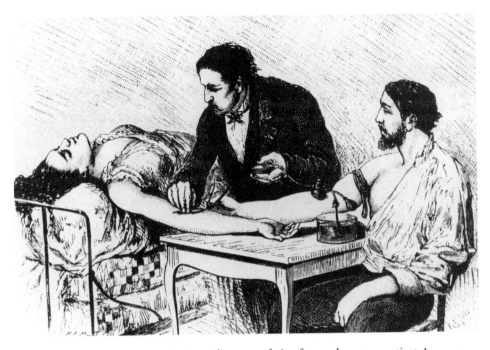

Blood Transfusion. A drawing showing a direct transfusion from a donor to a patient. LIBRARY OF CONGRESS

cation and occupational values, the development of a set of shared financial and political interests, and more extensive power to limit patient access to alternative sources of treatment. While professionalization has often been seen as an artificial control upon the free functioning of the medical marketplace, the changes it brought about resulted in the effective regulation of treatment and pharmaceuticals, and greatly enhanced the social influence of medical practice in America.

BIBLIOGRAPHY

Freidson, Eliot. *Profession of Medicine: A Study in the Sociology of Applied Knowledge.* New York: Dodd, Mead, 1972.

Starr, Paul. *The Social Transformation of American Medicine.* New York: Basic Books, 1982.

Aaron Mauck

See also **Health Care; Health Insurance; Medical Societies; Medicare and Medicaid; Medicine, Alternative; Medicine and Surgery.**

MEDICAL RESEARCH in the United States has been very dependent on research standards from overseas as well as American social, economic, and political issues. In the eighteenth century American medicine inherited two traditions: an ancient one of clinical observation, and a more recent one, associated with experimental science, in which conditions were modified and observations made in order to gain insights into possible causes. Most medical research was supported and undertaken by individuals.

In seventeenth century London and Paris the profession saw the introduction of scientific organizations for the presentation and discussion of research and journals for the publication of results. In America, Benjamin Franklin was a leader in founding the American Philosophical Society (1743), which, at least in part, served a similar purpose.

In 1818 the Army Medical Department was established along with the permanent position of Surgeon General of the Army. Joseph Lovell, the first to occupy the position, believed that physicians should increase medical knowledge. He required regular weather and disease incidence reports by all army physicians in an effort to correlate disease with climate, an ancient epidemiological observation. In the 1820s he encouraged the investigations of Dr. William Beaumont, who was studying the process of digestion by direct observation through a patient's fistula. Beaumont's book, *Experiments and observations on the gastric juice and the physiology of digestion* (1833), is a classic of physiology and was the first American contribution to basic medical research to be seriously noted by the European medical establishment.

During the antebellum period there were several abortive attempts to organize systematic medical research societies on the East Coast. Some physicians accumulated large pathology collections, which became research and teaching tools, but most did not have a sustained interest in research; it was something done while awaiting the development of practice. Only the Army had an institutional interest, which was given form during the Civil War with the creation of the Army Medical Museum (later the Armed Forces Institute of Pathology).

After the war, cities and states developed public health agencies, many of which funded laboratories where research was undertaken. Hospitals and reforming university medical schools also capitalized laboratories, some of which were used episodically for research in addition to their primary purposes of patient care, diagnostic service, and teaching. The single most important change was the conversion of the antebellum college into a research university. Although there were precursors, Johns Hopkins University in Baltimore is considered the oldest university in America because it was the first to adopt the German university ideal of creating new knowledge in addition to teaching what was known. By the end of the century there were research facilities in many American cities.

The changes in medical science at the end of the nineteenth century introduced new ambiguities in the medical research process, and scientists looked for ways to limit researcher bias. The idea of comparison and control was venerable, but it was applied erratically. In medical bacteriology Robert Koch provided what many considered the "gold standard" of animal modeling, but the problem of identifying animal disease was significant. Organizations for the discussion of medical research and refereed journals for publication became increasingly important to acceptance of the work.

Research scientists needed places to work, and philanthropists established them. The Rockefeller Institute for Medical Research (1901) was probably the most influential of a variety of similar private medical research institutes around the country. By 1930 there were over thirty foundations supporting medical research in one way or another.

A secondary source of research support was special-interest funding. The largest source of such funding was industry. Several corporations had internal laboratories by the 1920s, and drug companies also made grants and contracts with university-based researchers. The use of university-based researchers gave some physicians pause because of the presumed ethical conflicts generated by corporate research. There was considerable division of opinion on the ethics of medical patents: some schools refused to permit patenting of research done in their laboratories. The American Medical Association was opposed to pharmaceutical support of therapeutic research, believing such work inherently tainted.

Therapeutics quickly emerged as the most confusing area for the establishment of research standards. A medieval French saying highlights the task of the medical profession and captures the essence of the therapeutic research problem: *Guerir quelquefois, soulager souvent, consoler toujours* ("To cure sometimes, to relieve often, and to care always"). If the natural history of the disease is agreed upon and interrupted, then the patient might be judged

cured, but the natural history of many diseases was difficult to agree upon. Relief was a very difficult concept, confounded by the placebo effect: simply going to the doctor often made a patient feel better. The recognition that innovators sometimes interpreted things too optimistically led to a quest for repeatable results, but bias of various sorts, including spontaneous remissions, might obscure the reports of individual workers.

Confusion in therapeutic research led early-twentieth-century researchers into a variety of areas where their successors would wish they had not gone. The promise of pardons for prisoners led some to agree to serve as research subjects, and orphans and the insane were also exploited, all populations that provided large groups of easy-to-study patients who would later be found to be incapable of giving truly informed consent. After reports of Nazi atrocities committed in the name of "medical research" appeared in the late 1940s, Henry Beecher of Harvard University led a campaign to increase sensitivity to human use, and standards of conduct began to be part of all research protocols.

The role of science and technology during World War II led President Roosevelt to charter a study of the appropriate role of the federal government in scientific research in the coming postwar era. The U.S. Public Health Service, like other large public health agencies, had done some research since the nineteenth century. Its National Institutes of Health organized the Division of Research Grants (later renamed the Center for Scientific Review) to send federal research dollars to university medical research programs.

Bradford Hill, a British biostatistician, urged a new approach in evaluating therapy—the double-blinded clinical trial. The idea included the random assignment of patients to new-therapy and non-new-therapy groups without their knowing to which group they were assigned—this was the first blind. It also prevented observer bias by not letting the attending physician know to which therapeutic group the patient belonged—this was the second blind. Patients were evaluated and at the end of the trial the codes were read and the members of each group identified. Other methodological studies found a variety of biases in the collection and interpretation of data. By the 1990s these techniques were brought together under the rubric of "evidence-based medicine."

The traditional research approaches continued to pay dividends. Especially important was the progress in immunology. One of the greatest successes was the development of the polio vaccine in the 1950s, which was supported in large part by the National Foundation for Infantile Paralysis, a single-disease foundation. Providing seed funds and other grants, the special-interest foundations played an increasing role in medical research. Even more important, the special-interest foundations served as interest groups encouraging public research funding and charitable donations to combat specific problems.

From a largely derivative, independent activity of interested amateurs, medical research in the United States has become a multibillion-dollar professional activity, attracting worldwide attention and raising significant social issues. With public funding has come political and social issues ranging from the ethics of human experimentation, animal care and use, and fetal tissue research to fears of negative eugenics raised by the possibility of genomic modifications. Despite the difficulties, its promise of human relief supports the continued growth and development of medical research.

BIBLIOGRAPHY

Harvey, A. McGehee. *Science at the Bedside: Clinical Research in American Medicine 1905–1945*. Baltimore: Johns Hopkins University Press, 1981.

Lederer, Susan E. *Subjected to Science: Human Experimentation in America before the Second World War*. Baltimore: Johns Hopkins University Press, 1995.

Marks, Harry M. *The Progress of Experiment: Science and Therapeutic Reform in the United States, 1900–1990*. Cambridge: Cambridge University Press, 1997.

Shryock, Richard Harrison. *American Medical Research, Past and Present*. New York: Arno, 1980.

Strickland, Stephen P. *Politics, Science, and Dread Disease: A Short History of United States Medical Research Policy*. Cambridge, Mass.: Harvard University Press, 1972.

Dale C. Smith

See also **Human Genome Project; Laboratories; Microbiology; Molecular Biology.**

MEDICAL SOCIETIES. During the eighteenth and nineteenth centuries, the American medical profession emerged in a distinct fashion from its European counterparts. Political autonomy was in its infancy in the newly liberated colonies, and American wariness of centralized authorities discouraged the involvement of Congress and state legislatures in the regulation of the profession. Few universities had yet been established on American soil, leaving medical education to occur in a haphazard fashion. Proprietary schools offering medical degrees for fees thrived in this unregulated environment, despite the fact that the training they provided was of a highly questionable nature. In addition, the entrepreneurial spirit of the young country encouraged innovation, and free market forces drove the development of diverse forms of health care practices. Practitioners with varying levels of knowledge and skill therefore competed with each other to treat the public.

The establishment of medical societies provided one means by which physicians could separate themselves from the variety of health practitioners and be among like-minded and equally qualified colleagues. Because the effects of free-market competition were most intense at the local community level, local societies were the first to form. Many local societies adopted the name of their state, and the majority of their members came from nearby communities. The New Jersey Medical Society, composed of physicians from Essex and Middlesex Counties, was the first to form in 1766 and was the only colonial medical society to survive the Revolution. Boston followed in 1780, quickly expanding to the Massachusetts Medical Society (1781) as additional physicians from nearby communities sought membership. The College of Physicians formed in Philadelphia (1787) and the physicians of Charleston formed the Medical Society of South Carolina in 1789.

By the mid-nineteenth century, due to competition from the irregular and homeopathic physicians, it was becoming necessary for regular physicians to organize on a national basis. In 1847, the AMERICAN MEDICAL ASSOCIATION (AMA) was established as the first national association of practicing physicians. Its primary mission was to implement standards for physicians through a national reform of medical education. By 1901, the AMA reorganized to include a House of Delegates that included voting representatives from all state societies. In order to be a member of the AMA, a physician had to belong to the state medical society. Since county and state societies banned black physicians from becoming members until well into the twentieth century, these physicians were effectively barred from membership in the AMA as well. The first black physician delegate did not enter the AMA House of Delegates until 1949. In the late nineteenth century, therefore, black physicians formed their own medical societies at the local levels, consolidating to the National Medical Association in 1895. Recognizing the growing power of organized medicine in shaping medical policy for the country, the mission of the National Medical Society was to counter the discriminatory policies toward black physicians and black patients.

As scientific medicine began to produce more specialized knowledge in the nineteenth and twentieth centuries, medical specialists began to form their own groups. The goal of these societies was generally the advancement of specialized medical knowledge. These specialty societies include: the American Academy of Ophthalmology (1896), American Society of Anesthesiologists (1905), American Society of Pediatrics (1930), American Society for Reproductive Medicine (1944), American College of Cardiology (1949), and the Society of Nuclear Medicine (1954). By the end of the twentieth century, nearly 3,000 medical societies existed in the United States, with physicians participating in city, county, state, and national medical societies.

BIBLIOGRAPHY

Duffy, John. *From Humors to Medical Science: A History of American Medicine*. Chicago: University of Illinois Press, 1993.

Rothstein, William G. *American Physicians in the 19th Century: From Sects to Science*. Baltimore: Johns Hopkins University Press, 1992.

Starr, Paul. *The Social Transformation of American Medicine.* New York: Basic Books, 1982.

Karen E. Geraghty

See also **Medical Profession.**

MEDICARE AND MEDICAID. In most industrialized countries virtually everyone receives governmentally insured HEALTH CARE. The uniquely expensive U.S. medical system, however, consigns most citizens to private HEALTH INSURANCE or to none at all. Medicare (federal government health insurance covering the costs of private medical care for seniors and, after 1972, the long-term disabled) and Medicaid (means-tested coverage for the medical expenses of the poor, jointly paid for by federal and state governments) stand as notable exceptions, accounting for one of every three dollars spent on health care in the 1990s.

Since the 1910s major government reform of the U.S. health care system has often seemed just around the corner. Despite overwhelming public support, it has usually foundered on pressures from the medical establishment; claims that these programs were socialist vehicles that would confer undeserved benefits on many who could be perfectly well served by hospital charity wards, private health insurance, and the private market; and predictions of burdensome, unsustainable expense along with an impersonal bureaucracy that would undermine family responsibility and the sacred doctor-patient relationship. President Franklin D. Roosevelt thus omitted health insurance from his social security proposals in the 1930s. President Harry S. Truman's proposed National Health Act in 1945 for compulsory medical expense insurance succumbed to conservative partisanship and an attack from the arch enemy of government health care activism, the American Medical Association (AMA), the medical profession's well-funded organizational center.

With the vast expansion of private health insurance, particularly union-negotiated medical plans, in the 1940s, government plans seemed doomed, but in the 1950s key officials in the Social Security Administration, a group commonly at the core of U.S. welfare state expansion, shifted strategy. To make government health insurance more politically marketable, they proposed that it be confined to seniors and tied to the hugely popular old age insurance social security program. After all, older Americans, who had to stretch far smaller than average incomes to cover far greater than average medical needs, could scarcely be cast as unworthy welfare cheats. The private health care market for the elderly had clearly fallen short; almost half of them in 1965 possessed no health insurance at all.

By the late 1950s government health insurance for seniors was backed by organized labor and many Democrats, including the candidate and future president John F. Kennedy, who recognized Medicare as a popular mo-bilizing campaign issue. Kennedy never was able to push the program through either house of Congress, and even the clear commitment and legendary legislative skills of his successor Lyndon B. Johnson at first could only secure Senate passage. In 1965, however, Kennedy's martyred legacy plus a strong economy and the overwhelming Democratic congressional majority elected on the coattails of Johnson's 1964 landslide combined to pass by partisan votes the Social Security Amendments of 1965, which established both Medicaid and Medicare as part of Johnson's triumphant Great Society. To honor former president Truman, Johnson signed the bill at the Truman Library in Independence, Missouri, on 30 July 1965.

Medicaid

Medicaid's enactment proved less of a legislative struggle than Medicare's. Medical interests saw some virtue in the government picking up the tab for hospital or doctor bills of "charity cases," and confining government-funded health care to the poor was a common fallback position for opponents of more wide-ranging plans. As early as 1950, states had been allowed to make payments under federally subsidized welfare programs directly to hospitals, nursing homes, and doctors. An amendment to the Social Security Act in 1960 (the Kerr-Mills program) beefed up these so-called "vendor payments" for the elderly poor while adding coverage of the "medically indigent" elderly, whose health care expenses would otherwise leave them impoverished. In 1965 a new medical assistance program, administered by states but with federal matching grants funding 50 to 83 percent of expenditures, extended this coverage of medical costs from the elderly poor to low-income people of all ages.

This Medicaid program had a marked impact. By 2001 it paid for a third of all births and almost two-thirds of all nursing home patients, and it covered one-fifth of American children. It allowed the poor to receive much more care from doctors and hospitals (now desegregated, thanks in part to the financial leverage provided by Medicare and Medicaid) than previously, because the poor had often postponed treatment until they required emergency-room care. While two-thirds of its recipients by the 1990s were children and nonelderly low-income women, Medicaid served as a safety net for the American medical system, assisting in coverage ranging from the elderly poor's Medicare premiums and copayments to prescription drugs to long-term institutional services for the developmentally disabled and AIDS patients. It carried the stigma, however, of welfare, and wide disparities among state programs assured that many who needed medical treatment would receive inadequate coverage or none at all.

Medicare

Medicare, by contrast, was a federally administered, contributory, social insurance program, provided to Americans, rich and poor alike, aged sixty-five and over as a right they had purportedly earned through the earmarked social security hospital insurance taxes paid by their employers and themselves over their working lives. The AMA and other Medicare opponents sought to limit the government's role by proposing a last-ditch alternative of government-subsidized voluntary private insurance for needy seniors. This "eldercare" plan, they noted, would cover a wider range of medical services, including doctor bills, than the original Medicare bill. The rural Arkansas Democrat Wilbur Mills, the powerful and previously obstructive chair of the House Ways and Means Committee, cannily adapted this alternative into a new Part B of Medicare. Thus Medicare Part A, financed by payroll taxes on employers and employees, reimbursed recipients for ninety days of hospital care per single "spell of illness" and another hundred days of posthospitalization nursing home care plus additional home nursing visits. Part B, "Supplementary Medical Insurance," offered Medicare recipients a voluntary government insurance program that combined monthly premiums deducted from social security checks with even more substantial subsidies from federal general-revenue funds to pay for doctor visits, ambulance charges, and certain lab tests (though significantly not out-of-hospital prescription drugs, which eat up a sizable share of the out-of-pocket medical expenses that have long required more than a fifth of the annual incomes of Medicare beneficiaries).

Post-1965 History

Despite or perhaps because of the gap between the perception of Medicare as an earned benefit and the reality that most of this program's costs were financed from current social security taxes and government subsidies rather than from the accumulated lifetime contributions of the elderly themselves, Medicare became popular. But it also proved much more expensive than advocates had anticipated, even though the Social Security Administration's overhead to administer the program was gratifyingly low.

To gain the cooperation of medical interests who had opposed Medicare as intrusive "socialized medicine," Medicare originally had no cost-control provisions to speak of. Being guaranteed reimbursement of all customary or reasonable fees, hospitals and doctors cashed in, pushing up medical prices far faster than general inflation, and provided medical services, lab tests, and technologies that a more cost-conscious system might have precluded. Medicaid reimbursement rates were less generous, enough so that many doctors refused to participate. Even so, Medicaid expenditures also rocketed, fueled less by sensational cases of provider fraud than by a combination of greater use of medical services and a manyfold increase in the number of recipients (by 2001 it covered 44 million low-income Americans). With exceptions, such as the financial incentive provided for states to move the chronically mentally ill from state-supported mental hospitals to overcrowded but Medicaid-eligible nursing homes, this program growth was a boon for the health of the poor but an increasingly resented bust for state budgets (in 2001 Medicaid was the fastest-growing item in most state budgets, accounting for nearly a fifth of their outlays).

Also facing mounting costs, Medicare kept increasing payroll taxes, deductibles, and copayments; established systems to limit allowable charges by hospitals and doctors; and encouraged enrollment in HEALTH MAINTENANCE ORGANIZATIONS. Medical schools and their teaching hospitals, which had provided most of the free or below-cost charity ward care for the poor, were in turn transformed by these new streams of revenue, shifting faculty time from research and teaching toward now more lucrative clinical practice. As the United States entered the twenty-first century and faced the prospect of a declining ratio of contributing taxpayers to baby boom retirees, Medicare, Medicaid, and medical and pharmaceutical costs in general approached financial crisis, assuring further reform.

BIBLIOGRAPHY

Berkowitz, Edward D. *America's Welfare State: From Roosevelt to Reagan.* Baltimore: Johns Hopkins University Press, 1991.

———. *Mr. Social Security: The Life of Wilbur J. Cohen.* Lawrence: University Press of Kansas, 1995.

David, Sheri I. *With Dignity: The Search for Medicare and Medicaid.* Westport, Conn.: Greenwood Press, 1985.

Ludmerer, Kenneth M. *Time to Heal: American Medical Education from the Turn of the Century to the Era of Managed Care.* New York: Oxford University Press, 1999.

Sundquist, James L. *Politics and Policy: The Eisenhower, Kennedy, and Johnson Years.* Washington, D.C.: Brookings Institution, 1968.

Zelizer, Julian E. *Taxing America: Wilbur D. Mills, Congress, and the State, 1945–1975.* New York: Cambridge University Press, 1998.

Mark H. Leff

See also **Social Security**.

MEDICINE, ALTERNATIVE. Alternative medical practices have arisen in or have easily been transported to the United States, where social values and political infrastructure have encouraged many forms to flourish. The pervading American value placed in persons having autonomy with respect to making decisions over their own bodies; the skepticism toward any professional group having a monopoly on a given field; and Article 10 of the U.S. Constitution, which reserves to each state the exclusive power to set standards, make rules, and license practitioners in their jurisdictions, have enabled the public and small groups of unorthodox practitioners to shape laws that limit the powers of the dominant orthodox medical profession and protect the interests of alternative minority groups. In Europe and most other countries, licensure and medical policy are centralized, and alternative practitioners and their supporters must win one large battle to gain political recognition or face being marginalized. In the United States, alternative medical movements have been able to fight simultaneous battles in several states, winning some and using those successes to institutionalize, build followings, set standards, and continue their struggles in other jurisdictions.

Although alternative medicine has existed throughout the country's history, the greatest growth of alternative medical movements occurred during three eras, when more broad-based social ideologies nurtured the philosophical premises and political aims of such movements. These ideologies were Jacksonian Democracy (roughly the 1820s to the 1840s), populism (1880s–1910s), and New Age thought (1970s–1990s).

The Era of Jacksonian Democracy

President Andrew Jackson and many of his followers trumpeted the virtues of "the common man," feared large centralized institutions, and had a distrust of professionals, particularly when the latter sought special privileges or exclusive rights based upon expertise to practice in fields traditionally open to those with or without formal training. Consistent with these beliefs, three large alternative medical movements arose during this time.

Samuel Thomson, a self-trained root doctor from New Hampshire, believed that all disorders were caused by obstructed perspiration. He argued that fever was the body's effort to eliminate disease and that orthodox physicians, with their bleedings, blisterings, and use of drugs like mercury, arsenic, and antimony, were jeopardizing the lives of patients and causing many deaths. Thomson believed anyone could treat disease using six classes of remedies consisting of botanical drugs and the steam bath, all designed to produce great internal heat, eliminate the cold, and allow the body to reestablish its natural balance. Thomson wrote a popular book, prepared kits of his medicine, sold individual rights to his practice, and encouraged followers to defeat or repeal medical licensure laws that restricted the practice of medicine to formally trained physicians. Although Thomson was antiprofessional, other alternative groups that employed a wider range of botanical drugs emerged, including Eclectic Medicine, which established schools, journals, and hospitals and won status for its practitioners as physicians.

The second major group of medical reformers, part of the so-called popular health movement, believed that physicians were largely unnecessary because most diseases could be prevented by individuals adopting healthy habits. The most prominent American lecturer and writer in this movement, Sylvester Graham, maintained that disease resulted from excessive stimulation of the tissues. Any food that caused too much stimulation had to be avoided, including tea, coffee, alcohol, pastries, and all fleshy meats. Graham also used the doctrine of overstimulation to warn of the powerful dangers of too much sexual energy. Eating meat, he argued, produced a heightened sex drive, which was health destroying. One of his innovations was a cracker that still bears his name, which was initially designed in part to discourage overstimulation of this type.

The most significant European import during this era was HOMEOPATHY, a system of practice originated by the German physician Samuel Hahnemann. Brought to America in the 1820s, homeopathy encompassed two essential principles. The first principle was that the drug best able to cure a given illness would be that which could produce the symptoms of that illness in a healthy person. The second principle was that the smaller the dose, the more powerful the effect. One active part per hundred was shaken in a vial, and one part of that solution was mixed with another ninety-nine inactive parts, and so on, usually thirty times. By the end of the nineteenth century, homeopaths constituted 10 percent and the eclectics 5 percent of the physician and surgeon population in the United States.

The Era of Populism

Midwestern populism encompassed a distrust of large East Coast–controlled businesses and institutions, a belief that elites had gained too much power, and a sense that common people had too little say in shaping government and law in their own interests. As opposed to Jacksonian Democracy, many populists were not against creating laws governing the professions as long as the interests of competing groups were protected. In the 1870s and 1880s, new medical licensure laws were enacted; however, homeopathic and eclectic physicians were given the same rights as orthodox physicians. Challenging this hegemony were two groups—osteopathy and chiropractic.

OSTEOPATHY was founded by Andrew Taylor Still, an apprenticeship-trained Midwestern physician. Still, who had practiced for a time as a bonesetter, believed that disease was the result of an obstruction or imbalance of the fluids caused by misplaced bones, particularly of the spinal column. These misplacements could be corrected through physical manipulation. He established an infirmary and school in Kirksville, Missouri, in 1892. Still's followers relatively quickly gained some measure of legal protection, established other colleges, and gradually expanded osteopathy's scope of practice to incorporate drugs and surgery. Eventually, D.O.s (doctors of osteopathic medicine) won equal rights along with M.D.s as full-fledged physicians and surgeons in every state and equal recognition by the federal government. As homeopathic and eclectic medicine faded after the beginning of the twentieth century, osteopathy became, and remained, the only equivalent professional rival of allopathic medicine, although the differences between the two groups have faded considerably.

CHIROPRACTIC appeared within a decade of the emergence of osteopathy and was founded in Davenport, Iowa, by Daniel David Palmer. Like Still, Palmer believed that diseases were due to misplaced bones. Many early chiropractors or D.C.s (doctors of chiropractic) were initially charged with practicing osteopathy without a license, but they demonstrated to courts and eventually legislatures that their diagnostic and treatment techniques were different. Unlike osteopathic physicians, who grew to encompass the full range of medical training and skills, chiropractors, despite the addition of some adjuncts, continued to center their activities on spinal manipulation and quickly became associated in the public mind with that technique, though osteopathy had historical priority.

"New Age" Thought

Fueled by America's continued participation in the Vietnam War and frustration with the perceived failure of government to produce meaningful change consistent with their own beliefs, a growing number of middle-class Americans in the 1970s shifted their attention from reforming society by legislative action to focusing on the potential for personal improvement. Drawing upon the rich traditions of other cultures, and often incorporating metaphysical and spiritual understandings of the basis and meaning of life, millions of Americans turned to a variety of disparate health beliefs and practices, including traditional Chinese and Ayurvedic medicine; crystals and scented candles; rolfing and other body treatments; imaging and other psychological interventions; alternative diets; herbs, vitamins, and other supplements; and a rediscovery of homeopathic and botanical remedies. By the end of the twentieth century, more money was spent by Americans on alternative practitioners and remedies than on visits to the offices of conventional primary care physicians.

This movement also reflected a growing frustration with the way orthodox medicine was practiced. Too little time was spent listening to patients, and while science had contributed to the treatment of acute diseases, many patients with chronic illnesses wanted more relief from their conditions than conventional physicians could provide. The number of alternative treatments that became available provided patients with new choices and new hopes. Experience by physicians with some of these modalities, and later research indicating value in some forms of alternative treatment, encouraged a growing number of conventionally trained physicians to incorporate these methods under the banner of "holistic" or "integrative" medicine. The continued popularity of these most recent forms of alternative medicine will, as in earlier periods, depend not only on the perceived efficacy of the respective practices over time but also on the broader social trends and ideologies that facilitated the emergence and growth of these practices.

BIBLIOGRAPHY

Berman, Alex, and Michael A. Flannery. *America's Botanico-Medical Movements: Vox Populi.* New York: Pharmaceutical Products Press, 2001.

Gevitz, Norman. *The D.O.'s: Osteopathic Medicine in America.* Baltimore: Johns Hopkins University Press, 1991.

———, ed. *Other Healers: Unorthodox Medicine in America.* Baltimore: Johns Hopkins University Press, 1988.

Haller, John S. *Medical Protestants: The Eclectics in American Medicine, 1825–1939.* Carbondale: Southern Illinois University Press, 1994.

Kaufman, Martin. *Homeopathy in America: The Rise and Fall of a Medical Heresy.* Baltimore: Johns Hopkins University Press, 1971.

McGuire, Meredith. *Ritual Healing in Suburban America.* New Brunswick, N.J.: Rutgers University Press, 1988.

Moore, J. Stuart. *Chiropractic in America: The History of a Medical Alternative.* Baltimore: Johns Hopkins University Press, 1993.

Whorton, James C. *Crusaders for Fitness: The History of American Health Reformers.* Princeton, N.J.: Princeton University Press, 1982.

Norman Gevitz

See also **Homeopathy; Medical Profession; Medicine and Surgery; New Age Movement.**

MEDICINE, INDIAN, an ancient, intact, complex holistic healthcare system practiced and used by indigenous peoples worldwide, is more profound and more deeply rooted and complex than is commonly understood. Based upon a spiritual rather than a materialistic or Cartesian worldview, Indian medicine emphasizes the spirit world; supernatural forces; and religion, which is considered virtually identical to medicine. To some degree Indian medicine depends upon phenomena that can best be described as mystical, even magical. Indian medicine was not a primitive medicine that is embryonic modern medicine or a predecessor to Western medicine, but an entirely different entity. In the last third of the twentieth century and into the twenty-first, Indian medicine has become increasing popular with holistic and alternative medicine practitioners.

The healing traditions (passed down orally) of Indian medicine have been practiced on the North American continent for at least 12,000 years and possibly for more than 40,000 years. Indigenous peoples describe their medicine as an art practiced since time immemorial; some indigenous peoples use only Western medicine or only traditional medicine, some take advantage of both simultaneously or serially. Some decide which health system to use based upon the ailment.

An indigenous individual strives to restore and maintain excellent health and live in accordance with prescribed life ways or religion. While these various life ways differ among tribes, all suggest how to maintain wellbeing and a balanced life. Disease is associated with imbalance, while health suggests a state of balance, harmony, synchronicity, and wholeness in spiritual, mental, emotional, and physical realms; in life energy in the body; in ethical, reasonable, and just behavior; in relations within the family and community; and in relationships with nature and the universe. When illness occurs, the imbalance or disruption must be corrected to restore health.

Indigenous traditional healers, both men and women (gender depends on the tribe), have practiced the art of healing within their communities for centuries. Modern Indian medicine practitioners are little different from earlier native practitioners and may practice across tribes and provide healing to non-natives. Healing ability and knowledge can be acquired several ways, however, healers usually serve many years of apprenticeship.

Although the same beliefs related to healing are held by the more than 500 indigenous tribes scattered across the United States, methods of diagnosis, methodology, and treatment vary greatly from tribe to tribe and from healer to healer; methods used to correct imbalance include divination; use of elements such as water, fire, smoke, stones, or crystals as a projective field to help see the reason and/or cause of the imbalance; prayer; chanting; use of music, singing, drums, rattles; smudging with medicinal plants such as sage cedar or sweetgrass; laying on of hands, talking, counseling; making medicinal plants or botanical medicines into teas, salves, ointments, or purgatives; ceremony; sweat lodge; and shake tent. The Navajo also use star gazing, crystal gazing, and hand-tremblers. Traditional healers also use techniques such as sucking to remove a disease and blowing away a disease.

Traditional medicine was anything sacred, mysterious, or of wonderful power or efficacy in Indian life or belief. Thus, medicine has come to mean "supernatural power." From this usage came the terms: medicine man (which omits medicine women), medicine bag, good versus bad medicine, and so on. The origin of the word medicine can be traced to at least the seventeenth century when French Jesuit missionaries among the Huron, Montagnais, Ottawa, and other inhabitants of New France, documented and described indigenous healers using *homes-médecins* (*médecin* is French for doctor). The medicine man was long recognized by settlers as a principal barrier to the eradication of Indian culture. Traditional healing and use of Indian medicine was made illegal during early European contact and the art of Indian medicine was driven underground. In 1978, Congress passed the Indian Religious Freedom Act; this act gave American Indians the right to practice their spiritual and healing traditions. Today, some indigenous medicinal plants are becoming endangered because of excessive harvesting, global warming, private land ownership, and pesticide use.

BIBLIOGRAPHY

Avery, C. "Native American Medicine: Traditional Healing." *Journal of the American Medical Association* 265, no. 17 (1991): 2271, 2273.

Cohen, K. "B. H." "Native American Medicine." *Alternative Therapies* 4, no. 6 (1998): 45–57.

Lyon, W. S. *Encyclopedia of Native American Healing*. New York: Norton, 1996.

Rhoades, E. R., and D. A. Rhoades. "Traditional Indian and Modern Western Medicine." In *American Indian Health: Innovations in Health Care, Promotions, and Policy*. Edited by E. R. Rhoades. Baltimore: John Hopkins University Press, 2000.

Struthers, R. "The Lived Experience of Ojibwa and Cree Women Healers." Ph.D. diss., University of Minnesota, 1999.

Roxanne Struthers

See also **Indian Religious Life**.

MEDICINE, MILITARY, as a specialty, has focused on the surgical management of mass casualties; on the prevention and treatment of infectious diseases, especially tropical diseases; and, in the twentieth century, on the effects of operating military machines such as submarines and airplanes. As part of a military hierarchy, the organization of structured medical command and administrative systems has been important for interaction with the line and for function in combat.

Army Medicine

Medical support for an American army began on 27 July 1775 when the Continental Congress established a medical service for the army of Gen. George Washington during the siege of Boston. The organization followed the model of the British army. Military physicians wrote several texts on surgery, on preventive medicine, and on pharmacy during the Revolutionary War, the first American publications of their kind.

On 14 April 1818, Congress reorganized the staff departments of the army and established the present medical department. Medical officers gained military rank in 1847. A hospital corps, providing formal instruction for enlisted men as physicians' assistants, was formed in 1887; the present civilian programs for paramedical physician extenders have their philosophical base in this system. The army established the Nurse Corps in 1901, the Dental Corps in 1911, the Veterinary Corps in 1916, and the Sanitary Corps in 1917; the latter became the Medical Service Corps in 1947 when the Women's (since 1966, Army) Medical Specialist Corps enrolled dietitians and physical and occupational therapists. Corps functions had existed previously in the medical department, but organization into a corps not only formalized the position of the specialty in the military bureaucracy but also regularized the status of the individuals and provided for commissions, tenure, and pensions. Thus, because she was chief of her corps, it was possible for Col. Anna Mae Violet McCabe Hays of the Army Nurse Corps to become the first female general officer in American history in 1970. One consequence of formal organization, with command overview of health-care delivery, including the supporting infrastructure, was the development of a centrally managed health-care program outside the civilian fee-for-service system, which the Veterans Administration Hospital program later adapted to its needs.

The major military contributions of the surgical disciplines have been in mass casualty management, the evacuation of wounded, and in the treatment of battle wounds. Although the removal of the sick and wounded from the battlefield has always been a part of military operations, the development of an organized system did not come until 1862. Jonathan Letterman, the medical director of the Army of the Potomac, established the system that is now the practice of all armies: staged and echeloned medical care and forward treatment followed by evacuation of patients by medical elements in the rear. The next major advance was the use of airplanes for evacuating hospitalized patients in World War II, and of helicopters as forward tactical air ambulances in the Korean War. Later, having proved its worth in Vietnam, the helicopter was adopted by the civilian community for evacuating those injured in highway accidents. Army studies of wound ballistics, beginning in 1892, established the scientific rationale for wide debridement of wounds, and led to reduction in gas gangrene and wound infection, as well as to the development of individual body armor. Charles Drew, Douglas B. Kendrick, and others, developed systems for mass blood collection, distribution, and transfusion during World War II and introduced the civilian medical community to the concepts of massive blood transfusions for shock and trauma. An army burn research and treatment center, founded in 1947, was the first in the United States, and the use of Sulfamylon to prevent skin infection contributed greatly to the burn research program.

Communicable and infectious diseases have always been the major causes of morbidity among troops, and military medicine has made its greatest contributions in this area. In World War I, the application of infectious disease research to military sanitation produced a milestone in the history of war: lower mortality from disease than from battle wounds.

From 1818 to 1860, the army's medical department mostly concerned itself with patient care at the small army posts scattered over the southern and western frontiers. The department reported morbidity and mortality data in a uniform format, and published the collected reports, which included some civilian data, beginning in 1840; these national public-health statistics, the first of their kind, prompted the beginning of a national approach to public-health epidemiology. Because prevailing opinion believed disease etiology and occurrence were related to climate, post surgeons also included meteorological data with their reports. (The weather observations, separately published, were the only nationwide data of their kind, and the National Weather Service remained a medical department function until 1870.)

When bacteriology became a science in the 1860s, military physicians were among the first to explore this new field. Joseph J. Woodward and Edward Curtis in 1864 introduced aniline dyes in the United States for staining in microscopy, and pioneered photomicroscopy of tissues and bacteria. George M. Sternberg of the U.S. Army published the first American bacteriology textbook

in 1892; later, as surgeon general, he established and directed the two "Walter Reed boards" for the study of typhoid and yellow fever, in 1898 and 1900, respectively.

The history of Walter Reed's work on the transmission of yellow fever in 1900 is well known: he and his colleagues, using volunteer test subjects, took only a few months to disprove fomite infection, document mosquito transmission, and define the organism as nonbacterial. Less well known is the story of the "Typhoid Board" of 1898, which studied recruit camp epidemics, documented that contact mattered more than water in transmission, and suggested that a carrier state existed.

When Sternberg founded the Army Medical School in 1893—the first school of public health and preventive medicine in the United States—he began the trend of formal postgraduate education in the basic sciences for army medical officers. Renamed the Walter Reed Army Institute of Research, the organization became the largest tropical medicine research organization in the United States.

Tropical parasitic diseases occupied the attention of military physicians. Bailey K. Ashford, working in Puerto Rico after the Spanish-American War, isolated the American hookworm, *Necator americanus*, as the cause of anemia in Puerto Rican farm laborers. His program for detection, therapy, and prevention later became the model by which the Rockefeller Foundation attacked hookworm in the American South. Charles F. Craig wrote an early text on medical parasitology in 1911, developed serological tests for amebiasis, and described new intestinal parasites. Work at the Army Medical Research Board in the Philippines from 1900 to 1934 proved that dengue was a virus and that mosquitoes were the vector. The research also documented the usefulness of emetine in treating amebiasis; showed that *Aedes* mosquitoes were major vectors for equine encephalitis; and made critical contributions in new rabies and rinderpest vaccines, in the treatment of beriberi, and in zoonotic diseases.

Frederick F. Russell developed an American typhoid vaccine in 1909 at the Army Medical School. In 1911 the army immunized all its soldiers—the first time for an entire army—causing typhoid to disappear as a major cause of morbidity and mortality. Carl Rogers Darnall's introduction of anhydrous chlorine to purify drinking water in 1910 became the basis for present systems of municipal water purification. William C. Gorgas used the new findings on mosquito transmission to control yellow fever and MALARIA, permitting the building of the Panama Canal. In 1933, the Army Medical Research Board in Panama conducted the first American studies on the efficacy of atabrine as a prophylactic drug against malaria; it became the standard drug of World War II until the chloroquine-primaquine combination tablet replaced it following definitive studies in Korea in 1960. In 1963, the army's medical department began to support the only large international research program for the development of new antimalarial drugs.

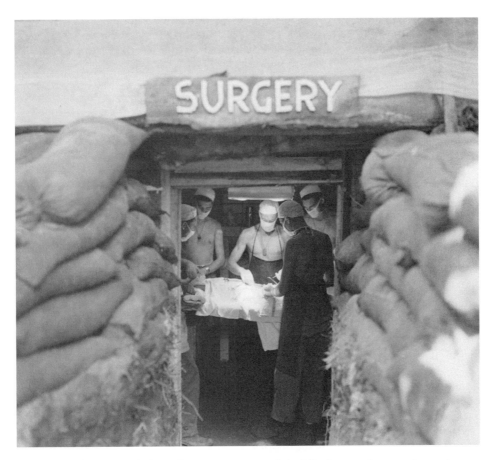

Military Medicine. A U.S. Army doctor treats a wounded soldier in an underground operating room behind the front lines on Bougainville, in the Solomon Islands, during World War II.

During World War II, the United States of America Typhus Commission, a joint military-civilian organization, did broad-scale work on the typhus fevers and was responsible for applying DDT to delouse populations and for field trials of vaccines. Similarly, military-civilian investigators of the Army Epidemiological Board investigated viral hepatitis, separated infectious and serum hepatitis as entities, and demonstrated the usefulness of gamma globulin for passive protection. After World War II, the concept of joint military-civilian teams persisted and led to such contributions as the use of chloramphenicol to treat typhoid fever and scrub typhus and the use of broad-spectrum antibiotics in the treatment of plague.

During and after the Korean War, members of the medical department studied communicable and infectious diseases, leading to the description of the ecology of the transmission cycle of Japanese B. encephalitis in 1955; the isolation of the Asian influenza virus in 1957; the isolation of the German measles virus in 1962, for later development of a vaccine by the National Institutes of Health; and the development of effective vaccines against adenovirus infection in recruit camps in 1967. Researchers also developed vaccines against meningococcal meningi-

tis, while Central American countries used a vaccine against Venezuelan equine encephalitis during epizootics in 1969 and 1970.

Other discoveries and contributions made by medical department members have been important to general medicine. In 1833, William Beaumont published his classic work on the physiology of digestion from his ten-year study of the gastric fistula of Alexis Saint Martin. In that decade, the surgeon general established a collection of medical books, which grew over time—and especially after the Civil War—to become the Army Medical Library; in 1956 it became the National Library of Medicine under the aegis of the Department of Health, Education, and Welfare.

The career of John Shaw Billings typifies military involvement in the mainstream of American medicine. In 1870 Billings's investigation and recommendations changed the Marine Hospital System to its present U.S. Public Health Service structure. He designed Johns Hopkins Hospital and was responsible for the selection of William H. Welch and William Osler as faculty for its medical school. As librarian of the Army Medical Library, he developed the *Index-Catalogue* and, with Dr. Robert Fletcher, developed and published the *Index-Medicus*. He recommended the use of electrically sorted punch cards for medical record-keeping, and oversaw Herman Hollerith's testing of such a system at the surgeon general's office. In retirement, Billings organized and built the New York Public Library and became its first director.

The Civil War period saw the founding of the Army Medical Museum, renamed the Armed Forces Institute of Pathology in 1949, from which, in the next thirty years, came the *Medical and Surgical History of the War of the Rebellion*, the first detailed account of the medical and surgical findings of the impact of war on an army. This era also saw the beginning of formal research in pathology in the United States.

Navy Medicine

Congressional appropriations on 2 November 1775 provided for surgeons on naval ships, but the navy did not establish its Bureau of Medicine and Surgery until 1842 and did not authorize flag rank for the surgeon general until 1898. The navy established its Nurse Corps in 1903 and its Dental Corps in 1912.

Edward R. Squibb, who later founded the pharmaceutical firm of the same name, founded a naval laboratory for the production of pure drugs in 1853. The Naval Medical School was established in 1902. The navy introduced annual physical examinations for officers in 1903, laying the foundation for programs of multiphasic health screening.

Edward R. Stitt, later surgeon general, wrote the first modern American text on tropical medicine in 1914. In 1958, navy physicians developed methods for fluid replacement in the treatment of CHOLERA, which became standard procedures, especially during epidemics. Toxicological research on trace-element effects in the closed environment of submarines produced some of the earliest data now useful for civilian pollution studies.

Aviation Medicine

Aviation medicine began in Europe as a medical problem of the army, and in 1917, with the entry of the United States into World War I, the army established a research laboratory and the School for Flight Surgeons. Louis H. Bauer, the first commandant of the school, wrote the first American textbook of aviation medicine in 1926 and became the first director of civil aviation medicine for the Department of Commerce. In 1936, Harry E. Armstrong, later surgeon general of the U.S. Air Force, built the first centrifuge to study the effects of acceleration on humans.

The Air Force established a separate medical department in 1949. In 1950, the School of Aerospace Medicine began biological research on the effects of space flight, and air force officers conducted the great majority of the medical work in the National Aeronautics and Space Administration. John Paul Stapp's studies in 1954 on abrupt deceleration founded the present field in crash injury. Air

force studies of anthropometry, human factors, designs of instruments, displays, and basic work in vibration effects and noise-level tolerance have had widespread application to design.

BIBLIOGRAPHY

Ashburn, Percy M. *A History of the Medical Department of the United States Army.* Boston: Houghton Mifflin, 1929.

Bayne-Jones, Stanhope. *The Evolution of Preventive Medicine in the United States Army, 1607–1939.* Washington, D.C.: Office of the Surgeon General, 1968.

Hume, Edgar Erskine. *Victories of Army Medicine: Scientific Accomplishments of the Medical Department of the United States Army.* Philadelphia: Lippincott, 1943.

Peyton, Green. *Fifty Years of Aerospace Medicine: Its Evolution since the Founding of the United States Air Force School of Aerospace Medicine in January 1918.* Brooks Air Force Base: U.S. Air Force School of Aerospace Medicine, 1968.

Roddis, Louis. *A Short History of Nautical Medicine.* New York and London: P. B. Hoeber, 1941.

Tobey, James A. *The Medical Department of the Army: Its History, Activities and Organization.* Baltimore: Johns Hopkins Press, 1927; New York: AMS Press, 1974.

Robert J. T. Joy/c. w.

See also **Epidemics and Public Health; Hospitals; Medical Profession; Medical Research; Medicine and Surgery; Pharmacy; Sanitation, Environmental; Weather Service, National.**

MEDICINE, OCCUPATIONAL, attempts to maintain workers' health, prevent disease, and treat the results of occupational disease or accident. The field of occupational medicine in its modern form developed largely through the efforts of women reformers during the Progressive Era, although preliminary efforts to ameliorate occupational ill-health date back to the nineteenth century. Adverse working conditions can cause acute and chronic illnesses and disabling accidents. Low wages, long hours of work, emotional stress, and inferior status or social role may also adversely affect the general health of the worker. Health counseling and health maintenance have evolved as important facets of contemporary occupational medicine, along with psychological testing and industrial psychiatry. As safety engineering has emerged as a key aspect of accident prevention, so environmental engineering has emerged as a concern of occupational medicine.

Occupational medicine is a relatively recent phenomenon, and although work hazards were many in early America, injured workers had little access to medicine directed toward their specific problems. In the United States before the Civil War, the worst and most dangerous work was usually performed by enslaved people, although free people also performed some extremely dangerous work—for instance, the building of the Erie Canal and many other of the large-scale projects of the nineteenth century. Some occupational diseases began to be recognized as such in the eighteenth century; for example, Benjamin Franklin noted that typesetters suffered from abdominal cramps and wrist or foot paralysis from the lead used in their work. However, recognition did not bring treatment, for the most part.

Access to health services was the first principal theme in occupational medicine. In 1798, the U.S. Congress created the Marine Hospital Service to provide care for American seamen, since their disabilities and illnesses had exceeded the abilities of local communities to handle them under poor-law arrangements. In the early nineteenth century, labor unions began to concern themselves with safe working conditions, among the earliest being the Pennsylvania Society of Journeymen Cabinetmakers, founded in 1806. In the cities, mutual benefit societies multiplied; 38,000 societies formed by 1867, although many were financially unstable and failed. A high proportion had a lodge doctor, and some built and administered hospitals. However, working women and numerous working men rarely had access to union membership, and the most exploited workers continued to labor under very dangerous conditions.

Not until 1837 was a systematic examination of occupations and related health problems published in the United States. In that year, a New York physician, Benjamin W. McCready, modeling his study after the work of the Englishman C. Turner Thackrah, wrote a prize essay for the Medical Society of the State of New York entitled "On the Influence of Trades, Professions and Occupations in the United States in the Production of Disease." McCready dealt with the health problems of agricultural workers, laborers, seamen, factory operatives, artisans, professionals, and literary men, and also discussed housing and "the general conditions of life" stemming from poverty and unhealthy cities. McCready identified long hours of work, slum living, and the effects of insufficient fresh food and sunshine as culprits. Far ahead of his time, he also commented on anxiety as a negative health factor.

As the nineteenth century unfolded, some diseases were diagnosed as occupational. In 1860, J. Addison Freeman of Orange, New Jersey, coined the expression "mad as a hatter" to describe mercury poisoning in hattery workers (clearly, hatters in C.S. Lewis's England also were known to exhibit these effects). In 1869, the *Transactions of the Medical Society of Pennsylvania* vividly described lung problems among anthracite coal miners, particularly the illness now known as black lung. In 1884, the *Saint Louis Medical Journal* described lead colic among lead miners. In the late nineteenth century, safety conditions were considered a national scandal. Railroads, factories, mines, the construction industry, and lumbering all vied for "worst place" in work-connected accidents. Safety inspection and compensation for the results of accidents became leading subjects of public discussion.

Some companies organized mandatory forms of health insurance for their employees, in which employees prepaid their care. The first major industrial medical-care prepayment plan to endure was organized by the Southern Pacific Railroad in 1868. The first company-financed medical department with a full-time staff providing complete medical care for employees and families was established by the Homestake Mining Company of Lead, South Dakota, in 1887. Although some U.S. coal miners had been prepaying their medical and accident care at $1 per month at least since 1869, the check-off for hospitalization, doctor care, and drugs became general throughout U.S. coalfields by the end of the century. It was a compulsory deduction required by the coal companies until the 1920s, after which it became voluntary in most places. The coal companies' doctors practiced both industrial medicine and family medical care. This system was a cause of much protest and dissatisfaction on the part of workers, who found it inadequate and paternalistic, and resented the payment requirement. Dr. Alice Hamilton (who died in 1970 at age 101) was the powerhouse behind creating the field of occupational medicine in the twentieth century. Hamilton, a resident of Jane Addams's Hull House settlement, wrote on lead poisoning in 1911, and followed it with work on coal-tar dye toxicities and many other hazards. Her *Industrial Toxicology* (1934), and Wilhelm Hueper's *Occupational Tumors and Allied Diseases* (1942), were crucial breakthroughs in identifying the toxic effects of numerous substances. Later in the century, Dr. Harriet Hardy, a protégée of Hamilton, detected the toxicity of beryllium as the cause of "Salem sarcoid" in workers in fluorescent bulb factories and in beryllium-smelter workers. Hamilton's contemporary, John Andrews, tackled the use of phosphorus in making matches in the United States, recognized as the cause of "phossy jaw." Andrews founded the American Association for Labor Legislation in 1906, and, in 1910, the first U.S. Conference on Industrial Diseases was held under its auspices. In 1911, an excessive prevalence of tuberculosis among garment workers in New York City was clearly demonstrated by a Public Health Service physician, J. W. Schereschewsky. Harvard University established the first American academic program in industrial medicine in 1917. In the following year, the *Journal of Industrial Hygiene* made its appearance, followed in 1932 by the *Journal of Industrial Medicine*. In 1914, the U.S. Public Health Service created a Division of Industrial Hygiene and Sanitation, which became the National Institute of Occupational Safety and Health. The 1935 Social Security Act stimulated the formation of state industrial hygiene units. In 1937, the American Medical Association created the Council on Industrial Health and joined in work with the National Safety Council.

State legislation, pushed largely by women Progressives from the settlement houses, began protecting workers to some extent, although inadequately, in the first half of the twentieth century. The first legislation took the form of protection for women workers, particularly limiting hours. Such protection was two-edged: Opponents of women's rights had long cited women's purported fragility as a reason for their political subordination ("protection"), and some women's rights advocates decried advocates of protective legislation particularly aimed at women, fearing it would perpetuate the stereotypes used to justify women's subordination. On the other hand, advocates of such legislation—most of whom were women themselves—argued that women carried much heavier home responsibilities than men, and feared that without laws limiting their paid work hours, women's burdens would prove overwhelming and physically dangerous. Furthermore, although many reformers also wished to improve conditions for working men, they viewed women's health as the wedge through which they could press through the first worker protection laws, since legislators and the public tended to view women as weaker and in need of protection. (Such views had not applied to enslaved women, nor to hardworking women farmers, or a host of other women, but pleas based on women's fragility resonated in late Victorian and Progressive urban America.) Reformers also used middle-class fears of the spread of disease to try to abolish practices such as "home work," in which manufacturers contracted out work to women and children who were paid by the piece and worked in their own homes uninspected and unprotected. Working mothers often resented reformers' interference, since such work was the only sort they could perform while caring for their children.

Legislation for workers came slowly and piecemeal. The first state to enact a workmen's compensation law was New York, in 1910, but not until 1955 had all the states enacted such legislation. By 1960, dissatisfaction with state workers' compensation and safety rules led Congress to pass the federal Coal Mine Safety Act. In 1970, Congress authorized the use of the Social Security system to compensate for industrial diseases by providing work-connected disability payments and required the inclusion of occupational health and safety inspection and occupational health services in the Industrial Health and Safety Act of 1970.

Labor organizations also began using collective bargaining contracts as sources for medical-care payment, a practice that grew rapidly during World War II and afterward. Mining has been dangerous to health throughout history. In 1947, the United Mine Workers of America began services to miners paralyzed from rock falls and to silicotics. It then developed a comprehensive medical care program. Lawsuits over coal miners' "black lung disease" had some success, but mining of all kinds remained highly hazardous. Although employers provided most industrial workers with insurance coverage for hospitalization costs in the 1970s, the coverage was inadequate, and agitation for a national health security or insurance program was widespread. Numerous occupational health hazards remain for workers in the United States (and elsewhere). Excessive heat, cold, noise, and vibration

are among the basic hazards. Each technical advance has tended to produce its own occupational and environmental problems. For example, radioactivity burst upon the scene as a killer of fluorescent wristwatch workers who painted luminous dials. After World War II, uranium mining and fallout from atomic bomb testing constituted a new health hazard. Radiation hazards remain a problem. Carbon tetrachloride, used in cleaning establishments, causes liver poisoning. Coal tar derivatives emerged as major contributors to cancer of the bladder, of the skin, and of the blood-forming organs. Hot metal fumes, which arise in the smelting of mercury cadmium, lead, nickel, and beryllium, have come to be recognized as major causes of occupational disease. Dusty trades, such as pottery-making, glassworking, quarrying, sandblasting, tunneling, and mining, cause the lung diseases silicosis and black lung. Textile industries tend to cause brown lung, or byssinosis. Exposure to asbestos fiber became a major problem, in some cases causing lung cancer; 3.5 million U.S. workers were exposed as of 1970, and fiberglass, too, is suspect. Organic solvents are common producers of skin disorders, called dermatoses. Polyvinyl chloride used in plastics is a cause of liver cancer.

Environmental hazards in the community and home, first broadly publicized in the 1970s in Rachel Carson's *Silent Spring*, are also widespread. In the 1990s, health hazards came to include what was termed "sick building syndrome," a range of illnesses, often undiagnosed, which plagued workers and residents in newly-built or renovated buildings—the glues and other substances used in construction combined with a lack of ventilation proved highly deleterious. The airtight character of some building strategies also produced a toxic mold, outbreaks of which panicked new homebuilders in the early 2000s.

The computer age has brought a new host of occupational health hazards to workers of many types. One highly publicized, and still prevalent, problem is carpal tunnel syndrome, a condition arising from excessive typing; other forms of tendinitis often accompany it. Sitting for hours on end typing at poorly designed workstations causes not only carpal tunnel syndrome but a host of back and neck problems, as well as eyestrain and headaches. Although publicized largely as a problem of white-collar office workers, the dangers are even more severe and widespread for the lowest-paid workers, mostly women, who work in the data-entry field. Unlike middle-class office workers, these workers are unlikely to be able to afford, or have the workplace clout to demand, the new ergonomically designed furniture and computer accessories that have arisen in response to the problem.

Even as office workers' occupational health problems command widespread publicity, huge numbers of other Americans continue to labor in dangerous conditions. Farm workers, some of the least protected of America's workers, often work in fields laden with toxic pesticides. Some consumers buy organic produce because they worry about the effects of those pesticide residues on their food, but the people picking the produce are immersed in such substances throughout their long workdays. The United Farm Workers of America is fighting to protect its members and improve farm work conditions, but migrant workers, sometimes undocumented immigrants, have a difficult time finding protection. Workers in America's meat-processing industry also labor under often highly dangerous and unhealthy conditions; chicken and seafood processors bend for hours on end in icy water, developing back and circulation problems in addition to chronically compromised immune systems, and meat-packers labor among sharp surfaces, on floors slippery with blood and feces, in an increasingly deregulated and uninspected industry. Throughout America's history, domestic workers—paid and unpaid—have been exposed to numerous hazards. In recent decades, those hazards have included not only backbreaking labor, but also increasing amounts and varieties of toxic chemicals. A movement to unionize office cleaners, called "Justice For Janitors," is seeking to ameliorate these and other poor work conditions for its constituents. Soldiers, too, face occupational health hazards, aside from the most obvious of battle fatality; they have been consistently exposed to dangerous toxins, from Agent Orange during the Vietnam War to radioactive poisoning and gas exposure in the Persian Gulf War. Usually from working-class backgrounds, these military workers have little political clout in matters of occupational health, despite their willingness to sacrifice their lives for their nation.

Occupational medicine has made huge strides in the past century, and numerous workers have access to both protections and medical treatment that did not exist in previous times. At the same time, many workers remain without access to those protections and treatment, and, while scientific advancements have solved some old workplace hazards, they also have created new ones. Occupational medicine thus remains a crucial and rapidly developing field.

BIBLIOGRAPHY

Berman, Daniel M. *Death on the Job: Occupational Health and Safety Struggles in the United States.* New York: Monthly Review Press, 1978.

Carone, Pasquale A., et al., eds. *History of Mental Health in Industry: The Last Hundred Years.* New York: Human Sciences Press, 1985.

Corn, Jacqueline K. *Response to Occupational Health Hazards: A Historical Perspective.* New York: Van Nostrand Reinhold, 1992.

Hamilton, Alice. *Exploring the Dangerous Trades: The Autobiography of Alice Hamilton, M.D.* Boston: Little, Brown, 1943; Boston: Northeastern University Press, 1985.

———. *Industrial Poisons in the United States.* New York: Macmillan, 1925.

Hepler, Allison L. *Women in Labor: Mothers, Medicine, and Occupational Health in the United States, 1890–1980.* Columbus: Ohio State University Press, 2000.

Rosner, David, and Gerald Markowitz, eds. *Dying for Work: Workers' Safety and Health in Twentieth-Century America.* Bloomington: Indiana University Press, 1987.

Sellers, Christopher C. *Hazards of the Job: From Industrial Disease to Environmental Health Science.* Chapel Hill: University of North Carolina Press, 1997.

Sicherman, Barbara. *Alice Hamilton, a Life in Letters.* Cambridge, Mass.: Harvard University Press, 1984.

Leslie A. Falk
Dorothea Browder

See also **Automobile Workers v. Johnson Controls, Inc.; Health Insurance; Medicine and Surgery; National Institutes of Health; Occupational Safety and Health Act; Progressive Movement; "Silent Spring"; United Mine Workers of America; United Steelworkers of America; United Textile Workers; Women in Public Life, Business and Professions; Women's Health; Workers' Compensation.**

MEDICINE AND SURGERY

The Colonial Period

The people who settled the New World were often seeking something that had eluded them in the Old World; thus few established practitioners of medicine were among the early settlers. The exceptions were the apprentice-trained midwives who were members of the religious minorities who came to America and the "surgeons" who accompanied the gentlemen adventurers of early Virginia. Surgeons in the early modern era were, in general, apprentice-trained practitioners without university education who used external treatment—baths, massage, and external ointments and salves—as well as the knife. However, many "surgeons" were general practitioners. Medicine was a university discipline read, not practiced, by those who took a medical degree but also by those taking arts and theology degrees. Physicians prescribed for patients after consultation; few examined their patients. If procedures were required, a surgeon was summoned. Because university education was expensive, the vast majority of physicians were from the successful middle orders of society. They practiced among those who could afford to pay for their expensive consultations. Physicians moved to the New World in significant numbers in the eighteenth century. Most were native sons who returned to the increasingly affluent colonies after a university education in Europe.

In the seventeenth and early eighteenth centuries, the highest concentrations of university-educated persons in the colonies were among the clergy and the political classes; not surprisingly, both groups gave medical advice. Among the most prominent of the medical political leaders were John Winthrop and his son, also named John. Both conducted an extensive medical advice correspondence among the population of the sparsely settled New England countryside. In the eighteenth century, John Wesley, the founder of the Methodist sect, wrote a guidebook, *Primitive Physick* (1747), for clergy and laypeople to use in the provision of health care. It remained popular through much of the nineteenth century.

Among the prominent clerical medical advisors was Cotton Mather, who contributed to the introduction of variolation, or smallpox inoculation, as a smallpox preventive. Smallpox had been regularly epidemic in Boston, and in 1721 Mather sent a letter to the medical practitioners of Boston urging them to collectively undertake inoculation. When they did not respond, Mather convinced Zabdiel Boylston to undertake the procedure without the concurrence of his colleagues. The reaction was vigorous, with most medical practitioners opposed and most of the clergy supportive.

Mather's experience and the subsequent history of inoculation reveal many things about medicine in colonial America. First and foremost, the idea of professional authority among physicians was in its infancy. As the university-trained physician Dr. William Douglass tried to get the apprentice-trained surgeon Boylston to discontinue an experimental intervention, the clergy decided to intervene. The local political leaders did not stop the practice, although they did mandate that inoculated persons be in quarantine as if they had natural smallpox. In Virginia in 1768, an inoculator started an epidemic by not confining his patients, and the legislature restricted the practice. In Marblehead, Massachusetts, in 1774, inoculation led to riots. Part of the problem was economic; Benjamin Franklin, a strong supporter of the practice, noted its cost was "pretty high," usually greater than a common tradesman "can well spare." In addition it was impractical to take several weeks away from work (there was no sick leave) to convalesce from the procedure. If inoculation was practiced when there was not a raging epidemic, it was the well-to-do class who received the benefits and the working classes who were put at risk of the spreading disease.

Smallpox was only one of many infectious diseases to plague the colonists. Others included the childhood diseases of measles, mumps, and especially diphtheria; epidemics of gastrointestinal diseases, sometimes typhoid fever, sometimes dysentery, and sometimes food poisoning; respiratory disease, which occurred every winter; and the yellow fever brought episodically to American ports by trade with Africa and the West Indies. But the most common disease was the so-called intermittent fever. After 1619, in South Carolina, outbreaks of a particularly malignant intermittent fever began to occur. Sometimes it was called remittent fever because the disease never seemed to completely leave the patient. The malignant fever spread with the continuing arrival of African slaves and is widely believed to be an African variant of malaria. In new settlements the experience was so common as to be called "seasoning," a normal part of moving there. The planter patterns of Low Country South Carolina—winter on the plantation and summer in the city, the Sea Islands, or the uplands—were shaped by fear of the seasonal disease. (The seasonal pattern would later be explained as a result of malaria being communicated by a mosquito vector.)

By 1750 the colonies had several significant towns, some of which were becoming cities. In these towns the medical profession began to organize following European models. Local practitioners formed medical societies, which sometimes provided for regulation. New Jersey and Massachusetts both chartered societies. They examined apprentices completing their training, and through admission to membership in the society following their success on the examination, the apprentices were certified as competent to practice. This provided a transportable credential, allowing apprentices to move away from masters to establish a practice. The colonial governments supported professional efforts by denying uncertified practitioners the use of the courts to recover fees. The "license" of the medical society was not required to practice, and many practitioners of varying competency and training practiced quite successfully without the license.

With increases in colonial wealth, more and more young practitioners opted to visit European cities for further education. Usually they went to Edinburgh for a medical degree or London to walk the wards of the new voluntary hospitals, and some went to the Continent. In 1765 two such students, William Shippen and John Morgan, convinced the College of Philadelphia trustees to open a medical department (later the University of Pennsylvania). In 1766, Thomas Bond, a founder of the Pennsylvania Hospital (1751), offered to give clinical lectures for the new medical program, and in June 1768 the first medical degrees were awarded in the colonies. The Pennsylvania Hospital was a typical eighteenth-century British voluntary hospital, built by subscription of wealthy individuals who held the right to nominate patients for admission; the medical staff served gratis. Shippen also offered instruction in midwifery, following a new pattern of anatomically based, physician-mediated childbirth practices that he had learned in London.

The Nineteenth Century

In 1800 the nation had four medical schools: the University of Pennsylvania (Philadelphia), the College of Physicians and Surgeons (New York City), Harvard's Massachusetts Medical College, and Dartmouth in New Hampshire. The standard of education was two courses of identical lectures (each of approximately four months), a final examination of indifferent rigor, a thesis, and a three-year apprenticeship. The value of the lectures was to introduce material the student would not see in the practical apprenticeship and provide some theoretical underpinnings to future reading. The vast majority of practitioners remained apprentice-trained, and states steadily followed the lead of Massachusetts in exempting medical school graduates from licensure examination. The M.D. was even more transportable than the state license, and as the country expanded westward it became increasingly important.

Practice was eclectic at best; therapy had changed little in the early modern period despite new scientific knowledge. The heavy metals introduced in the Renaissance had become increasingly common therapeutic agents and many practitioners and patients preferred the purgative calomel (mercurous chloride) as a means of depletion in place of bloodletting, particularly if the digestion was implicated. Botanical remedies were also common, and some practitioners favored indigenous remedies. Modern scholars often disparage the value of these remedies, but they seemed to be effective. The physician gave a name to the unusual and serious disease (diagnosis), he frequently could tell patient and family what to expect in the coming days (prognosis), and he prescribed a remedy that had obvious physiological activity and so presumably helped effect a cure. Since most patients get well from most diseases (a concept not understood in 1800), this approach worked to most people's satisfaction.

Challenges and reforms. The growth of scientific and medical societies in Europe in the eighteenth century had established that the community of practitioners determined the degree of theoretical and therapeutic innovation that one could advocate and remain within the profession. Samuel Hahnemann introduced homeopathy in the late eighteenth century, but most medical practitioners rejected his ideas. By 1844, however, there were enough homeopathic practitioners to sustain a national medical society, the American Institute of Homeopathy. Germans in Pennsylvania came under Hahnemann's influence, and in 1848 they obtained a charter for a medical college in Philadelphia, which was later named for Hahnemann. Many practitioners tried homeopathy as a result of the failure of traditional remedies, especially in the cholera pandemics of 1832 and 1849.

European ideas were not the only challenges to the medical profession in the early nineteenth century. A New England farmer, Samuel Thomson, developed a system of healing based on his understanding of indigenous plant remedies, which he patented in 1813. By 1840 Thomson had sold over 100,000 rights. Thomson's son, John, was the agent in Albany, New York, when in 1844 a patient died under his care. The medical society pressed the state to bring charges against John Thomson for practicing without a license and so being guilty of the untimely death of a fellow citizen. Thomson collected a petition with over 50,000 signatures requesting the repeal of the licensing law in New York, and the legislature complied. By 1850 the licensure legislation in every state except Massachusetts (where it was not enforced) had been repealed in the name of equity.

At the close of the eighteenth century the French republic had combined the ancient professions of physician and surgeon into a new unitary profession, trained in a medical school that had science teaching and hospital-based clinical experiences. These new practitioners made important observations in pathology, particularly the correlation of clinical signs and symptoms with changes in the tissues observed at postmortem. New means of physical diagnosis—auscultation and percussion—became increasingly popular. Dissections were frequent and practitioners began to fully document the natural history of various diseases. Americans visited Paris in large numbers, some for a brief period, others for extended study.

In 1835 Jacob Bigelow of Harvard advanced a radical idea: the therapies of the medical profession, regular or sectarian, did not change the natural course of most cases of disease. His classic essay, "On Self-Limited Diseases," documented that those who take no remedies recover at rates similar to those who take remedies of the various forms of practice. The idea of self-limited disease was strongly resisted by much of the profession—self-interest, self-esteem, and even feelings of humanity all combined to oppose the idea. Yet more and more physicians became increasingly skeptical with the accumulation of data and the passage of time. As medical leaders abandoned the older therapies but had no new ones to take the place of that which was discarded, a crisis of confidence was exacerbated between the patient, who had been comfortable being prescribed for, and the profession, which now had a reduced, relatively passive role. Charles Rosenberg has described the profound change produced by this crisis as the "therapeutic revolution" and suggests that it was one of the most important turning points in the history of medicine since it led to reforms in the study and practice of medicine that ultimately excluded educated laymen from the medical decision-making process. The physician's increasingly scientific knowledge meant that doctor and patient no longer had a shared understanding of the therapeutic encounter.

In the years leading up to the Civil War these changes would play out in a variety of ways. One was the "malpractice crisis," in which improvements in orthopedics had resulted in improved limb salvage after bad fractures but at the cost of some limb shortening and limping. Juries awarded oppressive damages on the assumption that all fractures could be healed perfectly. Another area of confusion was the role and nature of ether anesthesia, introduced in 1846. Did pain serve an important physiological function? Should it be relieved if the patient could stand the surgery without pain relief? Patients wanted anesthesia, but doctors were worried about the long-term success if the normal physiology was interrupted. The competition of increasing numbers of practitioners, the growth of sectarian practice, and the influence of new ideas from Paris resulted in a profound change in the nature of medical thinking in the 1830s and 1840s.

As some practitioners campaigned to "improve" the profession socially and scientifically, others were concerned about the propriety of the changes. The frustrations surrounding these controversies resulted in the organization of the American Medical Association in 1847. Essentially an organization of medical schools and interested practitioners, the AMA had as its primary goal the elevation of standards of practice through improved medical school education. Professor Martyn Paine of New York University, one of the strongest voices for an open and egalitarian profession, felt those who wished to increase requirements for medical students were self-interested elitists who were unfairly attacking the honor of the profession for personal aggrandizement. Under the then current system, America was the only country in the world where every citizen had the expectation of receiving care from a medical graduate with an M.D., and "reform" might put that distinction at risk. However, the schools had no incentive to raise standards.

Post–Civil War changes. During the Civil War the diversity of education, knowledge, and skill within the medical profession was increasingly apparent. The experience focused attention on several areas where improvement was possible. The use of ambulances to evacuate the wounded from the battlefield led some physicians to advocate hospital-based, urban ambulance systems after the war. The experience with camp diseases and the failures of camp hygiene encouraged the sanitary reform movement in the later part of the nineteenth century. The failures of surgical knowledge were recognized as heavily based in anatomical ignorance and inspired anatomy acts in many states in the generation following the war. Perhaps most important, many Americans gained a knowledge of and experience with hospitals as places of quality medical care for all classes.

While America was engaged in the Civil War, scientists in France and Germany were creating modern physiology, cellular pathology, and the germ theory of disease causation. The development of a postwar urban, industrial culture in the United States, when combined with the new germ theory as applied to antiseptic surgery, helped drive the rapid expansion of hospitals in American cities. With a little over 600 hospitals at the centennial, the nation developed over 2,000 by the beginning of the new century. The volunteer surgical staffs of the hospitals saw the advantage of allowing the charities to provide the capital investment for antiseptic and increasingly aseptic operating rooms, realizing that their paying, private patients would benefit from this new surgical environment. The traditional charities had never had staff practitioners charge patients, and so surgeons engaged in campaigns to have the rules changed and to get private, paying beds added to the institutions. In addition, surgeons were frequently the driving force behind the establishment of nurse-training programs in the hospitals.

The passage of anatomy acts, starting in Pennsylvania (1867), improved basic education in medical science. The increased need for clinical experience was also recognized, and medical schools built relationships with the expanding community of hospitals. Apprenticeship declined rapidly. As professional leaders encouraged investment in improved education, they saw value in external certification of their graduates to limit the influence of students on curricula and admissions. The reintroduction of state licensure provided the needed extramural authority.

As licensing examinations grew more common, old sectarian practitioners declined. However, there were (and are) always patients for whom medicine has no answers, and such failures supported new sectarian movements as medicine was making scientific progress. Andrew T. Still, a bonesetter, developed the system of osteopathic medicine in the 1870s, based on nervous energy distribution mediated by the spine. He used the science of the day and brought physiologists into the new school of thought in such a way that osteopathy was open to new ideas and scientific change; it would be largely reintegrated with regular medicine in the 1960s. D. D. Palmer's "invention" of chiropractic (1894) did not allow for changes in theory, nor did Mary Baker Eddy's "discovery" of Christian Science (1875).

That medical science was progressing faster than anyone could manage was beyond dispute; the AMA adopted sections for special interest programming at its meetings and published their discussions in its periodicals. Many of the leaders of the sections were involved with other kinds of specialty organizations, the most common of which was the limited membership society made up of professors who published in the specialty and devoted all or most of their time to its practice. Organized medicine at the close of the nineteenth century was dynamic, innovative, and successful in its attempt to portray medical progress as being beyond the understanding of the nonpractitioner, trustworthy to keep its own house in order, and of sufficient societal benefit for society to take the risk.

The 1896 war with Spain and the resulting colonial empire served as an excellent study of the possibilities of the new medicine in American society. As the war progressed and America's premier surgeons volunteered and publicized their successes, the power of surgery was obvious. William Borden took the new X-ray machine to war. Walter Reed went to Cuba and solved the puzzle of yellow fever—it was caused by a virus and transmitted by the bite of the mosquito. William Gorgas, the health officer in Havana, began a campaign to eliminate mosquitoes, and with military efficiency yellow fever went away. In the Philippines army doctors established health departments that controlled smallpox, plague, cholera, malaria, and a host of other tropical infections. The vital statistics of various cities and states confirmed what the army experience demonstrated: modern medicine saved lives through preventing illness. Modern surgeons could do amazing things—delivery by cesarean section, appendectomy, hernia repair—and new drugs such as antitoxins, aspirin, and nitroglycerine for the heart made other diseases much less fearsome and painful. So as the new century opened, the power of science was turning back disease, healthy people could be more productive and thus happier, and at least to many opinion molders the possibilities of the future seemed limitless.

The Twentieth Century

In 1901, John D. Rockefeller founded the Rockefeller Institute for Medical Research. Other new institutes followed, and hospitals and medical schools began to receive philanthropy of an order that America had never seen in the past. The AMA asked the Carnegie Institution in Washington to investigate medical education, and in 1910 its agent, Abraham Flexner, issued his muckraking sensation, *Report on Medical Education in the United States and Canada.* Reform of medical education, which had been struggling, took on new definition from Flexner's report. He adopted Johns Hopkins as his model and evaluated every school by how well they matched it; only one came close. Societal leaders urged the others to meet the new standard, a standard designed to educate practitioners who would keep pace with the best science. Philanthropy helped, both with endowments and capital improvements. Tax support followed rapidly. Among the difficult challenges was the new entry requirement of a college education; also expensive was a university-controlled teaching hospital. It would take almost forty years before all schools could provide educational opportunities like Johns Hopkins had in the early years of the century, but eventually the standard of educational excellence would be achieved. The costs were high; if you could not afford college and full-time study you could not become a doctor. Even more unfortunate was the funneling of the limited philanthropy into traditional white male institutions, leaving women's medical colleges and black schools without the funds to survive the new push toward excellent education for every medical student. The profession became better trained but more homogeneous as the new century progressed.

Because the progress of medical science had made it difficult to teach practitioners everything they needed to know in even four years, much of the practical training was gained in postgraduate hospital service. In 1904, Pennsylvania became the first of many states to mandate the completion of an internship year prior to licensure. The AMA issued standards for an approved internship in 1919, although a generation would pass before the experience became essentially universal.

The surgical hospital needed nursing staff to assist in surgery and to care for patients in recovery and convalescence. As the practice became more complex, more individuals played important roles: personnel were needed to give anesthetics, to do pathological tests and examinations, and to use the new X-ray machines and interpret the images that resulted. Many of these individuals seemed to require special education and training, often beyond the basic M.D. Hospitals were expensive to capitalize and operate, and patients frequently could not pay the actual costs. By the second decade of the twentieth century, the increasing costs associated with modern medical care were attracting political attention worldwide. Germany had introduced sickness insurance in the 1880s, and by 1911 the British adopted workmen's health insurance. In various states insurance proposals were made. While these proposals frequently included hospitalization insurance, they most commonly called for the payment of what would come to be called sick leave (temporary salary replacement) and workmen's compensation or medical and disability pay protecting the employer from liability. The medical profession was divided on the proposals, but in 1915, as World War I gathered fury and the proposals were labeled as German, the movement lost strength and faded before the end of the decade. During the 1920s malpractice suits grew exponentially as lawyers recommended a malpractice countersuit when patients were sued for uncollected hospital bills. Finally, as the decade drew to a close, Texas teachers agreed on hospitalization insurance with local hospitals, and the voluntary insurance program known as Blue Cross was born.

It was still better to stay healthy, and the early twentieth century saw continued progress in preventive medicine. Among the most dramatic changes was the study of industrial risks led by Alice Hamilton of Illinois. The rural South also saw rapid progress in public health, first through the Rockefeller hookworm eradication campaign and then through Public Health Service campaigns against malaria and pellagra. After proving that pellagra was a nutritional deficiency disease, Dr. Joseph Goldberger, a Public Health Service officer, attracted national attention in 1921 when he publicly charged that the southern system of subsistence tenant farming was starving the people of the South. However, the cure for the disease—a higher standard of living—was more difficult to achieve than the diagnosis. Rockefeller and Public Health Service trials as well as local public health initiatives sometimes made local progress in fighting malaria, which required capital investment in drainage and screens to limit the access of mosquitoes to humans, but its elimination (or at least that of its mosquito vector) was beyond the scope of public health expenditure. As the century progressed it became increasingly clear that the easy public health victories had been won, and further progress required participation of the people and changes in public priorities, neither easy to mobilize.

By the 1930s the problems of specialization had grown to become a significant issue in the self-governance of the profession. A group of concerned surgeons formed the American College of Surgeons in 1913, which was restricted to surgeons who could document satisfactory experience in both training and practice and who were certified by their peers to practice according to high ethical standards. The College grew steadily and after World War I became an important force in education and specialization in the practice of surgery. The ophthalmologists took a different approach; their concern was with a group of "specialized eye doctors," the optometrists, who were marketing themselves as trained exclusively in eye problems. Ophthalmologists established a separate examination in eye medicine for well-trained specialists so that they too were certified as more specialized in eye problems than the average doctor. In 1917 the American Board of Ophthalmic Examinations was chartered, soon to be renamed the American Board of Ophthalmology;

303

and otolaryngology followed in 1922. In 1930, gynecology and obstetrics formed a third board, and before 1940, all the basic specialty boards were formed. The common basis was three years of specialty training beyond internship and a satisfactory certifying examination.

Innovations after World War II. World War II fundamentally reshaped American medicine in many important ways: it changed the opinions of doctors on the virtues of specialty practice, it changed the opinion of many Americans on the importance of physician access, and it convinced many of the profound possibilities of medical research. Americans' expectations of medical care grew, as did the system for paying for that care. In 1940 about 9 percent of Americans were covered by hospitalization insurance; by 1950 that percentage was greater than half. Fringe benefits were made exempt from taxation in the war and, unlike wages, were not frozen, creating an incentive to increase fringe benefits to attract workers to war industry. In the military, Americans were referred to specialized care in the general hospitals. Those approved as specialists received higher rank and so better pay and quarters. Even more telling was the observation that the specialist in the hospital was in the rear while the generalist was in the front; there is no greater statement of social value than distance from bullets.

At the end of the war the Servicemen's Readjustment Act (GI Bill) paid tuition to enhance the education and training of servicemen returning to civil life. Under the act, hospitals and medical schools were paid tuition to employ residents, whom they needed to staff the hospital anyway. The result was a rapid, almost exponential, expansion of residency positions all across the nation. The greatest impact of the wartime medical experience was probably the faith created in the power of science to change the quality and perhaps the quantity of life for Americans. Penicillin was the most obvious of the medical miracles, but new immunizations, blood fractionation, DDT insecticide, and the bug bomb to repel mosquitoes all contributed to the sense of rapid progress. The wealth of the postwar economy solved many of the social problems that had undermined health in the prewar years, and postwar Americans began to expect medicine to deliver on demand.

Streptomycin, the second great antibiotic, was valuable in the fight against tuberculosis, the last great nineteenth-century killer. As new epidemics emerged, particularly polio, the mobilization of medical research led to an immunization within a decade. The early 1950s saw the introduction of the heart-lung machine and open-heart surgery, the Kolff artificial kidney and the possibility of dialysis, as well as exceptional progress in disability management within the Veteran's Administration. The reformation of the VA medical system led to the association of new VA medical centers with medical schools in an effort to enhance care for the veterans and increase the number of physicians available to serve the higher expectations of the public. Even more important was the growth

of federal financing of medical research through the National Institutes of Health. With federal money through the VA and the NIH, the Flexnerian vision of American medical education finally became a complete reality. In the following decades, therapeutic interventions, especially drugs to control metabolic diseases, combat cancer, prevent pregnancy, and limit psychiatric symptoms, all transformed illness. Diagnostic imaging and automated diagnostic tests transformed the doctor-patient encounter in ways both helpful to precision and harmful to the doctor's counseling role. For the first time in human history, life expectancy for those over sixty-five increased, fundamentally altering the demographic profile of American society.

With an increasingly scientific and specialized medical profession, the ancillary components of the health care system also changed. The goal of a professional nursing service became increasingly common, and with insurance the hospitals could pay these fully qualified nurses. However, professions in America were educated in the university, not trained on the job, and leaders of American nursing increasingly looked to the bachelor's degree as the standard of basic training in nursing. The technical assistants of radiologists and pathologists were also increasingly educated in universities. As the personnel increased so did the technical equipment required to practice the best medicine, such as new imaging and laboratory machines. This equipment, as well as changes in nurseries and operating rooms to control infections and more semiprivate rooms expected by suburbanites who had insurance, required more capital and more management. A profession of hospital administration began to grow, and hospitals looked for new sources of support. The federal government was the obvious place to find large sums of money, and the 1947 Hill-Burton Act created a program of matching grants to build hospitals in underserved areas. The underserved areas that could raise matching funds were in the suburbs, and Hill-Burton hospitals sprang up across the nation at the edges of cities.

Paying for health care. The federal government might build hospitals and pay for medical research, but it would not organize ways to pay for medical care. The Truman administration reintroduced national health insurance after the war and was defeated by the AMA. Through the 1950s the insurance system and the economy both expanded rapidly enough to give the appearance of moving toward universal coverage. By 1960 it had become obvious that voluntary insurance was meeting the needs of many but that some groups were left out, particularly the elderly. The Johnson administration's Great Society initiative provided both the elderly and the poor with new federal programs: Medicare for the elderly—an addition to the social security program that provided hospital insurance and, for a small fee, doctor's bill coverage—and Medicaid, a state grant program to provide coverage for the poor. The medical profession was convinced to participate by making the programs reimburse on a costs-plus basis like private insurance rather than using an imposed fee schedule as most national insurance programs required. By 1971 the upward spiral of costs forced the government to reconsider its costs-plus approach and look for ways to retrench.

By the late 1960s health care began to be discussed as a "right." Increasingly there were those who felt that a right implied responsibility, and so individuals needed to be encouraged to take better care of themselves. In 1964 the surgeon general of the United States, on the advice of an expert committee, determined that the association between cigarettes and lung cancer in men was sufficient to issue a public warning. The nation grappled with the difficult question of how to change legal, if harmful, habits that were generations in the making. Like Goldberger's prescription of a better diet for southern tenant farmers in the early twentieth century, modern public health advice frequently requires massive social changes.

By the late 1980s health insurance for business had become a major personnel expense, and corporate leaders looked for ways to limit their costs. The idea of health maintenance organizations (HMOs) had been introduced in the early 1970s as a market-driven way to reduce utilization: if physician incomes were determined in advance by the number of patients they cared for and they had to pay for referrals, they would have an interest in holding down the expenditures on patients in order to retain more of the money. As business turned increasingly to HMOs and fee-for-service declined as a percentage of the medical marketplace, the suspicion that medical decisions were made on the basis of cost rather than patient interest began to grow. But when President Clinton attempted to overhaul the entire health care system in 1993, the general opinion was that it was not broken enough to take the chance of making it worse. Concerns over affirmative action and equity in medical school admissions suggest that society does not wish to return to the days when the well to do were the only ones able to become physicians. Concern with the uninsured remains politically important. Research and practice associated with fetal issues and genetics generate debate. Technological improvements continue to fascinate, as replacement parts, miniaturized diagnostics, and the increasing engineering marvels associated with modern medicine bespeak a commitment to excellence in health care undiminished in the twenty-first century.

BIBLIOGRAPHY

Dowling, Harry Filmore. *Fighting Infection: Conquests of the Twentieth Century.* Cambridge, Mass.: Harvard University Press, 1977.

Duffy, John. *Epidemics in Colonial America.* Port Washington, NY: Kennikat Press, 1972.

———. *The Sanitarians: A History of American Public Health.* Urbana: University of Illinois Press, 1990.

Gevitz, Norman, ed. *Other Healers: Unorthodox Medicine in America.* Baltimore: Johns Hopkins University Press, 1988.

Grob, Gerald N. *The Mad Among Us.* New York: Free Press, 1994.

Kraut, Alan M. *Silent Travelers: Germs, Genes, and the Immigrant Menace.* New York: Basic Books, 1994.

Leavitt, Judith Walzer. *Brought to Bed: Childbearing in America, 1750 to 1950.* New York: Oxford University Press, 1986.

Ludmerer, Kenneth M. *Time to Heal: American Medical Education from the Turn of the Century to the Era of Managed Care.* Oxford and New York: Oxford University Press, 1999.

Maulitz, Russell C., and Diana E. Long, eds. *Grand Rounds: One Hundred Years of Internal Medicine.* Philadelphia: University of Pennsylvania Press, 1988.

Morantz-Sanchez, Regina. *Sympathy and Science: Women Physicians in American Medicine.* Chapel Hill: University of North Carolina Press, 2000.

Numbers, Ronald L., ed. *Compulsory Health Insurance: The Continuing American Debate.* Westport, Conn.: Greenwood Press, 1982.

Rosenberg, Charles E. *The Cholera Years: The United States in 1832, 1849, and 1866.* 1962. Reprint, Chicago: University of Chicago Press, 1987.

———. *The Care of Strangers: The Rise of America's Hospital System.* New York: Basic Books, 1987.

Ruktow, Ira M., and Stanley B. Burns. *American Surgery: An Illustrated History.* Philadelphia: Lippencott, 1998.

Savitt, Todd L., and James H. Young, eds. *Disease and Distinctiveness in the American South.* Knoxville: University of Tennessee Press, 1988.

Starr, Paul. *The Social Transformation of American Medicine.* New York: Basic Books, 1982.

Stevens, Rosemary. *In Sickness and in Wealth: American Hospitals in the Twentieth Century.* New York: Basic Books, 1989.

———. *American Medicine and the Public Interest.* Rev. ed. Berkeley: University of California Press, 1998.

Dale C. Smith

See also **American Medical Association; Anesthesia, Discovery of; Chemotherapy; Childbirth and Reproduction; Chiropractic; Clinical Research; Epidemics and Public Health; Health Care; Health Insurance; Health Maintenance Organizations; Homeopathy; Hospitals; Hygiene; Johns Hopkins University; Malaria; Medical Education; Medical Profession; Medical Research; Medical Societies; Medicare and Medicaid; Medicine, Alternative; Microbiology; Osteopathy; Smallpox.**

MEDICINE SHOW, an early-nineteenth-century technique for selling patent medicines. To sell this bottled magic, the showman provided a free show at town squares, street corners, or wherever he could draw a crowd. Claiming special herbal knowledge, he claimed to be Indian or part Indian, or was accompanied by someone of complexion and garb professedly Indian. He employed blackface comedians. Songs and repartee jokes were his stock in trade, and he was an artist at "kidding" the crowd while he mixed in praise of the supernal drug.

Medicine Show. The only known photograph of a Kickapoo Medicine Company "Indian Village," taken at Manchester Depot, Vt., in 1885. LIBRARY OF CONGRESS

BIBLIOGRAPHY

Anderson, Ann, and Heinrich R. Falk. *Snake Oil, Hustlers, and Hambones: The American Medicine Show.* Jefferson, N.C.: McFarland, 2000.

J. Frank Dobie / c. w.

See also **Medicine, Alternative; Minstrel Shows.**

MEETINGHOUSE. Reserving "church" to designate a covenanted ecclesiastical society, New England Puritans used "meetinghouse" to denote the assembly place used for church services, town meetings, and other public gatherings. Church membership was restricted, but attendance at church services was mandatory. Services included baptisms, sermons, prayers, psalm singing, and funerals for notable persons. Typically a white frame structure, the early square meetinghouse, with a central tower, gave way to an oblong style with an end tower topped by a spire. The pulpit dominated the simple but dignified interior. In much of New England, taxes as well as pew receipts supported the meetinghouses' religious activities. In late colonial times the meetinghouse became a center of revolutionary activities.

BIBLIOGRAPHY

Donnelly, Marian C. *The New England Meeting Houses of the Seventeenth Century.* Middletown, Conn.: Wesleyan University Press, 1968.

Von Rohr, John. *The Shaping of American Congregationalism, 1620–1957.* Cleveland, Ohio: Pilgrim Press, 1992.

Louise B. Dunbar / A. R.

See also **Covenant, Church; New England Way; Theocracy in New England.**

MEGAN'S LAW. The term refers to a type of statute passed following the 1994 death of a seven-year-old girl named Megan Kanka, who was raped and killed by a sex offender on parole who lived across the street from her in Hamilton, New Jersey. First New Jersey and then most other states adopted some version of "Megan's Law." These laws require public notice that a sex offender is moving into a neighborhood, on the theory that people on notice will take increased care to protect their children. The relevant portion of the federal Crime Control and Law Enforcement Act of 1994 was amended in 1996 to require states to adopt procedures for neighborhood notification. The information disclosed about individuals is quite specific, with distinctions made in various state statutes between different types of information (addresses, photographs, descriptions of modus operandi) and the degree of risk to the community. Many states have set up Web sites giving information about sex offenders.

Megan's Laws are highly controversial because of a conflict between the protection of the public and the protection of the privacy rights of offenders who have served their sentences and been released.

Carol Weisbrod

See also **Child Abuse; Children, Missing.**

MELTING POT is a term that originated in Israel Zangwill's 1908 drama, *The Melting Pot.* It examined the American dream, the acceptance of newcomers, and their subsequent Americanization. German immigrants had used the term *schmelztiegel* ("melting pot") in the early nineteenth century, but the term was not popularized until Zangwill's play. The term is flexible and could mean "melting" or the creation of the homogenous American; it also refers to the mixing of various elements that lead to homogeneity. In the mid-twentieth century, cultural theorists who disputed the homogeneity theory increased the elasticity of the term by arguing for a stew, salad, or orchestra metaphor.

BIBLIOGRAPHY

Gleason, Philip. *Speaking of Diversity: Language and Ethnicity in Twentieth-Century America.* Baltimore: Johns Hopkins University Press, 1992.

Jennifer Harrison

See also **Beyond the Melting Pot.**

MEMORIAL DAY (May 30), or Decoration Day, began in 1868 when members of the GRAND ARMY OF THE REPUBLIC heeded the request of their commander, General John A. Logan, to decorate the graves of their fallen compatriots. It has since become the day on which the United States honors the dead of all its wars and is observed as a legal holiday in most states. National services

Memorial Day. Americans who died in war are remembered overseas as well, at American military cemeteries like this one from World War I in the village of Brookwood, Surrey, England. ARCHIVE PHOTOS, INC.

are held at the Tomb of the Unknown Soldier in Arlington, Virginia. In 2000 President Bill Clinton asked the nation to endorse a humanitarian organization's addition of a moment of silence to the holiday, designating 3 P.M. local time for a minute of quiet reflection on the meaning of America's war dead.

BIBLIOGRAPHY

Litwicki, Ellen M. *America's Public Holidays, 1865–1920*. Washington, D.C.: Smithsonian Institution Press, 2000.

Seddie Cogswell / H. S.

See also **Holidays and Festivals; Nationalism.**

MEMORIAL DAY MASSACRE (1937). In the spring of 1937 the Steel Workers' Organizing Committee (SWOC), the first mass recruitment project of the newly formed Congress of Industrial Organizations (CIO), called its first nationwide strike. Just a few months earlier, on 1 March, the SWOC had signed a contract with the largest steel corporation in the world, U.S. Steel, and was confident that the smaller remaining companies, collectively known as "Little Steel," could be brought to similar terms. On 26 May 1937 the SWOC called out over eighty-five thousand workers in three companies: Republic, Youngstown Sheet and Tube, and Inland Steel. Republic's South Chicago facility was one of the few plants that remained in operation during the strike. About half the workers stayed on the job, and Republic housed them on the mill grounds.

From the beginning Chicago police aggressively disrupted picket lines and arrested strike leaders. Strike leaders called for a mass demonstration to protest police brutality and partiality in the strike. Police officials reinforced

their numbers to over 250 around the plant in anticipation of the march that was scheduled for Memorial Day, 30 May 1937.

Memorial Day dawned bright and hot, and by mid-afternoon the crowd of strikers and supporters, numbering well over a thousand, marched behind two American flags toward the factory gates chanting "CIO, CIO." When the marchers drew up along the line of police, a tense standoff ensued. The police ordered the crowd to disperse, and the marchers argued for their right to peacefully assemble. Sticks and stones began to fly, and police responded with tear gas. Without warning, police began firing wildly into the crowd. A hundred marchers fell. Ten eventually perished, all of them shot facing away from the police.

Later investigations by Robert La Follette Jr.'s Senate Civil Liberties Committee, dramatically punctuated with a graphic Paramount newsreel that authorities had suppressed, attributed little provocation to the marchers and found that police had wantonly attacked them. Nevertheless the police and corporate intimidation caused the strike to collapse. None of the three "Little Steel" companies recognized the unions of their workers until forced to do so by the federal government under the emergency powers it assumed in World War II.

BIBLIOGRAPHY

Clark, Paul F., Peter Gottlieb, and Donald Kennedy. *Forging a Union of Steel: Philip Murray, SWOC, and the United Steel Workers*. Ithaca, N.Y.: ILR Press, 1987.

Leab, Daniel J. "The Memorial Day Massacre." *Midcontinent American Studies Journal* 8, no. 2 (1967): 3–15.

U.S. Senate. Committee on Education and Labor. *Violations of Free Speech and Rights of Labor: The Chicago Memorial Day Incident*. 75th Cong., 1st sess. Report no. 46 (2), 1937.

Timothy Messer-Kruse

See also **American Federation of Labor–Congress of Industrial Organizations; Steel Strikes; Strikes; Violence.**

MEMPHIS, the largest city in Tennessee and the chief city on the Mississippi River between St. Louis and New Orleans. In 1819, Memphis was laid out by a trio of town site developers, one of whom was the future president Andrew Jackson. It was named for the ancient Egyptian capital on the Nile River. During the following four decades, it became a leading river port and a center for the cotton trade. Completed in 1857, the Memphis and Charleston Railroad provided a transportation link to the Atlantic Ocean, further enhancing the city's commercial advantages. Occupied by Union forces in 1862, Memphis escaped the destruction suffered by many other southern cities during the Civil War. During the 1870s, however, repeated yellow fever epidemics decimated the local population and retarded the city's development. By 1900, Memphis had recovered and, with a population of

W. C. Handy. The blues pioneer, bandleader, and cornetist, whose most enduring fame is from the music he composed. AP/WIDE WORLD PHOTOS

102,320, ranked as the second-largest city in the former Confederacy.

The Democratic organization of Boss Ed Crump dominated Memphis politics during the first half of the twentieth century. Devoted to low property taxes, Crump was reluctant to invest in the costly public works projects suggested by city planners. Although the city earned no national recognition as a showpiece of urban government, it did win a reputation as a center of blues music. In 1909, the black musician W. C. Handy wrote "Memphis Blues" as a campaign song for Crump, and the city's Beale Street became famous as the birthplace of the blues.

Between 1947 and 1977, Memphis annexed 230 square miles and almost doubled in population, claiming to have 674,000 residents in the latter year. That same year marked the death of the city's most famous resident, Elvis Presley. Presley began his rock and roll career in Memphis, recording with a small local company called Sun Records. In 1982, his home, Graceland, was opened to the public and became a pilgrimage site for more than 600,000 visitors annually; their spending gave a boost to the city's economy. Meanwhile, as the headquarters of Federal Express Corporation, Memphis claimed to be America's distribution center, and the city's airport boasted of being the world's busiest air cargo port. The city also became a major medical center and remained a hub of the cotton trade. Despite its enlarged boundaries, Memphis lost residents to growing suburban areas, and in the 1980s and 1990s, its population was relatively stable. In 2000, it was home to 650,100 people.

BIBLIOGRAPHY

Capers, Gerald M., Jr. *The Biography of a River Town: Memphis in Its Heroic Age.* 2d ed. Memphis: G. M. Capers, 1966.

Tucker, David M. *Memphis Since Crump: Bossism, Blacks, and Civic Reformers, 1948–1968.* Knoxville: University of Tennessee Press, 1980.

Jon C. Teaford

See also **Blues; Rock and Roll; Tennessee.**

MENÉNDEZ DE AVILÉS, PEDRO, COLONIZATION EFFORTS OF.

Pedro Menéndez de Avilés (1519–1574) was a mariner, explorer, colonizer, and governor of Florida. A prominent defender of Spain against French privateers in Europe, he served as captain general of the Indies fleet in 1554, 1560, and 1561.

In 1565, Menéndez contracted with King Phillip II to colonize and explore La Florida, which as conceived by Spain at that time, extended from the Florida Panhandle to Newfoundland. Pressured by French Huguenot fort-building in present-day Florida, the Spanish felt it imperative to quickly establish a settlement in the territory. In addition to expelling the French from their fort on the Saint John's River, Menéndez's objectives were to explore, to found settlements, to find a passage to the Pacific, and to convert the native peoples. He was to accomplish these goals at his own expense, with some royal troops provided by King Phillip.

Menéndez led his party of eight hundred soldiers, sailors, and settlers, including the wives and children of twenty-six of his men, to Saint Augustine in 1565. He claimed Florida for Spain on 8 September. After securing a place for the settlers in a Timucuan Indian village, Menéndez set out with his soldiers to attack the French fort, which he conquered on 20 September. After finishing off the French forces at Matanzas Inlet, he addressed his other objectives.

In 1565, Menéndez reconnoitered the east coast of Florida, preparing for the establishment of outposts, and then sailed to Cuba for supplies. In early 1566 he explored the southwestern coast of Florida. During these journeys, he discovered currents and channels that eased navigation for the Spanish fleets. Upon his return to Saint Augustine in 1566, he had to put down a mutiny among his troops before he could continue carrying out his plans. Later, he sent out expeditionary parties to roam the interior, map the coastline, and find a passage to the Pacific. He founded a number of garrison settlements in southern Florida and a promising settlement at Santa Elena in what became South Carolina.

In 1565 the first Catholic mission, Nombre de Dios, was established at Saint Augustine. Menéndez set up a tribute system whereby the local Indians would supply the colonists with corn, skins, pottery, and labor. Many of the men married Indian women and formed a new society based on Indian and Spanish culture. By the end of the sixteenth century, Saint Augustine had become a city based on Spanish planning principles. It did not, however, become economically self-sufficient during Menéndez's rule. Life for the colonists was one of privation and hardship. Its main purpose was military—to protect the Spanish treasure fleets as they sailed up the coast in the Gulf Stream.

Eventually, Indian resistance led Menéndez to give up Spanish outposts in southern Florida. After 1569 he focused on the development of Santa Elena, but soon exhausted his personal resources. Upon receiving a royal subsidy in 1570, he brought his family from Spain to Santa Elena. Menéndez intended to build an estate, but this plan was interrupted in 1574, when he was called home to help quell a rebellion in the Spanish Netherlands. As he was gathering his forces in Santander, Spain, he became ill with a fever and died.

Menéndez was always more interested in exploration than colonization, but his most important accomplishment was the founding of Saint Augustine, the first continuous European settlement in what became the United States. Although Saint Augustine never flourished under Menéndez's rule, it survived.

BIBLIOGRAPHY

Manucy, Albert. *Menéndez: Pedro Menéndez de Avilés, Captain General of the Ocean Sea*. Sarasota, Fla.: Pineapple Press, 1992.

Milanich, Jerald T., and Susan Milbrath, eds. *First Encounters: Spanish Explorations in the Caribbean and the United States, 1492–1570*. Gainesville: University of Florida Press, 1991.

Bonnie L. Ford

See also **Colonial Administration, Spanish; Exploration and Expeditions: Spanish; Florida; Indian Policy, Colonial; Saint Augustine; South Carolina; Spanish Borderlands.**

MENNONITES. A worldwide religious movement with some 1.2 million adult members in the year 2000, Mennonites are the direct descendants of the Anabaptists (re-baptizers), a radical wing of the Protestant Reformation of the early sixteenth century. Although sharing basic doctrines of the Lutheran and Reformed faiths, Anabaptists held that these Protestants were too closely aligned with coercive governments. Contending for full religious liberty, Anabaptists were the first of what were called the Free Churches. They rejected the ancient practice of infant baptism as nonscriptural, and hence baptized only adults who could freely confess their conversion faith. These converts joined in covenants with fellow believers,

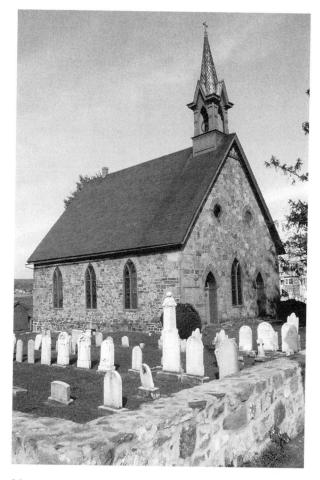

Mennonite Church. This plain stone structure and adjacent graveyard are in Lancaster, Pa. © LEE SNIDER/CORBIS

pledging to support each other both spiritually and materially. Because they refused to swear oaths or take up arms, Anabaptists were cruelly persecuted as societal rebels. Emerging first in the Swiss cantons and southern Germany, they were soon widely scattered throughout Europe, where at twentieth century's end they still lived in small numbers.

Anabaptists were first called Mennonites in the Low Countries after Menno Simons, a Catholic priest before his dramatic conversion in 1536 to the cause of these hunted heretics. His persistent pastoral visits and extensive writings served to gather, maintain, and unite the dissenters, who were badly dispersed and distressed by governmental and state church pressure, both Catholic and Protestant. Some Anabaptist bodies, however, long continued to use names other than Mennonite, such as Taufgesinnten or Doopsgezinden (that is, those who are baptism-minded).

Mennonites came early to North America, and are mentioned as being in the colony of New Amsterdam in 1653. The beginnings of mass migration to the New

World came in 1683 with the arrival in Philadelphia of some forty persons of Mennonite background. Later waves of migration took place throughout the eighteenth century, with most migrants settling in Pennsylvania before a dispersal southward and westward. In the nineteenth century large numbers of Mennonites came from northern Europe, some by way of Russia. Most Mennonite immigrants located in rural enclaves, where they lived in close-knit clusters to perpetuate their faith. The first Mennonites to migrate to Canada did so shortly after the beginning of the Revolutionary War, seeking relief as conscientious objectors to military pressures. Many Mennonites arrived in Canada after World War I and II after harrowing experiences as refugees.

Although Mennonites in Canada and the United States over the years have separated into a confusing number of small denominations, there are four major groupings: the (Old) Mennonites, largely of Swiss and German extraction; the General Conference Mennonites, largely of Dutch and Russian extraction; the Mennonite Brethren, the result of a schism in Russia in 1860 and heavily influenced by German Pietism; and the Amish, a conservative branch of Swiss and south German Mennonites who separated in 1693. In 2001, the Mennonite Church and the General Conference Mennonite Church united to form the new Mennonite Church USA, although some congregations departed in protest.

Until the mid-nineteenth century, Mennonites in North America largely spurned higher education and other institutions and agencies, but by the beginning of the twentieth century their life was marked by a surge of institution-building and creation of church programs. Among these institutions are Goshen College of Goshen, Indiana, and Eastern Mennonite University (Harrisonburg, Virginia), both sponsored by the Mennonite Church, and Bethel College of North Newton, Kansas, and Bluffton College of Bluffton, Ohio, sponsored by the General Conference Mennonite Church. Mennonites began missionary activity in Africa and Asia at that time and in South America and the Pacific region later on. That explains why in 2000 there were fewer active Mennonites in Europe and North America than in areas outside of those continents. Mennonites and associated groups form about ten thousand congregations in sixty-four nations, using eighty languages.

Mennonites are organized internationally in the Mennonite World Conference, which holds delegate conferences about every five years. Its office is in Strasbourg, France. The world gatherings cannot legislate for member bodies but work to further united witness and service.

A highly respected agency of social amelioration and development is the Mennonite Central Committee (with MCC USA offices in Akron, Pennsylvania, and MCC Canada offices in Winnipeg, Manitoba). The agency was founded in 1920 to coordinate the shipment of relief goods from North America to starving Mennonites in revolution-torn Ukraine. Following World War II, MCC

efforts burgeoned until in 2000 it had a combined budget of over $63 million, with 1,511 salaried and volunteer workers in many nations.

Traditionally, Mennonites were known as Plain People, farm families marked by uniformly severe garb and nonconformist ways. Today, most Mennonites are thoroughly integrated into North American society, with many working as teachers, physicians, social workers, and other professionals. Their Anabaptist heritage is most noticeable in their peace stance and vigorous response to human need, as in their Mennonite Disaster Service, which sends volunteer teams to areas of natural catastrophe to clean and rebuild. Once hated heretics, Mennonites have come to be widely known as compassionate and concerned fellow citizens.

BIBLIOGRAPHY

Bender, Harold S., et al., eds. *The Mennonite Encyclopedia.* 5 vols. Scottdale, Pa.: Herald Press, 1955–1990.

Dyck, Cornelius J. *An Introduction to Mennonite History: A Popular History of the Anabaptists and the Mennonites.* 3d ed. Scottdale, Pa.: Herald Press, 1993.

Hostetler, John A. *Amish Society.* 4th ed. Baltimore: Johns Hopkins University Press 1993.

Kraybill, Donald B., and C. Nelson Hostetter. *Anabaptist World USA.* Scottdale, Pa: Herald Press, 2001.

Kreider, Robert S., gen. ed. *The Mennonite Experience in America.* 4 vols. Scottdale, Pa.: Herald Press, 1985–1996.

Donald F. Durnbaugh

See also **Missions, Foreign; Pacifism; Religion and Religious Affiliation;** *and vol. 9:* **Earliest American Protest against Slavery.**

MENOMINEE. The name of the Menominee tribe refers to the wild rice that grew in the tribe's homeland, 10 million acres in what is now eastern Wisconsin. Although the Menominees were forced to cede their land in a series of treaties between 1817 and 1856 and were scheduled to be moved west, they negotiated a treaty in 1854 securing a reservation of nearly 300,000 acres in their ancestral homeland. Menominee history is marked by a continuing struggle to keep and protect their remaining land, where subsistence hunting, fishing, and gathering were supplemented by gardens of corn, beans, and squash. The people managed village and tribal affairs according to a patrilineal clan system and a hereditary chieftainship that changed to a system of elected tribal officials. Nominally Roman Catholic since their first significant European contacts with French fur traders and Jesuits in the 1650s, the tribe's native religious practices continue among an active enclave of traditionalists.

As they were drawn into a money economy, the Menominees recognized the value of their timberland. They strongly opposed clear-cutting and devised the sustained-yield forestry system now widely practiced. Resisting the

Menominees. Members of this economically hard-hit tribe waged a successful campaign in the early 1970s for restoration of their status as a federally recognized tribe and for reestablishment of their reservation. THE CAPITAL TIMES

federal allotment policy of the 1880s (see DAWES GENERAL ALLOTMENT ACT), the Menominees were the only reservation tribe in Wisconsin and one of the few across the nation to escape its disastrous consequences. Lumbering operations provided employment, financed reservation services, paid salaries of BUREAU OF INDIAN AFFAIRS (BIA) personnel, and supported the Catholic-run hospital and schools. The tribe also had nearly $10 million in working capital. Its relative prosperity made them appear "less Indian" than the many poor tribes and a prime candidate for the termination policy adopted in 1953 to eliminate reservations and force dispersal of the Indian tribes. The Termination Act was passed in 1954 over strenuous Menominee opposition; however, the tribe managed to delay its implementation until 1961. Meanwhile the tribe's lumber mill deteriorated and tribal resources were spent on a complicated self-management plan and to transfer tax-free federal land to county status for purposes of taxation. The tribe began termination with a $300,000 deficit. Their business operations were dominated by white government appointees, leaving the tribe with less control over their own affairs than under the BIA. Soon the hospital and schools closed, reservation services were abolished, and unemployment and health problems skyrock-

eted. Desperately needed revenue was raised through land sales. Termination also brought statutory genocide as tribal rolls were closed at 3,270 members in 1954.

A grassroots resistance movement to overturn termination began in late 1970 among urban Menominees, who then rallied the fearful reservation people. With legal help from Wisconsin Judicare and the NATIVE AMERICAN RIGHTS FUND, the Menominees united as a tribe, developing a successful lobbying campaign that resulted in the precedent-setting Menominee Restoration Act signed by President Richard Nixon on 22 December 1973. But the damage wrought by termination could not be undone by the historic Restoration Act alone. Three decades later the tribe, then numbering over 8,000 (according to the 2000 Census), was still striving for the social and economic well-being enjoyed before termination.

BIBLIOGRAPHY

Keesing, Felix M. *The Menomini Indians of Wisconsin: A Study of Three Centuries of Cultural Contact and Change.* Madison: University of Wisconsin Press, 1987.

Lurie, Nancy Oestreich. "To Save the Menominee People and Land." In *Approaches to Algonquian Archaeology: Proceedings of the Thirteenth Annual Conference, the Archaeology Association of the University of Chicago.* Edited by Margaret G. Hanna and Brian Kooyman. Calgary, Alberta, Canada: University of Calgary Press, 1982.

Peroff, Nicholas C. *Menominee Drums: Tribal Termination and Restoration, 1954–1974.* Norman: University of Oklahoma Press, 1982.

Shames, Deborah, ed. *Freedom with Reservation: The Menominee Struggle to Save Their Land and People.* Keshena, Wis.: College of the Menominee Nation Press, 1995.

Spindler, Louise S. "Menominee." In *Handbook of North American Indians.* Edited by William C. Sturtevant et al. Volume 15: *Northeast*, edited by Bruce G. Trigger. Washington D.C.: Smithsonian Institution, 1978.

Ada E. Deer

See also **Termination Policy; Tribes: Great Plains.**

MENOMINEE IRON RANGE, one of six iron ore ranges adjacent to Lake Superior. About two-thirds of the iron ore produced in the United States comes from these ranges. Three of them are in Michigan and three in Minnesota. Part of the Menominee Iron Range extends into parts of northern Wisconsin. Of these six ranges, the Menominee is the second to have been developed—the Marquette Range is the oldest. The other iron producing areas in Michigan include the Gogebic Iron Range, which also extends into Wisconsin, and the Marquette Range.

The Menominee Range is situated mainly in the valley of the Menominee River, which lies on the boundary between the Upper Peninsula of Michigan and northern Wisconsin. That iron was located here seems to have been known before the Civil War, but mining dates back only to the 1870s. The Breen Mine was opened in 1872, and other locations opened soon afterward. Active shipments, however, had to await construction of a branch of the Chicago and North Western Railroad from Powers, Michigan, on the main line of the Peninsular Division, which reached the district in 1877. The best outlet for the range was at Escanaba, on Little Bay De Noc of Lake Michigan, to which the North Western constructed a direct line. The Chicago, Milwaukee, and St. Paul Railroad also penetrated the region and shipped ore over the Escanaba and Lake Superior line until it reached a pooling agreement for shipment over the North Western. Mines were opened at Vulcan, Norway, Iron Mountain, and Iron River, Michigan, and at Florence, Wisconsin. The most remarkable producer was the Chapin Mine at Iron Mountain, which produced nearly 26 million tons of iron ore from its opening in 1879 to its closing in 1934. Most of this ore reached Lake Michigan at the ore docks at Escanaba. From there, bulk freighters carried the ore to lower lake ports. Between 1854 and 1972 the Michigan part of the Menominee Iron Range produced 297,883,000 long tons. Wisconsin produced considerably less—887,000 tons in 1972 as compared with 2,533,000 tons from the Michigan area of the range.

BIBLIOGRAPHY

Boyum, Burton H. *The Saga of Iron Mining in Michigan's Upper Peninsula.* Marquette, Mich.: John M. Longyear Research Library, 1983.

Hill, Jack. *A History of Iron County, Michigan.* Norway, Mich.: Norway Current, 1976.

Temin, Peter. *Iron and Steel in Nineteenth Century America.* Cambridge, Mass.: The Massachusetts Institute of Technology Press, 1964.

L. A. Chase / H. S.

See also **Iron and Steel Industry; Mesabi Iron Range.**

MENTAL ILLNESS

The Seventeenth through the Nineteenth Centuries

The history of mental illness in the United States reflects the ever-changing landscape of mental disorders and the medical specialties responsible for their management and treatment. Mental illness (psychiatric disorders) is a nebulous term that has evolved over time. Insanity, lunacy, madness, mental illness, derangement, or unreason are among the many labels used to describe those individuals who, for various reasons, are psychologically unable to successfully function in society and require some form of intervention or treatment. The underlying causality for mental illness may be either physical (as in senile dementia), psychological (as in depression), or a combination of both. Since the middle of the nineteenth century, medical science has revolutionized treatment for numerous medical conditions, including mental illness. Many conditions previously believed to be psychological have been determined to be organic and removed from psychiatric nomenclature (conditions caused by vitamin deficiency, for example). Other conditions, such as schizophrenia and bipolar disorders, are the subject of dispute as to whether or not they are organic or psychological. Consequently, psychiatric nosology (the use of diagnostic categories) has remained fluid, as has the reported incidence of mental illness, ranging from approximately 3 percent of the population for psychotic disorders to 50 percent of the population for depression. Treatment approaches have been fluid as well, ranging from the exclusively physical to the exclusively psychological. Most mental health professionals advocate a combination of physical (psychotropic medications) and psychological (counseling) for most forms of mental disturbance.

Attitudes toward, and treatment for, the mentally ill in the United States accompanied the colonists from Europe, particularly England. By the beginning of the colonial period in America, the mad in Europe were confined to a variety of facilities called workhouses or houses of correction, along with other deviant groups. Treatment for the mad was predicated on the belief that mental illness was either the result of some mysterious physical malady or punishment for sin. What constituted treatment was extreme: bleeding, cathartics, emetics, hot and cold showers, whipping, and chaining. The history of the insane in colonial America followed a similar pattern: the mad were confined together with other deviant groups, either at home or in institutions. However, "home confinement" meant detention within the community, which led to rigorous settlement laws for newcomers, intended to prevent economic dependency on the community. If the new settler or visitor could not satisfy the settlement laws, they were "warned out" or asked to leave the settlement. Thus many of the mentally afflicted, the poor, the disabled, and petty criminals were forced to wander from township to township, occasionally housed overnight in the town jail and then forced to leave the community. As population increased and communities became more urban, hospitals were established at Philadelphia (1751) and New York (1773) that accepted both the physically and the mentally ill. However, treatment for the mentally disturbed was unchanged. Benjamin Rush, the "father of American psychiatry" and a medical practitioner at the Pennsylvania Hospital, advocated the same "heroic" treatment procedures as had his predecessors.

The emergence of a radically different approach at the Retreat in York, England (founded in 1792; first patients in 1796), established by William Tuke, ushered in a new era in the management of the mad. Similar developments had been taking place about the same time in Paris, initiated by Philippe Pinel, who unchained the mad and imposed a more humanitarian treatment regimen. Labeled moral therapy, the new form of treatment for the mad became the dominant approach for more than one hundred years. Moral therapy, or moral management, included removing the mad from their environment and secluding them in facilities exclusively for them, providing a structured daily schedule and work therapy, and con-

Benjamin Rush. One of the founding fathers, a government official, a professor of chemistry and of medicine, a prominent physician in Philadelphia, and the author of several important works, including the first American psychiatric treatise.

fronting their "inappropriate" behavior for the purposes of reducing or eliminating such behavior. The goal of moral therapy was to restore the individual's sanity and to return the patient to society as a fully functioning, productive member of society through order, regularity, and discipline. Concurrently, the punitive treatments of the past were abolished. The introduction of moral therapy or management fostered a new optimism regarding treatment for the mad. Based on the new confidence, there followed an intense period of asylum building. Initially the new asylums were privately sponsored (corporate facilities), such as the one at the Charlestown branch of the Massachusetts General Hospital (1818; later renamed the McLean Asylum), the Bloomingdale Asylum (1821), and the Connecticut Retreat for the Insane (1824; later renamed the Hartford Retreat), but in short order, state governments began erecting public asylums. Although the first state asylum exclusively for the insane had been completed at Williamsburg, Virginia, in 1773, it remained a unique facility until 1824, when other states began to assume responsibility for the care and treatment of the insane. Between 1825 and 1865, fifty-three insane asylums were constructed, bringing the total in the United States to sixty-two. One individual, Dorothea Dix (1802–1887), had a significant influence on asylum construction. After a visit in 1841 to a local Massachusetts jail, where she observed the deplorable conditions for the insane inmates, Dix began a forty-year campaign to reform conditions for the mad. She appealed to various individuals

and government bodies with remarkable success. Dorothea Dix has been credited with the erection of thirty-two asylums, including Dorothea Dix Hospital in Raleigh, North Carolina (first patients in 1856). As state asylums were erected, they incorporated moral therapy as their treatment model, with unfortunate consequences. Whereas private, or corporate, asylums could limit patient population, public institutions could not. Populations in public facilities increased beyond the ability of the staff to realistically implement moral management. Consequently, public asylums became severely overcrowded and reduced to merely custodial institutions, a circumstance that was perpetuated well into the twentieth century.

The Association of Medical Superintendents of American Institutions for the Insane (AMSAII), organized in 1844, could do nothing to prevent or ameliorate the worsening problem of overcrowding and reduced funding. The Association was not an organization with an agreed-upon body of knowledge and theories concerning the causes and treatment of the insane that sought to inform and shape social attitudes toward the mentally ill. To the contrary, asylum superintendents and the facilities they administered had been assigned a role to play regarding a specific deviant group. Therefore, ideas articulated by the superintendents regarding the causes and treatment of mental illness were consistent with society's attitudes toward the asylum population. They were, first and foremost, agents of society and, second, physicians to the mad. Accordingly, there was a general consensus among the superintendents that most forms of madness were the consequence of some kind of physical trauma. Hallucinations, delusions, or disorders of the cognitive mind where observable aberrant behaviors were involved were easy to classify as madness and attribute to a blow to the head, fever, chronic illness, or some other easily discernible cause.

The difficulty with this theory lay in socially deviant behaviors where there was no observable mental or physical cause. How to diagnose, or classify, those individuals who committed apparently senseless, socially unacceptable acts? Were the individuals criminal, insane, or both? The answer was "moral insanity," an ambiguous label for various forms of social deviancy in the nineteenth century. The primary cause of "moral insanity" was a disordered society, the effect of urbanization and immigration. As a result, the asylum itself became the remedy for insanity and other forms of social deviancy. If insanity could not be "cured," at least it was confined and segregated from the remainder of society, where the mad would remain until 1964. From the beginning of the Civil War to the turn of the century, asylums continued to experience worsening overcrowding, decline in quality and quantity of personnel, reduced budgets, and a myriad of other problems.

Following the Civil War, neurology began to emerge as a new medical specialty and as one of the two major critics of asylum superintendents and asylum conditions.

While neurologists agreed with asylum superintendents that insanity was a disease of the brain and that the deplorable asylum conditions were due to budgetary issues, they were critical of the superintendents. Neurologists argued that the superintendents were no more than asylum administrators, certainly not physician-scientists concerned with clinical practice and medical research concerning the origins and treatment of aberrant mental conditions. The conflict between the two specialties culminated in 1894 when Silas Weir Mitchell addressed the American-Medico-Psychological Association (AMPA) (formerly the AMSAII; the new name was adopted in 1892). Mitchell declared that the asylum physicians were not collecting adequate case histories or mental status examinations, they were neglecting autopsy and laboratory work, and they were failing to properly care for their patients. Thereafter, the two medical specialties reached an accommodation that was perpetuated well into the twentieth century.

Allied with neurologists as the other significant critic of asylum management and inmate care were state boards of charities. Once state governments determined that asylum budgets were their single greatest expense, administrative and budgetary control of the asylums was transferred to the boards of charities. As a consequence, once again the mentally disordered were grouped together with other deviant groups, criminals, the indigent, and the disabled, as a function of centralizing and rationalizing public welfare.

Thus, by the end of the nineteenth century, treatment of the mentally ill in America had come full circle. Housed in separate facilities, the mad were once again the responsibility of a centralized agency, the public welfare departments of state governments. Moreover, the earlier optimism regarding moral management had been replaced by a renewed pessimism. By the end of the nineteenth century, the asylums had failed as a cure for madness. There was no recognized medical cure for madness; confinement had only removed the mad as a threat to social order ("out of sight, out of mind"). An impasse had been reached, with no effective treatment available; all that remained was the asylum.

The Twentieth Century
The origins of a new approach to mental disorders began in the decade preceding the turn of the century. The informal adoption of Emil Kraepelin's classification system by Adolf Meyer in 1896, accompanied by the new title for the official organization of asylum physicians (AMPA), signaled a change in the approach to the treatment of the mentally ill. Both developments suggested that the profession was moving toward a disease concept of mental illness, in keeping with growing influence of scientific medicine. However, the most significant catalyst for change was Sigmund Freud (1856–1939), the creator of psychoanalysis as a valid approach for the treatment of mental disorders. Freud's innovation was the develop-

ment of a systematic psychology of the mind and techniques to access the unconscious. Introduced to the American medical community during the first decade of the twentieth century, psychoanalytic techniques fundamentally altered treatment of the mentally ill. Freud and Carl G. Jung, the most prominent of Freud's followers, visited the United States to give a series of lectures at Clark University in 1909. Jung was one of the first psychoanalysts to employ psychoanalytic techniques with severely disturbed (psychotic) individuals, particularly schizophrenics. Freud's techniques were readily adapted to "office practice," whereas Jung's methods were particularly useful with more severely disturbed, hospitalized patients.

Psychoanalysis was modified and popularized by American physicians such as A. A. Brill, Freud's American translator; Adolf Meyer, the first director of the Henry Phipps Psychiatric Clinic (1913) at Johns Hopkins Medical Center; and William Alanson White, the superintendent (1903) of the federal psychiatric hospital, St. Elizabeth's, in Washington, D.C. From their respective positions, Meyer and White became two of the most influential members of the psychiatric specialty in America. Both men shaped the evolution of psychiatric concepts and training during the first half of the twentieth century. In their professional roles, Meyer and White supported a more general reform of treatment for the mentally ill, lending their support to the National Committee for Mental Hygiene, founded by Clifford Beers, a former mental patient, in 1909. The goals of the National Committee were to prevent mental illness and to improve institutional conditions for the mentally ill.

Meyer and White symbolized the revolution in psychiatry and, more generally, medicine at the beginning of the twentieth century. Medical science had a profound impact on psychiatry, as new developments in medicine altered treatment procedures for many psychiatric disorders, as it did for physical ailments. Physical and psychological medicine fused to become modern psychiatry, a legitimate, accepted medical science of the mind. In 1921, its professional organization adopted a new name, the American Psychiatric Association, changed the name of its professional journal to the *American Journal of Psychiatry*, and accepted Kraepelin's nosology as the standard nomenclature for classifying psychiatric disorders. In the decades that followed to the close of the twentieth century, there were three important developments: continuing developments in medicine that directly affected the treatment of mental illness; expanding government participation in funding and oversight of patient care; and a proliferation of psychotherapeutic "schools," most a response to the growing popularity of psychoanalysis.

Medical discoveries continued to redefine diagnostic categories and influence treatment for mental disorders. Therapeutic procedures appeared to revert to the former "heroic" measures of the past with the application of Metrazol, insulin, and electric shock therapies between 1937 and 1940. All three induced severe convulsions in the subject, who was typically chronically psychotic, with questionable results and at some risk to the patient. More effective and benign treatment appeared in the early 1950s in the form of chemical compounds known today as tranquilizers or, more accurately, psychotropic medication. The continuing evolution and effectiveness of these drugs has had a profound effect on treatment for the mentally ill, enabling many hospitalized patients to return to home and work or precluding hospitalization in the first place. As more effective treatment regimens appeared and as a response to public demand, government took a more active role in allocating funds for research and the establishment of model programs for the mentally ill. In 1946, the National Mental Health Act provided for the establishment of the National Institute of Mental Health; in 1963, the National Community Mental Health Centers Act was passed, which effectively "deinstitutionalized" most chronically ill patients and brought to an end reliance on custodial care facilities for the most severely disturbed individuals. The legislation anticipated that most former chronic patients would be managed by medications provided through local community mental health centers, but these expectations were not realized. The unfortunate consequence of this legislation has been to create an indigent homeless population in larger municipalities that absorbs law enforcement, medical, and other community resources. Nonetheless, state and federal governments have assumed a seemingly limitless role regarding mental disorders and the mentally ill.

Perhaps even more startling than any other development regarding mental illness in the United States has been an explosion in the number of mental health professionals during the past one hundred years. From an extraordinarily small group of psychiatrists, 222 in 1900, the number and variety of mental health professionals has grown enormously. No longer is psychiatry the only discipline concerned with treatment of the mentally ill. By the end of the twentieth century there were more than thirty-two thousand psychiatrists, seventy thousand psychologists, and many hundreds of thousands practicing in related professions—psychiatric social workers, pastoral counselors, sex therapists, marriage counselors, and a myriad of other quasi-professional and lay practitioners. Moreover, the number of psychotherapeutic approaches grew to nearly three hundred competing therapies, including various forms of psychoanalysis, individual and group psychotherapy, marriage and family counseling, "primal scream" therapy, "est," transactional analysis, Gestalt therapy, and so on. Public and private hospital expenditures surpassed $69 billion and continued to increase, while private out-patient expenditures were undetermined. A vast array of psychoactive medications became available, either over the counter or by prescription. What were once private, personal problems became the subject of radio and television talk shows and newspaper advice columns.

Mental illness in America was transformed during the twentieth century. The single therapeutic tool of the nineteenth century, the asylum, virtually disappeared. Once the stepchild of medicine, psychiatry became a recognized medical specialty, a requirement in most medical schools. Underlying causes for mental illnesses are now recognized as a combination of environment and biology. One constant remains: as the medical and natural sciences continue to make new discoveries, what constitutes mental illness continues to be redefined.

BIBLIOGRAPHY

Grob, Gerald N. *Mental Institutions in America, Social Policy to 1875.* New York: Free Press, 1973.

———. *Mental Illness and American Society, 1875–1940.* Princeton, N.J.: Princeton University Press, 1983.

———. *From Asylum to Community: Mental Health Policy in Modern America.* Princeton, N.J.: Princeton University Press, 1991.

Hale, Nathan G. *The Beginnings of Psychoanalysis in the United States, 1876–1917.* New York: Oxford University Press, 1971.

———. *The Rise and Crisis of Psychoanalysis in the United States: Freud and the Americans, 1917–1985.* New York: Oxford University Press, 1995.

Porter, Roy. *The Greatest Benefit to Mankind: A Medical History of Humanity.* Chapter XVI, "Psychiatry." New York: Norton, 1997.

Shorter, Edward. *A History of Psychiatry: From the Era of the Asylum to the Age of Prozac.* 2d ed. New York: Wiley, 1998.

William E. Wingfield

See also **Primal Therapy; Psychiatry; Psychology.**

MERCANTILISM is the name given to the economic doctrines and practices of major trading nations roughly from the fifteenth through the eighteenth centuries. Colonial empires such as those of England, France, and Spain were among those adhering to the mercantile system. Although specific practices regarding the doctrine varied from nation to nation, there were basic principles all mercantilists followed. Mercantilists practiced heavy state regulation of economic activity in order to boost national wealth. The wealth of the nation was based upon its stocks of gold and silver, rather than on its peoples' living conditions, for example. Thus the accumulation of national wealth was believed to be best achieved by creating as large an excess of exports over imports as possible, as the difference would be collected in gold from importing countries. Colonies in particular were seen as a valuable means of increasing exports and thereby enriching the mother country, as was the case with the British colonies.

One of the earliest navigation acts passed by the British Parliament to have a direct impact on the American colonies was in 1651. It is the modification of this law in

1660 that became known as the Navigation Act, which defined British colonial policy and its practice of mercantilism. Protecting its national interests, the law stated that trade within the British empire was to be conducted by English ships and English seamen. Those defined as English included residents of the colonies as well as England. This gave English ships a complete monopoly over trade within the British empire, greatly limited the trade of foreign vessels within England's ports, and excluded foreign vessels altogether from colonial ports.

Further revisions of the Act made British ports the hub for all trade within the empire. The revisions called for trade with foreign powers to be shipped from its point of production to England or a British colonial port before being shipped to its foreign destination. Conversely, foreign goods set for the colonies were required to stop first in England. This ensured England would be the center for all colonial trade and allowed for taxes to be levied as goods flowed through the country.

The next phase of the Navigation Acts specifically listed which products were to be shipped to ports within the British empire and which were to be shipped to foreign countries. They also regulated the manufacture and trade of colonial products. Those colonial products needed within the empire, like iron, lumber, and other raw materials, were highly supported by the British government. Direct bounties were used to promote the colonial production of hemp, tar, pitch, and other naval stores. Other colonial products benefited from bounties at various times, including raw silk, masts, lumber, and indigo. Large sums were paid for the production and trade of these items between 1705 and 1774, with payments averaging more than £15,000 a year in the decade preceding the Revolution alone. Other products, like tobacco, were given a monopoly of the market in England, as the government levied high tariffs on tobacco from Spain and other foreign markets. Sugar and molasses received similar treatment. When such products were not needed in the British market, the taxes were rolled back so that they could be exported to other markets with a minimum of British taxes.

As it actively supported some products, the British government also actively discouraged the production of colonial products that would compete with those produced at home. In 1699, prohibitive legislation was passed to restrict the transportation of raw wool from one colony to another because wool production and manufacturing would infringe upon the business practiced in England. Similar legislation restricting transportation between colonies was passed with regard to hats in 1732, as hat production was a valued craft in England. The Wrought Iron and Steel Bill of 1750 prohibited the creation within the colonies of new steel mills, slitting mills, and tilt hammers. In addition to these restrictions, taxes became the main issue of resentment of the American colonists living under the British mercantile system. With the Townshend Acts of 1767, Parliament levied duties on colonial imports of paper, glass, paint, and tea, to which one colonial response was the Boston Tea Party (1773).

It is widely asserted that among the causes of the American Revolution were these mercantilist laws. Revolutionary Americans resented the economic restrictions, finding them exploitative. They claimed the policy restricted colonial trade and industry and raised the cost of many consumer goods. In his 1774 pamphlet, "A Summary View of the Rights of British America," Thomas Jefferson asserted the Navigation Acts had infringed upon the colonists' freedom in preventing the "exercise of free trade with all parts of the world, possessed by the American colonists, as of natural right." Yet, as O. M. Dickerson points out, it is difficult to find opposition to the mercantile system among the colonists when the measures were purely regulatory and did not levy a tax on them. The British mercantile system did after all allow for colonial monopoly over certain markets such as tobacco, and not only encouraged, but with its 1660 regulation was instrumental in, the development of colonial shipbuilding. Indeed, the mercantile system was specifically approved by the First Continental Congress in the Declaration of Rights of 14 October 1774.

Comprehensive intellectual criticism of mercantilism as an economic doctrine began to arise in the 1750s and continued through the end of the century. Many intellectuals during the Enlightenment explored new ideas in political economy; Adam Smith in his 1776 *An Inquiry into the Nature and Causes of the Wealth of Nations* was one of the most influential figures for the Americans. Smith admitted the mercantile system worked, yet criticized its principles. Expounding a doctrine of individualism, Smith was one of many voices stating that the economy, like the individual, should be free from detailed regulation from the state. Economic, as well as individual, self-interest and its outcome in the market should be allowed to function without state regulation. Although it was indeed approved by the First Continental Congress, the practice of mercantilism was replaced with a Smith-oriented form of liberalism in post-Revolutionary America.

BIBLIOGRAPHY

Bruchey, Stuart Weems, ed. *The Colonial Merchant: Sources and Readings.* New York: Harcourt, Brace, 1966.

Crowley, John E. *The Privileges of Independence: Neomercantilism and the American Revolution.* Baltimore: Johns Hopkins University Press, 1993.

Dickerson, Oliver Morton. *Navigation Acts and the American Revolution.* Philadelphia: University of Pennsylvania Press, 1951.

Margaret Keady

See also **Boston Tea Party; Colonial Policy, British; Navigation Acts; Townshend Acts.**

MERCHANT ADVENTURERS. The term "merchant adventurer" had been applied to merchants since the early fifteenth century. While it originally referred to English merchants engaged in any export trade, it came to represent those who were willing to "adventure," or risk, their money in speculative ventures.

One of the most speculative adventures to be found in the seventeenth century was the colonization of North America, and merchants backed a handful of attempts to settle the New World beginning in 1583. The best-documented endeavor belonged to the London Merchant Adventurers, who backed the PILGRIMS as they established Plymouth Plantation in 1620.

The Pilgrims were a group of religious radicals, separatist Puritans, populating Nottinghamshire in England. Although Queen Elizabeth I did not seem to mind their existence, her successor, King James I, took strenuous issue with their beliefs. Seeking freedom to practice their religion, a group of Pilgrims, led by John Robinson, attempted to leave England illegally in 1607; their destination was the Netherlands. The captain of the ship they had hired betrayed them, and many of their goods and much of their money was confiscated in a raid as they boarded.

Eventually, many of the Pilgrims did make it to the Netherlands, but many of them were impoverished by the time they got there. Although they were able to practice their religion, they were still hounded by King James's spies. Additionally, many of the Pilgrims still wished to live under English rule rather than Dutch.

The New World seemed to offer the opportunity the Pilgrims needed, but the cash-strapped group had no means of getting across the ocean and establishing a colony. John Carver, a successful London merchant and brother-in-law of John Robinson's wife, joined the Pilgrims around 1610. Seven years later, he and Robert Cushman, a wool comber of some means, were dispatched to London to seek financial backing for a transoceanic journey.

While they were in London, Thomas Weston, an ironmonger from that city, visited Robinson in the Netherlands. A promoter who had heard of the Pilgrims' need for funds, he offered to put together a group of merchants to back the venture. Weston and his London Merchant Adventurers also recruited other people, not separatists and known as "strangers," to make the voyage to Virginia, as all of England's territory in America was then known. The merchants are believed to have invested about 7,000 pounds.

They formed with the colonists a joint-stock company, meaning the merchants would put up the money and the colonists the labor in a seven-year agreement. During those seven years, all land, livestock, and trade goods such as lumber, furs, and other natural resources were owned in partnership. At the conclusion of the seven-year period, the company was to be dissolved and the assets distributed.

The VIRGINIA COMPANY OF LONDON, itself a merchant adventurer group that had backed the ill-fated Jamestown colony under Captain John Smith in 1607, eventually issued a patent in 1619 allowing the Pilgrims to colonize in its territory. This patent was superseded in 1620 by one granted to John Peirce, a London clothier and associate of Weston's.

After the Pilgrims landed north of the territory claimed by the London company in December 1620, a second Peirce patent was issued in 1621 by the Council for New England, the rechartered Virginia Company of Plymouth, which held the rights to colonization in the northern end of England's New World holdings.

Weston and his fellow investors were dismayed when the *MAYFLOWER* returned to England in April 1621 without cargo. The malnourished Pilgrims had been subjected to "the Great Sickness" after the arrival at Plymouth, and the survivors had had little time for anything other than burying their dead and ensuring their own survival. Weston sold his London Merchant Adventurer shares in December, although he did send a ship, the *Sparrow*, in 1622 as his own private business venture.

The Pilgrims attempted to make their first payment by loading the *Fortune*, which had brought 35 additional settlers in November 1621, with beaver and otter skins and timber estimated to be worth 500 pounds. The ship was captured by French privateers and stripped of its cargo, leaving investors empty-handed again.

A second attempt, in 1624 or 1625, to ship goods to England failed when the *Little James* got caught in a gale in the English Channel and was seized by Barbary Coast pirates. Again the London Adventurers received nothing for their investment. Relations, always tempestuous between the colonists and their backers, faltered.

Facing a huge debt, the Pilgrims dispatched Isaac Allerton to England in 1626 to negotiate a settlement. The Adventurers, deciding their investment might never pay off, sold their shares to the Pilgrims for 1,800 pounds. Captain Smith, of the failed Jamestown venture, felt the London Merchant Adventurers had settled favorably, pointing out that the Virginia Company had invested 200,000 pounds in Jamestown and never received a shilling for their investment.

BIBLIOGRAPHY

Bartlett, Robert M. *The Pilgrim Way*. Philadelphia: Pilgrim Press, 1971.

Johnson, Richard R. *John Nelson: Merchant Adventurer: A Life between Empires*. New York: Oxford University Press, 1997.

"Plimoth-on-Web: The Library." Plimoth Plantation. Updated November 2001. Available from http://www.plimoth.org/ Library/library.htm.

T. L. Livermore
Michael Valdez

MERCHANT MARINE.

There was marked merchant marine activity, especially in New England, in the colonial period. Much of New England's cargo of lumber and fish went to the West Indies to be exchanged for sugar, molasses, or rum; some went along the coast to be exchanged for grain or flour; and some crossed the Atlantic. England's Navigation Laws, aimed at developing a self-sufficient empire, benefited the merchant marines, for a vessel built and manned on Massachusetts Bay or Casco Bay qualified as an English ship with an English crew; many of the cheaply built New England vessels, moreover, were sold to English owners. By 1700, Boston ranked third, after London and Bristol, among all English ports in the tonnage of its shipping. By 1730, Philadelphia passed it in commerce, but the New England coast remained the center of shipping activity.

The American Revolution brought short-lived dislocations of trade; then, during the long Anglo-French conflict, the merchant fleet quickly expanded and prospered. After the Revolution, American vessels no longer enjoyed British registry, could not be sold in England, and were barred from the profitable and mutually advantageous triangular trade with the British Caribbean sugar islands. On the other hand, American ships no longer had to buy all their return cargoes in Britain and were free to trade with countries in the Mediterranean and the Baltic, and with India and China. The long Anglo-French wars, starting in 1793, put a premium on the neutral status of American-flag shipping, which could visit ports where the belligerent British or French flags would be vulnerable. At the risk of occasional capture and confiscation in this "heroic age" as they ran afoul of belligerent regulations, the Americans reaped a rich profit. The registered tonnage of American ships rose from 346,000 in 1790 to 981,000 in 1810, while the combined exports and imports in those same years jumped from $43 to $152 million, about 90 percent of which was carried in American bottoms. Eventually, the American EMBARGO ACT and NON-INTERCOURSE ACT hurt the trade, while the British blockade during the War of 1812 eventually almost cut off the United States from the sea, forcing merchants to ship southern cotton and other goods over land.

In the relatively quiet period between 1815 and 1845, steam navigation and the performance of the transatlantic sailing packets laid the foundation for a long period of expansion of the merchant marine. Successful steam navigation is normally dated from the voyage of Robert Fulton's *Clermont* up the Hudson River from New York to Albany and back in 1807. New York quickly utilized the sheltered waters of Long Island Sound as a steam approach to New England, while other local uses of steam for ferries and tugs developed. The ability of steamboats to ascend the Mississippi and its tributaries revolutionized and promoted traffic on western waters. On the longer ocean runs, however, the early engines required so much coal—in contrast to wind, which was free—that steam was not profitable. The pioneer ocean crossing of the auxiliary steamer *Savannah* (1819) was unsuccessful. Permanent transatlantic steam navigation did not take off until 1838 when two British steamships, the *Sirius* and the *Great Western*, arrived at New York on the same day. American sailing packets from New York to Liverpool, London, and Le Havre, meanwhile, began dominating the North Atlantic run in 1818. These "square-riggers on schedule," sailing on specified dates with passengers, mail, and fine freight, demonstrated the value of regular line service previously unknown.

By the 1840s the Irish potato famine, Britain's repeal of its Corn Laws and Navigation Laws, and the discovery of gold in California were combining to bring the American merchant marine to its golden age in the early 1850s, almost equaling Britain's shipping in tonnage and surpassing it in quality. Irish immigrants arrived in America in huge numbers, followed shortly by a large migration of Germans. The Yankee ships that carried them could, with the repeal of the Corn Laws, carry back American grain. The California gold rush led to the construction of large numbers of fast clippers in which cargo capacity was sacrificed for speed, and to the establishment of subsidized steamship lines converging from New York and San Francisco upon the Isthmus of Panama. The British example of subsidizing the mail steamers of Samuel Cunard led Congress to support steamship lines to Bremen and Le Havre. Finally, Congress gave even more generous support to Edward K. Collins for a line to Liverpool to "beat the Cunardes." For a time, Collins was successful, but when speed led to the loss of two ships, Congress withdrew its support and the line failed.

This peak in American shipping was followed by a long depressed period accentuated by the panic of 1857. The clipper craze had been overdone, and the building of square-rigged ships, which reached its peak in 1855, fell off sharply. Moreover, depredations from British-built Confederate naval raiders sparked a panic disproportionate to the number of Union ships caught. War-risk insurance rates escalated such that shippers sought foreign flags that called for no such extra expense. Scores of the finest American square-riggers were consequently transferred to foreign registry and were not permitted to return afterward. After the war, the shift of the nation's interest and capital investment from the sea to westward expansion contributed to this decline.

One cause of the decline was the shift to steam. The development of the compound, reciprocating marine engine at last made it practicable to transport bulk cargoes, such as coal, wheat, and sugar, by steamship rather than by sailing vessel. The opening of the Suez Canal in 1869 furthered reliance on steamships, for sailing ships had great difficulty in traversing the Canal and the Red Sea. Steam gradually pushed sail off all but a few of the longest runs to Europe, such as those carrying grain from California, nitrates from Chile, jute from India, and wool and grain from Australia. The big American Down Easter square riggers found business on some of these runs but were gradually crowded out.

The most important cause of the new difficulties probably lay in the effect of the cost of iron or steel on steamship building. In the past, wooden vessels had been built more cheaply on the American side of the Atlantic because of the ample supplies of ship timber close to the seaboard, but Europe had gained the advantage of lower costs because of its iron deposits and technological advantages for manufacture. Although the value of foreign commerce between 1860 and 1910 grew from $762 million to nearly $3 billion, the share carried in American bottoms shrank from 66 percent to 8 percent.

Domestic trade, which had been protected by law from foreign competition since 1817, was a different story. From the 2,974,000 tons of enrolled and licensed shipping in 1860, a slight fall occurred during the 1860s and 1870s; however, by 1890, volume had climbed to 3,496,000 tons, continuing on to 6,726,000 by 1910—almost nine times the foreign trade total. The construction of certain river, Great Lakes, and Long Island Sound steamers was too specialized for oceangoing use, but, between the major coastal ports, some quite substantial and effective vessels performed regular cargo and passenger service, which long held its own against railroads parallel to the coast. Much of the coastal bulk cargo of lumber, granite, anthracite coal, and lime was still carried by sail, especially in the Northeast, in little two-masted schooners. Gradually, larger schooners came into use, with three- and four-masters carrying ice and southern lumber. Eventually, big five- and six-masters competed with barges and later with steam colliers in carrying bituminous coal northward from Hampton Roads. Tankers began to carry Gulf petroleum up around Florida to ports "north of Hatteras." On the West Coast, small "steam schooners" carried lumber southward to California, while big second-hand square-riggers brought the salmon catch down from Alaska.

The experiences of World War I produced a drastic transformation in the American merchant marine, leading it once more back to the distant sea routes. On the eve of the war, some 92 percent of the nation's foreign commerce was carried by British, German, and other ships that offered generally satisfactory service. When that was suddenly disrupted by World War I, the United States suddenly realized how serious it was to lack shipping flying its own flag. This was especially brought home to the nation when South America, Africa, Asia, and Australia suddenly offered rich opportunities for American exporters. American-owned vessels, which had been under foreign flags for reasons of economy, were glad to be admitted to neutral registry under the American flag, while sailing vessels had their last chance for large-scale useful service in supplying those distant markets.

An amazing expansion of American shipping resulted from the emergency building program undertaken in 1917 to offset the heavy Allied losses from Germany's unrestricted submarine warfare. The Shipping Board, which had been established by Congress in 1916, began an ambitious program to set up numerous new yards, the largest being at Hog Island just below Philadelphia. Much of this activity was continued after the war suddenly ended late in 1918. By 1921, the United States had overtaken Great Britain for first place among the world's merchant fleets; it had some 700 new large steel freighters and 575 smaller ones.

About a third of those new large ships found employment in a new intercoastal trade between the East and West coasts through the Panama Canal, opened in 1914, which cut the New York–San Francisco run from 13,122 to 5,263 miles. It was thus possible to carry steel, machinery, and similar heavy cargo westward and to bring back lumber and canned goods at rates about one-third cheaper than by rail.

More nearly permanent in national merchant-marine policy, however, was the use of many of the other new freighters on government-supported "essential trade routes" to all parts of the world. The wartime experience had shown how important it was to have regular service on certain runs to provide outlets for American exports and dependable sources of essential imports. At first, the new lines were operated directly for the Shipping Board, which absorbed the initial deficits. However, as soon as they were on a paying basis, the ships were auctioned off at bargain rates to private operators who agreed to maintain regular service on their lines for a period of years. In 1929, the JONES ACT provided generous grants, in the name of mail payments, to those approved lines that agreed to build new ships. The falling-off of trade during the depression that started that year left the shipping industry in difficulties, particularly because of competition against cheaper foreign operation and construction costs.

To address that situation, Congress in 1936 passed the Merchant Marine Act, which remained the basis of American shipping policy a quarter century later. The former supervisory functions of the Shipping Board passed to the Maritime Commission, which, in 1950, gave way to the Federal Maritime Board for policy and the Maritime Administration for operation. To enable American-flag vessels to compete with foreigners, Congress established "operating-differential" and "construction-differential" subsidies that were intended to meet the difference between American and foreign costs both in the operation and building of vessels.

The operating subsidies went only to lines approved for specific "essential trade routes"; there were usually from a dozen to fifteen such lines on thirty-odd routes from Atlantic, Gulf, or Pacific ports. To avoid excessive profits in boom periods, the government "recaptured" half of all profits in excess of 10 percent. About three-quarters of the operating subsidies went to meet the difference in pay between American and foreign officers and crews. Aggressive action on the part of new maritime unions in about 1936 began to push American wages far ahead of foreign wages; the daily wage cost on a medium-sized American-flag freighter rose from $141 in 1938 to $552 in 1948 and to $1,234 in 1960—about four times as much as in the principal foreign merchant marines. Consequently, unsubsidized vessels found it increasingly difficult to operate under the American flag, and large numbers of them shifted to the "flags of convenience" of Panama or Liberia.

The construction-differential subsidies, designed to keep American shipyards going, absorbed up to half the cost of construction in foreign yards. Lines receiving operating-differential subsidies had to build in American yards, and certain other ship owners were also eligible.

During World War II, the subsidized merchant marine fully demonstrated its high value through its adequate ships, trained mariners, overseas contacts, and operational skill, all of which did much to provide logistical support for the far-flung military operations across the Atlantic and Pacific. Once again, the government undertook a tremendous emergency building program, which produced 5,777 vessels, about half of them slow, capacious "Liberty ships."

The foreign services on the essential trade routes continued on a fairly successful basis after the war. Some of the other shipping also benefited by the congressional "50–50" stipulation that at least half of the cargo sent abroad in the various foreign-aid programs must be carried in American-flag vessels. Domestic shipping, however, fell off sharply in the coastal and intercoastal trades. Part of this decline was blamed by the shipping industry on the "railroad-minded" Interstate Commerce Commission, which in 1940 was given control of all transportation rates. Part of the trouble also arose from the still-mounting wages of mariners and longshoremen, and from the competition of trucks.

Continuing labor disputes with longshoremen, along with inefficiencies that accompanied marine shipping, prompted the invention of "containerization" in the 1950s by Malcolm McLean, a former truck driver and founder of McLean Trucking. (A container is a box up to forty feet long and eight feet wide that is transported on land by the use of a chassis pulled by a truck; containers are double-stacked without a chassis when hauled by train.) McLean sought an inexpensive way to return containers from New York to Texas, and fitted two tankers with platforms above the decks for carrying thirty-five-foot boxes. He purchased Pan-Atlantic Steamship Corporation and Waterman Steamship in 1955. In April the next year, Pan-Atlantic's *Ideal X*, the world's first container ship, sailed from Port Newark, New Jersey, to Houston. Pan-Atlantic announced that it would convert other ships into container ships. When these vessels went to sea, McLean told their captains not to bother him with nautical nonsense; they were ship drivers at sea. The first fully containerized vessel, *Gateway City*, began regular service between New York, Florida, and Texas in 1957. Pan-Atlantic Steamship Corporation changed its name to Sea-Land in 1960. In sending freight across the oceans, the container revolution proved as influential as the shift from sail to steam. The *Gateway City* had a capacity for 226 thirty-five-foot containers. It could be turned around in one day by two shore-based gantry cranes. With break-bulk, this would have taken weeks. Once the system came into full operation, damage and pilferage decreased dramatically. Matson Navigation helped to make containerization a familiar word in the shipping industry; the company developed a gantry crane that could handle 520 containers every twenty-four hours.

Other developments quickly followed. During the early 1960s, a division of American President Lines known as Pacific Far East Line (PFEL) transported military supplies to Vietnam. No one knew how long that war would last, and it seemed unwise to consider building docks and erecting gantry cranes at Cam Ranh Bay in South Vietnam. PFEL used a lighter aboard ship (LASH) system. Sea-Land, the original innovator, then introduced another novelty, this time in the pattern of trade employed by container ships voyaging to East Asia. Because Sea-Land ships were returning to Oakland, California, with empty containers, the company sought business in Japan, and, without waiting for cooperation from the Japanese government, arranged gantry cranes and other container equipment in a Japanese port, thereby giving Sea-Land a profitable back haul. The result was worldwide competition. After Sea-Land's move in Japan, local shipping firms installed U.S. equipment. In a short time, Japanese companies built container ships and were competing with U.S. companies. British shippers also moved to develop container capability.

McLean eventually overreached himself in attempting to create a worldwide line specializing in container ship commerce. After selling Sea-Land in May 1969 to the R. J. Reynolds Tobacco Company, which was seeking to diversify, McLean acquired the United States Lines and purchased another old American line, Moore McCormack. He signed contracts in 1983 for twelve new container ships, to be built in the huge Daewoo yards in South Korea. The $570 million order represented the largest single peacetime shipbuilding contract and the largest expansion of the U.S. Merchant Marine in its entire history. McLean conceived of a remarkable commerce, in which a Daewoo-built ship would depart an East Asian port for the Panama Canal, and after transit calls at East Coast ports, sail to Western Europe. After leaving the Mediterranean, passing through the Suez Canal, and calling at Middle Eastern ports, the ship would move on to the East Asian port of origin, thus completing a worldwide loop. He described the proposed route as his Sea Bridge. He intended to reach all areas of the world with the Sea Bridge except for West Africa, Australia, and New Zealand. The Sea Bridge operation began in December 1984, but after a few months of operation, McLean's venture turned into bankruptcy, with a loss of nearly $100 million in a single quarter. In 1987, the Econships, as they were known, were sold, then began operating under U.S. flag and Sea-Land ownership.

Shipping received a boost when Congress passed the Merchant Marine Act of 1970, which generously extended and liberalized the terms of the 1936 act. No longer were the fifteen or so lines of the specific "essential trade routes" to have a virtual monopoly of the subsidy benefits. The construction-differential subsidies were expanded to produce thirty new ships per year for the next ten years. Partly because of the growing need for oil and gas from overseas, bulk-cargo ships became potential beneficiaries. The act declared that "the bulk cargo carrying services should, for the promotion, development, expansion, and maintenance of the foreign commerce of the United States and for the national defense or other national requirements be provided by United States–flag vessels whether or not operating on particular services, routes, or lines." The construction subsidy was cut below the old 55 percent maximum; the operating-differential subsidy was extended in a more tentative and restrictive manner but was made to apply to areas rather than rigid lines, and the basis of computation was modified.

The act had an immediate quickening effect on merchant shipping; numerous applications for both kinds of subsidies were made, and plans were laid to build vessels far larger than any previously built in the United States, together with facilities to accommodate their construction. But the initial exuberance was suddenly dampened when President Richard M. Nixon's 1973 budget slashed funding of the program from $455 million to $275 million.

It was remarked that shipping underwent more drastic changes around 1970 than in any period since the mid-nineteenth century. The increased speed resulting from jet airplanes virtually drove out regular ocean passenger service (the transatlantic passage had dropped from five weeks with the sailing packets and five days with the crack liners to five hours in an airplane). The passenger liners were laid up, sold, or participated in the fast-growing development of pleasure cruises. The old economic self-sufficiency gave way to increasing need for seaborne cargoes. Oil tankers increased more than tenfold in size, special ships were developed for natural gas, and bulk carriers were developed to bring iron and other ore from overseas.

U.S. container ships continue to carry much world commerce. From 1985 to 1995, the volume of exports of containerized cargo from New York harbor alone jumped by 53 percent. The value of this shipping rose from $9.59 billion to $17.14 billion, a 32 percent increase after factoring in inflation. Part of the Port Authority's increase in business was caused by modernization, including new railway links, crucial because containers go directly from freighters onto trucks and trains all the while tracked by computers. Labor relations in the Port of New York area improved, but the principal reason for the resurgence of the New York–New Jersey area has been the efficiency of

container ships. The Port Authority of New York and New Jersey estimated that ocean shipping generated 166,000 regional jobs in 1998, and $20 billion in economic activity.

BIBLIOGRAPHY

Albion, Robert. G. *Seaports South of Sahara: The Achievements of an American Steamship Service*. New York: Appleton-Century-Crofts, 1959.

Butler, John A. *Sailing on Friday: The Perilous Voyage of America's Merchant Marine*. Washington, D.C.: Brassey's, 1997.

De La Pedraja, René. *The Rise and Decline of U.S. Merchant Shipping in the Twentieth Century*. New York: Twayne, 1992.

Gibson, Andrew, and Arthur Donovan. *The Abandoned Ocean: A History of United States' Maritime Policy*. Columbia: University of South Carolina Press, 2000.

Kendall, Lane C. *The Business of Shipping*. Centreville, Md: Cornell Maritime Press, 1793; 1992; 2001.

Kilmarx, Robert A., ed. *America's Maritime Legacy: A History of the U.S. Merchant Marine and Shipbuilding Industry since Colonial Times*. Boulder, Colo.: Westview Press, 1979.

Lawrence, Samuel H. *United States Merchant Shipping, Policies and Politics*. Washington, D.C.: Brookings Institution, 1966.

Niven, John. *The American President Lines and its Forebears, 1848–1984*. Newark: University of Delaware Press, 1986.

Robert G. Albion
Charles V. Reynolds Jr. / F. B.

See also **Maritime Commission, Federal; River and Harbor Improvements; River Navigation; Shipbuilding; Shipping, Ocean; Shipping Board, U.S.; Trade, Foreign.**

MERCHANTMEN, ARMED. Absence of INTERNATIONAL LAW at sea in the colonial and early national periods motivated American shipping interests to arm their vessels against piracy and privateering. Freedom of the seas was essential to the young republic's economic survival. Merchant ships like the *Ranger*, engaged in West Indian trade in 1782, carried seven guns, plus muskets and pikes.

To limit the possibility of international incident, Congress on 3 March 1805 required such ships to pledge that their ordnance would be used for defense only. During the War of 1812, U.S. merchant ships, typically armed with six-pounders, sailed clandestinely in and out of British ports, and traded in China, the West Indies, and South America.

The Declaration of Paris (16 April 1856) abolished privateering. This action, coupled with the gradual disappearance of piracy, obviated the need for armed merchantmen. Nevertheless, in 1877 and 1894, the U.S. Department of State, responding to threats against U.S. merchant ships, authorized ships to arm for self-defense.

During World War I, Germany announced on 31 January 1917 a policy of unrestricted submarine warfare.

Consequently, President Woodrow Wilson approved the arming of U.S. merchant ships with naval gun crews. Just prior to American entrance into World War II, German submarines had attacked U.S. ships in the Atlantic; on 13 November 1941 Congress authorized the use of naval armed guards aboard merchant ships similar to those of World War I. The convoy routes to Murmansk and to the Mediterranean were continually harried by German U-boats and bombing aircraft. The Allied combat campaigns would never have succeeded without the merchant ship convoys.

BIBLIOGRAPHY

Bunker, John. *Heroes in Dungarees: The Story of the American Merchant Marine in World War II.* Annapolis, Md.: Naval Institute Press, 1995.

Felknor, Bruce L., ed. *The U.S. Merchant Marine at War, 1775–1945.* Annapolis, Md.: Naval Institute Press, 1998.

Safford, Jeffrey J. *Wilsonian Maritime Diplomacy, 1913–1921.* New Brunswick, N.J.: Rutgers University Press, 1978.

Paul B. Ryan / A. R.

See also **Atlantic, Battle of the; Lend-Lease; Murmansk; Neutrality; Privateers and Privateering.**

MERGERS AND ACQUISITIONS.

Mergers and acquisitions are means by which corporations combine with each other. Mergers occur when two or more corporations become one. To protect shareholders, state law provides procedures for the merger. A vote of the board of directors and then a vote of the shareholders of both corporations is usually required. Following a merger, the two corporations cease to exist as separate entities. In the classic merger, the assets and liabilities of one corporation are automatically transferred to the other. Shareholders of the disappearing company become shareholders in the surviving company or receive compensation for their shares.

Mergers may come as the result of a negotiation between two corporations interested in combining, or when one or more corporations "target" another for acquisition. Combinations that occur with the approval and encouragement of the target company's management are called "friendly" mergers; combinations that occur despite opposition from the target company are called "hostile" mergers or takeovers. In either case, these consolidations can bring together corporations of roughly the same size and market power, or corporations of vastly different sizes and market power.

The term "acquisition" is typically used when one company takes control of another. This can occur through a merger or a number of other methods, such as purchasing the majority of a company's stock or all of its assets. In a purchase of assets, the transaction is one that must be negotiated with the management of the target company. Compared to a merger, an acquisition is treated differently for tax purposes, and the acquiring company does not necessarily assume the liabilities of the target company.

A "tender offer" is a popular way to purchase a majority of shares in another company. The acquiring company makes a public offer to purchase shares from the target company's shareholders, thus bypassing the target company's management. In order to induce the shareholders to sell, or "tender," their shares, the acquiring company typically offers a purchase price higher than market value, often substantially higher. Certain conditions are often placed on a tender offer, such as requiring the number of shares tendered be sufficient for the acquiring company to gain control of the target. If the tender offer is successful and a sufficient percentage of shares are acquired, control of the target company through the normal methods of shareholder democracy can be taken and thereafter the target company's management replaced. The acquiring company can also use their control of the target company to bring about a merger of the two companies.

Often, a successful tender offer is followed by a "cash-out merger." The target company (now controlled by the acquiring company) is merged into the acquiring company, and the remaining shareholders of the target company have their shares transformed into a right to receive a certain amount of cash.

Another common merger variation is the "triangular" merger, in which a subsidiary of the surviving company is created and then merged with the target. This protects the surviving company from the liabilities of the target by keeping them within the subsidiary rather than the parent. A "reverse triangular merger" has the acquiring company create a subsidiary, which is then merged into the target company. This form preserves the target company as an ongoing legal entity, though its control has passed into the hands of the acquirer.

Reasons for Mergers and Acquisitions

There are a number of reasons why a corporation will merge with, acquire, or be acquired by another corporation. Sometimes, corporations can produce goods or services more efficiently if they combine their efforts and facilities. These efficiency gains may come simply by virtue of the size of the combined company; it may be cheaper to produce goods on a larger scale. Collaborating or sharing expertise may achieve gains in efficiency, or a company might have underutilized assets the other company can better use. Also, a change in management may make the company more profitable. Other reasons for acquisitions have to do more with hubris and power. The management of an acquiring company may be motivated more by the desire to manage ever-larger companies than by any possible gains in efficiency.

Regulation of Mergers and Acquisitions

Mergers and acquisitions are governed by both state and federal laws. State law sets the procedures for the approval of mergers and establishes judicial oversight for the terms of mergers to ensure shareholders of the target company receive fair value. State law also governs the extent to which the management of a target company can protect itself from a hostile takeover through various financial and legal defenses. Generally, state law tends to be deferential to defenses as long as the target company is not acting primarily to preserve its own positions. Courts tend to be skeptical of defenses if the management of a target company has already decided to sell the company or to bring about a change of control. Because of the fear that mergers will negatively affect employees or other company stakeholders, most states allow directors at target companies to defend against acquisitions. Because of the number of state defenses now available, the vast majority of mergers and acquisitions are friendly, negotiated transactions.

The federal government oversees corporate consolidations to ensure that the combined size of the new corporation does not have such monopolistic power as to be unlawful under the SHERMAN ANTITRUST ACT. The federal government also regulates tender offers through the Williams Act, which requires anyone purchasing more than 5 percent of a company's shares to identify herself and make certain public disclosures, including an announcement of the purpose of the share purchase and of any terms of a tender offer. The act also requires that an acquirer who raises his or her price during the term of a tender offer, raise it for any stock already tendered, that acquirers hold tender offers open for twenty business days, and that acquirers not commit fraud.

History

Merger and acquisition activity in the United States has typically run in cycles, with peaks coinciding with periods of strong business growth. U.S. merger activity has been marked by five prominent waves: one around the turn of the twentieth century, the second peaking in 1929, the third in the latter half of the 1960s, the fourth in the first half of the 1980s, and the fifth in the latter half of the 1990s.

This last peak, in the final years of the twentieth century, brought very high levels of merger activity. Bolstered by a strong stock market, businesses merged at an unprecedented rate. The total dollar volume of mergers increased throughout the 1990s, setting new records each year from 1994 to 1999. Many of the acquisitions involved huge companies and enormous dollar amounts. Disney acquired ABC Capital Cities for $19 billion, Bell Atlantic acquired Nynex for $22 billion, WorldCom acquired MCI for $41.9 billion, SBC Communications acquired Ameritech for $56.6 billion, Traveler's acquired Citicorp for $72.6 billion, NationBank acquired Bank of America for $61.6 billion, Daimler-Benz acquired Chrysler for $39.5 billion, and Exxon acquired Mobil for $77.2 billion.

BIBLIOGRAPHY

Carney, William J. *Mergers and Acquisitions.* New York: Foundation Press, 2000.

Scherer, F. M., and David Ross. *Industrial Market Structure and Market Performance.* Chicago: Rand McNally, 1970.

Kent Greenfield

See also **Capitalism; Free Trade; Monopoly; Trusts.**

MERIAM REPORT, published in 1928, was a survey of conditions on Indian Reservations in twenty-six states. It was financed by the Rockefeller Foundation and supervised by Lewis Meriam of the Institute for Government Research (Brookings Institution). The survey team consisted of ten experts in various fields, including sociology, family life and women's activities, education, history, law, agriculture, health, and research methods.

Titled *The Problem of Indian Administration*, the Meriam Report was called the most important treatise on Indian affairs since Helen Hunt Jackson's *Century of Dishonor* (1881). The idea of commissioning a study of Indian administration began in 1913, when Acting Commissioner of Indian Affairs Frederick H. Abbott suggested to the BOARD OF INDIAN COMMISSIONERS that the government seek advice on how to make the Indian Office more efficient. In 1925 two members of the board, Warren K. Moorehead and Hugh Scott, offered separate plans for the office's reorganization. Others on the board urged the improvement of Indian health. Ultimately Secretary of the Interior Hubert Work proposed that the Rockefeller Foundation support a survey by the Institute for Government Research.

Scholars disagree over whether or not the Meriam Report was a harbinger of the Indian New Deal. Some regard it as a precursor of the Indian Reorganization Act of 1934. Margaret Szasz called it "the symbol of a definitive response to the failure of fifty years of assimilation policy." But Donald Critchlow claimed that Meriam and his associates were efficiency experts and that their recommendations contrasted sharply with the radical program of John Collier and the AMERICAN INDIAN DEFENSE ASSOCIATION (AIDA). The AIDA wanted to end individual ownership of land and to move toward tribal ownership by restoring allotments to the reservations from which they had been drawn. Rather than call for an end to allotments, the Meriam Report said allotments should be made with extreme conservatism.

BIBLIOGRAPHY

Brookings Institution, Institute for Government Research. *The Problem of Indian Administration.* Baltimore: Johns Hopkins Press, 1928.

Critchlow, Donald T. "Lewis Meriam, Expertise, and Indian Reform." *Historian* 43, no. 4 (1981): 325–344.

Fritz, Henry E. "The Board of Indian Commissioners and the Reform of Indian Affairs from the Late Progressive Era to the New Deal." Forthcoming in *Making United States Indian Policy, 1829–1933.* Norman: University of Oklahoma Press.

Szasz, Margaret. *Education and the American Indian: The Road to Self-Determination, 1928–1973.* Albuquerque: University of New Mexico Press, 1974.

Henry E. Fritz

See also **Indian Policy, U.S.**

MERITOR SAVINGS BANK V. MECHELLE VINSON,

477 U.S. 57 (1986), a Supreme Court decision that attempted for the first time to define what standard a court should use to determine sexual harassment under Title VII of the Civil Rights Act of 1964. The two main issues were whether a plaintiff's claim of sexual harassment could succeed if based on psychological aspects without tangible loss of an economic character, and whether employers are absolutely liable in cases of sexual harassment by supervisors.

Mechelle Vinson was an employee at Meritor Savings Bank under the supervision of the vice president and branch manager, Sidney Taylor, and Vinson had earned various promotions on the basis of merit. Vinson testified that Taylor invited her to dinner; repeatedly proposed sexual relations, leading to forty or fifty occasions of intercourse; fondled her in front of employees; followed her into the women's restroom; exposed himself to her; and raped her on several occasions. At first, Vinson resisted but ceased to do so out of fear of losing her job. She testified that she was afraid to report the incidents or use the bank's complaint procedure out of fear and because she would have to make the claim directly to her supervisor, Taylor. She said that Taylor stopped sexually harassing her when she began dating someone steadily. She was fired for taking an excessive leave of absence.

Subsequently, she filed a sexual harassment claim for violations of Title VII. Both the bank and Taylor denied Vinson's accusations and insisted that the claim arose from a business-related dispute. The bank asserted that if Vinson's claims were true, the supervisor's activities were unknown to the bank's executive managers and engaged in without its consent. The federal district court held that for a sexual harassment claim to prevail, the plaintiff had to demonstrate a tangible economic loss. The court also held that the bank was not liable for the misconduct of its supervisors. On both counts the circuit court reversed in favor of Vinson. The bank appealed to the Supreme Court, which in a unanimous decision decided for Vinson on the first point but held that employers were not automatically liable for sexual harassment by supervisors. Similarly, however, absence of notice to an employer did not insulate the business from liability for the acts of supervisors. In such cases the issue was one of fact, which required meeting a burden of proof. The case placed sexual harassment resulting in a hostile work environment on an equal footing with sexual harassment resulting in the loss of job or promotion. It put employers on notice that they must review supervisors' conduct because mere absence of notice of improper conduct is no longer a defense.

BIBLIOGRAPHY

Hartmann, Susan M. *From Margin to Mainstream: American Women and Politics since 1960.* Philadelphia: Temple University Press, 1989.

MacKinnon, Catharine A. *Sexual Harassment of Working Women: A Case of Sex Discrimination.* New Haven, Conn.: Yale University Press, 1979.

Tony Freyer / A. R.

See also **Discrimination: Sex; Sexual Harassment.**

MERRILL'S MARAUDERS.

In 1943, global priorities dictated that General Joseph W. Stilwell's command be scaled down from a 30,000-man corps to a three-battalion (3,000-man), all-volunteer force for his forthcoming operation to retake north Burma and reopen the land route to China. Coded GALAHAD and numbered the 5307th Provisional Unit, the force was nicknamed "Merrill's Marauders" by the press, after its field commander, General Frank D. Merrill. Merrill broke his three battalions down into two 472-man combat teams (the remainder had noncombat duties), plus pack animals.

Benefiting from the experience of British army officer Brigadier O. C. Wingate, GALAHAD's strengths lay in its tactical mobility, its potential to hit Japanese flanks and rear areas, and its unique air supply. The Marauders were to spearhead short envelopments while Stilwell's Chinese columns pushed back the enemy's front.

Entering combat on 24 February 1944, GALAHAD attacked down the Hukawng Valley and by March 29 entered the Mogaung Valley, gateway to the Irrawaddy River and its rail system. Stilwell aimed for Myitkyina, with a road to the Burma Road junction at Wanting. Reduced in numbers, the Marauders struck at Myitkyina's strategic airfield through a 6,100-foot mountain pass, surprising the 700-man Japanese garrison on 17 May. The Japanese retaliated with a force of 4,000 men, beginning a siege that would not end until 3 August. By 4 June, GALAHAD was spent: 123 dead, 293 wounded, 8 missing, 570 ill. Grievances that had mounted during a five-month, 500-mile campaign broke out dramatically at Myitkyina until Stilwell bestowed a Distinguished Unit Citation and explained how they had given heart to the Chinese soldiers to fight on to their homeland.

BIBLIOGRAPHY

Bjorge, Gary J. *Merrill's Marauders.* Fort Leavenworth, Kans.: Combat Studies Institute, 1996.

Hunter, Charles N. *GALAHAD.* San Antonio, Tex.: Naylor, 1963.

Charles F. Romanus
Christopher Wells

See also **Burma Road and Ledo Road; China, U.S. Armed Forces in.**

MERRIMAC, **SINKING OF** (3 June 1898). When the Cuban squadron of Pascual Cervera y Topete was blockaded by Adm. William T. Sampson at Santiago in the Spanish-American War, Assistant Naval Constructor Richmond Pearson Hobson, with seven men, volunteered to sink the collier *Merrimac* across the narrow entrance, blocking Cervera's escape. Under heavy enemy fire, the *Merrimac* was anchored in position about 2:00 A.M., but its steering gear was damaged and only two of its sinking charges exploded. The sunken vessel failed to close the channel effectively. Surviving almost miraculously, Hobson and his crew were taken prisoners and treated courteously until their exchange on 7 July.

BIBLIOGRAPHY

Hobson, Richard P. *The Sinking of the Merrimac.* New York: The Century Company, 1899; Annapolis, Md.: Naval Institute Press, 1988.

Long, John D. *The New American Navy.* New York: The Outlook Company, 1903; New York: Arno Press, 1979.

Allan Westcott / A. R.

See also **Navy, United States; Spanish-American War, Navy in.**

MESA, a flat-topped area of land with bluffy walls, sometimes hundreds of feet high, that stands above eroded terrain. A mesa may comprise an acre or a thousand acres. This geological formation is characteristic of the southwestern United States. Acoma, New Mexico, the "city in the sky," is a noted example.

BIBLIOGRAPHY

Shoumatoff, Alex. *Legends of the American Desert: Sojourns in the Greater Southwest.* New York: Knopf, 1997.

J. Frank Dobie / A. E.

See also **Ancestral Pueblo (Anasazi); Hopi; Navajo; Pueblo; Southwest.**

MESA VERDE, PREHISTORIC RUINS OF. Mesa Verde National Park (52,073 acres) in southwest Colorado was established in 1906 to preserve pre-Columbian cliff dwellings. Similar dwellings exist in adjacent parts of New Mexico, Arizona, and Utah, but Mesa Verde's are the most extensive and best-preserved structures. The builders were probably ancestors of today's Pueblos. For defense, they constructed their communal

Mesa Verde. These pre-Columbian cliff dwellings are the best preserved and most extensive in the United States. MESA VERDE NATIONAL PARK

houses in recesses high up steep canyon walls. The dwellings and temples consisted of stone, clay, and supporting poles. The cliff dwellers flourished in the eleventh and twelfth centuries, and severe drought probably forced them to abandon the mesa canyons in 1276.

BIBLIOGRAPHY

Ferguson, William M. *The Anasazi of Mesa Verde and the Four Corners.* Niwot, Colo.: University Press of Colorado, 1996.

Robert Phillips / J. H.

See also **Ancestral Pueblo (Anasazi); Architecture, American Indian.**

MESABI IRON RANGE   contained the richest deposit of iron ore in the United States, but the peculiar quality of the soft hematite ore (nonmagnetic and powdery rather than rock) delayed discovery and exploitation until the 1890s. The ore existed in some eighteen townships in northeastern Minnesota. When its great value became known, there was an unparalleled scramble to enter the land through abuse of the Preemption Act (1841) and the Homestead Act (1862) and for the choicer deposits with the rarer forms of land scrip. Leonidas Merritt and his seven brothers made some of the greatest finds, though, lacking capital to build a railroad to Lake Superior, they were unable to market their ore and lost their rich deposits to John D. Rockefeller. He, in turn, sold them to Andrew Carnegie, who transferred them to the United States Steel Corporation. More than 2.5 billion tons of ore have been mined from the Mesabi range, but by the mid-1960s the richest of the hematite ore was gone. Only then were the deposits of taconite appreciably valued.

BIBLIOGRAPHY

Goin, Peter, and Elizabeth Raymond. "Recycled Landscapes: Mining's Legacies in the Mesabi Iron Range." In *Technologies of Landscape: From Reaping to Recycling.* Edited by David E. Nye. Amherst, Mass.: University of Massachusetts Press, 1999.

Walker, David Allan. *Iron Frontier: The Discovery and Early Development of Minnesota's Three Ranges.* St. Paul, Minn.: Minnesota Historical Society Press, 1979.

Paul W. Gates / H. S.

See also **Iron and Steel Industry; Menominee Iron Range; U.S. Steel.**

MESQUAKIE.   When first encountered by the French, the Mesquakie (Fox) Indians were living along the Fox and Wolf Rivers, southwest of Green Bay, Wisconsin. Unlike many other Great Lakes tribes, the Mesquakies distrusted the French alliance and resented the emigration of French-allied tribes into Wisconsin in the mid-1600s. In 1710, the French administrator Antoine de

Mesquakie. Children and teachers pose outside the Mesquakie Day School, near Toledo, Iowa, in this early-twentieth-century photograph. LIBRARY OF CONGRESS

La Moth, Sierra de Cadillac, attempted to win Mesquakie allegiance by luring part of the tribe to the Detroit region, but there they quarreled with French-allied Indians and then attacked the French fort in 1712. The French and their allies retaliated and killed many Mesquakies near Detroit as the latter attempted to flee to the Iroquois. Most of the survivors returned to Wisconsin, where the Mesquakies disrupted the French fur trade, attacking French traders and raiding French and allied Indian villages in Illinois. In 1716, the Mesquakies defeated a French expedition that attacked their fortified villages in Wisconsin; and in 1728, although another French army burned their villages and cornfields, the Mesquakies retreated and suffered few casualties. Meanwhile, Mesquakie attacks upon French settlements in Illinois paralyzed the region and brought the fur trade to a standstill.

In 1728–1729, the Kickapoos and Winnebagos, former Mesquakie allies, defected to the French. Surrounded by enemies, the Mesquakies attempted to leave Wisconsin and migrate to New York where they hoped to seek refuge among the Iroquois. In August 1730, while en route across Illinois, they were intercepted by a large force of French and allied Indians and surrounded in a small grove of trees on the prairie. After a four-week siege, the Mesquakies attempted to flee during a thunderstorm but were followed and slaughtered on the prairie. The few survivors returned to Wisconsin, where in 1732 they were attacked again by French-allied Indians. The following year, the surviving Mesquakies were given refuge by the Sauk, who shielded them from further French attacks, and with whom part of the Mesquakies (Sauk and Fox Indians) have since resided.

Other Mesquakies established new villages in the Dubuque, Iowa, region, where their women mined and supplied lead to Spanish and American settlers. In 1856, the Iowa Mesquakies purchased eighty acres along the Iowa River, near Tama, Iowa. During the next century, adjoining lands were purchased, and in 2000 the settlement encompassed an area of almost 3,500 acres. Residents of the settlement community remained a conservative people, proudly retaining many of their old traditions and their continued identity as Mesquakies.

BIBLIOGRAPHY

Edmunds, R. David, and Joseph L. Peyser. *The Fox Wars: The Mesquakie Challenge to New France.* Norman: University of Oklahoma Press, 1993.

McTaggart, Fred. *Wolf that I Am: In Search of the Red Earth People.* Boston: Houghton Mifflin, 1976.

Murphy, Lucy Eldersveld. *A Gathering of Rivers: Indians, Metis, and Mining in the Western Great Lakes, 1737–1832.* Lincoln: University of Nebraska Press, 2000.

R. David Edmunds

See also **Indian Policy, Colonial; Sauk.**

MESQUITE, a spiny shrub or small tree characteristic of the American Southwest. Its astounding root system enables it to withstand the severest droughts and produce beans, which horses thrive on, cattle can exist on, and of which Indians and Mexicans make brew and bread. During the days of the open range, its leaves served as browse, its trunks as fence posts, and its limbs and roots as an aromatic fuel. Although mesquite is an attractive ornamental shrub and fixes nitrogen in the soil, it can also crowd out other vegetation, so many in the American Southwest now attempt to check its spread.

BIBLIOGRAPHY

Sowell, John. *Desert Ecology: An Introduction to Life in the Arid Southwest.* Salt Lake City: University of Utah Press, 2001.

J. Frank Dobie / A. E.

See also **Mohave; Tribes: Southwestern.**

METALWORK. Since the colonial period, craftspeople in America have worked with various metals, primarily silver, pewter, copper, brass, iron, and aluminum.

Silver

The designations "goldsmith" and "silversmith" were interchangeable in America throughout the seventeenth and eighteenth centuries. In England, silver- and gold-working skills were learned through apprenticeships that lasted from the ages of fourteen to twenty-one. City ordinances in Boston (1660) and New York City (1675) set down that no person could open a shop who was not of age and had not served a full seven-year apprenticeship. But no guilds were formed in the colonies.

At the time, working silver came from melted coins and was, in England and usually in America, assayed to the sterling standard (925 parts silver to which 75 parts of copper were added for hardness). Benjamin Silliman, a famous American scientist in the nineteenth century, recognized that the standard British silver was 8.3 percent

Pewter. This 1944 photograph shows a collection owned by Mr. and Mrs. T. Ferdinand Wilcox and displayed in their living room in New Canaan, Conn. Library of Congress

copper, while that for silver made in America was 10.8 percent copper. This difference in standards is now being used as a clue to the national origin of pieces of undocumented silver.

Working over stakes or anvils of different shapes and using forming hammers, silversmiths raised such objects as teapots from silver disks. Spouts, covers, and handles were hammered separately. Smaller pieces were cast. Moldings were made by drawing silver strips through shaped openings in a steel die. Planishing with a flat-faced hammer removed hammer marks. Then all parts could be assembled and soldered in preparation for decorating by chasing (removing no metal) or engraving (removing metal). Before the final finish, the maker's marks were struck on the piece.

The final step was to deal with oxidation, or tarnishing. It is not the silver but the copper that oxidizes, resulting in discoloration. Oxidation was cleverly inhibited by the silversmith who finished his masterpiece, in the words of Silliman, "by boiling the silver in a copper vessel containing very dilute sulfuric acid which dissolves out the copper of the alloy and leaves the silver dead white; it is then burnished and exhibits its proper beauty of color and lustre."

While it is very difficult to generalize about the social position of the eighteenth-century American silversmith, the most accomplished masters worked in cities and were socially well connected. Important silversmiths of the time included Paul Revere and Jacob Hurd in Boston, Myer Myers in New York City, and Joseph Richardson in Philadelphia.

Because a colonial silversmith was both manufacturer and retailer, his shop was often a workroom and a showroom. This practice continued until about 1840, when the discovery of the technique of electroplating led to the rise of large companies that produced and sold silver plate in stores. While not eliminating individual silversmiths, it did reduce their importance. By midcentury, silversmiths such as Edward Moore and William Gale, both of New York City, produced objects sold exclusively through establishments such as Tiffany and Company. Large corporations such as the Gorham Manufacturing Company and International Silver Company almost fully depersonalized the industry. Those who continued in individual shops specialized more in repair, chasing, and engraving than creation.

Until Europeans introduced silver into North America, it was unknown to the indigenous population. Small brooches of Iroquois and Seminole manufacture are known from the eighteenth century. Navajos first learned silversmithing about 1860, and they passed on their knowledge to the nearby Pueblo tribes. Southwestern silver was at first worn only as personal adornment, but as tourists arrived by railroad an industry was born. By the 1920s and 1930s, silversmithing provided regular income and became a full-time job for many in the Southwest.

Following the English model provided by Liberty and Company, Gorham Manufacturing introduced a self-consciously handcrafted line of silver in the 1890s, known by the trademark Martelé (a French word meaning "hammered," given by William C. Codman to mass-marketed silver produced by "hand"). This industrial process mass-produced the tenets of John Ruskin and William Morris at a time when Arts and Crafts societies mushroomed across America. By 1900, handcrafted silver was a choice, not a necessity. Women became silversmiths. After World War I, some Arts and Crafts silver shops survived the change in style, but new shapes and the economic difficulties of the 1930s proved harsh, and few survived World War II.

While the traditional silversmith tradition may have withered, the craft found new life in the hands of the academically trained artist-craftsperson. This change radically altered the nature of the craft, so that by the early 1950s, many colleges and universities offered programs in silversmithing. Most prominent silversmiths now are graduates of this system and themselves hold positions at universities, which allows them the artistic freedom to produce wares not possible in production work. The personal statement replaced the functionality of earlier times.

Pewter

Pewter is an alloy mostly of tin, with a small proportion of copper or lead or both. From the fourteenth century in England and much of Europe, "fine" or "plate" pewter consisted of ninety-seven parts tin to three parts copper, and "ley" or "lay" pewter was an alloy of tin with up to 20 percent lead. Cheapness encouraged the addition of lead, giving a soft dull alloy. Britannia metal is a later eighteenth-century pewter alloy that contains antimony (stibnite), not lead. It is also known as white metal. The distinction is in the method of fabrication. Britannia alloys are spun, stamped, or rolled, and articles are thin and light in construction. They require no annealing and take a shine like silver. Pewter is cast and turned and may be hammered to compact and strengthen it. Its low melting point allows for easy casting into intricate shapes in molds of plaster or more durable and expensive bronze.

British settlers introduced pewter into the American colonies. Richard Graves had a pewtering shop in Salem, Massachusetts, in 1635. In large cities such as Boston, Philadelphia, New York, and Newport, the high cost of materials led to the collection of discarded utensils for recasting. Skilled pewter craftsmen gravitated to these cities. Among them were John Bassett and Henry Will in New York, Samuel Danforth in Hartford, and William Will in Philadelphia.

Pewterware was essentially utilitarian and simple in concept, while keeping with the latest style. It was the common tableware for all but the wealthy. Its softness and low melting point kept pewter from being used for cooking vessels, but its cheapness and toughness made it ideal for tavern tankards, measuring cups, baby bottles, inkstands, candlesticks, furniture hardware, and religious service items.

Stamping pewter into shapes was introduced in America in 1829 by William Porter of Connecticut, who perfected single-drop stamping. Five years later, he patented the spinning technique. For many centuries the lathe had been an important tool in making pewter plates and goblets, but spinning made it possible to complete the whole process on the lathe. The result was a faster and more uniform assembly line for the production of pewter and Britannia vessels. As teapots, coffeepots, lamps, and candlesticks were produced cheaply in ever greater quantity, individual craftsmen quickly became a memory. With the advent of electroplating around 1840, Britannia was compromised by an even cheaper-to-produce silverlike look. Nevertheless, pewter has remained popular, both for fine historical replication and as a more pedestrian non-lead version of colonial ware, awkwardly replicated for a mass-market appeal.

Copper

A highly malleable metal, copper also takes well to other metals to form alloys. Paul Revere, famous for his nocturnal ride but a silversmith and bronze caster by profession, had an important influence on America's copper and brass production. In 1801, he set up some newly acquired British-made rollers in a converted powder mill in what would become Canton, Massachusetts, and built the first successful copper-rolling mill in the United States. Contracts for the dome of the Massachusetts statehouse and the resheathing of the USS *Constitution*, both in Boston, established him as America's leading coppersmith.

Until the 1850s, except for mined copper from Connecticut, the main raw material was used copper from ship sheathing, stills, and boilers. With the eventual discovery of vast copper reserves in the western United States, increased demands could be satisfied.

In his short-lived, fashionable San Francisco workshop, Dirk van Erp, born in Holland, combined hammered-copper bases with shades made of strong, translucent mica to veil the recently invented electric lightbulb. In Chicago, the Scottish-born Robert Riddle Jarvie made candlesticks, lanterns, light stands, and trophies in brass, copper, or patinated bronze. So many craftsmen tried to reproduce his candlesticks that Jarvie was compelled in 1903 to inform *House Beautiful* readers that all his future work would bear his incised signature.

Brass

Brass is an alloy of copper and zinc. In Shakespeare's day, and for some time thereafter, the word "brass" was applied to an alloy of copper and tin that is now known as bronze. While the distinction today is one of material, formerly it was one of purpose. If the metal was to be gilded it was bronze, and if not, it was brass.

The art of brass casting began in England in 1693, when a London merchant, John Lofting, was given a license for casting thimbles; these had previously been imported from Holland. During the eighteenth century, brass was made by alloying copper with metallic zinc imported from China under the name "tutenag." The smelting of indigenous zinc ore started in Europe about 1730. As brass became more plentiful, it received its own identity.

In colonial America, brass was commonly employed in churches for many-branched chandeliers and as horse fittings, candlesticks, andirons, and domestic containers. The new brass industry was centered in Connecticut's Naugatuck Valley. It grew fast, but not without serious foreign competition. The outcry against cheap imported brass was heard in Washington, and by 1816, the tariff stood at 20 percent, ad valorem. Two years later, the rate was raised to 25 percent. Late in the nineteenth century, brass casting was introduced to Detroit and then to Kenosha, Wisconsin.

The hardness and ductility of brass depends upon the amount of zinc. Most zinc for brass was imported until

Ironwork. This 1932 photograph by Samuel H. Gottscho shows a close-up of the iron grapevine decoration around a lamp at the Cosmopolitan Club in Manhattan. LIBRARY OF CONGRESS

about 1870. Brass with 30 percent zinc could be rolled and was ideal for cartridge cases. Brass with an alloy between 30 and 36 percent could also be rolled and would take a clear impression when cold-pressed or stamped into dies for making buttons for soldiers' uniforms. Above 36 percent, brass becomes harder and stronger but has less plasticity. It is shaped by hot-rolling or hot-forging. Fine plumbing fixtures are made from 40 to 60 percent alloy.

Iron

When iron in its malleable state is struck a square blow with the flat peen of a hammer, the metal tends to spread. Different-shaped hammers and skill in applying the blow can not only flatten the metal but also force it to move in the desired direction. This is the manual basis of decorative wrought iron.

Following English models, falling water–powered ironworks were established by 1619 in Falling Creek, Virginia, and on the Saugus River near Lynn, Massachusetts, in 1634. Ever since the sixteenth century, the English had sought to substitute coal and coke for charcoal fuel in a wide variety of industrial processes. After 1775, no new charcoal-fired blast furnace was built in England. By

1784, steam power and coal set the Industrial Revolution on its coal-powered way. The new technologies used coke, resulting in a very hard, high quality cast iron, which could be cast into countless shapes, competing with smiths who produced decorative wrought iron with traditional means and materials. While both Europe and the United States were slow to adopt English technologies, when the United States did begin to use coke in its blast furnaces in the 1850, it quickly surpassed the English. Spurred by the Civil War, railroads, bridges, and facades of buildings, from the 1860s on, America's iron industry developments pushed production to new heights, greater tonnage, and into ever-new shapes and forms.

To the great distress of critics such as A. W. N. Pugin and W. R. Lethaby, overall decoration of any number of patterns on cast-iron furniture, chimney pieces, mantels, stoves, gates, railings, fences, and other objects were exceptionally popular from the 1840s to the 1900s. Richmond, Virginia, has one of the finest public displays of nineteenth-century ironwork in the United States.

In Philadelphia, Frank Furness established an independent attitude toward the plastic forms of cast iron when he freely departed from Gothic or classic motifs and used it to resemble wood or stone. His student Louis H. Sullivan, working in Chicago, became the uncontested American master of original cast-iron designs.

Wrought iron's fortunes waned until the great surge in restoring authenticity to medieval monuments or medieval-looking buildings began in France and Germany in the 1850s. England and America quickly followed. In Philadelphia, the Polish immigrant Samuel Yellin based his work on medieval originals.

Steel was already on its way to mass production in the 1850s with the emergence of the Bessemer (England) and Siemens-Martin (Germany) processes. Both tough (like wrought iron) and hard (like cast iron), steel quickly put an end to the dominance of industrial iron. Adding carbon to wrought iron or reducing the carbon in cast iron produces steel. In May 1865, the first steel rails made in America were rolled at the North Chicago Rolling Mills. Rapid railroad development followed. In 1883–1885, using steel, William Le Baron Jenney, an architect and engineer, built Chicago's ten-story Home Insurance Building, generally known as the world's first steel skeleton–framed skyscraper.

Aluminum

Although it is never found as a metal in the earth, aluminum is plentiful in the earth's crust. The trick is to get it. With the announcement in 1808 by the Englishman Sir Humphry Davy that he believed that a plentiful compound, alumina, was the oxide of an undiscovered metal, the hunt was on. After many tries resulting in pinhead samples, in 1855 the French chemist Henri Sainte-Claire Deville made the first bar of aluminum. Soon the world began using minute amounts of costly aluminum for special purposes such as jewelry. On 23 February 1886,

Charles Martin Hall, a recent graduate of the Massachusetts Institute of Technology, melted cryolite in his crucible, dissolved a small amount of alumina, inserted two carbon electrodes, and connected them to a battery. A few hours later, he poured the crucible's contents into an iron skillet to "freeze" it. When it cooled, he broke it with a hammer. Among the pieces were several pellets of silvery aluminum. His low-cost process would turn the new metal into an enormous industry. In 1888, Hall set up the Pittsburgh Reduction Company. By 1891, the firm's aluminum was being used for heating grates, light fixtures, mailboxes, and, in Chicago's Monadnock Building, as staircase cladding. Brass-rolling experts were rolling aluminum sheet, and the company was selling aluminum wire to utilities in the American West while peddling aluminum pots, pans, kettles, and other utensils from coast to coast. In the 1920s, aluminum became the essential element of the American machine age. After World War II, aluminum became a byword for lawn furniture, children's toys, and the auto industry. In their 1950s furniture designs, Charles and Ray Eames used aluminum in influential ways.

BIBLIOGRAPHY

Carpenter, Charles H., Jr., and Mary Grace Carpenter. *Tiffany Silver*. New York: Dodd, Mead, 1978.

Darling, Sharon S. *Chicago Metalsmiths*. Chicago: Chicago Historical Society, 1977.

Kerfoot, J. B. *American Pewter*. New York: Houghton Mifflin, 1924. Reprint, Detroit: Gale Research Company, 1976.

Osborne, Harold, ed. *The Oxford Companion to the Decorative Arts*. New York: Oxford University Press, 1985.

Ward, Barbara McLean, and Gerald W. R. Ward, eds. *Silver in American Life*. Boston: D. R. Godine, 1979.

Rolf Achilles

See also **Arts and Crafts Movement.**

METEOROLOGY, the study of the atmosphere and, especially, of weather.

Colonial and Early America

Early settlers in the New World found the CLIMATE harsher and the storms more violent than in the Old World. Many colonial Americans kept weather journals but, compared to European standards, few had adequate instruments. The first prolonged instrumental meteorological observations, initiated by Dr. John Lining in Charleston in 1738, were related to his medical concerns.

In 1750 Benjamin Franklin hypothesized that grounded metal rods would protect buildings from lightning damage. Two years later he conducted his famous kite experiment. Franklin's investigations demonstrated that lightning is an electrical discharge and that most flashes originate in clouds. Franklin coined much of the vocabulary of modern electricity, including such terms as positive and negative charge. He was able to simulate many types of lightning damage and demonstrated that lightning rods would protect most structures from such effects. Franklin also suggested that the aurora borealis is of electrical origin and closely associated with terrestrial magnetism, that storms are progressive wind systems, and, on a practical note, that the government should set up an office to administer aid to citizens whose crops or property had been destroyed by hurricanes, tornadoes, blights, or pestilence. During several Atlantic crossings between 1746 and 1775, Franklin made observations of the warm current called the Gulf Stream and was able to chart its boundaries fairly accurately.

Thomas Jefferson and the Reverend James Madison made the first simultaneous meteorological measurements in America in 1778. Jefferson also exchanged observations regularly with his other numerous correspondents. He was a strong advocate for a national meteorological system, and encouraged the federal government to supply observers in each county of each state with accurate instruments. Although these plans did not materialize in his lifetime, within several decades voluntary observing systems were replaced by government-run meteorological services around the world.

The Nineteenth Century

Early in the nineteenth century the Army Medical Department, the General Land Office, and the academies of the State of New York established large-scale climatological observing programs. The information was used in a variety of ways: physicians studied the relationship between weather and health, farmers and settlers used the temperature and rainfall statistics, and educators brought meteorological observations into the classroom.

Between 1834 and 1859 the "American storm controversy" stimulated a meteorological crusade that transformed theory and practice. William Redfield, James Pollard Espy, and Robert Hare argued over the nature and causes of storms and the proper way to investigate them. Redfield focused on hurricanes as circular whirlwinds; Espy on the release of latent "caloric" in updrafts; and Hare on the role of electricity in storms. Espy also prepared the first long series of daily-analyzed weather charts and was the first official government meteorologist of the United States. While it came to no clear intellectual resolution, the controversy of the 1830s and 1840s stimulated the development of observational projects at the American Philosophical Society, Franklin Institute, and Smithsonian Institution. In the 1840s Matthew Fontaine Maury, superintendent of the U.S. Navy's Depot of Charts and Instruments prepared "pilot charts" of ocean winds and currents. The charts, compiled from navy logbooks and reports from ship captains, included sailing directions for mariners on all the world's oceans.

The Smithsonian meteorological project under the direction of Joseph Henry provided a uniform set of procedures and some standardized instruments to observers across the continent. Up to 600 volunteer observers filed reports monthly. In 1849 Henry began compiling weather reports collected from telegraph operators and displayed the results on a large map of the nation. In addition the Smithsonian established cooperative observing programs with the Navy Department, the states of New York and Massachusetts, the Canadian Government, the Coast Survey, the Army Engineers, the Patent Office, and the Department of Agriculture. The Smithsonian sponsored original research on storms, climatic change, and phenology (the study of recurring natural phenomena, especially in relation to climatic conditions); it also published and distributed meteorological reports, maps, and translations. James Coffin mapped the winds of the Northern Hemisphere and the winds of the globe using data collected through Smithsonian exchanges. William Ferrel used this information to develop his theory of the general circulation of the atmosphere. Elias Loomis improved weather-plotting methods and developed synoptic charts depicting winds, precipitation, isotherms, and lines of minimum pressure.

In 1870 Congress provided funds for a national weather service. Assigned to the Signal Service Corps within the War Department, the new service was called the Division of Telegrams and Reports for the Benefit of Commerce. General Albert J. Myer served as the first director of the service, which provided daily reports of current conditions and "probabilities" for the next day's weather. It employed civilian scientists Increase A. Lapham and Cleveland Abbe and more than 500 college-educated observer-sergeants. Its budget increased one hundredfold from 1869 to 1875. The *Monthly Weather Review*, begun in 1872, was still published in the early 2000s. Beginning in 1875, in cooperation with the weather services of other nations, the weather service issued a *Bulletin of International Simultaneous Observations*, which contained worldwide synoptic charts and weather observations. In 1891 the U.S. Weather Bureau moved to the Department of Agriculture.

The Twentieth Century

During World War I the bureau instituted the daily launching of upper-air sounding balloons, applied two-way radio communication to meteorological purposes, and developed marine and aviation weather services. The "disciplinary" period in meteorology began rather late compared with parallel developments in other sciences. University and graduate education, well-defined career paths, and specialized societies and journals began in the second decade of the twentieth century. The American Meteorological Society and the American Geophysical Union were both established in 1919.

In the 1930s a number of visiting scientists from Scandinavia, including Vilhelm Bjerknes, Jacob Bjerknes, C. G. Rossby, and Sverre Petterssen brought the new Bergen School methods of air-mass and frontal analysis to the United States. In 1940, to serve the growing needs of aviation, the Weather Bureau was transferred to the Department of Commerce. By this time the use of Bergen School methods and the acquisition of upper-air data by the use of balloon-borne radio-meteorographs had become routine.

During World War II meteorologists instituted crash education programs to train weather officers. Forecasters were needed for bombing raids, naval task forces, and other special operations. Many university departments of meteorology were established at this time. Testing and use of nuclear explosives also raised new issues for meteorologists. Scientists learned that radioactive fallout spreads in an ominous plume downwind and circles the globe at high altitudes in the jet stream. Atmospheric scientists played leading roles in promoting the Limited Test Ban Treaty of 1963, which banned atmospheric nuclear testing. That year, the original Clean Air Act was passed. It was substantially revised in 1970 and in 1990.

Following the war, surplus radar equipment and airplanes were employed in storm studies. At the Research Laboratory of the General Electric Company, Irving Langmuir, a Nobel Prize–winning chemist, and his associates Vincent Schaefer and Bernard Vonnegut experimented with weather modification using dry ice, silver iodide, and other cloud-seeding agents. Although these techniques did not result in their originally intended goal—large-scale weather control—they did provide impetus to the new field of cloud physics. Meanwhile, at the Institute for Advanced Study in Princeton, John von Neumann began experiments using digital computers to model and predict the weather. With the support of the weather bureau and the military weather services, operational numerical weather prediction became a reality by the mid-1950s. Viewing the earth from space had also become a reality. In 1947 cloud formations were photographed from high altitude using a V2 rocket. *Explorer 6* took the first photograph of the earth from space in 1959, while in the same year *Explorer 7* measured the radiation budget of the earth with a pair of infrared radiometers with spin-scan stabilization designed and built by Verner Suomi. *Tiros 1* (Television Infra-Red Observation Satellite), the world's first all-weather satellite, was launched into polar orbit by NASA in 1960.

Radio weather forecasts date to 1923, when E. B. Rideout began broadcasting in Boston. Televised weathercasts were first aired on the Weather Bureau Dumont Network in 1947 by James M. "Jimmie" Fidler. In 1982 the Weather Channel started round-the-clock cable operations. In 1965 the Weather Bureau became part of the Environmental Science Services Administration (ESSA); it was renamed the National Weather Service in 1970 as part of the new National Oceanic and Atmospheric Administration (NOAA).

Conclusion

New interdisciplinary problems, approaches, and techniques characterize the modern subdisciplines of the atmospheric sciences. Specialties in cloud physics, atmospheric chemistry, satellite meteorology, and climate dynamics have developed along with more traditional programs in weather analysis and prediction. The U.S. National Center for Atmospheric Research and many new departments of atmospheric science date from the 1960s. Fundamental contributions have been made by Edward Lorenz on the chaotic behavior of the atmosphere, by F. Sherwood Rowland and Mario Molina on potential damage to stratospheric ozone by chlorofluorocarbon (CFC) compounds, and by Charles David Keeling on background measurements of carbon dioxide, to name but a few.

Meteorology has advanced through theoretical understanding and through new technologies such as aviation, computers, and satellites, which have enhanced data collection and observation of the weather. Economic and social aspects of meteorology now include practical forecasting, severe weather warnings, and governmental and diplomatic initiatives regarding the health and future of the planet.

BIBLIOGRAPHY

Bates, Charles C., and John F. Fuller. *America's Weather Warriors, 1814–1985*. College Station: Texas A&M University Press, 1986.

Fleming, James Rodger. *Meteorology in America, 1800–1870*. Baltimore: Johns Hopkins University Press, 1990.

Fleming, James Rodger, ed. *Historical Essays on Meteorology, 1919–1995*. Boston: American Meteorological Society, 1996.

Nebeker, Frederik. *Calculating the Weather: Meteorology in the Twentieth Century*. San Diego, Calif.: Academic Press, 1995.

Whitnah, Donald R. *A History of the United States Weather Bureau*. Urbana: University of Illinois Press, 1961.

James Rodger Fleming
Malcolm Rigby

See also **Weather Satellites; Weather Service, National.**

METHODISM. In 1744 in England, John Wesley founded the Methodist church as a separate entity. He had initially hoped to reawaken the Church of England to the demands of vital piety. Wesley's theology was a warm-hearted evangelicalism that stressed the experience of Christ within the heart, humanity's capacity to accept Christ's offer of redemption, and the need for a disciplined life. In his later years, Wesley came to believe in the possibility of entire sanctification or holiness (a state of perfection) and taught that it should be the goal of every Christian. This latter doctrine has contributed to many of the divisions within Methodism.

Methodist ideas entered the American colonies informally at first, notably through the efforts of Robert Strawbridge in Maryland and Virginia, Philip Embury and Barbara Heck in New York, and Captain Thomas Webb in Pennsylvania. Their success prompted Wesley to send Richard Broadman and Joseph Pilmoor to America in 1769. Two years later, Wesley sent Francis Asbury, who was to become the great apostle of early Methodism in America. At first, Methodism was an extremely small movement that existed on the fringes of the Anglican church. Members listened to Methodist preachers but still received the sacraments from the Church of England because the Methodists were yet to ordain ministers of their own. Moreover, John Wesley's personal opposition to American independence made his emerging denomination unattractive to many who supported that cause. By the end of the the American Revolution, however, Methodism had become prominent enough to separate itself completely from the Church of England. The Christmas Conference, held in Baltimore in 1784, marks the beginning of the Methodist church in America. At that meeting, sixty preachers joined with Wesley's delegates Richard Vassey, Richard Whitcoat, and Thomas Coke in ordaining Francis Asbury and establishing an order for the church. The conference decided on a form of government by deacons, elders, and superintendents (later bishops); adopted the Book of Discipline, which regulated the life of the church and its members; and elected Coke and Asbury as its first superintendents.

Almost immediately after the Christmas Conference, Methodism entered a period of rapid expansion. The system of CIRCUIT RIDERS, which Wesley had experimented with in England, met the need for clergymen in outlying regions and allowed relatively uneducated men to enter the ministry. Wherever the circuit rider could gather a crowd, he would stop, preach a sermon, and organize a Methodist class to continue the work until he was able to return. Religious zeal rather than material reward motivated these circuit riders because remuneration was sparse. Methodist theology was also easy for the average person to understand, and the Methodist emphasis on discipline was invaluable to communities that were far from the ordinary restraints of civilization. The Methodist combination of simplicity, organization, and lay participation not only made it the largest Protestant denomination but also decisively influenced the other frontier churches. Other denominations, even those of Calvinist background, had to accept elements of Methodist theory and practice in order to survive.

The nineteenth century was a period in which the Methodists, like many other American denominations, experienced internal division. Despite Wesley's unequivocable distaste for slavery, the question of slavery became an important issue for Methodist churches in both the North and South. Mistreatment of black ministers and members by white Methodists led some African American Methodists to form their own churches, including the AFRICAN METHODIST EPISCOPAL CHURCH in 1816 and the African Methodist Episcopal Zion Church five years later. In 1843, the Wesleyan Methodist Connection, a small antislavery church, formed. The next year at the general conference of the Methodist Episcopal church, that branch

Anna Howard Shaw. The Methodist Protestant minister, doctor, and tireless suffragist, both as a persuasive lecturer and as president of the National American Woman Suffrage Association from 1904 to 1915. LIBRARY OF CONGRESS

split into two separate ecclesiastical bodies: the Methodist Episcopal church and the Methodist Episcopal church, South. At issue was whether or not one of the denomination's bishops could serve in that capacity while he owned slaves, and delegates from the slave states founded their own church when the general conference suspended the offending bishop. After the American Civil War, even more black Methodists formed their own denominations. In the same period, the increasingly middle-class nature of the church contributed to disputes over the issue of entire sanctification, and the lower-class membership largely withdrew into the "Holiness" or "Pentecostal" movement. Nevertheless, during the late nineteenth century, the various branches of American Methodism dramatically increased in both members and wealth.

In the twentieth century, Methodism was involved in both the ecumenical movement and the SOCIAL GOSPEL. In 1908, the Federal Council of Churchs adopted the Methodist Social Creed as its own statement of social principles. Methodism has also begun to heal the divisions within its own ranks. In 1939, the Methodist Episcopal church; the Methodist Episcopal church, South; and the Methodist Protestant church merged into the Methodist

Church, which resulted in a new denomination of almost eight million people. In 1968, the Methodist Church merged with the Evangelical United Brethren to form the United Methodist church with approximately eleven million members. The Evangelical United Brethen itself had come out of an earlier merger of two churches, the Church of the United Brethren in Christ and the Evangelical Association, in 1946. These two other denominations had arisen about the same time that Methodism emerged as a separate church and had always shared similar beliefs.

Like many mainstream Protestant churches, United Methodist faced falling membership in the second half of the twentieth century. In 1974, the United Methodist church had almost 10.2 million members, but that number had fallen to only 8.4 million by 1999. Nonetheless, the church remains the third largest Christian denomination in the United States and has substantially expanded its membership in Africa and Asia. Current membership levels for other prominent branches of Methodism, which have all grown over the last fifty years, include the African Methodist Episcopal church, 3.5 million members; the African Methodist Episcopal Zion church, 1.2 million members; and the Christian Methodist Episcopal church, 800,000 members.

BIBLIOGRAPHY

Andrews, Dee. *The Methodists and Revolutionary America, 1760–1800: The Shaping of an Evangelical Culture.* Princeton, N.J.: Princeton University Press, 2000.

Campbell, James T. *Songs of Zion: The African Methodist Episcopal Church in the United States and South Africa.* New York: Oxford University Press, 1995.

Richey, Russell E. *Early American Methodism.* Bloomington: Indiana University Press, 1991.

Schneider, A. Gregory. *The Way of the Cross Leads Home: The Domestication of American Methodism.* Bloomington: Indiana University Press, 1993.

Wigger, John H. *Taking Heaven by Storm: Methodism and the Rise of Popular Christianity in America.* New York: Oxford University Press, 1998.

Glenn T. Miller / A. E.

See also **African American Religions and Sects; Camp Meetings; Dissenters; Evangelicalism and Revivalism; Protestantism; Religion and Religious Affiliation.**

METROPOLITAN GOVERNMENT refers to the government of a metropolitan area as a whole, as opposed to the fragmentary rule of individual municipalities that constitute the area. Because of America's permissive municipal incorporation laws and the prevailing devotion to grassroots rule, governmental fragmentation has characterized most metropolitan areas in the United States. Scores of suburban municipalities surround central cities, especially in the Northeast and Midwest, and a multitude of special districts, each providing a single service, adds to the number of governmental units.

During the nineteenth century, aggressive annexation efforts eliminated some of the local units surrounding major cities. In 1854, Philadelphia annexed all of Philadelphia County; in 1889, Chicago's area increased fourfold; and in 1898, New York City combined with Brooklyn, Queens, Staten Island, and much of what is today The Bronx to form Greater New York. At the same time, state legislatures formed special-purpose metropolitan districts, thereby pioneering metropolitan-wide cooperation. In 1889, the Illinois legislature established the Chicago Sanitary District, enabling Chicago and its suburbs to work jointly to solve sewage disposal problems. Between 1889 and 1895, the Massachusetts legislature created metropolitan water supply, sewage disposal, and park districts to serve Boston and surrounding towns.

As suburban municipalities attracted more residents and wealth, they proved better able to provide services equal to those of the central cities. Thus, during the early twentieth century, suburbanites voted down an increasing share of proposals for consolidation with the core city. The number of suburban municipalities soared, much to the consternation of good-government reformers, who were devoted to efficient rule and abhorred the wasteful duplication and conflict that accompanied fragmentation. Such organizations as the National Municipal League and League of Women Voters as well as most political scientists staunchly supported metropolitan reform. Fearing economic decline in the suburb-ringed central cities, many business leaders also lined up behind metropolitan reform.

In the 1920s and 1930s, good-government reformers and business leaders in St. Louis, Pittsburgh, and Cleveland campaigned for a two-tier federative structure with an overarching metropolitan government exercising certain regional functions and the existing municipalities retaining local duties. Voters rejected the two-tier schemes, and they continued to veto federative plans in the decades after World War II. In 1957, however, Miami-area voters approved a proposal that shifted certain functions from municipalities to a metropolitan county government. During the late 1960s, Indiana's legislature created a unified city-county structure for Indianapolis, and Minnesota lawmakers established the Twin Cities Metropolitan Council to foster regional planning and coordination among the area's special-purpose metropolitan districts. Yet such victories over fragmentation were the exception, not the rule.

During the last decades of the twentieth century, public choice theorists in academia joined in the attack on metropolitan reform. They proclaimed the advantages of fragmentation, arguing that balkanization permitted citizens to shop around for a government that suited their needs. By the 1990s, however, a new generation of reformers was rallying behind a new regionalism movement and citing the need for metropolitan-wide cooperation to realize economic growth and social equity. Given the electorate's reluctance to support major reforms, even the new regionalists realized that dreams of consolidated metropolises or two-tier metropolitan federations were largely unrealistic.

BIBLIOGRAPHY

Hamilton, David K. *Governing Metropolitan Areas: Response to Growth and Change.* New York: Garland, 1999.

Teaford, Jon C. *City and Suburb: The Political Fragmentation of Metropolitan America, 1850–1970.* Baltimore: Johns Hopkins University Press, 1979.

Jon C. Teaford

See also **Municipal Government; Municipal Reform; Suburbanization; Urbanization.**

METROPOLITAN MUSEUM OF ART.

The founders of the Metropolitan Museum of Art hoped it would fill the need for a national art collection. Some had perceived this need for decades before the Civil War. In the 1860s sectional and industrial conflict intensified the desire of civic leaders to promote unification and class harmony through art. Thus, on 4 July 1866 diplomat John Jay proposed in Paris that New York City establish such a collection. In response the Union League, formed in 1863 to support Lincoln, sought to implement Jay's proposal, leading in 1869 to formation of a Provisional Committee assigned to establish such a museum. This committee, which included Union League members and other leading figures from New York's art world and social elite, elected a board of trustees for the new institution, which was incorporated in 1870 and soon housed in temporary quarters. Although from the beginning its board of trustees always has had a preponderance of businessmen, financiers, and lawyers, among the founders were poet William Cullen Bryant and artists such as Frederic E. Church and John Quincy Adams Ward.

During the Met's early decades, London's South Kensington Museum (later the Victoria and Albert) appealed to those who believed that the quality of American domestic life and manufacturing suffered from an absence of accessible examples of fine craftsmanship for study by artisans and others. However, because of the trustees' aesthetic preferences and their desire to present themselves and the United States as culturally advanced, the Met developed less as a design showcase than as a Louvre-like palace or temple of fine art. Mixed with hopes to use the museum's splendor to deepen faith in the existing social order was the more expansive idea, articulated by lawyer and founder Joseph H. Choate, that "knowledge of art in its higher forms of beauty would tend directly to humanize, to educate and refine a practical and laborious people."

These high expectations were backed by the Met's acquisitions, beginning with 174 European paintings in 1871, and by the efforts and donations of founders such as railroad millionaire John Taylor Johnston, the museum's first president. Yet when the Met moved to the site on the east side of Central Park between Eightieth and Eighty-fourth Streets where it has resided since 1880, it could not claim preeminence even among American museums, although they were few in number and mostly of recent origin. The appointment in 1879 of a paid director, Louis Palma di Cesnola, aided and complicated the quest for credibility. The vast collection of Cypriote antiquities that Cesnola sold to the museum in 1873 later occasioned embarrassing investigations that eventually confirmed the authenticity of most of the objects but revealed some careless reconstructions.

By the time Cesnola died in 1904, the Met had added an entrance on Fifth Avenue to the original one inside the park, and important collections such as the European paintings assembled by Henry G. Marquand. It had also created three curatorial departments, including one for casts and reproductions of art, mainly from antiquity and the Italian Renaissance, that was considered central to its early mission. It had also become rich, aided by a multimillion-dollar bequest from the New Jersey locomotive manufacturer Jacob Rogers.

Under J. P. Morgan's presidency (1904–1913), the museum moved away from an emphasis on individual collections and toward rigorous standards that involved arranging masterpieces in ways that depicted the development of art. In 1905 the museum's prominence and resources persuaded Sir Caspar Purdon Clarke to become director, for which he left a similar post at South Kensington. Edward Robinson resigned as director of the Boston Museum of Fine Arts, where he had built an especially strong Greek and Roman collection, to become assistant director. In 1910 Robinson became director, serving until 1931, and McKim, Mead and White completed a wing for decorative and medieval arts. Excavations in Egypt initiated by the Museum in 1906 contributed to a collection of ancient Egyptian artifacts that became the most important outside of Cairo. In 1913 the museum received thirteen Rembrandts and major works by Vermeer and others from a bequest of department store owner Benjamin Altman. Despite the new emphasis on integrating individual works into the general collection, they were displayed separately as the Altman collection. Several subsequently donated collections received similar treatment, leading critics such as artist Stuart Davis to conclude that the Met's primary concern remained glorifying the wealthy.

The wealthy responded; donations from the wealthy allowed the museum to establish a Far Eastern Art Department in 1915. Furthermore, perhaps the most valuable collection of all—medieval art acquired by Morgan and later installed in a Pierpont Morgan Wing—came the following year as a gift from his son. In the 1920s publisher Frank A. Munsey's bequest of approximately $10 million secured the Met's position as the wealthiest au-

Metropolitan Museum of Art. In 1880 the museum opened its building on the east side of Central Park between Eightieth and Eighty-Fourth streets. This photo shows the museum as it looked c. 1900, when it was just beginning to take its place as one of the world's best museums of art. LIBRARY OF CONGRESS

tonomous museum. Although the proliferation of American art museums vitiated the idea of a national collection, the Met provided a model for others. In his thirty-five years there beginning in 1905, most of them as secretary, Henry W. Kent created a card catalogue and photographic record of the collections, and established editorial and extension divisions. Curators such as William M. Ivins Jr., who headed the Department of Prints that was established in 1916, also set standards for museum practice.

Installing and Redefining the Canon

The issue of how to deploy the institution's growing power was a contentious one throughout the twentieth century. One consistent goal was building what an 1870 policy committee report called "a more or less complete collection of objects illustrative of the History of Art from the earliest beginnings to the present time." As the twenty-first century began, the first words on the homepage of the Met's Web site were: "5000 years of art." What deserved inclusion, however, was more disputed in 1910 than in 1870, and most intensely in the 1960s and after.

In 1910 modernist painting and sculpture, which challenged prevailing, assumptions about what constituted "art," presented the most troubling issues. Three years earlier conservative trustees, angered by the purchase of Renoir's *Madame Charpentier and Her Children* (1878), almost fired Roger Fry, whose brief tenure as curator of painting was turbulent but productive, and assistant Bryson Burroughs, who went on to serve as curator from 1909 to 1934. The Met purchased one Cezanne painting from the controversial 1913 Armory Show, but presented itself as the alternative to modernism's excesses.

Although trustee George A. Hearn established a fund for purchasing American art, like modern art it remained a low priority. The Met mounted an historical survey of American art in conjunction with Hudson-Fulton celebrations in 1909 and growing public interest in American decorative arts encouraged the opening of the American Wing in 1924. However, a few years later the museum turned down Gertrude Whitney's offer of her collection of American art, and it was not until 1949 that it formed the Department of American Paintings and Sculpture. With some exceptions, like the elimination of the galleries of casts, additions supplemented rather than replaced established areas, with canonical European painting and sculpture and Greek and Roman art at the core. The latter became an area of strength under professionals such as Cambridge-educated Gisela A. M. Richter, who served as a curator from 1925 to 1948. In 1921 attendance surpassed one million for first time, leaving the Met second only to the Louvre. In 1929 and later, donations from the H. O. Havemeyer Collection strengthened the Met's holdings in many areas. The collection reflected the influence of Mary Cassatt, who advised Louisine Havemeyer, and nudged trustees toward accepting impressionism and what followed.

Archaeologist Herbert Winlock served as director throughout the 1930s, spending much of his time in Egypt. In 1938, with support from John D. Rockefeller Jr., the museum opened The Cloisters at Fort Tryon Park in upper Manhattan. It was dedicated to medieval art and incorporated architectural elements from that period, many collected by the sculptor George Grey Barnard. From the 1930s to the 1960s the museum sponsored excavations in Iraq and Iran, from which the findings became part of the museum's collection. After World War II an experimental coalition with the Museum of Modern Art and the Whitney Museum of Art failed in part because the Met had less enthusiasm for American and modern art than did the other museums. Yet leading modernists, aware of the canonical status conferred by a presence in the Met, enriched the collections with bequests in 1946 by Gertrude Stein of Picasso's iconic portrait of her and by Alfred Stieglitz of several hundred photographs. In 1928 Stieglitz had given the Met the first photographs admitted into its collection, but not until 1992 did the museum create a separate department for photography, which had previously been grouped with prints. The museum created its first department dedicated to contemporary art in 1967. The opening in 1987 of the Lila Acheson Wallace Wing, funded by the co-founder of *Reader's Digest*, gave twentieth-century art a more prominent position within the museum.

Expanding the Audience

In 1961 the Met attracted five million visitors, helped by publicity related to purchase of Rembrandt's *Aristotle Contemplating the Bust of Homer* (1653) for a record price of $2.3 million. Equally important were the efforts of Francis Henry Taylor, director from 1940 to 1954, to make the Met attractive to a more diverse constituency. These efforts were maintained by James Rorimer, who had supervised the building of The Cloisters and who served as director from 1955 to 1966. They were taken to a new level by Thomas Hoving. A medievalist like Rorimer, Hoving had left the Met to serve briefly as New York City Parks Commissioner before returning as director from 1967 to 1977. He favored dramatic exhibitions, acquisitions, and building projects. Some, such as the acquisition of investment banker Robert Lehman's collection and the construction for it of one of several wings designed by Kevin Roche, John Dinkeloo and Associates, augmented the traditional core. Others broadened the Met's purview. The Met's century of neglect of work later grouped in the Department of the Arts of Africa, Oceania, and the Americas had led it to turn down Nelson Rockefeller's 1939 offer to finance an archaeological expedition to Mexico. In 1969, after the civil rights movement and Cold War concerns had redefined cultural significance, the museum accepted Rockefeller's gift of 3,300 works of non-Western art and supporting material, including a library.

Founders such as art historian George Fiske Comfort had imagined a museum that would innovate both in curatorial practices and in outward-looking activities such as programs for schoolchildren that would serve widely the city's population. Dependence on generous public funding, initially supported by William M. "Boss" Tweed just before his 1871 indictment, also encouraged democratic rhetoric. Often city contributions for operating expenses and construction accounted for over one-half of the Met's revenues. In the 1880s the museum had set up city schools for training in the crafts, but closed these in 1892. In 1897, when Cesnola defended the refusal of admission to a plumber in overalls because the Met was a "closed corporation" that set its own standards, critics declared this typical of the way it violated its charter requirement to furnish "popular instruction."

Slow steps toward broader access included, beginning in 1891, opening on Sundays despite conservative opposition on religious grounds. Like many institutions, in the 1930s the Met responded to economic and international crises with demonstrations of its Americanism, including an exhibition of 290 paintings called *Life in America*. After Pearl Harbor, fifteen-hundred works by American artists were featured in the *Artists for Victory Show*. The trustees added three women to their board in 1952. Two years later they added Dorothy Shaver, president of Lord and Taylor, who had guided the 1946 merger of the Met and the Costume Institute. White males remained dominant on the board, however, and in 1989 a poster by the Guerilla Girls—a feminist group formed in 1985 in New York to challenge the underrepresentation of women in collections and exhibitions—asked "Do women have to be naked to get into the Metropolitan Museum of Art?" and reported that "less than five percent of artists in the Modern Arts section are women, but 85 percent of the nudes are female."

The Guerilla Girls poster typified an era of cultural conflict initiated by the 1969 photographic and sound exhibition, *Harlem on My Mind: The Culture Capital of Black America, 1900–1968*. Detractors considered the exhibition an outsider's take on Harlem, organized around demeaning stereotypes and omitting work by painters and sculptors from the community. Defenders celebrated the unprecedented number of African American visitors that it attracted and the attention it gave to Harlem photographers, notably James Van DerZee. Remarks by a Harlem teenager in her essay in the exhibition catalogue also sparked a controversy over whether or not the catalogue was anti-Semitic. The show revealed that although a seat on the museum's board was prized by New York City's social elite, in many communities the Met had little credibility.

Hoving's successor, Philippe de Montebello, led the Met into the twenty-first century, trying to make the collection more accessible through, for example, video productions and the Internet. He also facilitated the use of the museum to create a favorable public image for large corporations, whose donations were becoming increasingly essential. Traditionalists approved of his observation, in response to a 2001 gift from the Annenberg Foundation of $20 million to purchase European art, that "it goes right to the heart of what this museum is about: acquisition." Yet none could predict precisely the impact that the Met's unsurpassed collection would have on the increasing number of virtual as well as actual visitors who selectively experienced it, sometimes responding in ways different from those that could have been imagined by collectors and curators. Such was the case in the days after the World Trade Center's destruction in September 2001, when the painter Helen Marden found comfort in coming to the Met's Islamic galleries "to see the good that people do." The issues of who these visitors were, what type of art they encountered and in what context, and how they looked at it, continued to matter.

BIBLIOGRAPHY

Dubin, Steven C. *Displays of Power: Memory and Amnesia in the American Museum*. New York: New York University Press, 1999. Includes a chapter on the *Harlem on My Mind* exhibition.

Duncan, Carol. *Civilizing Rituals: Inside Public Art Museums*. New York: Routledge, 1995.

Harris, Neil. *Cultural Excursions: Marketing Appetites and Cultural Tastes in Modern America*. Chicago: University of Chicago Press, 1990.

Hibbard, Howard. *The Metropolitan Museum of Art*. New York: Harper and Row, 1980.

Hoving, Thomas. *Making the Mummies Dance: Inside the Metropolitan Museum of Art*. New York: Simon and Schuster, 1993. The controversial director's controversial account of his tenure.

Lerman, Leo. *The Museum: One Hundred Years and the Metropolitan Museum of Art*. New York: Viking, 1969.

Tomkins, Calvin. *Merchants and Masterpieces: The Story of the Metropolitan Museum of Art.* New York: Dutton, 1970.

Wallach, Alan. *Exhibiting Contradictions: Essays on the Art Museum in the United States.* Amherst: University of Massachusetts Press, 1998. Includes an historical account of the collection of casts and reproductions.

George H. Roeder Jr.

See also **Art: Painting, Photography, Sculpture; Museums.**

MEUSE-ARGONNE OFFENSIVE

(26 September–11 November 1918). In April 1917, when the United States declared war against the Central Powers, the contending European powers had long been deadlocked in trench warfare. The entry of the United States gave hope to the French and British, but hostilities persisted for another bloody year and a half before the American Expeditionary Forces (AEF) were ready for a major part in the decisive Allied offensive.

When the war began in 1914, U.S. regulars consisted of only 5,033 officers and 93,511 soldiers. The National Guard had about 67,000 men; the U.S. Marines, a mere 10,386. The sinking of the *Lusitania* in May 1915 spurred Congress to enlarge the reserve and standing forces, but a concerted drive for battle readiness would not come until the formal declaration of war.

French and British leaders wanted the existing American regiments to replace veteran Allied divisions and for the new units to consist of infantrymen and machine gunners. Controversy smoldered over the U.S. decision—resolutely embodied by General John J. Pershing—to build the AEF into a power able to assume responsibility for a part of the front.

During the seemingly interminable buildup, American units reaching France were first trained by Allied in-

Early Tank. This primitive model of the armored mobile gun, introduced into warfare only two years earlier as Britain's secret weapon, had limited success during the final Allied push along the Western Front in World War I. © CORBIS

structors and then given front experience under Allied commanders in quiet sectors, starting near Saint-Mihiel on 5 February 1918. Meeting the Champagne-Marne crisis of May–July 1918, Americans at Château-Thierry and Belleau Wood sealed a German break through the French lines. In these operations, the French practice of ordering open attack rather than a dug-in defense wasted lives and vindicated Pershing's stubborn insistence on leading an organic, self-contained American force. (Pershing later compromised, allowing the gradual allocation of about one division in every three to serve under the French, the British, or the Belgians.) By early August, Pershing had formed the First American Army, nineteen divisions responsible for one hundred miles of the Lorraine front. Pershing made ready for what proved to be the grand Allied offensive that ended the war.

The Meuse-Argonne offensive began on 26 September 1918, when the First Army advanced northward with the ultimate goal of reaching Sedan, thirty-five miles distant and the strategic hub of German lateral railroad communications. The American left deployed via the Argonne forest, the center for the towering Montfaucon bastion, and the right mustered along the Meuse River. The German defenses were entrenched in four lines ten miles deep. The third German line checked the advance on 3 October. The First Army had destroyed sixteen German divisions. While Pershing planned his next offensive, Field Marshal Paul von Hindenburg advised Kaiser Wilhelm II to seek peace.

During a relatively slack period while he awaited fresh troops and supplies, Pershing formed the Second Army under Robert L. Bullard and gave the First Army to Hunter Liggett. Pershing in the meantime had been granted equality with the commander in chief of the French armies, Henri Philippe Pétain, and the British commander in chief in France, Douglas Haig. The Americans dispersed the third German line on 31 October. In the clearing of the deadly Argonne was the saga of the "Lost Battalion" and the unparalleled exploit of Sergeant Alvin C. York.

All along the western front, the Germans were near exhaustion. Forty-seven of their divisions, one-fourth of their force, had been committed in a hopeless attempt to halt the American advance. On 1 November the Americans pushed six miles through the last German line and onto the heights of Barricourt. Capture of that high ground compelled the Germans to retreat west of the Meuse. More than 1.2 million men in twenty-one divisions took part in Pershing's climactic Meuse-Argonne offensive. Overshadowed by the giant American drive, ten U.S. divisions simultaneously fought under Allied control in other sectors. On Armistice Day, 11 November 1918, as supreme U.S. commander, Pershing commanded 1,981,701 men.

BIBLIOGRAPHY

Cooke, James J. *Pershing and His Generals: Command and Staff in the AEF.* Westport, Conn.: Praeger, 1997.

Farwell, Byron. *Over There: The United States in the Great War, 1917–1918.* New York: Norton, 1999.

Kennedy, David M. *Over Here: The First World War and American Society.* New York: Oxford University Press, 1980.

Palmer, Frederick. *Our Greatest Battle: The Meuse-Argonne.* New York: Dodd, Mead, 1919.

Pershing, John J. *My Experiences in the World War.* New York: Stokes, 1931.

R. W. Daly / A. R.

See also **American Expeditionary Forces; Champagne-Marne Operation; Lost Battalion; Saint-Mihiel, Campaigns at.**

MEXICAN-AMERICAN WAR (1846–1848). The war's remote causes included diplomatic indiscretions during the first decade of American-Mexican relations, as well as the effects of the Mexican revolutions, during which American citizens suffered physical injury and property losses. Its more immediate cause was the annexation of TEXAS. The Mexican government refused to recognize Texas as independent or the RIO GRANDE as an international boundary. It first withdrew its minister from Washington, D.C., and then severed diplomatic relations in March 1845.

President James K. Polk anticipated military action and sent Brigadier General Zachary Taylor with his force from Louisiana to the Nueces River in Texas, but he also sought a diplomatic solution. Recognizing that the chief aim of American foreign policy was the annexation of CALIFORNIA, Polk planned to connect with that policy the adjustment of all difficulties with Mexico, including the dispute over jurisdiction in the territory between the Nueces River and the Rio Grande.

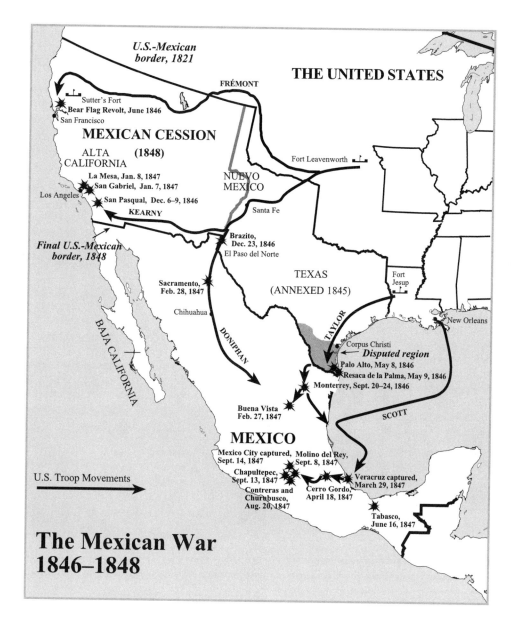

The Mexican War 1846–1848

In September 1845, assured through a confidential agent that the new Mexican government of José Joaquín Herrera would welcome an American minister, and acting on the suggestion of Secretary of State James Buchanan, Polk appointed John Slidell as envoy-minister on a secret mission to secure California and NEW MEXICO for $15 million to $20 million if possible, or for $40 million if necessary—terms later changed by secret instructions to $5 million for New Mexico and $25 million for California.

Mexico refused to reopen diplomatic relations. In January 1846, after the first news that the Mexican government, under various pretexts, had refused to receive Slidell, partly on the ground that questions of boundary and claims should be separated, Polk ordered Taylor to advance from Corpus Christi, Texas, to the Rio Grande, resulting shortly in conflicts with Mexican troops at the battle of Palo Alto on 8 May and the battle of Resaca de la Palma on 9 May. On 11 May, after arrival of news of the Mexican advance across the Rio Grande and the skirmish with Taylor's troops, Polk submitted to Congress a war message stating that war existed and that it was begun by Mexico on American soil. The United States declared war on 13 May, apparently on the ground that such action was justified by the delinquencies, obstinacy, and hostilities of the Mexican government; and Polk proceeded to formulate plans for military and naval operations to advance his goal of obtaining Mexican acceptance of his overtures for peace negotiations.

The military plans included an expedition under Colonel Stephen W. Kearny to New Mexico and from there to California, supplemented by an expedition to Chihuahua; an advance across the Rio Grande into Mexico by troops under Taylor to occupy the neighboring provinces; and a possible later campaign of invasion of the Mexican interior from Veracruz.

In these plans Polk was largely influenced by assurances received in February from Colonel A. J. Atocha, a friend of Antonio López de Santa Anna, then in exile from Mexico, to the effect that the latter, if aided in plans to return from Havana, Cuba, to Mexico, would recover his Mexican leadership and cooperate in a peaceful arrangement to cede Mexican territory to the United States. In June, Polk entered into negotiations with Santa Anna through a brother of Slidell, receiving verification of Atocha's assurances. Polk had already sent a confidential order to Commodore David Conner, who on 16 August permitted Santa Anna to pass through the coast blockade to Veracruz. Having arrived in Mexico, Santa Anna promptly began his program, which resulted in his own quick res-

Resaca de la Palma. This engraving shows the charge of Captain Charles May's dragoons against Mexican artillery on 9 May 1846—one of the clashes just north of the Rio Grande, in a disputed border area, that touched off the Mexican-American War. ARCHIVE PHOTOS, INC.

Buena Vista. This lithograph shows General Zachary Taylor during his triumph over a far larger Mexican force under General Antonio López de Santa Anna near Monterrey, Mexico, on 22–23 February 1847, ending the northern campaign of the war—and putting Taylor on the road to the White House two years later. LIBRARY OF CONGRESS

toration to power. He gave no evidences whatever of his professed pacific intentions.

On 3 July 1846 the small expedition under Kearny received orders to go via the SANTA FE TRAIL from Fort Leavenworth, Kansas, to occupy New Mexico. It reached Santa Fe on 18 August, and a part of the force (300 men) led by Kearny marched to the Pacific at San Diego. From there it arrived at Los Angeles to join the forces led by Commodore Robert Field Stockton, including John Charles Frémont's BEAR FLAG insurgents. Kearny and Stockton joined forces and defeated the Mexican army at Los Angeles on 8 and 9 January 1847. On 13 January, Frémont and Andres Pico, the leader of the Mexican forces in California, signed the Treaty of Cahuenga. Kearny went on to establish a civil government in California on 1 March.

Taylor's forces, meanwhile, began to cross the Rio Grande to Matamoros on 18 May 1846 and advanced to the strongly fortified city of Monterrey, which after an attack was evacuated by Mexican forces on 28 September. Later, in February 1847 at Buena Vista, Taylor stubbornly resisted and defeated the attack of Santa Anna's Mexican relief expedition.

Soon thereafter the theater of war shifted to Veracruz, from which the direct route to the Mexican capital seemed to present less difficulty than the northern route. In deciding on the campaign from Veracruz to Mexico City, Polk probably was influenced by the news of U.S. occupation of California, which reached him on 1 September 1846. The U.S. Navy had helped secure Monterrey, San Diego, and San Francisco in California and had continued blockades against Veracruz and Tampico. The Navy provided valuable assistance again when General Winfield Scott began a siege of Veracruz. After the capture of the fortress of Veracruz on 29 March 1847, Scott led the army westward via Jalapa to Pueblo, which he entered on 15 May and from which he began his advance to the mountain pass of Cerro Gordo on 7 August.

Coincident with Scott's operations against Veracruz, Polk began new peace negotiations with Mexico through a "profoundly secret mission." On 15 April, Buchanan had sent Nicholas P. Trist as a confidential peace agent to accompany Scott's army. In August, after the battles of Contreras and Churubusco, Trist arranged an armistice through Scott as a preliminary step for a diplomatic conference to discuss peace terms—a conference that began

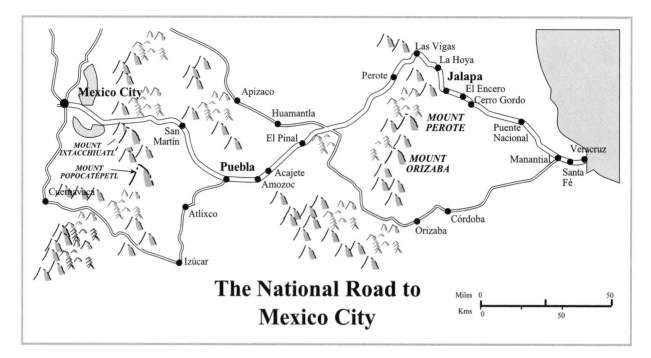

The National Road to Mexico City

Miles 0   50
Kms 0   50

on 27 August and closed on 7 September by Mexican rejection of the terms offered. Scott promptly resumed his advance. After hard fighting from 7 to 11 September at the battles of Molino del Rey and Chapultepec, he captured Mexico City on 14 September and with his staff entered the palace, over which he hoisted the American flag.

Practically, the war was ended. Santa Anna, after resigning his presidential office, made an unsuccessful attempt to strike at the American garrison Scott had left at Pueblo, but he was driven off and obliged to flee from Mexico.

The chief remaining American problem was to find a government with enough power to negotiate a peace treaty to prevent the danger of American annexation of all Mexico. Fortunately, Trist was still with the army and in close touch with the situation at the captured capital. Although recalled, he determined to assume the responsibility of remaining to renew efforts to conclude a peace treaty even at the risk of disavowal by his government. After some delay, he was able to conclude with the Mexican commissioners a treaty in accord with the instructions that had been annulled by his recall. The chief negotiations were conducted at Mexico City, but the treaty was completed and signed on 2 February 1848 at the neighboring town of Guadalupe Hidalgo. By its terms, which provided for cessation of hostilities, the United States agreed to pay $15 million for New Mexico and California. Polk received the treaty on 19 February and promptly decided to submit it to the Senate, which approved it on 10 March by a vote of thirty-eight to fourteen. Ratifications were exchanged on 30 May 1848.

Among the chief results of the war were expansion of American territory; a new population called MEXICAN AMERICANS; increased American interest in the problems of the Caribbean and the Pacific and in the opening and control of isthmian interoceanic transit routes at Panama, Nicaragua, and Tehuantepec; and outbursts of "manifest destiny" from 1848 to 1860. The acquisition of Mexico's northern lands also intensified debates over the extension of slavery into new territory and brought the Union a step closer to war.

BIBLIOGRAPHY

Connor, Seymour V., and Odie B. Faulk. *North America Divided: The Mexican War, 1846–1848.* New York: Oxford University Press, 1971.

Johannsen, Robert W. *To the Halls of the Montezumas: The Mexican War in the American Imagination.* New York: Oxford University Press, 1985.

McCaffrey, James M. *Army of Manifest Destiny: The American Soldier in the Mexican War, 1846 – 1848.* New York: New York University Press, 1992.

Robinson, Cecil, ed. and trans. *The View from Chapultepec: Mexican Writers on the Mexican-American War.* Tucson: University of Arizona Press, 1989.

Smith, George W., and Charles Judah, eds. *Chronicles of the Gringos: The United States Army in the Mexican War, 1846–1848.* Albuquerque: University of New Mexico Press, 1968.

J. M. Callahan / F. B.

See also **Hispanic Americans; Kearny's March to California; Manifest Destiny; Navy, United States;** *and vol. 9:* **Memories of the North American Invasion; Mexican Minister of War's Reply to Manuel de la Peña y Peña; National Songs, Ballads, and Other Patriotic Poetry, Chiefly Relating to the War of 1846; Message on the War with Mexico.**

MEXICAN-AMERICAN WAR CLAIMS were settled by a commission created under a convention of 1867 between the United States and Mexican governments. American citizens presented 1,017 claims against Mexico amounting to $470,126,613, and Mexicans countered with 998 claims totaling $86,661,891.15. To the former, 186 awards, totaling $4,125,622.20, were allowed; to the latter, 167 awards amounting to $150,498.41. Claims against the United States arose largely from Indian depredations and excesses committed by American soldiers. Those presented against Mexico were largely for the seizure and destruction of property, forced loans, illegal arrests and imprisonments, and murder. It took until November 1876 for the commission to complete its work.

BIBLIOGRAPHY

Francaviglia, Richard, and Douglas W. Richmond, eds. *Dueling Eagles: Reinterpreting the U.S.-Mexican War, 1846–1848*. Fort Worth: Texas Christian University Press, 2000.

Frank Freidel / c. w.

See also **Diplomatic Missions; Mexican-American War; Mexico, Relations with.**

MEXICAN AMERICAN WOMEN'S NATIONAL ASSOCIATION, a Hispanic women's advocacy group, renamed MANA, a national Latina organization. The group, whose mission statement calls for the empowerment of Latinas through leadership development, community service, and advocacy, was the largest pan-Latina organization in the United States in 2000, with membership exceeding two thousand in more than a dozen local chapters. Founded in 1974 with the aim of educational and economic advancement for Mexican American women, MANA runs leadership-training programs and stresses the importance of Latinas playing an active role in their communities. In 1994 it changed its name to better correspond with the diversity of its membership and broadened its mission to include all Latinas.

BIBLIOGRAPHY

de la Garza, Rodolpho O., Frank D. Bean, Charles M. Bonjean, Ricardo Romo, and Rodolfo Alvarez. *The Mexican American Experience: An Interdisciplinary Anthology*. Austin: University of Texas Press, 1985.

Garcia, Alma M., and Mario T. Garcia, eds. *Chicana Feminist Thought: The Basic Historical Writings*. New York: Routledge, 1997.

Eli Moses Diner

See also **Hispanic Americans.**

MEXICAN AMERICANS. A unique tradition characterizes the history of Mexican Americans in the United States in comparison to that of other ethnic groups. They have been both a conquered people and immigrants, in the classical sense of both terms. After prevailing in the Mexican-American War (1846–1848), the United States carved out what became the American Southwest and inherited approximately 80,000 Mexicans. The Treaty of Guadalupe Hidalgo assured Mexicans in the United States "all the rights of citizens," but this agreement was continuously violated as Mexicans lost their lands and their political rights.

Nonetheless, in areas where they dominated numerically, Mexicans maintained a modicum of political and economic influence. Americans and Mexicans in the Southwest had been trading with American interests in the East before the takeover, and Anglo-Americans and Europeans had actually lived among and intermarried with Mexicans. Following the transition to U.S. rule, the Gold Rush, military efforts to subdue and destroy the nomadic Indian tribes, and population growth created opportunities for merchants, farmers, livestock raisers, and transportation companies. This expanded economic activity engaged Anglo, European, and Mexican entrepreneurs, and involved Mexicans at every level; thus, migration from Mexico increased proportionally.

After 1880 a railroad network in the American Southwest and northern Mexico, built mainly with American capital, radically transformed the economy of both areas. The new economic structure was based on the production of industrial raw materials and linked the border region to markets of the industrial basin in the Midwest and the northeast. It also led to the decline of Mexican entrepreneurship and political power in the Southwest, as preindustrial economic activity lost its viability and the numbers of Hispanics declined in proportion to the non-Mexican population. But this transformation spurred a dramatic increase in immigration from Mexico. By 1900, 127,000 Mexicans had entered the United States—a number equaling more than a third of the population that had lived in the Southwest before the U.S. takeover. Rapid economic expansion in the Southwest meant that the settlement of Mexicans shifted beyond native-Hispanic centers. Numerous communities sprang up along the length of the railway lines in new agricultural sections and in the emerging mining districts that attracted Anglos and Mexicans alike. By 1915 Mexicans lived as far north as Kansas City and Chicago.

The Mexican Revolution, which began in 1910, forced an exodus of émigrés trying to escape turmoil and violence. All in all, Mexicans endured twenty years of interminable bloodshed. In the 1920s large numbers of middle-class Mexicans, a group critical to the formation of expatriate culture in the United States, joined the emigrant streams as refugees. Meanwhile, World War I spurred growth in every sector of the United States economy. Labor requirements had never been so great, yet disruption in transatlantic transportation, the restriction of immigration from southern and eastern Europe, and the drafting of American laborers to fight in the war created a labor vacuum. To fill this need, employers increasingly sought workers south of the border. Immigration policy also hindered the influx from Mexico, but Congress granted Mexicans a waiver to restrictions—a testimony to the importance of Mexicans in the labor market. During this era Mexicans migrated to labor sectors—in the urban Midwest cities or in rapidly growing Southwest cities—where they had never worked before.

For the majority of the one million Mexicans who entered the United States between 1910 and 1930, finding work, setting up homes and businesses, building churches, and organizing mutual aid societies dominated their lives. To contend with a hostile reception from Anglos, including intense police brutality, violence from civilians, segregation, abuse in the workplace, and general rejection from the mainstream community, the immigrants created organizations to defend themselves. In 1911, for example, they held El Primer Congreso Mexicanista (The First Mexican Congress) in Texas in order to implement a strategic plan to stem the tide of legal abuses and violence. One of the most painful abuses was the disproportionate subjection of Mexicans to imprisonment and capital punishment. In many parts of the United States, Mexicans formed organizations such as La Liga Protectora Mexicana (The Mexican Protective League), founded in Phoenix in 1915, and the Asamblea Mexicana, organized in Houston in 1924. When the 1921 depression caused severe destitution among unemployed Mexicans, the consular service formed Comisiones *Honoríficas* Mexicanas (Mexican Honorary Commissions; 1921–1942) to help ameliorate the problems faced by unemployment and destitution.

Immigrants from the Mexican urban middle classes, displaced as refugees during the revolution, promoted an immigrant nationalism, which was manifested through an often-stated desire to return to Mexico; maintaining Spanish; the celebration of Mexico's patriotic holidays; Catholicism, with special reverence to Our Lady of Guadalupe; and a symbolic identification with Mexico's pre-Columbian civilizations—in essence a nostalgic México Lindo (Pretty Mexico) expatriate nationalism. To partially offset a negative stigma and provide cohesion, Mexicans relied on cultural traditions such as live Mexican vaudeville, drama, and musical productions, activities that were just as important as religious, political, and economic institutions.

The Great Depression dramatically changed the evolution of the Mexican community in the United States. In 1930 about one and a half million ethnic Mexicans lived in the United States. Unemployed Mexicans were seen as a major problem. The federal government deported thousands of undocumented aliens, while local governments, charitable institutions, and employers organized massive repatriation drives, especially from large cities such as Los Angeles, Chicago, and Detroit. The Mexican government attempted to help by providing expatriates free transportation back to their homes. Those that resisted repatriation became more rooted and, in most cases, had families with children.

By the end of the 1930s thousands of young Mexican Americans were exposed to the greater Anglo society through formal education and through New Deal agencies designed to keep young people off the streets during the Great Depression. Mexicans born in the U.S. founded organizations such as the League of United Latin American Citizens (LULAC), in Texas, and other like groups emerged in other states. Basically they practiced "Mexican Americanism," an ideology that embraced assimilation to American values and a less faithful adherence to Mexican culture. These groups were committed to breaking down segregation codes in the school system and fighting discrimination in general. Mexicans also became involved in unionism in agriculture, mining, and in Midwest industries throughout the twentieth century, and became an integral part of this activity.

When the United States declared war in 1941, Mexican Americans enthusiastically enrolled in all branches of the armed forces, and Mexican American civilians not serving in the military engaged in "Home Front" efforts, such as bond drives. Mexican women, like their Anglo counterparts, worked in war industries. But after the war discrimination and rejection continued. In 1947 the American G.I. Forum, organized by Mexican American veterans, and LULAC became leading advocates for civil rights. A wartime need for labor prompted the Bracero program, which recruited thousands of Mexicans to work in agriculture and in railroad maintenance until the program ended in 1965. Since then, immigration has continued unabated.

In spite of the resurgence of Mexican immigration and the persistence of Mexican cultural modes, in the 1960s and 1970s many Mexican Americans were educated in Anglo systems, lived in integrated suburbs, and were subjected to Anglo-American mass media. Mexican Americans, now more integrated into mainstream society, made dramatic strides in breaking down obstacles, such as school segregation, to economic and social mobility. A crowning achievement of this generation was the formation of the "Viva Kennedy Clubs" in the 1960 presidential election; when John F. Kennedy was elected they took partial responsibility for his victory.

The late 1960s and early 1970s were a time of intellectual ferment and rebellion in the United States. Caught up in the mood, young Mexican Americans sought a new identity while struggling for the same civil-rights objectives of previous generations. This atmosphere generated the "Chicano Movement," which was fueled by the conviction that a racist American society deliberately subordinated Mexican Americans; its participants rejected assimilation, which they perceived the previous Mexican American generation had fostered. In the 1980s the term "Hispanic" took on a special generic meaning, referring to any person of Spanish American ancestry living in the United States. Many observers argue that the term represents a rejection by the Mexican American leadership of both cultural nationalism and the radical postures offered by the Chicano Movement.

In the early 2000s immigration from Mexico and Latin America continued unabated, a condition that has to be taken into account as we trace the continuing development of Mexican communities throughout the United States. Since the 1960s the massive influx of Hispanic immigrants reinforced Hispanic culture in the United States. The 2000 census counted about 35 million Latinos living in the United States, eighty percent of whom were ethnic Mexicans. All in all, the culture and identity of Mexican Americans will continue to change, reflecting both inevitable generational fusion with Anglo society and the continuing influence of immigrants, not only from Mexico, but from throughout Latin America.

BIBLIOGRAPHY

Gutiérrez, David G. *Walls and Mirrors: Mexican Americans, Mexican Immigrants, and the Politics of Ethnicity.* Berkeley: University of California Press, 1995.

Rosales, F. Arturo. *Chicano!: The History of the Mexican American Civil Rights Movement.* Houston, Tex.: Arte Público Press, 1996.

———. *Pobre Raza!: Violence, Justice, and Mobilization among México Lindo Immigrants, 1900–1936.* Austin: University of Texas Press, 1999.

F. Arturo Rosales

See also **Hispanic Americans; Immigration Restriction;** *and* vol. 9: **Pachucos in the Making.**

MEXICO, CONFEDERATE MIGRATION TO.

After the CIVIL WAR, many Confederate military and civil leaders, despondent and dreading RECONSTRUCTION, sought homes in Mexico. The exact number who went to Mexico will probably never be known, but an estimate of 2,500 seems reasonable. Southerners settled in all parts of the empire—on farms, in seaport towns, and in villages of the interior. Colonies were established in the provinces of Chihuahua, San Luis Potosí, Jalisco, and Sonora. The best known was the Cordova Valley Colony.

Ferdinand Maximilian encouraged migration to Mexico by offering low-priced public lands, free transportation for the needy, and tolerance for the Protestant churches and schools, but the movement failed because of unforeseen circumstances. There was a hostile Northern and Southern press; the U.S. government opposed the movement; and the settlers had little cash. The disturbed political conditions under Maximilian's regime aided in the downfall of the project. By 1867 most of the adventurers had returned to the United States.

BIBLIOGRAPHY

George D. Harmon. "Confederate Migration to Mexico." *Hispanic American Historical Review* 17.

George D. Harmon / A. R.

See also **Mexico, French in; Shelby's Mexican Expedition.**

MEXICO, FRENCH IN.

In October 1861, the United Kingdom, France, and Spain signed a treaty to undertake coercive action to secure reparation for their subjects and the execution of certain obligations contracted by Mexico. They agreed to refrain from intervention in Mexico's internal affairs and neither to make any territorial aggrandizements nor to influence its form of government. Spanish armed forces promptly seized Veracruz. After French and British soldiers arrived on the Mexican coast, a conference of commanders of the allied forces held at Orizaba could not agree. The British and Spaniards decided to withdraw from Mexico. The French army captured Mexico City in June 1862. The invaders convoked an assembly of notables, which decided to establish a Mexican monarchy headed by Ferdinand Maximilian, archduke of Austria, whom Napoleon III had selected.

Attracted by the glittering dream of a throne, Maximilian accepted the invitation. On 10 April 1864, he signed the Convention of Miramar, which specified that Napoleon III would support the exotic empire until 1867. After Maximilian's arrival in Mexico, he sought to secure recognition by the United States, but that government continued to support the republican leader, President Benito Juárez, who took refuge on the northern frontiers of his country.

The fortunes of Maximilian's empire largely depended on the outcome of the American CIVIL WAR. During that struggle, the United States made mild protests against French intervention in Mexico, but after the defeat of the Confederacy, the United States began to protest more strongly. France vainly attempted to secure the recognition of Maximilian's government by the United States or to postpone the withdrawal of its troops. Finally, on 12 March 1867, the last detachment of French soldiers left Mexican soil. The soldiers of Juárez soon captured Maximilian, and he faced a firing squad on 19 June 1867. Thus, the United States had repelled what it deemed a clear violation of the MONROE DOCTRINE, and republican government returned to Mexico.

BIBLIOGRAPHY

Leonard, Thomas M., ed. *United States-Latin American Relations, 1850–1903: Establishing a Relationship.* Tuscaloosa: University of Alabama Press, 1999.

Schoonover, Thomas D., ed. *Mexican Lobby: Matías Romero in Washington, 1861–1867.* Lexington: University Press of Kentucky, 1986.

Schoultz, Lars. *Beneath the United States: A History of U.S. Policy toward Latin America.* Cambridge, Mass.: Harvard University Press, 1998.

Weeks, Charles A. *The Juárez Myth in Mexico.* Tuscaloosa: University of Alabama Press, 1987.

William Spence Robertson / A. E.

See also **France, Relations with; Mexico, Confederate Migration to; Mexico, Relations with; Shelby's Mexican Expedition.**

MEXICO, GULF OF. Bounded by the southern United States, eastern Mexico, and Cuba, this oval-shaped body of water has played a central role in North America's economic and political development. The Gulf of Mexico and its coastal beaches, estuaries, and islands have supplied varied peoples with abundant food and minerals. A warm current, the Gulf Stream, enters the gulf from the Caribbean Sea at the Strait of Yucatán and flows into the Atlantic at the Straits of Florida. The gulf's large mass of warm water shapes weather across the region, creating long growing seasons and violent tropical storms. The 600,000-square-mile gulf has been the site of important trade routes and settlements and a pivotal arena for imperial contests since Europeans first arrived in the Americas.

Diverse native societies once ringed the gulf, including complex Maya and Aztec civilizations in Mesoamerica, and Calusa, Chickasaw, Choctaw, Natchez, and Karankawa peoples in what became the United States. Spain first explored the gulf in voyages by Juan Ponce de León in 1513 and Alonso Alvarez de Pineda in 1519, and colonial outposts such as Havana and Veracruz rapidly followed. The gulf was a Spanish sea for nearly two centuries, and Spanish galleons took great quantities of silver and gold from the region. The French entered the gulf in about 1700, and the heart of their colonial effort was the Mississippi River and New Orleans, founded in 1718.

Imperial rivalries between Spain, France, and England dominated the region in the eighteenth century. The eventual winner, the United States, entered the scene in 1803 with the Louisiana Purchase. The Americans continued earlier patterns of growing rice, sugar, and cotton using slave labor, and New Orleans became their major gulf port. A powerful desire for new lands led to American acquisition of Florida, completed between 1810 and 1819. Florida and Texas were granted statehood in 1845, and the admission of Texas led to war with Mexico. The American victory in the Mexican-American War in 1848 confirmed the Rio Grande as the western edge of America's Gulf Coast. Expansion along the gulf ended there, as antebellum efforts to purchase Cuba for its sugar plantations and strategic position failed.

The security and stability of the Gulf of Mexico remained a significant foreign policy concern during the twentieth century. In 1898 the American victory in the Spanish-American War gave Puerto Rico to the United States, and Cuba became an American protectorate. The PANAMA CANAL, begun in 1904, made shipping lanes in the gulf even more important. The United States intervened in the region many times in the twentieth century with its greatest focus on its complex Cold War relations with Cuba.

Military tensions in the gulf eased by the beginning of the twenty-first century, but environmental concerns increased as large numbers of Americans built homes along the Gulf or visited its beaches as tourists. In the twenty-first century the Gulf Coast remained a major agricultural region and the site of important fisheries, and after the 1940s it became a leader in oil, natural gas, and petrochemical production. The Gulf of Mexico has rich natural resources, but its many users put its productive waters and fragile coastlines and reefs at risk.

BIBLIOGRAPHY

Gore, Robert H. *The Gulf of Mexico: A Treasury of Resources in the American Mediterranean.* Sarasota, Fla.: Pineapple Press, 1992.

Weber, David J. *The Spanish Frontier in North America.* New Haven, Conn.: Yale University Press, 1992.

William C. Barnett

See also **Cuba, Relations with; Mexico, Relations with.**

MEXICO, PUNITIVE EXPEDITION INTO (1916–1917). On 9 March 1916, Francisco (Pancho) Villa, with 485 men, crossed the Mexican border and raided Columbus, New Mexico, killing eighteen people. The raid was the culmination of a series of border troubles resulting from the Mexican Revolution and possibly from Villa's mistaken belief that President Venustiano Carranza had traded Mexican independence for American military support. In hopes of quelling border unrest and punishing Villa, Brigadier General John J. Pershing was ordered into northern Mexico with a force that eventually numbered over 11,000. Initially, the United States concluded an agreement with Mexico, giving each country the right to cross the boundary in pursuit of bandits. Mexico understood the agreement to take effect in the event of future raids, whereas the United States interpreted it retroactively, to authorize the Pershing expedition. Carranza's government considered the uninvited Pershing force an infringement on its sovereignty, and Mexicans generally were hostile to the expedition. On two occasions American and Mexican troops clashed, and for a time, war seemed imminent. President Woodrow Wilson called out the NATIONAL GUARD of three border states on 9 May and that of the whole United States on 18 June. Negotiations between the governments took place from September 1916 to January 1917 but ended without a settlement. The United States ordered Pershing's force withdrawn in February 1917. Though Pershing never apprehended Villa, whose supporters had dwindled to a small band even before the expedition, the venture provided the U.S. military with training, served as a testing ground for equipment, and vaulted Pershing into his next post as head of the American Expeditionary Forces in World War I.

BIBLIOGRAPHY

Braddy, Haldeen. *Pershing's Mission in Mexico.* El Paso: Texas Western College Press, 1966.

Clendenen, Clarence C., *The United States and Pancho Villa: A Study in Unconventional Diplomacy.* Ithaca, N.Y.: Cornell University Press, 1961.

Katz, Friedrich. *The Life and Times of Pancho Villa.* Stanford, Calif.: Stanford University Press, 1998.

Donald Smythe/F. B.

See also **ABC Conference; Mexico, Relations with; Villa Raid at Columbus.**

MEXICO, RELATIONS WITH.

The relationship of the United States and Mexico has been greatly influenced by a long land border, asymmetry in economic and political power, deep-rooted social and economic ties, and a troublesome history of intervention and war associated with Washington's search for new territory, resources, security, and stability. By the end of the twentieth century, Mexico was the United States's second largest trading partner, a key member of the three-state North American Free Trade Agreement (NAFTA), the source of millions of immigrants to the United States, and a thorn in the side of Washington when it came to border crime, drug trafficking, corruption, and a set of foreign policy principles often out of sync with its neighbor to the north. The differences between the United States and Mexico do not mean that relations have not improved considerably since the end of the Cold War and the creation of NAFTA; but important legacies from a complex and difficult past continue to influence U.S.-Mexican relations, including a residual anti-Americanism in Mexico tied to the loss of over half its national territory in the nineteenth century and the way Mexico is often treated in the conduct of American foreign policy.

Relations between the United States and Mexico have evolved from a pattern of either conflict or indifference to a new partnership in their bilateral relations. From Mexico's independence from Spain in 1821 through the violence and turmoil of the Mexican Revolution (1910–1917), relations between the United States and Mexico were dominated by conflict and intervention. During this early period the United States was the dominant power, pursuing its interests—territorial expansion and national security concerns—through military force and diplomatic bluster. The conflict associated with the turmoil of the Mexican Revolution led President Woodrow Wilson to invade Mexico several times and to occupy it for brief periods in order to protect U.S. economic interests built up during the nineteenth century and to keep foreign powers from developing alliances with Mexico. Mexico and the United States formed a new relationship during World War II (1942–1945), eschewing the foreign policy of nonintervention and sensitivity to issues related to national sovereignty in favor of heightened collaboration on a broad range of wartime issues. During the Cold War the United States and Mexico developed a new style in which the two countries bargained on some issues and mostly neglected, or ignored, one another on other matters until the late 1980s. With the end of the Cold War the United States and Mexico began a period of extraordinary cooperation, marked by NAFTA and immigration,

debt relief, and antidrug efforts. Presidents George H. W. Bush and Carlos Salinas de Gortari not only championed the creation of NAFTA but also put in motion a new relationship based on a less ideological and more pragmatic approach to bilateral issues. Presidents Bill Clinton and Ernesto Zedillo met frequently to discuss bilateral issues of concern to the two countries during a period marked by strain over drug trafficking, migration, and Mexico's debt.

The 2000 defeat of the Institutional Revolutionary Party (PRI) after more than seventy years of continual rule caused a stir in Washington, uncertain as to how a relative unknown—President Vicente Fox and a coalition headed by the National Action Party (PAN)—would deal with the United States after years of predictability under PRI presidents. With the almost simultaneous election of Fox and George W. Bush in 2000, relations between the United States and Mexico showed further signs of continuing the historic shift to a more productive partnership based on the salience of bilateral issues such as trade, democracy, immigration, drug trafficking, economic stability, and the environment.

The analysis that follows examines five broad periods of U.S.-Mexican relations: (1) conflict, intervention, and turmoil between 1821 and 1940; (2) World War II and the beginnings of bilateral cooperation; (3) the Cold War, an era of bilateral bargaining and policy negligence; (4) constructing a more permanent relationship, 1988–2000; and (5) the new millennium.

Conflict, Intervention, and Turmoil: 1821–1940

Conflict and turmoil were the dominant traits in U.S.-Mexican relations for most of the nineteenth century and during the first four decades of the twentieth century. It was an unstable period during which Mexico struggled to create an effective political system with legitimate authority and a population with a common national identity, and the United States was interested mainly in territorial expansion and national security. Between 1836 and 1920 the United States intervened with military force at least fifteen times to protect American interests. The inability of Mexico to solve its internal political problems and Washington's expansionist desires in the 1840s contributed to a war with Mexico (1846–1848) in which the United States invaded Mexico and compelled it to yield a vast amount of its northern territory. Great Britain, France, and Spain also took an interest in Mexico for economic and political reasons. When France invaded and occupied Mexico between 1862 and 1867, the United States was helpless—largely due to the small size of its military and to an internal war driven by abolition and secession—and Mexico found that the Monroe Doctrine offered no guarantees against recolonization efforts by European powers in the Western Hemisphere. The Mexican-American War and the French invasion and occupation became a catalyst for Mexican resentment of the United States and the basis for a highly nationalistic foreign policy.

The repressive nature of the dictatorship of Porfirio Diaz and the hospitality offered foreign investment during the last two decades of the nineteenth century contributed to the beginning of the Mexican Revolution in 1910. Trade and foreign investment, the cornerstones of the Porfirian era (1876–1911), contributed to the antiforeign aspects of the revolution. By 1911 the United States controlled close to 40 percent of all foreign investment in Mexico, a figure almost equal to that of all U.S. investment in Latin America and the Caribbean. The positive benefits of foreign investment—mostly in railroads, mining, and real estate—could not offset the negative reactions to U.S. control of Mexico's destiny. U.S. involvement in Mexico's civil war contributed to further distrust of the northern neighbor and to postrevolutionary efforts to assert greater national sovereignty and reduce foreign control through the creation of new policies designed to fulfill the desires of those who fought in the Mexican Revolution. While President Franklin Roosevelt's Good Neighbor Policy helped erase some of the tensions in U.S.-Mexican relations through a pledge of nonintervention, reciprocity, and equality among states, the bilateral relationship did not improve until the onset of World War II.

World War II: The Beginnings of Bilateral Cooperation

The Good Neighbor Policy and the astute diplomatic handling of the conflict over Mexico's nationalization of U.S. oil properties and investments between 1938 and 1941 opened the way for greater collaboration during World War II and cordial relations at the beginning of the Cold War. The fact that the United States chose not to retaliate against Mexico's decision to expropriate foreign-owned oil companies, and thus run the risk of Mexico's aligning itself with Germany, Japan, or Italy during World War II, was a major turning point in U.S.-Mexican relations. After German submarines sank several Mexican tankers in the Gulf of Mexico in 1942, Mexico promptly declared war on the Axis powers, and Mexico and the United States became formal allies. This arrangement was a boon to both countries: it created the first military alliance between the two countries, provided the basis for a historic reconciliation, and created an era of good feelings during the war years. The United States gained access to Mexico's raw materials for the war effort and arranged to import lower-paid Mexican workers to fill a critical labor shortage in the United States because of the war. The wartime collaboration between U.S. and Mexican secret police and security bureaucracies continued after the war, particularly in antidrug and crime reduction efforts along the border.

The Cold War: Bilateral Bargaining and Policy Negligence

The period known as the Cold War brought relative harmony in U.S.-Mexican relations. Mexico emphasized economic growth and political stability while Washington worried about ways to combat communism in Latin America and establish order along its southern border. According to Domínguez and Fernández, between 1945 and 1988 a new style emerged in U.S.-Mexican bilateral relations that they refer to as "bargained negligence." What this means is that the two countries developed a tacit bargain in which Mexico rejected any overtures from the Soviet Union and kept its authoritarian political system from adopting communist practices while the United States pursued a noninterventionist policy toward Mexico. As long as Mexico supported capitalism and the containment of communism, the United States almost completely ignored its southern neighbor.

There were times during the Cold War when Mexico's revolutionary heritage of nationalism and antipathy toward outside intervention provided discordant tones in U.S.-Mexican relations. From 1954 until 1989 Mexico opposed U.S. intervention in Guatemala, Cuba, the Dominican Republic, Chile, El Salvador, Nicaragua, Grenada, and Panama. While the United States resented Mexico's refusal to sever diplomatic relations with Castro's Cuba during the Cold War (and its opposition to the collective sanctions imposed on the island by the Organization of American States), Mexico was not a foreign policy priority despite the growing interdependence of the two countries. Mexico also alienated Washington by extending aid to the Sandinista government in Nicaragua, opposing Ronald Reagan's Contras (terrorists, in the minds of many Mexicans), and recognizing the Salvadoran guerrillas and their political party as legitimate political actors. The United States complained about the durability of Soviet-Mexican relations during the Cold War, including the size and intelligence activities of the Soviet embassy in Mexico City, but Washington never found it necessary to invoke the Monroe Doctrine or intervene militarily in Mexico, as it did so readily elsewhere in Latin America. The paradox of Mexico's support for leftist governments abroad while it suppressed leftists at home did not seem to bother U.S. policymakers in charge of Latin America and the Caribbean.

However, there were critical times during the Cold War when the United States was forced to elevate Mexico to a foreign policy priority. In one way or another, all of the following conflicts contributed to a realization that "bargained negligence" could not be sustained as the predominant style of the bilateral relationship: (1) the domestic disturbances associated with the 1968 Olympic Games and the increasing authoritarianism of Mexico's one-dominant-party system; (2) the demands on worldwide supplies of petroleum and the discovery of huge petroleum reserves in the Gulf of Mexico; (3) the debt crisis of 1982 that led to near collapse of the Mexican economy and a growing realization that a new political economy might be needed to pump trade-based pesos into the ailing economic system; and (4) the crime and corruption associated with drug trafficking and money laundering that came with Mexico's growing economic problems.

Unable to service its foreign debt and experiencing a traumatic decline in petroleum revenues, Mexico was forced to begin a series of economic adjustment policies that eventually led to a free trade agreement with the United States and Canada in 1991. Throughout most of the Cold War it was difficult for Mexico to overcome its historical antipathy toward the predatory nature of its superpower neighbor and fully recognize the economic advantages of establishing a closer relationship with the United States. While it was possible to ignore the absence of democracy in Mexico during much of the Cold War, Washington's view of Mexico's ruling party as a bastion of stability could not be sustained once the Cold War was over.

Constructing a More Permanent Relationship: 1988–2000

The end of the Cold War and the elections of Carlos Salinas de Gortari and George H. W. Bush as presidents of their respective nations opened the way for constructing a new relationship, one based on greater collaboration through economic integration. The essence of the pact was the creation of NAFTA, a new partnership based on shared economic interests. While NAFTA was popular and easy to sell to the Mexican public, north of the border it faced major currents of opposition from organized labor, environmental interest groups, and the Democratic opposition in the U.S. Congress. However, both governments lobbied hard for NAFTA, and by late 1993 it had been constructed, albeit on somewhat narrow and shaky ground, in Congress and among the general public. Despite the ongoing debates about the benefits of NAFTA as a mechanism for economic integration, the passage of such a free trade agreement represents a serious change in the U.S.-Mexican relationship, and perhaps the most important bilateral agreement since the Treaty of Guadalupe-Hidalgo (1848) that ended the Mexican-American War.

The institutionalization of bilateral affairs continued through the presidencies of Bill Clinton and Ernesto Zedillo (1992–2000), despite challenges and turmoil on both sides of the border. The creation of NAFTA brought to light the emergence of the Zapatista movement in Chiapas, an indigenous revolt led by Subcommander Marcos, that complained of the negative consequences of economic integration and globalization for the plight of indigenous communities dispersed throughout Mexico. During the first six years of NAFTA, Mexico emerged as the United States' second-largest trading partner after Canada, with two-way trade approaching $210 billion in 2000. NAFTA also generated demand for the creation of more maquiladora assembly plants in the northern border region, but this trend exacerbated the growing gap between the wealth of the north and the poverty in southern Mexico. While NAFTA's benefits to the United States have been less than those for Mexico, American presidents continued to champion the benefits of "free trade" for Mexico and Latin America. Many blamed NAFTA for the increasing amount of drug-funded official corruption in Mexico during the 1990s, and there was growing concern over human rights abuses related to economic inequalities and the use of the Mexican military to suppress domestic insurgencies in the more impoverished parts of Mexico. There were still currents of opposition to the new economic partnership in the legislative branches of both countries. The emphasis on economic integration contributed to greater collaboration on matters of immigration, border security, and narcotrafficking; however, these were difficult and sensitive issues that often reflect images of conflict and suspicion from previous periods in bilateral relations.

The New Millennium: Democratization, Security, Partnership for Prosperity

The days of virtual single-party rule ended with the national elections that took place in Mexico on 2 July 2000. Vicente Fox, a charismatic businessman-politician from the interior of Mexico, defeated the ruling party (Partido Revolucionario Institucional—PRI) with a well-orchestrated coalition campaign led by the National Action Party (PAN). After seventy-one years of continual rule, the PRI lost the presidency but in the aftermath of the humiliating defeat retained a considerable amount of political power, particularly in both houses of the federal Congress, where it won the largest number of seats, and throughout the country, where it still controlled a majority of governorships in key states.

The fairness and accuracy of the 2000 election moved Mexico closer to a pluralist democracy with Vicente Fox at the helm, but with a party split between the executive and legislative branches of government, the new president's *sexenio* (six-year, nonrenewable term of office, 2000–2006) would be fraught with many challenges that his PRI predecessors never had to face. His rule enhanced with a greater sense of democratic legitimacy, and with a firm conviction of the importance of free trade, Fox pursued a foreign policy of closer ties with the United States and the rest of Latin America.

In order to achieve his foreign policy goal of a "Partnership for Prosperity" with the United States, President Fox faced a number of challenges. He managed to forge close ties with the new administration of George W. Bush and received positive reviews from the media and the attentive public in the United States. However, Fox faced a Congress that retained more of Mexico's traditional emphasis on nationalism and noninterference, and he soon realized that he would have to place greater emphasis on creating bureaucratic agencies to better manage the bilateral relationship. The Mexican ambassador to the United States and the Mexican embassy in Washington, D.C., were given enhanced power and coordinating responsibilities. President Fox chose as his foreign minister Jorge G. Castañeda, a highly competent but controversial figure with roots in the Mexican left. Castaneda quickly learned to adjust and adapt the major goals of Mexican foreign policy to the necessity of dealing with Republicans on Capitol Hill and the conservative members of the

George W. Bush administration. Between the time President Bush took office in January 2001 and early 2002, he and President Fox met to discuss important bilateral issues on four occasions, including the first state dinner at the White House for the Mexican delegation, just prior to the terrorist attacks on New York and Washington on 11 September 2001.

President Fox campaigned on several foreign policy issues that would provide a broader base of support for improving Mexican relations with the United States. A champion of free trade, Fox favored the creation of an amended NAFTA that would amount to a common market to allow a freer flow of workers and goods while adhering to provisions regarding labor, law enforcement, and workers' rights in the original agreement. The architect of this proposal was Foreign Minister Castañeda, a supporter of earlier opposition calls for a European-like arrangement that would facilitate free labor mobility in North America. On his three-nation Latin American tour in March 2002, President Bush unveiled a new security plan for the U.S.-Mexican border designed to "weed out those who we don't want in our country—the terrorists, the coyotes, the smugglers, those who prey on innocent life." He and President Fox signed a complex "smart border" plan that included expanded intelligence cooperation and special passes for Mexicans who make frequent border crossings. The hands-on, problem-solving process of reaching a bilateral agreement on a new border program was not matched by other initiatives on immigration—particularly the effort to increase the number of legal Mexican workers in the United States—and other thorny issues. In any case the meetings and conversations between presidents Bush and Fox suggested to some a new era of high-level cooperation. When pressed on the seriousness of his interest in Mexico, Bush responded, "A strong and prosperous Mexico is good for America." Now that Mexico has become more democratic, and the United States has come to realize that collaboration with Mexico is not a luxury but a necessity, the challenge for more productive United States–Mexico relations will most likely rest on confidence-building measures related to new and creative approaches to bilateral relations.

BIBLIOGRAPHY

Bailey, John, and Sergio Aguayo, eds. *Strategy and Security in U.S.-Mexican Relations: Beyond the Cold War.* San Diego: Center for U.S.-Mexican Studies, University of California San Diego, 1996.

Bethell, Leslie, ed. *Mexico Since Independence.* Cambridge, U.K.: Cambridge University Press, 1991.

Dent, David W. *Encyclopedia of Modern Mexico.* Lanham, Md.: Scarecrow Press, 2002.

Domínguez, Jorge I., and Rafael Fernández de Castro. *The United States and Mexico: Between Partnership and Conflict.* New York: Routledge, 2001.

Fernández de Castro, Rafael, et al., eds. *U.S.-Mexico: The New Agenda.* Austin: University of Texas Press, 1999.

Grayson, George W. *The United States and Mexico: Patterns of Influence.* New York: Praeger, 1984.

Green, Rosario, and Peter H. Smith, eds. *Foreign Policy in U.S.-Mexican Relations.* San Diego: Center for U.S.-Mexican Studies, University of California San Diego, 1989.

Mazza, Jacqueline. *Don't Disturb the Neighbors: The United States and Democracy in Mexico, 1980–1995.* New York: Routledge, 2001.

Pastor, Robert A., and Jorge G. Castañeda, *Limits to Friendship: The United States and Mexico.* New York: Vintage, 1988.

Roett, Riordan, ed. *Mexico and the United States: Managing the Relationship.* Boulder, Colo.: Westview Press, 1988.

Smith, Clint E. *Inevitable Partnership: Understanding Mexico-U.S. Relations.* Boulder, Colo.: Lynne Rienner, 2000.

David Dent

See also **Good Neighbor Policy; Mexican-American War; Mexican-American War Claims; Mexico City, Capture of; Mexico, Confederate Migration to; Mexico, Punitive Expedition into;** *and vol. 9:* **Mexican Minister of War's Reply to Manuel de la Peña y Peña; Message on the War with Mexico.**

MEXICO CITY, CAPTURE OF (13–14 September 1847). The fall of Chapultepec made possible a combined advance by the divisions of Gen. William J. Worth and Gen. John A. Quitman against the western gates of Mexico City. By dusk on 13 September, Worth, despite desperate resistance, arrived at the San Cosmé gate. Quitman, on the Belén Causeway, was held up before the citadel. During the night Antonio López de Santa Anna evacuated the city, the citadel surrendering to Quitman at dawn. Marching immediately to the plaza, Quitman raised the flag on the palace. Gen. Winfield Scott, arriving on the heels of Worth's troops, announced the capture of the capital.

BIBLIOGRAPHY

Eisenhower, John S. D. *Agent of Destiny: The Life and Times of General Winfield Scott.* New York: Free Press, 1997.

———. *So Far From God: The U.S. War with Mexico, 1846–1848.* New York: Anchor Books, 1990.

Elliott, Charles Winslow. *Winfield Scott, the Soldier and the Man.* New York: Macmillan, 1937; New York: Arno Press, 1979.

Johnson, Timothy. *Winfield Scott: The Quest for Military Glory.* Lawrence: University of Kansas Press, 1998.

Charles Winslow Elliott / A. R.

See also **Chapultepec, Battle of; Mexican-American War.**

MIAMI, founded in 1896, anchors a sprawling, four-county, South Florida metropolis of over 5 million people. The city has evolved through a series of quick character changes, including raw tropical frontier, vast real estate speculation, tourist playground for the rich and famous, retirement destination for the middle class, safe haven for Caribbean and Latin American exiles and refugees, and multicultural boiling pot. Few American cities have experienced such dramatic change so quickly. Few places captured the American imagination so completely and so consistently over the course of the twentieth century.

South Florida's forbidding distances and water-logged environment prevented the region from moving beyond the frontier stage until the early twentieth century. The railroad and hotel baron Henry Flagler made Miami the destination of his Florida East Coast Railway in 1896. In succeeding decades Flagler became the city's chief builder and promoter. Emphasizing Miami's seashore location and subtropical amenities, Flagler successfully cultivated the image of a "Magic City" in the Florida sunshine. Within two decades other fabulous promoters were grabbing national attention for their own Miami-area speculations. Carl Fischer created Miami Beach, George Merrick built suburban Coral Gables on city-beautiful principles, and dozens of smaller real estate speculators subdivided Miami and nearby communities. Even before the great Florida boom of the mid-1920s, tourists flocked to Miami and Miami Beach, some 150,000 a year by 1920.

The collapse of the Florida real estate boom in the late 1920s and the coming of the Great Depression in the 1930s only temporarily slowed Miami's growth. The glamorous vacation and resort image of Miami and Miami Beach kept the tropical twin cities in the national spotlight. Between 1920 and 1940 the Miami area grew in permanent population from 43,000 to 268,000, an increase of over 520 percent that placed Miami among the nation's fastest-growing metropolitan areas.

Metropolitan Miami's population growth slowed after 1940 but not by much, rising to 495,000 in 1950 and to 935,000 in 1960, a growth rate of 250 percent over two decades. Miami's upward growth spiral during the mid-century decades was sustained by powerful new forces for change. As in the rest of the emerging Sun Belt, the impact of World War II was far-reaching. The federal government established numerous military bases and training facilities in the Miami area. Defense spending and military payrolls provided a major boost to the local economy, attracted large numbers of civilian workers, and facilitated economic diversification. After the war thousands of servicepeople who had trained in Miami returned to live out their Florida dreams.

New technologies also brought growth and change to Miami. Rail transportation supported South Florida's tourist economy until the 1930s, when automobiles and then commercial air travel increasingly filled that role. The newly developed DC-3 airliner, introduced in 1935, set Miami on a new course as one of the nation's aviation centers and a major gateway to Latin American cities. By the 1980s Miami had one of the busiest airports in the world, and the aviation industry (airport, airlines, suppliers) had become the city's largest employer.

Other powerful forces for change emerged by the 1950s. The introduction of home air conditioning in 1955 revolutionized Miami home construction and made year-round living in South Florida appealing to larger numbers of people. Postwar demographic changes also altered Miami's population base considerably. Before the war Miami's population consisted primarily of southern whites and blacks as well as a large contingent of immigrant blacks from the Bahamas. After the war internal migration of Jews, Italians, and social-security retirees from the Northeast and Midwest brought new levels of ethnic diversity to the city. The Miami area's Jewish population rose from about 8,000 in 1940 to about 140,000 in 1960, a dramatic migration that rippled through Miami's politics and culture. Jews concentrated in Miami Beach, facing anti-Semitism but eventually coming to dominate that city's political structure. Liberal northern Jews, unaccustomed to racial segregation, worked with black activists in voter registration campaigns and lunch-counter sit-ins to achieve major civil rights breakthroughs by 1960. Miami's demographic transformation also underlay major governmental reforms, such as the introduction of a powerful countywide metropolitan government in 1957.

The decade of the 1960s brought still further change to Miami. The Cuban Revolution of 1959 toppled an unpopular dictatorship, but it also unleashed the first of many successive migration waves of Cuban exiles to South Florida. Over the next forty years, arriving by airlift, boatlift, and make-shift rafts, almost 1 million Cubans found a new home in the Miami area. The subsequent arrival of hundreds of thousands of Haitians, Nicaraguans, Colombians, and others from Latin America and the Caribbean quickly altered the city's ethnic composition. As the Latin population grew, the practice of exile politics resulted in Hispanic domination of Miami and Miami-Dade County. After 1972 Hispanic mayors predominated in Miami. Unsettled by the new immigration and its consequences, non-Hispanic whites began an exodus of their own from the Miami area by the 1980s. Most migrating northerners began to choose other Florida retirement destinations. However, international trade and finance boomed along with the local real estate market, as Miamians took advantage of the city's new Latin ambiance. By the 1980s Latin American and European tourists in Miami and Miami Beach outnumbered American vacationers.

Miami's new ethnic and racial diversity led to turmoil and conflict. Black Miamians suffered from job competition with Cuban arrivals in the 1960s and resented the special treatment and financial support the newcomers received from the federal government. Haitians complained about a double standard in American immigration policy that favored the mostly white exiles from communist Cuba but excluded black immigrants from Haiti. Four major race riots in Miami between 1980 and 1992 reflected these underlying tensions. The polarizing debate over Elian Gonzalez, the Cuban boy rescued from an overturned raft in 1999 and reunited with his father in

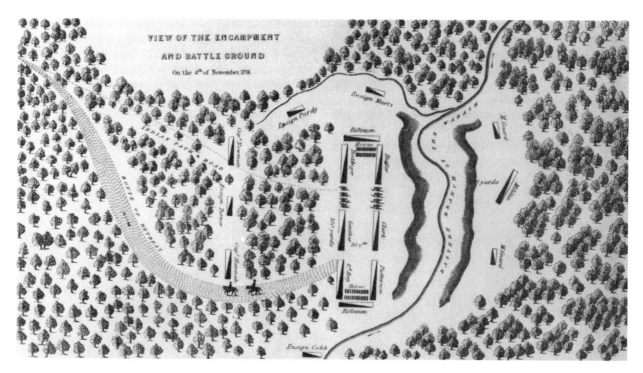

Miami Victory. A view of the American encampment along the Wabash River (at what is now Ohio's border with Indiana) where Little Turtle's Indians surprised the army of General Arthur St. Clair, the first governor of the Northwest Territory, on 4 November 1791, causing more than 900 casualties—an unprecedented defeat for the United States in the wars against Indian tribes. LIBRARY OF CONGRESS

Cuba in 2000, unleashed new tensions. Urban problems, such as high crime rates, a flourishing illegal drug trade, attacks on tourists, political corruption, and damage to an environmentally sensitive ecosystem, contributed to Miami's newest image as a lost paradise.

The 2000 census demonstrated the powerful impact of forty years of immigration on Miami and confirmed widely held perceptions of its boiling-pot cultural mix. Hispanics comprised 66 percent of the city of Miami's population of 362,470. Metro Miami's population of 2.2 million included 1.3 people of Hispanic background, or 57 percent of the total. About 650,000 of the Hispanics are of Cuban descent. Almost 60 percent of metro Miami residents speak Spanish at home, another testament to the power of Latin immigration. Transformed by twentieth-century technologies and shaped by economic and demographic changes, Miami nevertheless retains its tropical allure and cultural vitality.

BIBLIOGRAPHY

Dunn, Marvin. *Black Miami in the Twentieth Century.* Gainesville: University Press of Florida, 1997.

García, María Cristina. *Havana USA: Cuban Exiles and Cuban Americans in South Florida, 1959–1994.* Berkeley: University of California Press, 1996.

Grenier, Guillermo J., and Alex Stepick III, eds. *Miami Now! Immigration, Ethnicity, and Social Change.* Gainesville: University Press of Florida, 1992.

Mohl, Raymond A. "Miami: The Ethnic Cauldron." In *Sunbelt Cities: Politics and Growth since World War II.* Edited by Richard M. Bernard and Bradley R. Rice. Austin: University of Texas Press, 1983.

Portes, Alejandro, and Alex Stepick. *City on the Edge: The Transformation of Miami.* Berkeley: University of California Press, 1993.

Raymond A. Mohl

See also **Cuban Americans; Resorts and Spas; Sun Belt.**

MIAMI (INDIANS). In the 1670s, the Miamis first encountered the French in Wisconsin, where the tribe had fled to avoid the Iroquois, but by the 1740s they had returned to their homeland in the Maumee and Wabash valleys of Indiana. There they divided into four separate bands. The Miamis proper occupied the upper Maumee Valley, including the portage between the Wabash and Maumee rivers. The Eel Rivers maintained villages on the Wabash tributary, while the Ouiatenons or "Weas" dominated the central Wabash valley from towns near the mouth of the Tippecanoe. The Piankashaws established villages along the lower Wabash, near modern Vincennes.

In the colonial period, the Miamis were allied with the French, but between 1748 and 1752, dissident Miamis led by La Demoiselle (or Memeskia) established a pro-British trading village on Ohio's Miami River until French allied Indians forced them back to the Wabash. The Miamis supported the French during the Seven Years' War but were divided between the Americans and British during the American Revolution. During the 1790s, the Miami chief Little Turtle led the initial Indian resistance to American settlement north of the Ohio but made peace with the Americans following the Treaty of Greenville (1795).

Successful traders, the Miamis intermarried with the Creole French and adopted much of their culture. They were removed from Indiana to Kansas in the 1840s. At the beginning of the twenty-first century, the Miami Tribe of Oklahoma resided near tribal offices at Miami, Oklahoma, while the Indiana Miamis, although not "recognized" by the federal government, maintained tribal offices at Peru, Indiana.

BIBLIOGRAPHY

Anson, Bert. *The Miami Indians.* Norman: University of Oklahoma Press, 1970.

Kohn, Rita, and W. Lynwood Montell, eds. *Always a People: Oral Histories of Contemporary Woodland Nations.* Bloomington: Indiana University Press, 1997.

Rafert, Stewart. *The Miami Indians of Indiana: A Persistent People, 1654–1994.* Indianapolis: Indiana Historical Society, 1996.

R. David Edmunds

See also **Tribes: Northwestern.**

MIAMI PURCHASE, the next important colonization project in the Old Northwest after the grant to the Ohio Company of Associates, was first settled about eight months after Marietta (April 1788). The Miami purchase represented an important step in the incursion of white settlers into the Indian country on the north bank of the Ohio River. Extending northward from the Ohio, between the Miami and the Little Miami Rivers, it commanded not only the increasingly important Ohio River route but also the Miami–Maumee roadway to Lake Erie, while southward the Licking River gave ready access to the Kentucky bluegrass region. Benjamin Stites, an Indian trader, represented the possibilities of the Miami country to Judge John Cleves Symmes of Morristown, New Jersey, an influential member of the Continental Congress. After a personal inspection, Symmes enlisted the support of Jonathan Dayton, Elias Boudinot, and other important men to found a colony between the two Miamis. A contract with the Treasury Board on 15 October 1788 granted Symmes and his associates 1 million acres, for which, under the Land Ordinance of 1785, they agreed to pay $1 per acre. As in the Ohio Company purchase, section sixteen in each township was reserved for the support of education, and section twenty-nine for that of religion. Also, one entire township was set aside for a college. Symmes could not meet the payments in full, and in 1794 he received a patent for the Miami purchase that covered only 311,682 acres.

Symmes started for his new colony in July 1788 and made a temporary stop at Limestone, Kentucky. The first permanent settlement in the Miami purchase was made on 18 November 1788 by Benjamin Stites at Columbia, at the mouth of the Little Miami. The next settlement, on 28 December 1788, opposite the mouth of the Licking, was led by Israel Ludlow and Robert Patterson and was given the fanciful name Losantiville, which the first governor of the Northwest Territory, Arthur St. Clair, changed to Cincinnati, in honor of the Society of the Cincinnati. Symmes founded a third settlement on 2 February 1789 at North Bend. At first, the constant danger of Indian attacks confined the settlers, the majority of whom were from New Jersey, to the vicinity of Fort Washington, but gradually they went up the watercourses into the interior. Fort Hamilton, founded in 1791, became the nucleus of an advanced settlement, and after the Treaty of Greenville (1795), population spread quickly through the lands of the Miami purchase.

BIBLIOGRAPHY

Cayton, Andrew R. L. *The Frontier Republic: Ideology and Politics in the Ohio Country, 1780–1825.* Kent, Ohio: Kent State University Press, 1986.

The Correspondence of John Cleves Symmes. Edited by Beverly W. Bond Jr. New York: Macmillan, 1926.

Beverley W. Bond Jr./A. R.

See also **Cincinnati; Land Companies; Marietta; Proclamation of 1763; Westward Migration.**

MICHIGAN (population 9,938,444 in 2000) is bounded to the west by Wisconsin, Minnesota, and Lake Michigan; to the north by Lake Superior; to the east by Lakes Huron and St. Clair; and to the south by Ohio and Indiana. Though well into the interior of the nation, its two peninsulas are formed by the Great Lakes in such a way that provides an extensive coastline. Known as the "automobile state," its history is far more diverse than that nickname implies.

Government and Strategy, 1622–1796

During the period of exploration and colonial rule, the Michigan area had strategic and commercial value derived from its position in the Great Lakes region. Under the French, and later the British, the area proved an important source of furs easily transported on the extensive natural waterways. Based on early travel accounts, historians know that Samuel de Champlain sent Etienne Brûlé west along the upper parts of Lake Huron to search for a water route to the Pacific Ocean. Sometime in 1622, they surmise Brûlé reached the Sault Sainte Marie area. In 1668 the first formal settlement, a mission, was established by Rev. Jacques Marquette at the Sault, followed by a second at St. Ignace in 1671. Shortly thereafter, the French settlers claimed the land for Louis XIV. To secure their hold on the emerging and lucrative fur trade, the French Crown

Michigan

Miles 0 ___ 50 ___ 100
Kms 0 ___ 50 ___ 100

established forts at strategic points. Fort Ponchartrain at Detroit (meaning the straits), established in 1701, was the first permanent French settlement in the Lower Peninsula. Antoine de Cadillac established the fort and settlement as a fur center.

French control over the area passed to the British in 1763, who fortified Detroit and outposts at Michilimackinac. In 1780, in response to the revolution in the thirteen colonies, the British established a fortification at Mackinac Island that still stands today.

At the time of American independence, the area of Michigan was very much on the frontier. In 1787, the Northwest Ordinance made Michigan a part of the newly established Northwest Territory. In 1794, an American force under the command of Anthony Wayne defeated a British-inspired Native American confederacy. Although the British formally ceded the area of Michigan to the United States through the Treaty of Paris in 1783, the British did not actually leave Fort Mackinac and Detroit until 1796. Only then were the political institutions recognized by the Northwest Territory gradually implemented. By 1803, Michigan had become a part of the Indiana Territory. On 1 July 1805, in response to the petitions of Detroit residents, Congress authorized the creation of the Michigan Territory, with Detroit designated as its capital.

Agriculture and Market, 1796–1850

Though John Jacob Astor founded the American Fur Company with headquarters on Mackinac Island in 1808, the fur trade that had been the economic basis for European settlement in the Michigan area was already in decline. In the first decades of the nineteenth century, a project was begun to survey the lands of southern Michigan. Today's grid of townships was first laid out by the Surveyor General of the United States. Land offices

opened in Detroit and Monroe, where settlers could purchase a substantial farm for a very modest cost. The value of this opportunity increased enormously in 1825 when the Erie Canal opened to traffic and linked Michigan lands to the lucrative markets of the Northeast. The response was dramatic, as many chose to move to Michigan from the exhausted lands of upper New York State and elsewhere. Between 1820 and 1840, the population of European origin in Michigan increased from 8,767 to 212,267. Most of the settlement was east to west in the lower part of the state along the Chicago Road, which was developed between 1825 and 1835. Ann Arbor, Marshall, and Kalamazoo were among the market towns that were established. The prospects for farming in Michigan were promoted abroad by real estate interests, which attracted a diverse group of settlers that included Irish, German, and Dutch immigrants. These settlers brought with them a variety of religious beliefs and institutions. This diversity would continue to increase in scope and complexity throughout the subsequent history of the state.

The rapid population growth propelled arguments for statehood, and in 1835 it was authorized by territorial election. However, contention over the border with Ohio, finally resolved by the so-called Toledo War, delayed statehood to 1837 and ensured the inclusion of the Upper Peninsula as part of the new state. Stevens T. Mason, who had been appointed at the age of 19 in 1831 to succeed Lewis Cass as territorial governor, was appointed first governor of the new state in 1837. The new constitution provided for a university to be established, and offers of land were received from a number of towns. Ann Arbor was chosen for the institution. In 1817, three Native American tribes donated lands to the territorial university established in Detroit, but were sold to benefit the new campus in Ann Arbor. The spread of population across the lower part of state made Detroit impractical as a state capitol, and, after considerable debate, the more centrally located city of Lansing was selected in 1847.

Extracting Timber and Minerals, 1850–1910

Agriculture in Michigan flourished in the southernmost part of the state. However, with the expansion of a rail network and a good supply of Great Lakes shipping vessels, the state was in an excellent position to move heavier raw materials with relative ease. The lands in the northern two thirds of the state remained largely untouched and covered with timber. By 1860, Michigan had more than 800 timber mills and was shipping forest products throughout the Northeast. At its peak, in the years around 1890, Michigan was producing more than $60 million in timber per year. The lumber industry was largely homegrown, which meant that the revenue generated would remain, for the most part, in the state. Such was not the case with minerals extracted in the upper part of the state.

One of the first acts of the new state legislature was to commission Douglas Houghton, professor at the state-chartered university in Ann Arbor, to survey the geologic resources of Michigan. Houghton noted large deposits of copper in the Upper Peninsula. In 1844, iron was discovered. By the late 1860s, rail transport made it possible to move the iron and copper. The capital for many of the mines and the transport infrastructure came from the eastern states, most notably Massachusetts. Consequently, a significant portion of returns on those investments went east. By the late nineteenth century, copper and iron production nearly equaled the value of lumber production.

This extractive economy had a profound impact on the state. Whole cities were established to serve as centers for the finance and distribution of these raw materials. Bay City, Saginaw, and Traverse City, for example, were established as lumber centers. Houghton, Hancock, Marquette, and others were mining centers. The mines and the lumber trade drew immigrants from Italy, Finland, Sweden, Germany, and Ireland, among others.

The state's population was as diverse as any in the nation. As such, tensions were a part of the political landscape. In the mid-nineteenth century, nativist and anti-Catholic sentiment led to internal dissension in both the Whig and Democratic Parties. In 1854, a new political coalition, the Republican Party, emerged more tolerant and opposed to the extension of slavery. This new party would dominate politics in the state until the depression of the 1930s. At the time of the Civil War, Michigan supported the Union cause, sending ninety thousand men into service.

By the dawn of the twentieth century, the state's population had surged to 2,240,982, with more than 40 percent foreign-born or children of foreign-born. There were tensions within various groups. For example, the Dutch split between Christian Reformed and the Reformed Church in America in the mid-nineteenth century. The Polish community was split over the Kolasinski affair in the 1890s. There were conflicts within the German community at the time of World War I, chronicled in the pages of the daily *Detroiter Abend-Post*.

Automobile and Manufacturing, 1910 to the Present
Many manufacturing centers had been established in Michigan before the appearance of the automobile in the state. Most notably, Grand Rapids had emerged by the 1870s as a national center for furniture. Drawing from local and imported sources of lumber, as well as a population of expert craftsmen, its furniture could be shipped by rail to most destinations in the country. Kalamazoo had paper manufacturers, Battle Creek had health food factories that became the foundation for its famed breakfast food industry, and Detroit had factories that made rail cars, stoves, and other goods. However, it was only with the emergence of the automobile that Michigan became known as an urban industrial state.

At the turn of the twentieth century, Ransom Olds, Henry Ford, Henry Leland, David Buick, and Roy Chapin were among many in the state working on the idea of attaching a motor to wheels to make a personal transport vehicle. There were others working with the concept outside the state, but with well-established engine works and carriage manufacturers in Michigan, along with a transport infrastructure in place, the state was an ideal place to pursue these ideas on a large scale.

The auto manufacturers in Michigan came to dominate the industry through innovation and organization. Henry Ford's application of the assembly line so transformed the economies of production that what had been an expensively crafted luxury good became a mass-produced consumer good within reach of a large segment of the population. This innovation, more than any other, led to the dominance of Michigan in the automobile industry. Several independent auto producers amalgamated under a corporate framework called General Motors (conceived by William Durant of Flint, Michigan), and it, too, realized economies of scale and market power that raised significantly the barriers to entry for new mass producers of automobiles. By 1920, the automotive industry in Michigan employed 127,000 and had an output valued at $1,330,000,000.

While Michigan was well known as a manufacturing state by the 1920s, it was only in the 1940s that the world would come to realize the enormous industrial capacity of the state. In 1940, at the request of President Franklin D. Roosevelt, William Knudsen, then president of General Motors, directed the changeover of the auto plants to war production. The production output of tanks and planes earned the state the appellation "arsenal of democracy."

The transformation of Michigan from an agricultural and extractive economy to one of the leading industrial economies of the world was not without stress and cultural tensions. The demand for labor to work in the new auto factories and then to sustain production during two world wars brought a huge influx of workers into the state. These were from nearly every country in the world, but most notably Canada, Poland, and Germany. In response, many in the state embraced new ideas of the Progressive Era, which manifested in programs of change and reform as well as restriction and control. Hazen Pingree, as mayor of Detroit in the 1870s, was an early proponent of government regulation of public transport and utilities. Chase Osborn, a Progressive governor (1911–1912), introduced the concept of workers' compensation to the state, among other reform measures. The Detroit Citizens League, the Grand Rapids Furniture Manufacturers Association, and other groups formed to protect the interests of the urban elite in the face of changes brought on by rapid urban industrial growth.

The Detroit Urban League, along with a host of ethnic and church-based associations, helped maintain individual and group identities. These organizations structured urban and town life with a focus on assimilation. The demand for workers was so strong during World War II that many people, both white and African American, migrated from the South to work in the factories.

Though always a diverse state, Michigan by 1940 was among the most diverse in the country. With boom and bust cycles in the industrial economy, combined with cultures of intolerance, the population had its stresses—most notably manifested in the Detroit racial disturbances of 1943. There was also an elegance that emerged in Detroit and other cities in the 1920s. Detroit, a prosperous city and the fourth largest in America, built monuments, parks, museums, libraries, office towers, and great estates. During this time, stately houses were built in Grosse Pointe, Flint, Pontiac, Grand Rapids, and other industrial towns emblematic of the fruits of the new automobile industry. With railroads and highways leading north, grand houses and hotels appeared on the lakeshore along the coastline of Upper Michigan, a precursor to the vigorous travel industry that would emerge in the later half of the twentieth century.

As the industrial capacity of the state developed, so, too, did the size of the labor force. There had been tensions from the start, as indicated by the Grand Rapids Furniture strike of 1912, and the attempts to unionize the cereal industry in Battle Creek. Michigan became a real bulwark for the labor movement, with the establishment of the United Automobile Workers (UAW) in 1935. There had been a series of strikes and protests brought on by the severe economic depression of the 1930s. However, the "sit-down strike" of 1936–1937 in Flint was the event that brought recognition to the UAW as the sole bargaining representative for workers at General Motors. Soon thereafter, the union represented all workers employed with Ford Motor Company and other smaller firms.

By the 1930s, Michigan had an enormous industrial capacity. As a result, the effects of the depression were particularly difficult. A variety of voices emerged in the state. Frank Murphy became an early advocate of New Deal reform, first as mayor of Detroit (1930–1933) and later as governor (1937–1938). He eagerly worked with Franklin D. Roosevelt to establish governmental assistance to the many unemployed and dislocated. Another voice that arose from Detroit was that of Rev. Charles Coughlin. This Roman Catholic priest, from his pulpit in Royal Oak, Michigan, gained a huge national following for his radio broadcasts. At first a supporter of the New Deal, he was later discredited as his critiques became more harsh and anti-Semitic. Henry Ford, too, weighed in with extensive critiques in his *Dearborn Independent*, pushing his own particular notions of American values, which he was able to exemplify in his three-dimensional re-creation of the ideal American environment at his museum he called "Greenfield Village."

The end of World War II brought a rebirth of the strength of the Democratic Party in the state. Neil Staebler was the architect of a new strategy of reaching out to each segment of the population, combined with a high sense of morality in politics. G. Mennen Williams, known as "Soapy" because he was heir to the Mennen soap fortune, was the party's candidate for governor in 1948. Narrowly elected, he was able to establish the newly defined party and stay in office for six consecutive terms through 1960. Among his many achievements was the completion of the bridge at the straits of Mackinac in 1957, which linked the two peninsulas of the state.

Unionization proved an economic benefit for the state and set the foundation for middle-class prosperity that had a huge impact on Flint, Pontiac, Ypsilanti, as well as Detroit and its suburbs. The post–World War II economy was booming, bringing higher wages, new roads, and the automobile, significantly changing the urban and social landscape of the state. Many people in the cities relocated to the newly developed suburbs. The movement involved prosperous white residents almost entirely, leaving older residents and those of African American descent within the city limits. This exacerbated a racial divide that increasingly defined city and state politics. The population of Detroit began to decline until, in the year 2000, it was nearly half its high point of 1,849,568 in 1950. New shopping malls siphoned the retail trade from the city centers. The once elegant streets of downtown Flint, Grand Rapids, and Detroit became relatively sparsely populated.

This isolation of race and poverty within the cities erupted in a series of violent confrontations in 1967. Detroit's riot captured national attention; there were also disturbances in Pontiac, Flint, Grand Rapids, Lansing, and Kalamazoo, all of which further encouraged the abandonment of the cities. At the same time, throughout the latter half of the twentieth century the state population steadily grew, mostly in new suburban subdivisions, to the point that cities such as Southfield, Birmingham, Troy, Ann Arbor, and East Grand Rapids took on functions formerly associated with older urban downtowns. Also, a general prosperity in the Midwest increased the demand for lakefront property. A continuing building boom transformed Petoskey, Harbor Springs, Charlevoix, Traverse City, and Alpena.

The prosperity of the state, however, suffered in the later decades of the twentieth century. The lumber was exhausted, as were the mines of the Upper Peninsula. The value of agricultural production was at the same level as in the 1920s. The furniture industry had moved south, and foreign competition had severely challenged the automotive industry. Michigan became the very symbol of the "RUST BELT," with aging factories and a seeming inability to compete in a new global economy. Under George Romney and William Milliken, the Republican Party controlled the governorship from 1963 through 1983. During the late 1970s and early 1980s, the state's economy was in deep recession. A split in the state's Republican Party led to the election of the Democrat James Blanchard as the state continued a struggle to regain competitiveness in its old industries, while trying to diversify its economic base. In 1990, Republicans regained the governorship under John Engler, a representative of the more conservative wing of the party. His program of vigorous cost cutting and welfare reform, combined with the general economic boom in the country as a whole, restored Michigan to the point that, in 1993, it had achieved more growth than any industrial state in the union.

By the turn of the twenty-first century, the economy had rebounded due to the internationalization of the automobile industry, the development of high-tech activities, and the persistent growth of the tourist industry based on the state's extensive lakeshore. Michigan contained a large number of prosperous towns, characterized by new office buildings and a high rate of new residential construction. There were important initiatives to revive old downtowns, most notably with new cultural facilities in Grand Rapids and Detroit; the latter city also built a new stadium for major league baseball. The new century, however, brought new challenges. A stalled economy revived the need for cost cutting in state government and in the corporate sector. The effects of the attacks on the World Trade Center in New York and the Pentagon in Washington, D.C., on 11 September 2001 had a particular impact on the state of Michigan, which, in Dearborn, had the largest Arab American community in the country. The slowed economy, coupled with the national tragedies, again focused attention on the diversity of Michigan's population and on the historic reliance of the state on a single industry.

BIBLIOGRAPHY

Dunbar, Willis, and George May. *Michigan: A History of the Wolverine State.* 3d rev. ed. Grand Rapids, Mich.: W.B. Eerdmans, 1995.

Kern, John. *A Short History of Michigan.* Lansing: Michigan Department of State, 1977.

Hathaway, Richard J., ed. *Michigan: Visions of Our Past.* East Lansing: Michigan State University Press, 1989.

Poremba, David Lee, ed. *Detroit in Its World Setting: A Three-Hundred Year Chronology.* Detroit, Mich.: Wayne State University Press, 2001.

Francis X. Blouin

See also **Automobile Industry; Michigan, Upper Peninsula of; University of Michigan.**

MICHIGAN, UPPER PENINSULA OF shares a 344-mile border with Wisconsin to the southwest and arches northeastward, south of Lake Superior, north of Lake Michigan, and touches Lake Huron to the east. Before the Civil War, copper was discovered in the Keweenaw Peninsula of the Upper Peninsula, and until 1900, supplied about 75 percent of America's copper. The western 60 percent of the peninsula has heavily forested, rocky highlands; the eastern 40 percent has wetlands, flat lands, and hills. Annual snowfall averages over 160 inches, and sometimes tops 300 inches. The population of about 300,000 people is thinly scattered except for the cities of Marquette and Sault Ste. Marie on the north coast.

BIBLIOGRAPHY

Lassen, Tina. *Michigan Handbook: Featuring the Great Lakes and the Upper Peninsula.* Chico, Calif.: Moon Travel Handbooks, 1999.

McKee, Russell, ed. *A Most Superior Land: Life in the Upper Peninsula of Michigan.* Lansing, Mich.: Two Peninsula Press, 1983.

Kirk H. Beetz

See also **Michigan.**

MICROBIOLOGY is the study of organisms beyond the scope of human vision, particularly bacteria, viruses, algae, fungi, and protozoa. Since its founding in the nineteenth century, the science has largely focused on the isolation, identification, and elimination of pathogens from humans, animals, plants, food, and drinking water. Microbiologists have also examined nonpathogenic forms, seeking to understand their structure, function, and classification in order to control or exploit their activities.

Microbiology Arrives in America, 1878–1899

Microbiology gained a foothold in the United States after the discoveries of European researchers Ferdinand Cohn (1828–1898), Louis Pasteur (1822–1895), and Robert Koch (1843–1910) during the 1870s and early 1880s. While American physicians and biologists followed developments in the germ theory of disease (and the germ theory of fermentations) with great interest, few conducting original studies of their own. One exception was Thomas J. Burrill (1839–1916), a botanist and plant pathologist at the University of Illinois, who identified the etiological agent of pear blight in 1878. Burrill's discovery spawned little interest in bacteria as plant pathogens. Instead, microbiology first appeared in departments of pathology and veterinary medicine. William H. Welch (1850–1934), T. Mitchell Prudden (1894–1924), and Harold C. Ernst (1856–1922) each studied in Europe during the late 1870s, returning to the United States to begin instruction at Bellevue Medical College, Columbia University College of Physicians and Surgeons, Harvard, and Johns Hopkins University. By close of the nineteenth century, more than fifty American medical colleges required formal instruction in bacteriology, mostly intended to impart the techniques for isolating the pathogens responsible for tuberculosis, cholera, diphtheria, anthrax, plague, typhoid fever, and gonorrhea. While American medical colleges actively promoted bacteriological instruction, only William Welch's discovery of the gas-gangrene bacillus (1892) drew attention from European bacteriologists. Instead, American bacteriologists distinguished themselves in their contributions to public health practice and sanitary science.

In response to the global cholera epidemic of 1892, the New York City Health Department founded the first extensive laboratory for public health bacteriology. Under the direction of Hermann M. Biggs (1859–1923), William

357

H. Park (1863–1939), and Anna W. Williams (1863–1954), the department, in 1894, designed and distributed throat culture kits for diagnosing cases of diphtheria. The next year, Park and Williams refined methods of mass-producing diphtheria antitoxin, supplying it without charge to city physicians, and selling to outside public health departments. By 1899, more than twenty state and city departments of health established similar laboratories, aiding in the diagnoses of tuberculosis, typhoid fever, malaria, and gonorrhea.

Microbiologists also supported the field of sanitary science, helping to eliminate harmful microbes from drinking water, milk, and food. At Massachusetts Institute of Technology and the Lawrence Experiment Station, William T. Sedgwick (1855–1921) and his students designed methods of improving water filtration systems, reducing rates of typhoid fever in American cities by more than 70 percent. Sedgwick's colleagues, Samuel C. Prescott (1872–1962) and William L. Underwood (1864–1929), studied means of reducing food poisoning in commercially manufactured foods.

American microbiologists achieved their greatest successes in the fields of veterinary medicine, dairying, soil science, and plant pathology, under the aegis of the bureaus of the U.S. Department of Agriculture and the several state agricultural experiment stations. At the Bureau of Animal Industry, Daniel E. Salmon (1850–1914) and Theobald Smith (1859–1934) isolated the bacterial agent of swine plague, and developed the first heat-killed (as opposed to Pasteur's live-attenuated) vaccine. In the early 1890s, Salmon and Smith identified the protozoan responsible for Texas cattle fever, and established that a tick carried the parasite from host to host, the first demonstration of an insect vector in the spread of disease. In the field of dairying, Herbert W. Conn (1859–1917) at the Storrs Agricultural Experiment Station and Harry L. Russell (1866–1954) at the Wisconsin station detailed the function of bacteria in the formation and flavoring of hard cheeses and butter. In the late 1890s, researchers at the New Jersey and Delaware stations advanced the scientific understanding of soil fertility, defining the role of bacteria and fungi in the decomposition of manures, their action upon fertilizers, and their importance in the fixation of atmospheric nitrogen. American plant pathologists, in the 1880s and 1890s, contributed greatly to the understanding and prevention of various wilts, rusts, and blights of agricultural crops. While most plant diseases are fungal in origin, Erwin F. Smith (1854–1927), of the Bureau of Plant Industry, and Harry Russell were the first to identify bacterial diseases of plants.

The Flourishing of American Microbiology, 1900–1924

Microbiology flourished in the first quarter of the twentieth century. The Society of American Bacteriologists and the Laboratory Section of the American Public Health Association formed in 1899. In the first years of the new century, the Rockefeller Institute for Medical Research in New York, the John McCormick Institute in Chicago, and the U.S. Public Health Service Hygienic Laboratory began sponsoring original investigations in medical microbiology. By 1925, American researchers could point to notable advances in the comprehension and control of many infectious diseases, including: Walter Reed (1851–1902) and James Carroll (1854–1907) for demonstrating that mosquitoes transmitted yellow fever; Simon Flexner (1863–1946) for his discovery of a new variant of dysentery and devising a serum for treating meningitis; Howard T. Ricketts (1871–1910) for his research on Rocky Mountain spotted fever; George W. McCoy (1876–1952) and William B. Wherry (1875–1936) for identifying the bacteria of tularemia; and, F. Peyton Rous (1879–1970) for proposing a viral etiology of some cancers.

In the field of public health, bacteriology occupied an authoritative position. Increasingly, public health leaders shifted their focus from cleanup campaigns and municipal reforms to the bacteriological methods of identifying sick or susceptible individuals, including the control of "health carriers." In 1907, the New York City Health Department detained the immigrant cook Mary Mallon ("Typhoid Mary") for transmitting typhoid fever, even though she showed no signs of the illness herself. Health officials also lobbied for compulsory school vaccinations and mandatory tests for susceptibility to diphtheria and scarlet fever. By 1925, most municipalities distributed filtered or chlorinated water, mandated pasteurized milk, and inspected commercial canneries.

Veterinary microbiologists devised diagnostic tests, vaccines, and treatments for several economically devastating livestock diseases (e.g., hog cholera, blackleg in sheep, pullorum in chickens, and blackhead in turkeys). Regarding bovine tuberculosis and contagious abortion in cattle, these efforts carried implications for human health. In the first years of the new century, Theobald Smith, Harry Russell, and Mazyck P. Ravenel (1861–1946) documented that the dairy products made from tubercular cows could transmit the disease to infants. Similarly, Alice C. Evans (1881–1975) argued, in 1916, that cows suffering from contagious abortion could transmit undulant fever to humans. While Evans's claim drew initial skepticism, her work led to the recognition of a new class of infections, brucellosis. As a result, the Bureau of Animal Industry sponsored a national eradication movement, dramatically decreasing the incidence of both diseases.

The Triumph of Microbiology, 1925–1979

Throughout much of the twentieth century, American microbiologists led an age of scientific triumph. In the battle against infectious disease, researchers and pharmaceutical firms improved vaccines and therapeutic sera to control measles, diphtheria, mumps, rubella, and whooping cough. At Vanderbilt University and the Rockefeller Institute, Ernest W. Goodpasture (1886–1960), Thomas M. Rivers (1888–1962), and Richard E. Shope (1901–

1966) transformed the study of influenza, herpes, and encephalitis, developing methods of culturing these viruses in chick embryos. John F. Enders (1897–1985) and his colleagues at Harvard University devised a technique in 1949 for growing polio virus in cultures of tissue cells. Within a decade, Jonas E. Salk (1914–1995) and Albert B. Sabin (1906–1993) introduced two separate polio vaccines, largely eliminating the scourge of infantile paralysis. While penicillin was introduced as a therapeutic agent in the early 1940s by the British researchers Alexander Fleming, Howard Florey, and Ernst Chain, American scientists also studied the antagonisms between different microbes. In 1939, Rockefeller Institute researcher René Dubos (1901–1981) isolated a crystalline antibiotic, gramicidin, from a soil organism. Unfortunately, gramicidin proved too toxic for internal use. Dubos's former teacher, Selman Waksman (1888–1973), found another group of soil organisms showing anti-germicidal properties. Waksman and his students at Rutgers University identified streptomycin, the first effective antibiotic in the treatment of tuberculosis.

Microbiologists equally contributed to the development of molecular biology. In the 1930s and 1940s, Oswald T. Avery (1877–1955) and his colleagues at the Rockefeller Institute showed that DNA played a role in transforming non-virulent pneumococci into virulent forms, intimating that this substance might be generally involved in heredity. Employing a bacteriophage of *E. coli*, Max Delbruck (1906–1981) and Salvador Luria (1912–1991) revealed that bacteria and viruses followed normal principles of replication and mutation, thereby establishing phage as a model organism for genetic research. Joshua Lederberg (1925–) and Edward L. Tatum (1909–1975) showed that bacteria can exchange genes when cultured in direct contact. In 1952, Lederberg and Norton D. Zinder (1928–) elucidated the phenomenon of bacterial transduction, where a phage carries DNA from one bacterium to another. Their research suggested a mechanism for introducing genes into new cells, a technique now common in genetic engineering. In the 1960s and early 1970s, Matthew S. Meselson (1930–), David Baltimore (1938–), and Howard M. Temin (1934–1994) employed bacteriophages and other viruses to delineate the relationship among DNA, RNA, and protein synthesis.

Emerging Challenges, 1980–2002

In 1979, the World Health Organization declared that one of the most ancient and devastating diseases, smallpox, had been officially eliminated. Scientific optimism proved, however, to be short-lived, as medical researchers soon grappled with the emergence of AIDS. While Robert C. Gallo (1937–), of the National Institutes of Health, co-discovered the human immunodeficiency virus in 1983, and developed an accurate test for HIV infection, no vaccine or cure has been found. Microbiologists have also struggled against new microbial threats, from Rift Valley fever, dengue fever, ebola, and hanta virus abroad, to lyme disease and multiple-drug resistant

tuberculosis domestically. Even the class of infectious agents has expanded. In 1982, Stanley Prusiner (1942–) found evidence of infectious protein particles or "prions," and concluded that they were responsible for scrapie, a transmissible spongiform encephalopathy fatal to sheep. In the 1990s, Prusiner and others demonstrated that both mad cow disease in livestock and Creutzfeldt-Jakob disease in humans were likely caused by prions.

BIBLIOGRAPHY

American Society for Microbiology. "Celebrating a Century of Leadership in Microbiology." *ASM News* 65, no. 5 (1999): 258–380.

Clark, Paul F. *Pioneer Microbiologists in America*. Madison: University of Wisconsin Press, 1962.

Garrett, Laurie. *The Coming Plague: Newly Emerging Diseases in a World Out of Balance*. New York: Farrar, Straus and Giroux, 1994.

Parascandola, John, ed. *The History of Antibiotics: A Symposium*. Madison, Wisc.: American Institute of the History of Pharmacy, 1980.

Postgate, John. *Microbes and Man*. 4th ed. Cambridge, Mass.: Cambridge University Press, 2000.

Tomes, Nancy. *The Gospel of Germs: Men, Women, and the Microbe in American Life*. Cambridge, Mass.: Harvard University Press, 1998.

Eric D. Kupferberg

MICROSOFT. Founded in 1975, the Microsoft Corporation rose from having no assets to become one of the most valuable companies in the world, and in 2003 was the largest computer software company and one of the great success stories in American business.

The roots of the company go back to 1968, when the Lakeside Academy acquired access to a computer in downtown Seattle. Computer programming fired the imaginations of Bill Gates and Paul Allen, then thirteen and fifteen years old. At the time, access to computers was expensive. They took on local programming jobs to pay for more computer time. In 1971, they wrote a program called Traf-O-Data, analyzing patterns of traffic flow. This project earned them $20,000. The next opportunity to turn their skills into income was a major turning point. In 1974, Management Information Tools, Inc. (MITI), published an advertisement for the first mass-produced home computer, called the MITS Altair. The machine was primitive by today's standards. It took a soldering iron and hours of patience to assemble. Once assembled, it could only be programmed with the 1s and 0s of machine code, requiring the programmer to set toggle switches at the front of the machine.

Despite these limitations, Gates and Allen saw the potential of personal computing. But first, it had to be made practical for the nonspecialist. Their solution was to write a compact version of the BASIC language that could be loaded into the Altair's memory from tape. Once loaded, the program understood and responded to simple, quasi-English commands in BASIC, using a Teletype machine to communicate. To complete negotiations with MITI, Gates and Allen formed a partnership they called Micro-Soft, for microcomputer software. They later dropped the hyphen. As other companies produced personal computers of their own, Gates persuaded them to use Microsoft's BASIC. Microsoft hired additional programmers as it produced other languages for the new machines.

Bill Gates attended Harvard while trying to run the fledgling company. He had planned to major in law. Shortly, however, he quit to focus on the company full-time. While at Harvard, he met Steve Ballmer, a business major who would eventually join the company and later become its chief executive officer.

Microsoft's next triumphs came in the area of operating systems. An operating system is a resident program that enables a user to load, manage, and run other programs; it provides the computer's general look and feel.

In 1981, the International Business Machines Corporation (IBM) released its personal computer, or "PC." Microsoft grew tremendously after acquiring the MS-DOS operating system and licensing it to IBM. (Gates paid a programmer named Tim Patterson $50,000 for the system, although Microsoft added refinements.) IBM did not insist on exclusive rights to the software. As a hardware company, it believed that more money was to be made selling machines. Microsoft was therefore able to license the system to all the IBM "clones" and so reap hundreds of millions of dollars. The de facto designer of the PC environment became Microsoft in conjunction with chipmaker Intel. The main competition remaining in the personal computer market was Apple—although Microsoft also wrote the most popular applications for the Apple Macintosh.

Along with Apple, Microsoft saw the value of graphical user interface (GUI), using pictures, menus, and icons, instead of typed-in commands. While continuing to expand into many areas, Microsoft worked for years on a GUI operating system for IBM PCs and clones (now just known as PCs). That system was Windows, released in 1985. At first a failure—clumsy and awkward compared to the Macintosh—Windows eventually succeeded. Windows 3.0 was easy to use and took advantage of improvements in PC hardware, such as superior graphics, that had occurred since Windows 1.0. Microsoft also released a new version of BASIC—Visual Basic—making it easy to write programs for Windows.

Eventually, 90 percent of all personal computers ran Windows, and the leading applications (including word processing, database, and spreadsheets) were also Microsoft products. In the mid-1990s, it seemed that the emerging Internet might give rivals a chance to supplant Microsoft, whose software had always been based on the single-user model. By the late 1990s, however, Microsoft's integration of Internet technology into its products helped secure its dominance. Meanwhile, the company continued to devote its large research budget to new areas, such as interactive television.

But on 7 June 2000, the confidence and persistence that had served Microsoft in the past threatened to damage it, as Judge Thomas Penfield Jackson ordered the breakup of the company in a suit brought by the U.S. Justice Department and a number of states. The suit charged that Microsoft had an operating-system monopoly in Windows, which it exploited to its advantage in other product lines. Jackson reasoned that if Microsoft was two companies, the applications division could not take advantage of close ties to the designers of Windows. In the summer of 2001, an appellate panel overturned this penalty as too severe (citing Jackson's bias, as revealed in published interviews) and sent the case back to a lower court for rehearing.

BIBLIOGRAPHY

Andrews, Paul. *How the Web Was Won: Microsoft from Windows to the Web: The Inside Story of How Bill Gates and His Band of Internet Idealists Transformed a Software Empire*. New York: Random House, 1999.

Ichbiah, Daniel, and Susan L. Knepper. *The Making of Microsoft: How Bill Gates and His Team Created the World's Most Successful Software Company*. New York: St. Martin's, 1991.

Manes, Stephen, and Paul Andrews. *Gates: How Microsoft's Mogul Reinvented an Industry—and Made Himself the Richest Man in America*. New York: Doubleday, 1993.

Microsoft Corporation. *Inside Out: Microsoft—In Our Own Words*. New York: Warner Books, 2000.

Wallace, James, and Jim Erickson. *Hard Drive: Bill Gates and the Making of the Microsoft Empire*. New York: Wiley, 1992.

Brian Overland

See also **Computers and Computer Industry; Internet.**

MICROWAVE TECHNOLOGY. Microwave detection and communications systems have come to play a major, but little appreciated, role in American life since 1940. Perhaps the application best known to the public is the microwave oven, but microwaves have also made possible live television from space and between continents. Microwave technology is also essential for safe all-weather operation of commercial and military aircraft as well as for intercity telephone traffic. Before the 1970s the high cost of microwave systems tended to limit their use for mass-produced consumer products. This situation changed with the introduction of comparatively inexpensive solid-state microwave sources suitable for such applications as counter-top ovens, collision-avoidance devices for automobiles, burglar alarms, mobile telephones, and health-data telemetry.

Microwave technology has gone through several stages. European physicists did some theoretical and experimental work in the late nineteenth century, but interest languished because of the dominance of long waves in early radio communication. George C. Southworth, John R. Carson, and others at the Bell Telephone Laboratories made some fundamental advances in the transmission of microwaves during the 1930s. Researchers at Stanford University in 1939 developed an important new microwave generator known as the klystron. The waveguide, klystron, and cavity magnetron, brought to the United States in a famous "black box" by a British team in 1940, became key elements in a wide variety of radar systems developed by several groups, including the Radiation Laboratories formed at the Massachusetts Institute of Technology in 1941.

Bell System installed the prototype for a major microwave communications system by means of repeating stations separated by distances of about thirty miles between New York and Boston in 1947. By 1960, microwave chains carried about 40 percent of Bell's intercity traffic; the proportion of domestic communications handled through microwave networks increased steadily thereafter. Similar apparatus was adapted for use in satellite repeating stations, beginning with the launch of *Pioneer 3* in 1958. Further innovations and the increasing congestion of the electromagnetic spectrum aroused renewed interest in the use of Southworth's hollow pipes for communications by 1970. (A single circular pipe is believed capable of carrying 250,000 simultaneous conversations over long distances.) The discovery in the 1960s by J. B. Gunn of IBM and others that semiconductor devices such as the Gunn oscillator and IMPATT diode can generate and amplify microwave signals stimulated a variety of consumer and industrial applications of microwave technology.

In the 1940s Dr. Percy Spencer, an engineer with the Raytheon Corporation researching radars, noticed that microwaves emitted by a new vacuum tube called a magnetron caused food sitting nearby to heat up. The first commercial microwave oven—weighing more than 750 pounds and standing over five feet tall—hit the market in 1947. In the late 1960s, microwave ovens began appearing in stores as domestic appliances, and by 1975 their sales surpassed those of gas ranges. Although culinary purists avoided them, microwave ovens spurred a new industry in frozen prepared foods and vastly reduced the amount of time needed to cook food, further reducing Americans' dependence on a primary domestic laborer.

BIBLIOGRAPHY

Cowan, Ruth Schwartz. *More Work for Mother: The Ironies of Household Technology from the Open Hearth to the Microwave.* New York: Basic Books, 1983.

Veley, Victor F. C. *Modern Microwave Technology.* Englewood Cliffs, N.J.: Prentice Hall, 1987.

James E. Brittain / A. R.

See also **Physics: Solid-State Physics; Radar.**

MIDCONTINENT OIL REGION, a vast mineral fuel-producing region situated in the nation's heartland, extending from Nebraska to south Texas and flanked by the Mississippi River and the Rocky Mountains. Early in recorded history, individuals noted a sign of oil in the form of a green slick on springs and creeks at widely scattered locations. In the age before kerosine lamps and internal-combustion engines, oil slick was used as a lubricant and as medicine. Teamsters crossing the Plains from the Missouri settlements to the Rio Grande towns greased their wagon axles with oil slick. Before the Civil War, oil springs in the Chickasaw Nation in south-central Oklahoma and in north Texas served as spas. Oil was believed to have therapeutic properties, particularly in the treatment of rheumatism, dropsy, and other chronic diseases. Natural gas is a ubiquitous associate of oil in the midcontinent region. Indians in the region lighted their council grounds with surface leakage of natural gas, using gun barrels thrust into the gas seepage crevices as tubes to control the gas flow and to serve as burners.

Early discoveries of subsurface oil in the midcontinent region were inadvertent, largely the result of digging wells for water and saline solution used in salt manufacture. One of the earliest discoveries occurred in 1859 when Lewis Ross, an Indian operating a saltworks in the Cherokee Nation on Grand River in Mayes County in northeastern Oklahoma, dug a well to increase the flow from his salt springs. He struck oil, which flowed at the rate of ten barrels a day until the gas pressure producing the free flow dissipated. A year later at Paola, Kansas, oil was found in a well at a depth of about 300 feet. Thereafter, from Kansas to Texas, oil discoveries through digging water wells became a regular occurrence.

Prospecting for oil in the midcontinent region began in the 1880s. In 1882, H. W. Faucett from the Pennsylvania oil fields received a concession from the Choctaw tribal government for drilling rights in the Choctaw Nation in southeastern Oklahoma. On Boggy Creek near Atoka, he produced a shower of oil and gas 1,400 feet high. Successive discoveries in Kansas, Indian Territory, and Texas opened oil and gas fields. The production was used as a lubricant, an illuminant (kerosine, coal oil, and rock oil), and medicine. The natural gas fields of southern Kansas became an important source for fuel for smelters refining lead and zinc ores from the nearby Tri-State District, for ceramic manufacture, particularly bricks, and for other industrial purposes. Also, natural gas was widely used as a home fuel and an illuminant for lighting city streets and homes.

The premier oil well of the midcontinent region was Spindletop, a dramatic gusher brought in by Anthony F. Lucas near Beaumont, Texas, on 10 January 1901, which produced 75,000–100,000 barrels per day. The advent of the internal-combustion engine with the concomitant increase in demand for petroleum products led to a sustained flurry of exploration by drilling, called wildcatting, throughout the midcontinent region, opening new fields in every state of the region from Nebraska to Louisiana.

Sporadic efforts to control production from the late 1920s through the early 1930s met with resistance from operators, and in 1931, excessive production in East Texas brought prices to less than 10 cents per barrel. Under the 1933 National Recovery Act, representatives of the oil industry authorized the federal government to issue drilling permits and set production quotas. In 1935, however, the Supreme Court deemed the National Recovery Act unconstitutional. In response, oil-producing states formed and joined the Interstate Oil Compact to track and control production and shipping.

Around 1945, midcontinent petroleum production peaked and began to level off. However, the discovery of extensive new fields in eastern New Mexico, the Permian Basin in Texas, and the Wilburton Field in Oklahoma between the late 1940s and the early 1960s continued to dramatically increase the oil and gas resources of the region. Also, deeper drilling, environmental changes, and advances in petroleum technology allowed resumed production in previously abandoned wells, increased pool discovery, and augmented well production.

The oil industry of the midcontinent region has provided a legacy of bonanza wealth and boomtowns reminiscent of the California gold rush in 1848–49. The region's petroleum industry has been a major influence in state and regional economic development, urban and suburban evolution, and politics.

BIBLIOGRAPHY

Connelly, William L. *The Oil Business As I Saw It: Half a Century with Sinclair.* Norman: University of Oklahoma Press, 1954.

Olien, Diana Davids. *Oil in Texas: The Gusher Age, 1895–1945.* Austin: University of Texas Press, 2002.

Olien, Roger. *Oil and Ideology: The Cultural Creation of the American Petroleum Industry.* Chapel Hill: University of North Carolina Press, 2000.

Rister, Carl Coke. *Oil! Titan of the Southwest.* Norman: University of Oklahoma Press, 1949.

Williamson, Harold Francis, et al. *The American Petroleum Industry.* Evanston, Ill.: Northwestern University Press, 1959.

Arrell M. Gibson/ F. B.

See also **Automobile; Energy Industry; Oil Fields; Petroleum Industry; Petroleum Prospecting and Technology; Wildcat Oil Drilling.**

MIDDLE COLONIES, composed of Pennsylvania, Delaware, New York, and New Jersey, were a mix of both northern and southern features, creating a unique environment of early settlement by non-English Europeans, mostly Dutch and German, where English men and women composed the smallest minority. A combination of both urban and rural lifestyles made it more cosmopolitan, religiously pluralistic, and socially tolerant within a commercial atmosphere. They were all at one time proprietary colonies. After 1664, Anglos began to rush into East Jersey, and English Quakers settled Pennsylvania and West Jersey. Philadelphia, the second largest English city by the time of the American Revolution, was the Ellis Island of colonial America, and many indentured servants made their homes in the Middle Colonies. Established commercial networks from Ulster in Northern Ireland brought the Scotch-Irish Presbyterians to Philadelphia and New Castle and Wilmington, Delaware. These immigrants came mostly in family units that preserved a balanced sex ratio. During the eighteenth century the Middle Colonies' population grew at a higher rate than New England or the southern colonies.

The English established the township, an area twenty-five to thirty miles square, as the basic settlement type. Various rural neighborhoods along creeks and watercourses developed into townships that were spatially dispersed, like the southern colonies, but that pulled together merchandising and distribution recourses for both commercial and staple crops, like the New England colonies. Fords and crossroads connected the hinterland with Philadelphia and New York. The grain trade to Europe fed Philadelphia commerce.

The Middle Colonies had the highest ratio of churches to population of the three sections of colonial America. Settlement from the European states disrupted by the Protestant Reformation transplanted Dutch Mennonites, Dutch Calvinists, French Huguenots, German Baptists, and Portuguese Jews who joined larger established congregations of Dutch Reformed, Lutherans, Quakers, and Anglicans. Education in the Middle Colonies was mostly sectarian, as local churches sponsored schools. Pennsylvania's toleration allowed Anglicans, Moravians, and Quakers to open schools.

BIBLIOGRAPHY

Balmer, Randall H. *A Perfect Babel of Confusion: Dutch Religion and English Culture in the Middle Colonies.* New York: Oxford University Press, 1989.

Kavenagh, W. Keith, ed. *Foundations of Colonial America: A Documentary History.* New York: Chelsea House, 1973.

Neuenschwander, John A. *The Middle Colonies and the Coming of the American Revolution.* Port Washington, N.Y.: Kennikat Press, 1973.

Newcomb, Benjamin H. *Political Partisanship in the American Middle Colonies, 1700–1776.* Baton Rouge: Louisiana State University Press, 1995.

Michelle M. Mormul

See also **Delaware; New Jersey; New York Colony; Pennsylvania; Philadelphia; Proprietary Colonies.**

MIDDLE PASSAGE. Even before African slaves arrived on the shores of Virginia in 1619, the slave trade figured significantly in the economy of the Atlantic na-

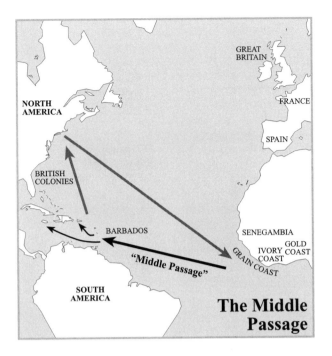

The Middle Passage

slave-catching raids to supply Europeans' demands, using firearms supplied by slavers.

Renaissance Europeans discovered the existence of the Americas in 1492 when Christopher Columbus stumbled upon the New World during an attempt to find a sea-trading route to the Far East. The subsequent conquest of the New World encouraged transatlantic slave trading as early as 1502 in support of plantations instituted in the Americas. Bartolomé de Las Casas, later the bishop of Chiapas, Mexico, proposed in 1517 the large-scale importation of African slaves to replace the local Indian slaves, whom he deemed unsuitable. The following year, the Spanish Crown authorized the first direct shipment of slaves from Africa to the Americas and, by 1595, began to grant the *asiento*, permits providing for slave-trading monopolies to Spanish dominions. The year 1619 saw the first African slaves in North American colonies.

Initially, Portuguese and Spanish colonies in South America and Central America bought slaves to work on sugar cane plantations, facilities known as the "seasoning stations" by the northern plantations because of the brutal conditioning that took place there. Although Portugal retained control of the southern transatlantic slave trade, several nations, especially England, challenged the Spanish for the northern Atlantic. In 1562, Sir John Hawkins became the first Englishman to carry a cargo of African slaves to the New World. His voyage netted such gains that Queen Elizabeth, who had publicly denounced slave-trading voyages, secretly invested heavily in Hawkins's subsequent slaving expeditions. Sir Francis Drake, Hawkins's cousin, commanded one of these ships.

In the late 1560s, Hawkins sailed his ships into the port of Veracruz on the Mexican coast, where he encountered a large and heavily armed Spanish fleet, which attacked and defeated the English vessels as part of their attempt to retain the monopoly over the northern transatlantic slave trade. British interest in the slave trade did not resume for a century, until after the English Civil War, when in 1672 Charles II chartered the Royal African Company, which quickly established England as the world's greatest slave trader. By the 1700s, due to increasing demand for African slaves, slave traders began to ship their cargo of Africans directly from Africa to North America.

The Middle Passage may have served to enrich many Europeans and Americans, but the enslaved Africans suffered extraordinary atrocities and inhuman conditions during these voyages. Estimates for the total number of Africans imported to the New World by the slave trade range from 25 million to 50 million; of these, perhaps as many as half died at sea during the Middle Passage experience. The journey from Africa to North America could take between thirty and ninety days. The vessels were called "loose packers" or "tight packers," where captives were laid side by side, coffin-like, beneath the deck. The ships carried the stench of diseased and decaying

tions. Established primarily by sea captains from England and New England, a system of trading routes developed among Europe, Africa, and North America and became known collectively as the triangular trade. Ships in these triangular lanes carried goods among the three continents, taking advantage of the fact that none of these regions was economically self-sufficient; each depended on the other two for goods they could not provide themselves. The so-called Middle Passage consisted of the leg across the Atlantic that connected Africa to the Americas.

The economics of such trafficking went something like this: England produced textiles and other manufactured goods like firearms and gunpowder, unavailable in either North America or Africa. This cargo made the voyage from England to the African "Slave Coast" to be traded for slaves and other riches such as gold and silver. The next leg sent these slaves and domestic goods to the West Indies and North American coast, where shippers traded their cargo for tobacco, fish, lumber, flour, foodstuffs, and rum distilled in New England before returning with these goods to England.

The inhabitants along the west coast of Africa had long recognized the practice of slavery; however, trafficking existed mainly to supply domestic slaves. Local kings would often sell surplus slaves, in addition to criminals, debtors, and prisoners of war, to European traders. However, the exportation of African slaves had its real origins in 1419, when Prince Henry the Navigator of Portugal began to send expeditions to explore the West African coast. By 1444, Europe began to buy African slaves, and the first leg of the slave trade triangle became established. Demand for slaves proved to be greater than the usual practices could provide, and coastal tribes resorted to

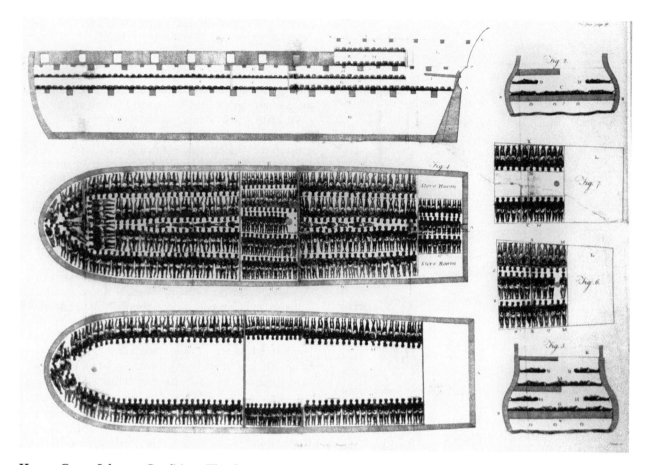

Human Cargo, Inhuman Conditions. This diagram, produced after the passage of the British Slavery Regulation Act of 1788—an attempt at bringing some order to the slave trade—shows the layout of the British slave ship *Brookes*, revealing the appalling living conditions to which captive Africans were subject during their forced voyage across the Atlantic. Slaves were usually chained side-by-side in tightly packed confines below decks, where they were left to live or die in their own waste. In case of water shortage or spreading illness, slavers would often murder slaves and throw them overboard to try to ensure the healthy delivery of the remaining slaves. LIBRARY OF CONGRESS

bodies, and slavers often threw unruly Africans overboard, which lured sharks along these shipping lanes.

Olaudah Equiano, of the Ibo tribe in what is now modern Nigeria, wrote an account of the horrors of the Middle Passage. Kidnapped and sold into slavery at the age of eleven, Equiano recounted the shock of seeing white people purchase slaves in Africa and the fear aroused by the claim that whites ate Africans or drank their blood. The few first-hand accounts that exist consistently report that the unsanitary conditions aboard ship on the longer journeys created high mortality rates, encouraged by the incidence of smallpox, eye infections, gastrointestinal disorders, and body sores. "Fever" and "flux" were the terms used to describe common causes of death during the ocean crossing, and some slaves committed suicide by refusing to eat or throwing themselves overboard. Ships sometimes reported slave rebellions, and the result became a maritime standard of even harsher and more brutal handling.

Slave-ship captains were given incentives for delivering only healthy, salable men and women to American slave markets. As a result, certain circumstances could lead to the mass murder of their African cargo at sea. When captives seemed too sick to survive the journey, slavers were known to hurl the weak and infirm into the sea. At other times, storms at sea or shortages of drinking water might lead to the mass execution of captives as well. In fact, records show that captains who ordered Africans overboard at sea often sought reimbursement from insurance companies for their losses.

In 1807, England became the first nation to abolish the African slave trade, but not even the mutiny aboard the slave ship *Amistad* in 1839 could put an end to the Middle Passage until the American Civil War came to a close in 1865. Only then did the United States outlaw slavery and end 300 years of Middle Passage horror and inhumanity.

364

TO BE SOLD on board the Ship *Bance-Island*, on tuesday the 6th of *May* next, at *Ashley-Ferry*; a choice cargo of about 250 fine healthy

NEGROES,

juft arrived from the Windward & Rice Coaft. —The utmoft care has already been taken, and fhall be continued, to keep them free from the leaft danger of being infected with the SMALL-POX, no boat having been on board, and all other communication with people from *Charles-Town* prevented.

Auftin, Laurens, & Appleby.

N. B. Full one Half of the above Negroes have had the SMALL-POX in their own Country.

Slave Trade. This advertising flier from 1780 announces the sale of 250 "fine healthy NEGROES" into slavery after their arrival on the ship *Bance-Island*—the slaver's sales pitch masking the extraordinary brutality and degradation of the Middle Passage, which claimed the lives of many Africans and destroyed the health and spirit of countless others. LIBRARY OF CONGRESS

BIBLIOGRAPHY

Alderman, Clifford L. *Rum, Slaves, and Molasses: The Story of New England's Triangular Trade.* New York: Crowell-Collier, 1972.

Dow, George Francis. *Slave Ships and Slaving.* New York: Dover, 1970.

Equiano, Olaudah. *Interesting Narrative of the Life of Olaudah Equiano.* New York: Negro Universities Press, 1969.

Howard, Thomas, ed. *Black Voyage: Eyewitness Accounts of the Atlantic Slave Trade.* Boston: Little, Brown, 1971.

Klein, Herbert S. *The Middle Passage: Comparative Studies in the Atlantic Slave Trade.* Princeton, N.J.: Princeton University Press, 1978.

Plimmer, Charlotte, and Denis Plimmer. *Slavery: The Anglo-American Involvement.* New York: Harper and Row, 1973.

Rawley, James A. *The Transatlantic Slave Trade: A History.* New York: Norton, 1981.

Thomas, Hugh. *The Slave Trade: The History of the Atlantic Slave Trade: 1440–1870.* New York: Simon and Schuster, 1997.

Mark Todd

See also **Amistad** Case; Antislavery; Slave Ships; Slave Trade.

MIDDLEBROW CULTURE.

Middlebrow culture is the offspring of universal education and the belief,

In Masscult, the trick is plain—to please the crowd by any means. But Midcult has it both ways: it pretends to respect the standards of High Culture while in fact it waters them down and vulgarizes them.

Dwight Macdonald

SOURCE: *Partisan Review,* Spring 1960.

unique to the United States, that education is a lifelong process. More than any other national group, Americans attend evening schools and community colleges, while also taking advantage of intensive educational efforts by museums, musical organizations, and theaters. The myth of American classlessness supports using culture as a ladder for upward mobility and status definition.

Until the end of the nineteenth century, American culture divided into high, for the few, and low, for the many. But the proliferation of media in the twentieth century fostered the development of a new cultural class, although decades would pass before it acquired a name. During the prosperous 1920s such new magazines as *Time, Reader's Digest,* and *The New Yorker* sought this audience, as did such enterprises as the BOOK-OF-THE-MONTH CLUB. Also marketed to this growing group were classical recordings and educational radio programs. In 1922 the cultural critic H. L. Mencken disparaged these stodgy, sheeplike consumers as the "booboisie," while the best-selling novelist Sinclair Lewis lampooned them in *Babbitt* (1922).

In the 1930s Americans began to define their own culture as being distinct from that of Europe. The central role of the United States in World War II and its emergence as a world leader reinforced perceptions of a uniquely American culture. But its expressions were criticized as parochial, conservative, and, particularly, as too middlebrow.

The spasm of fulminations over middlebrow culture was as brief as it was shrill. It erupted in 1939, on the eve of World War II, fanned by two radical followers of Leon Trotsky, Clement Greenberg, and Dwight Macdonald. Unlike Mencken, who had blamed the audience for its lack of interest in serious culture, the critics of the 1940s accused capitalist commercial culture of seducing naive consumers with kitsch. But the outcry quickly subsided; by 1949 "brow-beating" was more of a parlor game than an intense political issue.

The indictment of middlebrows was a symptom of the loss of cultural authority previously wielded by critics and specialists. But it also confronted the weakness of high culture in the face of the American public's lack of interest in political ideology and seemingly insatiable appetite for entertainment.

365

When America and Americans are characterized by foreigners and highbrows, the middlebrows are likely to emerge as the dominant group in our society—a dreadful mass of insensible back-slappers, given to sentimentality as a prime virtue, the willing victims of slogans and the whims of the bosses, both political and economic.

Russell Lynes

SOURCE: "Highbrow, Lowbrow, Middlebrow," *Harper's Magazine*, February 1949.

By the 1960s, most of those considering themselves highbrow were settling comfortably into academe, and other issues—Vietnam, civil rights, personal liberation—dominated public dialogue. Gone were the many generalists, people whom the social critic Russell Jacoby called "public intellectuals," who had previously set cultural standards.

During the early 1960s, the federal government stepped into this perceived cultural vacuum by funding public radio and television in the form of the Public Broadcasting Service (PBS), along with support for the NATIONAL ENDOWMENT FOR THE ARTS (NEA) and the NATIONAL ENDOWMENT FOR THE HUMANITIES (NEH). But these idealistic efforts failed to generate widespread lifting of Americans' general cultural level. To compete with commercial media, PBS had to appeal to the overwhelming middlebrow majority. Denounced and defunded when it attempted to foster avant-garde art, the NEA retreated to funding safely middlebrow opera, theater, music, and art. The NEH escaped criticism by sheltering most of its grants behind the walls of academe.

As the twentieth century was ending, the brow exercise abated in all but two surprisingly diverse nodes within the cultural spectrum: newspapers and the academic world. The two connect when journalists consult professors to learn the deeper meaning of such lowbrow fare as a remake of the 1968 film, *Planet of the Apes*. Objectively, the journalist dwells squarely in middlebrowland, a reasonably literate writer describing assorted lowbrow happenings: car thefts, politicians' poses, presidential foibles, felonies and misdemeanors, weddings, home runs, and bicycle races. By contrast, the academic strives for highbrow status by producing a respectable fifty-three pages (and eighty-four footnotes) obsessing on whether it is "all right" to enjoy reading the nineteenth-century middlebrow novelist Anthony Trollope. Ground between these two tectonic cultural plates, middlebrow gets pummeled, shrunk, and stretched.

Meanwhile, middlebrow culture has penetrated deeply into highbrow culture; only a determined highbrow remnant shelters in small magazines and on the margins of academe. Postmodernism has downgraded elitist high-culture values such as quality, beauty, truth, and authenticity in favor of democratic values that privilege multiculturalism, relevance, and equal opportunity. Speeding the decline is "camp," the conscious effort to bring a cynical smile to the consumer, who understands that the work before him is a mockery of something serious.

The Internet presents a growing obstacle to any individual, institution, or medium attempting to influence the public's cultural tastes. It is giving voices to millions of individuals, and provides a platform for every imaginable cultural offering, but its sheer size and diversity hinder formation of any coherent cultural standards. As a medium, it offers equal opportunity to purveyors of pornography, airline tickets, or medieval manuscripts. With easy access to myriad offerings of uncertain caliber, Internet users are challenged to develop their own cultural standards, whether high, low, or that comfortable old friend: middlebrow.

BIBLIOGRAPHY

Bloom, Allan. *The Closing of the American Mind*. New York: Simon and Schuster, 1987.

Fussell, Paul. *Class*. New York: Summit, 1983.

Greenberg, Clement. "Avant Garde and Kitsch." *Partisan Review* 6 (Fall 1939): 34–49.

Jacoby, Russell. *The Last Intellectuals: American Culture in the Age of Academe*. Rev. ed. New York: Basic Books, 2000.

Levine, Lawrence. *Highbrow/Lowbrow: The Emergence of Cultural Hierarchy in America*. Cambridge, Mass.: Harvard University, 1988.

Lynes, Russell. *The Tastemakers*. New York: Harper, 1954.

Macdonald, Dwight. *Against the American Grain*. New York: Random House, 1962.

Rubin, Joan Shelley. *The Making of Middlebrow Culture*. Chapel Hill: University of North Carolina, 1992.

Alice Goldfarb Marquis

See also **New York Intellectuals**.

MIDDLE-OF-THE-ROAD POPULISTS,

the name given during the 1896 presidential campaign to those members of the People's (Populist) Party who objected to fusion with the Democrats and who insisted that the party should "keep in the middle of the road." At their national convention in Saint Louis, they were unable to prevent the party from accepting the Democratic candidate, William Jennings Bryan, as its candidate for president, but they forced the convention to nominate a Populist, Thomas E. Watson of Georgia, for vice president. After 1896 the Middle-of-the-Road Populists formed a separate organization, which endured feebly for a dozen years.

BIBLIOGRAPHY

Goodwyn, Lawrence. *The Populist Moment: A Short History of the Agrarian Revolt in America.* New York: Oxford University Press, 1978.

Hicks, John D. *The Populist Revolt: A History of the Farmers' Alliance and the People's Party.* Lincoln: University of Nebraska Press, 1959.

John D. Hicks / A. G.

See also **Conventions, Party Nominating; Democratic Party; Populism.**

MIDNIGHT JUDGES refers to the judicial appointments made by President John Adams just before he was succeeded by President Thomas Jefferson. Adams saw the appointments as a way to preserve Federalist influence in the federal government during the Jeffersonian tenure. Congress, dominated in the next session by Jeffersonians, reconstructed the inferior courts and legislated most of the midnight judges out of their commissions. In the case of a justice of the peace for the District of Columbia, the delivery of his commission was refused. This act led to the famous Supreme Court case of *MARBURY V. MADISON.*

BIBLIOGRAPHY

Brown, Ralph Adams. *The Presidency of John Adams.* Lawrence: University Press of Kansas, 1975.

Cunningham, Noble E., Jr. *The Process of Government under Jefferson.* Princeton, N.J.: Princeton University Press, 1978.

William S. Carpenter / A. G.

See also **Federalist Party; Jeffersonian Democracy; Judiciary Act of 1801.**

MIDWAY, BATTLE OF (4–6 June 1942), a major engagement of aircraft carriers that reversed Japan's initial tactical successes in the Pacific during World War II. After ravaging the U.S. Battle Fleet at Pearl Harbor, the Japanese steamed unimpeded across the western Pacific, their progress delayed only briefly by the indecisive Battle of the Coral Sea (3–8 May 1942). Adm. Isoroku Yamamoto, commander of Japan's Combined Fleet, resolved to take Midway Island and force Adm. Chester W. Nimitz, commander of the U.S. Pacific Fleet, to commit his weakened forces to a final clash at sea.

At Nimitz's disposal were the carriers *Enterprise* and *Hornet* and their support ships under Rear Adm. Raymond A. Spruance, and a task force built around the carrier *Yorktown.* In overall sea command was Rear Adm. Frank J. Fletcher, who flew his flag from the *Yorktown.*

Late in May, Yamamoto's great fleet of 185 battleships, carriers, cruisers, destroyers, submarines, and auxiliary vessels steamed eastward from various Japanese bases, while a diversionary assault fleet steamed toward the Aleutians in a bid to draw the Americans away from the Midway area. Yamamoto planned to shatter Midway's

Battle of Midway. Japanese planes attack the USS *Yorktown,* which was subsequently torpedoed—but by then American dive-bombers had destroyed four Japanese aircraft carriers, effectively putting U.S. forces on the long road to victory in the Pacific. NATIONAL ARCHIVES AND RECORDS ADMINISTRATION

defenses with aircraft from the carriers *Akagi, Kaga, Hiryu,* and *Soryu* under Vice Adm. Chuichi Nagumo and clear the way for an invasion force of some 5,000 troops. Yamamoto steamed toward Midway, convinced through intelligence reports that there were no American carriers in the area of Midway.

Nimitz anticipated Yamamoto's battle plans precisely. He sent a few warships northward to cover the Aleutians, stationed his three carriers 350 miles northeast of Midway, and waited. On 3 June the Japanese mounted their deceptive strike at the Aleutians, and on 4 June the first wave of Japanese aircraft hit Midway. Shortly after 7 A.M., Spruance launched his air strike on the zigzagging Japanese fleet. Meanwhile, the flight leader of the returning Japanese air strike radioed Nagumo that one more bombing attack on Midway was needed. Accordingly, the Japanese admiral ordered his torpedo-laden reserve aircraft to re-arm with bombs for another strike at the island. This was the first fatal decision of the battle. When a scout plane sighted the U.S. naval force, Nagumo halted the re-arming operation and ordered part of his second wave to attack the American ships with torpedoes, the rest to hit Midway again with bombs. However, before launching these attacks, he decided to recover the planes of his returning first Midway strike. This was his second fatal decision. Shortly after recovery was made, Nagumo had to dodge U.S. torpedo attacks; the torpedo aircraft were massacred, but behind them came U.S. dive-bombers that struck the Japanese carriers while their flight decks were loaded with fueled and armed aircraft. The *Akagi, Kaga, Soryu,* and *Hiryu* burst into flame and sank with their planes.

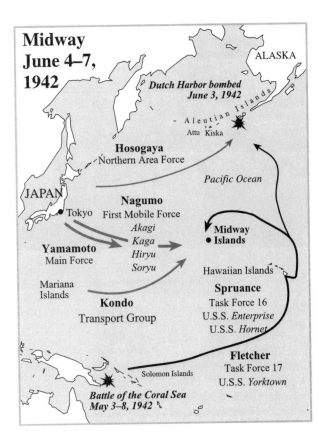

Midway June 4–7, 1942

ALASKA

Dutch Harbor bombed June 3, 1942

Aleutian Islands

Attu Kiska

Hosogaya ~Northern Area Force

Pacific Ocean

JAPAN

Tokyo

Nagumo First Mobile Force

Akagi
Kaga
Hiryu
Soryu

• Midway • Islands

Hawaiian Islands

Yamamoto Main Force

Mariana Islands

Kondo Transport Group

Spruance Task Force 16
U.S.S. *Enterprise*
U.S.S. *Hornet*

Fletcher Task Force 17
U.S.S. *Yorktown*

Solomon Islands

Battle of the Coral Sea May 3–8, 1942

MIDWAY ISLANDS, located 1,200 miles northwest of Honolulu, are part of a coral atoll containing two islands (Sand and Eastern), with a total area of about two square miles. Discovered in 1859, they were annexed by the United States in 1867. Attacked by the Japanese in WORLD WAR II, Midway was the scene of a naval aircraft battle (June 1942) that resulted in a severe defeat for Japan. By checking the Japanese advance toward Hawaii, the battle proved to be one of the decisive American victories of the war. Since World War II, the islands have served as a naval and air base and as a stopover point for commercial transpacific flights.

Seddie Cogswell / A. G.

See also **Aircraft Carriers and Naval Aircraft; Midway, Battle of; Navy, Department of the; World War II, Navy in.**

MIDWEST is a region extending north and west from the Ohio River to just west of the Mississippi River and includes the states of Ohio, Indiana, Illinois, Iowa, Michigan, Minnesota, and Wisconsin. The region is often referred to as the heartland of America. It was originally home to numerous Native American groups who had a mixed economy of hunting, fishing, and agriculture. The region included three of North America's predominate biomes, that is, conifer forest, deciduous forest, and prairie. The climate is typical of midcontinental positions. Winters and summers are characterized by extremes in temperature and precipitation.

The land east of the Mississippi was acquired from the British as part of the Treaty of Paris in 1783 and was designated the Northwest Territory. The land west of the Mississippi was acquired in the Louisiana Purchase of 1803. The region's geography and identity are rooted in its creation in the Land Ordinance of 1785, which created the orderly survey of land, and the Northwest Ordinance of 1787, which established a pattern of government for the new territory. These two federal acts laid the groundwork for rapid and orderly settlement in the nineteenth century.

The region was a productive fur trade area for over two hundred years. The timber industry moved west out of Maine and New England early in the nineteenth century. The rich and diverse forests of the region have made this a continuing and profitable industry. Early timber harvesting focused on pine, particularly white pine. As pine lands were exhausted the timber industry turned to hardwoods and pulpwood production. Settlers originally attempted to farm the cutover lands but found that conditions were not conducive to commodity agriculture. Second- and third-growth forests came to cover the land, and timber production and recreational uses came to predominate in the northern reaches of the Midwest.

Yankees, Pennsylvanians, and northern Europeans came throughout the nineteenth century. Agricultural settlement stretched out along the rivers first, then fol-

On 5 June, Yamamoto canceled the invasion of Midway. Spruance pressed further his attack on the retreating Japanese fleet and sank the cruiser *Mikuma*. The American naval triumph was flawed when a lurking Japanese submarine torpedoed the listing and vulnerable *Yorktown*, along with a lone ministering destroyer. On 7 June, the *Yorktown* succumbed to its many wounds and the Battle of Midway was over. The U.S. Navy, having inflicted enormous and irreparable damage on a vastly superior fleet, effectively turned the tide of the naval war in the Pacific.

BIBLIOGRAPHY

Levite, Ariel. *Intelligence and Strategic Surprises.* New York: Columbia University Press, 1987.

Lord, Walter. *Incredible Victory.* New York: Harper and Row, 1967; 1969; Short Hills, N.J.: Burford Books, 1997.

Morison, Samuel Eliot. *History of United States Naval Operations in World War II, Vol. 4: Coral Sea, Midway and Submarine Actions.* Edison, N.J.: Castle Books, 2001.

Prange, Gordon W., Donald M. Goldstein, and Katherine V. Dillon. *Miracle at Midway.* New York: McGraw-Hill, 1982; Norwalk, Conn.: Easton Press, 1990.

Spectre, Ronald H. *Eagle Against the Sun: The American War with Japan.* New York: Vintage Books, 1985.

Thaddeus V. Tuleja / A. R.

See also **Coral Sea, Battle of the; Navy, United States; Pearl Harbor; World War II, Navy in.**

lowed the railroad into the interior of the tall grass prairie. Commodity agricultural production, primarily grains and livestock, dominated the region from the start. Farming population rose dramatically until the early twentieth century but made a steady decline as mechanization increased. The rural character of the region is evident in the farms and small towns that dot the landscape.

Manufacturing and heavy industry also became prevalent in the region, particularly along major waterways and south of the Great Lakes. Early on waterpower and access to water transportation figured heavily in this development. The dramatic increase in iron mining in Michigan and Minnesota also contributed to development. Industrial development and mining attracted new immigrants in the first half of the twentieth century. African Americans fled the South during this period and were attracted to the Midwest by industrial jobs and greater freedom from "Jim Crow." Eastern Europeans also immigrated to work in the region's industrial and mining operations. Like other places across the United States, the region became home to a multitude of ethnic groups and immigrants from around the world.

While the region was originally blanketed by mixed forests and prairies, this is no longer the case. Forests have been cleared, the prairie has been plowed, and rivers have been dredged and straightened for commercial barge traffic. Agriculture, the timber industry, and heavy manufacturing have all left an indelible mark on the land.

BIBLIOGRAPHY

Cayton, Andrew R. L., and Peter S. Onuf. *The Midwest and the Nation: Rethinking the History of the Region.* Bloomington: Indiana University Press, 1990.

Polly Fry

See also **Illinois; Indiana; Iowa; Michigan; Minnesota; Ohio; Wisconsin.**

MIGRATION, AFRICAN AMERICAN.

The landing of Africans in America began nearly five hundred years ago. Between the fifteenth and nineteenth centuries, eight to twelve million Africans were transported to New World slave plantations via the transatlantic SLAVE TRADE in one of the largest forced migrations in history. About 6 percent (600,000 to 1 million) of the Africans sold into slavery were brought to the territory of the present United States. Since the slave trade, black people in America have continued to migrate in larger numbers, some self-initiated and some coerced.

The first English-speaking Africans arrived in Jamestown, Virginia, in 1619. Initially, British colonists and Africans coexisted, but developments in colonial America precipitated the enslavement of black people. Slavery spread, particularly in the South, and between the mid-1600s and 1865, most Africans in America were treated as chattel and denied the most basic of human rights.

After 1865, with slavery abolished, white supremacy continued to reign in the South. As Reconstruction collapsed, the treatment of black people in the region reached its nadir. Ninety-two percent of the black people in America lived in the South in 1865, and 95 percent of them were poor, unschooled, abused, and exploited rural farmers. They were denied social equality, land, education, and voting rights. Racist "social clubs" such as the KU KLUX KLAN terrorized anyone who challenged this system. These vicious and unequal circumstances prompted black people to search for a better life and vote "with their feet" against their mistreatment.

The first major black migration within the United States grew out of this quest. In May 1879, black leaders from fourteen states gathered in Nashville, Tennessee, and proclaimed that "colored people should emigrate to those states and territories where they can enjoy all the rights which are guaranteed by the laws and Constitution of the United States." Black leaders such as Benjamin "Pap" Singleton and Ida B. Wells-Barnett supported the declaration and called upon their supporters to do so as well. As a result, thousands of black people "quit the South" and headed north and west. Between 1865 and 1880, forty thousand black people moved to Kansas. The "Exodusters," as they became known, forged black towns like Nicodemus and Morton City.

African Americans also migrated to Arizona, California, Oklahoma, and Washington. By 1880, they had settled in this region as servants, farmers, fur trappers, entrepreneurs, and teachers, weaving themselves into the fabric of post–Civil War western communities. By 1900, some ten thousand black people had also migrated to the high plains, while others drove cattle up the Chisholm Trail or served on remote army outposts.

African Americans continued to migrate to the North and West in smaller numbers between 1900 and 1910. But World War I spurred the largest black migration in American history as wartime industrial needs increased the demand for labor. Between 1910 and 1940, some 1.75 million black people left the South and moved northward. Between 1910 and 1920 black populations expanded in Philadelphia (58 percent), New York (60 percent), Chicago (148 percent), and Detroit (611 percent). Most of the migrants were young people born during the 1880s and 1890s. Nevertheless, despite the magnitude of the "Great Migration," most African Americans remained in the South. Many simply migrated from the rural to the urban South.

During the 1910s, the southern economy buckled under the weight of several natural disasters. Between 1915 and 1916, floods ravished agriculture in Mississippi and Alabama, and the BOLL WEEVIL devastated southern crops. These events, coupled with the poverty and hopelessness associated with sharecropping, prompted many African Americans to leave southern agricultural regions. Continued racial discrimination and white supremacy also prompted African Americans to leave. Although

"The Migration Gained Momentum." Many southern African Americans—including the parents of the painter Jacob Lawrence—"voted with their feet" against poverty, discrimination, and racial violence, moving North in search of better conditions and jobs in northern industries. This painting is part of Lawrence's sixty-painting series, *The Migration of the Negro* (1941), which tells the story of African American migration during and after World War I. © THE MUSEUM OF MODERN ART black people encountered discrimination in the North and West, they found greater access to the ballot, better public schools, access to public accommodation, and justice in the courts.

Many migrants endeavored to help themselves and "uplift the race" in the North and West by joining organizations such as the NATIONAL ASSOCIATION FOR THE ADVANCEMENT OF COLORED PEOPLE and the NATIONAL ASSOCIATION OF COLORED WOMEN. African Americans often allied themselves with progressive whites in the NATIONAL URBAN LEAGUE, the Congress of Industrial Organizations, and the Communist Party. One of the most effective activist tactics was the "Don't Buy Where You Can't Work" campaign, which increased the number of blacks in white-collar jobs. Black migrants helped facilitate the flowering of African American art, literature, and music during the Harlem and Chicago Renaissances. Some became political leaders, while others found success in business. The promise of freedom and democracy in the North and West, however, was illusory: relocation was hard on African American families; migrants were often separated from their relatives while they searched for jobs and housing; and extended families were often squeezed into small living quarters. Families suffered economically, because black men rarely secured positions as skilled workers, and black women had even fewer opportunities for employment.

Discrimination, housing shortages, the movement of jobs and infrastructure to suburbs, the breakdown of family structures, crime, and the proliferation of drugs became serious and complex issues for African American communities. Moreover, the influx of large numbers of African Americans into northern and western cities often kindled the flames of white racism. The Civil Rights and BLACK POWER movements of the 1950s, 1960s, and 1970s, fought prejudice and racial inequality. Discrimination and antagonism continued throughout the remainder of the twentieth century as race riots rocked major cities, sparked by the apathy and rancor of whites and by the indignation and hopelessness of blacks.

As the twentieth century ended, African Americans continued to migrate, in large numbers, in search of opportunity. They now moved primarily to western cities and back to the South. After 1970 the number of new immigrants from Africa also increased dramatically to swell the numbers of those seeking freedom and democracy.

BIBLIOGRAPHY

Gomez, Michael Angelo. *Exchanging Our Country Marks: The Transition of African Identities in the Colonial and Antebellum South.* Chapel Hill: University of North Carolina Press, 1998.

Hunter, Tera W. *To 'Joy My Freedom: Southern Black Women's Lives and the Labors after the Civil War.* Cambridge, Mass.: Harvard University Press, 1997.

Painter, Nell Irvin. *Exodusters: Black Migration to Kansas after Reconstruction.* Revised, Lawrence: University Press of Kansas, 1986.

Taylor, Quintard. *In Search of the Racial Frontier: African Americans in the American West, 1528–1990.* New York: Norton, 1998.

Trotter, Joe William, Jr., ed. *The Great Migration in Historical Perspective: New Dimensions of Race, Class, and Gender.* Bloomington: Indiana University Press, 1991.

Matthew Whitaker

See also **African Americans; Harlem Renaissance; Sharecroppers; Suffrage: African American Suffrage.**

MIGRATION, INTERNAL, is the habit of the American people, whom foreign observers have described as restless migrants for at least the past three centuries.

The Western Frontier, Seventeenth Century to Nineteenth Century

From the times of the earliest European settlements to 1890, when the U.S. Census Bureau declared the frontier closed, a western-moving edge of newly available land triggered waves of migratory European-descended Americans in pursuit.

The people who participated in these successive migrations usually traveled in groups linked by kinship, business interests, or geographic proximity in their former communities. Most were motivated by opportunities for economic gain, while a minority, such as the Shakers and the Mormons, sought to live out their religious and social ideals in isolated communities of their own devising. Though they set out with widely varying assets, most came from the middle ranges of the economic spectrum. The most prosperous members of the populace "back home" would have had little reason to leave their comfortable circumstances, and the poorest members would not have had the means to purchase the supplies and equipment for the journey. At the same time European Americans were moving in, Indians migrated out. From pre–Revolutionary War (1775–1783) days, when "the west" lay just beyond the eastern seaboard, to the settlement of the Great Plains in the 1870s, European Americans first had to contend with the removal of Indians from their ancestral lands. Indians were considered little more than dangerous obstacles in the path of progress, and the story of their forced migrations is a shameful one.

Generally, settlers moved west from adjacent areas in the East. The fledgling U.S. government had offered veterans of the Revolutionary War land west of the Alleghenies in lieu of wages. With the resolution of the original states' conflicting land claims and the organization of the Northwest Territory in 1787, settlers poured into the Ohio River valley. Southerners chose lands closer to the Ohio River, while New Englanders headed almost due west for the northern sections of Ohio and, later, Indiana and Illinois. Many were farmers fleeing overworked soil and high land prices at home; plantation-style agriculture

371

"Emigrant-Car." Since the post–Revolutionary War days, when soldiers were given land west of the Allegheny Mountains in lieu of pay, Americans pushed the boundaries of their new country and continually moved into new areas, usually to the west. The engraving by Jim Murphy called "Across America on an Emigrant Train" shows people trying to sleep on a crowded "emigrant-car" of a train taking them to a new life. © Denver Public Library

also encroached on small landholders in the South, urging them north. At this time, the first settlers in an area were often squatters, who cleared some land, put up a simple shelter, and then sold it as "improved" to someone else—often a wealthy land speculator—before moving on to the next wilderness edge, where they would repeat the process.

Though the routes they took (the Wilderness Road and Zane's Trace, for example) into the Ohio country were called roads, they were little more than rough trails, prohibiting overland transport in anything other than small carts. As the decades from 1800 progressed, roads improved, but any part of the journey in which water-borne transport was unavailable must have been one of considerable hardship. The Louisiana Purchase (1803) incorporated French settlements along the Mississippi and Missouri watersheds into the United States at this time.

Transportation improvements made migration easier when an all-water route opened up from the East Coast to the Great Lakes states. The Erie Canal opened in 1825, making it possible to float from the Hudson River to Buffalo in western New York. From there, ships carried passengers on to Detroit.

Waves of non-English-speaking newcomers from Europe joined the national migration and, by 1850, the United States had been settled all the way to the Mississippi. Germans were the most plentiful; many established enclaves in burgeoning cities such as Cincinnati, Milwaukee, and St. Louis, while others came with large extended families, even villages, to settle the rural Midwest. By midcentury, railroads had supplanted canals and the "frontier" lay along the Pacific coast, while the Great Plains and Rocky Mountains were still hostile territory inhabited by Indians. Though a mass overland migration (the Oregon Trail) to Oregon's Willamette Valley began in 1843, European Americans had already sailed around the tip of South America to settle in the Spanish-dominated area that now comprises California. Gold lured men to the Southwest, too, on the first of many gold rushes beginning in 1848. Irish and Chinese immigrants made a pool of potential laborers for the hard, dangerous, low-paying jobs on the new railroads surging west. The coming of the railroad (the Transcontinental Railroad was completed in 1869) established a pattern that would be repeated, not just across the prairies of the Great Plains, but in cities as well. Typically, a company would obtain large quantities of land at reasonable rates for the railroad right-of-way. The railroad would then sell the surplus land at a higher price, while enticing farmers to settle along these ready-made routes to markets back east.

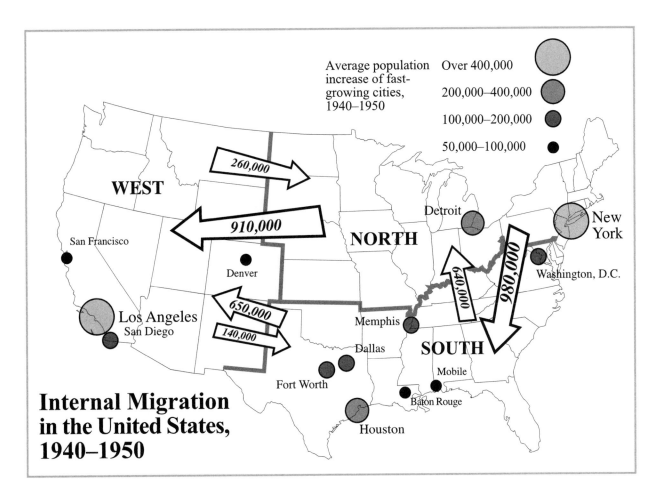

Average population
increase of fast-
growing cities,
1940–1950

Over 400,000

200,000–400,000

100,000–200,000

50,000–100,000

260,000

WEST

910,000

NORTH

San Francisco

Denver

Los Angeles
San Diego

650,000

140,000

Memphis

Dallas

Fort Worth

Detroit

New York

Washington, D.C.

980,000

640,000

SOUTH

Mobile

Baton Rouge

Houston

**Internal Migration
in the United States,
1940–1950**

Migration to the Cities

While some nineteenth-century Americans sought the wide open spaces of the frontier, others migrated to the growing urban centers. In America's largest eighteenth-century cities—Charleston, Philadelphia, New York, and Boston—as in Europe, the most desirable place to live was the center of the city. Whatever amenities, such as sewers, a city had to offer were most likely to be centrally located, and most people walked to work. Nasty trades such as slaughterhouses and tanneries located on the fringes, as did the workers who toiled there. The elite lived in large townhouses in proximity to less affluent tradesmen and artisans. However, the majority of people lived in rural areas; in 1790 only 5.1 percent of the population lived in cities.

The industrial revolution reversed that trend. New jobs in industries spawned by steam power brought migrants into the cities from played-out farms and accommodated the flood of foreign immigrants too poor to travel far from their port of arrival. By 1890, one-third of all Americans lived in cities, but two-thirds of all immigrants did. African Americans, too, poured into northern cities from the rural South. In the years since 1920, the black population has changed from being almost entirely rural to more than 90 percent urban.

From Urban to Suburban

The same technological advances that built the great cities also created an escape route. By the 1870s cities offered street lighting, municipal water, and police and fire services, but many white Protestants increasingly viewed cities as centers of crime, immorality, and disease as non-English-speaking immigrants crowded into dangerously run-down housing, and factories spread noise and pollution.

Property outside the central city became more attractive as transportation to and from work became more reliable. At midcentury a few suburbs, such as Lewellyn Park, New Jersey, and Riverside, Illinois, designed specifically for rich businessmen and their families, appeared outside New York, Chicago, and other major cities. These imitated the Romantic ideal of an uncorrupted retreat in the country with winding, irregular roads and large lots that followed the contours of the land.

In the years following the Civil War (1861–1865), commuter railroads were built across the nation, allowing workers to live miles away from their jobs in the central cities. Philadelphia's "Main Line" suburbs such as Swarthmore, Villanova, Radnor, and Stratford date from this era. In the 1860s and 1870s the Pennsylvania Railroad decided it would be easier to improve its line to Pittsburgh by purchasing outright the farms in its way. Like the rail companies out west, the railroad kept the rights-of-way and sold the rest of the land to developers, who found ready customers for private homes located within walking distance of the new commuter lines. At first, only the affluent could afford the daily round-trip fares, but soon satellite neighborhoods and even whole suburbs sprang up to accommodate the low-wage labor pool that served richer suburbanites.

Suburbanization accelerated in the twentieth century, propelled by the advances of the trolley system and later the automobile. Some of the migration to the suburbs resulted from racial and cultural insecurities; "white flight," the exodus of white families from cities in the wake of school desegregation, began in the mid-1950s. As of 2002, many suburbanites no longer commuted into the city at all, as corporate headquarters have followed them beyond the city's edge. In 1950, 23 percent of the population lived in suburbs; in 1998, 50 percent lived there.

The suburban ideal—owning a private dwelling and surrounding land—taps into a longstanding American idea that land ownership means wealth. Whether they came as victims of the Scottish land clearances of the eighteenth century or as refugees from the turmoil of central Europe in the twentieth, few European American immigrants owned land in their homelands. For three centuries Americans have migrated to the locations where that ideal could become a reality. Home ownership still equals security in American culture.

Sun Belt Migration

Since 1960 Americans have migrated south and west to the band of states known as the Sun Belt, following jobs, a warmer climate, and sometimes a lower cost of living. Hundreds of thousands of retirees have settled there as well. Florida has always had a large retired population, but from 1990 to 1998, Nevada's over-65 population jumped 55 percent, while Arizona's gained 29 percent, Utah's grew by 22 percent, and the elderly in Colorado and New Mexico increased by 21 percent.

Migrant Workers

The United States also hosts a population of migrant agricultural workers who follow the harvest. Nine out of ten of these workers are foreign born; it is estimated that about half do not have authorization to work in the United States.

BIBLIOGRAPHY

Billington, Ray Allen, and Martin Ridge. *Westward Expansion: A History of the American Frontier.* 5th ed. New York: Macmillan, 1982.

Fischer, David Hackett. *Albion's Seed: Four British Folkways in America.* New York: Oxford University Press, 1989.

Flanders, Stephen A. *The Atlas of American Migration.* New York: Facts On File, 1998.

Jackson, Kenneth T. *Crabgrass Frontier: The Suburbanization of the United States.* New York: Oxford University Press, 1985.

Tanner, Helen Hornbeck, ed. *The Settling of North America: The Atlas of the Great Migrations in North America from the Ice Age to the Present.* New York: Macmillan, 1995.

Jennifer Maier

See also **Suburbanization; Sun Belt; Wagon Trains; Westward Migration.**

MILITARY ACADEMY. During his presidency, George Washington pushed Congress to create a military academy for professional military training of promising youths. In 1794 Congress established a School for Artillerists and Engineers at West Point, New York, but it was a training school, not a professional one. The establishment of a true military academy did not occur until 1802, when President Thomas Jefferson provided for a formal military academy at West Point. Jonathan Williams was the first superintendent (1801–1803, 1805–1812), followed by Joseph G. Swift (1812–1814) and Alden Partridge (1815–1817).

The academy initially languished for lack of congressional support. When the WAR OF 1812 began, the academy existed only on paper. Spurred to action, Congress passed an act on 29 April 1812 providing for a reorganization, a maximum of 250 cadets, and age and mental requirements for admission. Not until Major Sylvanus Thayer took over as superintendent on 28 July 1817 did the academy begin truly to fulfill the purposes envisioned by its founders. Thayer, known as the father of the military academy, was superintendent for sixteen years (1817–1833). He expanded the curriculum, introduced a new system of order, organization, and discipline, and left a lasting mark on the academy.

The U.S. Military Academy was for many years the only engineering school in the country, and its graduates, working both as civil and military engineers, were largely responsible for planning and directing the building of major canals, roads, and railroads in the period before the CIVIL WAR. The MEXICAN-AMERICAN WAR meanwhile proved the value of West Point education in the training of army officers; academy graduates in the middle and lower officer ranks were largely responsible for the new professionalism demonstrated by the U.S. Army in Mexico. In the Civil War, West Point graduates dominated the higher positions on both sides, furnishing about 150 Confederate and 300 Union generals.

After the Civil War, with the rise of civilian engineering schools, the Military Academy lost its preeminent position in this field and, with appropriate curriculum changes, became an institution for training officers of all branches of the army. An act of Congress on 13 July 1866 transferred supervision from the Corps of Engineers to the War Department. From 1865 to 1914, most academy graduates pursued military careers, and in WORLD WAR I they nearly monopolized the higher ranks. During WORLD WAR II, graduates of the RESERVE OFFICERS' TRAINING CORPS (ROTC) claimed an increasing place in the sun, though 70 percent of full generals and 65 percent of all lieutenant generals were graduates of West Point.

After each of the world wars there were extensive curriculum changes to keep abreast of new developments in military art and technology. After World War II there was a progressive increase in the use of modern technology in the cadet's education. The academy introduced electives and fields of concentration. In 1975 the academy began admitting women, who by the 1990s made up more than 10 percent of the school's cadets. Enrollment has grown progressively from 10 students in 1802 and 250 in 1812 to 1,960 in 1935, 2,496 in 1942, and 4,417 in 1975. In the 1990s, enrollment was capped at roughly 4,000, but the military academy has seen a growing number of applicants interested in the discipline of army training. The United States Military Academy will celebrate its bicentennial in 2002.

BIBLIOGRAPHY

Ambrose, Stephen E. *Duty, Honor, Country: A History of West Point.* Baltimore: Johns Hopkins University Press, 1966.

Ellis, Joseph J. *School for Soldiers: West Point and the Profession of Arms.* New York: Oxford University Press, 1974.

Franke, Volker. *Preparing for Peace: Military Identity, Value Orientations, and Professional Military Education.* Westport, Conn: Praeger, 1999.

Ruggero, Ed. *Duty First: West Point and the Making of American Leaders.* New York: HarperCollins, 2001.

Robert W. Coakley / H. S.

See also **Air Force Academy; Army, United States; Engineering Education; Engineers, Corps of; Naval Academy.**

MILITARY BASE CLOSINGS. By the late 1980s the United States had approximately 3,800 military installations within its borders, including army forts, navy and air force bases, and federally owned supply depots and building and repair facilities. Many of these had been established less to meet military needs than as a matter of national politics, because members of Congress regarded the establishment of a military base within their state or district as a way of attracting federal money and jobs, and a way of creating additional employment for those who provided services for the base's population.

In the late 1980s this protective attitude toward bases started to change. The conclusion of the Cold War, with the collapse of both the Warsaw Pact and the Soviet Union, ended a major threat to U.S. national security. A mounting federal budget deficit and a desire to redirect federal spending into domestic programs reinforced arguments favoring cuts in national defense spending. As a consequence, military base closings began, along with reductions in military personnel and weapons. Congress chose neither to allow the president or the Department of Defense to decide which bases to close nor to make such decisions itself. Instead, it voted in 1988 to create an independent, bipartisan advisory commission to the Pentagon to propose lists of bases for closure. The secretary of defense would announce the proposed list, and, provided Congress did not reject it within forty-five legislative days, the schedule for closings would become official. Congress established and authorized the actions of three subsequent defense base closure and realignment commissions in 1991, 1993, and 1995. While some bases ceased their operations entirely, others actually grew through realignment or the shifting of personnel and functions among installations.

In 1989 Secretary of Defense Frank Carlucci announced, and Congress accepted, the first commission's list. This list targeted eighty-six bases for closure, five for partial closure, and fifty-four for realignment. The bases had at least four years advance notice, except for Pease Air Force Base in New Hampshire, which closed in 1991. In 1990, Secretary of Defense Richard Cheney announced a second list of proposed base closings without relying on a commission. This caused an outcry in Congress, where the Democratic majority believed that the list contained too many bases in states or districts represented by Democrats. The chair of the House Armed Services Committee, Les Aspin of Wisconsin, recommended that a second commission propose another list, and in October 1990 Congress approved the creation of such a commission. In 1991 the commission presented its list, which called for the closure of thirty-four bases and the realignment of another forty-eight. Congress accepted these recommendations and stated that the secretary of defense must consider closing overseas bases as well.

Even though Congress had created the commission format, some senators and representatives were concerned about the impact of these closures on their particular state and local economies. Legislators from the Philadelphia area who opposed the closing of that city's naval shipyard, for example, turned to the federal courts to determine whether base closure decisions should be subject to judicial review. In May 1994, the Supreme Court unanimously ruled against this idea.

The 1993 commission faced similar difficulties. Concerned about the loss of jobs and the economic impact of base closures on communities and states, Congress closely scrutinized the proposed list. Aspin, now secretary of defense, rebutted allegations that some of the closings were politically motivated. The third list affected 175 military installations, with some thirty major U.S. bases to be closed, twelve other major bases subject to realignment, and additional smaller bases being closed, realigned, or relocated. Congress accepted the list in 1993. In June 1995, the commission recommended closing seventy-nine bases and realigning twenty-six others. Although President Bill Clinton expressed strong concern about the economic impact of base closings in Texas and California, he approved the recommendations in July. Later that month, the House National Security Committee rejected legislation that, if accepted, would have overturned the recommendations.

Base closings in themselves did not substantially reduce the annual defense budget. For example, closures announced in 1991 would save about $1.5 billion annually after 1997, and the 1993 list would save about $2.3 billion annually after 1999. It was more difficult to estimate the effects of base closings on local economies. States such as California, with more than 300,000 people employed at sixty-seven bases in 1991, felt the loss of jobs and income disproportionately. Including all base closures through the 1995 recommendations, Senator Diane Feinstein of California estimated that 108,900 Californians employed at these bases would lose their jobs. Evidence suggested, however, that base closings did not affect communities as seriously as layoffs in the defense industry because military bases tended not to be as integrated into local economies as defense manufacturing concerns. Many communities even hoped to benefit from base closings by acquiring the land once occupied by bases, although federal regulations often slowed up this process. A greater problem in this regard was perhaps the serious environmental hazards at military installations that the extensive storage of solvents, fuels, and explosives posed. In the 1990s the cleanup of such hazards depended on the availability of federal funding. President George W. Bush's administration proposed a round of base closings in 2001 that would have reduced active-duty military by another 60,000 persons, only a modest decrease compared to the decline in active-duty personnel of 600,000 since the Berlin Wall fell in 1989. However, these plans were scuttled by the September 2001 terrorist attack on the World Trade Center and Pentagon, which strengthened the hand of those hoping to slow the pace of post–Cold War demobilization. In December 2001 Congress agreed to delay any further consideration of base closings and realignments until 2005.

BIBLIOGRAPHY

Mayer, Andrew C., and George H. Siehl. *Military Base Closures: Issues for the 104th Congress.* Washington, D.C.: Penny Hill Press, 1995.

U.S. Congress, Office of Technology Assessment. *After the Cold War: Living with Lower Defense Spending.* OTA-ITE-524. Washington, D.C.: U.S. Government Printing Office, 1992.

Wallensteen, Peter, ed. *Experiences in Disarmament: On Conversion of Military Industry and Closing of Military Bases.* Uppsala, Sweden: Uppsala University, 1978.

Kenneth B. Moss / c. w.

See also **Air Force, United States; Army, United States; Marine Corps, United States; Navy, United States; Unemployment.**

MILITARY-INDUSTRIAL COMPLEX.

The term "military-industrial complex" (MIC) was coined by President Dwight D. Eisenhower in his farewell address of 1961. Great and sustained spending for defense and war, he warned, created power groups that could disastrously harm the nation's future. He was referring to the years after 1950 when Cold War military and related budgets reached as high as 10 percent of the gross national product (GNP). Agitation against the MIC became most intense in the 1960s and 1970s as protest against the Vietnam War peaked. The term began to fade in usage during the 1980s, despite huge increases in the armed forces' budgets under the presidency of Ronald Reagan. Even though at the beginning of the twenty-first century the military continued to be comparatively large and expensive—totaling around 3 percent of the GNP—its size and influence was no longer the matter of great controversy that it was in the past.

MIC Theory

According to MIC theorists, prolonged international conflict after World War II produced high levels of military expenditure, creating powerful domestic interest groups that required a Cold War ideology to safeguard their power and prestige within the state's political and economic structure. These interest groups, which arose among the military services, corporations, high government officials, members of Congress, labor unions, scientists and scholars, and defense societies (private organizations that combine industrialists, financiers, and business people involved in weapons production, acquisition, and the like and members of the armed forces), came to occupy powerful positions within the state. They became mutually supportive, and, on defense-related matters, their influence exceeded that of any existing countervailing coalitions or interests. Theorists differed over whether civilians or the military dominated a MIC or whether they shared power. But most agreed that civilians could match and even surpass those in uniform in their dedication to military creeds. Most scholars pointed out that MIC operations constituted military Keynesianism, a means of stimulating the economy; others went further, proposing defense spending as an industrial policy, albeit a limited and economically distorting one. Some critics of vast and continued spending on the armed forces worried that military professionalism was undermined by focusing inordinate attention on institutional growth and the advancement of careers instead of defending the nation.

Since most MIC theorists regarded Cold War ideology as either false or exaggerated, they maintained that its adherents either deliberately engaged in deception in order to further their own interests or falsely believed themselves to be acting in broader public or national interests—or some combination of the two. Whatever the case, proponents of arms without end, so-called hawks, served to perpetuate Cold War ideological strains. The close connection between the MIC and U.S. Cold War ideology notwithstanding, some MIC theorists maintained that capitalism had no monopoly on defense and war complexes. The former Soviet Union, they argued, had its own complex, and the U.S. and Soviet MICs interacted to perpetuate a mutually advantageous but in fact enormously dangerous and ultimately destructive state of heightened competition.

Opponents of MIC theory insisted that arms spending genuinely reflected, rather than in any way created, national security threats. The armed services and their weapons were essential, they argued, for deterring formidable and aggressive foes. Most analysts, however, believed that an accurate assessment of a MIC rests somewhere between the assessments of proponents and critics of MIC theory. Such a viewpoint asserted that, while national defense spending and the industrial and political interests associated with it can exacerbate tensions between the United States and its adversaries, they do not themselves cause these tensions, nor do they prevent their resolution. It is likely that much of the general population subscribed to this more measured view.

Historical Background

Cold War–era debate over a MIC actually obscured understanding of a critical subject by removing it from its proper historical context. Military spending has created special problems since the nation's origins. Vested interests made it exceptionally difficult to close down, consolidate, or move military and naval bases. Too often, national defense and armed forces' welfare were subordinated to economic and political purposes. These corrupting forces were kept under control principally by limiting—often drastically so—military expenditures during peacetime. Special circumstances began to alter that pattern at the end of the nineteenth century. As the United States began expanding abroad, it built a new navy starting in the 1880s of steel, steam, propeller, armor, and modern ordnance. To build this navy required assembling a production team of political leaders, naval officers, and industrialists. Here are to be found the origins of a MIC. Such teams, which continued to exist at the beginning of the twenty-first century, grew out of the need to apply modern science and technology to weaponry on a continuing basis. Private and public production teams were particularly important in the development and growth of aircraft between the two world wars and aerospace in the post–World War II period. And scientists, of course, were indispensable in nearly all nuclear developments.

During World War I, the United States had to plan its economy to meet the massive and increasingly sophisticated supply demands of the armed services. That reality revealed the country's unique and complicated civil–military relations. Emergency conditions led private interests to combine their power with that of the military in order to influence, and even shape, national defense and war policies. In the absence of a higher civil service system, it fell upon business people, professionals, and others to devise methods of harnessing the economy for war. The ultimate result was the creation of the War Industries Board

(WIB) in 1917. The board was staffed and directed largely by private industrialists serving the public for a token salary, while remaining on the payroll of their private firms. Organizing the supply side of economic mobilization, WIB could function properly only after the demand side, and especially the armed services, were integrated into it. Fearful of and unwilling to accept their dependence upon civilian institutions for the fulfillment of the military mission, the armed services resisted joining WIB. They did so only when threatened with losing control of supply operations entirely. Once industrial and military elements joined their operations in WIB, the board was able to maintain stable economic conditions in a planned wartime economy.

Concerned about the military disruption of future economics of warfare, Congress in 1920 authorized the War Department to plan for procurement and economic mobilization. Carrying out these responsibilities with the Navy Department and under the guidance of industry, business, and finance, the army wrote and submitted for public review a series of industrial mobilization plans, the last and most important of which was published in 1939. Based principally on WIB, this plan outlined how the economy would be organized for World War II.

The economics of World War II, however, became intensely controversial. Interwar developments had anticipated this controversy over the formalized alliance between the military and industrial interests. Throughout the 1920s and 1930s, and culminating in the Senate Special Committee Investigating the Munitions Industry (Nye Committee) in 1934–1936, antiwar critics insisted that modern warfare was creating an "unhealthy alliance" between economic and military groups that threatened both the peace and the country's economic future. During World War II, New Dealers, organized labor, small businesses, consumer advocates, and others constantly challenged the War Production Board (WPB), which, like its predecessors, was dominated by a conservative coalition made up principally of corporations and the military. These challenges met with little success, although they managed to make war mobilization exceptionally tumultuous. Overall, however, conservative mobilization patterns and wartime prosperity severely weakened New Deal reform instincts.

MIC in Operation

Except in the aircraft, shipbuilding, and machine tool industries, businessmen after World War II favored a return to the familiar American pattern of reducing military spending to minimal levels. Only after the administration of Harry Truman (1945–1953) developed its Cold War containment polices did Department of Defense (DOD) budgets, which had been declining steadily since 1945, begin dramatically rising in 1950. In the context of military expenditures running into the hundreds of billions of dollars, there emerged patterns associated with a full-blown MIC: defense firms such as Lockheed Aircraft

Corporation wholly or significantly dependent upon DOD contracts; armed services committed to weapons systems in which military careers are at stake; states like California heavily tied to military spending; "think tanks" such as the Rand Corporation and university research projects funded by the DOD; a high percentage of scientific and engineering talent and research and development dollars devoted to weaponry; industrial executives and military officers circulating among government posts, defense contractors, and related institutions; charges of massive waste, duplication, cost overruns, useless and malfunctioning weapons, some so far as to be dangerous to their users; all while funding for health, education, welfare, and other civilian needs suffered by comparison. Nuclear weapons capable of destroying civilization and creating enormous problems of waste disposal and pollution greatly complicated all MIC problems. So, too, did the fact that the United States emerged as the world's principal exporter of arms, ranging from the simplest to the most sophisticated, and extended its reach throughout the globe. All of these trends raised grave problems for and led to intense disputes about the free flow of scientific information, academic freedom, and matters of loyalty, security, and secrecy in a democratic society.

Although the Cold War ended, numerous experts insisted that the United States did not realistically adjust its defense mission accordingly; strong and entrenched interests tenaciously resist change. Hence, a relatively large military establishment and a vast nuclear arsenal continued to exist to cover the remote possibility of fighting two major regional wars simultaneously, while also engaging in peacemaking. At the same time, the United States pursued highly questionable antimissile defense systems that could end up costing trillions of dollars. Although the issue is no longer headline news, many contended that a military-industrial complex still existed, even thrived, despite the much less hospitable circumstances.

BIBLIOGRAPHY

Greider, William. *Fortress America: The American Military and the Consequences of Peace.* New York: Public Affairs, 1998.

Koistinen, Paul A. C. *The Military-Industrial Complex: A Historical Perspective.* New York: Praeger, 1980.

Lowen, Rebecca S. *Creating the Cold War University: The Transformation of Stanford.* Berkeley: University of California Press, 1997.

Markusen, Ann, and Joel Yudken. *Dismantling the Cold War Economy.* New York: Basic Books, 1992.

McNaugher, Thomas L. *New Weapons, Old Politics: America's Military Procurement Muddle.* Washington, D.C.: Brookings Institution, 1989.

Schwartz, Stephen I., ed. *Atomic Audit: The Costs and Consequences of U.S. Nuclear Weapons Since 1940.* Washington, D.C.: Brookings Institution, 1998.

Waddell, Brian. *The War against the New Deal: World War II and American Democracy.* DeKalb: Northern Illinois University Press, 2001.

Paul A. C. Koistinen

See also **Arms Race and Disarmament; Defense, National;** *and* vol. 9: **Eisenhower's Farewell Address.**

MILITARY LAW. A nation's armed forces are governed by and subject to military law. In the United States, military law includes statutes enacted by Congress as well as regulations promulgated by the president as commander in chief, by the Department of Defense, or by the individual branches of the military (the army, navy, air force, marine corps, and coast guard), as well as relevant federal constitutional provisions and the inherent authority of military commanders. Military law is one type of military jurisdiction and is distinct from MARTIAL LAW, which is the temporary governance of the civilian population by the military, and from military government, which is the governance of the civilian population in enemy territory by a belligerent military force. Sources of military law in the United States are the Constitution and international law, including the law of war or national security law.

The U.S. Constitution confers broad powers on both Congress and the president with respect to military law. Article I grants Congress the power to declare war, to raise and support armies, to create and maintain a navy, and to provide disciplinary regulations and administrative procedures applicable to the uniformed services. The militia clauses allow Congress to call up state militias to enforce federal laws (as in the 1957 Little Rock school desegregation struggle), as well as to suppress insurrections and to repel invasions. Militias, now known as the national guard, remain under state control until called into federal service.

National security powers are divided between Congress and the president: Congress has the power to initiate or recognize war ("declare war"), while the power to conduct war belongs to the president. The Charter of the United Nations, a treaty that under the supremacy clause of the Constitution is part of U.S. law, plays a role in modern declarations of war. Because Article 2(4) of the Charter outlaws aggressive war, the United States no longer declares war at the commencement of hostilities, but rather engages in hostilities under Article 51 of the U.N. Charter, which recognizes the right to individual or collective self-defense. (Congress may authorize the use of force under the War Powers Resolution [1973] as it did against Iraq in Operation Desert Storm, or not—for example, military actions during the fall of Saigon in 1975. No president has conceded the constitutionality of the War Powers Resolution.)

Codification

Primarily a body of criminal law and criminal procedure, including the Military Rules of Evidence (MRE), military law is codified in the Constitution; the UNIFORM CODE OF MILITARY JUSTICE (UCMJ), a federal statute; and the Manual for Courts-Martial (MCM). (Civil issues, such as divorce and child custody, inheritance, property disputes, torts, and contract disputes are not addressed by military law and are handled in civilian courts.)

Military law governs those who have military status, for example, those enlisted or commissioned into the armed forces, and may continue after retirement or while serving a sentence imposed by court martial. Members of the armed forces reserves or the army or air national guard are subject to federal military law only when in federal service.

Beginnings and Evolution

Military law in the United States began on 30 June 1775, with the adoption by Congress of Articles of War for the regulation and discipline of members of the Continental Army. In 1775, William Tudor, a prominent Boston lawyer, became the first judge advocate of the army; in 1776, the title changed to judge advocate general, a designation of the chief legal officer in each branch of service that continues to the present. Tudor was involved in several prominent prosecutions in the Revolutionary War, including those of generals Benedict Arnold, Charles Lee, and Philip Schuyler. John Laurance, who succeeded Tudor in 1777, was involved in the prosecution of the British Maj. John André who conspired with Benedict Arnold for the surrender of WEST POINT.

In 1806, the Articles of War were revised to include new, distinctly military offenses, for example, the use of contemptuous or disrespectful language directed at the president (now Art. 88 of the UCMJ). The modern Code retains a number of peculiarly military offenses such as absence without leave or "AWOL" (Art. 86), conduct unbecoming an officer and gentleman (Art. 133), and violations of the general article (Art. 134), which include "disorders and neglects to the prejudice of good order and discipline" and service-discrediting conduct.

Civilian Issues

Jurisdiction over civilians under military law is generally disfavored as a result of the Supreme Court's ruling in *Ex parte Milligan* (1866). In that case, the Court ruled that civilians could not be tried in military tribunals in areas where regular courts continue to function. The Milligan ruling is subject to four exceptions: civilians are subject to military law during occupation by a belligerent nation due to the obligation to preserve the security of civilians during a state of war (*Leitensdorfer vs. Webb* [1857]); spies and saboteurs can be tried under military law either by court-martial or by military tribunal; service-connected civilians, or "persons serving with, employed by, or accompanying the armed forces" abroad are subject to military law. In 1957, the Supreme Court ruled against military jurisdiction over civilian dependents (*Reid vs. Covert*), and, in 1960, over civilian employees (*McElroy vs. United

States ex rel. Guagliardo), leaving little to this exception. The fourth exception relates to "persons serving with or accompanying an armed force in the field . . . in time of war." During the Vietnam War, this provision was narrowly construed by a military appellate court to apply only to wars declared by Congress (*United States vs. Averette* [1970]). Service members abroad provide a special challenge for military law since under international law nations have jurisdiction over persons and events occurring within their borders. Unless provided for by an international agreement, service members who are nonbelligerent guests in a foreign state would be subject only to the laws of the host nation and not to the military law of the nation they are serving. To address this issue of authority, nations enter into Status of Forces Agreements (SOFA) with each other. Such agreements allocate jurisdiction between the host country and the guest military. For example, SOFAs allow the United States to retain court-martial jurisdiction over members of the armed services with respect to military offenses but allow host-country jurisdiction over other serious offenses.

Enforcement of military law is in the hands of commanders. Minor offenses may be handled by nonpunitive disciplinary measures under Article 15 of the UCMJ. Article 15 includes due process rights such as the rights to remain silent, to call witnesses and cross-examine adverse witnesses, to consult with counsel and have a spokesperson, and to appeal. The privilege against self-incrimination under military law practice predates the adoption of the Fifth Amendment of the Constitution; it was incorporated in Article 6 of the 1786 Articles of War. Nonjudicial procedure or trial by a commander under Article 15 developed after World War II in response to a perceived need for a process to dispose of minor offenses without permanently stigmatizing the person convicted.

Courts-Martial

There are three types of COURTS-MARTIAL: summary courts-martial with jurisdiction limited to enlisted personnel and limited authority to punish; special courts-martial, which may try serious but noncapital crimes or those that do not carry the death penalty; and general courts-martial, which may try any person subject to the UCMJ or any offense punishable by the Code and may impose a full range of punishments including death, dishonorable discharge, total forfeiture of all pay and allowances, and confinement. Trials by general court-martial include most rights familiar to civilian jurisprudence, including a right to counsel, to call and confront witnesses, and the right to remain silent. These rights are guaranteed by military law.

Reviews and Reform

Review of convictions by courts-martial evolved over time. Under current practice, convictions are reviewed by the convening authority, or commander who ordered the court-martial of the accused, often with the advice of a staff judge advocate or military lawyer who is part of the commander's staff. A commander may not change a finding of not guilty but may reverse a finding of guilty and reduce, mitigate, or disapprove a sentence. The role of the commander in the exercise of military law remains controversial, and command influence is a persisting issue. Each branch of the service has a Court of Criminal Appeals to which appeals may be taken. From there, further review may be sought in a civilian court or the three-judge United States Court of Appeals for the Armed Forces. From there, review may be sought by *certiorari* in the Supreme Court.

Major themes of reform of military law involved conforming of military law to civilian concepts of justice, including the right of appeal and the replacement of military officers lacking legal training with trained lawyers who could ensure the fairness and integrity of the judicial process. For example, outrage over the authority of individual commanders to impose and carry out sentences without higher approval or effective review in the case of African American troops tried and summarily executed following the Fort Sam Houston mutiny of 1917 prompted reforms.

BIBLIOGRAPHY

Bishop, Joseph W., Jr. *Justice Under Fire: A Study of Military Law.* New York: Charterhouse, 1974.

Generous, William T., Jr. *Swords and Scales: The Development of the Uniform Code of Military Justice.* New York: Kennikat Press, 1973.

Lurie, Jonathan. *Arming Military Justice: The Origins of the United States Court of Military Appeals, 1775–1950.* Princeton, N.J.: Princeton University Press, 1992.

———. *Pursuing Military Justice: The History of the United States Court of Appeals for the Armed Forces, 1951–1980.* Princeton, N.J.: Princeton University Press, 1998.

Shanor, Charles A., and L. Lynn Hogue. *Military Law in a Nutshell.* 2d ed. St. Paul, Minn.: West Publishing, 1996.

United States. Army. Judge Advocate General's Corp. *The Army Lawyer: A History of the Judge Advocate General's Corps, 1775–1975.* Washington, D.C.: Government Printing Office, 1975.

L. Lynn Hogue

MILITARY MEDALS. *See* **Decorations, Military.**

MILITARY MEDICINE. *See* **Medicine, Military.**

MILITARY ORDER OF THE LOYAL LEGION OF THE U.S.A., an organization resembling the Society of the Cincinnati, was established at Philadelphia in 1865 by a group of officers who had served in the Union army during the Civil War. The founders originally limited membership to such officers and their eldest male descendants, according to the laws of primogeniture; in subsequent years the society opened its membership rolls to all male descendants of Union officers. The order, whose headquarters are still in Philadelphia, publishes the *Loyal Legion Historical Journal.*

BIBLIOGRAPHY

Military Order of the Loyal Legion of the United States (series). Wilmington, N.C.: Broadfoot, 1991.

Alvin F. Harlow / c. w.

See also **Army, Union; Cincinnati, Society of the.**

MILITARY PHOTOGRAPHY. *See* **Photography, Military.**

MILITARY SERVICE AND MINORITIES

This entry includes 3 subentries:
African Americans
Hispanics
Homosexuals

AFRICAN AMERICANS

From the beginning of the nation's history, African Americans have served in the vanguard of the country's military, fighting its enemies as well as racism and discrimination in their own armed forces. At the beginning of the Revolutionary War in 1775, they made up 500,000 of the budding nation's population of 2.5 million. About five thousand blacks served in the ranks of the Continental Army. During the War of 1812, blacks made up between 10 and 20 percent of the United States Navy. New York organized two regiments of one thousand former slaves and free blacks each, while Louisiana and Philadelphia organized a battalion.

The Civil War and Spanish-American War

By the beginning of the Civil War in 1861, there were 3.5 million African Americans living in the South and 250,000 living in the North. Blacks joined the Union army in large numbers and participated in 449 military engagements. Some 180,000 African American soldiers served in the Union army during the Civil War; 38,000 died, 3,000 to combat-related fatalities. At the end of the Civil War, 122,000 black troops were on active duty. Almost 30,000 blacks served in the integrated Union navy and a few vessels were manned predominantly by black sailors. Blacks won 23 of the 1,523 Medals of Honor awarded during the Civil War, 8 after the Civil War, and 17 during the Indian campaigns from 1861 to 1898.

Twenty-two African American sailors, 9 percent of the ship's complement, perished with the USS *Maine* when it was sunk in Havana Harbor, Cuba, on 15 February 1898, igniting the Spanish-American War. Because of the war's brevity, the only black units to see combat were the 1,700 men of the 9th and 10th Cavalry and the

24th and 25th Infantry Regiments. These were the only African American units to survive military cutbacks after the Civil War. Black soldiers and sailors won 6 of the 109 Medals of Honor awarded during the war.

The World Wars

At the beginning of World War I, there were twenty-thousand African Americans serving in the military. In October 1917 the War Department authorized the organization of the first black division, the 92d. Fear of concentrating too many black soldiers in any one place, however, resulted in the division being scattered to seven different locations in France. Under the command of the more racially tolerant French, the men of the division won fifty-seven Distinguished Service Crosses. The success of the 92d resulted in the formation of the 93d Division. The latter division's 369th Infantry Regiment became the most famous African American unit in World War I. The French awarded the Croix de Guerre and the Legion of Merit to 170 officers and men of the regiment.

Early Twentieth Century. Prior to World War I, African Americans were joining the military in increasing numbers. By the start of that war, there were 23,000 black soldiers serving in the various branches of the military; by the end, 140,000 African Americans had served in France, and more than 400,000 had served in the military in some capacity. This photo, taken in 1910, shows the African American soldiers of the Army's 368th Infantry marching down a dirt road. © CORBIS

Free Black Militia. African Americans have a long and distinguished history of military service in the United States that dates back to the Continental Army, in which five thousand African American soldiers battled the British. Shown here is a drawing of two members of the Free Black Militia in Havana, Cuba, in 1795. The men are in full uniform, with one wearing a tall hat and one a tricorner hat, both of which were common for soldiers of that time. LIBRARY OF CONGRESS

Eighty-nine officers and men of the division's 370th Infantry Regiment won the American Distinguished Service Cross or the French Croix de Guerre. Some 140,000 black soldiers served in France during the war, but only 40,000 saw combat. The bulk of the 400,000 African Americans who served during the war were assigned to service and supply duties. Corporal Freddie Stowers of the 93d Division was the only black to win the Medal of Honor during the war.

In August 1939 there were only 3,640 African Americans in the army. By the end of November 1941, this figure had grown to 97,725, and one year after the Japanese attack on Pearl Harbor to 467,833. World War II marked the advent of blacks in the air and signal corps. Overall, twenty-two African American combat units served in Europe during World War II, including the 92d Infantry Division, which saw protracted combat in Italy and suffered 2,735 battle casualties. Other units, like the 93d Infantry Division and the 24th Infantry Regiment, fought in the Pacific. Most black army and marine units, however, never saw combat and the majority of black soldiers, sailors, and marines served as stevedores, truck drivers, wiremen, cooks, and mess stewards. Those that engaged in combat, however, proved themselves superb fighters. The army's 761st Tank Battalion, the first black unit to go into combat, fought for 183 days in France, the Netherlands, Belgium, Luxembourg, Germany, and Austria, inflicting tens of thousands of enemy casualties and liberating thirty major towns while suffering 50 percent losses. It was awarded a Presidential Unit Citation thirty

The Famed Tuskegee Airmen. By December 1942 the U.S. military had more than 467,000 African American servicemembers active in Europe, Africa, and the Pacific. While most did not see combat, blacks were allowed for the first time to serve in the air and signal corps. The air force's 99th Fighter Squadron, also known as the Tuskegee Airmen (named after the historically black Tuskegee University), won 150 Distinguished Flying Crosses for action in North Africa and Europe. Here six members of the airmen's paratrooper corps gather for a photo. © CORBIS

years after the war. The air force's famed 99th Fighter Squadron, the Tuskegee Airmen, won 150 Distinguished Flying Crosses for service over North Africa and Europe. The black sailors of the destroyer escort USS *Mason* won special praise for their outstanding seamanship and determination in the North Atlantic. By the end of the war the U.S. Army had 8,268,000 men organized into eighty-nine divisions. Of these, 694,333 men were black. In comparison, the navy had only 7,000 black officers and sailors in its ranks. Nine out of ten were mess stewards. In all, some 1.1 million African Americans served in the U.S. military during World War II. Only seven African Americans won the Medal of Honor during the war.

Post–World War II Conflicts and the Desegregation of the Armed Forces

By the beginning of the Korean War on 25 June 1950, the army had 591,000 men in uniform; 1,317 officers and 56,446 enlisted men were African American, 9.8 percent of ground force strength and 10.9 percent of enlisted strength. Most still served in support units. Between September 1950 and September 1951, almost one hundred black units served in Korea, including the 24th Infantry Regiment, the 64th Tank Battalion, and the 58th, 96th, and 999th Field Artillery Battalions. Heavy infantry losses early in the war, the resulting shortage of white infantrymen, and a surplus of black replacements however, prompted General Matthew B. Ridgway, the Eighth Army commander, to integrate the army in Korea in 1951. Two 24th Infantry soldiers won the Medal of Honor during the war.

African Americans made up about 10 percent of the approximately 8,744,000 service members in Vietnam. A total of 7,115 of the 58,151 Americans killed in Vietnam, or 12.2 percent, were black, a figure equal to the proportion of African Americans in the U.S. population. By the end of the war there were twelve black generals in the army, three in the air force, and one black admiral in the navy. African Americans won 20 of the 239 Medals of Honor awarded during the war. They made up about 30 percent of the U.S. military during Operations Urgent Fury in Grenada (1983), Just Cause in Panama (1989), Desert Storm-Desert Shield in the Persian Gulf (1990–1991), Restore Hope in Somalia (1992), and Uphold Democracy in Haiti (1994–1996). In 1999 African Americans made up 13 percent of the U.S. population and 22 percent of the military. After two centuries of national history, they were finally serving as full and equal partners, defending their country.

BIBLIOGRAPHY

Black Americans in Defense of Our Nation. Washington, D.C.: Department of Defense, 1991.

Bowers, William T., William M. Hammon, and George L. MacGarrigle. *Black Soldier, White Army: The 24th Infantry Regiment in Korea.* Washington, D.C.: Center of Military History, U.S. Army, 1996. The army's candid and controversial history of the African American 24th Infantry Regiment in the Korean War.

Lanning, Michael Lee. *The African-American Soldier: From Crispus Attucks to Colin Powell.* Secaucus, N.J.: Carol Publishing Group, 1997. A detailed history of African Americans in the U.S. military. The author highlights the racism that existed even while African Americans were fighting alongside whites in America's wars.

Lee, Ulysses. *The Employment of Negro Troops.* Washington, D.C.: Center of Military History, U.S. Army, 1963. The official army history of African American troops in World War II.

MacGregor, Morris J., Jr. *Integration of the Armed Forces, 1940–1965.* Washington, D.C.: Center of Military History, U.S. Army, 1981. Official army history of the integration of African Americans into the U.S. military.

Moore, Brenda L. *To Serve My Country, To Serve My Race: The Story of the Only African-American WACs Stationed Overseas during World War II.* New York: New York University Press, 1996. The story of the first African American Women's Army Corps unit to serve overseas.

Trudeau, Noah Andre. *Like Men of War: Black Troops in the Civil War, 1862–1865.* Boston: Little, Brown, 1998. An excellent history of African Americans in the Civil War.

Wilson, Joe, Jr. *The 761st "Black Panther" Tank Battalion in World War II: An Illustrated History of the First African American Armed Unit to See Combat.* Jefferson, N.C.: McFarland, 1999. A superb battle history.

Gilberto Villahermosa

See also **African Americans; Desegregation; Segregation;** *and* vol. 9: **Black Power Speech.**

At Ease. Two Mexican American soldiers play guitars while the soldiers around them sing in a moment of rest during World War II, 18 February 1943. © UPI/CORBIS-BETTMANN

HISPANICS

Hispanics have served in the U.S. military since the Revolutionary War. The Civil War, however, was the first conflict in which they were represented in large numbers. At its outbreak in 1861, some 2,500 Mexican Americans joined the Confederates, while about 1,000 joined the Union forces. By 1865 more than 10,000 Hispanics had fought in the war and two had won the Medal of Honor, the nation's highest combat award. Union admiral David G. Farragut, the most famous Hispanic of the war, is best remembered for his command, "Damn the torpedoes! Full speed ahead!" at Mobile Bay in Alabama on 5 August 1864.

During the Spanish-American War in 1898, Hispanics served in volunteer units, mostly from the southwestern United States. The First U.S. Volunteer Cavalry (the Rough Riders), for example, contained a number of Hispanic officers and soldiers. After the war, a battalion of Puerto Rican volunteers was organized in Puerto Rico. It later entered the Regular Army as the Puerto Rico Regiment. Private France Silvia, a Mexican American in the U.S. Marines, was the only Hispanic to win the Medal of Honor during the 1900 Boxer Rebellion in China.

More than 200,000 Hispanics were mobilized for World War I. Puerto Rico alone provided the Army with 18,000 soldiers. Most of the latter served in the island's seven segregated infantry regiments on Puerto Rico and in the Panama Canal Zone. Three regiments were combined to form the Provisional Division of Puerto Rico. Private David Barkley, of the 89th Infantry Division's 356th Infantry Regiment, was the only Hispanic to win the Medal of Honor during the war. Between 250,000 and 500,000 Hispanics served in World War II, mostly Mexican Americans. General Douglas MacArthur called the 158th Infantry Regiment, or Bushmasters—a unit with a large number of Hispanics—one of the greatest fighting combat teams ever deployed for battle. The regiment served with distinction in the Pacific theater. The 141st Infantry Regiment, another unit with many Hispanics, fought in Europe, suffering almost seven thousand battle casualties in 361 days of combat and winning three Medals of Honor, thirty-one Distinguished Service Crosses, 492 Silver Stars, and 1,685 Bronze Stars. Some 65,000 Puerto Ricans served during World War II, most with the 65th Infantry Regiment and the Puerto Rican National Guard's 295th and 296th Infantry Regiments in the Caribbean, North Africa, Europe, and the Pacific. Many also served in medical, transportation, and quartermaster units, including two hundred Puerto Rican women of the Women's Army Corps. Hispanics won 12 of the

383

431 Medals of Honor awarded during the war. Shortages of infantrymen during the war might have been alleviated had the United States taken better advantage of the large numbers of Hispanics that registered for service.

Nearly twenty thousand Puerto Ricans were serving in the army and marines at the beginning of the Korean War. Puerto Rico's 65th Infantry Regiment arrived in Korea in September 1950 and fought in every major campaign of the war, winning 4 Distinguished Service Crosses and around 130 Silver Stars in three years of fighting. The regiment killed six thousand Communist soldiers and captured two thousand. It received the Presidential Unit Citation and two Republic of Korea Presidential Unit Citations. About 60,000 Puerto Ricans served in the army during the Korean War. More than three thousand were killed and wounded. By end of 1953 Puerto Ricans had been integrated throughout the army. Nearly 148,000 Hispanics served in the military in Korea, winning 9 of the 131 Medals of Honor awarded during the war.

Some eighty-thousand Hispanics served during the country's involvement in Vietnam (1963–1973), winning 13 of the 239 Medals of Honor awarded during the war. About twenty thousand took part in Operation Desert Shield and Desert Storm (1990–1991). In 1997 Hispanics made up almost one-third of the infantry, artillery crews, and specialists deployed to Bosnia for peacekeeping operations. At the time they constituted nearly 11 percent of the U.S. population and 8 percent of the U.S. military. By November 2000, Hispanics constituted almost 11 percent of the military, but still accounted for only four percent of all the officers. The marines had the highest representation with almost 14 percent, while the air force had the lowest with slightly more than 7 percent. The army and navy both had about 11 percent.

Over the years Hispanics have slowly risen to the top of the military profession. In 1964 Admiral Horacio Rivero, a Puerto Rican, became the navy's first Hispanic four-star admiral. In 1982 General Richard E. Cavazos, a Mexican American, became the army's first Hispanic four-star general. On 2 July 1998 Luis Caldera, a Mexican American, became the highest-ranking Hispanic ever when he was appointed secretary of the army. Caldera sought to increase the number of Hispanics in the military. The failure of nearly half of all Hispanics to graduate from high school, however, continues to be a major obstacle to greater representation in the military.

BIBLIOGRAPHY

Arthur, Anthony. *The Bushmasters: America's Jungle Warriors of World War II.* New York: St. Martin's Press, 1987. A history of the 158th Infantry Regiment in World War II.

Harris, W. W. *Puerto Rico's Fighting 65th U.S. Infantry: From San Juan to Chorwan.* San Raphael, Calif.: Presidio Press, 1980. A history of the 65th Infantry Regiment in Korea by its commander.

Hispanics in America's Defense. Washington, D.C.: Office of the Deputy Assistant Secretary of Defense for Military Man-power and Personnel Policy, 1990. The only existing military history of Hispanics in the U.S. military.

Into the Storm. The Story of the Puerto Rican National Guard in Operation Desert Shield/Desert Storm. Puerto Rico: Arteaga and Arteaga, 1992.

Population Representation in the Military Services, Fiscal Year 1999. Washington, D.C.: Office of the Assistant Secretary of Defense for Force Management Policy, November 2000.

Thompson, Jerry D. *Vaqueros in Blue and Gray.* New ed. Austin, Tex.: State House Press, 2000. A history of Hispanics in the Civil War.

Villahermosa, Gilberto. "Glory, Defeat, and the Road Back." *Army Magazine.* September 2001, pp. 81–85. A review of the history of the Regular Army's only Hispanic regiment in Korea.

Gilberto Villahermosa

See also **Desegregation; Hispanic Americans; Segregation.**

HOMOSEXUALS

The U.S. military's ban on homosexual conduct, later applied to homosexual service members themselves, has from its beginning been nebulously defined and inconsistently applied. The first soldier discharged for homosexual conduct in the U.S. military was Lieutenant Gotthold Frederick Enslin, ceremonially drummed out of the Continental Army at Valley Forge on 27 February 1778.

Letters, diaries, and other historical documents from the late-eighteenth century and the nineteenth century record homosexual conduct and relationships amid the ranks. The first documented female homosexual service members were among the approximately four hundred women who passed as men to serve in the Civil War. Homosexual conduct in the military prior to the twentieth century was neither explicitly banned nor sought out by official policy, although once exposed, the customary result was immediate discharge and public humiliation and sometimes even institutionalization or suicide.

The first codified law prohibiting homosexual conduct in the U.S. military appeared during World War I. The Articles of War of 1916 listed assault with the intent to commit sodomy as a felony crime, and by 1919 sodomy itself, consensual or otherwise, was named as a felony crime. During World War II homosexuals were first categorized as a particular group of people unfit for military service due to what psychologists regarded as a pathological sexual orientation. Regulations banning homosexual persons from all branches of the U.S. military went into effect in 1943.

In the 1950s homosexuals were characterized as a threat to national security and the nation's moral welfare. Military investigators turned to so-called "witch hunts," detaining suspects and subjecting them to lengthy and repeated interrogations for the purpose of rooting out other suspected homosexuals. As a result service members were coerced into admitting their homosexuality against their will, and many quietly accepted dishonorable discharges before even being formally charged to escape the harassment of investigators.

Throughout the 1950s and 1960s investigations and discharges of homosexual personnel were applied largely at the discretion of commanders. Relatively few homosexuals were discharged during the conflicts in Korea and Vietnam, with far greater numbers discharged during peacetime. The first lawsuit challenging the ban was brought in 1973 and was followed by several others in subsequent years, although none was successful in overturning it.

In 1982 the Department of Defense established a policy that mandated exclusion of homosexuals without exception, stating that service by open homosexuals under any circumstance was detrimental to unit cohesion, individual privacy, recruitment, and public acceptance of military policy. The department supplied no data to back up these claims, and homosexuals were investigated, interrogated, and discharged at a faster rate than in previous years, costing the government nearly half a billion dollars between 1982 and 1992.

The 1990s brought greater public attention to the military's ban on homosexuals. The 1992 murder of Seaman Allen Schindler by his shipmates for his alleged homosexuality was followed by public outrage and inquiry into the policy and its implementation. In 1993 President Bill Clinton proposed a compromise on the homosexual ban, resulting in the "Don't Ask, Don't Tell, Don't Pursue" policy. After the 1999 murder of Private First Class Barry Winchell by fellow soldiers who perceived him to be homosexual, the Department of Defense surveyed some seventy-five thousand service members the following year and found that antihomosexual harassment was prevalent throughout the military. The policy was amended to also include "Don't Harass."

Military policy has sought to eradicate and exclude homosexuals for reasons that have reflected the prevailing antihomosexual sentiments of the day. Since the first internal report prepared for the secretary of the navy in 1957, numerous official studies have concluded that no credible evidence supports the ban on homosexuals in the U.S. military. The ban remained in place in the early twenty-first century.

BIBLIOGRAPHY

Bérubé, Allan. *Coming Out under Fire: The History of Gay Men and Women in World War Two.* New York: Free Press, 1990.

Halley, Janet E. *Don't: A Reader's Guide to the Military's Anti-Gay Policy.* Durham, N.C.: Duke University Press, 1999.

RAND. *Sexual Orientation and U.S. Military Personnel Policy: Options and Assessment.* Santa Monica, Calif.: RAND/National Defense Research Institute, MR-323-OSD, 1993.

Scott, Wilbur J., and Sandra Carson Stanley, eds. *Gays and Lesbians in the Military: Issues, Concerns, and Contrasts.* New York: Aldine de Gruyter, 1994.

Shilts, Randy. *Conduct Unbecoming: Gays and Lesbians in the U.S. Military.* New York: St. Martin's Press, 1993.

Williams, Colin J., and Martin S. Weinberg. *Homosexuals and the Military: A Study of Less Than Honorable Discharge.* New York: Harper and Row, 1971.

Kristen L. Rouse

See also **"Don't Ask, Don't Tell"; Gay and Lesbian Movement; Sexual Orientation.**

MILITIA MOVEMENT. Catapulted into the public eye after the 1995 bombing of the Murrah Federal Building in Oklahoma City because early, exaggerated reports linked the bombers to the Michigan Militia, the militia movement combined conspiracy theories with a fascination for paramilitary activity. Ideologically, militias are an offshoot of the Posse Comitatus (roughly 1970–1989), a right-wing group whose philosophy combined extreme libertarianism with a conviction that the government was illegitimate. By the 1980s, the Posse's influence had helped create the loosely organized antigovernment "Patriot" movement. In the 1990s, militia groups surfaced as its newest component.

Many factors, including the end of the Cold War and the rapidly changing U.S. economy, led to the militias' emergence. Specific catalysts included the election of Bill Clinton (1992) and the passage of the North American Free Trade Agreement (1993), the Brady Law (1994), and the Assault Weapons Ban (1994). Most important, however, were two controversial and deadly standoffs involving federal agents at Ruby Ridge, Idaho (1992), and Waco, Texas (1993). Far-right activists held that the Weaver family in Idaho and the Branch Davidians in Texas had been targeted by the federal government. The desire to prevent more standoffs, by force if necessary, led by 1994 to the formation of paramilitary groups. The term "militia" not only evoked memories of the American Revolution but also allowed the groups to claim legitimacy as the statutory militia, whose purpose they claimed was to act as a check on tyrannical government.

The movement spread quickly, drawing support from beyond the traditional right-wing fringe, especially among gun-rights activists and libertarians. That it represented something new can be seen in its leadership, which consisted of people not previously active in leadership roles. Some observers, pointing to members with ties to racist organizations, initially claimed that the movement was just a cover for white supremacy. Such ties certainly existed; in particular, militias had many members who were adherents of the racist and anti-Semitic religious sect Christian Identity. However, the ideological thrust of the militia movement remained antigovernment in nature; militia rhetoric stressed not race but rather conspiracy theories about an attempt to institute a one-world government or "new world order." Members repeated rumors about United Nations soldiers hiding in national parks, secret concentration camps established by the government, and plans for door-to-door gun confiscation.

Militia members held rallies and sometimes ran for public office, but their illegal activities brought them the most attention. Many adherents amassed illegal weapons and explosives and some plotted to use such weapons against the government. Major arrests of militia members for possession of weapons or explosives or on conspiracy charges occurred in Oklahoma, Arizona, Georgia, Washington, West Virginia, California, and elsewhere. Some militia members engaged in confrontations or even shoot-outs with law enforcement. Arrests involving militias had a dampening effect on more timid members of the movement; at the same time, the movement saw the exodus of radical members disgusted at the lack of militia involvement in the eighty-one-day Montana Freeman standoff against FBI agents in 1996 and the Republic of Texas standoff near Fort Davis in 1997. Consequently, beginning in 1997, the militia movement experienced a decline in membership and activity, accelerating after the "Y2K" computer bug failed to live up to expectations. By the early 2000s, the militia movement was much smaller than in 1995, although in some parts of the country, such as the Midwest, it was still quite active.

BIBLIOGRAPHY

Pitcavage, Mark. "Camouflage and Conspiracy: The Militia Movement from Ruby Ridge to Y2K." *American Behavioral Scientist* 44 (February 2001): 957–981.

Snow, Robert L. *The Militia Threat: Terrorists among Us.* New York: Plenum, 1999.

Stern, Kenneth S. *A Force upon the Plain: The American Militia Movement and the Politics of Hate.* New York: Simon and Schuster, 1996.

Mark Pitcavage

See also **Oklahoma City Bombing; Ruby Ridge; Waco Siege.**

MILITIAS, a form of citizen-based defense that shaped early American history and created an American tradition of citizen soldiery. Early American colonies faced dangers from Native American and European foes. Colonial governments quickly established universal military obligation for white males. At its simplest, men were armed or ordered to arm themselves, organized into units, and trained.

In practice, the compulsory militia system worked poorly. Participants viewed it at best as an unpleasant obligation and at worse as something to be avoided. Moreover, militia mobilization placed strain on the labor and economic resources of the underpopulated and underdeveloped colonies. Further, the militia had limited military value: it was ill armed, ill trained, and ill disciplined, able to compete neither with European soldiers nor with Native American guerrilla tactics. Consequently, the militia system tended toward decay, though revived or reformed during slave revolts, Indian conflicts, or colonial wars. The system functioned most effectively as a bureaucratic framework for obtaining military manpower. In Connecticut, for example, colonial authorities often used the militia system to recruit volunteers for military service or to draft colonists when volunteers proved wanting.

The American Revolution gave new life to the militia. As unrest grew, revolutionary governments formed that subverted the militia away from royal governors. The militia formed a major portion of patriot forces, achieving fame at Lexington and Bunker Hill in 1775, and playing important roles in American victories throughout the war, such as Saratoga (1777) and Cowpens (1781). Just as often, however, militias proved unreliable, breaking in battle or leaving before a battle could even be fought. George Washington penned a famous lament about the militia in 1776: "They come in you cannot tell how, go you cannot tell when, and act you cannot tell where, consume your provisions, exhaust your stores, and leave you at last at a critical moment." Yet Washington himself had a shrewd understanding of how to use militias as auxiliary and partisan forces in his campaigns. In addition to strictly military concerns, the militia played an important role in securing the countryside and subduing Loyalist sentiment.

The militia emerged from the Revolution with its military reputation mixed but its symbolic importance enhanced immeasurably. Americans no longer viewed the militia solely as a practical necessity; instead, republican thought imbued the militia with an ideological role as a guarantor of liberty, particularly in opposition to standing armies. The symbolic role of the militia complicated its practical role in the new Republic immensely. Nationalists hoped to rely on the militia for the nation's defense, backed by a small standing army. They sought increased federal control over the militia to increase its effectiveness. Antifederalists, though, feared the federal government would deliberately weaken the militia, leaving states defenseless to tyranny. This debate, manifested in the Constitution and in the first federal militia law passed in 1792, resulted in a system that awkwardly divided control of the militia between federal and state governments and had few teeth for enforcement.

Despite federal-state tensions, the militia system might have remained intact for many years had it not been for increasing social strains within the institution itself. Although the ideal remained universal compulsory military service, the reality was far different. The burdens of militia service rested primarily on the young and the poorer classes. The wealthy could escape militia service by obtaining exemptions or simply paying fines for nonattendance. Militiamen complained that the militia system was unequal and unfair. After the War of 1812—in which the militia performed poorly—these sentiments increased as foreign threats receded. Unhappiness with the militia was widespread, including on the frontier, where the militia was ineffective and militia service particularly burdensome, because of the distances involved, the low populations, the difficulty in procuring arms, and the undeveloped economies.

Militia. Members of the Seventh New York State Militia rest at Camp Cameron in the District of Columbia, soon after the start of the Civil War. LIBRARY OF CONGRESS

Militia reformers were numerous, but their plans tended to emphasize military effectiveness and ignored the social factors that weakened the existing system. The most commonly advocated plan, "classification," involved changing federal law to divide the militia into classes by age, placing additional burdens of service on the younger classes. Classification thus increased rather than soothed discontent among those younger people dissatisfied with the system. In the face of discontent and lack of federal reform, state governments often responded by creating age-based exemptions from militia service. Yet because such exemptions left those most hostile to militia service—younger men—in the militia, opposition never really ceased. In the 1840s, consequently, many states began dismantling compulsory militia service. Instead, they relied on volunteer militia companies, which had long coexisted with the compulsory militia. In some states, particularly in the South, where the threat of slave revolt made it impolitic to overtly dismantle compulsory militia service, the laws remained on the books but were largely ignored.

The volunteer militia system outlasted strains put on it by the Mexican War, which caused antiwar sentiment to sweep the Northeast, and the California gold rush, which lured many young men westward, but it did not survive the Civil War intact. In the late 1850s, many states began strengthening their militia systems in anticipation of sectional conflict. However, the civil war that broke out was so large in scale that it quickly swallowed up the volunteer militia companies. In the North, for example, Abraham Lincoln called for the mobilization of 75,000 militia to quell the rebellion; 93,000 responded to the call, including most of the volunteer militia. Subsequently, both the Union and the Confederacy relied not on militias but on volunteer regiments organized by states and mustered into national service. Northern and southern states alike had to recreate their militia systems, but these new state militias played only a very limited role in the Civil War.

After the Civil War, states reestablished the volunteer militias, increasingly calling them National Guards. The National Guard Association, a lobbying organization, formed in 1879. The primary role of the National Guard in many states was to quell civil disorder, a task often defined to include strikebreaking. This was, however, a distasteful duty to many in the National Guard who thought of themselves as playing an important role in national defense. Such guardsmen were rudely awakened in 1898, when the U.S. Army successfully excluded the guard from participation (except as individuals) in the Spanish-American War. This exclusion and its political repercussions led to a major reform of the militia with the Dick Act of 1903, which replaced the Uniform Militia Act of 1792. The Dick Act solidified the militia (soon formally renamed the National Guard) with increased federal funds for training and arms, as well as greater federal control. Subsequent laws in 1916 and 1933 further strengthened federal control over the National Guard, establishing it as a reserve component of the army and allowing it to be deployed overseas. These reforms made the guard viable militarily.

Tensions between the National Guard and the regular army never evaporated, but the compromises maintained both military utility and the American tradition of the citizen-soldier. National Guardsmen (and, since 1945, members of the Air National Guard) have served in every major military conflict since World War II, in addition to serving their states in situations ranging from riots to natural disasters.

BIBLIOGRAPHY

Mahon, John K. *History of the Militia and the National Guard.* New York: Macmillan, 1983.

McCreedy, Kenneth Otis. "Palladium of Liberty: The American Militia System, 1815–1861." Ph.D. diss., University of California at Berkeley, 1991.

Pitcavage, Mark. "An Equitable Burden: The Decline of the State Militias, 1783–1858." Ph.D. diss., Ohio State University, 1995.

Riker, William H. *Soldiers of the States: The Role of the National Guard in American Democracy.* New York: Arno, 1979.

Selesky, Harold E. *War and Society in Colonial Connecticut.* London and New Haven, Conn.: Yale University Press, 1990.

Shea, William L. *The Virginia Militia in the Seventeenth Century.* Baton Rouge: Louisiana State University Press, 1983.

Mark Pitcavage

See also **National Guard.**

MILLENNIALISM, or millenarianism, focuses on a thousand-year period of unprecedented peace and righteousness that some Christians believe will either precede or follow the return of Christ to earth, marking the end of history. Millennial thinking has traditionally followed one of two patterns. For the premillennialists, God alone would choose the time of the Second Coming; final judgment would come swiftly and without warning; and human beings could do nothing to postpone or hasten it. Postmillennialists, on the other hand, downplayed the apocalyptic nature of the end time, stressed the one-thousand years of bliss promised in Revelations, and theorized that mankind could demonstrate its fitness for Christ's return by remaking the world in His image. The more optimistic outlook of postmillennial thinking made it the preferred theological position for nineteenth-century reformers. More recently, those wishing for radical change have been drawn to premillennialism. Inspired especially by events in the Middle East since the creation of the state of Israel in 1948, premillennialism has produced a vast literature speculating about current events and the end of history. Some believers watch current events carefully and set dates for Christ's coming (later to revise their predictions), as in Harold Camping's *1994?* (1992) or Edgar Whisenant's *Eighty-Eight Reasons Why the Rapture Will Be in 1988* (1988).

BIBLIOGRAPHY

Bloch, Ruth H. *Visionary Republic: Millennial Themes in American Thought 1756–1800.* Cambridge, N.Y.: Cambridge University Press, 1985.

Boyer, Paul S. *When Time Shall Be No More: Prophecy Belief in Modern American Culture.* Cambridge, Mass.: Belknap Press of Harvard University Press, 1992.

Weber, Timothy P. *Living in the Shadow of the Second Coming: American Premillennialism, 1875–1925.* New York: Oxford University Press, 1979; Chicago: University of Chicago Press, 1987.

Edith Blumhofer / A. R.

See also **Adventist Churches; Disciples of Christ; Jehovah's Witnesses; Shakers; Social Gospel.**

MILLS. *See* **Flour Milling; Gristmills; Sawmills; Textiles.**

MILWAUKEE is the largest city in Wisconsin and the nineteenth largest in the United States. Known as the Cream City (for the cream-colored bricks produced there), Brew City (for its many breweries), and the German Athens (for its once-dominant German population), Milwaukee was still known at the end of the twentieth century for its bratwurst, ethnic festivals, and innovative city government. Milwaukee's history has been marked by the long terms of its mayors. The nonpartisan format of local elections (a socialist reform) produced remarkable stabil-

Milwaukee. The fourteen-story Pabst Building (photographed early in the twentieth century), the tallest in the city when it was built in 1892 to house a bank run by the brewing tycoon Captain Frederick Pabst; many places in Milwaukee were named for him. LIBRARY OF CONGRESS

ity in the mayoralty, as only three men held the job between 1948 and 2000.

The area now known as Milwaukee (opinions differ as to the exact Native American meaning of the name, but the most likely is "gathering place") was the home to various settlements after at least A.D. 400. The first permanent white settlements began in the early 1830s, following the lead of the French Canadian fur trader Solomon Juneau. Other early noteworthies included Byron Kilbourn and George Walker, whose names persisted in street and neighborhood names. In its early years, Milwaukee vied with Chicago as a Great Lakes port, but the coming of the railroad cemented Chicago's place as the predominant metropolis of the Middle West.

The late nineteenth century saw the arrival of a large Polish population to rival the Germans, Irish, and British who had arrived earlier; this new group left its mark on the landscape of the city's South Side, although relatively few Poles remained at the end of the twentieth century. Additions to Milwaukee's ethnic mix during that century included large Hispanic and African American populations, as well as other small groups.

Economically, the 1970s and 1980s saw the steady erosion of the industrial base that had once powered Milwaukee's economy. Established firms such as Allis-Chalmers, Allen-Bradley, Briggs and Stratton, Harley-Davidson, Milwaukee Power Tools, Pabst Brewing Company, and Schlitz Brewing Company either slashed workforces or were bought out, resulting in a painful period of adjustment. The election of John Norquist as mayor in 1988 signaled a new direction and the 1990s were a decade of rejuvenation for the appearance, if not the population, of Milwaukee. (The population declined 5 percent from 1990 to 596, 974 in 2000.) At the end of the decade, the economy was anchored by some old names (Miller Brewing, Harley-Davidson, Northwestern Mutual) and some new ones (M and I Data Services, Firstar Bank, Manpower Professional), and the metropolitan area had entered a period of slow but stable growth.

BIBLIOGRAPHY

Alderman, Ralph M. *From Trading Post to Metropolis: Milwaukee County's First 150 Years.* Milwaukee, Wisc.: Milwaukee County Historical Society, 1987.

Gurda, John. *The Making of Milwaukee.* Milwaukee, Wisc.: Milwaukee County Historical Society, 1999.

Still, Bayrd. *Milwaukee: The History of a City.* Madison: State Historical Society of Wisconsin, 1948.

Christopher Miller

See also **Midwest; Wisconsin.**

MIMS, FORT, MASSACRE AT took place on 30 August 1813 during the Creek Indian War. This "fort" was little more than a log stockade surrounding the home of Samuel Mims. The militia captain Daniel Beasley and a force of some 170 had occupied the post. In early August, the captain divided his forces among several nearby stockades, leaving only forty defenders at Mims. Beasley, a lawyer with no military knowledge, owed his position to political patronage. On 29 August 1813, he received word from two slaves that they had seen Creek Indians nearby. When a militia patrol failed to confirm the sighting, Beasley had the slaves flogged. Less than twenty-four hours later, around noon, a force of approximately one thousand Creek warriors assaulted the gates, which Beasley had left wide open, believing he could hold the fort against "any number of hostiles." The fighting and post-battle slaughter killed approximately 250 settlers. Word of the massacre became a rallying cry for regional settlers and helped seal the fate of the Creek.

BIBLIOGRAPHY

Halbert, Henry S., and Timothy H. Ball. *The Creek War of 1813 and 1814.* Tuscaloosa: University of Alabama, 1995. First published 1895, this reprint is edited, with introductions and notes, by Frank L. Owsley Jr. Material reflects social and cultural biases of initial publication date.

Robert L. Bateman

See also **Creek; Creek War.**

MINERAL PATENT LAW. The discovery of gold in California in 1848 occurred in a legal vacuum. The regulation of the race for wealth on the public domain was accomplished by rules growing out of the needs of the miners through the organization of districts and the adoption of bylaws for those districts. It gradually became apparent that a national policy for the administration and disposal of the mineral resources of the public lands was essential. The resulting Mining Law of 1866 adopted the idea of open mineral exploitation of the public lands. A claimant who discovered a mineral lode, made a minimum investment in labor and improvements, and complied with filing and posting prerequisites could secure a patent from the United States on the lands covered by his claim. In 1870 similar legislation was enacted that specifically covered placers—that is, surface deposits of gravels of mineral value, as opposed to lodes or veins of ore.

The laws of 1866 and that of 1870 were combined in the Mining Law of 1872. Locations based on discovery of a lode were limited to fifteen hundred feet by six hundred feet, while placer claims were limited to twenty acres. Patents were issued upon payment of $5.00 per acre for lode claims and $2.50 per acre for placers. Although oil and gas were included under the placer mining provisions, the Mineral Leasing Act of 1920 provided that exploration and production of these substances was to be leased, with royalties paid to the United States, and not patented.

Although there were a number of supplementing land limiting statutes, such as the Wilderness Act of 1964, the 1872 act still governs most of the public domain of the United States. In the 1990s, however, the 1872 act came under intense criticism from environmental groups and the administration of President William J. Clinton. In 1992, in order to reduce speculation and clear unworked claims, legislation was enacted to require a $100 annual holding fee per claim. Congress also imposed an effective patent moratorium by enacting legislation prohibiting the Bureau of Land Management from spending any funds to process mineral patent applications. As of 2001, this prohibition remained in effect.

BIBLIOGRAPHY

Miller, Charles Wallace, Jr. *Stake Your Claim!: The Tale of America's Enduring Mining Laws.* Tucson, Ariz.: Westernlore Press, 1991.

John A. Kidwell
Richard C. Maxwell

See also **Mines, U.S. Bureau of; Mining Towns; Public Domain; Western Lands.**

MINERAL SPRINGS, naturally occurring, often heated waters that are relatively high in certain dissolved substances. The occurrence of mineral springs depends on geologic structure. Most occur along fault lines or corrugated regions, none in undisturbed regions, and few in

Ulysses S. Grant. The former Civil War commander and postwar president, dying of cancer, hurries to finish his memoirs at his home near the mineral springs of Saratoga, N.Y.; he died at home on 23 July 1885—four days after completing the posthumously acclaimed book. LIBRARY OF CONGRESS

regions of little disturbance. Range of temperature is far higher in western regions than eastern, and they are more numerous in the west, where mountains are younger. About 10,000 mineral springs have been mapped in the United States. The most famous springs were at Saratoga, New York, and White Sulphur Springs, West Virginia.

BIBLIOGRAPHY

Albu, Marius, David Banks, and Harriet Nash, eds. *Mineral and Thermal Groundwater Resources.* New York: Chapman and Hall, 1997.

Stearns, Noah D., Harold T. Stearns, and Gerald A. Waring. *Thermal Springs in the United States.* Washington, D.C.: Government Printing Office, 1937.

Mary Anne Hansen

See also **Geology; Resorts and Spas.**

MINERALOGY. Observations on minerals in the New England and Virginia colonies appear in the writings of John Josselyn and other early-seventeenth-century travelers. In the mid-seventeenth century John Winthrop, son of the first governor of the Massachusetts Bay Colony, actively engaged in the search for and development of mineral deposits. His grandson, John Winthrop Jr., formed a notable mineral collection that was presented to

the Royal Society of London in 1734 and later incorporated into the British Museum. Throughout the colonial period, questions about the nature and use of minerals and rocks and about the development of known mineral deposits were usually answered by sending specimens or trial shipments of ore abroad or by importing experts from Europe. The first professional study of mineralogy in America began after the Revolution—led by Adam Seybert, Gerard Troost, and the mineral chemist James Woodhouse, all of Philadelphia. The first mineral collections of scientific importance began to be acquired at about the same time. Most of the specimens were brought from Europe, chiefly by Americans traveling abroad for educational purposes and by immigrants of scientific or technological bent. It was the acquisition of these European collections, with their store of correctly identified and labeled material illustrating European textbooks, that provided the basis for American study instruction.

The formal teaching of mineralogy—the term then usually included earth history and other aspects of geology—began in American colleges shortly before 1800. Benjamin Waterhouse, a Rhode Island Quaker who had been trained in medicine and the natural sciences in Leyden and London, lectured on mineralogy and botany at Rhode Island College (later Brown University) in 1786 and at the medical school at Harvard between 1788 and 1812.

The first textbook on mineralogy written in the United States, Parker Cleaveland's *Elementary Treatise on Mineralogy and Geology,* was published in Boston in 1816. Cleaveland, a Harvard graduate of 1799, was self-taught in mineralogy. The work received good reviews in Europe and remained a standard text for many years. In 1837 James Dwight Dana of Yale brought out the *System of Mineralogy,* which became an international work of reference, reaching a sixth edition in 1892. Both of these books drew heavily on European works, especially those of the German Friedrich Mohs and of the French crystallographer R. J. Haüy.

The most rapid progress in mineralogy in the United States took place in the first three decades of the nineteenth century, as New England colleges sought to add the sciences to their theological and classical curricula. The leading figure was Benjamin Silliman, appointed professor of chemistry and natural science at Yale in 1802. Silliman was active as a teacher, editor, and public lecturer, rather than as a researcher. Among his students, Amos Eaton, Charles Upham Shepard, and Dana became important in the further development of the geological sciences.

The marked growth of the geological sciences in American colleges in the early nineteenth century was accompanied by the formation of numerous state and local academies, lyceums, and societies concerned with natural history. These organizations afforded public platforms from which such men as Silliman and Eaton and, later, Louis Agassiz spread scientific ideas. The Academy of

Natural Sciences of Philadelphia, organized in 1812, was a leading factor; it began the publication of its journal in 1817 and of its proceedings in 1826. The Boston Society of Natural History, formed in 1830—the year the first state geological survey was begun, in Massachusetts—and the Lyceum of Natural History of New York, organized in 1817, also were important. The *American Journal of Science and Arts*, started by Silliman in 1818, published the bulk of American mineralogical contributions for the next five decades. (A forerunner, the *American Mineralogical Journal*, edited by Archibald Bruce of New York City, had published only four issues, 1810–1814.)

Toward the middle of the nineteenth century, courses in analytical chemistry, emphasizing ores, minerals, and agricultural materials, were introduced into many colleges and medical schools. Mineral chemistry and geochemistry developed strongly during the late 1800s, fostered especially by the U.S. Geological Survey, organized in 1879, and American work on minerals and rocks was outstanding in those fields. The publications of the U.S. Geological Survey and of the state geological surveys carried much descriptive mineralogical and petrographic material. Toward the end of the nineteenth century, as the organization and interests of science enlarged and specialized, the various academies and their attendant periodicals were joined and ultimately virtually supplanted by national and regional professional societies. The Mineralogical Society of America was founded in 1919 and continues today. The *American Mineralogist*, an independent journal first published in 1916, became its official journal.

The great private mineral collections, to which public museums and universities are deeply indebted, were developed during the last decades of the nineteenth century and the first decades of the twentieth century, a period coinciding with the major development of America's mineral resources and the accumulation of fortunes from mining in the West. Commercial dealing in mineral specimens, as by A. E. Foote of Philadelphia, developed on a large scale. Exhibits at national and international fairs, notably at the St. Louis World's Fair of 1904, also spread interest.

Crystallography, particularly in its theoretical aspects, did not attract much attention in the United States during the nineteenth century, when American interest in minerals was primarily concerned with chemical composition, occurrence, and use. It was not until the early twentieth century that advanced instruction and research in the formal aspects of crystallography became widespread. Charles Palache of Harvard was one of the leaders.

Over the course of the twentieth century, the boundaries of the discipline of mineralogy shifted with the change in economic and social priorities. As scientific interest in the traditional extractive resources—particularly iron ore and precious metals—declined in relation to research in oil exploration, nuclear waste storage, and earthquake and volcano prediction, mineralogy became an um-

brella term for an array of highly technical fields, including petrology, crystallography, geochemistry, and geophysics.

BIBLIOGRAPHY

Chandos, Michael Brown. *Benjamin Silliman: A Life in the Young Republic.* Princeton, N.J.: Princeton University Press, 1989.

Greene, John C., and John G. Burke. *The Science of Minerals in the Age of Jefferson.* Philadelphia: American Philosophical Society, 1978.

Oldroyd, David R. *Sciences of the Earth: Studies in the History of Mineralogy and Geology.* Brookfield, Vt.: Ashgate, 1998.

*Clifford Frondel/*A. R.

See also **Geological Survey, U.S.; Geological Surveys, State; Geology.**

MINES, U.S. BUREAU OF. In 1910, Congress passed the Organic Act (Public Law 179), officially creating the U.S. Bureau of Mines (USBM). Dr. Joseph A. Holmes, a geologist and professor, was the bureau's first director. The bureau's first priority under Holmes's direction was the reduction of the alarmingly high number of deaths in mining accidents. In 1913, however, the bureau's scope of authority expanded to include the collection, analysis, and dissemination of economic data within the mining industry. In 1925, the USBM was moved from the Department of the Interior to the Department of Commerce, where it became the principal collector of mineral statistics and acquired the responsibility of producing, conserving, and exploiting helium gas, important at the time to national defense.

The influence of the labor movement in the late 1930s paved the way for the Coal Mine Inspection Act of 1941. This act gave the USBM authority to inspect mines for safety conditions and recommend corrective measures, although enforcement power remained limited until Congress passed the Federal Coal Mine Health and Safety Act of 1969, establishing mandatory standards and making it possible for the USBM to research alternative mining procedures. The Federal Coal Mine Safety and Health Amendments Act of 1977 addressed for the first time regulatory procedures concerning coal, metal, and nonmetal mining operations, as well as research germane to all three types of mining.

USBM scientists and industry personnel initially worked together to develop new equipment and technologies, but because of concern over potential conflicts of interest the Mining Enforcement and Safety Administration (MESA) was created in 1973 to handle regulatory functions, such as enforcing health and safety regulations, assessing penalties when violations occurred, developing safety and health standards, and providing training and education. MESA later became the Mine Safety and Health Administration under the Department of Labor, while the USBM retained responsibility for research and development. The Office of Coal Research was created in 1960 under the Department of the Interior, and then became part of the Energy Research and Development Administration (ERDA) in 1974, which ultimately became part of the Department of Energy.

During World War II, USBM research focused on minerals critical to national defense, and eventually developed an international research program in 1961 to follow and study mineral resources around the world (the Mineral Attaché program), with a staff of country specialists surveying information from more than 160 countries. The Division of Mineral Information Systems, created in 1979, became in 1990 the Division of Statistics and Information Services, responsible for collecting, analyzing, and disseminating data on mineral commodities around the world, including data on exploration, production, consumption, pricing, recycling, and mineral reserves and inventories.

The USBM also had an advisory role in making policy regarding mineral resources, the economic use of public land, and the preservation of natural resources. The USBM's assistant director of policy, in the late 1970s; the Division of Policy Analysis, in the early 1980s; the Office of Regulatory Projects Coordination, in the late 1980s; and the division of regulatory and policy analysis, in the 1990s; trace the increasing importance of the USBM's contribution to national policy. Beginning in 1970, the state liaison program employed specialists to coordinate the flow of information and material between mining-related industries in the states and the USBM.

The USBM's extensive list of pragmatic accomplishments include significantly reducing the number of mine fatalities; discovering a method to remove sulfur from smelter fumes so as not to harm national forests (1911); developing a cost-effective method of extracting radium from domestic ores for use in the treatment of cancer (1912–1915); developing gas masks for American soldiers during World War I; doing research (1920s) on exhaust gases making it possible to properly ventilate the Holland Tunnel between New York and New Jersey; and developing technologies for the safe handling of radioactive materials (1940s), which ultimately led to the creation of the first atomic-powered submarine. In addition, during the 1960s and 1970s, the USBM evaluated vast areas of American wilderness in field studies and mineral surveys; developed a smokeless incinerator for use in burning junked automobiles; developed safer methods of treating mine drainage to protect drinking water sources and aquatic life; developed and implemented a variety of measures to stabilize the earth around mining cites, to control and extinguish fires at abandoned mines, and restore and reclaim mined lands; worked with the Bureau of Indian Affairs to identify mineral resources on Indian lands and negotiated production lease agreements that corresponded with tribal organization goals; and researched, in conjunction with the Federal Highway Commission, the use

of synthetic ceramic aggregates to improve the surfaces of paved roads.

The USBM created and utilized various programs in order to carry out its work. The Commodities and Materials Program analyzed domestic and international trends in materials use, from exploration through disposal; the International Mineral Studies Program addressed global issues important to mining-dependent industries; the Land and Mineral Resources Program studied the potential for future mineral supplies; the Regulatory Impact Analysis Program provided scientific information to policymakers searching for effective and efficient solutions to environmental problems; the Statistics and Information Services Program provided critical information to legislative bodies and other federal agencies; research conducted by the Environmental Technology Program contributed scientific data for the development of new environmental technologies to reduce toxic waste products, decontaminate hazardous waste sites, and alleviate the adverse effects of coal mining; the Health, Safety, and Mining Technology program focused on research to find solutions to a variety of health and safety problems experienced by miners; the Minerals and Materials Science Program addressed possible ways to ensure a long-term supply of materials.

In 1995, a committee of members from both the U.S. Senate and the House of Representatives recommended that the USBM be abolished within ninety days, citing budgetary concerns. After eighty-five years of performing extensive research and analysis, of gathering and disseminating information, and of contributing to policymaking, industry, and environmental, health, and safety legislation, the USBM officially closed on 30 September 1996. The Health and Safety Research Program and the Materials Research Program were transferred to the U.S. Department of Energy. The Land and Mineral Resources Program was transferred to the Bureau of Land Management. Part of the Information and Analysis Program was transferred to the U.S. Geological Survey. The Helium Program was transferred initially to the Bureau of Land Management, but was finally closed in 1998. The USBM occupied a unique position, serving as a source of and conduit for information between industry and labor, between environmentalists and capitalists, between government and the people. The bureau's annual publications *Minerals Yearbook* and *Mineral Facts and Problems* were both internationally recognized reference works. The USBM enjoyed a reputation, free of many of the political machinations of other federal agencies, for conducting unbiased research and providing scientific data and analyses to leaders of both industry and government throughout its existence.

BIBLIOGRAPHY

Ball, Howard. *Cancer Factories: America's Tragic Quest for Uranium Self-Sufficiency.* Westport, Conn.: Greenwood Press, 1993.

Curran, Daniel J. *Dead Laws for Dead Men: The Politics of Federal Coal Mine Health and Safety Legislation.* Pittsburgh, Pa.: University of Pittsburgh Press, 1993.

Derickson, Alan. *Black Lung: Anatomy of a Public Health Disaster.* Ithaca, N.Y.: Cornell University Press, 1998.

Kirk, William S. *The History of the U.S. Bureau of Mines.* Washington, D.C.: U.S. Department of the Interior, Bureau of Mines, 1995.

Smith, Duane A. *Mining America: The Industry and the Environment, 1800–1980.* Lawrence: University Press of Kansas, 1987.

Christine E. Hoffman

See also **Coal; Coal Mining and Organized Labor; Mineralogy; Mining Towns.**

MINESWEEPING, the systematic clearance of mines from an area where submarines, surface ships, or aircraft have planted them. Most minesweeping involves towing various devices behind a ship: serrated wires to cut the mooring lines of contact mines to bring them to the surface; noisemakers to detonate acoustic mines; and cables with a pulsating current to set off magnetic mines. No method for sweeping pressure mines exists, but generally they are set to sterilize themselves after a certain period, when they become harmless.

Minesweeping is a tedious and dangerous operation. During the Civil War, Union forces dragged for Confederate mines with chains strung between boats but failed to make mined areas completely safe. After World War I, during which the United States and Great Britain laid some 56,000 mines in a stretch of the North Sea 230 miles long and from fifteen to thirty-five miles wide, minesweepers spent months incompletely clearing the mines.

During WORLD WAR II, combatants laid an estimated 500,000 mines in all the world's oceans. In European waters alone, more than 1,900 minesweepers spent approximately two years clearing mines. American minesweepers cleared some 17,000 square miles of water in the Japanese area.

No extensive mining operations have been conducted since World War II, although the North Koreans laid mines off both Korean coasts during the KOREAN WAR, and the U.S. Air Force dropped mines in Haiphong harbor during the VIETNAM WAR. Minesweepers subsequently cleared both areas. HELICOPTERS, which are faster, safer, and more efficient than ships, have virtually taken over minesweeping.

BIBLIOGRAPHY

Lott, Arnold S. *Most Dangerous Sea; A History of Mine Warfare and an Account of U.S. Navy Mine Warfare Operations in World War II and Korea.* Annapolis, Md.: U.S. Naval Institute, 1959.

Marolda, Edward J., ed. *Operation End Sweep: A History of Minesweeping Operations in North Vietnam.* Washington, D.C.: Naval Historical Center, Department of the Navy, 1993.

Arnold S. Lott / c. w.

MINIATURE. In Europe, about 1520, the independent miniature, or "limning," evolved from the illuminated manuscript. In eighteenth-century America, a portrait painting was sometimes referred to as a miniature or a limning. Both terms refer to a small painting on a wafer-thin oval of ivory; parchment or paper were also used. At a price, a miniature could be set in a suitable frame of ivory, silver, or gold; others were framed in pinchbeck, pewter, brass, iron, steel, wood, or finely machine-tooled leather. In competent hands, miniatures became objects of great elegance and sophistication, often stippled and painted in thin, translucent layers of a subtle array of watercolors, which allows the milky glow of the ivory to show through the veils of paint. While most miniatures served as personal, portable, visual tokens of affection and keepsakes, others were patriotic, depicting symbolic images such as Lady Liberty.

In America, the portrait miniature became popular in the second half of the eighteenth century and continued through the 1860s. John Watson, a Scot, was among the first documented miniaturists. His small portraits are in pencil and India ink. Most well-known eighteenth-century American painters, such as John Singleton Copley, filled their time between larger commissions with miniature painting and, presumably, signed them. Few have survived. Other distinguished American painters who also did miniature work include Gilbert Stuart, Thomas Sully, and John Trumbull. Trumbull contracted with Yale University in 1831 to supply portraits and miniatures in return for an annuity. He also designed Trumbull Gallery there. Completed in 1832, it was America's first art museum. It was demolished in 1901.

One of America's most sought-after portrait painters, Charles Wilson Peale, who had studied in London, did miniatures in a stipple technique. His younger brother and pupil James Peale painted miniatures in a linear style. Miniatures survive from the hand of John Wesley Jarvis, a respected painter in New York State. Anson Dickinson, a trained silversmith, gained renown for his miniatures. Joseph Wood began his miniature career in New York State, and then painted in Philadelphia and Washington, D.C. The Museum of Worcester, Massachusetts, has a fine miniature portrait of Captain Charles Tyler Savage by Wood's talented follower Nathaniel Rogers, who was a founding member of the National Academy of Design.

Probably the finest American miniaturist was Edward Greene Malbone. Born in Newport, Rhode Island, he studied and trained under the painter Benjamin West at the Royal Academy, London. Admired as a fine draftsman, Malbone worked in Boston, New York, Philadelphia, Charleston, and Savannah. *A Portrait of Charles In-*

Miniature. A portrait of Mungo Park, the British explorer of Africa until his premature death in 1806. GRANGER COLLECTION, LTD.

glis, in the National Portrait Gallery at Washington, D.C., represents Malbone's artistry. Françoise M. Guyol de Guiran, a Frenchman, was active in St. Louis and New Orleans between about 1812 and 1828. His only known miniature is *Portrait of a Gentleman and His Daughter* (1800/25), now in the collection of the Metropolitan Museum of Art, New York.

When daguerreotypes made the personal image both popular and cheap, the miniature hand-painted image was quickly replaced.

BIBLIOGRAPHY

Colding, Torben Holck. *Aspects of Miniature Painting.* Copenhagen: Munksgaard, 1953.

Johnson, Dale T. *American Portrait Miniatures in the Manney Collection.* New York: Metropolitan Museum of Art, 1990.

Rolf Achilles

See also **Art: Painting.**

MINIMUM-WAGE LEGISLATION. These laws specify the minimum amount that employers may pay their employees for doing a specified type of work. The first minimum-wage laws in the United States were passed by state legislatures in the mid-nineteenth century and applied only to women and children. For example, in 1842 Connecticut passed a wage and hour law for children.

The concept of minimum-wage legislation gained popularity during the first two decades of the twentieth century, often referred to as the Progressive Era. In general, people who considered themselves progressives advocated using governmental authority to limit some of the negative effects of rapid industrialization and urbanization brought about by the growth of large-scale corporate capitalism. One of the evils they hoped to combat through legislation consisted of hourly wages that were often below the minimum necessary for subsistence.

The Problem of Liberty of Contract

During the Progressive Era minimum-wage legislation generally did not grant protections to men in ordinary occupations, but only to women and children, or to men in especially dangerous occupations. Men did not fall within the scope of legislation regulating the pay or conditions of employment because they were thought to possess the constitutional right to enter into any contract they chose. This right was known as "liberty of contract." This doctrine held that parties who were legally able to enter into contracts should not have their freedom interfered with by the state unless such interference was necessary to protect the health, welfare, or morals of the community. For example, in *Lochner v. New York* (1905), the Supreme Court struck down a New York law limiting the working hours of bakers. While the case did not involve a minimum-wage law, it did establish that legislation regulating the terms of employment contracts represented an unconstitutional interference by government into the marketplace and thus violated the Fourteenth Amendment.

Despite the doctrine of liberty of contract, legislators and courts believed that contracts involving women could be governmentally regulated because of women's status as mothers. For example, in *Muller v. Oregon* (1908) the U.S. Supreme Court upheld an Oregon statute that set a maximum limit to the number of hours that women could work. This case demonstrated that the constitutional right to liberty of contract was a right possessed only by men. Nevertheless, even minimum-wage laws directed toward female employees remained controversial. Such legislation was held invalid in New York in 1901, Indiana in 1903, and Nebraska in 1914. Between 1914 and 1920, however, judges in Oregon, Minnesota, Arkansas, Washington, and Massachusetts upheld minimum-wage laws for women, reasoning that the physical condition of women required special legislative protection through the use of the state's police powers.

After women gained the right to vote in 1920, the Supreme Court altered its jurisprudence and held in *Adkins v. Children's Hospital* (1923) that a federal minimum-wage provision for women unconstitutionally violated their right to freedom of contract. Adkins involved a minimum-wage rate set by the District of Columbia that was based on detailed studies of prices for food, housing, clothing, and other budget items. The defendant, Children's Hospital, claimed it could not afford to pay its female housekeepers the statutory minimum wage. In *Adkins*, a majority of the Supreme Court, in a close decision, refused to follow the *Muller* decision and made no reference to the burdens of motherhood on women workers. Instead it relied on the *Lochner* case for authority for its decision, stating that the legal and political differences between the sexes "have now come almost, if not quite, to the vanishing point." The Court majority relied on the passage of the Nineteenth Amendment giving women the right to vote to demonstrate this legal and political equality. According to the Court, this revolutionary change in women's legal status now granted women the same rights to liberty of contract as men, including the right to agree to work for less than the state-sanctioned minimum wage.

Passage of Federal Minimum-Wage Legislation

As the economy worsened during the Depression, many states once again attempted to enact minimum-wage legislation. The federal government also became an advocate of a national minimum wage. In 1933 as a part of President Franklin Roosevelt's NEW DEAL, Congress passed the National Industrial Recovery Act (NIRA). This legislation attempted to stimulate business recovery by allowing individual industries to draft codes of fair competition. A number of these codes set minimum-wage levels for particular types of work. In 1935 the Supreme Court struck down the NIRA in *Schechter Poultry Corp. v. United States*, finding that among other defects, the legislation could not be supported by Congress's power under the commerce clause because the employees and the company violating the code were not engaged in interstate commerce.

Soon afterward the Court demonstrated that it was willing to strike down state as well as national legislation imposing a minimum wage. In 1936 in *Morehead v. New York ex rel. Tipaldo*, the Supreme Court narrowly voted to strike down a New York minimum-wage law for women and children. Relying on Adkins, the Court again held that the right to contract freely for wages is protected by the Constitution, and that this right applied to women and children as well as to men. One of the dissenters in the case, Justice Harlan Fiske Stone, noted that "there is grim irony in speaking of the freedom of contract of those who, because of their economic necessities, give their services for less than is needful to keep body and soul together." Many members of the public strongly criticized the decision.

The following year in a dramatic reversal of policy, the Court upheld a Washington State minimum-wage law for women. The law at issue in *West Coast Hotel v. Parrish* (1937) closely resembled the law the Court had struck down in *Morehead v. New York ex rel. Tipaldo* only the year before. Justice Roberts, the key swing vote in the Morehead case, switched sides and voted to uphold the law.

Many observers attributed Jackson's decision to change his vote to the fact that the decision was handed down less than two months after President Franklin D. Roosevelt announced his plan to pack the Supreme Court with justices more supportive of New Deal economic regulation. For this reason the decision is sometimes called "the switch in time that saved nine." Yet whether a direct causal link actually existed between the two events is less than clear.

In *Parrish*, the Court explicitly overruled the *Adkins* decision, holding that liberty of contract, while protected by the Constitution, was subject to reasonable regulation in the interest of the community. Justice Hughes, who authored the opinion, stated that "the Constitution does not speak of freedom of contract" and noted that "the Constitution does not recognize an absolute and uncontrollable liberty."

The decision in *Parrish* opened the door for both states and the federal government to pass legislation regulating the wages and hours of employees. In 1938 Congress passed the FAIR LABOR STANDARDS ACT (FLSA) that established a federal minimum wage. The FLSA originally applied to industries whose combined employment represented only about one-fifth of the labor force. In those industries it banned oppressive child labor and set the minimum hourly wage at 25 cents and the maximum work week at 44 hours. In 1941 the Supreme Court upheld the constitutionality of the FLSA. Because the FLSA covered only employees engaged in activities in interstate commerce, many states also enacted their own minimum wage laws. The FLSA provides that when state and federal minimum wage legislation both apply, the higher standard governs.

After passage of the FLSA, questions arose as to which types of work-related activities were covered by the act. In 1947 Congress amended the FLSA by enacting the Portal-to-Portal act, which overturned a Supreme Court decision permitting extra pay for employees engaged in preparation and clean-up work. Under the act, only work that is an integral and indispensable part of the employee's principal activities is entitled to compensation. Over the years Congress has amended the FLSA to add categories of employees covered by its provisions and to raise the level of the minimum wage. The minimum was raised to $5.15 hour, effective as of 1 September 1997.

In 1963 Congress passed the Federal EQUAL PAY ACT, which provides that men and women must receive equal pay for equal work in any industry engaged in interstate commerce. Congress has also passed additional legislation that covers the federal government as both an employer and a purchaser of goods and services. This legislation requires it to pay preestablished minimum wages to its employees (Davis-Bacon Act of 1931) and requires that parties holding government contracts do the same (Walsh Healey Public Contracts Act of 1936).

BIBLIOGRAPHY

Cox, Archibald, et al., eds. *Labor Law: Cases and Materials.* 13th ed. New York: Foundation Press, 2001.

Hall, Kermit L. *The Magic Mirror: Law in American History.* New York: Oxford University Press, 1989.

Irons, Peter H., and Howard Zinn. *A People's History of the Supreme Court: The Men and Women Whose Cases and Decisions Have Shaped Our Constitution.* New York: Penguin, 2000.

Katherine M. Jones

See also **National Recovery Administration;** *and vol. 9:* **Women in Industry (Brandeis Brief).**

MINING INDUSTRY. *See* **Coal Mining** *and individual metals.*

MINING TOWNS. In the nineteenth and twentieth centuries, mining towns were central to industrialization and the economic growth of the United States. Mining towns grew up around numerous ores, and the particular minerals and the technologies required to remove them from the earth had different impacts on the development of social relations within the towns.

Mining towns arose quickly once a mineral deposit was discovered. This was particularly true in the case of gold and silver because people understood the direct link between the amount one could extract and one's wealth. "Gold Rush" towns were notorious for a quick rise and, often, an equally dramatic fall. These temporary towns were often dominated by young, single men who came from all over the United States as well as from around the world to take their chances at striking it rich.

Not all mining towns experienced the boom-and-bust cycle. Those that surrounded large metal deposits, like the gold and silver in Nevada's Comstock Lode and in Cripple Creek, Colorado, and the copper at Butte, Montana, expanded and became more permanent. Coal mining towns in central Illinois, southwestern Pennsylvania, and West Virginia produced for decades and ensured railroad development across the continent. Permanency changed the demography as well as the conditions of mining communities. Mining towns often became family towns where male, female, and child labor became essential for production and profits.

Mining towns became famous for working-class struggles and militant unionism. Some of the nation's most important labor battles occurred in mining towns, such as the great anthracite strike of 1902, the strike that led to the

Mining Town. Miners during a gold rush; many towns like this one were short-lived, though others became permanent settlements even when the nearby deposits dwindled. GETTY IMAGES

1914 massacre of coal workers at Ludlow, Colorado, and the 1917 forcible removal from the state of Arizona of International Workers of the World members and sympathizers in Bisbee, Arizona. Indeed the Western Federation of Miners and the United Mine Workers of America were dominated by progressive U.S.- and European-born miners whose beliefs were molded in America's mining towns.

BIBLIOGRAPHY

Francaviglia, Richard V. *Hard Places: Reading the Landscape of America's Historic Mining Districts.* Iowa City: University of Iowa Press, 1991.

Long, Priscilla. *Where the Sun Never Shines: A History of America's Bloody Coal Industry.* New York: Paragon House, 1989.

Rickard, T. A. *A History of American Mining.* New York: McGraw-Hill, 1932.

Waszkis, Helmut. *Mining in the Americas: Stories and History.* Cambridge, U.K.: Woodhead, 1993.

Caroline Waldron Merithew

See also **Boomtowns; Ghost Towns.**

MINNEAPOLIS–ST. PAUL,

located in southeastern Minnesota, with a regional population of close to three million, is the nation's fifteenth-largest metropolitan area. Minneapolis is Minnesota's largest city, St. Paul the state capital. Historically noted for flour milling and progressive politics, the cities began as Fort Snelling, an early nineteenth century military outpost. The nearby settlement of St. Paul was named in 1841 after a recently built chapel and its patron saint; a contest named Minneapolis—the Sioux word *minne*, "water," combined with the Greek *polis*, "city."

As steamboats brought settlers and trade goods upriver, St. Paul became the head of navigation on the Mississippi and headquarters for the American Fur Company and the Great Northern Railroad. By the 1880s, a new flour milling technique made Minneapolis the nation's largest milling center. Railroads moved farm machinery and trade goods from Minneapolis to the large western wheat-growing areas.

Drawing early migrants from New England and Canada, and by the 1880s from Germany, Sweden, Norway, and Denmark, Minneapolis–St. Paul's population swelled to over 350,000 by 1900. One of the nation's most homogeneous (and Lutheran) regions well into the 1980s, the core city population was approximately one-third nonwhite at the beginning of the twenty-first century. Traditionally small African American and Native American populations increased, while recent immigrants from Vietnam, Cambodia, Laos, Mexico, Somalia, and Ethiopia added to the region's diversity. In the 1990s, the core cities of Minneapolis-St.Paul gained population for the first time since 1960 (4 to 5 percent).

Old and New in Minneapolis. In this 1973 photograph by Donald Emmerich, the 775-foot IDS Center towers over the 447-foot Foshay Tower, the city's tallest building for four decades after it opened in 1929. NATIONAL ARCHIVES AND RECORDS ADMINISTRATION

From its nineteenth-century milling and food processing (General Mills) and railroading (Burlington Northern) origins, the regional economy has diversified and become service-oriented, with corporate headquarters ranging from Target to 3M. "High-tech" industries, media/graphic and other arts, banking and insurance, and other services abound, while overall manufacturing capacity has declined. St. Paul's largest employer is state government.

The Minneapolis–St. Paul area has numerous higher education institutions, most notably the University of Minnesota's main campus, with over 40,000 students. Nationally regarded as a leading cultural center with a vibrant theater, music, and dance scene, Minneapolis is home to the Institute of Arts, the Guthrie Theater, the Walker Art Center, and numerous other cultural venues. St. Paul is home to the state's largest museum, the History Center Museum, as well as the Science Museum of Minnesota, the Minnesota Museum of American Art, and the Minnesota Children's Museum. The lake-dotted region attracts outdoor enthusiasts year-round.

BIBLIOGRAPHY

Adams, John S., and Barbara J. VanDrasek. *Minneapolis-St. Paul: People, Place and Public Life*. Minneapolis: University of Minnesota Press, 1993.

Lanegran, David, and Judith A. Martin. *Where We Live*. Minneapolis: University of Minnesota Press, 1983.

Judith A. Martin

See also **Snelling, Fort.**

MINNESOTA. The state of Minnesota lies nearly at the center of the North American continent. Issuing from one of its many lakes, the Mississippi River rises and flows south to the Gulf of Mexico. On its western border the Red River flows north through Lake Winnipeg to Hudson Bay, and the streams that drain eastward into Lake Superior ultimately reach the Atlantic Ocean. It is a transition zone, divided among northern pine forests, the midwestern corn belt, and the Great Plains. The name Minnesota, derived from a Dakota word meaning "cloud-colored water," has become the popular designation "Land of Sky Blue Waters."

Except for a small area in the southeastern corner, the state's modern topography was shaped by the ice sheets of the last (Wisconsin) glacial advance, which melted away between ten and fifteen thousand years ago. From that era come the first signs of human occupation and for most of the period until the arrival of Europeans some 350 years ago the area was a part of the Archaic and Woodland traditions and lay on the northwestern fringe of the Hopewell and Mississippian cultures that dominated the Ohio and Mississippi valleys. French traders and missionaries arriving in the late seventeenth century found it a land dotted with burial mounds and other ceremonial earthworks.

Colonial Occupation

In advance of the French came migrating OTTAWA, HURON, and OJIBWE (Chippewa) Indians driven westward by the Iroquois wars and seeking to trade European goods for the furs gathered by the Dakota (Sioux) and other tribes beyond the Great Lakes. The first Frenchmen to leave a record of reaching the area, Pierre D'Esprit, Sieur de Radisson, and Medart Chouart, Sieur de Groseilliers, accompanied a group of Ottawas at some time between the years 1654 and 1660. They were soon followed by others: Daniel Greysolon, Sieur du Luth (1679), Father Louis Hennepin (1680), Pierre Charles le Sueur (1700), and Pierre Gaultier, Sieur de la Verendrye (1731).

These men and many more licensed by the French crown took over and expanded the fur-trading network created by Indian middlemen. After Britain acquired French Canada in 1763, control of this trade passed to the North West Company and its various offshoots. Indian tribes meanwhile continued to move westward. The introduction of horses from Spain had produced a new buffalo-hunting culture that drew the Cheyennes and the western bands of Dakotas (Sioux) onto the open plains, even as the forests of northern Minnesota were being occupied by the Ojibwes.

Following the purchase of Louisiana Territory in 1803, the American government not only dispatched Meriwether Lewis and William Clark to the west coast, but also sent an expedition under Lieutenant Zebulon M. Pike to explore the headwaters of the Mississippi and assert American authority there. In 1805 Pike purchased from the eastern bands of Dakotas the right to locate a fort at the mouth of the Minnesota River along with land that also encompassed the nearby Falls of Saint Anthony.

American Conquest

The War of 1812 intervened, and not until 1820 did the building of the fort commence. Named for Colonel Josiah Snelling, who saw it to completion, the outpost became the focus for American influence throughout the region during the next thirty years. The first steamboat, the *Virginia*, reached Fort Snelling in 1823, and a small trading and farming community grew, dominated by the regional headquarters of the American Fur Company. In 1837 the United States acquired by treaties with the Ojibwes and the Sioux the land on the east bank of the Mississippi, where settlers who had been forced off the military reservation established the village of Saint Paul in 1840.

After Iowa was admitted to statehood in 1846 and Wisconsin in 1848, the area that remained in those two territories, extending north to the British border and west to the Missouri River, became Minnesota. At this time, however, all but a small triangle between the Mississippi and Saint Croix Rivers was still Indian land. The new territory owed its creation in 1849 to the influence of Illinois Senator Stephen A. Douglas and to an influx of New England lumbermen eager to exploit its vast stands of pine. Saint Paul, located at the practical head of steamboat navigation on the Mississippi, became its capital.

In the nine years that followed, Minnesota rode the crest of a boom in western land speculation. Its population increased from barely 5,000 to 150,000, many of whom were new immigrants from Germany, Scandinavia, and Ireland. Treaties forced on the Dakota Indians in 1851 gave all of southern Minnesota except a narrow reservation along the Minnesota River to the United States, and even before the treaties were ratified, settlers poured into the southeastern counties and the Minnesota River Valley. In 1858, on the eve of the Civil War, Minnesota became the thirty-second state of the Union. Its north-south orientation, including a potential port at the head of Lake Superior and a common boundary with Canada, was dictated by expansionist ambitions and by railroad interests, for which Douglas was again the spokesman.

Saint Paul, a natural hub of future transportation routes, remained the capital. Henry Hastings Sibley, who for twenty years had managed the Minnesota trade of the American Fur Company, became the state's first governor. He was the last Democrat to hold the office for thirty years.

Swept by abolitionist and Republican sentiment in the election of 1860, the state was the first to volunteer troops to the Union. In 1862, however, Minnesota was engulfed by its own war. A faction among the Dakota tribe, enraged at forced assimilation and broken promises and led by Chief Little Crow, launched a surprise attack, slaying nearly 500 settlers. Vengeance was swift and terrible. All Indians, including not only the entire Dakota tribe but also the peaceful Winnebagos, were removed from southern Minnesota, and those who fled were pursued onto the northern plains, where intermittent warfare ended only with the massacre at Wounded Knee, South Dakota, in 1890.

Forty Years of Statehood
By the close of the nineteenth century, Minnesota's prairies and hardwood forests had been transformed into farmland. The pine forests were nearly exhausted, and lumbering, the state's first great extractive industry, was at its peak of productivity. It would cease abruptly after 1905. Already, however, timber was being replaced in the northeastern corner of Minnesota by a second great resource. Iron mining had begun on the Vermilion Range in the 1880s and on the richer Mesabi Range in 1890.

Agriculture also had its extractive aspects. Soaring wheat prices during the Civil War years tied Minnesota farming from the outset to a cash crop system and world markets. With luck and a limited investment, pioneer farmers could pay for their land in a year or two. Single-crop farming, however, exhausted even the richest prairie soil, and diversification demanded more capital. Those without access to it sold out and went on to new land, thus producing a moving "wheat frontier" that by the 1880s had reached the Red River Valley and the Dakota plains.

Minnesota grew with the railroad era. Just as it owed its early organization to the dreams of railroad promoters, so the shape and location of its towns and cities were determined by steel rails. Government land grants to railroad companies comprised more than one-fifth of the state's area. Its own most prominent railroad promoter was James J. Hill, who built the St. Paul, Minneapolis, and Manitoba line in 1878 and completed the transcontinental Great Northern Road in 1890.

Minnesota industry centered on the processing of raw materials and agricultural products. Sawmilling gained an early start in towns along the Saint Croix and Mississippi Rivers. The largest concentration was at the Falls of Saint Anthony. Industry powered by the falls produced the city of Minneapolis, which by 1880 had surpassed St. Paul in population. By then sawmilling was giving way

to flour milling, and Minneapolis boasted of being the country's breadbasket. Firms like Washburn Crosby and Pillsbury had the most advanced flour-milling technology in the world, while the Minneapolis Millers Association, through its connection with rail lines and grain storage facilities, dictated the price of wheat to farmers across the region.

The stream of immigrants from Europe had continued to swell. By 1880, 71 percent of the population was either foreign-born or had an immigrant parent. The greatest number were from Germany, but Norway was a close second, and the Scandinavian countries together far outnumbered any single group. Native-born Anglo-Americans continued to control most of the seats of power in business and government, but in 1892 Minnesota elected Knute Nelson as its first foreign-born governor.

The Early Twentieth Century
The opening decades of the twentieth century saw the high tide of small-town life in Minnesota. Communities like Sauk Centre, which was bitterly satirized by its native son Sinclair Lewis in his novel *Main Street* (1920), thrived on rural prosperity, and in 1900 they were served by a railroad network that reached to every corner of the state. Soon, however, automobiles and the initiation of a state highway system, together with a prolonged agricultural depression in the 1920s, brought the decline and disappearance of many small towns.

In the same decades, the cities of Minneapolis and St. Paul merged into a twin-headed metropolis. Spreading suburbs were served by a single system of electric streetcars. Enlarged city newspapers circulated throughout the state, and with the arrival of commercial radio in 1922, city stations dominated the airwaves. The business and financial sway of the Twin Cities was recognized in 1912, when Minneapolis became the seat of the Ninth Federal Reserve District, extending from Upper Michigan to the Rocky Mountains. In the meantime Minnesota had gained yet a third urban center as iron mining expanded. Duluth and its surrounding communities, supported by shipbuilding, ore docks, and a steel mill, reached a population of 150,000 in 1920.

The Progressive Era in Minnesota, with its public concern over urbanization and industry, brought the election of the Democratic governor John Lind in 1898 and the passage of laws to open up the political system and expand the regulatory powers of government. Suffrage for women, however, was blocked until 1919 because of its association with the temperance movement in the minds of German voters and the brewing interests.

Industrialization also brought an emerging labor movement. The Minnesota State Federation of Labor was formed in 1890, but the major struggles of the next decades were led by groups like the WESTERN FEDERATION OF MINERS and the INDUSTRIAL WORKERS OF THE WORLD. Low pay and dangerous working conditions among immigrant miners in the great open pits of the Mesabi Range brought on two bitter strikes, in 1907 and in 1916. In Minneapolis, employers and bankers formed a semisecret organization called the Citizens Alliance, that held down wages and preserved an open-shop city until passage of the NATIONAL LABOR RELATIONS ACT in 1935.

The perceived threat of labor activism and the hysteria accompanying World War I led to a dark period of nativism and red-baiting that scarred Minnesota for a generation. Antiwar sentiment within the state's large German population was met with open persecution and mob violence, and a wartime Committee of Public Safety used its near-absolute power to register all aliens, break strikes, and eliminate civil liberties such as freedom of speech.

Depression and World War II

In Minnesota the depression of the 1930s was a continuation of the agricultural crisis that had begun in 1920. Combined with increased mechanization during World War I, it had already eliminated thousands of small farms. Drought and depression in the 1930s only exacerbated the effects.

Minnesota industry had already begun to change. Papermaking and the manufacture of wood products had replaced lumbering. The state had lost its dominance in flour-making, and the large milling firms were turning to brand-name consumer products and intensive marketing. Meatpackers like the Hormel Company, along with other food processors, were doing likewise. With the decline of railroads, the Twin Cities were becoming a center for trucking and interstate buses and also home to the new Northwest Orient Airline.

New political alliances had been forged by the heat of wartime repression, and in the 1920s the Farmer-Labor Party replaced the Democrats as the state's second major party. In 1930 its candidate, Floyd B. Olson, was elected governor. A charismatic leader, Olson described himself as a radical but drew widespread support for policies that essentially mirrored those of the New Deal. His early death from cancer in 1936 left the Farmer-Labor Party divided, and his successor, Elmer A. Benson, met defeat in 1938 from the young Republican Harold E. Stassen.

The years preceding World War II revived bitter memories of the last war. Antiwar sentiment was strong, and there was significant support for former Minnesotan Charles A. Lindbergh and his "America First" campaign. Until 1940 both Minnesota senators opposed all moves toward intervention, and one of them, Henrik Shipstead, stayed on to cast his vote against the United Nations charter in 1945. That the war had reversed these attitudes in Minnesota was shown by his defeat in the next primary election.

The Postwar Era

The three decades after World War II saw more Minnesotans rise to prominence in national politics and public life than at any other period. Most notable was Hubert H. Humphrey, United States senator, vice president under Lyndon B. Johnson and Democratic candidate for president in 1968. Others included former governor Stassen, an architect of the United Nations charter and advisor to President Dwight D. Eisenhower; Orville Freeman and Robert Bergland, both secretaries of agriculture; Maurice Stans, secretary of commerce; Warren E. Burger, chief justice of the United States; Eugene J. McCarthy, United States senator and candidate for president; and Eugenie M. Anderson, the first woman to serve as a United States foreign ambassador. They were followed in the 1970s by Walter E. Mondale, vice president under Jimmy Carter (1976–1980) and Democratic candidate for president in 1984.

This unusual record reflected in part the health of both Minnesota's political parties. In 1944 the Farmer-Labor and Democratic Parties merged to form what became known as the Democratic Farmer-Labor Party (DFL). Four years later Humphrey and a group of young Democrats dedicated to internationalism, the Cold War, and civil rights assumed party leadership. Led by Stassen and his successors, Minnesota Republicans were in substantial agreement with the DFL on these issues and other more local ones, such as support for education and human services. Rivalry between the parties remained keen, nevertheless; power was evenly divided, and Minnesota acquired a national reputation for clean politics and citizen participation.

Minnesota's economy also emerged from World War II stronger than ever before. Wartime retooling had laid the foundations for a new manufacturing sector. The state found itself especially strong in precision industries such as computers and medical devices and later in electronics. High prices had restored farm prosperity, and the green revolution in plant genetics and chemistry soon led to record crops. Although this new agriculture demanded ever greater capital investment and presaged the end of the family farm, its even darker side, including environmental damage, did not become evident until the 1980s.

Yet the postwar period brought hard times to the iron ranges, for reserves of high-grade ore had been exhausted. Abundant iron was locked in the hard rock known as taconite, but the investment required for its extraction was enormous. Prosperity slowly returned to northern Minnesota with the opening of the Saint Lawrence Seaway in 1959, the development of tourism, and passage of a state constitutional amendment in 1964 that limited the taxation of taconite plants.

In August 1973 *Time* magazine celebrated what it called "The Good Life in Minnesota." This included a broad array of cultural phenomena. A mushrooming of theater, art, and music groups in the 1960s was accompanied by founding of the Guthrie Theater and the Minnesota Symphony Orchestra; small presses flourished; major league sports came to the state. Minnesota became a mecca for canoeists and outdoors enthusiasts with expansion of its wilderness area on the Canadian border and establishment of Voyageurs National Park (1975). In the 1970s nationwide popularity of the radio show *A Prairie Home Companion* made mythical Lake Wobegon Minnesota's best-loved small town.

Demographic and Social Change

Until the mid-twentieth century Ojibwe Indians clustered on seven reservations in northern Minnesota were the state's largest racial minority. A small African American community centered in the Twin Cities found employment in service industries. Hispanics, mostly Mexican, included migratory workers in agriculture and a few permanent residents near the packinghouses of South Saint Paul. Asians numbered only a few hundred.

Immediately after World War II, migration to cities along with national and international shifts in population brought great change. By the year 2000, nonwhites, including Hispanics, accounted for about 10 percent of the state's 4,919,000 people. Among minority groups Africans, both African Americans and recent immigrants from the continent, were the most numerous at 171,000. Asians and Pacific Islanders together numbered nearly 144,000, while Hispanics (of any race) were a close third at 143,000. American Indians, including members of various tribes living in the Twin Cities, came to just under 55,000.

Meanwhile Minnesota had become an urban state. Most minority immigrants stayed in the Twin Cities, and as early as 1970 more than half the population lived in the sprawling metropolitan area. The proportion grew as consolidation of farms into ever larger industrial-style operations brought depopulation to rural counties, especially those in the southern and western parts of the state.

Other forms of diversity accompanied these demographic changes in the state's ethnicity. The women's and gay rights movements of the 1970s and 1980s encountered growing resistance among conservatives rooted in the state's powerful religious traditions. Deep political rifts resulted, and after 1973, when Minnesotan Harry A. Blackmun wrote the United States Supreme Court's decision in the case of *Roe v. Wade*, abortion laws dominated each legislative session. Nevertheless, the number and power of women in public life grew steadily. The number of women representatives in the legislature increased from none from 1945 to 1950 to 61 in 1996. In 1977 Rosalie Wahl became the first woman to serve on the Minnesota Supreme Court, and from 1990 to 1994 women held a majority on the court. Social and demographic change were both evident in Minneapolis, where an African American woman, Sharon Sayles Belton, served as mayor from 1993 to 2001.

BIBLIOGRAPHY

Clark, Clifford E., Jr., ed. *Minnesota in a Century of Change: The State and Its People Since 1900*. St. Paul: Minnesota Historical Society Press, 1989.

Gilman, Rhoda R. *The Story of Minnesota's Past*. St. Paul: Minnesota Historical Society Press, 1991. For general readers. Heavily illustrated.

Graubard, Stephen R., ed. *Minnesota, Real and Imagined: Essays on the State and Its Culture*. St. Paul: Minnesota Historical Society Press, 2001. Originally published as the summer 2000 (vol. 129, no. 3) issue of *Daedalus*.

Holmquist, June Drenning, ed. *They Chose Minnesota: A Survey of the State's Ethnic Groups*. St. Paul: Minnesota Historical Society Press, 1981.

Lass, William E. *Minnesota: A History*. New York: Norton, 2d ed., 1998.

Rhoda R. Gilman

See also **Demography and Demographic Trends; Explorations and Expeditions: French; Farmer-Labor Party of Minnesota; Immigration; Iron and Steel Industry; Midwest; Minneapolis–St. Paul; Railroads.**

MINNESOTA MORATORIUM CASE, or *Home Building and Loan Association v. Blaisdell et al.*, 290 U.S. 398 (1934), upheld the constitutionality of a Minnesota moratorium on mortgage foreclosures passed in 1933 amid the economic crisis of the depression, which began in 1929. Critics of the law contended that it constituted a violation of the contract clause in the federal Constitution (*see* FLETCHER V. PECK) and of the due process and equal protection clauses of the Fourteenth Amendment. The Supreme Court found the act was justified by the emergency conditions and concurred with the view that such measures were temporary.

BIBLIOGRAPHY

Leuchtenburg, William E. *The Supreme Court Reborn: The Constitutional Revolution in the Age of Roosevelt*. New York: Oxford University Press, 1995.

McConnell, Grant. *Private Power and American Democracy*. New York: Knopf, 1966.

W. Brooke Graves/A. R.

See also **Constitution of the United States; Contract Clause; Government Regulation of Business; Mortgage Relief Legislation; New Deal.**

MINOR V. HAPPERSETT, 21 Wallace 162 (1875). The Fourteenth Amendment provides in part that "No State shall make or enforce any law which shall abridge the privileges or immunities of citizens of the United States." When Virginia L. Minor of Missouri was rebuffed in 1866 in her attempt to register as a voter, she maintained that the right of suffrage was a privilege of U.S. citizenship. In rejecting this contention, the Supreme Court held that the right of suffrage was not coextensive with CITIZENSHIP—that the Fourteenth Amendment did not add to the privileges or immunities of citizens of the

United States, but merely furnished an additional guarantee for those in existence.

BIBLIOGRAPHY

Kerber, Linda K. *No Constitutional Right to be Ladies: Women and the Obligations of Citizenship.* New York: Hill and Wang, 1998.

Rogers, Donald W., and Christine Scriabine, eds. *Voting and the Spirit of American Democracy: Essays on the History of Voting Rights in America.* West Hartford, Conn.: University of Hartford, 1990; Urbana: University of Illinois Press, 1992.

Thomas S. Barclay / A. R.

See also **Civil Rights and Liberties; Suffrage: Exclusion from the Suffrage; Suffrage: Woman's Suffrage; Voting; Women's Rights Movement: The Nineteenth Century.**

MINSTREL SHOWS evolved from early nineteenth-century theatrical performances of Negro "delineators," most famously Thomas D. Rice, the original "Jim Crow." Rice was not the first white actor to appear on stage in blackface, but his imitation of African American song, dance, and dialect introduced a style of entertainment that broadly influenced American popular culture. Unlike

Edwin P. Christy. The founder of the Christy Minstrels in the mid-1840s, and its interlocutor until he retired about a decade later; the troupe standardized many minstrel routines and commissioned songs by Stephen Foster. LIBRARY OF CONGRESS

Rice's song and dance acts, the minstrel show offered full evenings of blackface entertainment and became known for its standard characters from the opening scene. The interlocutor appeared in blackface but did not speak in dialect. He directed the row of seated musicians and elicited jokes in dialect from the two end men, Mr. Tambo, who played the tambourine, and Mr. Bones, who played the bone castanets. Among the most popular minstrel troupes by the mid-nineteenth century were Daniel Emmett's traveling Virginia Minstrels and the Christy Minstrels of New York City, who introduced the works of Stephen Foster. The widely performed stage production of *Uncle Tom's Cabin* also incorporated elements of the minstrel show, albeit with a greater air of solemnity.

In the late nineteenth century minstrel shows declined in popularity in cities, and theatrical companies, including African American groups, took their shows on the road to rural areas. By the 1930s, as minstrel shows faded from view, the minstrel banjo style had become a central element in the new "country" music disseminated to audiences by radio broadcasts.

Although much of the genre of minstrelsy was highly sentimental and sympathetic toward the plight of slaves, minstrel shows also sustained nostalgia for the Old South among northern white audiences and presented to them grotesque stereotypes of African American culture. However, the theatricality of racial doubling served no single purpose. As part of a complex tradition of masquerade, minstrelsy shaped popular culture across the American barrier of race.

BIBLIOGRAPHY

Hans, Nathan. *Dan Emmett and the Rise of Early Negro Minstrelsy.* Norman: University of Oklahoma Press, 1962.

Lott, Eric. *Love and Theft: Blackface Minstrelsy and the American Working Class.* New York: Oxford University Press, 1993.

Rehin, George. "Harlequin Jim Crow." *Journal of Popular Culture* 9 (Winter 1975): 682–701.

Louis S. Gerteis

See also **Music: Country and Western; Theater.**

MINT, FEDERAL. The first American Secretary of Finance, Robert Morris, first urged the Continental Congress to establish a mint in 1782. In 1786, Congress ordered the Board of the Treasury to study the subject, but not until 2 April 1792, three years after the Constitution, did the new government authorize the creation of a mint. The mint was set up in 1793 in Philadelphia, then the national capital, and remained there permanently after other government agencies moved to Washington, D.C. Silver coinage began in 1794 and gold coinage in 1795. The staff at first consisted of eleven officers and clerks, nineteen workmen in the coining department, and seven men at the furnaces. The total coinage produced in 1794–1795 was less than $500,000. By 1807, the output exceeded $1 million. In 1851, the mint struck nearly $63.5 million, all of it gold except for about $800,000. In the earlier years, the mint often lacked gold and silver with which to work. In 1820, it operated only part of the time because of this scarcity and the small demand for copper coins.

In 1835, Congress established three branch mints—one at New Orleans and two in new goldfields in Charlotte, North Carolina, and Dahlonega, Georgia. The mint at New Orleans was taken over by the Confederates at the beginning of the Civil War and operated by them between 26 January and 31 May 1861, when they suspended operations. The New Orleans mint did not resume work until 1879, and, in 1909, it ceased to coin and became an assay office. The mint at Dahlonega closed in 1861 and the mint at Charlotte was used as barracks by Confederate soldiers and never operated after that. A branch mint was installed at San Francisco in 1854 and operated until 1955. Another mint was legally established at Denver in 1862, but no coins had yet been made there when in 1870 it was turned into an assay office. In 1895, it was again authorized to coin, but no MONEY was made there until 1906. A sixth branch mint began work at Carson City, Nevada, in 1870, but its production was not great, and it closed in 1893. Another mint, authorized in 1864 at Dalles, Oregon, was in the process of construction in 1871 when it was destroyed by fire, and the project was abandoned. A mint authorized in 1902 at Manila, in the Philippines, had a comparatively small output. By acts of 1846 and later, the various mints were made public depositories. The Bureau of the Mint was created by Congress on 12 February 1873, as a division of the Treasury Department. In 1984, the name of the Bureau of the Mint changed to the United States Mint. Currently, the mint supervises the four remaining coinage mints in Denver, Philadelphia, San Francisco, and West Point as well as a bullion depository in Fort Knox, Kentucky.

The minting of gold coins ceased in 1934. In 1979, the United States Mint began producing the Susan B. Anthony dollar, the first American coin to feature a non-mythological woman, but it proved unpopular because it too closely resembled a quarter. In 2000, the United States Mint replaced that unsuccessful dollar with another dollar coin featuring a woman: Sacagawea, who helped guide the Lewis and Clark expedition. The mint hoped that the gold color, smooth edge, and wide, raised border around the edge of the Sacagawea dollar would distinguish it from other currency denominations. At the end of the twentieth century, the United States Mint introduced the Fifty State Quarters program, which will mint one style of quarter for each state in the United States.

BIBLIOGRAPHY

Birdsall, Clair M. *The United States Branch Mint at Charlotte, North Carolina: Its History and Coinage.* Easley, S.C.: Southern Historical Press, 1988.

Head, Sylvia. *The Neighborhood Mint: Dahlonega in the Age of Jackson.* Macon, Ga.: Mercer University Press, 1986.

Stewart, Frank H. *History of the First United States Mint.* Lawrence, Mass.: Quarterman Publications, 1974.

Alvin F. Harlow / H. S.; A. E.

See also **Currency and Coinage; Financial Panics; Hard Money; Legal Tender; Pieces of Eight; Specie Payments, Suspension and Resumption of.**

MINTS, PRIVATE, frequently appeared in new gold-producing areas—first in Georgia and North Carolina, later in the West—when there was a scarcity of U.S. minted coins. In California, from 1849 to 1851, government money was so scant that several private mints were set up; though not legal tender, their coins circulated widely and were accepted on deposit by banks. A little later, private mints functioned in Oregon, Utah, and Colorado. With the establishment of the U.S. mint at San Francisco in 1854, the need for privately minted coins disappeared. The federal government has never requested a private mint to produce U.S. coins.

BIBLIOGRAPHY

Adams, Edgar H. *Private Gold Coinage of California, 1849–55.* New York: E. H. Adams, 1913.

Alvin F. Harlow / A. R.

See also **Currency and Coinage; Gold Mines and Mining; Gold Rush, California; Mint, Federal; Treasury, Department of the.**

MINUTEMEN were citizen soldiers in the American colonies who volunteered to fight the British at a "minute's" notice during the years before the American Revolution. The most famous minutemen were those who figured in the battles at Lexington and Concord, though minutemen militias were organized in other New England colonies as well.

While the term "minuteman" goes back at least to 1756, the famous body that developed under that name first appearing in the reorganization of the MASSACHUSETTS militia by the Worcester convention and the Provincial Congress in 1774. To rid the older militia of Tories, resignations of officers were called for in September. The Massachusetts Provincial Congress called for a reorganization of regiments and enrolled the minutemen as an organized militia. The Provincial Congress, meeting in October, found the same process voluntarily going on in the militia of other counties, and directed its completion. Thus a system of regiments was established in the province, with the minutemen to be ready for any emergency. The formation of the minuteman regiments proceeded slowly. On 14 February 1775, the Provincial Congress set 10 May for a complete return. None was ever made, and only scattered records show that while Marblehead organized its company on 7 November 1774, Woburn, though close to Boston, did not vote to establish

Minutemen. *The Struggle at Concord Bridge*, a depiction of the second clash on the first day of the American Revolution, is a copy of an engraving based on a painting by Alonzo Chappel, c. 1859.

its minutemen until 17 April 1775, two days before the outbreak of war. No complete list of minuteman companies and regiments was possible, and only from town records, a few lists, and the "Lexington alarm lists" of minutemen and militia can a fragmentary roster be patched together of an organization that never was completed.

On 19 April, militia and minutemen turned out together to resist the British in Lexington and Concord, Massachusetts, in the first battles of the American Revolution. After news traveled through the countryside that the minutemen engaged in a skirmish with the British at Lexington, the colonial forces met with little opposition as they moved to the Concord bridge to meet the British expedition later that day. Both militia forces and minutemen participated in these conflicts. The minuteman organization was abandoned by the Provincial Congress when they organized Washington's Eight Months Army. As this was formed, it drew men from both minutemen and militia. Those who could not join went back into the militia, and the minutemen thenceforth disappeared in Massachusetts.

Other colonies organized their minutemen on the recommendation of the Continental Congress in July 1775. Maryland, New Hampshire, and Connecticut used minutemen for rounds of service on special brief enlistments. Most notably, the Connecticut minutemen resisted William Tryon's expedition against Danbury.

The battle site in Concord, Massachusetts, is the present-day site of the Minute Man National Historic Park.

BIBLIOGRAPHY

Gross, Robert A. *The Minutemen and their World.* New York: Hill and Wang, 1976, 2001.

Hoffman, Ronald, and Peter J. Albert, eds. *Arms and Independence: The Military Character of the American Revolution.* Charlottesville: University Press of Virginia, 1984.

Shy, John W. *A People Numerous and Armed: Reflection on the Military Struggle for American Independence.* New York: Oxford University Press, 1976; Ann Arbor: University of Michigan Press, 1990.

Allen French/h. s.

See also **Militias; Provincial Congresses; Revolution, American: Military History.**

MIRANDA V. ARIZONA, 384 U.S. 436 (1966). One of the core concerns of the Fifth Amendment's guarantee against self-incrimination is the use of coerced confessions. In *Miranda v. Arizona,* the Supreme Court codified this concern by prescribing rules for police interrogation. Specifically, any person who is in custody must be warned, before questioning begins, that: "he has the right to remain silent," "anything he says can be used against him in a court of law," "he has the right to an attorney," and he may consult with his attorney at any time. Only if the individual "knowingly and intelligently" waives these rights—a waiver that may be withdrawn at any stage of questioning—may his statements be used against him.

The 5–4 *Miranda* ruling has always been controversial. Critics contend that these rules hamstring law enforcement, despite Ernesto Miranda's conviction at a retrial where his confession was excluded. The Court created numerous exceptions to the Miranda rules, and Congress attempted to overturn them in a rarely used provision of the 1968 Crime Control Act. The Supreme Court struck down that provision in *United States v. Dickerson* (2000), saying that the Miranda rules "have become part of our national culture."

BIBLIOGRAPHY

Brooks, Peter. *Troubling Confessions: Speaking Guilt in Law and Literature.* Chicago: University of Chicago Press, 2000.

Leo, Richard A., and George C. Thomas III, eds. *The Miranda Debate: Law, Justice, and Policing.* Boston: Northeastern University Press, 1998.

White, Welsh S. *Miranda's Waning Protections: Police Interrogation Practices after Dickerson.* Ann Arbor: University of Michigan Press, 2001.

Jonathan L. Entin

See also **Civil Rights and Liberties; Police Power.**

MISCEGENATION is the intermarriage of people of different races. In the United States the term is primarily used to describe the marriage between a black person and a white person. Miscegenation is an American word, and it is difficult to translate into other languages. It is derived from the Latin *"miscere"* (to mingle) and *"genus"* (kind or category). Miscegenation plays a larger role in American history than perhaps in any other nation's history. The states, plagued by racial division between blacks and whites, codified the racial divide by prohibiting mingling of the races in marriage with antimiscegenation laws during colonial times. Prohibition of interracial marriage did not exist under the common law or by statute in England when the American colonies were established. Antimiscegenation laws were first drafted in colonial America.

The enactment of antimiscegenation laws can be attributed to a variety of factors, including economic considerations and a desire on the part of some for the maintenance of so-called "racial purity." The first antimiscegenation statute appears to have been enacted in Maryland in 1661, in part for economic reasons. The statute forbidding interracial marriage in effect gave slave owners the ability to increase their number of slaves through birth. The statute deemed any child born of a free mother and slave father to be a slave of the father's

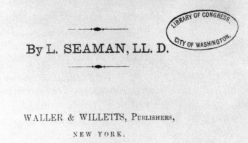

What Miscegenation Is! The title page of L. Seaman's 1864 book features the subtitle "What We Are to Expect Now That Mr. Lincoln Is Re-elected." © CORBIS

master. The statute was designed to deter free white women from marrying black men. Before the statute, the freedom of a child was determined by her or his mother's free or enslaved status. If the mother was a free woman, the children would also be free. The 1661 statute changed this and increased the number of children born into slavery. The effect of the statute, however, was to increase forced interracial marriages because of the economic incentive for slave owners to force indentured white female servants to marry black male slaves to produce more slaves by birth from a slave father. Many other states in both the south and the north followed suit. America's first federal naturalization act, passed in 1790, limited the right to become citizens to "free white persons."

Some states' antimiscegenation laws prohibited marriage between any races, but most laws were more concerned with preserving white racial purity. Many antimiscegenation laws were enacted at a time when slavery and notions of white supremacy had already become fixtures in the epic of American history. The notion of white supremacy and preserving "whiteness" encompassed the idea that marriage between races producing "mixed" children would "muddle" the purity of the white race. The "one drop rule" of classifying a person as black because the person had one drop of black blood exemplified the concern of some in the United States for preserving whiteness. To preserve white racial purity and prevent production of mixed offspring, many American states forbade the marriage between whites and blacks. This view was vindicated in the Supreme Court's opinion in *Plessy v. Ferguson* (1896), in which Homer A. Plessy, whose only nonwhite ancestor was one of his eight great-grandparents, was determined to be black in the eyes of the law. Other states, such as California in 1909, added people of Japanese descent to the list of those banned from marrying whites.

Antimiscegenation laws remained in effect in many states from colonial days until 1967, when the Supreme Court declared Virginia's antimiscegenation law unconstitutional in *Loving v. Virginia*. The Supreme Court found that Virginia's law, which specifically prohibited and prevented the recognition of marriage between blacks and whites, denied citizens the fundamental right to marry. Soon after *Loving v. Virginia* was decided, most states repealed their own antimiscegenation statutes. Others kept these now unenforceable laws on their books, and some even kept the prohibition in their constitutions. The people of Alabama voted in November 2000 to remove the section of their constitution that prohibited interracial marriage. South Carolina took a similar step in 1998. While "mixed race" couples and their offspring continued to suffer DISCRIMINATION in the twenty-first century, no state is allowed to deny recognition of a marriage between a black person and a white person or between persons of any different races.

BIBLIOGRAPHY

Ferber, Abby L. *White Man Falling: Race, Gender, and White Supremacy.* Lanham, Md.: Rowman and Littlefield, 1998.

Sollors, Werner, ed. *Interracialism: Black-White Intermarriage in American History, Literature, and Law.* Oxford: Oxford University Press, 2000.

Williamson, Joel. *New People: Miscegenation and Mulattoes in the United States.* New York: Free Press, 1980.

Akiba J. Covitz
Esa Lianne Sferra
Meredith L. Stewart

See also **Loving v. Virginia; Plessy v. Ferguson; Race.**

MISS AMERICA PAGEANT, which set the standard for American BEAUTY CONTESTS, began in 1921 as a typical "bathing beauty" contest in Atlantic City, New Jersey. The hotelier H. Conrad Eckholm staged the Inter-City Beauty Pageant as a tourist attraction. A city newspaper sponsored each of the seven contestants, and sixteen-year-old Margaret Gorman from Washington, D.C., won the title "Miss America." The spectacle was repeated the

following year, and by 1923 the contest attracted over seventy contestants. Despite its success, by the late 1920s women's religious and civic groups protested the pageant as a display of lax morals. A combination of bad press and the Great Depression caused the pageant to cease between 1929 and 1932. The contest was revived in Wildwood, New Jersey, and returned to Atlantic City in 1933. The changing roles of women wrought by World War II and the advent of television professionalized and popularized the pageant. Where early pageants were considered the path to Hollywood and stardom, the Miss America Pageant of the 1950s gave queens better access to education. The pageant was televised for the first time in 1954, and in 1955 Bert Parks, a popular television personality, became the master of ceremonies, a position he held until 1980. Also in 1955 the song "There She Is, Miss America" was introduced, and it became the pageant's enduring theme.

In the 1960s the all-white contest became controversial for enforcing stereotypes of racial superiority and gender. The pageant began to include members of racial minorities in the 1970s, and in 1983 Vanessa Williams was the first African American woman crowned Miss America. Subsequent pageant winners have represented various racial and ethnic groups as well as people with handicaps and illnesses. Despite this diversity, critics assert that the Miss America Pageant, still a popular television event every September in the early twenty-first century, enforces a beauty stereotype that does not accurately represent the face of America.

BIBLIOGRAPHY

Banner, Lois W. *American Beauty.* Chicago: University of Chicago Press, 1983.

Goldman, William. *Hype and Glory.* New York: Villard Books, 1990.

Savage, Candace. *Beauty Queens: A Playful History.* New York: Abbeville Press, 1998.

Deirdre Sheets

MISSILE DEFENSE. *See* **Strategic Defense Initiative.**

MISSILE GAP, the presumed strategic disparity between the Soviet Union and the United States believed to have been created by the USSR's technological achievements in the late 1950s.

Beginning in late 1957, media observers claimed that the Soviet Union's successful test of an intercontinental ballistic missile and the launch of the *Sputnik* space satellites had created a "missile gap." The missile gap became an important political issue, with critics charging that President Dwight D. Eisenhower had allowed the Soviets to gain a dangerous military advantage over the United States by refusing to spend enough money on missile programs. Building on these claims, John F. Kennedy won the presidential election of 1960 by calling for bold action to restore American prestige that had been tarnished in the wake of the missile gap.

Despite dire warnings that the missile gap would pose a threat to citizens in the United States and to U.S. interests abroad, the missile gap was a myth. Eisenhower had explained that there was no gap, but many doubted the president's claims. Concerns over the missile gap did not recede until after October 1961, when members of the Kennedy administration declared that the United States possessed overwhelming military strength.

BIBLIOGRAPHY

Divine, Robert A. *The* Sputnik *Challenge: Eisenhower's Response to the Soviet Satellite.* New York: Oxford University Press, 1993.

McDougall, Walter A. *The Heavens and the Earth.* New York: Basic Books, 1985.

Roman, Peter J. *Eisenhower and the Missile Gap.* Ithaca, N.Y.: Cornell University Press, 1997.

Christopher A. Preble

See also **Arms Race and Disarmament; Cold War.**

MISSILES, MILITARY, include the spectrum of rockets and jet vehicles, ballistic or winged in flight, capable of carrying destructive payloads ranging from tactical weapons to "nation buster" thermonuclear warheads at intercontinental ranges (intercontinental ballistic missiles, or ICBMs). World War II saw the development of missilery by the major participants: the U.S. hand-held bazooka antitank weapon; the artillery-like Soviet Katyusha and U.S. naval barrage rocket; a variety of antiaircraft missiles for air and ground forces; the innovative German V-1 pulse-jet buzz bomb; and the German supersonic, liquid-fuel V-2 ballistic missile with a range of 200 miles, launched by the hundreds against London and Antwerp. Military missilery after 1945, its evolution, and its influence on American security policies and international crises—for example, the Cuban missile crisis in 1962—were compounded by dynamic technological advances and interactions of the Cold War.

American military needs for the North Atlantic Treaty Organization (NATO) and the Korean War in the 1950s, and for the Vietnam War in the 1960s, forced accelerated development of improved tactical rockets. Missiles designed to destroy aircraft included the Falcon (radar-guided), the Sidewinder (heat-seeker homing, effective against jet aircraft), and the Genie (nuclear warhead). Missiles fired from aircraft to attack surface targets included the Bullpup, Hound Dog, Maverick, Walleye (television-guided glide bomb), and later the "smart bomb" (laser-guided). Operational decoys, such as the Quail subsonic missile, were also developed. Antiaircraft and antimissile missiles included the U.S. Army Nike-Hercules and the

U.S. Air Force Bomarc, as well as the shorter-range Redeye, Sea Sparrow, Hawk, and Terrier. Missiles for continental defense against ICBMs were under development in the early 1970s; one such missile was the Safeguard. An antisubmarine missile, the Asroc, and the Subroc, a missile to be fired from submarines, were also developed. Missiles developed for battlefield support of ground forces included the Lance, Dragon, Honest John, Sergeant, SS-11B1, and TOW (antitank or antihelicopter). Missiles saw service during the Vietnam War when applicable; prominent among them were the Soviet SAM antiaircraft missiles massively deployed in North Vietnam and the numerous small rockets of guerrilla forces fired into South Vietnamese cities.

The German V-2 and the American atomic bomb proved the major innovations of World War II, leading directly to the development of strategic missile weapons systems by the 1960s. Lacking a long-range bomber and the atomic bomb in 1947, the Soviet Union immediately gave highest priority to the development of an intercontinental-range missile, nuclear weapons, and long-range jet aircraft. Premier Josef Stalin is reported to have said that such a policy "could be an effective strait jacket for that noisy shopkeeper, Harry Truman." By 1954, the United States was faced with a much altered situation, both because of Soviet missile progress and because of the invention of the thermonuclear warheads, far more powerful although of reduced size. Thereupon President Dwight D. Eisenhower initiated priority development of 5,000-mile ICBMs and 1,500-mile intermediate-range ballistic missiles (IRBMs). When the USSR launched Sputnik 1 on 4 October 1957, it was clear that it had already developed an ICBM rocket as announced in August, quite apart from launching the first man-made space satellite to orbit the earth. Thus, the first generation of ICBMs (Atlas and Titan 1) and IRBMs (Jupiter, Thor, and nuclear-powered submarine-carried Polaris A1) were quickly followed by subsequent generations. In 1959 Thors were deployed to England and Jupiters to Turkey for NATO. Second-generation ICBMs by the mid-1960s included a solid-propellant and silo-sited Minuteman 1 and 2. In the third generation, the Minuteman 3, with MIRV (multiple, independently targeted reentry vehicle) warheads and the submarine-based Polaris A3 (2,500-mile range) were developed. They were to be followed by the Poseidon (2,500-mile-range MIRV warhead, for an advanced Trident submarine) in the late 1970s.

Strategic missile weapons systems—deployed in hardened sites or on ocean-legged nuclear-powered submarines, each carrying sixteen missiles and held in readiness to retaliate instantly against nuclear attack—came to serve during the 1960s as the fulcrum of the strategic balance of military power between the United States and the Soviet Union. In the 1970s lateral negotiations between Washington and Moscow were undertaken to consider the control and limit the development and deployment of strategic weapons. These were known as the SALT (Stra-

Mission Indians. This 1877 illustration by Paul Frenzeny depicts "Mission Indians of southern California making baskets and hair ropes." NORTH WIND PICTURE ARCHIVES

tegic Arms Limitation Treaty) talks. A limited agreement on "basic principles" was reached in May 1972 between the United States and the Soviet Union.

The United States had installed MIRVs in most of its then-current sixteen missiles on each of forty-one Polaris submarines and 550 of its 1,000 Minuteman land-based ICBMs, while the Soviet Union was constructing additional missile-firing submarines. In June 1975, the Soviets demonstrated new large strategic missiles, each with five or six MIRV accurate warheads, according to the U.S. secretary of defense. The Space Treaty of 1968 had previously outlawed nuclear weapons in space. SALT talks continued after 1972, while the Soviet Union greatly increased, as expected, the number of its warheads.

The development of nuclear warhead missiles by the People's Republic of China increasingly erected a tripolar strategic world for the 1970s, but the existence of nuclear weapons continued to enforce an uneasy peace among the major nations. The United States endeavored to avoid possible strategic surprise, partly by means of passive military satellites and by the establishment of direct communications ("hot lines") with Moscow and Peking. Since 1945, no nuclear weapons involving missile technology have been exploded in anger.

In the 1980s and 1990s nuclear proliferation emerged as a major threat to global security. South Asia, in particular, became a site of international concern as both India and Pakistan developed nuclear missile technology. Even more troubling, international renegade states such as North Korea, Iraq, and Iran began ballistic missile programs of their own. In the early 1980s the Reagan administration proposed a strategic defense system to defend the United States from a ballistic missile attack, but exorbitant costs and technological obstacles have thus far prevented such a system from being implemented.

BIBLIOGRAPHY

Fitzgerald, Frances. *Way Out There in the Blue: Reagan, Star Wars, and the End of the Cold War.* New York: Simon and Schuster, 2000.

Hughes, Robert C. *SDI: A View from Europe.* Washington, D.C.: National Defense University Press, 1990.

Parson, Nels A. *Missiles and the Revolution in Warfare.* Cambridge, Mass.: Harvard University Press, 1962.

Worden, Simon. *SDI and the Alternatives.* Washington, D.C.: National Defense University Press, 1991.

Eugene M. Emme / A. G.

See also **Air Force, United States; Air Power, Strategic; Bombing; Chemical and Biological Warfare; Munitions; Ordnance; Russia, Relations with; Strategic Arms Limitation Talks.**

MISSING IN ACTION CONTROVERSY. *See* **Prisoners of War.**

MISSION INDIANS OF CALIFORNIA. Beginning in 1769, the first of twenty-one Franciscan missions was established in California. The missions ranged from San Diego north to San Francisco and were a means for the Spanish to control the Indians. Soldiers rounded up Indians who, once taken inside the missions, became slaves. Those who tried to escape were severely punished;

some were killed. Indians' tribal names were usually forgotten, and instead they became known by the names of the missions they served. During the sixty-five years of the missions, Indians were inflicted with disease and despair, and their numbers were depleted by over 80 percent.

Previously these Indians had lived a nomadic life, hunting with bows and arrows and unearthing roots with digging sticks. Under mission control, they were taught Catholicism, ranching, agriculture, and trades such as weaving, blacksmithing, hide tanning, and candle making.

In 1834, thirteen years after Mexican independence from Spain, the missions were dissolved and their lands were turned into huge ranches by settlers. The Indians were technically free, but in fact, only their masters changed, as they were dependent on local ranchers for employment. Today descendants of the Mission Indians live on twenty-eight tiny reservations in southern California.

BIBLIOGRAPHY

Jackson, Robert H., and Edward Castillo. *Indians, Franciscans, and Spanish Colonization: The Impact of the Mission System on California Indians*. Albuquerque: University of New Mexico Press, 1995.

Veda Boyd Jones

See also **Indian Missions; Tribes: California.**

MISSIONARY SOCIETIES, HOME,

are voluntary associations for the advancement of Christian piety and domesticity in poor areas of the United States. In the eighteenth century, small-scale missions to new settlements were sponsored by Presbyterian synods and Baptist and Congregational associations. The revival of evangelical religion in the early nineteenth century, along with the growing spirit of humanitarian reform and continuing westward settlement, led to the proliferation of local missionary societies. In 1826, members of four Protestant denominations formed the American Home Missionary Society, but conflicts within the alliance forced its dissolution. Unlike the sabbatarian and abolition movements in which an ecumenical spirit prevailed, denominational associations like the Missionary and Bible Society of the Methodist Episcopal Church (1819) and the Baptist Home Mission Society (1832) handled most of the home missionary work. As a further obstacle to ecumenical cooperation, the slavery controversy divided home missionaries into the antislavery American Missionary Association (1846) and societies affiliated with the southern churches.

Throughout most of the nineteenth century, the home missionary societies sent preachers to the western frontier; later more attention was paid to the foreign-born in the cities, to African Americans, and to rural communities in the East. White, middle-class women dominated the home missionary movement, exemplifying their new voice in public affairs. Many colleges and academies in the West trace their roots to home missionaries. During the 1930s,

following a study by the Institute of Social and Religious Research, home missionary societies deemphasized church programs and began to follow more closely the secular, bureaucratic model of government welfare agencies.

BIBLIOGRAPHY

Pascoe, Peggy. *Relations of Rescue: The Search for Female Moral Authority in the American West, 1874–1939*. New York: Oxford University Press, 1990.

Yohn, Susan M. *A Contest of Faiths: Missionary Women and Pluralism in the American Southwest*. Ithaca, N.Y.: Cornell University Press, 1995.

Colin B. Goodykoontz/A. R.

See also **Baptist Churches; Congregationalism; Episcopalianism; Iowa Band; Presbyterianism; Women in Churches.**

MISSIONS. See **Indian Missions.**

MISSIONS, FOREIGN,

were the primary means by which American Christians spread their religion and worldview across cultures in the nineteenth and twentieth centuries. In sending missionaries, denominations and parachurch organizations sought at various times to convert people to Christianity, found churches, translate the Bible into vernaculars, establish schools and hospitals, dispense relief and development aid, and support human rights. Missionaries were the first scholars to study other religions and to conduct ethnographic studies of tribal peoples. As bridges between American Christians and non-Western cultures, missionaries also worked to shape government policy, for example through defending Asians' rights to American citizenship in the early twentieth century or opposing military aid to Central America in the late twentieth century. Views of missions often reflected popular opinions about projections of American power abroad. They therefore received widespread support in the decades before World War I but were accused of imperialism during the Vietnam War era.

In 1812 the American Board (Congregationalists, Presbyterians, and Reformed) sent the first American foreign missionaries to India. Other Protestant denominations soon organized for mission activity and selected their own "mission fields." By 1870 approximately two thousand Americans had gone as missionaries to India, Burma, the South Pacific, Liberia, Oregon, the Near East, China, and other locations. In the late nineteenth century women founded over forty denominational societies to send unmarried women as teachers, doctors, and evangelists to women in other cultures, and female missionaries began to outnumber males. With the United States itself a Catholic "mission field" until 1908, American Catholics only began supporting significant numbers of foreign missionaries after World War I. Priests and sisters planted churches, ran schools and orphanages, and founded Native religious congregations. During the 1960s

Aimee Semple McPherson. A missionary in China (for a year) before settling in Los Angeles and becoming a hugely successful—and very controversial—Pentecostal preacher on the radio and at revival meetings across the United States in the 1920s; evangelists like her have spread their message to "mission fields" all over the world, particularly in Latin America, Asia, and the South Pacific. GETTY IMAGES

Catholics responded to a call by Pope John XXIII to send 10 percent of church personnel to Latin America. Subsequent missionary experiences living among the poor of the continent were a major factor behind the spread of liberation theology.

Until the 1950s, when Communists conquered China and India and Pakistan broke from British rule, China and South Asia were the largest sites of American mission activity. By the late 1960s a decline in denominational vitality, relativism and self-criticism, and a commitment to partnerships with non-Western churches caused the number of missionaries to drop among older Protestant denominations like Presbyterians, Disciples of Christ, Episcopalians, and Methodists. Simultaneously the center of the world Christian population shifted from the Northern Hemisphere to sub-Saharan Africa, Latin America, and parts of Asia. Churches in former "mission fields" began

sending missionaries to the United States to accompany their own immigrant groups. Yet interest in sending missionaries remained high among conservative evangelicals, Pentecostals, and nontraditional groups like Mormons, whose combined personnel outnumbered those from older denominations from the late 1960s. In 1980 roughly thirty-five thousand American career missionaries were in service. As the end of the millennium neared, evangelistic missions around the world organized the "A.D. 2000 and Beyond" movement to begin churches among every "people group" by the year 2000. The largest American Protestant mission-sending agencies by the 1990s were the Southern Baptist Convention and the Wycliffe Bible Translators.

BIBLIOGRAPHY

Dries, Angelyn. *The Missionary Movement in American Catholic History.* Maryknoll, N.Y.: Orbis Books, 1998.

Hutchison, William R. *Errand to the World: American Protestant Thought and Foreign Missions.* Chicago: University of Chicago Press, 1987.

Robert, Dana L. *American Women in Mission: A Social History of Their Thought and Practice.* Macon, Ga.: Mercer University Press, 1997.

Dana L. Robert

See also **Religion and Religious Affiliation.**

MISSISSIPPI. Located in the heart of the South, Mississippi is one of five southern states that border the Gulf of Mexico. Its total area consists of 47,689 square miles, ranking it the second smallest Gulf-South state and the thirty-first in population nationally. Despite its size, the region has been blessed with perhaps the South's most fertile soil, though there are marked contrasts in several infertile belts. Its brown loam soil region in the central interior, its loess soil in the southwestern corridor, and its rich east-central prairie have continued to be productive cotton and grazing lands and, in the early and mid-nineteenth century, were dominant economic centers before major development of the even more fertile Yazoo-Mississippi Delta in the decades surrounding the Civil War.

Long before the arrival of Europeans and Africans, numerous native groups made Mississippi their home. Three tribes dominated, however: the Choctaws, Chickasaws, and the Natchez. While their worlds were hardly tranquil or their civilizations as technologically developed as that of the Europeans, they lived in harmony with nature and, even as the Europeans intruded, continued to develop their culture. In both positive and negative ways, life would never be the same for them thereafter. For example, after the early 1730s, the Natchez, with one of the most complex and highly developed civilizations north of Mexico, no longer existed in Mississippi following a long period of confrontations with the colonial French.

European interest in Mississippi began soon after New World discovery. The Spaniard Hernando de Soto, seeking to reclaim the glory and increase the wealth that he had achieved with Francisco Pizarro in Peru, was the first European explorer of Mississippi. He failed in his efforts, eventually dying in his quest. But the conquistador left an enduring legacy of his journey through Mississippi's wilderness when, in 1541, he happened upon the Mississippi River to become the first known white man to approach its banks overland. Other aspects of his expedition through the Southeast are far less admirable because of the inhumane tolls that he inflicted on Native peoples along the way, including the Chickasaws with whom he quartered during the winter of 1540–1541.

It was, however, the French who first laid substantive claims to Mississippi. René-Robert Cavelier, Sieur de La Salle, an ambitious French explorer and fur trader interested in both personal gain and French expansion in North America, claimed the Mississippi countryside in 1682 for King Louis XIV as an integral part of the Louisiana colony. Thirteen years later, Pierre Le Moyne, Sieur d'Iberville, led a group of settlers to the Gulf Coast, where he constructed Fort Maurepas (later named Ocean Springs), the first permanent white settlement on Mississippi soil.

France's settlements in Mississippi soon expanded to included Natchez on the Mississippi and Biloxi near Ocean Springs. Its colonial experience in the Lower Mississippi Valley, however, proved an immense failure. A misguided imperial policy, punctuated by a weak economy, an inadequate immigration flow, and poor Indian relations influenced its regional instability. A rivalry with England for colonial domination culminated with the French and Indian War (1754–1763) and eventually led to France's expulsion from North America. For nearly two decades thereafter, England controlled Mississippi as part of its West Florida province and sought to develop a tobacco culture in the Natchez region, but it, too, met only limited success. Although the Mississippi region did not revolt against England in the American Revolution, England lost West Florida to Spain soon after Spain entered the conflict. It was a propitious situation for Spain, which added the east bank of the Mississippi to its west bank holdings, an area acquired prior to the French and Indian War.

An American dispute with Spain over West Florida's northern boundary remained a diplomatic issue until the 1795 signing of Pinckney's Treaty. The agreement ceded to the United States the coveted Yazoo Strip and resulted in the establishment of the Mississippi Territory, ceremoniously declared in Natchez on 7 April 1798. Congress fixed the northern and southern boundaries at thirty-two degrees and twenty-eight minutes north latitude and thirty-one degrees north latitude, respectively. The Mississippi and Chattahoochee Rivers bounded the territory in the west and in the east. Excluding the Gulf Coast region, which remained in Spanish West Florida, southern Mississippi and Alabama lay essentially within the territory. However, by 1804, the territory's northern limits had reached the Tennessee line; eight years later, expansion to the south incorporated the Gulf Coast, the result of presidential decree shortly after borderland inhabitants successfully revolted against Spanish authority. Natchez, with its advantageous location, great economic potential, and larger population was the clear choice over Alabama settlements to seat the territorial government.

Mississippi's government was established under guidelines similar to legislation that organized the Old Northwest Territories in 1787. A federally appointed governor, with the assistance of a secretary and three judges, comprised the initial structure until the territory met higher population standards. With slavery long established in the area, however, provisions in the Northwest Ordinance that banned the institution there could not apply to Mississippi. Winthrop Sargent served as the first governor, a contentious tenure that lasted until President Thomas Jefferson replaced him in 1801. Sargent was a Federalist appointee and, like three of his four Democratic-Republican Party successors, governed during a period when politics in Mississippi was extremely partisan. Eastern Mississippi's yeoman farmers found much to differ over with the Mississippi River area's aristocratic planters and creditor classes, who dominated governmental and economic affairs. Political turmoil was so disruptive that it influenced Governor W. C. C. Claiborne, Sargent's successor, to seek a solution by moving the territorial capital to Washington, a small village several miles north of Natchez. Only under the administration of the more tractable Virginian David Holmes, the last territorial governor, did Mississippi find relief from the political infighting, prompting a unity certainly influenced by exigencies from the War of 1812 and the volatile Creek War of 1813.

The peace that followed sparked a period of massive population growth, particularly in the eastern areas. Rapidly upon the heels of this great migration of 1816, Mississippi successfully lobbied Congress for statehood. On 10 December 1817, President James Monroe signed legislation that admitted Mississippi to the Union as the twentieth state. By then, the Alabama settlements had gone their separate way and soon followed Mississippi into statehood.

It was clear from the outset that Mississippi's constitutional framers were uninterested in establishing a broad-based democracy. Persistent sectional problems had disrupted the constitutional convention, and eastern territorial delegates could not prevent westerners from maintaining their political dominance over the state. Only men of considerable real property were eligible to hold office and vote, though militia service could qualify one for the franchise. Occasionally, the backcountry commoners' pleas for a greater voice were heard, as they were in 1822, when efforts to end a long-standing grievance moved the capital to the centrally located and politically neutral site that became Jackson. Universal white manhood suffrage and other democratic changes resulted from a new constitution in 1832, inspired by the widening national influence of Jacksonian democracy; yet constitutional reform hardly negated the power of the wealthy ruling class of planters and businessmen.

The 1830s—Mississippi's "flush times"—were also years of unparalled prosperity. Much of this stimulation came at the expense of Native Americans, who, after experiencing years of territorial shrinkage, lost title to all of their remaining lands. Removal of the Mississippi Choctaws and Chickasaws to Indian Territory opened vast new fertile lands to white exploitation. Banks proliferated through easy credit policies and paper currency and helped to fuel the boom. Speculators prospered through high land prices. Land-hungry farmers and planters poured into Mississippi and rapidly filled the empty spaces, primarily the state's northern half. The 1840 census revealed a ten-year white population increase of 175 percent and of black, 197 percent, almost entirely slaves. But a change in federal monetary and credit policies ended this golden age, prompting the panic of 1837. Unable to meet their obligations, many Mississippians lost their possessions and suffered through the depression; numerous others sought to escape by migrating to Texas.

Some Mississippians certainly benefited from the cyclical upswing that began in the mid-1840s. The spread of the cotton culture into Indian cession lands increased the size and power of the planter elite. Corn, not cotton, was the largest crop in acreage, but it neither generated the income nor enhanced the image and prestige of its producers as "white gold" did for planters. The disparity between the affluent and poor naturally increased. None were, of course, more impoverished than the thousands of slaves, who by 1840 comprised a 52 percent population majority. They toiled in virtually every capacity, but cotton and fieldwork were their major calling and, by 1860, their labor had helped to make Mississippi one of the five richest states in the nation.

More than any other, it was the slave issue that proved to be the most decisive in Mississippi's justification for secession. To be sure, disunion was hardly endorsed enthusiastically everywhere, but even for Mississippians in areas with fewer slaves, such as the Piney Woods and the Northeastern Hills, Abraham Lincoln's election in 1860 and the Republican Party's opposition to slavery's expansion seemed threatening to a familiar way of life. Consequently, the state left the union by a large majority on 9 January 1861.

The enthusiasm and optimism that Mississippians expressed at the onset of Southern nationhood soon gave way to the realities of war. Food, materials, and labor shortages affected both the military and civilian populations. Numerous battles occurred in Mississippi, but none compared to Vicksburg and the significance it held for the Confederacy as a railway supply center for the Deep South, and for the Union's goal to control the strategically important Mississippi River. For the Confederacy and Mississippi, Vicksburg's loss on 4 July 1863 was costly in human life and morale and certainly influenced the war's outcome. The siege at Vicksburg severely damaged the town, but Mississippi as a whole did not experience the extensive physical devastation that occurred elsewhere. Few communities, and fewer families, however, were left untouched in some way by the war. More than 78,000 white men went off to fight; 27,000 never returned, and, for many who did, disability was often a reminder of their commitment and sacrifice. A year after the war, Mississippi devoted one-fifth of its budget to purchase artificial limbs for veterans.

Black Mississippians, too, saw activity in the war; 17,000 fought to help save the Union and free their people. Months into the conflict, slavery's fate seemed sealed; by war's end, emancipation was assured. In Mississippi, 436,000 former slaves would join more than 3 million from other states in freedom. At the outset, however, it was unclear exactly what their status would be, beyond legal freedom. In the years that followed emancipation, their challenges proved formidable, as federal and state officials sought to define African American citizenship, while simultaneously wrestling with the politics and economics of Reconstruction (1865–1877) and North–South reconciliation.

Federal policy gave Mississippi freedmen no land and only a fleeting opportunity to experience citizenship. But they responded enthusiastically. They influenced a temporary return to Mississippi's two-party system by helping the newly formed Republican Party. They voted, helped to shape and implement constitutional reform, and served in offices at all government levels, including both houses of Congress. The seating of Hiram R. Revels and Blanche K. Bruce as U.S. senators, for example, represented unprecedented nineteenth-century accomplishments. Not until 1986 would another Mississippian, Mike Espy, become the second African American to follow John R. Lynch into the House of Representatives.

Reconstruction gains were short-lived for freedmen, however. This was largely because the Republican Party's ascendancy was brief. Democrats regained elective hegemony in 1875 through their "Mississippi plan," a counterrevolution campaign of widespread violence, economic intimidation of freedmen, and balloting fraud. Thereafter, through impeachment they quickly purged most remaining Republicans from state offices.

The outcome proved crucial to the former slaves and, like elsewhere, they fell victim to an insidious political and racial backlash that relegated them to less than second-class citizens. To be sure, the overthrow of Republican rule—a period that hardly equaled the Reconstruction excesses in some former Confederate states—and its replacement with the redemption (1876–1900) did not immediately submerge the freedmen into near total subordination, but by the end of the century, such results were certainly evident.

Demand for their suppression came from white farmers in the hills counties. These common men were dissatisfied with conservative democrats—so-called BOURBONS, or Redeemers—because of their promotion and alliance with the railroad and industrial establishment. Railroading and timber production dramatically increased but afforded economic opportunity for only a small minority. Tied ever more to "king cotton" and one-crop agriculture, with its farm tenancy, crop lien credit system, farmers had sweltered economically in an agriculturally depressed postwar period, largely dominated by the success of northern industrial expansion. From their perspective, federal economic and monetary policies exacerbated agrarian woes. The white majority, seeking greater empowerment and believing it possible only through ousting the Bourbons and the black vote they controlled, supported a Democratic party leadership that insisted on a new constitution in 1890, which would legally deprive blacks of the vote. This disfranchisement coalesced with rigid Jim Crowism and a stifling sharecropping system that pushed blacks ever deeper into impoverishment and ensured white supremacy well beyond the mid-twentieth century.

The 1902 Primary Election Law helped propel James K. Vardaman—representative of this new "redneck" faction—into the governorship in 1903. Vardaman was popularly known as the "white chief" because of his white supremacy views, and, along with his demagogue successors, he championed white commoners' elevation through a progressive agenda of social justice, limitations on business and industry, and adherence to white supremacy and classism. Medical and juvenile care, prison reform, and transportation all progressed; improvements in education occurred only minimally. Although these leaders enjoyed immense popularity, they had their detractors, and perhaps none aroused as much controversy and criticism as did Theodore Bilbo, twentieth-century Mississippi's most rabid race baiter, who was elected governor in 1915 and 1927 and three times to the U.S. Senate.

The influence of the redneck leadership waned after the onset of the Great Depression during the 1930s and with the emergence of business-oriented governors such as Martin Sennett Conner (1932–1936) and Hugh White (1936–1940, 1952–1956). Motivated as much by the need to lessen the effects of the depression on the nation's poorest state as they were to create a more diversified economy, these leaders instituted creative measures such as the sales tax and lucrative state incentives to attract industry. Light industrial expansion in furniture and clothing manufacturing could not compare to the arrival of a major shipbuilding corporation on the Gulf Coast in 1938—which was still the state's largest private employer in the early 2000s—but collectively they added promise to the prospects of Mississippi's economic future.

Much needed to be done. Federal depression-era measures certainly helped, but conditions hardly improved for most landless farmers, black or white, who were further affected adversely by mechanization and a declining need for manual labor. For many, migration to northern industrial states or nearby cities like Memphis, Mobile, and New Orleans held the greatest promise. One result was that, by 1940, blacks had become a minority, a downward spiral that continued into the 1960s. World War II sparked a similar intrastate "pull" factor for Jackson, which assumed a distinctively urban character, and for Hattiesburg and the Gulf Coast, attractive because of demands from recently established military installations.

War put 23,700 Mississippians into military uniforms. Their service exposed them to a world that was very different from Mississippi. Veterans' benefits provided them opportunities for college and better housing. The farm and rural life appealed less to them as cities and towns continued their slow but steady growth. Some veterans had certainly been influenced by one of the war's goals—to end Nazi racism—but Mississippi found it difficult to break from its past. Opposed to black Mississippians' demands for equal rights and the national Democratic Party's increasingly liberal support of civil rights, between 1948 and 1970 the state was frequently a center of attention because of its determined stand to maintain racial orthodoxy.

Governor Hugh White's unrealistic proposals to equalize black and white schools in the early 1950s inevitably failed and forecast the historic 1954 Supreme Court school desegregation decision. Mississippi was perhaps the South's most segregated state, and many certainly believed they had much to defend; others understood the importance of cracking the monolith, for success there might make gains easier to achieve elsewhere. Forces such as the White Citizens Council—the so-called Uptown Klan—first emerged in Mississippi before its regional spread to fight "race-mixers" through political and economic intimidation. But change was inevitable, though it occurred grudgingly and not without frequent bloody consequences. In 1962, rioting erupted over the black student James Meredith's admission to the University of Mississippi, and beatings of civil rights workers by both citizens and law officials occurred throughout the state. Nothing, however, equaled the international revulsion that resulted from the manhunt and grave discovery of three young activists, two of whom were white college students, brutally murdered in the 1964 Freedom Summer voting rights campaign. By the end of the 1960s, however, nearly all white colleges and universities enrolled black students; the federal courts ordered statewide public school desegregation in the early 1970s; and, a decade after its passage, the 1965 Voting Rights Act had resulted in more African Americans in Mississippi government offices than in any other state in the nation. Undeniably, disparities endured, as revealed by a 2002 state settlement of a twenty-seven year black plaintiffs college funding discrimination suit. At the end of the twentieth century, however, the race question was no longer the political, social, and economically divisive issue that had retarded Mississippi's development throughout much of its history.

Other adjustments also appeared in the last third of the twentieth century. A viable two-party system functioned for the first time since Reconstruction, as Republicans won elective offices to all levels of government, including the governorship and Congress. The state ended its dependence on cotton as soybean production rivaled it. The early vision of governors such as Hugh White, Paul Johnson Sr. (1940–1943), and Paul Johnson Jr. (1964–1968), all of whom had worked to achieved a more balanced economy, showed remarkable fruition as industry, for the first time, provided Mississippians with more jobs and wages than did agriculture. Opportunities in extracting and developing Mississippi's major natural resources of oil, timber, coal, bauxite, sand, and gravel expanded. Oil refining, furniture and paper manufacturing, and diverse service-related jobs joined with tourism and the new casino industry to invigorate Mississippi's economy. Employment from a major automobile manufacturing plant would open in 2003 and add further economic growth in central Mississippi. A massive ongoing highway building program, initiated in the 1980s, has significantly improved the infrastructure and quality of transportation. Finally, education reform in the establishment of kindergartens, smaller classrooms, and teacher aides and the institution of more equitable funding through the Adequate Education Program have improved an education system that long lagged behind other states.

Progress notwithstanding, in 2000 Mississippi remained one of the nation's poorest states, its citizens earning 71 percent of the national median income. For every tax dollar that Mississippi sent to the federal government in the early 2000s it received three back through various programs. With a relatively small population of 2.8 million people as of 2002, the state's modest growth in the previous decade would result in the loss of one of five congressional seats and, perhaps accordingly, the loss of substantive influence in ensuring Mississippi's continued receipt of vital federal dollars.

BIBLIOGRAPHY

Bartley, Numan V. *The New South, 1945–1980: The Story of the South's Modernization.* Baton Rouge: Louisiana State University Press, 1995.

Bettersworth, John K. *Confederate Mississippi: The People and Politics of a Cotton State in Wartime.* Philadelphia: Porcupine Press, 1978.

Bond, Bradley. *Political Culture in the Nineteenth-Century South: Mississippi, 1830–1900.* Baton Rouge: Louisiana State University Press, 1995.

Carpenter, Barbara, ed. *Ethnic Heritage in Mississippi.* Jackson: University Press of Mississippi, 1992.

Dittmer, John. *Local People: The Struggle for Civil Rights in Mississippi.* Chicago: University of Illinois Press, 1994.

Foner, Eric. *Reconstruction: America's Unfinished Revolution.* New York: Perennial Classics, 2002.

Harris, William C. *The Day of the Carpetbagger.* Baton Rouge: Louisiana State University Press, 1979.

James, D. Clayton. *Antebellum Natchez.* Baton Rouge: Louisiana State University Press, 1968.

Kirwan, Albert D. *Revolt of the Rednecks: Mississippi Politics, 1876–1925.* Gloucester, Mass.: P. Smith, 1964.

McLemore, Richard A., ed. *A History of Mississippi.* 2 vols. Hattiesburg: University Press of Mississippi. 1973.

McMillen, Neil. *Dark Journey: Black Mississippians in the Age of Jim Crow.* Urbana: University of Illinois Press, 1989.

———. *The Citizen's Council: Organized Resistance to the Second Reconstruction, 1954–1964.* Urbana: University of Illinois Press, 1994.

Miles, Edwin A. *Jacksonian Democracy in Mississippi.* New York: Da Capo Press, 1970.

Moore, John Hebron. *The Emergence of the Cotton Kingdom in the Old Southwest: Mississippi, 1770–1860.* Baton Rouge: Louisiana State University Press, 1988.

Robert Jenkins

See also **Reconstruction; Tribes: Southeastern; Vicksburg in the Civil War;** *and vol. 9:* **An Interview with Fannie Lou Hamer; Black Code of Mississippi, November, 1865.**

MISSISSIPPI BUBBLE refers to the disastrous failure of John Law's scheme for exploiting the resources of French Louisiana. Law, a Scot who had previously gained an enviable reputation in France as a successful banker and financier, organized a trading company to assume control of LOUISIANA. In 1719, the company founded a colony at New Biloxi, Mississippi. Law's reputation and aggressive promotion of the company's stock led to wild speculation that drove the price of shares to high figures without any sound basis in tangible assets. In December 1720 the company failed and the "bubble" burst, wiping out investors throughout Europe. By then, many of the colonists had also lost their lives. Those who remained waited for relief ships to take them back to France.

BIBLIOGRAPHY

Fortier, Alcée. *A History of Louisiana.* 4 vols. New York: Goupil and Company of Paris, 1904; Baton Rouge, La.: Claitor's Book Store, 1966.

Murphy, Antoin E. *John Law: Economic Theorist and Policy-Maker.* New York: Oxford University Press, 1997.

Walter Prichard / c. p.

MISSISSIPPI PLAN, the name given to two attempts in the South to disfranchise AFRICAN AMERICANS. The first Mississippi Plan arose in the 1870s after federal troops withdrew from the southern states. On election day, bands of whites carrying firearms would menace black voters. The second, adopted by the Mississippi constitutional convention of 1890, required every citizen from twenty-one to sixty to display his POLL TAX receipt. It also required the would-be voter to both read and interpret the U.S. Constitution, allowing registration officials to discriminate between white and black illiterates. The Supreme Court upheld the practice in *WILLIAMS V. MISSISSIPPI* (1896), and six other southern states adopted similar suffrage provisions between 1895 and 1910. However, in *Harper v. Virginia Board of Elections* (1966), the Court invalidated the poll tax as a requirement for voting in state elections. Two years earlier, the Twenty-Fourth Amendment eliminated the poll tax in federal elections. These actions, along with federal legislation passed in 1957, 1960, 1964, and 1965, have neutralized the Mississippi Plan as an instrument for disfranchisement.

BIBLIOGRAPHY

Berry, Mary Frances. *Black Resistance, White Law: A History of Constitutional Racism in America.* New York: Appleton-Century-Crofts, 1971; New York: Lane, Penguin, 1994.

Dittmer, John. *Local People: The Struggle for Civil Rights in Mississippi.* Urbana: University of Illinois Press, 1994.

Perman, Michael. *The Road to Redemption: Southern Politics, 1869–1879.* Chapel Hill: University of North Carolina Press, 1984.

Woodward, C. Vann. *The Strange Career of Jim Crow.* New York: Oxford University Press, 1957, 1965, 1966.

Gerald M. Capers Jr.
Oscar S. Dooley / A. R.

See also **Civil Rights Act of 1875; Disfranchisement; South, the: The New South; Suffrage: African American Suffrage.**

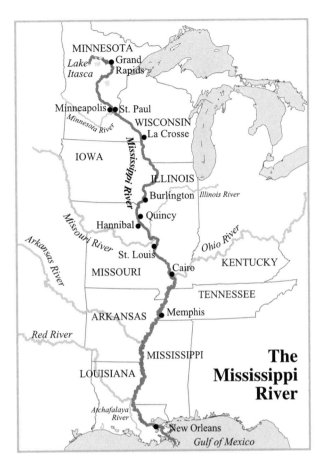

The Mississippi River

MISSISSIPPI RIVER.

One of the major rivers of North America, the Mississippi River has been a focal point in American history, commerce, agriculture, literature, and environmental awareness. The length of the Mississippi River from its source in Lake Itasca in northwestern Minnesota to its mouth in the Gulf of Mexico flows 2,348 miles; it is the second longest river in the United States behind the Missouri (2,466 miles). The Mississippi River system drains the agricultural plains between the Appalachian Mountains to the east and the Rocky Mountains to the west. This drainage basin (approximately 1,234,700 square miles) covers about 40 percent of the United States and ranks as the fifth largest in the world.

Mississippi River's Course

The Mississippi River actually begins as a small stream flowing from Lake Itasca, Minnesota. The river initially flows north and then east as the means of connecting several lakes in northern Minnesota. The river begins to flow southward near Grand Rapids, Minnesota, and is joined with the Minnesota River between the cities of Minneapolis and Saint Paul. The muddy waters of the Missouri River flow into the clear waters of the Mississippi River just north of St. Louis, Missouri. At this point, the Mis-

sissippi becomes brown and muddy for the rest of the journey south.

At Cairo, Illinois, the Ohio River flows into the Mississippi, doubling its volume and creating the point that divides the Upper Mississippi from the Lower Mississippi. The Lower Mississippi Valley is a wide and fertile region. In this area, the river meanders its way south and over time has continuously changed its course, leaving behind numerous oxbow lakes as remnants of its past. As it flows in this southern region, the Mississippi deposits rich silt along its banks. In many areas, the silt builds up to create natural levees. South of Memphis, Tennessee, the Arkansas River junctions with the Mississippi River. Near Fort Adams, Mississippi, the Red River joins with the Mississippi, diverting with it about a quarter of the flow of the Mississippi into the Atchafalaya River.

As the Mississippi River nears the Gulf of Mexico it creates a large delta with its silt. The Mississippi River delta covers approximately 13,000 square miles. South of the city of New Orleans, the Mississippi creates several channels, known as distributaries, which then flow separately into the Gulf of Mexico. The most prominent of these are known as the North Pass, South Pass, Southwest Pass, and Main Pass. Annually, the Mississippi River discharges about 133 cubic miles of water (approximately 640,000 cubic feet per second).

Jacques Marquette. This engraving depicts the French explorer and Jesuit missionary standing in a canoe guided by his companions along the Mississippi River in 1673; not shown is the second canoe, with fellow explorer Louis Jolliet. GETTY IMAGES

History

The Mississippi River played an important role in the lives of many Native Americans who lived in the Upper Mississippi Valley, such as the Santee Dakota, the Illinois, the Kickapoo, and the Ojibwe, as well as those tribes in the southern valley, such as the Chicksaw, the Choctaw, the Tunica, and the Natchez. The name "Mississippi," meaning "great river" or "gathering of water," is attributed to the Ojibwe (Chippewa).

The first known European to travel on the Mississippi River was the Spaniard Hernando de Soto, who crossed the river near present-day Memphis in May 1541. Over a century later, in 1673, the French explorers Louis Jolliet and Father Jacques Marquette entered the Mississippi River from the Wisconsin River and traveled by canoe downriver to a point near the mouth of the Arkansas River. Less than a decade later, another Frenchman, René-Robert Cavelier, Sieur de La Salle, explored the Mississippi River from the Illinois River to the Gulf of Mexico. La Salle declared on 9 April 1682 that the Mississippi Valley belonged to France, and he named the region Louisiana. It was not until 1718 that the French were actually established at New Orleans. They maintained control over the lower Mississippi until the end of the French and Indian War (1754–1763). In 1762 and 1763, the French made cessions that established the Mississippi River as an international boundary with Spanish territory to the west and British territory to the east.

During the American Revolution (1775–1783), the river served as the supply line for George Rogers Clark, allowing him to maintain control of the Illinois country.

The Peace of Paris of 1783 outlined the new country of the United States as extending to the Mississippi River between Spanish Florida and the Canadian border. Additionally, the United States was entitled to free navigation of the Mississippi River. Spain, though not party to the treaty, controlled the mouth of the Mississippi and, through high duties, maintained actual power over the river and, in essence, over the entire Mississippi Valley. Not until Pinckney's Treaty with Spain in 1795 was the river truly free to American navigation. This freedom was short-lived, however, for when Spain ceded Louisiana back to France in 1800, the French again closed the Mississippi to American river traffic. Finally, the Louisiana Purchase (1803) made the Mississippi an American river, and it rapidly became a major route of trade and commerce for the entire Mississippi Valley.

Western settlers and traders traversed the Mississippi in flatboats (on which farmers floated their produce downstream to market) and keelboats (which could be pushed upstream with great effort). Certainly the most significant change in river transportation on the Mississippi came in 1811 when the steamboat *New Orleans* made its legendary trip from Pittsburgh to New Orleans. This event opened the Mississippi River to two-way traffic, essentially doubling the carrying capacity of the river. By 1860, more than 1,000 steamboats were actively engaged in transport along the Mississippi River system, and the cities of Cincinnati (Ohio), Louisville, (Kentucky), St. Louis, Memphis, and New Orleans became important cities in the movement west.

During the Civil War (1861–1865) both the Union and the Confederacy recognized the importance of the Mississippi River, and the fight over its control was a major part of the war. A decisive victory for the Union came with the fall of Vicksburg, Mississippi (1863), which essentially gave the Union full possession of the river, reopening the trade routes down the Mississippi from the Ohio Valley and splitting the Confederacy.

Following the war, life on the Mississippi did not return to the golden years so richly described in Mark Twain's writings. The faster and more convenient railroads replaced much of the commercial traffic on the Mississippi. In 1879, the U.S. Congress established the Mississippi River Commission as a means of maintaining and improving the river as a commercial waterway. In the years that followed, the commission deepened and widened several channels along the river, making it more navigable for larger boats and barges. These changes promoted increased transport on the Mississippi, particularly of heavy and bulky freight.

At the turn of the twenty-first century, the Mississippi River carried more than half of the freight transported on American inland water. Nearly 460 million short tons of freight were transported on the Mississippi River each year. Most of this freight was carried on large barges pushed by tugboats. The upper Mississippi traffic was predominantly composed of agricultural products such as wheat, corn, and soybeans. Coal and steel freight traveled down the Ohio River and onto the lower Mississippi River. At Baton Rouge, Louisiana, petroleum, petrochemical products, and aluminum joined the freight being moved south. It is at this point that the depth of the Mississippi River increases, allowing for larger ships to traverse upriver to this point.

Flooding

People living along the Mississippi River are well aware of the flooding potential of the river. During de Soto's exploration of the Mississippi, he noted much flooding. Evidence from Native American Mississippi Valley settlement locations (on higher land) and the creation of mounds on which they placed their dwellings indicate Native American awareness of and adaptation to flooding of the Mississippi. Significant flooding of the Mississippi Valley in 1927 prompted national discussion of flood control along the Mississippi. Other severe flooding events occurred in 1937, 1965, 1973, 1982, and 1993. The severe flooding in 1993 is considered to be the most devastating in recorded U.S. history. It affected the upper and middle Mississippi Valley from late June until mid-August 1993 with record levels on the Mississippi River and most of its tributaries from Minnesota to Missouri. At St. Louis, the river remained above flood stage for over two months and crested at 49.6 feet (19 feet above flood stage). Industry and transportation along the Mississippi were virtually at a standstill during the summer months of 1993. In all, over 1,000 of the 1,300 levees in the Mississippi

River system failed, over 70,000 people were displaced, nearly 50,000 homes were either destroyed or damaged, 12,000 square miles of agricultural land was unable to be farmed, and 52 people died. Fortunately, larger cities along the Mississippi remained protected by floodwalls. The cost of the flood was enormous. Most estimates of total flood damage run to nearly $20 billion. Flood events are certain to remain a part of life along the Mississippi River.

Human Influence

Humans have influenced the flow of the Mississippi and the quality of its water. Historically, the river and its tributaries meandered across the floodplain, and erosion, sedimentation, and flooding were natural processes. During the twentieth century, however, humans interrupted these processes. In the 1930s, twenty-nine navigation dams were built between St. Louis and Minneapolis. These dams impound the water to improve navigation. One cost of damming, however, is increased retention of sediment in the river. Flood-control levees have been built in order to manage the seasonal flooding. Much of the Mississippi floodplain has been converted to agriculture. This change has two serious consequences for the Mississippi River. First, the loss of prairie wetlands and floodplain forest decreases the biodiversity of the region. Second, conversion of land to agriculture often leads to increased runoff of fertilizers and pesticides. The presence of high rates of nitrogen and phosphorus can be directly attributed to farming practices in the Mississippi Valley. At the end of the twentieth century, many experts suggested that agricultural pollution in the Mississippi River was directly responsible for the creation of the "dead zone," an area in the Gulf of Mexico where there is little aquatic life due to abnormally low levels of oxygen.

Industrial pollution is also a concern along the Mississippi River. Industries have contributed significant amounts of oil, aluminum, lead, and other industrial wastes such as sulfur dioxide, hydrogen sulfide, and benzene to the flow of the Mississippi. A study in 2000 estimated that 58 million pounds of toxic discharge travels down the Mississippi annually. At the turn of the twenty-first century, much of the river remained unswimmable and unfishable, despite the fact that it serves as the primary source of drinking water for 18 million people. Growing awareness of environmental processes and increased concern for the state of the Mississippi River system that began during the last decade of the twentieth century may prove to have a positive influence in the life of the great river.

BIBLIOGRAPHY

Badt, Karin. *The Mississippi Flood of 1993.* Chicago: Children's Press, 1994.

Geus, Theodor. *The Mississippi.* Lexington: University Press of Kentucky, 1989.

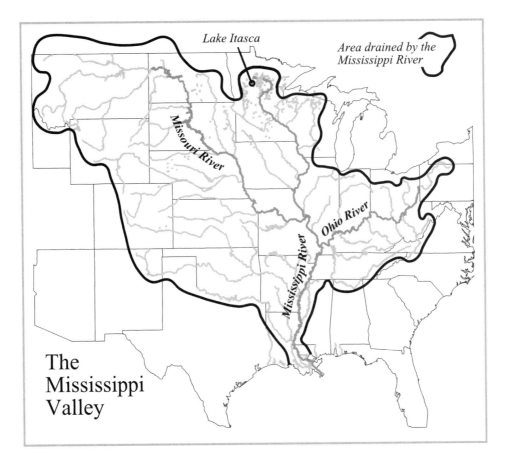

The
Mississippi
Valley

Haites, Erik, James Mak, and Gary Walton. *Western River Transportation: The Era of Early Internal Development, 1810–1860.* Baltimore: Johns Hopkins University Press, 1975.

Lauber, Patricia. *Flood: Wrestling with the Mississippi.* Washington, D.C.: National Geographic Society, 1996.

Janet S. Smith

See also **Mexico, Gulf of; Missouri River; River Navigation; Water Pollution; Water Supply and Conservation.**

BIBLIOGRAPHY
Fairman, Charles. *Reconstruction and Reunion, 1864–88.* Vol. 1. New York: Macmillan, 1971.

Kutler, Stanley I. *Judicial Power and Reconstruction Politics.* Chicago: University of Chicago Press, 1968.

William M. Wiecek

See also **Georgia v. Stanton; Marbury v. Madison; Reconstruction; Separation of Powers.**

MISSISSIPPI V. JOHNSON, 4 Wallace (71 U.S.) 475 (1867), Chief Justice Salmon P. Chase's opinion for a unanimous U.S. Supreme Court denied Mississippi's request for an injunction to prohibit President Andrew Johnson from enforcing the Military Reconstruction Acts of 1867. Chase held that under *Marbury v. Madison* (1803), courts could enjoin only ministerial duties of the president, not the exercise of discretionary authority vested in the president by statute. Together with *Georgia v. Stanton* (1868) and the unreported *Mississippi v. Stanton* (1868), this case marked the Court's refusal to use judicial authority to frustrate congressional Republican Reconstruction. The decision remains a pillar of separation-of-powers doctrine.

MISSISSIPPI VALLEY occupies the center of the United States. It stretches 2,348 miles from Lake Itasca in northern Minnesota to the mouth of the Mississippi River in the Gulf of Mexico. Originally the river meandered significantly through its broad valley, but flood control and improving the river for transportation have resulted in significant straightening by the U.S. Army Corps of Engineers. These and other changes to the river have combined with agricultural, industrial, and urban runoff to significantly impair the ecological health of the river and its valley.

The river valley was originally home to numerous Native American groups. By A.D. 1000 many of these groups were engaged in agricultural production in the rich bottomland. Hernando De Soto was the first European to document seeing the Mississippi Valley in 1541. He was followed by Father Jacques Marquette and Louis Jolliet in 1673, Louis Hennepin in 1679, and Robert Cavelier, Sieur de La Salle in 1682. France, Spain, and England claimed portions of the valley, and it served as the western boundary of the United States after 1783. The entire valley was acquired by the United States in the LOUISIANA PURCHASE of 1803.

The river valley's bottomlands have been used extensively for agriculture. The river has also served a key role in transportation and commerce throughout the center of the United States.

BIBLIOGRAPHY

Scarpino, Philip. *Great River: An Environmental History of the Upper Mississippi, 1890–1950.* Columbia: University of Missouri Press, 1985.

Polly Fry

MISSOURI. Missouri's diversity marks it as a microcosm of the nation. Located in the center of the country and drained by the great Mississippi River on its eastern border and bisected by the Missouri River, Missouri's land area is 68,886 square miles. In 2000, the state's population stood at 5,595,211, with 11.2 percent being African American, just short of the 12.3 percent in the nation.

With rich farmlands north of the Missouri River devoted to general agriculture, a 200-day growing season in the Mississippi Delta of the southeast portion of the state for cotton, melons, soybeans, and rice, the Osage Plains in the southwest for dairying and cattle raising, and the Ozark Highlands occupying 31,000 square miles of the rest, Missouri offers a wide range of landforms. The Boston Mountains that make up the Ozarks are one of the oldest mountain ranges in the nation. The free-flowing Jack's Fork, Current, and Eleven Points Rivers provide opportunities for floating that places one in the natural beauty of the Ozarks. The Gasconade, White, and Osage Rivers add further to the charm of the region. Meramec, Round, and Big are some of the springs found in Missouri. Numerous caves add further to the attraction of the state.

The leading producer of lead in the world, Missouri also produces many minerals, including an abundance of coal, zinc, limestone, silica, barite, clay for brick-making, and Carthage marble, from which the State Capitol is constructed. Timber resources are abundant as well, and only the absence of oil in any quantity keeps Missouri from having all of the important natural resources.

Missouri's two major cities represent the urban dimension to its status as a microcosm of the nation. St. Louis, with more than 2.5 million people in its metropolitan area, retains the look and feel of an eastern city. Kansas City, with its more than 1.7 million metropolitan area residents, broad avenues, and expansive boundaries, is clearly a western city. Branson, in the southwest corner of the state, is an entertainment capital that surpasses Nashville, Tennessee, in its live performances and attraction of more than 6 million visitors a year. Diversity marks Missouri.

People

The people of the state also represent the citizens of the nation. Native Americans, particularly the Osage, dominated the area called Missouri before European explorers entered the region. Preceded by Mound Builders of the Mississippian period (A.D. 900–1500), who left their imprint on the earth still to be seen at Cahokia Mounds in Illinois, the Osage dominated the area when Father Jacques Marquette and Louis Jolliet, early French explorers, came to the area in the 1670s. The state takes its name from the Missouri Indians, who succumbed to attacks from their enemies, the Sauk Indians, and from smallpox epidemics. Remnants of the Missouri eventually blended with the Oto tribe of Kansas. Other French explorers, including René Robert Cavelier, sieur de La Salle, Claude Du Tisne, and Etienne De Bourgmont, added to European knowledge and promoted settlement in the area. In 1720, Phillipe Renault introduced African American slaves into the area as the labor force for mining lead. In 1750, the French made the first permanent European settlement in the state at Ste. Genevieve. Just fourteen years later, Pierre Laclede Liguest and his adopted son, Auguste Chouteau, founded St. Louis, some one hundred miles north and also on the Mississippi River. Liguest and the other early French settlers sought to either profit from the fur trade with the Indians or to gain riches from mineral resources. Fur interested Chouteau and his descendants, and for the next sixty years, the Chouteau family explored, traded, and moved across Missouri. Even after Spain took over the area in 1762 through the Treaty of Fontainebleau, the French remained dominant. In 1800, Spain relinquished political control back to France through the Treaty of San Ildefonso. Three years later, Napoleon Bonaparte sold the entire Louisiana Territory, which included Missouri, to the United States. By then, other towns included St. Charles (1769), Cape Girardeau (1793), and New Madrid (1789).

Territorial Period

Disputed land claims accompanied the establishment of control by the United States. Spanish governors had been lavish in rewarding their friends with large grants. When Americans began entering the region in great numbers between 1803 and 1810, they began disputing these claims. To confuse the matter further, when the great earthquake hit the New Madrid area in 1811–1812, the territorial government offered those devastated by the quake the right to claim land in central Missouri called the Boonslick area (named for the famous frontiersman Daniel Boone and his sons, who had come to Missouri in 1799). A land commission settled some of the claims and the first territorial secretary, Frederick Bates, settled others between 1812 and 1820, but it took until 1880 for the last claim to be resolved.

President Thomas Jefferson, who had purchased Louisiana, decided to explore and lay claim to as much area as possible. In 1804, he sent an expedition led by Meriwether Lewis and William Clark on one of the greatest adventures in American history. The intrepid travelers went up the Missouri River to its origins and then along the Columbia River to the Pacific Coast. They returned in 1806 with broad knowledge of the Native Americans and the plants and animals that lived in this vast region. They also drew maps of the area. News of their findings spurred settlement and the establishment of extensive fur trading operations throughout the west. Fur trading became Missouri's first important industry.

Between 1804 and 1810, Missouri's population doubled from 10,000 to 20,000. It moved through the stages of territorial administration established by the Northwest Ordinance and became a third-class territory in 1816. By 1820, the population reached 67,000, and Missourians sought statehood.

Many settlers came from Kentucky, Tennessee, and Virginia. They brought slaves with them and quickly established a predominantly Southern culture in the Boonslick area, which became known as "Little Dixie." Still other settlers from those states and North Carolina began to enter the Ozarks, but they reflected their hill origins and brought few slaves with them.

The Missouri Compromise

The question of Missouri's entrance into the union of states evoked the first national debate over slavery. Through the efforts of Kentucky senator Henry Clay, a compromise that left the number of states even allowed Missouri to come into the Union as a slave state, for Maine to enter the Union as a free state, and for there to be no more slave states allowed north of the southern boundary of Missouri. Missouri became the twenty-fourth state to enter the Union in 1821.

The convention that drew up the constitution and the first general assembly met in St. Louis. The assembly designated St. Charles as temporary capital, and then on 31 December 1821 it decided to locate a new capitol on the banks of the Missouri River about 12 miles from the mouth of the Osage River. Named after Thomas Jefferson, the City of Jefferson became Missouri's seat of government.

The Age of Benton

Elected as one of the two United States senators in 1821, Thomas Hart Benton and his central Missouri supporters dominated Missouri politics for the next thirty years. A spokesman for the interests of hard money and cheap land, Benton became synonymous with Jacksonian Democracy, the party of President Andrew Jackson. During the 1840s, as the question of slavery and its expansion

reached its zenith with the annexation of Texas, Benton took the side of free soil. His former supporters in central Missouri found new leaders in Claiborne Fox Jackson and David Rice Atchison, who associated Missouri's interests with the Southern states. Through a series of resolutions that passed the legislature in 1849, the supporters of slavery tried to force Benton's hand. His refusal to accept the resolutions caused him to lose his reelection campaign, and Missouri became so politically divided that for a period in the 1850s, only David Rice Atchison represented the state in the Senate, because a majority of the General Assembly could not decide on anyone.

In 1854, Congress passed the Kansas-Nebraska Act, which opened the territories to slavery and negated the Missouri Compromise. Contention over slavery and its extension led to fighting in Kansas, with Missourians along the border supporting slavery and the forces of abolition supporting a free Kansas. This fighting represented a prelude to the Civil War (1861–1865).

The *Dred Scott* Decision and the Civil War

While "Bleeding Kansas" gripped the nation's attention, the Supreme Court in 1857 decided that Dred Scott and his wife Harriet must stay in slavery. During the 1840s, Dred and Harriet, Missouri slaves, sued for their freedom on the grounds that they had been taken to free territories by their master. Reversing precedent and quite divided, the court ruled against the Scotts. Chief Justice Roger B. Taney went even further in the majority opinion, when he wrote that African Americans had no right to citizenship rights, thus making any suit invalid. A minority of justices wrote dissenting opinions, revealing the deep divisions within the country.

The election of 1860 further indicated that division. Four major candidates ran for president, and, Abraham Lincoln, the candidate of a purely regional party, won. Even before Lincoln's inauguration, South Carolina and other Southern states began to secede. Claiborne Jackson and Thomas Reynolds, the newly elected governor and lieutenant governor of Missouri, had run as moderates, but they attempted to lead Missouri into the Confederacy. Jackson called a convention to decide on secession, and the elected delegates surprised him by voting unanimously to stay in the Union. Federal forces led by Nathaniel Lyon and Frank Blair took forceful action and drove Jackson and Reynolds from the state. The pro-Confederates eventually established a government in exile and sent representatives to the Confederate government. Meanwhile, a provisional governor, Hamilton R. Gamble, ran the state government.

During the war, some 50,000 Missourians fought for the Confederacy and more than 100,000 fought for the Union. Some 8,000 of Missouri's 115,000 African Americans fought for their freedom. Only Virginia and Tennessee surpassed Missouri in the number of battles fought during the war. "Civil War" found its true meaning in Missouri as fathers fought sons and brothers fought each other. The intensity of guerrilla fighting on the western border involving such infamous figures as Frank and Jesse James and William Quantrill on the South's side, and the notorious General James Lane on the North's side went unsurpassed in brutality.

The influx of German immigrants into Missouri, and especially St. Louis, during the 1840s and 1850s helped greatly in keeping Missouri in the Union. The German immigrants hated slavery. A number of the new immigrants had left Germany because they fought on the losing side during the Revolution of 1848. Between 1850 and 1860, St. Louis's population more than doubled, going from 77,000 to 160,773, and 50,000 of these people had been born in Germany. Ireland also sent many of its sons and daughters to Missouri, and they represented the second most important immigrant group in the state's population.

The end of the war brought Radical Republican domination in Missouri, and five years of Reconstruction. Again, Missouri experienced, as it had in the Civil War, the nation's experiences in microcosm. Missouri officially freed its slaves before the Thirteenth Amendment was ratified, but the 1865 Constitution provided for segregated schools. But through the leadership of white Republicans and black James Milton Turner, a statewide school system was established in Missouri. Also, court cases in the late 1860s ruled against segregation of the state's public transportation facilities. And once African Americans achieved the right to vote through the Fifteenth Amendment, they never lost it in Missouri. The mixed pattern of race relations in Missouri reflected the complexity of race relations in the nation as a whole.

Industrial Missouri

Railroads transformed Missouri and led to the growth of cities. In 1870, Missouri had completed 1,200 miles of track. By 1920, more than 8,529 miles of track carried goods and people to all but four of the 114 counties in the state. New towns blossomed, manufacturing greatly increased, and employment opportunities spurred immigration from throughout Europe. St. Louis grew from 160,000 in 1860 to more than 575,000 by 1900. Kansas City changed from a village in 1860 to a city of 163,000 by the end of the century. With the growth of its two major cities came organized labor. In 1877, St. Louis experienced the first general strike in the nation's history. Missouri's greatest writer, Samuel Clemens, known as Mark Twain, commented on this era in his coauthored, *The Gilded Age*, and made some failed investments in this industrial age. Machine politics also accompanied industrialization.

Ed Butler, a former blacksmith, created a political machine in St. Louis. Future Democratic Governor Joseph W. Folk made his reputation by attacking Butler's political corruption. He went from circuit attorney to governor in only three years and became nationally famous for reform. Progressives across the nation recognized Folk's efforts.

In Kansas City, Boss Tom Pendergast controlled city politics from the 1920s until his conviction for income tax invasion in 1939. Besides lining his pockets, Pendergast allowed a wide-open city where musicians could find lucrative employment and play all night. The Kansas City sound with such bands as Count Basie's influenced jazz nationally. Building upon this heritage, Kansas Citian Charles "Bird" Parker helped invent a jazz form called bebop in the 1940s. Of course, jazz built on the ragtime music of Sedalia and St. Louis composer Scott Joplin.

World War I–World War II

Missouri supported World War I (1914–1918) and sent General John J. Pershing to lead United States forces in Europe. Future President Harry S. Truman gained significant leadership experience as a Captain in the Great War, as it was called. During the 1920s, Missourians reflected the trends of the nation by electing Republicans as governors. With the spread of good roads, educational opportunities greatly increased during the decade. Woman's suffrage provided activists such as Emily Newell Blair with new opportunities for leadership. Missouri women such as Sara Teasdale and Fanny Hurst became nationally known writers, and not long afterward, Mary Margaret McBride began her remarkable radio career.

During the 1930s, Democratic governors attacked the depression. The January 1939 roadside demonstrations of former sharecroppers in southeast Missouri demonstrated how difficult conditions remained even after six years of the New Deal. In Missouri as in the nation, only World War II (1939–1945) relieved depression conditions. No business in Missouri benefited more from the war than the company founded by James S. McDonnell, who built airplanes in St. Louis. In addition, Truman gained a national reputation as the watchdog of defense contracts, which propelled him into the vice presidency and then in 1945, when Franklin Roosevelt died, into the presidency.

The Postwar World

The years after World War II brought school consolidation to Missouri, beginning in 1947, integration of the public schools during the 1950s, and major tests of the efficacy of busing to improve racial diversity in St. Louis and Kansas City during the 1980s and 1990s. Higher education expanded through the creation of the University of Missouri system in 1963 and the addition of four-year campuses in Joplin and St. Joseph during the late 1960s. A full-fledged junior college system and the takeover of Harris-Stowe College by the state completed the expansion of higher education. During the 1990s, in an effort to equalize funding for schools, Democratic leaders created a new formula for allocating state money to school districts.

In politics, Missouri remained a bellwether state, reflecting almost exactly the nation's preferences for candidates. During the 1960s, Democrats governed, with Governor Warren Hearnes becoming the first Missourian to serve two terms in that office because of a change in the state constitution. In the 1968 election, Hearnes won his second term, but in the same election John Danforth, a Republican, became attorney general. Danforth recruited other likely candidates and led in a Republican takeover of the governor's office in 1972 with the election of Christopher "Kit" Bond. In 1976, Bond lost to Democrat Joe Teasdale, as Missouri reflected national politics again. But in 1980, the state went for Ronald Reagan and Kit Bond won reelection. Meanwhile, John Danforth had replaced Democrat Stuart Symington in the Senate. Future United States Attorney General John Ashcroft served as governor after Bond, and Bond joined Danforth in the Senate. With Danforth's retirement, Ashcroft won his seat and two Republicans represented Missouri in the Senate. In 1992, just as Bill Clinton broke Republican dominance in the presidency, so did Democrat Mel Carnahan win election as governor of Missouri. He won again in 1996, and ran against Ashcroft for the Senate in 2000. A plane crash took his life and the lives of his son and an aide less than a month before the election, which led to an unprecedented development. Missouri voters elected the deceased Carnahan to the Senate. Roger Wilson, who had succeeded Carnahan in the governor's chair, appointed Carnahan's wife, Jean, to the office. Jean Carnahan became the first woman to represent Missouri in the Senate, although during the 1980s, Lieutenant Governor Harriet Woods came very close to defeating Kit Bond for the same office.

Finally, to complete the analogy of Missouri as a microcosm of the nation, it suffered urban sprawl during the 1980s and 1990s. While St. Louis's metropolitan population greatly expanded, the city's population declined from a high of 850,000 in 1950 to only 348,189 in 2000. Kansas City, with the boundaries of a western city, encompassed the sprawl within its borders, and surpassed St. Louis as the state's largest city. In 2000, its population stood at 441,545. The state's third largest city reflected growth in the Ozarks. Springfield counted 151,500 people in 2000. Indeed, except for population growth north of St. Louis, over the last twenty years, the Ozarks region has grown the fastest, replicating rapid growth of resort areas across the nation.

BIBLIOGRAPHY

Brownlee, Richard S. *Gray Ghosts of the Confederacy: Guerilla Warfare in the West 1861–1865.* Baton Rouge: Louisiana State University Press, 1958.

Christensen, Lawrence O., William E. Foley, Gary R. Kremer, and Kenneth H. Winn, eds. *The Dictionary of Missouri Biography.* Columbia: University of Missouri Press, 1999.

Fellman, Michael. *Inside War: The Guerrilla Conflict in Missouri During the American Civil War.* New York: Oxford University Press, 1989.

Foley, William E. *The Genesis of Missouri: From Wilderness Outpost to Statehood.* Columbia: University of Missouri Press, 1989.

Greene, Lorenzo, Gary R. Kremer, and Antonio F. Holland. *Missouri's Black Heritage.* 2d ed. Columbia: University of Missouri Press, 1993.

Hurt, R. Douglas. *Agriculture and Slavery in Missouri's Little Dixie.* Columbia: University of Missouri Press, 1992.

March, David D. *The History of Missouri.* 4 vols. Chicago: Lewis Publishing, 1967.

Meyer, Duane. *The Heritage of Missouri.* 3d ed. St. Louis, Mo.: The River City, 1982.

Parrish, William E., ed. *A History of Missouri.* 5 vols. Columbia: University of Missouri Press, 1971–1997.

Parrish, William E., Charles T. Jones, Jr., and Lawrence O. Christensen. *Missouri: The Heart of the Nation.* 2d ed. Arlington Heights, Ill.: Harlan Davidson, 1992.

Lawrence O. Christensen

MISSOURI COMPROMISE, legislation enacted by the U.S. Congress in 1820 settling the first serious American sectional crisis over slavery's expansion: the Maine statehood act of 3 March ("An Act for the admission of the state of Maine into the Union") and the Missouri enabling act of 6 March ("An Act to authorize the people of the Missouri territory to form a constitution and state government, and for the admission of such state into the Union on an equal footing with the original states, and to prohibit slavery in certain territories"). The crisis, in conjunction with economic disputes deriving from the panic of 1819, helped to undermine American national unity in the so-called "Era of Good Feelings" following the War of 1812.

Background

The Missouri controversy erupted unexpectedly in 1819, when northern congressmen objected to the Missouri Territory, part of the 1803 Louisiana Purchase from France, being admitted to the Union as a new slave state. Previously, northern congressmen had not obstructed the

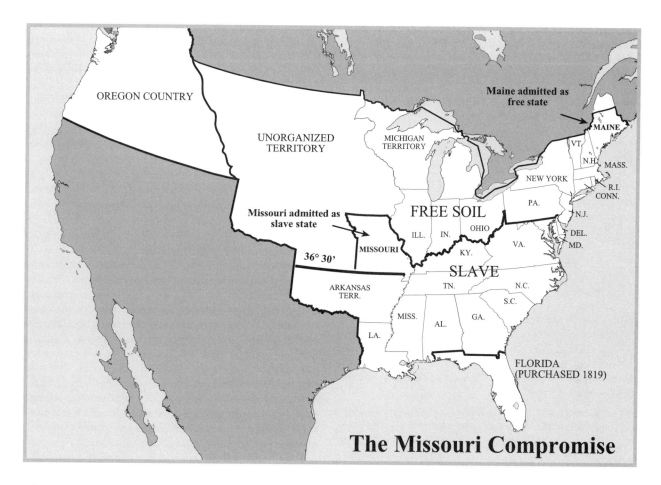

OREGON COUNTRY

UNORGANIZED
TERRITORY

Maine admitted as
free state

MAINE

MICHIGAN
TERRITORY

VT.

N.H. MASS.

NEW YORK

R.I.
CONN.

PA.

N.J.

Missouri admitted as
slave state

FREE SOIL

OHIO

ILL.   IN.

DEL.

MD.

MISSOURI

VA.

36° 30'

KY.

SLAVE

ARKANSAS
TERR.

TN.

N.C.

S.C.

MISS.

AL.

GA.

LA.

FLORIDA
(PURCHASED 1819)

The Missouri Compromise

admission of new slave states. Later that year, Congress would grant statehood to Alabama by a joint resolution that left its slave labor system intact. However, some northern congressmen took exception to Missouri becoming a slave state, apparently less because slavery was already entrenched in the territory (bondspeople were approximately 16 percent of its population) than because Missouri was located directly west of a free state (Illinois) as well as west of the Mississippi River. Their unwillingness to countenance slavery's encroachment northward and westward initiated a struggle that endangered the Union.

The Congressional Impasse

New York Representative James Tallmadge Jr. ignited the dispute on 13 February 1819, when during the Fifteenth Congress's second session he moved an amendment to a House bill permitting the Missouri Territory to take preparatory steps for statehood. Tallmadge's amendment proposed gradually ending slavery in Missouri by prohibiting the "further introduction" of slaves there and by freeing the children of slaves already in Missouri at statehood when those children reached the age of twenty-five. The House, dominated 105 to 80 by representatives from nonslave states (because population growth in the free states had outstripped the growth rate in slave states), twice that session passed the Missouri bill with Tall-

madge's amendment. However, in both instances the more southern-oriented Senate demurred. The Senate was far more evenly divided than the House, reflecting the Union's composition at that time of eleven free states and ten slave states, with free Illinois having a system of black apprentice labor that amounted to quasi-slavery. During the same session, southerners also narrowly defeated a northern effort to prohibit slavery in the Arkansas Territory, that part of the Louisiana Purchase territory below Missouri.

Congress again took up the Missouri question in December 1819, when the Sixteenth Congress convened. With Alabama now a state, southerners had even more power in the Senate. Earlier that year, however, the government of Massachusetts had authorized the district of Maine to separate from it and seek statehood (provided that Congress authorize it by 4 March 1820). Maine's admission promised to augment the number of free states in the country and free-state influence in the Senate. Maine's petition for statehood also came before Congress in December 1819. The Missouri and Maine issues ignited the angriest exchanges among national leaders over slavery's morality and its appropriateness in a democratic republic since the U.S. Constitutional Convention. On 26 January 1820, in the midst of predictions of disunion and war, Representative John W. Taylor of New York offered an even more radically antislavery amendment than Tallmadge's to the House enabling bill for Missouri. This proposal, which would have made all children of slaves in the new state free at birth, received the House's endorsement on 25 February. Meanwhile, the Senate considered its own measures respecting Maine and Missouri.

The Compromise
The breakthrough occurred on 2 March, when, following the recommendation of a House-Senate conference committee, the House voted 90 to 87 to delete the Taylor amendment from its Missouri bill and 134 to 42 to substitute for it an amendment to a competing Senate bill that had been offered by Senator Jesse B. Thomas of Illinois. Thomas's amendment, which had passed the Senate by a 34 to 10 vote on 17 February, prohibited slavery throughout the Louisiana Purchase territory, excepting Missouri, north of 36 degrees 30 minutes. On 3 March, the House and Senate concurred in a conference committee report on statehood for Maine. According to the act approved that day, Maine's statehood would occur on 15 March. The Missouri enabling act, with the Thomas amendment embedded within it as section 8, received President James Monroe's signature and became law on 6 March.

The Missouri question was not completely settled, however, until the Sixteenth Congress's second session (which began on 14 November 1820), after Missouri's proposed state constitution came under consideration. Although most of the document was virtually copied from the constitution of Kentucky and thus was unexceptional, the proposed constitution's twenty-sixth section included wording that called upon the new state's assembly to adopt legislation to prevent "free negroes and mulattoes" from entering and residing in Missouri "under any pretext whatsoever." A select Senate committee endorsed Missouri's admission under this constitution, but the controversial provision sparked heated debate in the full Senate not only on race in America but also, again, on slavery. Missouri's stipulation especially raised the issue of whether blacks were or could be U.S. citizens.

The Senate ultimately evaded the issue by passing on 12 December, without a recorded vote, a resolution endorsing Missouri's statehood, with a proviso previously introduced by Senator John Eaton of Tennessee, stipulating that congressional consent should not be construed as endorsing any clause in Missouri's constitution contravening the "privileges and immunities"—or equal citizenship—clause of the federal constitution. Missouri's constitution encountered more resistance in the House of Representatives, which refused to accept the Senate's resolution, not only delaying Missouri's admission but also throwing into question whether Missouri's three electoral votes should be counted on 14 February 1821, when the electoral votes for the 1820 presidential election were totaled by Congress. In a chaotic scene, the president of the Senate announced the results both with and without Missouri's inclusion. That same month, Representative and former speaker Henry Clay played a key role in resolving the imbroglio over Missouri's constitution, by using his influence to get the matter referred to a joint House-Senate committee. The committee then recommended a resolution (subsequently approved) incorporating the substance of Eaton's proviso, with the added stipulation, sometimes designated the Second Missouri Compromise, that Missouri's state legislature confirm in "a solemn public act" that its constitution abided by Eaton's requirement. Although Missouri's subsequent 26 June declaration denied Congress's right to require such a statement, President Monroe proclaimed Missouri's statehood on 10 August 1821.

Significance of the Compromise
Some historians suggest that the Missouri Compromise is a misnomer because majorities of northerners and southerners did not alike endorse all its key elements. In the House vote deleting Taylor's antislavery provision from the Missouri bill, for example, free-state congressmen voted overwhelmingly, 87 to 14, in favor of retaining the constraint. It was only because four free-staters abstained that compromise forces carried the day. Some historians, moreover, have echoed southern charges at the time and interpreted Tallmadge's initiative as an attempt to revive the fortunes of the fading Federalist Party, since some of the most vehement antislavery diatribes in Tallmadge's support came from Federalist congressmen, most notably Senator Rufus King of New York. If the majority Republican Party split along sectional lines, it might pave the way for a Federalist resurgence. But both Tallmadge and King had earlier demonstrated antislavery tendencies, and historians have yet to uncover documents proving that the amendment originated as a partisan cabal.

Historians further disagree over how to interpret the ringing defenses of slavery issued by southern congressmen in the heat of the debates. One can see such rhetoric as evidence that the northern assault on slavery influenced a gradual shift in southern public opinion from conceding that slavery was evil to proclaiming it a positive good, and that it thus backfired by provoking southerners to relinquish an earlier receptivity to slavery's ultimate abolition. However, the breakdown of voting on the Missouri measures also shows that some southerners remained uncertain about slavery's future. For instance, border slave state representatives voted 16 to 2 for Thomas's barrier against slavery's expansion. Further, as William W. Freehling argues in *The Road to Disunion*, some southerners who endorsed slavery's continued access to the West argued that this would help diffuse the institution into extinction. What historians do agree on is that northern attacks were prompted, in no small measure, by resentment of the political advantage given the slave states by the three-fifths clause in the U.S. Constitution (which allowed slaves to be counted as population for the purposes of political representation but did not allow them to vote), that northerners and southerners alike felt that the sectional balance of power hinged on the outcome of the dispute, and that significant numbers of southern congressmen had reservations about the precedent set by Thomas's limitation on slavery's future expansion. House Virginians voted 18 to 4 against the 36 degrees 30 minutes provision. Some southerners who endorsed Thomas's constraint apparently did so to get a slave state (Missouri) west of the Mississippi River at a time when only Florida remained for slavery's expansion in the East, and because of a belief that much of the remaining land in the West was desert.

The compromise's 36 degrees 30 minutes line helped to preserve sectional peace for more than thirty years, and might have done so longer had not Texan annexation and the Mexican War greatly enlarged the national domain and caused new sectional divisions over slavery's expansion. Without Congress's repeal of Thomas's provision in the Kansas-Nebraska Act of 1854, it is conceivable that the Civil War would have been considerably delayed, or even prevented. In a postmortem commentary on the Missouri Compromise, U.S. Supreme Court Chief Justice Roger B. Taney's opinion in the *Dred Scott* case (1857) contended that the already repealed 36 degrees 30 minutes line had been unconstitutional because it violated the property rights of southerners guaranteed by the Fifth Amendment of the U.S. Constitution. Taney's ruling outraged many northerners, contributing to pre–Civil War sectional tensions.

BIBLIOGRAPHY

Cooper, William J. *Liberty and Slavery: Southern Politics to 1860.* New York: Knopf, 1983.

Dangerfield, George. *The Era of Good Feelings.* New York: Harcourt, Brace and World, 1952.

Freehling, William W. *The Road to Disunion.* Vol. 1, *Secessionists at Bay, 1776–1854.* New York: Oxford University Press, 1990.

Moore, Glover. *The Missouri Controversy, 1819–1821.* Lexington: University of Kentucky Press, 1953.

Morrison, Michael A. *Slavery and the American West: The Eclipse of Manifest Destiny and the Coming of the Civil War.* Chapel Hill: University of North Carolina Press, 1997.

Remini, Robert V. *Henry Clay: Statesman for the Union.* New York: Norton, 1991.

Zeitz, Joshua Michael. "The Missouri Compromise Reconsidered: Rhetoric and the Emergence of the Free Labor Synthesis." *Journal of the Early Republic* 20, no. 3 (Fall 2000): 447–485.

Robert E. May

See also **Civil War; Dred Scott Case; Kansas-Nebraska Act; Mason-Dixon Line; Sectionalism; Slavery; Tallmadge Amendment.**

MISSOURI EX REL GAINES V. CANADA, 305 U.S 337 (1938). *Gaines* was the first major victory won in the U.S. Supreme Court by the National Association for the Advancement of Colored People in its campaign against racial segregation in public education. In a 6-2 decision, Chief Justice Charles Evans Hughes struck down a Missouri scheme whereby the state excluded African Americans from its state university's law school and paid their tuition to attend a public law school in a contiguous state. (There was no law school at Lincoln University, the state's black public college.) Hughes held that this violated the Fourteenth Amendment's guarantee of equal protection of the law. While *Gaines* did not question the separate-but-equal doctrine of *Plessy v. Ferguson* (1896), it was the first case in which the Court refused to accept segregation and exclusion in public universities. The Court left states the option of creating segregated professional and graduate schools, but in *Sweatt v. Painter* (1950), it also foreclosed that possibility, holding that such schools failed to provide true equality for their prospective students. After *Brown v. Board of Education I* (1954) held segregated public education unconstitutional per se, it became apparent that *Gaines* had marked the beginning of segregation's downfall at all levels of public schooling.

BIBLIOGRAPHY

Kluger, Richard. *Simple Justice: The History of Brown v. Board of Education and Black America's Struggle for Equality.* New York: Random House, 1975.

William M. Wiecek

See also **Brown v. Board of Education of Topeka; Plessy v. Ferguson; Segregation.**

MISSOURI RIVER, in the central and northwest central United States, is a major tributary of the MISSISSIPPI RIVER and the longest river in the United States (2,466 miles). It drains a watershed of approximately 580,000 square miles. Father Jacques Marquette and Louis Jolliet reached the mouth of the Missouri in 1673. It was known to them as Peki-tan-oui, so named on some of the early maps, and later as Oumessourit. From its source in southwestern Montana, where the Jefferson, Gallatin, and Madison Rivers join together, it winds around hills and bluffs, through one of the most fertile valleys in the world, to its junction with the Mississippi (ten miles north of SAINT LOUIS).

The lower part of the Missouri was known to the French trappers, traders, and voyageurs, who ascended it as far as the Kansas River in 1705. In 1720 a Spanish caravan was sent from Santa Fe to the Missouri to drive back the French. The early French called the river Saint Philip. They probably did not go higher than the Platte, which was considered the dividing line between the upper and lower river. In 1719 Claude Charles du Tisne and party went up the Missouri in canoes as far as the Grand River. Credited with being the first white man to visit the upper Missouri country, Pierre Gaultier de Varennes, Sieur de La Vérendrye, led a party from one of the posts of the Hudson's Bay Company in 1738 to the Mandan villages. Other explorations followed, searching for the "Western

Sea" by way of the Missouri River. The Missouri was first explored from its mouth to its source by Meriwether Lewis and William Clark (1804–1805).

Although it was thought for years that no keelboat could ascend the Missouri, it later became the great highway into the West. Gregoire Sarpy is said to have first introduced the keelboat, but the real father of navigation on the Missouri was Manuel Lisa. The first steamboat ever to ascend the river was the *Independence*, which pushed off from Saint Louis in 1819, reached Old Franklin in thirteen days, and turned back at Old Chariton, in MISSOURI. In 1831, Pierre Chouteau succeeded in ascending the Missouri in his steamboat *Yellowstone*. As a result of steamboating, many cities grew up along the edge of the river and several states built their capitals on its bank. Steamboating on the river reached its peak in the late 1850s and declined following the completion in 1859 of the Hannibal and Saint Joseph Railroad.

The Missouri River has always carried in suspension an immense amount of solid matter, mostly very fine light sand, discoloring the water and justifying the name of "Big Muddy." It is said that the yearly average of solid matter carried into the Mississippi by this river is over 500 million tons, brought along for an average distance of 500 miles. While the Missouri has a greater annual flow of water than the Mississippi above its mouth, it is subject to greater fluctuations. These have affected its navigability in certain seasons and caused the shoreline to shift, some farms and villages to disappear, and others to be left far back through deposits of the soil in front of them.

In 1944 Congress authorized a Missouri River basin project to control flooding of the Missouri, improve navigation, develop hydroelectric power, irrigate more than 4.3 million acres in the basin, halt stream pollution, and provide recreation areas. By the 1970s there were seven dams on the Missouri and eighty on its tributaries. The Missouri Basin Interagency Committee, with representatives from seven federal agencies and the governors of the ten Missouri basin states (North Dakota, South Dakota, Wyoming, Nebraska, Kansas, Minnesota, Missouri, Colorado, Iowa, and Montana), oversees the project. In the late twentieth century, the urbanization, soil erosion, and pollution had made the Missouri River one of the nation's most endangered rivers.

BIBLIOGRAPHY

Brower, Jacob V. *The Missouri River and Its Utmost Source; Curtailed Narration of Geologic, Primitive and Geographic Distinctions Descriptive of the Evolution and Discovery of the River and Its Headwaters.* St. Paul, Minn.: Pioneer Press, 1896, 1897.

Indians Killing Buffaloes in the Missouri River. A print after a drawing by W. M. Cary. NORTH WIND PICTURE ARCHIVES

The Missouri River

DeVoto, Bernard A. *Across the Wide Missouri: 1897–1955*. Boston: Houghton Mifflin, 1947, 1987; New York: American Legacy Press, 1981.

Griffith, Cecil R. *The Missouri River: The River Rat's Guide to Missouri River History and Folklore*. Leawood, Kans.: Squire Publishers, 1974.

Stella M. Drumm / A. G.

See also **Kansas City; Lewis and Clark Expedition.**

MISSOURI RIVER FUR TRADE. The fur trade was the principal form of commerce in the early days of European migration to the West, and it was able to develop to such a great extent because of the MISSOURI RIVER. Although the Missouri was difficult to navigate, it was the most dependable medium of transportation for furs. Late eighteenth-century expeditions by such men as Sieur de La Vérendrye, Pierre Menard, and Jean Truteau demonstrated its usefulness in this regard.

The river and its tributaries constituted one of the three great river systems of importance to the fur trader and trapper. First, the Spanish Commercial Company and Saint Louis Missouri Fur Company, and later, the Missouri Fur Company, the Columbia Fur Company, the American Fur Company, and, to a limited extent, the Rocky Mountain Fur Company, all operated in the Missouri and Mississippi watersheds.

These fur companies established some of the earliest European settlements in this region. The most important early post was that of the Saint Louis Missouri Fur Company. Known as Fort Lisa, it was located in Nebraska, near Council Bluffs, Iowa. Other early posts included Truteau's Post, erected in 1794, and Cedar Post, established in 1800, thirty-five miles south of the present site of Pierre, South Dakota.

The Missouri River also made SAINT LOUIS the greatest center of the fur trade in the nineteenth century. All the early expeditions were outfitted and started from this point, and, by 1843, its tributary reached 150 fur trading posts, a great majority of which lay along the Missouri River.

BIBLIOGRAPHY

Chittenden, Hiram M. *The American Fur Trade of the Far West: A History of the Pioneer Trading Posts and Earl Fur Companies of the Missouri Valley and the Rocky Mountains and the Overland Commerce with Santa Fe*. New York: Harper, 1902; New York: Press of the Pioneers, 1935; New York: Wilson, 1936; Stanford, Calif: Academic Reprints, 1954; Fairfield, N.J.: Kelley, 1976; Lincoln: University of Nebraska Press, 1986.

Hafen, LeRoy R., ed. *Fur Traders, Trappers, and Mountain Men of the Upper Missouri*. Lincoln: University of Nebraska Press, 1995.

Sunder, John E. *The Fur Trade on the Upper Missouri, 1840–1865.* Norman: University of Oklahoma Press, 1965, 1993.

Stella M. Drumm / T. D.

See also **French Frontier Forts; Fur Companies; Fur Trade and Trapping; Western Exploration.**

MISSOURI V. HOLLAND, 252 U.S. 416 (1920), was a 7 to 2 Supreme Court decision establishing that the treaty-making power allows the exercise of federal power in areas not specifically delegated to the national government. Following ratification of the Migratory Bird Treaty between the United States and Great Britain, Congress enacted legislation to enforce its provisions. The state of Missouri challenged the act as an encroachment on the jurisdiction reserved to the states by the Tenth Amendment, a claim the Court rejected. *Missouri v. Holland* figured prominently in mid-twentieth-century debates over U.S. participation in organizations such as the United Nations and is also significant for its conception of the Constitution as a "living document," allowing decisions to be based on historical practice instead of strict reliance on original intent.

BIBLIOGRAPHY

Bickel, Alexander M., and Benno C. Schmidt Jr. *History of the Supreme Court of the United States.* Volume 9: *The Judiciary and Responsible Government 1910–21.* New York: Macmillan, 1984.

R. Volney Riser

See also **Constitution of the United States.**

MIXED COMMISSIONS. Under international law, mixed commissions are instruments of ARBITRATION that have been established by bilateral or multilateral treaties. They are made up of members of different nationalities for the purpose of settling international disputes peacefully. These bodies may function as mixed claims commissions, conciliation commissions, or commissions of inquiry.

The concept of mixed commissions is generally regarded to have begun with JAY's TREATY of 1794 between the United States and Great Britain. This treaty included provisions for the establishment of three mixed commissions to resolve a number of issues that they had been unable to settle through negotiation. These commissions were made up of both American and British nationals, and while not strictly bodies of third-party mediation, they did function to some extent as tribunals and served to help revive interest in arbitration as a means of resolving international quarrels. Perhaps more important from the American perspective, the agreement to use these mixed commissions to resolve disagreements implied equality between the young United States and Great Britain. In the following decades, mixed commissions and arbitration were used often by the Americans and British to resolve their disagreements, as well as by other European and American nations.

Resolution of the ALABAMA CLAIMS between the United States and Great Britain established a precedent for successful arbitration. In order to adjudicate claims arising from a dispute from alleged breaches of neutrality on England's part during the Civil War, a mixed commission made up of representatives from Italy, Brazil, and Switzerland was created. Ultimately the commission awarded damages to the United States. The United States also took part in mixed claims commissions with Mexico in 1868 and Germany after World War I.

Conciliation commissions, such as those provided for in the twenty "cooling-off" treaties negotiated by Secretary of State William Jennings Bryan with various European states between 1913 and 1915, were designed to determine facts in a dispute and offer recommendations for settlement. Bryan's treaties each involved the appointment of a five-member commission to investigate the facts and offer a recommendation for a cordial resolution of the dispute. Although similar to conciliation commissions, a commission of inquiry simply endeavors to determine the facts in an international dispute. The United States was a participant in the Lytton Commission, which investigated the Japanese invasion of Manchuria in 1931 and whose report led to Japan's withdrawal from the League of Nations.

Mixed commissions do not always bring about a successful resolution of a dispute or claims for damages. Following the IRAN HOSTAGE CRISIS of November 1979–January 1981, the financial claims resulting from the dispute were submitted to the Iran–United States Claims Tribunal, which convened in May 1981. Made up of nine members, three each appointed by the United States and Iran, with the remainder chosen on the basis of mutual agreement, the commission failed to produce a resolution of any of the major issues after two years of effort.

BIBLIOGRAPHY

Boyle, Francis Anthony. *The Foundations of World Order: The Legalist Approach to International Relations, 1898–1921.* Durham, N.C.: Duke University Press. 1999.

Clement, Kendrick A. *William Jennings Bryan: Missionary Isolationist.* Knoxville: University of Tennessee Press. 1982.

Merrill, J.G. *International Dispute Settlement.* 3rd ed. New York: Cambridge University Press. 1998.

Wolfe, James H. *Modern International Law: An Introduction to the Law of Nations.* Upper Saddle River, N.J.: Prentice Hall, 2002.

Gregory Moore

MOBILE BAY, BATTLE OF (5 August 1864). A Union fleet of four monitors and fourteen wooden vessels under Adm. David G. Farragut forced an entrance into

Mobile Bay in Alabama through a narrow passage protected by mines, the guns of Fort Morgan, and the ironclad *Tennessee* and three small wooden gunboats, commanded by Adm. Franklin Buchanan. The Union monitor *Tecumseh* was sunk by a mine; "Damn the torpedoes!" cried Farragut, as his *Hartford* took the lead. Surrounded, the *Tennessee* was forced to surrender. Farragut lost fifty-two killed, ninety-three drowned, and 170 wounded. Buchanan lost twelve killed and twenty wounded. Fort Morgan surrendered on 23 August and the city of Mobile was completely blockaded.

BIBLIOGRAPHY

Duffy, James P. *Lincoln's Admiral: The Civil War Campaigns of David Farragut.* New York: Wiley, 1997.

Hearn, Chester G. *Mobile Bay and the Mobile Campaign: The Last Great Battles of the Civil War.* Jefferson, N.C.: McFarland, 1993.

Lewis, C. L. *Admiral Franklin Buchanan.* Baltimore: Norman, Remington, 1929.

Mahan, Alfred Thayer. *Admiral Farragut.* New York: Appleton, 1892, 1895, 1901; New York, Greenwood Press, 1968.

Charles Lee Lewis / A. R.

See also **"Damn the Torpedoes"; Navy, Confederate; Torpedo Warfare; Warships.**

MOBILIZATION is the process of assembling and organizing troops and matériel for the defense of a nation in time of war or national emergency. It has become a central factor in warfare since the French Revolution and the rise of nationalism. Whereas eighteenth-century powers most often hired mercenaries to fight limited wars, nineteenth-century nations increasingly demanded that every able-bodied citizen respond to mobilization calls. American attitudes toward war further reinforced the concept of total war because threats to public tranquility were interpreted as being illegal and immoral and thus as calling for nothing short of total war to reestablish the peace. In twentieth-century wars, it has been necessary to mobilize not only men and matériel but also psychological support, as illustrated by President Woodrow Wilson's vow to "make the world safe for democracy" and President Franklin D. Roosevelt's call for Germany's "unconditional surrender."

While embracing the notion of total war, the United States, until the twentieth century, was notoriously inept at mobilizing troops and retaining them for the duration of the wars it fought. Congress was ever suspicious of standing armies and of all efficient means that would enable the executive to mobilize the state militia forces, feeling that these instruments might serve partisan causes.

The mobilization problems experienced in the War of 1812 and the Mexican-American War (1846–1848) continued to plague U.S. military efforts throughout the nineteenth century. For instance, the militia system was never workable. This fact, together with the unreliability of the volunteers and the vices of the bounty system, demonstrated the necessity for conscription in any extended war in which the United States was involved. Furthermore, the tendency to mobilize manpower before mobilizing matériel was to create confusion down to World War I.

In the Mexican-American War, mobilization was based largely upon an expansible standing army and the calling of volunteers, because the militia's poor performance in the War of 1812 had demonstrated that the militia system was irredeemable. There were traces of pre-planning in this first foreign war, as arms and supplies were provided by the federal government based on the needs of the entire mobilized army.

The Civil War was a total war and thus a modern conflict, although many of the mobilization mistakes of previous wars were repeated. At the outset, few were able to perceive the conflict's full dimensions, and thus mobilization proceeded sporadically. Initially, President Abraham Lincoln called 75,000 state militia troops. But since this element had not been called since 1836 at the outset of the second Seminole War, the 2,471,377 troops on its rolls represented only a paper force in 1861. Next, a call was issued for volunteers; with no effective mobilization plan, the war department was unable to process the overwhelming number of recruits. Later, when the ardor of volunteering cooled, other methods of raising troops were resorted to, such as the draft implemented by the Conscription Act of 1863. Although the act netted few draftees, it forced many to volunteer who otherwise would not have. Other extraordinary measures employed to mobilize manpower included accepting African Americans for army service and organizing special service units to receive invalid volunteers for noncombatant duty.

All the old nightmares of poor mobilization were present in the Spanish-American War (1898), plus some new ones. With no plan of mobilization, there was no integration of manpower with matériel and no training in combined naval and military operations. Only the fact that the war was short and successful helped to ameliorate some of the potentially disastrous problems. A series of postwar reforms was instituted to remedy the worst mobilization shortcomings, among which was the founding of the Army War College in 1901 to study the mobilization process.

U.S. participation in World War I (1917–1918) and World War II (1941–1945) introduced speed into the war-making equation. Although the urgency of mobilization was slightly cushioned by the prior entry of America's allies into both wars, the gigantic scale of mobilization, the increased importance of technology, the total absorption of a sophisticated industrial economy into the war effort, and the huge number of troops, all raised mobilization planning to the highest councils of war.

By the National Defense Act of 1916, the United States avoided some of the desperate measures used to raise manpower in previous wars: uncertain calls for militiamen and volunteers were no longer to be relied on, and draftees were not to make substitutions, purchase exemptions, or receive bounties. Whereas in earlier American wars estimates of manpower requirements had been based largely on guesses of what public sentiment would allow, in World War I, the calls for manpower were limited only by the manpower requirements for industry. Therefore, the great mobilization problems of World War I were not those of recruiting, but of equipping, training, organizing, and transporting the army to the front.

The Japanese attack on Pearl Harbor in 1941 catapulted the United States into the most massive mobilization effort in history. As in World War I, the armed forces and the war industries were in competition for manpower. In addition, there were the requirements of not one but five theaters of war, the need of maintaining lines of communication to each theater, and the need to dovetail efforts with coalition partners. The squeeze upon American manpower extended the search for able hands to the enlisting of women, indigenous personnel, prisoners of war, and the physically handicapped.

The leading role of the United States in the Cold War significantly altered its traditional mobilization techniques. Although never implemented, universal military training, authorized in principle by the Universal Military Training and Service Act of 1951, was intended to provide a peacetime pool of manpower that could be drafted in time of national emergency. Until the Korean War (1950–1953), the emphasis on air power and nuclear arms allowed the army's manpower strength to slip.

Selective-service legislation passed in 1955 assured that reserve units would be manned by trained men; but instead of the reserves being called for the Vietnam War, as had been done in the Korean War, forces were raised through increased draft calls. As the war became increasingly unpopular at home, millions of young men sought college deferments to avoid service in Vietnam. Others engaged in open draft evasion, including fleeing to Canada and Europe. The draft created so much political controversy and domestic turmoil that the Nixon administration replaced it with an all-volunteer military in the early 1970s. The U.S. military continues to rely exclusively on volunteers to fill the needs of its fighting forces. Nevertheless, all young men are still required by law to register for selective service upon their eighteenth birthday.

BIBLIOGRAPHY

Chambers, John W. *To Raise an Army: The Draft Comes to Modern America.* New York: Free Press, 1987.

Kreidberg, Marvin A., and Merton G. Henry. *History of Military Mobilization in the United States Army, 1775–1945.* Washington D.C.: Department of the Army, 1953, 1955; Westport, Conn.: Greenwood, 1975; Washington, D.C.: U.S. Government Printing Office, 1984.

Millett, Alan R. *For the Common Defense: A Military History of the United States of America.* New York: Free Press, 1984, 1994.

Don E. McLeod / A. G.

See also **Bounties, Military; Conscription and Recruitment; Military Law; Preparedness; Quartering Act; Reserve Officers' Training Corps; War Costs; Women in Military Service.**

MOBY-DICK, Herman Melville's sixth book, was published in 1851. It was a work in which, as the novelist Walker Percy has written, Melville first fully felt "the happiness of the artist discovering, breaking through into the freedom of his art." *Moby-Dick* began as yet another young-man-goes-to-sea story, but it grew into an encyclopedic work in which the first-person voice of the narrator, Ishmael, fractures into multiple voices. The highly digressive narrative about the whaleship *Pequod* incorporates meticulous descriptions of the whaling business (from its wage structure to its inventory of weapons and tools), bawdy sailor songs, lyric celebrations of seafaring life, as well as flights of speculation about human destiny. This wonderfully multifarious book, however, is eventually taken over by the "monomaniac" Captain Ahab, who turns the *Pequod* into an instrument for achieving his singular and focused purpose: to hunt and kill the great white whale that, on a previous voyage, had dashed his boat to splinters and ripped him half to death.

Although a few critics recognized the imaginative power of *Moby-Dick*, most recoiled from what one reviewer called its strange "horrors and . . . heroics." Melville's reputation continued to decline until the 1920s, when *Moby-Dick* was rediscovered as a protomodernist work. Readers in the 1930s and 1940s, shocked by the rise of totalitarian dictators in their own time, felt an eerie prescience in Melville's story of how a demagogue fuses his personal need for vengeance with the popular will. More recently, scholars have noticed that *Moby-Dick* is not only a book that touches with prophetic insight on timeless themes of human cruelty, but that it was also a careful political allegory tied to the ominous events of its own time—a meditation on the American ship of state heading for doom.

Today, *Moby-Dick* is probably the most discussed work in American literary history. It probes many themes that remain salient in our time—religious, philosophical, environmental, and sexual, as when Melville celebrates the love between an American boy (Ishmael) and a tattooed cannibal (the harpooner Queequeg). The scholar Harry Levin remarked that "the investigation of *Moby-Dick* might almost be said to have taken the place of whaling among the industries" of the United States.

BIBLIOGRAPHY

Hardwick, Elizabeth. *Herman Melville*. New York: Viking, 2000.

Parker, Hershel, and Harrison Hayford, eds. *Moby-Dick as Doubloon: Essays and Extracts 1851–1970*. New York: Norton, 1970.

Andrew Delbanco

MODERNISTS, PROTESTANT.

Protestant modernism, or the conscious adaptation of the Christian religion to modern conditions of life, has a long lineage in American history. It shares many important features with the ideas more generally known as liberal Christianity—notably the belief that God acts in the world and a conviction that history is progressing ever upwards toward the Kingdom of God. Modernist Christianity, however, differed from liberal Protestantism in that it grappled directly with issues that previously fell outside the traditional scope of American churches. Modernists were not content to simply update doctrine but made sustained and explicit efforts to "modernize" Christianity by applying it to the most pressing political and social concerns of the day. Accordingly, the high tide of Protestant modernism in the United States came during the 1890s through 1920s, when the country transformed itself from an agricultural nation into an industrial powerhouse and global political leader. Although its pervasive optimism was dealt a severe blow by the horrors of World War I, and its influence was eroded by the continued de-Christianization of American life, modernist Christianity retained considerable cultural and political power well into the twentieth century.

Nineteenth-Century Background

The religious impulses that flowered into modernist Christianity found their antecedents in the liberal Christianity of the early nineteenth century, particularly in New England. The development of Unitarianism, a liberal denomination formally organized in 1825, moved a subset of highly educated and influential Protestants away from the dogmatism of their Puritan ancestors, and toward a more flexible, rational Christianity. Unitarianism provided a cerebral alternative to the more emotional, evangelistic denominations that were gathering strength in the South during this time, such as the Baptists and the Methodists. Although Unitarians were most notably successful in the Boston area, their influence was felt throughout the country, because so many of the nineteenth century's preeminent religious leaders and theologians hailed from the Harvard–Boston–New England cultural nexus.

Although he was a Congregationalist minister, Horace Bushnell provides a good example of this liberal tendency, for he harmonized many long-standing tensions in New England religion. Bushnell exerted an influence far beyond his local Connecticut parish due to the success of his books, including *Christian Nurture* (1847) and *God in Christ* (1849). In *Christian Nurture*, Bushnell outlined a specific program of childrearing and religious education

that proved popular throughout the century. In *God in Christ*, he argued that language (and by extension, Scripture) was best understood on a symbolic, organic, or poetic level, rather than literally. Bushnell's theology drew upon currents of German Romanticism that were becoming increasingly influential among educated Americans; his ideas were often controversial but seldom ignored. With his emphasis on the social and corporate nature of religious belief, Bushnell paved the way for widespread Christian engagement with social problems in the latter part of the century.

Social Gospel

In the decades following the Civil War, the leaders of the Protestant establishment participated in a movement known as the social gospel and brought their religious perspective to bear on the problems of a dawning industrial age. According to the movement's foremost proponents—ministers such as Walter Rauschenbusch, Washington Gladden, and Josiah Strong—Christians were obligated to address pressing social problems such as labor exploitation, factory conditions, and urban poverty. In his influential *Christianity and the Social Crisis* (1908), Rauschenbusch argued that Christians must take control of social forces in order to promote harmony and defeat evil. Primarily a city-based movement, the social gospelers exhorted their congregations to recognize the Christian fellowship that tied them to the new immigrants who were pouring into the United States. In the widespread social disorder, disease, and apparent immorality of the immigrant slums, social gospelers heard a clarion call to Christian action. Committed reformers like Jane Addams started settlement houses in the blighted neighborhoods, while others advocated legislation to blunt the impact of industrialization.

The same impetus behind the social gospel movement led to increased interest in overseas missionary work and proselytization, which peaked in the first decades of the twentieth century. Liberal Protestants, influenced by the doctrine of postmillennialism—which taught that human effort could help inaugurate a 1,000-year golden age after which Christ would return to earth—remained convinced that the kingdom of God could be achieved in this world. The social gospel might hasten this process by addressing problems in America, while missionary work spread the light of Christ across the globe. To advance this agenda, Protestants formed organizations such as the Student Volunteer Movement (1888) and the Intercollegiate Young Men's Christian Association (1877). Despite their enthusiasm and effort, these organizations failed to achieve their stated goal of "The Evangelization of the World in This Generation"; while they met with some success, they by no means converted even a majority of the foreign peoples they encountered. Missionary work, however, did lead to a cosmopolitan outlook that would later help the Protestant elite achieve significant political power in a century focused on international affairs.

431

The social gospel and missionary movements were the most obvious demonstrations of Protestantism's refocusing toward modernity. Neither sought to escape from the complexities and troubles of modern life but claimed instead that Christianity would be a central part of any new order. Their firm belief in progress helped alleviate the anxieties of industrialization. According to this religious perspective, uneven economic development, with all its hardships, was only a temporary stage on the way to greater social equality and prosperity.

The Fundamentalist-Modernist Controversy

Potentially more serious threats to Christianity than industrialization were developments in science, particularly the growing popularity of Darwinian theories. By providing a convincing alternative to the Biblical creation narrative, the theory of evolution expounded by Charles Darwin in 1859 threatened to undermine a central basis of the Christian faith. However, Protestant modernizers were not daunted by the new science and remained convinced that evolution could be easily accommodated to religious belief. These thinkers found it easy to interpret biblical accounts of Genesis as providing rough metaphors for the process of evolution. Furthermore, they saw no reason why God could not act as the driving force behind the processes Darwin described. But the advent of evolution created sharp divisions between those Christians who thought it possible to reconcile religion to modernity and the new science, and those who rejected the new intellectual developments outright. While men such as Harvard biologist Asa Gray, Princeton President James McCosh, or New York minister Lyman Abbott were quite content to call themselves both Darwinists and Christians, others would vehemently reject the new scientific theories and call for the strengthening of traditional Protestantism. Christians who rejected the conclusions of Darwin were known as "fundamentalists," after a series of pamphlets published in 1910–1915, *The Fundamentals*. This countervailing current burst onto the American scene in 1925 with the Scopes trial, the most famous by-product of what would be known as the fundamentalist-modernist controversy. Regardless of who "won" this conflict, the very existence of such a public battle pointed to growing fissures in American Christian identity.

World War I and After

World War I was a watershed event for liberal Christians because it challenged their underlying belief in progress and human goodness. If God were truly present in history, then what explained the bloody clash that had just overtaken and nearly destroyed European civilization? A young generation of Christian students became firmly committed to pacifism but continued to support missionary work, albeit in a slightly chastened form.

From his perch at the Chicago School of Divinity, Shailer Mathews became one of the country's most important modernizers in the 1920s. He firmly rebutted the fundamentalist claim to true Christianity, arguing instead that liberalism was closer to the animating spirit of Christ. According to Mathews, liberals alone accepted the true spiritual essence of Christianity. They were also the only hope and future of Christianity, for unless religion learned to adapt itself to the modern age, it would perish. Mathews was influential, yet feared by some Christians who saw him as a dire threat to their faith.

The fundamentalist-modernist controversy also continued to simmer in the career of Harry Emerson Fosdick, who advanced ideas similar to those of Mathews. Ousted from his original pulpit for his liberal views, by 1931 Fosdick was triumphantly installed in New York City's grand new interdenominational center, Riverside Church, which had been funded by John D. Rockefeller Jr. Over the next fifteen years, Fosdick became the most famous and oft-quoted preacher of the age. Yet at the same time, members of his denomination, the Northern Baptists, were energetic organizers of numerous fundamentalist groups and seminaries.

World War I devastated the assumptions of Protestant liberalism but created several advantages for Protestant modernizers. Shorn of their unrealistic optimism, in the 1930s a new generation of theologians such as Reinhold Niebuhr were able to make Christianity relevant to modern times by drawing connections between current events and traditional Christian ideas of sin. Drawing upon the international infrastructure created by missions and employing the considerable cultural capital of Christianity, these thinkers came to prominence in the years before and after World War II.

While the Protestant establishment that had nourished modernism began to wane in the 1960s and 1970s, it continued to exercise episodic influence, as seen in the case of Harvey Cox, who published his best-selling *The Secular City* in 1965. In this work, Cox argued that the secular world—particularly its urban spaces—was not a place Christians should flee but rather a vital locus they should understand, accept, and learn to engage. Cox's conclusion, in which he suggested Christians wait for the next manifestation of the spirit, adumbrated later radical religious movements such as liberation and feminist theology.

Other new social and political currents, however, threatened to sweep the theology of Protestant modernizers to the periphery. Postmodernism, decolonization of the Third World, and multiculturalism, combined with the electoral resurgence of fundamentalism, suggested that liberalism's strength at midcentury had perhaps been illusory. Regardless of the complexity involved, however, it was clear that the project of adapting Protestant Christianity to the modern world remained vitally important to many Americans.

BIBLIOGRAPHY

Ahlstrom, Sydney E. *A Religious History of the American People.* New Haven, Conn.: Yale University Press, 1972. See especially chapters 24–25, 46–47.

Carpenter, Joel A., and Wilbert R. Shenk, eds. *Earthen Vessels: American Evangelicals and Foreign Missions, 1880–1980.* Grand Rapids, Mich.: W. B. Eerdmans, 1990.

Handy, Robert T., ed. *The Social Gospel in America, 1870–1920.* New York: Oxford University Press, 1966.

Hutchison, William R. *The Modernist Impulse in American Protestantism.* 2d rev. ed. Durham, N.C.: Duke University Press, 1992.

Larson, Edward J. *Summer for the Gods: The Scopes Trial and America's Continuing Debate over Science and Religion.* Cambridge, Mass.: Harvard University Press, 1997.

May, Henry F. *The End of American Innocence: A Study of the First Years of Our Time, 1912–1917.* New York: Columbia University Press, 1992.

Warren, Heather A. *Theologians of a New World Order: Reinhold Niebuhr and the Christian Realists, 1920–1948.* New York: Oxford University Press, 1997.

Jennifer Burns

See also **Fundamentalism; Protestantism; Social Gospel.**

MODOC WAR (1872–1873). One of the costliest of the nineteenth-century Indian Wars, the Modoc War officially began on 29 November 1872 because of a misunderstanding between the Modoc Indians and the United States. Settlers, who began moving through Modoc territory as early as 1843, set off conflicts that led eventually to war. In 1864 the Modocs signed a treaty with the United States whereby the Modocs would receive goods and protection once they moved to the Klamath Reservation in Oregon. When agency officials ignored Modoc grievances, approximately two hundred Modocs fled the reservation under the leadership of Kintpuash (Captain Jack). They resettled along Lost River, their ancestral home.

Between 1865 and 1869 Kintpuash and his followers moved three times to their assigned reservation, but they were treated poorly there and did not always remain within its boundaries. Pressure to force the Modocs to comply with the treaty's provisions increased after the document was ratified in 1869. By 1871, 159 Modocs still refused to move back to the Oregon reservation. In November 1872 President Ulysses S. Grant gave orders to force the Modocs back. On 29 November the war began with the Battle of Lost River. The United States cavalry, commanded by Captain James Jackson, opened fire on Kintpuash's camp, forcing the Modocs to split up and flee to the Lava Beds in Northern California. En route, Hooker Jim and his men killed eleven male settlers. Kintpuash learned of these killings when Hooker Jim reached the Lava Beds. Over the next two months three major battles occurred as U.S. troops sought to infiltrate the Lava Beds: Battle of Land's Ranch, First Battle for the Stronghold, First Battle of Scorpion Point.

On 29 January 1873 President Grant appointed a peace commission, headed by General Edward R. S. Canby, to meet with the Modocs to cease hostilities and persuade them to return to the reservation. Between February and March negotiations continued with the assistance of two primary interpreters, Winema (Toby Riddle) and her husband Frank Riddle. In April, Winema visited the Lava Beds and returned to warn Canby of the Modocs' intentions to kill the peace commissioners if they did not comply with Modoc demands of a reservation along Lost River and exoneration for the murderers of the settlers. Canby ignored Winema's warnings and proceeded with the meeting on 11 April 1873. At this meeting Kintpuash and his men tried to negotiate, but Canby refused to listen, demanding their unconditional surrender. The Modocs carried out their plans, killing Canby (the highest ranking officer killed in the Indian Wars of the nineteenth century), Reverend Eleasar Thomas, and L. S. Dyar, and wounding Alfred Meacham.

Four battles that followed (Second Battle for the Stronghold, Second Battle of Scorpion Point, Battle of Dry Lake, and Battle of Willow Creek Ridge) brought the army closer to the Modocs' stronghold, forcing them to disperse. Kintpuash surrendered on 1 June 1873. He and five other Modocs (John Schonchin, Boston Charley, Black Jim, Slolux, and Barncho) stood trial and were sentenced to hang. Slolux and Barncho's sentences were commuted to life imprisonment at the military prison on Alcatraz; the other four Modocs were hanged on 3 October. The government exiled the remaining 153 Modocs to Indian Territory.

During eight months of warfare 159 Modoc men, women, and children fought 1,000 U.S. soldiers. In all 83 U.S. soldiers, 3 Modocs, and 14 other Native Americans died in the war.

BIBLIOGRAPHY

Landrum, Francis S., comp. *Guardhouse, Gallows, and Graves: The Trial and Execution of Indian Prisoners of the Modoc Indian War by the U.S. Army, 1873.* Klamath Falls, Ore.: Klamath County Museum, 1988.

Murray, Keith A. *The Modocs and Their War.* Norman: University of Oklahoma Press, 1959.

Riddle, Jeff C. *The Indian History of the Modoc War.* Eugene, Ore.: Urion Press, 1974.

Rebecca Bales

See also **Indian Policy, U.S., 1830–1900.**

MOHAVE. The Mohaves are the northernmost of three culturally related groups living along the lower Colorado River. All three speak related Yuman languages. Traditional Mohave territory extends roughly forty-five miles upriver and seventy-five miles downriver from the modern city of Needles, California. To their south, in the area of the Colorado-Gila confluence, are the Quechans; farther south, straddling the modern international boundary, are the Cocopas. (Between 1827 and 1829 a fourth

Mohave. This illustration depicts members of this tribe of farmers and warriors in loincloths and war paint. ARCHIVE PHOTOS, INC.

Yuman group, the Halchidhomas, were driven out of the area between the Mohaves and the Quechans and absorbed by groups to the east.) The Mohaves are probable descendents of the more widespread ancient culture known archaeologically as Hakatayan or Lowland Patayan. Their own origin narratives declare this river region has always been their home, anchored by the sacred Spirit Mountain nearby.

They briefly met Spaniards in 1604, and again in 1776. In the late 1850s, after three decades of encounters with various white expeditions, the U.S. Army built Fort Mohave in their territory and subjugated them. Factionalism erupted in the 1860s and divided the Mohaves into two groups now on two separate reservations: Fort Mohave (just north of Needles, California) and, about forty miles south, the Colorado River reservation. Mohave population in the eighteenth and nineteenth centuries was estimated at between three and four thousand.

Like their lower Colorado Yuman relatives, the Mohaves traditionally maintained a strong sense of tribal identity despite their scattered and shifting settlement pattern and flexible leadership. They mounted tribal military campaigns, for example, sometimes allied with Quechans.

Their livelihood was linked to the Colorado: they farmed corn, beans, and pumpkins in the rich silt deposited during spring flooding. They lived as scattered extended families under sunshade shelters close by their family farm plots. Low, earth-covered winter houses squatted on elevations above the floodplain. Besides their crops, the Mohaves relied heavily on wild mesquite and screwbean pods, which they ground into meal for gruel or baking. The pods became even more vital when there was no spring flooding. Fish were an important source of animal protein; deer and rabbit were less significant.

The scattered families were loosely clustered into larger settlements or rancherias, usually separated from one another by about four or five miles. Each rancheria in turn belonged to one of three larger named geographical subdivisions of the tribe. The tribe also included about twenty patrilineal clans, each of which had some totemic affiliation with an animal or plant (for example, frog, corn, or snake). The clans were exogamous, but their other functions remain unknown; they were not localized groups. Leadership was not highly structured; each rancheria recognized one or more leading men whose wise actions and generosity revealed their personal dream power. This informal civil leadership may or may not have included some members of a separate special category of benevolent orator-ritualists, who were endowed with extraordinary dream power. The title of tribal chief recognized by whites may not have been traditional. Especially skilled and courageous warriors belonged to a category of brave men. Other statuses included shamans, capable of curing or harm, and singers; all required power dreams.

The dominant theme of the Mohave worldview emphasized spiritual power derived from dreaming and from war. Individual spiritual power came from dreams whose specific content followed general scenarios and whose significance was publicly pondered (and sometimes underscored in long song cycles). Evidently a collective tribal spiritual power waxed and waned; victories over traditional enemies (including principally Yuman-speaking Maricopas to the east and Cocopas to the south, as well as Halchidhoma, Pima, and Tohono O'odam groups) were a primary means of increasing the tribal power.

War parties were of two types: small-scale surprise raids and larger tribal campaigns. In tribal wars the opposing lines drew up to fling verbal insults at each other before loosing arrows and closing for hand-to-hand combat with heavy wooden clubs and short staffs. In the postcontact period, at least, these larger battles were not usually ignited to seize more territory. (The expulsion of the Halchidhomas was a qualified exception.) The small raids were more frequent, and evidently launched by younger men seeking to build their reputations and spread consternation among the enemy.

The most elaborate tribal ritual commemorated the deaths of prominent people during the preceding year or so. Its scenario portrayed successive phases of an epic war expedition as well as cremation segments of the origin narrative.

About 1,175 people live on the modern Fort Mohave Reservation, on a land base of 23,699 acres in Arizona and

5,582 acres in Nevada; 15,000 of these are under cultivation. The Colorado River Reservation includes about 2,400 people representing four ethnic groups: the Mohaves (the most numerous); the Chemehuevis; and Navajo and Hopi families who were moved on to the land in 1945. About 84,500 of the reservation's 278,000 acres are cultivated. Both reservations feature casinos.

BIBLIOGRAPHY

Kroeber, Alfred L. *Handbook of the Indians of California.* Washington, D.C.: Government Printing Office, 1925. American Ethnology Bureau Bulletin 78 (1925). Reprinted by Dover Publications, New York (1976).

Kroeber, Alfred L., and Clifton B. Kroeber. *A Mohave War Reminiscence, 1854–1880.* Vol. 10, University of California Publications in Anthropology. Berkeley and Los Angeles: University of California Press (1973).

Stewart, Kenneth M. "Mohave." In *Handbook of North American Indians.* Edited by William C. Sturtevant et al. Volume 10, *Southwest,* edited by Alfonso Ortiz. Washington, D.C.: Smithsonian Institution Press, 1983.

Wallace, William J. "The Mohave Indians of the Lower Colorado River." In *The Native Americans* 2d edition. Edited by Robert F. Spencer, Jesse D. Jennings et al. New York: Harper and Row, 1977.

Robert L. Bee

See also **Tribes: Southwestern.**

MOHAWK VALLEY. Situated in east central New York State, the Mohawk Valley runs 148 miles (east-west) and is created by the Mohawk River. The Mohawk Valley has played an influential historical role in human settlement, migration, and transportation. Home to many nations of the Iroquois Confederacy, the Mohawk Valley was the location of numerous battles during the French and Indian War (1754–1763) as well as during the American Revolution (1775–1783) because of its strategic importance—it served as the only natural east-west passage through the Appalachian Mountains. The ERIE CANAL, completed in 1825, follows part of the course of the Mohawk River and created the first water route between the eastern United States and the Midwest. This geographic fact was exploited by thousands of settlers as they migrated west. In addition, the Mohawk Valley served as the main route by which agricultural products from the Midwest were transported east and industrial goods made their way west. The New York Central Railroad also followed a course through the Mohawk Valley. During the twentieth century, the Mohawk Valley was a prime location for new industries in the United States. Some historians maintain that the importance of the valley with regard to migration, transportation, industrialization, and commerce contributed to the growth of New York City as a world city.

BIBLIOGRAPHY

Phelan, Thomas. *The Hudson-Mohawk Gateway: An Illustrated History.* Northridge, Calif.: Windsor, 1985.

Janet S. Smith

MOHEGAN. The Mohegans, an Eastern Algonquian-speaking people located in southeastern Connecticut, first appear on a 1614 Dutch map that shows them located close to the Pequots. If not part of the Pequot tribe, the Mohegan village was under Pequot control until the outbreak of hostilities between the English and Pequots in the 1630s. By the commencement of the English-Pequot War (1636–1638), the Mohegans, under the leadership of Uncas, had broken with the Pequots and joined the English against them.

After the war, Uncas became the most important pro-English Indian leader in New England, but his loyalty did not prevent the English from acquiring most of his tribe's lands. By the 1750s the tribe was split over issues of leadership, which were exacerbated by the last tribal sachem Ben Uncas III. The opposition was led by Samson Occom, Mohegan minister, who after Uncas's death in 1769, organized the Brothertown movement.

The tribe held some 2,000 acres until 1861 when the state legislature divided the land among the tribal members, with the title and citizenship being granted in 1872. Only the plot on which the Mohegan Church was located remained tribal.

The tribe continued to function throughout the twentieth century, centering its activities around the church. It brought suit in the 1970s for the land lost in 1861, and in 1994 it was granted federal recognition and settled its land claim.

BIBLIOGRAPHY

Conkey, Laura E., Ethel Boissevain, and Ives Goddard "Indians of Southern New England and Long Island: Late Period." In *Handbook of North American Indians.* Vol. 15: *Northeast.* Edited by Bruce Trigger. Washington, D.C.: Smithsonian Institution, 1978.

DeForest, John W. *History of the Indians of Connecticut from the Earliest Known Period to 1850.* Hamden, Conn.: Archon, 1964. Originally published in 1851.

Jack Campisi

See also **Tribes: Northeastern.**

MOLASSES ACT, a British law put into effect on 25 December 1733, laid prohibitive duties of six pence per gallon on molasses, nine pence per gallon on rum, and five shillings for every one hundred weight on sugar imported from non-British colonies into Great Britain's American mainland colonies. The duty had to be paid before the ships landed. The act also stipulated that these products could only be imported into Ireland on British ships, in accordance with the Navigation Acts.

The Molasses Act originated in the vying economic interests of the British continental and island colonies. In 1717, France permitted French West Indies sugar to supersede the British product in European markets, and it competed successfully in the markets of the English colonies. At the same time, France prohibited the importation of rum into France to protect French brandy production. This obliged the molasses producers in the French colonies to develop markets in New England and New York. The mainland colonial merchants involved in the considerable rum industry in New England found it more lucrative to deal with the French, Dutch, or Spanish sugar interests in the West Indies than with the costly English suppliers. Boston alone produced more than a million gallons of rum per year by the 1730s. From 1730 to 1733, the planters in the British West Indies sugar colonies, led by Barbados, which had highly placed political connections, petitioned Parliament to disallow the mainland colonies from carrying on commerce with the foreign West Indies. The British West Indies planters insisted they were suffering from soil exhaustion, a recent hurricane, burdensome export taxes, and the restraints of the Navigation Acts. The mainland colonies argued that the British West Indies could not consume all of the fish, lumber, flour, cheese, and other agricultural products of the Bread Colonies (the mainland colonies) or provide the amount of rum the mainland colonies demanded.

Colonial smuggling minimized the act's effects. Lax enforcement within the negligible customs bureaucracy allowed colonial commerce to follow previous routes without coercion. Illicit trade with the enemy, even during wartime, had become a way of life for the colonists. Estimates indicate that New England distilled considerably more rum than could have been produced with legally imported molasses, so rum production in New England could only survive by circumventing the act. The act continued in force for five years and was renewed five times. As the Molasses Act was about to expire, George Grenville, the first lord of the treasury and chancellor of the exchequer, replaced it in 1764 with the Sugar Act. A more effective tariff, the sugar duty collected a greater amount of revenue than any other duty in the next decade, because it lowered the levy on molasses from six pence to three pence, making molasses less profitable to smuggle. Any ships in violation of the Sugar Act were subject to immediate seizure by British customs commissioners and were placed under the authority of the Vice Admiralty Court in Nova Scotia.

BIBLIOGRAPHY

Barrow, Thomas C. *Trade and Empire: The British Customs Service in Colonial America, 1660–1775.* Cambridge, Mass.: Harvard University Press, 1967.

Dickerson, Oliver M. *The Navigation Acts and the American Revolution.* New York: A. S. Barnes, 1963.

Pares, Richard. *Yankees and Creoles: The Trade between North America and the West Indies before the American Revolution.* Cambridge, Mass.: Harvard University Press, 1956.

Taussig, Charles William. *Rum, Romance, and Rebellion.* New York: Minton, Balch, 1928.

Walton, Gary M., and James F. Shepherd. *The Economic Rise of Early America.* New York: Cambridge University Press, 1979.

Michelle M. Mormul

See also **Colonial Commerce; Navigation Acts; Rum Trade; Sugar Acts; West Indies, British and French.**

MOLASSES TRADE was the keystone of colonial commerce, as it supplied a product that enabled the colonists to offset their unfavorable balance of trade with England. Except for experimental attempts to produce molasses locally from corn, the source of supply was the West Indies. It centered at first in the English sugar colonies in Barbados and Jamaica, but by the early eighteenth century it had shifted to the other West Indies, such as Spain's Santo Domingo and France's Martinique.

The main significance of molasses was to provide a "money cargo," almost as current as cash. Once it was exported from the islands, there was little trade in molasses as such. Its real potency came once the NEW ENGLAND distillers turned it into rum. Most important, it served as the basis for the TRIANGULAR TRADE in rum, slaves, and molasses. New England traders carried rum to Africa in exchange for slaves. These slaves were transported and sold to the West Indies to work in the sugar plantations that produced the molasses. Traders then returned with molasses to New England and sold the goods to rum producers.

At first the trade was unrestrained except for local taxes, but in 1704 Parliament confined the exportation of molasses to England or its colonies. In order to force a British monopoly of the molasses trade on the colonies, Parliament passed a MOLASSES ACT (1733), which unsuccessfully attempted to eliminate trade with the foreign West Indies by prohibitive taxes. At first colonists tried to protest such measures. Rather than comply with these taxes, however, colonial merchants found it far simpler to smuggle molasses, beginning a robust clandestine trade in the good that lasted several decades.

When the British tried to assert their influence over the colonies following the FRENCH AND INDIAN WAR, the new prime minister George Grenville began a strict policy of customs law enforcement. Parliament revived the Molasses Act as the Sugar Act of 1764. This act created strong customs enforcement of duties on molasses imported into the colonies on non-British ships, in effect granting a monopoly of the molasses trade to British West Indies sugar planters. Though colonial protests against this act resulted in a lowering of the tax, the heavy fines and penalties frustrated the colonial commerce in imported sugar and molasses. Independence freed the thirteen colonies from such restraints, but hampered their trade with the British West Indies. Modifications of the law permitted the direct importation of molasses, but the NAVIGATION ACTS continued to limit American shipping until 1830.

BIBLIOGRAPHY

McCusker, John J. *Rum and the American Revolution: The Rum Trade and the Balance of Payments of the Thirteen Continental Colonies.* New York: Garland, 1989.

Lawrence A. Harper / H. S.

See also **Rum Trade; Slave Trade; Sugar Acts; West Indies, British and French.**

MOLECULAR BIOLOGY is the science, or cluster of scientific activities, that seeks to explain the phenomena of life through investigation of the molecules found in living things. The term was apparently invented in the late 1930s by Warren Weaver, a mathematician-turned-official of the Rockefeller Foundation, who from 1933 through World War II (1939–1945) channeled much of this philanthropy's considerable resources into a program to promote medical advances by making the life sciences more like physics in intellectual rigor and technological sophistication. There is considerable debate about the extent to which Weaver successfully altered the intellectual direction of the wide range of life sciences with which he interacted. However, there can be little doubt that his program made important new instruments and methods available for biologists. For instance, Rockefeller support greatly furthered the development of X-ray crystallography, ultracentrifuge and electrophoresis instrumentation, and the electron microscope, all used for analyzing the structure and distribution in organisms of proteins, nucleic acids, and other large biomolecules. In the 1930s and 1940s, these biological macromolecules were studied not mainly by biochemists, since the traditional methods of biochemistry were adequate only for the study of compounds orders of magnitude smaller (with molecular weights in the hundreds), but rather by scientists from the ill-defined fields known as "biophysics" and "general physiology."

A general postwar enthusiasm for science made rich resources available to biologists from federal agencies such as the National Science Foundation and the National Institutes of Health. Thanks to this new funding, and also to a postatomic urge to make physics benefit mankind peacefully, the research topics and methods of biophysicists made great headway in the 1950s. New radioisotopes and accelerators spurred radiobiology. Electron microscopes were turned on cells and viruses. Protein structure was probed by crystallography, electrophoresis, and ultracentrifugation; furthermore, chemical methods were developed allowing determination of the sequence of the string of amino acids making up smaller proteins. This kind of macromolecule-focused research in the 1950s has been described as the "structural school of molecular biology" (or biophysics). In the immediate postwar era, another approach also developed around Max Delbrück, a physicist-turned-biologist fascinated since the 1930s with explaining the gene, who attracted many other physicists to biology. Now regarded as the beginning of molecular genetics, this style has been called the "informational school of molecular biology," since during the 1940s and 1950s the school probed the genetic behavior of viruses and bacteria without any attempt to purify and characterize genes chemically. To the surprise of many, largely through the combined efforts of James Watson and Francis Crick—a team representing both schools—in the mid-1950s, the gene was found to be a double-helical form of nucleic acid rather than a protein. From this point through the early 1960s, molecular geneticists concentrated much of their efforts on "cracking" the "code" by which sequences of nucleic acid specify the proteins that carry out the bulk of biological functions. After the "coding" problem was settled in the mid-1960s, they turned mainly to the mechanisms by which genes are activated under particular circumstances, at first in viruses and bacteria, and from the 1970s, in higher organisms. While the extent to which physics actually influenced the development of molecular biology is controversial, some impact can clearly be seen in the use of cybernetic concepts such as feedback in explaining genetic control, as well as in early thinking about genetics as a cryptographic problem.

Although many projects associated with biophysics flourished in the 1950s, the field as a whole did not. Rather, some areas pioneered by biophysicists, such as protein structure, were partly absorbed by biochemistry, while others split off in new disciplines. For example, electron microscopists studying cell structure split when they established cell biology, and radiobiologists largely left biophysics to join (with radiologists) in the newly emerging discipline of nuclear medicine. By the later 1960s, departments bearing the name "molecular biology" were becoming more common, typically including molecular genetics as well as certain types of "structural" biophysics. In the 1970s a new generation of convenient methods for identifying particular nucleic acids and proteins in biological samples (RNA and DNA hybridization techniques, monoclonal antibodies) brought the study of genes and their activation to virtually all the experimental life sciences, from population genetics to physiology to embryology. Also in the 1970s, methods to determine the sequence of nucleic acids making up genes began to be developed—culminating during the 1990s in the government-funded, international Human Genome Project—as well as methods for rearranging DNA sequences in an organism's chromosomes, and then reintroducing these altered sequences to living organisms, making it possible for molecular geneticists to embark upon "genetic engineering." In the early twenty-first century, there is virtually no branch of life science and medicine that is not "molecular," in that all explain biological phenomena partly in terms of nucleic acid sequences and protein structure. Thus, from its beginnings, molecular biology has resisted definition as a discipline. But however defined—as a style of investigation, a set of methods or questions, or a loosely knit and overlapping set of biological fields based in several disciplines—the enterprise of explaining life's properties through the behavior of its constituent molecules has, since its origins in the interwar era, become one of the most intellectually fruitful and medically useful movements ever to engage the life sciences.

BIBLIOGRAPHY

Abir-Am, Pnina. "The Discourse of Physical Power and Biological Knowledge in the 1930's: A Reappraisal of the Rockefeller Foundation's 'Policy' in Molecular Biology," *Social Studies of Science* 12: 341–382 (1982).

———. "Themes, Genres and Orders of Legitimation in the Consolidation of New Scientific Disciplines: Deconstructing the Historiography of Molecular Biology." *History of Science* 23 (1985): 73–117.

Chadarevian, Soraya de. *Designs for Life: Molecular Biology After World War II*. Cambridge, UK: Cambridge University Press, 2002.

Creager, Angela N. H. *The Life of a Virus: Tobacco Mosaic Virus As an Experimental Model, 1930–1965*. Chicago: University of Chicago Press, 2002.

Kay, Lily E. *The Molecular Vision of Life: Caltech, the Rockefeller Vision, and the Rise of the New Biology*. New York: Oxford University Press, 1993.

———. *Who Wrote the Book of Life?: A History of the Genetic Code*. Stanford, Calif.: Stanford University Press, 2000.

Keller, Evelyn Fox. *Refiguring Life: Metaphors of Twentieth-Century Biology*. New York: Columbia University Press, 1995.

Kohler Jr., Robert E. "The Management of Science: The Experience of Warren Weaver and the Rockefeller Foundation Program in Molecular Biology." *Minerva* 14 (1976): 279–306.

Olby, Robert C. *The Path to the Double Helix*. Seattle: University of Washington Press, 1974.

Pauly, Philip. "General Physiology and the Discipline of Physiology, 1890–1935," in G. L. Geison, ed., *Physiology in the American Context, 1850–1940*. Baltimore: American Physiological Society, 1987, 195–207.

Rasmussen, Nicolas. "The Midcentury Biophysics Bubble: Hiroshima and the Biological Revolution in America, Revisited." *History of Science* 35 (1997): 245–293.

———. *Picture Control: The Electron Microscope and the Transformation of Biology in America, 1940–1960*. Stanford, Calif.: Stanford University Press, 1997.

Nicolas Rasmussen

See also **DNA; Genetic Engineering; Genetics; Human Genome Project.**

MOLLY MAGUIRES.

The Molly Maguires were a group of Irish mine workers who terrorized the anthracite region of Pennsylvania from about 1865 until a series of sensational murder trials between 1875 and 1877. The Molly Maguires was neither an ordered secret society nor a vast conspiracy. Rather, the workers engaged in sporadic collective violent protest characteristic of particular rural areas of Ireland from 1760 to 1850. In Ireland the protests were directed at landlords and their agents who disrupted traditional land use practices; in Pennsylvania the protests were directed at agents and conditions of industrial exploitation—the Welsh miners for whom the Irish worked, mine officials, the bob-tailed check (payment by means of goods from the overpriced company store instead of cash), and figures of local authority. The Molly Maguire protests included industrial sabotage, beatings, and assassinations. Violence directed against them included gang warfare, deployment of local militias and the National Guard during labor disputes, vigilante committees, and execution by hanging. The name Molly Maguires has become a bogeyman deployed in some efforts to demonize and suppress trade-union activism in the area.

BIBLIOGRAPHY

Aurand, Harold W., and William Gudelunas. "The Mythical Qualities of Molly Maguire." *Pennsylvania History* 49 (1982): 91–105.

Kenny, Kevin. *Making Sense of the Molly Maguires*. New York: Oxford University Press, 1998.

John Bakeless
Cynthia R. Poe

See also **Coal Mining and Organized Labor; Irish Americans; Labor; Secret Societies.**

MONEY

is any item of value that can be exchanged and accepted as payment for goods, services, or debts. Historically, money had taken many forms, but today the most common types include paper and coin issued by a government and personal or bank checks that constitute a promise to pay and that can readily be converted into currency. Money makes it possible to bypass the practice known as bartering, in which a person trades either goods or services in order to receive other needed goods or services. Although its value may fluctuate on currency markets, money, unlike perishable or exhaustible commodities, also constitutes "stored value"; it can be acquired in the present expressly to be used in the future.

The Properties of Money

Good money is made of a material that is durable, easily stored, lacking in bulk, and light in weight. Small coins and paper are ideal for these purposes. Money is created by a government and also by private institutions under the direct supervision and control of a government. The Constitution of the United States, for instance, grants Congress the "power to coin money and regulate the value thereof." Congress has delegated this authority to the United States Treasury Department, the Federal Reserve System, and through it to privately owned commercial banks.

Some money also serves as legal tender. This money by law must be accepted as payment for debts. Currency and coin are considered legal tender because they are created by a government or by government authority and must be accepted in payment for all debts, public and private. Checks, however, are products of commercial banks and, although considered a form of money, they are not legal tender. A merchant or debtor has the legal right to refuse to accept a personal check and, instead, to demand payment in cash.

Money also has the ability to affect prices. Because money finances almost all economic activity, the total money supply in circulation at any given time exercises an impact not only on the price of goods and services but also on the price of money itself in the form of interest rates charged for borrowing. If for some reason the quantity of money doubles, it usually follows that prices will increase as well.

The Functions of Money
Money performs four basic functions. It is a medium of exchange, a measure or standard of value, a store of value, and a standard of deferred payment. As an instrument of exchange, money serves as an asset that enables consumers, whether they are individuals, corporations, or governments, to acquire goods and services. In this way, money facilitates both conversion and growth. If, for example, a farmer grows and then sells soybeans for money, that money can, in turn, be converted into other goods and services. A series of related transactions fuels the growth of the economy.

As a standard of value, money acts as what economists call the "unit of account." In this capacity, money serves as the common denominator of value because the price of all goods and services is stated in monetary terms, regardless of how the value of money changes or affects the price charged for goods and services.

Economists define money that is earned from services provided or labor completed as a store of value because it can be kept for future use as purchasing power rather than immediately expended. Money in a savings or checking account, however, is not the only store of value. Value can also be stored in stocks, bonds, real estate, and even such commodities as wheat or corn. In some cases, money, held in the form of cash, is actually inferior to interest- or dividend-bearing assets as a store of value, since cash by itself yields no return and is subject to its value being eroded by inflation. Money is easily stored, however, because it is not bulky and will not physically deteriorate.

As a standard of deferred payment, money in the form of credit permits consumers to acquire goods and services now and to pay for them over a specified period of time. The ability to access credit and defer full payment enhances purchasing power.

Money. The Federal Reserve system of the United States oversees the country's money supply, including the total amount of money available for circulation or borrowing. Here employees of the Federal Reserve Bank of New York City stack gold bars in a subterranean vault located eighty feet below the street surface. © AP/WIDE WORLD PHOTOS

Coins, currency, and checking accounts are the only items that perform all four of these monetary functions. However, in recent years, some economists have extended their definition of money to include what they called "near money" or money substitutes. These items have become known simply as M1, M2, and M3 and refer to the different levels of the money supply.

The Money Supply
The debate over how to define the "money supply" of the United States centers primarily on the question of whether savings deposits should be included in it. To that end, economists have identified the following levels for the money supply. M1 is the traditional money supply consisting only of coin, currency, and checking accounts. M2 includes M1 plus deposits in commercial savings banks, both passbook accounts and certificates of deposit. However, negotiable certificates worth $100,000 or more are not part of M2. M3 consists of M2 plus savings deposits in savings and loan associations, banks, and credit unions. It also excludes certificates valued at $100,000 or more.

Once the money supply has been determined, the next question is who will manage it and to what end. In the United States the Federal Reserve oversees the money supply. It does so by controlling the dollar amount of commercial bank reserves and, through these reserves, the total supply of money available for circulation or borrowing. Among the objectives of the Federal Reserve is the maintenance of price stability and control of the rate of economic growth.

The Circulation of Money
The speed with which money circulates, or changes hands, is one of the most important factors determining economic health. Economists call this characteristic the "velocity of money." If a dollar changes hands five times per year, the velocity of money is five. Overall price levels are determined by the quantity of money multiplied by the velocity of its circulation. Increases in either the quantity or velocity of money will cause prices to rise. Decreases will bring a decline in prices. If the quantity of money in circulation or the velocity at which it circulates is such that one rises while the other falls, there is little or no impact on prices.

The Money Market
Institutions that bring the borrowers and lenders of short-term funds together on an impersonal basis are known collectively as the money market, a highly competitive arena in which borrowers pay whatever the going interest rate may be to access available funds. Commercial banks are the most important source of short-term funds in the money market. The Federal Reserve, working through member banks, also supplies funds. At times, life insurance companies, pension funds, savings and loan associations, credit unions, and mutual funds also supply funds in the money market.

Common borrowers in the money market include businesses looking to finance short-term expansion often in response to economic conditions, as well as the U.S. Treasury Department, which seeks funds to finance the federal deficit. Treasury bills are the major money market instrument used by the Treasury to finance the deficit. These T-bills, as they are known, represent short-term obligations sold at a discount and redeemed at face value upon maturity. The two major instruments that corporations use to satisfy short-term needs are commercial paper and bankers' acceptances. They, too, are sold at a discount and then appreciate to face value at maturity.

The Monetary System of the United States
The monetary system of the United States is made up of two government agencies, the United States Treasury and the FEDERAL RESERVE SYSTEM (the Fed), along with 14,700 privately owned commercial banks. These institutions create the money supply. The U.S. Treasury and the Federal Reserve can strike coins, print paper money, or write checks as outlined in their duties by the United States Congress. Commercial banks can create bank money or checking accounts, but only under the close supervision of the Federal Reserve. Commercial banks must first have adequate reserves before they can make loans and set up new accounts for borrowers. The Federal Reserve controls the dollar amount of these reserves and, in that way, also controls the volume of money in circulation and the costs of borrowing.

The Fed implements monetary policy through this control and manipulation of the money supply. By increasing or decreasing the amount of money flowing through the economy, monetary policy can accelerate or slow the rate of economic growth. The object of monetary policy is, thus, to influence the performance of the economy as reflected in such factors as inflation, productivity, and employment. It works by affecting demand across the economy, that is, consumers' willingness or ability to pay for goods, services, and credit.

There are several methods by which the Fed implements monetary policy. The Fed adjusts bank reserve requirements by buying and selling U.S. government securities. By raising or lowering the reserve requirements, the Board of Governors at the Fed can either encourage or discourage the expansion of credit.

The most powerful and efficient entity within the Fed for shaping monetary policy, however, is the Federal Open Market Committee (FOMC). This group, headed by the Chairman of the Federal Reserve Board, who in 2002 was Alan Greenspan, sets interest rates either directly (by changing the discount rate) or through the use of "open market operations," the buying and selling of government securities to affect the federal funds rate. The discount rate is the rate the Federal Reserve Bank charges member banks for overnight loans. The Fed actually controls this rate directly, but adjustment tends to have little impact on the activities of banks because funds are available elsewhere. This rate is agreed upon during the FOMC meetings by the directors of the regional banks and the Federal Reserve Board.

The federal funds rate is the interest rate at which banks lend excess reserves to each other. Although the Fed cannot directly influence this rate, it effectively controls the rate through buying and selling Treasury bonds to banks. During the course of eight regularly scheduled meetings, the FOMC sets the federal funds rate by determining a plan of open market operations. The group also sets the discount rate, which technically is established by the regional banks and approved by the Board.

In the early twenty-first century, the FOMC began announcing its decisions at the end of every meeting. The committee can increase or decrease the discount rate, or leave it unchanged. Increasing the interest rates is called "tightening" the money supply because this action reduces the amount of money flowing through the economy. Lowering interest rates is called "easing" because this action increases the money supply. Generally, analysts believe that changes in the discount rate will have little direct effect on the economy because banks can get credit from outside sources with ease.

The Fed has the same three options with the federal funds rate. By carefully buying and selling government securities, the Fed can actually change what other banks charge each other for short-term loans. Over time, changes in the money supply will affect the economy as a whole. Most analysts believe that monetary policy takes at least six months to have an impact, and by that time the economic circumstances that the policy was designed to address may have changed. Consequently, the members of the FOMC must predict what the conditions will be when the rate changes begin to exercise an influence over the rate of economic growth. Needless to say, such foresight can be difficult.

As a consequence, the Fed also routinely announces it current "bias," indicating its present thinking about the future direction the economy will take. Such an announcement usually explains whether the Fed will continue to be concerned about inflation (a tightening bias), about slow growth (a loosening bias), or about neither (a neutral bias). In this way, the Federal Reserve tries to maintain a sustainable level of economic growth, without allowing growth to proceed too rapidly or, on the contrary, without allowing the economy to become sluggish and stagnant.

If growth is too fast, inflation will rise, prices will fluctuate upward and, as wages also rise, unemployment will eventually ensue. These three factors, inflation, rising prices, and unemployment, will short-circuit economic growth. If, by contrast, economic growth is too slow, unemployment will also rise as workers are laid off, leaving growing numbers of consumers without adequate reserve capital to spend their way out of the recession. The Fed, therefore, tries to use monetary policy to maintain a sustainable level of growth for the economy that will keep inflation, prices, and unemployment at manageable levels.

The monetary policy of the United States affects the kinds of economic decisions people make, from obtaining a loan to buying a new home to starting a business. Because the U.S. economy is the largest and most prosperous in the world, American monetary policy also has a significant impact on economies around the world. As economic circumstances change at home and around the world, the Fed adjusts its policies to stimulate, sustain, or slow growth. When the Japanese economy began to fall apart in the mid-1990s, for example, it greatly diminished the volume of American exports to Japanese markets and threatened to short-circuit the unprecedented economic boom that the United States was then experiencing. To counteract this development, the Fed cut interest rates to stimulate economic growth or at least to slow decline and to execute what economists call "soft landing."

Monetary Theory: The Prevailing Models

There are two predominant theories about how best to manage the money supply. One of these is associated with

SUPPLY-SIDE ECONOMICS. According to the basic principles of supply-side economics, the growth and operation of the economy depends almost entirely on factors affecting supply rather than demand. In terms of monetary theory and policy, supply-side economists embrace such measures as cuts in the interest and tax rates to encourage investment and, at the same time, favor restricting the growth of the money supply to dampen inflation.

Supply-side economists generally hold that if people had more cash in hand, they would spend more on goods and services, thereby increasing the aggregate demand for those goods and services and stimulating economic growth. Since there are natural limits to the amount of goods and services people require, they would invest their surplus assets in interest- or dividend-bearing securities, thus making additional capital available for investment and further driving down interest rates. Lower interest rates, coupled with higher aggregate demand, would prompt businesses to borrow to fund expansion, a development that also quickens economic growth. According to monetarist theory, even a small reduction in taxes and interest rates would increase consumer spending, aggregate demand, and capital investment and, as a consequence, ensure economic growth.

An alternative to the monetary theory of supply-side economies emerged when economist James Tobin criticized the narrow emphasis on money. Tobin argued that there was a range of financial assets that investors might be willing to hold in their portfolios besides money, including bonds and equities. Their preferences were rationally determined by calculating potential gains against potential risks. Tobin, following John Maynard Keynes, showed how government economic and fiscal policy could impinge on productivity and employment.

Keynes had argued that a drop in prices would increase the value of money in real terms. Simply put, without raising wages, falling prices would mean that consumers enjoyed greater purchasing power. An increase in the real value of money would also make available a greater surplus of capital for investment and bring about a consequent decline in interest rates, thus prompting additional investment and stimulating economic growth. In the Keynesian system, the quantity of money determined prices. Interest rates brought savings and investment into balance, while the interest rate itself was set by the quality of money people desired to hold (liquidity preference) in relation to the money supply. Government monetary policy, therefore, ought to aim at keeping money in the hands of consumers and investors, either through increasing wages to counter the effects of inflation or by lowering prices if wages remained stable. Lowering wages to cut business costs, increase profit margins, and stimulate employment, Keynes suggested, was counterproductive. Lower wages only served to decrease income, depress aggregate demand, and retard consumption, all of which would more than offset any benefits that accrued to business from a reduction in wages. During economic hard times, when the private sector could not absorb the costs of labor, the government could take over the role of business by spending money on public works projects to reduce unemployment.

The Future of Money

By the 1990s, Americans were already becoming immersed in the technology of the digital economy. The idea of digital money, e-cash, is simple. Instead of storing value in paper, e-cash saves it in a series of digits and codes that are as portable and exchangeable as paper, but more secure and even "smarter." If e-cash is lost or stolen, its proponents maintain, the card can easily be canceled via computer and its value transferred to another card. E-cash is also more mutable and controllable than paper money. It enables individuals to send funds over the Internet, encoded in an e-mail message rather than sending cash, checks, or wire transfers. Digital currency can also be programmed so that it can be spent only in specific ways; money budgeted for food cannot be used to go to the movies or visit the local pub. Finally, e-cash, unlike paper money when withdrawn from an account, continues to earn interest until it is used.

This characteristic of e-cash gave rise to another extraordinary aspect of the digital financial revolution: the dissolution of the government monopoly on money. Digital cash has no boundaries. Cardholders are free to acquire e-cash from worldwide lenders willing to pay higher interest rates than banks in the United States. As long as e-cash is easily convertible and widely accepted, customers will find that there is no reason to limit themselves to the currency of a single government. Government-issued money will not cease to exist, but it will have to compete with dozens of other currencies, each tailored to meet specific needs of customers. "In the electronic city, the final step in the evolution of money is being taken," explained Howard M. Greenspan, president of Heraclitus Corporation, a management consulting firm. "Money is being demonetized. Money is being eliminated."

BIBLIOGRAPHY

Ando, Albert, and R. Farmer Eguchi and Y. Suzuki, eds. *Monetary Policy in Our Times*. Cambridge, Mass.: MIT Press, 1985.

Auerbach, Robert D. *Money, Banking, and Financial Markets*. New York: Macmillan 1985.

Block, Valerie. "Atlanta Conference Previews the Future of Money." *American Banker* 161 (May 14, 1996): 14.

Davidson, William. "Does Money Exist?" *Forbes* 157 (June 3, 1996): 26.

"E-Cash." *The Economist* 354 (February 2000): 67.

Friedman, Milton, and Anna Schwartz. *A Monetary History of the United States, 1867–1960*. Princeton, N.J.: Princeton University Press, 1963.

Hahn, Frank. *Money and Inflation*. Cambridge, Mass.: MIT Press, 1983.

Hutchinson, Harry D. *Money, Banking, and the United States Economy*. 5th ed. Englewood Cliffs, N.J.: Prentice Hall, 1984.

Lacker, Jeffrey M. "Stored Value Cards: Costly Private Substitutes for Government Currency." *Economic Quarterly* 82 (Summer 1996): 25.

Niehans, Jurg. *The Theory of Money*. Baltimore: Johns Hopkins University. Press, 1978.

Nixon, Brian. "E-Cash." *America's Community Banker* 5 (June 1996): 34–38.

Ritter, Lawrence S., and William L. Silber. *Money*. 5th rev. ed. New York: Basic Books, 1984.

Meg Greene Malvasi

See also **Currency and Coinage; Keynesianism; Treasury, Department of the.**

MONITOR AND *MERRIMACK*, BATTLE OF.

The French introduced the principle of the ironclad ship during the Crimean War, and about a hundred ironclads were built or projected—none in the United States—before the American CIVIL WAR. When Stephen Mallory, chairman of the Senate Committee on Naval Affairs since 1851, became Confederate secretary of the navy, he saw ironclads as the Confederacy's only chance of beating the North. Although his program was initially subordinated to the greater needs of equipping the Confederate army, Mallory commissioned thirty-two ironclads, of which fewer than a dozen were ever fully ready.

The Confederates salvaged the U.S.S. *Merrimack*, which had been scuttled in the Union evacuation of Norfolk. Upon its sound hull the Confederates built a sloping iron casemate to house an artillery battery. The conversion dragged on for months, time that allowed the Union to recognize the danger and begin its own program. The *Merrimack* was rechristened the C.S.S. *Virginia*, a name that did not gain contemporary usage. It had no captain, inasmuch as Flag Officer Franklin Buchanan preferred to have it commanded by its able young executive officer, Lt. Catesby Jones.

On 8 March 1862 the *Merrimack* sortied from Norfolk to gain control of Hampton Roads and the James River, which would aid Maj. Gen. John Magruder in expelling Union forces from the lower Yorktown peninsula. The wooden warships *Cumberland* and *Congress* protected the water flanks of the Union position at Newport News, and Buchanan sank them easily, although he was wounded by imprudent exposure during the fight with the *Congress*. After driving back a Union squadron on duty at the blockading station outside the Roads, Jones brought the ironclad to anchor for the night off Sewell's Point. Buchanan resolved to finish off the *Minnesota*, stranded in shallow water and helpless, in the morning.

During the night, the U.S.S. *Monitor* arrived after a dramatic dash from New York. When Jones got up steam on 9 March to destroy the *Minnesota*, it was no longer

Battle of the Ironclads. Shortly after they were commissioned, the Union ironclad ship *Monitor* and its Confederate counterpart the *Merrimack* (also known as the *Virginia*) met in battle on 9 March 1862. This view from the deck of the *Monitor* was taken just after the two ships fought to a bloody draw. NATIONAL ARCHIVES AND RECORDS ADMINISTRATION

raised in 1998 and a ten-foot section of the shaft in 2000. In the summer of 2002, the salvage team was close to raising the ship's 160-ton gun turret. All the recovered artifacts of the *Monitor* will go on display in a planned $30 million museum.

BIBLIOGRAPHY
Broad, William J. "Retrieval Efforts Aim to Bring *Monitor* Back to Life." *New York Times*, 30 July 2002 (www.nytimes.com/2002/07/30/science/30MONI.html).

Davis, William C. *Duel between the First Ironclads.* Mechanicsburg, Pa.: Stackpole Books, 1994.

De Kay, James T. *Monitor: The Story of the Legendary Civil War Ironclad and the Man Whose Invention Changed the Course of History.* New York: Walker, 1997.

Hoehling, Adolph A. *Thunder at Hampton Roads.* Englewood Cliffs, N.J.: Prentice-Hall, 1976.

Still, William N., Jr. "Confederate Naval Strategy: The Ironclad." *The Journal of Southern History* 27 (1961): 330–343.

R. W. Daly / A. R.

See also **Ironclad Warships; Monroe, Fortress; Navy, Confederate; Navy, United States; Peninsular Campaign.**

alone. The *Monitor,* under Lt. John Worden, successfully engaged the *Merrimack* until tide and cumulative damage required Jones to head for Norfolk. Worden was blinded by a shell explosion.

Union claims of victory were founded on the misconception that the *Merrimack* was trying to break the blockade. Buchanan aimed only to clear Hampton Roads and did so. By naval semantics, both antagonists won: the *Monitor* tactically because Worden kept the *Merrimack* from destroying the *Minnesota,* and the *Merrimack* strategically because it frightened the Union navy away from the Roads. Gen. George B. McClellan, who had initially planned using the Roads and the James River for a swift stab at Richmond, was compelled to rely on the limited wharfage of Fort Monroe, safely outside the Roads, to mount his famously unsuccessful Peninsular Campaign.

The career of the *Merrimack* is an example of a successful strategic deterrent. A hugely exaggerated notion of its power was responsible for McClellan's self-defeating decision to use the Union-controlled York River for his supplies. The *Merrimack* was destroyed by its own crew when the Confederates evacuated Norfolk on 11 May 1862.

Nine months after its famous clash with the *Merrimack,* the *Monitor* sank in a violent storm while under tow off Cape Hatteras. In 1973 scientists discovered its remains lying 230 feet deep off the Cape Hatteras coast. Sporadic salvage efforts began in 1975 and were later brought under the supervision of the National Oceanic and Atmospheric Administration. The propeller was

MONMOUTH, BATTLE OF.

The British army, en route from Philadelphia to New York, arrived at Monmouth Courthouse (Freehold, New Jersey) on 26 June 1778. George Washington ordered Maj. Gen. Charles Lee to attack the British rear guard, but Lee delayed and the attack failed. His division of more than four thousand men retreated until halted by Washington, two and one-half miles to the rear. Washington skillfully re-formed his lines to meet the British, now heavily reinforced. One of the war's fiercest contests followed. Repeated assaults failed to break the American lines, and the British withdrew. Washington reported his loss at 69 killed and 161 wounded; the Americans buried 249 British on the field. A court-martial sustained charges against Lee of disobeying orders and making an unnecessary retreat.

BIBLIOGRAPHY
Smith, Samuel Stelle. *The Battle of Monmouth.* Trenton, N.J.: New Jersey Historical Commission, 1975.

Walling, Richard S. *Men of Color at the Battle of Monmouth, June 28, 1778.* Hightstown, N.J.: Longstreet House, 1994.

C. A. Titus / A. R.

See also **Courts-Martial; Revolution, American: Military History.**

MONONGAHELA, BATTLE OF THE

(9 July 1755). In the opening stages of the French and Indian War, a vanguard of British Gen. Edward Braddock's expedition encountered a band of French and Indian soldiers near Braddock, Pa., surprising both sides. The British opened fire immediately, scattering the enemy. The

Indians occupied a commanding hill and worked through a gully on the other British flank. Surrounded, the vanguard retreated, abandoning its guns. Meanwhile, the main body rushed forward hastily, and the whole army became an unmanageable huddle. Most of the officers were killed or wounded, but Lt. Col. George Washington, who was one of Braddock's aides, was almost miraculously unscathed. Braddock, mortally wounded, ordered a retreat; the soldiers fled in disorder.

BIBLIOGRAPHY

Hamilton, Charles, Ed. *Braddock's Defeat.* Norman: University of Oklahoma Press, 1959.

Kopperman, Paul E. *Braddock at the Monongahela.* Pittsburgh, Pa.: University of Pittsburgh Press, 1977.

Pargellis, Stanley McCrory. "Braddock's Defeat." *American Historical Review* (1936).

Parkman, Francis. *Montcalm and Wolfe.* New York: Collier Books, 1962.

Solon J. Buck / A. R.

See also **Braddock's Expedition; Colonial Wars; French and Indian War.**

MONONGAHELA RIVER, an important tributary of the upper Ohio, drains the western slopes of the Allegheny Mountains in northern West Virginia, Maryland, and southern Pennsylvania. Long used by Indians and fur traders, the river played a significant role in the imperial wars of the eighteenth century. After the expedition of Pierre Joseph de Céloron de Blainville along the river in 1749 claimed much of the Ohio River Valley for the French, anxious British land companies began more active expeditions along the same route. During and after the French and Indian War, settlers from Pennsylvania, Virginia, and Maryland pushed west to the Monongahela. Much of the later westward migration traveled down the river.

BIBLIOGRAPHY

Bissell, Richard Pike. *The Monongahela.* New York: Rinehart, 1952.

Parker, Arthur. *The Monongahela: River of Dreams, River of Sweat.* University Park: Pennsylvania State University Press, 1999.

Alfred P. James / H. S.

See also **French and Indian War; Ohio Company of Virginia; Ohio River.**

MONOPOLY occurs when a single seller or provider supplies all of a particular product or service. Typically, the term is used to describe a private, commercial situation—a market containing only one seller in a private enterprise economic system. Non-business sources of supply also can hold monopoly power, such as when the government owns the only provider of a product and precludes others by law. Government also can grant exclusive right to a single business entry or group to produce a product or service, thereby creating a monopoly, albeit a private one. A monopoly thus can be legal when a government determines who will produce. Other monopolies may be technological, whereby economies of scale in production lead to decreasing average cost over a large range of output relative to demand. Under these conditions, one producer can supply the entire market at lower cost per unit than could multiple producers. This is the case of a "natural monopoly," which reflects the underlying cost structure for firms in the industry. Monopoly also can stem from mergers of previously independent producers.

The definition of monopoly requires definition of a "product" to determine whether alternative suppliers exist. With no close substitutes, the supplier has monopoly power. The price elasticity of demand, measured as the percentage change in quantity of the product demanded, divided by percentage change in price, indicates the likely proximity of near substitutes; the lower the price elasticity of demand in absolute value, the greater is the ability of the monopolist to raise the price above the competitive level.

A social and political hostility toward monopoly had already developed in Western Europe long before economists developed a theoretical analysis connecting monopoly power to inefficient use of resources. Aristotle, for example, called it unjust. Large-scale enterprise was rare in manufacturing before the nineteenth century, but local producers and workers sought to protect their incomes through restrictions on trade. Capitalism evolved over time, superimposed on preexisting economic and social relationships. During this evolution, economic literature focused frequently on the abuses of monopoly, but without specificity. Well before large manufacturing firms formed, the nation-state granted monopoly rights to colonial trade and domestic activities, often creating resentment toward all forms of monopoly related to royal favoritism. England's Statute of Monopolies (1623) reflected this resentment by limiting governmental grant of monopoly power.

The writings of Adam Smith, his contemporaries, and his nineteenth-century descendents display antipathy toward monopoly, an antagonism perhaps more pronounced in England than elsewhere. This antagonism extended to situations of a few sellers and to practices designed to limit entry into an industry, as well as monopoly per se. English common law generally found abuses of monopoly illegal, but the burden fell upon the aggrieved to bring suit. The United States followed English common law, though that law was really a multitude of laws.

In the 1830s, August Cournot formalized the economic analysis of monopoly and duopoly, apparently the first to do so. His analysis—not very well known among economists of the nineteenth century—showed that profit-maximizing, monopoly firms produce less and charge a higher price than would occur in competition, assuming that both industry structures have the same cost condition. It also led eventually to the demonstration, within the context of welfare economics, that single-price monopoly reflects underlying cost structures. Price discrimination, though prohibited and vilified, might lead to a competitive, single-price level of output and efficiency. Cournot's static analysis did not take into account the effect of firm size on technological change, one potential benefit of large firms able to invest in research and development.

Public outcry about trusts—an organizational form associated with mergers that create large firms with substantial market power in many industries—led American legislators to pass the Sherman Antitrust Act in 1890. This act was the first major federal antitrust legislation in the United States and remains the dominant statute, having two main provisions. Section one declares illegal every contract or combination of companies in restraint of trade. Section two declares guilty of misdemeanor any person who monopolizes, or attempts to monopolize, any part of trade or commerce. The Clayton Act of 1914 prohibited a variety of actions deemed likely to restrict competition. Early legislation and enforcement of antitrust law reflected popular opposition to monopoly. Better understanding of economic theory and the costs of monopoly, however, gradually transformed the policy of simply opposing monopoly (antitrust) into one that more actively promotes competition. When the promotion of competition was likely to result in firms too small to exhaust economies of scale, public policy moved to regulate the natural monopoly, presumably to protect consumers from abuse of monopoly power.

Formal economic analysis of monopoly locates that industry structure at the far end of the spectrum from competition. Both are recognized as stylized types, useful in determining the extreme possibilities for industry price and output. Competitive and monopolistic models are relatively simple, because each participant is assumed to act independently, pursuing optimizing behavior without consideration of the likely reaction of other participants. The limitations of monopoly theory in predicting behavior of actual firms stimulated work on imperfect competition. Numerous case studies of American industry structure in the mid-twentieth century yielded detail about firm behavior, but no universally accepted theory.

More recently, developments in game theory permit better analysis of the interdependent behavior of oligopolistic firms. Game theory analyses during the last two decades of the twentieth century—though lacking a unique solution and easy generalizations—also permit more dynamic examination of behavior. This includes considering how a monopolist might behave strategically to maintain monopoly position. Thus, a firm might behave so as to forestall entry. Game theory models have led to reevaluation of the effects of various practices, creating a more complex interpretation of the relationship between industry structure and economic efficiency.

BIBLIOGRAPHY

Church, Jeffrey, and Roger Ware. *Industrial Organization: A Strategic Approach.* Boston: Irwin McGraw-Hill, 2000.

Cournot, Antoine Augustin. *Researches into the Mathematical Principles of the Theory of Wealth.* New York: Augustus M. Kelley, 1971.

Ellis, Howard, ed. *A Survey of Contemporary Economics.* Philadelphia: Blakiston, 1948. See especially the article by John Kenneth Galbraith, "Monopoly and the Concentration of Economic Power."

Neale, A. D., and D. G. Goyder. *The Antitrust Laws of the U.S.A.: A Study of Competition Enforced by Law.* New York: Cambridge University Press, 1980.

Schumpeter, Joseph A. *History of Economic Analysis.* New York: Oxford University Press, 1994.

Stigler, George, and Kenneth Boulding, eds. *Readings in Price Theory: Selected by a Committee of the American Economic Association.* Chicago: Richard D. Irwin, 1952. See especially the article by J. R. Hicks, "Annual Survey of Economic Theory: The Theory of Monopoly."

Tirole, Jean. *The Theory of Industrial Organization.* Cambridge, Mass.: MIT Press, 1988.

Ann Harper Fender

See also **Antimonopoly Parties; Antitrust Laws: Business, Big; Economics; Government Regulation of Business; Sherman Antitrust Act; Supply-Side Economics; Trickle-Down Economics.**

MONOPOLY is a board game in which players try to enrich themselves by developing Atlantic City, New Jersey, real estate. Unemployed sales representative Charles B. Darrow of Germantown, Pennsylvania, invented the game in 1934. Darrow sold five thousand handmade sets to a Philadelphia department store before selling the rights to Parker Brothers. By 1935 *Monopoly* had become the best-selling game in America. By century's end, some 200 million *Monopoly* sets had been sold in eighty countries worldwide and in twenty-six different languages, spawning a variety of derivative products, including a twenty-five-thousand-dollar gold and silver set built by Alfred Dunhill of London in 1974.

BIBLIOGRAPHY

Orbanes, Philip. *The Monopoly Companion.* Boston: Bob Adams, 1988.

Philippe R. Girard

See also **Toys and Games.**

MONROE, FORTRESS. Construction on Fortress Monroe, sited on a strategic position overlooking the entrance to the Chesapeake Bay, began in 1819 and was completed in 1834. The Confederates made no attempt to capture it, and it remained in Union hands. The action of the *Monitor* and *Merrimack,* on 9 March 1862, took place just off the fort. Gen. George B. McClellan began the Peninsular campaign from it in 1862. Jefferson Davis was confined in Fortress Monroe from 1865 to 1867. During World Wars I and II the nation's harbor defense system was headquartered at the fort. Since 1973 it has been the home of the Army Training and Doctrine Command.

BIBLIOGRAPHY

Chapman, Anne W. *The Army's Training Revolution, 1973–1990: An Overview.* Fort Monroe, Va.: Office of the Command Historian, United States Army Training and Doctrine Command, 1991.

Weinert, Richard P., and Robert Arthur. *Defender of the Chesapeake: The Story of Fort Monroe.* Shippensburg, Pa.: White Mane Publishing Company, 1989.

H. J. Eckenrode / A. R.

See also **Davis, Imprisonment and Trial of; Defense, National; Fortifications;** *Monitor* **and** *Merrimack,* **Battle of; Peninsular Campaign.**

MONROE DOCTRINE. Four years after the ratification of the Adams-Onís Transcontinental Treaty, President James Monroe announced the Monroe Doctrine in a message to Congress in December 1823. While few countries paid much attention to its pronouncement, the doctrine captured the American belief that the New and Old Worlds greatly differed and that the United States had a special role to play. It presaged Manifest Destiny, and, as the years passed, the Monroe Doctrine increasingly became a tenet of American foreign policy, although its international acceptance and significance is still debated.

In the aftermath of the French Revolution (1787–1799) and the Napoleonic Wars (1805–1814), conservative European powers—Russia, Prussia, Austria, and, to a lesser extent, England—sought to prop up the old monarchies and stamp out revolution. The result, in 1813, was the Quadruple Alliance, which France joined after Louis XVIII returned to Paris.

At this time, Spanish America was throwing off its imperial yoke. Inspiring nationalists like Simón Bolívar, José San Martín, and Bernardo O'Higgins led their respective peoples to independence. The situation then became very complicated. At first, the U.S. government welcomed these independence movements, hoping to establish commercial ties and open new markets for American goods. France then invaded Spain and acted, at least initially, as if it would seek to reestablish Spain's former colonial empire in the Americas. There were even rumors that Spain would cede Cuba to France for its help in reestablishing Spain's empire in the New World! The British also had cause to oppose any reestablishment of Spain's empire, because Great Britain had moved to a concept of maintaining an informal empire—based on trade and avoiding the costs of a more formal empire, which included stationing of troops and maintaining of bases—in

Latin America, China, and elsewhere. Britain therefore wanted to economically exploit these newly independent lands.

So the British foreign minister, George Canning, suggested that the United States stand against such foreign intervention in the Americas, and with much input from the American Secretary of State, John Quincy Adams, Monroe worked out his doctrine. To be sure, Monroe's warning against European intervention in the Americas only had force, if it had any force, because of British naval power and behind-the-scenes support. Still, the American people enthusiastically received the message, although it had little practical influence at the time.

Over the years, the Monroe Doctrine became a tenet of American foreign policy, and there were additions by later presidents. On 2 December 1845, President James K. Polk reiterated the principles of Monroe in his condemnation of the intrigues of Great Britain and France in seeking to prevent the annexation of Texas to the United States and in contesting with Great Britain over the vast Oregon Territory ("54'40" or fight!"). And, on 29 April 1848, Polk declared that an English or Spanish protectorate over the Mexican Yucatan would be a violation of the Monroe Doctrine principles and could compel the United States to assume control over that area. Polk thus made the doctrine the basis for expansion, although ultimately he took no such action. During the American Civil War (1861–1865), France tried to establish an empire in Mexico under Austrian Archduke Maximilian. As the North's victory became assured, the U.S. secretary of state used this power to rebuff the French and helped cause France to withdraw its troops; the regime in Mexico collapsed.

One of the more dramatic extensions of the doctrine was President Grover Cleveland's assertion that its principles compelled Great Britain to arbitrate a boundary dispute with Venezuela over the limitations of British Guiana. Cleveland's views produced a diplomatic crisis, but British moderation helped bring about a peaceful solution. And, later, President Theodore Roosevelt expanded upon Cleveland's views to produce the so-called Roosevelt Corollary to the Monroe Doctrine. The joint intervention of Great Britain, Germany, and Italy against Venezuela looking to recover unpaid loans upset many in the United States. President Roosevelt on the one hand believed that such bills needed to be paid, but did not want foreign intervention to compel timely repayment. So he moved to the position that the United States must assume a measure of control over more unruly Latin American states to prevent European action. Although Senate approval of this corollary was delayed for three years until 1907, Roosevelt produced a view that seemingly justified frequent American interventions in Caribbean affairs, which certainly smacked of imperialism and "White Man's Burden," and did not burnish the image of the United States with its southern neighbors.

During the two decades following World War I (1914–1918), a change took place. Increasing resentment against American interference in the affairs of the republics of Latin America helped bring about the liquidations of U.S. interventions in Santo Domingo in 1924 and in Haiti in 1934. The intervention in Nicaragua begun in Calvin Coolidge's presidency was relatively short-lived. President Franklin D. Roosevelt gave proof of this retreat from an expansive view of the Monroe Doctrine by pledging against armed intervention, and by signing a treaty not to intervene in the internal and external affairs of various Latin American countries at the seventh Pan-American Conference in Montevideo, Uruguay, in December 1933.

The Monroe Doctrine never obtained a true international status. At the Versailles Peace Conference in 1919, President Woodrow Wilson, to win over domestic opponents to his cherished League of Nations covenant, incorporated into the language of the document an article declaring that nothing therein affected the validity of a regional understanding such as the Monroe Doctrine. It was not clear that this either met with European support or placated more nationalistic supporters of Monroe's principles in the United States.

In more modern times, the Monroe Doctrine has undergone change. The Inter-American Conference on Problems of War and Peace, called to strengthen arrangements for collective security in the Western Hemisphere during World War II (1939–1945) and to discuss problems resulting from Argentina's neutrality against the Axis powers, met in February 1945. Participants adopted the Act of Chapultepec, which broadened the Monroe Doctrine with the principle that an attack on any country of the hemisphere would be viewed as an act of aggression against all countries of the hemisphere. The act also had a provision for negotiation of a defense treaty among American states after the war. Meeting at Petrópolis, outside Rio de Janeiro, from 15 August through 2 September 1947, the United States and nineteen Latin American republics (Canada was a member of the British Commonwealth and did not directly participate) drew up the so-called Rio Pact, a permanent defensive military alliance that legally sanctioned the principle from the Act of Chapultepec and foreshadowed the establishment of the North Atlantic Treaty Organization two years later.

The United States would justify its action in Guatemala in 1954, its continuing opposition to Fidel Castro's regime in Cuba, and its intervention in the Dominican Republic in 1965 with the view that communism as a movement was foreign to the Americas. This provided the basis for intervention reaching back as far as the Monroe Doctrine and as recent as the Rio Pact.

In the end, the Monroe Doctrine as an international policy has only been as effective as the United States' power to support it.

BIBLIOGRAPHY

Dozer, Donald Marquand, ed. *The Monroe Doctrine: Its Modern Significance.* rev. ed. Tempe: Arizona State University Press, 1976.

Merk, Frederick. *The Monroe Doctrine and American Expansionism, 1843–1849.* New York: Alfred A. Knopf, 1966.

Perkins, Dexter. *A History of the Monroe Doctrine.* Boston: Little, Brown & Co., 1963.

Smith, Gaddis. *The Last Years of the Monroe Doctrine, 1945–1993.* New York: Hill and Wang, 1994.

Charles M. Dobbs

See also vol. 9: **The Monroe Doctrine and the Roosevelt Corollary.**

MONROE-PINKNEY TREATY. On 31 December 1806, James Monroe (the American minister at London) and William Pinkney (a special envoy from President Thomas Jefferson) signed the Monroe-Pinkney Treaty in London. Jefferson had instructed Monroe and Pinkney to seek a British pledge not to interfere with American neutral shipping. This had been a long-standing source of Anglo-American dispute. Jefferson sought to redress John Jay's failure in 1794 to attain this outcome through the controversial JAY's TREATY. In return for British concessions on American neutral shipping, Jefferson promised to repeal the Non-Importation Act (1806) and other legislation that prohibited U.S. imports from England.

Monroe and Pinkney could not convince British leaders to accept this bargain. Instead, Lord Holland and Lord Auckland offered the Americans extended trading rights within the British Empire, including renewal of those granted by Jay's Treaty. Holland and Auckland also promised that the British would exercise "the greatest caution" when considering interference with American ships headed to France and other British enemies. Monroe and Pinkney accepted this arrangement as the best compromise they could attain from a position of weakness.

Unsatisfied with the treaty, Jefferson refused to send it to the Senate for ratification in 1807. He pursued a policy of commercial warfare against Great Britain. This policy contributed to the WAR OF 1812.

BIBLIOGRAPHY

Kaplan, Lawrence S. *Thomas Jefferson: Westward the Course of Empire.* Wilmington, Del.: Scholarly Resources, 1999.

Perkins, Bradford. *The Creation of a Republican Empire, 1776–1865.* Vol. 1: *Cambridge History of American Foreign Relations,* edited by Warren I. Cohen. New York: Cambridge University Press, 1993.

Jeremi Suri

See also **Nonimportation Agreements.**

MONTANA. A land of contrast, Montana's 147,138 square miles contain both vast prairies and towering heights (including the 12,799-foot Granite Peak, the state's highest elevation). Much of the history of the state, which is poor in water but rich in natural resources, has been connected to the extractive industries and the problem of aridity.

First Peoples

More than twelve thousand years ago, small bands of hunters and gatherers lived in present-day Montana in the northern Rocky Mountain foothills and in the Great Plains that lie east of the Continental Divide. The region was part of the Louisiana Purchase when the Lewis and Clark Expedition crossed it in 1805, following the Missouri River to its headwaters and later exploring the Marias and Yellowstone Rivers. The expedition spent one quarter of its journey within the state's current borders. In the Rocky Mountains, the expedition met probable descendants of Montana's early inhabitants as well as some of the area's more recent Native immigrants. Native cultures changed in the eighteenth century because of two major stimuli: the introduction of horses (brought or traded north by southwestern Indians who had obtained them from the Spanish) and guns (brought or traded west and south by eastern tribes who acquired them from British and French fur traders). European settlements to the east also indirectly affected the region's peoples as displaced eastern tribes pushed west. The resultant competition for rich hunting grounds, cultural factors (such as the honor accorded successful warriors), and the desire for the guns and horses owned by competing tribes combined to produce a period of intense intertribal warfare that lasted well into the nineteenth century.

The Fur Trade

Fur traders likely entered Montana before the arrival of Lewis and Clark, but competition for fur heightened after that expedition. In 1807, the St. Louis–based trader Manuel Lisa built a trading post at the confluence of the Bighorn and Yellowstone Rivers, the first permanent building constructed in Montana. A year later, the Canadian North West Company established a trading post near present-day Libby, Montana. The race for fur was on.

The fur trade was the dominant European industry in the region from 1807 through the 1850s and radically transformed tribal life. Tribes such as the Crows and the Blackfeet joined a global market economy as they began to hunt for furs—first beaver and then buffalo—to trade with the Europeans. The fur economy created new routes to status within the tribes and transformed internal tribal politics. Exposure to diseases such as smallpox, to which Native Americans had little immunity, decimated many bands; for example, an estimated 50 percent of the Blackfeet died in an 1837 epidemic. In addition, the trade brought easy access to liquor, which quickly became a destructive force.

Although the fur trade had a tremendous impact on Native Americans, it brought relatively few non-Indians

to the region. Administratively, the eastern two-thirds of Montana was part of Missouri Territory until 1821, Indian Country until 1854, and Nebraska Territory until 1861, but in fact, there was little government presence with the exception of occasional road building and military expeditions.

The Mining Frontier

White settlement began in earnest following the discovery of gold in 1862 in present southwest Montana at Bannack, now a state park. An 1863 strike in Alder Gulch produced an estimated $35 million in gold during the first five years of mining. Gold fever brought approximately ten thousand people to the region by 1865, many of them from the goldfields of Idaho and California. Booming population expansion created the need for additional governmental services; to provide them, the federal government carved Idaho Territory from the Washington, Nebraska, and Dakota territories in 1863. Continuing growth led to the organization of Montana Territory on 26 May 1864, with first Bannack and then Virginia City as its capital. Other gold strikes followed, including in 1864 a major discovery in Last Chance Gulch (later called Helena), which became Montana's third territorial capital in 1875.

Although the image of the lone prospector dominates the myth of western mining, industrialized mining arrived early on the scene. Hydraulic mining, which used water from high-pressure hoses to wash away whole stream banks, and floating dredges, which mined the bottom of the rivers, required heavy capital investment and caused substantial environmental damage. Even more labor and capital intensive was quartz-lode mining, with its enormous stamp mills, smelters, and other expensive equipment.

In the 1870s, silver replaced gold as Montana's principle source of mineral wealth. The state became the nation's second largest producer of silver by 1883. Silver mining suffered a serious blow during the panic of 1893, however, when President Grover Cleveland ended mandatory government purchases of silver. Thereafter, copper dominated Montana's mining economy.

Mining wealth encouraged railroad construction, which in turn made possible larger mining operations. In 1881 the Union Pacific entered Butte (the heart of Montana's copper enterprises). The Northern Pacific crossed Montana in 1883; the Great Northern connected Butte to St. Paul in 1889. The Milwaukee Road, a relative latecomer, completed its line through Montana in 1909.

As railroads raced across the Plains and miners and the merchants who "mined the miners" poured into Montana Territory, tribal peoples found themselves under increasing pressure. Racism abounded and food was increasingly scarce, as the availability of game (particularly buffalo) declined due to overhunting, competition with horses and cattle for grazing land, and the introduction of exotic bovine diseases. Although the tribes most often negotiated political solutions, two legendary acts of Indian resistance to white incursion occurred in Montana

Territory during the 1870s: the Great Sioux War of 1876–1877, which included the most famous battle in the Indian wars, the Battle of the Little Bighorn; and the Nez Perce War of 1877.

Neither resistance nor negotiation worked particularly well. Montana's Indian tribes lost most of their lands—including much of the territory guaranteed by early treaties as permanent reserves. For example, an 1855 treaty recognized the Blackfeet's claim to two-thirds of eastern Montana (although the tribe, in turn, agreed to allow whites to live in and cross their territory). A series of subsequent treaties and executive orders reduced their reservation to a fraction of its former size. And when the buffalo approached extinction in the 1880s, starvation was the result. According to the historian John Ewers, an estimated one-sixth to one-fourth of the Piegan Blackfeet died of hunger in 1883–1884.

Another blow to Montana's Indians was the 1887 Dawes General Allotment Act, which opened reservation lands to white settlement after "allotting" 160-acre parcels to Indian heads of households. Applied unevenly and at various times, the policy of allotment affected each tribe differently. On the Flathead Indian Reservation in northwestern Montana, for example, the sale of "excess" land to non-Indians during the homestead boom of the 1910s left members of the Salish and Kootenai tribes owning less than half of the land on their reservation. In 2000, enrolled tribal members made up only 26 percent of the reservation's population.

Indians, primarily from ten tribes (Assiniboine, Blackfeet, Chippewa, Cree, Crow, Gros Ventre, Kootenai, Lakota or Sioux, Northern Cheyenne, and Salish), were the state's largest minority in 2000, at 7.3 percent of the population. Many lived on one of Montana's seven Indian reservations (Blackfeet, Crow, Flathead, Fort Belknap, Fort Peck, Northern Cheyenne, and Rocky Boy's), though tribal members also live in Missoula, Great Falls, Billings, and other Montana communities.

The Cattle Boom and Sheep Industry

Territory opened by the removal of Indians to reservations included rich grazing land. Large, corporate ranches—financed mainly by wealthy speculators—brought longhorns from Texas to feed on the area's expansive grasslands in the 1880s, supplementing older cattle operations established primarily by former prospectors. According to one source, at the peak of the open-range boom in 1886, approximately 664,000 cattle and 986,000 sheep grazed on Montana rangelands.

The legendary days of the open range—commemorated by Montana's "cowboy artist" Charles M. Russell—suffered a blow during 1886–1887, when summer drought and a long, cold winter struck the overcrowded range to cause the death of approximately 60 percent of Montana's cattle. Cattle remained an important industry, but increasingly ranchers began to grow hay to see their animals through the winters. The homesteading boom decreased the availability of open range, but the 1934 Taylor Grazing Act provided a boon to ranchers hard hit by the depression by allowing livestock to graze on public land.

Less celebrated than the cattle industry, the sheep industry in Montana also thrived and then declined. In 1900, Montana's six million sheep made it the biggest wool-producing state in the union. Eventually, however, foreign competition, the popularity of synthetic fibers, and an end to wool subsidies caused the number of sheep in Montana to drop from 5.7 million head in 1903 to 370,000 head in January 2000.

The Rise of Copper

Even at their height, the sheep and cattle industries could not rival the growth brought by copper. The discovery of rich veins of copper in Butte in the 1880s coincided with an expanding demand for the metal fueled by the electrical revolution and the growing need for copper wire. By 1889, Butte was the nation's largest copper producer and the biggest city between Minneapolis and Seattle. Perhaps the most ethnically diverse city in the intermountain west, Butte was known as the "Gibraltar of Unionism." The Western Federation of Miners, whose leaders later helped found the Industrial Workers of the World, was founded there in 1893. In 1912 even Butte's two chimneysweeps had their own union. Twenty-six miles west, Butte's sister town of Anaconda, founded by the Anaconda Copper Company in 1884, processed the ore wrested from the "richest hill on earth," while poisonous gases bellowing from its stacks killed crops, cattle, and forests for miles around.

Rivalry between two of Butte's "copper kings" profoundly effected statewide politics. Marcus Daly, owner of the Anaconda Company, successfully opposed copper magnate William Clark's 1888 run for territorial delegate and 1893 senate campaign, a race marked by massive corruption. Clark retaliated in 1894, successfully backing Helena as the permanent site of the state capital in opposition to Daly's choice of Anaconda.

Copper continued as a force in Montana politics after the state's copper mines and smelters were consolidated under the control of the directors of Standard Oil in 1899. The Company, as the conglomerate was often called, offered its most naked display of power in 1903 when it closed its operations and put 15,000 men out of work until the governor called a special session of the legislature to enact the legislation it demanded. In addition to its mining interest, the Company operated large logging operations to feed the mines' voracious appetite for lumber.

Even after it severed its ties to Standard Oil in 1915, the Company remained a political force. It controlled most of the state's major newspapers until 1959, and, some believed, many of the state's politicians. Unlike Clark and Daly, the directors of the Company in the teens actively opposed unionism. With the help of state and federal troops, which occupied Butte six times between 1914 and

1920, the Company completely crippled the miners' unions until a resurgence of labor activity during the 1930s.

Open-pit mining—initiated in the 1950s after the richest copper veins had played out—transformed Butte. While Butte shrank (open-pit mining employed fewer people than did traditional hardrock mining), the Company's Berkeley Pit grew, consuming entire neighborhoods. Low copper prices, declining concentrations of ore, reduced industrial use of copper, and increasing global competition led to the closure of the Anaconda smelter in 1980 and the shutdown of mining activity in Butte in 1983, leaving Butte and Anaconda economically and environmentally devastated. When mining resumed in the mid-1980s, it was as a small-scale, nonunion operation. In 2000, mining operations again ceased, due to high energy costs and low copper prices. The Butte and Anaconda region hosted the largest Superfund cleanup site in the United States, and jobs in reclamation were an important part of the area's sluggish economy.

The Homestead Era

With the homestead boom of 1909 to 1919, agriculture surpassed mining as the state's major source of income. The Enlarged Homestead Act of 1909 offered farmers 320 acres of free land. A second law passed in 1912 made it easier for homesteaders to "prove up." The railway companies, which foresaw a lucrative business in transporting crops to market and supplying settlers, conducted a massive advertising campaign and Montana quickly became "the most homesteaded state in the union." As the state's population ballooned from approximately 243,000 in 1900 to a high of approximately 770,000 in 1918, local governments multiplied, from sixteen counties at the time of statehood in 1889 to fifty-six by 1926.

Wartime inflation, resultant high prices, and relatively wet years through 1917 produced unprecedented prosperity for Montana's farmers. However, a six-year drought beginning in 1918 and the collapse of commodity prices in 1920 exposed the weakness of the homesteading economy. Montana's arid lands simply could not support small-scale farming. Between 1919 and 1925, more than half of Montana farmers lost their land and over 60,000 people left the state.

Wet weather after 1926 provided some help to those who stayed, but the agricultural depression of the 1920s grew into the Great Depression of the 1930s, when drought and falling prices again pushed farmers from the land. Nevertheless, agriculture—primarily wheat and beef—still dominates the landscape: Montana is second among states in the number of acres devoted to agriculture. However, as the depopulation of the eastern two-thirds of Montana attests, this increasingly industrialized enterprise requires fewer and fewer workers. In 2000, agriculture employed less than 6 percent of Montanans.

The Great Depression

The Great Depression hit Montana hard, as mining, smelting, and logging slowed to a halt. President Franklin Roosevelt's New Deal programs provided welcome relief. The federal government sent over $523 million to Montana (approximately 27 percent in loans), making Montana the union's second most subsidized state. The money arrived through payments to farmers; construction projects such as the massive Fort Peck Dam, which in 1936 employed more than 10,000 people; rural electrification loans to farmers' cooperatives; and direct relief. Federal jobs programs, according to the historian Michael Malone, provided income to a quarter of Montana households by 1935.

The New Deal also brought a shift in federal Indian policy. After decades of trying to "assimilate" Native Americans, the federal government recognized the value of tribal sovereignty with the Wheeler-Howard Act, cosponsored by Montana senator Burton K. Wheeler. In addition, the New Deal brought employment and infrastructure improvements to Montana's reservations through the formation of the Indian Conservation Corps.

Post–World War II Montana

Commodity prices rose with the beginning of World War II, bringing economic recovery to Montana. The state, however, lost population as young men and women joined the armed forces or found work in the war industries on the West Coast. Malmstrom Air Force Base in Great Falls—which employed approximately 4,000 people in 2001—was established during World War II, but the military-industrial complex had less impact on Montana's economy than it did on other western states.

The 1950s through the 1970s saw booms in petroleum, tourism, wood products, and coal industries. The oil industry—concentrated along the "hi-line" (Montana's northern tier) in the 1910s and 1920s—moved east with the discovery of the oil-rich Williston Basin. Three large refineries opened in Billings, which became the state's largest city by 1960. Jobs in government, tourism, and healthcare helped the city maintain this status despite the oil market crash in the 1980s.

Tourism boomed in the prosperous postwar period, building on its earlier significance to the state (Yellowstone National Park was established in 1872, Glacier National Park in 1910). In the 1950s, the timber industry, centered in the rich forests west of the Continental Divide, transformed into a genuine wood-products industry (manufacturing plywood, cardboard, and particle board), making it one of Montana's few value-added industries, albeit one with a large environmental cost. The construction of missile silos and dams and the infusion of highway money played a major role in the state's economy during the 1950s and 1960s. The 1970s energy crisis encouraged coal production in southeastern Montana, which claims 13 percent of the nation's coal reserves. In 1971, 7 million tons of coal were mined in Montana; by 1980, that figure had skyrocketed to 30 million, well over half of it from federally owned land.

The Role of the Federal Government

The federal government has always been important to Montana. Examples of early federal policies that have shaped Montana include Indian removal, railroad subsidies, an 1872 mining law (still in effect today, and the source of much controversy) that encourages the development of mineral resources, the homestead acts, timber sales at below-market value from the national forests, and the creation of national parks and wilderness areas. Despite the myth of the independent westerner and many Montanans' deep-seated distrust of "big government," the federal government remains crucial in shaping Montana's economy. In 1969, Montana received $1.88 from Washington ($1.59 in 2000) for every $1.00 its residents paid in taxes. Federal payments to farmers, for example, made up 22 percent of total agricultural receipts in 1999.

Politics

Remarkably corrupt and dominated by copper, Montana has displayed what many have deemed "political schizophrenia" through much of its history, sending conservatives to Helena and liberals to Washington. Many of Montana's representatives on the national level have become quite prominent: Senator Thomas Walsh, who led the investigation into the Teapot Dome scandal; Representative Jeannette Rankin, the first woman elected to Congress; and Senator Mike Mansfield, the Senate's longest-ruling majority leader.

Since state senators were elected by county, rather than by population, rural Montana dominated the legislature through the 1960s, leading to charges of "one cow, one vote" and court-ordered reapportionment. A constitutional convention to revise the original 1889 state constitution followed. A remarkably progressive document, the 1972 constitution enshrined the rights to privacy and "a clean and healthful environment," and committed the state to the preservation of "the unique and distinct cultural heritage of American Indians."

At the end of the twentieth century, Montana's politics moved increasingly rightward, as evidenced by the election of the conservative senator Conrad Burns in 1988, and his reelections in 1994 and 2000. Another political trend was tribal governments' determination to assert sovereignty on the reservations and their increasing willingness to resort to the courts when necessary to accomplish it.

Facing a New Century

At the beginning of the twenty-first century, Montana remained a low-population, high-acreage state, the most "non-metropolitan state in the nation," according to a 1999 study. The fourth largest state in the union, Montana ranks forty-fourth in population, with (according to the 2000 census) 902,195 residents. Energy deregulation,

passed by the legislature in 1997, was followed by soaring energy prices and shutdowns in the wood-products, mining, and refining industries. Tourism—which barely trailed agriculture as the second largest segment of the economy—continued to grow in importance. Remaining dependent on the federal government, beset by frequent droughts, and prey to the cyclical nature of an economy based on natural resource extraction, the state—listed as forty-seventh in per capita income in 1999—faced an uncertain economic future.

BIBLIOGRAPHY

Bennett, John W., and Seena B. Kohl. *Settling the Canadian-American West, 1890–1915: Pioneer Adaptation and Community Building.* Lincoln: University of Nebraska Press, 1995.

Bryan, William L., Jr. *Montana's Indians, Yesterday and Today.* 2nd rev. ed. Helena, Mont.: American World and Geographic, 1996.

Dobb, Edwin. "Pennies from Hell: In Montana, the Bill for America's Copper Comes Due." *Harper's* 293 (October 1996): 39–54.

Greene, Jerome A. *Nez Perce Summer, 1877: The U.S. Army and the Nee-Me-Poo Crisis.* Helena: Montana Historical Society Press, 2000.

MacMillan, Donald. *Smoke Wars: Anaconda Copper, Montana Air Pollution, and the Courts, 1890–1920.* Helena: Montana Historical Society Press, 2000.

Malone, Michael P. *Montana: A Contemporary Profile.* Helena, Mont.: American World and Geographic, 1996.

Malone, Michael P., ed. *Montana Century: 100 Years in Pictures and Words.* Helena, Mont.: Falcon, 1999.

Malone, Michael P., Richard B. Roeder, and William L. Lang. *Montana: A History of Two Centuries.* Rev. ed. Seattle: University of Washington Press, 1991.

Murphy, Mary. *Mining Cultures: Men, Women, and Leisure in Butte, 1914–41.* Urbana: University of Illinois Press, 1997.

Rankin, Charles E., ed. *Legacy: New Perspectives on the Battle of the Little Bighorn.* Helena: Montana Historical Society Press, 1996.

Martha Kohl

See also **Anaconda Copper; Billings; Buffalo; Cattle; Cheyenne; Copper Industry; Dawes General Allotment Act; Fur Companies; Fur Trade and Trapping; Gold Mines and Mining; Helena Mining Camp; Homestead Movement; Indian Removal; Indian Territory; Little Bighorn, Battle of; Nez Perce War; Sheep; Silver Prospecting and Mining; Yellowstone National Park;** *and* vol. 9: **The Vigilantes of Montana.**

MONTE CASSINO, a mountain fifty miles north of Naples topped with a famous Benedictine abbey, was the site of fierce fighting in World War II during the first five months of 1944. German troops in mountaintop gun posts observed the entire Liri Valley, the Allies' chosen route to Rome. Under the mistaken belief that Germans occupied the abbey, the Allies, on 15 February, destroyed the buildings and their artistic and cultural treasures with an air bombardment by 250 planes. Not until a powerful spring offensive broke the GUSTAV LINE did the Allies gain entrance into the Liri Valley and, on 18 May, capture the mountain. The abbey and the town of Cassino (also bombed) were rebuilt after the war, but controversy continued about whether the destruction had been justified.

BIBLIOGRAPHY

Blumenson, Martin. *Salerno to Cassino.* Washington, D.C.: Office of the Chief of Military History, U. S. Army, 1969.

Graham, Dominick. *Cassino.* New York: Ballantine Books, 1971.

Majdalany, Fred. *The Battle of Cassino.* Boston: Houghton Mifflin, 1957.

Smith, E. D. *The Battles for Cassino.* New York: Scribners, 1975.

Martin Blumenson/A. R.

See also **Anzio; Salerno; World War II.**

MONTERREY, BATTLES OF.

In the MEXICAN-AMERICAN WAR, Gen. Zachary Taylor's invading army of six thousand men attacked Monterrey, Mexico, which was defended by Gen. Pedro de Ampudia's force of nine thousand. The first day's fight outside the city paved the way for the assault on three fortified hills that guarded the approach and that was carried before daybreak on 22 September. On that day and the next the Americans completed the conquest of the city. An eight-weeks armistice was agreed on but repudiated by Congress, and the fighting was renewed within six weeks.

BIBLIOGRAPHY

Bauer, K. Jack. *Zachary Taylor.* Baton Rouge: Louisiana State University Press, 1985.

———. *The Mexican War, 1846–1848.* Lincoln: University of Nebraska Press, 1993.

Clayton, Lawrence R., and Joseph E. Chance. *The March to Monterrey: The Diary of Lieutenant Rankin Dilworth, U. S. Army.* El Paso: Texas Western Press, 1996.

Alvin F. Harlow/A. R.

See also **Manifest Destiny; Mexico, Relations with.**

MONTGOMERY CONVENTION.

The Montgomery Convention assembled at Montgomery, ALABAMA, on 4 February 1861, to organize the Confederate States of America. Representatives from six states (South Carolina, Georgia, Alabama, Mississippi, Florida, and Louisiana) declared the convention a provisional legislature, established a government without waiting for constitutional ratification, and selected provisional leaders. The convention sat in Montgomery until 20 May 1861, when it adjourned to Richmond, Virginia. In Richmond it completed a permanent constitution (adopted 11 March 1861),

supervised its ratification, directed congressional and presidential elections in November 1861, and adapted the existing laws and machinery of government to the needs of the new government. With the inauguration of the permanent government (22 February 1862), it adjourned.

BIBLIOGRAPHY

McPherson, James M. *Battle Cry of Freedom: The Civil War Era.* New York: Oxford University Press, 1988.

Hallie Farmer/c. w.

See also **Civil War; Confederate States of America.**

MONTICELLO

(constructed between 1769 and 1809) was designed and built by Thomas Jefferson to be his home, farm, and plantation. Construction progressed through two stages, the first beginning in 1769, and the second in 1796, after Jefferson's presidency and travels in Europe.

Altered throughout most of Jefferson's life, the brick house embodies the ideals of the American Enlightenment, as well as the moral, aesthetic, political, and scientific motives of its designer. Located southwest of Charlottesville, Virginia, and surrounded by thousands of acres devoted to agriculture and industry, the house was built on the leveled summit of "Little Mountain." More than one hundred enslaved African Americans and paid laborers supported the cultivation of elaborate vegetable gardens, a variety of crops and livestock, fruit trees, a vineyard, and a terraced, picturesque garden. Twenty-six years old when Monticello was begun, Jefferson pursued an urbane, aristocratic, and educated life in this rural setting, where he was inspired by his study of ancient Roman architecture, the writings of Pliny, and the neoclassical villa architecture of Andrea Palladio. The orderly landscape, carefully arranged shops and outbuildings, and the balanced planning of Monticello's interior spaces demonstrated Jefferson's belief that architecture must be both practical and symbolic, a visible instrument of a new nation's purposes. Monticello reflects both the private country gentleman's family and the plantation's social structure.

Choosing the scenic mountaintop for his plantation house, Jefferson made clear his understanding of how a house and its natural landscape interact. From 1768 onward, Jefferson worked out the plan, elevations, materials, and details of his house in numerous ink on laid paper drawings. By 1770, the site was cleared, lumber was prepared, and bricks were made to build a small brick house (still standing), shaped after regional vernacular buildings. By 1771, the general plan of the main house and its dependencies had been drawn, derived from typical plans for country villas in Robert Morris's *Select Architecture* (1757), an illustrated volume in Jefferson's substantial collection of architecture books. Monticello's cruciform plan, balanced proportions, and classical ornamental details demonstrate Jefferson's familiarity with the prevailing ar-

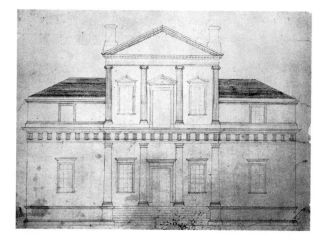

Monticello. An architect's drawing (elevation) of Thomas Jefferson's elaborately planned, eclectically neoclassical, and never completely finished estate in Virginia. © BETTMANN/CORBIS

chitectural aesthetic derived from the sixteenth-century Italian architect Andrea Palladio. Seeking constant refinements and originality, the eclectic Jefferson combined his own sense of practicality and beauty with Palladio's use of the Doric and Ionic orders, pedimented roofs, and classical proportions, all of which Jefferson had studied in Palladio's *Four Books of Architecture* (1570). This earliest phase of Monticello featured a double portico, one of Palladio's most well known classical elements.

For classical details, Jefferson turned to James Gibbs's *Rules for Drawing the Several Parts of Architecture* (1738). The classical Roman villa and the cultivated lifestyle of its inhabitants occupied Jefferson's imagination, fostered as well by his study of Pliny, whose description of ancient Roman interiors, cultivated landscapes, and villa architecture informed American Palladianism. Jefferson brought his wife to Monticello in 1772, and the house's construction continued for the next ten years under the direct supervision of its architect. In designing the various public and private spaces, Jefferson unified beauty and function. The untimely death of his wife in 1782, and Jefferson's departure to Paris in 1784, ended this first phase of construction.

In France, Jefferson immersed himself in French neoclassical studies, acquired important architecture books, and visited ancient Roman sites in France and Italy. His fascination with numbers and precise measurement is reflected in his writings and travel sketches. The authentic Roman buildings tempered Jefferson's attachment to Palladio and, for solving the practical household needs at Monticello, Jefferson also carefully studied French domestic architecture. In particular, he was impressed by the Hotel de Salm, a modern townhouse combining neoclassical order and modern rational planning. When Jefferson resumed construction at Monticello in 1796, the second phase of design showed dramatically the impact of Roman antiquity, Palladio's villas, French neoclassicism, and his visits to English country houses, especially Lord Burlington's Chiswick House (1725) near London. Palladio's Villa Rotunda, near Vicenza, was memorable for its centralized plan and dome. Monticello's two-story portico was replaced by a low octagonal dome, and the dependencies were drawn horizontally across the site to emphasize the much-desired view of the surrounding Blue Ridge Mountains. Monticello was mostly finished by 1809, when Jefferson retired from his public life, but Jefferson continued to tinker with his dwelling until his death in 1826.

BIBLIOGRAPHY

Burstein, Andrew. *The Inner Jefferson: Portrait of a Grieving Optimist.* Charlottesville: University Press of Virginia, 1996.

Cunningham, Noble E., Jr. *In Pursuit of Reason: The Life of Thomas Jefferson.* Baton Rouge: Louisiana State University Press, 1987.

Guinness, Desmond, and Julius Trousdale Sadler, Jr. *Mr. Jefferson, Architect.* New York: Viking, 1973.

Kimball, Fiske. *Thomas Jefferson, Architect: Original Designs in the Coolidge Collection of the Massachusetts Historical Society.* New York: DaCapo, 1968.

McLaughlin, Jack. *Jefferson and Monticello: The Biography of a Builder.* New York: Holt, 1988.

Stein, Susan R. *The Worlds of Thomas Jefferson at Monticello.* New York: Abrams, 1993.

R. Stephen Sennott

See also **Architecture.**

MONTREAL, CAPTURE OF (1760).

The spirits of the French had been raised by the success of François Gaston de Lévis at Sainte Foy on 28 April 1760, but not for long. On 15 May the vanguard of the English ships appeared below Quebec. Lévis, abandoning hope of help from France, raised the siege and retreated up the river. The British plan to take Montreal had been carefully prepared. While Gen. Geoffrey Amherst descended the SAINT LAWRENCE RIVER, Gen. James Murray, with another army and the fleet, moved up the river, and Col. William Haviland approached by way of LAKE CHAMPLAIN. At Amherst's demand, on 8 September 1760 the governor, Pierre François de Rigaud, Marquis de Vaudreuil-Cavagnal, surrendered Montreal, and with it Canada.

BIBLIOGRAPHY

Wrong, George M. *The Fall of Canada: A Chapter in the History of the Seven Years' War.* Oxford: Clarendon Press, 1914.

Lawrence J. Burpee / A. R.

See also **Canada, Relations with; French and Indian War; Montreal, Capture of (1775).**

MONTREAL, CAPTURE OF (1775).

After Ethan Allen's failed *coup de main* in September 1775, the main body of the American force under Gen. Richard Montgomery took Saint John's, Newfoundland, on 2 November and pushed on toward Montreal. Because the city's fortifications were weak, Gov. Guy Carleton made no attempt to defend it, and, on 11 November, slipped away with the garrison down the river toward Quebec. American batteries at Sorel barred the way, and the flotilla and the troops were captured; but Carleton himself reached Quebec safely. On 13 November the American troops marched into Montreal without encountering resistance. The city remained in American hands until 15 June 1776.

BIBLIOGRAPHY

Burt, Alfred LeRoy. *The Old Province of Quebec.* Toronto: McCelland and Stewart, 1968.

George M. Wrong, *Canada and the American Revolution.* New York: Cooper Square Publishers, 1935.

C. P. Stacey / A. R.

See also **Canada, Relations with; Montreal, Capture of (1760).**

MOODY'S.

One of the two best-known bond rating services, Moody's was created by American financial writer John Moody (1868–1958). Moody's also rates commercial paper, preferred and common stock, and municipal short-term bond issues. There are six Moody's manuals published annually, with weekly updates containing information on issuers and securities. The quarterly *Moody's Handbook of Common Stocks* follows more than 500 companies and analyzes the historical and present financial condition and the future outlook of each. Moody's Investment Grade Rating provides ratings such as MIG-1,2,3,4, to investment-grade or bank-quality municipal short-term debt securities. The ratings signify, respectively, best, high, favorable, and adequate quality.

BIBLIOGRAPHY

Pollock, John Charles. *Moody.* Chicago: Moody Press, 1983.

Meg Greene Malvasi

MOON LANDING.

On 16 July 1969, half a million people gathered near Cape Canaveral (then Cape Kennedy), Florida. Their attention was focused on three astronauts—Neil A. Armstrong, Edwin E. Aldrin Jr., and Michael Collins—who lay in the couches of an Apollo spacecraft bolted atop a Saturn V launch vehicle, awaiting ignition of five clustered rocket engines to boost them toward the first lunar landing. This event took place eight years after President John F. Kennedy, in the wake of Soviet Sputnik and Vostok successes, issued a challenge to land men on the moon before 1970 and thus give the United States preeminence in space exploration. After twenty manned missions—two to the vicinity of the moon

First Man on the Moon. Astronaut Neil Armstrong faces the American flag placed on the lunar surface, 20 July 1969.

itself—the National Aeronautics and Space Administration was ready to achieve that goal.

At 9:32 A.M., the *Apollo 11* crew fired the 200,000-pound-thrust Saturn S-IVB stage to escape earth's gravitational field. On their way to the moon, the astronauts monitored systems, ate, and slept. Several times via television they showed scenes of the receding earth and their own cabin activities.

Early Saturday afternoon (19 July), the crew slowed their ship while on the back side of the moon to enter lunar orbit. Following this maneuver, Aldrin slid through a passageway into the lunar module, called Eagle, to test its systems and then returned to the command module Columbia so that he and the other crew members could sleep before the descent to the lunar surface.

On Sunday, Armstrong and Aldrin cut loose from the command module and headed toward the surface of the moon. Armstrong set the craft down at 4:17 P.M. (EDT), reporting, "Houston, Tranquility Base here. The Eagle has landed." Six and one-half hours later, after donning a protective suit and life-sustaining backpack, Armstrong climbed down and set foot on lunar soil, saying, "That's one small step for [a] man, one giant leap for mankind." Aldrin soon followed. Half a billion people watched on television as the two astronauts moved about on the lunar surface with its gravity one-sixth that of earth's.

While on the Sea of Tranquility, Armstrong and Aldrin deployed a television camera, raised the American flag, collected about forty-seven pounds of samples, talked with President Richard M. Nixon, set up scientific equipment, and gave millions of listeners a description of their experiences. After two hours of exploring, they returned to the lunar module, rested for eight hours, and then started the engine of the ascent stage to rejoin Collins, who was orbiting the moon in Columbia, late Monday afternoon. Discarding the Eagle, the astronauts fired the service module engine shortly after noon the next day to escape the lunar gravitational field for the return to earth.

Apollo 11 splashed down in the Pacific Ocean on Thursday, 24 July, a week and a day (195 hours) after departing the Florida launch site. The astronauts, greeted by Nixon aboard the U.S.S. *Hornet*, were kept in quarantine for sixteen days because scientists feared the introduction of pathogens from outer space (none was found).

BIBLIOGRAPHY

Launius, Roger D. *NASA: A History of the U.S. Civil Space Program.* Malabar, Fla.: Krieger, 1994.

Lewis, Richard S. *Appointment on the Moon.* New York: Viking, 1969.

McDougall, Walter A. *The Heavens and the Earth: A Political History of the Space Age.* New York: Basic Books, 1985.

James M. Grimwood/A. R.

See also **National Aeronautics and Space Administration; Petrography; Space Program;** *and vol. 9:* **Voice from Moon: The Eagle Has Landed.**

MOONEY CASE. On 22 July 1916 a bomb killed ten and wounded forty during a Preparedness Day parade in SAN FRANCISCO. Thomas J. Mooney and Warren K. Billings, labor leaders who had been accused of unlawful possession of explosives in 1913, were among those charged. Mooney was sentenced to death, and Billings received a life sentence. Some evidence was so questionable that even the presiding judge became convinced the trial had been unfair. In 1918, at President Woodrow Wilson's request, Gov. William Stephens of California commuted Mooney's sentence to life imprisonment. Governor after governor received petitions for pardon until 1939, when Gov. Culbert L. Olson pardoned Mooney and released Billings.

BIBLIOGRAPHY

Ward, Estolv. *The Gentle Dynamiter: A Biography of Tom Mooney.* Palo Alto, Calif.: Ramparts Press, 1983.

Alvin F. Harlow/c. w.

See also **Bombing; Labor; Terrorism.**

MOONSHINE, an old English term for smuggled liquor, indicating its customary transportation by night, evolved into "moonshiners" in the nineteenth century to describe illicit distillers in southern APPALACHIA. Because moonshiners' stills were located among thickets or rocks, their products were known locally as "brush whiskey" and "blockade"; few described the liquor itself as "moonshine." "Blockaders," as moonshiners were also known, viewed whiskey production as a natural right and as the only way to obtain a fair monetary return on mountain corn crops. Despite intensified campaigns against moonshining after 1877 involving armed patrols of revenue officers, frequent killings, and pitched battles, the business was never quite eliminated. During Prohibition, the term "moonshine" came to be popularly applied to liquor illicitly made anywhere, even in the home.

BIBLIOGRAPHY

Dabney, Joseph E. *Mountain Spirits: A Chronicle of Corn Whiskey from King James' Ulster Plantation to America's Appalachians and the Moonshine Life.* New York: Scribners, 1974.

———. *More Mountain Spirits: The Continuing Chronical of Moonshine Life and Corn Whiskey, Wines, Ciders, and Beers in America's Appalachians.* Ashville, N.C.: Bright Mountain Books, 1985.

Alvin F. Harlow/c. w.

See also **Alcohol, Regulation of; Bootlegging; Prohibition.**

MORAL MAJORITY. The Reverend Jerry Falwell, an evangelical Christian, formed the Moral Majority, a civic advocacy and a political action group, in 1979. The name was meant to project strength by highlighting and validating the ethical and numerical supremacy of ordinary Americans, especially in rural areas and religious communities, over affluent, urban, and more educated people. Of particular concern were secular, individualistic, liberal movements—including pacifist, gay, and feminist groups—and their impact on private life, popular culture, and public policy. The members of the Moral Majority frequently perceived the modern lifestyle as decadent, promiscuous, self-indulgent, and vacuous. They wanted to challenge its prevalence and its influence.

The essence of the Moral Majority was its religious fundamentalism, which insisted upon reliance on a strict interpretation of the Christian version of the Bible, a belief in God's moral authority as conveyed to people and imparted by the clergy, and an awareness of His close supervision of human deeds. The agenda was socially conservative, anticommunist, populist, and nationalist. It exuded pride in the traditional American heritage of freedom and piety, but also reacted against the perceived excesses of the 1960s often embodied in the Democratic Party.

The Moral Majority supported collective prayer in public schools, the widespread teaching of Christian scriptures as superior to the findings of modern science, as in its support of creationism, and lobbied for these goals throughout the United States. The group took a strict pro-life stance, advocating the reversal of the U.S. Supreme Court's decision in *Roe v. Wade* (1973) that permitted abortions. Although that campaign failed, a growing public awareness of the claim that life begins at conception was achieved and a dismay at abortions—especially those performed in the last trimester of the pregnancy—grew measurably.

The Moral Majority also played a role in blocking the adoption of the Equal Rights Amendment, which was supported by women's organizations, as defending vulnerable members of society. The Moral Majority objected to the promotion and the protection of homosexual rights, with varying results in individual states. It denounced nuclear disarmament agreements with the Soviet Union, notably the two phases of the Strategic Arms Limitation Treaty, SALT I and II. The group's major accomplishment was its voter registration and fund-raising activities in 1980, which propelled conservative candidates, primarily Republicans—including presidential nominee Ronald Reagan—to local and national offices.

On 10 June 1989, Falwell announced that "our mission is accomplished" and dissolved the Moral Majority, effective 31 August 1989. The surviving organization most resembling it was the Liberty Foundation.

BIBLIOGRAPHY

Wilcox, Clyde. *Onward Christian Soldiers? The Religious Right in American Politics.* 2d ed. Boulder, Colo.: Westview Press, 2000.

Itai Sneh

See also **Christian Coalition; Fundamentalism; Pro-Life Movement.**

MORAL SOCIETIES were formed in the United States to combat "vice and immorality," particularly during the first two decades of the nineteenth century. Based on English and colonial precedent of seventeenth-century societies to reform manners, hundreds of moral societies were established, mostly in New York and New England. Linked to the established churches and the Federalist Party, they thrived during the War of 1812, when anxieties about the future of New England increased. Considering Puritan morality to be synonymous with republican virtue, they often supplemented or even replaced churches as guardians of what they deemed a moral society. Linking religious moral tradition and the reform movement of the early-nineteenth century, many moral societies concentrated on temperance and slavery, but they also regarded Sabbath-breaking, cockfights, gambling, profanity, and horseracing as dangerous. Society members tried to persuade citizens to lead a "moral" life and, if this was not successful, often acted as informers to the local authorities who would prosecute offenders. Opposition against moral societies increased after the end of the War of 1812. Forc-

ing members of the community to lead a "moral" life was increasingly regarded as intolerant and as an abridgement of citizens' liberties. By the 1820s, moral societies had gone into sharp decline.

BIBLIOGRAPHY

Bernard, Joel. "Between Religion and Reform: American Moral Societies, 1811–1821." *Proceedings of the Massachusetts Historical Society* 105 (1993): 1–38.

Walters, Ronald G. *American Reformers, 1815–1860.* Rev. ed. New York: Hill and Wang, 1997.

Michael Wala

See also **Federalist Party.**

MORATORIUM, HOOVER. The ominous financial situation throughout the world in the spring of 1931 and its disastrous effects on American economic conditions led President Herbert Hoover, on 20 June, to propose a one-year international postponement "of all payments on intergovernmental debts, reparations, and relief debts, both principal and interest, of course not including obligations of governments held by private parties." He hoped that this measure, which came to be known as the "Hoover moratorium," would promote a worldwide restoration of confidence and economic stability. By 6 July all fifteen of the nations involved had accepted the proposal.

BIBLIOGRAPHY

Kennedy, David M. *Freedom from Fear: The American People in Depression and War.* New York: Oxford University Press, 1999.

W. A. Robinson / c. w.

See also **Debt, Public; Debt and Investment, Foreign; Great Depression.**

MORAVIAN BRETHREN. The Moravian Church (Unity of Brethren) originated in a Bible-centered group that formed in Bohemia and Moravia in 1457 and later became known as the Unitas Fratum (Unity of Brethren). Exiled to Poland at the time of the Thirty Years War, the Brethren were reborn in Saxony in 1722 under the leadership of Count Nicholas Zinzendorf. Moravians stressed the humanity of Jesus Christ, the power of divine grace in effecting a change of heart, mind, and disposition, and the love of God in Christ, rather than his sovereignty or justice. They refrained from authoritative definitions of doctrine and tried to avoid approaching Scripture in a dogmatic way, stressing religious tolerance and an evangelical vision rather than theological conformity.

The first Moravians settled in Georgia in 1735, although within five years they had relocated to Pennsylvania, where they ministered to German Protestant exiles. Under Bishop August Spangenberg, they made a major

Board was created in 1855 and the Church expanded its mission work to the Midwest.

During the twentieth century, Moravians in the North, most notably Paul de Schweinitz, expressed strong support for religious cooperation and church union. There has been some decline of Moravian religious traditions and the adoption of main-line church practices such as vacation Bible school. During the 1910s, the Church established commissions to conduct work in rural areas and to focus evangelistic effort. Authority in the Church was decentralized in 1930, and bishops became subject to election by ballot in 1936. In the South, the Moravians grew rapidly and have been much involved in the religious culture of Winston-Salem, winning much approval for their support for women's education.

Cooperation between the Northern and Southern Provinces has been fostered by Moravian College and Moravian Theological Seminary in Bethlehem, Pennsylvania, and by the Interprovincial Board of Education, created in 1936. In 1946, the Moravian World Peace Committee was established to encourage overseas relief and secure the banning of atomic weapons. The Moravian Church in America has remained comparatively small, with only 26,103 members in 1999, and most Moravian congregations are found in Tanzania and the Caribbean.

BIBLIOGRAPHY

Hamilton, John Taylor, and Kenneth G. Hamilton. *History of the Moravian Church: The Renewed Unitas Fratrum, 1722–1957*. Bethlehem, Pa: Interprovincial Board of Christian Education, Moravian Church in America, 1967.

Sawyer, Edwin A. *All About the Moravians: History, Beliefs, and Practices of a Worldwide Church*. Bethlehem, Pa: Moravian Church in America, 1990.

Jeremy Bonner

See also **Religion and Religious Affiliation.**

MORGAN-BELMONT AGREEMENT was a contract (8 February 1895) between the U.S. Treasury Department and the banking houses of J. P. Morgan and August Belmont, American representative of the Rothschilds of Paris. In 1893 the American economy sank into a serious depression, creating a rapid flight of foreign investment. With shrinking gold reserves threatening to worsen the crisis, the Cleveland administration turned to Morgan and Belmont for help. Under the contract, these financiers agreed to buy $62 million worth of thirty-year government bonds and pay for them in gold, thus replenishing the government's rapidly diminishing gold reserve. By 1897, the depression ended.

BIBLIOGRAPHY

Black, David. *The King of Fifth Avenue: The Fortunes of August Belmont*. New York: Dial Press, 1981.

Brands, H. W. *The Reckless Decade: America in the 1890s*. New York: St. Martin's Press, 1995.

Count Nicholas Zinzendorf. The eighteenth-century leader of the reorganized Moravian Church in Saxony; he subsequently established congregations in other European countries and then in Pennsylvania (1741–43). GETTY IMAGES

contribution to the GREAT AWAKENING during the 1740s. The Moravian Church operated a communal system known as the "Economy," whereby it controlled all enterprises and real estate and assigned duties to its members. In 1766, the Moravians settled Salem, North Carolina, and in 1771, the Northern and Southern congregations were administratively separated. During the Revolution, the Brethren adopted a neutral stance, refusing to bear arms, but paying taxation and ministering to the wounded.

The Church's evangelistic effectiveness was limited by a 1779 decision of the United Brethren General Synod in Europe to adopt strict standards of admission. Congregations were required to conform to regulations demanding a quietist form of piety. American Moravians, however, soon challenged the General Synod's positions on military service and pastoral control of the temporal affairs of a congregation and demanded a democratic election structure for church offices. In the 1840s, restrictions on exclusive Church ownership of land and business in Moravian communities were lifted, and in 1848, the General Synod sanctioned provincial synods for the Northern and Southern Provinces. A provincial Home Missions

Brodsky, Alyn. *Grover Cleveland: A Study in Character*. New York: St. Martin's Press, 2000.

Strouse, Jean. *Morgan: American Financier*. New York: Random House, 1999.

P. Orman Ray / A. G.

See also **Debt and Investment, Foreign; Gold Exchange; Gold Standard; Laissez-Faire; Treasury, Department of the.**

MORGAN'S RAIDS.

After seeing minor action as a Confederate cavalry leader, Col. John Hunt Morgan embarked on a career as a raider in July 1862 with a spectacular dash from Knoxville, Tennessee, into Kentucky with 1,200 men. He pushed as far as Georgetown and Cynthiana, caused alarm in Cincinnati and Lexington, and destroyed quantities of Union arms and supplies. He also assisted Edmund Kirby-Smith's northward advance in September 1862, captured a Union force at Hartsville, Tennessee, in December and continued his activities the next spring. His most spectacular achievement came in July 1863, when he led 2,460 men across Kentucky, reaching the Ohio River in five days. Without authority from his superiors and pursued by Union cavalry, he crossed the Ohio River at Brandenburg, Kentucky, drove off some Indiana militia, dashed northeastward into Ohio at Harrison, and, passing through the suburbs of Cincinnati at night, bewildered Union and state forces by the speed and boldness of his attack. His Ohio raid ended disastrously in a battle at the ford at Buffington Island, but Morgan and 1,200 men escaped, only to be captured on 26 July. After several months' confinement in Ohio, Morgan escaped to resume his military career as commander of the Department of Southwestern Virginia. His raiding activities ended suddenly when he was surprised and killed in eastern Tennessee in September 1864. His raid of 1863 had given Indiana and Ohio a bad fright, had inflicted property damages of more than $500,000 in Ohio, and had helped relieve the pressure on the Confederate forces in Tennessee.

BIBLIOGRAPHY

Duke, Basil W. *Morgan's Cavalry*. New York: Neale Publishing Company, 1906.

Ramage, James A. *Rebel Raider: The Life of General John Hunt Morgan*. Lexington: University Press of Kentucky, 1986.

Taylor, David L. *"With Bowie Knives & Pistols": Morgan's Raid in Indiana*. Lexington, Ind.: TaylorMade Write, 1993.

Eugene H. Roseboom / A. R.

See also **Civil War; Perryville, Battle of.**

MORMON BATTALION.

The Mormon Battalion was a company of U.S. soldiers serving in the war with Mexico (1846–1848). Enlisted from Mormon camps in the Iowa Territory and furnished by Brigham Young, they numbered 549 persons. Under the command of Col. Philip St. George Cooke, the Mormon volunteers marched to California via Santa Fe and the Gila River. Because of short rations, lack of water, and excessive toil in road-making and well digging, many fell sick and some died. They reached San Diego, California, in January 1847, where they disbanded. Most of the members joined Brigham Young's Mormon company that had arrived in Utah in July 1847.

BIBLIOGRAPHY

Powell, Allan Kent, ed. *Utah History Encyclopedia*. Salt Lake City: University of Utah Press, 1994.

L. E. Young / c. w.

See also **Mexican-American War.**

MORMON EXPEDITION.

The Mormon Expedition of 1857–1858 was a federal force sent by President James Buchanan to force the Mormons, led by Brigham Young, to obey federal laws. The initial party of about 1,500 infantry and artillery failed to subdue them. Using guerilla tactics, the Mormons held off the troops, forced them to camp out in Wyoming through the winter, and raided federal supplies. Eventually, promises of amnesty by Buchanan, coupled with the threat of federal military intervention, induced Young and his followers to submit, and, on 26 June 1858, the federal expedition marched into Salt Lake City, UTAH, without bloodshed.

BIBLIOGRAPHY

Allen, James B., and John W. Welch, eds. *Coming to Zion*. Provo, Utah: BYU Studies, Brigham Young University, 1997.

Brown, S. Kent, Donald Q. Cannon, and Richard H. Jackson, eds. *Historical Atlas of Mormonism*. New York: Simon and Schuster, 1994.

Schindler, Harold, ed. *Crossing the Plains: New and Fascinating Accounts of the Hardships, Controversies, and Courage Experienced and Chronicled by the 1847 Pioneers on the Mormon Trail*. Salt Lake City, Utah: Salt Lake Tribune, 1997.

C. A. Willoughby / D. B.

See also **Latter-day Saints, Church of Jesus Christ of; Mormon Trail; Mormon War; Nauvoo, Mormons at.**

MORMON HANDCART COMPANIES.

Not all Mormons migrating to UTAH in the mid-nineteenth century could afford horses for the journey. Ingeniously, some resorted to the use of handcarts. One or two persons were assigned to each handcart, which the migrants pushed and pulled across the plains from Iowa to the Salt Lake Valley. Most of these companies successfully made the journey, but two companies that started late in the summer of 1856 were caught in the early winter storms, and some of the members perished. Travel with handcarts began in 1856 and continued until 1860.

Mormon Emigration. Led by Brigham Young, the Mormons first made the long journey west to Utah in 1846, arriving in July 1847. Later travelers, such as Mormons in the caravan shown above (c. 1879), followed the same route from Illinois, through Iowa and the Nebraska Territory, into Wyoming, and southwest into Utah. National Archives and Records Administration

BIBLIOGRAPHY

Stegner, Wallace E. *The Gathering of Zion: The Story of the Mormon Trail.* New York: McGraw-Hill, 1964.

J. F. Smith/A. R.

See also **Latter-day Saints, Church of Jesus Christ of; Mormon Trail; Salt Lake City.**

MORMON TRAIL. The Mormon Trail refers to the route the Mormons took after their expulsion from Nauvoo, Illinois, in February 1846. They took a well-beaten trail westward, through what is now Iowa, crossing the Missouri River into Nebraska Territory by permission of the Omaha Indians. In April 1847 Brigham Young led 143 men, 3 women, and 2 children west along the Platte River to Fort Laramie, Wyoming, over the old Oregon Trail to Fort Bridger, Wyoming, southwest through Echo Canyon to the Weber River, through East Canyon, and across the Big and Little Mountains of the Wasatch Range. They entered the valley of the Great Salt Lake in Utah through Emigration Canyon on 24 July 1847.

BIBLIOGRAPHY

Allen, James B., and John W. Welch, eds. *Coming to Zion.* Provo, Utah: BYU Studies, Brigham Young University, 1997.

Brown, S. Kent, Donald Q. Cannon, and Richard H. Jackson, eds. *Historical Atlas of Mormonism.* New York: Simon and Schuster, 1994.

Schindler, Harold, ed. *Crossing the Plains: New and Fascinating Accounts of the Hardships, Controversies, and Courage Experienced and Chronicled by the 1847 Pioneers on the Mormon Trail.* Salt Lake City, Utah: Salt Lake Tribune, 1997.

L. E. Young/D. B.

See also **Latter-day Saints, Church of Jesus Christ of; Mormon Expedition; Mormon War; Nauvoo, Mormons at.**

MORMON WAR. The Mormon War (1844–1846) was a series of disorders between the Mormon residents of Nauvoo in Hancock County, Illinois, and the non-Mormon population of the neighboring territory. The non-Mormon population had welcomed the Mormons upon their 1839 arrival but soon resented their city charter, feared their political power, and envied their apparent prosperity. By June 1844 the Mormon militia was under arms in Nauvoo. At at least 1,500 armed men had assembled to expel the Mormons, and Governor Thomas had taken charge. The Mormon leader Joseph Smith surrendered on a charge of riot, but a mob murdered him and his brother Hyrum in the Carthage jail on 27 June. The

Mormons began migrating in February 1846 and were nearly gone by the year's end.

BIBLIOGRAPHY

Allen, James B., and John W. Welch, eds. *Coming to Zion*. Provo, Utah: BYU Studies, Brigham Young University, 1997.

Hallwas, John E., and Roger D. Launius, eds. *Cultures in Conflict: A Documentary History of the Mormon War in Illinois*. Logan: Utah State University Press, 1995.

Schindler, Harold, ed. *Crossing the Plains: New and Fascinating Accounts of the Hardships, Controversies, and Courage Experienced and Chronicled by the 1847 Pioneers on the Mormon Trail*. Salt Lake City, Utah: Salt Lake Tribune, 1997.

Paul M. Angle / D. B.

See also **Latter-day Saints, Church of Jesus Christ of; Mormon Expedition; Mormon Trail; Nauvoo, Mormons at.**

MORMONS. *See* **Latter-day Saints, Church of Jesus Christ of.**

MORRILL ACT. After decades of agitation by agricultural societies, farm journals, and other advocates of vocational training for farmers and mechanics, Senator Justin S. Morrill of Vermont introduced into Congress a bill for the establishment of agricultural and mechanical arts colleges in every state. The measure passed Congress in 1858, but President James Buchanan vetoed it. The Morrill Act, signed by President Abraham Lincoln in 1862, offered states thirty thousand acres of land for each sitting federal representative and senator as an endowment for the proposed schools. Some states, most notably Wisconsin, elected to give the land to existing institutions; others used it to establish new agricultural and technical colleges.

BIBLIOGRAPHY

Cross, Coy F. *Justin Smith Morrill: Father of the Land-Grant Colleges*. East Lansing: Michigan State University Press, 1999.

Simon, John Y. "The Politics of the Morrill Act," *Agricultural History* 37 (1963): 103–111.

Williams, Roger L. *The Origins of Federal Support for Higher Education: George W. Atherton and the Land-Grant College Movement*. University Park: Pennsylvania State University Press, 1991.

Paul W. Gates / A. R.

See also **Agriculture; Cornell University; Education; Land Grants: Land Grants for Education; Universities, State; University of Wisconsin.**

MORSE, JEDIDIAH, GEOGRAPHIES OF. The first edition of *Geography Made Easy* by Jedidiah Morse, a New England politician and divine, appeared in 1784. The little book was the first geography published in the United States. As the title implies, *Geography Made Easy* attempted to simplify existing notions about American GEOGRAPHY, which British books treated poorly. More than twenty-five editions followed during the author's lifetime. In 1789, Morse, the "father of American geography," also published an enlarged work, *The American Geography*, later called *The American Universal Geography*. In 1795, a child's book, *Elements of Geography*, appeared, and in 1797 *The American Gazetteer* was published.

BIBLIOGRAPHY

Moss, Richard J. *The Life of Jedidiah Morse: A Station of Peculiar Exposure*. Knoxville: University of Tennessee Press, 1995.

Phillips, Joseph W. *Jedidiah Morse and New England Congregationalism*. New Brunswick, N.J.: Rutgers University Press, 1983.

Randolph G. Adams / A. E.

See also **Education; Encyclopedias.**

MORTARS, CIVIL WAR NAVAL. CIVIL WAR naval mortars were heavy guns designed to throw shells with a high angle of fire; they were first built in 1862 for use in the New Orleans campaign. In April 1862 twenty mortars bombarded Forts Jackson and Saint Philip, the principal defenses below New Orleans, with thirteen-inch shells, allowing Adm. David G. Farragut's Union fleet to pass them. After the surrender of New Orleans, the flotilla ascended the Mississippi and bombarded Vicksburg, Mississippi, enabling Farragut's fleet to run past the city. During the siege of Vicksburg the following year, a mortar fleet bombarded the city for forty-two days prior to its surrender.

BIBLIOGRAPHY

Ryan, J. W. *Guns, Mortars, and Rockets*. New York: Brassey's Publishers, 1982.

Louis H. Bolander / C. W.

See also **Mississippi River; Navy, Confederate; Navy, United States; New Orleans, Capture of; Vicksburg in the Civil War.**

MORTGAGE RELIEF LEGISLATION is legislation meant to help borrowers. Since the early nineteenth century the relationship between mortgagor and mortgagee in the United States has undergone substantial modification—not continuously, but as the result of emergency measures taken at times of widespread financial distress arising from economic or natural causes. The alterations were usually to the apparent advantage of the borrower and thus are referred to as relief for mortgage debtors, or, when statutory, simply as mortgage relief legislation.

Because the states govern real property law (including mortgage law), they have passed most mortgage relief.

The major episodes of mortgage debtor relief followed periods of farm mortgage distress in the late nineteenth century and in the period between World War I and World War II, especially in the 1930s.

One feature of the Plains states settlement of the 1870s and 1880s was a large-scale overextension of farmer indebtedness, primarily in land mortgages. When farm incomes deteriorated and land values declined in subsequent years, mortgage debt became very burdensome to the borrower. As a result, many borrowers found themselves forced into delinquency, default, and finally foreclosure or some other form of distress transfer. The inevitable agitation for debtor relief included demands for inflation of the money supply (such as the FREE SILVER movement) and for public regulation of business monopolies. Two kinds of mortgage relief legislation, in the narrow sense, emerged from this period of farm mortgage distress: the establishment of statutory periods of redemption that continued after foreclosure sale and the requirement of appraisal of mortgaged property prior to sale and the prohibition of sale at less than a specified proportion of the appraised value. Such legislation resulted from criticism of sales at unreasonably low prices and deficiency judgments based on those sales.

A similar period of farm mortgage distress occurred in the 1920s, primarily in the High Plains region. There, after agriculture expanded rapidly during the World War I years, farm income deteriorated and farm land value declined; numerous foreclosures and other distress transfers of mortgaged farms resulted. After 1929 the GREAT DEPRESSION—in conjunction with severe drought in some areas—made mortgage distress a national concern. As a result of the extent and severity of the problem in both rural and urban areas, mortgage relief legislation reached a peak in the 1930s.

Although debtors and creditors reached voluntary adjustments, in which creditors gave debtors more time to repay and refinance their loans, these remedies proved insufficient in the face of the economic catastrophe of the 1930s. The states were the first to take legislative action. By early 1936, twenty-eight states had passed mortgage relief legislation in one or more of the following forms: moratoria on foreclosures, extensions of redemption periods, and restrictions on the use of deficiency judgments. A moratorium halted foreclosure proceedings for a temporary period identified as an economic emergency. Legislation extending the period of redemption specified a definite period during which the debtor continued to have the right to redeem the mortgaged property. These new laws restricted the use of deficiency judgments in any of several ways. For example, they might establish a minimum sales price, require creditors to use an appraised "fair value" rather than a sales value as a base for figuring the amount of deficiency, and limit the time within which a deficiency judgment could be executed. Courts generally upheld state mortgage relief legislation as long as it afforded relief only on a temporary basis, dependent on the existence of the economic emergency; did not impair the integrity of the mortgage indebtedness contract; and assured creditors appropriate compensation in the form of rental payments during the period of relief. The U.S. SUPREME COURT made the key decision on constitutionality in *Home Building and Loan Association v. Blaisdell*, 290 U.S. 398 (1934), when it upheld the Minnesota Moratorium Act of 1933.

State mortgage relief legislation did not fully solve the mortgage distress problems of the 1930s, partly because the measures were not enacted until after much of the damage had been done. More important, the problem of mortgage distress was only part of the much larger problem of general economic depression. In the mortgage relief area, as in so many others, the federal government took over from the states the search for solutions. In 1935 the Court declared unconstitutional an attempt at a federal moratorium, the Frazier-Lemke Farm Bankruptcy Act of 1934; but in 1937 it approved an amended version. The federal farm-credit agencies took the more effective action of refinancing mortgage loans—a policy that benefited lenders by providing welcome liquidity while enabling debtors to escape foreclosure. The federal government took similar steps in the field of urban mortgage finance.

When WORLD WAR II pulled the nation out of the general economic depression and into prosperity, the farm sector returned to relative well-being. No widespread mortgage distress calling for mortgage relief legislation occured in the postwar period. Farm ownership transfers by foreclosures, assignments, bankruptcies, and related defaults averaged twenty-two per thousand farms annually from 1929 through 1938, and peaked at thirty-nine per thousand in 1933. Such distress transfers averaged about 1.5 per thousand farms annually from 1950 through 1974.

In the 1980s and 1990s, farms fell upon hard times again, with huge numbers forced to foreclose. A more conservative federal government encouraged large-scale "factory" farming and did not protect smaller farmers with mortgage relief legislation. In 1996 President Bill Clinton signed the Farm Credit System Reform Act of 1996, which aimed to lower costs for farmers and ranchers. However, small farmers continued to go bankrupt at very high rates.

BIBLIOGRAPHY

Government Sponsorship of the Federal National Mortgage Association and the Federal Home Loan Mortgage Corporation. Washington, D.C.: U.S. Dept. of the Treasury, 1996.

Rucker, Randal R., and Lee J. Alston. "Farm Failures and Governmental Intervention: A Case Study of the 1930s." *American Economic Review* 77 (1987): 724–731.

Wallison, Peter J., and Bert Ely. *Nationalizing Mortgage Risk: The Growth of Fannie Mae and Freddie Mac.* Washington, D.C. AEI Press, 2000.

Glenn H. Miller Jr. / D. B.

461

See also **Bankruptcy Laws; Cooperatives, Farmers'; Farm Security Administration; Frazier-Lemke Farm Bankruptcy Act; Minnesota Moratorium Case.**

MOSBY'S RANGERS.

During the CIVIL WAR Mosby's Rangers were an irregular body of Confederate troops under the command of Col. John S. Mosby. They operated from 1863 to 1865 south of the Potomac, behind the Union lines. This organization began with a scouting assignment from Confederate Gen. J. E. B. Stuart in January 1863. From a few troopers the rangers gradually grew to eight companies by 1865. Apart from participation with Stuart in the Gettysburg, Pennsylvania, campaign, their main activities consisted of sudden attacks on Union outposts, followed, when pursued, by quick dispersion. To Gen. Philip H. Sheridan, Gen. George A. Custer, and others, Mosby's men were a thorn in the flesh. Efforts to destroy the rangers invariably failed.

BIBLIOGRAPHY

Williamson, James J. *Mosby's Rangers, A Record of the Forty-Third Battalion Virginia Cavalry from Its Organization to the Surrender.* Alexandria, Va.: Time-Life Books, 1982.

Alfred P. James/c. w.

See also **Cavalry, Horse; Gettysburg, Battle of; Rangers.**

MOST-FAVORED-NATION PRINCIPLE

is an agreement between two parties that each will extend to the other trading terms at least as good as those given any third country. It has been one of the fundamental objectives of American FOREIGN POLICY since independence. The first expression of this principle was the conditional most-favored-nation article in the Treaty of Amity and Commerce with France of 1778, which was inserted at the request of French negotiators.

One of the more famous uses of this principle was in the Wangxia Treaty of 1844 with China, in which the United States received most-favored-nation status, thus gaining all of the development and trading rights that Britain and France had wrested from the declining Qing dynasty. Most-favored-nation status would become a standard feature of imperialist treaties with the Qing for the remainder of the nineteenth century. Indeed, the Open Door Policy, which the United States articulated at the century's end, reflected this principle, declaring that the United States would press for the same commercial and industrial rights won by Japan and the western European powers, which had carved out spheres of influence in China.

Over the years, this principle ran up against the former British system of imperial preferences and other efforts at closed trading blocs or protective trade rules that favor one industry or one geographic region over another. In the 1990s most-favored-nation status figured prominently in trade negotiations between the United States and former Soviet bloc nations. It was also an issue of contention in U.S.-Chinese relations, with a number of American interest groups and members of Congress wanting to link most-favored-nation status to Chinese improvements in human rights.

BIBLIOGRAPHY

Ghosh, Madanmohan, Carlo Perroni, and John Whalley. *The Value of MFN.* Cambridge, Mass.: National Bureau of Economic Research, 1998.

Snyder, Richard C. *The Most-Favored-Nation Clause: An Analysis with Particular Reference to Recent Treaty Practice and Tariffs.* New York: King's Crown Press, 1948.

Charles M. Dobbs

MOTELS

developed in the second decade of the twentieth century to fill the need for functional, accessible, and economical sleeping accommodations catering to the burgeoning number of automobile travelers. Variously known as "tourist cabins," "motor courts," or "cabin camps," individually operated cabin complexes sprang up along highways, especially in the South and West.

The term "motel," a contraction of "motor" and "hotel," was coined in the mid-1920s. By the mid-1930s motels were more decorative, with quaint exteriors mimicking local architectural motifs. A few entrepreneurs experimented with luxurious or exotic designs, including accommodations adapted from aircraft or modeled on log cabins, historic structures, even wigwams.

The number of motels exploded following World War II (1939–1945), tripling from about 20,000 in 1940

Motels. In the 1920s motels, also known as "tourist cabins" or "motor courts," became popular for their inexpensive, clean overnight accommodations. Shown in the photo is a row of small motels in Lake George Village, New York, located in the Adirondack Forest Preserve. The large number of signs detracts somewhat from the area's rustic feel. NATIONAL ARCHIVES AND RECORDS ADMINISTRATION to over 60,000 by 1960. More economical and standardized attached units, individualized by absurdly garish signs, gradually replaced cabins as the preferred motel design.

In the second half of the twentieth century, the individually owned motel gave way to corporate chains such as Best Western and Holiday Inn. Motels are increasingly similar to the hotels that they once challenged, locating in urban areas, adding stories, and, especially, creating elegant spaces and business centers to accommodate private and corporate events.

BIBLIOGRAPHY

Jakle, John A., Keith A. Sculle, and Jefferson S. Rogers. *The Motel in America.* Baltimore and London: Johns Hopkins University Press, 1996.

Margolies, John. *Home Away from Home: Motels in America.* Boston: Little, Brown, Bulfinch Press, 1995.

Sculle, Keith A. "Frank Redford's Wigwam Village Chain: A Link in the Modernization of the Roadside." In *Roadside America: The Automobile in Design and Culture.* Edited by Jan Jennings. Ames: Iowa State University Press for the Society for Commercial Archeology, 1990.

Perry Frank

See also **Transportation and Travel; Vacation and Leisure.**

MOTHER'S DAY AND FATHER'S DAY

are annual observances saluting the contributions of parents in American life. Celebrated on the second Sunday of May, Mother's Day was first observed on 10 May 1908 in Grafton, West Virginia, and Philadelphia, Pennsylvania, and was soon celebrated nationwide following a campaign by the activist Anna Jarvis. (Others, including the social reformer Julia Ward Howe, had proposed similar celebrations in the 1800s.) Father's Day originated in Spokane, Washington, in 1910 at the urging of Sonora Louise Smart Dodd, the daughter of a Civil War veteran. It is celebrated on the third Sunday of June. On both days, children may prepare meals or give their parents gifts and greeting cards.

BIBLIOGRAPHY

Christianson, Stephen G. *The American Book of Days.* 4th ed. New York: Wilson, 2000.

Cohen, Hennig, and Tristram Potter Coffin. *The Folklore of American Holidays.* 2d ed. Detroit: Gale Research, 1991.

Phelan, Mary Kay. *Mother's Day.* New York: Crowell, 1965. Fine source for younger students.

Ryan F. Holznagel

MOTION PICTURES. *See* **Cartoons; Film.**

MOTOR CARRIER ACT.

On 1 July 1980, President Jimmy Carter signed into law the Motor Carrier Regulatory Reform and Modernization Act (MCA). The act significantly reduced the control of the Interstate Commerce Commission (ICC) over the trucking industry and truckers. The trucking industry had been regulated by the ICC since Congress passed the Motor Carrier Act of 1935. That act required new truckers to seek a certificate of public convenience and necessity from the ICC. The MCA made it considerably easier for a trucker to obtain these certificates, by shifting the burden of proof needed to receive a certificate from the applicant to the party challenging the issuance of the certificate. It also gave the trucking industry greater freedom to set rates, by creating a zone of reasonableness, meaning that truckers could increase or decrease rates from the 1980 levels by 15 percent without challenge. The act forced the ICC to eliminate many of their restrictions on the kinds of goods that could be carried, on the routes that truckers could use, and on the geographic region they could serve. Passage of the MCA was part of a wave a deregulation beginning in 1978 of numerous areas of transportation including air freight, air passengers, and railroads.

BIBLIOGRAPHY

Barrett, Colin. *Shippers, Truckers, and the Law: How to Live With the New Motor Carrier Act, 1980.* Reston, Va.: Barrett, 1980.

McMullen, B. Starr, ed. *Transportation After Deregulation.* Amsterdam, N.Y.: JAI, 2001.

Shira M. Diner

See also **Trucking Industry.**

MOULTRIE, FORT, BATTLE OF.

Throughout a ten-hour bombardment on 28 June 1776, Fort Moultrie—a palmetto fort on Sullivan's Island in Charleston Harbor in South Carolina commanded by Col. William Moultrie—successfully beat off a British attack under Sir Henry Clinton and Peter Parker. The American loss was slight, while that of the British, both in lives and damage to ships, was large. The victory kept the British out of the South for the next two years.

BIBLIOGRAPHY

Lipscomb, Terry W. *The Carolina Lowcountry, April 1775–June 1776.* Columbia: South Carolina Department of Archives and History, 1991.

Nadelhaft, Jerome J. *The Disorders of War: The Revolution in South Carolina.* Orono, Me.: University of Maine at Orono Press, 1981.

Robert S. Thomas/A. R.

See also **Charleston; Revolution, American: Military History.**

MOUNDS AND MOUND BUILDERS. *See* **Indian Mounds.**

MOUNT HOLYOKE COLLEGE. Located in South Hadley, Massachusetts, Mount Holyoke College is the oldest institution of higher education for women in the United States never to have closed its doors and the first of the "Seven Sister" liberal arts schools. Founded as Mount Holyoke Female Seminary by Mary Lyon in 1837 to produce well-qualified teachers, the institution initially met some opposition from those who subscribed to the prevailing view that women were constitutionally unfit to withstand the mental and physical demands of higher education. Lyon countered by promoting women's education as the means by which women might best fulfill their responsibilities to furnish good citizens to the nation. After marshalling public support for the school, Lyon wanted to guarantee Mount Holyoke's financial stability and was determined not to leave the college dependent on a small base of wealthy donors. By soliciting small donations from a large number of New England women, she made Mount Holyoke the first privately endowed school for women in the United States. A permanent endowment allowed the school to offer quality education to the daughters of the middle class at a cost within their means.

With an enrollment of eighty, Mount Holyoke Female Seminary officially opened on 8 November 1837. It followed a three-year curriculum and embodied major innovations in female education by instituting rigorous academic entrance requirements and a curriculum free of instruction in domestic pursuits. Patterned more after the colleges than the contemporary female seminaries, Mount Holyoke gave generous place to the sciences, including Lyon's specialty of chemistry.

Upon Lyon's death in 1849, the school continued to flourish. In 1861, as Lyon had planned, a four-year course of study was instituted. In 1888, the institution obtained collegiate status and the seminary curriculum began to be phased out. The school formally became Mount Holyoke College in 1893. Mary Emma Woolley, a noted advocate for international women's rights, served as president for thirty-seven years beginning in 1900.

Through the years, no other institution has been as closely associated with women missionaries. The success of Mount Holyoke students in organizing and teaching in mission schools, and in garnering support from women at home, figured importantly in the explosion of American Protestant influence around the world. At the start of the twenty-first century, approximately 2,000 students took classes at the 800-acre campus. Mount Holyoke alumnae include Emily Dickinson, poet; Frances Perkins, the first woman to serve in a presidential cabinet; Virginia Apgar, a physician who developed a score for evaluating newborns; and Wendy Wasserstein, a Pulitzer Prize–winning playwright.

BIBLIOGRAPHY

Cole, Arthur. *A Hundred Years of Mount Holyoke College: The Evolution of an Educational Ideal.* New Haven, Conn.: Yale University Press, 1940.

Porterfield, Amanda. *Mary Lyon and the Mount Holyoke Missionaries.* New York: Oxford University Press, 1997.

Stow, Sarah D. (Locke). *History of Mount Holyoke Seminary, South Hadley, Massachusetts During its First Half Century, 1837–1887.* South Hadley, Mass.: Mount Holyoke, 1887.

Thomas, Louise Porter. *Seminary Militant: An Account of the Missionary Movement at Mount Holyoke Seminary and College.* South Hadley, Mass.: Mount Holyoke College, 1937.

Caryn E. Neumann

See also **Education, Higher: Women's Colleges; Schools, Single-Sex; Seven Sisters Colleges.**

MOUNT HOPE, a hill in the present town of Bristol, RHODE ISLAND, was, in 1676, in the colony of Plymouth. It was the headquarters of the WAMPANOAG sachem Metacom (King Philip), the leading spirit in King Philip's War. On the east side of the hill are his spring and "King Philip's Chair," a rocky ledge from which Metacom watched for enemy ships on the bay. Metacom was slain in a swamp at the west foot of the hill on 12 August 1676. The hill lent its name to Mount Hope Bay, which it overlooks.

BIBLIOGRAPHY

Munro, Wilfred Harold. *The History of Bristol, R.I.* Providence, R.I.: Reid, 1880.

Howard M. Chapin / L. T.

See also **King Philip's War; Narragansett Bay; Plymouth Colony.**

MOUNT RUSHMORE is the world's largest sculpture and foremost mountain carving. Located about twenty-five miles southwest of Rapid City, South Dakota, in the BLACK HILLS National Forest, the memorial commemorates the foundation, preservation, and expansion of the United States and features the faces of four of the nation's most famous presidents, George Washington, Thomas Jefferson, Abraham Lincoln, and Theodore Roosevelt. Each of the sculpted faces is over sixty feet high. Carved out of a granite cliff atop the 5,725-foot-high mountain, the memorial is visible from miles away.

In 1923 the South Dakota state historian Doane Robinson initially proposed a memorial of giant sculptures in the Black Hills as a way to commemorate heroes of the old West, like the explorers Meriwether Lewis and William Clark and the Sioux Indian leader Red Cloud. Robinson understood that, in the era of the beginnings of widespread automobile ownership and the development of a vacation industry in America, such a monument would attract tourists and bring extra revenue to the region. He contacted the sculptor Gutzon Borglum, who was then famous for his work on a Confederate memorial at Stone Mountain in Georgia. Borglum traveled to South Dakota in 1924 and endorsed the project but introduced

Mount Rushmore. Workers are dwarfed by the face of George Washington, c. 1932, partway through the fourteen-year project. LIBRARY OF CONGRESS

a fundamental change in its scope. Rather than a western memorial of regional interest, the fiercely patriotic Borglum envisioned a memorial national in character that would appeal to all Americans. In fact, Borglum suggested the memorial feature carvings of the four presidents. After surveying the Black Hills for a suitable cliff in 1925, Borglum chose Mount Rushmore, and carving began in 1927.

Fourteen years later, in October 1941, work at Mount Rushmore finally came to an end, though less than half that time was actually spent on carving and sculpting the monument. Lack of money for the project was a constant problem, which often shut down operations for whole seasons at a time. The fact that Mount Rushmore was meant as a national memorial did help, however. South Dakota senator Peter Norbeck and Borglum himself often successfully lobbied Congress for funds, even during the Great Depression. Of the nearly $1 million total cost of carving Mount Rushmore, more than $800,000 came from federal sources.

In 1933, President Franklin Roosevelt placed the project under the jurisdiction of the National Park Service, which continued to administer the memorial. "The Shrine to Democracy," as Mount Rushmore National Memorial is often called, is visited by more than 2.6 million sightseers annually, fulfilling both Robinson's dream

of a historical tourist attraction in the Black Hills and Borglum's vision of a lasting monument to America's majesty.

BIBLIOGRAPHY

Price, Willadene. *Gutzon Borglum, Artist and Patriot.* Chicago: Rand, 1961.

Smith, Rex Alan. *The Carving of Mount Rushmore.* New York: Abbeville Press, 1985.

Noah Gelfand

See also **Art: Sculpture; National Park System.**

MOUNT ST. HELENS is a stratovolcanic peak in southwest Washington State. Dormant since 1857, Mount St. Helens erupted on 18 May 1980, after a series of earthquakes below the volcano's peak. It released a mushroom cloud of gases 63,000 feet high and sent a lavalike mixture of glass, gas, and ash down the mountainside at speeds up to a hundred miles per hour, killing sixty people, decimating several native animal populations, and destroying $500 million worth of timber. Economic losses totaled $3 billion. Subsequent minor eruptions occurred on 25 May 1980 and 11 April 1981. In 1982 Mount St. Helens was declared a national volcano monument.

BIBLIOGRAPHY

Caroline D. Harnly, Caroline D., and David A. Tyckoson. *Mount St. Helens: An Annotated Bibliography.* Metuchen, N.J.: Scarecrow Press, 1984.

Carolyn Bronstein / c. w.

See also **Disasters; Volcanoes; Washington, State of;** *and picture (overleaf).*

MOUNT VERNON, George Washington's home, lies on the south bank of the Potomac River, near Alexandria, VIRGINIA. The Washington family acquired Mount Vernon in 1690. The central part of the house was built about 1743 for Lawrence Washington, George's half-brother. Lawrence died in 1752, and the property passed to George a short time later.

In 1759 Washington and his wife, Martha, established household at Mount Vernon, and George lived as a tobacco planter there until the outbreak of war in 1775. After the revolution he returned to his home and completed improvements that he had begun earlier, including additions to buildings, gardens, and grounds. At the end of his presidency in 1797, Washington returned again to Mount Vernon, where he died in 1799. He and Martha Washington, who died in 1802, are interred there in the family vault.

The Mount Vernon Ladies' Association, founded in 1856, assumed responsibility for restoration and maintenance at Mount Vernon. This organization acquired the

Mount St. Helens. After lying dormant for 123 years, this volcanic peak in the Cascade Range in Washington State erupted on 18 May 1980. With Mount Hood in the background, the volcano unleashes some of the millions of tons of earth and ash that rose as high as 65,000 feet in the air.
© CORBIS

property from the last private owner, Col. John Augustine Washington, in 1858. The wood mansion and thirteen subsidiary structures have survived, and several others have been reconstructed. Together they constitute one of the best remaining examples of the eighteenth-century plantations that were the center of a highly developed social and economic life.

BIBLIOGRAPHY

Dalzell, Robert F. *George Washington's Mount Vernon: At Home in Revolutionay America.* New York: Oxford University Press, 1998.

West, Patricia. *Domesticating History: The Political Origins of America's House Museums.* Washington, D.C.: Smithsonian Institution Press, 1999.

Charles C. Wall / s. b.

See also **Gardening; Landscape Architecture; Museums; National Trust for Historic Preservation; Preservation Movement.**

MOUNTAIN CLIMBING, or mountaineering, the practice of ascending to elevated points or peaks, is historically a quest for the challenges of new routes and peaks. Most often a group sport, mountain climbing requires teamwork and skill. Mountain climbing can be divided into three types with varying degrees of difficulty. Trail climbing or hiking is the least difficult type. More

commonly associated with mountaineering are the more difficult practices of rock climbing and ice climbing. Although some rock climbers engage in the more dangerous form of free climbing, most use equipment that may include special shoes, ropes, and steel spikes (pitons) that are driven into the rock to assist the climber. Ice climbing, performed on the highest peaks, uses an ice axe and attachable boot spikes (crampons).

Early attempts to ascend mountain peaks were motivated by scientific, geographic, or spiritual quests, but mountain climbing evolved into a sport by the mid-eighteenth century. By that time, techniques for snow, ice, and rock climbing had developed, and an elite class of professional guides had become established. The Swiss Alps were especially popular with early climbers, but with the successful scaling of the Matterhorn in 1865, climbers began to seek other peaks, turning to the more distant Andes, Caucasus, North American Rockies, African peaks, and finally the Himalayas. In 1852, Mount Everest was determined the world's highest peak, but climbers did not successfully summit Everest until 1953, when the New Zealander Sir Edmund Hillary and the Sherpa Tenzing Norgay reached the top. The first American to ascend Everest was James Whittaker in 1963.

Mountain climbing became popular in the United States after World War II. American interest in wilderness exploration can be traced to the early eighteenth century. By the nineteenth century, new ideologies about nature,

Mount Vernon. This Currier & Ives lithograph shows George Washington (center left) and French General Lafayette (center right) with Washington's family in front of Mount Vernon, the family plantation that was acquired in 1690. Washington inherited the house from his brother and lived there from 1759 until his death in 1799. © CORBIS

promoted especially by educated, upper-class East Coast nature lovers and bird watchers, began to develop. They extolled the virtues of wild areas as places to reflect and rejuvenate. This ideology was born of the intrinsic values and scientific curiosities of such places and a reaction to rapid urbanization and industrialization. Nature lovers celebrated the idea of the "noble savage" much as European Enlightenment thinkers had a century earlier.

During the Progressive Era, a "cult of wilderness" emerged, spearheaded by Theodore Roosevelt, that extolled the virtues of rigorous outdoor sports. The Sierra range was explored in the 1860s and 1870s, especially by the naturalist John Muir. Grand Teton, the highest peak in the Teton Range, was climbed in 1872. In Alaska, Mount Saint Elias was climbed in 1897, and Mount Blackburn and Mount McKinley were ascended in 1912 and 1913, respectively.

Between 1947 and 1970 advancements in technology, skill, and climbing routes made the sport accessible to greater numbers of people. By the end of the twentieth century, novice climbers, relying on equipment, technology, and guides rather than individual abilities, attempted dangerous peaks. The results were dramatic losses of life, such as the deaths of clients and experienced guides on Mount Everest in 1996.

BIBLIOGRAPHY

Krakauer, Jon. *Into Thin Air.* New York: Villard, 1997.

Nash, Roderick. *Wilderness and the American Mind.* 3d ed. New Haven, Conn.: Yale University Press, 1982.

Reuther, David, and John Thorn, eds. *The Armchair Mountaineer.* New York: Scribner's, 1984.

Deirdre Sheets

See also **Sports.**

MOUNTAIN MEADOWS MASSACRE, the worst slaughter of white civilians on the westward trek. In 1857, a wagon train of some thirty families moved through Utah on the way west. Tension was high between Utah's governor Brigham Young, spiritual leader of the Church of Jesus Christ of Latter-day Saints, or Mormons, and the federal government, with the widespread expectation of an invasion by U.S. troops. As the emigrants, numbering as many as 150 people, including dozens of children, rolled west, they clashed with local Mormons and Indians. Mormon leaders incited the Indians to attack the train at Mountain Meadows in September 1857. The emigrants circled their wagons and drove off the first attack; when a second assault also failed, the Mormon elder John D. Lee and others promised the emigrants a safe conduct if they would leave all their goods behind. When the emigrants followed Lee out of the circle of wagons, a mixed force of Indians and Mormons, lying in wait, rose up and slaughtered all save seventeen children believed to be too young to remember. John D. Lee was later tried and executed for the act; he went to his grave claiming he was a scapegoat. Complicity of the Mormon hierarchy has never been conclusively proven.

BIBLIOGRAPHY

Brooks, Juanita. *The Mountain Meadows Massacre*. Rev. ed. Norman: University of Oklahoma Press, 1991.

Smith, Christopher. "Unearthing Mountain Meadows Secrets: Backhoe at a S. Utah Killing Field Rips Open 142-Year-Old Wound." *Salt Lake Tribune* (12 March 2000).

Cecelia Holland

See also **Latter-day Saints, Church of Jesus Christ of; Mormon War.**

MOUNTAIN MEN, as early-nineteenth-century fur trappers were called, first came west to the ROCKY MOUNTAINS, drawn by their search for the pelts of beavers, which they lured to traps by castor bait. Virgin streams producing the prize catches rewarded trailblazing and transformed trappers into explorers of the FAR WEST. French traders, the most experienced nonnative fur gatherers, mingled with Americans, American Indians, and Spaniards at SAINT LOUIS in the first decades of the nineteenth century and made this the great western emporium of the fur trade. Trapping parties and trading company caravans laden with supplies and goods for the mountain trade left from Saint Louis. After a season or two of trapping, the adventurer boasted the sobriquet of "mountain man."

Trappers cultivated trade relationships with the local Indian groups, who controlled the areas and had the power to evict unwanted visitors. The interactions between traders and American Indians changed both groups. Trapper life held an irresistible appeal to a variety of men—to the restless and daring it offered adventure; to the homeless, a home; to the lawless, an asylum. Fur traders of European extraction often married American Indian women. Their children served as a bridge among the various groups, routinely working as translators and intermediaries. The mixed cultural strains produced a polyglot jargon, spiced with metaphor and known to some as "mountain talk." Mountain men adopted some aspects of their Indian trading partners' manner of life, including their approaches to food, shelter, morals, and even some aspects of religion. At the same time the local Indian communities became increasingly accustomed to goods that they could not easily produce for themselves, such as copper kettles, metal spear points, and guns. Jim Bridger, Christopher ("Kit") Carson, Thomas Fitzpatrick, and Bill Williams were famous examples of the fraternity of "mountain men." There were three classes: the hired trapper, paid annual wages by a fur company; the skin trapper, who dealt with one company only; and the free trapper, who trapped and disposed of his furs when and where he pleased.

The summer rendezvous at Green River, Wyoming, or at some other appointed mountain valley became the most interesting and typical institution of fur-trading days. Trappers and Indians gathered there. Fur companies from Missouri brought out their supplies and goods, and barter flourished. With drinking, gambling, racing, and contests of skill, the mountain man had a holiday. His regular meat diet was now augmented with limited supplies of flour, coffee, and similar luxuries from the "states." In a few days of prodigal living, he frequently spent his year's earnings.

With the introduction of the silk hat and the consequent decline in beaver-skin prices—from six or eight dollars apiece to two dollars or less—the the mountain men gradually forsook their traps. Buffalo robes replaced beaver pelts, and the trading post supplanted the rendezvous. With the coming of emigrant homeseekers, government exploring, and military expeditions, the trapper-trader became scout and guide to lead newcomers over the paths he knew. Advancing European-American settlements eliminated the mountain man's economic niche.

BIBLIOGRAPHY

Barbour, Barton H. *Fort Union and the Upper Missouri Fur Trade.* Norman: University of Oklahoma Press, 2001.

Ekbreg, Carl J. *French Roots in the Illinois Country: The Mississippi Frontier in Colonial Illinois.* Urbana: University of Illinois Press, 1998.

Foley, William E., and C. David Rice. *The First Chouteaus, River Barons of Early St. Louis.* Urbana: University of Illinois Press, 1983.

Nestor, William R. *From Mountain Man to Millionaire: The "Bold and Dashing Life" of Robert Campbell.* Columbia: University of Missouri Press, 1999.

Sleeper-Smith, Susan. *Indian Women and French Men: Rethinking Cultural Encounter in the Western Great Lakes.* Amherst: University of Massachusetts Press, 2001.

LeRoy R. Hafen / s. c.

See also **Fur Companies; Fur Trade and Trapping; Indian Intermarriage; Indian Trade and Traders; West, American.**

MOURT'S RELATION, printed in London in 1622, a valuable source of information on the Pilgrims' first months in America, was naively propagandist as it described the "safe arival" of these "English Planters" and their "joyful building of . . . the now well defended Towne of New Plimoth." G. Mourt, signer of the recommendatory preface, is identified as George Morton, who settled in Plymouth in 1623. Most scholars have taken William Bradford and Edward Winslow to be the chief authors of the book.

BIBLIOGRAPHY
Dexter, Henry M., ed. *Mourt's Relation or Journal of the Plantation in Plymouth: With an Introduction and Notes by Henry Martin Dexter.* Boston: J. K. Wiggin, 1865.

Louise B. Dunbar / A. R.

See also **New England; Massachusetts; Plymouth Colony.**

MRI. *See* **Magnetic Resonance Imaging.**

MS. MAGAZINE. A product of the women's movement in the early 1970s, *Ms.* magazine has stood as the single mainstream publication dedicated to voicing feminist issues. Initially tested as a "one-shot" supplement to the December 1971 issue of *New York* magazine, *Ms.* was in part the brainchild of Gloria Steinem, in part the product of a rising feminist publishing industry in the early 1970s, and in part the logical outcome of a decade of activism. The freelance journalist and activist Steinem joined forces with the longtime publishing executive Patricia Carbine, among others, to create a magazine sharing the diverse consciousness of feminist ideology with women across America.

While names such as "Lilith," "Sisters," and "Everywoman" were considered, the publication took its title from the emerging, status-neutral form of address "Ms.," a moniker it hoped to help mainstream. The test issue sold out its 300,000 copies in eight days and galvanized its editorial team to move forward on their own. The premiere, stand-alone issue of *Ms.* in July 1972 celebrated a revitalized image of female superhero, Wonder Woman, on its cover and featured the provocative articles that would become its hallmark and subsequently earn the magazine awards for journalistic excellence. Despite fears that it would be anti-motherhood and anti-men, the founding editors, Letty Cottin Pogrebin, Suzanne Braun Levine, Carbine, and Steinem, encouraged topics ranging from date rape and black feminism to "Welfare Is a Woman's Issue," "How to Write Your Own Marriage Contract," and "Raising Kids without Sexual Roles." *Ms.* was the first mainstream publication to advocate for passage of the Equal Rights Amendment and repeal of laws criminalizing abortion. In 1974, *Ms.* also produced the *Woman Alive!* documentary series with PBS. It later published several books on its own, and over the years enhanced the growing visibility of feminist writers, including Alice Walker, Susan Faludi, Barbara Ehrenreich, and Maxine Hong Kingston.

Money troubles would plague *Ms.* throughout its history. Initial investments included checks for $126.67 from various principals and $1 million from Warner Communications—a third of what the startup needed. Securing advertising was troublesome for a publication that focused on politics and refused to cover fashion and beauty, mainstays of other women's magazines. Advertisers often

Ms. Gloria Steinem stands in front of the White House with a mock-up of her feminist magazine. AP/WIDE WORLD PHOTOS

balked at stories on abortion, violence, and pornography. The magazine also rejected ads it found insulting or demeaning to women. With 26,000 subscribers after the premiere issue and circulation that reached 550,000 in 1989, *Ms.* stretched every dollar, only turning its red ink black in 1974 and again briefly in the 1990s.

By 1978, the struggle to survive led *Ms.* to seek nonprofit status, placing the magazine under the rubric of the newly formed *Ms.* Foundation for Education and Communication until 1987. Strapped for cash again, in 1988 *Ms.* magazine was sold, first to the Australian publishing company Fairfax Ltd. and six months later to a new firm, Matilda Publications, which reinvented *Ms.* as a "general interest magazine for women," combining feminist perspectives on news with articles on personal finance and cover stories on celebrities.

Ms.'s ownership changed again in 1989 and 1996. Steinem returned to help save the magazine, convincing the feminist poet, activist, and author Robin Morgan to take the helm. As editor-in-chief, Morgan inaugurated a new, reader-supported, advertising-free *Ms.* She banished celebrity features and restored *Ms.*'s feminist core, boosting circulation from 75,000 to 200,000 before resigning the top spot to Marcia Ann Gillespie in 1993. In 1998, Steinem and Gillespie created a consortium of feminist investors, Liberty Media for Women, LLC, which purchased *Ms.* for an estimated $3 million. Ongoing financial problems led *Ms.* to change hands again in November 2001, when it transferred ownership to the nonprofit Feminist Majority Foundation. Although *Ms.*'s history has been marked by the occasional gaffe—like the cover that misspelled "feminism" in 1996—the magazine survived the twists and turns of American and feminist politics by steadfastly serving as "the voice of responsible feminism."

BIBLIOGRAPHY

Choo, Kristen. "Milestone for Ms.: Bold and Controversial Magazine Turns 25." *Chicago Tribune* (26 January 1997).

Thom, Mary. *Inside "Ms.": Twenty-five Years of the Magazine and the Feminist Movement.* New York: Henry Holt, 1997.

Debra Michals

See also **Magazines, Women's.**

MUCKRAKERS. Writers whose exposés of corruption in business and government aroused public opinion and helped spur Progressive-Era reforms. Theodore Roosevelt popularized the term in a 14 April 1906 speech, in which he compared them to the Man with the Muckrake in Bunyan's *Pilgrim's Progress,* who remained so intent on raking the filth at his feet that he failed to look up and behold the celestial crown. Likewise, Roosevelt argued, the muckrakers remained so focused on the evils in society they failed to reaffirm the vision of America's promise. The usage stuck, and henceforth the term was applied to all those engaged in uncovering scandal and corruption.

Lincoln Steffens's "Tweed Days in St. Louis," appearing in the October 1902 issue of *McClure's Magazine,* is generally regarded as the first true muckraking article. Noteworthy precedents, however, included Henry Demarest Lloyd's *Wealth Against Commonwealth* (1894), Jacob Riis's *How the Other Half Lives* (1890), and Josiah Flynt's *World of Graft* (1901). The classic pieces of muckraking's golden age included Steffens's series on municipal corruption (collectively titled *Shame of the Cities*), Ida Tarbell's *The History of the Standard Oil Company* (1902), Upton Sinclair's *The Jungle* (1906), David Graham Phillips's *Treason of the Senate* (1906), Ray Stannard Baker's *Following the Color Line* (1908), and renegade financier Thomas Lawson's *Frenzied Finance* (1904). All were initially serialized in popular journals, a fact revealing the close connection between the muckrakers and a new generation of mass periodicals. Established near the turn of the century, journals including *McClure's, Cosmopolitan, Collier's, Everybody's,* and the revamped *Ladies' Home Journal* quickly supplanted the older established literary magazines by featuring popular, attention-grabbing stories. Editors such as S. S. McClure and *Cosmopolitan*'s John Brisben Walker combined their commitment to reform with their drive to reach a new readership and boost circulation, thus providing fertile ground for the muckrakers' talents. The genre these writers developed merged elements of investigative, advocacy, sensationalist, and yellow journalism.

The muckrakers' best work provided hard-hitting, factual revelations of wrongdoing in the nation's most powerful institutions. What distinguished the muckrakers from previous reform-minded writers was their emphasis on concrete detail rather than moral suasion. It was the revelation of fact based on verifiable information and firsthand experience that gave the genre its impact. At its worst, however, muckraking degenerated into sensationalism and yellow journalism, lending credence to Roosevelt's criticism.

The Father of Muckraking. Joseph Lincoln Steffens, widely known as Lincoln, is considered by most to be the first of the muckraking journalists. In 1902 his article "Tweed Days in St. Louis" appeared in the October edition of *McClure's Magazine;* from there, Steffens proceeded to tackle municipal corruption in America's cities. His series of articles on the subject was published as the book *Shame of the Cities.*

Ida Tarbell. A pioneering woman journalist, Tarbell was also one of the earliest practitioners of the muckraker's craft—although she disliked the label. Her 1902 *History of the Standard Oil Company* exposed John D. Rockefeller's illegal monopolistic practices. LIBRARY OF CONGRESS

The muckrakers' influence reached its zenith between 1904 and 1908, when the exposés on patent-medicine fraud, meat processing, insurance swindles, monopolies, political corruption, and racial violence led to criminal indictments and reform legislation, which included the Pure Food and Drug Act, the breakup of Standard Oil, the direct election of senators, investigations into the insurance and finance industries, and the founding of the National Association for the Advancement of Colored People. Their fortunes began to fade with the accession of the conservative William Howard Taft to the presidency in 1909, and by 1911 most of the journals were feeling the pinch of a concerted effort by business and political foes to silence their attacks. Advertiser boycotts forced some magazines to close, while others found their loans recalled and creditors insisting on immediate payment. Still others, including *McClure's* and *Cosmopolitan*, were bought out and transformed into noncontroversial entertainment publications.

BIBLIOGRAPHY

Chalmers, David Mark. *The Social and Political Ideas of the Muckrakers.* New York: Citadel Press, 1964.

Filler, Louis. *Crusaders for American Liberalism.* Yellow Springs, Ohio: Antioch Press, 1950.

Miraldi, Robert, ed. *The Muckrakers: Evangelical Crusaders.* Westport, Conn.: Praeger, 2000.

C. Wyatt Evans

See also **Corruption, Political; *Jungle, The*.**

MUGLER V. KANSAS, 123 U.S. 623 (1887). Kansas had passed an act in 1881 that forbade the manufacture and sale, except for medicinal purposes, of all intoxicating liquors. Convicted under this act, Mugler argued that since he had invested his money in a brewing business incorporated under the authority of the state government, he could not be denied the right to continue the operation of his business. The SUPREME COURT refused to accept this position. Because of its relevance to "the public health, the public morals, and the public safety," the Kansas law met the Court's standard that a regulation passed under a state's POLICE POWER bears a substantial relation to the public welfare it claims to protect.

BIBLIOGRAPHY

Roettinger, Ruth Locke. *The Supreme Court and State Police Power: A Study in Federalism.* Washington, D.C.: Public Affairs Press, 1957.

W. Brooke Graves
Andrew C. Rieser

See also **Epidemics and Public Health; Prohibition.**

MUGWUMP. A Natick Indian word signifying "great chief" and used by the Puritan missionary John Eliot in his Algonquian Bible (1661–1663) to translate the English words "duke" and "centurion." It entered the American popular lexicon in the early nineteenth century as a humorous term for a person in authority. Its most famous application came in 1884, when *New York Sun* editor Charles A. Dana labeled as "little mugwumps" those liberal Republicans who bolted the party to support Democrat Grover Cleveland for president. Their defection contributed to James G. Blaine's defeat, and party leaders considered the mugwumps hypocritical turncoats and fence-sitters. Many dissident Republicans accepted the term proudly as marking their opposition to the SPOILS SYSTEM and party corruption in general. In contemporary usage the term is often synonymous with "genteel reformers," designating upper-class, native-born reformers of the same era. Noted mugwumps include Samuel Clemens, Thomas Wentworth Higginson, and Carl Schurz. Although past historians have tended to view them as elitist, reactionary, ineffective, and idealistic in their efforts to reform American politics, more recent assessments have pointed out their links to Civil War abolitionism and their efforts in pushing for civil service reform and independent voting, seeing the activities of mugwumps as important preludes to the achievements of the Progressive Era.

BIBLIOGRAPHY

Hofstadter, Richard. *The Age of Reform: From Bryan to F.D.R.* New York: Knopf, 1955.

McFarland, Gerald W. *Mugwumps, Morals, and Politics, 1844–1920.* Amherst: University of Massachusetts Press, 1975.

C. Wyatt Evans

MULE. A mule is a cross between a male donkey and a female horse. The male mule is called a jack and the female is a jennet or a jenny. A smaller cross, the hinny, is from a male horse and a female donkey. Both mules and hinnies are nearly always sterile.

In the formative years of the United States, the attributes of mules, horses, and oxen were the subject of much debate. Mules traveled at 2½ miles per hour. Oxen were slower, at 2 m.p.h. The faster speed could save a week or more over that of oxen when going long distances. However, a pair of oxen cost $40 to $160, and mules from $200 up to $400 for a pair. Oxen could graze along the trail, but mules had to be fed grain to supplement the grazing. Grain had to be taken on the wagons; therefore, less paying freight could be hauled. Speed and distance were the main parts of the equation.

Mules could go twenty-four hours without water when they had a light load of under 300 pounds. The standard army mule load was about 150 pounds. A mule was used to pack loads on its back, pull wagons, or be ridden. Mules had more stamina and were more surefooted than horses and were resistant to disease. Oxen could be slaughtered and eaten when meat was low and wild game impossible to find.

Mules. While carrying a load of under 300 pounds, a mule can travel for twenty-four hours without water. Packs of mules can travel at two and one-half miles per hour, faster than a team of oxen. Here a mule carries a full load of corkboard out of a cork forest while his young master walks beside him. © CORBIS

George Washington used his influence to get embargoes removed so mules could be imported from France and Spain. He much preferred mules over horses as work animals. Washington spoke disparagingly of horses when he pronounced, "Horses eat too much, work too little, and die too young." Washington's support of mules and his mule-breeding program was well known. At MOUNT VERNON, Washington's plantation, many individuals came to observe the mules and later went into the mule business.

Mules were important to the settling of MISSOURI. The overgrowth of trees and brush had to be cleared enough to make trails and roads, logs had to be cut for houses, and land for fields needed to be reclaimed. Mules were the perfect work animals for these jobs. By the 1871 census, Missouri was ranked as the state with the most mules, 110,000. Nearly half of Missouri farmers either used mules on their farms or bred them as a business. The mule has been the official state animal of Missouri since 1995.

BIBLIOGRAPHY

Marcy, Randolph B. *The Prairie Traveler: The Best-Selling Handbook for America's Pioneers.* Old Saybrook, Conn.: Applewood Books, Globe Pequot Press, 1994. Originally published in 1859.

Stamm, Mike. *The Mule Alternative: The Saddle Mule in the American West.* Battle Mountain, Nev.: Medicine Wolf Press, 1992.

Peggy Sanders

MULE SKINNER. Mule skinners (or mule drivers) and their complements, the bullwhackers (freighters with OXEN), flourished from the 1850s through the 1870s, when millions of tons of freight were being pulled by mules and oxen across the GREAT PLAINS. In the early 1860s the great firm of Russell, Majors and Waddell operated 6,250 wagons and 75,000 oxen pulling freight west of the Missouri River. Mules and mule skinners were probably as numerous as oxen and bullwhackers at that time. The mule skinner used a long whip with which he could, aided by "language," take the skin off a mule.

BIBLIOGRAPHY

Pelzer, Louis. "Pioneer Stage-Coach Travel." *The Mississippi Valley Historical Review* 23 (1936): 3–26.

Taylor, George Rogers. *The Transportation Revolution.* New York: Rinehart, 1951.

J. Frank Dobie / T. D.

See also **Mule.**

MULLER V. OREGON (1908), 208 U.S. 412. In *Muller* the United States Supreme Court unanimously upheld an Oregon statute limiting the hours that women could labor in factories and laundries to ten a day. In a brief, conclusory opinion, Justice David J. Brewer, normally a foe of laws that interfered with the liberty of employment contracts exalted by *Lochner v. New York* (1905), found the Oregon limits compatible with *Lochner* because "this liberty is not absolute." Brewer justified the limits because of "woman's physical structure" and the "maternal functions" she performs in society. "Healthy mothers are essential to vigorous offspring" and thus to the "strength and vigor of the race."

In paternalistic passages, Brewer emphasized women's "disadvantage in the struggle for subsistence." Because of differences in physical strength and emotional temperament, a woman "is not an equal competitor" in the social-Darwinist struggle. "Woman has always been dependent on man," yet laws must "protect her from the greed as well as the passion of man."

Despite its now discarded presumptions, Muller had a far-reaching influence on subsequent constitutional doctrine. Though its authority was eclipsed for a time by *Adkins v. Children's Hospital* (1923) and *Morehead v. New York ex rel. Tipaldo* (1936), the court vindicated its holding after 1937. It was one of the first Supreme Court opinions to acknowledge the relevance of what are now called "constitutional facts." These are questions of fact that are necessary for an appellate court to know to be able to make a ruling on a constitutional issue. Most importantly, it was a turning point in constitutional law because the court for the first time accepted the persuasive authority of the "Brandeis brief," thereby admitting the relevance of the social sciences into constitutional adjudication.

BIBLIOGRAPHY

Fiss, Owen M. *Troubled Beginnings of the Modern State, 1888–1910.* New York: Macmillan, 1993.

Mason, Alpheus T. "The Case of the Overworked Laundress." In *Quarrels that Have Shaped the Constitution.* Edited by John A. Garraty. New York: Harper and Row, 1964.

William M. Wiecek

See also **Adkins v. Children's Hospital; Lochner v. New York;** and *vol. 9:* **Women in Industry (Brandeis Brief).**

MULLIGAN LETTERS. Between 1864 and 1876, James G. Blaine wrote a series of letters to a Boston businessman, Warren Fisher Jr., that indicated Blaine had used his official power as Speaker of the House of Representatives to promote the fortunes of the Little Rock and Fort Smith Railroad. James Mulligan, an employee of Fisher's, testified before a congressional committee that he had such letters in his possession. After Blaine obtained possession of the letters, he read them on the floor of the House to defend himself, and his friends claimed he was vindicated. When Blaine ran as the Republican candidate for president in 1884, however, the publication of the letters most likely contributed to his narrow defeat.

BIBLIOGRAPHY

McFarland, Gerald. *Mugwumps, Morals, and Politics.* Amherst: University of Massachusetts Press, 1975.

Summers, Mark Wahlgren. *Rum, Romanism, and Rebellion: The Making of a President, 1884.* Chapel Hill: University of North Carolina Press, 2000.

*J. Harley Nichols/*A. G.

See also **Corruption, Political; Political Scandals; Speaker of the House of Representatives.**

MULTICULTURALISM. American multiculturalism long predated the widespread use of the term. A 1965 report by the Canadian Commission on Bilingualism and Biculturalism used "multiculturalism" to represent that nation's diverse peoples, and after 1971 Canada used the term as a policy to preserve its myriad cultures. The word appeared in the American press in the early 1970s, and multiculturalism became commonplace by the 1980s. It was a flashpoint for controversy in the late 1980s and early 1990s, especially in relation to educational curricula and government policies, and remained troublesome in 2001. Multiculturalism has been provocative because it represented intensely held, conflicting perceptions of American society, principles, and standards. Many viewed it as the fulfillment of America's quest for equality of racial and ethnic groups and women. Many others have seen it as the subversion of the nation's unifying values.

The movement for multiculturalism was the culmination of a number of defining events. Challenges to inequality following World War II sparked the civil rights movement of the 1950s and 1960s, initiating the institutionalization of the principle of equality of all Americans, men and women. The 1968 Bilingual Education Act, the related 1974 *Lau v. Nichols* decision, and the 1972 Ethnic Heritage Studies Program Act bolstered the multicultural movement, awakening many groups to seek their cultural roots, proclaim the value of their cultures, and call for the inclusion of group histories and cultures in educational programs. The goals have been to overcome historic invisibility and to nurture group pride, and some have believed schools have the obligation to help preserve such cultures.

But as some spokespersons became more strident in their insistence on such curricula reforms, repudiating the long-held American belief in assimilation, their demands generated equally intense opposition among those who already perceived threats to American core culture and values, especially in the emerging affirmative action policies. Multiculturalism became the focal point of the battles over group rights versus individual rights, ethnic cultures versus the common culture, pluralism versus assimilation, and particularly the diversity content in school curricula.

Placing diversity at the center of the American polity and educating all children about the richly varied components of the nation's heritage were viewed by advocates of multiculturalism as the fulfillment of America's promise of respect, opportunity, and equality. Others perceived a lack of a consistent definition of multiculturalism and felt that culture was being made synonymous with race. In addition, they argued, ethnic cultures were fading in the United States. They also maintained that proponents used curriculum changes for separatist political ends, retarding the education of non-English-speaking children and posing a threat to the common center that bound the nation together.

Some people have explored a middle ground. They accepted the multiplicity of heritages and cultures and have seen pluralism as a part of the core culture and values, but they deemphasized contemporary ethnicity and have viewed Americans as possessing flexible and fluid identities because they lived in multiple "worlds." That approach prompted an emphasis on cosmopolitanism and universalism over the particularism of ethnicity. The conflicting visions of the nation's mission ensured that the controversy did not end with the beginning of the twenty-first century.

BIBLIOGRAPHY

Gordon, Avery F., and Christopher Newfield, eds. *Mapping Multiculturalism*. Minneapolis: University of Minnesota Press, 1996.

Higham, John. *Hanging Together: Unity and Diversity in American Culture*. Edited by Carl J. Guarneri. New Haven, Conn.: Yale University Press, 2001.

King, Desmond. *Making Americans: Immigration, Race, and the Origins of the Diverse Democracy*. Cambridge, Mass.: Harvard University Press, 2000.

Nash, Gary. "Multiculturalism and History: Historical Perspectives and Present Prospects." In *Public Education in a Multicultural Society: Policy, Theory, Critique*. Edited by Robert K. Fullinwinder. Cambridge, UK, and New York: Cambridge University Press, 1996, pp. 183–202.

Elliott R. Barkan

See also **Civil Rights and Liberties; Education, Bilingual; Race Relations.**

MUNICIPAL GOVERNMENT refers to the institution created by states to govern incorporated localities—particularly cities. States grant powers to municipal governments so that they might provide basic services, such as police and fire protection, as well as solve the special problems associated with urban localities, as various as affordable housing, environmental quality, and parking shortages. As with other levels of government, the powers granted to municipalities have increased dramatically over time. However, the expansion of municipal power came only as cities faced new or growing problems, and municipal officials always seemed to lack the authority or means to solve the crises that faced American cities.

Following English political traditions, many cities functioned under special city charters in the colonial era.

Other cities, particularly in New England, retained their town governments, even as they grew quite large. Early municipal governments concerned themselves largely with commercial issues, administering local marketplaces and wharves, and they provided the barest of services to residents, if any at all. While colonial cities often had democratically elected aldermen, colonial governors generally appointed powerful mayors to run municipalities. By the mid-1700s, resident concerns over crime, public drunkenness, and other moral shortcomings did encourage municipal responses to urban disorder, but municipal governments continued to be a minor force in the late colonial era. America remained predominantly rural, and as late as 1750 only fourteen municipal governments existed.

Nineteenth-Century Expansion of Power

After independence, national democratic trends brought more directly elected mayors and other political reforms. While state governments dominated by rural representatives continued to express concern about potential urban evils, city residents gained more say in choosing those who would govern their cities, and those who governed gradually gained more power to do so. Through the early 1800s provision of services continued to expand with the establishment of fire companies, school systems, municipal water supplies, and regular garbage collection. Only problems that posed the gravest of threats to cities received sufficient governmental attention, however. With dense concentrations of wooden structures and water supplies with limited pressure, fires posed a continuous threat to American cities. This threat led to a number of reforms, including regulating against wooden buildings, which New York City had done as early as 1776, and the creation of professional fire-fighting forces, which became common by the 1840s.

With epidemic diseases such as yellow fever and cholera causing periodic crises, municipal governments expanded efforts to control public health. Given the inadequate knowledge of how diseases spread and how to cure them, municipalities focused on prevention, particularly through the improvement of the urban environment. Since streets were the most important urban spaces, municipalities placed new emphasis on street cleaning and paving. Comments concerning the persistence of inadequate and filthy street surfaces, however, suggest the limited nature of public power to improve the urban environment in the mid-1800s. Because epidemic diseases were capable of shutting down cities—the 1849 cholera epidemic in St. Louis, Missouri, killed nearly a tenth of the city's residents—public health at least attracted the attention of municipal governments. Other urban problems, like concentrated poverty and inadequate housing, still gained little governmental attention.

As the national economy alternately boomed and busted through the decades between 1870 and 1910, municipal governments served both as scapegoats for urban problems and as the primary mechanism through which these problems could be solved. Urban populations exploded, particularly in the industrial heartland, and so too did urban problems. With large immigrant populations, particularly from southern and eastern Europe, cities faced new concerns associated with extremely diverse and dynamic populations. Immigrants poured into cramped and unsafe slums, and cities generally failed to meet the housing needs of their growing populations. Most municipal governments took little action to improve housing quality. The American conception of the proper role of municipal government failed to keep pace with the growing need for municipal regulation. At the same time, the concentration of industrial jobs in cities created a host of environmental threats, including polluted air and water, as well as occupational safety concerns. After the 1911 Triangle Shirtwaist factory fire killed 146 workers, New York City and other municipalities rewrote building codes in an effort to prevent further disasters.

This era did witness some successes. Reflecting a new understanding of the importance of parks, playgrounds, and other open spaces, most cities attempted to follow the example of New York City and its remarkable Central Park, begun in 1856. Cities around the nation created large landscaped parks, parkways, and smaller open spaces within extensive park systems. In addition, a new movement to create beautiful cities encouraged the construction of new, substantial civic buildings, and many of the nation's finest courthouses, public libraries, and city halls date from the turn of the century. To meet demands for better services, municipalities gained new means of raising taxes, and despite a series of sharp economic downturns cities proved remarkably successful in borrowing to make major improvements and in repaying those debts in a timely manner. Indeed, the safety of investing in municipal bonds suggests at least a degree of success in municipal governance.

Bossism and Corruption

Municipal government may be best known not for its accomplishments, but for its corruption. By the late 1800s political machines provided a sense of order in many large cities, as elected officials allied themselves with bosses who dispensed favors and reaped the benefits of kickbacks and other corruption. The boss system provided some benefits to otherwise underrepresented groups, perhaps most famously providing municipal jobs to Irish immigrants in Eastern cities. Still, bossism became notorious for the corruption upon which it was built. In addition, as its opponents liked to point out, bossism subverted democracy within cities, as urban elections were often decided through the dispensation of cash, gifts, and alcohol.

Perhaps due in part to perceptions of municipal corruption, as well as revulsion to the increasingly diverse and impoverished urban population, many wealthier communities on the edges of cities chose not to join municipalities through annexation. In deciding to create or keep their own local governments, these suburbs sought to keep out the disorder of the city simply by choosing not to join with it. By the early twentieth century the permanent incorporation of suburban municipalities impeded the growth of central cities and contributed to the developing distance between wealth and poverty in American metropolises. Despite boss control in many American cities and increasing difficulties in expanding city boundaries, however, the creation of park commissions, police and fire commissions, boards of health, and boards of education, spoke to the growing complexity of municipal governance, and to the complexity of cities themselves.

Governmental Response to Urban Decline

In another era of dramatic urban change, from the 1960s through the 1980s, municipal government again attracted considerable attention. In this era, however, rapid urban decline, particularly in older industrial cities, stressed municipal budgets and challenged urban leadership. With increasingly concentrated poverty, rising crime rates, and a series of drug epidemics, municipal governments from Boston to Detroit to Los Angeles found themselves confronting intractable problems. As wealth flowed out of central cities and into suburbs, many large municipalities found their tax bases dwindling. Greater concentrations of African Americans did allow the rapid increase of minority mayors, including Maynard Jackson in Atlanta and Coleman Young in Detroit, both elected in the 1970s. Still, many of America's finest cities, including New York City and Washington, D.C., faced real crises. Congress responded by passing legislation that allowed the federal government to bypass municipalities in offering its own solutions, but federal education, housing, and antipoverty programs proved largely ineffective and often problematic. For example, huge housing projects designed and funded by the Department of Housing and Urban Development (HUD), created in 1965, generally left municipalities with the many problems associated with concentrated poverty. By the 1990s federal funds funneled through HUD helped demolish many of these high-rise projects, clearing the way for mixed-income housing and more open space.

By the 1980s and 1990s, many central-city governments sought revitalization by creating amenities designed to attract middle-class residents and visitors. Often taking on large debts and passing special taxes, municipal governments pumped billions of dollars into stadiums, malls, and their failing school systems in an attempt to stem the movement of people and money into more and more distant suburbs. Improvements in Baltimore's Inner Harbor and Cleveland's Flats, for example, suggested that city governments might tap the great potential that lay in postindustrial landscapes.

Suburban Governance and the Metropolis

While many central cities declined in the late twentieth century, suburban municipalities around the nation found themselves challenged by the problems of success: managing growth, providing adequate transportation infrastructure, and building schools for burgeoning populations. As many suburban communities began to look more and more like cities, their governments sought expanded powers to solve existing or anticipated problems. In increasingly complex metropolitan regions, some with more than one hundred different municipal governments, regional planning proved challenging, if not impossible. With neighboring municipalities competing for jobs and development, local governments made promises of tax abatements and infrastructure improvements, all to the benefit of employers but often to the detriment of residents. By the end of the twentieth century, fragmented metropolitan governance ensured the persistence of transportation, housing, and environmental problems in America's urban regions.

BIBLIOGRAPHY

Curry, Leonard P. *The Corporate City: The American City as a Political Entity, 1800–1850.* Westport, Conn.: Greenwood Press, 1997.

Goldfield, David R., and Blaine A. Brownell. *Urban America: A History.* Boston: Houghton Mifflin, 1990.

Griffith, Ernest S., and Charles R. Adrian. *A History of American City Government: The Formation of Traditions, 1775–1870.* Washington, D.C.: University Press of America, 1983.

Monkkonen, Eric H. *America Becomes Urban: The Development of U.S. Cities and Towns, 1780–1980.* Berkeley: University of California Press, 1988.

Teaford, Jon C. *The Unheralded Triumph: City Government in America, 1870–1900.* Baltimore: Johns Hopkins University Press, 1984.

———. *Post-Suburbia: Government and Politics in the Edge Cities.* Baltimore: Johns Hopkins University Press, 1997.

David Stradling

See also **Charters, Municipal; City Councils; City Manager Plan; Metropolitan Government; Municipal Reform; Town Government.**

MUNICIPAL OWNERSHIP refers to city government's control and operation of property, services, and systems. In the late 1800s and early 1900s the term took on special meaning, however, as reformers, eager for better and more affordable services, encouraged the expansion of municipal ownership of key urban systems, including water, electricity, and mass transportation. At the same time, demands for more and better open spaces forced cities to control more land within their boundaries and to provide better recreational outlets for their residents.

Private Enterprise and Municipal Acquiescence

In early American history, cities often owned and operated key economic sites, particularly marketplaces and wharves, and, of course, municipalities have always controlled streets and public squares. Still, in the first half of the 1800s municipalities rarely owned a significant portion of the land within their boundaries. Most cities had modest parks, such as Philadelphia's Rittenhouse and Washington Squares, but they made little effort to provide sufficient open space for ever-growing populations. With the notable exception of Charleston, South Carolina, most cities grew with little attention to municipal control of space. The encouragement of growth being paramount, municipal economic strategies included laying out regular streets, usually in a grid pattern, and allowing the market to determine the best use of urban land. As a result, many booming American cities became densely settled, with industrial, commercial, and residential space mingled in and around busy urban cores. In the 1830s cramped urbanites took to private developments to seek refuge, including expansive, landscaped urban cemeteries (ironically called rural cemeteries), usually created just at the outskirts of the city, and to private parks, most famously New York City's Gramercy Park, developed beginning in 1833.

Beyond the issue of public open space, the failure to provide basic utilities haunted many cities, particularly as suspect water supplies endangered public health and safety, with both epidemic diseases and uncontrollable fires threatening urban residents. The history of the Manhattan Company, organized by Aaron Burr in 1798, best illustrates the problems associated with the reliance on private enterprise for the provision of basic services. Ostensibly created to supply potable water to New York City, then reliant on a polluted pond called the Collect, the Manhattan Company never gave this duty sufficient attention, concentrating instead on creating a successful bank, later known as Chase Manhattan. Meanwhile, the booming New York population remained dependent on its old, suspect source of water, and in 1832 a cholera epidemic killed more than 3,500 New Yorkers, revealing the dire consequences of municipal neglect of the water supply. The following year, a state bill allowed New York to develop a city-owned system using a Westchester County source, and by 1842 an aqueduct brought fresh Croton waters to a thirsty city. By the turn of the century, municipally owned water systems had become the norm rather than the exception around the nation; forty-one of the largest fifty municipalities owned their systems in 1897.

Emphasis on private enterprise in the mid-1800s led to the development of significant inefficiencies, including the duplication of facilities and awkward placement of transportation hubs. It was common practice, for example, for each railroad line to build its own station or terminal. This made for very awkward transfers for passengers coming into town on one line and going out on another. Perhaps more important to city residents, the growth of competing lines often brought excessive interference in streets, as trolley lines and railroad tracks were laid in an effort to attract business. This market approach to transportation did leave many cities with very extensive streetcar systems, and track mileage in American cities far exceeded that of comparatively sized European cities.

Seeking greater profits, transportation companies were quick to innovate as well, and American streetcar systems converted to cleaner, faster electricity much more quickly than European systems. Still, as trolleys clogged streets and companies were afforded monopoly rights to certain lines, by the turn of the century reformers came to suspect that the city itself could organize a more efficient system.

The Progressive Era, Monopoly, and Reform
With the rise of big business in the late 1800s came a growing concern over the power of monopolies. As federal trustbusters concerned themselves with huge industrial corporations, municipalities turned their attention to local monopolies, particularly utilities. Political machines found large municipal contracts for services to be valuable in their efforts to build allies and profits through kickbacks. But, increasingly, reformers pointed to service contracts as a source of corruption and as evidence of municipal inefficiency. Municipal ownership of key services became a hallmark of Progressive Era reform in the effort to both rationalize city administration and diminish corruption.

During his administration from 1901 to 1909, reform mayor Tom Johnson launched a multifront battle against Cleveland's political machine, including a broad effort to increase municipal ownership. By the end of his term, Johnson had brought garbage collection, street cleaning, and major utilities under municipal control. In areas where municipal ownership was not complete, Johnson made better contracts with corporations, including those who supplied natural gas and operated streetcars. After 1903, Jersey City's mayor Mark Fagan followed Johnson's example, advocating municipal ownership of utilities and passing strict regulation of other key services, particularly in limiting streetcar fares.

Municipalities also increased efforts to provide open space, especially through the provision of parks and the creation of parkways that laced the city. Although this effort dated back to the mid-1800s and had already seen great successes, including New York's Central Park and the design and creation of Chicago's extensive park system, the Progressive Era witnessed greater emphasis on access, particularly for poor residents. Thus, cities created more "pocket" parks and playgrounds in the densest neighborhoods, not just the large landscaped parks that had become so popular with the wealthier classes.

Despite calls for regulation of streetcars, municipal ownership in transportation remained limited. By 1919 Seattle had fully municipalized its trolleys, but most cities fell far short of this goal. The consequences of this failure became evident slowly as streetcar systems gradually went out of business. Some failed due to strict limitations on fares, while many others met with early demise as General Motors and Firestone Tire Company purchased established lines, dismantled them, and replaced them with bus lines. Although the buses did promise some advantages, including flexibility of routes and a less obstructive presence in city streets, in the end the loss of thousands of miles of trolley lines proved devastating to urban transportation systems. In the postwar era, a greater emphasis on automobiles, the ultimate in private transportation, led to persistent, seemingly permanent traffic problems, particularly in the many cities with no municipally controlled transportation infrastructure offering an alternative to auto-clogged streets.

By the end of the Progressive reform decades, municipal ownership of some basic services was widely accepted as both proper and efficient. Municipal governments assumed prominent roles in the provision of fresh water, and in most large cities the government provided garbage collection services, if not through direct ownership then through citywide contracts with private companies. But for other services, particularly utilities, private ownership remained widespread. Although some cities provided their residents with gas and electricity, most urban residents relied on private companies for these services.

City Ownership and Urban Recovery
After World War II, city governments found themselves operating in increasingly dispersed and fragmented metropolises. In a partial attempt to keep the city attractive to middle-class commuters, more and more cities took it upon themselves to build and operate city parking lots and garages. Cities also expanded ownership or involvement in other urban amenities once controlled by private interests, including the development of arts centers, stadiums, and convention centers. Thus, particularly in central business districts, municipalities continued to expand their ownership and control of space and services. In one major exception, however, transportation systems, long since requiring extramunicipal expansion, took on regional approaches and moved beyond municipal control. Many private bus systems experienced financial hardships, particularly in the poor economy of the 1970s, and governmental transit authorities gained in popularity. For rail systems, where capital investments were much steeper, regional transit authorities became nearly requisite; the successes of the Port Authority of New York and New Jersey and of San Francisco's Bay Area Rapid Transit reveal the importance of providing regional transportation solutions.

Even as cities increased ownership to court middle-class residents and visitors, they also increased involvement in the lives of poor residents, particularly through the development of municipally owned and operated housing. Most large cities have faced perpetual shortages of affordable housing, and after World War II municipalities, with the aid of the federal government, increasingly sought to provide housing for low-income residents. Generally operated through housing authorities, these projects have been controversial and many have failed by any measure. Indeed, the simple negative connotation of the word "projects" suggests the failure of municipal involvement in housing. While many politicians have pointed to this obvious disappointment as indicative of a broader failure of interventionist government, the much more popular municipal ownership of urban amenities, such as parks and stadiums, suggests a more complicated rationale for and judgment of municipal ownership.

BIBLIOGRAPHY

Judd, Dennis R., and Todd Swanstrom. *City Politics: Private Power and Public Policy.* New York: HarperCollins College Publishers, 1994.

Melosi, Martin V. *The Sanitary City: Urban Infrastructure in America from Colonial Times to the Present.* Baltimore: Johns Hopkins University Press, 2000.

Schuyler, David. *The New Urban Landscape: The Redefinition of City Form in Nineteenth-Century America.* Baltimore: Johns Hopkins University Press, 1986.

Teaford, Jon C. *The Unheralded Triumph: City Government in America, 1870–1900.* Baltimore: Johns Hopkins University Press, 1984.

David Stradling

See also **Housing; Monopoly.**

MUNICIPAL REFORM refers to changes in city governments made to encourage greater efficiency, honesty, and responsiveness. Although municipal governments have been in flux since their creation, the greatest era of municipal reform came in the late 1800s and early 1900s. In this era, many city residents, particularly middle-class businessmen, organized against the corruption and inefficiency that they thought plagued their cities. This movement was particularly strong in cities controlled by political machines, the undemocratic and corrupt arrangements through which bosses could profit by controlling city governments.

In 1894 urban professionals interested in improving municipal governance formed the National Municipal League, designed to promote the creation of more efficient city administrations. The Municipal League and other supporters of good government, derisively called "goo-goos" by those who found them patrician or naive, encouraged a national dialogue on city governance, supported appropriate reforms, and encouraged the development of better governmental systems.

In many cities municipal reformers made significant changes. Reform mayors in several cities provided good alternatives to the corrupt machines, including Hazen Pingree in Detroit, who served from 1890 to 1897, and Tom Johnson in Cleveland, who served from 1901 to 1909. Reformers sought improvements in city services, particularly through the reform of contracts or through the development of city-owned services. Pingree, for example, led successful fights to reform the city's relationship with the Detroit City Railway Company and the Detroit Gas Company. These reforms, and others like them around the nation, both improved services and decreased costs to residents.

Reformers also struggled for permanent structural changes in city government. In an attempt to impede machine control of city council, reformers devised a number of changes. Some cities adopted at-large voting for council members, decreasing the possibility that a machine controlling some city wards could control the entire council. This reform may have hindered the revival of machines in some cities, but it certainly impeded the growth of minority representation in many others, as African Americans had difficulty electing black representatives in citywide elections. Most cities adopted extensive civil service requirements for municipal jobs, with some positions requiring specific education or experience and others requiring acceptable scores on qualifying exams. These changes diminished the ability of bosses to distribute government jobs to cronies, while simultaneously encouraging the development of a more professional bureaucracy.

Business leaders pushed for even more dramatic reforms in some cities, most famously in Galveston, Texas, which struggled to recover from a hurricane in 1900. In the wake of the storm, the city developed a five-member commission that held legislative and administrative powers, all in an effort to improve city responsiveness. Other cities, finding government unnecessarily politicized, adopted a city manager system, in which a nonelected official took responsibility for day-to-day operations of city departments.

While the heyday of municipal reform passed in the 1920s, reformism never ended. Beginning in the 1960s, for example, African Americans lobbied for changes in electoral rules that would lead to better representation on city councils. Other municipalities have worked to recreate strong mayor positions with the power to take quick action to improve the city's performance vis-à-vis growing suburbs.

BIBLIOGRAPHY

Fox, Kenneth. *Better City Government: Innovation in American Urban Politics, 1850–1937.* Philadelphia: Temple University Press, 1977.

Schiesl, Martin J. *The Politics of Efficiency: Municipal Administration and Reform in America: 1880–1920.* Berkeley: University of California Press, 1977.

David Stradling

See also **Municipal Government.**

MUNITIONS. Derived from a Latin word meaning "fortification," "munitions," through long usage, has come to mean, in a strict sense, weapons and ammunition, although broadly it embraces all war materials. "Ammunition" has the same derivation, but it has come to apply strictly to propellants, projectiles, and explosives. Neutrality legislation and embargoes, along with definitions of contraband of war, invest the broader term "munitions" with legal significance. But in legal language it almost never stands alone. In treaties, legislative acts, and proclamations it usually forms part of a redundancy as "arms and munitions of war" or gives way to the synonymous triplet "arms, ammunition, or implements of war."

In March 1912 the attorney general issued a "practical working definition" of "arms or munitions of war" for the use of border officials in enforcing an embargo on such items to Mexico. His list included

> weapons of every species used for the destruction of life, and projectiles, cartridges, ammunition of all sorts, and other supplies used or useful in connection therewith, including parts used for the repair or manufacture of such arms, and raw material employed in the manufacture of such ammunition; also dynamite, nitroglycerin, or other explosive substances; also gun mountings, limber boxes, limbers, and military wagons; field forges and their component parts, comprising equipment of a distinctively military character; articles of camp equipment and their distinctive component parts; and implements manufactured exclusively for the manufacture of implements of war, or for the manufacture or repair of arms or war material.

President Franklin D. Roosevelt's list of items to be considered as arms, ammunition, and implements of war prohibited for export to belligerents under the Neutrality Act of 1935 included firearms, MACHINE GUNS, ARTILLERY, bombs, torpedoes, mines, tanks, war vessels of all types, aircraft, aircraft engines and certain parts, and poison gas.

During the American Revolution the colonial militia and Continental forces depended largely on British and European models of muskets and artillery, although some American innovations were already apparent. Perhaps the most storied of these was the RIFLE, especially the Pennsylvania or Kentucky rifles. Made practical by the use of a greased patch that would permit muzzle loading with a tightly fitting ball down the grooved bore, these rifles, in the hands of those who had them, possessed a range and accuracy superior to smooth-bore muskets. The principal artillery pieces of the period were cast-iron, bronze, and brass cannon, taking shot of four, nine, twelve, or thirty-two pounds—and thus known as four-pounders, nine-pounders, and so on—and siege mortars.

The first major improvements in small arms after the Revolution and the WAR OF 1812 were in breech-loaders and repeaters. Although the first breech-loading rifle, the Hall, made its appearance in 1819 and was adjusted to percussion ammunition in 1833, the muzzle-loading musket remained the standard infantry arm in the U.S. Army until the end of the MEXICAN-AMERICAN WAR. In fact, muzzle loaders remained the Army's chief weapon during the opening phase of the Civil War.

The quality and quantity of the Union infantry's and cavalry's repeating rifles and carbines gave it one of the greatest advantages of the CIVIL WAR, although these were slow in winning acceptance. At first, those armed with Springfield rifles converted them to breechloaders, which were still single-shot. But the spectacular success of Colt revolvers (pistols) in the Mexican-American War made nothing seem more reasonable than the development of a repeating rifle that operated on the same principle—the use of a rotating cylinder. Colt introduced the first repeating rifle in 1858. The missing link was the metallic cartridge, just being developed, which was much safer than the paper cartridges that sometimes accidentally ignited in the cylinder, causing severe burns on the hands or face. The Sharps repeating rifle tested well in 1860, but it still used paper cartridges. The fifteen-shot Henry and the seven-shot Spencer—"the seven-forked lightning"—proved to be the best of the newer models and had a great impact on the last year of the war.

Even after the demonstrated success of repeating rifles in the Civil War, U.S. soldiers still carried single-shot Springfields twenty-five years later. The Winchester model of 1873 became famous throughout the West, and everyone except the army used it. The army tested but did not accept other models by Remington and by the Springfield Armory. Government policies so discouraged the Winchester Company that it did not even enter the competition in 1890, when the army finally accepted a repeating rifle, the Danish-designed Krag-Jörgensen magazine rifle, which became the standard shoulder weapon of U.S. forces in the SPANISH-AMERICAN WAR.

The all-time favorite U.S. rifle among marksmen was the .30-caliber Springfield Model 1903, but it found only slight use in WORLD WAR I, when the U.S. Army mainly used an adaptation of the British Enfield in the interest of making maximum use of industrial capacity. During WORLD WAR II and the KOREAN WAR, the eight-shot Garand, or M-1, a semiautomatic rifle that was not as accurate as the 1903 but fired more rapidly and with less "kick," was the standard rifle. In the VIETNAM WAR the army favored the M-16, a lighter rifle that used .22-caliber ammunition. Ironically, the United States had adopted the M-14 rifle, which took the standardized NATO 7.62 mm (.30-caliber) cartridge, and then proceeded to go into mass production of the M-16, which used a different-sized cartridge.

Probably the most significant change in artillery during the period immediately preceding the Civil War was the adoption in 1857 of the "Napoleon" gun, a smooth-bore bronze cannon that had proved itself in the Crimean War. Introduced by Napoleon III in an effort to simplify his field artillery system with a single general-purpose weapon that could perform the functions of howitzers as well as guns, this twelve-pounder was efficient enough and maneuverable enough to reduce the need for other calibers. Its ammunition included solid shot, cannister, grape, explosive shell, spherical case, and carcass (incendiary).

Artillery improvements during the Civil War mostly moved in the direction of greater size and strength and in the introduction of rifled cannon on a large scale. A process devised by Maj. Thomas J. Rodman for casting guns on a hollow core and cooling from the inside added considerable strength to the Dahlgren gun. Robert P. Parrott found that it was possible to add great strength to the breech of a gun—and so to its power and range—by encasing it with coiled wrought-iron hoops mounted red hot and then shrunk to a tight fit by cooling. Some of these guns were of tremendous size and strength. The "Swamp Angel," which Parrott built, hurled two-hundred-pound shells more than four miles into Charleston, South Carolina. With one 4.2-inch (30-pound) gun, Parrott fired 4,605 rounds before the tube burst. At that time the greatest limitation on artillery was the lack of a good recoil mechanism.

Inventors overcame that deficiency before World War I, the war of artillery par excellence. By far the best recoil system and "recuperators" were those on the French seventy-five-millimeter gun the Allied forces used as their main field artillery weapon. This gun fired a sixteen-pound shell over a range of three miles at thirty rounds per minute. Combatants mounted many heavy guns on railroad cars for long-range bombardment. The American Expeditionary Force, while relying on the French for most of its artillery, did bring in a number of U.S. fourteen-inch naval guns for use in land warfare.

The other weapon that dominated the battlefield in World War I and remained prominent until after World War II was the machine gun, which had its beginning in the multibarreled Gatling gun of the Civil War. Hiram S. Maxim, an American inventor, developed the first practical automatic machine gun. John M. Browning developed his recoil-operated machine gun in 1900, and in 1917 the U.S. Army adopted this "best of all machine guns"—a .30-caliber, recoil-operated, belt-fed, watercooled, heavy weapon fired from a tripod mount. A version of this gun with an air-cooling jacket served as a light machine gun, but the army favored the Browning automatic rifle, introduced near the end of World War I and widely used in World War II. Soldiers usually used a bipod to fire the Browning rifle, a gas-operated, air-cooled, magazine-fed, shoulder weapon, with a cyclic rate of 550 rounds a minute. Turned down by the U.S. Army just before the outbreak of World War I, the Lewis light machine gun, fed from a revolving drum, came into widespread use in the British Army early in that war. Airplanes used it widely, and the Marine Corps adopted it, but the U.S. Army never adopted it for general ground use.

The tank, the airplane, and poison gas marked the other major developments in munitions during World War I. Both the tank and the plane were the results of American inventions, but the United States was slow to adopt both.

World War II relied largely on improved versions of World War I weapons. The numbers and effectiveness of tanks and airplanes—including especially the long-range heavy bombers—characterized the military operations of that war. Jet fighter planes had come into use by the time of the Korean War, and helicopters became a favorite for supply and medical evacuation. In Vietnam the jet bomber, the B-52, having a range of more than 12,000 miles and carrying a weapons load of 75,000 pounds, was the chief instrument of heavy aerial bombing.

Naval vessels have gone through periods of swift change. Steam power came into use during the Mexican and Civil wars, and the Civil War saw the introduction of the ironclad. The "Great White Fleet" of U.S. armored cruisers and battleships impressed the world in the round-the-world cruise of the battle fleet in 1907–1909. The 1906 British battleship *Dreadnought*, carrying ten twelve-inch guns in center-line turrets and having a speed of twenty-one knots, established a new standard for battleships. This same period saw the conversion from coal to oil and the introduction of the steam turbine for the propulsion of vessels.

The widespread use of the submarine provided the greatest innovation of World War I in naval warfare , and in World War II became a major weapon. Development has been continual and spectacular since the advent of nuclear propulsion gave submarines practically unlimited range. By the 1970s about 60 percent of the U.S. attack submarine fleet of more than ninety vessels relied on nuclear power.

After World War I the aircraft carrier began to come into prominence. During World War II battleships were used more for providing support for landing operations than for direct ship-to-ship combat. By the end of the war, the battleship had given way almost completely to the aircraft carrier. In the post–World War II period nuclear power came into use in the 76,000-ton supercarrier *Enterprise*, and in 1973 Congress authorized its use in another supercarrier that would be the world's first billion-dollar weapon system.

The most spectacular development of all in munitions was the intercontinental ballistic missile with its nuclear warhead. The atomic bomb introduced near the close of World War II had a rating of twenty kilotons; that is, its explosive force equaled that of twenty thousand tons of TNT. In 1961 the Soviet Union deployed the SS-7 Saddler missile, said to have a warhead with a yield of five megatons, the equivalent of 5 million tons of TNT. The U.S. Titan, deployed a year later, was of equal or greater magnitude, but in 1965 the Soviets claimed their SS-9 Scarp had a warhead of twenty to twenty-five megatons. The race was on.

Manufacture

A major problem of public policy has always been the determination of what kind of industry should provide munitions of war and what measures should be instituted for encouragement, on the one hand, and control, on the other. The usual assumption in the United States has been that the munitions industry should combine public and private ownership—that government armories, arsenals, and shipyards should set standards of quality, provide experience for accurate pricing, and fill essential needs for armaments for peacetime military forces but that private contractors should provide most of the capacity and flexibility needed for war mobilization.

The vast majority of the weapons that American colonists used in the colonial wars came from England. Several colonial foundries cast cannons, and colonial gunpowder mills supplied some powder. These activities increased during the revolution, but most munitions came from French and other European sources and from the raids of privateers against British ships.

After the revolution, American leaders were anxious to free the country of dependence on Europe for the means of defense. Two men of genius, Alexander Hamilton and Eli Whitney led the way in setting the course for the national arms policy of the United States. In his report of 1783 on a military peace establishment, Hamilton urged the founding of "public manufactories of arms, powder, etc." In his celebrated report on manufactures eight years later, he once again stressed the importance of the development of domestic industries for national security. In 1794 Congress authorized the construction of some national armories, and four years later it authorized contracting for the private manufacture of arms. Congress chose Springfield, Massachusetts, as the site for the first national armory, and George Washington himself chose the site for the second: Harpers Ferry, Virginia, where the manufacture of muskets began in 1797.

Whitney's great contribution—a contribution indeed to the whole of American industry—was to pursue the manufacture of muskets with interchangeable parts. At his arms plant in New Haven, Connecticut, he sought to substitute machinery for much of the skill of individual gunsmiths when he set to work on his first government contract in 1798, establishing a principle that later became one of the key ideas underlying the system of mass production.

One of the most important steps in the development of a domestic arms industry in the United States was the enactment, in 1808, of a bill that provided for the appropriation of an annual sum of $200,000 "for the purpose of providing arms and military equipment for the whole body of the militia of the United States," either by purchase or by manufacture. Nineteen firms signed contracts to produce 85,200 muskets in five years. None of the guns were delivered satisfactorily on schedule, but the effort set a pattern for encouraging private arms manufacture over the next forty years. Six private armories enjoyed contract renewals until the late 1840s: Whitney; Lemuel Pomeroy of Pittsfield, Massachusetts; and Asa Waters of Sutton, Massachusetts, all of whom specialized in muskets. Contracts also went to Henry Deringer of Philadelphia, who made small arms; Simeon North of Middletown, Connnecticut, who specialized in pistols; and Nathan Starr, also of Middletown, who made swords.

The War of 1812 also helped place the production of artillery on a more secure basis. The West Point Foundry began to make cannon in 1816 under the direction of Gouverneur Kemble and quickly became the leading supplier of heavy ordnance. Government assurances of continued support convinced the entrepreneurs behind this and several other projects to establish and maintain foundries. While depending on private manufacturers for guns, the government itself went into the business of constructing carriages, limbers, and caissons at arsenals in Washington, D.C.; Pittsburgh, Pennsylvania; and Watervliet, New York.

The biggest munitions contractor of the Civil War was Parrott (West Point Arms and Cannon Foundry), to which Congress awarded 2,332 contracts with a value of $4,733,059. Close behind was Samuel Colt's Patent Fire Arms Company at Hartford, Connecticut, which held 267 contracts for a total value of $4,687,031. No fewer than fifteen companies—including such names as J. T. Ames, Herman Baker and Company, Alfred Jenks and Son, Naylor and Company, E. Remington and Sons, Sharpe's Rifle Manufacturing Company, Starr Arms Company, and Spencer Arms Company—had contracts amounting to at least $1 million each. The old firm of Eli Whitney of Whitneyville remained in the picture, but only to the extent of $353,647. Private industry supplied all the artillery (although the federal arsenals manufactured carriages and caissons), all the gunpowder, and a large part of the small arms that the government needed. The Springfield Armory turned out 802,000 rifled muskets, some of which used parts manufactured by private industry. Private arms makers produced 670,600 of these Springfield weapons. Other purchases, from domestic industry and from abroad, included nearly 1,225,000 muskets and rifles, more than 400,000 carbines, and 372,800 revolvers.

With the advent of World War I, American leaders looked for every possible facility, government or private, that they could put to use. Not only did the government expand its arsenals and factories, but it stimulated the construction of vast new government-owned or government-financed plants. Probably the most ambitious, disappointing, dramatic, and controversial production story of the war was that of aircraft. And the brightest spot in that story was the development and production of the Liberty engine. Packard, Ford, General Motors (Buick and Cadillac), Nordyke and Marman, Willys-Overland, Olds, and Trego Motors shared in this mass-production effort, which was ensnared in all of the difficulties of trying to start an aircraft industry almost from scratch. In addition to the problems of finding aeronautical engineers, building factories, developing designs, and organizing production, planners had to overcome serious shortages of materials. They had to develop long-staple cotton cloth, used for covering the airplanes, to replace linen; create a new dope for applying to the cloth for weatherproofing; cultivate castor beans to supply the necessary lubricants until a satisfactory mineral oil could be developed; and increase the supplies of spruce, the principal wood used in airframes.

The Liberty engine's design incorporated all the best features of known engines in a way suited to mass production. Less than six weeks after engineers began drawing plans in May 1917, the government received the first working model of an eight-cylinder Liberty engine, and within another six weeks a twelve-cylinder model had completed its fifty-hour test. By August 1917 the Aircraft Production Board had placed contracts with Ford for 10,000 of the eight-cylinder engines, and with Packard for 22,500 of the twelve-cylinder. Total orders surpassed 64,000, although actual production to the date of the armistice amounted only to 13,500, of which 4,400 reached the American Expeditionary Forces overseas and 1,000 reached the Allies.

Industrial mobilization and production of munitions during World War II generally followed the pattern of World War I, but on a vastly larger scale. The biggest and most complex single project of the war undoubtedly was the making of the atomic bomb. This was a $2.2 billion undertaking under the direction of the Manhattan Project of the Corps of Engineers. It involved the coordinated efforts of scientists, engineers, and laborers; of universities; and of industrial corporations. Secretary of War Henry L. Stimson called it "the greatest achievement of the combined efforts of science, industry, and the military in all history."

But production of war materials on a great scale has always brought questions about profiteering, corrupt bargains, the selling of influence, and the influence of special interests on national policy in a way that might be contrary to the national interest. Such serious charges have arisen in every war, and the seriousness tends to be proportional to the magnitude and duration of the war, although peacetime arms production may be equally subject to such practices or suspicions.

One of the most dramatic appeals against the munitions makers as "merchants of death" came in 1935–1936 with the hearings of the Senate's Special Committee Investigating the Munitions Industry, under the chairmanship of Senator Gerald P. Nye of North Dakota. Although the committee failed in its aim to establish that munitions makers were a major cause of war, it probably fanned the flames of isolationist sentiment then rising in the country. This sentiment produced the arms embargo provisions in the neutrality acts of 1935, 1936, and 1937. Secretary of State Cordell Hull later wrote in his *Memoirs*: "It is doubtful that any Congressional committee has ever had a more unfortunate effect on our foreign relations, unless it be the Senate Foreign Relations Committee considering the Treaty of Versailles submitted by President Wilson." Others would minimize its influence on legislation.

In the ever-growing complexities of munitions manufacture since World War II, nagging questions remain about the extent to which companies dependent on government contracts for their very existence influence national security policy, urging the government to retain, adopt, or emphasize certain weapon systems—whether aircraft, naval vessels, or missiles—in which they have a direct financial interest. President Dwight D. Eisenhower himself brought this question into focus when, in his farewell speech, he warned,

> In the councils of Government, we must guard against the acquisition of unwarranted influence, whether sought or unsought, by the military-industrial complex. The potential for the destructive use of misplaced power exists and will persist. . . . Only an alert and knowledgeable citizenry can compel the proper meshing of the huge industrial and military machinery of defense with our peaceful methods and goals, so that security and liberty may prosper together.

BIBLIOGRAPHY

Armstrong, David A. *Bullets and Bureaucrats: The Machine Gun and the United States Army, 1861–1916*. Westport, Conn.: Greenwood Press, 1982.

Bellesiles, Michael A. *Arming America: The Origins of a National Gun Culture*. New York: Knopf, 2000.

Bush, Vannevar. *Modern Arms and Free Men*. Westport, Conn.: Greenwood Press, 1985.

Craven, Wesley F., and James L. Cate, eds. *The Army Air Forces in World War II*. Vol. 6: *Men and Planes*. Washington, D.C.: Office of Air Force History, 1983.

Dillin, John G. W., and Kendrick Scofield. *The Kentucky Rifle*. 5th ed. York, Pa.: G. Shumway, 1967.

Green, Constance. *Eli Whitney and the Birth of American Technology*. Boston: Little, Brown, 1956.

Hicks, James E. *U.S. Military Firearms, 1776–1956*. La Canada, Calif.: J. E. Hicks, 1962.

Hogg, Ian V., ed. *The American Arsenal*. Mechanicsburg, Pa.: Stackpole Books, 2001.

Hooks, Gregory Michael. *Forging the Military-Industrial Complex: World War II's Battle of the Potomac*. Urbana: University of Illinois Press, 1991.

Johnson, Melvin M., Jr., and Charles T. Haven. *Ammunition: Its History, Development, and Use, 1600 to 1943*. New York: W. Morrow, 1943.

Williamson, Harold Francis. *Winchester: The Gun That Won the West*. Washington, D.C.: Combat Forces Press, 1952.

Wiltz, John Edward. *In Search of Peace: The Senate Munitions Inquiry, 1934–36*. Baton Rouge: Louisiana State University Press, 1963.

James A. Huston / c. w.

See also **American System; Bombing; Colt Six-Shooter; Fortifications; Military-Industrial Complex; Missiles, Military; Mobilization; Nuclear Weapons; Ordnance.**

MUNN V. ILLINOIS, 94 U.S. 113 (1876), upheld state regulation of grain elevator prices. Chief Justice Morrison Waite's majority opinion rejected a commerce clause claim on the grounds that the grain elevators were wholly intrastate and Congress has taken no action to regulate any interstate commerce effects. The Court rejected a Fourteenth Amendment claim on the theory that the state could regulate private property devoted to public use and in the nature of a virtual monopoly. It suggested, however, that in other situations the prices of private contracts might be judicially reviewable under a reasonableness standard. Justice Stephen Field, joined by Justice William Strong, dissented, viewing the statute as "subversive of the rights of private property" as guaranteed by the Constitution. In the 1930s supporters of the New Deal would use *Munn* as an example of proper judicial restraint and appropriate deference to the judgments of legislative bodies.

BIBLIOGRAPHY

Nowark, John E., and Ronald D. Rotunda. *Constitutional Law.* St. Paul, Minn: West, 2000.

Richard L. Aynes

See also **Government Regulation of Business.**

MURALS.

A mural is art painted directly on a wall, making it a visual component of a building. Throughout history, murals have been created for a spectrum of environments, including caves, churches, state capitals, factories, corporations, schools, libraries, post offices, courthouses, and residences. By nature of the medium, mural painting is typically restricted by several conditions, including scale, orientation, fixed spatial requirements, the purpose of the architectural structure, and the appropriateness of its subject matter for its patron or audience. Unlike an easel painter, the muralist must consider and overcome all or several of these factors in the construction of his or her imagery. Mural painting involves inherent social obligations and formal strategies that extend beyond the scope of a purely personal vision to a broader form of communication that is often rooted in shared social beliefs.

By the early 1900s, academic mural painting was flourishing in the United States and reflected many of the Progressive Era's themes, including big business, U.S. international involvement, conservation of the natural environment, and social issues concerning the poor, laborers, and women. Many of these issues, which were vigorously opposed during the 1920s, eventually became reemphasized during the NEW DEAL era, often in the form of a mural. The New Deal mural movement exposed and affirmed the social role of mural art like no other period in American history.

The transformation that took place in the history of mural art during the 1920s and 1930s was highly influenced by the government sponsorship of public murals in Mexico. The Mexican president Alvaro Obregon began a nationalist cultural program in the 1920s. As part of this program, the Mexican Ministry of Education and other government entities commissioned artists to create public murals. The most prominent muralists were Diego Rivera, Jose Clemente Orozco, and David Alfaro Siqueiros, often referred to as "Los Tres Grandes" (the Three Giants), who later received private commissions in the United

States. The program in Mexico became a model for the U.S. government's New Deal efforts beginning in 1933. The careers, styles, and techniques of the Mexican muralists inspired the emerging muralists of the New Deal era.

Franklin Delano Roosevelt's New Deal began in 1933 after four years of a devastating economic depression. Echoing Theodore Roosevelt's SQUARE DEAL, it reinstated Progressive Era priorities and expanded on the original Square Deal goals. In addition to these goals, it established a series of art programs dedicated to indigent artists, starting with the Public Works of Art Project (1933–1934) and continuing with the Works Progress Administration's famous Federal Art Project (1935–1943), which sponsored a wide range of art activities, including a massive program to create murals in public institutions such as schools, libraries, hospitals, and courthouses. The unprecedented production of murals in the United States during this period remains a testimony to the government's effort to bring art to the American people. Mural art has continued to flourish since this period, and the murals seen on public walls throughout America serve as a reminder of art's ability to act as a record of a people, place, and time.

BIBLIOGRAPHY

Becker, Heather. *Art for the People.* San Francisco: Chronicle Books, 2002.

O'Connor, Francis V., ed. *Art for the Millions.* Greenwich, Conn.: New York Graphic Society, 1973.

Heather Becker

MURMANSK,

an ice-free Russian port on the Barents Sea, became important in WORLD WAR I with the completion by prisoner-of-war labor of a railway from there to Petrograd (later Leningrad). After the 1917 Russian Revolution the Allies landed a guard in Murmansk to protect their stockpiles of military goods. In 1918 some 720 U.S. military engineers helped to improve and maintain the new railroad. In WORLD WAR II the "Murmansk run" was the most perilous route for convoys delivering LEND-LEASE supplies to the Soviet Union. In July 1942 only thirteen of the thirty-six merchantmen in Convoy PQ 17 reached Murmansk.

BIBLIOGRAPHY

Herring, George C., Jr. *Aid to Russia, 1941–1946: Strategy, Diplomacy, the Origins of the Cold War.* New York: Columbia University Press, 1973.

Van Tuyll, Hubert P. *Feeding the Bear: American Aid to the Soviet Union, 1941–1945.* New York: Greenwood Press, 1989.

*R. W. Daly/*A. R.

See also **Archangel Campaign; Merchantmen, Armed.**

MUSCLE SHOALS SPECULATION.

During the Confederation period, the Muscle Shoals region on the

Tennessee River in Alabama was considered valuable as an alternative waterway to the Mississippi River, which was blocked by the Spanish. John Sevier, William Blount, and others purchased land and received a grant from Georgia to settle the Muscle Shoals region as a colony of that state. They were resisted by Native Americans and the Confederation government. In 1785, the project was supposed to become part of the new state of Franklin, and when these plans came to naught, Sevier and others offered to secede from the union in return for Spanish support. Spain rejected the proposal and Sevier became a loyal supporter of the new federal government.

BIBLIOGRAPHY
Whitaker, A. P. "The Muscle Shoals Speculation, 1783–1789." *Mississippi Valley Historical Review* 13 (1927).

Michael Wala

MUSEUM OF MODERN ART.

Through exhibitions, educational programs, publications, and ever-expanding permanent collections, the Museum of Modern Art, a nonprofit educational institution popularly known as MoMA, has been a leading shaper and challenger of American public taste. MoMA was the brainchild of Lillie P. Bliss, Abby Aldrich Rockefeller, and Mary Quinn Sullivan, who in May 1929 asked A. Conger Goodyear, the museum's first president, to chair a committee to organize a museum dedicated to contemporary art and its immediate predecessors. They appointed Alfred H. Barr Jr. director in August, and MoMA opened with its first loan exhibition on 8 November 1929. Barr, who retired as director of collections in 1967, was MoMA's intellectual guiding light.

MoMA includes six collecting departments: Painting and Sculpture, Architecture and Design (est. 1932 as the Architecture Department), Film and Media (est. 1935 as the Film Library), Photography (est. 1940), Prints and Illustrated Books (est. 1969), and Drawings (est. 1971). The Architecture and Design, Film, and Photography departments were the first of their kind in a museum. Several departments are among the world's strongest in depth and quality. Among MoMA's iconic paintings are Vincent van Gogh's *Starry Night* (1889), Pablo Picasso's *Les Demoiselles d'Avignon* (1907), and Salvador Dali's *Persistence of Memory* (1931). Groundbreaking exhibitions organized by MoMA have included *Fantastic Art, Dada, Surrealism* (1936), *The Family of Man* (1955), and *"Primitivism" in 20th Century Art* (1984). Educational programs have included tours, lectures, lending programs, the publication of guides and exhibition catalogs, and, during World War II, a number of war programs. Funding comes primarily through admission and membership fees, sales of services and publications, and contributions. MoMA has been particularly well endowed with donations of art from trustees and supporters, beginning with Bliss and Rockefeller.

Since 1932, MoMA's address has been 11 West Fifty-third Street in New York City, though it has expanded enormously by repeatedly acquiring adjacent property and undergoing major building projects completed in 1939, 1964, 1984, and (anticipated) 2005.

BIBLIOGRAPHY
Kantor, Sybil Gordon. *Alfred H. Barr, Jr. and the Intellectual Origins of the Museum of Modern Art.* Cambridge, Mass.: MIT Press, 2001.
Lynes, Russell. *Good Old Modern: An Intimate Portrait of the Museum of Modern Art.* New York: Atheneum, 1973.
Museum of Modern Art. *The History and the Collection.* New York: Abrams and the Museum of Modern Art, 1984.

Craig Bunch

MUSEUM OF SCIENCE AND INDUSTRY

(MSI) occupies the structure built as the Palace of Fine Arts for the 1893 World's Columbian Exposition in Chicago; until 1920, the site in Jackson Park housed the Field Columbian Museum. Inspired by the hands-on displays at the Deutsches Museum in Munich, Germany, Julius Rosenwald, the chairman of Sears, Roebuck and Company and a prolific philanthropist, donated several million dollars to found a similar industrial museum for Chicago. When MSI opened to the public on 1 July 1933, most of the building renovations were still incomplete, but a reconstructed southern Illinois coal mine was ready for visitors in the basement.

During the depression of the 1930s, the staff collected spectacular artifacts more successfully than they balanced the budget. It was not until Lenox Lohr became the full-time president (1940–1968) that the museum achieved financial stability. Lohr, former president of the National Broadcasting Company, forged a close relationship between MSI and the companies whose research and products the museum celebrated. Corporations like General Motors and International Harvester signed long-term agreements to develop and sponsor exhibits about achievements in their fields. To assure these companies that their public relations dollars were well spent, Lohr increased museum attendance with interactive displays, blockbuster exhibits such as a lavish "Fairy Castle" donated by the silent-movie star Colleen Moore and a German submarine captured intact during World War II, and annual festivities such as the "Christmas Around the World Celebration," begun in 1941.

Lohr's successors sought to broaden the museum's popular and financial bases. They encouraged attendance by African Americans, Latinos, and girls by running programs featuring their artistic, cultural, and scientific endeavors. They also located noncorporate funds, raising new money from wealthy individuals, private foundations, and the museum's first general admission fee.

BIBLIOGRAPHY

Kogan, Herman. *A Continuing Marvel: The Story of the Museum of Science and Industry.* Garden City, N.Y.: Doubleday, 1973.

Pridmore, Jay. *Inventive Genius: The History of the Museum of Science and Industry, Chicago.* Chicago: Museum of Science and Industry, 1996.

Amanda I. Seligman

See also **Science Museums.**

MUSEUMS define relationships between life, community, the nation, and the world through the interpretation of objects, experience, and the environment. These institutions range from community-based museums, such as the Japanese American National Museum in Los Angeles, and Chinatown History Museum and the Lower East Side Tenement Museum in New York, to house museums like MOUNT VERNON and MONTICELLO. Among other developments are historic sites, reconstructed towns and villages such as the Boston African American National Historic Site and Lowell National Historic Park in Massachusetts; the HENRY FORD MUSEUM AND GREENFIELD VILLAGE, Michigan; and Colonial Williamsburg in Virginia. There are also national museums of art and science that include the National Museums of the SMITHSONIAN INSTITUTION, METROPOLITAN MUSEUM OF ART, AMERICAN MUSEUM OF NATURAL HISTORY, Field Museum of Chicago, Boston Museum of Fine Arts, and the MUSEUM OF MODERN ART in New York, among thousands of others.

The sheer variety of museums evinces the need to address different constituencies and to engage different interpretations of historic events that recover the multiplicity of cultures that constitute American identity. In the United States, the provision of social and civic spaces by government, private, and nonprofit organizations points to the complex nature of the relationship between knowledge and identity that has developed in the last fifty years. A 1997 study of state museum organizations revealed an estimated 16,000 museums in operation. Because several hundred new institutions appear each year, this estimate may have risen to over 20,000. According to a 1999 census report, museums average 865 million visits per year, or 2.3 million visits a day, a statistic suggestive of their importance in American life.

Emergence of Museums in America

While thousands of museums exist in contemporary rural and urban landscapes, their precedents in the United States extend to the late eighteenth century. The history of this earlier museum era begins after the 1770s and offers a different starting point for the founding of museums in the United States. Museums and cabinets existed nearly a century before the "great age" of museum building from 1870 to 1920, which resulted in the creation of large beaux-arts structures with classically inspired exteriors that housed collections of art and natural history. Instead of exhibiting the grand collections belonging to an aristocracy or monarchy, the museum in America has much humbler beginnings. In 1773, the Charleston Library Society founded a private museum that featured a collection of artifacts, birds, and books available to its members, until it was destroyed in wartime three years later. Once the Revolutionary War (1775–1783) was over, attention was turned toward the development of useful knowledge, and collections were one way of displaying the natural materials that could support the growth of industry and promote a sense of unity. Access to such early collections, also known as "cabinets," was possible through membership in philosophical societies or through courses taken in college. For some, awareness of a need to establish a sense of collective identity prompted them to open their collections to a paying public.

In 1780s Philadelphia, Dr. Abraham Chovet, Pierre Eugene Du Simitiere, and Charles Willson Peale each formed their own semiprivate cabinets accessible to a public made of the professional class for an admission fee. Such businesses offered their owners opportunities for pursuing nontraditional employment as an entrepreneur. In running them, they honed their skills in dealing with the public, and by experiment and experience, developed their respective displays. A public largely composed of merchants, government bureaucrats, and military officers paid admission fees equal to a laborer's daily wage. Sometimes admission fees were deliberately kept high, which effectively worked as a filter mechanism that limited the visitors to a specific group. Dr. Abraham Chovet maintained a cabinet of anatomical waxworks as a means of training physicians about the body at a time when actual subjects were in short supply. High admission fees ensured that students of physick (medicine) remained its main audience.

General museums of natural history and art charged admission fees of a half or quarter of a dollar to see examples of natural history, portraiture, waxworks, and trade goods. In port cities like New York, Boston, Philadelphia, or New Haven, such extensive collections were entirely housed under a single roof. In 1784, Swiss expatriate Pierre Eugene Du Simitiere opened his cabinet for admission to the public in his Arch Street, Philadelphia, home, which he advertised in newspapers and broadsides as "The American Musaeum." For half of a dollar at an appointed time, he offered audiences tours of books, prints, archival collections, and the artifacts and antiquities of indigenous peoples. Everything was auctioned off after his death in 1785. Artist and saddle maker Charles Willson Peale was familiar with Du Simitiere's failed effort. He began his museum by building extensions onto his home, first building a portrait gallery to display his work to prospective clients, and then adding rooms to accommodate his collections of natural history. He maintained his practice of portraiture, thereby ensuring an in-

"The Artist in His Museum." Self-portrait by Charles Willson Peale, 1822. © The Pennsylvania Academy of Fine Arts

come to support his large family, and he developed a style for the portraits of national heroes he displayed above cases of specimens. Peale continued to expand his home to house a growing collection. In 1794 he was able to rent rooms in the American Philosophical Society building and later, in 1802, the museum was moved to the Pennsylvania State House (Independence Hall), where it remained until 1829. Peale's Museum developed differently than museums in New York and Boston that catered more to popular entertainment. In part this was due to Peale's duties as curator of the American Philosophical Society and the desire of leaders to maintain Philadelphia's prominence as a cultural capital of the United States. Professors of natural philosophy at the University of Pennsylvania used the museum collections in courses on natural history, and Peale also delivered a series of lectures on natural history at the University. By the 1810s, the end of this mutual arrangement arrived. The University built its own museum and collections, which marked the growing divide between higher education, the rise of specialized societies, and popular efforts to educate citizens about natural history. Peale built a lecture room in his museum, used for scientific demonstrations and lectures on natural history. Other universities and colleges developed their own museums, where professors employed teaching collections in courses on anatomy and natural philosophy. This presaged the development of entertainment rather than science as a means of attracting customers to the museum.

When New York became the capital of the United States in 1790, the Tammany Society founded its own museum, dedicated to the collection of American Indian artifacts. First located in a rented room in City Hall, the museum quickly outgrew its initial home and was moved to the Old Exchange Building. In 1795, unable to maintain the museum, the Society transferred ownership to the museum keeper, Gardiner Baker. Baker's Tammany or American Museum (1795–1798) was dedicated to waxworks displays, paintings and collections of American Indian artifacts, automata, coins, fossils, insects, mounted animals, and a menage of live animals. Such a program of selected materials was followed by other museums. Aside from the entertainment, displays fell into two large categories—natural or artificial curiosities—the second designating objects that were made by people.

When Baker died in 1798, the museum collections were auctioned off and became part of Edward Savage's Museum, which was, in turn, sold to John Scudder for his American Museum in the 1820s, and by the 1840s, these collections were incorporated into Barnum's American Museum. In Boston, Daniel Bowen established his Columbian Museum (1795–1803), which featured extensive waxworks displays, paintings, and collections of animals, like those of Baker's and Peale's Museums. Bowen exited the museum business after three disastrous fires and worked with his nephew, the engraver Abel Bowen.

In this formative period between 1785 and 1820, museums gained additional support. City and state government provided support through the charge of a nominal fee ("one peppercorn" or minimal rent) for the lease of an available vacant building. For example, Scudder's American Museum began by renting the old New York Almshouse in City Hall Park in 1810. In 1816, Peale solicited the help of Philadelphia's City Corporation, newly owner of the State House, to establish a reasonable rent for his museum. Often, the interior of an older building was completely modified to hold display cases for arrangements of mounted specimens of the animal kingdom. Less frequently, a museum edifice was designed and built to order, as was the short-lived Philadelphia Museum (1829), Bowen's Columbian Museum in Boston (1803), and Peale's Museum in Baltimore (1814–1829), the latter operated by Peale's sons as a private business for profit. Fiercely competitive and dependent on profits from admission fees, museums were difficult to maintain given the uncertainty of an economy that suffered periodic depressions. Support from the federal government was negligible. Not until the formation of the National Park Service in the 1920s and the establishment of the Smithsonian did the U.S. government provide complete support for a public museum.

Changes in Collecting

Collecting became institutionalized between 1819 and 1864, and institutions dealing with the past—museums, historical societies, and collections—began to systematically develop their record keeping of acquisitions, inventories, and displays. Different fields of study branched from the humanities and the sciences, and institutions became more specific in their focus. Popular interest in the natural sciences spurred a broad range of activities and a market for lectures, textbooks, and journals channeled through the lyceum circuit by the 1840s. A decade later, many secondary schools and colleges featured their own collection of specimens, created by teachers and students. The growth of cities saw an increase in the number of museums in other national regions.

In general, two main types of museum emerged after midcentury—those devoted to the natural sciences, and those devoted to the arts. Not included in the histories of these large institutions is the "dime museum," which ranged from curio halls to storefronts that exhibited living anomalies, magic shows, plays, waxworks, or menageries. The predecessor of the dime museum was P. T. Barnum's American Museum (1841–1865) in downtown New York. Barnum's Museum became a national attraction that offered visitors displays of natural and scientific specimens along with live animal shows, plays, waxworks, sideshows, and plays in one location, for a quarter of a dollar. Together with Moses Kimball, proprietor of the Boston Museum, Barnum purchased the collections of museums at auction, recycling the contents of previous institutions unable to survive periodic depressions. Although Barnum left the museum business after three fires destroyed his collections in New York, the success of his institution inspired other museum entrepreneurs to follow his lead.

In the Midwest, museums were established near the waterfront in Cincinnati and St. Louis in the early 1800s. William Clark, Governor and Secretary of Indian Affairs at St. Louis, built an Indian council chamber and museum in 1816, filled with portraits by George Catlin and artifacts of various Native American peoples. Until his death in 1838, Clark's museum served as an introduction for visitors to the West and its resources. Part of Clark's collections was incorporated into Albert Koch's St. Louis Museum and dispersed after 1841, when Koch departed for Europe. Cincinnati's Western Museum (1820–1867) began as a scientific institution and was doing poorly by 1823; its new owner, Joseph Dorfeuille, transformed the museum into a successful popular entertainment. The Western Museum's most successful draw was the "Infernal Regions," a display that featured waxworks and special effects designed by the artist Hiram Powers. Low admission fees, central locations, and a wide variety of entertainment under one roof offered another option for spending leisure time in expanding industrial centers.

The display of industrial achievement had a profound influence on exhibition culture in the antebellum period. In 1853, the first U.S. World's Fair, the New York Crystal Palace, opened, followed by the Sanitary Fairs of the Civil War era. Fairs highlighted national achievement, rather than focusing on an individual artist, through participation in these venues. These events exposed larger segments of the population to the arts of painting and sculpture in addition to displays of manufacturing and industrial power. The rise of exhibitions and world's fairs offered opportunities for many to purchase reproductions, if not the original works on display. Expositions offered opportunities for public education. As instruments of social control, fairs and museums reiterated the racial and cultural hierarchy of white dominance. Access to museums by people of color was often restricted, and even specified in admission policy as early as 1820 at Scudder's American Museum. Beginning with the 1876 Philadelphia Centennial Exposition, this restriction was expressed through the organization of living ethnological displays. Indigenous groups from the Philippines and the United States were housed in reservations surrounded by fences and guards, while visitors moved around the areas to watch performances of everyday life. Between 1876 and 1939, fairs took place in St. Louis, Omaha, Cleveland, New Orleans, Dallas, and Seattle. World's fairs and expositions had a close relationship to museums, like that between the Smithsonian and the Philadelphia CENTENNIAL EXPOSITION. Materials on display became part of museum collections; elements of exposition displays, such as the period room, were developments incorporated into museums. Frequently, former fair buildings became homes for new museums.

Boston, New York, Philadelphia, and Washington, D.C., developed into important centers for the arts and the natural sciences. The architecture of larger institutions featured an imposing exterior executed in a classical or gothic style that symbolized power on a federal level. In New York, the American Museum of Natural History opened in 1869, and the Metropolitan Museum of Art opened in 1870. The Castle, the Smithsonian Institution's original red brick gothic building, was visible for a distance from its bare surroundings in Washington, D.C. Its rapidly increasing collections of specimens, some of which came from the 1876 Exposition, were contained in a series of glass cases that lined the walls of the Castle's Great Hall. By the 1880s, the Smithsonian comprised the U.S. National Museum and the Arts and Industries Building. Museums of natural history featured large collections arranged according to the latest scientific taxonomy, supported research, and expeditions for fossils and living specimens. Interest in prehistoric life-forms increased, and the skeletons of large dinosaurs, wooly mammoths, and giant sloths remained immensely popular with the public for the next seventy-five years.

Large science museums were not simply sites for educating students about biology, geology, or chemistry, but illustrated the place of America in the larger world, through the featured display of large collections of specimens culled from around the globe by official exploring expeditions sponsored by the United States government. Smaller regional organizations also formed museums, and their members gave courses in ornithology, geology, mineralogy, or conchology to a local public, as did the Worcester Natural History Society in Massachusetts. Such organizations frequently lacked the staff and collection resources of larger urban institutions, but offered access to natural history through shelves of natural specimens or guided field trips to the surrounding area.

Curators of natural history museums were also involved in another collection activity as anthropology became a distinct discipline, and interest in acquiring the material culture and remains of various indigenous peoples intensified. By the end of the nineteenth century, interest in anthropology led to the development of ethnographic exhibit techniques, some influenced by the villages of World's Columbian Exposition of 1893. Much of this material was donated to public museums. Although the displays of objects or dioramas of native life received scientific treatment, they also contained a moral dimension. Underpinning approaches to the study of indigenous cultures was a sense of Americans as inheritors of civilization, and the ongoing population decline of many American Indian peoples precipitated interest in the development of representative collections. Little changed until the 1990s, when Native and non-Native curators and scholars began to reevaluate the interpretation and presentation of Native American peoples in museums.

Over the course of the twentieth century, cities increased in physical size, population, and wealth. Museums and related institutions developed and were shaped by the public response to education as entertainment. Gradually, more funds, more services, and more equipment was dedicated to museums and their programs as municipal and state governments realized how tourism contributed to their regions. Higher education and training programs developed the study of art and cultural production, which in turn, shaped the acquisition and display of antiquities, paintings, and sculpture in museums.

Wealthy industrialists contributed to their own collections, which ultimately became a privately or publicly run museum. For two industrialists, objects were seen as the means of conveying history. Henry Ford believed that objects told the story of American history more accurately than texts, and was the largest buyer of Americana in the country, collecting objects and entire buildings, which he moved to Dearborn, Michigan, to create Greenfield Village. Henry Mercer held similar ideas to Ford concerning objects, and sought to create an encyclopedic collection of every implement used by European Americans before 1820. Mercer's museum, built in 1916 in Doylestown, Pennsylvania, focused on tools, and his collection of 25,000 artifacts is housed in a seven-story building of his own design in reinforced concrete. Industrialists also worked to found large institutions that later housed numerous private collections displayed for the benefit of public audiences. This specialization began in the early twentieth century, with the emergence of institutions such as the Museum of Modern Art, the WHITNEY MUSEUM OF American Art, and the Boston Institute of Contemporary Art.

In the 1930s, museum management shifted; the federal government increasingly became a source of support for museums through grants, and businesses supported and programmed science museums. In the post–World War II era, collectors and philanthropists turned their attention to founding institutions, which focused on national culture, business, and industry. Museums were not just one structure, but could constitute a number of buildings. A particular and specific image of the past was evoked by clustering old buildings in danger of demolition on a new site, renamed and declared an authentic link to the past. Examples of this include Greenfield Village, Old Sturbridge Village, and Colonial Williamsburg. But like many institutions of that time, displays offered a segregated history geared for white audiences. Audiences at these sites are introduced to another reading of the past, visible in a comparison of programming with that a half century earlier. For example, the William Paca House in Annapolis, Maryland, and Monticello, Thomas Jefferson's home in Charlottesville, Virginia, make visible the relationship of slavery to the structure and history of the site, restoring visibility to people fundamental to the economy in the Colonial period and in the early Republic. Sites run by the National Park Service have also undergone similar shifts in interpretation, which changes the perception and understanding of history for the public. There remains much to be done. Museums are responsive rather than static sites of engagement.

In the early twenty-first century, the history of museums and collection practices are studied in terms of their larger overlapping historical, cultural, and economic contexts. No longer anchored to a national ideal, the architecture of new museums instead attracts tourists, workers, and students and invites connections with local institutions. Programming, outreach, and work with artists and communities have brought museums further into the realm of public attention, sparking support, controversy, or concession over the links between the present and the past. Exhibitions such as the *Enola Gay* at the Smithsonian Air and Space Museum or the artists exhibited in the Brooklyn Museum of Art's show *Sensation* make visible the social tensions that surround the display and the ways in which particular narratives are told. The thousands of museums that exist in the United States today testify to the power of material culture and the increasingly central role display maintains across the country.

BIBLIOGRAPHY

Adams, Bluford. *E Pluribus Barnum: The Great Showman and the Making of U.S. Popular Culture.* Minneapolis: University of Minnesota Press, 1997.

Alderson, William T., ed. *Mermaids, Mummies, and Mastodons: The Emergence of the American Museum.* Washington, D.C.: American Association of Museums, 1992.

"America's Museums." *DAEDALUS: Journal of the American Academy of Arts and Sciences.* Summer 1999. Issued as Volume 128, Number 3, of the *Proceedings of the American Academy of Arts and Sciences.*

Brigham, David R. *Public Culture in the Early Republic: Peale's Museum and Its Audience.* Washington, D.C.: Smithsonian Institution Press, 1995.

The Changing Presentation of the American Indian: Museums and Native Cultures. National Museum of the American Indian, Washington, D.C.: Smithsonian Institution/University of Washington Press, 2000.

Conn, Steven. *Museums and American Intellectual Life, 1876–1926.* Chicago: University of Chicago Press, 1998.

Dennett, Andrea Stulman. *Weird and Wonderful: The Dime Museum in America.* New York: New York University Press, 1997.

Eichstedt, Jennifer L., and Stephen Small. *Representations of Slavery: Race and Ideology in Southern Plantation Museums.* Washington, D.C., and London: Smithsonian Institution Press, 2002.

Handler, Richard, and Eric Gable. *The New History in an Old Museum: Creating the Past at Colonial Williamsburg.* Durham, N.C.: Duke University Press, 1997.

Hinsley, Curtis M. *The Smithsonian and the American Indian: Making a Moral Anthropology in Victorian America.* Washington, D.C., and London: Smithsonian Institution Press, 1981.

Jones, H. G., ed. *Historical Consciousness in the Early Republic: The Origins of State Historical Societies, Museums, and Collections, 1791–1861.* Chapel Hill: North Caroliniana Society Inc., and North Carolina Collection, 1995.

Kretch III, Shepard, and Barbara A. Hail, eds. *Collecting Native America, 1870–1960.* Washington, D.C.: Smithsonian Institution Press, 1999.

Leon, Warren, and Roy Rosenzweig, eds. *History Museums in the United States: A Critical Assessment.* Urbana: University of Illinois Press, 1989.

Orosz, Joel J. *Curators and Culture: The Museum Movement in America, 1740–1870.* Tuscaloosa and London: University of Alabama Press, 1990.

Phillips, Ruth B., and Christopher Steiner, eds. *Unpacking Culture: Art and Commodity in Colonial and Postcolonial Worlds.* Berkeley and Los Angeles: University of California Press, 1999.

Rivinus, E. F., and E. M. Youssef. *Spencer Baird of the Smithsonian.* Washington, D.C.: Smithsonian Institution Press, 1992.

Wallach, Alan. *Exhibiting Contradiction: Essays on the Art Museum in the United States.* Amherst: University of Massachusetts Press, 1998.

West, Patricia. *Domesticating History: The Political Origins of America's House Museums.* Washington, D.C.: Smithsonian Institution Press, 1999.

Ellen Fernandez-Sacco

See also **Collecting; National Park System; World's Fairs;** *and individual museums; fairs; and expositions.*

MUSIC

This entry includes 10 subentries:
African American
Bluegrass
Classical
Country and Western
Early American
Folk Revival
Gospel
Indian
Popular
Theater and Film

AFRICAN AMERICAN

Among the defining features of African American music are the mix of cultural influences from African to European, the presence of both syncopation and improvisation, and the pull between city and country, spiritual and secular. These characteristics eventually led black Americans to create what is widely believed to be America's greatest cultural achievement: jazz.

When Africans first arrived in America in 1619, they brought with them only memories. Among those memories, the drumming, singing, and dancing of their West African homes. Although music was often forbidden to the slaves, they sometimes found ways of using it to communicate, as well as to commemorate occasions, especially deaths. Work songs and sorrow songs, or spirituals, were the first music to grow out of the African experience in America. These songs were often performed a cappella; when instruments were used, they were largely fiddles and banjos.

Some slave owners felt that blacks should be Christianized, though this was far from universal, as many slaveholders felt that slaves should not be treated as humans or beings with souls. However, in New England in the late seventeenth century, blacks often did attend church services and learn church songs. In the South, those slaves who were sent to church services were taught to obey their masters; good behavior would result in heavenly rewards. As life on earth was clearly without hope, many slaves found solace in this message and in the Christian hymns that accompanied it. At the same time, they built their own repertory of songs, both religious and secular. Often the songs combined a mix of influences, including the Middle Eastern nuances of West African music, the Spanish accent in Creole music, and the anguish drawn from everyday experience. Black music has always been appreciated; there are many reports of slave entertainment on plantations and of street vendors who made up original songs to hawk their wares. In the 1820s white performers began to capitalize on the accomplishments of black performers by using their songs in minstrel shows. Whites—and later blacks as well—performed in black face, using burnt cork to create a parody of an African. The minstrels altered their songs from the original African American versions to suit the taste of whites, a tradition that endured well into the twentieth century when white artists made covers of songs by African Americans. Between 1850 and 1870, minstrel shows reached the peak of their popularity. The two main characters, often called "Jim Crow" and "Zip Coon," represented country and city dwellers, respectively. Minstrelsy continued its popularity long after the Civil War, until the early twentieth century.

Around the turn of the twentieth century, the two major precursors of jazz came into popularity: ragtime and blues. Scott Joplin was the premier composer of ragtime, a form that reflected the taste of the newly formed black bourgeois, who preferred pianos over banjos and fiddles. Ragtime took its name from the practice of "ragging" tunes; the left hand of the pianist added the syncopation that was provided in earlier music by foot stomping. At about the same time, American blacks were innovating the blues. City versus country is again a factor in blues music; often a third category, "classic" blues, is used. While the best-known ragtime tunes are instrumental, memorable blues songs are meant to be sung. Country blues is widely deemed an older form and derives from folk music. It was originally accompanied by folk instruments including strings, crockery jugs, and harmonicas and sometimes had a sound near to that of spirituals. Urban blues tends to be more complex and played by a band with a rhythm section. Chicago is the capital of urban blues. Classic blues has a woman singer, such as Ma Rainey or Bessie Smith, in front. Both ragtime and blues were created by more musically sophisticated blacks who often knew how to write music and were knowingly fusing the music of their African roots with European-influenced composition. At this time, brass bands, boogie-woogie piano bars, and dance orchestras flourished throughout the country. African American music was not recorded until the 1920s, though it did find many proponents at the close of the nineteenth century, including the Czech composer Antonín Dvořák.

The New Orleans brass bands developed Dixieland jazz, with trumpeter Louis Armstrong the first to stress on-the-spot innovations while playing. At the same time, Kansas City jazz was developing under Count Basie and his orchestra, and, perhaps the greatest American jazz composer, Duke Ellington, was conducting his swing band on the East Coast. Billie Holliday influenced music by using blues and jazz touches in popular songs and by singing with white orchestras. By the 1950s Charlie Parker and Dizzie Gillespie were making "bebop" jazz in New York City.

The 1940s and 1950s saw the rise of rhythm-and-blues (R&B), a combination of both jazz and blues. By the 1950s, some black artists (T-Bone Walker, Louis Jordan, Bo Diddley) had become popular with mainstream audiences—but what often happened was that white performers made a sanitized cover version of a black artist's work and sold many more records. Still, R&B stars such as Little Richard and Chuck Berry had a huge influence on the then-burgeoning rock and roll. The 1950s also brought the popularity of doo-wop, a gospel-based vocal style that emphasized harmonizing.

Gospel was the basis for soul music, which began its development in the 1950s and peaked in popularity during the Black Power movement of the 1960s. In 1959 Ray Charles combined contemporary R&B with the call and response of the church in "What'd I Say." Aretha Franklin also drew on her gospel roots, starting with 1967's "Respect." The 1960s brought the first multimillion-dollar black-owned recording company, Motown. Detroit producer Berry Gordy Jr. introduced the world to such crossover groups as the Supremes, Marvin Gaye, the Temptations, and the Jackson Five, all of whom received massive airplay on top-40 radio stations. Michael Jackson's 1982 album "*Thriller*" sold forty million copies and gave Jackson a spot as the first black artist on MTV.

Both Jackson and James Brown are known for their dancing. Brown's version of soul was funk. He used African polyrhythms to sing 1969's "Say It Loud—I'm Black and I'm Proud" and in turn influenced other socially conscious groups, as well as disco in the 1970s and rap in the 1980s.

Funk, soul, and R&B mix in rap, which grew out of the hip-hop movement. Some early rappers such as The Last Poets, Grandmaster Funk, and Public Enemy commented on racial issues. At the same time, other rappers were largely interested in the entertainment value of break dancing and producing music that was nonmelodic and almost entirely dependent on syncopation. Gangster rap spawned another subculture as artists such as Snoop Doggy Dogg and Tupac Shakur ran into real life trouble with the law and sometimes, as with Shakur who was murdered in 1994, with other gangsters.

BIBLIOGRAPHY

Charlton, Katherine. *Rock Music Styles: A History*. 3d ed. Boston: McGraw Hill, 1998.

Jones, LeRoi (Amiri Baraka). *Blues People: Negro Music in White America*. New York: Morrow, 1963.

Ogg, Alex, with David Upshal. *The Hip Hop Years: A History of Rap*. New York: Fromm, 2001.

Southern, Eileen. *The Music of Black Americans: A History*. New York: Norton, 1971.

Stambler, Irwin. *The Encyclopedia of Rock, Pop, and Soul*. Rev. ed. New York: St. Martin's Press, 1989.

White, Newman I. *American Negro Folk-Songs*. Cambridge, Mass.: Harvard University Press, 1928.

Rebekah Presson Mosby

See also **Blues; Jazz; Minstrel Shows; Ragtime.**

BLUEGRASS

Bluegrass music is a form of country music that emerged in the 1940s and 1950s from a group known as the Blue Grass Boys headed by Grand Ole Opry star Bill Monroe,

Roy Acuff. The country and bluegrass star (second from right) plays fiddle with his band, the Crazy Tennesseans (later renamed the Smoky Mountain Boys), c. 1938. SOUTHERN FOLKLIFE COLLECTION, UNIVERSITY OF NORTH CAROLINA AT CHAPEL HILL

who came to be known as "the father of bluegrass." The music in its definitive form was first heard in NASHVILLE, Tennessee. Early bluegrass was distinctively flavored by APPALACHIA, where such groups as the Stanley Brothers and their Clinch Mountain Boys, Lester Flatt, Earl Scruggs, and the Foggy Mountain Boys performed on radio station WCYB in Bristol on the Tennessee-Virginia border. As elsewhere in country music, white performers predominated in professional settings, but the music took its inspiration from both white and black musicians. Several characteristics define bluegrass style. A typical band consists of four to seven players and singers who use acoustic rather than electrical instruments. Early bluegrass musicians tuned their instruments a half note above standard, a practice still used by some groups today, and bluegrass generally uses high-pitched vocals and requires more than one voice to sing something other than harmony parts. The guitar, mandolin, banjo, string bass, and fiddle play both melody and provide rhythm and background for vocal soloists. Through recordings, television, tours, and festivals, bluegrass performers have gained a national and even international constituency. An establishment consisting of several recording companies (Country, Rebel, Rounder, Sugar Hill, and others), clubs, and magazines, such as *Bluegrass Unlimited*, developed as the bluegrass festival movement spread in the 1960s. In the 1970s performances departed from the traditional form with "new grass," using rock repertoire and techniques. The formation of the International Bluegrass Association in 1985 and the creation of the Americana Record chart in 1995 carved out radio time for late twentieth-century bluegrass musicians and expanded the music's popularity.

BIBLIOGRAPHY

Cantwell, Robert. *Bluegrass Breakdown: The Making of the Old Southern Sound.* Urbana: University of Illinois Press, 1984.

Ewing, Tom, ed. *The Bill Monroe Reader.* Urbana: University of Illinois Press, 2000.

Rosenberg, Neil V. *Bluegrass: A History.* Urbana: University of Illinois Press, 1985.

Charles A. Weeks / F. H.

See also **Bluegrass Country.**

CLASSICAL

Early American Classical Music

Classical music encompasses instrumental and vocal music written by trained composers, expressing cultivated artistic and intellectual values, as opposed to music of an essentially commercial nature (popular) or music that develops anonymously and is transmitted aurally (folk). In the eighteenth century, classical music could be heard in Boston, Philadelphia, New York, Williamsburg, Charleston, New Orleans, and elsewhere in the homes of talented amateur musicians (most notably Francis Hopkinson and Thomas Jefferson) and in occasional public and private concerts (beginning in the 1730s) performed by local or touring musicians. Nearly all of the art music heard during this period was that of European masters such as George Frideric Handel, Arcangelo Corelli, Antonio Vivaldi, Luigi Boccherini, Jean-Philippe Rameau, Franz Joseph Haydn, and Thomas Arne. A few Americans, including Hopkinson and immigrant professional musicians Alexander Reinagle, Rayner Taylor, James Hewitt, and Benjamin Carr, composed and published songs and instrumental music in the style of their European contemporaries. German-speaking Moravian or Unitas Fratrum settlers in Pennsylvania and North Carolina had perhaps the most active musical communities of the period. A large part of their music was composed locally by European-trained members.

A movement to regularize psalm singing in New England Protestant meeting houses led to the formation of singing schools that fostered the development of musical skill in a wider population. Groups of amateurs formed musical societies for the recreational singing of sacred music, including psalm settings by Boston composer William Billings. In the nineteenth century, hymn singing gradually replaced psalm singing in popularity. Massachusetts composer Lowell Mason, along with writing his own hymn melodies, adapted music from classical composers such as Handel and Mozart to fit hymn texts.

The nineteenth century produced new audiences, performing venues, and important musical organizations. The Boston Handel and Haydn Society (established 1815) promoted the performance of choral music. The Philharmonic Society, predecessor of the New York Philharmonic Orchestra, gave its first concert in 1842. As early as the 1790s, operas were performed in New Orleans and Philadelphia. In New York City, opera was performed in theaters and at the Academy of Music (beginning in the 1850s). A concert circuit developed during the 1840s, introducing solo performers and musical troupes to cities and towns throughout America. The most famous of these performers was the Swedish singer Jenny Lind, promoted by the greatest of all entertainment entrepreneurs of the century, Phineas T. Barnum. In 1853, New Orleans composer Louis Gottschalk returned from studies in Paris to pursue a successful career as a touring concert pianist, which provided him opportunities to perform his own music.

Early American performers and composers lacked the main sources of patronage that supported the European tradition of art music, such as the aristocracy and the Catholic church, and depended on entrepreneurs willing to market classical music to the public. In spite of efforts by musicians such as Philadelphia composer William Henry Fry in the 1850s to champion the cause of American music, orchestras and other performing groups felt that the financial risk remained too high to allow performances of unknown American pieces in place of proven European masterworks. Fry further noted that only composers with independent means could afford to devote time and resources to writing music. Following the Civil War, however, the idea of supporting music as an artistic and educational endeavor became popular, and a stable, professional musical culture finally took root in America. Subsidies supported resident orchestras and opera companies, helping to pay for music halls and touring expenses. Orchestras were established in St. Louis (1880), Boston (1881), Chicago (1891), and Cincinnati (1895). The New York Metropolitan Opera House opened in 1883. In 1870 a landmark event occurred when Harvard College hired composer John Knowles Paine as assistant professor of music. Later, Horatio Parker joined the faculty at Yale (1894), Edward MacDowell came to Columbia (1896), and George Whitefield Chadwick became the director of the New England Conservatory (1897). Since then, such teaching positions have provided financial security for many composers and performers.

An important group of American composers active at the end of the nineteenth century—including Paine, Parker, and Chadwick, sometimes labeled the "New England School" or the "Boston Classicists"—were related by background, interest, and age: each had studied in Germany, lived in Boston where their works were frequently performed, interacted in the same social circles, and composed in a primarily German Romantic style. New York composer MacDowell also spent time in Boston but was more widely recognized and also advocated a kind of musical nationalism. He incorporated American landscapes and indigenous music into his style, as in the *Woodland Sketches* (1896) and his *Indian Suite* (1896), which includes several Native American melodies. At the end of the century the German influence began to fade. The works of two early twentieth-century composers, Charles Martin Loeffler and Charles Tomlinson Griffes,

instead display primarily French impressionist and Russian influences.

Twentieth-Century American Music

American composers produced a wealth of music over the course of the twentieth century. Some sought to innovate; others enriched European tradition. Most taught at universities or such conservatories as Juilliard (established 1905), the Eastman School of Music (1921), and the New England Conservatory (1867). The most unique of American composers at the turn of the century was Charles Ives, who prospered as the founder of an insurance firm and made musical composition his avocation. His orchestral and chamber works, choral music, and songs often predate similar experiments by European composers, employing innovative techniques such as polytonal effects, multilayered structures, tone clusters, microtones, and free, unmetrical rhythms. Ives often quotes American hymn and song tunes, and his descriptive pieces for orchestra are closely related to the American scene, including his *Three Places in New England* and *The Housatonic at Stockbridge* (which quotes the hymn tune "Dorrnance").

In the period following World War I, a group of composers arose who, although largely trained in the European tradition, were distinctly American in outlook: Aaron Copland, Roy Harris, Virgil Thomson, Marc Blitzstein, and Roger Sessions. Most studied with the French teacher Nadia Boulanger, who believed a non-European perspective would produce innovative musical ideas. Copland, in particular, was an advocate of American music and at times fused jazz and folk elements into his compositions to create an audibly American style. Some African American composers, such as William Grant Still in his *Afro American Symphony* (1930), also practiced greater compositional diversity in an effort to express their heritage. Important symphonists in the traditional vein include Howard Hanson, Samuel Barber, Walter Piston, and William Schumann.

The most notable aspect of music in the twentieth century was an unparalleled diversity of musical styles resulting from the breakdown of the traditional tonal system and the disintegration of the idea of a universal musical language. Some composers, such as Milton Babbit, extended the serial techniques of Arnold Schoenberg and Anton Webern's "Viennese School." But many (including Henry Cowell, Harry Partch, and Edgar Varèse), inspired by Ives, largely abandoned traditional formal or technical practices and experimented with sound and other musical materials. John Cage continued this exploration with a technique termed "indeterminacy" that intentionally included some degree of chance in composition or performance. Others made notational innovations and sought out new instrumental resources, such as percussion (George Crumb), introduced rhythmic and textural innovations (Elliott Carter), and investigated the sounds of language (Babbitt). In the 1960s a group of composers, including Philip Glass and Steve Reich, attempted to bring music back to its most basic elements by working with drastically reduced means—a practice known as "minimalism." Experimentation reached its climax in the 1960s, but in the 1970s musicians including David Del Tredici and George Rochberg began to reintroduce tonality into their music. Electronic and synthesizer music have also been explored by Varèse, Cage, Babbitt, Morton Subotnick, and others.

During earlier periods in America when concerts were rare, particularly for people outside of cosmopolitan areas, most classical music was heard in the home, primarily in the performance of songs and piano pieces. After the Civil War, classical music found larger audiences because of the growing numbers of American symphony orchestras—1,400 by the late twentieth century. New halls and cultural centers opened in New York, Washington, Atlanta, San Francisco, Los Angeles, Dallas, and other cities; older halls, including former movie theaters, were renovated and restored in Detroit, Pittsburgh, Oakland, and St. Louis. Enrollment in conservatories and music schools and attendance at a growing number of summer music festivals increased. Many orchestras expanded their seasons, encouraged new music through composer-in-residence programs, and showed a remarkable ability to innovate in programming and format. Radio and television further disseminated music, as illustrated by the Metropolitan Opera's Saturday afternoon radio broadcasts beginning in 1940 and such public television series as "Great Performances" and "Live from Lincoln Center." Recordings have allowed unprecedented variety in musical consumption, allowing classical works, both new and old, by Americans and others, to be heard by anyone. Even in competition with the many other pursuits possible today, classical music remains a vital part of the musical culture of the United States.

BIBLIOGRAPHY

Chase, Gilbert. *America's Music: From the Pilgrims to the Present.* 3rd. rev. ed. Chicago: University of Illinois Press, 1992.

Crawford, Richard. *The American Musical Landscape: The Business of Musicianship from Billings to Gershwin.* Berkeley, Calif.: University of California Press, 2000.

———. *America's Musical Life: A History.* New York: W. W. Norton, 2001.

Levin, Monroe. *Clues to American Music.* Washington, D.C.: Starrhill Press, 1992.

Sadie, Stanley, and H. Wiley Hitchcock, eds. *The New Grove Dictionary of American Music.* 4 vols. New York: Grove's Dictionaries of Music, 1986.

Martina B. Bishopp
Charles A. Weeks

COUNTRY AND WESTERN

Country and western music often referred to just as country music, eludes precise definition because of its many sources and varieties. It can best be understood as a style of popular music that originated in the folk culture of the rural south, a culture of European and African origin. Fid-

Patsy Cline. The country-music legend, who was killed in a plane crash in 1963. GETTY IMAGES/FRANK DRIGGS COLLECTION

dlers, banjo players, string bands, balladeers, and gospel singers drew upon existing music to develop materials suitable for performance at family and community events. As southerners migrated to northern cities in the early twentieth century, their music went with them; and, beginning in the 1920s, radio and recordings did much to popularize and diversify this music. In 1934, when a radio hillbilly singer from Texas named Orvon Gene Autry went to Hollywood, the era of the great cowboy singer in the movies began. The Grand Ole Opry in Nashville, Tennessee, beginning in the 1940s, made that city a mecca for country music fans, many of whom listened religiously to its performances on the radio. The popularity of rock and roll through the revolution in popular music begun by Elvis Presley in the mid-1950s posed a challenge to country music, but the development of a new style known as country pop or the Nashville Sound countered it in part. By the 1990s country and western music had an international following.

BIBLIOGRAPHY

Ching, Barbara. *Wrong's What I Do Best: Hard Country Music and Contemporary Culture.* New York: Oxford University Press, 2001.

Malone, Bill C. *Country Music, U.S.A.* Austin: University of Texas Press, 1985.

———. *Don't Get Above Your Raisin': Country Music and the Southern Working Class.* Urbana: University of Illinois Press, 2002.

Peterson, Richard A. *Creating Country Music: Fabricating Authenticity.* Chicago: University of Chicago Press, 1997.

Charles A. Weeks / A. E.

See also **Ballads; Cowboy Songs; Music Festivals; Music: Bluegrass, Popular; Nashville.**

EARLY AMERICAN

By the early eighteenth century, the English colonies on the eastern seaboard stretched from Maine to Georgia. They were replicas of English culture in terms of language, religion, social institutions, and customs, including music. While the population at this time included many Native Americans and newly arrived Africans, the colonists seemed little influenced by their cultures. The middle colonies were the most ethnically diverse, attracting people from all over Europe, including Germany, Sweden, France, and Holland. Nevertheless, the New England Puritans had considerable influence in shaping both the American ethos and American music. While the Puritans considered secular music frivolous and attempted to limit its place in society, they considered the singing of psalms the highest form of spiritual expression.

The music of the colonists was based on British and other European genres, which included sacred music of the Protestant Church, classical music, and popular music, including ballads, madrigals, theater songs, dance music, and broadsides. While the musical life of each colonist depended on socio-economic factors, religious beliefs, and geographical location, there was much crossover of musical traditions. The same repertories passed through all strata of society, although performed differently according to context. The performance of religious music, especially in New England, gave rise to the first music schools in America and the first truly American composers.

Sacred Music in the Eighteenth Century

The a cappella singing of vernacular translations of the psalms by a whole congregation was common in Protestant England during the sixteenth and seventeenth centuries. Both Puritans and Anglicans continued this tradition in the American colonies. Some of the earliest books in the Colonies were Psalters, which include texts of the Psalms. The Puritans who landed at Plymouth Rock in 1620 brought with them the Book of Psalms, published in Holland by Henry Ainsworth in 1612.

By the beginning of the eighteenth century, New England church leaders were dissatisfied with the state of hymn singing among their congregations. Many of the colonists did not read music, which led them to rely on the practice of "lining out," a call and response form originating in England, whereby the music was taught orally. While Psalters were readily available, including the popular *Bay Psalm Book* first published in America in 1642, most included text without musical notation. Therefore, new versions of the musical settings began to emerge through the process of oral tradition. Leaders in the church deplored this lack of standardization and the low level of musical literacy.

By the mid-eighteenth century, singing schools were established in New England. Boston became the first center for singing schools in the 1720s, and the practice gradually spread. The teachers were mostly itinerant singing masters who were the first professional musicians in New England. They typically spent several weeks in a community teaching participants to read music and to learn psalm tunes. The classes were designed as both a religious and a secular activity, primarily for teenagers and young adults. Participants learned the art of singing within the church setting, but hymn singing also took place outside the church—in homes, in taverns, and at parties. It became a social pastime and a form of amateur entertainment. As the general level of singing improved, singing provided a new expression of community.

The singing schools helped to raise the level of music literacy, expanded the repertoire, increased the demand for new books, and encouraged American composers to create new music. One of the most influential New England composers of this period was the musician, songwriter, and singing master William Billings (1746–1800), who published numerous collections of religious music, including the *New England Psalm Singer* (1770) and *The Singing Master's Assistant* (1778).

In the South, singing schools were maintained well into the nineteenth century. The schools took two paths of development. One was the regular singing of hymns and psalms, which led to the formation of choirs and choral societies, while the other was a more rural, folk-oriented style. This form of communal singing became part of the outdoor, religious camp meetings of the early nineteenth century, a period known as the "Great Awakening."

Secular Music in the Eighteenth Century

Most secular music performed in the colonies also originated in England. Until after the Revolution, musicians, music, instruments, and music books were imported, and this had a tremendous impact on home entertainment and what was performed on concert stages. While theater performances were restricted for religious reasons, especially in the North, by the 1730s, almost all American cities held public concerts. Charleston, South Carolina, was one of the most musical cities in the colonies before the Revolution, and the oldest musical society in North America, the St. Cecilia Society, was founded there in 1762. As cities grew and became more prosperous, music making grew closer to its counterpart in England, where classical music, plays, ballad operas, and dancing were extremely popular. The music there became more like that in England, where the rage was classical music, plays, ballad operas, and dancing. By the 1750s and 1760s, there were theater performances in most major cities.

One of the most popular types of entertainment throughout the colonies was country-dancing, another import from England. Although thought to have originated with rural folk, by the sixteenth century country-dances had been appropriated by the upper classes and moved into a ballroom setting. Both men and women performed these figure dances in line, square, and circle formations. By the eighteenth century, lines of men and women faced each other in the most popular form, the "longways for as many as will" country-dance.

Country-dancing took place regularly at balls, assemblies, private parties, and taverns in the colonies and provided entertainment for all social classes, though urban dance events for the elite were usually held in elegant ballrooms. As in England, dancing was regarded as a necessary social skill for social advancement. Itinerant dancing masters taught both dancing and etiquette throughout the colonies. John Griffiths, a dancing master who traveled and taught between Boston and New York in the 1780s and 1790s, published the first collection of country-dances in America, *A Collection of Figures of the Newest and Most Fashionable Country-Dances* (1786).

The tunes associated with the country-dance came from a variety of sources. While some tunes were part of the common repertory handed down by oral tradition in England, Scotland, Ireland, and America, others were new. They were found not only in country-dance books, but also on broadsides, in collections of theater, instrumental, and vocal music, and in tutors for various instruments. Country-dances were often performed at the end of theater productions, and dancing masters borrowed popular tunes and songs from the stage to create new dances. Some of the country-dance tunes from this period, such as "Fisher's Hornpipe," "Irish Wash Woman," and "St. Patrick's Day in the Morning" are still found in the repertories of traditional dance musicians today.

Music in America: 1780–1860

After the Revolution, there was an increase in musical activity, and a new demand for instruments, instruction tutors, and printed copies of pieces performed on stage and in concert halls. American printing also increased, especially in the form of sheet music. Movable type became more common in the 1780s and marked the rise of specialty publishing. While the printing of Psalm tune anthologies burgeoned in the 1760s and 1770s, major anthologies of secular instrumental music did not appear until the 1780s.

The first American publishers of secular music were established in Philadelphia, including Benjamin Carr (1768–1831), who arrived from England in 1791 and quickly became known as a singer in ballad operas, as well as a composer, arranger, and publisher. Carr and his son imported much of their music from Europe, but also published music by local musicians, including the first edition of the patriotic song, "Hail Columbia" (1798), with music by Philip Phile and lyrics by John Hopkinson.

New York and Boston also became important publishing centers. The publishing houses in these cities had close ties with the theaters, and their early catalogues consisted largely of theater songs. By 1840, publishing as a whole was concentrated in New York, Boston, and Philadelphia. Major publishers, such as the Oliver Ditson Company of Boston, had near monopolies on the new music industry, including ownership of retail stores, publishing, distribution of music and musical supplies, and the manufacture of musical instruments.

The tremendous social and regional diversity of nineteenth-century America led to more clear-cut distinctions between traditional, popular, and classical music. For example, the Irish and Scottish immigrants who settled in the Appalachian Mountains during the late eighteenth century continued to pass down a distinct repertory of old ballads and tunes through oral tradition well into the twentieth century, partly because of their geographical isolation. Music on the western frontier was by necessity different from urban centers on the Eastern seaboard. The first Italian opera performances, such as the 1818 Philadelphia premier of Rossini's *Barber of Seville*, were restricted to the major cities, where new musical organizations and patrons made such productions possible.

The period before the Civil War saw both the growth of classical music performance and the creation of the first orchestras (The Philharmonic Society of New York was the first, in 1842) and the rise of popular entertainment genres. Military and civic bands proliferated throughout the country and played for all kinds of ceremonial events. With the introduction of keyed brass instruments in the 1830s, all-brass ensembles soon replaced the Revolutionary-era ensembles of clarinets, flutes, bassoons, trumpets, and drums. Band repertories included military, patriotic, and popular pieces of the day.

The nineteenth century also saw the rise of social dance ensembles called quadrille bands. The quadrille, a social dance performed in sets of four couples in square formation, was exported from France to England in 1815, and soon after to America. By the mid-nineteenth century, the quadrille and variant forms—such as the Lancers and the Polka Quadrille—were extremely popular in both urban and rural settings. A large body of music repertory was published for the typical ensemble of first violin, second violin, clarinet, two coronets, bass, flute, viola, cello, trombone, and piano.

Popular songs were also an important part of theater productions, concerts, and home entertainment. The first songs published in America in the 1780s were in the form of sheet music and arranged for solo voice and piano. Irish and Scottish songs were popular at the beginning of the nineteenth century, and the growing consumer market was flooded by arrangements of new songs set to traditional airs by Irishmen Thomas Moore (1779–1852) and Samuel Lover (1797–1868).

As the century progressed, the minstrel song emerged as one of the first distinctly American genres. Created by white Americans in blackface for the entertainment of other white people, minstrel songs caricatured slave life on the plantation, creating and maintaining grotesque stereotypes of African American customs and behavior. While the first performers in the 1820s were solo acts, by the 1840s, blackface performers toured in troupes. The most famous of these groups was Christy's Minstrels, who first performed in New York in 1846. Like other groups of the period, all of their music was from the Anglo-American tradition. By the 1850s, black performers formed minstrel troupes, and many groups were touring by the 1870s.

The most famous songwriter to emerge from this period was Stephen Foster (1826–1864), whose "Oh Susanna" (1848), "Old Folks at Home" (1851), "My Old Kentucky Home" (1853), and "Jeanie With the Light Brown Hair" (1854) are considered classics. Foster was influenced by both the lyrical Anglo-Irish song repertory and the minstrel song tradition. His songs range from nostalgic, sentimental songs about love and loss to typical minstrel songs in dialect. His songs in the early 1850s were more in the mold of earlier songwriters such as Thomas Moore, and it was these works that influenced a whole generation of songwriters after the Civil War.

BIBLIOGRAPHY

Chase, Gilbert. *America's Music: From the Pilgrims to the Present.* 3d ed. Urbana: University of Illinois Press, 1987.

Crawford, Richard. *The American Musical Landscape.* Berkeley: University of California Press, 1993.

Davis, Ronald L. *A History of Music in American Life: The Formative Years, 1620–1865.* Huntington, N.Y.: Krieger, 1982.

Hamm, Charles. *Music in the New World.* New York: Norton, 1983.

Hast, Dorothea. *Music, Dance, and Community: Contra Dance in New England.* Doctoral dissertation, Wesleyan University, 1994.

Hitchcock, H. Wiley. *Music in the United States: A Historical Introduction.* Upper Saddle River, N.J.: Prentice Hall, 2000.

Krummel, D. W. "Publishing and Printing of Music." In *The New Grove Dictionary of American Music.* Edited by H. Wiley Hitchcock and Stanley Sadie. New York: Grove's Dictionaries of Music, 1986.

MacPherson, William A. *The Music of the English Country Dance 1651–1728.* Doctoral dissertation, Harvard University, 1984.

Van Cleef, Joy, and Kate Keller. "Selected American Country Dances and Their English Sources." In *Music in Colonial Massachusetts 1630–1830: Music in Public Places.* Boston: The Colonial Society of Massachusetts, 1980.

Dorothea E. Hast

See vol. 9: **National Songs, Ballads, and Other Patriotic Poetry, Chiefly Relating to the War of 1846.**

FOLK REVIVAL

The American folk music revival began in the early twentieth century with collectors and folklorists who sought to preserve regional American music traditions, and composers and performers who wanted to bring these traditions into the concert hall. From the late 1920s until World War II, the work of folklorists and performers took two paths: the first was to promote and encourage rural musicians who were considered tradition bearers, such as Leadbelly and Molly Jackson, and the second was to use music to raise political consciousness, as in the performances of such artists as Woody Guthrie and the Almanac Singers. Between 1928 and 1934, four large folk festivals were organized in the rural South in an effort to bring performers out of isolation and to create new audiences. Interest in regional American music was also fueled by

Pete Seeger. A 1955 photograph by Fred Palumbo of the highly influential folksinger, as a member of the Weavers and on his own; songwriter, including the classics "If I Had a Hammer" (with fellow Weaver, Lee Hays) and "Where Have All the Flowers Gone?"; and political and environmental activist, who was blacklisted in the 1950s. LIBRARY OF CONGRESS

the creation of numerous government-sponsored folklore projects of the Works Progress Administration. During this same period, folk music became ideologically associated with protest music, especially among left-wing urbanites. Drawing on both the music of earlier protest movements and newly composed repertory, performers such as Woody Guthrie, Leadbelly, Pete Seeger, Cisco Huston, Josh White, Sonny Terry, Brownie McGee, and Lee Hays performed at union rallies, hootenannies, and for a variety of social causes throughout the 1940s.

The movement gained momentum after World War II and adopted three routes for its development: the cultivation of a variety of world folk musics and dances, a rediscovery and appreciation of rural American music, and the growth of new urban styles devoted to political issues and social commentary. Publications and organizations such as *The People's Song Book* (1948 and 1956) and *Lift Every Voice* (1953) disseminated political music through print media, recordings, and performances. In the 1950s, the commercial success of the Weavers, Harry Belafonte, and the Kingston Trio ushered in a new relationship between folk music and the mass media. The Weavers' rendition of "Goodnight Irene" is estimated to have sold over four million records in 1952.

At the peak of the revival in the 1960s, civil rights activism, resistance to the Vietnam War, and a youth subculture gave rise to new and mixed folk genres that entered into the mainstream. The increased visibility of acoustic folk music among college youth and others created a boom in concerts, folk festivals, recordings, broadcasts, instrument sales, and informal music making. Many college-educated musicians were drawn into the serious study and recreation of folk styles, including old time, bluegrass, blues, New England contra dance, and Cape Breton fiddling. Although folk music was perceived as "people's music," in the 1960s it was in many ways no less a commercial genre than country music and rock and roll. The major figures associated with this period include Pete Seeger; Bob Dylan; Joan Baez; and Peter, Paul, and Mary.

BIBLIOGRAPHY

Cantwell, Robert. *When We Were Good: The Folk Revival.* Cambridge, Mass.: Harvard University Press, 1996.

Denisoff, R. Serge. *Great Day Coming: Folk Music and the American Left.* Urbana: University of Illinois Press, 1971.

Hast, Dorothea. *Music, Dance, and Community: Contra Dance in New England.* Ph.D. diss., Wesleyan University, 1994.

Slobin, Mark. "Fiddler Off the Roof: Klezmer Music as an Ethnic Musical Style." In *The Jews of North America.* Edited by Moses Rischin. Detroit: Wayne State University Press, 1987.

Whisnant, David E. *All That Is Native and Fine: The Politics of Culture in an American Religion.* Chapel Hill: University of North Carolina Press, 1983.

Dorothea E. Hast

Mahalia Jackson. The very popular and critically acclaimed gospel singer, as well as civil rights activist, who performed her joyful hymns in churches, music festivals, and concert halls, and on the radio and television, for decades. AP/WIDE WORLD PHOTOS

GOSPEL

Gospel hymns originated within the Protestant evangelical church in the last two decades of the nineteenth century, popularized through the revival meetings conducted by Dwight L. Moody and his musical partner Ira D. Sandkey. The popularity of expressing one's religious experience through song convinced Sandkey to create a publication designed to bring the gospel hymn to a wider audience. With business partner Phillip P. Bliss, in 1875 Sankey published *Gospel Hymns and Sacred Songs.* The hymns were especially successful in the South, where songs like "What A Friend We Have In Jesus" demonstrated both the religious and commercial appeal of gospel music. For the next four decades, the classic southern gospel quartet—four men and a piano—dominated revival and secular gospel singing. Thomas Dorsey, an African American from Chicago, challenged that traditional arrangement when he introduced the sounds of ragtime and the blues to accompany the religious text of the hymn. The founder and creative force behind the National Convention of Gospel Choirs and Choruses, Dorsey composed some 500 hymns, including the hit "Move On Up a Little Higher," performed by Mahalia Jackson in 1947. Gospel music continued to attract a larger audience over the next two decades, including the popularity of James Cleveland's traditional-sounding Gospel Choir tour and Edwin Hawkins's rhythm and blues "Oh Happy Day," which reached number one on *Billboard's* Top Fifty Chart in 1969. Between 1970 and 2000, gospel music, sometimes referred to as "praise music" or simply "Christian music" had become a billion-dollar industry.

BIBLIOGRAPHY

Blackwell, Lois S. *The Wings of the Dove: The Story of Gospel Music in America*. Norfolk, Va.: Donning Press, 1978.

Harris, Michael W. *The Rise of Gospel Blues: The Music of Thomas Andrew Dorsey in the Urban Church*. New York: Oxford University Press, 1992.

David O'Donald Cullen

INDIAN

Through the twentieth century and in earlier times, music has been a major marker of ethnicity and nationality and an indispensable component of the ceremonial, spiritual, and social life of Native American cultures. Ubiquitous in the daily cycle of tribal activity and in the year and life cycles of typical societies, music became in the twentieth century a significant part of the arsenal of cultural survival and revival, and has made a distinctive contribution to mainstream American popular and concert music. The importance of music is illustrated by its prominent appearance in virtually every event in which Native Americans mark or celebrate their cultural traditions.

Comparative study suggests that in distant, prehistoric times, virtually all ceremonies included music and dance; that music was thought to possess great spiritual and medicinal powers; that the creation of music was seen as the result of contact with the supernatural; that songs played a major role in recreational activities such as intra- and inter-tribal games; and that distinctions were made between songs available to everyone and songs available only to particular groups of shamans or priests, or that were owned by clans, families, or individuals. Songs were transmitted through aural tradition and learned from hearing, but nevertheless maintained consistency. Depending on aesthetic and cultural values, some societies permitted individual singers to develop personal variants of songs, while others prohibited and punished mistakes and creative departures. With significant exceptions—and in contrast to South America—men played a quantitatively greater role in musical life than women. While varying enormously, the words of songs might consist of brief spiritual statements ("This grass, it is powerful"), accounts of visions ("Bird is here; it makes the sky yellow"), and the hopes of a team in a gambling game ("It is hidden in one of these"); they might also be extended complex poems narrating history and myth.

Each tribe had its own complement of instruments, but virtually all had various kinds of drums, rattles, and other percussion and many used flutes of various sorts and whistles. The vast preponderance of musical performance was, however, vocal.

Historical Native American music is stylistically unified and easily distinguished from other world traditions. In sound it is most like native South American music, and like that of tribal societies in northern and easternmost Asia, underscoring historical relationships. The early contact map of North American societies suggests a number of related but distinct musical areas that roughly parallel cultural areas. However, songs associated with children, children's games, adult gambling games, and love charms were stylistically identical throughout the continent.

The traditional songs of all tribes were typically short and repeated many times in performance, melodic without harmony, and accompanied by percussion. Music of different areas differed in structure (for example, aabbcc in some Great Basin tribes, aa bcd bcd in Plains music, call-and-response patterns in the Southeast, and so on); in preferred melodic contour (sharply descending in Plains music, undulating with an occasional ascent in Yuman cultures, very complex in Pueblo music); and most important, in the singing style and type of vocal sound preferred (high and harsh in the Northern Plains, nasal-sounding in some Apache and Navajo singing, deep and raspy in some Pueblo genres).

North American Indian musical culture has changed enormously since it was first recorded around 1890. Disappearance of tribes and cultures and their musics was balanced by the development of intertribal, continent-wide musical genres. Significant among these was the music of the GHOST DANCE movement, derived from music of the Great Basin area, and from peyote songs, which are shared by many tribes that have members in the NATIVE AMERICAN CHURCH.

The most vigorous musical development, dating from the mid-twentieth century and continuing into the twenty-first century, accompanies powwows and social events celebrating tribal or broadly Native identity and culture and consists largely of singing and dancing. Adopted (by 1970) by virtually all American Indian peoples, the dance costume and song styles of POWWOWS are derived from historical Plains practices. Featuring singing groups of from six to eight men (and, since about 1980, also women) sitting around a drum (the groups therefore called Drums), powwows often permit participation by non-Natives and may have the function of introducing Native American culture to non-Indians.

Native American musicians made distinctive contributions to mainstream American forms of music in the late twentieth century. Popular singers of the 1960s and 1970s such as Buffy Sainte-Marie, Jim Pepper, and Peter LaFarge sang about oppression and other subjects of currency, with music referring to Indian styles and instruments. In the 1980s and 1990s, rock groups such as Xit and Ulali fashioned distinctive sounds combining European and Indian elements. A number of musicians, prominently the Navajo-Ute artist Carlos Nakai, have developed Native-oriented flute music. In the world of classical music, Louis Ballard is most prominent.

BIBLIOGRAPHY

Frisbie, Charlotte J., ed. *Southwestern Indian Ritual Drama.* Albuquerque: University of New Mexico Press, 1980.

Levine, Victoria. *Writing American Indian Music: Historic Transcriptions, Notations, and Arrangements.* Middleton, Wisc.: A-R Editions, 2002. An anthology, with detailed annotations, illustrating the way Indian songs were notated by scholars and musicians starting in the nineteenth century.

Merriam, Alan P. *Ethnomusicology of the Flathead Indians.* Chicago: Aldine, 1967. A landmark study providing information on music and its cultural context in one tribal society.

"Music of the American Indians/First Nations in the United States and Canada." In *The Garland Encyclopedia of World Music.* Volume 3: *The United States and Canada*, edited by Ellen Koskoff. New York: Garland, 2001. A reference book consisting of short essays by a number of authorities, for the nonspecialist.

Vander, Judith. *Songprints: The Musical Experience of Five Shoshone Women.* Urbana: University of Illinois Press, 1988.

Bruno Nettl

See also **Dance, Indian; Music: Popular;** *and vol. 9:* **Land of the Spotted Eagle.**

POPULAR

Popular music is embraced by the populace and includes almost all forms except classical and JAZZ, which are considered to be more elite. In America, the early white settlers had a low regard for music because of their religious beliefs, in contrast with the Native population, which used music for communication and ceremony. Among Native Americans there was neither "high" nor "low" music—music was simply a part of community life. Thus, popular music did not take root in the United States until the eighteenth century, primarily in the form of theatrical entertainments, including ballad operas drawn from European influences, and MINSTREL SHOWS that were racist parodies of black life. Minstrels were generally white artists who darkened their faces with burnt cork.

In the nineteenth century, the most popular American songwriter was Stephen Foster, whose nostalgic songs "Beautiful Dreamer" and "Jeannie with the Light Brown Hair" were staples in white American homes. During the Civil War, minstrelsy continued to be popular along with a new form of entertainment, vaudeville. By the end of the nineteenth century, the music that came from the New York City sheet music publishers located in "Tin Pan Alley" captured much popular attention. Among the crazes at the beginning of the twentieth century was ragtime, whose premier composer was Scott Joplin. Ragtime took its name from the practice of "ragging" tunes, or improvising them into lively, syncopated dance music.

In the meantime, former slaves were streaming into cities and developing new forms of their indigenous music, spirituals and BLUES. Until the twentieth century, this music was not generally published or written down, but rather passed on from person to person. Early blues were based on a variety of musical sources ranging from African to Middle Eastern and Spanish. There were both country blues, including delta blues, and urban blues, named after various cities including Chicago. While ragtime and the blues were primarily the forerunners of jazz, they also inspired rock and roll.

In 1879, Gilbert and Sullivan's *H.M.S. Pinafore* opened in America and began a long love affair with the musical theater. Show tunes were hummed and sung in homes and in the movies. Among the greatest show tune composers were George and Ira Gershwin, Cole Porter, Irving Berlin, and later, Stephen Sondheim.

By about 1930, phonographs and radios became widely available and popular music—as performed by professional musicians—became accessible to the masses, not just those who lived in big cities or could afford to buy tickets for performances in theaters and nightclubs. It was common for families to gather around the radio and listen to the swing music performed by big bands such as those led by Glenn Miller, Benny Goodman, and sometimes even black musicians such as Duke Ellington. While the bands were mostly segregated, some race mixing occurred in solo performances since, after all, no one could see the performers on the radio. Bing Crosby and Perry Como were among the best-known singers to work with big bands.

Radio also enabled white audiences to listen to stations intended for black audiences. The black music, then called "race" music, was especially exciting to young white people who were enthralled by the edgy rawness of blues and rhythm and blues. By 1945, many white teenagers had become enamored of "jumpin' jive," played by such artists as Louis Jordan. As teens started to buy the records, the recording industry went into a tailspin. The industry's response to white interest in black music was twofold. In some instances, white artists made covers of black songs. For example, in 1956, singer Pat Boone recorded a sanitized version of Little Richard's 1955 rhythm-and-blues classic "Tutti Frutti," and Boone's version vastly outsold the original. In other instances, the white recording establishment decided to go head-to-head with the sexually open lyrics and staccato beat of black musicians. Thus, the hip-gyrating, southern-roots sound of Elvis Presley was born.

Before long, radio stations were playing racially mixed music, which caused outrage in some white circles, and was vehemently denounced in white newspapers and from the pulpits. Nevertheless, Elvis Presley became an enormous star, British musicians including the Beatles and the Rolling Stones immersed themselves in rhythm and blues, and ROCK AND ROLL became an unstoppable phenomenon.

Over the years, rock has become a catchall term for a wide range of popular music styles such as pop, country rock, doo-wop, surf music, folk rock, bubblegum music, jazz rock, psychedelic rock, funk, disco, glitter and glam rock, hard rock, heavy metal, punk rock, new wave, and alternative and underground rock. Popular music styles played mostly by black musicians, such as soul, Motown, ska, reggae, hip hop, and rap music, are also considered rock.

BIBLIOGRAPHY

Charlton, Katherine. *Rock Music Styles: A History*. Boston: Mc-Graw Hill, 1998.

Ward, Geoffrey C. *Jazz: A History of America's Music*. New York: Knopf, 2000.

Londré, Felicia Hardison, and Daniel J. Watermeier. *The History of North American Theater: The United States, Canada, and Mexico from Pre-Columbian Times to the Present*. New York: Continuum, 1999.

Luther, Frank. *Americans and Their Songs*. New York: Harper and Brothers, 1942.

Rebekah Presson Mosby

See also **Tin Pan Alley;** *and vol. 9:* **Lyrics of Over There.**

THEATER AND FILM

Some of the richest strains of American music have emerged from stage and screen. Puritan culture and foreign influences retarded the development of a native stage musical tradition, but the late nineteenth century saw the emergence of genuinely American music theater from Reginald De Koven (*Robin Hood*, 1890), John Philip Sousa (*El Capitan*, 1896), George M. Cohan (*Little Johnny Jones*, 1904), and Victor Herbert (*Naughty Marietta*, 1910). In the niche between European operetta and theatrical burlesque emerged composers like Jerome Kern (*Show Boat*, 1927) and George Gershwin, both of whom drew upon black musical traditions, as in Kern's "Ol' Man River" and the whole of Gershwin's operatic *Porgy and Bess* (1935). Vincent Youmans (*No, No, Nanette*, 1923), Sigmund Romberg (*The Desert Song*, 1926), and Cole Porter (*Anything Goes*, 1934) furthered the popularity of original musical theater.

The "Broadway musical," integrating story, dance, and song, achieved supreme popularity and influence in the mid-twentieth-century collaborations of Richard Rodgers and Oscar Hammerstein, including *Oklahoma!* (1943), *Carousel* (1945), and *South Pacific* (1949). These works helped to inspire a golden age of musicals by the likes of Irving Berlin (*Annie Get Your Gun*, 1946), Frank Loesser (*Guys and Dolls*, 1950), Frederick Loewe (*My Fair Lady*, 1956), Leonard Bernstein (*West Side Story*, 1957), and Jule Style (*Gypsy*, 1959). Stephen Sondheim, lyricist for the last two shows, went on to a successful composing career of his own in increasingly ambitious works like *A Little Night Music* (1973) and *Sweeney Todd* (1979). By the end of the century, rising production costs, demand for theatrical spectacle, and the narrowing of the popular musical mainstream led to renewed foreign domination of Broadway (e.g., *Cats, The Phantom of the Opera, Les Misérables*), although native composers enjoyed striking successes with

A Chorus Line (Marvin Hamlisch, 1975), *Dreamgirls* (Henry Krieger, 1981), and *Rent* (Jonathan Larson, 1996).

Many Broadway classics, including all of Rodgers and Hammerstein's key works, were adapted as Hollywood films to great domestic success, although film musicals did not export as well as other Hollywood product. There was also a thriving tradition of original screen musicals from the beginning of the sound era (*42nd Street, Dames, Meet Me in St. Louis, Singin' in the Rain*), although most of these films drew heavily upon the existing body of popular song. *The Wizard of Oz* (Harold Arlen, 1939) has become one of the best-loved of all American movies.

Moviemakers have always used music to heighten drama and set the scene. The "silent era" was never without sound. Sometimes a pianist would play along; at other times an orchestra played classical selections. Studios hired libraries of "mood" music for theaters. Occasionally, a major production such as D. W. Griffith's *The Birth of a Nation* (1915) used specially composed music, played by teams of musicians traveling with the film.

The innovation of "talkies" in the late 1920s sealed the marriage of film and music. Studios employed full orchestras and hired eminent composers to create original scores. By 1940, film music had become a highly specialized compositional form. In the golden age of film music (c. 1935–1960), such composers as the immigrants Max Steiner, Erich Wolfgang Korngold, Franz Waxman, Dimitri Tiomkin, and Miklós Rózsa and the native-born Alfred Newman, Roy Webb, Bernard Herrmann, and later Alex North, Henry Mancini, Elmer Bernstein, and Jerry Goldsmith created compelling symphonic and jazz-based film scores.

The advent of rock and roll inspired a trend of incorporating pop songs into films, beginning with Richard Brooks's use of Bill Haley's "Rock Around the Clock" in *Blackboard Jungle* (1955). Elvis Presley's strong screen presence made hits of a mostly mediocre string of movie musicals from 1956 to 1972. The integration of popular songs by Paul Simon and Art Garfunkel was central to the huge success of *The Graduate* (1967). The disco movement of the late 1970s spawned such film scores as the Bee Gees songs for *Saturday Night Fever* (1977). Director Spike Lee gave African American music greater prominence in *Do the Right Thing* (1989), which employed a radical rap and blues soundtrack.

America's characteristic musical eclecticism continued in the early 2000s. The symphonic tradition revived mightily in the hands of the enormously popular John Williams (*Star Wars* [1977], *Schindler's List* [1993]), who became a sort of unofficial American composer laureate. And the movie musical was revitalized by the influence of MUSIC TELEVISION's video style in *Moulin Rouge* (2001).

BIBLIOGRAPHY

Gänzl, Kurt. *The Encyclopedia of the Musical Theatre*. 2d ed. New York: Schirmer Books, 2001.

Gänzl, Kurt, and Andrew Lamb. *Gänzl's Book of the Musical Theatre.* New York: Schirmer Books, 1989.

Palmer, Christopher. *The Composer in Hollywood.* London: Marion Boyars, 1990.

Prendergast, Roy M. *Film Music, A Neglected Art.* 2d ed. New York: Norton, 1992.

Romney, Jonathan, and Adrian Wooten, eds. *Celluloid Jukebox: Popular Music and the Movies since the Fifties.* London: BFI Press, 1995.

John Fitzpatrick
Graham Russell Hodges

See also **Film; Theater.**

Boston Globe Jazz and Blues Festival. Inspired by the famous Newport Jazz Festival, the *Boston Globe* sponsored its first music festival in 1966. Top performers such as Dizzy Gillespie, Dave Brubeck, and, here, the Marcus Roberts Group, have played the popular festival over the years.

MUSIC FESTIVALS commemorate anniversaries, celebrate religious or ethnic traditions, or offer music of a composer, period, or type; they can range from a single event to many events encompassing days or even a season. The earliest festivals in the United States date from the eighteenth century and had religious, social, or pedagogical functions. The first were associated with singing schools, to promote the singing of psalms according to established rules and order. Folk music began in the eighteenth century in the form of fiddlers' contests, many expanding to several days and involving instrumental music and community audiences.

Several large events took place beginning in the middle of the nineteenth century. In 1856 the Boston Handel and Haydn Society presented three major choral works—Haydn's *The Seasons*, Handel's *Messiah*, and Mendelssohn's *Elijah*. In 1869 the bandmaster Patrick S. Gilmore arranged a National Peace Jubilee in Boston with 20,000 instrumentalists. During the 1876 centennial of independence, Philadelphia sponsored a major music festival. Worcester, Massachusetts, in 1858 and Cincinnati, Ohio, in 1873 inaugurated festivals that have continued to the present day. Four festivals that came out of the tradition of singing schools continued into the twentieth century: the Messiah Festival in Lindsborg, Kansas (1882); the Big Singing Day in Benton, Kentucky (1884); the Ann Arbor May Festival (1894); and the Bethlehem, Pennsylvania, Bach Festival (1900).

Festivals proliferated in the twentieth century. Many occur in rural settings during summer months. Commercial motives and entrepreneurial talent have been a significant force in their promotion. Major symphony orchestras that employ musicians year-round include summer seasons that have become festivals. Since 1936 the Chicago Symphony Orchestra has played in Ravinia Park north of Chicago. The Tanglewood Music Center, in the Berkshire Hills of western Massachusetts, has been the summer home of the Boston Symphony Orchestra since 1936, featuring regular summer programming, and the Blossom Music Center between Cleveland and Akron became the summer residence of the Cleveland Orchestra in 1968. In 1966 the annual Mostly Mozart Festival became a major offering of the Lincoln Center for the Performing Arts in New York City. Many of these summer centers have expanded to offer jazz, folk, and rock music. Smaller festivals have grown out of centers that specialize in the study of particular styles of music. The Marlboro School in Vermont has stressed chamber music since 1950, whereas the Cincinnati Summer Opera Festival has offered a series of opera productions since 1920. New Music Across America began as a festival in New York in 1979 and has emphasized works by composers using new techniques and new instruments; in 1992 the festival took place simultaneously in many sites across the country.

Also frequently held during summer months in the open air, festivals organized around other types of music, including folk, bluegrass, blues, jazz, and rock, proliferated in the twentieth century. Building on the tradition of fiddlers' contests, the Old Time Fiddler's Convention began in North Carolina in 1924. The National Folk Festival first took place in St. Louis in 1934 and in 1971 moved to Wolf Trap Farm Park southwest of Washington, D.C. The Kool Jazz Festival, founded in 1954 as the Newport Jazz Festival in Rhode Island, moved to New York City in 1972, and, on the Pacific coast, the Monterey Jazz Festival began in 1958. Smaller annual jazz and blues festivals are held in numerous cities around the country, including venues as diverse as Sacramento, California, and Madison, Wisconsin. Rock music promoters staged big events in the 1960s, notably California's Monterey International Pop Festival in 1967 and New York State's WOODSTOCK in 1969. The Woodstock event, among the largest rock concerts ever organized, took on iconic status for many and was commemorated in 1994 by a second concert. The Womyn's Music Festival has been held each summer in Michigan since 1975 and has been an important site for women's organizing. Festivals have become so plentiful and diverse at the end of the twentieth century that publishers issue music festival guide books, which offer a listing of events around the country.

BIBLIOGRAPHY

Clynes, Tom. *Music Festivals from Bach to Blues: A Traveler's Guide*. Detroit: Visible Ink Press, 1996.

McAll, Reginald. *The Hymn Festival Movement in America*. New York: Hymn Society of America, 1951.

Morris, Bonnie J. *Eden Built by Eves: The Culture of Women's Music Festivals*. Los Angeles: Alyson Books, 1999.

Rabin, Carol Price. *Music Festivals in America*. 4th ed. Great Barrington, Mass.: Berkshire Traveller Press, 1990.

Santelli, Robert. *Aquarius Rising: The Rock Festival Years*. New York: Dell Publishing Company, 1980.

Charles A. Weeks / L. T.

See also **Music Industry; Music: African American, Classical, Popular.**

MUSIC INDUSTRY. The music industry involves the production, distribution, and sale of music in a variety of forms as well as the promotion of live musical performance. People arguably have bought, sold, and bartered music for as long as it has been made. Street singers, roving minstrels, broadside sellers, and traveling music teachers developed makeshift grassroots music industries that differed more in scale than in kind when compared to the modern music business.

In the mid-nineteenth century, printed sheet music was the industry's primary product. Publishers marketed sentimental ballads and parlor songs for use by the growing number of private piano owners. Advertised nationally, sheet music sales were boosted by the inclusion of songs in touring musical reviews. Blackface minstrelsy, the most popular form of live entertainment in the United States through much of the nineteenth century, provided one of the central vehicles for publishers to acquaint audiences with their wares. Large minstrel companies became celebrities by touring relentlessly through established national theater circuits. Their endorsement of a song could result in significant sales throughout the nation.

Beginning in the early 1880s, publishing firms became concentrated around Manhattan's 28th Street, dubbed Tin Pan Alley by the newspaper writer and songwriter Monroe H. Rosenfeld. The city's publishers perfected the mass production and distribution of songs. Usually paying staff or freelance composers a flat rate per song, Tin Pan Alley firms issued thousands of titles in the hope that a few would hit with the nation's public. Publishers courted popular vaudeville singers, often paying them handsomely to include a song of choice in their act.

Thomas Edison invented the phonograph in 1877. Few initially imagined the invention would be used primarily for music. Yet by the 1890s, "nickel-in-the-slot" talking machines graced urban arcades, introducing the nation to the novelty of mechanically reproduced music. A few companies controlled the patents to competing phonograph technologies. Edison controlled his wax cylinder playback technology. He licensed it to the fledgling Columbia Phonograph Company and the two introduced the first talking machines designed for home use in 1896. By this time, the competing gramophone disk machines and records made by Emile Berliner were already liberally distributed. In 1901, Eldridge Johnson, a Camden, New Jersey, engineer, formed the Victor Talking Machine Company to market Berliner's technology.

These firms raced to establish their technology as the consumer standard throughout the United States and the world. Victor eventually won the technology wars by focusing on the home consumer trade, creating celebrity recording artists such as the opera singer Enrico Caruso, and expanding internationally. In 1901, Victor and licensee Gramophone divided the globe into distinct markets and established distribution networks, retail outlets, and recording operations from China to Latin America. Other companies quickly followed suit.

In 1917, the end of initial patent restrictions resulted in the creation of a number of small firms that catered to previously marginalized consumers. African American and southern white vernacular artists introduced blues, jazz, country, and folk to the industry. In 1919, the Radio Corporation of America (RCA) was founded and began to market consumer-friendly radios. The United States had over one million sets by the early 1920s. Radio raised concerns among copyright holders, especially as broadcasters started selling airtime. Yet phonograph companies soon realized the advertising potential of the new medium. In 1929, RCA acquired Victor and the phonograph and the radio industries continued to increase their ties. Recording artists demanded compensation for the broadcast of their material through the American Society of Composers, Authors, and Publishers (ASCAP).

The Great Depression decimated the industry. Record sales plummeted from 150 million in 1929 to 10 million in 1933. Businesses failed, and the industry was again comprised of a few powerhouse corporations. ASCAP, overseeing royalty collection for the vast majority of published music, continued to demand compensation for radio broadcasts. In 1941, they forbade radio stations to play the music they represented. Their rival, Broadcast Music, Inc. (BMI), offered stations its collection of music that had not been accepted by ASCAP—music by African American composers and artists, working-class styles, and industry unknowns. The result was another wave of decentralization within the industry, as previously scorned artists, styles, and companies gained access to the airwaves and recording studios. The shift opened the door for African American styles to be the guiding force behind the industry's postwar expansion.

Throughout the century, musicians organized to protect their rights and promote their careers. Musician unions typically failed—or refused—to bring most recording and performing artists into their ranks, yet garnered rights for their members, including closed shops and union pay scales in established theater circuits, symphony orchestras, society dance networks, and recording studios. They were less successful in countering the loss of jobs to new technologies and garnering higher royalty rates for record sales.

The postwar decade witnessed three developments that again transformed the music industry: tape recording, the long-playing (LP) record, and the rise of rock and roll. Magnetic tapes finally enabled the easy recording of long segments of music, and the LP allowed their playback. With the concurrent introduction of the 45-rpm single and the growing jukebox trade, the LP heightened sales of new consumer technology, as it would again with the introduction of stereo in the late 1950s. Hundreds of independent labels entered the industry during the era, many promoting regional styles ignored by the majors. Often embraced by smaller radio stations, disks from small startups such as Chess Records and Sun Records introduced the sounds of black rhythm and blues to young audiences throughout the country, contributing to the rise of rock and roll and the reorientation of the industry toward the youth market.

By the late 1960s, the LP dominated industry profits. Major labels soon perfected promotional strategies that combined well-advertised albums, large-scale tours, and airplay on "album-oriented rock" stations. Industry profits increasingly derived from a small number of high-selling artists. The 1981 advent of MTV added the music video to the list of powerful marketing tools at the industry's disposal.

In the last decades of the twentieth century, the music industry was characterized by a wave of corporate mergers and transnational expansion. In 1994, 90 percent of worldwide gross music sales accrued to six multinational corporations. The century ended much as it had begun, even as the industry giants grappled with the copyright repercussions of the digital revolution.

BIBLIOGRAPHY

Burnett, Robert. *The Global Jukebox: The International Music Industry.* London: Routledge, 1996.

Gronow, Pekka, and Ilpo Saunio. *An International History of the Recording Industry.* London: Cassell, 1998.

Hamm, Charles. *Yesterdays: Popular Song in America.* New York: Norton, 1979.

Sanjek, Russell. *Pennies from Heaven: The American Popular Music Business in the Twentieth Century.* Updated by David Sanjek. New York: Da Capo, 1996.

Karl Hagstrom Miller

See also **Compact Discs; Music; Music Television; Radio.**

MUSIC TELEVISION. MTV (Music Television) is a cable channel launched by Warner Amex Satellite Entertainment in 1981 and acquired by Viacom in 1987. Supported by advertising, it began as a service providing music videos twenty-four-hours per day in programs hosted by "video jockeys" (VJs), a term coined by MTV. Before long, programming diversified as the channel introduced game shows (*Remote Control, Singled Out*); animated series (*Beavis and Butt-Head, Daria*); news programs; and later, a soap opera, *Undressed.*

Perhaps more than any other channel, MTV helped launch the cable explosion in America. Many viewers who had been reluctant to sign up for pay cable services ultimately capitulated to the pleas of their children and teenagers who could find on MTV what was not available on broadcast channels. MTV typified cable's approach to television by targeting specific audiences (in this case, persons from twelve to thirty-four years old) rather than aiming for the undifferentiated mass audience of broadcast TV. Reality TV shows like *Survivor* and *Big Brother*, which would emerge in Europe in the 1990s and in the United States in 2000, owe their heritage to the MTV series *The Real World*, a show that taped seven strangers living together in an apartment and was introduced on MTV in 1992.

Although many parents and educators decried the negative influences of MTV on youth, pointing most often to videos and programming with sexual content, the channel had an important civic dimension as well. Its *Rock the Vote* and *Choose or Lose* campaigns advocated voting among young people and presidential candidates made MTV a stop on their campaign trails beginning in the 1990s.

BIBLIOGRAPHY

Denisoff, R. Serge. *Inside MTV.* New Brunswick, N.J.: Transaction, 1988.

Goodwin, Andrew. *Dancing in the Distraction Factory: Music Television and Popular Culture.* Minneapolis: University of Minnesota Press, 1987.

Kaplan, E. Ann. *Rocking around the Clock: Music Television, Postmodernism, and Consumer Culture.* New York: Methuen, 1987.

Robert Thompson

See also **Music Industry; Music: Popular; Rock and Roll; Television: Programming and Influence.**

MUSSEL SLOUGH INCIDENT. Known locally as the Mussel Slough tragedy, an outbreak of gunfire in 1880, seven miles northwest of Hanford, California, brought to a head a long controversy between settlers on railroad lands and the Southern Pacific Company. In the end, seven men were killed.

In 1866, Congress voted to give the Southern Pacific Company a huge land grant in California to help subsidize a rail line. If the company met the terms and built the line, then it could sell the odd-numbered sections in the grant to cover costs. Southern Pacific encouraged settlement of the grant lands with promotional pamphlets that promised the land would eventually sell for $2.50 to $5.00 an acre, without additional charges for improvements. These prices were close enough to government rates to convince people to settle the arid Mussel Slough district beginning in the late 1860s. Within a few years the cooperative efforts of hundreds of families helped irrigate thousands of acres, and in 1880 the area boasted a population of four thousand people centered around the towns of Hanford, Grangeville, and Lemoore. By then, however, land ownership in the district was hotly contested.

In the mid-1870s, Southern Pacific stunned settlers by announcing that it would charge market value, $20 to $35 an acre, for homestead lands within the district. The prices were well above those stated in the pamphlets and above what the company charged in other areas. Hundreds of families who had already improved the land were told they could either pay the established prices or vacate. At first the settlers responded nonviolently by petitioning Congress to enact a law to force the railroads to sell the land at the government rate of $2.50 an acre. They also argued that the railroad should forfeit the land because it had violated its contract terms by not completing an agreed-upon rail line. When these efforts failed, six hundred Mussel Slough residents formed the Settlers' League on 12 April 1878. Although initially nonviolent, the league's approach shifted after Southern Pacific brought suit against settlers living on lands in odd-numbered sections. Beginning in November 1878, masked vigilantes rode through the district at night, intimidating residents who sided with the railroad.

Tensions peaked in spring 1880, when Southern Pacific brought suits of ejectment against twenty-three members of the Settlers' League. The league responded with heightened vigilance and posted warnings against the purchase of railroad lands. On 11 May 1880, Southern Pacific took advantage of the settlers' preoccupation with a league-sponsored picnic and sent the U.S. marshal Alonzo Poole, the land appraiser Walter Clark, and the residents Walter Crow and Mills Hartt to dispossess several settlers. The four met a group of league members in a wheat field near Hanford. Although the railroad men were heavily armed, they were severely outnumbered. Within minutes an argument erupted, followed by a sudden burst of gunfire. The source of the first shots was unclear, but in the end Hartt and five settlers were killed. Crow initially escaped but was caught and killed by an unknown gunman later in the day, thus bringing the death toll to seven. After the tragedy, tensions relaxed significantly. Some settlers purchased the lands they occupied, but many did not. In 1886 the Mussel Slough area was renamed Lucerne Valley.

BIBLIOGRAPHY

Brown, James Lorin. *The Mussel Slough Tragedy*. n.p., 1958.

Brown, Richard Maxwell. *No Duty to Retreat: Violence and Values in American History and Society*. Norman: University of Oklahoma Press, 1994.

Conlogue, William. "Farmers' Rhetoric of Defense: California Settlers versus the Southern Pacific Railroad." *California History* 78, no. 1 (1999): 40–55, 73–76.

Jennifer L. Bertolet

See also **California; Railroads.**

MUSTANGS. Many mustangs are descendants of sixteenth-century Spanish explorers' imported horses that had escaped and adapted to wilderness conditions. Modern feral horses represent hybrids of numerous breeds and primarily live in western states.

Books and movies usually depict mustangs sentimentally as symbols of freedom. In fact, mustangs often suffer starvation because fires, droughts, and urbanization destroy grazing sites. Pathogens spread fatal diseases in mustang herds. Mustangs occasionally die during natural disasters. Wild animals prey on mustangs. Humans sometimes poach mustangs to sell their carcasses.

The federal government approved extermination of the estimated 2 million mustangs living on public ranges in the 1930s. During the 1950s, Velma "Wild Horse Annie" Johnston (1912–1977) lobbied Congress to halt mustang slaughtering. Nevada legislation forbade contamination of water sources and use of aircraft to hunt mustangs. The federal government designated the Pryor Mountain Wild Horse Range in 1968. By 1971, Congress passed the Wild Free-Roaming Horse and Burro Act to protect mustangs in the Bureau of Land Management's (BLM) jurisdiction. The BLM established Herd Management Areas (HMA). The Wild Horse and Burro Preservation and Managment Act of 1999 assured additional federal protection. BLM personnel round up mustangs for public adoption. The Spanish Mustang Registry, Incorporated, and North American Mustang Association and Registry document mustangs. Sanctuaries protect some mustangs, including two HMAs that help Kiger Mustangs, which genetic tests indicate possess distinctive Spanish Barb traits.

BIBLIOGRAPHY

Bureau of Land Management. Home page at http://www.blm .gov/whb/.

Dines, Lisa. *The American Mustang Guidebook: History, Behavior, State-by-State Directions on Where to Best View America's Wild Horses*. Minocqua, Wis.: Willow Creek Press, 2001.

Kiger Mesteno Association. Home page at http://www.kiger mustangs.org.

Spragg, Mark, ed. *Thunder of the Mustangs: Legend and Lore of the Wild Horses*. San Francisco: Sierra Club Books, 1997.

Elizabeth D. Schafer

See also **Horse.**

MUSTER DAY. Under the militia act of 1792, in effect for more than a century, every able-bodied citizen between the ages of eighteen and forty-five was a member of the militia. The annual muster day accomplished actual enrollment of the members. Muster day also served as a significant social event in early America, at least for men. Since militia commanders often attempted to win their men's cooperation by providing them with alcohol, muster day frequently degenerated into an annual drunken spree. After the Civil War, muster day generally lost importance.

BIBLIOGRAPH

Stone, Richard G., Jr. *The Brittle Sword: The Kentucky Militia, 1776–1912.* Lexington: University Press of Kentucky, 1978.

Don Russell/A. E.

See also **Conscription and Recruitment; Militias; Revolution, American: Military History.**

MUTINY ACT. The Mutiny Act of 1765 was a routine parliamentary measure that included a provision for quartering of troops in the American colonies. This feature, like the STAMP ACT, was designed to shift the burden of supporting British troops in America from British taxpayers to the colonists. It required provincial legislatures to provide barracks, fuel, and other necessities for soldiers stationed in their colonies. Colonial Whigs feared that the Mutiny Act would pave the way for a standing army to enforce the Stamp Act, but after the repeal of the Stamp Act, colonists protested that the Mutiny Act violated the principle of no taxation without representation. Most colonies attempted to evade the act.

BIBLIOGRAPHY

Edgar, Gregory T. *Reluctant Break with Britain: From Stamp Act to Bunker Hill.* Bowie, Md.: Heritage Books, 1997.

Middlekauff, Robert. *The Glorious Cause: The American Revolution, 1763–1789.* New York: Oxford University Press, 1982.

John C. Miller/s. B.

See also **Billeting; Coercive Acts; Colonial Policy, British; Parliament, British; Quartering Act.**

"MY COUNTRY, TIS OF THEE." Samuel Francis Smith received several German books from Lowell Mason, a friend, who had himself been given them by William Woodbridge on his return from Europe in 1831. Looking through the German hymnals in early 1832, Smith was moved to write a poem he called "America," which he intended to be a national song dedicated to the United States. He wrote the words with the melody of the British song "God Save the King," that country's national anthem, in mind. The melody was popular in many European countries, where different words had been written for it since its origin, which has been dated from as early as the seventeenth century to the 1740s. The melody was also not new in the United States. Previous to Smith's version, the tune had been sung in the United States to lyrics with titles such as "God Save the Thirteen States" and "God Save the President."

The first public performance of "My Country, Tis of Thee" reportedly was at Park Street Church in Boston, at a children's Sunday school celebration of Independence Day in 1832. At the beginning of the twenty-first century the song was still performed at patriotic occasions, though it was not as popular as the U.S. national anthem the "STAR-SPANGLED BANNER" (1814) or the patriotic hymn "AMERICA THE BEAUTIFUL" (1863).

BIBLIOGRAPHY

James, Robert Branham, and Stephen J. Hartnett. *Sweet Freedom's Song: "My Country 'Tis of Thee" and Democracy in America.* New York: Oxford University Press, 2002.

Smith, Samuel Francis. Papers, 1834–1936. Library of Congress, Washington, D.C.

Todd, Mike. "America." *An American Encyclopedia.* Available at http://miketodd.net/encyc/americasong.htm

Connie Ann Kirk

MY LAI INCIDENT. On 16 March 1968, U.S. Army soldiers of Company C, First Battalion, Twentieth Infantry of the Eleventh Infantry Brigade, Twenty-third (Americal) Infantry Division, while searching for a Vietcong force at My Lai hamlet in Son My Village, Quang Ngai Province, South Vietnam, massacred two hundred to five hundred South Vietnamese civilians. Following revelations of the atrocity a year later, an army investigation headed by Lieutenant General William R. Peers implicated thirty soldiers in the commission and cover-up of the incident. Fourteen soldiers were charged with war crimes. All had their charges dismissed or were acquitted by courts-martial except First Lieutenant William L. Calley Jr., a Company C platoon leader, who was convicted of murdering twenty-two civilians and sentenced in March 1971 to life imprisonment. The public viewed Calley as a scapegoat, and his sentence was eventually reduced to ten years. After serving forty months of his sentence, all but three months confined to quarters, Calley was paroled by President Richard M. Nixon in November 1974. The My Lai incident increased disillusionment with the army's conduct of the Vietnam War, fueled growing antiwar sentiment, and underscored concerns within the army itself regarding the professionalism and ethics of its officer corps.

BIBLIOGRAPHY

Hersh, Seymour M. *Cover-up: The Army's Secret Investigation of the Massacre at My Lai.* New York: Random House, 1972.

Peers, William R. *The My Lai Inquiry.* New York: Norton, 1979.

Vincent H. Demma

See also **Atrocities in War; Vietnam War;** *and picture (overleaf).*

My Lai. An American soldier enters a hut in the South Vietnamese hamlet where a U.S. Army company murdered hundreds of civilians on 16 March 1968. NATIONAL ARCHIVES AND RECORDS ADMINISTRATION

MYERS V. UNITED STATES. In 1920 President Woodrow Wilson removed Frank S. Myers, the Portland, Oregon, postmaster, without first obtaining the consent of the Senate. Myers sued in the Court of Claims, challenging the president's right to remove him. He lost, and on appeal the SUPREME COURT held, in *Myers v. United States* (272 U.S. 52 [1926]) that officers named by the president were subject to removal at his pleasure. In an opinion written by Chief Justice William Howard Taft, the Supreme Court declared unconstitutional the law that had been passed in 1876 limiting removal of postmasters.

Although presidential authority to appoint carries with it the right to remove, exceptions have been made by the Court after *Myers* with respect to members of several independent regulatory and administrative agencies, such as the FEDERAL TRADE COMMISSION and the War Claims Commission. These exceptions apply if the Congress has decreed in the statute creating the office that removal is subject only to specific cause made explicit by the statute and if the official involved exercises adjudicatory function. The cases of *HUMPHREY'S EXECUTOR V. UNITED STATES* (1935) and *Wiener v. United States* (1958) distinguished between officials like Myers, who exercised only ministerial and administrative authority, and those

like W. E. Humphrey, a member of the Federal Trade Commission, and Wiener, a member of the War Claims Commission, who functioned in a quasi-judicial capacity.

BIBLIOGRAPHY

Corwin, Edward S. *The President: Office and Powers.* New York: New York University Press, 1984.

Fisher, Louis. *Constitutional Conflicts between Congress and the President.* Lawrence: University Press of Kansas, 1997.

Paul Dolan / A. R.

See also **Civil Service; Congress, United States; Postal Service, U.S.; President, U.S.; Removal, Executive Power of.**

MYSTICISM has many meanings in the study of the history of religions. In general it refers to a type of faith that emphasizes the direct experience of unity with the Divine. Theologically, mystical faiths tend to stress the divine immanence, and they often identify God with the structure of being. In the United States mystical forms of faith can be seen as a protest against the dominant religious tradition. Often centered around charismatic leaders, many of whom have been women, important strains of American mysticism have also set themselves explicitly outside Christianity.

The most famous mystic in early American history was Anne Hutchinson, whose mysticism evolved from the Puritan emphasis on the Holy Spirit as the means of grace. Her teachings were inflammatory, and for stating that she had communicated directly with God, she was exiled from Massachusetts Bay Colony in 1637.

Although Jonathan Edwards, a leading preacher of the GREAT AWAKENING, was primarily interested in traditional forms of religious experience, many elements in his writings suggest mystical leanings. The description of his wife's religious experience in *Some Thoughts Concerning the Present Revival* (1792) is one of the classic accounts of mystical experience in American literature. Edwards's own theology presented a view of the world as filled with shadows and images of things divine and had elements in it similar to those found in mystical faiths.

Ralph Waldo Emerson was perhaps the most prominent proponent of nineteenth-century Romantic mysticism in the United States. Building on ideas ultimately derived from German philosophy and—in his later years—from the religions of the East, Emerson evolved a unique American mysticism that stressed the unity of humans with all nature. Through humans' communication with the world, Emerson argued, they could come to transcend it and recognize themselves as part of it at the same time.

In the years after the Civil War a variant of mysticism known as theosophy gained in popularity. Theosophy focused both on humans' ability to experience God and on the power of the human mind. Drawing on ideas from Hindu and Buddhist scriptures, charismatic leaders, such

Thomas Merton. Priest and poet, he was an insightful and influential advocate of Catholic mysticism, meditation, and social justice. NEW DIRECTIONS PUBLISHING CORP.

as Madame Helena Petrovna Blavatsky and Annie Wood Besant, attracted both numerous followers and considerable controversy. In 1875 Blavatsky helped found the Theosophical Society and Universal Brotherhood in New York City. Mysticism also became better known to Americans through the World Parliament of Religions, held in Chicago in 1893. Representatives of Eastern religions and Western mysticism presented their views of the religious life to large audiences.

In the Native American tradition, mysticism had always played a central role, and this tendency increased under the pressure of persecution and displacement from ancestral lands. The most famous example of this phenomenon is the rise of the Ghost Dance movement among the Plains Indians in the late 1880s. Inspired by the Paiute

prophet Wovoka, who claimed transcendent experiences in the afterworld, Sioux believing themselves invincible to bullets came into conflict with the U.S. Army. In 1890 over three hundred Sioux were killed in what became known as the Battle of Wounded Knee. Although this massacre brought the Ghost Dance movement to an end, the ideas that had animated it lived on and became part of the NATIVE AMERICAN CHURCH, founded in 1918. Native American mysticism after Wounded Knee often revolved around peyote, a hallucinogenic plant that was used as a sacrament in ceremonies.

The Roman Catholic Church has always had more of a place for mysticism than the Protestant churches, and the mystical experience has continued to be important in the lives of many Roman Catholic religious orders. Thomas Merton, a convert to Catholicism, was one of the influential voices for Catholic mysticism in the United States in the twentieth century. His exposition of the mystical way was marked by clarity and philosophical insight, and his works reveal a deep concern for social justice and a keen analysis of political issues.

The drug culture of the 1960s created a widespread interest in mysticism among the young. Many who tried mind-expanding drugs found the states they induced were remarkably similar to or even identical with the experiences of the great mystics of the past. This led many to explore or become followers of non-Christian faiths, such as Hinduism, Zen Buddhism, and Native American religions.

BIBLIOGRAPHY

Merton, Thomas. *The Seven Storey Mountain.* New York: Harcourt, Brace, 1948.

Miller, Perry. *Jonathan Edwards.* New York: W. Sloane, 1949.

Moore, R. Laurence. *In Search of White Crows: Spiritualism, Parapsychology, and American Culture.* New York: Oxford University Press, 1977.

Underhill, Evelyn. *Mysticism: A Study in the Nature and Development of Man's Spiritual Consciousness.* London: Methuen, 1962.

Jennifer Burns

See also **Ghost Dance; Indian Religious Life; Spiritualism; Theosophy; Transcendentalism.**

MYTHS. *See* **Folklore.**

NADER'S RAIDERS. In 1968, the consumer advocate Ralph Nader and seven law students began investigating the Federal Trade Commission (FTC). The *Washington Post* dubbed this group "Nader's Raiders" after they testified before an FTC hearing. For the next several years, Nader recruited hundreds of idealistic college students and lawyers to work with his Center for Study of Responsive Law. This organization criticized the INTERSTATE COMMERCE COMMISSION and FOOD AND DRUG ADMINISTRATION and focused national attention on a variety of issues, such as elder care, occupational safety, and the misuse of natural resources. "Nader's Raiders" stimulated important reforms, particularly in the FTC, and spearheaded the American consumer movement during the 1970s.

BIBLIOGRAPHY

Nader, Ralph. *The Ralph Nader Reader.* New York: Seven Stories Press, 2000.

Richard R. Benert / E. M.

See also **Automobile Industry; Consumer Protection; Distribution of Goods and Services; Lebanese Americans; Trusts.**

NAFTA. *See* **North American Free Trade Agreement.**

NAMING. American personal names typically include a given name, middle name, surname, and occasionally suffixes. Anglo-American surnames can be traced back to the English adoption of surnames after the Crusades in the thirteenth century. Traditionally, American surnames were transmitted along the male line only. The practice of giving children the mother's surname, or a hyphenated or composite version of both parents' names, was becoming more common by the end of the twentieth century. The assumption that women will assume their husband's surname remains unquestioned in many communities; many other women, however, retain their natal surnames after MARRIAGE or hyphenate their surname with that of their husband. Middle names appeared in the United States and Great Britain at the end of the eighteenth century. By the end of the nineteenth century most Americans received middle names, and by the end of the twentieth century, fewer than 5 percent of Anglo-American children lacked such names. Middle names and suffixes were first popular among the elite and later were adopted generally.

Most twentieth-century American given names trace to three sources: a small stock of traditional Anglo-Saxon names popular in England before the Norman Conquest in 1066, a stock of Norman names introduced following the Conquest, and a stock of biblical names from both the Old and New Testaments. Throughout the nineteenth century the stock of American given names continued to grow as names were introduced by immigrant groups (especially German and Scotch-Irish), surnames occasionally were used as given names, masculine names were transformed to feminine forms (Roberta, Michelle), and many new names were coined. In the twentieth century the pool of American given names greatly expanded, especially since the 1970s. While many traditional names continued in popularity, especially among religious groups who preferred biblical names or those of saints, names gained and lost popularity with increasing speed. In the 1990s the ten most popular names for men and women were given to 20 to 30 percent of children, down from 50 percent or more two centuries ago.

There were two notable trends in naming in the late twentieth century. First, while parents continued to name children after relatives (especially sons after fathers), FAMILY names were more often used as middle names and less often as first names. Second, Americans increasingly selected names that expressed identification with or pride in ethnic, racial, or religious groups. AFRICAN AMERICANS, for example, after a century of preference for traditional given names, began to draw names from a wider variety of sources and to coin new names. Many chose African names as a means of reclaiming an ancestral link to Africa. Religious conversion to ISLAM, in its various American forms, added another incentive to import names from non-Western sources. The renaming of boxing champion Cassius Clay (Muhammad Ali) and the basketball star Lew Alcinder (Kareem Abdul Jabar) brought this practice into the mainstream. Self-naming could also serve ostensibly political purposes. After his release from prison in Massachusetts in 1952, Malcolm Little joined the Nation of Islam, then led by Elijah Muhammad. Considering "Little" a "slave name," he chose his new name, Malcolm X, to dramatize the negation of black identity and manhood under slavery ("X" represented his lost tribal name).

BIBLIOGRAPHY

Richard D. Alford, Richard D. *Naming and Identity: A Cross-Cultural Study of Personal Naming Practices.* New Haven, Conn.: HRAF Press, 1988.

Mehrabian, Albert. *The Name Game: The Decision That Lasts a Lifetime.* Bethesda, Md.: National Press, 1990.

Richard D. Alford/A. R.

See also **Kinship**.

NANTUCKET. An island twenty-five miles south of Cape Cod, Massachusetts, Nantucket was first explored in 1602 by Bartholomew Gosnold and settled by English Quakers in 1659 with permission of the native WAMPA-NOAG people. Poor soil led colonists after 1670 to fishing, WHALING, and raising sheep. Deep-sea vessels made possible long cruises hunting whales in the Atlantic Ocean and after 1790 in the Pacific Ocean. Nantucket enterprise and hardihood also led to profitable trade in Asia, Polynesia, and South America. By 1842 the island fleet had grown to eighty-six ships that went on whaling voyages lasting as long as six years. However, the California gold rush, the discovery of petroleum, and the Civil War contributed to the decline of Nantucket whaling. In 1869 the last whaling ship cleared port and brought to a close a brilliant chapter in American economic history.

After the Civil War the sandy beaches, good fishing, and picturesque bluffs of Nantucket brought it a new reputation as an artist colony and summer resort, and tourism became its principal industry. The painter Eastman Johnson depicted the landscape in a memorable series dealing with cranberry picking on the island in 1870–1880. The town of Nantucket, incorporated in 1687, has many historic features, including cobblestone streets, fine nineteenth-century homes, and a whaling museum. The population by 2000 increased to 9,520.

BIBLIOGRAPHY

Gambee, Robert. *Nantucket Island.* 2d ed. New York: Norton, 1993.

Schneider, Paul. *The Enduring Shore: A History of Cape Cod, Martha's Vineyard, and Nantucket.* New York: Henry Holt, 2000.

Peter C. Holloran

NARCOTICS TRADE AND LEGISLATION. Narcotics are habit-forming drugs that relieve pain or induce sleep; in excess, they can cause convulsions or actuate coma. In the legal sense, narcotics refers to a class of controlled, criminalized drugs that most commonly includes opium, cocaine, heroin, and marijuana, as well as many synthetic drugs that also have psychoactive effects.

Early Regulation and Legislation

In the nineteenth century, narcotics use was an unregulated activity, limited only by community mores and social stigma. Narcotics were available at grocery stores and through mail order, and cocaine was a key ingredient in many medicine remedies, as well as soda pop. Many veterans of the Civil War became addicted to the battlefield morphine. Addiction among members of the middle and upper classes was viewed more as a weakness of character than criminal behavior, although Chinese in the West and blacks in the South were readily stigmatized for drug use. Estimates of drug addiction ranged from 2 to 4 percent of the population at the end of the nineteenth century.

Opium was the first drug that was subject to regulation and trade restrictions. In the West, where many Chinese immigrants resided, xenophobic state governments instituted bans on opium use. Congress raised the tariff on opium importation in the 1880s and 1890s, and finally banned the importation of smoking-grade opium with the passage of the Opium Exclusion Act of 1909. Much of the legislation regarding opium at the time sought to create domestic concurrence with international treaties regulating the world opium trade.

An important step toward federal control of narcotics use was the Food and Drug Act of 1906, which required proper labeling of drugs sold to consumers. The muckrakers of the Progressive Era warned that many of the remedies marketed to cure a variety of ills were medical quackery. As a result of the act, over-the-counter sales of products that used narcotics as ingredients slumped. Narcotics users turned to doctors to get their products.

The Harrison Narcotics Act of 1914

The Harrison Narcotics Act of 1914 was the federal government's first move toward the regulation of narcotics as a class of drugs. The act required that producers and distributors of narcotics register with the Internal Revenue Service, record their sales, and pay a federal tax. Under the Harrison Act, drug users could obtain narcotics with a doctor's prescription. The major forces behind the legislation were pharmaceutical and medical associations that wanted to increase their control of narcotics regulation; antidrug crusaders—led by Dr. Hamilton Wright, a U.S. representative at many international drug conferences; and the U.S. State Department, which sought to move U.S. domestic policy in line with the international agreements they were pursuing with countries in Asia. Their lobbying overcame the opposition of those in Congress who worried about federal usurpation of state government power.

The punitive nature of the Harrison Act was not evident until the Treasury Department began implementing its statutory provisions. The narcotics division of the Bureau of Internal Revenue issued regulations prohibiting physicians from prescribing maintenance doses to addicts. Doctors who refused to obey were targeted for prosecution and fines by the Bureau to such an extent that by the early 1920s, most doctors refused treatment of addicts.

The punitive approach toward narcotics use and addiction gathered strength in the era of alcohol prohibition. In 1922 Congress passed the Narcotic Drugs Import and Export Act, which banned the importation of refined narcotics and criminalized narcotic possession. A year later Congress passed a resolution calling on the president to pressure opium producing countries to curtail production.

In the 1930s responsibility for drug policy enforcement fell to a new bureaucracy within the Treasury Department, the Federal Bureau of Narcotics (FBN). Under the leadership of Commissioner Harry Anslinger, the FBN spearheaded an antidrug crusade, and persuaded most state governments to adopt uniform codes that criminalized narcotics possession. Anslinger was an important force behind passage of the Marijuana Tax Act of 1937. Modeled after the Harrison Act, the legislation brought marijuana within the regulatory framework of harder drugs by requiring sellers and users to register with the IRS and pay taxes. The high tax rate shut the legal marijuana market down and forced many users to buy marijuana in illegal black markets.

After World War II attention turned to the demand-side of the drug trade. The Boggs Act of 1951 imposed a mandatory minimum two-year sentence for possession. The Narcotic Control Act of 1956 raised the minimum sentence for a third offense to ten to forty years, and permitted death sentences for drug sellers who dealt to minors.

Nixon's War on Drugs

Despite the criminal penalties imposed on the buying and selling of drugs, in the late 1960s drug abuse was widely perceived as a growing social problem. In 1969 President Richard M. Nixon, declaring the illegal use of narcotics the most pressing problem the country faced, launched the War on Drugs, a political initiative to curb the supply of illegal drugs as well as a public relations drive to discourage use. The Nixon White House cited studies showing a sixfold increase in the number of heroin users in the late 1960s, as well as close links between rising drug use and crime. High profile drug interdiction efforts were established like the well-publicized but short-lived "Operation Intercept" that allowed federal law enforcement agencies to police the Mexican-American border with heightened vigilance for one week in 1969. Efforts to restrict heroin routes were an important part of diplomatic work in the early 1970s. Payments were made to Turkey to destroy its poppy crops, and a new pesticide—paraquat—was developed to eliminate marijuana in Mexico.

During the Nixon years a new antidrug bureaucracy was created. In 1973, federal drug enforcement agencies in the Departments of Justice, Treasury and Health, Education and Welfare were consolidated into a new agency,

the Drug Enforcement Administration (DEA). Drug enforcement spending increased from $43 million in 1970 to $321 million in 1975.

The 1980s and 1990s: Further Escalation

The 1980s saw a further escalation in federal efforts to stop the entrance of drugs into the United States. The DEA organized twelve regional task forces to coordinate state, local, and federal drug interdiction efforts. To demonstrate the Reagan administration's commitment, the biggest—the South Florida Task Force—was organized by Vice President George Bush. The National Narcotics Border Interdiction System was created to coordinate efforts to seal off U.S. borders from drug trafficking. President Ronald Reagan issued an executive order to increase the participation of the Central Intelligence Agency and the military in drug interdiction efforts. In a series of bills in the 1980s, Congress expanded police power and increased drug-related sentencing. The number of prisoners in federal detention increased from 36,000 in 1985 to 93,000 in 1996. The combined prison population rose from 744,000 to 1.6 million over the same period. Half of the rapid growth in the prison population from 1985 to 1996 is attributed to drug related crimes, both selling and possession.

The 1988 Anti-Drug Abuse Act again reorganized the bureaucracy, with the establishment of the Office of National Drug Control Policy (ONDCP). President Bush appointed William Bennett director with the mandate to serve as a "drug czar," the national leader of antidrug policy. Bennett established a national strategy that focused on targeting drug users, even occasional ones. Bennett's work had little long-term impact, and subsequent directors of the office—former Florida Governor Robert Martinez, and, in the Clinton administration, former New York City Police Commissioner Lee Brown and General Barry McCaffrey—maintained a lower profile.

Initially, the Clinton administration seemed open to rethinking drug policy. The surgeon general, Jocelyn Elders, suggested publicly that drug legalization merited examination. As drug czar, Lee Brown sought to refocus policy on providing medical assistance to the "hard-core" users who, although they composed only 20 percent of the drug user population, consumed 80 percent of the drug product. But members of Congress from both the Democratic and Republican Parties blocked efforts to redirect funds away from criminal justice–oriented approaches. While medical approaches that focused on providing assistance to addicts were not discounted, they were widely viewed by policymakers as an adjunct to, rather than a replacement for, criminal justice approaches.

The cumulative impact of the successive attempts to eliminate the drug trade created a bureaucracy—a group of local, state, and federal agencies that in 1995 (a representative year) spent $8.2 billion to stop the supply of drugs. (An additional $5 billion was spent on treatment and education programs.) More than forty federal agen-

Major Narcotics Trafficking Routes

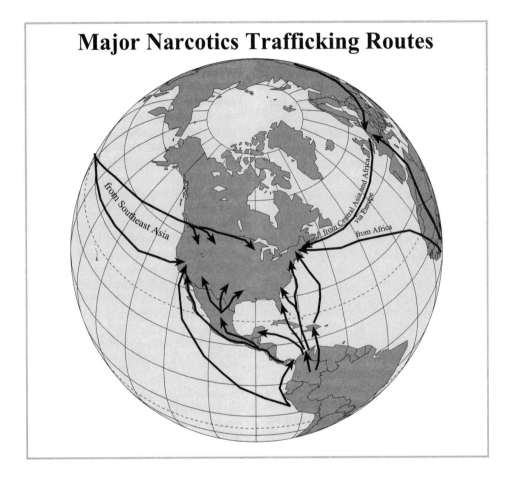

cies participated in drug enforcement efforts. The lead agency, the DEA, carried out a broad range of work, including programs to eradicate domestic marijuana crops, gather intelligence about drug trafficking, and cooperate with foreign governments to carry out enforcement. The FBI investigated drug-running operations, and the Pentagon established special task forces that used military personnel and technology to detect drug smugglers. Other important agencies involved in 1990s drug enforcement included the U.S. Customs office, the Immigration and Naturalization Service, and the State Department. In addition, state and local police departments and courts enforced their own penal codes and funded treatment and abstinence programs. Estimates of sub-federal government spending are difficult to calculate, but generally ran ahead of federal spending. According to a federal study, in 1992 state and local governments spent $15.9 million on drug enforcement and treatment and the federal government spent $11.9 billion.

The Logic of the War on Drugs

The goal of government drug policy from the 1960s through the early 2000s was to control and reduce the incidence of illegal use, operating on the assumption that drugs impose substantial costs on the user (addiction,

poor health, death) and society (drug influenced crime and violence). To that end, resources were devoted to working with or pressuring foreign governments to destroy drug crops, and sealing off U.S. borders from illegal drug smuggling. While interdiction policies were at work as early as 1914, it was not until the spike in both casual and serious drug use in the 1960s that the control of illegal narcotics trade became a serious foreign policy and federal law enforcement matter. Nixon's pressure on Turkey, as well as foiling the "French Connection" smuggling route into the United States, cut off the import of heroin from the west. However, production (the growing of poppies) simply moved to Mexico and Southeast Asia. The shift of production of narcotics to other nations and regions after the application of U.S. pressure marred subsequent interdiction and drug destruction efforts.

In the 1980s, enforcement efforts concentrated on South American production of coca, from which cocaine and its smokable derivative, crack, are derived. In 2002 military and economic aid continued to be directed to Colombia, Bolivia, and Peru to destroy crops as well as eliminate production facilities. Appropriations for the "Andes Initiative" totaled $1.8 billion in 2000. U.S. efforts at controlling drug production in Latin America during the 1980s and 1990s were ineffective. In the case of Bolivia, for example, crop elimination efforts in the 1980s were thwarted by widespread corruption among high-ranking government officials, successful efforts of farmers to avoid detection, and the country's overwhelming dependence on drug trade revenue. In 1990, the Bolivian drug trade employed 500,000 workers and financed half of the country's imports. The ineffectiveness of interdiction efforts can be seen in the decrease in the street value of hard drugs during the 1980s and 1990s, despite the federal government's efforts to increase the costs and risks of selling drugs. Efforts to destroy foreign marijuana production also proved unsuccessful, having little impact on street price as crackdowns on production in foreign countries encouraged domestic cultivation.

Interdiction efforts involved the use of sophisticated technology as well agents from the DEA, the U.S. Customs Service, the Border Patrol, and soldiers of the U.S. military. But in the late twentieth century these efforts captured only a small percentage of the drugs entering the United States each year. Smugglers became increasingly sophisticated in evading detection, in some cases smuggling drugs in the steel containers of cargo ships. An effort to concentrate interdiction in one region simply diverted the traffic to another. Successful interdiction efforts in southern Florida in the 1980s, for example, shifted smuggling to the northern Mexico routes.

Longer jail terms for users as well as crackdowns on street selling characterized drug policy from the 1980s to the early 2000s, with little effect. Jail time was not a strong deterrent to addicts, and sellers assumed the significant risks of incarceration because of the profits that drug sales created. Punitive policies may have discouraged the casual use of drugs, since two thirds of all drug related arrests were for possession (the remaining third for drug sale). But the decline in drug use among casual users since 1978 may be attributed not only to stiffer sentencing for possession, but also to a changing social and economic context, improved public health education, or a combination of all three factors. The number of hard core drug users remained relatively constant during the period 1980–2000 despite the acceleration in incarceration rates.

Between 1988 and 1995, Americans spent $57.3 billion on criminal drug enforcement and each year during that period made 1.23 million arrests for drug related offenses. Nevertheless, illegal drug sales and use did not decline. The political economy of the drug trade makes the eradication of illegal narcotics virtually impossible. Studies estimated that even if the government had been able to seize 50 percent of the cocaine from Latin America, U.S. street prices would have risen only 3 percent. Most of the value of drugs was added after the product entered the United States. The cost to drug dealers from interdiction or crop destruction was easily absorbed because of the healthy profits enjoyed in the black market.

The Politics of Narcotics Policy

The crackdown on drug use by the Nixon administration was part of broader political strategy to secure middle class voters with law and order policies at a time when the Democratic Party was under criticism for being "soft on crime." Seeking to undermine the president's efforts to differentiate the two major parties on the crime issue, congressional Democrats supported the president's drug initiatives. The same dynamic was at work during the Reagan and Bush years. President Bill Clinton made modest attempts to redirect resources from enforcement to drug treatment, but was rebuffed by members of his own party.

In the 1990s many libertarians within the Democratic and Republican Parties, as well as public heath and medical professionals, argued to varying degrees for the decriminalization of narcotics. George Soros, a financier, in 1994 established the Lindesmith Center to lobby for reductions in criminal penalties for drug use. In 1996 the editorial board of *The National Review* labeled U.S. drug policy a failure and called for a public heath–oriented approach to policy. Opponents of the status quo were especially critical of laws that prevented the distribution of clean needles to heroin addicts in order to prevent the spread of AIDS. Still, in the late 1990s and early 2000s most law enforcement associations and elected officials resisted any major legislative changes in U.S. drug policy.

BIBLIOGRAPHY

Meir, Kenneth J. *The Politics of Sin: Drugs, Alcohol, and Public Policy.* Armonk, N.Y.: M. E. Sharpe, 1994.

Bertram, Eva, et al. *Drug War Politics: The Price of Denial.* Berkeley: University of California Press,1996.

Musto, David. *The American Disease: Origins of Narcotic Control,* 3d ed. New York: Oxford University Press, 1999.

Richard M. Flanagan

See also **Drug Trafficking, Illegal; Substance Abuse.**

NARRAGANSETT. Narragansetts first encountered Europeans in 1524. Relatively unaffected by the massive epidemic of 1616–1617, they became players in the fur trade and a major power in southern New England. In 1636 the tribe allowed Roger Williams and other Puritan dissidents to settle in their territory (now southern Rhode Island), and then joined the English in the PEQUOT WAR. Their relationship quickly soured, although negotiators managed to prevent war. But when KING PHILIP'S WAR erupted in 1675, an English preemptive strike drove the tribe into the conflict. Ninigret, sachem of the neighboring Niantics, remained neutral; his community drew many survivors and gradually became known as Narragansett. By 1750 Ninigret's descendents were selling tribal lands to pay for their rich lifestyle, alienating most in the tribe. After the Revolution many left for Brothertown in New York. Those remaining became the last autonomous tribe

Narrows. Tall ships and naval vessels lead the parade of watercraft through the Narrows of New York Harbor during Operation Sail, which was part of the nationwide U.S. Bicentennial celebration in 1976.

in the region, governed by an elected council. In 1880 Rhode Island decided to terminate the tribe and sell its reserve. But kinship and gatherings continued to bring Narragansetts together; the tribe incorporated in 1934 and in 1978 won 1,800 acres from the state. In April 1983 the Narragansett tribe was the first in southern New England to win federal recognition, and in 2000 counted about 2,400 members.

BIBLIOGRAPHY

Campbell, Paul R., and LaFantosie, Glenn W. "Scattered to the Winds of Heaven: Narrangansett Indians, 1676–1880." *Rhode Island History* 37, no. 3 (1978): 66–83.

Simmons, William S. "Narragansett." In *Handbook of North American Indians.* Edited by William C. Sturtevant et al. Volume 15: *The Northeast,* edited by Bruce G. Trigger. Washington, D.C.: Smithsonian Institution, 1978.

Daniel R. Mandell

See also **Indian Claims Commission.**

NARRAGANSETT BAY. An inlet of the Atlantic Ocean in southeastern RHODE ISLAND, Narragansett Bay was so named by English explorers after the Indians who lived on its western shore.

The bay served as a primary artery of colonial maritime commerce. Trade and shipbuilding were the most prominent businesses. By the early 1700s, ships built in Newport and other bayside towns were available for sale to other colonies and Europe. During the American Revolution the Bay, integral to trade in restricted goods such as molasses, was the site of several key confrontations between the colonists and British officials. In 1772 HMS *Gaspee,* charged with pursuing colonial smugglers, was burned to the waterline.

BIBLIOGRAPHY

Daniels, Bruce Colin. *Dissent and Conformity on Narragansett Bay: The Colonial Rhode Island Town.* Middletown, Conn.: Wesleyan University Press, 1983.

Hale, Stuart O. *Narragansett Bay: A Friend's Perspective.* Narragansett, R.I.: Marine Advisory Service, University of Rhode Island, 1980.

Leslie J. Lindenauer

See also **Narragansett.**

NARRAGANSETT PLANTERS. The Narragansett Planters were a group of wealthy landowners who settled on the fertile lands in southern and southwestern RHODE ISLAND. Their planter culture more closely resembled southern plantation life than that of the New England yeoman farmer. They raised cattle and bred horses, including the renowned Narragansett Pacer, on estates that in some cases exceeded several thousand acres. The planters also cultivated tobacco for a time. Motivated by the search for profit, they relied upon both African slaves and white indentured servants to cultivate this labor-intensive crop. In the mid-eighteenth century, slave laborers constituted over 10 percent of the Narragansett or South County population, the highest concentration in New England.

BIBLIOGRAPHY

Fitts, Robert K. *Inventing New England's Slave Paradise: Master-Slave Relations in Eighteenth-Century Narragansett, Rhode Island.* New York: Garland, 1998.

Leslie J. Lindenauer

See also **New England Colonies; Providence Plantations, Rhode Island and; Slavery; Tobacco Industry.**

NARROWS, a strait connecting the upper and lower New York Bays, was entered by the Italian explorer Giovanni da Verrazano in 1524, and first shown on a map made by the Italian scholar Giambattista Ramusio in 1556. It was fortified about 1710, and more strongly for the War of 1812, providing for an effective defense of New York Harbor. A semaphore telegraph, to announce the sighting of vessels, was erected there in 1812. In 1964 the Narrows were spanned by the world's longest suspension bridge (4,260 feet), the Verrazano-Narrows Bridge.

BIBLIOGRAPHY

Stokes, Isaac Newton Phelps. *The Iconography of Manhattan Island, 1498–1909.* New York: Arno Press, 1967.

Alvin F. Harlow / D. B.

See also **Bridges; New York City; War of 1812.**

NASA. *See* **National Aeronautics and Space Administration.**

NASHVILLE, the capital of Tennessee, is in the north-central region of the state. In many ways a typically "New South" metropolis, the city has always exercised disproportionately large political and cultural influence over the mid-South. Nineteenth-century American presidents Andrew Jackson, James Polk, and Andrew Johnson all adopted Nashville as their hometowns, as did Vanderbilt University's "Fugitives," a southern literary movement led by Robert Penn Warren and John Crowe Ransom.

Grand Ole Opry. The main stage, since 1925, at the center of the country music industry: Nashville. GRAND OLE OPRY

Nashville was founded by a group of settlers led by James Robertson in the winter of 1779/80. Investors and speculators from North Carolina and Virginia were soon attracted to Nashville's prime location in the fertile Cumberland River Valley, and by 1806, the fledging town was officially incorporated. The city grew steadily throughout the nineteenth century, never booming like neighboring Memphis and Atlanta, but growing in population from 17,000 in 1860 to 80,000 by 1900. During this time, Nashville became known as the "Athens of the South" for its cultural institutions and highly regarded universities such as Fisk and Vanderbilt, and the city gained somewhat of a genteel reputation.

Nashville began to grow into a major metropolis with the onset of the Great Depression and the subsequent New Deal programs like the Tennessee Valley Authority, which provided cheap and plentiful power. The city's economy boomed throughout the remainder of the twentieth century. Never a major industrial center, Nashville's banking, insurance, and entertainment industries allowed it to take advantage of the national shift to a more service-centered economy. The entertainment industry provided Nashville with a new image, as the Grand Ole Opry helped make Nashville into "Music City," the center of the country music recording industry.

After World War II, the civil rights movement forced the South to end segregation de jure, and Nashville followed suit somewhat more peacefully than other Southern cities. In contrast to many American cities in the postwar era, Nashville's population rose the fastest during the 1960s, from 170,000 to 426,000, largely because of the city's governmental functions merged with Davidson County.

As of 2000, the Nashville-Davidson population had risen to 569,891, an eleven percent increase from 1990. The metropolitan area reached 1,231,311, a twenty-five percent increase, making Nashville the fastest-growing metropolitan area between Atlanta and Dallas. The city's economy remains diverse, with religious publishing joining tourism, banking, auto manufacturing, and health care as major growth sectors.

BIBLIOGRAPHY

Doyle, Don Harrison. *Nashville in the New South: 1880–1930.* Knoxville: University of Tennessee Press, 1985.

———. *Nashville since the 1920s.* Knoxville: University of Tennessee Press, 1985.

John McCarthy

See also **Music: Country and Western; Tennessee.**

NASHVILLE, BATTLE OF.

The Battle of Nashville (15–16 December 1864) was a dramatic winter conflict in which Gen. George H. Thomas, with a hastily organized army of heterogeneous troops, moved out of Nashville and fell upon the Confederate forces of Gen. John B. Hood. On the first day the Confederates were pushed back. On the following day, while feinting and holding on his left wing, Thomas pressed forward on his right and drove the Confederates in disorderly retreat from the battlefield. Sometimes described as exemplifying perfect tactics, Thomas's victory freed Tennessee of organized Confederate forces and marked the end of Hood's Tennessee campaign.

BIBLIOGRAPHY

Hay, Thomas Robson. *Hood's Tennessee Campaign.* Dayton, Ohio: Morningside Bookshop, 1976.

Sword, Wiley. *Embrace an Angry Wind: The Confederacy's Last Hurrah.* New York: HarperCollins, 1991.

Alfred P. James / A. R.

See also **Civil War; Hood's Tennessee Campaign; Tennessee, Army of.**

NASHVILLE CONVENTION

of delegates from the southern states met in two sessions from 3 to 12 June and 11 to 18 November 1850. As sectional tensions deepened following the opening of the first session of the new Congress of December 1849, many southern politicians, led by the aging senator John C. Calhoun of South Carolina, believed that a united front was necessary if slavery and southern rights were to be maintained within the Union. Calls for concerted action were made throughout the South, and in October 1849, strongly prompted by Calhoun, the Mississippi state convention, in a bipartisan move, resolved "that a convention of the slave-holding States should be held in Nashville, Tenn. . . . to devise and adopt some mode of resistance to [northern] aggressions." In response to this call, delegates from nine states—chosen by popular vote, by conventions, by state legislatures, or by governors—assembled at Nashville on 3 June 1850. The majority of delegates present came from Tennessee itself, but of the main slave states, only Loui-

siana and North Carolina were unrepresented. Although delegates from both parties were chosen, Democrats dominated the proceedings. Wary of Calhounite calls for cross-party unity, and fortified by the introduction in Congress of Henry Clay's compromise program in January 1850, the majority of southern Whigs had come to regard the proposed convention as a cloak for Democratic disunionism.

In truth, the Nashville Convention proved a failure for Democratic radicals. At the close of its first session, the convention unanimously adopted twenty-eight resolutions but issued no ultimatums on southern rights in the territories, the main bone of sectional dispute. The resolutions maintained that slavery existed independent of, but was recognized by, the Constitution; that the territories belonged to the people of the states; that the citizens of the several states had equal rights to migrate to the territories; and that Congress had no power to exclude a citizen's property but was obligated to protect it. In its eleventh resolution, the convention demonstrated its moderation by expressing a willingness to settle the territorial matter by extending the Missouri Compromise line to the Pacific, albeit as an "extreme concession." Finally, delegates adopted an address to the people of the southern states that condemned Clay's compromise resolutions, then being debated by Congress. Reassembling on 11 November, the convention, with a much reduced attendance, rejected the compromise that had been agreed by Congress six weeks earlier and affirmed the right of secession while calling for a further meeting. With southern sentiment rapidly crystallizing in support of the compromise, the second session proved a fiasco. A week after the delegates concluded their work, voters in Georgia voted by a clear majority in support of the compromise, evidence of the changed political sentiment that had undermined the convention's appeal.

BIBLIOGRAPHY

Cooper, William J., Jr. *The South and the Politics of Slavery, 1828–1856.* Baton Rouge: Louisiana State University Press, 1978.

Jennings, Thelma. *The Nashville Convention: Southern Movement for Unity, 1848–1851.* Memphis, Tenn.: Memphis State University Press, 1980.

Martin Crawford
Fletcher M. Green

See also **Missouri Compromise.**

NAT TURNER'S REBELLION

was the most significant slave revolt in United States history. Under the leadership of Nat Turner, a thirty-one-year-old religious mystic, a group of enslaved people in Southampton County, Virginia, conspired to strike a blow to the system. On 21 August 1831 Turner and six followers attacked and killed Turner's owner and the owner's family, gathered arms and ammunition, and set out to gain support from other slaves. Turner's force grew to about seventy-five,

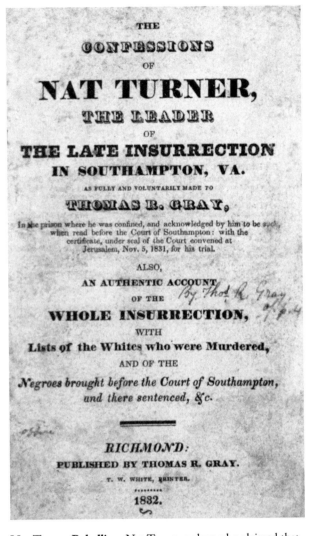

Nat Turner Rebellion. Nat Turner, a slave who claimed that he had received divine guidance, led an insurrection in 1831 that resulted in the deaths of approximately sixty white people and dozens of slaves, some of whom were bystanders. Captured in October, Turner gave this confession before he was hanged on 11 November.

and they killed approximately sixty whites. On 23 August, while en route to the county seat at Jerusalem, the rebels encountered a large force of white volunteers and trained militia and were defeated. Turner escaped and attempted unsuccessfully to gather other supporters. He was captured on 30 October, sentenced to death by hanging on 5 November after a brief trial, and executed on 11 November. Several of his followers had been hanged earlier.

The incident sparked a reign of terror resulting in the murder of a number of innocent blacks, the passage of more stringent slave laws, and the more vigorous enforcement of existing statutes. The immediate effect of the rebellion on the attitudes of blacks toward slavery and toward themselves is difficult to document, but there is evidence that Turner's example of resistance lived on in the collective memory of the black community.

BIBLIOGRAPHY

Herbert Aptheker, *Nat Turner's Slave Rebellion.* Prometheus Books: New York, 1966.

Foner, Eric. *Nat Turner.* Englewood Cliffs, N.J.: Prentice-Hall, 1971.

Oates, Stephen B. *The Fires of Jubilee: Nat Turner's Fierce Rebellion.* New York: Harper and Row, 1976.

Tragle, Henry Irving. *The Southampton Slave Revolt of 1831: A Compilation of Source Material.* Amherst: University of Massachusetts Press, 1971.

Henry N. Drewry/A. R.

See also **African American Religions and Sects; Education, African American; Insurrections, Domestic; Slave Insurrections; South, the: The Antebellum South;** *and* vol. 9: **The Nat Turner Insurrection.**

NATCHEZ. The Natchez, existing from circa A.D. 700 until they were dispersed by the French in 1731, stood out among other southeastern tribes for their class-like organization of society and for the power and privileges of their premier lineage, the Suns. French observers left accounts that, rich as they are, did not provide a clear record of Natchez society's many unique features. The Natchez language is a linguistic isolate not clearly related to other languages.

The Natchez population declined rapidly in the first quarter of the 1700s from an initial recorded estimate of about 5,000. Likewise, in precontact times, archaeological evidence reveals that the Natchez's ancestors occupied up to five mound centers, but in the eighteenth century European disease reduced the polity to a single mound center, Natchez proper, and nine smaller communities. Despite this contraction, the Natchez remained militarily powerful, and they resisted French domination in a series of rebellions between 1715 and 1730. However, tribal solidarity became fatefully compromised when they split into a French faction led by the chief of the Grand Village, and a British faction led by the upstart chief of the White Apple village.

The name "Natchez" actually refers to the Grand Village. "Theocloel," the name by which the polity was known to its members, meant "people of Thé," or the descendants of this founding ancestor-deity. The French used the name Natchez to refer to the polity as a whole, not understanding the degree of autonomy that individual villages could exercise. Village chief authority was despotic to those residing nearby, but chiefs of more distant places such as the White Apple village operated independently of each other in postcontact times.

The Natchez had a complex social hierarchy. Membership in one of three social ranks was by birth, with an additional "honored" rank that generally was achieved

Natchez. This 1732 illustration by Alexandre de Batz shows the Tunica chief Buffalo Tamer *(left)*—along with the widow and son of his predecessor, who was killed by the Natchez—holding a coup stick bearing three Natchez scalps; by then, the French, with Tunica help, had killed, captured, or dispersed the Natchez people. NATIONAL ARCHIVES AND RECORDS ADMINISTRATION

Lorenz, Karl G. "The Natchez of Southwest Mississippi." In *Indians of the Greater Southeast.* Edited by Bonnie G. McEwan. Gainesville: University Press of Florida, 2000.

Stern, Theodore. "The Natchez." In *The Native Americans.* Edited by Robert F. Spencer et al. New York: Harper and Row, 1965.

James A. Brown

See also **Tribes: Southeastern.**

NATCHEZ CAMPAIGN OF 1813.

The Natchez Campaign of 1813 was waged by U.S. forces against the Creeks of the Tombigbee and Alabama Rivers region, then the eastern frontier of the Mississippi Territory. The Creeks threatened hostilities early in 1813, and a brigade of volunteers from NATCHEZ country, commanded by Gen. F. L. Claiborne, was ordered to Fort Stoddert, on the Tombigbee. Following the Creek attack on Fort Mims on the east bank of the Alabama River about thirty-five miles above Mobile, 30 August 1813, Claiborne was reinforced and was able to destroy the Creek stronghold at the Holy Ground in present-day Lowndes County, Alabama, on 23 December 1813.

BIBLIOGRAPHY

Halbert, Henry S., and T. H. Ball. *The Creek War of 1813 and 1814.* University: University of Alabama Press, 1969.

Owsley, Frank L. *Struggle for the Gulf Borderlands.* Tuscaloosa: University of Alabama Press, 2000.

Edgar B. Nixon / A. R.

See also **Creek War; Indian Policy, U.S.: 1775–1830; Indian Removal; Mississippi; Native Americans.**

through merit. The topmost lineage was the Suns, who were senior descendents of a line of mothers from the tribal deity. Three influential positions were monopolized by the Suns. The eldest male held the chiefship, "Great Sun," and controlled access to the ancestral godhead in the shrine that was erected atop the principal platform mound. The mother of the Great Sun, or the senior female Sun, was called "White Woman," and the younger brother of the Sun was called "Tattooed Serpent," and held the office of war chief. The funeral rites of these privileged individuals captured the attention of the earliest French observers. Junior members of the Sun lineage possessed the same ancestral rights and exercised authority as chiefs in their own villages. In the second rank were the "Nobles," who were children of male Suns. Children of male nobles dropped in rank to that of "Stinkards," or commoners.

BIBLIOGRAPHY

Hudson, Charles M. *The Southeastern Indians.* Knoxville: University of Tennessee Press, 1976.

NATCHEZ TRACE,

a road running more than five hundred miles from Nashville, Tennessee, to Natchez, Mississippi, on the MISSISSIPPI RIVER, roughly follows an old Indian trail. After the United States purchased Louisiana in 1803, the economic and military necessity spurred the government to build ROADS. In 1806, Congress authorized construction to begin on the Natchez Trace. For several decades most of its traffic was northward, since settlers would float their produce down the Mississippi to market on flatboats and return over the Trace by foot or on horseback. Construction of a 450-mile parkway following the trace began in 1934. In 1938 it was designated the Natchez Trace National Parkway.

BIBLIOGRAPHY

Adams, Katherine J., and Lewis L. Gould. *Inside the Natchez Trace Collection: New Sources for Southern History.* Baton Rouge: Louisiana State University Press, 1999.

Daniels, Jonathan. *The Devil's Backbone: The Story of the Natchez Trace.* New York: McGraw-Hill, 1962.

Davis, William C. *A Way through the Wilderness: The Natchez Trace and the Civilization of the Southern Frontier.* New York: Harper Collins, 1995.

Gerald M. Capers Jr. / H. S.

See also **Louisiana Purchase.**

NATION OF ISLAM. The Nation of Islam (NOI), whose members are widely referred to as Black Muslims, was founded in Detroit in 1930 by Wallace D. Fard. An enigmatic figure with mysterious origins, Fard surfaced in the city in 1929 and attracted the attention of poor blacks as he walked the streets selling fabrics and expounding novel religious and political messages. Fard skillfully blended tenets of traditional Islam with antiwhite preachments that resonated with the psychological and social needs of economically strapped blacks. This group, frustrated by the inability of traditional religions to generate change in their lives and keenly aware of the impact of racism on their opportunities, was drawn to Fard's message.

The cosmology of the NOI was exotic but carefully crafted to offer a millenarian vision to African Americans, promising a future apocalypse for the evil (whites) and salvation to the true believers (blacks or "Original People"). According to Fard's theology, an insane scientist, Yakub, who lived 6,000 years ago, grafted a new human species from the Original People. Over time, the grafted species mutated and became white. An angry God looked with disfavor on the manipulations of Yakub and decreed that the white race of people he created would rule for 6,000 years and then be vanquished. At that point, the Original People would inherit a world where true nirvana would reign.

Early Leadership

Researchers in the 1990s who examined state and federal records concluded that Fard was born Wallace Dodd Ford on 25 February 1891. Despite the uneven quality of record keeping in the period, most researchers conclude that he was white. Public records reveal that he grew up in southern California and became involved in petty crime at an early age. In 1926 he was sentenced to serve time in San Quentin prison for selling narcotics to an undercover policeman. FBI records show that after his release from San Quentin in 1929 he headed east, spent a brief period in Chicago, then settled in Detroit.

As Fard began constructing his religious and political message, one of his most ardent followers was Elijah Poole. After repeated clashes with white officials in his hometown of Sandersville, Georgia, Poole joined the thousands of blacks who fled the South to search for greater freedom and economic opportunity. Elijah was a tireless and loyal lieutenant to Fard and slowly gained authority within the mosque. He established the Southside Mosque in Chicago in 1932, and in 1933, Fard granted Elijah the surname "Muhammad."

Elijah Muhammad. The longtime leader of the Nation of Islam in 1966, the year after the assassination of his former protégé Malcolm X. © CORBIS

The Muslims, with their antiwhite rhetoric, soon became prime targets for law enforcement. In 1933, Fard abruptly told his followers that God had preordained that he leave Detroit, and that he was passing on the mantle of leadership to his faithful student, Elijah. Despite Fard's claim of divine direction, evidence since disclosed suggests that the worsening relationship with Detroit police officers was the primary impetus for Fard's departure. Under Elijah Muhammad's direction, the NOI survived, but grew slowly in northern cities. Bitter contests over leadership and finances plagued the NOI's viability through the depression years.

After the bombing of Pearl Harbor in 1941, Muhammad was drafted into the army but refused to serve, citing his Islamic religious beliefs and expressing sympathy for the nonwhite Japanese. He was convicted of draft evasion and served three years in the federal prison at Milan, Michigan. His bold antigovernment stand earned him martyr status among the faithful and helped solidify his position in the Muslim community, where competition for standing was constant. While in prison, Muhammad noted that through inmate labor and cooperation, the facility was able to produce food to meet the needs of the prison population. Elijah expanded this insight into an economic strategy for the Nation of Islam. When released in 1946, Elijah returned to Chicago, and with enhanced personal authority he began rebuilding the NOI, which had languished during his detention. Consistent with the goal of racial self-reliance, Elijah established farms, dairies, retail food outlets, and a number of small Muslim-owned businesses.

Rejuvenation

In 1948, Malcolm Little, serving time in a Michigan prison for petty larceny, became attracted to the Muslim ideology and from prison began a correspondence with Muhammad. Shortly after his release in 1952, he visited the leader in Chicago; soon afterward he converted and was designated "Malcolm X." The frail and diminutive Muhammad was not a formidable presence on public podiums; however, he recognized Malcolm's talent as a spokesperson and organizer. Malcolm X's skill and unwavering dedication to Muhammad led to a swift ascent within the Muslim organization. In succession, he revitalized and headed mosques in Boston, Philadelphia, and New York. Malcolm was responsible for a slow but steady upsurge in membership. However, in July 1959, the television documentary *The Hate that Hate Produced* propelled the Nation of Islam and Malcolm X into America's consciousness.

The CBS network and the show's producers, Mike Wallace and Louis Lomax, calculated that sensational publicity about the antiwhite ideology of the Black Muslims would prompt hostile reactions in the black communities and arrest the development of the NOI. Instead, the show sparked a sharp upsurge of black interest in the Muslims and their eloquent spokesman, Malcolm X. Soon, Malcolm was a sought-after commentator on America's racial morass. The media cast him as counterpoint to the moderation of civil rights leaders. Essentially self-taught, Malcolm became skilled in public debate and held his own against political and intellectual adversaries on campuses and in broadcast studios. He consistently expressed views ridiculing civil rights leaders and their integrationist assumptions. Malcolm was contemptuous of nonviolence and distrustful of a constitutional system that had coexisted for centuries with bigotry and black oppression.

Malcolm X's effectiveness as a national spokesperson was key in the growth of the NOI to approximately 20,000 members by the early 1960s, though estimates vary. Importantly, the NOI founded a nationally distributed newspaper, *Muhammad Speaks*, that offered news and opinion consistent with the Muslim program. With a circulation of 600,000 (largely through street corner sales by members) by 1966, it was the most widely read black newspaper in the United States.

The most notable Muslim convert was the heavyweight boxing champion (1964–1967) Cassius Clay. Recruited by Malcolm X, Clay converted to the NOI in 1964, and Elijah gave him the name Muhammad Ali. The charismatic and loquacious celebrity gained fame internationally when, in 1967 at the height of the Vietnam War, he refused to be inducted into the army, claiming conscientious objector status. His lawyers argued unsuccessfully that as a Muslim minister he had the same rights as other religious leaders. In explaining his decision, Ali further politicized the dispute by remarking, "no Vietcong ever called me Nigger." Under pressure from con-

gressional powers, U.S. boxing officials stripped Ali of his championship title. Thus, at the height of his pugilistic prowess he was effectively banned from the sport. The actions of officials generated broad sympathy for Ali among African Americans as well as among critics of the war. Ali's position was vindicated when in 1971 the Supreme Court overturned his 1967 conviction for draft evasion.

Tensions grew within the NOI between Malcolm X and the venerable Elijah Muhammad. In 1963, Muhammad disciplined Malcolm when he characterized the assassination of President John F. Kennedy as a case of "chickens coming home to roost." Malcolm accepted Muhammad's sanctions but bridled under what he thought were unnecessary niceties in the face of federal government inaction in the civil rights arena.

The conflicts exploded into violence when Malcolm X was assassinated in Harlem's Audubon Ballroom on 21 February 1965. Three men with ties to Elijah Muhammad's faction were arrested, tried, and sentenced to long prison terms. Speculations about the motives behind Malcolm X's murder centered on his increasingly public statements about his longtime mentor's morality. Elijah had fathered at least ten out-of-wedlock children with Muslim women.

The public perception of the NOI as a radical and aggressive group finds little support in its social and cultural practices. The group was fundamentally conservative in organizational structure, economic outlook, and political matters. Muhammad functioned as an autocratic leader, issuing direction from the top of a rigid hierarchy. Women's roles in the NOI were restricted and subordinated to those of men. The NOI was thoroughly capitalistic in economic matters, holding out hope that its small business initiatives could provide jobs and subsistence needed by poor African Americans. The failure of

Louis Farrakhan. The fiery head of the new Nation of Islam and chief organizer of the 1995 "Million Man March." AP/ WIDE WORLD PHOTOS

an all-black group to actively participate in the black liberation struggles that were taking place in the United States helped reinforce the suspicions of many that the Muslims' antiwhite rhetoric was never coupled with action. Muhammad deferred to what he believed to be God's divine scheme and discouraged his followers from voting and taking any direct action on behalf of other blacks. Malcolm X cited the NOI's political passivity as a factor in his separation from the organization.

More Transformations

When Elijah died of heart failure on 25 February 1975, the group did not undergo the disruptive factionalism that NOI had experienced in the 1930s and 1960s. Muhammad had named his son Wallace Muhammad as his successor, and the Muslim faithful coalesced around his leadership. Wallace soon announced a new direction for the Nation of Islam, one more closely aligned with orthodox Islam. The organization downplayed the antiwhite theme that for years had been an important drawing card for NOI recruiters. Voting and political participation was endorsed. In 1976, Wallace changed the name of the group to the World Community of Islam in the West (WCIW).

In 1979, the minister Louis Farrakhan, leader of the New York Mosque, announced his departure from Wallace's WCIW and his plans to establish a group under his leadership, reclaiming the name "Nation of Islam." Farrakhan had become skeptical about the reforms instituted by Wallace and vowed that the new NOI would resuscitate the ideology of Wallace's father. Farrakhan's fiery public preachments reflected the style of Malcolm X and attracted the attention of many non-Muslims (especially young people) who admired his bold critiques. During the 1980s and 1990s, few African American leaders stepped forward to express the anger shared by millions of blacks suffering from racial oppression.

Farrakhan's comments about Jews led some critics to accuse him of anti-Semitism, but the charges had little impact on his core constituency. In 1995, Farrakhan spearheaded the drive for a "Million Man March" in Washington, D.C., to encourage black males to acknowledge and atone for past failings and rededicate themselves to social and family responsibilities. Contrary to the predictions of black and white officials, approximately one million black men participated in the demonstration and heard Farrakhan deliver the keynote address.

From the brief tenure of W. D. Fard though the Farrakhan period, the Nation of Islam rhetorically highlighted the drama of black racial identity in the United States. However, Black Muslims held that the tension could only be resolved by racial separatism and group self-help—not civil rights and integration. Although the encompassing demands of formal membership in the NOI assured that the organization would remain small, the fusillades against white supremacy launched by figures like Malcolm X and the philosophy of group self-help earned Black Muslims the respect, if not allegiance, of millions of black Americans.

BIBLIOGRAPHY

Clegg, Claude Andrew. *An Original Man: The Life and Times of Elijah Muhammad.* New York: St. Martin's Press, 1997.

Evanzz, Karl. *The Messenger: The Rise and Fall of Elijah Muhammad.* New York: Pantheon, 1999.

Gardell, Mattias. *In the Name of Elijah Muhammad: Louis Farrakhan and the Nation of Islam.* Durham, N.C.: Duke University Press, 1996.

Lee, Martha F. *The Nation of Islam: An American Millenarian Movement.* Syracuse, N.Y.: Syracuse University Press, 1996.

William M. Banks

See also **African American Religions and Sects; Black Nationalism; Islam.**

NATION, THE, a weekly journal of opinion founded in New York in 1865. America's oldest weekly magazine, *The Nation* has been distinctive since its inception for its independent and often dissenting voice. Its political commentary, cultural criticism, and, in later years, investigative reporting have often been far more influential than its modest circulation and frequently tenuous finances might suggest. Among its "main objects," *The Nation's* prospectus listed: "The discussion of the topics of the day. . . . The maintenance and diffusion of true democratic principles. . . . Sound and impartial criticism of books and works of art." The magazine was originally funded by a group interested in aiding freed slaves, though under its first editor, the Irish-born journalist E. L. Godkin, it soon shifted its political emphasis to civic reform with particular attention to the abuses of Boss Tweed and Tammany Hall in New York City.

The Nation under Godkin was notable for its classic laissez-faire liberalism, its commitment to a "higher standard" of literary criticism, and its moral seriousness. Lord Bryce remarked that Godkin's intimates admired him less for his "intellectual gifts" than for the "moral qualities" that directed them. And while those qualities could draw criticism—for example, Charles A. Dana, editor of the raffish and popular daily *New York Sun*, dismissed Godkin as "priggish and self-complacent"—the magazine gained a devoted following among the small but influential readership Godkin cared most to win, which he described as "thoughtful, educated, high-minded men—gentlemen in short." Into that category also fell most of his contributors, among them William James, Henry James, William Dean Howells, Charles S. Peirce, Frederick Law Olmsted, William Graham Sumner, and John W. De Forest. De Forest is said to have launched the term "great American novel" in a *Nation* essay in 1868.

After Godkin was named editor of Henry Villard's *New York Evening Post* in 1881, *The Nation*, incorporated into the newspaper as a weekly supplement, underwent a slow leakage of freshness, edge, and influence. At one point, H. L. Mencken called it "perhaps, the dullest publication of any sort ever printed in the world." In 1918, Oswald Garrison Villard sold the *Post* and became editor of *The Nation*, which he transformed so starkly that, he later recalled, many old readers were said to "have perished from shock and heart failure." New readers, however, more than filled whatever void those left, and by 1920, its circulation had jumped more than fivefold to 38,087. A longtime pacifist and reformer, Villard crusaded for civil rights, workers' rights, the impeachment of Attorney General A. Mitchell Palmer, and a new trial for the convicted anarchist-murderers Nicola Sacco and Bartolomeo Vanzetti. Villard opposed U.S. adventurism in Haiti and Nicaragua, and he supported the Progressive Party candidate Robert La Follette in 1924.

In 1932, Villard was succeeded as editor by Freda Kirchwey, who as a young staffer had edited the magazine's 1923 series "New Morals for Old," a bold exploration of marriage, sexuality, and the role of women. Kirchwey, who bought the magazine in 1937, maintained its liberal and crusading spirit. *The Nation* backed the Loyalists in Spain and the rescue of European refugees, and it supported the New Deal even while pressing the president to move further left. But Kirchwey's growing belief that fascism was a greater evil than war led to a bitter break with Villard, who accused her of "prostituting" the magazine. After the war, Kirchwey claimed credit for influencing President Harry Truman to recognize the State of Israel, but the magazine's fierce resistance to McCarthyism and its support for détente with the Soviet Union made it a frequent target of criticism, including from some of its own contributors and staffers and other members of the splintered left.

Among the goals of Carey McWilliams, the editor from 1955 to 1975, was what he called the revival of the muckraking tradition at a time when it had publicly been pronounced dead. The magazine investigated such topics as the Bay of Pigs disaster, welfare, the Central Intelligence Agency, blacklisting, the death penalty, business corruption, the Robert Oppenheimer and Julius and Ethel Rosenberg cases, and the beginnings of U.S. involvement in Vietnam. It was the first to publish Ralph Nader's articles on car safety. It also returned to its earliest roots with a vigorous campaign on behalf of the civil rights of African Americans.

Ownership of the magazine took many forms over the years, including individuals, the nonprofit group of Nation Associates, and groups of large and small investors in limited partnership with the publisher. The audited circulation in 2000 was 97,213. The Nation Institute, a nonprofit arm founded in 1966, supported investigative reporting projects, First Amendment and civil rights issues, and public education. Victor Navasky became editor in 1978 and was succeeded in that post by Katrina vanden Heuvel in 1995, when Navasky assumed the positions of publisher and editorial director. He has said that the mag-azine has not yet, to his knowledge, turned a profit. Rumor has it the publication once made money for three years, but no one, he said, can figure out when that was.

BIBLIOGRAPHY

Alpern, Sara. *Freda Kirchwey, a Woman of the "Nation."* Cambridge, Mass.: Harvard University Press, 1987.

vanden Heuvel, Katrina, ed. *The "Nation" 1865–1990: Selections from the Independent Magazine of Politics and Culture.* New York: Thunder's Mouth Press, 1990.

McWilliams, Carey. *The Education of Carey McWilliams.* New York: Simon and Schuster, 1979.

Ogden, Rollo, ed. *Life and Letters of Edwin Lawrence Godkin.* New York: Macmillan, 1907.

Andie Tucher

See also **Magazines**.

NATIONAL ACADEMY OF SCIENCES

NATIONAL ACADEMY OF SCIENCES was established by Congress on 3 March 1863 as a private organization to investigate and report on any subject of science or art (technology) whenever called upon by any department of the government. Largely a creation of the Civil War, the academy proved its usefulness immediately when in 1864 it helped the Union navy design a compass that would work inside the new ironclad warships. In 1871 the academy drew up instructions for the government-sponsored Arctic expedition of the *Polaris*, commanded by Charles F. Hall.

The National Research Council was established by the academy in 1916 at the request of President Woodrow Wilson. Two years later, an executive order made the National Research Council a permanent agency of the National Academy of Sciences to aid the military and civil branches of the government during World War I, and afterward to stimulate research—particularly cooperative research—in both pure and applied science. Since that time, the research council, supported by both public and private funds, has acted as the principal operating arm of the academy. In 1950 the National Academy of Sciences and its research council became a single administrative and operating unit, the National Academy of Sciences-National Research Council.

The National Academy of Engineering was created by Congress in 1964 under the original 1863 charter of the National Academy of Sciences as a private, permanent agency through which engineers could advise the government on the needs and uses of technology and engineering as it affected public policy. The National Academy of Engineering was organized with twenty-five founding members and with no limitation on membership. The parent organization, the National Academy of Sciences, had originally been limited by its charter to fifty members. In 1870 that restriction in the enabling act was removed, and membership was limited only by the maximum number that could be elected annually. Prominent members of the National Academy of Sciences have included Louis Agassiz, Albert Einstein, and Leo Szilard. The National Research Council drew its membership from scientists, engineers, and other professionals in universities, industry, and government to serve on its several hundred study committees. Because the four divisions of the academy are related but independent, when referred to as a group they are called the National Academies.

The National Academies played a central role in organizing the International Geophysical Year of 1958–1959, a worldwide scientific investigation that included the launching of Explorer I, the first American satellite. Both the National Academy of Sciences and the National Academy of Engineering annually elect foreign associates who meet the qualifications for membership. In 1970 the parent academy established an Institute of Medicine to provide advisory services in the areas of medicine and public health on a national scale. Based in Washington, D.C., the National Academies oversee hundreds of research projects run by its volunteer members, publish scientific and policy papers through the National Academy Press, and issue an annual report to Congress on the scientific, technological, and medical dimensions of pressing policy issues.

BIBLIOGRAPHY

Cochrane, Rexmond C. *The National Academy of Sciences: The First Hundred Years, 1863–1963.* Washington, D.C.: The Academy, 1978.

Kohlstedt, Sally G. *The Formation of the American Scientific Community.* Urbana: University of Illinois Press, 1976.

Rexmond C. Cochrane / a. r.

See also **American Association for the Advancement of Science; Engineering Societies; Learned Societies.**

NATIONAL AERONAUTICS AND SPACE ADMINISTRATION

(NASA) is the unit of the federal government charged with operating the nation's space exploration and aeronautics programs. The administrator of NASA, an independent agency, is appointed by the president, subject to Senate confirmation. NASA came into existence on 1 October 1958, after Congress passed the National Aeronautics and Space Act of 1958, at the recommendation of President Dwight D. Eisenhower. Many Americans had been highly alarmed when, on 4 October 1957, the Soviet Union put into orbit *Sputnik*, the first man-made satellite. In the midst of the Cold War, Americans feared that the Soviets might develop superior missile and space technology and use it against the United States. The new agency absorbed the National Advisory Committee for Aeronautics, a poorly funded research agency formed in 1915.

Even though much of NASA's early political support stemmed from America's Cold War competition with the Soviet Union, NASA was designed as an explicitly civilian agency to pursue peaceful space activities. Overseeing the military applications of space technology was left to the Department of Defense. In practice, however, the distinction has sometimes blurred. From the beginning, NASA and the military have cooperated in a variety of ways, and many astronauts have come from military backgrounds.

Projects Mercury and Gemini

NASA designed its first major program, Project Mercury, to study human abilities in space and to develop the technology required for manned space exploration. The program and the original seven astronauts received tremendous public attention, and the astronauts became national heroes. One of those seven, Alan Shepard, became the first American in space with his suborbital flight on 5 May 1961. On 20 February 1962, John Glenn became the first American to orbit the earth (Soviet cosmonaut Yuri A. Gagarin was the first human in space and the first to orbit the Earth, on 12 April 1961).

President John F. Kennedy congratulated the astronauts and NASA but said that the nation needed "a substantially larger effort" in space. Speaking to Congress on 25 May 1961, Kennedy declared what that effort should be: "I believe that this nation should commit itself to achieving the goal, before this decade is out, of landing a man on the moon and returning him safely to the Earth." Kennedy admitted that the lunar program would be expensive and risky, but the public came to support it enthusiastically. Congress approved the program—called Project Apollo—with very little debate. Apollo became the most expensive civilian project in American history.

Kennedy's dramatic goal exhilarated NASA. Under the skillful leadership of administrator James Webb, NASA set out to achieve the goal. The Mercury flights (a total of six from 1961 to 1963) and the subsequent Project Gemini (ten flights from 1965 to 1966) served as preliminary steps to going to the moon. The larger and more advanced Gemini spacecraft allowed astronauts to practice maneuvers that would be essential in the Apollo program.

Project Apollo

Ironically, as NASA worked toward fulfilling its exciting goal, public support for the agency began to decline. After it became clear that the United States was not really losing the "space race" to the Soviet Union, many Americans wondered whether the lunar program was worth its cost. Then, on 27 January 1967, three astronauts conducting tests inside a sealed Apollo capsule died when a fire broke out in the spacecraft. A review board found that NASA had not paid adequate attention to safety.

After several unmanned Apollo test flights and one manned mission that orbited the Earth, NASA was ready to send a spacecraft into lunar orbit. Circling the moon on Christmas Eve, 1968, the crew of *Apollo 8* beamed back to Earth spectacular pictures of the moon's surface. NASA

Second Man on the Moon. Edwin "Buzz" Aldrin Jr. joins Neil Armstrong in fulfilling the primary goal of NASA's Project Apollo. ASSOCIATED PRESS/WORLD WIDE PHOTOS

sent two more test flights into lunar orbit and was then ready to land on the moon. *Apollo 11* lifted off on 16 July 1969 and landed on the moon four days later. As much of the world watched televised coverage in awe, Neil Armstrong became the first human to walk on the moon. Just after he stepped from his spacecraft onto the lunar surface, Armstrong spoke his immortal line: "That's one small step for [a] man, one giant leap for mankind." The crew of *Apollo 11* returned safely to earth on 24 July.

Apollo 12 made a smooth journey to the moon and back, but the next mission—*Apollo 13*—encountered serious problems. On the way to the moon in April 1970, one of the spacecraft's oxygen tanks exploded, crippling the ship and leaving doubt whether the crew could return safely. Some ingenious work by the astronauts and the NASA engineers on the ground brought the crew of *Apollo 13* home alive. NASA conducted four more successful expeditions to the moon, but dwindling public interest and congressional support led to the cancellation of the final two planned flights.

The Space Shuttle

NASA's next major project was the space shuttle, which the agency promoted as a means of reliable and economical access to space. As it developed the shuttle during the 1970s, NASA also pursued the Apollo-Soyuz Test Project

with the Soviets, Skylab, and a series of unmanned exploratory missions, including the Viking probe of Mars. The shuttle began flying in 1981. Although the shuttle proved not to be as efficient as NASA promised, more than twenty flights had taken place by the end of 1985.

On 28 January 1986, tragedy struck. The shuttle *Challenger* exploded seventy-three seconds after liftoff, killing all seven astronauts aboard. The disaster stunned NASA and the nation. A presidential commission investigating the accident sharply criticized NASA's management and safety procedures. After revamping the program, shuttle flights resumed in 1988.

The Space Station

The 1990s saw NASA make significant improvements to the shuttle program, pursue a variety of unmanned missions (including the impressive Hubble Space Telescope), continue research in aeronautics and space science, and work on its next major project, an orbiting space station. Hampered by budgetary restraints and widespread criticisms of the initial station design, the project progressed slowly. In the mid-1980s, NASA had announced that the station would be a cooperative effort. Fifteen other nations—including Russia, America's former rival in space—eventually joined with the United States to develop the International Space Station (ISS). Russia's own space station, Mir, orbited the Earth from 1986 to 2001.

In late 1998, the first of more than forty space flights needed to transport and assemble the station in orbit took place. Plans originally called for international crews of up to seven astronauts to stay on the station for three to six months at a time. However, unexpectedly high development costs, plus unexpectedly low financial contributions from Russia, forced NASA to scale back the project to save money. The first crew to inhabit the station arrived in November 2000. Assembly of the station was scheduled for completion around 2004.

BIBLIOGRAPHY

Bilstein, Roger E. *Orders of Magnitude: A History of the NACA and NASA, 1915–1990.* Washington, D.C.: NASA, 1989.

Byrnes, Mark E. *Politics and Space: Image Making by NASA.* Westport, Conn.: Praeger, 1994.

Launius, Roger D. *NASA: A History of the U.S. Civil Space Program.* Malabar, Fla.: Krieger, 1994.

Walsh, Patrick J. *Echoes Among the Stars: A Short History of the U.S. Space Program.* Armonk, N.Y.: M.E. Sharpe, 2000.

Mark E. Byrnes

See also **Challenger Disaster; Hubble Space Telescope; Space Program; Space Shuttle.**

NATIONAL ARCHIVES. The National Archives and Records Administration (NARA) is America's national record keeper. By law NARA is charged with safeguarding records of all three branches of the federal government. Its mission is to assure federal agencies and the American public ready access to essential evidence documenting the rights of citizens, the actions of government officials, and the national experience.

NARA appraises, accessions, arranges, describes, preserves, and provides access to the essential documentation of the three branches of government; manages the presidential libraries; and publishes laws, regulations, and presidential and other public documents. It also assists the Information Security Oversight Office, which manages federal classification and declassification policies, and the National Historical Publications and Records Commission, which makes grants nationwide to help provide access to materials that document American history.

While the need for a central, safe repository for government records was acknowledged from the early days of the republic, storage systems before the twentieth century were decentralized and haphazard. The offices that created the records also stored them, keeping them in whatever space happened to be available. Over the years, records were lost, destroyed by fire, or otherwise made nearly inaccessible. The National Archives Act, signed by President Franklin Roosevelt on 19 June 1934, established a new agency to care for the records of the federal government and ensure that they endured for future generations. In 1949 the National Archives was put under the control of the General Services Administration, but it became an independent agency again—the National Archives and Records Administration—in 1985.

NARA currently holds approximately 7 billion pages of textual records; 5.5 million maps, charts, and architectural and engineering drawings; 35 million still photographs and graphics; 16 million aerial photographs; 56,000 machine-readable data sets; and hundreds of thousands of motion picture films and video and sound recordings. Much of the archival material, including special media such as still and motion pictures, sound recordings, maps, and electronic records, is housed in the National Archives at College Park, Maryland, and in the original National Archives Building in Washington, D.C.

Eighteen regional records services facilities located across the country house records from the federal courts and the regional offices of federal agencies in the geographic areas they serve. More material resides in NARA's records centers, where agency-owned records are held as long as legally required before destruction or transfer to the National Archives.

Providing storage for inactive records in these centers is part of NARA's records-management operation. To ensure proper documentation of the organization, policies, and activities of the government, NARA develops standards and guidelines for the management and disposition of recorded information. NARA also appraises federal records and approves records-disposition schedules, inspects agency records and records management practices, develops training programs, and provides guidance and assistance on proper records management.

In addition, NARA contains a unique resource in its presidential libraries and presidential materials projects, which document the administrations of Presidents Hoover to Clinton. These institutions, though not strictly libraries, contain—in addition to museums—archival collections of records (textual, electronic, visual, and audio) from the Office of the President and presidential commissions, along with personal papers of the president, his family and associates, and members of his administration.

Another part of NARA, the Office of the Federal Register, publishes the daily *Federal Register*, a record of government proclamations, orders, and regulations; the weekly *Compilation of Presidential Documents*; and the annual *Code of Federal Regulations*, along with *The U.S. Government Manual and Public Papers of the Presidents*. It is also responsible for receiving and documenting Electoral College certificates for presidential elections and state ratifications of proposed constitutional amendments.

The National Historical Publications and Records Commission is NARA's grant-making affiliate. Its grants help state and local archives, universities, historical societies, and other nonprofit organizations strengthen archival programs, preserve and process records collections, and provide access to them through the publication of finding aids and documentary editions of papers related to the Founding Era, to other themes, and to various historical figures.

NARA is continually expanding the availability of its resources through the Internet. The NARA home page directs visitors to such resources as the "Research Room" (offering guidance on using NARA records), the "Exhibit Hall" (bringing NARA exhibits to a wider audience), the "Digital Classroom" (presenting resources for students and teachers), the *Federal Register*, and *Prologue*, NARA's quarterly magazine. The Archival Research Catalog, an online database, will eventually describe all of NARA's holdings and make the descriptions accessible through an easy-to-use search form.

NARA also offers a variety of public programs to bring its resources to a wide audience. In the Washington area, at regional archives, and at presidential libraries, visitors may attend lectures, exhibits, film screenings, and conferences.

Records held by NARA are arranged into numbered "record groups." A record group comprises the records of a major government entity, such as a Cabinet department, a bureau, or an independent agency. For example, Record Group 59 contains General Records of the Department of State, and Record Group 29 holds Records of the Bureau of the Census. Most record groups also contain records of predecessors of the organization named in the title.

A great number of records have been recorded on microfilm both to preserve them and to make them more available to researchers. NARA has microfilmed more than 3,000 series of federal records, and copies are located at the two Washington-area archives buildings and in the various regional archives around the country.

The federal government documents people's lives in many ways, not only in censuses, court records, and records of immigration, military service, and employment but also in records such as scientific surveys or diplomatic correspondence. Records in all NARA locations provide information on government actions that have affected the entire nation and the individual home.

The *Guide to Federal Records in the National Archives of the United States* is the single major work that briefly describes the holdings of the National Archives. It is published in print format and on the web. The online version is regularly updated.

BIBLIOGRAPHY

U.S. National Archives and Records Administration. Home page at http://www.archives.gov/index.html.

National Archives and Records Administration

See also **Archives.**

NATIONAL ASSOCIATION FOR THE ADVANCEMENT OF COLORED PEOPLE.

African American communities, usually through their churches, made several attempts to organize in the late nineteenth century. The only national organization to last from these efforts was the National Association for the Advancement of Colored People (NAACP), founded in 1909. The NAACP was originally founded by an interracial group of white progressives and black militants belonging to the Niagara Movement. In response to the Springfield, Illinois, race riot of August 1908, a distinguished gathering that included the journalist William English Walling, the social worker Mary White Ovington, the newspaper editor Oswald Garrison Villard, and the scholar W. E. B. Du Bois issued "The Call" for a national conference on black rights to meet on 12 February 1909, the centennial of Abraham Lincoln's birth. The conference formed the National Negro Committee, out of which the NAACP emerged in May 1910.

At its formation, the NAACP adopted a militant program of action based on the platform of its radical forerunner, the Niagara Movement, demanding equal educational, political, and civil rights for blacks and the enforcement of the Fourteenth and Fifteenth Amendments. The NAACP initially employed two basic methods in its protest philosophy—the legal approach and public education. Relying on an integrated and middle-class approach to reform, the NAACP stressed corrective education, legislation, and litigation rather than more radical, disruptive protest. The first years of the NAACP were dedicated to the problems of mob violence and lynching. Between 1915 and 1936, under the leadership of Arthur B. Spingarn, white and black attorneys for the NAACP, including Moorfield Story, Louis Marshall, and

Clarence Darrow, attacked four areas of injustice: suffrage, residential segregation ordinances, restrictive covenants, and due process/equal protection for African Americans accused of crimes. The NAACP legal committee joined other organizations, such as the National Urban League, and won its first important victory before the U.S. Supreme Court in *Guinn and Beal v. United States* (1915), which overturned the amendment to Oklahoma's state constitution that exempted from literacy tests those or the descendents of those who had been eligible to vote prior to 1 January 1867. Other states had enacted similar "grandfather clauses," the clear intent of which was to deny blacks the vote. A second case, *Buchanan v. Warley* (1917), nullified Jim Crow housing ordinances in Louisville, Kentucky, as they were found to be in violation of the Fourteenth Amendment.

During the post–World War I period, the organization, led by its African American executive secretary James Weldon Johnson, focused its attention on antilynching legislation. Although no federal antilynching bills were passed by Congress, in an age of increasing racism and the national rise to prominence of the Ku Klux Klan, the NAACP's aggressive campaign heightened public awareness of and opposition to mob violence against blacks and firmly established the organization as the national spokesman for African Americans.

Over the next three decades, the NAACP directed its attention to voting rights, housing, and the desegregation of public education. In the 1930s, under the leadership of Charles Houston, former dean of the Howard University Law School, the NAACP prepared its first cases aimed at "the soft underbelly" of Jim Crow—graduate schools. In 1935, NAACP lawyers Charles Houston and Thurgood Marshall won the legal battle to admit an African American student, Donald Gaines Murray, to the University of Maryland Law School. Building on the strategy and issues used in the Murray case, the NAACP legal counsel finally argued its first case involving education and the "separate but equal" doctrine before the Supreme Court in *Missouri ex. rel. Gaines v. Canada* in 1938. Although the court decision reaffirmed the doctrine that separate educational facilities were legal if equal, the road to the 1954 Brown decision had been paved.

During the depression, the NAACP had notable successes, the most famous of which was in response to the barring of the acclaimed soprano Marian Anderson from performing at the Constitution Hall in Washington, D.C., by the Daughters of the American Revolution. The NAACP helped to have her concert moved to the Lincoln Memorial, where over 75,000 people attended.

Between 1940 and 1950, the NAACP fought in the courts in two areas, racial injustice in court procedures and discrimination in the voting process. The first case, involving a forced confession of a crime, *Lyons v. Oklahoma* (1944), resulted in a setback for the NAACP legal team, but the second case, *Smith v. Allwright* (1944), resulted in banning the all-white primary in Texas. During

World War II, the NAACP led the effort to ensure that President Franklin Roosevelt ordered a nondiscrimination policy in war-related industries and federal employment. In 1946, the NAACP won the *Morgan v. Virginia* case, which banned states from having laws that sanction segregated facilities in interstate travel by train and bus. The NAACP was also influential in pressuring President Harry Truman to sign Executive Order 9981 banning discrimination by the federal government and subsequently integrating the armed forces in 1948.

With Thurgood Marshall as its special legal counsel, the NAACP figured prominently in a series of Supreme Court decisions that outlawed residential covenants against black homebuyers (*Shelley v. Kraemer,* 1948) and ordered the integration of the University of Oklahoma (*Sipuel v. University of Oklahoma,* 1948) and the University of Texas (*Sweatt v. Painter,* 1950). These successful cases on higher education issues helped lead to the landmark case *Brown v. Board of Education of Topeka* of May 1954, which finally declared segregated schools unequal and unconstitutional. The Brown decision marked the beginning of the end of the formal aspects of Jim Crow and ushered in a new and stormy course for race relations in the form of the civil rights movement. Although it worked with a variety of newly formed African American–led groups such as the Student Nonviolent Coordinating Committee, the NAACP's hegemony as the country's major civil rights group was unchallenged.

After one of his many successful mass rallies for civil rights, the NAACP's first field director, Medgar Evers, was assassinated in front of his house in Jackson, Mississippi, in 1963; five months later, President John F. Kennedy was also assassinated, setting the course of the civil rights movement in a different direction, through legislative action. The NAACP achieved its goals by playing a leading role in the passage of the Civil Rights Act of 1957, which established the Civil Rights Division of the Department of Justice and the Commission on Civil Rights. The NAACP worked for passage of the Civil Rights Act of 1964, which not only forbade discrimination in public places, but also established the Equal Employment Opportunity Commission (EEOC).

As the NAACP entered the fourth quarter of the twentieth century, it remained an active force among African Americans committed to racial integration, and it continued to work successfully to fight discrimination in housing and strengthen the penalties for violations of civil rights. The organization helped win extensions of the Voting Rights Act of 1965 and led successful efforts in 1972 to increase the power of the EEOC. Under its executive secretary, Roy Wilkins, the NAACP had a membership of 433,118 in 1,555 branches located in all fifty states by 1975.

In 1982, the NAACP registered more than 850,000 voters, and its protests helped prevent President Ronald Reagan from giving a tax break to the racially segregated Bob Jones University. The NAACP led a massive anti-apartheid rally in New York in 1985 and launched a campaign that helped defeat the nomination of Judge Robert Bork to the Supreme Court in 1987. In 1996, Maryland congressman Kweisi Mfume left Congress and became the NAACP's president. As the twenty-first century started, the NAACP continued to follow its original goals of fighting social injustice through legal and political action.

BIBLIOGRAPHY

Harris, Jacqueline L. *History and Achievement of the NAACP.* New York: Watts, 1992.

National Association for the Advancement of Colored People. Web site http://www.naacp.org/.

Ovington, Mary W. *Black and White Sat Down Together: The Reminiscences of an NAACP Founder.* New York: Feminist Press, 1995.

Tushnet, Mark V. *NAACP's Legal Strategy against Segregated Education, 1925–1990.* New York: Oxford University Press, 1987.

Zangrando, Robert L. *The NAACP Crusade against Lynching, 1909–1950.* Philadelphia: Temple University Press, 1980.

James F. Adomanis

See also **Brown v. Board of Education of Topeka**; **Civil Rights Movement; Integration; Jim Crow Laws; Niagara Movement; Race Relations.**

NATIONAL ASSOCIATION OF COLORED WOMEN.

In 1896, two national African American women's organizations joined to form the National Association of Colored Women's Clubs under the leadership of Josephine Ruffin, Margaret Murray Washington, Mary Church Terrell, and Victoria Earle Matthews. The association's goals were to protect the reputation of African American women, while also improving social conditions in their communities. With a membership of over 100,000 by 1916, they created kindergartens, nurseries, settlements, and homes for working girls, dependent children, and the elderly. Their later focus on civil rights included military and school desegregation, voter registration, and anti-lynching legislation. They also restored Frederick Douglass's home in Anacostia, Washington, D.C.

BIBLIOGRAPHY

Wesley, Charles H. *The History of the National Association of Colored Women's Clubs: A Legacy of Service.* Washington, D.C: The Association, 1984.

White, Deborah Gray. *Too Heavy a Load. Black Women in Defense of Themselves, 1894–1994.* New York: Norton, 1999.

Williams, Lillian Serece, ed. *The Records of the National Association of Colored Women's Clubs.* Bethesda, Md.: University Publications of America, 1994, 1995.

Anne Meis Knupfer

NATIONAL ASSOCIATION OF MANUFACTURERS (NAM) was founded in Cincinnati, Ohio, in

1895. Most fundamentally, the organization sought to give business an authoritative voice in the determination of governmental policy. More particularly, born in the midst of the serious depression of the mid-1890s, the NAM was dedicated initially to the protection of the home market via the tariff and to the expansion of foreign trade by such means as reform of the counselor service, the construction of an isthmian canal, and a revamping of the U.S. merchant marine. In the wake of the anthracite coal strike of 1902–1903, the association increasingly turned its attention to combating the rise of organized labor. During the 1920s, the NAM became a national leader in the business drive for the open shop. The Great Depression hit the organization hard, however, and its membership and revenues dropped precipitously.

The NAM retrenched and reasserted itself in the mid-1930s as the chief business opponent of New Deal liberal activism. Its shrill nay-saying failed to stop the torrent of reform legislation, but the organization gained an enduring reputation for ideological rigor in its denunciation of government regulation and the emergent welfare state.

In the postwar era the NAM played a significant role in the passage of the Taft-Hartley Act of 1947, which placed new limits on organized labor. Thereafter, the association remained one of the nation's most prominent business lobbies, usually taking a harder, more ideological line than such accommodationist, big-business groups as the Business Roundtable. In 1974 the NAM moved its national headquarters from New York City to Washington, D.C. At the end of the twentieth century the organization had 14,000 member firms, including 10,000 small and midsize companies, and 350 member associations.

BIBLIOGRAPHY

Collins, Robert M. *The Business Response to Keynes, 1929–1964.* New York: Columbia University Press, 1981.

Steigerwalt, Albert K. *The National Association of Manufacturers, 1895–1914: A Study in Business Leadership.* Ann Arbor: University of Michigan Press, 1964.

Vogel, David. *Fluctuating Fortunes: The Political Power of Business in America.* New York: Basic Books, 1989.

Robert M. Collins

See also **Business Unionism; Taft-Hartley Act; Tariff; Trade, Foreign.**

NATIONAL BANK NOTES. The National Bank Act of 1863 (amended in 1864) was a congressional act that authorized the issuance of bank notes by national banks. Each national bank was required to deposit with the Treasury U.S. bonds in the amount of at least one-third of its capital stock. Circulating notes, guaranteed by the government, might be issued up to 90 percent of the par value of deposited bonds. Passed by northern Republicans in the absence of southern legislators, the National

Bank Act raised much-needed cash for the war effort. It was also a substantial step toward a national banking system. The notes issued under it constituted the sole banknote currency of the United States until 1914 and remained in circulation until 1935.

BIBLIOGRAPHY

Hammond, Bray. *Sovereignty and an Empty Purse: Banks and Politics in the Civil War.* Princeton, N.J.: Princeton University Press, 1970.

Frederick A. Bradford/A. R.

See also **Banking; Civil War; Cooke, Jay, and Company; Federal Reserve System; Greenbacks; Legal Tender; Ten-forties.**

NATIONAL BUREAU OF ECONOMIC RESEARCH. The National Bureau of Economic Research was founded in 1920 in Cambridge, Massachusetts, "to conduct . . . exact and impartial investigations in the field of economic, social, and industrial science." The private, nonprofit bureau has sought to maintain a disinterested stance on public issues and has made no policy recommendations. The first set of bureau studies developed a conceptual system for analyzing national income and wealth and presented national income estimates, a line of work that led to the official estimates now prepared by the Department of Commerce. The national accounts have remained central to the research of the bureau and have figured prominently in the studies of the business cycle and economic growth in which the bureau has been chiefly engaged since the 1930s. In the 1960s and 1970s several new lines of work opened up that had to do with current problems of urban economics, health, education, income distribution, and population. By 2002 it served as a clearinghouse for the research of more than six hundred scholars around the country.

BIBLIOGRAPHY

Bernstein, Michael A. *A Perilous Progress: Economists and Public Purpose in Twentieth-Century America.* Princeton, N.J.: Princeton University Press, 2001.

Robert E. Gallman/A. E.

See also **Business Cycles; Productivity, Concept of.**

NATIONAL BUREAU OF STANDARDS. The question of standards first arose with the union of the thirteen colonies. In a predominantly agricultural nation, the power to coin money, to regulate the alloy and value of coin, and to fix the standard of weights and measures throughout the United States, granted to Congress in the Articles of Confederation in 1776 and in the Constitution, were deemed sufficient to serve a simple economy. Both George Washington and Thomas Jefferson had advocated for a uniform system of weights and measures at a time when a variety of systems, many of them remnants of methodologies employed during medieval times in England, were still in varying use in industry and commerce. As early as 1821, John Quincy Adams, then secretary of state, advised Congress to consider adopting the metric system, which was then being used in France. However, the United States opted instead to adopt a version of the English system, culminating in the creation of the Office of Standard Weights and Measures in 1824. Despite some degree of standardization, the system was cumbersome, at best, using such constructs as "Queen Anne's gallon" (231 cubic inches), the "avoirdupois pound" (7,000 grains), the "troy pound" (5,760 grains), and the "U.S. bushel" (2,150.42 cubic inches), a derivation of the fifteenth century "Winchester bushel." In 1836, responsibility for the construction of weights and measures was transferred from Congress to the secretary of the Treasury, who was already maintaining standards in the customs houses. The new office was set up in the Treasury Department's Coast and Geodetic Survey. The use of the metric system was first authorized in the United States in 1866, but its genesis goes back to 1670 in France, where it was generally recognized that there was a need for a uniform system to facilitate scientific communication.

Originally known as the Office of Standard Weights and Measures, Congress created an agency in 1824 within the Treasury Department to establish and promote the consistent use of uniform weights and measures. In 1890, Congress established the Office of Construction of Weights and Measures, and in 1894, it authorized that office to define and establish the units of electrical measure. In 1901, the name was changed to the National Bureau of Standards, where its responsibilities were expanded to address the growing use of electricity. In 1903, it was moved to the Department of Commerce and became involved in promoting the use of technology as a means of increasing the international competitiveness of American businesses. In 1988, the name was again changed to the National Institute of Standards and Technology (NIST).

By 1900, when U.S. exports exceeded imports for the first time, the industrialization of America was well underway. When the National Bureau of Standards was founded the next year, with a staff of twelve, the secretary of the Treasury appointed a visiting committee of five distinguished scientists and industrialists to report annually to the secretary on the work of the bureau. That same year, construction began on the first of its laboratories in Washington, D.C. Augmenting its staff and planning new laboratories, the bureau began establishing more accurate and stable standards, launched a crusade for the use of honest weights and measures in the marketplace, began testing materials and supplies purchased for government agencies, and developed test methods for use in evaluating consumer products.

In succeeding decades, through its fundamental research in measurement and materials on behalf of government, industry, science, and the public, the bureau developed thousands of new standards of quality, safety, performance, and precision measurement. These standards played a significant role in the development of the radio, radio propagation, automotive technology, aviation, cryogenics, electronics, nuclear physics, and space science. The National Bureau of Standards thus became one of the largest institutions for scientific research in the world.

At the beginning of the twenty-first century, the NIST developed and promoted the use of measurement, standards, and technology designed to facilitate trade, enhance productivity, and improve the quality of life. A staff of approximately 4,600 scientists, engineers, technicians, visiting researchers, manufacturing specialists, and support and administrative personnel, with an annual budget in excess of $800 million, conducted research in engineering, chemistry, physics, and information science through four main programs: the NIST Laboratories (in Gaithersburg, Maryland and Boulder, Colorado), the Baldrige National Quality Program, the Manufacturing Extension Partnership, and the Advanced Technology Program (all located in Gaithersburg). The Baldrige National Quality Program promotes performance excellence in manufacturing, services, education, and health care. The Manufacturing Extension Partnership provides technical and business assistance to small manufacturers, and the Advanced Technology Program supports research and development of innovative technologies with the potential for broad-based national benefit.

NIST researchers, responding to industry needs and in collaboration with industry colleagues, academic institutions, and government agencies, carry out their work in specialized laboratories. The building and fire research laboratory addresses issues of construction quality and productivity, as well as loss due to fires, earthquakes, wind, and other potentially damaging natural occurrences. The Chemical Science and Technology Laboratory strives to improve public health and safety and American industrial competitiveness in the global market by developing universal reference standards, models, and measurements for chemical, biochemical, and chemical engineering applications. The electronics and electrical engineering laboratory establishes and maintains all electrical measurements in the United States, with applications in the fields of microelectronics, optoelectronics, radio frequency technology, semiconductor electronics, electromagnetic and magnetic technologies, and law enforcement. The information technology laboratory focuses its research on rapidly changing information technologies to improve the reliability and security of computers and computer networks. Research areas include mathematics and computational sciences, convergent information systems, software diagnostics and conformance testing, advanced network technologies, information access, and statistical engineering. The Manufacturing Engineering Laboratory develops measurement methods, standards, and technologies aimed at improving U.S. manufacturing capabilities, efficiency, and productivity. In addition to maintaining the basic units for measuring mass and length in the United States, this lab conducts research in the areas of precision engineering, intelligent systems, fabrication technology, manufacturing metrology, and manufacturing systems integration. The Materials Science and Engineering Laboratory provides technical leadership and expertise in the use of ceramics, polymers, metallurgy, neutron characterization, and materials reliability, which are critical in the microelectronics, automotive, and health care industries. This laboratory contains the first cold neutron research facility in the country (the NIST Center for Neutron Research), as well as the Center for Theoretical and Computational Materials Science. The Physics Laboratory, in collaboration with industry, works to implement commercial and industrial solutions to problems encountered in the fields of electron and optical physics, optical technology, atomic physics, ionizing radiation, quantum physics, and time and frequency. The Technology Services division provides several products and services to both industry and the public, including standard reference materials and data, weights and measures information and data, laboratory accreditation, and the training of foreign standards officials.

BIBLIOGRAPHY

Passaglia, Elio, and Karma A. Beal. *A Unique Institution: The National Bureau of Standards, 1950–1969*. Washington, D.C.: Government Printing Office, 1999.

Snyder, Wilbert F., and Charles L. Bragaw. *Achievement in Radio: Seventy Years of Radio Science, Technology, Standards, and Measurement at the National Bureau of Standards*. Boulder, Colo. National Bureau of Standards, 1986.

Christine E. Hoffman

See also **Laboratories**.

NATIONAL CIVIC FEDERATION. The United States was a country of small businesses and family farms when the Civil War ended in 1865. Forty years later, however, railroads, gigantic industrial corporations, and financial institutions had transformed the nation. It was not a peaceful transformation, however. In 1877, starving workers furiously attacked railroad and other corporate property and were gunned down by company militias. Fifteen years later, southern and midwestern farmers rose against the political power of eastern banks and northern manufactures in the Populist revolt. By 1900, all such movements had been defeated, but the nation was still rife with social discontent.

After observing the hostility of Kansas Populists and Chicago Socialists toward corporate domination, Ralph M. Easley, a self-styled conservative Republican, became a crusader to rationalize and stabilize the new economic system. In 1900, he organized the National Civic Federation (NCF) to bring top business and labor leaders together in harmony. Above all, this was an organization of business leaders who believed, like J. P. Morgan's partner George W. Perkins, that unless the new trust system spread its benefits to workers, it could not survive. Agreeing, the coal baron and Ohio Senator Marcus A. Hanna, NCF's first president, hoped, by accommodating labor, to "lay the foundation stone of a structure that will last for all time." Top American Federation of Labor (AFL) leaders were happy to cooperate, including Samuel Gompers, NCF's first vice president. And prominent public figures, including former U.S. presidents Grover Cleveland and William H. Taft also joined this project of class cooperation.

Together—under the guidance of corporate leaders who had transcended a narrow interest-consciousness and were emerging as class-conscious leaders of the nation—these men sought to legitimize trade unions and foster cooperation between workers and employers. For almost twenty years—from 1900 to 1918—they had mixed success, until, during the war, the Wilson administration made them obsolete.

BIBLIOGRAPHY

Weinstein, James. *The Corporate Ideal in the Liberal State, 1900–1918*. Westport, Conn.: Greenwood Press, 1981.

James Weinstein

NATIONAL COLLEGIATE ATHLETIC ASSOCIATION (NCAA) began following a meeting of college presidents on 9 December 1905, called by the New York University chancellor Henry M. McCracken to alleviate the dangers of intercollegiate football. The presidents organized a national convention on 28 December attended by sixty-two colleges that formed the Intercollegiate Athletic Association of the United States (IAA), chaired by Captain Palmer E. Pierce of the U.S. Military Academy at West Point. The IAA developed standards of conduct for members, conferences, and a rules committee to open up the game. In 1910, it renamed itself the NCAA to reflect its national scope, and added new rules, including those requiring seven men on the line of scrimmage, allowing forward passes from any point behind the line of scrimmage, and eliminating penalties for incompletions. By 1919, the NCAA had 170 members and supervised eleven sports. It staged its first championship in track and field in 1919.

The NCAA had serious jurisdictional disputes with the Amateur Athletic Union (AAU) over playing rules (each had different rules for basketball until 1915), eligibility (the AAU forbade collegians from competing against non-AAU athletes), and especially international competition. This was never fully resolved until the federal government intervened with the Amateur Sports Act of 1978, taking power from the AAU and dividing it among the federations that governed Olympic sports.

The early NCAA could not alleviate the problems of big-time college sports, including commercialization, professionalization, and hypocrisy, amply revealed in the Carnegie Report of 1930. Football had become a huge spectator sport, with seven stadiums seating 70,000 fans, and athletes were subsidized by easy jobs and facile academic programs. Institutions maintained complete autonomy and the NCAA had little disciplinary power.

In 1939, because of growing concern over recruiting, gambling, and postseason bowl games, NCAA members voted overwhelmingly for a "purity code" affirming the principles of institutional responsibility, academic standards, financial aid controls, and recruiting restrictions. A new constitution authorized investigations of alleged violations and expulsions of rules violators. The 1948 "sanity code" permitted only institutionally supported aid based on need and permitted athletes to hold jobs. However, it was repealed in 1951, because members wanted to determine aid only on athletic ability.

In 1952, the NCAA took further steps toward becoming a cartel. It placed some colleges on probation, set up rules for postseason bowls, established its national headquarters in Kansas City, Missouri, hired Walter Byers as full-time executive director, and signed its first national football contract with the National Broadcasting Company for $1.1 million. But in 1981, when the television package with American Broadcasting Company (ABC) was worth $29 million, the Supreme Court struck down the package system as an antitrust violation, and this empowered individual colleges to negotiate their own rights. Nonetheless, in 1982 a combined package from ABC, the Columbia Broadcasting System, and Turner Broadcasting brought in $74.3 million. The NCAA rights to its basketball championship, first contested in 1939, became extremely lucrative. Television revenues from the "Final Four" basketball tournament tripled from $49 million in 1987 to $150 million in 1994, and then to nearly $220 million annually through 2002.

The NCAA's major issues at the beginning of the twenty-first century involved recruitment, retention, and graduation of athletes; gender-based inequities; drug use; and cost containment. The Presidents Commission, established in 1983 to promote reform, secured stricter penalties for institutional violations including the "death penalty" that closed Southern Methodist University's athletic program in 1985. The NCAA has curtailed booster activities, reduced athletic scholarships and coaching staffs, and shortened the recruiting season, and in 1986, it instituted Proposition 48, setting minimal test scores and high school grades for incoming freshmen athletes. The NCAA opposed Title IX (1972), which mandated women's equal access to athletic facilities and programs, fearing its negative impact on revenue-producing sports. Nonetheless, in 1982 it took over control of women's sport when the Association of Intercollegiate Athletics for Women folded, unable to compete with the NCAA's prestige, wealth, and television exposure, and since then has taken major strides to promote gender equity.

BIBLIOGRAPHY

Falla, Jack. *The NCAA: The Voice of College Sports: A Diamond Anniversary History, 1906–1981.* Mission, Kans.: NCAA, 1981.

Watterson, John Sayle. *College Football: History, Spectacle, Controversy.* Baltimore: Johns Hopkins University Press, 2000.

Steven A. Riess

See also **Baseball; Basketball; College Athletics; Football; Hockey; Sports; Swimming; Track and Field.**

NATIONAL CONFERENCE OF PUERTO RICAN WOMEN,

an advocacy group concerned with the advancement of Puerto Rican women. Founded in 1972, the organization is dedicated to achieving greater political, economic, and social participation in the United States and Puerto Rico for Puerto Rican and other Hispanic women. In 1994 it had more than three thousand members in thirteen state chapters. The national headquarters, in Washington, D.C., works with other like-minded advocacy groups as a political lobbying force and promotes the creation of local chapters. Three times a year they publish their newsletter, *Ecos Nacionales* (National Echoes), which covers Puerto Rican and other Hispanic women's issues.

BIBLIOGRAPHY

Acosta-Belén, Edna, ed. *The Puerto Rican Woman: Perspectives on Culture, History, and Society.* 2d ed. New York: Praeger, 1986.

Chabrán, Rafael, and Richard Chabrán, eds. *The Latino Encyclopedia.* New York: Marshall Cavendish, 1996.

Matos Rodríguez, Félix V., and Linda C. Delgado, eds. *Puerto Rican Women's History: New Perspectives.* Armonk, N.Y.: M.E. Sharpe, 1998.

Eli Moses Diner

See also **Hispanic Americans; Puerto Ricans in the United States.**

NATIONAL CONGRESS OF AMERICAN INDIANS.

The founding of the National Congress of American Indians (NCAI) in Denver, Colorado, in 1944 represented a milestone in Indian history, because it signified the first successful national intertribal political organization controlled by Indians. By 1944, the legacy of off-reservation boarding schools and the Indian New Deal, coupled with recent wartime experience, had convinced a new generation of Indians of the need to organize themselves to make their voices heard in Congress and elsewhere. In particular, D'Arcy McNickle (Flathead), Archie Phinney (Nez Perce), and Charles Heacock (Lakota) largely conceived and helped organize the NCAI.

In all, eighty Indian delegates from twenty-seven states and representing more than fifty tribes, groups, and associations attended the first convention. One year later, the NCAI claimed members from nearly all the tribes of the United States. Although at the outset men largely comprised the organization, by 1955 women made up at least half of the delegates. Delegates attending the founding convention represented a fairly representative cross section of Indian leadership west of the Mississippi River. On the whole, the convention attendees represented an equal blend of young and old, full-bloods and mixed-bloods, and both highly educated and less formally educated, distinguished professionals and lesser known Indians.

In its earliest years the NCAI battled to protect the rights of Alaskan natives, to end voting discrimination, to create the Indian Claims Commission (established in 1946), to promote the right to independent counsel without federal government interference or control, to stop termination legislation to end tribal governance, and to push for greater Indian participation in the government's decision-making processes. By passing broad resolutions, the founders mapped a political strategy that appealed to many Indians. Also, by steering a moderate course, the NCAI leadership decreased the risk of distancing the reservation Indians from the urban, the more assimilated from the less, the older Native Americans from the younger, and individuals from tribal groups.

The NCAI played a significant role in late-twentieth-century Indian affairs. Its emphasis on treaty rights, tribal sovereignty, and identity issues had no equals in earlier intertribal efforts. The NCAI was less preoccupied than previous twentieth-century Indian intertribal movements had been with the benefits of Indian assimilation and more concerned with the group rights of Indians and with interests within tribal communities. In practice, the group offered tribes legal aid and information and lobbied for Indian interests before the courts, Congress, and the Bureau of Indian Affairs. Its leaders used the conventional weapons of politics to promote the interests of Indian peoples. Not strictly confined to national issues, it also fought campaigns on the local and regional level.

More importantly, the limited success of the NCAI helped open a broader political arena within which contemporary Indian activists have spoken out and agendas have been engaged. Beginning in the 1960s, new Indian activist groups like the American Indian Movement and the National Indian Youth Council used the NCAI's energy as a springboard to forge new political movements that employed direct confrontation and civil disobedience. The NCAI's influence diminished slightly in the 1980s and the 1990s as Indian activism shifted from the legislative arena to the courts, but it remained one of the most important Indian organizations.

BIBLIOGRAPHY

Cowger, Thomas W. *The National Congress of American Indians: The Founding Years.* Lincoln: University of Nebraska Press, 1999.

Hertzberg, Hazel. *The Search for an American Indian Identity: Modern Pan-Indian Movements.* Syracuse, N.Y.: Syracuse University Press, 1971.

Thomas W. Cowger

See also **American Indian Movement; Bureau of Indian Affairs; Indian Claims Commission; Indian Policy, U.S., 1900–2000; Indian Political Life; National Indian Youth Council; Society of American Indians.**

NATIONAL COUNCIL OF CHURCHES. The National Council of Churches (NCC), formally known as the National Council of Churches of Christ in the United States of America, was founded in Cleveland, Ohio, in 1950. Conceived as an umbrella association exerting no formal control over its members, the NCC has facilitated cooperation among the major Protestant denominations and several Orthodox communions, and has relayed the concerns of its member groups to the United Nations. Historians consider it the voice of the Protestant establishment, though it has always counted non-Protestant Christians among its members. The NCC was born of the ecumenical impulse that had been building in America since the nineteenth century, when Protestants forged interdenominational ties around issues such as the missionary enterprise, abolitionism, temperance, and urban reform. The EVANGELICAL ALLIANCE was the largest and most powerful of these organizations until the formation of the Federal Council of Churches (FCC) in 1908.

During the FCC's lifetime, activities such as religious education and missions at home and abroad remained the province of independent interdenominational groups. However, this lack of centralization became increasingly intolerable to many Protestant leaders in the post–World War II atmosphere of universalism and institution building. The proliferation of interdenominational groups seemed to perpetuate the problems of DENOMINATIONALISM, including duplication of effort and communication difficulties. Rising interfaith tensions in the politicized religious climate of the early Cold War years also convinced many Protestants of the need for a centralized agency to represent the major Protestant denominations in negotiations with other religious groups. The 1948 inaugural meeting of the World Council of Churches, an international ecumenical organization unprecedented in its scope, inspired a group of American Protestant leaders to fully consolidate their interdenominational activities at the national level.

The NCC was a merger of the Federal Council of Churches and seven interdenominational agencies, including the Foreign Missions Conference of North America, the Home Missions Council of North America, and the International Council of Religious Education. At its inception, the organization represented twenty-nine Christian bodies: twenty-five from major Protestant denominations (Presbyterian, Reformed, Methodist, Baptist, Lutheran, Moravian, Quaker, Episcopal, Congregational, Christian

Ecumenical Alliance. After Martin Luther King Jr.'s "I Have a Dream" speech at the March on Washington, 28 August 1963, Eugene Carson Blake of the National Council of Churches is part of a group of rally organizers to meet with President John F. Kennedy at the White House. AP/WIDE WORLD PHOTOS

Church, and Church of the Brethren) and four Eastern Orthodox communions. Neither the Roman Catholic Church nor the fundamentalist Protestant members of the National Association of Evangelicals, founded in 1942, joined the NCC.

Since its founding, the NCC's functions have expanded steadily, and its internal structure, originally comprising divisions of Home Missions, Foreign Missions, Christian Education, and Christian Life and Work, has been altered several times. In the early twenty-first century, the NCC continued to provide day-by-day support to its member groups in their basic tasks of evangelism, education, missionary work, and social welfare by offering consultation and sponsoring conferences, workshops, publications, public lobbies, and service agencies. Driven by the conviction that Christian faith demands social action, the NCC has worked nationally and internationally to promote brotherhood between Christians and non-Christians, cross-cultural understanding, peace, human rights, and anti-poverty measures. Because it brings together Christians with a wide range of political perspectives, the NCC has always been subject to internal tensions regarding controversial social issues and policy questions. Nevertheless, though its cultural influence has declined since 1970, the NCC sustains a broad coalition of moderate to liberal, non–Roman Catholic Christians.

BIBLIOGRAPHY

Cavert, Samuel McCrea. *The American Churches in the Ecumenical Movement, 1900–1968.* New York: Association Press, 1968.

The Christian Century, vol. 67, no. 50 (December 13, 1950). This volume is devoted to the founding of the National Council of Churches. Available from http://www.ncccusa.org.

Findlay, James F., Jr. *Church People in the Struggle: The National Council of Churches and the Black Freedom Movement, 1950–1970.* New York: Oxford University Press, 1993.

Hutchison, William R., ed. *Between the Times: The Travail of the Protestant Establishment in America, 1900–1960.* New York: Cambridge University Press, 1989.

Marty, Martin E. *Modern American Religion, Volume 3: Under God, Indivisible, 1941–1960.* Chicago: University of Chicago Press, 1996.

K. Healan Gaston

See also **Christianity; Missionary Societies, Home; Missions, Foreign; Protestantism; Religion and Religious Affiliation.**

NATIONAL COUNCIL OF JEWISH WOMEN.

The National Council of Jewish Women (NCJW) was founded in 1893 as a result of the Jewish Women's Congress held at the Chicago World's Fair. Early leaders included Hannah G. Solomon, Rebekah Kohut, and Sadie American. The group dedicated itself to promoting Judaism, philanthropy, and education through aid to Jewish immigrants and educational programs for Americans. During both world wars, it provided assistance to JEWS overseas and to refugees. Throughout its history the group has supported many issues, including civil and reproductive rights, children's education and welfare, and the Equal Rights Amendment. Early in the twentieth century the NCJW was the largest Jewish women's organization. Today, the group has sections in over five hundred American communities.

BIBLIOGRAPHY

Elwell, Ellen Sue Levi. "The Founding and Early Programs of the National Council of Jewish Women: Study and Practice as Jewish Women's Religious Expression." Ph.D. diss., Indiana University, 1982.

Hyman, Paula. "The Jewish Body Politic: Gendered Politics in the Early Twentieth Century." *Nashim: A Journal of Jewish Women's Studies and Gender Issues* 1, no. 2 (1999): 37–51.

Rogow, Faith. *Gone to Another Meeting: The National Council of Jewish Women, 1893–1993.* Tuscaloosa: University of Alabama Press, 1993.

Mary McCune

NATIONAL COUNCIL OF NEGRO WOMEN.

Mary McLeod Bethune founded the National Council of Negro Women in 1935 to consolidate the activism of African American female professional and political organizations. The council emphasized national politics, African American female employment, and civil rights. During World War II, the organization helped recruit African American women into the Women's Army Corps. By 1949 its membership was 850,000. During the 1950s, the council worked for voter registration, anti-lynching legislation, and the Fair Employment Practices Commission. During the 1960s and 1970s, the council promoted self-help programs for poor southerners. In 1979 it established the Mary McLeod Bethune Memorial Museum and the National Archives for Black Women's History.

BIBLIOGRAPHY

Collier-Thomas, Bettye. *N.C.N.W., 1935–1980.* Washington, D.C.: National Council of Negro Women, 1981.

McCluskey, Audrey Thomas, and Elaine M. Smith, eds. *Mary McLeod Bethune, Building A Better World: Essays and Selected Documents.* Bloomington: Indiana University Press, 1999.

Anne Meis Knupfer

See also **National Association of Colored Women.**

NATIONAL EDUCATION ASSOCIATION

(NEA), the largest professional educational organization in the United States, grew out of the National Teachers Association (NTA), which was established in 1857. Through the activity of the NTA, the Office of Education was established in the federal government in 1867. The NTA was reorganized as the National Education Association in 1871, and in 1906 it was chartered by Congress. Initially representing the ideals and interests of the nation's leading educators, including public school officials, college and university leaders, and educational journalists, the organization experienced a significant transformation after 1917, when the national office moved to Washington, D.C., where it could hopefully influence federal policies. Thereafter, emphasis was placed on recruiting and serving the needs of classroom teachers, mostly female; membership grew from 8,466 in 1917 to 220,000 in 1931. The Research Division was founded in 1922, serving the interests of both teachers and administrators. The NEA survived the Great Depression, but with a significant loss of membership and increasing competition from the AMERICAN FEDERATION OF TEACHERS (AFT). While not challenging the authority of school administrators, the NEA created a committee on equal opportunity in 1935 to study gender and racial salary inequities, with most attention devoted to assisting female teachers. The association grew during World War II, when it linked education to the war effort with the creation of the Commission on the Defense of Democracy in Education. Membership escalated through the decade, reaching 454,000 in 1950, with increasing emphasis from the national office on strengthening the local and state associations.

Continuing its conservative approach during the 1950s, the NEA had little organizing success in the larger cities. Beginning in the 1960s, this would change when the organization transformed itself from a professional organization to something resembling a teachers' union in response to the increasing number of teachers' strikes led by the AFT. While the NEA had a membership of 1.1 million in 1970 (compared to the AFT's 205,000), it had growing difficulty in mobilizing teachers at the local level. The NEA leadership initially shied away from sanctioning collective bargaining, but substituted what it termed "professional negotiations," which amounted to the same thing. The publication by the NEA of the *Negotiations Research Digest* in 1967 also indicated an increased commitment to collective bargaining. Another sign of change was the creation in 1972 of a national political action committee to enhance political lobbying and campaigning, giving the NEA increasing national clout.

The NEA had little interest in civil rights matters until the 1960s. Starting in 1926, the organization formed a relationship with American Teachers Association (ATA), the national organization of black teachers, but membership remained segregated, particularly among the southern affiliates. The NEA officially supported integration in 1963 and the number of segregated southern affiliates gradually decreased, although there were still eleven the following year. The NEA and the ATA officially merged in 1966 and by decade's end, only the Mississippi and Louisiana affiliates had refused to accept the merger, for which they were expelled from the NEA in 1970. Merger was not completed in these two states until the late 1970s. The NEA, meanwhile, strongly supported school desegregation.

By the 1980s, the NEA had become a progressive, activist, integrated teachers' union with strong presidential leadership and an active political agenda; it generally supported the Democratic Party's candidates and policies. Merger with the AFT was increasingly broached but uncompleted as of 2002, when the NEA had 2.7 million members distributed in all fifty states and 13,000 communities. It continued its commitment to improving teachers' salaries and school programs, while issuing *NEA Today* and numerous other publications, all within the context of protecting urban public schools from political pressure for increased school privatization.

BIBLIOGRAPHY

Murphy, Marjorie. *Blackboard Unions: The AFT and the NEA, 1900–1980*. Ithaca, N.Y: Cornell University Press, 1990.

Urban, Wayne J. *Gender, Race, and the National Education Association: Professionalism and Its Limitations*. New York: Routledge Falmer, 2000.

Wesley, Edgar B. *NEA: The First Hundred Years*. New York: Harper, 1957.

Ronald D. Cohen

NATIONAL ENDOWMENT FOR THE ARTS

(NEA). An independent agency of the federal government, the NEA was first envisioned by President John F. Kennedy, and created in 1965 along with the National Endowment for the Humanities (NEH).

The NEA funds an array of works and activities in music, theater, and the visual and performance arts. The National Council on the Arts, a panel of artists and cultural leaders headed by the NEA's chairman, serves as the endowment's advisory board, reviewing grant applications and making policy recommendations. NEA grants range from $5,000 to $100,000, but all grant recipients must obtain matching private funding. Most grants fall into one of five main categories: creativity, organizational capacity, access, arts learning, and heritage/preservation. At its inception in 1965, the NEA had a budget of $2.5 million; the endowment's highest level of federal funding was its $175 million budget in 1991. But controversy over grant recipients led to major budget reductions in the final five years of the twentieth century, when annual funding dipped below $100 million. The budget eventually began to rebound, reaching $115.2 million in 2002.

The NEA's support for the arts has had a marked impact on American culture. For example, between 1990 and 2002, the NEA provided support to thirty-five recipients of National Book Awards, National Book Critics Circle Awards, and Pulitzer Prizes in fiction and poetry. It also funded the regional theatrical production of *A Chorus Line* that went on to become a Broadway smash in 1975 and Maya Lin's design of the Vietnam Veteran's Memorial, dedicated in Washington, D.C., in 1982. The NEA has also made a special effort to recognize American jazz masters through a series of fellowships.

Controversial Artistry

Yet the NEA has always had its critics, especially among those who questioned the artistic merit and morality of some of the grant recipients. These issues came to a head in 1989, when opponents shined the spotlight on a handful of NEA-funded exhibitions featuring artworks they termed obscene and immoral. Among the works they found objectionable were photographer Andres Serrano's *Piss Christ*, which depicted a plastic crucifix immersed in a jar of the artist's urine; art student Scott Tyler's *What Is the Proper Way to Display a U.S. Flag?*, which allowed people to comment on the title question while walking over an American flag on the gallery floor; and photographer Robert Mapplethorpe's sadomasochistic and homoerotic images and pictures of nude children.

Some members of Congress, most notably Sen. Jesse Helms and Rep. Dana Rohrabacher, attacked NEA funding head-on, while other conservative legislators and right-wing groups endorsed funding cuts and grant restrictions. These measures were vigorously opposed by artists, arts organizations, free-speech advocates, and gay and lesbian alliances. Over the protests of these groups, the NEA began requiring grant recipients to sign an "obscenity pledge," promising that their work would be free of obscenities. In addition, John Frohnmayer, the NEA chairman appointed by President George H. W. Bush in 1989, drew fire from artists and arts organizations for denying certain grants recommended by NEA panels. Critics accused Frohnmayer of using political criteria in denying the funding.

Taking It to the Courts

Soon, the battles over funding and the arts moved to the courts. In 1990, in the first of several high-profile cases related to the NEA, Dennis Barrie, director of Cincinnati's Contemporary Art Center, was arrested and tried on obscenity charges for exhibiting Mapplethorpe's work—an exhibition that had been partially supported by an NEA grant. Barrie was subsequently acquitted, but the NEA's grant-making process remained in the spotlight on Capitol Hill as Sen. Helms continued to introduce bills and amendments to limit funding for artworks of a sexual or sacrilegious nature.

In 1990, after a heated debate, Congress passed a three-year reauthorization of the NEA that eliminated restrictions on the kinds of art the endowment might fund. But a new provision required the NEA to use as its grant-making guidelines the "general standards of decency and respect for the diverse beliefs and values of the American public." While the NEA eliminated its obscenity pledge, a few organizations, artists, and panel members continued to protest by declining endowment funding.

In 1994 Congress renewed its attack after conservative hackles were raised by an appearance at the Walker Art Center in Minneapolis by HIV-positive performance artist Ron Athey, who incorporated bloodletting into his act. Although only $150 of NEA money (out of a $100,000 grant to the Walker Art Center) had gone to support the performance, outraged lawmakers sliced deeply into the endowment's budget; the areas of visual arts, theater, performance art, and photography were particularly hard hit as a result of the cuts.

In 1992, the NEA was sued for a violation of First Amendment rights by four performance artists—Karen Finley, John Fleck, Holly Hughes, and Tim Miller—whose grants were initially recommended for approval but then subsequently denied after the NEA's congressionally mandated "standards of decency" provision were implemented. Although the suit was rejected by lower courts, the case was appealed to the Supreme Court in 1997, where the "NEA Four" were joined in their suit by the National Association of Artists' Organizations. The amended suit included a constitutional challenge to the decency provision on the grounds that it was vague and viewpoint-based. The U.S. Supreme Court upheld the decision to reject the lawsuit.

Changing with the Times

During the Clinton Administration actress Jane Alexander led the NEA. The most activist chairman the NEA had ever known, Alexander traveled the country, visiting arts centers and attending performances and exhibitions, spreading the word about the positive impact of the NEA. In 1995, to emphasize the NEA's value to the nation, Alexander testified before the U.S. Senate that the per capita contribution to the endowment was a mere sixty-four cents, but that without such federal matching funds, arts organizations would be far less able to raise private money. Still, opponents argued that the endowment needed to better monitor its funding policies, and some also argued for privatization of the endowment, or for funding its mandate through copyright fees.

As a result of the controversy that dogged the NEA during the 1990s, at the beginning of the twenty-first century the endowment no longer funded individual visual or performance artists (although writers still received fellowships). Its mission was refocused to include a heavier emphasis on arts education and cultural heritage, including the promotion of cultural tourism.

BIBLIOGRAPHY

Alexander, Jane. *Command Performance: An Actress in the Theater of Politics*. New York: Public Affairs Press, 2000.

Biddle, Livingston. *Our Government and the Arts: A Perspective from the Inside*. New York: Americans for the Arts, 1988.

Bolton, Richard, ed., *Culture Wars: Documents from the Recent Controversies in the Arts*. New York: New Press, 1992.

Brenson, Michael. *Visionaries and Outcasts: The NEA, Congress, and the Place of the Visual Arts in America*. New York: New Press, 2001.

Dowley, Jennifer, and Nancy Princenthal. *A Creative Legacy: A History of the National Endowment for the Arts Visual Artists' Fellowship Program*. New York: Abrams, 2001.

Dubin, Steven C. *Arresting Images: Impolitic Art and Uncivil Actions*. New York: Routledge, 1992.

The National Endowment for the Art. Home page at http://www.nea.gov.

Wallis, Brian, Marianne Weems, and Philip Yenawine, eds. *Art Matters: How the Culture Wars Changed America*. New York: New York University Press, 1999.

Zeigler, Joseph Wesley. *Arts in Crisis: The National Endowment for the Arts Versus America*. Pennington, N.J.: A Cappella Books, 1994.

Laura A. Bergheim
Kathleen B. Culver

See also **National Endowment for the Humanities.**

NATIONAL ENDOWMENT FOR THE HUMANITIES.

A federal role in culture received early endorsement with the creation of the Library of Congress in 1800 and with Congress's acceptance in 1836 of the Smithson bequest that eventually became the Smithsonian Institution. In the twentieth century New Deal–era legislation creating the Works Progress Administration (WPA) provided support for artists, writers, dramatists, and musicians. In so doing the federal government stamped cultural activity with a public purpose.

In 1954 Health Education and Welfare Undersecretary Nelson Rockefeller crafted a bill with the support of the Eisenhower administration that would create a national arts council. Modeled after the national arts council of Great Britain, the bill failed but established the concept of a national foundation. President John Kennedy marked the arts as a priority early in his administration, while private foundations had begun advocating for a national arts foundation. In 1964 a blue-ribbon commission organized by the American Council of Learned Societies, Phi Beta Kappa, and the Council of Graduate Schools in the United States issued a report calling for the creation of a national humanities foundation. This momentum culminated with the passage in 1965 of the National Foundation for the Arts and Humanities Act. Senator Claiborne Pell of Rhode Island introduced the bill in Congress for the administration. While the first appropriation for the National Endowment for the Arts (NEA) and the National Endowment for the Humanities (NEH) was modest ($2.9 million and $5.9 million, respectively), of real importance was the public recognition of a linkage among the vitality of civilization, the health of democracy, and a federal role. President Lyndon Johnson's choice to head the NEH was Barnaby Keeney, president of Brown University.

From its inception the National Endowment for the Humanities functioned as a competitive grant-making foundation with programmatic funding categories (these change periodically), funding levels, and application guidelines. The NEH definition of the humanities is congressionally mandated and includes the core disciplines of history, literature, and philosophy and the humanistic aspects of other forms of knowledge. The legislation asserts a "relevance of the humanities to the current conditions of national life." The agency early adopted an outside review process made up of rotating panels of professionals and experts who review each submitted application. The final award of funds is subject to preliminary approval of the National Council on the Humanities with ultimate authority resting in the chairperson of the agency. The chairperson and membership of the national council are presidential appointees subject to the confirmation of the Senate, and they serve for a set term of years or until replaced. The NEH is by far the most significant humanities funding source in the United States. It supports major research projects, centers for advanced study, research fellowships, and grants-in-aid of scholarship. The American Council for Learned Societies was the first recipient in 1972.

Federal funding fills a critical gap in cultural resources in the United States. The true value of NEH, beyond the numbers of projects it funds or the audience figures it can point to, is its role in nurturing scholarship and public learning. The state humanities councils are an indispensable complement to the agency. At the instigation of Congress, between 1971 and 1979 NEH organized state-based programs in each of the fifty states. Begun as an experiment, the councils soon evolved into independent nonprofit grant-making organizations that function as partners of the NEH at the state and local levels. They rank as the most remarkable and far-reaching of the NEH–sponsored endeavors. While Congress specifically authorizes and earmarks funds in the NEH appropriation process for award to the councils, the NEH chairperson has final authority in devising standards and conditions for the award of funds.

Humanities councils are boards made up of scholars, members of the public, and gubernatorial appointees. Councils are charged with developing plans that serve the people of their states. Great innovators, the councils have pioneered programs that successfully engage grassroots audiences, including library-based reading and discussion programs, exhibitions, oral histories, lecture series, family reading programs, a modern Chautauqua movement, book festivals, cultural tourism, community symposia, and the electronic state encyclopedia. They have also stimulated significant levels of public involvement by college and university humanities faculty, who serve as project scholars in council-funded programs. One noticeable byproduct of the councils' work has been the creation of a substantial base of public support for, and involvement in, the humanities.

NEH has acquired a reputation for excellence, and for the most part it has remained above the political fray. Still, its fortunes have been subject to some political wildfires. In the first year of President Ronald Reagan's administration, the Office of Management and Budget targeted both NEH and NEA for 50 percent reductions (they were cut 14 percent) amidst charges of "politicization." Later that same year the Senate confirmed the president's nomination of William Bennett, a critic of NEH and current trends in humanities scholarship, as chairperson.

The off-year election of 1994 swept the Republicans into power in the House and the Senate. When the 104th Congress convened in January, the new Republican House leadership slated both agencies, along with public television and radio, for elimination. Strengthened, opponents pointed to some of the controversial grants made by NEA as a rationale for elimination. Two former NEH chairs, William Bennett and Lynne Cheney, testified that NEH had become politically tainted. Other opponents included some members of Congress who resisted any federal role at all in the funding of culture.

That neither agency was eliminated (after some dramatic up-or-down votes in the House) reflected the presence of bipartisan support for NEH and the state humanities councils. Key was the public outcry against elimination at the grassroots level and NEH's record of accomplishment that held it in good stead with congressional leaders. The cost was staggering, however. NEH sustained a cut of 34 percent and NEA 40 percent, among the most severe reductions of any federal agency in the 1996 budget year. In 1981 NEH funding was $151.3 million, and NEA funding was $158.8 or $1.35 per capita. In 1996 funding for both endowments dropped to $110 million and $99.5 million, respectively, or about $.80 per capita—a cost even greater when the dollar's valuation since 1981 is factored.

Subsequent developments signal that a corner may have been turned. Consecutive budget increases in 1999 and 2000—and these in the Republican-dominated House and Senate—followed President Clinton's nomination of William Ferris as NEH chairperson in 1997. In 2001 President George W. Bush nominated Bruce Cole for NEH chairperson. A professor of art history and a former member of the National Council, Cole was a knowledgeable advocate of the endowment and the humanities councils.

In their histories NEH and NEA have traced the tension between public funding and private vision. Joined at the legislative hip by the original authorizing legislation, the agencies have experienced conflicts that reflect political and intellectual currents in society and Congress and issues surrounding the appropriateness of federal sponsorship, especially in the arts. While these tensions are not likely to end, the maturation of the agencies and the continuing education of the publics they serve would seem to have placed the necessity of a federal role beyond question. Proponents who rank NEH with the National Science Foundation advocate funding for NEH and NEA equal to the need.

BIBLIOGRAPHY

Commission on the Humanities. *Report.* New York: American Council of Learned Societies, Council of Graduate Schools in the United States, and United Chapters of Phi Beta Kappa, 1964.

Miller, Stephen. *Excellence and Equity: The National Endowment for the Humanities.* Lexington: University Press of Kentucky, 1984.

National Foundation on the Arts and Humanities Act of 1965 (Public Law 89-209).

Jamil Zainaldin

See also **Federal Agencies; National Endowment for the Arts.**

NATIONAL FEDERATION OF BUSINESS AND PROFESSIONAL WOMEN'S CLUBS,

the first national organization for professional women, has been dedicated to achieving equity for women in the workplace and providing professional women with resources and educational programs since the 1920s. The Organization was founded 15 July 1919. In the 1930s it became a charter member of the International Federation of Business and Professional Women. It has been a driving force behind significant national legislation, such as the War Classification Act (1923), the Equal Pay Act (1963), the Civil Rights Act (1964), the Federal Jury Selection and Service Act (1968), the Educational Equity Act (1974), and the Retirement Equity Act (1983).

BIBLIOGRAPHY

Kwolek-Folland, Angel. *Incorporating Women: A History of Women and Business in the United States.* New York: Twayne, 1998.

Zophy, Angela Howard, ed. *Handbook of American Women's History.* New York: Garland, 1990.

Eli Moses Diner

NATIONAL GALLERY OF ART.

In December 1936, Andrew W. Mellon offered to build an art gallery for the United States in Washington, D.C., and to donate his superb art collection to the nation as the nucleus of its holdings. President Franklin D. Roosevelt recommended acceptance of this gift, described as the largest to the national government up to that time. On 24 March 1937, the Seventy-fifth Congress approved a joint resolution to establish the National Gallery of Art as an independent bureau of the Smithsonian Institution.

The Genesis of the National Gallery of Art

Andrew W. Mellon (1855–1937), one of America's most successful financiers, came to Washington in 1921 as sec-

retary of the treasury, a position he held until 1932. While in Washington, he came to believe that the United States capital needed a great art museum to serve Americans and visitors from abroad. He had begun to collect paintings early in life, yet he made his most important purchases after his plans for the national art gallery began to take shape. Most notably, in 1930 and 1931 Mellon purchased twenty-one paintings from the Hermitage Museum in Leningrad, USSR. He paid a total of more than $6.6 million for the works, including *The Annunciation* by Jan van Eyck, *The Alba Madonna* by Raphael, and *A Polish Nobleman* by Rembrandt. In 1930, he formed the A. W. Mellon Educational and Charitable Trust to hold works of art and funds to build the new museum.

The institution that Mellon envisioned was to blend private generosity with public ownership and support. He laid out his proposals in two letters of 22 December 1936 and 31 December 1936 to President Franklin D. Roosevelt. These letters became the basis for the museum's enabling legislation. Mellon believed the museum should belong to the people of the United States and that the entire public "should forever have access" to it. To accomplish this, it should be open to the public without charge and maintained by annual Congressional appropriation. At the same time, however, Mellon believed the museum, which would be built with private funds, should grow through gifts of works of art from private citizens. To encourage such gifts, Mellon stipulated that the museum not bear his name but be called "the national gallery of art or such other name as would identify it as a gallery of art of the National Government." To ensure its excellence, he also stipulated that all works of art in the museum be of the same high standard of quality as his own extraordinary collection.

Reflecting the combined public and private character of the museum, its enabling legislation specifies that the National Gallery of Art will be governed by a board of nine trustees consisting of four public officials: the Chief Justice of the United States, the Secretary of State, the Secretary of the Treasury, and the Secretary of the Smithsonian Institution, and five private citizens.

Mellon selected architect John Russell Pope (1874–1937), one of the best known architects of his generation, to design the museum's original West Building. The building Pope planned is classic in style, but thoroughly modern in its proportions and structure.

The location of the museum was of particular concern to Mellon. He believed that it should be close to other museums and accessible for visitors. After considering various alternatives, he selected a site on the north side of the national Mall, close to the foot of Capitol Hill near the intersection of Constitution and Pennsylvania Avenues. Construction of the West Building began in June 1937. In August 1937, less than three months later, Andrew W. Mellon died. John Russell Pope died less than twenty-four hours later. The building was completed by Pope's associates, architects Otto Eggers and Daniel P.

Higgins, under the direction of the A. W. Mellon Educational and Charitable Trust.

Dedication

On the evening of 17 March 1941, the National Gallery of Art was dedicated before a gathering of roughly nine thousand invited guests. Andrew Mellon's son Paul presented the gift of the museum and the Mellon Collection to the nation on behalf of his father. In accepting the gift for the people of the United States, President Franklin D. Roosevelt concluded the ceremonies: "The dedication of this Gallery to a living past and to a greater and more richly living future, is the measure of the earnestness of our intention that the freedom of the human spirit shall go on."

In keeping with Andrew Mellon's vision for the National Gallery of Art, by the time of the museum's dedication, its collections were already being augmented by gifts from other donors. In July 1939, Samuel H. Kress (1863–1955), founder of the chain of five and dime stores, had offered the museum his large collection of mostly Italian Renaissance art. The great Widener Collection, including paintings by Rembrandt, Vermeer, El Greco, Degas, and others, also had been promised. Nonetheless, vast possibilities remained for further expansion.

The War Years

The museum opened on the eve of World War II. Less than ten months after its dedication, on 1 January 1942, the Gallery's most important works of art were moved for safekeeping to Biltmore House in Asheville, North Carolina. The museum remained open throughout the war and made every effort to make its rooms welcoming to men and women of the armed services. Following the example of the National Gallery in London, the museum began a series of Sunday afternoon concerts to entertain and inspire visitors. The concerts proved so successful that they were extended throughout the war and continue to the present.

The National Gallery of Art was instrumental in the establishment and work of the American Commission for the Protection and Salvage of Artistic and Historic Monuments in War Areas (the Roberts Commission). At the request of a number of organizations and individuals in the American cultural and intellectual community, on 8 December 1942 Chief Justice of the United States Harlan Stone, then Chairman of the Board of Trustees of the National Gallery of Art, wrote President Roosevelt to ask him to set up a commission to help in protecting historic buildings and monuments, works of art, libraries, and archives in war areas. The Commission was formed as a result of this request. Its headquarters was in the National Gallery building.

In December 1945, shortly after the close of hostilities, the United States Army asked the National Gallery to accept temporary custody of 202 paintings from Berlin museums until conditions permitted their return to Ger-

Paul Mellon. The philanthropist, art collector, and longtime trustee of the National Gallery of Art; his father, Andrew W. Mellon, created the museum and donated his art collection to grace its walls. © CORBIS

many. The move proved highly controversial. Nonetheless, the works remained in secure storage at the museum until March 1948 when they were placed on public display for 40 days. Nearly a million people viewed the works during this brief period. Following the exhibition, paintings on panel were transferred to Germany and the remaining works toured to twelve other museums in the United States before being returned.

The Collections

During the war and afterward, the collections of the National Gallery of Art continued to grow. In 1943, Lessing J. Rosenwald (1891–1979) gave his collection of old master and modern prints and drawings. He continued to enlarge and enhance the collection until his death in 1979, when his gifts to the Gallery totaled some 22,000 prints and drawings. In 1943, Chester Dale (1883–1962), who eventually assembled one of the greatest collections of French impressionist and post-impressionist paintings, gave his first gift to the museum. When Dale died in 1962, he left the Gallery a bequest that included 252 masterworks of painting and sculpture.

Andrew Mellon's own children, Ailsa Mellon Bruce (1901–1969) and Paul Mellon (1907–1999) became the museum's most important supporters and benefactors. Throughout her life, Ailsa gave the museum works of art and funds that were used for the purchase of such masterpieces as Leonardo da Vinci's *Ginevra de'Benci.* Her brother Paul served as a trustee for more than 40 years before retiring in 1985. Paul Mellon also was an important collector, especially of British and French impressionist works. By the time of his death, he had given more than 1,000 works of art and generous endowments to the museum his father founded.

The East Building

By the time of its twenty-fifth anniversary in 1966, the National Gallery of Art had outgrown the original West Building. Additional space was needed for the display of the permanent collection, including large modern paintings and sculpture; for temporary exhibitions; and for new library and research facilities. Realizing these needs, in 1967 Paul Mellon and Ailsa Mellon Bruce offered funds for a second museum building. Architect Ieoh Ming Pei (1917–) was selected to design the new building, which was to be built on the trapezoidal site immediately to the east of the original building. The site had been set aside for the museum in its enabling legislation. Pei designed a dramatic modernist building, whose public spaces are centered around a grand atrium enclosed by a sculptural space frame. The ground breaking took place in 1971, and the East Building was dedicated and opened to the public in 1978.

Special Exhibitions

Even as the East Building was being designed and built, museums were becoming ever more popular destinations for the public and temporary exhibitions began to receive enormous public attention. At the National Gallery of Art, the exhibition *Treasures of Tutankhamun* attracted more than 800,000 visitors during the four months it was on view from November 1976 to March 1977. *The Treasure Houses of Britain: 500 Years of Patronage and Collecting*, the largest and most complicated exhibition undertaken by the Gallery, was on view from November 1985 to April 1986. It attracted nearly a million visitors who viewed some 700 works of art in 17 specially constructed period rooms.

The museum attracted national attention between November 1995 and February 1996 when an unprecedented Vermeer exhibition brought together 21 of the existing 35 works known to have been painted by the Dutch artist. The exhibition was closed for a total of 19 days during its showing due to two Federal budget-related shutdowns and a major blizzard.

In recent decades, the museum's collection also continued to grow. In 1991, to celebrate the museum's fiftieth anniversary, over 320 works of art were given or committed to the National Gallery by more than 150 donors.

National Gallery of Art Sculpture Garden

With the opening of the National Gallery of Art Sculpture Garden in 1999, the museum added an area for the outdoor display of large sculpture to its campus. Designed by landscape architect Laurie D. Olin in cooperation with the National Gallery of Art, the garden was a gift of the Morris and Gwendolyn Cafritz Foundation. The garden's design is centered on a circular pool, which is transformed into an ice skating rink in winter.

Museum Programs

As the museum enters its seventh decade, it continues an active exhibition program, presenting approximately fifteen temporary shows annually. It also lends its own works of art widely to make the national collections available beyond Washington.

With its superb collection of works of art and outstanding library and research facilities, the National Gallery of Art has become an important center for the scholarly study of art. Its Center for Advanced Study in the Visual Arts (CASVA) was created in 1977 to promote research in the history of art, architecture, and urbanism. The Center supports fellowships and sponsors lectures and symposia on specialized topics intended to shape new directions in research.

Education programs are an important part of the museum's activities. Regular public lectures, tours, and film programs help interpret works of art for visitors. An extensive docents program provides guided tours and other activities for school groups. Films and videos are loaned to schools throughout the United States through an extension program. The MicroGallery, an interactive computer information center, is available to visitors on-site.

The National Gallery of Art web site (www.nga.gov) is among the most extensive art museum sites available on the Internet. It was among the first to provide access to complete, searchable information about the collection on-line. Extensive features and information relating to the museum's history, buildings, collections, and special exhibitions are included.

The museum operates an art conservation laboratory that monitors the condition of paintings, sculpture, and works on paper, and develops methodology to ensure the security of art during transportation. Since 1950, the museum has sponsored a program to conduct scientific research into conservation methods and artists' materials. Research analyzing the physical materials of works of art and the causes and prevention of deterioration continues to the present.

To date, there have been four directors of the National Gallery of Art, including David Finley (1939–1956), John Walker (1956–1969), and J. Carter Brown (1969–1992). Earl A. Powell III became director in 1992.

BIBLIOGRAPHY

Finley, David Edward. *A Standard of Excellence: Andrew W. Mellon Founds the National Gallery of Art at Washington.* Washington, D.C.: Smithsonian Institution Press, 1973.

Kopper, Philip. *America's National Gallery of Art: A Gift to the Nation.* New York: Harry N. Abrams, 1991.

Mellon, Paul, with John Baskett. *Reflections in a Silver Spoon: A Memoir.* New York: William Morrow, 1992.

Nicholas, Lynn H. *The Rape of Europa: The Fate of Europe's Treasures in the Third Reich and the Second World War.* New York: Alfred A. Knopf, 1994.

Walker, John. *Self-Portrait with Donors: Confessions of an Art Collector.* Boston: Little, Brown, 1974.

———. *National Gallery of Art, Washington.* New York: Harry N. Abrams, 1984.

Maygene F. Daniels

See also **Philanthropy.**

NATIONAL GEOGRAPHIC SOCIETY, the world's largest scientific and educational organization, was founded in Washington, D.C., on 13 January 1888 by a group of thirty-three teachers, explorers, cartographers, military officers, financiers, and others. They had met to discuss creating an organization to serve their mutual interests in geography. Two weeks later, on 27 January, the National Geographic Society was officially incorporated and later that year the first issue of *National Geographic Magazine* was published, with an announcement stating,

> The National Geographic Society has been organized to increase and diffuse geographic knowledge, and the publication of a Magazine has been determined upon as one means of accomplishing these purposes. As it is not intended to be simply the organ of the Society, its pages will be open to all persons interested in geography, in the hope that it may become a channel of intercommunication, stimulate geographic investigation and prove an acceptable medium for the publication of results.

The society's first president was Gardiner Greene Hubbard, a lawyer, financier, and philanthropist, who helped fund the experiments of his son-in-law, Alexander Graham Bell. During Hubbard's tenure as president from 1888 to 1897, membership grew to about fourteen hundred, although the society remained financially unsuccessful. Hubbard died in December 1897, and the following month, Bell took the helm as the society's second president. Bell believed that the future of the society depended on the success of the magazine.

For the first decade, the magazine was a studious, scientific journal with a dull brown cover. Bell felt that people would be more inclined to read geography if it was light and entertaining. As a first step, in 1899 he hired Gilbert Hovey Grosvenor to do editing and promote membership. Grosvenor made changes in promotion and marketing, and began rejecting articles that he considered too technical or uninteresting, even when they were approved by the editorial board. He also began to slowly change the magazine's look. He insisted upon short paragraphs, enlarged the page size, and switched to two columns of type on each page. Perhaps the most striking changes were his generous use of photographs, something that was practically nonexistent in serial publications at

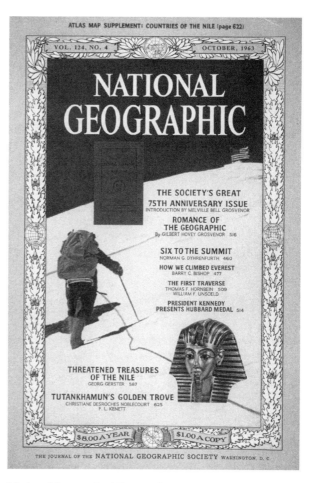

National Geographic. The October 1963 cover (featuring the first American expedition to Mount Everest) of the National Geographic Society's magazine, which has been renowned worldwide for its photography—and maps—for more then a century. NATIONAL GEOGRAPHIC SOCIETY

the time, and early use of color graphics. All of this provoked a fierce debate among the society's trustees between those who wanted to reach out to a larger audience through the popularization of the magazine and the traditionalists who felt the changes compromised the scientific scholarship. Grosvenor prevailed and won praise when the magazine, and consequently membership, began to grow. In 1905, it more than doubled from 3,400 to 11,000 members.

Grosvenor was guided by what he referred to as the "Seven Principles," which included striving for absolute accuracy, printing only what is of a "kindly nature about any country or people," and avoiding partisan or controversial issues. By the end of World War I, the National Geographic Society had become an American institution. In 1920, the circulation of *National Geographic Magazine* stood at 750,000.

The increased revenues allowed the society to act on its mission to increase geographic knowledge through supporting research. One of its first major awards was to

541

Robert E. Peary for his unsuccessful attempt to reach the North Pole in 1906; it sponsored his eventual conquest of the pole in 1909. On the heels of Peary's success, the society helped sponsor Hiram Bingham's exploration of the lost Inca capital of Machu Picchu in the Peruvian Andes in 1911. Through the magazine, the society played an instrumental role in the creation of Sequoia National Park in California and Carlsbad National Monument in New Mexico in the early 1920s. Also in the 1920s, the society gave financial support to Admiral Robert E. Byrd in his successful effort to become the first person to fly over the South Pole.

In keeping with their commitment to present only what is of a "kindly nature" about countries or people, some of the articles about Europe during the late 1930s were openly sympathetic to the National Socialist agenda. However, when the United States entered World War II, the society fully backed the Allied powers. It published detailed maps of the European and Pacific theaters, and every issue of *National Geographic Magazine* contained at least one major article on the war. Its 1944 map of Japan was used for planning air offensives. The society was presented with an almost impossible challenge during the Cold War. Favorable portrayals of communist countries would have been unpatriotic, yet to focus on the evils of such states would have violated editorial policy. For this reason, there was absolutely no coverage of the Soviet Union between 1945 and 1959, and stories about China were rare between 1950 and 1976.

Gilbert H. Grosvenor retired as president of the society and editor of the magazine to become the chairman of the society's board in 1954, a job created for him. His son, Melville Bell Grosvenor, who had already spent thirty-three years with the society, assumed the lead role in 1957. The elder Grosvenor's philosophy remained the guiding light of *National Geographic Magazine* under Melville. The editorship was then handed down to his son, Gilbert Melville Grosvenor, in 1970. The Grosvenor dynasty at the magazine came to an end in 1980 with the appointment of Wilbur E. Garrett as editor, with Gilbert Melville Grosvenor becoming the society's president.

BIBLIOGRAPHY

Abramson, Howard S. *National Geographic: Behind America's Lens on the World*. New York: Crown, 1987.

Grosvenor, Gilbert. *The National Geographic Society and Its Magazine*. Washington, D.C.: National Geographic Society, 1957.

Lutz, Catherine A., and Jane L. Collins. *Reading National Geographic*. Chicago: University of Chicago Press, 1993.

Timothy Bawden

See also **Science Journalism and Television.**

NATIONAL GUARD. The modern counterpart of the militia has the longest continuous history of any American military component. The guard's original units were organized in December 1636 as the North, South, and East Regiments of the Massachusetts Bay Colony Artillery. They served at the beginning of the twenty-first century as components of the Massachusetts Army National Guard. The name "National Guard" was first used in 1824 by New York units to honor the Marquis de Lafayette, commander of the Garde Nationale de Paris, during his visit to the newly established United States. The Marquis de Lafayette greatly assisted General George Washington during the Revolutionary War. After 1889, the term "National Guard" was adopted gradually by the militias of the various states.

From the Militia Act of 1792 to the Dick Act of 1903, the United States lacked a uniformly enforced militia policy. The modern National Guard began with the Dick Act, which divided the militia into the organized militia, or National Guard, and the unorganized militia. Units were to conform to the standards of the regular army and receive increased state and federal aid, but they were separate from the army. A 1908 amendment authorized the president to send guard units outside the country. The National Defense Act of 1916 made the guard a component of the army while in federal service and provided for regular training. The National Defense Act of 1920 established a three-component army: the regular army, the National Guard, and the organized reserves. Although the guard was considered the first-line reserve, it still was not a full-time component of the army. An amendment in 1933 created the National Guard of the United States (NGUS) as a full-time reserve component of the army. Although the composition of this force was identical to that of the state National Guard, it was subject to a call to active duty by the president without his having to go through the governor. In 1940, just prior to the outbreak of World War II, nineteen guard divisions along with their air "observation squadrons" were activated. They served in all theaters of war, garnering campaign credits and honors. After the cessation of hostilities in 1945, the WAR DEPARTMENT established the guard as a twenty-seven-division force, available for immediate service in the event of war. Under terms of the Reserve Forces Act of 1955, the army became responsible for training guard recruits for at least six months.

Upon the creation of a separate air force in 1947, the Air National Guard was formed. Many Air Guard units were formed from those that previously existed as division observation squadrons and from units that had earned campaign credits and battle honors during World War II. Both Army and Air Guard units were called to federal service in the Korean War, the Vietnam War, and the Persian Gulf War. The Air Guard has served as an integral part of the U.S. Air Force since the beginning of the Vietnam War, when airlift units were added to its (Air Guard) flying inventory of mostly fighter units.

Reorganization in 1962 cut four divisions from authorized guard strength. In 1965, Secretary of Defense

Robert S. McNamara tried to amalgamate the guard with the reserves, but he encountered powerful opposition from Congress. Two years later fifteen divisions were cut from the force structure, leaving six infantry and two armored divisions. All National Guard unit members must serve at least forty-eight drills and fifteen days of field training annually. They must also conform to the regulations and requirements of the Departments of the Army and Air Force. From the 1980s into the twenty-first century, Army and Air National Guard units have been called to serve in all of the major contingency operations that have involved the United States.

Aside from being used in wartime, guard units have also given aid in times of natural disasters and maintained order during civil disturbances.

BIBLIOGRAPHY

Doubler, Michael D. *Closing with the Enemy: How GIs Fought the War in Europe, 1944–1945.* Lawrence: University Press of Kansas, 1994.

Mahon, John K. *History of the Militia and the National Guard.* New York, Macmillan, 1983.

Gary Gault

See also **Militias.**

NATIONAL INDIAN YOUTH COUNCIL. The National Indian Youth Council, an all-Indian organization, was started in 1961 by Indian college students and recent college graduates. The council is more militant than the National Congress of American Indians, which it has criticized as being too conservative. It manifests the influence of the CIVIL RIGHTS MOVEMENT of the period of its founding and has used tactics of demonstration and confrontation. It favors the abolition of the Bureau of Indian Affairs. The National Indian Youth Council and the National Congress of American Indians both predate the AMERICAN INDIAN MOVEMENT (AIM) and share its focus on a national unity that respects tribal sovereignty.

BIBLIOGRAPHY

Hoxie, Frederick E., Peter C. Mancall, and James H. Merrell, eds. *American Nations: Encounters in Indian Country, 1850 to the Present.* New York: Routledge, 2001.

National Indian Youth Council. *ABC: Americans before Columbus.* Denver, Colo.: National Indian Youth Council, 1963–.

Smith, Paul Chaat, and Robert Allen Warrior. *Like a Hurricane: The Indian Movement from Alcatraz to Wounded Knee.* New York: New Press, 1996.

Kenneth M. Stewart / D. B.

National Guard. Bayonets fixed, and aided by tanks, these troops—called out after looters disrupted a march on 28 March 1968 by striking black sanitation workers in Memphis, Tenn.—block Beale Street the next day. © BETTMANN/CORBIS

See also **American Indian Defense Association; Youth Movements.**

NATIONAL INSTITUTE FOR THE PROMOTION OF SCIENCE. *See* **American Association for the Advancement of Science.**

NATIONAL INSTITUTES OF HEALTH (NIH), established at the Marine Hospital, Staten Island, N.Y., in 1887 as the Laboratory of Hygiene, for research on cholera and other infectious diseases. In 1891 it was renamed the Hygienic Laboratory and moved to Washington, D.C., and in 1930, as a result of the Ransdell Act, it became the National Institute of Health. In 1937 it incorporated the National Cancer Institute, and the following year Congress authorized the construction of new, larger laboratory facilities and the transfer of the National Institute of Health (NIH) to Bethesda, Md. Legislation in 1948 established a National Heart Institute and changed the name of the National Institute of Health to National Institutes of Health.

An agency of the Department of Health, Education and Welfare since that department's establishment in 1953, NIH has the mission of improving the health of all Americans. To achieve this goal it conducts biomedical research; provides grants to individuals, organizations, and institutions for research, training, and medical education; assists in the improvement and construction of library facilities and resources; and supports programs in biomedical communications. From its beginnings in a one-room laboratory, NIH has developed into a large research center. The NIH campus consists of over 300 acres and includes laboratories, libraries, and clinical facilities for highly sophisticated research into the biomedical sciences. NIH also has annual lectures, honors, exhibits, and symposia.

Its intramural program supports research in NIH laboratories on the Bethesda, Md., campus, and its extramural program distributes grants to university investigators across the United States and makes collaborative arrangements with researchers in other countries. The NIH annual budget in the early 1990s was more than $8 billion, and personnel on the Bethesda campus numbered more than 16,000. In 1993 Congress directed the NIH to include more women in research designs and analysis instead of continuing to concentrate on studies involving only men. By 1994 the NIH consisted of seventeen institutes (Aging; Alcohol Abuse and Alcoholism; Allergy and Infectious Diseases; Arthritis and Musculoskeletal and Skin Diseases; Cancer; Child Health and Human Development; Deafness and Other Communication Disorders; Dental Research; Diabetes and Digestive and Kidney Diseases; Drug Abuse; Environmental Health Sciences; Eye; General Medical Sciences; Heart, Lung, and Blood; Mental Health; Neurological Disorders and Stroke;

and Nursing Research); two divisions (Computer Research and Technology and Research Grants); four centers (Center for Research Resources; John E. Fogarty International Center; National Center for Human Genome Research; and Warren Grant Magnuson Clinical Center); three offices (Women's Health; Alternative Medicine; and Minority Health); the National Library of Medicine; and the Children's Inn at NIH. The NIH also funds three field units (the Gerontology Research Center in Baltimore, Md.; the Rocky Mountain Laboratories in Hamilton, Mont.; and the NIH Animal Center in Poolesville, Md.). NIH has joined with other agencies to advance biomedical research. In one of the larger projects, NIH and the Howard Hughes Medical Institute launched a multimillion-dollar cooperative program to encourage physicians to enter research.

BIBLIOGRAPHY

Ahrens, Edward H., Jr. *The Crisis in Clinical Research: Overcoming Institutional Obstacles.* New York: Oxford University Press, 1992.

Kelley, William N., et al. *Emerging Policies for Biomedical Research.* Washington, D.C.: Association of Academic Health Centers, 1993.

National Institutes of Health (U.S.) Division of Public Information. *NIH Almanac.* Bethesda, Md.: U.S. Department of Health, Education and Welfare, Public Health Service, National Institutes of Health, 1975.

———. *NIH Almanac.* Bethesda, Md.: U.S. Department of Health, Education and Welfare, Public Health Service, National Institutes of Health, 1992.

Reagan, Michael D. *The Accidental System: Health Care Policy in America.* Boulder, Colo.: Westview Press, 1999.

Manfred Waserman / c. w.

See also **Clinical Research; Health and Human Services, Department of; Hygiene; Laboratories; Medical Research.**

NATIONAL LABOR RELATIONS ACT. The National Labor Relations Act (NLRA), enacted in 1935, was a major component of President Franklin D. Roosevelt's NEW DEAL, and represented a sea change in national labor policy. Known initially as the Wagner Act, it followed three decades of debate over the role the federal government should play in labor policy. Its authors intended it as a law to extend democratic rights in the workplace by guaranteeing workers the rights to organize and to bargain collectively with their employers. It provided for the establishment of the National Labor Relations Board (NLRB) to administer its provisions.

The Wagner Act stipulated that workers had the right to collective bargaining, outlawed company unions, listed unfair labor practices, and provided governmental processes for the selection of employee bargaining representatives. Because it prohibited employers from interfering with, restraining, or coercing employees in the exercise of their rights to form unions, to bargain collectively, and to engage in other concerted activities, it also protected employees' right to strike. It prohibited discrimination in employment to encourage or discourage membership in a labor organization but permitted "closed shops" established by collective-bargaining agreements between employers and unions with exclusive bargaining rights. It protected employees who file charges or give testimony under the act from being fired or otherwise discriminated against. It also made it unlawful for an employer to refuse to bargain collectively with the representative chosen by a majority of employees in a group appropriate for collective bargaining.

Workers and their advocates initially hailed the Wagner Act as a milestone, for it made union recognition a right rather than an issue decided through overt conflict between labor and management. In the years following the act, numerous large industries such as automobile, electric, rubber, and steel were forced to allow their workforces to unionize. However, the act soon fell under attack, and was seriously compromised in 1947, after which its interpretation and enforcement varied widely along with the political tide. During President Ronald Reagan's administration in the 1980s, further changes brought federal labor law far indeed from the premises of the original National Labor Relations Act.

The first major blow to the NLRA came in 1947, when the Labor Management Relations Act, commonly known as the TAFT-HARTLEY ACT, shifted the legal conception of workers' rights from a collective one to an individualistic one. Taft-Hartley passed amid the first stirrings of the Cold War, was born of accusations that organized labor had become too strong and corrupt and was permeated by communists. Where the Wagner Act had protected workers' right to unionize, the Taft-Hartley amendment emphasized their right *not* to organize. Taft-Hartley outlawed closed shops, authorized the president to intervene in labor disputes with a "national emergency" injunction, required the National Labor Relations Board to seek injunctions against unions involved in secondary boycotts or jurisdictional strikes, and required union officials to sign affidavits swearing they were not and never had been communists. Another proviso stated that union-shop agreements could not be authorized in states where they were forbidden by state law, thus giving antiunion states the power to supersede federal protection of workers. In all other respects the NLRA preempted state laws. The 1947 amendments also reorganized the NLRB, providing for the president to appoint the general counsel, who was assigned statutory responsibility for the investigation of charges of unfair labor practice, the issuance of complaints, and the prosecution of complaints before the board. Thus, the National Labor Relations Board's administration of federal labor law became largely a matter of the political ideology of whichever president was in office. Employers and others who believed unions had too much power hailed the act. Taft-Hartley prompted outrage on the part of labor advocates

and liberals, who continue to view it as an antilabor watershed in American labor history and an opening shot in the Cold War era war of suppression of activism and labor rights.

The NLRA was amended again in 1959 by the Labor-Management Reporting and Disclosure Act, commonly known as the Landrum-Griffin Act. These amendments forbade unions from picketing or threatening to picket to force recognition by the employer, or to force the employees to accept the union as their representative, if the union was not certified to represent the employees. The act followed upon a decade of well-publicized Congressional hearings that emphasized union corruption and presented the public with the image of powerful, antidemocratic union leaders, with the Teamsters' Jimmy Hoffa as their poster child. Rather than empowering the rank-and-file union members, however, Landrum-Griffin turned over more power to the National Labor Relations Board, which, as of 2002, was composed of five members appointed (since 1947) by the president subject to approval by the Senate, with each member having a term of five years. The general counsel, whose appointment also must be approved by the Senate, has a term of four years. Headquartered in Washington, D.C., the agency has more than thirty regional offices and eleven smaller field offices throughout the country, and thousands of staff members.

The board members act primarily as a quasi-judicial body in deciding cases on formal records, generally upon review of findings of fact and decisions by its administrative law judges (formerly called trial examiners) in cases of unfair labor practice or upon review of regional-director decisions in representation cases. The NLRB has no independent statutory power of enforcement of its orders, but it may seek enforcement in the U.S. courts of appeals; parties aggrieved by board orders also may seek judicial review.

At the turn of the twenty-first century, most labor historians viewed the National Labor Relations Board as a far cry from what the Wagner Act's authors envisioned. Some labor advocates argue that the NLRB should have more power to protect workers' right to organize. Others argue that rank-and-file union members need to have more control over their unions and that centralizing worker protection in a federal board is inimical to industrial democracy, the original goal of the Wagner Act.

BIBLIOGRAPHY

Gould, William B. *Labored Relations: Law, Politics, and the NLRB: A Memoir.* Cambridge, Mass.: MIT Press, 2000.

Gross, James A. *Broken Promise: The Subversion of U.S. Labor Relations Policy, 1947–1994.* Philadelphia: Temple University Press, 1995.

O'Brien, Ruth Ann. *Workers' Paradox: The Republican Origins of New Deal Labor Policy, 1886–1935.* Chapel Hill: University of North Carolina Press, 1998.

Taylor, Benjamin J., and Fred Witney. *U.S. Labor Relations Law: Historical Development.* Englewood Cliffs, N.J.: Prentice Hall, 1992.

Tomlins, Christopher L. *The State and the Unions: Labor Relations, Law, and the Organized Labor Movement in America, 1880-1960.* New York: Cambridge University Press, 1985.

Frank M. Kleiler / D. B.

See also **American Federation of Labor–Congress of Industrial Organizations; Clayton Act, Labor Provisions; Closed Shop; Fair Labor Standards Act; Injunctions, Labor; Labor Legislation and Administration; Lockout;** *National Labor Relations Board v. Jones and Laughlin Steel Corporation;* **Wages and Hours of Labor, Regulation of.**

NATIONAL LABOR RELATIONS BOARD V. JONES AND LAUGHLIN STEEL CORPORATION,

301 U.S. 1 (1937), a Supreme Court decision that, by a five-to-four decision, upheld the validity of the NATIONAL LABOR RELATIONS ACT of 1935. The Jones and Laughlin Corporation was engaged in interstate commerce, argued the Court, and thus, "Congress had constitutional authority to safeguard the right of respondent's employees to self-organization and freedom in the choice of representatives for collective bargaining." The Court thus reversed the lower court, which had ruled that the federal government had no constitutional right to regulate labor relations in a manufacturing establishment. This was the first of fifteen formal decisions won by the National Labor Relations Board.

BIBLIOGRAPHY
Cortner, Richard C. *The Jones and Laughlin Case.* New York: Knopf, 1970.

Erik McKinley Eriksson
Andrew C. Rieser

See also **Commerce Clause; Wages and Hours of Labor, Regulation of.**

NATIONAL LABOR UNION

(NLU) was begun at a conference in Baltimore in 1866. The organization was a pioneering coalition of trade unionists, feminists, and social reformers, oriented toward changing the American political and economic systems. In 1868, William Sylvis, leader of the Iron Molder's International Union, was elected as its first president. The NLU had some success in attracting members until 1869, when Sylvis died suddenly. After that, the NLU divided over politics and the issue of beginning a third party. In 1872, the organization, by then called the National Labor Reform Party, collapsed when its chosen presidential candidate backed out of the race.

BIBLIOGRAPHY
Commons, John R., et al. History of Labour in the United States. 4 vols. New York: Macmillan, 1918–1935.

Jonathan Rees

NATIONAL LAWYERS GUILD,

a progressive legal organization founded in 1937 by lawyers opposed to the American Bar Association (ABA), which was then politically conservative and did not admit African Americans. Early guild members included prominent liberals like Morris Ernst, New Dealers like Solicitor General Robert H. Jackson, African Americans like Charles Houston, and women like the radical labor lawyer Carol Weiss King. In addition, many members had ties to other reformist organizations, including the American Civil Liberties Union and the International Labor Defense. Whereas in the 1930s the ABA supported property rights and laissez-faire, the guild championed New Deal economic and legal reforms, declaring that "human rights" should be "more sacred than property rights," and the group accordingly supported President Franklin Roosevelt's controversial court-packing plan. Guild lawyers represented the Congress of Industrial Organizations during the 1937 sit-down strikes and in *Hague v. Congress of Industrial Organizations* (1939), which established workers' free speech rights to use public streets to demonstrate and organize. The early guild also advocated legal aid for poor people. Government-supported legal aid did not appear until the 1960s, but some local guild chapters operated privately funded law clinics in the 1940s that helped nonelite attorneys gain a professional foothold, and brought legal help to people not otherwise able to afford it.

The general conservative reaction against the New Deal in the late 1930s brought specific charges from guild opponents that it was a subversive organization. This accusation exacerbated internal tensions, with liberal guild members increasingly demanding statements from other members endorsing democracy and disavowing "dictatorships," whether fascist, nazi, or communist. Radical members (including many who were communists) resisted these calls, opposing what they saw as unfair conflations of fascism and communism. In 1940, liberal and New Dealer members began resigning from the guild over this issue.

The guild's public standing improved during World War II, and subsequently, its president was officially invited to the United Nations' founding and the Nuremberg trials. However, the guild became reentangled in the national debate over communism when its members represented many prominent McCarthy era defendants, including several of the Hollywood Ten and the leaders of the Communist Party, USA. The House Committee on Un-American Activities responded by denouncing the guild as "the legal bulwark of the Communist Party," and the Justice Department attempted to list it as a subversive organization. No guild wrongdoing was ever found, but the accusations reduced membership by 80 percent in the 1950s.

Guild membership recovered in the 1960s when it represented civil rights organizations such as the Mississippi Freedom Project and antiwar protesters like the Chicago Seven. The guild remained active in left-progressive legal causes from the 1970s onward, including immigrant rights, gay and lesbian rights, death penalty repeal, and Palestinian statehood.

BIBLIOGRAPHY

Auerbach, Jerold S. *Unequal Justice: Lawyers and Social Change in Modern America.* New York: Oxford University Press, 1976.

Bailey, Percival R. "The Case of the National Lawyers Guild, 1939–1958." In *Beyond the Hiss Case: The FBI, Congress, and the Cold War.* Edited by Athan G. Theoharis. Philadelphia: Temple University Press, 1982.

Ginger, Ann Fagan, and Eugene M. Tobin, eds. *The National Lawyers Guild: From Roosevelt through Reagan.* Philadelphia: Temple University Press, 1988.

Charles F. Bethel

See also **American Bar Association; Communist Party, United States of America; Legal Profession; McCarthyism.**

NATIONAL MONETARY COMMISSION, a

commission established by the ALDRICH-VREELAND ACT of 30 May 1908 to "inquire into and report to Congress . . . what changes are necessary or desirable in the monetary system of the United States or in the laws relating to banking and currency."

The commission, composed of nine members of the Senate and nine members of the House of Representatives, with Senator Nelson Aldrich as chairman, was duly appointed and proceeded to carry out its designated task. It appointed experts to make studies of banking history and existing conditions in the United States and other countries, and in the summer of 1908 members of the commission visited England, France, and Germany to ascertain their banking arrangements, methods, and practices by personal observation and interviews.

On 8 January 1912 the commission submitted its report to Congress. The report contained a summary of the work done by the commission, and by experts and others employed by it, as well as a description and text of a proposed law to remedy a number of existing defects as enumerated in the report. The proposed law contained provisions for the establishment of a National Reserve Association with branches to act as a central bank for the United States (*see* FEDERAL RESERVE SYSTEM). The monographs and articles, prepared for the commission by experts and published in conjunction with the report, numbered more than forty and constituted, at the time, one of the most comprehensive banking libraries available.

BIBLIOGRAPHY

Broz, J. Lawrence. *The International Origins of the Federal Reserve System.* Ithaca, N.Y.: Cornell University Press, 1997.

Degen, Robert A. *The American Monetary System: A Concise Survey of Its Evolution since 1896.* Lexington, Mass.: Lexington Books, 1987.

Frederick A. Bradford / c. w.

See also **Banking.**

NATIONAL MUSEUM OF THE AMERICAN INDIAN.

The National Museum of the American Indian of the Smithsonian Institution (NMAI) began as the private collection of a wealthy New York banker, George Gustav Heye (1874–1957). In 1903 Heye began a half century of voracious acquisition of Native American artifacts, during which he dispatched agents throughout the Western Hemisphere to obtain objects and collections from Native peoples. In the first decade, Heye worked in collaboration with the University Museum in Philadelphia and with Franz Boas at Columbia University. In 1916, however, Heye established, over Boas's strenuous objections, his independent institution in Manhattan: the Heye Foundation and the Museum of the American Indian. The goal of the new museum was as simple as it was comprehensive: "the preservation of everything pertaining to our American tribes." Over the next fifteen years Heye established a publication series, an anthropological library, a storage facility in the Bronx, and a research and collecting agenda in archaeology and ethnography.

The death of two of Heye's major benefactors in 1928 and the onset of economic depression a year later effectively ended Heye's ambitious program of acquisition. Over the next twenty-five years Heye continued collecting and sponsoring expeditions, but on a greatly reduced level. After his death in 1957, Heye's institution fell into disrepair; when the museum's sad state came to public attention in the mid-1970s, nearly fifteen years of debate and negotiation ensued. This resulted finally, in 1990, in the transfer of the Heye artifact collection, archives, and library in their entirety to the SMITHSONIAN INSTITUTION, where they constitute the core of the National Museum of the American Indian. The transfer also stipulated that human remains and funerary objects from the Heye collection be repatriated to Native peoples where possible.

Building upon its core collection of nearly one million artifacts, the Smithsonian's National Museum of the American Indian preserves, studies, and exhibits the histories and cultures of Native American peoples; the NMAI also works in close collaboration with Native peoples to protect, sustain, and reaffirm traditional beliefs and encourage artistic expression.

There are several NMAI facilities. Opened in 1994, the George Gustav Heye Center of NMAI, located at the Alexander Hamilton U.S. Custom House in lower Manhattan, is an educational and exhibition facility with public programs of music, dance, and film. The Cultural Resources Center outside Washington, D.C., in Suitland, Maryland, invites Native and non-Native scholars to utilize its library and archival collections. The central facility—the Smithsonian's last museum on the Mall—was scheduled to open in 2003 and serve as the major exhibition space, as well as a venue for ceremony and education. Finally, a "virtual museum" is available through the NMAI Web sites.

BIBLIOGRAPHY

Force, Roland W. *Politics and the Museum of the American Indian: The Heye and the Mighty.* Honolulu, Hawaii: Mechas Press, 1999.

"The History of the Museum." *Indian Notes and Monographs*, Miscellaneous Series No. 55. New York: Museum of the American Indian, Heye Foundation, 1956.

Kidwell, Clara Sue. "Every Last Dishcloth: The Prodigious Collecting of George Gustav Heye." In *Collecting Native America, 1870–1960.* Edited by Shepard Krech III and Barbara A. Hail. Washington, D.C.: Smithsonian Institution Press, 1999, 232–258.

National Museum of the American Indian. Home page at http://www.nmai.si.edu.

National Museum of the American Indian Act, Public Law 101–185, 101st Congress (28 November 1989).

Wallace, Kevin. "Slim-Shin's Monument." *New Yorker* (19 November 1960).

Curtis M. Hinsley

See also **Native Americans.**

NATIONAL ORGANIZATION FOR WOMEN

(NOW). NOW was founded in 1966 when the third annual meeting of the federal Equal Employment Opportunity Commission (EEOC) refused to consider a resolution insisting that it enforce Title VII of the 1964 Civil Rights Act outlawing discrimination in job advertising and hiring practices. Fifteen women who were in Washington to promote this resolution met at the suggestion of the feminist author and activist Betty Friedan to discuss founding a new feminist civil rights organization. On 29 October that year, 300 women met in Washington, D.C., as the founding convention of NOW. The convention drafted a statement of purpose that emphasized that U.S. women's demands for equality were part of an international human rights movement and challenged the United States to pay attention to women's grievances and demands. It also criticized the U.S. government for falling behind other industrialized nations in providing health care, child care, and pregnancy leave for women and labeled these as social needs, not individual problems. The convention chose Friedan as NOW's first president. In 1970, NOW members elected the African American union leader and former EEOC commissioner, Aileen Hernandez, as president.

NOW's first national convention in 1967 adopted a Bill of Rights whose demands were all aimed at dismantling institutionalized gender discrimination. These demands included passage of the Equal Rights Amendment, EEOC enforcement of laws banning gender discrimination in employment, protection of the right of each woman to control her reproductive life, and child day care centers with tax deductions for child care expenses for working parents. One of NOW's first victories came in 1968 when the EEOC finally agreed to bar gender-specific job ads.

NOW as a Political Action Group

Leaders of NOW regularly appear before Congress, lobby officeholders, and organize letter-writing campaigns. Its overall strategy has been to work to pressure the political and legal systems to promote gender equality. Its leadership has come largely from the ranks of professional women who have focused much of the organization's attention on promoting and developing the leadership and organizing skills that would make women good lobbyists, organizers, and strategists. As such, other feminist groups have challenged it for being too reformist. NOW, for instance, had sought to be gender inclusive in its statement of purpose, which began with the words "we men and women." Other feminist groups rejected this inclusivity. Minority groups have challenged NOW for being overly focused on the needs of middle-class white women. At the same time, NOW has been denounced by conservative groups as "anti-family" for its 1970 definition of marriage as an equal partnership in which both parents should share equally the economic, household, and child-care responsibilities.

NOW's persistent pursuit of its strategy of political action working within the system has produced numerous victories for women's rights. In the 1970s, it forced 1,300 corporations doing federal business to compensate female employees for past pay discrimination. It helped prevent the confirmation of a conservative nominee, Harold Carswell, to the Supreme Court by documenting a past record of discrimination. In the 1990s, it helped secure the federal Violence Against Women Act (VAWA; 1994) that resulted in the institution of the Violence Against Women Office in the Justice Department. The VAWA and the Family Violence Prevention and Services Act (1984) have also resulted in federal funding for women and family victims of violence. In 2000, NOW began a campaign to extend the VAWA to include funding to train police, law enforcement, and court personnel to better handle issues of violence against women.

As a public action organization, NOW conducts national awareness, agitation, and legal campaigns and political lobbying against discrimination of every type. In 1978 it organized a pro-Equal Rights Amendment march in Washington, D.C., that drew 100,000 participants. In 1992, 750,000 people participated in NOW's abortion rights rally in Washington. It rallied 250,000 to protest violence against women in 1995. The following year, 50,000 demonstrators marched in San Francisco in NOW's rally to support affirmative action. NOW has been a staunch supporter of lesbian rights and held a Lesbian Rights Summit in 1999.

Legal and Educational Defense Fund

NOW takes its issues to court. To pursue its legal cases, NOW established a Legal and Educational Defense Fund in 1971. One of the fund's first cases was in support of southern working women against Colgate-Palmolive and Southern Bell Telephone for job discrimination. One of its most recent legal successes came in *NOW v. Scheidler* (1998), when a Chicago jury convicted the anti-abortion group Operation Rescue and its leader Joseph Scheidler under the statutes of the federal Racketeer-Influenced and Corrupt Organization Act, making the group responsible for tripling the cost for damages done to women's health clinics.

NOW Funding

NOW raises the money to support its various causes and campaigns from a dues-paying membership, voluntary contributions to an equality action fund, fund-raising campaigns, and grants from national foundations. In 1986 it also established a NOW Foundation, as a tax-deductible education and litigation organization affiliated with NOW.

NOW and Politics

NOW campaigns vigorously to elect feminists to public office. In 1992, it endorsed and financially supported the election of Carol Moseley Braun as senator from Illinois. Braun was the first African American woman elected to the Senate. It formed an umbrella political action committee (PAC) in 1978 called NOW/PAC under which it has organized specific PACs to target specific campaign drives and to support both female and male candidates who have a feminist agenda. The NOW/PAC screens political candidates for their stand on feminist issues, which the organization defines broadly as abortion rights; women's economic equality, especially pay equity; and, fair treatment of poor women, especially their right to Medicaid. In 2000 NOW/PAC launched a major political drive titled Victory 2000—the Feminization of Politics Campaign.

NOW Membership

In 1978, NOW had 125,000 members. NOW reported that anger over the treatment of Anita Hill during congressional hearings on the Supreme Court nomination of Clarence Hill gained the organization 13,000 new members in the closing months of 1991. In 2001, NOW elected Kim Gandy, a Louisiana lawyer and long-time NOW activist, to the office of president. By 2002 its membership had grown to 500,000 contributing members and 550 chapters across the country.

BIBLIOGRAPHY

Ford, Lynne E. *Women and Politics: The Pursuit of Equality.* New York: Houghton Mifflin, 2002.

Hartmann, Susan M. *The Other Feminists: Activists in the Liberal Establishment.* New Haven, Conn.: Yale University Press, 1998.

Rosen, Ruth. *The World Split Open: How the Modern Women's Movement Changed America.* New York, Penguin, 2000.

Maureen A. Flanagan

See also **Equal Rights Amendment; Women, President's Commission on the Status of;** *and vol. 9:* **NOW Statement of Purpose.**

NATIONAL PARK SYSTEM. The national park system preserves the natural and cultural resources of the United States for the benefit of present and future generations. A total of 384 units, spanning 83.6 million acres in forty-nine states, fall under the jurisdiction of the National Park Service (NPS), the federal bureau responsible for the protection, management, and maintenance of designated areas. National parks are customarily established by act of Congress on the advice of the secretary of the interior, although the president retains the right to create national monuments under the Antiquities Act. Preserved by virtue of their natural, recreational, or historic value, the national park system encompasses an array of sites including parks, monuments, battlefields, and scenic rivers, as well as structures such as the White House and the Statue of Liberty. Wrangell–St. Elias National Park and Preserve in Alaska represents the largest unit in the system at 13.2 million acres, while the Thaddeus Kosciuszko National Memorial in Pennsylvania comprises the smallest at one-fiftieth of an acre. The first person to describe the reserves under NPS tutelage as part of a system was the service's assistant director Horace M. Albright in 1918, although only in 1970 did Congress officially recognize the individual units and their united purpose as "cumulative expressions of a single national heritage." The national park ideal is regarded by many as America's greatest contribution to world culture; according to western novelist Wallace Stegner, it is "the best idea we ever had." By the end of the twentieth century, a global national park movement predicated on preserving scenic and historic landscapes counted 1,200 reserves worldwide.

The Birth of the National Park Movement

The nineteenth-century artist George Catlin is usually credited as the original exponent of the national park ideal. Concerned at the rapid decimation of indigenous peoples and wildlife brought about by westward expansionism, Catlin proposed the creation of "A *nation's park,* containing man and beast, in all the wild and freshness of their nature's beauty!" during a trip to the Dakotas in 1832. The same year, Congress moved to protect a natural feature for the first time, establishing Hot Springs National Reservation, Arkansas, for the purposes of public medicinal use. The dedication of Mount Auburn rural cemetery, Boston (1831), and New York City's Central Park (1861) attested to a growing perception amongst nineteenth-century Americans of nature as a bucolic refuge from city life. The tenets of romanticism, as manifested in the writings of Henry David Thoreau and the paintings of Thomas Cole, celebrated wild nature as a sublime venue for contemplation and spiritual renewal. From the 1850s onward, cultural nationalists looked to the grandeur of western scenery as a harbinger of national greatness, with pure and imposing vistas evincing a proud heritage to rival the cathedrals of Europe.

A newfound appreciation of rugged landscapes as natural and cultural treasures, allied with a desire to avoid the profligate commercialism that had sullied the natural resplendence of Niagara Falls, underscored the early American national park movement. Mindful of attempts by businessmen to capitalize on the popularity of the Yosemite Valley and the Mariposa Grove of Big Trees since their discovery in the early 1850s, Congress ceded forty square miles in the High Sierras to the State of California for "public use, resort, and recreation" in 1864. Eight years later, in 1872, the government withdrew 3,300 square miles of rocky terrain, spouting geysers, and plunging waterfalls in Wyoming and Montana territories to create Yellowstone National Park. The establishment of Yellowstone "as a public park or pleasuring-ground for the benefit and enjoyment of the people" is generally regarded as the formal beginning of the national park system. While the protective ideals encompassed in the Yellowstone Act resembled the Yosemite example, the size of the Rocky Mountain reserve, together with its federal jurisdiction, proved unprecedented. The setting aside of vast swaths of land under the auspices of governmental protection represented a significant exception to the culture of acquisition and conquest that predominated in nineteenth-century American society, although the smooth passage of the Yellowstone bill in part reflected the worthlessness of the high country for extractive or agricultural purposes.

Despite the precedent established in Yellowstone, it took eighteen years for Congress to found another park that endured into the twentieth century, as Mackinac National Park, Michigan (1875), was abolished in 1895. Aided by railroad companies eager to profit from park-related tourism, the movement to furnish additional national parks gained momentum in the 1890s. Yosemite, General Grant, and Sequoia, all in California, attained national park status in 1890, reflecting burgeoning desires to protect grandiose western scenery. Dedicated in 1899, Mount Rainier, Washington, became the first reserve to be labeled a national park in its enabling legislation.

Congress also acquired an interest in preserving Native American ruins and artifacts during this period. Motivated by concerns over wanton vandalism and looting of prehistoric sites in the Southwest, Congress enacted legislation to protect Casa Grande Ruin, Arizona (1889), and Mesa Verde National Park, Colorado (1906). The Antiq-

uities Act, passed in 1906, allowed the president to establish national monuments for the preservation of archaeological sites, historic structures, and features of scientific merit. During his presidency, Theodore Roosevelt designated eighteen national monuments, notably Devils Tower, Wyoming (1906), and Grand Canyon, Arizona (1908).

The National Park Service and the Consolidation of a System

By 1916, the United States boasted fourteen national parks and twenty-one national monuments. However, no presiding institution existed to manage them effectively. Lacking national policy directives, superintendents administered preserves independently, rarely coordinating their actions with equivalent officials in other park units. Compromised management in the fledgling preserves allowed poaching and vandalism to proliferate. Flouting of regulations became so acute that the secretary of the interior dispatched the U.S. Army to Yellowstone and the California parks to thwart market and souvenir hunters. The controversial damming of Yosemite's Hetch Hetchy Valley in 1913 further revealed the vulnerability of national parks to material interests and demonstrated a need for an institutional framework to ensure their protection. In 1916, a cadre of influential conservationists, including the Chicago businessman Stephen T. Mather, the landscape architect Frederick Law Olmsted Jr., J. Horace McFarland from the American Civic Association, and the publicist Robert Sterling Yard, successfully lobbied for the creation of a federal agency to administer park areas. President Woodrow Wilson signed the bill creating the National Park Service (NPS) within the Department of the Interior on 25 August 1916. The purpose of the bureau, as outlined in its enabling legislation (usually described as the Organic Act), was to "promote and regulate the use of Federal areas known as national parks, monuments, and reservations . . . [and] conserve the scenery and the natural and historic objects and the wild life therein and to provide for the enjoyment of the same in such manner and by such means as will leave them unimpaired for the enjoyment of future generations." As only the second agency in the world charged with managing protected environments (the first being Canada's Dominion Parks Branch, founded in 1911), the National Park Service articulated an important commitment to conservation in the United States.

Stephen T. Mather was the first director of the NPS (1916–1929) and was assisted by the California lawyer Horace M. Albright. Together, the two men defined the principal tenets and administrative methodology of the National Park Service. Mather and Albright readily endorsed the agency's dual mandate of preservation and use, firmly believing that securing a rosy future for the NPS depended on rendering the parks popular, and economically lucrative, tourist destinations. Lavish publications such as the *National Parks Portfolio* (1916), guidebooks, and promotional leaflets advertised America's preserves as scenic playgrounds. The bureau stressed the role of en-

Bryce Canyon National Park. Visitors follow a trail at the bottom of this canyon in southern Utah in 1929, not long after it became a national park. NATIONAL ARCHIVES AND RECORDS ADMINISTRATION

tertainment in the national park experience. Vacationers savored the delights of bear-feeding shows, Indian rodeos, outdoor sports, and the famous summer firefall at Yosemite's Glacier Point. Administrators advocated the construction of rustic hotels and forged alliances with railroad companies and the American Automobile Association. By 1919, nearly 98,000 vehicles journeyed through the parks, leading two asphalt enthusiasts to herald the automobile as "the greatest aid" to the parks' "popularity and usefulness."

By promoting national parks as valuable recreational resources, Mather and Albright secured appropriations from Congress and fended off attempts by timber, mining, and grazing lobbies to encroach on protected areas. When Albright retired following a term as director (1929–1933), the national parks had achieved popular success along with security. However, the focus on entertainment had led early authorities into a series of ill-advised management policies. Styling the parks as idyllic resorts, staff engaged in programs of fire suppression, vista clearing, exotic species introduction, and predator control. Early

administrators failed to anticipate the problems inherent in promoting preservation alongside use, and subsequent park managers struggled with an array of thorny management issues deriving from the contradictory nature of the dual mandate.

Expansion, Ecology, and Wartime Retrenchment

The 1930s represented a dynamic period of expansion for the national park system. Following a pivotal meeting between Horace Albright and Franklin D. Roosevelt in April 1933, the president signed a decree transferring authority for fifty-six parks and monuments under the auspices of the Agriculture and War Departments to the National Park Service. The reorganization of 10 August 1933 significantly expanded the size and the range of the national park system, conferring authority on the NPS to manage historic as well as natural features. Progress in the realm of historic preservation continued under the direction of Arno B. Cammerer (1933–1940), who presided over an exhaustive survey of nationally significant buildings mandated by the Historic Sites Act (1935). The

NPS also broadened its responsibilities for recreational provision with a series of newly designated parks, including Blue Ridge Parkway, North Carolina/Virginia (1933), and Cape Hatteras National Seashore, North Carolina (1937). Extant national parks received investment in infrastructure as part of New Deal public relief programs. Thousands of unemployed workers attached to the Civilian Conservation Corps serviced the preserves, leading to the construction of roads, trails, and visitor facilities.

With the park system consolidated, staff commenced a detailed appraisal of traditional management priorities. Influenced by the emergent discipline of ecological science, a new generation of resource managers strongly expressed a need to preserve representative landscapes as well as monumental scenery. Advocates stressed the essential role of parks as scientific laboratories, arguing for areas to be protected in their natural condition. Early park programs such as animal shows and predator extermination came under severe criticism. George Wright, Ben Thompson, and Joseph Dixon, biologists in the employ of the newly created Wildlife Division (1933), emerged as champions of "total preservation." In their influential 1933 report, *The Fauna of the National Parks*, Wright, Thompson, and Dixon raised pertinent questions about the arbitrary boundaries and biotic sustainability of many parks, and extolled "nature itself" rather than inanimate scenery as "perhaps our greatest natural heritage." Scientific reports by Adolph and Olaus Murie in turn demonstrated the contribution of persecuted species such as wolves and coyotes to healthy ecosystems. Subsequent policy changes reflected the rise of ecological thought in NPS philosophy. Predators earned protection as "special charges" of the parks, while personnel phased out bear-feeding events, caged menageries, and the Yosemite firefall. The dedication of Everglades National Park (1934), a flat coastal swamp in Florida, communicated a fresh commitment to the preservation of biological systems irrespective of their scenic splendor.

The appointment of Newton B. Drury, a conservationist with the California-based Save the Redwoods League, as NPS director (1940–1951) signified a departure from the Mather-Albright management tradition. Drury's administration represented an era of retrenchment for the national park system. As a result of wartime exigencies, funding plummeted from $21.1 million in 1940 to $4.6 million in 1944, while personnel faced demands that the national parks be opened to forestry, mining, and grazing. The NPS headquarters relocated from Washington, D.C., to Chicago for the duration of World War II, and only reconvened in October 1947. The park system survived such challenges, although Drury resigned in protest over Bureau of Reclamation plans to dam Dinosaur National Monument, Utah.

Mission 66 and the Environmental Revolution

Faced with a national park system suffering from financial neglect and insufficient facilities, Conrad L. Wirth, a landscape architect who had worked in the preserves during the 1930s as part of the Civilian Conservation Corps, became director (1951–1963) and embarked on a massive program of development and investment. Labeled Mission 66, Wirth's ambitious ten-year plan committed more than $1 billion to improving park infrastructure and visitor resources. Park personnel constructed 2,800 miles of new roads, 575 campgrounds, 936 miles of trails, and 114 visitor centers as part of the scheme. The major overhaul came in response to a vast surge in visitation during the post-1945 era, facilitated by increased affluence, affordable transportation, and rising interest in outdoor vacationing. The number of tourists who visited the parks in 1950 reached 33 million, compared to 6 million in 1942.

The environmental movement of the 1960s and 1970s exerted a defining influence on the national park system. Influential staff reports during this period articulated a growing environmental ethic shaped by scientific discovery and citizen advocacy. Concerned at the overpopulation of elk in Jackson Hole, Wyoming, Secretary of the Interior Stewart Udall convened an advisory board on wildlife management under the chairmanship of biologist A. Starker Leopold. When the committee delivered its report in 1963, it stated that "biotic associations within each park [should] be maintained, or where necessary recreated, as nearly as possible in the condition that prevailed when the area was first visited by the white man." Advertising the preserves as "vignette[s] of primitive America," the report emphasized the importance of natural regulation allied with the restoration of ecological processes. These findings helped refine official NPS philosophy and contributed to diverse management imperatives, from the reinstitution of natural fire regimes to predator reintroduction schemes. During the 1960s and 1970s, an active public environmental lobby, led by the Sierra Club and the National Parks Conservation Association, highlighted the fate of protected areas and their wildlife. Environmentalists pressured the NPS to promote wilderness values and criticized the agency for its historic focus on leisure promotion. In his 1968 book *Desert Solitaire*, the part-time ranger and radical ecologist Edward Abbey berated the rise of "industrial tourism" and called for the banning of automobiles from national parks, areas that he defined as "holy places."

The national park system underwent a major expansion under the directorship of George B. Hartzog (1964–1972). Congress inaugurated a series of newly created parks, including Ozark National Scenic Riverways, Missouri (1964), Pictured Rocks National Lakeshore, Michigan (1966), and North Cascades National Park, Washington (1968). The Gateway National Recreation Area, New York City (1972), and the Golden Gate National Recreation Area, San Francisco (1972), satiated demands for open spaces in urban areas.

In 1980, the national park system received a dramatic boost with the addition of forty-seven million acres of Alaskan lands. The dedication of new units under the

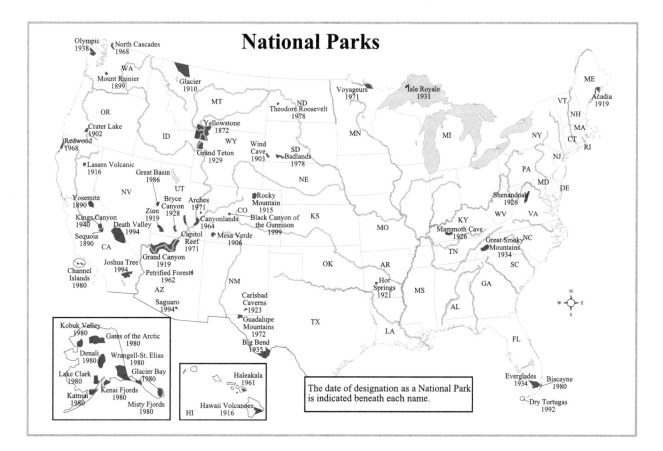

National Parks

Olympic 1938
North Cascades 1968
WA
Mount Rainier 1899
OR
Crater Lake 1902
Redwood 1968
Lassen Volcanic 1916
ID
MT
Glacier 1910
Yellowstone 1872
WY
Grand Teton 1929
Wind Cave 1903
ND
Theodore Roosevelt 1978
SD
Badlands 1978
NE
Voyageurs 1971
Isle Royale 1931
MN
MI
ME
Acadia 1919
VT
NH
MA
NY
CT
RI
NJ
PA
MD
DE
Great Basin 1986
Yosemite 1890
NV
UT
Bryce Canyon 1928
Zion 1919
Arches 1971
CO
Rocky Mountain 1915
Canyonlands 1964
Black Canyon of the Gunnison 1999
KS
Shenandoah 1926
WV
VA
Kings Canyon 1940
Death Valley 1994
Sequoia 1890
CA
Capitol Reef 1971
Mesa Verde 1906
MO
KY
Mammoth Cave 1926
TN
Great Smoky Mountains 1934
NC
SC
Grand Canyon 1919
Joshua Tree 1994
Channel Islands 1980
Petrified Forest 1962
AZ
Saguaro 1994
NM
OK
AR
Hot Springs 1921
MS
AL
GA
N
W E
S
Carlsbad Caverns 1923
Guadalupe Mountains 1972
Big Bend 1935
TX
LA
FL
Kobuk Valley 1980
Gates of the Arctic 1980
Denali 1980
Wrangell-St. Elias 1980
Lake Clark 1980
Glacier Bay 1980
Kenai Fjords 1980
Katmai 1980
Misty Fjords 1980
Haleakala 1961
Hawaii Volcanoes 1916
HI

The date of designation as a National Park is indicated beneath each name.

Alaskan National Interest Lands Conservation Act more than doubled the existing park system. Significantly, national preserves allowed the continuance of Native American subsistence activities such as trapping and hunting within their borders, an important recognition of historic indigenous land-use rights in national park territories.

The Challenges of Preservation

By the 1980s, the national park system had grown to encompass a multitude of different units and responsibilities. However, resource allocation failed to keep pace. Funding cutbacks, which proved especially acute under the administration of Ronald Reagan in the 1980s, contributed to a $5 billion backlog in park infrastructure improvements and repair projects by the mid-1990s. During the so-called "Sagebrush Rebellion" of the early 1980s, staff dealt with western interest groups and their powerful political representatives who argued for the parks to be opened to commercial and industrial uses. Budgetary constraints and political machinations led to declining morale, evident in the critical appraisal of the system offered by the government-sponsored Vail Report (1991). Resource managers engaged in long-term, and often contentious, strategies for ecological restoration and faced an uphill struggle establishing public-transport systems inside park boundaries. The popularity of national parks as tourist destinations led to concerns over Americans "loving the parks to death." At Grand Canyon National Park, car drivers lined up to catch a glimpse of the famous ra-

vine, while helicopters and light aircraft buzzed overhead. The proliferation of exotic species and encroaching urban development jeopardized the biotic health of many preserves. Sulfur and nitrogen clouds from fossil fuel power plants resulted in declining air quality and the defoliation of native spruce trees at Great Smoky Mountains National Park, Tennessee. Many park units proved too small to serve as sustainable environments for vulnerable species such as the grizzly bear, while peripheral development rendered many preserves "ecological islands." At the end of the twentieth century, the national park system remained arguably incomplete, with a number of ecological zones, including George Catlin's grasslands, lacking protection.

Despite its shortcomings, the national park system nonetheless received capacious popular support, with the National Park Service consistently rated one of the most respected federal agencies. The intense media attention devoted to the Yellowstone fires of 1988 and the Yellowstone wolf reintroduction scheme of 1995 testified to the cultural allure of national parks. The controversial debates that frequently attended park management issues reflected on issues of governmental power, resource use, national pride, and environmental responsibility. Meanwhile, the preserves retained status as ideal vacation destinations, attracting almost 286 million visitors in 2000.

BIBLIOGRAPHY

Dilsaver, Lary M., ed. *America's National Park System: The Critical Documents.* Lanham, Md.: Rowman and Littlefield, 1994.

Frome, Michael. *Regreening the National Parks.* Tucson: University of Arizona Press, 1992.

Ise, John. *Our National Park Policy: A Critical History.* Baltimore: Johns Hopkins Press, 1961.

Kaufman, Polly Welts. *National Parks and the Woman's Voice.* Albuquerque: University of New Mexico Press, 1996.

Rettie, Dwight F. *Our National Park System: Caring for America's Greatest Natural and Historic Treasures.* Urbana: University of Illinois Press, 1995.

Runte, Alfred. *National Parks: The American Experience.* 2d rev. ed. Lincoln: University of Nebraska Press, 1987.

Sellars, Richard West. *Preserving Nature in the National Parks: A History.* New Haven, Conn.: Yale University Press, 1997.

Karen Jones

See also individual entries such as **Everglades National Park; Mount Rushmore; Yosemite National Park.**

NATIONAL PUBLIC RADIO (NPR) is a private, nonprofit corporation serving more than 640 member radio stations throughout the United States. At the start of the twenty-first century, National Public Radio served 16 million listeners weekly via its U.S. stations; ran NPR Worldwide for listeners in Europe, Asia, Australia, and Africa, and American Forces Network for overseas military personnel; and broadcast throughout Japan via cable. It had news bureaus in Chicago, New York, Los Angeles, London, and Moscow, and part-time correspondents worldwide. Music programming included classical music, jazz, blues, and contemporary African music. Talk shows included the humorous *Car Talk*, as well as political and social programs.

NPR formed in response to the Public Broadcasting Act of 1967, which authorized federal financing of public television and radio. Founded in 1970, NPR initially served primarily as a producer and distributor of programs for public RADIO stations. It won critical acclaim for its thoughtful, in-depth news programming, such as the evening news magazine *All Things Considered,* which debuted in 1971, and *Morning Edition,* which began in 1979. In the late 1970s, NPR began providing its member stations with program promotion, training, and management assistance, and in 1979 it set up a satellite system for program distribution. In its early days NPR established a reputation with news and information programming. *All Things Considered* combined news headlines with reports from NPR staff members and part-time correspondents, and often included offbeat features. Reporters did lengthy profiles of prominent newsmakers and covered such topics as rural life and the ravages of drug addiction, bringing about a new style of radio reporting that relied on sound, not just narrative. Many of the NPR reporters credited the influence of Edward R. Murrow, the noted CBS correspondent of earlier years who had placed a microphone in the London street to allow audiences to hear World War II bombings. Murrow's style

of reporting had disappeared from commercial radio, where tight formats discouraged long stories.

From its widely heralded early decades, NPR has made changes that some critics charge have compromised its originality and even its integrity. From 1983 to 1986, the organization underwent a severe financial crisis that nearly bankrupted it. In order to survive, NPR dismissed more than a hundred employees and instituted tough financial controls. The crisis also prompted a fundamental change in the financing of public radio. The federal Corporation for Public Broadcasting (CPB) granted a loan to NPR and then began funneling public money to individual public radio stations, which used the money to acquire national programming. The move was intended to give public stations a greater voice in the governance of NPR and other program suppliers. Since the early 1980s public radio as a whole has relied less on government support and more on contributions. By the early twenty-first century, critics of NPR charged that its increasing corporate sponsorship had softened its news, which was becoming more like commercial news outlets, and that it increasingly focused on entertainment.

BIBLIOGRAPHY

Collins, Mary, Murray Bognovitz, and Jerome Liebling. *National Public Radio: The Cast of Characters.* Washington, D.C.: Seven Locks Press, 1993.

Eksterowicz, Anthony J., and Robert N. Roberts, eds. *Public Journalism and Political Knowledge.* Lanham, Md.: Rowman and Littlefield Publishers, 2000.

McCourt, Tom. *Conflicting Communication Interests in America: The Case of National Public Radio.* Westport, Conn.: Praeger, 1999.

Wertheimer, Linda, ed. *Listening to America: Twenty-Five Years in the Life of a Nation, as Heard on National Public Radio.* Boston: Houghton Mifflin, 1995.

James Kates/ D. B.

See also **Mass Media; Talk Shows, Radio and Television.**

NATIONAL RECOVERY ADMINISTRATION (NRA). The National Recovery Administration was the most ambitious effort ever to enact federal planning of the economy during peacetime. As such, it was the culmination of interest in planning that arose during the Progressive Era and climaxed during World War I when the WAR INDUSTRIES BOARD (WIB) mobilized agriculture, industry, and transportation for the war effort. After the wartime planning ended, the urge to have expert, cooperative management of the economy, rather than competition held in check by antitrust legislation, remained strong. In the private sector it resulted in the creation of management and labor councils in several industries, the rise of organizations dedicated to planned conservation of natural resources, and expressions of admiration for state planning in revolutionary nations, especially Fascist Italy and Soviet Russia. Within the federal government, Herbert Hoover focused his work as secretary of commerce and then as president on fostering voluntary association between industry and government as a way to establish fair and efficient business practices.

Franklin Roosevelt also developed an interest in planning during his government service in World War I and was quick during his 1932 campaign for the presidency to endorse the recovery plan of the president of General Electric, Gerard Swope, to set up trade associations under the direction of the Federal Trade Commission and a national workmen's compensation law to provide a financial cushion for unemployed, disabled, and retired workers. After taking office Roosevelt summoned Swope to Albany for a talk and listened attentively to Rexford Tugwell and others in his "brains trust" who favored measures that would go beyond the self-regulation urged by Swope to outright government coordination of the economy. Out of those discussions arose the design for the National Industrial Recovery Act (NIRA), which was voted into law by Congress on 16 June 1933.

The NIRA and its implementing agency, the NRA, struck a balance between industrial self-regulation and governmental planning in an effort to serve the interests of all parties. The act authorized councils composed of representatives from industry, government, and consumer groups to draw up codes of fair wages and prices for each industry. To foster cooperative integration of the economy, rather than competition, the act suspended antitrust laws for those whose codes were accepted by the government. A group offering a code had to be truly representative of the trade or industry involved, and no code could be designed to promote monopoly or oppress or eliminate small enterprises. Every code also had to provide for maximum hours and minimum wages and abide by section 7a, guaranteeing freedom for workers to join their own unions. Within a year nearly all American industry was codified.

The NRA failed to live up to hopes that it would fundamentally reform the economy and lead to recovery with full employment. One problem was that the chief administrator, Hugh Johnson, chosen because of his energetic service in the WIB during World War I, proved to be unstable and failed to inspire cooperation. As Johnson engaged in promotional campaigns, feuds, and drinking bouts, businessmen exerted their advantage within the councils. They knew their industries' operations far better than government officials and consumer advocates and were well organized to advance self-interest. As a result, the 541 codes eventually completed tended to maintain high prices, low wages, and long hours. Consumer desire for more affordable goods was thwarted, as were plans to reduce unemployment by spreading the work around through shorter hours. Workers also soured on the promises of section 7a as NRA officials repeatedly allowed industries to form company unions, rather than deal with independent labor organizations.

The failure of the NRA dashed progressive hopes for a planned economy. Yet it did demonstrate that active governmental involvement in the running of the economy was possible. In particular, the NRA established the principle of maximum hours and minimum wages on a national basis, abolished child labor, and made collective bargaining a national policy, setting the stage for the transformation of organized labor.

By the time the authorization of the NIRA approached its end in early 1935, public support had dwindled, and the chances for renewal in Congress were in doubt. The Supreme Court then delivered the death blow in the case of SCHECHTER POULTRY CORPORATION v. UNITED STATES (1935), which ruled that NRA codes were an unconstitutional delegation of legislative power and further violated the Constitution by regulating commerce within sovereign states. Although Congress acceded to the president's wish for renewal, the NRA had lost its powers and was terminated on 1 January 1936.

BIBLIOGRAPHY

Brand, Donald R. *Corporatism and the Rule of Law: A Study of the National Recovery Administration.* Ithaca, N.Y.: Cornell University Press, 1988.

Hawley, Ellis W. *The New Deal and the Problem of Monopoly: A Study in Economic Ambivalence.* Princeton, N.J.: Princeton University Press, 1966. The classic work on the importance of the NRA to New Deal policy.

Himmelberg, Robert F. *The Origins of the National Recovery Administration.* New York: Fordham University Press, 1976.

Alan Lawson

See also **New Deal.**

NATIONAL REPUBLICAN PARTY, an outcome of the controversy surrounding the election of 1824. When none of the presidential candidates in 1824 won a majority in the electoral college, the election was thrown into the House of Representatives to select a winner. Although Andrew Jackson had won a plurality of the popular vote, John Quincy Adams won election in the House on the first ballot. Jackson's supporters protested the results, claiming that a corrupt bargain had been struck between Adams and a third candidate, Henry Clay. Adams had indeed owed his election in part to the fact that Clay had instructed his supporters in the House to vote for Adams. The charge that a "corrupt bargain" had taken place gained credence when Adams selected Clay to serve in the cabinet as secretary of state. The controversy divided the Jeffersonian Republicans so severely that they devolved into two parties, one supporting the Adams-Clay faction and the other supporting the Jackson faction. The Adams party eventually became known as the National Republicans and the Jackson party assumed the name Democratic-Republicans. In 1834 the National Republican Party was absorbed by the new and larger Whig Party, and Democratic-Republicans took on the name Democrats.

BIBLIOGRAPHY

Hargreaves, Mary. *The Presidency of John Quincy Adams*. Lawrence: University Press of Kansas, 1985.

Watson, Harry L. *Liberty and Power: The Politics of Jacksonian America*. New York: Hill and Wang, 1990.

William O. Lynch / A. G.

See also **Corrupt Bargain; Democratic Party; Elections: Presidential.**

NATIONAL REVIEW, founded in 1955, was the flagship journal of American political conservatism throughout the late twentieth century. The journal was conceived by William F. Buckley Jr., then in his late twenties and already the author of two books, one a lament at the secularization of Yale University, the other a defense of Senator Joseph McCarthy. He raised funds and brought together a talented group of contributors who shared his view that President Dwight Eisenhower's "modern Republicanism" was inadequate. Some were former communists, including James Burnham, Whittaker Chambers, Max Eastman, and Frank Meyer. They believed that communism threatened the existence of civilization itself and that "coexistence" with Soviet Russia, symbolized by Nikita Khrushchev's visit to America in 1959, was a fatal mistake. Others, like Henry Hazlitt, were free-market conservatives or "classical liberals" who believed that political manipulation of the economy, practiced on a large scale since the New Deal, was inefficient and unethical. A third group included social and educational conservatives such as Russell Kirk, who decried the decline of manners and America's widespread acceptance of progressive educational techniques under the influence of John Dewey. Buckley deftly settled internal disputes among these factions, enabling the journal to present a bitingly polemical and often entertaining critique of liberalism and communism.

Most contributors, apart from the libertarians, were religious, with Catholics predominating, though *National Review*'s religious affairs editor Will Herberg was another former communist who had returned to the Judaism of his birth. The Catholic influence did nothing to soften their antagonism to John F. Kennedy in the presidential election of 1960, however; neither did it restrain their criticism of Popes John XXIII and Paul VI for their peace initiatives in the era of the Second Vatican Council. *National Review* campaigned hard for Barry Goldwater, the unsuccessful Republican candidate in the presidential election of 1964, and supported American intervention in Vietnam. In the late 1960s, it objected not to the escalation of this intervention but to the fact that the U.S. government's war aims were too limited. The army, it argued, should be fighting to win and seizing this opportunity to "roll back" communism. At the same time, it opposed President Lyndon Johnson's Great Society programs and the continuous expansion of the federal government.

On racial issues, *National Review* could be surprising. In an early issue, for example, it said that the Montgomery bus boycott in Alabama was defensible on free-market grounds. If black bus riders were dissatisfied with the service, they were entitled to withhold their custom until the provider improved the service. On the other hand, as the civil rights movement escalated, *National Review* provided a platform for such highbrow defenders of segregation as Donald Davidson and James J. Kilpatrick. Unenthusiastic about the civil rights laws of 1964 and 1965 at the time of their passage, the magazine nevertheless cited them in later editorials against affirmative action, which it regarded as a violation of the principle of equality.

National Review was lukewarm about President Richard Nixon, just as it had been about Eisenhower. At first, nevertheless, it defended him against the Watergate allegations, assuming them to be no more than Democratic efforts to discredit the incumbent in an election year. As the evidence against Nixon mounted in 1973 and 1974, however, *National Review* also abandoned Nixon. Its political star in those days was Buckley's brother, James Buckley, who ran a successful campaign for the Senate from New York as a conservative. The rapid growth of neoconservatism in the 1970s and 1980s made *National Review*, by contrast, headquarters of the paleoconservatives, and the two groups sparred over the future of the movement. Nevertheless, from the election of President Ronald Reagan in 1980 onward, *National Review* felt that the original objective of reorienting American politics in a conservative direction had been fulfilled.

BIBLIOGRAPHY

Allitt, Patrick. *Catholic Intellectuals and Conservative Politics in America, 1950–1985*. Ithaca, N.Y.: Cornell University Press, 1993.

Diggins, John P. *Up from Communism: Conservative Odysseys in American Intellectual History*. New York: Harper and Row, 1975.

Nash, George H. *The Conservative Intellectual Movement in America since 1945*. New York: Basic Books, 1976.

Patrick N. Allitt

See also **Conservatism; Magazines; Neoconservatism.**

NATIONAL RIFLE ASSOCIATION (NRA) is a voluntary group dedicated to the promotion and proper use of firearms in the United States. It was founded in 1871 in New York City by William Church and George Wingate. Its original purpose was to teach marksmanship to the New York National Guard for riot control in the city. The association languished until the twentieth century, when the deadly accuracy of untrained farmers with rifles in the Boer War awakened military interest in the NRA in 1901. The U.S. Army began funding NRA-sponsored shooting matches in 1912 at the NRA firing range on Long Island, New York. The army also gave away surplus or outdated weapons and ammunition to NRA chapters for their members' use.

Beginning with the National Firearms Act of 1934, the association began lobbying Congress to prevent firearms control legislation. Despite the public outcries over the indiscriminate use of firearms by criminals, this law barred only machine guns and sawed-off shotguns from interstate commerce. In the National Firearms Act of 1936, the NRA succeeded in getting handguns, including the infamous Saturday night specials, exempted from interstate prohibitions.

After World War II, the NRA became more of a leisure and recreation club than a lobbying organization. Its espoused purposes during this time included firearm safety education, marksmanship training, and shooting for recreation. Its national board floated suggestions to change the NRA's name to the National Outdoors Association. After three high-profile assassinations using firearms—John F. Kennedy (1963), Robert Kennedy (1968), and Martin Luther King Jr. (1968)—the Democratic-controlled Congress passed the Gun Control Act of 1968, ending mail-order sales of weapons. The army ceased providing funds and guns for the NRA-sponsored shooting matches in 1977. In response, conservative hard-liners demanded the NRA's return to legislative lobbying. Led by the Texan Harlan Carter, they staged the Cincinnati Revolt at the annual membership meeting in 1977, stripping power from the elected president and giving it to the appointed executive director—Harlan Carter. As part of the nationwide conservative surge in 1980, Carter turned the NRA's moribund Institute for Legislative Action (ILA) over to professional lobbyists Wayne LaPierre and James Jay Baker. These changes turned the NRA into a single-issue lobbying organization par excellence. Its membership had jumped to three million by 1984, with fifty-four state chapters and fourteen hundred local organizations. The locals became a grassroots political power, ready to inundate newspapers with letters to the editor and politicians' offices with progun ownership materials.

Most of the membership espoused conservative causes generally. Their reward for supporting Ronald Reagan was the Firearms Owners' Protection Act of 1986, which weakened the 1968 law's gun availability restraints. Nevertheless, in 1987 the NRA refused to endorse Robert Bork's nomination to the U.S. Supreme Court by claiming itself first and foremost a progun group, not a conservative organization. In addition, as a federal judge Bork had failed—in NRA eyes—to protect retail gun sales to the full. After seven years of maneuvering, NRA lobbying helped limit the provisions of the Handgun Violence Prevention Act of 1993—known as the Brady Bill—to just a five-day waiting period and a federal record-keeping system for all gun purchases. During the 2000 presidential election, the NRA spent approximately $20 million. Democratic Party analysts credited the NRA with swinging at least two states—Arkansas and Tennessee—and thus the election, to the Republican candidate.

The NRA also worked other political venues in its single-minded efforts to thwart government gun controls. At the NRA's annual meeting in Kansas City in 2001, its firearms law seminar offered legal advice, strategies, and theories for undermining local government enforcement of existing gun laws. The new attorney general, NRA life member John Ashcroft, also initiated Department of Justice and Federal Bureau of Investigation rule changes weakening waiting periods and record-keeping requirements for firearm ownership.

BIBLIOGRAPHY

Davidson, Osha Gray. *Under Fire: The NRA and the Battle for Gun Control.* Iowa City: University of Iowa Press, 1998.

Bill Olbrich

See also **Brady Bill; Gun Control.**

NATIONAL ROAD. See **Cumberland Road.**

NATIONAL SCIENCE FOUNDATION. The National Science Foundation (NSF), a federal agency that subsidizes scientific research and education, was created in 1950 after several years of debate over the proper organization of national science policy. Vannevar Bush, the head of the wartime Office of Scientific Research and Development, and the West Virginia Senator Harley Kilgore both felt that an extensive federal commitment to scientific research would ensure postwar prosperity and military strength. But Bush wanted to keep control of the new agency in the hands of leading scientists, fearing that any incursion on the self-organization of researchers would jeopardize their results, while the populist Kilgore argued that the government should direct research toward pressing social and economic issues, retain ownership of patents, and redistribute resources away from the top northeastern schools.

Bush originally gained the upper hand with an influential 1945 report entitled *Science—The Endless Frontier* and worked out a compromise bill with Kilgore in the spring of 1946. But some prominent scientists protested that government support of science was socialistic, while others chafed at the elitist and militaristic focus of the proposed agency. Meanwhile, army and navy leaders wanted to gain control of military research for themselves. Congress managed to pass a research bill in 1947 despite such opposition, but President Harry S. Truman vetoed it, probably because he was suspicious of Bush's drive to give experts so much freedom from government oversight.

The National Science Foundation Act of 1950 applied a strict budget cap of $15 million and authorized an initial allocation of only $225,000. The organization's scope was also limited, as the expanded NATIONAL INSTITUTES OF HEALTH (NIH) and new agencies such as the Office of Naval Research, the Research and Development

Board, and the Atomic Energy Commission had captured important areas of research while NSF supporters fought among themselves. Nor could the NSF support the social sciences, which Kilgore had hoped to include. The budget cap was lifted in 1953, but annual expenditures remained in the low tens of millions until the Soviet launch of the *Sputnik* satellite in 1957 drew Americans' attention to the nation's scientific capacities. The NSF appropriation jumped to $134 million in 1959 and reached almost half a billion dollars by the end of the 1960s.

Despite its slow start, the NSF came to play a critical role in funding basic research in the nation's universities. In the mid-1990s, for example, the NSF provided nearly a quarter of the government's support for university research, though its research budget was only 3 percent of total federal research spending—far smaller than the shares of the Department of Defense, the NIH, and the National Aeronautics and Space Administration. The agency's mission has also expanded since its inception. Congress changed its charter in 1968 to include applied research and the social sciences, and President Richard M. Nixon actively pushed the agency in this direction. Engineering was added in 1986, reflecting a new desire to spur industrial growth in the face of overseas competition. President Bill Clinton redoubled this industrial emphasis after 1993, but the NSF soon became embroiled in a broad debate over the role of the state, as a new class of Republican congressmen sought to reduce the size of the federal government.

BIBLIOGRAPHY

England, J. Merton. *A Patron for Pure Science: The National Science Foundation's Formative Years, 1945–1957.* Washington, D.C.: National Science Foundation, 1983.

Leslie, Stuart W. *The Cold War and American Science: The Military-Industrial-Academic Complex at MIT and Stanford.* New York: Columbia University Press, 1993.

Smith, Bruce L. R. *American Science Policy since World War II.* Washington, D.C.: Brookings Institution, 1990.

Wang, Jessica. "Liberals, the Progressive Left, and the Political Economy of Postwar American Science: The National Science Foundation Debate Revisited." *Historical Studies in the Physical and Biological Sciences* 26 (Fall 1995): 139–166.

Andrew Jewett

See also **Office of Scientific Research and Development.**

NATIONAL SECURITY AGENCY

NATIONAL SECURITY AGENCY (NSA) is a key institution within the U.S. intelligence community. The NSA's predecessor, the Armed Forces Security Agency (AFSA), was established within the Department of Defense (DOD) under the command of the Joint Chiefs of Staff on 20 May 1949 by Secretary of Defense Louis Johnson. In theory, the AFSA was to direct the communications intelligence and electronic intelligence activities of the signals intelligence units of the army, navy, and air force. In practice, the AFSA had little power.

On 24 October 1952 President Harry S. Truman signed a (later declassified) top-secret, eight-page memorandum entitled "Communications Intelligence Activities," which abolished the AFSA and transferred its personnel to the newly created National Security Agency. The creation of NSA had its origins in a 10 December 1951 memo from Director of Central Intelligence Walter Bedell Smith to National Security Council executive secretary James B. Lay stating that "control over, and coordination of, the collection and processing of Communications Intelligence had proved ineffective" and recommending a survey of communications intelligence activities. The study was completed in June 1952 and suggested a need for much greater coordination and direction at the national level. As the change in the agency's name indicated, the role of the NSA was to extend beyond the armed forces, to be "within but not part of DOD." In 1958, the NSA was also assigned responsibility for directing and managing the electronics intelligence activities of the military services.

Communications and Electronic Intelligence Operations

The charter for the NSA is National Security Council Intelligence Directive (NSCID) 6, "Signals Intelligence" (SIGINT), of 17 January 1972. It directed the NSA to produce SIGINT "in accordance with the objectives, requirements and priorities established by the Director of Central Intelligence Board." The directive also authorized the director of the NSA "to issue direct to any operating elements engaged in SIGINT operations such instructions and assignments as are required" and states that "all instructions issued by the Director under the authority provided in this paragraph shall be mandatory, subject only to appeal to the Secretary of Defense."

SIGINT includes two components: communications intelligence (COMINT) and electronic intelligence (ELINT). COMINT includes diplomatic, military, scientific, and commercial communications sent via telephone, radio-telephone, radio, or walkie-talkie. The targeted communications might be relayed via satellites, ground stations, or cables. ELINT includes the signals emitted by radar systems as well as by missiles during testing.

At the end of the twentieth century, NSA's headquarters at Fort George G. Meade in Maryland housed approximately twenty thousand civilian employees in three buildings. The NSA budget was approximately $4 billion annually. The NSA has two major directorates: the Directorate for Signals Intelligence and the Directorate for Information Assurance. In addition to the employees serving at NSA headquarters and NSA facilities oversees, the director of the NSA also guided (through the Central Security Service that he also heads) the SIGINT activities of approximately eighteen thousand army, navy, and air force signals intelligence personnel. Those military personnel were largely responsible for manning U.S. SIG-

INT ground stations around the world, some of which control and receive data from signals intelligence satellites, while others intercept signals from a variety of antennae at those sites.

The most important U.S. signals intelligence satellites are those in geosynchronous orbit, which essentially hover 22,300 miles above points on the equator. From that vantage point they can collectively intercept a vast array of signals from most of the earth. Some ground stations intercept the communications passing through civilian communications satellites. Other ground stations, such as those located in Korea and Japan, target high-frequency military communications in their part of the world.

Military personnel from air force and navy SIGINT units (the Air Intelligence Agency and Naval Security Group Command) also occupy key positions on board aircraft used to collect signals intelligence, including the air force's RC-135 RIVET JOINT aircraft and the navy's EP-3 ARIES reconnaissance planes. Both planes intercept communications and electronic signals. Another version of the RC-135, designated COMBAT SENT, focuses purely on electronic signals such as radar emanations.

Naval vessels, including surface ships and submarines, have been employed for decades to monitor communications and electronic signals. Ships were employed to intercept Nicaraguan communications during the Reagan administration (1981–1989) while submarines conducted highly secret intercept operations near and within Soviet waters from 1960 until the end of the Cold War. In addition a joint CIA-NSA organization, the Special Collection Service, conducts eavesdropping operations from U.S. embassies and consulates across the world, partly in support of CIA operations in those countries and partly for strategic intelligence purposes.

Specific Operations

Although the details of NSA intercepts are generally highly classified, information about some successes have leaked out over the years. The NSA intercepted Britain's communications during the 1956 Suez Crisis, Iraq's communications to its embassy in Japan in the 1970s, and Libya's communications to its East Berlin People's Bureau prior to the bombing of a West Berlin nightclub in 1986. Eavesdropping operations from the U.S. embassy in Moscow during the 1970s, the intelligence from which was designated Gamma Gupy, picked up conversations from senior Soviet leaders as they spoke from their limousines.

In addition, intercepts allowed the United States to piece together the details concerning the sinking of a Soviet submarine in the North Pacific in 1983. In 1988, intercepted Iraqi military communications led U.S. officials to conclude that Iraq had used chemical weapons in its war with Iran. After the Iraqi invasion of Kuwait in August 1990, COMINT and other intelligence reports indicated that some Saudi leaders were considering attempts to pay off Saddam Hussein.

The NSA's eavesdropping operations were often highly risky. In 1967 the USS *Liberty*, a ship operated by the navy on behalf of the NSA, was bombed by Israeli aircraft during the Six Day War in the Mideast. In January 1968, North Korea captured the USS *Pueblo*, holding its crew for approximately a year. In April 1969, North Korea shot down an EC-121 SIGINT aircraft. In 2001, the People's Republic of China detained the crew of an EP-3 after it was forced to land on Chinese territory after a collision with a Chinese fighter.

Assuring the Integrity of Intelligence

The NSA has a second major mission, originally known as Communications Security (COMSEC), but renamed Information Security (INFOSEC) in the 1980s and, subsequently, Information Assurance. In its information assurance role, NSA performs the same basic COMSEC functions as it did in the past. It creates, reviews, and authorizes the communications procedures and codes of a variety of government agencies, including the State Department, the DOD, the CIA, and the FBI. This includes the development of secure data and voice transmission links on such satellite systems as the Defense Satellite Communications System (DSCS). Likewise, for sensitive communications FBI agents use a special scrambler telephone that requires a different code from the NSA each day. The NSA's COMSEC responsibilities also include ensuring communications security for strategic weapons systems so as to prevent unauthorized intrusion, interference, or jamming. In addition, the NSA is responsible for developing the codes by which the president must identify himself to order the release of nuclear weapons. As part of its information assurance mission, the NSA is also responsible for protecting national security data banks and computers from unauthorized access by individuals or governments.

BIBLIOGRAPHY

Aid, Matthew M. "The Time of Troubles: The US National Security Agency in the Twenty-First Century." *Intelligence and National Security* 15, no. 3 (Autumn 2000): 1–32.

Aid, Matthew M., and Cees Wiebes, eds. *Secrets of Signals Intelligence during the Cold War and Beyond.* London: Frank Cass, 2001.

Bamford, James. *The Puzzle Palace: A Report on America's Most Secret Intelligence Organization.* New York: Penguin, 1983.

———. *Body of Secrets: Anatomy of the Ultra-Secret National Security Agency from the Cold War to the Dawn of a New Century.* New York: Doubleday, 2001.

Jeffrey Richelson

See also **Central Intelligence Agency; Defense, Department of; Intelligence, Military and Strategic.**

NATIONAL SECURITY COUNCIL.

The National Security Council (NSC) is a product of World War II and the Cold War. The world war highlighted the need for a system that coordinated foreign, defense, and international economic policies. U.S. military and national security coordinating committees established during World War II included the Joint Chiefs of Staff in 1942 and the State-War-Navy Coordinating Committee (SWNCC), founded late in 1944 at the assistant secretary level to improve coordination between the State Department and the U.S. military on politico-military matters. To expedite communication about such matters between the secretaries of state, war, and navy, a Committee of Three was established during the war and subsequently abolished. It was a forerunner of the NSC.

After the war individuals and groups examined the problem of national security coordination. One solution, many believed, was the creation of a high-level coordinating mechanism. A study conducted in September 1945 for Secretary of the Navy James Forrestal was the first to suggest "National Security Council" as the name for the coordinating body.

Establishment of such a council took some time. In December 1945, President Harry S. Truman first asked Congress to create a unified military establishment along with a national defense council. In November 1946, officials in the War and Navy departments hammered out the membership for the proposed council, then designated the "Council of Common Defense." Creation of such a council was again requested by Truman in February 1947. Both the House and Senate substituted "national security" for "common defense" in the organization's title.

Functions and Personnel

The National Security Act, establishing the NSC, the Central Intelligence Agency (CIA), the National Security Resources Board, along with a unified military establishment, was approved by Congress on 25 July 1947 and signed by President Truman the next day. The legislation specified that the NSC would "advise the President with respect to the integration of domestic, foreign, and military policies relating to the national security . . . to enable the military services and other departments and agencies . . . to cooperate more effectively in matters involving the national security." In addition, subject to the direction of the president, the NSC would "assess and appraise the objectives, commitments, and risks of the United States in relation to our actual and potential military power" and "consider policies on matters of common interest to the departments and agencies of the Government concerned with the national defense" for the purpose of making recommendations to the president.

The act also specified the council's membership: the president; the secretaries of state, defense, army, navy, and air force; and the chairman of the National Security Resources Board. The president was also authorized to designate the secretaries of executive departments and the chairpersons of the Munitions Board and the Research and Development Board as members. In addition, the act

provided for the creation of a career staff headed by a civilian executive secretary to be appointed by the president.

Evolution

The NSC and its staff have evolved in a number of ways. The composition of the NSC itself has changed. At the beginning of the twenty-first century, membership consisted of the president, vice president, and the secretaries of state, defense, and the Treasury, along with the assistant to the president for National Security Affairs. The director of Central Intelligence and chairman of the Joint Chiefs of Staff served as advisers.

The post of special assistant to the president for National Security Affairs was established in 1953 to provide the leader for an NSC policy planning unit. Since then the role of the special assistants has expanded. Along with directing the operations of the NSC staff, they have generally served as the president's primary national security adviser.

The role of the NSC and its staff has also changed over time. Under McGeorge Bundy, President John F. Kennedy's national security adviser, the staff's role with regard to substantive as opposed to administrative matters grew, as did its influence. President Kennedy encouraged an activist White House role and he relied on direct personal access to Bundy and a number of NSC staffers as well. Under Kennedy and Bundy the NSC staff became a direct instrument of the president.

Six functions that the special assistant and the NSC staff have performed since that time are routine staff support and information; crisis management; policy advice; policy development; policy implementation; and operations. Staff support includes the preparation of routine presidential speeches and messages, coordination of presidential trips outside the United States, and management of state visits. The NSC staff, through the national security adviser, also serves as a channel for information (including intelligence data) from agencies and departments.

Since the Cuban Missile Crisis of 1962, the NSC has played a role in crisis management. The need for an organization with direct ties to the president to coordinate the foreign policy and military aspects of crisis management made the NSC a logical choice. Over the years presidential directives have established NSC committees or working groups to handle various issues, including crises.

Policy development can involve serving as an impartial broker of ideas generated by government departments or identifying policy issues and framing presidential policy initiatives. The policy development role can include studies and analyses conducted wholly within the NSC or the tasking of departments to produce studies relevant to policy. Upon receipt of the studies, a staff can simply specify the alternative options produced by the departments and identify the strengths and weaknesses of each option. Alternatively, it can seek to develop a policy proposal that would draw on the different responses to the NSC staff's tasking. In 1969, one the first tasks of the Nixon administration's NSC staff was to synthesize contributions from a variety of agencies concerning U.S. policy on Vietnam.

The NSC staff can also aid in policy implementation. It can draw up detailed guidance to implement presidential policy decisions as well as ask agencies to provide information on how they have implemented presidential policy.

Policy advice has become a standard part of the national security adviser's job and, through him or her, of the NSC staff. The national security adviser serves as a logical adviser for a president to consult in the event of disagreement between cabinet officials. In addition, the day-to-day proximity of the national security adviser can serve to establish a strong relationship with the president.

The most controversial aspects of the NSC's staff functions have been some of its operational activities. For a considerable period of time these have included diplomatic missions (some public, some secret), consultations with U.S. ambassadors, meetings with foreign visitors, public appearances by the national security adviser, and press briefings. During the Reagan administration the NSC staff also became involved in covert action operations related to support of the Contras in Nicaragua and attempts to free American hostages held in Lebanon, operations that would normally be the responsibility of the CIA.

BIBLIOGRAPHY

Brzezinski, Zbigniew. *Power and Principle: Memoirs of the National Security Adviser, 1977–1981.* New York: Farrar, Straus, Giroux, 1983.

———. "The NSC's Midlife Crisis." *Foreign Policy* 69 (Winter 1987–1988): 80–99.

Lord, Carnes. *The Presidency and the Management of National Security.* New York: Free Press, 1988.

———. "NSC Reform for the Post–Cold War Era." *Orbis* 44 (2000): 433–450.

Prados, John. *Keepers of the Keys: A History of the National Security Council from Truman to Bush.* New York: Morrow, 1991.

Jeffrey Richelson

See also **Cold War; Cuban Missile Crisis; Foreign Policy; Iran-Contra Affair;** *and vol. 9:* **Report on the Iran-Contra Affair.**

NATIONAL TRADES' AND WORKERS' ASSOCIATION,

an organization begun in 1910 in Battle Creek, Michigan, by Charles Williams Post, head of the Postum Cereal Company, to fight trade unions. Post's company produced such well-known products as Postum breakfast beverage and Grape-Nuts and Post Toasties cereals. The National Trades' and Workers' Association replaced the Citizens' Industrial Association, which Post had founded in 1902. *The Square Deal*, the new association's organ, provided accounts of the evils of organized labor. It advocated arbitration for labor disputes and opposed closed shops, strikes, lockouts, boycotts, and blacklisting. Only a few locals were established, and the association came to an end soon after Post's death in 1914.

BIBLIOGRAPHY

Fine, Sidney. *Without Blare of Trumpets: Walter Drew, the National Erectors' Association, and the Open Shop Movement, 1903–57.* Ann Arbor: University of Michigan Press, 1995.

*James D. Magee/*A. E.

See also **Cereals, Manufacture of; Labor; Trade Unions.**

NATIONAL TRADES' UNION.

In the mid-1830s, hard times and frustration with the inutility of their expanded voting rights drove tens of thousands of urban wage earners toward unionism. By 1836 as many as fifty local unions had formed in Philadelphia and New York, with more in Baltimore; Boston; Albany, Schenectady, and Troy, New York; Washington, D.C.; Newark and New Brunswick, New Jersey; Cincinnati, Ohio; Pittsburgh, Pennsylvania; Louisville, Kentucky; and elsewhere. While some organized national unions within their crafts, most participated in citywide "trades' unions," which established the short-lived National Trades' Union in 1834 under the presidencies of first Ely Moore then John Commerford. The NTU collapsed with most of its constituent bodies during the panic of 1837.

BIBLIOGRAPHY

Pessen, Edward. *Most Uncommon Jacksonians: The Radical Leaders of the Early Labor Movement.* Albany: State University of New York Press, 1967.

Mark A. Lause

See also **Trade Unions.**

NATIONAL TRAFFIC AND MOTOR VEHICLE SAFETY ACT.

Signed into law by President Lyndon Johnson on 9 September 1966, this act created the first mandatory federal safety standards for motor vehicles. Implementation authority was assigned to the Department of Commerce and, shortly thereafter, to the National Highway Safety Bureau within the newly formed Department of Transportation. The act, intended to reduce driving fatalities, reflected a growing consensus that faulty vehicles cause accidents, not (simply) faulty drivers—an approach popularized by consumer advocate Ralph Nader and his 1965 book, *Unsafe at Any Speed*.

After initial hesitation, the automobile industry supported the act and moderated bureau attempts to impose stringent standards. Recodified in the early 1980s, the law has undergone numerous revisions.

BIBLIOGRAPHY
Harfst, David L., and Jerry L. Mashaw. *The Struggle for Auto Safety.* Cambridge, Mass.: Harvard University Press, 1990.

Kimberly A. Hendrickson

See also **Consumer Protection.**

NATIONAL TRUST FOR HISTORIC PRESERVATION. "Protecting the Irreplaceable" is the motto of the National Trust for Historic Preservation, a multifaceted organization that advocates on behalf of historic properties and districts, serves as a resource for professionals in the field, and educates the public, policymakers, and legislators about issues related to historic preservation. The wide ranging and eclectic nature of its work becomes apparent from the array of properties the trust has accumulated since its founding in 1949—from President Woodrow Wilson's home in Washington, D.C., to the studio and home of Frank Lloyd Wright in Chicago, Illinois, to the Cooper-Molera adobe compound built by a New England sea captain in what was once Mexican California. Trust programs, including a National Main Street Center focused on revitalizing historic business districts, a community partners' program that identifies historic residential neighborhoods, and a rural heritage program that seeks to preserve historic structures, landscapes, and sites in small towns and rural communities, are no less diverse. With a staff of 300, an annual budget of more than $40 million, and 250,000 members, the National Trust for Historic Preservation is a formidable presence in contemporary American society.

When Congress passed legislation more than fifty years ago to create the National Trust for Historic Preservation, its intention was to provide a means by which historic properties could be acquired and properly cared for. The trust now owns twenty such properties, has eight field offices throughout the nation, and a preservation services fund that can support specific projects at the local level. A range of publications figure prominently in the work of the trust, with *Preservation* magazine—aimed at educating the public—beginning in 1952. *Forum News*, a bimonthly newsletter, *Forum Journal*, a quarterly journal, and *Forum Online* are designed for the preservation professional, providing venues for airing key issues, identifying resources, and offering models for solving problems. An annual Preservation Leadership Training Institute also provides experience and training for practitioners in the field. In addition to an annual meeting the trust also offers more specialized conferences such as the recent series on "Preserving the Historic Road in America," as well as other educational and organizational resources for local communities through its website at www.nationaltrust.org.

Though it received federal funds from 1966 to 1998, the trust is a nonprofit organization funded mainly through membership dues, sales, and grants. It lobbies for specific legislation and policies at the federal, state, and local level and has undertaken litigation to ensure preservation laws are enforced. "Save America's Treasures," an outgrowth of the 1998 White House Millennium initiative to protect the nation's cultural heritage, has continued as a partnership of the National Trust for Historic Preservation and the National Park Foundation and has led to the designation of several hundred preservation projects throughout the nation.

Since 1988, the trust has issued an annual list of "America's Most Endangered Historic Places," a leadership effort that, while it has had mixed success in assuring the preservation of particular buildings and sites, has created a growing public consciousness. In the late 1980s, the trust was able, for example, to convince the state of Maryland to acquire preservation easements that stopped the encroachments of developers at the site of Antietam National Battlefield Park. Similar threats to the integrity of Little Big Horn Battlefield Monument in Montana have been publicized, but the outcome remains in doubt. At Ellis Island National Monument, the trust has worked with the New York Landmarks Conservancy, the U.S. Congress, and the presidential Save America's Treasures effort to save many historic buildings from deterioration. With trust publicity the town of Bennington, Vermont, was able to persuade a Wal-Mart store to depart from its typical "big box" retail center outside of downtown, and instead use an older building in the downtown area. In Downey, California, the trust helped convince the McDonald's Corporation not to demolish its oldest surviving restaurant. Similarly the city of Dallas, Texas, has provided tax incentives for developers to rehabilitate, rather than demolish, historic properties. Central High School, once a center of desegregation efforts in Little Rock, Arkansas, was badly in need of rehabilitation when the trust placed it on the endangered list in 1996, but its prospects have brightened as President Clinton signed legislation making it a National Historic Site two years later. These and dozens of other trust-led efforts have inspired thousands of citizens to take seriously the historic places in their communities and to fight to save them.

BIBLIOGRAPHY
Finley, David E. *History of the National Trust for Historic Preservation, 1947–1963.* Washington D.C.: National Trust for Historic Preservation, 1965.
Hosmer, Charles B., Jr. *Preservation Comes of Age: From Williamsburg to the National Trust, 1926–1949.* Charlottesville: University Press of Virginia, 1981.
Mulloy, Elizabeth. *The History of the National Trust for Historic Preservation 1963–1973.* Washington, D.C.: Preservation Press, 1976.

Arnita A. Jones

NATIONAL UNION (ARM-IN-ARM) CONVENTION. The National Union (Arm-in-Arm) Convention, held in Philadelphia, 14–16 August 1866, was an effort by President Andrew Johnson's supporters to unite Democratic and moderate Republican opposition to the Radical Republicans. The convention platform called for sectional reconciliation, equality among the states, acceptance of the results of the CIVIL WAR, and the election of conservatives to Congress. Copperhead delegates, who had been tainted with charges of disloyalty during the Civil War, withdrew to preserve harmony. Although the convention was widely acclaimed at first, Radical Republican successes in the congressional elections of 1866 demonstrated its failure. Johnson's support grew so weak that in 1868 his Radical Republican opponents impeached him.

BIBLIOGRAPHY

Foner, Eric. *Reconstruction: America's Unfinished Revolution, 1863–1877.* New York: Perennial Classics, 2002.

McKitrick, Eric L. *Andrew Johnson and Reconstruction.* New York: Oxford University Press, 1988.

Charles H. Coleman / A. G.

See also **Democratic Party; Impeachment Trial of Andrew Johnson; Radical Republicans; Reconstruction; Sectionalism.**

NATIONAL UNION FOR SOCIAL JUSTICE,

organized by Charles E. Coughlin, a Roman Catholic priest and popular radio speaker, was one of the strongest movements to challenge President Franklin D. Roosevelt's NEW DEAL policies. The union both denounced communism and advocated the nationalization of banks and utilities. Coughlin's rhetoric drew a large constituency, especially from northeastern urban immigrant Catholics, and the union forged ties with the movement for the Townsend pension plan, among others. Though the union officially disbanded in 1938, some units functioned for a few more years. The union's magazine, *Social Justice,* ceased publication in 1942 after it was barred from the U.S. mails for anti-Semitic and pro-Nazi statements.

BIBLIOGRAPHY

Brinkley, Alan. *Voices of Protest: Huey Long, Father Coughlin, and the Great Depression.* New York: Knopf, 1982.

Fried, Albert. *FDR and His Enemies.* New York: St. Martin's Press, 1999.

Alvin F. Harlow / D. B.

See also **Anticommunism; Anti-Semitism; Catholicism; Townsend Plan.**

NATIONAL URBAN LEAGUE.

Founded in New York in 1911 through the consolidation of the Committee for Improving the Industrial Condition of Negroes in New York (1906), the National League for the Protection of Colored Women (1906), and the Committee on Urban Conditions Among Negroes (1910), the National Urban League quickly established itself as the principal agency to serve as a resource for the black, urban population. An interracial organization committed to integration, it relied on tools of negotiation, persuasion, education, and investigation to accomplish its economic and social goals. The League was founded by Mrs. Ruth Standish Baldwin, the widow of a railroad magnate and philanthropist, and Dr. George Edmund Haynes, the first African American to receive a doctorate from Columbia University. The National Urban League was concerned chiefly with gaining jobs for blacks. It placed workers in the private sector, attacked the color line in organized labor, sponsored programs of vocational guidance and job training, and sought for the establishment of governmental policies of equal employment opportunity.

During the GREAT DEPRESSION, the National Urban League lobbied for the inclusion of AFRICAN AMERICANS in federal relief and recovery programs. It worked to improve urban conditions through boycotts against firms refusing to employ blacks, pressures on schools to expand vocational opportunities, and a drive to admit blacks into previously segregated labor unions. During the 1940s, the league pressed for an end to discrimination in defense industries and for the desegregation of the armed forces.

As much concerned with social welfare as with employment, the Urban League conducted scientific investigations of conditions among urban blacks as a basis for practical reform. It trained the first corps of professional black social workers and placed them in community service positions. It worked for decent housing, recreational facilities, and health and welfare services, and it counseled African Americans new to the cities on behavior, dress, sanitation, health, and homemaking.

In the 1960s the Urban League supplemented its traditional social service approach with a more activist commitment to civil rights. It embraced direct action and community organization and sponsored leadership training and voter-education projects. Though the League's tax-exempt status did not permit protest activities, activists such as A. Philip Randolph and Martin Luther King Jr. used the group's headquarters to help organize massive popular demonstrations in support of the enforcement of civil rights and economic justice, including the MARCH ON WASHINGTON of 1963 and the Poor People's Campaign of 1968. The League's executive director, Whitney M. Young Jr., called for a domestic Marshall Plan, a ten-point plan designed to close the economic gap between white and black Americans, which influenced the WAR ON POVERTY of the Johnson administration.

Since the 1960s the Urban League has continued working to improve urban life, expanding into community programs that provide services such as health care, housing and community development, job training and placement, and AIDS education. It remains involved in national politics and frequently reports on issues such as equal employment and welfare reform.

BIBLIOGRAPHY

Hamilton, Charles V. *The Struggle for Political Equality.* New York: National Urban League, 1976.

Moore, Jesse Thomas, Jr. *A Search for Equality: The National Urban League, 1910–1961.* University Park: Pennsylvania State University Press, 1981.

Parris, Guichard, and Lester Brooks. *Blacks in the City: A History of the National Urban League.* Boston: Little, Brown, 1971.

Wiess, Nancy J. *The National Urban League, 1910–1940.* New York: Oxford University Press, 1974.

———. *Whitney M. Young, Jr., and the Struggle for Civil Rights.* Princeton, N.J.: Princeton University Press, 1989.

Nancy J. Weiss / H. S.

See also **African Americans; Civil Rights Movement; National Association for the Advancement of Colored People.**

NATIONAL WAR LABOR BOARD, WORLD WAR I

(NWLB) was appointed by President Woodrow Wilson on 8 April 1918 to adjudicate labor disputes. Its members had already served in Washington, D.C., on the War Labor Conference Board, convened on 28 January 1918 by the secretary of labor to devise a national labor program. They included five labor representatives from the American Federation of Labor, five employer representatives from the National Industrial Conference Board, and two public representatives, the labor lawyer Frank P. Walsh and former Republican president William Howard Taft, who acted as cochairs.

Until its demise on 31 May 1919, the board ruled on 1,245 cases. Almost 90 percent of them sprang from worker complaints, and five skilled trades accounted for 45 percent. Of the cases, 591 were dismissed, 315 were referred to other federal labor agencies, and 520 resulted in formal awards or findings. In reaching their decisions the board was aided by an office and investigative staff of 250 people. Approximately 700,000 workers in 1,000 establishments were directly affected.

NWLB judgments were informed by principles that aimed to balance labor agitation for change with employer support for the status quo, yet its judgments generally favored labor's position. According to board policy, workers had the right to organize and bargain collectively and could not be dismissed for "legitimate trade union activities" so long as they rejected "coercive measures" in recruitment and bargaining. The eight-hour day was upheld where currently mandated by law, though otherwise it was open to negotiation. Wages and hours were set with regard to "conditions prevailing in the localities involved" rather than a national standard. Women hired during the war were to receive equal pay for equal work, and all workers had a right to "a living wage" sufficient to guarantee "the subsistence of the worker and his family in health and reasonable comfort."

As a voluntary agency without legal authority, the NWLB could never be certain how employers and employees would react to its judgments. Wartime public opinion provided crucial leverage, at least before the armistice on 11 November 1918, but Wilson's active support was also significant. On 16 July 1918, for example, the president signed a joint congressional resolution to nationalize the Western Union Company after executives rejected attempts at unionization. On 13 September 1918 he successfully threatened ten thousand striking machinists in Bridgeport, Connecticut, with loss of draft exemptions for war production unless they complied with board orders to return to work.

Employees gained more than employers from NWLB rulings. The board's commitment to labor's right to organize stirred workers' hopes and sparked dramatic increases in union membership, both in industries where unions were represented before the war and in those where they had been excluded. Workers were also gratified by NWLB calls for higher minimum wages, for displacement of individual employee contracts by collective bargaining, and for shop committees elected under board supervision. The NWLB's effectiveness weakened dramatically in 1919, but the prolabor actions it took during its thirteen-month tenure were without precedent in the history of federal labor policy.

BIBLIOGRAPHY

Conner, Valerie Jean. *The National War Labor Board: Stability, Social Justice, and the Voluntary State in World War I.* Chapel Hill: University of North Carolina Press, 1983.

McCartin, Joseph A. *Labor's Great War: The Struggle for Industrial Democracy and the Origins of Modern American Labor Relations, 1912–1921.* Chapel Hill: University of North Carolina Press, 1997. The NWLB in a social setting.

Robert Cuff

See also **Labor Legislation and Administration; National War Labor Board, World War II.**

NATIONAL WAR LABOR BOARD, WORLD WAR II.

To arbitrate labor disputes during World War II, the National War Labor Board (NWLB) was established by President Franklin D. Roosevelt on 12 January 1942 under Executive Order No. 9017. Composed of four labor leaders (from both the American Federation of Labor and the Congress of Industrial Organizations), four corporate executives, and four public representatives, it inherited personnel and policies from the National Defense Mediation Board (19 March 1941–12 January 1942) and gained strength from a pledge made in December 1941 by employee and employer representatives to avoid strikes and lockouts during the war. On 3 October 1942 the board's jurisdiction was extended by Executive Order No. 9250 to cover all wage rate adjustments. On 25 June 1943 its authority was strengthened by congressional passage of the War Labor Disputes Act.

As a result of increased caseloads from wage stabilization policy, the NWLB in December 1942 decentralized decision-making authority to ten regional war labor boards and to special commissions on individual industries, including aircraft, meat packing, and shipbuilding. Before its official termination on 31 December 1945, this quasi-judicial network, supported by 2,613 full-time staff, received 20,692 cases and disposed of 17,650. The central board settled 16 percent, affecting 29 percent of the 12.2 million workers involved.

More than 80 percent of the disputes involved wages. Rising living costs were a central concern. In responding to them the board applied the so-called Little Steel formula. Announced in July 1942, this policy limited general wage increases for groups of employees to not more than 15 percent of their hourly earnings in January 1941. The board also sanctioned wage increases in order to improve low standards of living, correct interplant and intraplant inequities, and ensure women war workers equal pay for equal work.

Only 17 percent of cases involved nonwage issues. Of these, union security generated the most debate. Labor leaders wanted closed shops, with union membership a condition of employment; employers wanted open shops, with freedom to hire at will. The board struck a compromise with the maintenance-of-membership clause. Under this policy, current and new employees were not required to join a union, but those who were or became union members had to remain members and pay dues, often through an automatic checkoff, during the life of a contract. A fifteen-day escape period was eventually provided so workers could quit unions without forfeiting jobs.

The maintenance-of-membership clause offended employers but strengthened CIO unions in mass-production industries. NWLB rulings also reinforced peacetime patterns of collective bargaining and augmented various fringe benefits, including sick leaves, holidays, and vacations. On the other hand, board efforts to fight inflation by capping wages alienated many workers. In 1943, for example, the United Mine Workers defied NWLB rulings and struck four times; subsequent work stoppages, especially in the auto industry, reached record numbers in 1944 and 1945. Subsequently, the NWLB staff of arbitrators, labor lawyers, and academics would draw on their wartime experiences to define the theory and practice of employer-employee relations in postwar decades.

BIBLIOGRAPHY

Atleson, James B. *Labor and the Wartime State: Labor Relations and Law during World War II.* Urbana: University of Illinois Press, 1998.

Lichtenstein, Nelson. *Labor's War at Home: The CIO in World War II.* New York: Cambridge University Press, 1982.

Robert Cuff

See also **American Federation of Labor–Congress of Industrial Organizations; Labor Legislation and Administration; Wages and Hours of Labor, Regulation of.**

NATIONAL WATERWAYS COMMISSION. Congress established the commission on 3 March 1909, upon recommendation of the INLAND WATERWAYS COMMISSION, to investigate water transportation and river improvements and report to Congress. The commission of twelve congressmen submitted a preliminary report in 1910 on GREAT LAKES and inland waterways commerce. It urged continuance of investigations by army engineers and completion of projects under way and opposed improvements not essential to navigation. A final report in 1912 favored the Lake Erie–Ohio River Canal, suggested further study on the Lake Erie–Lake Michigan Canal, opposed the Anacostia-Chesapeake Canal, and urged regulation of all water carriers by the INTERSTATE COMMERCE COMMISSION.

BIBLIOGRAPHY

Hull, William J., and Robert W. Hull. *The Origin and Development of the Waterways Policy of the United States.* Washington, D.C.: National Waterways Conference, 1967.

Hunchey, James R., et al. *United States Inland Waterways and Ports.* Fort Belvoir, Va.: U.S. Army Engineers Institute for Water Resources, 1985.

William J. Petersen / c. p.

See also **Canals; Conservation; River and Harbor Improvements; Waterways, Inland.**

NATIONAL WOMAN'S PARTY. Inspired by her experience with English suffragettes, Alice Paul led a group of women out of the National American Woman Suffrage Association in 1914 to form a new organization, the Congressional Union, renamed the National Woman's Party in 1916. Its purpose was to put pressure on the Democratic Party, which controlled both houses of Congress as well as the White House, to secure the right of women to the suffrage.

Beginning on 14 July 1917 (the anniversary of the fall of the Bastille in France), women began picketing in Washington, D.C., under purple, white, and gold banners using such slogans as "Liberty, Equality, Fraternity" and "Kaiser Wilson, have you forgotten your sympathy with the poor Germans because they were not self-governing? Twenty million American women are not self-governing. Take the beam out of your own eye." Mobs attacked the women and destroyed their banners without interference from the police. Picketing continued through October of that year. Although the demonstrations were peaceful, many women were jailed and drew attention to their campaign through hunger strikes. This period was climaxed by the attempted burning in effigy of President Woodrow Wilson on New Year's Day 1917.

President Wilson finally did give official support to the Nineteenth Amendment, which was the object of the women's campaign, and eventually persuaded the one senator whose vote was needed to pass it (1920). Subsequently the activities of the Woman's Party were oriented toward passage of further legislation to end discrimination against women and toward ratification of enfranchisement by state legislators.

BIBLIOGRAPHY

Flexner, Eleanor. *Century of Struggle: The Woman's Rights Movement in the United States.* Cambridge, Mass.: Belknap Press of Harvard University Press, 1975.

Kraditor, Aileen S. *The Ideas of the Woman Suffrage Movement, 1890–1920.* New York: Norton, 1981.

Carol Andreas/A. G.

See also **Bill of Rights in U.S. Constitution; Progressive Movement; Suffrage: Exclusion from the Suffrage, Woman's Suffrage; Women's Rights Movement.**

NATIONAL WOMEN'S POLITICAL CAUCUS.

Frustrated with legislative opposition to the Equal Rights Amendment, in 1971 Bella Abzug, Gloria Steinem, Shirley Chisholm, and Betty Friedan held an organizing conference in Washington, D.C., attended by more than 320 women from twenty-six states. That conference resulted in the formation of the National Women's Political Caucus (NWPC), a national, bipartisan, grassroots membership organization dedicated to increasing the number of women in all levels of political life. At that time, there were 362 women in state legislatures, compared with 1,656 in 2001, and 15 women in the 92nd Congress, compared with 72 in the 107th Congress. In 1975, the NWPC formed the Candidate Support Committee to give campaign funds to women candidates; it was the first political action committee for that purpose. A year later the NWPC organized the Coalition for Women's Appointments (CWA) specifically to increase the number of pro-choice women in policymaking positions. By 1979, the number of women in such posts had grown by 10 percent since CAW's formation.

The NWPC was instrumental in getting Geraldine Ferraro named as the Democratic vice presidential nominee (1984), in defeating the Robert Bork nomination to the U.S. Supreme Court (1987), pressuring Congress to allow Anita Hill to be heard at Clarence Thomas's U.S. Supreme Court confirmation hearings in the Senate (1991), in getting Janet Reno (attorney general), Donna Shalala (secretary of health and human services), and Madeleine Albright (secretary of state) appointed to cabinet-level positions (1993), as well as Ann Veneman (secretary of agriculture), Elaine Chao (secretary of labor), and Gale Norton (secretary of the Interior) appointed to the Bush cabinet (2001).

The NWPC identifies, recruits, trains, and supports pro-choice women for electoral races and for appointive political positions. Meanwhile, it works to ensure equality for all women in all spheres of life.

BIBLIOGRAPHY

Freeman, Jo. *A Room at a Time: How Women Entered Party Politics.* Lanham, Md.: Rowman and Littlefield, 2000.

Thomas, Sue, and Clyde Wilcox, eds. *Women and Elective Office: Past, Present, and Future.* New York: Oxford University Press, 1998.

Christine E. Hoffman

See also **Women in Public Life, Business, and the Professions; Women's Rights Movement: The Twentieth Century.**

NATIONALISM is the ideological apparatus by which citizens and the nation-state find common loyalties and identification. While citizens may discern a generalized vision of government, nationalism spurs them to identify with a particular country. Because the United States is a secular, free society, the components of nationalism arise from rituals and symbolic images that change in meaning over time and are relentlessly politicized. Rituals such as those performed on the Fourth of July and personalities such as George Washington originated with the founding of the United States in 1776, but have values and uses that rise and fall and change according to the era and the section of the country in which they are celebrated. This essay combines the creation of American nationalism with attention to the time and place of the use of imagery and ritual.

Roots of Nationalism

Nationalism may have been born in Europe with the modern nation-state, but it reached its broadest flowering in the multicultural United States. The American Revolution transformed loyal colonialists into patriotic Americans. It also changed monarchial identification into love for the first president, George Washington, and charged ritual commemoration of revolutionary events and figures with quasi-religious passion. In 1783, after the peace treaty legitimized the boundaries of the new nation, Americans had the requisite qualities to establish their own ideology. Americans were highly literate and had a burgeoning number of newspapers and book publishers. The desire to commemorate the American Revolution inspired fledgling historians to write chronicles of the conflict and create a hagiography of heroes. Most literature was written in English, which became the predominate language after the Revolution. Building upon monarchial and religious holidays, Americans celebrated the great events and accomplishments of the Revolution to instill patriotism. Americans high and low adopted Europeans' conceptions of republicanism to inscribe a self-sacrificing love for the new nation and the responsibilities of citizenship.

The Constitutional Procession of 1788 is a good example of how these values coalesced across the classes. After a spirited national debate in newspapers, pamphlets, and public orations over the contours of the new Constitution, American white male freeholders voted to adopt it. In city after city, Americans celebrated the adoption of the Constitution with orderly marches replete with occupational banners praising the agreement and the financial plans of the "Good Ship Hamilton." In the New York City procession, butchers participated by herding two oxen down Broadway. One ox had a banner with the word "Anarchy" between its horns; the other was emblazoned with "Confusion." The butchers themselves held a banner that proclaimed, "The Death of Anarchy and Confusion Shall Feed the Poor." After the parade, the butchers slaughtered the oxen and fed them to the poor. The butchers were making a point about their daily contribution to the health of the new nation, showing the importance of their productive labor, and demonstrating their political clout. In the same procession over 1,000 cart men demonstrated their loyalty to the Constitution, a number no politician could ignore. In Philadelphia, organizers conducted a "temperance" march as an alternative to the inebriated parades elsewhere as a demonstration that clear-minded citizens were free of the diabolical powers of rum. Among all, the process emphasized civic responsibility for the "middling class" of people. Women may have watched these proceedings from the sidelines but soon learned to claim the mantle of virtue as their own. Similarly, African Americans instilled holidays with their own frustrated claims for citizenship, creating alternative political festivals.

America's Founding Fathers and the Birth of the Hero

As American white males gained universal suffrage by the early 1820s, they coalesced a variety of symbols into a nationalism based upon revolutionary unity. The United States became personified by eidolons, or ideal figures in human form. As Americans softened their memories of the violence of the American Revolution and saw their liberty as fragile and in need of protection, Miss Liberty stood for such values. Brother Jonathan, who stood for the country bumpkin whose crudeness disguised a cunning and ambitious mentality, had a brief popularity. Uncle Sam, whose red, white, and blue top hat shaded shrewd eyes, replaced Brother Jonathan in the 1840s. As Wilbur Zelinksy observes in his book *Nation into State: The Shifting Symbolic Foundations of American Nationalism* (1988), Uncle Sam came to personify the American state, a concept that transcends the bureaucratic apparatus of government. Uncle Sam's lanky body resembles President Abraham Lincoln, who was both the savior of the American nation and the formulator of the modern American state.

The revolutionary era inspired national heroes. George Washington personified all that was good about America. The first president and hero of the Revolution, Washington became a charismatic hero who, as Zelinsky notes, inspired devotion through his physical bearing, character, and mind. Washington is credited with tying together the fractious thirteen colonies-turned-states and surviving military defeats to best the hated British. As the

name of the national capital indicates, Washington's memory is imprinted upon the national landscape in the decades after his death; scores of counties and towns adopted his name. His image became ubiquitous on currency, statues, newspapers, and an infinite variety of media. Although some scholars comment about Washington's loss of place in contemporary society, the plethora of commemorations ensure at least memory of him. His freeing of his slaves also gives him a cachet denied to the more intellectual founding father Thomas Jefferson, whose popularity seems in decline. Benjamin Franklin soon joined Washington in the pantheon. Franklin's humble visage inspired a generation of clubs devoted to the meaning of his memory. Franklin stood for wisdom, thrift, humility, and a restless, striving intellect. Alexander Hamilton personifies the commercial, political American, especially in those decades when businessmen are in charge of government.

Americans perceived the French statesman and officer Lafayette as an example of the American mission and the spread of republican principles throughout the world. When Lafayette made his triumphal return to the United States in 1824, he made special contact with African Americans, as if to emphasize the incomplete nature of the American Revolution. Thomas Jefferson is among the most controversial of the early national heroes. Viewed grudgingly as the "sage of Monticello," he held little meaning for antebellum Americans. His standing fell sharply in the Gilded Age. When Franklin D. Roosevelt enshrined Jefferson to push his New Deal in the decades after the 1930s, Jefferson became a national hero, with emphasis on his sharp intellect and philosophic probing. Jefferson's writings have gotten him into trouble, however. Antebellum racists sized upon his allegations on the intellectual inferiority of African Americans as proof of the need for slavery. In a twenty-first-century multicultural society, they seem mean-spirited. Combined with the proof of his paternity of a child with Sally Hemmings, his black servant, Jefferson's writings have sent his reputation downward again.

The antebellum period gave birth to fewer American saints. Davy Crockett, though a real person and congressman, became closer to an eidolon that stood for frontiersmen who maintained an unsteady relationship, often through women, with civilization. Crockett's image, together with Daniel Boone and, later, Buffalo Bill, is tailor-made for popular American literature, film, and television. More substantial an image is that of Andrew Jackson, who redirected the American presidency from the neocolonial Virginia dynasty into a modern, political machine replete with patronage. Jackson's presidency combines the support of the common (white) man with the fierce, combative individual vision of the imperial presidency. A link between Washington and Lincoln, Jackson was profoundly popular after Word War II because of the connection between a strong president and popular support. However, Jackson's popularity has taken a dive because of his race prejudices. As some scholars have shown, Jackson's administration did not open economic doors for the common man; reconsideration of the frontier myth has had a side effect emphasizing Jackson as an irrational, murderous Indian-hater.

Holidays, National Events, and Conflicts

Americans celebrated their heroes and the memory of the American Revolution on the Fourth of July, also known as Independence Day. A day of parades and barbecues, the Fourth of July remains the paramount American political holiday. While Americans enjoyed fireworks and food for generations, they listened carefully to commemorative orations and to a ritualized, moving reading of the Declaration of Independence. In the twenty-first century, the Fourth of July is more of a holiday for workers and a time for eating hot dogs; however, the Declaration is still printed in full in most American newspapers. Other American holidays from the first decades of the nation have not fared as well. Evacuation Day, when the British troops turned over New York City on 25 November 1783, was marked by a festival for about a century, but finally fell into disuse after the United States and England became allies in the 1880s.

American nationalism was not restricted to drums and barbecues. The completion of the stalemated War of 1812 with England saw an upsurge of nationalism. Despite the sour memory of the New England Federalists who endorsed secession, Americans such as Albert Gallatin viewed their fellow citizens as "more American, they feel and act more like a nation; and I hope the permanency of the Union is better secured," as the statesman wrote to his friend Matthew Lyon in 1816. Other observers were more cautious. George Templeton Strong, the New York diarist, concluded that Americans "are so young a people that we feel the want of nationality."

There were sizable obstacles to a national consensus. Federal power was relatively weak. From the 1830s on, controversies over slavery wracked the nation. North and South found support in religious arguments. Northerners determined that it was impossible to be a slaveholder and a good Christian; southerners found justification for chattel bondage in the Bible. That split played out in Manifest Destiny, by which the United States extended political and military authority over much of North America. As God's chosen people, Americans had a divinely inspired right to expand across the continent. Southerners in turn viewed expansion, as Susan-Mary Grant argues in her book, *The American Civil War: Explorations and Reconsiderations* (2000), as an insurance policy to sustain slavery and combat the encroachments of centralized power. Americans increasingly saw an inevitable conflict. Southerners in particular came to see their section as "The South," a kind of "southern nationalism." These divergent conceptions of national purpose yawned wider after the bloody clashes in Kansas-Nebraska and the Supreme Court's disastrous *Dred Scott* decision of 1857.

The watershed event was the Civil War. The last major conflict fought solely in the territorial United States, the Civil War cost more lives than any other American war. Out of its ashes came a new American saint, Abraham Lincoln, and retirement of the American Revolution as the engine of nationalism in favor of a new understanding of American nationalism based upon a disciplined, organized nation-state with immense power and capabilities. A brilliant orator, whose speeches encapsulated the need for a Union at a time of treasonous rebellion by the South, Lincoln became the symbol of this new nationalism. Aside from Franklin and Washington, Lincoln remains paramount among American heroes. Lincoln rose from Davy Crockett's frontier to take on the imperial power of Washington, the sagacity of Franklin, and the racial ambivalence of Jefferson (Lincoln favored colonization, or repatriation of blacks to Africa). Lincoln guided the North through the bloody years of the Civil War, rose to the occasion by stating the Emancipation Proclamation, and enrolled thousands of black troops and sent them into the South to vanquish their former oppressors. His deification was completed by his assassination on Good Friday after the Union had been redeemed by great blood sacrifice. At each stop, tens of thousands of Americans viewed his funeral procession up through the northern states and out to the Midwest for burial. Zelinsky refers aptly to this event as a "religious catharsis."

After his death, Lincoln was commemorated in every conceivable way. As with Washington, his birthday became a national holiday; every genre of literature dealt with his manifold meaning. Even more than Jackson, Lincoln is credited with the creation of the ennobling of the presidency and the placing of the national trust in the nation's chief executive. Lincoln's death joined him with the tens of thousands of other men who gave their lives for the Union. Constitutionally, Lincoln's legacy was stamped into the Thirteenth and Fourteenth Amendments that ended slavery, gave the vote to African American males, and endorsed a new concept of national citizenship. No longer was it permissible to say that one was a South Carolinian or New Yorker first. Now, the term "American" became foremost. The Civil War also saw the stars and stripes become the true national flag.

Lincoln's and the Civil War's legacy was evident in the decades that followed. Politicians of every stripe tried to identify themselves with Lincoln and "waved the bloody shirt," to pair their candidacy or program with the sacrifice of the fallen soldiers. Contesting the meaning of the Civil War and citizenship sharpened in late nineteenth century. As southerners used terrorism and northern indifference to reaffix African Americans into a form of bondage through sharecropping and the rapid construction of penal institutions, they took away the citizenship rights of blacks and left a legacy of racial and sectional bitterness that continues to divide the American landscape.

Nationalism in the Twentieth Century

Notwithstanding the politicized conflicts over nationalism, Americans at the onset of the twentieth century adapted its multiple symbols. The flag became mandatory; the Great Seal was everywhere. Organizations such as the Grand Army of the Republic commemorated the Civil War. The new media of film and recorded popular music permitted widespread and rapid nationalist messages. In 1915 D. W. Griffith's *The Birth of a Nation* combined a new southern view of the Civil War and American destiny with a racial view of the conflict.

At the same time, Americans began to shift their gaze from political to business heroes. Theodore Roosevelt combined intellectual activism with physical fitness to become the archetype of twentieth-century presidents. Roosevelt's devotion to fitness gave sports a national heritage. Baseball became the "national pastime," and its championship round is called the "World Series," though no teams from Japan, Korea, Mexico, or Latin America, all hotbeds of baseball, are eligible to take part. Teddy's fifth cousin, Franklin D. Roosevelt, became the "Lincoln" of the Great Depression era by devising Hamiltonian programs to lift the nation out of economic despair. But more and more, Americans found equal meaning in inventors such as Thomas Edison and Henry Ford. The publisher Henry Luce attempted to persuade Americans of his brand of nationalism through his widespread newsmagazines, including the ever-popular *Time*. Franklin D. Roosevelt may have epitomized the strong presidency, but after him the office took a great fall. Able if ruthless politicians such as Lyndon Johnson and Richard Nixon became villains in the 1960s and 1970s. Later, Ronald Reagan and George Bush campaigned against the office of the presidency, even if their actual policies further extended the reach of government power.

As human heroes proved vulnerable, the imprint of nationalism spread across the country. Beginning with the Works Progress Administration in the 1930s, the federal government spawned post offices in every town. The Tennessee Valley Authority became the first federal utility. Physical representation of the national government became evident everywhere in bland, mammoth regional offices of federal bureaucracies. Federal prisons and military bases dotted the landscape. In front of each was the requisite American flag.

The Twenty-First Century

At the beginning of the twenty-first century, historical American nationalism was represented by pageantry and the rise of a heritage industry. Re-creations of colonial days in Williamsburg, Virginia, were matched by the huge popularity of Civil War reenactments in which men and boys in copycat uniforms mimicked the battles fought in the mid-1800s. Their enthusiasm for such representation of American nationalism was a reflection of a stronger military comprehension of nationalism. The American military presence was felt globally as American soldiers resided on bases around the world. The war on terrorism ensured that, if anything, the American military presence globally would increase rather than decline. The acts of terrorism committed on 11 September 2001 were followed by a huge upswing in nationalist sentiment, symbolized by the ubiquity of American flags and the swoop of a bald eagle at the start of nearly every major sporting event.

BIBLIOGRAPHY

Anderson, Benedict. *Imagined Communities: Reflections on the Origin and Spread of Nationalism.* New York: Verso Books, 1993.

Fousek, John. *To Lead the Free World: American Nationalism and the Cultural Roots of the Cold War.* Chapel Hill: University of North Carolina Press, 2000.

Grant, Susan-Mary. "From Union to Nation? The Civil War and the Development of American Nationalism." In *The American Civil War: Explorations and Reconsiderations.* Edited by Susan-Mary Grant and Brian Holden Reid. London: Longman, 2000.

Waldstreicher, David. *In the Midst of Perpetual Fetes: The Making of American Nationalism, 1776–1820.* Chapel Hill: University of North Carolina Press, 1997.

Zelinsky, Wilbur. *Nation into State: The Shifting Symbolic Foundations of American Nationalism.* Chapel Hill: University of North Carolina Press, 1988.

Graham Russell Hodges

See also **Black Nationalism; Nativism; New Nationalism;** *and* vol. 9: **Chicano Nationalism: The Key to Unity for La Raza.**

ISBN 0-684-80527-8

90000